Interest Amortization Tables

JACK C. ESTES

McGRAW-HILL BOOK COMPANY

New York   St. Louis   San Francisco   Auckland   Düsseldorf
Johannesburg   Kuala Lumpur   London   Mexico   Montreal
New Delhi   Panama   Paris   São Paulo   Singapore   Sydney
Tokyo   Toronto

5 6 7 8 9 10 MU MU 7 9

Library of Congress Cataloging in Publication Data

Estes, Jack C   1922-
  Interest amortization tables.

  (McGraw-Hill paperbacks)
  1. Interest and usury—Tables, etc.
I. Title.
HG1634.E79   332.8′2′0212   76-7035
ISBN 0-07-019680-X

These tables have been prepared as accurately as possible; the publishers do not, however, guarantee complete freedom from error.

PREFACE

"How much will my payments be?" and "How much do I still owe on my ten-year-old loan?" are often asked questions.

This book is designed for the real estate salespersons, officials of financial institutions and other professionals who are asked these questions. It is also designed to answer the questions for the many members of the public who wish to be informed regarding this vital factor of their economic life.

For over 20 years in real estate, as a salesman, sales manager and broker-owner, the author was faced with answering the above questions. Very often, rate books available did not cover the specific rate or amount sought, forcing interpolations, which are often not accurate. Or, if the proper information could be found, it was presented in type too small to read. These problems have increased in recent years because of fluctuating and rapidly rising interest rates. Rate books have just not kept up with the market.

Upon learning that other brokers and officials of financial institutions were encountering the same problems, the author decided to prepare a set of tables covering most normally used fractional parts of a percent, with coverage large enough to satisfy present and future needs. The result is this book containing four of the most needed tables presented in a type size, style and format to make them easy to read and use. Preceding each of the four tables is a brief description of the table, with easily understood examples showing how to use them.

Repayment of a mortgage or other real estate loan and most long-term installment loans can be made by using several plans. The most popular is the monthly amortizing plan with level or constant, systematic repayment of both principal and interest, sometimes referred to as a direct reduction loan. In this plan, monthly payments to principal and interest are fixed at the equal, constant payment amount necessary to amortize or fully repay the original loan, with interest, during the term of the loan. In this type of loan, interest is paid only on the unpaid balance of the principal amount as of each payment due date. As the amount of the principal decreases, a smaller amount of interest is charged; therefore, a larger percentage of each total monthly payment is available to reduce the principal balance. The first table with rates of 5.00 to 25.75 percent in increments of one-quarter percent, terms up to 40 years, and amounts up to $100,000 covers this type of loan.

All FHA-insured, VA-guaranteed and almost all conventional real estate loans in the United States are amortizing, constant payment loans. Tables in this book are for use with this type of loan, with payments in arrears (at the end of each payment period), as is the usual practice for payments on mortgages and most other long-term installment loans. *Note:* For FHA-insured loans, a mortgage insurance premium (MIP) would be added to the principal and interest payments shown here.

Extreme care has been taken to insure accuracy in these tables. Each calculation was computed with "double precision accuracy" (computer programmed with 14 decimals, before rounding). Because of this, you may find some variation from other, less accurate tables. One deviation from absolute accuracy has been made in the rounding procedure. Normally, when computing payments or interest, any half cent or greater would be rounded up, and anything less than a half cent would be dropped. In these tables any portion of a cent has been rounded up. This was done to insure that any loan would be fully paid within the time periods specified, without a large lump sum payment becoming necessary at the end. This may not seem of importance. However, at the higher rates, failure to do so can make a vast difference.

My sincere thanks to Robert A. Arnold, of Computer Sciences Corporation, and Sandor Rosenberg, a computer programmer, whose knowledge and dedication to precision and accuracy have made these tables possible. Also to W. Z. Smith, Jr., Director—Systems, Airline Tariff Publishing Company, for the use of unique printing equipment, which made possible the presentation of these tables in clear, easy-to-read type.

JACK C. ESTES

PUBLISHER'S NOTE

The author of these tables died suddenly on December 1, 1975, on the eve of their publication.

Mr. Estes enjoyed a long and successful career in real estate, and he was truly a professional in every sense of the word. His loss will be felt keenly by his associates and by his former students, who number in the thousands. These tables are but one example of his lifelong desire "to find a better way," and to some small degree they will be something of a continuing testimonial to these efforts.

CONTENTS

Table 1 MONTHLY PAYMENT REQUIRED TO AMORTIZE A LOAN

These tables give the dollar amount of equal monthly payments, combined principal and interest, to amortize a loan at a specified rate of interest by the end of the term shown.

Examples:

1. What monthly payment would be required to repay the principal and interest on a loan of $11,000 at 5.00 percent per annum interest in a 10-year period?

    Ans. By referring to the 5.00 percent table under the 10-year column opposite $11,000, you will find the payment required is $116.68.

2. What monthly payment would be required to repay the principal and interest on a loan of $15,500 at 5.00 percent per annum interest in a 30-year period?

    Ans. By referring to the 5.00 percent table under the 30-year column opposite $15,000, you will find the payment required is $80.53; to this would be added $2.69, the payment required for $500. Total payment is $83.22.

Anytime you interpolate or add two amounts, you magnify the variations caused by rounding. In any amortization schedule the last payment is always different from the regular payments to correct for these variations.

Table 1

5.00%

MONTHLY
PAYMENT REQUIRED TO AMORTIZE A LOAN

TERM AMOUNT	1 YEAR	2 YEARS	3 YEARS	4 YEARS	5 YEARS	6 YEARS	7 YEARS	8 YEARS	9 YEARS	10 YEARS	11 YEARS	12 YEARS
50	4.29	2.20	1.50	1.16	.95	.81	.71	.64	.58	.54	.50	.47
100	8.57	4.39	3.00	2.31	1.89	1.62	1.42	1.27	1.16	1.07	.99	.93
200	17.13	8.78	6.00	4.61	3.78	3.23	2.83	2.54	2.31	2.13	1.98	1.85
300	25.69	13.17	9.00	6.91	5.67	4.84	4.25	3.80	3.46	3.19	2.96	2.78
400	34.25	17.55	11.99	9.22	7.55	6.45	5.66	5.07	4.61	4.25	3.95	3.70
500	42.81	21.94	14.99	11.52	9.44	8.06	7.07	6.33	5.76	5.31	4.94	4.63
600	51.37	26.33	17.99	13.82	11.33	9.67	8.49	7.60	6.92	6.37	5.92	5.55
700	59.93	30.71	20.98	16.13	13.21	11.28	9.90	8.87	8.07	7.43	6.91	6.48
800	68.49	35.10	23.98	18.43	15.10	12.89	11.31	10.13	9.22	8.49	7.90	7.40
900	77.05	39.49	26.98	20.73	16.99	14.50	12.73	11.40	10.37	9.55	8.88	8.33
1000	85.61	43.88	29.98	23.03	18.88	16.11	14.14	12.66	11.52	10.61	9.87	9.25
2000	171.22	87.75	59.95	46.06	37.75	32.21	28.27	25.32	23.04	21.22	19.73	18.50
3000	256.83	131.62	89.92	69.09	56.62	48.32	42.41	37.98	34.56	31.82	29.60	27.75
4000	342.43	175.49	119.89	92.12	75.49	64.42	56.54	50.64	46.07	42.43	39.46	37.00
5000	428.04	219.36	149.86	115.15	94.36	80.53	70.67	63.30	57.59	53.04	49.33	46.25
6000	513.65	263.23	179.83	138.18	113.23	96.63	84.81	75.96	69.11	63.64	59.19	55.50
7000	599.26	307.10	209.80	161.21	132.10	112.74	98.94	88.62	80.63	74.25	69.06	64.75
8000	684.86	350.98	239.77	184.24	150.97	128.84	113.08	101.28	92.14	84.86	78.92	74.00
9000	770.47	394.85	269.74	207.27	169.85	144.95	127.21	113.94	103.66	95.46	88.79	83.25
10000	856.08	438.72	299.71	230.30	188.72	161.05	141.34	126.60	115.18	106.07	98.65	92.49
11000	941.69	482.59	329.68	253.33	207.59	177.16	155.48	139.26	126.70	116.68	108.51	101.74
12000	1027.29	526.46	359.66	276.36	226.46	193.26	169.61	151.92	138.21	127.28	118.38	110.99
13000	1112.90	570.33	389.63	299.39	245.33	209.37	183.75	164.58	149.73	137.89	128.24	120.24
14000	1198.51	614.20	419.60	322.42	264.20	225.47	197.88	177.24	161.25	148.50	138.11	129.49
15000	1284.12	658.08	449.57	345.44	283.07	241.58	212.01	189.90	172.76	159.10	147.97	138.74
16000	1369.72	701.95	479.54	368.47	301.94	257.68	226.15	202.56	184.28	169.71	157.84	147.99
17000	1455.33	745.82	509.51	391.50	320.82	273.79	240.28	215.22	195.80	180.32	167.70	157.24
18000	1540.94	789.69	539.48	414.53	339.69	289.89	254.42	227.88	207.32	190.92	177.57	166.49
19000	1626.55	833.56	569.45	437.56	358.56	306.00	268.55	240.54	218.83	201.53	187.43	175.73
20000	1712.15	877.43	599.42	460.59	377.43	322.10	282.68	253.20	230.35	212.14	197.29	184.98
21000	1797.76	921.30	629.39	483.62	396.30	338.21	296.82	265.86	241.87	222.74	207.16	194.23
22000	1883.37	965.18	659.36	506.65	415.17	354.31	310.95	278.52	253.39	233.35	217.02	203.48
23000	1968.98	1009.05	689.34	529.68	434.04	370.42	325.08	291.18	264.90	243.96	226.89	212.73
24000	2054.58	1052.92	719.31	552.71	452.91	386.52	339.22	303.84	276.42	254.56	236.75	221.98
25000	2140.19	1096.79	749.28	575.74	471.79	402.63	353.35	316.50	287.94	265.17	246.62	231.23
26000	2225.80	1140.66	779.25	598.77	490.66	418.73	367.49	329.16	299.45	275.78	256.48	240.48
27000	2311.41	1184.53	809.22	621.80	509.53	434.84	381.62	341.82	310.97	286.38	266.35	249.73
28000	2397.01	1228.40	839.19	644.83	528.40	450.94	395.75	354.48	322.49	296.99	276.21	258.97
29000	2482.62	1272.28	869.16	667.85	547.27	467.05	409.89	367.14	334.01	307.59	286.08	268.22
30000	2568.23	1316.15	899.13	690.88	566.14	483.15	424.02	379.80	345.52	318.20	295.94	277.47
31000	2653.84	1360.02	929.10	713.91	585.01	499.26	438.16	392.46	357.04	328.81	305.80	286.72
32000	2739.44	1403.89	959.07	736.94	603.88	515.36	452.29	405.12	368.56	339.41	315.67	295.97
33000	2825.05	1447.76	989.04	759.97	622.76	531.47	466.42	417.78	380.08	350.02	325.53	305.22
34000	2910.66	1491.63	1019.02	783.00	641.63	547.57	480.56	430.44	391.59	360.63	335.40	314.47
35000	2996.27	1535.50	1048.99	806.03	660.50	563.68	494.69	443.10	403.11	371.23	345.26	323.72
36000	3081.87	1579.38	1078.96	829.06	679.37	579.78	508.83	455.76	414.63	381.84	355.13	332.97
37000	3167.48	1623.25	1108.93	852.09	698.24	595.89	522.96	468.42	426.14	392.45	364.99	342.21
38000	3253.09	1667.12	1138.90	875.12	717.11	611.99	537.09	481.08	437.66	403.05	374.86	351.46
39000	3338.70	1710.99	1168.87	898.15	735.98	628.10	551.23	493.74	449.18	413.66	384.72	360.71
40000	3424.30	1754.86	1198.84	921.18	754.85	644.20	565.36	506.40	460.70	424.27	394.58	369.96
41000	3509.91	1798.73	1228.81	944.21	773.73	660.31	579.50	519.06	472.21	434.87	404.45	379.21
42000	3595.52	1842.60	1258.78	967.24	792.60	676.41	593.63	531.72	483.73	445.48	414.31	388.46
43000	3681.13	1886.47	1288.75	990.26	811.47	692.52	607.76	544.38	495.25	456.09	424.18	397.71
44000	3766.73	1930.35	1318.72	1013.29	830.34	708.62	621.90	557.04	506.77	466.69	434.04	406.96
45000	3852.34	1974.22	1348.70	1036.32	849.21	724.73	636.03	569.70	518.28	477.30	443.91	416.21
46000	3937.95	2018.09	1378.67	1059.35	868.08	740.83	650.16	582.36	529.80	487.91	453.77	425.45
47000	4023.56	2061.96	1408.64	1082.38	886.95	756.94	664.30	595.02	541.32	498.51	463.64	434.70
48000	4109.16	2105.83	1438.61	1105.41	905.82	773.04	678.43	607.68	552.83	509.12	473.50	443.95
49000	4194.77	2149.70	1468.58	1128.44	924.70	789.15	692.57	620.34	564.35	519.73	483.36	453.20
50000	4280.38	2193.57	1498.55	1151.47	943.57	805.25	706.70	633.00	575.87	530.33	493.23	462.45
55000	4708.42	2412.93	1648.40	1266.62	1037.92	885.78	777.37	696.30	633.46	583.37	542.55	508.69
60000	5136.45	2632.29	1798.26	1381.76	1132.28	966.30	848.04	759.60	691.04	636.40	591.87	554.94
65000	5564.49	2851.65	1948.11	1496.91	1226.64	1046.83	918.71	822.90	748.63	689.43	641.20	601.18
70000	5992.53	3071.00	2097.97	1612.06	1320.99	1127.35	989.38	886.20	806.21	742.46	690.52	647.43
75000	6420.57	3290.36	2247.82	1727.20	1415.35	1207.87	1060.05	949.50	863.80	795.50	739.84	693.67
80000	6848.60	3509.72	2397.68	1842.35	1509.70	1288.40	1130.72	1012.80	921.39	848.53	789.16	739.92
85000	7276.64	3729.07	2547.53	1957.49	1604.06	1368.92	1201.39	1076.10	978.97	901.56	838.49	786.16
90000	7704.68	3948.43	2697.39	2072.64	1698.42	1449.45	1272.06	1139.40	1036.56	954.59	887.81	832.41
95000	8132.72	4167.79	2847.24	2187.79	1792.77	1529.97	1342.73	1202.70	1094.15	1007.63	937.13	878.65
100000	8560.75	4387.14	2997.09	2302.93	1887.13	1610.50	1413.40	1266.00	1151.73	1060.66	986.45	924.90

Table 1

MONTHLY
5.00%
PAYMENT REQUIRED TO AMORTIZE A LOAN

TERM / AMOUNT	13 YEARS	14 YEARS	15 YEARS	16 YEARS	17 YEARS	18 YEARS	19 YEARS	20 YEARS	25 YEARS	30 YEARS	35 YEARS	40 YEARS
50	.44	.42	.40	.38	.37	.36	.35	.33	.30	.27	.26	.25
100	.88	.83	.80	.76	.73	.71	.69	.66	.59	.54	.51	.49
200	1.75	1.66	1.59	1.52	1.46	1.41	1.37	1.32	1.17	1.08	1.01	.97
300	2.62	2.49	2.38	2.28	2.19	2.11	2.05	1.98	1.76	1.62	1.52	1.45
400	3.50	3.32	3.17	3.04	2.92	2.82	2.73	2.64	2.34	2.15	2.02	1.93
500	4.37	4.15	3.96	3.79	3.65	3.52	3.41	3.30	2.93	2.69	2.53	2.42
600	5.24	4.98	4.75	4.55	4.38	4.22	4.09	3.96	3.51	3.23	3.03	2.90
700	6.12	5.81	5.54	5.31	5.11	4.93	4.77	4.62	4.10	3.76	3.54	3.38
800	6.99	6.64	6.33	6.07	5.83	5.63	5.45	5.28	4.68	4.30	4.04	3.86
900	7.86	7.46	7.12	6.82	6.56	6.33	6.13	5.94	5.27	4.84	4.55	4.34
1000	8.74	8.29	7.91	7.58	7.29	7.04	6.81	6.60	5.85	5.37	5.05	4.83
2000	17.47	16.58	15.82	15.16	14.58	14.07	13.61	13.20	11.70	10.74	10.10	9.65
3000	26.20	24.87	23.73	22.74	21.86	21.10	20.41	19.80	17.54	16.11	15.15	14.47
4000	34.93	33.16	31.64	30.31	29.15	28.13	27.22	26.40	23.39	21.48	20.19	19.29
5000	43.66	41.45	39.54	37.89	36.44	35.16	34.02	33.00	29.23	26.85	25.24	24.11
6000	52.39	49.74	47.45	45.47	43.72	42.19	40.82	39.60	35.08	32.21	30.29	28.94
7000	61.12	58.03	55.36	53.04	51.01	49.22	47.62	46.20	40.93	37.58	35.33	33.76
8000	69.85	66.31	63.27	60.62	58.30	56.25	54.43	52.80	46.77	42.95	40.38	38.58
9000	78.58	74.60	71.18	68.20	65.58	63.28	61.23	59.40	52.62	48.32	45.43	43.40
10000	87.31	82.89	79.08	75.77	72.87	70.31	68.03	66.00	58.46	53.69	50.47	48.22
11000	96.04	91.18	86.99	83.35	80.16	77.34	74.84	72.60	64.31	59.06	55.52	53.05
12000	104.77	99.47	94.90	90.93	87.44	84.37	81.64	79.20	70.16	64.42	60.57	57.87
13000	113.50	107.76	102.81	98.50	94.73	91.40	88.44	85.80	76.00	69.79	65.61	62.69
14000	122.23	116.05	110.72	106.08	102.02	98.43	95.24	92.40	81.85	75.16	70.66	67.51
15000	130.96	124.34	118.62	113.66	109.30	105.46	102.05	99.00	87.69	80.53	75.71	72.33
16000	139.69	132.62	126.53	121.23	116.59	112.49	108.85	105.60	93.54	85.90	80.76	77.16
17000	148.43	140.91	134.44	128.81	123.88	119.52	115.65	112.20	99.39	91.26	85.80	81.98
18000	157.16	149.20	142.35	136.39	131.16	126.55	122.45	118.80	105.23	96.63	90.85	86.80
19000	165.89	157.49	150.26	143.96	138.45	133.58	129.26	125.40	111.08	102.00	95.90	91.62
20000	174.62	165.78	158.16	151.54	145.74	140.61	136.06	132.00	116.92	107.37	100.94	96.44
21000	183.35	174.07	166.07	159.12	153.02	147.64	142.86	138.60	122.77	112.74	105.99	101.27
22000	192.08	182.36	173.98	166.69	160.31	154.67	149.67	145.20	128.61	118.11	111.04	106.09
23000	200.81	190.65	181.89	174.27	167.60	161.70	156.47	151.79	134.46	123.47	116.08	110.91
24000	209.54	198.93	189.80	181.85	174.88	168.73	163.27	158.39	140.31	128.84	121.13	115.73
25000	218.27	207.22	197.70	189.43	182.17	175.76	170.07	164.99	146.15	134.21	126.18	120.55
26000	227.00	215.51	205.61	197.00	189.46	182.79	176.88	171.59	152.00	139.58	131.22	125.38
27000	235.73	223.80	213.52	204.58	196.74	189.82	183.68	178.19	157.84	144.95	136.27	130.20
28000	244.46	232.09	221.43	212.16	204.03	196.85	190.48	184.79	163.69	150.32	141.32	135.02
29000	253.19	240.38	229.34	219.73	211.32	203.88	197.29	191.39	169.54	155.68	146.36	139.84
30000	261.92	248.67	237.24	227.31	218.60	210.92	204.09	197.99	175.38	161.05	151.41	144.66
31000	270.65	256.95	245.15	234.89	225.89	217.95	210.89	204.59	181.23	166.42	156.46	149.49
32000	279.38	265.24	253.06	242.46	233.17	224.98	217.69	211.19	187.07	171.79	161.51	154.31
33000	288.11	273.53	260.97	250.04	240.46	232.01	224.50	217.79	192.92	177.16	166.55	159.13
34000	296.85	281.82	268.87	257.62	247.75	239.04	231.30	224.39	198.77	182.52	171.60	163.95
35000	305.58	290.11	276.78	265.19	255.03	246.07	238.10	230.99	204.61	187.89	176.65	168.77
36000	314.31	298.40	284.69	272.77	262.32	253.10	244.90	237.59	210.46	193.26	181.69	173.60
37000	323.04	306.69	292.60	280.35	269.61	260.13	251.71	244.19	216.30	198.63	186.74	178.42
38000	331.77	314.98	300.51	287.92	276.89	267.16	258.51	250.79	222.15	204.00	191.79	183.24
39000	340.50	323.26	308.41	295.50	284.18	274.19	265.31	257.39	228.00	209.37	196.83	188.06
40000	349.23	331.55	316.32	303.08	291.47	281.22	272.12	263.99	233.84	214.73	201.88	192.88
41000	357.96	339.84	324.23	310.65	298.75	288.25	278.92	270.59	239.69	220.10	206.93	197.71
42000	366.69	348.13	332.14	318.23	306.04	295.28	285.72	277.19	245.53	225.47	211.97	202.53
43000	375.42	356.42	340.05	325.81	313.33	302.31	292.52	283.79	251.38	230.84	217.02	207.35
44000	384.15	364.71	347.95	333.38	320.61	309.34	299.33	290.39	257.22	236.21	222.07	212.17
45000	392.88	373.00	355.86	340.96	327.90	316.37	306.13	296.99	263.07	241.57	227.11	216.99
46000	401.61	381.29	363.77	348.54	335.19	323.40	312.93	303.58	268.92	246.94	232.16	221.82
47000	410.34	389.57	371.68	356.12	342.47	330.43	319.74	310.18	274.76	252.31	237.21	226.64
48000	419.07	397.86	379.59	363.69	349.76	337.46	326.54	316.78	280.61	257.68	242.26	231.46
49000	427.80	406.15	387.49	371.27	357.05	344.49	333.34	323.38	286.45	263.05	247.30	236.28
50000	436.53	414.44	395.40	378.85	364.33	351.52	340.14	329.98	292.30	268.42	252.35	241.10
55000	480.19	455.88	434.94	416.73	400.77	386.67	374.16	362.98	321.53	295.26	277.58	265.21
60000	523.84	497.33	474.48	454.61	437.20	421.83	408.17	395.98	350.76	322.10	302.82	289.32
65000	567.49	538.77	514.02	492.50	473.63	456.98	442.19	428.98	379.99	348.94	328.05	313.43
70000	611.15	580.21	553.56	530.38	510.06	492.13	476.20	461.97	409.22	375.78	353.29	337.54
75000	654.80	621.66	593.10	568.27	546.50	527.28	510.21	494.97	438.45	402.62	378.52	361.65
80000	698.45	663.10	632.64	606.15	582.93	562.43	544.23	527.97	467.68	429.46	403.76	385.76
85000	742.11	704.55	672.18	644.03	619.36	597.58	578.24	560.97	496.91	456.30	428.99	409.87
90000	785.76	745.99	711.72	681.92	655.79	632.74	612.25	593.97	526.14	483.14	454.22	433.98
95000	829.41	787.43	751.26	719.80	692.23	667.89	646.27	626.96	555.37	509.99	479.46	458.09
100000	873.06	828.88	790.80	757.69	728.66	703.04	680.28	659.96	584.60	536.83	504.69	482.20

Table 1

5.25%

MONTHLY
PAYMENT REQUIRED TO AMORTIZE A LOAN

TERM AMOUNT	1 YEAR	2 YEARS	3 YEARS	4 YEARS	5 YEARS	6 YEARS	7 YEARS	8 YEARS	9 YEARS	10 YEARS	11 YEARS	12 YEARS
50	4.29	2.20	1.51	1.16	.95	.82	.72	.64	.59	.54	.50	.47
100	8.58	4.40	3.01	2.32	1.90	1.63	1.43	1.28	1.17	1.08	1.00	.94
200	17.15	8.80	6.02	4.63	3.80	3.25	2.86	2.56	2.33	2.15	2.00	1.88
300	25.72	13.20	9.03	6.95	5.70	4.87	4.28	3.84	3.50	3.22	3.00	2.82
400	34.29	17.60	12.04	9.26	7.60	6.49	5.71	5.12	4.66	4.30	4.00	3.75
500	42.87	22.00	15.05	11.58	9.50	8.12	7.13	6.39	5.82	5.37	5.00	4.69
600	51.44	26.40	18.05	13.89	11.40	9.74	8.56	7.67	6.99	6.44	6.00	5.63
700	60.01	30.79	21.06	16.20	13.30	11.36	9.98	8.95	8.15	7.52	7.00	6.57
800	68.58	35.19	24.07	18.52	15.19	12.98	11.41	10.23	9.32	8.59	8.00	7.50
900	77.15	39.59	27.08	20.83	17.09	14.60	12.83	11.51	10.48	9.66	8.99	8.44
1000	85.73	43.99	30.09	23.15	18.99	16.23	14.26	12.78	11.64	10.73	9.99	9.38
2000	171.45	87.97	60.17	46.29	37.98	32.45	28.51	25.56	23.28	21.46	19.98	18.75
3000	257.17	131.96	90.25	69.43	56.96	48.67	42.76	38.34	34.92	32.19	29.97	28.13
4000	342.89	175.94	120.34	92.58	75.95	64.89	57.01	51.12	46.56	42.92	39.96	37.50
5000	428.62	219.92	150.42	115.72	94.93	81.11	71.26	63.90	58.20	53.65	49.95	46.88
6000	514.34	263.91	180.50	138.86	113.92	97.33	85.52	76.68	69.83	64.38	59.94	56.25
7000	600.06	307.89	210.59	162.00	132.91	113.55	99.77	89.46	81.47	75.11	69.93	65.63
8000	685.78	351.87	240.67	185.15	151.89	129.77	114.02	102.24	93.11	85.84	79.92	75.00
9000	771.50	395.86	270.75	208.29	170.88	146.00	128.27	115.02	104.75	96.57	89.90	84.38
10000	857.23	439.84	300.84	231.43	189.86	162.22	142.52	127.80	116.39	107.30	99.89	93.75
11000	942.95	483.82	330.92	254.57	208.85	178.44	156.77	140.58	128.03	118.03	109.88	103.13
12000	1028.67	527.81	361.00	277.72	227.84	194.66	171.03	153.36	139.66	128.76	119.87	112.50
13000	1114.39	571.79	391.09	300.86	246.82	210.88	185.28	166.14	151.30	139.48	129.86	121.88
14000	1200.11	615.77	421.17	324.00	265.81	227.10	199.53	178.91	162.94	150.21	139.85	131.25
15000	1285.84	659.76	451.25	347.15	284.79	243.32	213.78	191.69	174.58	160.94	149.84	140.63
16000	1371.56	703.74	481.34	370.29	303.78	259.54	228.03	204.47	186.22	171.67	159.83	150.00
17000	1457.28	747.72	511.42	393.43	322.77	275.76	242.28	217.25	197.86	182.40	169.81	159.38
18000	1543.00	791.71	541.50	416.57	341.75	291.99	256.54	230.03	209.49	193.13	179.80	168.75
19000	1628.72	835.69	571.59	439.72	360.74	308.21	270.79	242.81	221.13	203.86	189.79	178.13
20000	1714.45	879.67	601.67	462.86	379.72	324.43	285.04	255.59	232.77	214.59	199.78	187.50
21000	1800.17	923.66	631.75	486.00	398.71	340.65	299.29	268.37	244.41	225.32	209.77	196.88
22000	1885.89	967.64	661.84	509.14	417.70	356.87	313.54	281.15	256.05	236.05	219.76	206.25
23000	1971.61	1011.62	691.92	532.29	436.68	373.09	327.79	293.93	267.68	246.78	229.75	215.63
24000	2057.34	1055.61	722.00	555.43	455.67	389.31	342.05	306.71	279.32	257.51	239.74	225.00
25000	2143.06	1099.59	752.09	578.57	474.65	405.53	356.30	319.49	290.96	268.23	249.72	234.38
26000	2228.78	1143.57	782.17	601.72	493.64	421.76	370.55	332.27	302.60	278.96	259.71	243.75
27000	2314.50	1187.56	812.25	624.86	512.63	437.98	384.80	345.05	314.24	289.69	269.70	253.13
28000	2400.22	1231.54	842.34	648.00	531.61	454.20	399.05	357.82	325.88	300.42	279.69	262.50
29000	2485.95	1275.52	872.42	671.14	550.60	470.42	413.30	370.60	337.51	311.15	289.68	271.88
30000	2571.67	1319.51	902.50	694.29	569.58	486.64	427.56	383.38	349.15	321.88	299.67	281.25
31000	2657.39	1363.49	932.59	717.43	588.57	502.86	441.81	396.16	360.79	332.61	309.66	290.62
32000	2743.11	1407.48	962.67	740.57	607.56	519.08	456.06	408.94	372.43	343.34	319.65	300.00
33000	2828.83	1451.46	992.75	763.71	626.54	535.30	470.31	421.72	384.07	354.07	329.63	309.37
34000	2914.56	1495.44	1022.84	786.86	645.53	551.52	484.56	434.50	395.71	364.80	339.62	318.75
35000	3000.28	1539.43	1052.92	810.00	664.51	567.75	498.81	447.28	407.34	375.53	349.61	328.12
36000	3086.00	1583.41	1083.00	833.14	683.50	583.97	513.07	460.06	418.98	386.26	359.60	337.50
37000	3171.72	1627.39	1113.09	856.29	702.49	600.19	527.32	472.84	430.62	396.98	369.59	346.87
38000	3257.44	1671.38	1143.17	879.43	721.47	616.41	541.57	485.62	442.26	407.71	379.58	356.25
39000	3343.17	1715.36	1173.25	902.57	740.46	632.63	555.82	498.40	453.90	418.44	389.57	365.62
40000	3428.89	1759.34	1203.34	925.71	759.44	648.85	570.07	511.18	465.54	429.17	399.56	375.00
41000	3514.61	1803.33	1233.42	948.86	778.43	665.07	584.32	523.96	477.17	439.90	409.54	384.37
42000	3600.33	1847.31	1263.50	972.00	797.42	681.29	598.58	536.73	488.81	450.63	419.53	393.75
43000	3686.05	1891.29	1293.59	995.14	816.40	697.51	612.83	549.51	500.45	461.36	429.52	403.12
44000	3771.78	1935.28	1323.67	1018.28	835.39	713.74	627.08	562.29	512.09	472.09	439.51	412.50
45000	3857.50	1979.26	1353.75	1041.43	854.37	729.96	641.33	575.07	523.73	482.82	449.50	421.87
46000	3943.22	2023.24	1383.84	1064.57	873.36	746.18	655.58	587.85	535.36	493.55	459.49	431.25
47000	4028.94	2067.23	1413.92	1087.71	892.35	762.40	669.83	600.63	547.00	504.28	469.48	440.62
48000	4114.67	2111.21	1444.00	1110.86	911.33	778.62	684.09	613.41	558.64	515.01	479.47	450.00
49000	4200.39	2155.19	1474.09	1134.00	930.32	794.84	698.34	626.19	570.28	525.73	489.45	459.37
50000	4286.11	2199.18	1504.17	1157.14	949.30	811.06	712.59	638.97	581.92	536.46	499.44	468.75
55000	4714.72	2419.09	1654.58	1272.85	1044.23	892.17	783.85	702.87	640.11	590.11	549.39	515.62
60000	5143.33	2639.01	1805.00	1388.57	1139.16	973.27	855.11	766.76	698.30	643.76	599.33	562.49
65000	5571.94	2858.93	1955.42	1504.28	1234.09	1054.38	926.36	830.66	756.49	697.40	649.27	609.37
70000	6000.55	3078.85	2105.83	1619.99	1329.02	1135.49	997.62	894.55	814.68	751.05	699.22	656.24
75000	6429.16	3298.76	2256.25	1735.71	1423.95	1216.59	1068.88	958.45	872.87	804.69	749.16	703.12
80000	6857.77	3518.68	2406.67	1851.42	1518.88	1297.70	1140.14	1022.35	931.07	858.34	799.11	749.99
85000	7286.38	3738.60	2557.08	1967.14	1613.81	1378.80	1211.40	1086.24	989.26	911.98	849.05	796.86
90000	7714.99	3958.51	2707.50	2082.85	1708.74	1459.91	1282.66	1150.14	1047.45	965.63	898.99	843.74
95000	8143.60	4178.43	2857.92	2198.56	1803.67	1541.01	1353.91	1214.04	1105.64	1019.28	948.94	890.61
100000	8572.21	4398.35	3008.33	2314.28	1898.60	1622.12	1425.17	1277.93	1163.83	1072.92	998.88	937.49

Table 1

5%

MONTHLY

PAYMENT REQUIRED TO AMORTIZE A LOAN

5.25%

TERM AMOUNT	13 YEARS	14 YEARS	15 YEARS	16 YEARS	17 YEARS	18 YEARS	19 YEARS	20 YEARS	25 YEARS	30 YEARS	35 YEARS	40 YEARS
50	.45	.43	.41	.39	.38	.36	.35	.34	.30	.28	.27	.25
100	.89	.85	.81	.78	.75	.72	.70	.68	.60	.56	.53	.50
200	1.78	1.69	1.61	1.55	1.49	1.44	1.39	1.35	1.20	1.11	1.05	1.00
300	2.66	2.53	2.42	2.32	2.23	2.15	2.09	2.03	1.80	1.66	1.57	1.50
400	3.55	3.37	3.22	3.09	2.97	2.87	2.78	2.70	2.40	2.21	2.09	2.00
500	4.43	4.21	4.02	3.86	3.72	3.59	3.48	3.37	3.00	2.77	2.61	2.50
600	5.32	5.06	4.83	4.63	4.46	4.30	4.17	4.05	3.60	3.32	3.13	3.00
700	6.21	5.90	5.63	5.40	5.20	5.02	4.86	4.72	4.20	3.87	3.65	3.50
800	7.09	6.74	6.44	6.17	5.94	5.74	5.56	5.40	4.80	4.42	4.17	4.00
900	7.98	7.58	7.24	6.94	6.68	6.45	6.25	6.07	5.40	4.97	4.69	4.49
1000	8.86	8.42	8.04	7.71	7.43	7.17	6.95	6.74	6.00	5.53	5.21	4.99
2000	17.72	16.84	16.08	15.42	14.85	14.34	13.89	13.48	11.99	11.05	10.42	9.98
3000	26.58	25.26	24.12	23.13	22.27	21.50	20.83	20.22	17.98	16.57	15.63	14.97
4000	35.44	33.68	32.16	30.84	29.69	28.67	27.77	26.96	23.97	22.09	20.83	19.96
5000	44.30	42.09	40.20	38.55	37.11	35.84	34.71	33.70	29.97	27.62	26.04	24.95
6000	53.15	50.51	48.24	46.26	44.53	43.00	41.65	40.44	35.96	33.14	31.25	29.94
7000	62.01	58.93	56.28	53.97	51.95	50.17	48.59	47.17	41.95	38.66	36.46	34.93
8000	70.87	67.35	64.32	61.68	59.37	57.33	55.53	53.91	47.94	44.18	41.66	39.91
9000	79.73	75.77	72.35	69.39	66.79	64.50	62.47	60.65	53.94	49.70	46.87	44.90
10000	88.59	84.18	80.39	77.10	74.21	71.67	69.41	67.39	59.93	55.23	52.08	49.89
11000	97.44	92.60	88.43	84.81	81.63	78.83	76.35	74.13	65.92	60.75	57.29	54.88
12000	106.30	101.02	96.47	92.52	89.05	86.00	83.29	80.87	71.91	66.27	62.49	59.87
13000	115.16	109.44	104.51	100.23	96.47	93.16	90.23	87.60	77.91	71.79	67.70	64.86
14000	124.02	117.86	112.55	107.93	103.89	100.33	97.17	94.34	83.90	77.31	72.91	69.85
15000	132.88	126.27	120.59	115.64	111.31	107.50	104.11	101.08	89.89	82.84	78.12	74.84
16000	141.74	134.69	128.63	123.35	118.74	114.66	111.05	107.82	95.88	88.36	83.32	79.82
17000	150.59	143.11	136.66	131.06	126.16	121.83	117.99	114.56	101.88	93.88	88.53	84.81
18000	159.45	151.53	144.70	138.77	133.58	128.99	124.93	121.30	107.87	99.40	93.74	89.80
19000	168.31	159.95	152.74	146.48	141.00	136.16	131.87	128.04	113.86	104.92	98.95	94.79
20000	177.17	168.36	160.78	154.19	148.42	143.33	138.81	134.77	119.85	110.45	104.15	99.78
21000	186.03	176.78	168.82	161.90	155.84	150.49	145.75	141.51	125.85	115.97	109.36	104.77
22000	194.88	185.20	176.86	169.61	163.26	157.66	152.69	148.25	131.84	121.49	114.57	109.76
23000	203.74	193.62	184.90	177.32	170.68	164.82	159.63	154.99	137.83	127.01	119.78	114.75
24000	212.60	202.03	192.94	185.03	178.10	171.99	166.57	161.73	143.82	132.53	124.98	119.73
25000	221.46	210.45	200.97	192.74	185.52	179.16	173.51	168.47	149.82	138.06	130.19	124.72
26000	230.32	218.87	209.01	200.45	192.94	186.32	180.45	175.20	155.81	143.58	135.40	129.71
27000	239.18	227.29	217.05	208.16	200.36	193.49	187.39	181.94	161.80	149.10	140.61	134.70
28000	248.03	235.71	225.09	215.86	207.78	200.65	194.33	188.68	167.79	154.62	145.81	139.69
29000	256.89	244.12	233.13	223.57	215.20	207.82	201.27	195.42	173.79	160.14	151.02	144.68
30000	265.75	252.54	241.17	231.28	222.62	214.99	208.21	202.16	179.78	165.67	156.23	149.67
31000	274.61	260.96	249.21	238.99	230.04	222.15	215.15	208.90	185.77	171.19	161.44	154.65
32000	283.47	269.38	257.25	246.70	237.47	229.32	222.09	215.64	191.76	176.71	166.64	159.64
33000	292.32	277.80	265.28	254.41	244.89	236.48	229.03	222.37	197.76	182.23	171.85	164.63
34000	301.18	286.21	273.32	262.12	252.31	243.65	235.97	229.11	203.75	187.75	177.06	169.62
35000	310.04	294.63	281.36	269.83	259.73	250.82	242.91	235.85	209.74	193.28	182.27	174.61
36000	318.90	303.05	289.40	277.54	267.15	257.98	249.85	242.59	215.73	198.80	187.47	179.60
37000	327.76	311.47	297.44	285.25	274.57	265.15	256.79	249.33	221.73	204.32	192.68	184.59
38000	336.61	319.89	305.48	292.96	281.99	272.31	263.73	256.07	227.72	209.84	197.89	189.58
39000	345.47	328.30	313.52	300.67	289.41	279.48	270.67	262.80	233.71	215.36	203.09	194.56
40000	354.33	336.72	321.56	308.38	296.83	286.65	277.61	269.54	239.70	220.89	208.30	199.55
41000	363.19	345.14	329.59	316.09	304.25	293.81	284.55	276.28	245.70	226.41	213.51	204.54
42000	372.05	353.56	337.63	323.79	311.67	300.98	291.49	283.02	251.69	231.93	218.72	209.53
43000	380.91	361.98	345.67	331.50	319.09	308.14	298.43	289.76	257.68	237.45	223.92	214.52
44000	389.76	370.39	353.71	339.21	326.51	315.31	305.37	296.50	263.67	242.97	229.13	219.51
45000	398.62	378.81	361.75	346.92	333.93	322.48	312.31	303.23	269.67	248.50	234.34	224.50
46000	407.48	387.23	369.79	354.63	341.35	329.64	319.25	309.97	275.66	254.02	239.55	229.49
47000	416.34	395.65	377.83	362.34	348.78	336.81	326.19	316.71	281.65	259.54	244.75	234.47
48000	425.20	404.06	385.87	370.05	356.20	343.97	333.13	323.45	287.64	265.06	249.96	239.46
49000	434.05	412.48	393.91	377.76	363.62	351.14	340.07	330.19	293.64	270.58	255.17	244.45
50000	442.91	420.90	401.94	385.47	371.04	358.31	347.01	336.93	299.63	276.11	260.38	249.44
55000	487.20	462.99	442.14	424.02	408.14	394.14	381.71	370.62	329.59	303.72	286.41	274.38
60000	531.49	505.08	482.33	462.56	445.24	429.97	416.41	404.31	359.55	331.33	312.45	299.33
65000	575.79	547.17	522.53	501.11	482.35	465.80	451.11	438.00	389.52	358.94	338.49	324.27
70000	620.08	589.26	562.72	539.65	519.45	501.63	485.81	471.70	419.48	386.55	364.53	349.21
75000	664.37	631.35	602.91	578.20	556.55	537.46	520.51	505.39	449.44	414.16	390.56	374.16
80000	708.66	673.44	643.11	616.75	593.66	573.29	555.21	539.08	479.40	441.77	416.60	399.10
85000	752.95	715.53	683.30	655.29	630.76	609.12	589.91	572.77	509.37	469.38	442.64	424.04
90000	797.24	757.62	723.49	693.84	667.86	644.95	624.61	606.46	539.33	496.99	468.67	448.99
95000	841.53	799.71	763.69	732.39	704.97	680.78	659.31	640.16	569.29	524.60	494.71	473.93
100000	885.82	841.80	803.88	770.93	742.07	716.61	694.01	673.85	599.25	552.21	520.75	498.88

5.50%

MONTHLY
PAYMENT REQUIRED TO AMORTIZE A LOAN

Table 1

TERM AMOUNT	1 YEAR	2 YEARS	3 YEARS	4 YEARS	5 YEARS	6 YEARS	7 YEARS	8 YEARS	9 YEARS	10 YEARS	11 YEARS	12 YEARS
50	4.30	2.21	1.51	1.17	.96	.82	.72	.65	.59	.55	.51	.48
100	8.59	4.41	3.02	2.33	1.92	1.64	1.44	1.29	1.18	1.09	1.02	.96
200	17.17	8.82	6.04	4.66	3.83	3.27	2.88	2.58	2.36	2.18	2.03	1.91
300	25.76	13.23	9.06	6.98	5.74	4.91	4.32	3.87	3.53	3.26	3.04	2.86
400	34.34	17.64	12.08	9.31	7.65	6.54	5.75	5.16	4.71	4.35	4.05	3.81
500	42.92	22.05	15.10	11.63	9.56	8.17	7.19	6.45	5.88	5.43	5.06	4.76
600	51.51	26.46	18.12	13.96	11.47	9.81	8.63	7.74	7.06	6.52	6.07	5.71
700	60.09	30.87	21.14	16.28	13.38	11.44	10.06	9.03	8.24	7.60	7.08	6.66
800	68.67	35.28	24.16	18.61	15.29	13.08	11.50	10.32	9.41	8.69	8.10	7.61
900	77.26	39.69	27.18	20.94	17.20	14.71	12.94	11.61	10.59	9.77	9.11	8.56
1000	85.84	44.10	30.20	23.26	19.11	16.34	14.38	12.90	11.76	10.86	10.12	9.51
2000	171.68	88.20	60.40	46.52	38.21	32.68	28.75	25.80	23.52	21.71	20.23	19.01
3000	257.52	132.29	90.59	69.77	57.31	49.02	43.12	38.70	35.28	32.56	30.35	28.51
4000	343.35	176.39	120.79	93.03	76.41	65.36	57.49	51.60	47.04	43.42	40.46	38.01
5000	429.19	220.48	150.98	116.29	95.51	81.69	71.86	64.50	58.80	54.27	50.57	47.51
6000	515.03	264.58	181.18	139.54	114.61	98.03	86.23	77.40	70.56	65.12	60.69	57.02
7000	600.86	308.67	211.38	162.80	133.71	114.37	100.60	90.30	82.32	75.97	70.80	66.52
8000	686.70	352.77	241.57	186.06	152.81	130.71	114.97	103.20	94.08	86.83	80.92	76.02
9000	772.54	396.87	271.77	209.31	171.92	147.05	129.34	116.10	105.84	97.68	91.03	85.52
10000	858.37	440.96	301.96	232.57	191.02	163.38	143.71	129.00	117.60	108.53	101.14	95.02
11000	944.21	485.06	332.16	255.83	210.12	179.72	158.08	141.90	129.36	119.38	111.26	104.52
12000	1030.05	529.15	362.36	279.08	229.22	196.06	172.45	154.80	141.12	130.24	121.37	114.03
13000	1115.88	573.25	392.55	302.34	248.32	212.40	186.82	167.70	152.88	141.09	131.49	123.53
14000	1201.72	617.34	422.75	325.60	267.42	228.74	201.19	180.60	164.64	151.94	141.60	133.03
15000	1287.56	661.44	452.94	348.85	286.52	245.07	215.56	193.49	176.40	162.79	151.71	142.53
16000	1373.39	705.54	483.14	372.11	305.62	261.41	229.93	206.39	188.16	173.65	161.83	152.03
17000	1459.23	749.63	513.34	395.37	324.72	277.75	244.30	219.29	199.92	184.50	171.94	161.53
18000	1545.07	793.73	543.53	418.62	343.83	294.09	258.67	232.19	211.68	195.35	182.06	171.04
19000	1630.90	837.82	573.73	441.88	362.93	310.42	273.04	245.09	223.44	206.20	192.17	180.54
20000	1716.74	881.92	603.92	465.13	382.03	326.76	287.41	257.99	235.20	217.06	202.28	190.04
21000	1802.58	926.01	634.12	488.39	401.13	343.10	301.78	270.89	246.96	227.91	212.40	199.54
22000	1888.41	970.11	664.31	511.65	420.23	359.44	316.15	283.79	258.72	238.76	222.51	209.04
23000	1974.25	1014.21	694.51	534.90	439.33	375.78	330.52	296.69	270.48	249.62	232.63	218.54
24000	2060.09	1058.30	724.71	558.16	458.43	392.11	344.89	309.59	282.24	260.47	242.74	228.05
25000	2145.92	1102.40	754.90	581.42	477.53	408.45	359.26	322.49	294.00	271.32	252.85	237.55
26000	2231.76	1146.49	785.10	604.67	496.64	424.79	373.63	335.39	305.76	282.17	262.97	247.05
27000	2317.60	1190.59	815.29	627.93	515.74	441.13	388.00	348.29	317.52	293.03	273.08	256.55
28000	2403.44	1234.68	845.49	651.19	534.84	457.47	402.37	361.19	329.28	303.88	283.20	266.05
29000	2489.27	1278.78	875.69	674.44	553.94	473.80	416.74	374.09	341.04	314.73	293.31	275.55
30000	2575.11	1322.87	905.88	697.70	573.04	490.14	431.11	386.98	352.80	325.58	303.42	285.06
31000	2660.95	1366.97	936.08	720.96	592.14	506.48	445.48	399.88	364.56	336.44	313.54	294.56
32000	2746.78	1411.07	966.27	744.21	611.24	522.82	459.85	412.78	376.32	347.29	323.65	304.06
33000	2832.62	1455.16	996.47	767.47	630.34	539.16	474.22	425.68	388.08	358.14	333.76	313.56
34000	2918.46	1499.26	1026.67	790.73	649.44	555.49	488.59	438.58	399.84	368.99	343.88	323.06
35000	3004.29	1543.35	1056.86	813.98	668.55	571.83	502.96	451.48	411.60	379.85	353.99	332.57
36000	3090.13	1587.45	1087.06	837.24	687.65	588.17	517.33	464.38	423.36	390.70	364.11	342.07
37000	3175.97	1631.54	1117.25	860.49	706.75	604.51	531.70	477.28	435.12	401.55	374.22	351.57
38000	3261.80	1675.64	1147.45	883.75	725.85	620.84	546.07	490.18	446.88	412.40	384.33	361.07
39000	3347.64	1719.74	1177.65	907.01	744.95	637.18	560.44	503.08	458.64	423.26	394.45	370.57
40000	3433.48	1763.83	1207.84	930.26	764.05	653.52	574.81	515.98	470.40	434.11	404.56	380.07
41000	3519.31	1807.93	1238.04	953.52	783.15	669.86	589.18	528.88	482.16	444.96	414.68	389.58
42000	3605.15	1852.02	1268.23	976.78	802.25	686.20	603.55	541.78	493.92	455.82	424.79	399.08
43000	3690.99	1896.12	1298.43	1000.03	821.35	702.53	617.92	554.68	505.68	466.67	434.90	408.58
44000	3776.82	1940.21	1328.62	1023.29	840.46	718.87	632.29	567.58	517.44	477.52	445.02	418.08
45000	3862.66	1984.31	1358.82	1046.55	859.56	735.21	646.66	580.47	529.20	488.37	455.13	427.58
46000	3948.50	2028.41	1389.02	1069.80	878.66	751.55	661.03	593.37	540.96	499.23	465.25	437.08
47000	4034.33	2072.50	1419.21	1093.06	897.76	767.89	675.40	606.27	552.72	510.08	475.36	446.59
48000	4120.17	2116.60	1449.41	1116.32	916.86	784.22	689.77	619.17	564.48	520.93	485.47	456.09
49000	4206.01	2160.69	1479.60	1139.57	935.96	800.56	704.14	632.07	576.24	531.78	495.59	465.59
50000	4291.84	2204.79	1509.80	1162.83	955.06	816.90	718.51	644.97	588.00	542.64	505.70	475.09
55000	4721.03	2425.27	1660.78	1279.11	1050.57	898.59	790.36	709.47	646.80	596.90	556.27	522.60
60000	5150.21	2645.74	1811.76	1395.39	1146.07	980.28	862.21	773.96	705.60	651.16	606.84	570.11
65000	5579.40	2866.22	1962.74	1511.68	1241.58	1061.97	934.06	838.46	764.40	705.43	657.41	617.62
70000	6008.58	3086.70	2113.72	1627.96	1337.09	1143.66	1005.91	902.96	823.20	759.69	707.98	665.13
75000	6437.76	3307.18	2264.70	1744.24	1432.59	1225.35	1077.76	967.45	882.00	813.95	758.55	712.63
80000	6866.95	3527.66	2415.68	1860.53	1528.10	1307.04	1149.61	1031.95	940.80	868.22	809.12	760.14
85000	7296.13	3748.14	2566.66	1976.81	1623.60	1388.73	1221.46	1096.45	999.60	922.48	859.69	807.65
90000	7725.52	3968.61	2717.64	2093.09	1719.11	1470.41	1293.31	1160.94	1058.40	976.74	910.26	855.16
95000	8154.50	4189.09	2868.62	2209.37	1814.62	1552.10	1365.16	1225.44	1117.20	1031.00	960.83	902.67
100000	8583.68	4409.57	3019.60	2325.65	1910.12	1633.79	1437.01	1289.94	1176.00	1085.27	1011.40	950.18

Table 1

MONTHLY

5.50%

PAYMENT REQUIRED TO AMORTIZE A LOAN

TERM	13 YEARS	14 YEARS	15 YEARS	16 YEARS	17 YEARS	18 YEARS	19 YEARS	20 YEARS	25 YEARS	30 YEARS	35 YEARS	40 YEARS
AMOUNT												
50	.45	.43	.41	.40	.38	.37	.36	.35	.31	.29	.27	.26
100	.90	.86	.82	.79	.76	.74	.71	.69	.62	.57	.54	.52
200	1.80	1.71	1.64	1.57	1.52	1.47	1.42	1.38	1.23	1.14	1.08	1.04
300	2.70	2.57	2.46	2.36	2.27	2.20	2.13	2.07	1.85	1.71	1.62	1.55
400	3.60	3.42	3.27	3.14	3.03	2.93	2.84	2.76	2.46	2.28	2.15	2.07
500	4.50	4.28	4.09	3.93	3.78	3.66	3.54	3.44	3.08	2.84	2.69	2.58
600	5.40	5.13	4.91	4.71	4.54	4.39	4.25	4.13	3.69	3.41	3.23	3.10
700	6.30	5.99	5.72	5.50	5.29	5.12	4.96	4.82	4.30	3.98	3.76	3.62
800	7.19	6.84	6.54	6.28	6.05	5.85	5.67	5.51	4.92	4.55	4.30	4.13
900	8.09	7.70	7.36	7.06	6.81	6.58	6.38	6.20	5.53	5.12	4.84	4.65
1000	8.99	8.55	8.18	7.85	7.56	7.31	7.08	6.88	6.15	5.68	5.38	5.16
2000	17.98	17.10	16.35	15.69	15.12	14.61	14.16	13.76	12.29	11.36	10.75	10.32
3000	26.97	25.65	24.52	23.53	22.67	21.91	21.24	20.64	18.43	17.04	16.12	15.48
4000	35.95	34.20	32.69	31.38	30.23	29.22	28.32	27.52	24.57	22.72	21.49	20.64
5000	44.94	42.75	40.86	39.22	37.79	36.52	35.40	34.40	30.71	28.39	26.86	25.79
6000	53.93	51.29	49.03	47.06	45.34	43.82	42.48	41.28	36.85	34.07	32.23	30.95
7000	62.91	59.84	57.20	54.91	52.90	51.13	49.56	48.16	42.99	39.75	37.60	36.11
8000	71.90	68.39	65.37	62.75	60.45	58.43	56.64	55.04	49.13	45.43	42.97	41.27
9000	80.89	76.94	73.54	70.59	68.01	65.73	63.71	61.91	55.27	51.11	48.34	46.42
10000	89.87	85.49	81.71	78.44	75.57	73.04	70.79	68.79	61.41	56.78	53.71	51.58
11000	98.86	94.04	89.88	86.28	83.12	80.34	77.87	75.67	67.55	62.46	59.08	56.74
12000	107.85	102.58	98.06	94.12	90.68	87.64	84.95	82.55	73.70	68.14	64.45	61.90
13000	116.83	111.13	106.23	101.96	98.23	94.95	92.03	89.43	79.84	73.82	69.82	67.06
14000	125.82	119.68	114.40	109.81	105.79	102.25	99.11	96.31	85.98	79.50	75.19	72.21
15000	134.81	128.23	122.57	117.65	113.35	109.55	106.19	103.19	92.12	85.17	80.56	77.37
16000	143.79	136.78	130.74	125.49	120.90	116.86	113.27	110.07	98.26	90.85	85.93	82.53
17000	152.78	145.33	138.91	133.34	128.46	124.16	120.35	116.95	104.40	96.53	91.30	87.69
18000	161.77	153.87	147.08	141.18	136.01	131.46	127.42	123.82	110.54	102.21	96.67	92.84
19000	170.75	162.42	155.25	149.02	143.57	138.77	134.50	130.70	116.68	107.88	102.04	98.00
20000	179.74	170.97	163.42	156.87	151.13	146.07	141.58	137.58	122.82	113.56	107.41	103.16
21000	188.73	179.52	171.59	164.71	158.68	153.37	148.66	144.46	128.96	119.24	112.78	108.32
22000	197.71	188.07	179.76	172.55	166.24	160.67	155.74	151.34	135.10	124.92	118.15	113.47
23000	206.70	196.61	187.93	180.39	173.80	167.98	162.82	158.22	141.25	130.60	123.52	118.63
24000	215.69	205.16	196.11	188.24	181.35	175.28	169.90	165.10	147.39	136.27	128.89	123.79
25000	224.67	213.71	204.28	196.08	188.91	182.58	176.98	171.98	153.53	141.95	134.26	128.95
26000	233.66	222.26	212.45	203.92	196.46	189.89	184.06	178.86	159.67	147.63	139.63	134.11
27000	242.65	230.81	220.62	211.77	204.02	197.19	191.13	185.73	165.81	153.31	145.00	139.26
28000	251.63	239.36	228.79	219.61	211.58	204.49	198.21	192.61	171.95	158.99	150.37	144.42
29000	260.62	247.90	236.96	227.45	219.13	211.80	205.29	199.49	178.09	164.66	155.74	149.58
30000	269.61	256.45	245.13	235.30	226.69	219.10	212.37	206.37	184.23	170.34	161.11	154.74
31000	278.60	265.00	253.30	243.14	234.24	226.40	219.45	213.25	190.37	176.02	166.48	159.89
32000	287.58	273.55	261.47	250.98	241.80	233.71	226.53	220.13	196.51	181.70	171.85	165.05
33000	296.57	282.10	269.64	258.83	249.36	241.01	233.61	227.01	202.65	187.38	177.22	170.21
34000	305.56	290.65	277.81	266.67	256.91	248.31	240.69	233.89	208.79	193.05	182.59	175.37
35000	314.54	299.19	285.98	274.51	264.47	255.62	247.77	240.77	214.94	198.73	187.96	180.52
36000	323.53	307.74	294.16	282.35	272.02	262.92	254.84	247.64	221.08	204.41	193.33	185.68
37000	332.52	316.29	302.33	290.20	279.58	270.22	261.92	254.52	227.22	210.09	198.70	190.84
38000	341.50	324.84	310.50	298.04	287.14	277.53	269.00	261.40	233.36	215.76	204.07	196.00
39000	350.49	333.39	318.67	305.88	294.69	284.83	276.08	268.28	239.50	221.44	209.44	201.16
40000	359.48	341.94	326.84	313.73	302.25	292.13	283.16	275.16	245.64	227.12	214.81	206.31
41000	368.46	350.48	335.01	321.57	309.80	299.43	290.24	282.04	251.78	232.80	220.18	211.47
42000	377.45	359.03	343.18	329.41	317.36	306.74	297.32	288.92	257.92	238.48	225.55	216.63
43000	386.44	367.58	351.35	337.26	324.92	314.04	304.40	295.80	264.06	244.15	230.92	221.79
44000	395.42	376.13	359.52	345.10	332.47	321.34	311.47	302.68	270.20	249.83	236.29	226.94
45000	404.41	384.68	367.69	352.94	340.03	328.65	318.55	309.55	276.34	255.51	241.66	232.10
46000	413.40	393.22	375.86	360.78	347.59	335.95	325.63	316.43	282.49	261.19	247.03	237.26
47000	422.38	401.77	384.03	368.63	355.14	343.25	332.71	323.31	288.63	266.87	252.40	242.42
48000	431.37	410.32	392.21	376.47	362.70	350.56	339.79	330.19	294.77	272.54	257.77	247.57
49000	440.36	418.87	400.38	384.31	370.25	357.86	346.87	337.07	300.91	278.22	263.14	252.73
50000	449.34	427.42	408.55	392.16	377.81	365.16	353.95	343.95	307.05	283.90	268.51	257.89
55000	494.28	470.16	449.40	431.37	415.59	401.68	389.34	378.34	337.75	312.29	295.36	283.68
60000	539.21	512.90	490.26	470.59	453.37	438.19	424.74	412.74	368.46	340.68	322.21	309.47
65000	584.15	555.64	531.11	509.80	491.15	474.71	460.13	447.13	399.16	369.07	349.07	335.26
70000	629.08	598.38	571.96	549.02	528.93	511.23	495.53	481.53	429.87	397.46	375.92	361.04
75000	674.01	641.12	612.82	588.23	566.71	547.74	530.92	515.92	460.57	425.85	402.77	386.83
80000	718.95	683.87	653.67	627.45	604.49	584.26	566.31	550.31	491.27	454.24	429.62	412.62
85000	763.88	726.61	694.53	666.66	642.27	620.77	601.71	584.71	521.98	482.63	456.47	438.41
90000	808.82	769.35	735.38	705.88	680.05	657.29	637.10	619.10	552.68	511.02	483.32	464.20
95000	853.75	812.09	776.23	745.09	717.83	693.81	672.50	653.50	583.39	539.40	510.17	489.99
100000	898.68	854.83	817.09	784.31	755.61	730.32	707.89	687.89	614.09	567.79	537.02	515.78

Table 1

5.75%

MONTHLY
PAYMENT REQUIRED TO AMORTIZE A LOAN

TERM	1 YEAR	2 YEARS	3 YEARS	4 YEARS	5 YEARS	6 YEARS	7 YEARS	8 YEARS	9 YEARS	10 YEARS	11 YEARS	12 YEARS
AMOUNT												
50	4.30	2.22	1.52	1.17	.97	.83	.73	.66	.60	.55	.52	.49
100	8.60	4.43	3.04	2.34	1.93	1.65	1.45	1.31	1.19	1.10	1.03	.97
200	17.20	8.85	6.07	4.68	3.85	3.30	2.90	2.61	2.38	2.20	2.05	1.93
300	25.79	13.27	9.10	7.02	5.77	4.94	4.35	3.91	3.57	3.30	3.08	2.89
400	34.39	17.69	12.13	9.35	7.69	6.59	5.80	5.21	4.76	4.40	4.10	3.86
500	42.98	22.11	15.16	11.69	9.61	8.23	7.25	6.52	5.95	5.49	5.13	4.82
600	51.58	26.53	18.19	14.03	11.54	9.88	8.70	7.82	7.13	6.59	6.15	5.78
700	60.17	30.95	21.22	16.36	13.46	11.52	10.15	9.12	8.32	7.69	7.17	6.75
800	68.77	35.37	24.25	18.70	15.38	13.17	11.60	10.42	9.51	8.79	8.20	7.71
900	77.36	39.79	27.28	21.04	17.30	14.81	13.05	11.72	10.70	9.88	9.22	8.67
1000	85.96	44.21	30.31	23.38	19.22	16.46	14.49	13.03	11.89	10.98	10.25	9.63
2000	171.91	88.42	60.62	46.75	38.44	32.92	28.98	26.05	23.77	21.96	20.49	19.26
3000	257.86	132.63	90.93	70.12	57.66	49.37	43.47	39.07	35.65	32.94	30.73	28.89
4000	343.81	176.84	121.24	93.49	76.87	65.83	57.96	52.09	47.53	43.91	40.97	38.52
5000	429.76	221.05	151.55	116.86	96.09	82.28	72.45	65.11	59.42	54.89	51.21	48.15
6000	515.71	265.25	181.86	140.23	115.31	98.74	86.94	78.13	71.30	65.87	61.45	57.78
7000	601.67	309.46	212.17	163.60	134.52	115.19	101.43	91.15	83.18	76.84	71.69	67.41
8000	687.62	353.67	242.48	186.97	153.74	131.65	115.92	104.17	95.06	87.82	81.93	77.04
9000	773.57	397.88	272.78	210.34	172.96	148.10	130.41	117.19	106.95	98.80	92.17	86.67
10000	859.52	442.09	303.09	233.71	192.17	164.56	144.90	130.21	118.83	109.77	102.41	96.30
11000	945.47	486.29	333.40	257.08	211.39	181.01	159.38	143.23	130.71	120.75	112.65	105.93
12000	1031.42	530.50	363.71	280.45	230.61	197.47	173.87	156.25	142.59	131.73	122.89	115.56
13000	1117.38	574.71	394.02	303.82	249.82	213.92	188.36	169.27	154.48	142.70	133.13	125.19
14000	1203.33	618.92	424.33	327.19	269.04	230.38	202.85	182.29	166.36	153.68	143.37	134.82
15000	1289.28	663.13	454.64	350.56	288.26	246.83	217.34	195.31	178.24	164.66	153.61	144.45
16000	1375.23	707.33	484.95	373.93	307.47	263.29	231.83	208.33	190.12	175.64	163.85	154.08
17000	1461.18	751.54	515.25	397.30	326.69	279.74	246.32	221.35	202.01	186.61	174.09	163.71
18000	1547.13	795.75	545.56	420.68	345.91	296.20	260.81	234.37	213.89	197.59	184.33	173.34
19000	1633.08	839.96	575.87	444.05	365.12	312.65	275.30	247.39	225.77	208.57	194.57	182.97
20000	1719.04	884.17	606.18	467.42	384.34	329.11	289.79	260.41	237.65	219.54	204.81	192.60
21000	1804.99	928.37	636.49	490.79	403.56	345.56	304.27	273.43	249.54	230.52	215.05	202.23
22000	1890.94	972.58	666.80	514.16	422.77	362.02	318.76	286.45	261.42	241.50	225.29	211.86
23000	1976.89	1016.79	697.11	537.53	441.99	378.47	333.25	299.47	273.30	252.47	235.53	221.49
24000	2062.84	1061.00	727.42	560.90	461.21	394.93	347.74	312.49	285.18	263.45	245.77	231.12
25000	2148.79	1105.21	757.72	584.27	480.42	411.38	362.23	325.51	297.07	274.43	256.01	240.75
26000	2234.75	1149.41	788.03	607.64	499.64	427.84	376.72	338.53	308.95	285.40	266.25	250.38
27000	2320.70	1193.62	818.34	631.01	518.86	444.29	391.21	351.55	320.83	296.38	276.49	260.00
28000	2406.65	1237.83	848.65	654.38	538.07	460.75	405.70	364.57	332.71	307.36	286.73	269.63
29000	2492.60	1282.04	878.96	677.75	557.29	477.20	420.19	377.59	344.60	318.34	296.97	279.26
30000	2578.55	1326.25	909.27	701.12	576.51	493.66	434.68	390.61	356.48	329.31	307.21	288.89
31000	2664.50	1370.45	939.58	724.49	595.72	510.11	449.16	403.63	368.36	340.29	317.45	298.52
32000	2750.46	1414.66	969.89	747.86	614.94	526.57	463.65	416.65	380.24	351.27	327.69	308.15
33000	2836.41	1458.87	1000.20	771.23	634.16	543.02	478.14	429.67	392.13	362.24	337.93	317.78
34000	2922.36	1503.08	1030.50	794.60	653.38	559.48	492.63	442.69	404.01	373.22	348.17	327.41
35000	3008.31	1547.29	1060.81	817.98	672.59	575.93	507.12	455.71	415.89	384.20	358.41	337.04
36000	3094.26	1591.49	1091.12	841.35	691.81	592.39	521.61	468.73	427.77	395.17	368.65	346.67
37000	3180.21	1635.70	1121.43	864.72	711.03	608.84	536.10	481.75	439.66	406.15	378.89	356.30
38000	3266.16	1679.91	1151.74	888.09	730.24	625.30	550.59	494.77	451.54	417.13	389.13	365.93
39000	3352.12	1724.12	1182.05	911.46	749.46	641.76	565.08	507.79	463.42	428.10	399.37	375.56
40000	3438.07	1768.33	1212.36	934.83	768.68	658.21	579.57	520.81	475.30	439.08	409.61	385.19
41000	3524.02	1812.53	1242.67	958.20	787.89	674.67	594.05	533.83	487.19	450.06	419.85	394.82
42000	3609.97	1856.74	1272.97	981.57	807.11	691.12	608.54	546.85	499.07	461.04	430.09	404.45
43000	3695.92	1900.95	1303.28	1004.94	826.33	707.58	623.03	559.87	510.95	472.01	440.33	414.08
44000	3781.87	1945.16	1333.59	1028.31	845.54	724.03	637.52	572.89	522.83	482.99	450.57	423.71
45000	3867.83	1989.37	1363.90	1051.68	864.76	740.49	652.01	585.91	534.72	493.97	460.81	433.34
46000	3953.78	2033.58	1394.21	1075.05	883.98	756.94	666.50	598.93	546.60	504.94	471.05	442.97
47000	4039.73	2077.78	1424.52	1098.42	903.19	773.40	680.99	611.95	558.48	515.92	481.29	452.60
48000	4125.68	2121.99	1454.83	1121.79	922.41	789.85	695.48	624.97	570.36	526.90	491.53	462.23
49000	4211.63	2166.20	1485.14	1145.16	941.63	806.31	709.97	637.99	582.25	537.87	501.77	471.86
50000	4297.58	2210.41	1515.44	1168.53	960.84	822.76	724.46	651.01	594.13	548.85	512.01	481.49
55000	4727.34	2431.45	1666.99	1285.39	1056.93	905.04	796.90	716.11	653.54	603.74	563.21	529.63
60000	5157.10	2652.49	1818.53	1402.24	1153.01	987.31	869.35	781.21	712.95	658.62	614.41	577.78
65000	5586.86	2873.53	1970.08	1519.09	1249.09	1069.59	941.79	846.31	772.37	713.50	665.61	625.93
70000	6016.61	3094.57	2121.62	1635.95	1345.18	1151.86	1014.24	911.41	831.78	768.39	716.81	674.08
75000	6446.37	3315.61	2273.16	1752.80	1441.26	1234.14	1086.68	976.51	891.19	823.27	768.01	722.23
80000	6876.13	3536.65	2424.71	1869.65	1537.35	1316.42	1159.13	1041.61	950.60	878.16	819.21	770.37
85000	7305.89	3757.69	2576.25	1986.50	1633.43	1398.69	1231.57	1106.71	1010.02	933.04	870.41	818.52
90000	7735.65	3978.73	2727.80	2103.36	1729.51	1480.97	1304.02	1171.81	1069.43	987.93	921.61	866.67
95000	8165.40	4199.77	2879.34	2220.21	1825.60	1563.24	1376.46	1236.91	1128.84	1042.81	972.81	914.82
100000	8595.16	4420.81	3030.88	2337.06	1921.68	1645.52	1448.91	1302.01	1188.25	1097.70	1024.01	962.97

Table 1

MONTHLY   5.75%

PAYMENT REQUIRED TO AMORTIZE A LOAN

TERM / AMOUNT	13 YEARS	14 YEARS	15 YEARS	16 YEARS	17 YEARS	18 YEARS	19 YEARS	20 YEARS	25 YEARS	30 YEARS	35 YEARS	40 YEARS
50	.46	.44	.42	.40	.39	.38	.37	.36	.32	.30	.28	.27
100	.92	.87	.84	.80	.77	.75	.73	.71	.63	.59	.56	.54
200	1.83	1.74	1.67	1.60	1.54	1.49	1.45	1.41	1.26	1.17	1.11	1.07
300	2.74	2.61	2.50	2.40	2.31	2.24	2.17	2.11	1.89	1.76	1.67	1.60
400	3.65	3.48	3.33	3.20	3.08	2.98	2.89	2.81	2.52	2.34	2.22	2.14
500	4.56	4.34	4.16	3.99	3.85	3.73	3.61	3.52	3.15	2.92	2.77	2.67
600	5.47	5.21	4.99	4.79	4.62	4.47	4.34	4.22	3.78	3.51	3.33	3.20
700	6.39	6.08	5.82	5.59	5.39	5.21	5.06	4.92	4.41	4.09	3.88	3.74
800	7.30	6.95	6.65	6.39	6.16	5.96	5.78	5.62	5.04	4.67	4.43	4.27
900	8.21	7.82	7.48	7.19	6.93	6.70	6.50	6.32	5.67	5.26	4.99	4.80
1000	9.12	8.68	8.31	7.98	7.70	7.45	7.22	7.03	6.30	5.84	5.54	5.33
2000	18.24	17.36	16.61	15.96	15.39	14.89	14.44	14.05	12.59	11.68	11.08	10.66
3000	27.35	26.04	24.92	23.94	23.08	22.33	21.66	21.07	18.88	17.51	16.61	15.99
4000	36.47	34.72	33.22	31.92	30.78	29.77	28.88	28.09	25.17	23.35	22.15	21.32
5000	45.59	43.40	41.53	39.90	38.47	37.21	36.10	35.11	31.46	29.18	27.68	26.65
6000	54.70	52.08	49.83	47.87	46.16	44.66	43.32	42.13	37.75	35.02	33.22	31.98
7000	63.82	60.76	58.13	55.85	53.86	52.10	50.54	49.15	44.04	40.86	38.75	37.31
8000	72.94	69.44	66.44	63.83	61.55	59.54	57.76	56.17	50.33	46.69	44.29	42.64
9000	82.05	78.12	74.74	71.81	69.24	66.98	64.98	63.19	56.62	52.53	49.82	47.96
10000	91.17	86.80	83.05	79.79	76.93	74.42	72.20	70.21	62.92	58.36	55.36	53.29
11000	100.29	95.48	91.35	87.76	84.63	81.86	79.42	77.23	69.21	64.20	60.89	58.62
12000	109.40	104.16	99.65	95.74	92.32	89.31	86.63	84.26	75.50	70.03	66.43	63.95
13000	118.52	112.84	107.96	103.72	100.01	96.75	93.85	91.28	81.79	75.87	71.96	69.28
14000	127.64	121.52	116.26	111.70	107.71	104.19	100.07	98.30	88.08	81.71	77.50	74.61
15000	136.75	130.20	124.57	119.68	115.40	111.63	108.29	105.32	94.37	87.54	83.03	79.94
16000	145.87	138.88	132.87	127.65	123.09	119.07	115.51	112.34	100.66	93.38	88.57	85.27
17000	154.99	147.56	141.17	135.63	130.78	126.51	122.73	119.36	106.95	99.21	94.10	90.60
18000	164.10	156.24	149.48	143.61	138.48	133.96	129.95	126.38	113.24	105.05	99.64	95.92
19000	173.22	164.92	157.78	151.59	146.17	141.40	137.17	133.40	119.54	110.88	105.17	101.25
20000	182.33	173.60	166.09	159.57	153.86	148.84	144.39	140.42	125.83	116.72	110.71	106.58
21000	191.45	182.28	174.39	167.54	161.56	156.28	151.61	147.44	132.12	122.56	116.24	111.91
22000	200.57	190.96	182.70	175.52	169.25	163.72	158.83	154.46	138.41	128.39	121.78	117.24
23000	209.68	199.64	191.00	183.50	176.94	171.16	166.04	161.48	144.70	134.23	127.31	122.57
24000	218.80	208.32	199.30	191.48	184.63	178.61	173.26	168.51	150.99	140.06	132.85	127.90
25000	227.92	217.00	207.61	199.46	192.33	186.05	180.48	175.53	157.28	145.90	138.38	133.23
26000	237.03	225.68	215.91	207.43	200.02	193.49	187.70	182.55	163.57	151.73	143.92	138.56
27000	246.15	234.36	224.22	215.41	207.71	200.93	194.92	189.57	169.86	157.57	149.45	143.88
28000	255.27	243.04	232.52	223.39	215.41	208.37	202.14	196.59	176.15	163.41	154.99	149.21
29000	264.38	251.72	240.82	231.37	223.10	215.81	209.36	203.61	182.45	169.24	160.52	154.54
30000	273.50	260.40	249.13	239.35	230.79	223.26	216.58	210.63	188.74	175.08	166.06	159.87
31000	282.62	269.08	257.43	247.33	238.48	230.70	223.80	217.65	195.03	180.91	171.59	165.20
32000	291.73	277.76	265.74	255.30	246.18	238.14	231.02	224.67	201.32	186.75	177.13	170.53
33000	300.85	286.44	274.04	263.28	253.87	245.58	238.24	231.69	207.61	192.58	182.66	175.86
34000	309.97	295.12	282.34	271.26	261.56	253.02	245.46	238.71	213.90	198.42	188.20	181.19
35000	319.08	303.80	290.65	279.24	269.26	260.46	252.67	245.73	220.19	204.26	193.73	186.52
36000	328.20	312.48	298.95	287.22	276.95	267.91	259.89	252.76	226.48	210.09	199.27	191.84
37000	337.31	321.16	307.26	295.19	284.64	275.35	267.11	259.78	232.77	215.93	204.80	197.17
38000	346.43	329.84	315.56	303.17	292.33	282.79	274.33	266.80	239.07	221.76	210.34	202.50
39000	355.55	338.51	323.86	311.15	300.03	290.23	281.55	273.82	245.36	227.60	215.87	207.83
40000	364.66	347.19	332.17	319.13	307.72	297.67	288.77	280.84	251.65	233.43	221.41	213.16
41000	373.78	355.87	340.47	327.11	315.41	305.11	295.99	287.86	257.94	239.27	226.94	218.49
42000	382.90	364.55	348.78	335.08	323.11	312.56	303.21	294.88	264.23	245.11	232.48	223.82
43000	392.01	373.23	357.08	343.06	330.80	320.00	310.43	301.90	270.52	250.94	238.01	229.15
44000	401.13	381.91	365.39	351.04	338.49	327.44	317.65	308.92	276.81	256.78	243.55	234.48
45000	410.25	390.59	373.69	359.02	346.18	334.88	324.87	315.94	283.10	262.61	249.08	239.80
46000	419.36	399.27	381.99	367.00	353.88	342.32	332.08	322.96	289.39	268.45	254.62	245.13
47000	428.48	407.95	390.30	374.97	361.57	349.76	339.30	329.98	295.69	274.28	260.15	250.46
48000	437.60	416.63	398.60	382.95	369.26	357.21	346.52	337.01	301.98	280.12	265.69	255.79
49000	446.71	425.31	406.91	390.93	376.96	364.65	353.74	344.03	308.27	285.96	271.22	261.12
50000	455.83	433.99	415.21	398.91	384.65	372.09	360.96	351.05	314.56	291.79	276.76	266.45
55000	501.41	477.39	456.73	438.80	423.11	409.30	397.06	386.15	346.01	320.97	304.43	293.09
60000	546.99	520.79	498.25	478.69	461.58	446.51	433.15	421.26	377.47	350.15	332.11	319.74
65000	592.58	564.19	539.77	518.58	500.04	483.72	469.25	456.36	408.92	379.33	359.78	346.38
70000	638.16	607.59	581.29	558.47	538.51	520.92	505.34	491.46	440.38	408.51	387.46	373.03
75000	683.74	650.99	622.81	598.36	576.97	558.13	541.44	526.57	471.83	437.68	415.13	399.67
80000	729.32	694.38	664.33	638.25	615.44	595.34	577.53	561.67	503.29	466.86	442.81	426.32
85000	774.91	737.78	705.85	678.15	653.90	632.55	613.63	596.78	534.75	496.04	470.48	452.96
90000	820.49	781.18	747.37	718.03	692.36	669.76	649.73	631.88	566.20	525.22	498.16	479.60
95000	866.07	824.58	788.89	757.92	730.83	706.97	685.82	666.98	597.66	554.40	525.83	506.25
100000	911.65	867.98	830.42	797.81	769.29	744.17	721.92	702.09	629.11	583.58	553.51	532.89

Table 1

6%

6.00%

MONTHLY
PAYMENT REQUIRED TO AMORTIZE A LOAN

AMOUNT	1 YEAR	2 YEARS	3 YEARS	4 YEARS	5 YEARS	6 YEARS	7 YEARS	8 YEARS	9 YEARS	10 YEARS	11 YEARS	12 YEARS
50	4.31	2.22	1.53	1.18	.97	.83	.74	.66	.61	.56	.52	.49
100	8.61	4.44	3.05	2.35	1.94	1.66	1.47	1.32	1.21	1.12	1.04	.98
200	17.22	8.87	6.09	4.70	3.87	3.32	2.93	2.63	2.41	2.23	2.08	1.96
300	25.82	13.30	9.13	7.05	5.80	4.98	4.39	3.95	3.61	3.34	3.12	2.93
400	34.43	17.73	12.17	9.40	7.74	6.63	5.85	5.26	4.81	4.45	4.15	3.91
500	43.04	22.17	15.22	11.75	9.67	8.29	7.31	6.58	6.01	5.56	5.19	4.88
600	51.64	26.60	18.26	14.10	11.60	9.95	8.77	7.89	7.21	6.67	6.23	5.86
700	60.25	31.03	21.30	16.44	13.54	11.61	10.23	9.20	8.41	7.78	7.26	6.84
800	68.86	35.46	24.34	18.79	15.47	13.26	11.69	10.52	9.61	8.89	8.30	7.81
900	77.46	39.89	27.38	21.14	17.40	14.92	13.15	11.83	10.81	10.00	9.34	8.79
1000	86.07	44.33	30.43	23.49	19.34	16.58	14.61	13.15	12.01	11.11	10.37	9.76
2000	172.14	88.65	60.85	46.98	38.67	33.15	29.22	26.29	24.02	22.21	20.74	19.52
3000	258.20	132.97	91.27	70.46	58.00	49.72	43.83	39.43	36.02	33.31	31.11	29.28
4000	344.27	177.29	121.69	93.95	77.34	66.30	58.44	52.57	48.03	44.41	41.47	39.04
5000	430.34	221.61	152.11	117.43	96.67	82.87	73.05	65.71	60.03	55.52	51.84	48.80
6000	516.40	265.93	182.54	140.92	116.00	99.44	87.66	78.85	72.04	66.62	62.21	58.56
7000	602.47	310.25	212.96	164.40	135.33	116.02	102.26	92.00	84.05	77.72	72.57	68.31
8000	688.54	354.57	243.38	187.89	154.67	132.59	116.87	105.14	96.05	88.82	82.94	78.07
9000	774.60	398.89	273.80	211.37	174.00	149.16	131.48	118.28	108.06	99.92	93.31	87.83
10000	860.67	443.21	304.22	234.86	193.33	165.73	146.09	131.42	120.06	111.03	103.68	97.59
11000	946.74	487.53	334.65	258.34	212.67	182.31	160.70	144.56	132.07	122.13	114.04	107.35
12000	1032.80	531.85	365.07	281.83	232.00	198.88	175.31	157.70	144.07	133.23	124.41	117.11
13000	1118.87	576.17	395.49	305.31	251.33	215.45	189.92	170.84	156.08	144.33	134.78	126.87
14000	1204.94	620.49	425.91	328.80	270.66	232.03	204.52	183.99	168.09	155.43	145.14	136.62
15000	1291.00	664.81	456.33	352.28	290.00	248.60	219.13	197.13	180.09	166.54	155.51	146.38
16000	1377.07	709.13	486.76	375.77	309.33	265.17	233.74	210.27	192.10	177.64	165.88	156.14
17000	1463.13	753.46	517.18	399.25	328.66	281.74	248.35	223.41	204.10	188.74	176.24	165.90
18000	1549.20	797.78	547.60	422.74	348.00	298.32	262.96	236.55	216.11	199.84	186.61	175.66
19000	1635.27	842.10	578.02	446.22	367.33	314.89	277.57	249.69	228.11	210.94	196.98	185.42
20000	1721.33	886.42	608.44	469.71	386.66	331.46	292.18	262.83	240.12	222.05	207.35	195.18
21000	1807.40	930.74	638.87	493.19	405.99	348.04	306.78	275.98	252.13	233.15	217.71	204.93
22000	1893.47	975.06	669.29	516.68	425.33	364.61	321.39	289.12	264.13	244.25	228.08	214.69
23000	1979.53	1019.38	699.71	540.16	444.66	381.18	336.00	302.26	276.14	255.35	238.45	224.45
24000	2065.60	1063.70	730.13	563.65	463.99	397.75	350.61	315.40	288.14	266.45	248.81	234.21
25000	2151.67	1108.02	760.55	587.13	483.33	414.33	365.22	328.54	300.15	277.56	259.18	243.97
26000	2237.73	1152.34	790.98	610.62	502.66	430.90	379.83	341.68	312.15	288.66	269.55	253.73
27000	2323.80	1196.66	821.40	634.10	521.99	447.47	394.44	354.82	324.16	299.76	279.91	263.48
28000	2409.87	1240.98	851.82	657.59	541.32	464.05	409.04	367.97	336.17	310.86	290.28	273.24
29000	2495.93	1285.30	882.24	681.07	560.66	480.62	423.65	381.11	348.17	321.96	300.65	283.00
30000	2582.00	1329.62	912.66	704.56	579.99	497.19	438.26	394.25	360.18	333.07	311.02	292.76
31000	2668.06	1373.94	943.09	728.04	599.32	513.76	452.87	407.39	372.18	344.17	321.38	302.52
32000	2754.13	1418.26	973.51	751.53	618.65	530.34	467.48	420.53	384.19	355.27	331.75	312.28
33000	2840.20	1462.59	1003.93	775.01	637.99	546.91	482.09	433.67	396.19	366.37	342.12	322.04
34000	2926.26	1506.91	1034.35	798.50	657.32	563.48	496.70	446.81	408.20	377.47	352.48	331.79
35000	3012.33	1551.23	1064.77	821.98	676.65	580.06	511.30	459.96	420.21	388.58	362.85	341.55
36000	3098.40	1595.55	1095.19	845.47	695.99	596.63	525.91	473.10	432.21	399.68	373.22	351.31
37000	3184.46	1639.87	1125.62	868.95	715.32	613.20	540.52	486.24	444.22	410.78	383.59	361.07
38000	3270.53	1684.19	1156.04	892.44	734.65	629.77	555.13	499.38	456.22	421.88	393.95	370.83
39000	3356.60	1728.51	1186.46	915.92	753.98	646.35	569.74	512.52	468.23	432.98	404.32	380.59
40000	3442.66	1772.83	1216.88	939.41	773.32	662.92	584.35	525.66	480.23	444.09	414.69	390.35
41000	3528.73	1817.15	1247.30	962.89	792.65	679.49	598.96	538.80	492.24	455.19	425.05	400.10
42000	3614.80	1861.47	1277.73	986.38	811.98	696.07	613.56	551.95	504.25	466.29	435.42	409.86
43000	3700.86	1905.79	1308.15	1009.86	831.32	712.64	628.17	565.09	516.25	477.39	445.79	419.62
44000	3786.93	1950.11	1338.57	1033.35	850.65	729.21	642.78	578.23	528.26	488.50	456.15	429.38
45000	3872.99	1994.43	1368.99	1056.83	869.98	745.78	657.39	591.37	540.26	499.60	466.52	439.14
46000	3959.06	2038.75	1399.41	1080.32	889.31	762.36	672.00	604.51	552.27	510.70	476.89	448.90
47000	4045.13	2083.07	1429.84	1103.80	908.65	778.93	686.61	617.65	564.28	521.80	487.26	458.65
48000	4131.19	2127.39	1460.26	1127.29	927.98	795.50	701.22	630.79	576.28	532.90	497.62	468.41
49000	4217.26	2171.71	1490.68	1150.77	947.31	812.08	715.82	643.94	588.29	544.01	507.99	478.17
50000	4303.33	2216.04	1521.10	1174.26	966.65	828.65	730.43	657.08	600.29	555.11	518.36	487.93
55000	4733.66	2437.64	1673.21	1291.68	1063.31	911.51	803.48	722.78	660.32	610.62	570.19	536.72
60000	5163.99	2659.24	1825.32	1409.11	1159.97	994.38	876.52	788.49	720.35	666.13	622.03	585.52
65000	5594.32	2880.84	1977.43	1526.53	1256.64	1077.24	949.56	854.20	780.38	721.64	673.86	634.31
70000	6024.66	3102.45	2129.54	1643.96	1353.30	1160.11	1022.60	919.91	840.41	777.15	725.70	683.10
75000	6454.99	3324.05	2281.65	1761.38	1449.97	1242.97	1095.65	985.61	900.44	832.66	777.53	731.89
80000	6885.32	3545.65	2433.76	1878.81	1546.63	1325.84	1168.69	1051.32	960.46	888.17	829.37	780.69
85000	7315.65	3767.26	2585.87	1996.23	1643.29	1408.70	1241.73	1117.03	1020.49	943.68	881.20	829.48
90000	7745.98	3988.86	2737.98	2113.66	1739.96	1491.56	1314.77	1182.73	1080.52	999.19	933.04	878.27
95000	8176.32	4210.46	2890.09	2231.08	1836.62	1574.43	1387.82	1248.44	1140.55	1054.70	984.87	927.06
100000	8606.65	4432.07	3042.20	2348.51	1933.29	1657.29	1460.86	1314.15	1200.58	1110.21	1036.71	975.86

Table 1

MONTHLY

6.00%

PAYMENT REQUIRED TO AMORTIZE A LOAN

TERM / AMOUNT	13 YEARS	14 YEARS	15 YEARS	16 YEARS	17 YEARS	18 YEARS	19 YEARS	20 YEARS	25 YEARS	30 YEARS	35 YEARS	40 YEARS
50	.47	.45	.43	.41	.40	.38	.37	.36	.33	.30	.29	.28
100	.93	.89	.85	.82	.79	.76	.74	.72	.65	.60	.58	.56
200	1.85	1.77	1.69	1.63	1.57	1.52	1.48	1.44	1.29	1.20	1.15	1.11
300	2.78	2.65	2.54	2.44	2.35	2.28	2.21	2.15	1.94	1.80	1.72	1.66
400	3.70	3.53	3.38	3.25	3.14	3.04	2.95	2.87	2.58	2.40	2.29	2.21
500	4.63	4.41	4.22	4.06	3.92	3.80	3.69	3.59	3.23	3.00	2.86	2.76
600	5.55	5.29	5.07	4.87	4.70	4.55	4.42	4.30	3.87	3.60	3.43	3.31
700	6.48	6.17	5.91	5.69	5.49	5.31	5.16	5.02	4.52	4.20	4.00	3.86
800	7.40	7.05	6.76	6.50	6.27	6.07	5.89	5.74	5.16	4.80	4.57	4.41
900	8.33	7.94	7.60	7.31	7.05	6.83	6.63	6.45	5.80	5.40	5.14	4.96
1000	9.25	8.82	8.44	8.12	7.84	7.59	7.37	7.17	6.45	6.00	5.71	5.51
2000	18.50	17.63	16.88	16.23	15.67	15.17	14.73	14.33	12.89	12.00	11.41	11.01
3000	27.75	26.44	25.32	24.35	23.50	22.75	22.09	21.50	19.33	17.99	17.11	16.51
4000	36.99	35.25	33.76	32.46	31.33	30.33	29.45	28.66	25.78	23.99	22.81	22.01
5000	46.24	44.07	42.20	40.58	39.16	37.91	36.81	35.83	32.22	29.98	28.51	27.52
6000	55.49	52.88	50.64	48.69	46.99	45.49	44.17	42.99	38.66	35.98	34.22	33.02
7000	64.74	61.69	59.07	56.81	54.82	53.08	51.53	50.16	45.11	41.97	39.92	38.52
8000	73.98	70.50	67.51	64.92	62.65	60.66	58.89	57.32	51.55	47.97	45.62	44.02
9000	83.23	79.32	75.95	73.03	70.48	68.24	66.25	64.48	57.99	53.96	51.32	49.52
10000	92.48	88.13	84.39	81.15	78.32	75.82	73.61	71.65	64.44	59.96	57.02	55.03
11000	101.72	96.94	92.83	89.26	86.15	83.40	80.97	78.81	70.88	65.96	62.73	60.53
12000	110.97	105.75	101.27	97.38	93.98	90.98	88.33	85.98	77.32	71.95	68.43	66.03
13000	120.22	114.57	109.71	105.49	101.81	98.57	95.70	93.14	83.76	77.95	74.13	71.53
14000	129.47	123.38	118.14	113.61	109.64	106.15	103.06	100.31	90.21	83.94	79.83	77.03
15000	138.71	132.19	126.58	121.72	117.47	113.73	110.42	107.47	96.65	89.94	85.53	82.54
16000	147.96	141.00	135.02	129.84	125.30	121.31	117.78	114.63	103.09	95.93	91.24	88.04
17000	157.21	149.82	143.46	137.95	133.13	128.89	125.14	121.80	109.54	101.93	96.94	93.54
18000	166.46	158.63	151.90	146.06	140.96	136.47	132.50	128.96	115.98	107.92	102.64	99.04
19000	175.70	167.44	160.34	154.18	148.79	144.06	139.86	136.13	122.42	113.92	108.34	104.55
20000	184.95	176.25	168.78	162.29	156.63	151.64	147.22	143.29	128.87	119.92	114.04	110.05
21000	194.20	185.06	177.21	170.41	164.46	159.22	154.58	150.46	135.31	125.91	119.74	115.55
22000	203.44	193.88	185.65	178.52	172.29	166.80	161.94	157.62	141.75	131.91	125.45	121.05
23000	212.69	202.69	194.09	186.64	180.12	174.38	169.30	164.78	148.19	137.90	131.15	126.55
24000	221.94	211.50	202.53	194.75	187.95	181.96	176.66	171.95	154.64	143.90	136.85	132.06
25000	231.19	220.31	210.97	202.86	195.78	189.55	184.03	179.11	161.08	149.89	142.55	137.56
26000	240.43	229.13	219.41	210.98	203.61	197.13	191.39	186.28	167.52	155.89	148.25	143.06
27000	249.68	237.94	227.85	219.09	211.44	204.71	198.75	193.44	173.97	161.88	153.96	148.56
28000	258.93	246.75	236.28	227.21	219.27	212.29	206.11	200.61	180.41	167.88	159.66	154.06
29000	268.17	255.56	244.72	235.32	227.10	219.87	213.47	207.77	186.85	173.87	165.36	159.57
30000	277.42	264.38	253.16	243.44	234.94	227.45	220.83	214.93	193.30	179.87	171.06	165.07
31000	286.67	273.19	261.60	251.55	242.77	235.04	228.19	222.10	199.74	185.87	176.76	170.57
32000	295.92	282.00	270.04	259.67	250.60	242.62	235.55	229.26	206.18	191.86	182.47	176.07
33000	305.16	290.81	278.48	267.78	258.43	250.20	242.91	236.43	212.62	197.86	188.17	181.58
34000	314.41	299.63	286.92	275.89	266.26	257.78	250.27	243.59	219.07	203.85	193.87	187.08
35000	323.66	308.44	295.35	284.01	274.09	265.36	257.63	250.76	225.51	209.85	199.57	192.58
36000	332.91	317.25	303.79	292.12	281.92	272.94	264.99	257.92	231.95	215.84	205.27	198.08
37000	342.15	326.06	312.23	300.24	289.75	280.53	272.36	265.08	238.40	221.84	210.98	203.58
38000	351.40	334.87	320.67	308.35	297.58	288.11	279.72	272.25	244.84	227.83	216.68	209.09
39000	360.65	343.69	329.11	316.47	305.41	295.69	287.08	279.41	251.28	233.83	222.38	214.59
40000	369.89	352.50	337.55	324.58	313.25	303.27	294.44	286.58	257.73	239.83	228.08	220.09
41000	379.14	361.31	345.99	332.69	321.08	310.85	301.80	293.74	264.17	245.82	233.78	225.59
42000	388.39	370.12	354.42	340.81	328.91	318.43	309.16	300.91	270.61	251.82	239.48	231.09
43000	397.64	378.94	362.86	348.92	336.74	326.01	316.52	308.07	277.05	257.81	245.19	236.60
44000	406.88	387.75	371.30	357.04	344.57	333.60	323.88	315.23	283.50	263.81	250.89	242.10
45000	416.13	396.56	379.74	365.15	352.40	341.18	331.24	322.40	289.94	269.80	256.59	247.60
46000	425.38	405.37	388.18	373.27	360.23	348.76	338.60	329.56	296.38	275.80	262.29	253.10
47000	434.63	414.19	396.62	381.38	368.06	356.34	345.96	336.73	302.83	281.79	267.99	258.61
48000	443.87	423.00	405.06	389.50	375.89	363.92	353.32	343.89	309.27	287.79	273.70	264.11
49000	453.12	431.81	413.49	397.61	383.72	371.50	360.69	351.06	315.71	293.78	279.40	269.61
50000	462.37	440.62	421.93	405.72	391.56	379.09	368.05	358.22	322.16	299.78	285.10	275.11
55000	508.60	484.68	464.13	446.30	430.71	416.99	404.85	394.04	354.37	329.76	313.61	302.62
60000	554.84	528.75	506.32	486.87	469.87	454.90	441.65	429.86	386.59	359.74	342.12	330.13
65000	601.08	572.81	548.51	527.44	509.02	492.81	478.46	465.69	418.80	389.71	370.63	357.64
70000	647.31	616.87	590.70	568.01	548.18	530.72	515.26	501.51	451.02	419.69	399.14	385.15
75000	693.55	660.93	632.90	608.58	587.33	568.63	552.07	537.33	483.23	449.67	427.65	412.67
80000	739.78	704.99	675.09	649.16	626.49	606.53	588.87	573.15	515.45	479.65	456.16	440.18
85000	786.02	749.06	717.28	689.73	665.64	644.44	625.68	608.97	547.66	509.62	484.67	467.69
90000	832.26	793.12	759.48	730.30	704.80	682.35	662.48	644.79	579.88	539.60	513.18	495.20
95000	878.49	837.18	801.67	770.87	743.95	720.26	699.28	680.61	612.09	569.58	541.69	522.71
100000	924.73	881.24	843.86	811.44	783.11	758.17	736.09	716.44	644.31	599.56	570.19	550.22

Table 1

MONTHLY

6%

6.25%

PAYMENT REQUIRED TO AMORTIZE A LOAN

TERM / AMOUNT	1 YEAR	2 YEARS	3 YEARS	4 YEARS	5 YEARS	6 YEARS	7 YEARS	8 YEARS	9 YEARS	10 YEARS	11 YEARS	12 YEARS
50	4.31	2.23	1.53	1.18	.98	.84	.74	.67	.61	.57	.53	.50
100	8.62	4.45	3.06	2.36	1.95	1.67	1.48	1.33	1.22	1.13	1.05	.99
200	17.24	8.89	6.11	4.72	3.89	3.34	2.95	2.66	2.43	2.25	2.10	1.98
300	25.86	13.34	9.17	7.08	5.84	5.01	4.42	3.98	3.64	3.37	3.15	2.97
400	34.48	17.78	12.22	9.44	7.78	6.68	5.90	5.31	4.86	4.50	4.20	3.96
500	43.10	22.22	15.27	11.80	9.73	8.35	7.37	6.64	6.07	5.62	5.25	4.95
600	51.71	26.67	18.33	14.16	11.67	10.02	8.84	7.96	7.28	6.74	6.30	5.94
700	60.33	31.11	21.38	16.52	13.62	11.69	10.32	9.29	8.50	7.86	7.35	6.93
800	68.95	35.55	24.43	18.88	15.56	13.36	11.79	10.62	9.71	8.99	8.40	7.92
900	77.57	40.00	27.49	21.24	17.51	15.03	13.26	11.94	10.92	10.11	9.45	8.90
1000	86.19	44.44	30.54	23.60	19.45	16.70	14.73	13.27	12.13	11.23	10.50	9.89
2000	172.37	88.87	61.08	47.20	38.90	33.39	29.46	26.53	24.26	22.46	20.99	19.78
3000	258.55	133.31	91.61	70.80	58.35	50.08	44.19	39.80	36.39	33.69	31.49	29.67
4000	344.73	177.74	122.15	94.40	77.80	66.77	58.92	53.06	48.52	44.92	41.98	39.56
5000	430.91	222.17	152.68	118.00	97.25	83.46	73.65	66.32	60.65	56.15	52.48	49.45
6000	517.09	266.61	183.22	141.60	116.70	100.15	88.38	79.59	72.78	67.37	62.97	59.34
7000	603.27	311.04	213.75	165.20	136.15	116.84	103.11	92.85	84.91	78.60	73.47	69.22
8000	689.46	355.47	244.29	188.80	155.60	133.53	117.83	106.11	97.04	89.83	83.96	79.11
9000	775.64	399.91	274.82	212.40	175.05	150.23	132.56	119.38	109.17	101.06	94.46	89.00
10000	861.82	444.34	305.36	236.00	194.50	166.92	147.29	132.64	121.30	112.29	104.95	98.89
11000	948.00	488.77	335.89	259.60	213.95	183.61	162.02	145.90	133.43	123.51	115.45	108.78
12000	1034.18	533.21	366.43	283.20	233.40	200.30	176.75	159.17	145.56	134.74	125.94	118.67
13000	1120.36	577.64	396.96	306.80	252.85	216.99	191.48	172.43	157.69	145.97	136.44	128.55
14000	1206.54	622.07	427.50	330.40	272.29	233.68	206.21	185.69	169.82	157.20	146.93	138.44
15000	1292.73	666.51	458.04	354.00	291.74	250.37	220.94	198.96	181.95	168.43	157.43	148.33
16000	1378.91	710.94	488.57	377.60	311.19	267.06	235.66	212.22	194.08	179.65	167.92	158.22
17000	1465.09	755.37	519.11	401.20	330.64	283.75	250.39	225.48	206.21	190.88	178.42	168.11
18000	1551.27	799.81	549.64	424.80	350.09	300.45	265.12	238.75	218.34	202.11	188.91	178.00
19000	1637.45	844.24	580.18	448.40	369.54	317.14	279.85	252.01	230.47	213.34	199.41	187.88
20000	1723.63	888.67	610.71	472.00	388.99	333.83	294.58	265.27	242.60	224.57	209.90	197.77
21000	1809.81	933.11	641.25	495.60	408.44	350.52	309.31	278.54	254.73	235.79	220.40	207.66
22000	1896.00	977.54	671.78	519.20	427.89	367.21	324.04	291.80	266.86	247.02	230.89	217.55
23000	1982.18	1021.97	702.32	542.80	447.34	383.90	338.77	305.07	278.99	258.25	241.39	227.44
24000	2068.36	1066.41	732.85	566.40	466.79	400.59	353.49	318.33	291.12	269.48	251.88	237.33
25000	2154.54	1110.84	763.39	590.00	486.24	417.28	368.22	331.59	303.25	280.71	262.38	247.21
26000	2240.72	1155.27	793.92	613.60	505.69	433.98	382.95	344.86	315.38	291.93	272.87	257.10
27000	2326.90	1199.71	824.46	637.20	525.14	450.67	397.68	358.12	327.51	303.16	283.37	266.99
28000	2413.08	1244.14	854.99	660.80	544.58	467.36	412.41	371.38	339.64	314.39	293.86	276.88
29000	2499.27	1288.57	885.53	684.40	564.03	484.05	427.14	384.65	351.77	325.62	304.36	286.77
30000	2585.45	1333.01	916.07	708.00	583.48	500.74	441.87	397.91	363.90	336.85	314.85	296.66
31000	2671.63	1377.44	946.60	731.60	602.93	517.43	456.59	411.17	376.03	348.07	325.35	306.54
32000	2757.81	1421.87	977.14	755.20	622.38	534.12	471.32	424.44	388.16	359.30	335.84	316.43
33000	2843.99	1466.31	1007.67	778.80	641.83	550.81	486.05	437.70	400.29	370.53	346.34	326.32
34000	2930.17	1510.74	1038.21	802.40	661.28	567.50	500.78	450.96	412.42	381.76	356.83	336.21
35000	3016.35	1555.17	1068.74	826.00	680.73	584.20	515.51	464.23	424.55	392.99	367.33	346.10
36000	3102.53	1599.61	1099.28	849.60	700.18	600.89	530.24	477.49	436.68	404.21	377.82	355.99
37000	3188.72	1644.04	1129.81	873.20	719.63	617.58	544.97	490.75	448.81	415.44	388.32	365.87
38000	3274.90	1688.47	1160.35	896.80	739.08	634.27	559.70	504.02	460.94	426.67	398.81	375.76
39000	3361.08	1732.91	1190.88	920.40	758.53	650.96	574.42	517.28	473.07	437.90	409.31	385.65
40000	3447.26	1777.34	1221.42	944.00	777.98	667.65	589.15	530.54	485.20	449.13	419.80	395.54
41000	3533.44	1821.77	1251.95	967.60	797.42	684.34	603.88	543.81	497.33	460.35	430.30	405.43
42000	3619.62	1866.21	1282.49	991.20	816.87	701.03	618.61	557.07	509.45	471.58	440.79	415.32
43000	3705.80	1910.64	1313.02	1014.80	836.32	717.72	633.34	570.34	521.58	482.81	451.29	425.20
44000	3791.99	1955.07	1343.56	1038.40	855.77	734.42	648.07	583.60	533.71	494.04	461.78	435.09
45000	3878.17	1999.51	1374.10	1062.00	875.22	751.11	662.80	596.86	545.84	505.27	472.28	444.98
46000	3964.35	2043.94	1404.63	1085.60	894.67	767.80	677.53	610.13	557.97	516.49	482.77	454.87
47000	4050.53	2088.37	1435.17	1109.20	914.12	784.49	692.25	623.39	570.10	527.72	493.27	464.76
48000	4136.71	2132.81	1465.70	1132.80	933.57	801.18	706.98	636.65	582.23	538.95	503.76	474.65
49000	4222.89	2177.24	1496.24	1156.40	953.02	817.87	721.71	649.92	594.36	550.18	514.26	484.54
50000	4309.07	2221.67	1526.77	1180.00	972.47	834.56	736.44	663.18	606.49	561.41	524.75	494.42
55000	4739.98	2443.84	1679.45	1298.00	1069.71	918.02	810.08	729.50	667.14	617.55	577.23	543.87
60000	5170.89	2666.01	1832.13	1415.99	1166.96	1001.47	883.73	795.81	727.79	673.69	629.70	593.31
65000	5601.79	2888.17	1984.80	1533.99	1264.21	1084.93	957.37	862.13	788.44	729.83	682.18	642.75
70000	6032.70	3110.34	2137.48	1651.99	1361.45	1168.39	1031.01	928.45	849.09	785.97	734.65	692.19
75000	6463.61	3332.51	2290.16	1769.99	1458.70	1251.84	1104.66	994.77	909.74	842.11	787.13	741.63
80000	6894.52	3554.67	2442.83	1887.99	1555.95	1335.30	1178.30	1061.08	970.39	898.25	839.60	791.07
85000	7325.42	3776.84	2595.51	2005.99	1653.19	1418.75	1251.94	1127.40	1031.03	954.39	892.08	840.52
90000	7756.33	3999.01	2748.19	2123.99	1750.44	1502.21	1325.59	1193.72	1091.68	1010.53	944.55	889.96
95000	8187.24	4221.17	2900.86	2241.99	1847.68	1585.66	1399.23	1260.04	1152.33	1066.67	997.03	939.40
100000	8618.14	4443.34	3053.54	2359.99	1944.93	1669.12	1472.88	1326.35	1212.98	1122.81	1049.50	988.84

Table 1

MONTHLY

6.25%

6%

PAYMENT REQUIRED TO AMORTIZE A LOAN

TERM AMOUNT	13 YEARS	14 YEARS	15 YEARS	16 YEARS	17 YEARS	18 YEARS	19 YEARS	20 YEARS	25 YEARS	30 YEARS	35 YEARS	40 YEARS
50	.47	.45	.43	.42	.40	.39	.38	.37	.33	.31	.30	.29
100	.94	.90	.86	.83	.80	.78	.76	.74	.66	.62	.59	.57
200	1.88	1.79	1.72	1.66	1.60	1.55	1.51	1.47	1.32	1.24	1.18	1.14
300	2.82	2.69	2.58	2.48	2.40	2.32	2.26	2.20	1.98	1.85	1.77	1.71
400	3.76	3.58	3.43	3.31	3.19	3.09	3.01	2.93	2.64	2.47	2.35	2.28
500	4.69	4.48	4.29	4.13	3.99	3.87	3.76	3.66	3.30	3.08	2.94	2.84
600	5.63	5.37	5.15	4.96	4.79	4.64	4.51	4.39	3.96	3.70	3.53	3.41
700	6.57	6.27	6.01	5.78	5.58	5.41	5.26	5.12	4.62	4.32	4.11	3.98
800	7.51	7.16	6.86	6.61	6.38	6.18	6.01	5.85	5.28	4.93	4.70	4.55
900	8.45	8.06	7.72	7.43	7.18	6.96	6.76	6.58	5.94	5.55	5.29	5.11
1000	9.38	8.95	8.58	8.26	7.98	7.73	7.51	7.31	6.60	6.16	5.88	5.68
2000	18.76	17.90	17.15	16.51	15.95	15.45	15.01	14.62	13.20	12.32	11.75	11.36
3000	28.14	26.84	25.73	24.76	23.92	23.17	22.52	21.93	19.80	18.48	17.62	17.04
4000	37.52	35.79	34.30	33.01	31.89	30.90	30.02	29.24	26.39	24.63	23.49	22.71
5000	46.90	44.74	42.88	41.26	39.86	38.62	37.52	36.55	32.99	30.79	29.36	28.39
6000	56.28	53.68	51.45	49.52	47.83	46.34	45.03	43.86	39.59	36.95	35.23	34.07
7000	65.66	62.63	60.02	57.77	55.80	54.07	52.53	51.17	46.18	43.11	41.10	39.75
8000	75.04	71.57	68.60	66.02	63.77	61.79	60.04	58.48	52.78	49.26	46.97	45.42
9000	84.42	80.52	77.17	74.27	71.74	69.51	67.54	65.79	59.38	55.42	52.84	51.10
10000	93.80	89.47	85.75	82.52	79.71	77.23	75.04	73.10	65.97	61.58	58.71	56.78
11000	103.17	98.41	94.32	90.78	87.68	84.96	82.55	80.41	72.57	67.73	64.58	62.46
12000	112.55	107.36	102.90	99.03	95.65	92.68	90.05	87.72	79.17	73.89	70.45	68.13
13000	121.93	116.30	111.47	107.28	103.62	100.40	97.56	95.03	85.76	80.05	76.32	73.81
14000	131.31	125.25	120.04	115.53	111.59	108.13	105.06	102.33	92.36	86.21	82.20	79.49
15000	140.69	134.20	128.62	123.78	119.56	115.85	112.56	109.64	98.96	92.36	88.07	85.17
16000	150.07	143.14	137.19	132.04	127.53	123.57	120.07	116.95	105.55	98.52	93.94	90.84
17000	159.45	152.09	145.77	140.29	135.50	131.29	127.57	124.26	112.15	104.68	99.81	96.52
18000	168.83	161.03	154.34	148.54	143.47	139.02	135.08	131.57	118.75	110.83	105.68	102.20
19000	178.21	169.98	162.92	156.79	151.44	146.74	142.58	138.88	125.34	116.99	111.55	107.88
20000	187.59	178.93	171.49	165.04	159.41	154.46	150.08	146.19	131.94	123.15	117.42	113.55
21000	196.96	187.87	180.06	173.30	167.38	162.19	157.59	153.50	138.54	129.31	123.29	119.23
22000	206.34	196.82	188.64	181.55	175.35	169.91	165.09	160.81	145.13	135.46	129.16	124.91
23000	215.72	205.77	197.21	189.80	183.33	177.63	172.60	168.12	151.73	141.62	135.03	130.59
24000	225.10	214.71	205.79	198.05	191.30	185.36	180.10	175.43	158.33	147.78	140.90	136.26
25000	234.48	223.66	214.36	206.30	199.27	193.08	187.60	182.74	164.92	153.93	146.77	141.94
26000	243.86	232.60	222.93	214.56	207.24	200.80	195.11	190.05	171.52	160.09	152.64	147.62
27000	253.24	241.55	231.51	222.81	215.21	208.52	202.61	197.36	178.12	166.25	158.52	153.29
28000	262.62	250.50	240.08	231.06	223.18	216.25	210.12	204.66	184.71	172.41	164.39	158.97
29000	272.00	259.44	248.66	239.31	231.15	223.97	217.62	211.97	191.31	178.56	170.26	164.65
30000	281.38	268.39	257.23	247.56	239.12	231.69	225.12	219.28	197.91	184.72	176.13	170.33
31000	290.76	277.33	265.81	255.82	247.09	239.42	232.63	226.59	204.50	190.88	182.00	176.01
32000	300.13	286.28	274.38	264.07	255.06	247.14	240.13	233.90	211.10	197.03	187.87	181.68
33000	309.51	295.23	282.95	272.32	263.03	254.86	247.64	241.21	217.70	203.19	193.74	187.36
34000	318.89	304.17	291.53	280.57	271.00	262.58	255.14	248.52	224.29	209.35	199.61	193.04
35000	328.27	313.12	300.10	288.82	278.97	270.31	262.64	255.83	230.89	215.51	205.48	198.71
36000	337.65	322.06	308.68	297.07	286.94	278.03	270.15	263.14	237.49	221.66	211.35	204.39
37000	347.03	331.01	317.25	305.33	294.91	285.75	277.65	270.45	244.08	227.82	217.22	210.07
38000	356.41	339.96	325.83	313.58	302.88	293.48	285.16	277.76	250.68	233.98	223.09	215.75
39000	365.79	348.90	334.40	321.83	310.85	301.20	292.66	285.07	257.28	240.13	228.96	221.42
40000	375.17	357.85	342.97	330.08	318.82	308.92	300.16	292.38	263.87	246.29	234.84	227.10
41000	384.55	366.80	351.55	338.33	326.79	316.65	307.67	299.69	270.47	252.45	240.71	232.78
42000	393.92	375.74	360.12	346.59	334.76	324.37	315.17	306.99	277.07	258.61	246.58	238.46
43000	403.30	384.69	368.70	354.84	342.73	332.09	322.68	314.30	283.66	264.76	252.45	244.13
44000	412.68	393.63	377.27	363.09	350.70	339.81	330.18	321.61	290.26	270.92	258.32	249.81
45000	422.06	402.58	385.85	371.34	358.68	347.54	337.68	328.92	296.86	277.08	264.19	255.49
46000	431.44	411.53	394.42	379.59	366.65	355.26	345.19	336.23	303.45	283.23	270.06	261.17
47000	440.82	420.47	402.99	387.85	374.62	362.98	352.84	343.54	310.05	289.39	275.93	266.84
48000	450.20	429.42	411.57	396.10	382.59	370.71	360.20	350.85	316.65	295.55	281.80	272.52
49000	459.58	438.36	420.14	404.35	390.56	378.43	367.70	358.16	323.24	301.71	287.67	278.20
50000	468.96	447.31	428.72	412.60	398.53	386.15	375.20	365.47	329.84	307.86	293.54	283.87
55000	515.85	492.04	471.59	453.86	438.38	424.77	412.72	402.02	362.82	338.65	322.90	312.26
60000	562.75	536.77	514.46	495.12	478.23	463.38	450.24	438.56	395.81	369.44	352.25	340.65
65000	609.64	581.50	557.33	536.38	518.08	502.00	487.76	475.11	428.79	400.22	381.60	369.04
70000	656.54	626.23	600.20	577.64	557.94	540.61	525.28	511.65	461.77	431.01	410.96	397.42
75000	703.43	670.96	643.07	618.90	597.79	579.23	562.80	548.20	494.76	461.79	440.31	425.81
80000	750.33	715.69	685.94	660.16	637.64	617.84	600.32	584.75	527.74	492.58	469.67	454.20
85000	797.22	760.42	728.81	701.42	677.49	656.45	637.84	621.29	560.72	523.36	499.02	482.58
90000	844.12	805.15	771.69	742.68	717.35	695.07	675.36	657.84	593.71	554.15	528.37	510.97
95000	891.01	849.88	814.56	783.94	757.20	733.68	712.88	694.39	626.69	584.94	557.73	539.36
100000	937.91	894.62	857.43	825.20	797.05	772.30	750.40	730.93	659.67	615.72	587.08	567.74

Table 1

6% | 6.50%

MONTHLY
PAYMENT REQUIRED TO AMORTIZE A LOAN

TERM / AMOUNT	1 YEAR	2 YEARS	3 YEARS	4 YEARS	5 YEARS	6 YEARS	7 YEARS	8 YEARS	9 YEARS	10 YEARS	11 YEARS	12 YEARS
50	4.32	2.23	1.54	1.19	.98	.85	.75	.67	.62	.57	.54	.51
100	8.63	4.46	3.07	2.38	1.96	1.69	1.49	1.34	1.23	1.14	1.07	1.01
200	17.26	8.91	6.13	4.75	3.92	3.37	2.97	2.68	2.46	2.28	2.13	2.01
300	25.89	13.37	9.20	7.12	5.87	5.05	4.46	4.02	3.68	3.41	3.19	3.01
400	34.52	17.82	12.26	9.49	7.83	6.73	5.94	5.36	4.91	4.55	4.25	4.01
500	43.15	22.28	15.33	11.86	9.79	8.41	7.43	6.70	6.13	5.68	5.32	5.01
600	51.78	26.73	18.39	14.23	11.74	10.09	8.91	8.04	7.36	6.82	6.38	6.01
700	60.41	31.19	21.46	16.61	13.70	11.77	10.40	9.38	8.58	7.95	7.44	7.02
800	69.04	35.64	24.52	18.98	15.66	13.45	11.88	10.71	9.81	9.09	8.50	8.02
900	77.67	40.10	27.59	21.35	17.61	15.13	13.37	12.05	11.03	10.22	9.57	9.02
1000	86.30	44.55	30.65	23.72	19.57	16.81	14.85	13.39	12.26	11.36	10.63	10.02
2000	172.60	89.10	61.30	47.43	39.14	33.62	29.70	26.78	24.51	22.71	21.25	20.04
3000	258.89	133.64	91.95	71.15	58.70	50.43	44.55	40.16	36.77	34.07	31.88	30.06
4000	345.19	178.19	122.60	94.86	78.27	67.24	59.40	53.55	49.02	45.42	42.50	40.08
5000	431.49	222.74	153.25	118.58	97.84	84.05	74.25	66.94	61.28	56.78	53.12	50.10
6000	517.78	267.28	183.90	142.29	117.40	100.86	89.10	80.32	73.53	68.13	63.75	60.12
7000	604.08	311.83	214.55	166.01	136.97	117.67	103.95	93.71	85.79	79.49	74.37	70.14
8000	690.38	356.38	245.20	189.72	156.53	134.48	118.80	107.09	98.04	90.84	85.00	80.16
9000	776.67	400.92	275.85	213.44	176.10	151.29	133.65	120.48	110.30	102.20	95.62	90.18
10000	862.97	445.47	306.50	237.15	195.67	168.10	148.50	133.87	122.55	113.55	106.24	100.20
11000	949.27	490.01	337.14	260.87	215.23	184.91	163.35	147.25	134.80	124.91	116.87	110.22
12000	1035.56	534.56	367.79	284.58	234.80	201.72	178.20	160.64	147.06	136.26	127.49	120.24
13000	1121.86	579.11	398.44	308.30	254.36	218.53	193.05	174.03	159.31	147.62	138.11	130.25
14000	1208.15	623.65	429.09	332.01	273.93	235.34	207.90	187.41	171.57	158.97	148.74	140.27
15000	1294.45	668.20	459.74	355.73	293.50	252.15	222.75	200.80	183.82	170.33	159.36	150.29
16000	1380.75	712.75	490.39	379.44	313.06	268.96	237.60	214.18	196.08	181.68	169.99	160.31
17000	1467.04	757.29	521.04	403.16	332.63	285.77	252.45	227.57	208.33	193.04	180.61	170.33
18000	1553.34	801.84	551.69	426.87	352.20	302.58	267.29	240.96	220.59	204.39	191.23	180.35
19000	1639.64	846.38	582.34	450.59	371.76	319.39	282.14	254.34	232.84	215.75	201.86	190.37
20000	1725.93	890.93	612.99	474.30	391.33	336.20	296.99	267.73	245.10	227.10	212.48	200.39
21000	1812.23	935.48	643.63	498.02	410.89	353.01	311.84	281.12	257.35	238.46	223.10	210.41
22000	1898.53	980.02	674.28	521.73	430.46	369.82	326.69	294.50	269.60	249.81	233.73	220.43
23000	1984.82	1024.57	704.93	545.45	450.03	386.63	341.54	307.89	281.86	261.17	244.35	230.45
24000	2071.12	1069.12	735.58	569.16	469.59	403.44	356.39	321.27	294.11	272.52	254.98	240.47
25000	2157.42	1113.66	766.23	592.88	489.16	420.25	371.24	334.66	306.37	283.87	265.60	250.49
26000	2243.71	1158.21	796.88	616.59	508.72	437.06	386.09	348.05	318.62	295.23	276.22	260.50
27000	2330.01	1202.75	827.53	640.31	528.29	453.87	400.94	361.43	330.88	306.58	286.85	270.52
28000	2416.30	1247.30	858.18	664.02	547.86	470.68	415.79	374.82	343.13	317.94	297.47	280.54
29000	2502.60	1291.85	888.83	687.74	567.42	487.49	430.64	388.21	355.39	329.29	308.09	290.56
30000	2588.90	1336.39	919.48	711.45	586.99	504.30	445.49	401.59	367.64	340.65	318.72	300.58
31000	2675.19	1380.94	950.12	735.17	606.56	521.11	460.34	414.98	379.89	352.00	329.34	310.60
32000	2761.49	1425.49	980.77	758.88	626.12	537.92	475.19	428.36	392.15	363.36	339.97	320.62
33000	2847.79	1470.03	1011.42	782.60	645.69	554.73	490.04	441.75	404.40	374.71	350.59	330.64
34000	2934.08	1514.58	1042.07	806.31	665.25	571.54	504.89	455.14	416.66	386.07	361.21	340.66
35000	3020.38	1559.12	1072.72	830.03	684.82	588.35	519.74	468.52	428.91	397.42	371.84	350.68
36000	3106.68	1603.67	1103.37	853.74	704.39	605.16	534.58	481.91	441.17	408.78	382.46	360.70
37000	3192.97	1648.22	1134.02	877.46	723.95	621.97	549.43	495.30	453.42	420.13	393.08	370.72
38000	3279.27	1692.76	1164.67	901.17	743.52	638.78	564.28	508.68	465.68	431.49	403.71	380.74
39000	3365.57	1737.31	1195.32	924.89	763.08	655.59	579.13	522.07	477.93	442.84	414.33	390.75
40000	3451.86	1781.86	1225.97	948.60	782.65	672.40	593.98	535.45	490.19	454.20	424.96	400.77
41000	3538.16	1826.40	1256.61	972.32	802.22	689.21	608.83	548.84	502.44	465.55	435.58	410.79
42000	3624.45	1870.95	1287.26	996.03	821.78	706.02	623.68	562.23	514.69	476.91	446.20	420.81
43000	3710.75	1915.49	1317.91	1019.75	841.35	722.83	638.53	575.61	526.95	488.26	456.83	430.83
44000	3797.05	1960.04	1348.56	1043.46	860.92	739.64	653.38	589.00	539.20	499.62	467.45	440.85
45000	3883.34	2004.59	1379.21	1067.18	880.48	756.45	668.23	602.39	551.46	510.97	478.07	450.87
46000	3969.64	2049.13	1409.86	1090.89	900.05	773.26	683.08	615.77	563.71	522.33	488.70	460.89
47000	4055.94	2093.68	1440.51	1114.61	919.61	790.07	697.93	629.16	575.97	533.68	499.32	470.91
48000	4142.23	2138.23	1471.16	1138.32	939.18	806.88	712.78	642.54	588.22	545.04	509.95	480.93
49000	4228.53	2182.77	1501.81	1162.04	958.75	823.69	727.63	655.93	600.48	556.39	520.57	490.95
50000	4314.83	2227.32	1532.46	1185.75	978.31	840.50	742.48	669.32	612.73	567.74	531.19	500.97
55000	4746.31	2450.05	1685.70	1304.33	1076.14	924.55	816.72	736.25	674.00	624.52	584.31	551.06
60000	5177.79	2672.78	1838.95	1422.90	1173.97	1008.60	890.97	803.18	735.28	681.29	637.43	601.16
65000	5609.27	2895.51	1992.19	1541.48	1271.80	1092.65	965.22	870.11	796.55	738.07	690.55	651.25
70000	6040.75	3118.24	2145.44	1660.05	1369.64	1176.70	1039.47	937.04	857.82	794.84	743.67	701.35
75000	6472.24	3340.97	2298.68	1778.63	1467.47	1260.75	1113.71	1003.97	919.09	851.61	796.79	751.45
80000	6903.72	3563.71	2451.93	1897.20	1565.30	1344.80	1187.96	1070.90	980.37	908.39	849.91	801.54
85000	7335.20	3786.44	2605.17	2015.78	1663.13	1428.85	1262.21	1137.83	1041.64	965.16	903.03	851.64
90000	7766.68	4009.17	2758.42	2134.35	1760.96	1512.90	1336.45	1204.77	1102.91	1021.94	956.14	901.73
95000	8198.17	4231.90	2911.66	2252.93	1858.79	1596.95	1410.70	1271.70	1164.18	1078.71	1009.26	951.83
100000	8629.65	4454.63	3064.91	2371.50	1956.62	1681.00	1484.95	1338.63	1225.46	1135.48	1062.38	1001.93

Table 1

MONTHLY
PAYMENT REQUIRED TO AMORTIZE A LOAN

6.50%

6%

TERM / AMOUNT	13 YEARS	14 YEARS	15 YEARS	16 YEARS	17 YEARS	18 YEARS	19 YEARS	20 YEARS	25 YEARS	30 YEARS	35 YEARS	40 YEARS
50	.48	.46	.44	.42	.41	.40	.39	.38	.34	.32	.31	.30
100	.96	.91	.88	.84	.82	.79	.77	.75	.68	.64	.61	.59
200	1.91	1.82	1.75	1.68	1.63	1.58	1.53	1.50	1.36	1.27	1.21	1.18
300	2.86	2.73	2.62	2.52	2.44	2.36	2.30	2.24	2.03	1.90	1.82	1.76
400	3.81	3.64	3.49	3.36	3.25	3.15	3.06	2.99	2.71	2.53	2.42	2.35
500	4.76	4.55	4.36	4.20	4.06	3.94	3.83	3.73	3.38	3.17	3.03	2.93
600	5.71	5.45	5.23	5.04	4.87	4.72	4.59	4.48	4.06	3.80	3.63	3.52
700	6.66	6.36	6.10	5.88	5.68	5.51	5.36	5.22	4.73	4.43	4.23	4.10
800	7.61	7.27	6.97	6.72	6.49	6.30	6.12	5.97	5.41	5.06	4.84	4.69
900	8.57	8.18	7.84	7.56	7.31	7.08	6.89	6.72	6.08	5.69	5.44	5.27
1000	9.52	9.09	8.72	8.40	8.12	7.87	7.65	7.46	6.76	6.33	6.05	5.86
2000	19.03	18.17	17.43	16.79	16.23	15.74	15.30	14.92	13.51	12.65	12.09	11.71
3000	28.54	27.25	26.14	25.18	24.34	23.60	22.95	22.37	20.26	18.97	18.13	17.57
4000	38.05	36.33	34.85	33.57	32.45	31.47	30.60	29.83	27.01	25.29	24.17	23.42
5000	47.56	45.41	43.56	41.96	40.56	39.33	38.25	37.28	33.77	31.61	30.21	29.28
6000	57.08	54.49	52.27	50.35	48.67	47.20	45.90	44.74	40.52	37.93	36.25	35.13
7000	66.59	63.57	60.98	58.74	56.78	55.06	53.54	52.20	47.27	44.25	42.30	40.99
8000	76.10	72.65	69.69	67.13	64.89	62.93	61.19	59.65	54.02	50.57	48.34	46.84
9000	85.61	81.73	78.40	75.52	73.01	70.80	68.84	67.11	60.77	56.89	54.38	52.70
10000	95.12	90.81	87.12	83.91	81.12	78.66	76.49	74.56	67.53	63.21	60.42	58.55
11000	104.64	99.90	95.83	92.30	89.23	86.53	84.14	82.02	74.28	69.53	66.46	64.41
12000	114.15	108.98	104.54	100.69	97.34	94.39	91.79	89.47	81.03	75.85	72.50	70.26
13000	123.66	118.06	113.25	109.08	105.45	102.26	99.44	96.93	87.78	82.17	78.55	76.11
14000	133.17	127.14	121.96	117.48	113.56	110.12	107.08	104.39	94.53	88.49	84.59	81.97
15000	142.68	136.22	130.67	125.87	121.67	117.99	114.73	111.84	101.29	94.82	90.63	87.82
16000	152.20	145.30	139.38	134.26	129.78	125.85	122.38	119.30	108.04	101.14	96.67	93.68
17000	161.71	154.38	148.09	142.65	137.90	133.72	130.03	126.75	114.79	107.46	102.71	99.53
18000	171.22	163.46	156.80	151.04	146.01	141.59	137.68	134.21	121.54	113.78	108.75	105.39
19000	180.73	172.54	165.52	159.43	154.12	149.45	145.33	141.66	128.29	120.10	114.79	111.24
20000	190.24	181.62	174.23	167.82	162.23	157.32	152.98	149.12	135.05	126.42	120.84	117.10
21000	199.75	190.71	182.94	176.21	170.34	165.18	160.62	156.58	141.80	132.74	126.88	122.95
22000	209.27	199.79	191.65	184.60	178.45	173.05	168.27	164.03	148.55	139.06	132.92	128.81
23000	218.78	208.87	200.36	192.99	186.56	180.91	175.92	171.49	155.30	145.38	138.96	134.66
24000	228.29	217.95	209.07	201.38	194.67	188.78	183.57	178.94	162.05	151.70	145.00	140.51
25000	237.80	227.03	217.78	209.77	202.79	196.65	191.22	186.40	168.81	158.02	151.04	146.37
26000	247.31	236.11	226.49	218.16	210.90	204.51	198.87	193.85	175.56	164.34	157.09	152.22
27000	256.83	245.19	235.20	226.56	219.01	212.38	206.52	201.31	182.31	170.66	163.13	158.08
28000	266.34	254.27	243.92	234.95	227.12	220.24	214.16	208.77	189.06	176.98	169.17	163.93
29000	275.85	263.35	252.63	243.34	235.23	228.11	221.81	216.22	195.82	183.30	175.21	169.79
30000	285.36	272.43	261.34	251.73	243.34	235.97	229.46	223.68	202.57	189.63	181.25	175.64
31000	294.87	281.51	270.05	260.12	251.45	243.84	237.11	231.13	209.32	195.95	187.29	181.50
32000	304.39	290.60	278.76	268.51	259.56	251.70	244.76	238.59	216.07	202.27	193.33	187.35
33000	313.90	299.68	287.47	276.90	267.67	259.57	252.41	246.04	222.82	208.59	199.38	193.21
34000	323.41	308.76	296.18	285.29	275.79	267.44	260.06	253.50	229.58	214.91	205.42	199.06
35000	332.92	317.84	304.89	293.68	283.90	275.30	267.70	260.96	236.33	221.23	211.46	204.91
36000	342.43	326.92	313.60	302.07	292.01	283.17	275.35	268.41	243.08	227.55	217.50	210.77
37000	351.95	336.00	322.31	310.46	300.12	291.03	283.00	275.87	249.83	233.87	223.54	216.62
38000	361.46	345.08	331.03	318.85	308.23	298.90	290.65	283.32	256.58	240.19	229.58	222.48
39000	370.97	354.16	339.74	327.24	316.34	306.76	298.30	290.78	263.34	246.51	235.63	228.33
40000	380.48	363.24	348.45	335.64	324.45	314.63	305.95	298.23	270.09	252.83	241.67	234.19
41000	389.99	372.32	357.16	344.03	332.56	322.50	313.60	305.69	276.84	255.75	247.71	240.04
42000	399.50	381.41	365.87	352.42	340.68	330.36	321.24	313.15	283.59	265.47	253.75	245.90
43000	409.02	390.49	374.58	360.81	348.79	338.23	328.89	320.60	290.34	271.79	259.79	251.75
44000	418.53	399.57	383.29	369.20	356.90	346.09	336.54	328.06	297.10	278.11	265.83	257.61
45000	428.04	408.65	392.00	377.59	365.01	353.96	344.19	335.51	303.85	284.44	271.87	263.46
46000	437.55	417.73	400.71	385.98	373.12	361.82	351.84	342.97	310.60	290.76	277.92	269.32
47000	447.06	426.81	409.43	394.37	381.23	369.69	359.49	350.42	317.35	297.08	283.96	275.17
48000	456.58	435.89	418.14	402.76	389.34	377.55	367.14	357.88	324.10	303.40	290.00	281.02
49000	466.09	444.97	426.85	411.15	397.45	385.42	374.78	365.34	330.86	309.72	296.04	286.88
50000	475.60	454.05	435.56	419.54	405.57	393.29	382.43	372.79	337.61	316.04	302.08	292.73
55000	523.16	499.46	479.11	461.50	446.12	432.61	420.68	410.07	371.37	347.64	332.29	322.01
60000	570.72	544.86	522.67	503.45	486.68	471.94	458.92	447.35	405.13	379.25	362.50	351.28
65000	618.28	590.27	566.22	545.40	527.23	511.27	497.16	484.63	438.89	410.85	392.71	380.55
70000	665.84	635.67	609.78	587.36	567.79	550.60	535.40	521.91	472.65	442.45	422.91	409.82
75000	713.40	681.08	653.34	629.31	608.35	589.93	573.65	559.18	506.41	474.06	453.12	439.10
80000	760.96	726.48	696.89	671.27	648.90	629.25	611.89	596.46	540.17	505.66	483.33	468.37
85000	808.52	771.89	740.45	713.22	689.46	668.58	650.13	633.74	573.93	537.26	513.54	497.64
90000	856.08	817.29	784.00	755.17	730.01	707.91	688.38	671.02	607.69	568.87	543.74	526.92
95000	903.64	862.70	827.56	797.13	770.57	747.24	726.62	708.30	641.45	600.47	573.95	556.19
100000	951.20	908.10	871.11	839.08	811.13	786.57	764.86	745.58	675.21	632.07	604.16	585.46

15

Table 1

6%

6.75%

MONTHLY
PAYMENT REQUIRED TO AMORTIZE A LOAN

TERM / AMOUNT	1 YEAR	2 YEARS	3 YEARS	4 YEARS	5 YEARS	6 YEARS	7 YEARS	8 YEARS	9 YEARS	10 YEARS	11 YEARS	12 YEAR.
50	4.33	2.24	1.54	1.20	.99	.85	.75	.68	.62	.58	.54	.51
100	8.65	4.47	3.08	2.39	1.97	1.70	1.50	1.36	1.24	1.15	1.08	1.02
200	17.29	8.94	6.16	4.77	3.94	3.39	3.00	2.71	2.48	2.30	2.16	2.04
300	25.93	13.40	9.23	7.15	5.91	5.08	4.50	4.06	3.72	3.45	3.23	3.05
400	34.57	17.87	12.31	9.54	7.88	6.78	5.99	5.41	4.96	4.60	4.31	4.07
500	43.21	22.33	15.39	11.92	9.85	8.47	7.49	6.76	6.20	5.75	5.38	5.08
600	51.85	26.80	18.46	14.30	11.82	10.16	8.99	8.11	7.43	6.89	6.46	6.10
700	60.49	31.27	21.54	16.69	13.78	11.86	10.48	9.46	8.67	8.04	7.53	7.11
800	69.13	35.73	24.62	19.07	15.75	13.55	11.98	10.81	9.91	9.19	8.61	8.13
900	77.78	40.20	27.69	21.45	17.72	15.24	13.48	12.16	11.15	10.34	9.68	9.14
1000	86.42	44.66	30.77	23.84	19.69	16.93	14.98	13.51	12.39	11.49	10.76	10.16
2000	172.83	89.32	61.53	47.67	39.37	33.86	29.95	27.02	24.77	22.97	21.51	20.31
3000	259.24	133.98	92.29	71.50	59.06	50.79	44.92	40.53	37.15	34.45	32.27	30.46
4000	345.65	178.64	123.06	95.33	78.74	67.72	59.89	54.04	49.53	45.93	43.02	40.61
5000	432.06	223.30	153.82	119.16	98.42	84.65	74.86	67.55	61.91	57.42	53.77	50.76
6000	518.47	267.96	184.58	142.99	118.11	101.58	89.83	81.06	74.29	68.90	64.53	60.91
7000	604.89	312.62	215.35	166.82	137.79	118.51	104.80	94.57	86.67	80.38	75.28	71.06
8000	691.30	357.28	246.11	190.65	157.47	135.44	119.77	108.08	99.05	91.86	86.03	81.21
9000	777.71	401.94	276.87	214.48	177.16	152.37	134.74	121.59	111.43	103.35	96.79	91.36
10000	864.12	446.60	307.63	238.31	196.84	169.30	149.71	135.10	123.81	114.83	107.54	101.52
11000	950.53	491.26	338.40	262.14	216.52	186.23	164.68	148.61	136.19	126.31	118.29	111.67
12000	1036.94	535.92	369.16	285.97	236.21	203.16	179.65	162.12	148.57	137.79	129.05	121.82
13000	1123.36	580.58	399.92	309.80	255.89	220.08	194.62	175.63	160.95	149.28	139.80	131.97
14000	1209.77	625.24	430.69	333.63	275.57	237.01	209.60	189.14	173.33	160.76	150.55	142.12
15000	1296.18	669.89	461.45	357.46	295.26	253.94	224.57	202.65	185.71	172.24	161.31	152.27
16000	1382.59	714.55	492.21	381.29	314.94	270.87	239.54	216.16	198.09	183.72	172.06	162.42
17000	1469.00	759.21	522.97	405.12	334.62	287.80	254.51	229.67	210.47	195.21	182.81	172.57
18000	1555.41	803.87	553.74	428.95	354.31	304.73	269.48	243.18	222.85	206.69	193.57	182.72
19000	1641.82	848.53	584.50	452.78	373.99	321.66	284.45	256.69	235.23	218.17	204.32	192.87
20000	1728.24	893.19	615.26	476.61	393.67	338.59	299.42	270.20	247.61	229.65	215.07	203.03
21000	1814.65	937.85	646.03	500.44	413.36	355.52	314.39	283.71	259.99	241.14	225.83	213.18
22000	1901.06	982.51	676.79	524.27	433.04	372.45	329.36	297.22	272.37	252.62	236.58	223.33
23000	1987.47	1027.17	707.55	548.10	452.72	389.38	344.33	310.73	284.75	264.10	247.34	233.48
24000	2073.88	1071.83	738.32	571.94	472.41	406.31	359.30	324.24	297.13	275.58	258.09	243.63
25000	2160.29	1116.49	769.08	595.77	492.09	423.24	374.27	337.75	309.51	287.07	268.84	253.78
26000	2246.71	1161.15	799.84	619.60	511.77	440.16	389.24	351.26	321.89	298.55	279.60	263.93
27000	2333.12	1205.81	830.60	643.43	531.46	457.09	404.22	364.77	334.27	310.03	290.35	274.08
28000	2419.53	1250.47	861.37	667.26	551.14	474.02	419.19	378.27	346.65	321.51	301.10	284.23
29000	2505.94	1295.13	892.13	691.09	570.83	490.95	434.16	391.78	359.03	332.99	311.86	294.38
30000	2592.35	1339.78	922.89	714.92	590.51	507.88	449.13	405.29	371.41	344.48	322.61	304.54
31000	2678.76	1384.44	953.66	738.75	610.19	524.81	464.10	418.80	383.79	355.96	333.36	314.69
32000	2765.17	1429.10	984.42	762.58	629.88	541.74	479.07	432.31	396.17	367.44	344.12	324.84
33000	2851.59	1473.76	1015.18	786.41	649.56	558.67	494.04	445.82	408.55	378.92	354.87	334.99
34000	2938.00	1518.42	1045.94	810.24	669.24	575.60	509.01	459.33	420.93	390.41	365.62	345.14
35000	3024.41	1563.08	1076.71	834.07	688.93	592.53	523.98	472.84	433.31	401.89	376.38	355.29
36000	3110.82	1607.74	1107.47	857.90	708.61	609.46	538.95	486.35	445.69	413.37	387.13	365.44
37000	3197.23	1652.40	1138.23	881.73	728.29	626.39	553.92	499.86	458.07	424.85	397.88	375.59
38000	3283.64	1697.06	1169.00	905.56	747.98	643.32	568.89	513.37	470.45	436.34	408.64	385.74
39000	3370.06	1741.72	1199.76	929.39	767.66	660.24	583.86	526.88	482.83	447.82	419.39	395.90
40000	3456.47	1786.38	1230.52	953.22	787.34	677.17	598.84	540.39	495.21	459.30	430.14	406.05
41000	3542.88	1831.04	1261.28	977.05	807.03	694.10	613.81	553.90	507.59	470.78	440.90	416.20
42000	3629.29	1875.70	1292.05	1000.88	826.71	711.03	628.78	567.41	519.97	482.27	451.65	426.35
43000	3715.70	1920.36	1322.81	1024.71	846.39	727.96	643.75	580.92	532.35	493.75	462.40	436.50
44000	3802.11	1965.02	1353.57	1048.54	866.08	744.89	658.72	594.43	544.73	505.23	473.16	446.65
45000	3888.52	2009.67	1384.34	1072.37	885.76	761.82	673.69	607.94	557.11	516.71	483.91	456.80
46000	3974.94	2054.33	1415.10	1096.20	905.44	778.75	688.66	621.45	569.49	528.20	494.67	466.95
47000	4061.35	2098.99	1445.86	1120.04	925.13	795.68	703.63	634.96	581.87	539.68	505.42	477.10
48000	4147.76	2143.65	1476.63	1143.87	944.81	812.61	718.60	648.47	594.25	551.16	516.17	487.25
49000	4234.17	2188.31	1507.39	1167.70	964.49	829.54	733.57	661.98	606.63	562.64	526.93	497.41
50000	4320.58	2232.97	1538.15	1191.53	984.18	846.47	748.54	675.49	619.01	574.13	537.68	507.56
55000	4752.64	2456.27	1691.97	1310.68	1082.60	931.11	823.40	743.04	680.91	631.54	591.45	558.31
60000	5184.70	2679.56	1845.78	1429.83	1181.01	1015.76	898.25	810.58	742.81	688.95	645.21	609.07
65000	5616.76	2902.86	1999.59	1548.98	1279.43	1100.40	973.10	878.13	804.71	746.36	698.98	659.82
70000	6048.81	3126.16	2153.41	1668.13	1377.85	1185.05	1047.96	945.68	866.61	803.77	752.75	710.58
75000	6480.87	3349.45	2307.22	1787.29	1476.26	1269.70	1122.81	1013.23	928.51	861.19	806.52	761.33
80000	6912.93	3572.75	2461.04	1906.44	1574.68	1354.34	1197.67	1080.78	990.41	918.60	860.28	812.09
85000	7344.99	3796.05	2614.85	2025.59	1673.10	1438.99	1272.52	1148.32	1052.31	976.01	914.05	862.84
90000	7777.04	4019.34	2768.67	2144.74	1771.52	1523.63	1347.37	1215.87	1114.21	1033.42	967.82	913.60
95000	8209.10	4242.64	2922.48	2263.90	1869.93	1608.28	1422.23	1283.42	1176.11	1090.83	1021.59	964.35
100000	8641.16	4465.94	3076.30	2383.05	1968.35	1692.93	1497.08	1350.97	1238.01	1148.25	1075.35	1015.11

Table 1

MONTHLY
PAYMENT REQUIRED TO AMORTIZE A LOAN

6.75%

6%

TERM AMOUNT	13 YEARS	14 YEARS	15 YEARS	16 YEARS	17 YEARS	18 YEARS	19 YEARS	20 YEARS	25 YEARS	30 YEARS	35 YEARS	40 YEARS
50	.49	.47	.45	.43	.42	.41	.39	.39	.35	.33	.32	.31
100	.97	.93	.89	.86	.83	.81	.78	.77	.70	.65	.63	.61
200	1.93	1.85	1.77	1.71	1.66	1.61	1.56	1.53	1.39	1.30	1.25	1.21
300	2.90	2.77	2.66	2.56	2.48	2.41	2.34	2.29	2.08	1.95	1.87	1.82
400	3.86	3.69	3.54	3.42	3.31	3.21	3.12	3.05	2.77	2.60	2.49	2.42
500	4.83	4.61	4.43	4.27	4.13	4.01	3.90	3.81	3.46	3.25	3.11	3.02
600	5.79	5.54	5.31	5.12	4.96	4.81	4.68	4.57	4.15	3.90	3.73	3.63
700	6.76	6.46	6.20	5.98	5.78	5.61	5.46	5.33	4.84	4.55	4.35	4.23
800	7.72	7.38	7.08	6.83	6.61	6.41	6.24	6.09	5.53	5.19	4.98	4.83
900	8.69	8.30	7.97	7.68	7.43	7.21	7.02	6.85	6.22	5.84	5.60	5.44
1000	9.65	9.22	8.85	8.54	8.26	8.01	7.80	7.61	6.91	6.49	6.22	6.04
2000	19.30	18.44	17.70	17.07	16.51	16.02	15.59	15.21	13.82	12.98	12.43	12.07
3000	28.94	27.66	26.55	25.60	24.76	24.03	23.39	22.82	20.73	19.46	18.65	18.11
4000	38.59	36.87	35.40	34.13	33.02	32.04	31.18	30.42	27.64	25.95	24.86	24.14
5000	48.23	46.09	44.25	42.66	41.27	40.05	38.98	38.02	34.55	32.43	31.08	30.17
6000	57.88	55.31	53.10	51.19	49.52	48.06	46.77	45.63	41.46	38.92	37.29	36.21
7000	67.53	64.52	61.95	59.72	57.78	56.07	54.57	53.23	48.37	45.41	43.50	42.24
8000	77.17	73.74	70.80	68.25	66.03	64.08	62.36	60.83	55.28	51.89	49.72	48.27
9000	86.82	82.96	79.65	76.78	74.28	72.09	70.16	68.44	62.19	58.38	55.93	54.31
10000	96.46	92.17	88.50	85.31	82.54	80.10	77.95	76.04	69.10	64.86	62.15	60.34
11000	106.11	101.39	97.35	93.84	90.79	88.11	85.75	83.65	76.01	71.35	68.36	66.37
12000	115.75	110.61	106.19	102.37	99.04	96.12	93.54	91.25	82.91	77.84	74.57	72.41
13000	125.05	119.83	115.04	110.91	107.30	104.13	101.33	98.85	89.82	84.32	80.79	78.44
14000	135.05	129.04	123.89	119.44	115.55	112.14	109.13	106.46	96.73	90.81	87.00	84.47
15000	144.69	138.26	132.74	127.97	123.80	120.15	116.92	114.06	103.64	97.29	93.22	90.51
16000	154.34	147.48	141.59	136.50	132.06	128.16	124.72	121.66	110.55	103.78	99.43	96.54
17000	163.98	156.69	150.44	145.03	140.31	136.17	132.51	129.27	117.46	110.27	105.65	102.58
18000	173.63	165.91	159.29	153.56	148.56	144.18	140.31	136.87	124.37	116.75	111.86	108.61
19000	183.28	175.13	168.14	162.09	156.82	152.19	148.10	144.47	131.28	123.24	118.07	114.64
20000	192.92	184.34	176.99	170.62	165.07	160.20	155.90	152.08	138.19	129.72	124.29	120.68
21000	202.57	193.56	185.84	179.15	173.32	168.21	163.69	159.68	145.10	136.21	130.50	126.71
22000	212.21	202.78	194.69	187.68	181.58	176.22	171.49	167.29	152.01	142.70	136.72	132.74
23000	221.86	211.99	203.53	196.21	189.83	184.23	179.28	174.89	158.91	149.18	142.93	138.78
24000	231.50	221.21	212.38	204.74	198.08	192.24	187.07	182.49	165.82	155.67	149.14	144.81
25000	241.15	230.43	221.23	213.28	206.34	200.25	194.87	190.10	172.73	162.15	155.36	150.84
26000	250.80	239.65	230.08	221.81	214.59	208.26	202.66	197.70	179.64	168.64	161.57	156.88
27000	260.44	248.86	238.93	230.34	222.84	216.27	210.46	205.30	186.55	175.13	167.79	162.91
28000	270.09	258.08	247.78	238.87	231.10	224.28	218.25	212.91	193.46	181.61	174.00	168.94
29000	279.73	267.30	256.63	247.40	239.35	232.28	226.05	220.51	200.37	188.10	180.22	174.98
30000	289.38	276.51	265.48	255.93	247.60	240.29	233.84	228.11	207.28	194.58	186.43	181.01
31000	299.02	285.73	274.33	264.46	255.86	248.30	241.64	235.72	214.19	201.07	192.64	187.05
32000	308.67	294.95	283.18	272.99	264.11	256.31	249.43	243.32	221.10	207.56	198.86	193.08
33000	318.32	304.16	292.03	281.52	272.36	264.32	257.23	250.93	228.01	214.04	205.07	199.11
34000	327.96	313.38	300.87	290.05	280.62	272.33	265.02	258.53	234.91	220.53	211.29	205.15
35000	337.61	322.60	309.72	298.58	288.87	280.34	272.81	266.13	241.82	227.01	217.50	211.18
36000	347.25	331.81	318.57	307.11	297.12	288.35	280.61	273.74	248.73	233.50	223.71	217.21
37000	356.90	341.03	327.42	315.64	305.38	296.36	288.40	281.34	255.64	239.99	229.93	223.25
38000	366.55	350.25	336.27	324.18	313.63	304.37	296.20	288.94	262.55	246.47	236.14	229.28
39000	376.19	359.47	345.12	332.71	321.88	312.38	303.99	296.55	269.46	252.96	242.36	235.31
40000	385.84	368.68	353.97	341.24	330.14	320.39	311.79	304.15	276.37	259.44	248.57	241.35
41000	395.48	377.90	362.82	349.77	338.39	328.40	319.58	311.75	283.28	265.93	254.79	247.38
42000	405.13	387.12	371.67	358.30	346.64	336.41	327.38	319.36	290.19	272.42	261.00	253.41
43000	414.77	396.33	380.52	366.83	354.90	344.42	335.17	326.96	297.10	278.90	267.21	259.45
44000	424.42	405.55	389.37	375.36	363.15	352.43	342.97	334.57	304.01	285.39	273.43	265.48
45000	434.07	414.77	398.21	383.89	371.40	360.44	350.76	342.17	310.92	291.87	279.64	271.52
46000	443.71	423.98	407.06	392.42	379.66	368.45	358.55	349.77	317.82	298.36	285.86	277.55
47000	453.36	433.20	415.91	400.95	387.91	376.46	366.35	357.38	324.73	304.85	292.07	283.58
48000	463.00	442.42	424.76	409.48	396.16	384.47	374.14	364.98	331.64	311.33	298.28	289.62
49000	472.65	451.63	433.61	418.01	404.42	392.48	381.94	372.58	338.55	317.82	304.50	295.65
50000	482.30	460.85	442.46	426.55	412.67	400.49	389.73	380.19	345.46	324.30	310.71	301.68
55000	530.52	506.94	486.71	469.20	453.93	440.54	428.71	418.21	380.01	356.73	341.78	331.85
60000	578.75	553.02	530.95	511.85	495.20	480.58	467.68	456.22	414.55	389.16	373.85	362.02
65000	626.98	599.11	575.20	554.51	536.47	520.63	506.65	494.24	449.10	421.59	403.93	392.19
70000	675.21	645.19	619.44	597.16	577.73	560.68	545.62	532.26	483.64	454.02	435.00	422.35
75000	723.44	691.27	663.69	639.82	619.00	600.73	584.60	570.28	518.19	486.45	466.07	452.52
80000	771.67	737.36	707.93	682.47	660.27	640.78	623.57	608.30	552.73	518.88	497.14	482.69
85000	819.90	783.44	752.18	725.12	701.53	680.83	662.54	646.31	587.28	551.31	528.21	512.86
90000	868.13	829.53	796.42	767.78	742.80	720.87	701.51	684.33	621.83	583.74	559.28	543.03
95000	916.36	875.61	840.67	810.43	784.07	760.92	740.49	722.35	656.37	616.17	590.35	573.19
100000	964.59	921.70	884.91	853.09	825.33	800.97	779.46	760.37	690.92	648.60	621.42	603.36

17

Table 1

7.00%

MONTHLY
PAYMENT REQUIRED TO AMORTIZE A LOAN

7%

TERM AMOUNT	1 YEAR	2 YEARS	3 YEARS	4 YEARS	5 YEARS	6 YEARS	7 YEARS	8 YEARS	9 YEARS	10 YEARS	11 YEARS	12 YEARS
50	4.33	2.24	1.55	1.20	1.00	.86	.76	.69	.63	.59	.55	.52
100	8.66	4.48	3.09	2.40	1.99	1.71	1.51	1.37	1.26	1.17	1.09	1.03
200	17.31	8.96	6.18	4.79	3.97	3.41	3.02	2.73	2.51	2.33	2.18	2.06
300	25.96	13.44	9.27	7.19	5.95	5.12	4.53	4.10	3.76	3.49	3.27	3.09
400	34.62	17.91	12.36	9.58	7.93	6.82	6.04	5.46	5.01	4.65	4.36	4.12
500	43.27	22.39	15.44	11.98	9.91	8.53	7.55	6.82	6.26	5.81	5.45	5.15
600	51.92	26.87	18.53	14.37	11.89	10.23	9.06	8.19	7.51	6.97	6.54	6.18
700	60.57	31.35	21.62	16.77	13.87	11.94	10.57	9.55	8.76	8.13	7.62	7.20
800	69.23	35.82	24.71	19.16	15.85	13.64	12.08	10.91	10.01	9.29	8.71	8.23
900	77.88	40.30	27.79	21.56	17.83	15.35	13.59	12.28	11.26	10.45	9.80	9.26
1000	86.53	44.78	30.88	23.95	19.81	17.05	15.10	13.64	12.51	11.62	10.89	10.29
2000	173.06	89.55	61.76	47.90	39.61	34.10	30.19	27.27	25.02	23.23	21.77	20.57
3000	259.59	134.32	92.64	71.84	59.41	51.15	45.28	40.91	37.52	34.84	32.66	30.86
4000	346.11	179.10	123.51	95.79	79.21	68.20	60.38	54.54	50.03	46.45	43.54	41.14
5000	432.64	223.87	154.39	119.74	99.01	85.25	75.47	68.17	62.54	58.06	54.43	51.42
6000	519.17	268.64	185.27	143.68	118.81	102.30	90.56	81.81	75.04	69.67	65.31	61.71
7000	605.69	313.41	216.14	167.63	138.61	119.35	105.65	95.44	87.55	81.28	76.19	71.99
8000	692.22	358.19	247.02	191.57	158.41	136.40	120.75	109.07	100.06	92.89	87.08	82.28
9000	778.75	402.96	277.90	215.52	178.22	153.45	135.84	122.71	112.56	104.50	97.96	92.56
10000	865.27	447.73	308.78	239.47	198.02	170.50	150.93	136.34	125.07	116.11	108.85	102.84
11000	951.80	492.50	339.65	263.41	217.82	187.54	166.02	149.98	137.57	127.72	119.73	113.13
12000	1038.33	537.28	370.53	287.36	237.62	204.59	181.12	163.61	150.08	139.34	130.61	123.41
13000	1124.85	582.05	401.41	311.31	257.42	221.64	196.21	177.24	162.59	150.95	141.50	133.69
14000	1211.38	626.82	432.28	335.25	277.22	238.69	211.30	190.88	175.09	162.56	152.38	143.98
15000	1297.91	671.59	463.16	359.20	297.02	255.74	226.40	204.51	187.60	174.17	163.27	154.26
16000	1384.43	716.37	494.04	383.14	316.82	272.79	241.49	218.14	200.11	185.78	174.15	164.55
17000	1470.96	761.14	524.92	407.09	336.63	289.84	256.58	231.78	212.61	197.39	185.03	174.83
18000	1557.49	805.91	555.79	431.04	356.43	306.89	271.67	245.41	225.12	209.00	195.92	185.11
19000	1644.01	850.68	586.67	454.98	376.23	323.94	286.77	259.05	237.62	220.61	206.80	195.40
20000	1730.54	895.46	617.55	478.93	396.03	340.99	301.86	272.68	250.13	232.22	217.69	205.68
21000	1817.07	940.23	648.42	502.88	415.83	358.03	316.95	286.31	262.64	243.83	228.57	215.97
22000	1903.59	985.00	679.30	526.82	435.63	375.08	332.04	299.95	275.14	255.44	239.46	226.25
23000	1990.12	1029.77	710.18	550.77	455.43	392.13	347.14	313.58	287.65	267.05	250.34	236.53
24000	2076.65	1074.55	741.06	574.71	475.23	409.18	362.23	327.21	300.16	278.67	261.22	246.82
25000	2163.17	1119.32	771.93	598.66	495.03	426.23	377.32	340.85	312.66	290.28	272.11	257.10
26000	2249.70	1164.09	802.81	622.61	514.84	443.28	392.41	354.48	325.17	301.89	282.99	267.38
27000	2336.23	1208.86	833.69	646.55	534.64	460.33	407.51	368.12	337.67	313.50	293.88	277.67
28000	2422.75	1253.64	864.56	670.50	554.44	477.38	422.60	381.75	350.18	325.11	304.76	287.95
29000	2509.28	1298.41	895.44	694.45	574.24	494.43	437.69	395.38	362.69	336.72	315.64	298.24
30000	2595.81	1343.18	926.32	718.39	594.04	511.48	452.79	409.02	375.19	348.33	326.53	308.52
31000	2682.33	1387.95	957.20	742.34	613.84	528.52	467.88	422.65	387.70	359.94	337.41	318.80
32000	2768.86	1432.73	988.07	766.28	633.64	545.57	482.97	436.28	400.21	371.55	348.30	329.09
33000	2855.39	1477.50	1018.95	790.23	653.44	562.62	498.06	449.92	412.71	383.16	359.18	339.37
34000	2941.91	1522.27	1049.83	814.18	673.25	579.67	513.16	463.55	425.22	394.77	370.06	349.65
35000	3028.44	1567.05	1080.70	838.12	693.05	596.72	528.25	477.19	437.72	406.38	380.95	359.94
36000	3114.97	1611.82	1111.58	862.07	712.85	613.77	543.34	490.82	450.23	418.00	391.83	370.22
37000	3201.49	1656.59	1142.46	886.02	732.65	630.82	558.43	504.45	462.74	429.61	402.72	380.51
38000	3288.02	1701.36	1173.33	909.96	752.45	647.87	573.53	518.09	475.24	441.22	413.60	390.79
39000	3374.55	1746.14	1204.21	933.91	772.25	664.92	588.62	531.72	487.75	452.83	424.48	401.07
40000	3461.07	1790.91	1235.09	957.85	792.05	681.97	603.71	545.35	500.26	464.44	435.37	411.36
41000	3547.60	1835.68	1265.97	981.80	811.85	699.01	618.80	558.99	512.76	476.05	446.25	421.64
42000	3634.13	1880.45	1296.84	1005.75	831.66	716.06	633.90	572.62	525.27	487.66	457.14	431.93
43000	3720.66	1925.23	1327.72	1029.69	851.46	733.11	648.99	586.25	537.77	499.27	468.02	442.21
44000	3807.18	1970.00	1358.60	1053.64	871.26	750.16	664.08	599.89	550.28	510.88	478.91	452.49
45000	3893.71	2014.77	1389.47	1077.59	891.06	767.21	679.18	613.52	562.79	522.49	489.79	462.78
46000	3980.24	2059.54	1420.35	1101.53	910.86	784.26	694.27	627.16	575.29	534.10	500.67	473.06
47000	4066.76	2104.32	1451.23	1125.48	930.66	801.31	709.36	640.79	587.80	545.71	511.56	483.34
48000	4153.29	2149.09	1482.11	1149.42	950.46	818.36	724.45	654.42	600.31	557.33	522.44	493.63
49000	4239.82	2193.86	1512.98	1173.37	970.26	835.41	739.55	668.06	612.81	568.94	533.33	503.91
50000	4326.34	2238.63	1543.86	1197.32	990.06	852.46	754.64	681.69	625.32	580.55	544.21	514.20
55000	4758.98	2462.50	1698.25	1317.05	1089.07	937.70	830.10	749.86	687.85	638.60	598.63	565.61
60000	5191.61	2686.36	1852.63	1436.78	1188.08	1022.95	905.57	818.03	750.38	696.66	653.05	617.03
65000	5624.24	2910.22	2007.02	1556.51	1287.08	1108.19	981.03	886.20	812.91	754.71	707.47	668.45
70000	6056.88	3134.09	2161.40	1676.24	1386.09	1193.44	1056.49	954.37	875.44	812.76	761.89	719.87
75000	6489.51	3357.95	2315.79	1795.97	1485.09	1278.68	1131.96	1022.53	937.98	870.82	816.31	771.29
80000	6922.14	3581.81	2470.17	1915.70	1584.10	1363.93	1207.42	1090.70	1000.51	928.87	870.73	822.71
85000	7354.78	3805.67	2624.56	2035.44	1683.11	1449.17	1282.88	1158.87	1063.04	986.93	925.15	874.13
90000	7787.41	4029.54	2778.94	2155.17	1782.11	1534.42	1358.35	1227.04	1125.57	1044.98	979.57	925.55
95000	8220.05	4253.40	2933.33	2274.90	1881.12	1619.66	1433.81	1295.21	1188.10	1103.04	1033.99	976.97
100000	8652.68	4477.26	3087.71	2394.63	1980.12	1704.91	1509.27	1363.38	1250.63	1161.09	1088.42	1028.39

Table 1

MONTHLY

PAYMENT REQUIRED TO AMORTIZE A LOAN

7.00%

7%

TERM AMOUNT	13 YEARS	14 YEARS	15 YEARS	16 YEARS	17 YEARS	18 YEARS	19 YEARS	20 YEARS	25 YEARS	30 YEARS	35 YEARS	40 YEARS
50	.49	.47	.45	.44	.42	.41	.40	.39	.36	.34	.32	.32
100	.98	.94	.90	.87	.84	.82	.80	.78	.71	.67	.64	.63
200	1.96	1.88	1.80	1.74	1.68	1.64	1.59	1.56	1.42	1.34	1.28	1.25
300	2.94	2.81	2.70	2.61	2.52	2.45	2.39	2.33	2.13	2.00	1.92	1.87
400	3.92	3.75	3.60	3.47	3.36	3.27	3.18	3.11	2.83	2.67	2.56	2.49
500	4.90	4.68	4.50	4.34	4.20	4.08	3.98	3.88	3.54	3.33	3.20	3.11
600	5.87	5.62	5.40	5.21	5.04	4.90	4.77	4.66	4.25	4.00	3.84	3.73
700	6.85	6.55	6.30	6.08	5.88	5.71	5.56	5.43	4.95	4.66	4.48	4.36
800	7.83	7.49	7.20	6.94	6.72	6.53	6.36	6.21	5.66	5.33	5.12	4.98
900	8.81	8.42	8.09	7.81	7.56	7.34	7.15	6.98	6.37	5.99	5.75	5.60
1000	9.79	9.36	8.99	8.68	8.40	8.16	7.95	7.76	7.07	6.66	6.39	6.22
2000	19.57	18.71	17.98	17.35	16.80	16.32	15.89	15.51	14.14	13.31	12.78	12.43
3000	29.35	28.07	26.97	26.02	25.19	24.47	23.83	23.26	21.21	19.96	19.17	18.65
4000	39.13	37.42	35.96	34.69	33.59	32.63	31.77	31.02	28.28	26.62	25.56	24.86
5000	48.91	46.78	44.95	43.37	41.99	40.78	39.71	38.77	35.34	33.27	31.95	31.08
6000	58.69	56.13	53.93	52.04	50.38	48.94	47.66	46.52	42.41	39.92	38.34	37.29
7000	68.47	65.48	62.92	60.71	58.78	57.09	55.60	54.28	49.48	46.58	44.72	43.51
8000	78.25	74.84	71.91	69.38	67.18	65.25	63.54	62.03	56.55	53.23	51.11	49.72
9000	88.03	84.19	80.90	78.05	75.57	73.40	71.48	69.78	63.62	59.88	57.50	55.93
10000	97.81	93.55	89.89	86.73	83.97	81.56	79.42	77.53	70.68	66.54	63.89	62.15
11000	107.59	102.90	98.88	95.40	92.37	89.71	87.37	85.29	77.75	73.19	70.28	68.36
12000	117.37	112.25	107.86	104.07	100.76	97.87	95.31	93.04	84.82	79.84	76.67	74.58
13000	127.15	121.61	116.85	112.74	109.16	106.02	103.25	100.79	91.89	86.49	83.06	80.79
14000	136.94	130.96	125.84	121.41	117.56	114.18	111.19	108.55	98.95	93.15	89.44	87.01
15000	146.72	140.32	134.83	130.09	125.95	122.33	119.13	116.30	106.02	99.80	95.83	93.22
16000	156.50	149.67	143.82	138.76	134.35	130.49	127.08	124.05	113.09	106.45	102.22	99.43
17000	166.28	159.02	152.81	147.43	142.75	138.64	135.02	131.81	120.16	113.11	108.61	105.65
18000	176.06	168.38	161.79	156.10	151.14	146.80	142.96	139.56	127.23	119.76	115.00	111.86
19000	185.84	177.73	170.78	164.77	159.54	154.95	150.90	147.31	134.29	126.41	121.39	118.08
20000	195.62	187.09	179.77	173.45	167.94	163.11	158.84	155.06	141.36	133.07	127.78	124.29
21000	205.40	196.44	188.76	182.12	176.33	171.26	166.79	162.82	148.43	139.72	134.16	130.51
22000	215.18	205.79	197.75	190.79	184.73	179.42	174.73	170.57	155.50	146.37	140.55	136.72
23000	224.96	215.15	206.74	199.46	193.13	187.57	182.67	178.32	162.56	153.02	146.94	142.93
24000	234.74	224.50	215.72	208.13	201.52	195.73	190.61	186.08	169.63	159.68	153.33	149.15
25000	244.52	233.86	224.71	216.81	209.92	203.88	198.55	193.83	176.70	166.33	159.72	155.36
26000	254.30	243.21	233.70	225.48	218.32	212.04	206.50	201.58	183.77	172.98	166.11	161.58
27000	264.09	252.56	242.69	234.15	226.71	220.19	214.44	209.34	190.84	179.64	172.50	167.79
28000	273.87	261.92	251.68	242.82	235.11	228.35	222.38	217.09	197.90	186.29	178.88	174.01
29000	283.65	271.27	260.67	251.50	243.51	236.50	230.32	224.84	204.97	192.94	185.27	180.22
30000	293.43	280.63	269.65	260.17	251.90	244.66	238.26	232.59	212.04	199.60	191.66	186.43
31000	303.21	289.98	278.64	268.84	260.30	252.81	246.20	240.35	219.11	206.25	198.05	192.65
32000	312.99	299.33	287.63	277.51	268.70	260.97	254.15	248.10	226.17	212.90	204.44	198.86
33000	322.77	308.69	296.62	286.18	277.09	269.12	262.09	255.85	233.24	219.55	210.83	205.08
34000	332.55	318.04	305.61	294.86	285.49	277.28	270.03	263.61	240.31	226.21	217.22	211.29
35000	342.33	327.40	314.59	303.53	293.89	285.43	277.97	271.36	247.38	232.86	223.60	217.51
36000	352.11	336.75	323.58	312.20	302.28	293.59	285.91	279.11	254.45	239.51	229.99	223.72
37000	361.89	346.10	332.57	320.87	310.68	301.74	293.86	286.87	261.51	246.17	236.38	229.94
38000	371.67	355.46	341.56	329.54	319.08	309.90	301.80	294.62	268.58	252.82	242.77	236.15
39000	381.45	364.81	350.55	338.22	327.47	318.05	309.74	302.37	275.65	259.47	249.16	242.36
40000	391.23	374.17	359.54	346.89	335.87	326.21	317.68	310.12	282.72	266.13	255.55	248.58
41000	401.02	383.52	368.52	355.56	344.27	334.36	325.62	317.88	289.78	272.78	261.94	254.79
42000	410.80	392.87	377.51	364.23	352.66	342.52	333.57	325.63	296.85	279.43	268.32	261.01
43000	420.58	402.23	386.50	372.90	361.06	350.67	341.51	333.38	303.92	286.09	274.71	267.22
44000	430.36	411.58	395.49	381.58	369.46	358.83	349.45	341.14	310.99	292.74	281.10	273.43
45000	440.14	420.94	404.48	390.25	377.85	366.98	357.39	348.89	318.06	299.39	287.49	279.65
46000	449.92	430.29	413.47	398.92	386.25	375.14	365.33	356.64	325.12	306.04	293.88	285.86
47000	459.70	439.64	422.45	407.59	394.65	383.29	373.28	364.40	332.19	312.70	300.27	292.08
48000	469.48	449.00	431.44	416.26	403.04	391.45	381.22	372.15	339.26	319.35	306.66	298.29
49000	479.26	458.35	440.43	424.94	411.44	399.60	389.16	379.90	346.33	326.00	313.04	304.51
50000	489.04	467.71	449.42	433.61	419.84	407.76	397.10	387.65	353.39	332.66	319.43	310.72
55000	537.95	514.48	494.36	476.97	461.82	448.53	436.81	426.42	388.73	365.92	351.38	341.79
60000	586.85	561.25	539.30	520.33	503.80	489.31	476.52	465.18	424.07	399.19	383.32	372.86
65000	635.75	608.02	584.24	563.69	545.78	530.08	516.23	503.95	459.41	432.45	415.26	403.94
70000	684.66	654.79	629.18	607.05	587.77	570.86	555.94	542.71	494.75	465.72	447.20	435.01
75000	733.56	701.56	674.13	650.41	629.75	611.63	595.65	581.48	530.09	498.98	479.15	466.08
80000	782.46	748.33	719.07	693.77	671.73	652.41	635.36	620.24	565.43	532.25	511.09	497.15
85000	831.37	795.10	764.01	737.13	713.72	693.18	675.07	659.01	600.77	565.51	543.03	528.22
90000	880.27	841.87	808.95	780.49	755.70	733.96	714.78	697.77	636.11	598.78	574.98	559.29
95000	929.18	888.64	853.89	823.85	797.68	774.73	754.49	736.54	671.45	632.04	606.92	590.36
100000	978.08	935.41	898.83	867.21	839.67	815.51	794.20	775.30	706.78	665.31	638.86	621.44

Table 1

7.25%

MONTHLY
PAYMENT REQUIRED TO AMORTIZE A LOAN

7%

TERM	1 YEAR	2 YEARS	3 YEARS	4 YEARS	5 YEARS	6 YEARS	7 YEARS	8 YEARS	9 YEARS	10 YEARS	11 YEARS	12 YEARS
AMOUNT												
50	4.34	2.25	1.55	1.21	1.00	.86	.77	.69	.64	.59	.56	.53
100	8.67	4.49	3.10	2.41	2.00	1.72	1.53	1.38	1.27	1.18	1.11	1.05
200	17.33	8.98	6.20	4.82	3.99	3.44	3.05	2.76	2.53	2.35	2.21	2.09
300	26.00	13.47	9.30	7.22	5.98	5.16	4.57	4.13	3.79	3.53	3.31	3.13
400	34.66	17.96	12.40	9.63	7.97	6.87	6.09	5.51	5.06	4.70	4.41	4.17
500	43.33	22.45	15.50	12.04	9.96	8.59	7.61	6.88	6.32	5.88	5.51	5.21
600	51.99	26.94	18.60	14.44	11.96	10.31	9.13	8.26	7.58	7.05	6.61	6.26
700	60.65	31.43	21.70	16.85	13.95	12.02	10.66	9.64	8.85	8.22	7.72	7.30
800	69.32	35.91	24.80	19.25	15.94	13.74	12.18	11.01	10.11	9.40	8.82	8.34
900	77.98	40.40	27.90	21.66	17.93	15.46	13.70	12.39	11.37	10.57	9.92	9.38
1000	86.65	44.89	31.00	24.07	19.92	17.17	15.22	13.76	12.64	11.75	11.02	10.42
2000	173.29	89.78	61.99	48.13	39.84	34.34	30.44	27.52	25.27	23.49	22.04	20.84
3000	259.93	134.66	92.98	72.19	59.76	51.51	45.65	41.28	37.90	35.23	33.05	31.26
4000	346.57	179.55	123.97	96.25	79.68	68.68	60.87	55.04	50.54	46.97	44.07	41.68
5000	433.22	224.44	154.96	120.32	99.60	85.85	76.08	68.80	63.17	58.71	55.08	52.09
6000	519.86	269.32	185.95	144.38	119.52	103.02	91.30	82.56	75.80	70.45	66.10	62.51
7000	606.50	314.21	216.95	168.44	139.44	120.19	106.51	96.31	88.44	82.19	77.11	72.93
8000	693.14	359.09	247.94	192.50	159.36	137.36	121.73	110.07	101.07	93.93	88.13	83.35
9000	779.78	403.98	278.93	216.57	179.28	154.53	136.94	123.83	113.70	105.67	99.15	93.76
10000	866.43	448.87	309.92	240.63	199.20	171.70	152.16	137.59	126.34	117.41	110.16	104.18
11000	953.07	493.75	340.91	264.69	219.12	188.87	167.37	151.35	138.97	129.15	121.18	114.60
12000	1039.71	538.64	371.90	288.75	239.04	206.04	182.59	165.11	151.60	140.89	132.19	125.02
13000	1126.35	583.52	402.89	312.82	258.96	223.21	197.80	178.86	164.24	152.63	143.21	135.43
14000	1212.99	628.41	433.89	336.88	278.88	240.38	213.02	192.62	176.87	164.37	154.22	145.85
15000	1299.64	673.30	464.88	360.94	298.80	257.54	228.23	206.38	189.50	176.11	165.24	156.27
16000	1386.28	718.18	495.87	385.00	318.71	274.71	243.45	220.14	202.14	187.85	176.25	166.69
17000	1472.92	763.07	526.86	409.07	338.63	291.88	258.66	233.90	214.77	199.59	187.27	177.10
18000	1559.56	807.95	557.85	433.13	358.55	309.05	273.88	247.66	227.40	211.33	198.29	187.52
19000	1646.20	852.84	588.84	457.19	378.47	326.22	289.09	261.42	240.04	223.07	209.30	197.94
20000	1732.85	897.73	619.84	481.25	398.39	343.39	304.31	275.17	252.67	234.81	220.32	208.36
21000	1819.49	942.61	650.83	505.32	418.31	360.56	319.52	288.93	265.30	246.55	231.33	218.77
22000	1906.13	987.50	681.82	529.38	438.23	377.73	334.74	302.69	277.94	258.29	242.35	229.19
23000	1992.77	1032.38	712.81	553.44	458.15	394.90	349.95	316.45	290.57	270.03	253.36	239.61
24000	2079.41	1077.27	743.80	577.50	478.07	412.07	365.17	330.21	303.20	281.77	264.38	250.03
25000	2166.05	1122.16	774.79	601.57	497.99	429.24	380.38	343.97	315.84	293.51	275.40	260.44
26000	2252.70	1167.04	805.78	625.63	517.91	446.41	395.60	357.72	328.47	305.25	286.41	270.86
27000	2339.34	1211.93	836.78	649.69	537.83	463.58	410.81	371.48	341.10	316.99	297.43	281.28
28000	2425.98	1256.81	867.77	673.75	557.75	480.75	426.03	385.24	353.74	328.73	308.44	291.70
29000	2512.62	1301.70	898.76	697.81	577.67	497.91	441.25	399.00	366.37	340.47	319.46	302.11
30000	2599.27	1346.59	929.75	721.88	597.59	515.08	456.46	412.76	379.00	352.21	330.47	312.53
31000	2685.91	1391.47	960.74	745.94	617.51	532.25	471.68	426.52	391.64	363.95	341.49	322.95
32000	2772.55	1436.36	991.73	770.00	637.42	549.42	486.89	440.28	404.27	375.69	352.50	333.37
33000	2859.19	1481.24	1022.73	794.06	657.34	566.59	502.11	454.03	416.90	387.43	363.52	343.78
34000	2945.83	1526.13	1053.72	818.13	677.26	583.76	517.32	467.79	429.54	399.17	374.54	354.20
35000	3032.48	1571.02	1084.71	842.19	697.18	600.93	532.54	481.55	442.17	410.91	385.55	364.62
36000	3119.12	1615.90	1115.70	866.25	717.10	618.10	547.75	495.31	454.80	422.65	396.57	375.04
37000	3205.76	1660.79	1146.69	890.31	737.02	635.27	562.97	509.07	467.44	434.39	407.58	385.45
38000	3292.40	1705.67	1177.68	914.38	756.94	652.44	578.18	522.83	480.07	446.13	418.60	395.87
39000	3379.04	1750.56	1208.67	938.44	776.86	669.61	593.40	536.58	492.70	457.87	429.61	406.29
40000	3465.69	1795.45	1239.67	962.50	796.78	686.78	608.61	550.34	505.34	469.61	440.63	416.71
41000	3552.33	1840.33	1270.66	986.56	816.70	703.95	623.83	564.10	517.97	481.35	451.64	427.12
42000	3638.97	1885.22	1301.65	1010.63	836.62	721.12	639.04	577.86	530.60	493.09	462.66	437.54
43000	3725.61	1930.10	1332.64	1034.69	856.54	738.29	654.26	591.62	543.24	504.83	473.68	447.96
44000	3812.25	1974.99	1363.63	1058.75	876.46	755.45	669.47	605.38	555.87	516.57	484.69	458.38
45000	3898.90	2019.88	1394.62	1082.81	896.38	772.62	684.69	619.14	568.50	528.31	495.71	468.80
46000	3985.54	2064.76	1425.62	1106.88	916.30	789.79	699.90	632.89	581.14	540.05	506.72	479.21
47000	4072.18	2109.65	1456.61	1130.94	936.21	806.96	715.12	646.65	593.77	551.79	517.74	489.63
48000	4158.82	2154.53	1487.60	1155.00	956.13	824.13	730.33	660.41	606.40	563.53	528.75	500.05
49000	4245.46	2199.42	1518.59	1179.06	976.05	841.30	745.55	674.17	619.04	575.27	539.77	510.47
50000	4332.11	2244.31	1549.58	1203.13	995.97	858.47	760.76	687.93	631.67	587.01	550.79	520.88
55000	4765.32	2468.74	1704.54	1323.44	1095.57	944.32	836.84	756.72	694.84	645.71	605.86	572.97
60000	5198.53	2693.17	1859.50	1443.75	1195.17	1030.16	912.92	825.51	758.00	704.41	660.94	625.06
65000	5631.74	2917.60	2014.45	1564.06	1294.76	1116.01	988.99	894.30	821.17	763.11	716.02	677.15
70000	6064.95	3142.03	2169.41	1684.37	1394.36	1201.86	1065.07	963.10	884.33	821.81	771.10	729.23
75000	6498.16	3366.46	2324.37	1804.69	1493.96	1287.70	1141.14	1031.89	947.50	880.51	826.18	781.32
80000	6931.37	3590.89	2479.33	1925.00	1593.55	1373.55	1217.22	1100.68	1010.67	939.21	881.25	833.41
85000	7364.58	3815.32	2634.29	2045.31	1693.15	1459.40	1293.30	1169.47	1073.83	997.91	936.33	885.50
90000	7797.79	4039.75	2789.24	2165.62	1792.75	1545.24	1369.37	1238.27	1137.00	1056.61	991.41	937.59
95000	8231.00	4264.18	2944.20	2285.93	1892.34	1631.09	1445.45	1307.06	1200.17	1115.31	1046.49	989.67
100000	8664.21	4488.61	3099.16	2406.25	1991.94	1716.94	1521.52	1375.85	1263.33	1174.02	1101.57	1041.76

Table 1

MONTHLY 7.25%

PAYMENT REQUIRED TO AMORTIZE A LOAN

7%

TERM / AMOUNT	13 YEARS	14 YEARS	15 YEARS	16 YEARS	17 YEARS	18 YEARS	19 YEARS	20 YEARS	25 YEARS	30 YEARS	35 YEARS	40 YEARS
50	.50	.48	.46	.45	.43	.42	.41	.40	.37	.35	.33	.32
100	1.00	.95	.92	.89	.86	.84	.81	.80	.73	.69	.66	.64
200	1.99	1.90	1.83	1.77	1.71	1.67	1.62	1.59	1.45	1.37	1.32	1.28
300	2.98	2.85	2.74	2.65	2.57	2.50	2.43	2.38	2.17	2.05	1.97	1.92
400	3.97	3.80	3.66	3.53	3.42	3.33	3.24	3.17	2.90	2.73	2.63	2.56
500	4.96	4.75	4.57	4.41	4.28	4.16	4.05	3.96	3.62	3.42	3.29	3.20
600	5.96	5.70	5.48	5.29	5.13	4.99	4.86	4.75	4.34	4.10	3.94	3.84
700	6.95	6.65	6.40	6.18	5.98	5.82	5.67	5.54	5.06	4.78	4.60	4.48
800	7.94	7.60	7.31	7.06	6.84	6.65	6.48	6.33	5.79	5.46	5.26	5.12
900	8.93	8.55	8.22	7.94	7.69	7.48	7.29	7.12	6.51	6.14	5.91	5.76
1000	9.92	9.50	9.13	8.82	8.55	8.31	8.10	7.91	7.23	6.83	6.57	6.40
2000	19.84	18.99	18.26	17.63	17.09	16.61	16.19	15.81	14.46	13.65	13.13	12.80
3000	29.76	28.48	27.39	26.45	25.63	24.91	24.28	23.72	21.69	20.47	19.70	19.20
4000	39.67	37.97	36.52	35.26	34.17	33.21	32.37	31.62	28.92	27.29	26.26	25.59
5000	49.59	47.47	45.65	44.08	42.71	41.51	40.46	39.52	36.15	34.11	32.83	31.99
6000	59.51	56.96	54.78	52.89	51.25	49.82	48.55	47.43	43.37	40.94	39.39	38.39
7000	69.42	66.45	63.91	61.71	59.79	58.12	56.64	55.33	50.60	47.76	45.96	44.78
8000	79.34	75.94	73.03	70.52	68.33	66.42	64.73	63.24	57.83	54.58	52.52	51.18
9000	89.26	85.43	82.16	79.34	76.88	74.72	72.82	71.14	65.06	61.40	59.09	57.58
10000	99.17	94.93	91.29	88.15	85.42	83.02	80.91	79.04	72.29	68.22	65.65	63.97
11000	109.09	104.42	100.42	96.97	93.96	91.32	89.00	86.95	79.51	75.04	72.22	70.37
12000	119.01	113.91	109.55	105.78	102.50	99.63	97.09	94.85	86.74	81.87	78.78	76.77
13000	128.92	123.40	118.68	114.59	111.04	107.93	105.18	102.75	93.97	88.69	85.35	83.16
14000	138.84	132.90	127.81	123.41	119.58	116.23	113.27	110.66	101.20	95.51	91.91	89.56
15000	148.76	142.39	136.93	132.22	128.12	124.53	121.37	118.56	108.43	102.33	98.48	95.96
16000	158.67	151.88	146.06	141.04	136.66	132.83	129.46	126.47	115.65	109.15	105.04	102.35
17000	168.59	161.37	155.19	149.85	145.21	141.13	137.55	134.37	122.88	115.97	111.60	108.75
18000	178.51	170.86	164.32	158.67	153.75	149.44	145.64	142.27	130.11	122.80	118.17	115.15
19000	188.42	180.36	173.45	167.48	162.29	157.74	153.73	150.18	137.34	129.62	124.73	121.54
20000	198.34	189.85	182.58	176.30	170.83	166.04	161.82	158.08	144.57	136.44	131.30	127.94
21000	208.26	199.34	191.71	185.11	179.37	174.34	169.91	165.98	151.79	143.26	137.86	134.34
22000	218.17	208.83	200.83	193.93	187.91	182.64	178.00	173.89	159.02	150.08	144.43	140.73
23000	228.09	218.33	209.96	202.74	196.45	190.94	186.09	181.79	166.25	156.91	150.99	147.13
24000	238.01	227.82	219.09	211.55	204.99	199.25	194.18	189.70	173.48	163.73	157.56	153.53
25000	247.92	237.31	228.22	220.37	213.54	207.55	202.27	197.60	180.71	170.55	164.12	159.92
26000	257.84	246.80	237.35	229.18	222.08	215.85	210.36	205.50	187.93	177.37	170.69	166.32
27000	267.76	256.29	246.48	238.00	230.62	224.15	218.45	213.41	195.16	184.19	177.25	172.72
28000	277.67	265.79	255.61	246.81	239.16	232.45	226.54	221.31	202.39	191.01	183.82	179.11
29000	287.59	275.28	264.74	255.63	247.70	240.76	234.63	229.21	209.62	197.84	190.38	185.51
30000	297.51	284.77	273.86	264.44	256.24	249.06	242.73	237.12	216.85	204.66	196.95	191.91
31000	307.42	294.26	282.99	273.26	264.78	257.36	250.82	245.02	224.08	211.48	203.51	198.30
32000	317.34	303.75	292.12	282.07	273.32	265.66	258.91	252.93	231.30	218.30	210.07	204.70
33000	327.26	313.25	301.25	290.89	281.87	273.96	267.00	260.83	238.53	225.12	216.64	211.10
34000	337.17	322.74	310.38	299.70	290.41	282.26	275.09	268.73	245.76	231.94	223.20	217.49
35000	347.09	332.23	319.51	308.52	298.95	290.57	283.18	276.64	252.99	238.77	229.77	223.89
36000	357.01	341.72	328.64	317.33	307.49	298.87	291.27	284.54	260.22	245.59	236.33	230.29
37000	366.92	351.22	337.76	326.14	316.03	307.17	299.36	292.44	267.44	252.41	242.90	236.68
38000	376.84	360.71	346.89	334.96	324.57	315.47	307.45	300.35	274.67	259.23	249.46	243.08
39000	386.76	370.20	356.02	343.77	333.11	323.77	315.54	308.25	281.90	266.05	256.03	249.48
40000	396.67	379.69	365.15	352.59	341.65	332.07	323.63	316.16	289.13	272.88	262.59	255.87
41000	406.59	389.18	374.28	361.40	350.20	340.38	331.72	324.06	296.36	279.70	269.16	262.27
42000	416.51	398.68	383.41	370.22	358.74	348.68	339.81	331.96	303.58	286.52	275.72	268.67
43000	426.42	408.17	392.54	379.03	367.28	356.98	347.90	339.87	310.81	293.34	282.29	275.06
44000	436.34	417.66	401.66	387.85	375.82	365.28	355.99	347.77	318.04	300.16	288.85	281.46
45000	446.26	427.15	410.79	396.66	384.36	373.58	364.09	355.67	325.27	306.98	295.42	287.86
46000	456.17	436.65	419.92	405.48	392.90	381.88	372.18	363.58	332.50	313.81	301.98	294.25
47000	466.09	446.14	429.05	414.29	401.44	390.19	380.27	371.48	339.72	320.63	308.54	300.65
48000	476.01	455.63	438.18	423.10	409.98	398.49	388.36	379.39	346.95	327.45	315.11	307.05
49000	485.92	465.12	447.31	431.92	418.52	406.79	396.45	387.29	354.18	334.27	321.67	313.44
50000	495.84	474.61	456.44	440.73	427.07	415.09	404.54	395.19	361.41	341.09	328.24	319.84
55000	545.42	522.07	502.08	484.81	469.77	456.60	444.99	434.71	397.55	375.20	361.06	351.82
60000	595.01	569.54	547.72	528.88	512.48	498.11	485.45	474.23	433.69	409.31	393.89	383.81
65000	644.59	617.00	593.37	572.95	555.18	539.62	525.90	513.75	469.83	443.42	426.71	415.79
70000	694.17	664.46	639.01	617.03	597.89	581.13	566.35	553.27	505.97	477.53	459.53	447.78
75000	743.76	711.92	684.65	661.10	640.60	622.63	606.81	592.79	542.11	511.64	492.36	479.76
80000	793.34	759.38	730.30	705.17	683.30	664.14	647.26	632.31	578.25	545.75	525.18	511.74
85000	842.93	806.84	775.94	749.24	726.01	705.65	687.71	671.82	614.39	579.85	558.00	543.73
90000	892.51	854.30	821.58	793.32	768.71	747.16	728.17	711.34	650.53	613.96	590.83	575.71
95000	942.09	901.76	867.22	837.39	811.42	788.67	768.62	750.86	686.67	648.07	623.65	607.69
100000	991.68	949.22	912.87	881.46	854.13	830.18	809.07	790.38	722.81	682.18	656.47	639.68

Table 1

7.50%

7%

MONTHLY
PAYMENT REQUIRED TO AMORTIZE A LOAN

TERM AMOUNT	1 YEAR	2 YEARS	3 YEARS	4 YEARS	5 YEARS	6 YEARS	7 YEARS	8 YEARS	9 YEARS	10 YEARS	11 YEARS	12 YEARS
50	4.34	2.25	1.56	1.21	1.01	.87	.77	.70	.64	.60	.56	.53
100	8.68	4.50	3.12	2.42	2.01	1.73	1.54	1.39	1.28	1.19	1.12	1.06
200	17.36	9.00	6.23	4.84	4.01	3.46	3.07	2.78	2.56	2.38	2.23	2.12
300	26.03	13.50	9.34	7.26	6.02	5.19	4.61	4.17	3.83	3.57	3.35	3.17
400	34.71	18.00	12.45	9.68	8.02	6.92	6.14	5.56	5.11	4.75	4.46	4.23
500	43.38	22.90	15.56	12.09	10.02	8.65	7.67	6.95	6.39	5.94	5.58	5.28
600	52.06	27.00	18.67	14.51	12.03	10.38	9.21	8.34	7.66	7.13	6.69	6.34
700	60.74	31.50	21.78	16.93	14.03	12.11	10.74	9.72	8.94	8.31	7.81	7.39
800	69.41	36.00	24.89	19.35	16.04	13.84	12.28	11.11	10.21	9.50	8.92	8.45
900	78.09	40.50	28.00	21.77	18.04	15.57	13.81	12.50	11.49	10.69	10.04	9.50
1000	86.76	45.00	31.11	24.18	20.04	17.30	15.34	13.89	12.77	11.88	11.15	10.56
2000	173.52	90.00	62.22	48.36	40.08	34.59	30.68	27.77	25.53	23.75	22.30	21.11
3000	260.28	135.00	93.32	72.54	60.12	51.88	46.02	41.66	38.29	35.62	33.45	31.66
4000	347.03	180.00	124.43	96.72	80.16	69.17	61.36	55.54	51.05	47.49	44.60	42.21
5000	433.79	225.00	155.54	120.90	100.19	86.46	76.70	69.42	63.81	59.36	55.75	52.77
6000	520.55	270.00	186.64	145.08	120.23	103.75	92.03	83.31	76.57	71.23	66.89	63.32
7000	607.31	315.00	217.75	169.26	140.27	121.04	107.37	97.19	89.33	83.10	78.04	73.87
8000	694.06	360.00	248.85	193.44	160.31	138.33	122.71	111.08	102.09	94.97	89.19	84.42
9000	780.82	405.00	279.96	217.62	180.35	155.62	138.05	124.96	114.85	106.84	100.34	94.98
10000	867.58	450.00	311.07	241.79	200.38	172.91	153.39	138.84	127.62	118.71	111.49	105.53
11000	954.34	495.00	342.17	265.97	220.42	190.20	168.73	152.73	140.38	130.58	122.63	116.08
12000	1041.09	540.00	373.28	290.15	240.46	207.49	184.06	166.61	153.14	142.45	133.78	126.63
13000	1127.85	585.00	404.39	314.33	260.50	224.78	199.40	180.50	165.90	154.32	144.93	137.18
14000	1214.61	630.00	435.49	338.51	280.54	242.07	214.74	194.38	178.66	166.19	156.08	147.74
15000	1301.37	675.00	466.60	362.69	300.57	259.36	230.08	208.26	191.42	178.06	167.23	158.29
16000	1388.12	720.00	497.70	386.87	320.61	276.65	245.42	222.15	204.18	189.93	178.37	168.84
17000	1474.88	765.00	528.81	411.05	340.65	293.94	260.76	236.03	216.94	201.80	189.52	179.39
18000	1561.64	810.00	559.92	435.23	360.69	311.23	276.09	249.91	229.70	213.67	200.67	189.95
19000	1648.40	855.00	591.02	459.40	380.73	328.52	291.43	263.80	242.46	225.54	211.82	200.50
20000	1735.15	900.00	622.13	483.58	400.76	345.81	306.77	277.68	255.23	237.41	222.97	211.05
21000	1821.91	945.00	653.24	507.76	420.80	363.10	322.11	291.57	267.99	249.28	234.11	221.60
22000	1908.67	990.00	684.34	531.94	440.84	380.39	337.45	305.45	280.75	261.15	245.26	232.15
23000	1995.43	1035.00	715.45	556.12	460.88	397.68	352.79	319.33	293.51	273.02	256.41	242.71
24000	2082.18	1080.00	746.55	580.30	480.92	414.97	368.12	333.22	306.27	284.89	267.56	253.26
25000	2168.94	1124.99	777.66	604.48	500.95	432.26	383.46	347.10	319.03	296.76	278.71	263.81
26000	2255.70	1169.99	808.77	628.66	520.99	449.55	398.80	360.99	331.79	308.63	289.85	274.36
27000	2342.46	1214.99	839.87	652.84	541.03	466.84	414.14	374.87	344.55	320.50	301.00	284.92
28000	2429.21	1259.99	870.98	677.01	561.07	484.13	429.48	388.75	357.31	332.37	312.15	295.47
29000	2515.97	1304.99	902.09	701.19	581.11	501.42	444.82	402.64	370.07	344.24	323.30	306.02
30000	2602.73	1349.99	933.19	725.37	601.14	518.71	460.15	416.52	382.84	356.11	334.45	316.57
31000	2689.48	1394.99	964.30	749.55	621.18	536.00	475.49	430.40	395.60	367.98	345.59	327.13
32000	2776.24	1439.99	995.40	773.73	641.22	553.29	490.83	444.29	408.36	379.85	356.74	337.68
33000	2863.00	1484.99	1026.51	797.91	661.26	570.58	506.17	458.17	421.12	391.72	367.89	348.23
34000	2949.76	1529.99	1057.62	822.09	681.30	587.87	521.51	472.06	433.88	403.59	379.04	358.78
35000	3036.51	1574.99	1088.72	846.27	701.33	605.16	536.84	485.94	446.64	415.46	390.19	369.33
36000	3123.27	1619.99	1119.83	870.45	721.37	622.45	552.18	499.82	459.40	427.33	401.33	379.89
37000	3210.03	1664.99	1150.94	894.62	741.41	639.74	567.52	513.71	472.16	439.20	412.48	390.44
38000	3296.79	1709.99	1182.04	918.80	761.45	657.03	582.86	527.59	484.92	451.07	423.63	400.99
39000	3383.54	1754.99	1213.15	942.98	781.48	674.32	598.20	541.48	497.68	462.94	434.78	411.54
40000	3470.30	1799.99	1244.25	967.16	801.52	691.61	613.54	555.36	510.45	474.81	445.93	422.10
41000	3557.06	1844.99	1275.36	991.34	821.56	708.90	628.87	569.24	523.21	486.68	457.07	432.65
42000	3643.82	1889.99	1306.47	1015.52	841.60	726.19	644.21	583.13	535.97	498.55	468.22	443.20
43000	3730.57	1934.99	1337.57	1039.70	861.64	743.48	659.55	597.01	548.73	510.42	479.37	453.75
44000	3817.33	1979.99	1368.68	1063.88	881.67	760.77	674.89	610.90	561.49	522.29	490.52	464.30
45000	3904.09	2024.99	1399.78	1088.06	901.71	778.06	690.23	624.78	574.25	534.16	501.67	474.86
46000	3990.85	2069.99	1430.89	1112.23	921.75	795.35	705.57	638.66	587.01	546.03	512.81	485.41
47000	4077.60	2114.99	1462.00	1136.41	941.79	812.64	720.90	652.55	599.77	557.90	523.96	495.96
48000	4164.36	2159.99	1493.10	1160.59	961.83	829.93	736.24	666.43	612.53	569.77	535.11	506.51
49000	4251.12	2204.99	1524.21	1184.77	981.86	847.22	751.58	680.31	625.29	581.64	546.26	517.07
50000	4337.88	2249.98	1555.32	1208.95	1001.90	864.51	766.92	694.20	638.06	593.51	557.41	527.62
55000	4771.66	2474.98	1710.85	1329.84	1102.09	950.96	843.61	763.62	701.86	652.86	613.15	580.38
60000	5205.45	2699.98	1866.38	1450.74	1202.28	1037.41	920.30	833.04	765.67	712.22	668.89	633.14
65000	5639.24	2924.98	2021.91	1571.63	1302.47	1123.86	996.99	902.46	829.47	771.57	724.63	685.90
70000	6073.02	3149.98	2177.44	1692.53	1402.66	1210.31	1073.68	971.88	893.28	830.92	780.37	738.66
75000	6506.81	3374.97	2332.97	1813.42	1502.85	1296.76	1150.38	1041.30	957.08	890.27	836.11	791.42
80000	6940.60	3599.97	2488.50	1934.32	1603.04	1383.21	1227.07	1110.71	1020.89	949.62	891.85	844.19
85000	7374.39	3824.97	2644.03	2055.21	1703.23	1469.66	1303.76	1180.13	1084.69	1008.97	947.59	896.95
90000	7808.17	4049.97	2799.56	2176.11	1803.42	1556.12	1380.45	1249.55	1148.50	1068.32	1003.33	949.71
95000	8241.96	4274.97	2955.10	2297.00	1903.61	1642.57	1457.14	1318.97	1212.30	1127.67	1059.07	1002.47
100000	8675.75	4499.96	3110.63	2417.90	2003.80	1729.02	1533.83	1388.39	1276.11	1187.02	1114.81	1055.23

Table 1

MONTHLY
PAYMENT REQUIRED TO AMORTIZE A LOAN

7.50%

7%

TERM / AMOUNT	13 YEARS	14 YEARS	15 YEARS	16 YEARS	17 YEARS	18 YEARS	19 YEARS	20 YEARS	25 YEARS	30 YEARS	35 YEARS	40 YEARS
50	.51	.49	.47	.45	.44	.43	.42	.41	.37	.35	.34	.33
100	1.01	.97	.93	.90	.87	.85	.83	.81	.74	.70	.68	.66
200	2.02	1.93	1.86	1.80	1.74	1.69	1.65	1.62	1.48	1.40	1.35	1.32
300	3.02	2.89	2.79	2.69	2.61	2.54	2.48	2.42	2.22	2.10	2.03	1.98
400	4.03	3.86	3.71	3.59	3.48	3.38	3.30	3.23	2.96	2.80	2.70	2.64
500	5.03	4.82	4.64	4.48	4.35	4.23	4.13	4.03	3.70	3.50	3.38	3.30
600	6.04	5.78	5.57	5.38	5.22	5.07	4.95	4.84	4.44	4.20	4.05	3.95
700	7.04	6.75	6.49	6.28	6.09	5.92	5.77	5.64	5.18	4.90	4.72	4.61
800	8.05	7.71	7.42	7.17	6.95	6.76	6.60	6.45	5.92	5.60	5.40	5.27
900	9.05	8.67	8.35	8.07	7.82	7.61	7.42	7.26	6.66	6.30	6.07	5.93
1000	10.06	9.64	9.28	8.96	8.69	8.45	8.25	8.06	7.39	7.00	6.75	6.59
2000	20.11	19.27	18.55	17.92	17.38	16.90	16.49	16.12	14.78	13.99	13.49	13.17
3000	30.17	28.90	27.82	26.88	26.07	25.35	24.73	24.17	22.17	20.98	20.23	19.75
4000	40.22	38.53	37.09	35.84	34.75	33.80	32.97	32.23	29.56	27.97	26.97	26.33
5000	50.27	48.16	46.36	44.80	43.44	42.25	41.21	40.28	36.95	34.97	33.72	32.91
6000	60.33	57.79	55.63	53.75	52.13	50.70	49.45	48.34	44.34	41.96	40.46	39.49
7000	70.38	67.43	64.90	62.71	60.81	59.15	57.69	56.40	51.73	48.95	47.20	46.07
8000	80.43	77.06	74.17	71.67	69.50	67.60	65.93	64.45	59.12	55.94	53.94	52.65
9000	90.49	86.69	83.44	80.63	78.19	76.05	74.17	72.51	66.51	62.93	60.69	59.23
10000	100.54	96.32	92.71	89.59	86.88	84.50	82.41	80.56	73.90	69.93	67.43	65.81
11000	110.60	105.95	101.98	98.55	95.56	92.95	90.65	88.62	81.29	76.92	74.17	72.39
12000	120.65	115.58	111.25	107.50	104.25	101.40	98.89	96.68	88.68	83.91	80.91	78.97
13000	130.70	125.21	120.52	116.46	112.94	109.85	107.14	104.73	96.07	90.90	87.66	85.55
14000	140.76	134.85	129.79	125.42	121.62	118.30	115.38	112.79	103.46	97.90	94.40	92.13
15000	150.81	144.48	139.06	134.38	130.31	126.75	123.62	120.84	110.85	104.89	101.14	98.72
16000	160.86	154.11	148.33	143.34	139.00	135.20	131.86	128.90	118.24	111.88	107.88	105.30
17000	170.92	163.74	157.60	152.30	147.69	143.65	140.10	136.96	125.63	118.87	114.63	111.88
18000	180.97	173.37	166.87	161.25	156.37	152.10	148.34	145.01	133.02	125.86	121.37	118.46
19000	191.03	183.00	176.14	170.21	165.06	160.55	156.58	153.07	140.41	132.86	128.11	125.04
20000	201.08	192.63	185.41	179.17	173.75	169.00	164.82	161.12	147.80	139.85	134.85	131.62
21000	211.13	202.27	194.68	188.13	182.43	177.45	173.06	169.18	155.19	146.84	141.60	138.20
22000	221.19	211.90	203.95	197.09	191.12	185.90	181.30	177.24	162.58	153.83	148.34	144.78
23000	231.24	221.53	213.22	206.05	199.81	194.35	189.54	185.29	169.97	160.82	155.08	151.36
24000	241.29	231.16	222.49	215.00	208.50	202.80	197.78	193.35	177.36	167.82	161.82	157.94
25000	251.35	240.79	231.76	223.96	217.18	211.25	206.02	201.40	184.75	174.81	168.57	164.52
26000	261.40	250.42	241.03	232.92	225.87	219.70	214.27	209.46	192.14	181.80	175.31	171.10
27000	271.46	260.05	250.30	241.88	234.56	228.15	222.51	217.52	199.53	188.79	182.05	177.68
28000	281.51	269.69	259.57	250.84	243.24	236.60	230.75	225.57	206.92	195.79	188.79	184.26
29000	291.56	279.32	268.84	259.80	251.93	245.05	238.99	233.63	214.31	202.78	195.54	190.85
30000	301.62	288.95	278.11	268.75	260.62	253.50	247.23	241.68	221.70	209.77	202.28	197.43
31000	311.67	298.58	287.38	277.71	269.30	261.95	255.47	249.74	229.09	216.76	209.02	204.01
32000	321.72	308.21	296.65	286.67	277.99	270.40	263.71	257.79	236.48	223.75	215.76	210.59
33000	331.78	317.84	305.92	295.63	286.68	278.85	271.95	265.85	243.87	230.75	222.51	217.17
34000	341.83	327.47	315.19	304.59	295.37	287.30	280.19	273.91	251.26	237.74	229.25	223.75
35000	351.88	337.11	324.46	313.54	304.05	295.75	288.43	281.96	258.65	244.73	235.99	230.33
36000	361.94	346.74	333.73	322.50	312.74	304.20	296.67	290.02	266.04	251.72	242.73	236.91
37000	371.99	356.37	343.00	331.46	321.43	312.65	304.91	298.07	273.43	258.71	249.47	243.49
38000	382.05	366.00	352.27	340.42	330.11	321.09	313.15	306.13	280.82	265.71	256.22	250.07
39000	392.10	375.63	361.54	349.38	338.80	329.54	321.40	314.19	288.21	272.70	262.96	256.65
40000	402.15	385.26	370.81	358.34	347.49	337.99	329.64	322.24	295.60	279.69	269.70	263.23
41000	412.21	394.89	380.08	367.29	356.18	346.44	337.88	330.30	302.99	286.68	276.44	269.81
42000	422.26	404.53	389.35	376.25	364.86	354.89	346.12	338.35	310.38	293.68	283.19	276.39
43000	432.31	414.16	398.62	385.21	373.55	363.34	354.36	346.41	317.77	300.67	289.93	282.98
44000	442.37	423.79	407.89	394.17	382.24	371.79	362.60	354.47	325.16	307.66	296.67	289.56
45000	452.42	433.42	417.16	403.13	390.92	380.24	370.84	362.52	332.55	314.65	303.41	296.14
46000	462.48	443.05	426.43	412.09	399.61	388.69	379.08	370.58	339.94	321.64	310.16	302.72
47000	472.53	452.68	435.70	421.04	408.30	397.14	387.32	378.63	347.33	328.64	316.90	309.30
48000	482.58	462.31	444.97	430.00	416.99	405.59	395.56	386.69	354.72	335.63	323.64	315.88
49000	492.64	471.95	454.24	438.96	425.67	414.04	403.80	394.75	362.11	342.62	330.38	322.46
50000	502.69	481.58	463.51	447.92	434.36	422.49	412.04	402.80	369.50	349.61	337.13	329.04
55000	552.96	529.73	509.86	492.71	477.80	464.74	453.25	443.08	406.45	384.57	370.84	361.94
60000	603.23	577.89	556.21	537.50	521.23	506.99	494.45	483.36	443.40	419.53	404.55	394.85
65000	653.50	626.05	602.56	582.29	564.67	549.24	535.66	523.64	480.35	454.49	438.26	427.75
70000	703.76	674.21	648.91	627.08	608.10	591.49	576.86	563.92	517.30	489.46	471.97	460.65
75000	754.03	722.36	695.26	671.88	651.54	633.73	618.06	604.20	554.25	524.42	505.69	493.56
80000	804.30	770.52	741.61	716.67	694.97	675.98	659.27	644.48	591.20	559.38	539.40	526.46
85000	854.57	818.68	787.97	761.46	738.41	718.23	700.47	684.76	628.15	594.34	573.11	559.37
90000	904.84	866.83	834.32	806.25	781.84	760.48	741.68	725.04	665.10	629.30	606.82	592.27
95000	955.11	914.99	880.67	851.04	825.28	802.73	782.88	765.32	702.05	664.26	640.54	625.17
100000	1005.38	963.15	927.02	895.83	868.71	844.98	824.08	805.60	739.00	699.22	674.25	658.08

23

Table 1

7.75%

MONTHLY
PAYMENT REQUIRED TO AMORTIZE A LOAN

7%

TERM / AMOUNT	1 YEAR	2 YEARS	3 YEARS	4 YEARS	5 YEARS	6 YEARS	7 YEARS	8 YEARS	9 YEARS	10 YEARS	11 YEARS	12 YEARS
50	4.35	2.26	1.57	1.22	1.01	.88	.78	.71	.65	.61	.57	.54
100	8.69	4.52	3.13	2.43	2.02	1.75	1.55	1.41	1.29	1.21	1.13	1.07
200	17.38	9.03	6.25	4.86	4.04	3.49	3.10	2.81	2.58	2.41	2.26	2.14
300	26.07	13.54	9.37	7.29	6.05	5.23	4.64	4.21	3.87	3.61	3.39	3.21
400	34.75	18.05	12.49	9.72	8.07	6.97	6.19	5.61	5.16	4.81	4.52	4.28
500	43.44	22.56	15.62	12.15	10.08	8.71	7.74	7.01	6.45	6.01	5.65	5.35
600	52.13	27.07	18.74	14.58	12.10	10.45	9.28	8.41	7.74	7.21	6.77	6.42
700	60.82	31.58	21.86	17.01	14.11	12.19	10.83	9.81	9.03	8.41	7.90	7.49
800	69.50	36.10	24.98	19.44	16.13	13.93	12.37	11.21	10.32	9.61	9.03	8.56
900	78.19	40.61	28.10	21.87	18.15	15.68	13.92	12.61	11.61	10.81	10.16	9.62
1000	86.88	45.12	31.23	24.30	20.16	17.42	15.47	14.01	12.89	12.01	11.29	10.69
2000	173.75	90.23	62.45	48.60	40.32	34.83	30.93	28.02	25.78	24.01	22.57	21.38
3000	260.62	135.35	93.67	72.89	60.48	52.24	46.39	42.03	38.67	36.01	33.85	32.07
4000	347.50	180.46	124.89	97.19	80.63	69.65	61.85	56.04	51.56	48.01	45.13	42.76
5000	434.37	225.57	156.11	121.48	100.79	87.06	77.31	70.05	64.45	60.01	56.41	53.44
6000	521.24	270.69	187.33	145.78	120.95	104.47	92.78	84.06	77.34	72.01	67.69	64.13
7000	608.12	315.80	218.55	170.08	141.10	121.88	108.24	98.07	90.23	84.01	78.97	74.82
8000	694.99	360.91	249.77	194.37	161.26	139.30	123.70	112.08	103.12	96.01	90.26	85.51
9000	781.86	406.03	281.00	218.67	181.42	156.71	139.16	126.09	116.01	108.01	101.54	96.20
10000	868.73	451.14	312.22	242.96	201.57	174.12	154.62	140.10	128.90	120.02	112.82	106.88
11000	955.61	496.25	343.44	267.26	221.73	191.53	170.09	154.11	141.79	132.02	124.10	117.57
12000	1042.48	541.37	374.66	291.55	241.89	208.94	185.55	168.12	154.68	144.02	135.38	128.26
13000	1129.35	586.48	405.88	315.85	262.05	226.35	201.01	182.13	167.57	156.02	146.66	138.95
14000	1216.23	631.59	437.10	340.15	282.20	243.76	216.47	196.14	180.46	168.02	157.94	149.64
15000	1303.10	676.71	468.32	364.44	302.36	261.18	231.93	210.15	193.35	180.02	169.22	160.32
16000	1389.97	721.82	499.54	388.74	322.52	278.59	247.40	224.16	206.24	192.02	180.51	171.01
17000	1476.84	766.93	530.76	413.03	342.67	296.00	262.86	238.17	219.13	204.02	191.79	181.70
18000	1563.72	812.05	561.99	437.33	362.83	313.41	278.32	252.18	232.02	216.02	203.07	192.39
19000	1650.59	857.16	593.21	461.62	382.99	330.82	293.78	266.19	244.91	228.03	214.35	203.08
20000	1737.46	902.27	624.43	485.92	403.14	348.23	309.24	280.20	257.79	240.03	225.63	213.76
21000	1824.34	947.39	655.65	510.22	423.30	365.64	324.71	294.21	270.68	252.03	236.91	224.45
22000	1911.21	992.50	686.87	534.51	443.46	383.06	340.17	308.22	283.57	264.03	248.19	235.14
23000	1998.08	1037.61	718.09	558.81	463.62	400.47	355.63	322.23	296.46	276.03	259.47	245.83
24000	2084.95	1082.73	749.31	583.10	483.77	417.88	371.09	336.24	309.35	288.03	270.76	256.52
25000	2171.83	1127.84	780.53	607.40	503.93	435.29	386.55	350.25	322.24	300.03	282.04	267.20
26000	2258.70	1172.95	811.76	631.69	524.09	452.70	402.02	364.26	335.13	312.03	293.32	277.89
27000	2345.57	1218.07	842.98	655.99	544.24	470.11	417.48	378.27	348.02	324.03	304.60	288.58
28000	2432.45	1263.18	874.20	680.29	564.40	487.52	432.94	392.28	360.91	336.03	315.88	299.27
29000	2519.32	1308.29	905.42	704.58	584.56	504.94	448.40	406.29	373.80	348.04	327.16	309.95
30000	2606.19	1353.41	936.64	728.88	604.71	522.35	463.86	420.30	386.69	360.04	338.44	320.64
31000	2693.06	1398.52	967.86	753.17	624.87	539.76	479.33	434.31	399.58	372.04	349.72	331.33
32000	2779.94	1443.63	999.08	777.47	645.03	557.17	494.79	448.32	412.47	384.04	361.01	342.02
33000	2866.81	1488.75	1030.30	801.76	665.18	574.58	510.25	462.33	425.36	396.04	372.29	352.71
34000	2953.68	1533.86	1061.52	826.06	685.34	591.99	525.71	476.34	438.25	408.04	383.57	363.39
35000	3040.56	1578.97	1092.75	850.36	705.50	609.40	541.17	490.35	451.14	420.04	394.85	374.08
36000	3127.43	1624.09	1123.97	874.65	725.66	626.82	556.64	504.36	464.03	432.04	406.13	384.77
37000	3214.30	1669.20	1155.19	898.95	745.81	644.23	572.10	518.37	476.92	444.04	417.41	395.46
38000	3301.17	1714.31	1186.41	923.24	765.97	661.64	587.56	532.38	489.81	456.05	428.69	406.15
39000	3388.05	1759.43	1217.63	947.54	786.13	679.05	603.02	546.39	502.70	468.05	439.98	416.83
40000	3474.92	1804.54	1248.85	971.83	806.28	696.46	618.48	560.40	515.58	480.05	451.26	427.52
41000	3561.79	1849.65	1280.07	996.13	826.44	713.87	633.95	574.41	528.47	492.05	462.54	438.21
42000	3648.67	1894.77	1311.29	1020.43	846.60	731.28	649.41	588.42	541.36	504.05	473.82	448.90
43000	3735.54	1939.88	1342.52	1044.72	866.75	748.70	664.87	602.43	554.25	516.05	485.10	459.59
44000	3822.41	1984.99	1373.74	1069.02	886.91	766.11	680.33	616.44	567.14	528.05	496.38	470.27
45000	3909.28	2030.11	1404.96	1093.31	907.07	783.52	695.79	630.45	580.03	540.05	507.66	480.96
46000	3996.16	2075.22	1436.18	1117.61	927.23	800.93	711.25	644.46	592.92	552.05	518.94	491.65
47000	4083.03	2120.33	1467.40	1141.90	947.38	818.34	726.72	658.47	605.81	564.05	530.23	502.34
48000	4169.90	2165.45	1498.62	1166.20	967.54	835.75	742.18	672.48	618.70	576.06	541.51	513.03
49000	4256.78	2210.56	1529.84	1190.50	987.70	853.16	757.64	686.49	631.59	588.06	552.79	523.71
50000	4343.65	2255.67	1561.06	1214.79	1007.85	870.58	773.10	700.50	644.48	600.06	564.07	534.40
55000	4778.01	2481.24	1717.17	1336.27	1108.64	957.63	850.41	770.55	708.93	660.06	620.48	587.84
60000	5212.38	2706.81	1873.27	1457.75	1209.42	1044.69	927.72	840.60	773.37	720.07	676.88	641.28
65000	5646.74	2932.37	2029.38	1579.23	1310.21	1131.75	1005.03	910.65	837.82	780.07	733.29	694.72
70000	6081.11	3157.94	2185.49	1700.71	1410.99	1218.80	1082.34	980.70	902.27	840.08	789.70	748.16
75000	6515.47	3383.51	2341.59	1822.19	1511.78	1305.86	1159.65	1050.75	966.72	900.08	846.10	801.60
80000	6949.84	3609.07	2497.70	1943.66	1612.56	1392.92	1236.96	1120.80	1031.16	960.09	902.51	855.04
85000	7384.20	3834.64	2653.80	2065.14	1713.35	1479.98	1314.27	1190.85	1095.61	1020.10	958.91	908.48
90000	7818.56	4060.21	2809.91	2186.62	1814.13	1567.03	1391.58	1260.90	1160.06	1080.10	1015.32	961.92
95000	8252.93	4285.77	2966.02	2308.10	1914.92	1654.09	1468.89	1330.95	1224.51	1140.11	1071.73	1015.36
100000	8687.29	4511.34	3122.12	2429.58	2015.70	1741.15	1546.20	1401.00	1288.95	1200.11	1128.13	1068.80

Table 1

MONTHLY 7.75%

PAYMENT REQUIRED TO AMORTIZE A LOAN

7%

ERM UNT	13 YEARS	14 YEARS	15 YEARS	16 YEARS	17 YEARS	18 YEARS	19 YEARS	20 YEARS	25 YEARS	30 YEARS	35 YEARS	40 YEARS
50	.51	.49	.48	.46	.45	.43	.42	.42	.38	.36	.35	.34
100	1.02	.98	.95	.92	.89	.86	.84	.83	.76	.72	.70	.68
200	2.04	1.96	1.89	1.83	1.77	1.72	1.68	1.65	1.52	1.44	1.39	1.36
300	3.06	2.94	2.83	2.74	2.66	2.58	2.52	2.47	2.27	2.15	2.08	2.03
400	4.08	3.91	3.77	3.65	3.54	3.44	3.36	3.29	3.03	2.87	2.77	2.71
500	5.10	4.89	4.71	4.56	4.42	4.30	4.20	4.11	3.78	3.59	3.47	3.39
600	6.12	5.87	5.65	5.47	5.31	5.16	5.04	4.93	4.54	4.30	4.16	4.06
700	7.14	6.85	6.59	6.38	6.19	6.02	5.88	5.75	5.29	5.02	4.85	4.74
800	8.16	7.82	7.54	7.29	7.07	6.88	6.72	6.57	6.05	5.74	5.54	5.42
900	9.18	8.80	8.48	8.20	7.96	7.74	7.56	7.39	6.80	6.45	6.23	6.09
1000	10.20	9.78	9.42	9.11	8.84	8.60	8.40	8.21	7.56	7.17	6.93	6.77
2000	20.39	19.55	18.83	18.21	17.67	17.20	16.79	16.42	15.11	14.33	13.85	13.54
3000	30.58	29.32	28.24	27.31	26.51	25.80	25.18	24.63	22.66	21.50	20.77	20.30
4000	40.77	39.09	37.66	36.42	35.34	34.40	33.57	32.84	30.22	28.66	27.69	27.07
5000	50.96	48.86	47.07	45.52	44.18	43.00	41.97	41.05	37.77	35.83	34.61	33.84
6000	61.16	58.64	56.48	54.62	53.01	51.60	50.36	49.26	45.32	42.99	41.54	40.60
7000	71.35	68.41	65.89	63.73	61.84	60.20	58.75	57.47	52.88	50.15	48.46	47.37
8000	81.54	78.18	75.31	72.83	70.68	68.80	67.14	65.68	60.43	57.32	55.38	54.13
9000	91.73	87.95	84.72	81.93	79.51	77.40	75.54	73.89	67.98	64.48	62.30	60.90
10000	101.92	97.72	94.13	91.04	88.35	86.00	83.93	82.10	75.54	71.65	69.22	67.67
11000	112.11	107.49	103.55	100.14	97.18	94.59	92.32	90.31	83.09	78.81	76.14	74.43
12000	122.31	117.27	112.96	109.24	106.02	103.19	100.71	98.52	90.64	85.97	83.07	81.20
13000	132.50	127.04	122.37	118.35	114.85	111.79	109.10	106.73	98.20	93.14	89.99	87.97
14000	142.69	136.81	131.78	127.45	123.68	120.39	117.50	114.94	105.75	100.30	96.91	94.73
15000	152.88	146.58	141.20	136.55	132.52	128.99	125.89	123.15	113.30	107.47	103.83	101.50
16000	163.07	156.35	150.61	145.66	141.35	137.59	134.28	131.36	120.86	114.63	110.75	108.26
17000	173.26	166.13	160.02	154.76	150.19	146.19	142.67	139.57	128.41	121.80	117.67	115.03
18000	183.46	175.90	169.43	163.86	159.02	154.79	151.07	147.78	135.96	128.96	124.60	121.80
19000	193.65	185.67	178.85	172.97	167.86	163.39	159.46	155.99	143.52	136.12	131.52	128.56
20000	203.84	195.44	188.26	182.07	176.69	171.99	167.85	164.19	151.07	143.29	138.44	135.33
21000	214.03	205.21	197.67	191.17	185.52	180.58	176.24	172.40	158.62	150.45	145.36	142.10
22000	224.22	214.98	207.09	200.27	194.36	189.18	184.63	180.61	166.18	157.62	152.28	148.86
23000	234.41	224.76	216.50	209.38	203.19	197.78	193.03	188.82	173.73	164.78	159.21	155.63
24000	244.61	234.53	225.91	218.48	212.03	206.38	201.42	197.03	181.28	171.94	166.13	162.39
25000	254.80	244.30	235.32	227.58	220.86	214.98	209.81	205.24	188.84	179.11	173.05	169.16
26000	264.99	254.07	244.74	236.69	229.69	223.58	218.20	213.45	196.39	186.27	179.97	175.93
27000	275.18	263.84	254.15	245.79	238.53	232.18	226.60	221.66	203.94	193.44	186.89	182.69
28000	285.37	273.61	263.56	254.89	247.36	240.78	234.99	229.87	211.50	200.60	193.81	189.46
29000	295.56	283.39	272.97	264.00	256.20	249.38	243.38	238.08	219.05	207.76	200.74	196.22
30000	305.76	293.16	282.39	273.10	265.03	257.98	251.77	246.29	226.60	214.93	207.66	202.99
31000	315.95	302.93	291.80	282.20	273.87	266.58	260.16	254.50	234.16	222.09	214.58	209.76
32000	326.14	312.70	301.21	291.31	282.70	275.17	268.56	262.71	241.71	229.26	221.50	216.52
33000	336.33	322.47	310.63	300.41	291.53	283.77	276.95	270.92	249.26	236.42	228.42	223.29
34000	346.52	332.25	320.04	309.51	300.37	292.37	285.34	279.13	256.82	243.59	235.34	230.06
35000	356.72	342.02	329.45	318.62	309.20	300.97	293.73	287.34	264.37	250.75	242.27	236.82
36000	366.91	351.79	338.86	327.72	318.04	309.57	302.13	295.55	271.92	257.91	249.19	243.59
37000	377.10	361.56	348.28	336.82	326.87	318.17	310.52	303.76	279.48	265.08	256.11	250.35
38000	387.29	371.33	357.69	345.93	335.71	326.77	318.91	311.97	287.03	272.24	263.03	257.12
39000	397.48	381.10	367.10	355.03	344.54	335.37	327.30	320.17	294.58	279.41	269.95	263.89
40000	407.67	390.88	376.52	364.13	353.37	343.97	335.69	328.38	302.14	286.57	276.88	270.65
41000	417.87	400.65	385.93	373.24	362.21	352.57	344.09	336.59	309.69	293.73	283.80	277.42
42000	428.06	410.42	395.34	382.34	371.04	361.16	352.48	344.80	317.24	300.90	290.72	284.19
43000	438.25	420.19	404.75	391.44	379.88	369.76	360.87	353.01	324.80	308.06	297.64	290.95
44000	448.44	429.96	414.17	400.54	388.71	378.36	369.26	361.22	332.35	315.23	304.56	297.72
45000	458.63	439.73	423.58	409.65	397.54	386.96	377.66	369.43	339.90	322.39	311.48	304.48
46000	468.82	449.51	432.99	418.75	406.38	395.56	386.05	377.64	347.46	329.55	318.41	311.25
47000	479.02	459.28	442.40	427.85	415.21	404.16	394.44	385.85	355.01	336.72	325.33	318.02
48000	489.21	469.05	451.82	436.96	424.05	412.76	402.83	394.06	362.56	343.88	332.25	324.78
49000	499.40	478.82	461.23	446.06	432.88	421.36	411.22	402.27	370.12	351.05	339.17	331.55
50000	509.59	488.59	470.64	455.16	441.72	429.96	419.62	410.48	377.67	358.21	346.09	338.31
55000	560.55	537.45	517.71	500.68	485.89	472.95	461.58	451.53	415.44	394.03	380.70	372.15
60000	611.51	586.31	564.77	546.20	530.06	515.95	503.54	492.57	453.20	429.85	415.31	405.98
65000	662.47	635.17	611.83	591.71	574.23	558.94	545.50	533.62	490.97	465.67	449.92	439.81
70000	713.43	684.03	658.90	637.23	618.40	601.94	587.46	574.67	528.74	501.49	484.53	473.64
75000	764.38	732.89	705.96	682.74	662.57	644.93	629.42	615.72	566.50	537.31	519.14	507.47
80000	815.34	781.75	753.03	728.26	706.74	687.93	671.38	656.76	604.27	573.13	553.75	541.30
85000	866.30	830.61	800.09	773.77	750.91	730.92	713.35	697.81	642.03	608.96	588.35	575.13
90000	917.26	879.46	847.15	819.29	795.08	773.92	755.31	738.86	679.80	644.78	622.96	608.96
95000	968.22	928.32	894.22	864.81	839.26	816.91	797.27	779.91	717.57	680.60	657.57	642.79
100000	1019.18	977.18	941.28	910.32	883.43	859.91	839.23	820.95	755.33	716.42	692.18	676.62

Table 1

8.00%

MONTHLY
PAYMENT REQUIRED TO AMORTIZE A LOAN

8%

TERM AMOUNT	1 YEAR	2 YEARS	3 YEARS	4 YEARS	5 YEARS	6 YEARS	7 YEARS	8 YEARS	9 YEARS	10 YEARS	11 YEARS	12 YEAR
50	4.35	2.27	1.57	1.23	1.02	.88	.78	.71	.66	.61	.58	.55
100	8.70	4.53	3.14	2.45	2.03	1.76	1.56	1.42	1.31	1.22	1.15	1.09
200	17.40	9.05	6.27	4.89	4.06	3.51	3.12	2.83	2.61	2.43	2.29	2.17
300	26.10	13.57	9.41	7.33	6.09	5.26	4.68	4.25	3.91	3.64	3.43	3.25
400	34.80	18.10	12.54	9.77	8.12	7.02	6.24	5.66	5.21	4.86	4.57	4.33
500	43.50	22.62	15.67	12.21	10.14	8.77	7.80	7.07	6.51	6.07	5.71	5.42
600	52.20	27.14	18.81	14.65	12.17	10.52	9.36	8.49	7.82	7.28	6.85	6.50
700	60.90	31.66	21.94	17.09	14.20	12.28	10.92	9.90	9.12	8.50	8.00	7.58
800	69.60	36.19	25.07	19.54	16.23	14.03	12.47	11.31	10.42	9.71	9.14	8.66
900	78.29	40.71	28.21	21.98	18.25	15.78	14.03	12.73	11.72	10.92	10.28	9.75
1000	86.99	45.23	31.34	24.42	20.28	17.54	15.59	14.14	13.02	12.14	11.42	10.83
2000	173.98	90.46	62.68	48.83	40.56	35.07	31.18	28.28	26.04	24.27	22.84	21.65
3000	260.97	135.69	94.01	73.24	60.83	52.60	46.76	42.42	39.06	36.40	34.25	32.48
4000	347.96	180.91	125.35	97.66	81.11	70.14	62.35	56.55	52.08	48.54	45.67	43.30
5000	434.95	226.14	156.69	122.07	101.39	87.67	77.94	70.69	65.10	60.67	57.08	54.13
6000	521.94	271.37	188.02	146.48	121.66	105.20	93.52	84.83	78.12	72.80	68.50	64.95
7000	608.92	316.60	219.36	170.90	141.94	122.74	109.11	98.96	91.14	84.93	79.91	75.78
8000	695.91	361.82	250.70	195.31	162.22	140.27	124.69	113.10	104.15	97.07	91.33	86.60
9000	782.90	407.05	282.03	219.72	182.49	157.80	140.28	127.24	117.17	109.20	102.74	97.43
10000	869.89	452.28	313.37	244.13	202.77	175.34	155.87	141.37	130.19	121.33	114.16	108.25
11000	956.88	497.51	344.71	268.55	223.05	192.87	171.45	155.51	143.21	133.47	125.57	119.07
12000	1043.87	542.73	376.04	292.96	243.32	210.40	187.04	169.65	156.23	145.60	136.99	129.90
13000	1130.85	587.96	407.38	317.37	263.60	227.94	202.63	183.78	169.25	157.73	148.41	140.72
14000	1217.84	633.19	438.71	341.79	283.87	245.47	218.21	197.92	182.27	169.86	159.82	151.55
15000	1304.83	678.41	470.05	366.20	304.15	263.00	233.80	212.06	195.29	182.00	171.24	162.37
16000	1391.82	723.64	501.39	390.61	324.43	280.54	249.38	226.19	208.30	194.13	182.65	173.20
17000	1478.81	768.87	532.72	415.02	344.70	298.07	264.97	240.33	221.32	206.26	194.07	184.02
18000	1565.80	814.10	564.06	439.44	364.98	315.60	280.56	254.47	234.34	218.39	205.48	194.85
19000	1652.79	859.32	595.40	463.85	385.26	333.14	296.14	268.60	247.36	230.53	216.90	205.67
20000	1739.77	904.55	626.73	488.26	405.53	350.67	311.73	282.74	260.38	242.66	228.31	216.50
21000	1826.76	949.78	658.07	512.68	425.81	368.20	327.32	296.88	273.40	254.79	239.73	227.32
22000	1913.75	995.01	689.41	537.09	446.09	385.74	342.90	311.01	286.42	266.93	251.14	238.14
23000	2000.74	1040.23	720.74	561.50	466.36	403.27	358.49	325.15	299.44	279.06	262.56	248.97
24000	2087.73	1085.46	752.08	585.92	486.64	420.80	374.07	339.29	312.45	291.19	273.98	259.79
25000	2174.72	1130.69	783.41	610.33	506.91	438.34	389.66	353.42	325.47	303.32	285.39	270.62
26000	2261.70	1175.91	814.75	634.74	527.19	455.87	405.25	367.56	338.49	315.46	296.81	281.44
27000	2348.69	1221.14	846.09	659.15	547.47	473.40	420.83	381.70	351.51	327.59	308.22	292.27
28000	2435.68	1266.37	877.42	683.57	567.74	490.94	436.42	395.83	364.53	339.72	319.64	303.09
29000	2522.67	1311.60	908.76	707.98	588.02	508.47	452.01	409.97	377.55	351.86	331.05	313.92
30000	2609.66	1356.82	940.10	732.39	608.30	526.00	467.59	424.11	390.57	363.99	342.47	324.74
31000	2696.65	1402.05	971.43	756.81	628.57	543.54	483.18	438.24	403.59	376.12	353.88	335.57
32000	2783.63	1447.28	1002.77	781.22	648.85	561.07	498.76	452.38	416.60	388.25	365.30	346.39
33000	2870.62	1492.51	1034.11	805.63	669.13	578.60	514.35	466.52	429.62	400.39	376.71	357.21
34000	2957.61	1537.73	1065.44	830.04	689.40	596.14	529.94	480.65	442.64	412.52	388.13	368.04
35000	3044.60	1582.96	1096.78	854.46	709.68	613.67	545.52	494.79	455.66	424.65	399.55	378.86
36000	3131.59	1628.19	1128.11	878.87	729.96	631.20	561.11	508.93	468.68	436.78	410.96	389.69
37000	3218.58	1673.41	1159.45	903.28	750.23	648.73	576.69	523.06	481.70	448.92	422.38	400.51
38000	3305.57	1718.64	1190.79	927.70	770.51	666.27	592.28	537.20	494.72	461.05	433.79	411.34
39000	3392.55	1763.87	1222.12	952.11	790.78	683.80	607.87	551.34	507.73	473.18	445.21	422.16
40000	3479.54	1809.10	1253.46	976.52	811.06	701.33	623.45	565.47	520.75	485.32	456.62	432.99
41000	3566.53	1854.32	1284.80	1000.93	831.34	718.87	639.04	579.61	533.77	497.45	468.04	443.81
42000	3653.52	1899.55	1316.13	1025.35	851.61	736.40	654.63	593.75	546.79	509.58	479.45	454.64
43000	3740.51	1944.78	1347.47	1049.76	871.89	753.93	670.21	607.88	559.81	521.71	490.87	465.46
44000	3827.50	1990.01	1378.81	1074.17	892.17	771.47	685.80	622.02	572.83	533.85	502.28	476.28
45000	3914.48	2035.23	1410.14	1098.59	912.44	789.00	701.38	636.16	585.85	545.98	513.70	487.11
46000	4001.47	2080.46	1441.48	1123.00	932.72	806.53	716.97	650.29	598.87	558.11	525.12	497.93
47000	4088.46	2125.69	1472.81	1147.41	953.00	824.07	732.56	664.43	611.88	570.24	536.53	508.76
48000	4175.45	2170.92	1504.15	1171.83	973.27	841.60	748.14	678.57	624.90	582.38	547.95	519.58
49000	4262.44	2216.14	1535.49	1196.24	993.55	859.13	763.73	692.70	637.92	594.51	559.36	530.41
50000	4349.43	2261.37	1566.82	1220.65	1013.82	876.67	779.32	706.84	650.94	606.64	570.78	541.23
55000	4784.37	2487.51	1723.51	1342.72	1115.21	964.33	857.25	777.52	716.03	667.31	627.85	595.35
60000	5219.31	2713.64	1880.19	1464.78	1216.59	1052.00	935.18	848.21	781.13	727.97	684.93	649.48
65000	5654.25	2939.78	2036.87	1586.84	1317.97	1139.67	1013.11	918.89	846.22	788.63	742.01	703.60
70000	6089.20	3165.92	2193.55	1708.91	1419.35	1227.33	1091.04	989.57	911.32	849.30	799.09	757.72
75000	6524.14	3392.05	2350.23	1830.97	1520.73	1315.00	1168.97	1060.26	976.41	909.96	856.16	811.84
80000	6959.08	3618.19	2506.91	1953.04	1622.12	1402.66	1246.90	1130.94	1041.50	970.63	913.24	865.97
85000	7394.02	3844.32	2663.60	2075.10	1723.50	1490.33	1324.83	1201.62	1106.60	1031.29	970.32	920.09
90000	7828.96	4070.46	2820.28	2197.17	1824.88	1578.00	1402.76	1272.31	1171.69	1091.95	1027.40	974.21
95000	8263.91	4296.60	2976.96	2319.23	1926.26	1665.66	1480.70	1342.99	1236.78	1152.62	1084.47	1028.33
100000	8698.85	4522.73	3133.64	2441.30	2027.64	1753.33	1558.63	1413.67	1301.88	1213.28	1141.55	1082.46

Table 1

MONTHLY
PAYMENT REQUIRED TO AMORTIZE A LOAN

8.00%

8%

TERM / AMOUNT	13 YEARS	14 YEARS	15 YEARS	16 YEARS	17 YEARS	18 YEARS	19 YEARS	20 YEARS	25 YEARS	30 YEARS	35 YEARS	40 YEARS
50	.52	.50	.48	.47	.45	.44	.43	.42	.39	.37	.36	.35
100	1.04	1.00	.96	.93	.90	.88	.86	.84	.78	.74	.72	.70
200	2.07	1.99	1.92	1.85	1.80	1.75	1.71	1.68	1.55	1.47	1.43	1.40
300	3.10	2.98	2.87	2.78	2.70	2.63	2.57	2.51	2.32	2.21	2.14	2.09
400	4.14	3.97	3.83	3.70	3.60	3.50	3.42	3.35	3.09	2.94	2.85	2.79
500	5.17	4.96	4.78	4.63	4.50	4.38	4.28	4.19	3.86	3.67	3.56	3.48
600	6.20	5.95	5.74	5.55	5.39	5.25	5.13	5.02	4.64	4.41	4.27	4.18
700	7.24	6.94	6.69	6.48	6.29	6.13	5.99	5.86	5.41	5.14	4.98	4.87
800	8.27	7.94	7.65	7.40	7.19	7.00	6.84	6.70	6.18	5.88	5.69	5.57
900	9.30	8.93	8.61	8.33	8.09	7.88	7.70	7.53	6.95	6.61	6.40	6.26
1000	10.34	9.92	9.56	9.25	8.99	8.75	8.55	8.37	7.72	7.34	7.11	6.96
2000	20.67	19.83	19.12	18.50	17.97	17.50	17.10	16.73	15.44	14.68	14.21	13.91
3000	31.00	29.74	28.67	27.75	26.95	26.25	25.64	25.10	23.16	22.02	21.31	20.86
4000	41.33	39.66	38.23	37.00	35.94	35.00	34.19	33.46	30.88	29.36	28.42	27.82
5000	51.66	49.57	47.79	46.25	44.92	43.75	42.73	41.83	38.60	36.69	35.52	34.77
6000	61.99	59.48	57.34	55.50	53.90	52.50	51.28	50.19	46.31	44.03	42.62	41.72
7000	72.32	69.40	66.90	64.75	62.88	61.25	59.82	58.56	54.03	51.37	49.72	48.68
8000	82.65	79.31	76.46	74.00	71.87	70.00	68.37	66.92	61.75	58.71	56.83	55.63
9000	92.98	89.22	86.01	83.25	80.85	78.75	76.91	75.28	69.47	66.04	63.93	62.58
10000	103.31	99.14	95.57	92.50	89.83	87.50	85.46	83.65	77.19	73.38	71.03	69.54
11000	113.64	109.05	105.13	101.75	98.81	96.25	94.00	92.01	84.90	80.72	78.13	76.49
12000	123.97	118.96	114.68	111.00	107.80	105.00	102.55	100.38	92.62	88.06	85.24	83.44
13000	134.30	128.88	124.24	120.25	116.78	113.75	111.09	108.74	100.34	95.39	92.34	90.40
14000	144.64	138.79	133.80	129.49	125.76	122.50	119.64	117.11	108.06	102.73	99.44	97.35
15000	154.97	148.70	143.35	138.74	134.74	131.25	128.18	125.47	115.78	110.07	106.54	104.30
16000	165.30	158.62	152.91	147.99	143.73	140.00	136.73	133.84	123.50	117.41	113.65	111.25
17000	175.63	168.53	162.47	157.24	152.71	148.75	145.27	142.20	131.21	124.74	120.75	118.21
18000	185.96	178.44	172.02	166.49	161.69	157.50	153.82	150.56	138.93	132.08	127.85	125.16
19000	196.29	188.36	181.58	175.74	170.67	166.25	162.36	158.93	146.65	139.42	134.95	132.11
20000	206.62	198.27	191.14	184.99	179.66	175.00	170.91	167.29	154.37	146.76	142.06	139.07
21000	216.95	208.18	200.69	194.24	188.64	183.75	179.45	175.66	162.09	154.10	149.16	146.02
22000	227.28	218.10	210.25	203.49	197.62	192.50	188.00	184.02	169.80	161.43	156.26	152.97
23000	237.61	228.01	219.80	212.74	206.60	201.25	196.54	192.39	177.52	168.77	163.37	159.93
24000	247.94	237.92	229.36	221.99	215.59	210.00	205.09	200.75	185.24	176.11	170.47	166.88
25000	258.27	247.83	238.92	231.24	224.57	218.75	213.63	209.12	192.96	183.45	177.57	173.83
26000	268.60	257.75	248.47	240.49	233.55	227.50	222.18	217.48	200.68	190.78	184.67	180.79
27000	278.93	267.66	258.03	249.73	242.53	236.24	230.72	225.84	208.40	198.12	191.78	187.74
28000	289.27	277.57	267.59	258.98	251.52	244.99	239.27	234.21	216.11	205.46	198.88	194.69
29000	299.60	287.49	277.14	268.23	260.50	253.74	247.81	242.57	223.83	212.80	205.98	201.65
30000	309.93	297.40	286.70	277.48	269.48	262.49	256.36	250.94	231.55	220.13	213.08	208.60
31000	320.26	307.31	296.26	286.73	278.46	271.24	264.90	259.30	239.27	227.47	220.19	215.55
32000	330.59	317.23	305.81	295.98	287.45	279.99	273.45	267.67	246.99	234.81	227.29	222.50
33000	340.92	327.14	315.37	305.23	296.43	288.74	281.99	276.03	254.70	242.15	234.39	229.46
34000	351.25	337.05	324.93	314.48	305.41	297.49	290.54	284.39	262.42	249.49	241.49	236.41
35000	361.58	346.97	334.48	323.73	314.39	306.24	299.08	292.76	270.14	256.82	248.60	243.36
36000	371.91	356.88	344.04	332.98	323.38	314.99	307.63	301.12	277.86	264.16	255.70	250.32
37000	382.24	366.79	353.60	342.23	332.36	323.74	316.17	309.49	285.58	271.50	262.80	257.27
38000	392.57	376.71	363.15	351.48	341.34	332.49	324.72	317.85	293.30	278.84	269.90	264.22
39000	402.90	386.62	372.71	360.73	350.33	341.24	333.26	326.22	301.01	286.17	277.01	271.18
40000	413.23	396.53	382.27	369.98	359.31	349.99	341.81	334.58	308.73	293.51	284.11	278.13
41000	423.57	406.45	391.82	379.22	368.29	358.74	350.35	342.95	316.45	300.85	291.21	285.08
42000	433.90	416.36	401.38	388.47	377.27	367.49	358.90	351.31	324.17	308.19	298.31	292.04
43000	444.23	426.27	410.94	397.72	386.26	376.24	367.44	359.67	331.89	315.52	305.42	298.99
44000	454.56	436.19	420.49	406.97	395.24	384.99	375.99	368.04	339.60	322.86	312.52	305.94
45000	464.89	446.10	430.05	416.22	404.22	393.74	384.53	376.40	347.32	330.20	319.62	312.90
46000	475.22	456.01	439.60	425.47	413.20	402.49	393.08	384.77	355.04	337.54	326.73	319.85
47000	485.55	465.92	449.16	434.72	422.19	411.24	401.62	393.13	362.76	344.87	333.83	326.80
48000	495.88	475.84	458.72	443.97	431.17	419.99	410.17	401.50	370.48	352.21	340.93	333.75
49000	506.21	485.75	468.27	453.22	440.15	428.74	418.71	409.86	378.19	359.55	348.03	340.71
50000	516.54	495.66	477.83	462.47	449.13	437.49	427.26	418.23	385.91	366.89	355.14	347.66
55000	568.20	545.23	525.61	508.71	494.05	481.23	469.98	460.05	424.50	403.58	390.65	382.43
60000	619.85	594.80	573.40	554.96	538.96	524.98	512.71	501.87	463.09	440.26	426.16	417.19
65000	671.50	644.36	621.18	601.21	583.87	568.73	555.43	543.69	501.69	476.95	461.67	451.96
70000	723.16	693.93	668.96	647.45	628.78	612.48	598.16	585.51	540.28	513.64	497.19	486.72
75000	774.81	743.49	716.74	693.70	673.70	656.23	640.88	627.34	578.87	550.33	532.70	521.49
80000	826.46	793.06	764.53	739.95	718.61	699.98	683.61	669.16	617.46	587.02	568.21	556.25
85000	878.12	842.63	812.31	786.19	763.52	743.72	726.33	710.98	656.05	623.70	603.73	591.02
90000	929.77	892.19	860.09	832.44	808.44	787.47	769.06	752.80	694.64	660.39	639.24	625.79
95000	981.43	941.76	907.87	878.68	853.35	831.22	811.78	794.62	733.23	697.08	674.75	660.55
100000	1033.08	991.32	955.66	924.93	898.26	874.97	854.51	836.45	771.82	733.77	710.27	695.32

27

Table 1

8.25%

MONTHLY
PAYMENT REQUIRED TO AMORTIZE A LOAN

8%

AMOUNT	TERM 1 YEAR	2 YEARS	3 YEARS	4 YEARS	5 YEARS	6 YEARS	7 YEARS	8 YEARS	9 YEARS	10 YEARS	11 YEARS	12 YEARS
50	4.36	2.27	1.58	1.23	1.02	.89	.79	.72	.66	.62	.58	.55
100	8.72	4.54	3.15	2.46	2.04	1.77	1.58	1.43	1.32	1.23	1.16	1.10
200	17.43	9.07	6.30	4.91	4.08	3.54	3.15	2.86	2.63	2.46	2.32	2.20
300	26.14	13.61	9.44	7.36	6.12	5.30	4.72	4.28	3.95	3.68	3.47	3.29
400	34.85	18.14	12.59	9.82	8.16	7.07	6.29	5.71	5.26	4.91	4.63	4.39
500	43.56	22.68	15.73	12.27	10.20	8.83	7.86	7.14	6.58	6.14	5.78	5.49
600	52.27	27.21	18.88	14.72	12.24	10.60	9.43	8.56	7.89	7.36	6.94	6.58
700	60.98	31.74	22.02	17.18	14.28	12.36	11.00	9.99	9.21	8.59	8.09	7.68
800	69.69	36.28	25.17	19.63	16.32	14.13	12.57	11.42	10.52	9.82	9.25	8.77
900	78.40	40.81	28.31	22.08	18.36	15.90	14.14	12.84	11.84	11.04	10.40	9.87
1000	87.11	45.35	31.46	24.54	20.40	17.66	15.72	14.27	13.15	12.27	11.56	10.97
2000	174.21	90.69	62.91	49.07	40.80	35.32	31.43	28.53	26.30	24.54	23.11	21.93
3000	261.32	136.03	94.36	73.60	61.19	52.97	47.14	42.80	39.45	36.80	34.66	32.89
4000	348.42	181.37	125.81	98.13	81.59	70.63	62.85	57.06	52.60	49.07	46.21	43.85
5000	435.53	226.71	157.26	122.66	101.99	88.28	78.56	71.33	65.75	61.33	57.76	54.82
6000	522.63	272.05	188.72	147.19	122.38	105.94	94.27	85.59	78.90	73.60	69.31	65.78
7000	609.73	317.39	220.17	171.72	142.78	123.59	109.98	99.85	92.05	85.86	80.86	76.74
8000	696.84	362.74	251.62	196.25	163.18	141.25	125.69	114.12	105.19	98.13	92.41	87.70
9000	783.94	408.08	283.07	220.78	183.57	158.91	141.40	128.38	118.34	110.39	103.96	98.66
10000	871.05	453.42	314.52	245.31	203.97	176.56	157.12	142.65	131.49	122.66	115.51	109.63
11000	958.15	498.76	345.98	269.84	224.36	194.22	172.83	156.91	144.64	134.92	127.06	120.59
12000	1045.25	544.10	377.43	294.37	244.76	211.87	188.54	171.17	157.79	147.19	138.61	131.55
13000	1132.36	589.44	408.88	318.90	265.16	229.53	204.25	185.44	170.94	159.45	150.16	142.51
14000	1219.46	634.78	440.33	343.43	285.55	247.18	219.96	199.70	184.09	171.72	161.71	153.47
15000	1306.57	680.13	471.78	367.96	305.95	264.84	235.67	213.97	197.24	183.98	173.26	164.44
16000	1393.67	725.47	503.23	392.49	326.35	282.49	251.38	228.23	210.38	196.25	184.81	175.40
17000	1480.77	770.81	534.69	417.02	346.74	300.15	267.09	242.49	223.53	208.51	196.36	186.36
18000	1567.88	816.15	566.14	441.55	367.14	317.81	282.80	256.76	236.68	220.78	207.91	197.32
19000	1654.98	861.49	597.59	466.08	387.53	335.46	298.52	271.02	249.83	233.04	219.46	208.28
20000	1742.09	906.83	629.04	490.61	407.93	353.12	314.23	285.29	262.98	245.31	231.01	219.25
21000	1829.19	952.17	660.49	515.14	428.33	370.77	329.94	299.55	276.13	257.58	242.57	230.21
22000	1916.29	997.52	691.95	539.67	448.72	388.43	345.65	313.81	289.28	269.84	254.12	241.17
23000	2003.40	1042.86	723.40	564.21	469.12	406.08	361.36	328.08	302.42	282.11	265.67	252.13
24000	2090.50	1088.20	754.85	588.74	489.52	423.74	377.07	342.34	315.57	294.37	277.22	263.09
25000	2177.61	1133.54	786.30	613.27	509.91	441.39	392.78	356.61	328.72	306.64	288.77	274.06
26000	2264.71	1178.88	817.75	637.80	530.31	459.05	408.49	370.87	341.87	318.90	300.32	285.02
27000	2351.81	1224.22	849.20	662.33	550.70	476.71	424.20	385.14	355.02	331.17	311.87	295.98
28000	2438.92	1269.56	880.66	686.86	571.10	494.36	439.91	399.40	368.17	343.43	323.42	306.94
29000	2526.02	1314.91	912.11	711.39	591.50	512.02	455.63	413.66	381.32	355.70	334.97	317.91
30000	2613.13	1360.25	943.56	735.92	611.89	529.67	471.34	427.93	394.47	367.96	346.52	328.87
31000	2700.23	1405.59	975.01	760.45	632.29	547.33	487.05	442.19	407.61	380.23	358.07	339.83
32000	2787.34	1450.93	1006.46	784.98	652.69	564.98	502.76	456.46	420.76	392.49	369.62	350.79
33000	2874.44	1496.27	1037.92	809.51	673.08	582.64	518.47	470.72	433.91	404.76	381.17	361.75
34000	2961.54	1541.61	1069.37	834.04	693.48	600.29	534.18	484.98	447.06	417.02	392.72	372.72
35000	3048.65	1586.95	1100.82	858.57	713.87	617.95	549.89	499.25	460.21	429.29	404.27	383.68
36000	3135.75	1632.30	1132.27	883.10	734.27	635.61	565.60	513.51	473.36	441.55	415.82	394.64
37000	3222.86	1677.64	1163.72	907.63	754.67	653.26	581.31	527.78	486.51	453.82	427.37	405.60
38000	3309.96	1722.98	1195.17	932.16	775.06	670.92	597.03	542.04	499.65	466.08	438.92	416.56
39000	3397.06	1768.32	1226.63	956.69	795.46	688.57	612.74	556.30	512.80	478.35	450.47	427.53
40000	3484.17	1813.66	1258.08	981.22	815.86	706.23	628.45	570.57	525.95	490.62	462.02	438.49
41000	3571.27	1859.00	1289.53	1005.75	836.25	723.88	644.16	584.83	539.10	502.88	473.57	449.45
42000	3658.38	1904.34	1320.98	1030.28	856.65	741.54	659.87	599.10	552.25	515.15	485.13	460.41
43000	3745.48	1949.69	1352.43	1054.81	877.04	759.19	675.58	613.36	565.40	527.41	496.68	471.37
44000	3832.58	1995.03	1383.89	1079.34	897.44	776.85	691.29	627.62	578.55	539.68	508.23	482.34
45000	3919.69	2040.37	1415.34	1103.87	917.84	794.51	707.00	641.89	591.70	551.94	519.78	493.30
46000	4006.79	2085.71	1446.79	1128.41	938.23	812.16	722.71	656.15	604.84	564.21	531.33	504.26
47000	4093.90	2131.05	1478.24	1152.94	958.63	829.82	738.42	670.42	617.99	576.47	542.88	515.22
48000	4181.00	2176.39	1509.69	1177.47	979.03	847.47	754.14	684.68	631.14	588.74	554.43	526.18
49000	4268.10	2221.73	1541.14	1202.00	999.42	865.13	769.85	698.94	644.29	601.00	565.98	537.15
50000	4355.21	2267.07	1572.60	1226.53	1019.82	882.78	785.56	713.21	657.44	613.27	577.53	548.11
55000	4790.73	2493.78	1729.86	1349.18	1121.80	971.06	864.11	784.53	723.18	674.59	635.28	602.92
60000	5226.25	2720.49	1887.11	1471.83	1223.78	1059.34	942.67	855.85	788.93	735.92	693.03	657.73
65000	5661.77	2947.20	2044.37	1594.49	1325.76	1147.62	1021.22	927.17	854.67	797.25	750.79	712.54
70000	6097.29	3173.90	2201.63	1717.14	1427.74	1235.89	1099.78	998.49	920.41	858.57	808.54	767.35
75000	6532.81	3400.61	2358.89	1839.79	1529.72	1324.17	1178.33	1069.81	986.16	919.90	866.29	822.16
80000	6968.33	3627.32	2516.15	1962.44	1631.71	1412.45	1256.89	1141.13	1051.90	981.23	924.04	876.97
85000	7403.85	3854.02	2673.41	2085.09	1733.69	1500.73	1335.45	1212.45	1117.64	1042.55	981.80	931.78
90000	7839.37	4080.73	2830.67	2207.74	1835.67	1589.01	1414.00	1283.77	1183.39	1103.88	1039.55	986.59
95000	8274.89	4307.44	2987.93	2330.40	1937.65	1677.28	1492.56	1355.09	1249.13	1165.20	1097.30	1041.40
100000	8710.41	4534.14	3145.19	2453.05	2039.63	1765.56	1571.11	1426.41	1314.87	1226.53	1155.05	1096.21

28

Table 1

MONTHLY

PAYMENT REQUIRED TO AMORTIZE A LOAN

8.25%

8%

TERM AMOUNT	13 YEARS	14 YEARS	15 YEARS	16 YEARS	17 YEARS	18 YEARS	19 YEARS	20 YEARS	25 YEARS	30 YEARS	35 YEARS	40 YEARS
50	.53	.51	.49	.47	.46	.45	.44	.43	.40	.38	.37	.36
100	1.05	1.01	.98	.94	.92	.90	.87	.86	.79	.76	.73	.72
200	2.10	2.02	1.95	1.88	1.83	1.79	1.74	1.71	1.58	1.51	1.46	1.43
300	3.15	3.02	2.92	2.82	2.74	2.68	2.61	2.56	2.37	2.26	2.19	2.15
400	4.19	4.03	3.89	3.76	3.66	3.57	3.48	3.41	3.16	3.01	2.92	2.86
500	5.24	5.03	4.86	4.70	4.57	4.46	4.35	4.27	3.95	3.76	3.65	3.58
600	6.29	6.04	5.83	5.64	5.48	5.35	5.22	5.12	4.74	4.51	4.38	4.29
700	7.33	7.04	6.80	6.58	6.40	6.24	6.09	5.97	5.52	5.26	5.10	5.00
800	8.38	8.05	7.77	7.52	7.31	7.13	6.96	6.82	6.31	6.02	5.83	5.72
900	9.43	9.06	8.74	8.46	8.22	8.02	7.83	7.67	7.10	6.77	6.56	6.43
1000	10.48	10.06	9.71	9.40	9.14	8.91	8.70	8.53	7.89	7.52	7.29	7.15
2000	20.95	20.12	19.41	18.80	18.27	17.81	17.40	17.05	15.77	15.03	14.57	14.29
3000	31.42	30.17	29.11	28.19	27.40	26.71	26.10	25.57	23.66	22.54	21.86	21.43
4000	41.89	40.23	38.81	37.59	36.53	35.61	34.80	34.09	31.54	30.06	29.14	28.57
5000	52.36	50.28	48.51	46.99	45.67	44.51	43.50	42.61	39.43	37.57	36.43	35.71
6000	62.83	60.34	58.21	56.38	54.80	53.41	52.20	51.13	47.31	45.08	43.71	42.85
7000	73.30	70.39	67.91	65.78	63.93	62.32	60.90	59.65	55.20	52.59	51.00	49.99
8000	83.77	80.45	77.62	75.18	73.06	71.22	69.60	68.17	63.08	60.11	58.28	57.14
9000	94.24	90.51	87.32	84.57	82.19	80.12	78.30	76.69	70.97	67.62	65.57	64.28
10000	104.71	100.56	97.02	93.97	91.33	89.02	87.00	85.21	78.85	75.13	72.85	71.42
11000	115.18	110.62	106.72	103.37	100.46	97.92	95.70	93.73	86.73	82.64	80.14	78.56
12000	125.65	120.67	116.42	112.76	109.59	106.82	104.39	102.25	94.62	90.16	87.42	85.70
13000	136.12	130.73	126.12	122.16	118.72	115.72	113.09	110.77	102.50	97.67	94.71	92.84
14000	146.60	140.78	135.82	131.56	127.85	124.63	121.79	119.29	110.39	105.18	101.99	99.98
15000	157.07	150.84	145.53	140.95	136.99	133.53	130.49	127.81	118.27	112.69	109.28	107.13
16000	167.54	160.90	155.23	150.35	146.12	142.43	139.19	136.34	126.16	120.21	116.56	114.27
17000	178.01	170.95	164.93	159.75	155.25	151.33	147.89	144.86	134.04	127.72	123.85	121.41
18000	188.48	181.01	174.63	169.14	164.38	160.23	156.59	153.38	141.93	135.23	131.13	128.55
19000	198.95	191.06	184.33	178.54	173.52	169.13	165.29	161.90	149.81	142.75	138.42	135.69
20000	209.42	201.12	194.03	187.94	182.65	178.03	173.99	170.42	157.70	150.26	145.70	142.83
21000	219.89	211.17	203.73	197.33	191.78	186.94	182.69	178.94	165.58	157.77	152.99	149.97
22000	230.36	221.23	213.44	206.73	200.91	195.84	191.39	187.46	173.46	165.28	160.27	157.12
23000	240.83	231.29	223.14	216.12	210.04	204.74	200.08	195.98	181.35	172.80	167.56	164.26
24000	251.30	241.34	232.84	225.52	219.18	213.64	208.78	204.50	189.23	180.31	174.84	171.40
25000	261.77	251.40	242.54	234.92	228.31	222.54	217.48	213.02	197.12	187.82	182.13	178.54
26000	272.24	261.45	252.24	244.31	237.44	231.44	226.18	221.54	205.00	195.33	189.41	185.68
27000	282.72	271.51	261.94	253.71	246.57	240.34	234.88	230.06	212.89	202.85	196.70	192.82
28000	293.19	281.56	271.64	263.11	255.70	249.25	243.58	238.58	220.77	210.36	203.98	199.96
29000	303.66	291.62	281.35	272.50	264.84	258.15	252.28	247.10	228.66	217.87	211.27	207.11
30000	314.13	301.67	291.05	281.90	273.97	267.05	260.98	255.62	236.54	225.38	218.55	214.25
31000	324.60	311.73	300.75	291.30	283.10	275.95	269.68	264.15	244.42	232.90	225.84	221.39
32000	335.07	321.79	310.45	300.69	292.23	284.85	278.38	272.67	252.31	240.41	233.12	228.53
33000	345.54	331.84	320.15	310.09	301.37	293.75	287.08	281.19	260.19	247.92	240.41	235.67
34000	356.01	341.90	329.85	319.49	310.50	302.66	295.77	289.71	268.08	255.44	247.69	242.81
35000	366.48	351.95	339.55	328.88	319.63	311.56	304.47	298.23	275.96	262.95	254.98	249.95
36000	376.95	362.01	349.26	338.28	328.76	320.46	313.17	306.75	283.85	270.46	262.26	257.09
37000	387.42	372.06	358.96	347.68	337.89	329.36	321.87	315.27	291.73	277.97	269.55	264.24
38000	397.89	382.12	368.66	357.07	347.03	338.26	330.57	323.79	299.62	285.49	276.83	271.38
39000	408.36	392.18	378.36	366.47	356.16	347.16	339.27	332.31	307.50	293.00	284.12	278.52
40000	418.84	402.23	388.06	375.87	365.29	356.06	347.97	340.83	315.39	300.51	291.40	285.66
41000	429.31	412.29	397.76	385.26	374.42	364.97	356.67	349.35	323.27	308.02	298.69	292.80
42000	439.78	422.34	407.46	394.66	383.55	373.87	365.37	357.87	331.15	315.54	305.97	299.94
43000	450.25	432.40	417.17	404.05	392.69	382.77	374.07	366.39	339.04	323.05	313.26	307.08
44000	460.72	442.45	426.87	413.45	401.82	391.67	382.77	374.91	346.92	330.56	320.54	314.23
45000	471.19	452.51	436.57	422.85	410.95	400.57	391.46	383.43	354.81	338.07	327.83	321.37
46000	481.66	462.57	446.27	432.24	420.08	409.47	400.16	391.96	362.69	345.59	335.11	328.51
47000	492.13	472.62	455.97	441.64	429.22	418.37	408.86	400.48	370.58	353.10	342.40	335.65
48000	502.60	482.68	465.67	451.04	438.35	427.28	417.56	409.00	378.46	360.61	349.68	342.79
49000	513.07	492.73	475.37	460.43	447.48	436.18	426.26	417.52	386.35	368.13	356.97	349.93
50000	523.54	502.79	485.08	469.83	456.61	445.08	434.96	426.04	394.23	375.64	364.25	357.07
55000	575.90	553.07	533.58	516.81	502.27	489.59	478.46	468.64	433.65	413.20	400.68	392.78
60000	628.25	603.34	582.09	563.80	547.93	534.09	521.95	511.24	473.08	450.76	437.10	428.49
65000	680.60	653.62	630.61	610.78	593.59	578.60	565.45	553.85	512.50	488.33	473.52	464.20
70000	732.96	703.90	679.10	657.76	639.25	623.11	608.94	596.45	551.92	525.89	509.95	499.90
75000	785.31	754.18	727.61	704.74	684.92	667.62	652.44	639.05	591.34	563.45	546.37	535.61
80000	837.67	804.46	776.12	751.73	730.58	712.12	695.93	681.66	630.77	601.02	582.80	571.32
85000	890.02	854.74	824.62	798.71	776.24	756.63	739.43	724.26	670.19	638.58	619.22	607.02
90000	942.37	905.01	873.13	845.69	821.90	801.14	782.92	766.86	709.61	676.14	655.65	642.73
95000	994.73	955.29	921.64	892.67	867.56	845.65	826.42	809.47	749.03	713.71	692.07	678.44
100000	1047.08	1005.57	970.15	939.66	913.22	890.15	869.91	852.07	788.46	751.27	728.50	714.14

Table 1

8.50%

MONTHLY

PAYMENT REQUIRED TO AMORTIZE A LOAN

8%

TERM / AMOUNT	1 YEAR	2 YEARS	3 YEARS	4 YEARS	5 YEARS	6 YEARS	7 YEARS	8 YEARS	9 YEARS	10 YEARS	11 YEARS	12 YEARS
50	4.37	2.28	1.58	1.24	1.03	.89	.80	.72	.67	.62	.59	.56
100	8.73	4.55	3.16	2.47	2.06	1.78	1.59	1.44	1.33	1.24	1.17	1.12
200	17.45	9.10	6.32	4.93	4.11	3.56	3.17	2.88	2.66	2.48	2.34	2.23
300	26.17	13.64	9.48	7.40	6.16	5.34	4.76	4.32	3.99	3.72	3.51	3.34
400	34.89	18.19	12.63	9.86	8.21	7.12	6.34	5.76	5.32	4.96	4.68	4.45
500	43.61	22.73	15.79	12.33	10.26	8.89	7.92	7.20	6.64	6.20	5.85	5.56
600	52.34	27.28	18.95	14.79	12.31	10.67	9.51	8.64	7.97	7.44	7.02	6.67
700	61.06	31.82	22.10	17.26	14.37	12.45	11.09	10.08	9.30	8.68	8.19	7.78
800	69.78	36.37	25.26	19.72	16.42	14.23	12.67	11.52	10.63	9.92	9.35	8.89
900	78.50	40.92	28.42	22.19	18.47	16.01	14.26	12.96	11.96	11.16	10.52	10.00
1000	87.22	45.46	31.57	24.65	20.52	17.78	15.84	14.40	13.28	12.40	11.69	11.11
2000	174.44	90.92	63.14	49.30	41.04	35.56	31.68	28.79	26.56	24.80	23.38	22.21
3000	261.66	136.37	94.71	73.95	61.55	53.34	47.51	43.18	39.84	37.20	35.06	33.31
4000	348.88	181.83	126.28	98.60	82.07	71.12	63.35	57.57	53.12	49.60	46.75	44.41
5000	436.10	227.28	157.84	123.25	102.59	88.90	79.19	71.97	66.40	62.00	58.44	55.51
6000	523.32	272.74	189.41	147.89	123.10	106.68	95.02	86.36	79.68	74.40	70.12	66.61
7000	610.54	318.19	220.98	172.54	143.62	124.45	110.86	100.75	92.96	86.79	81.81	77.71
8000	697.76	363.65	252.55	197.19	164.14	142.23	126.70	115.14	106.24	99.19	93.50	88.81
9000	784.98	409.11	284.11	221.84	184.65	160.01	142.53	129.53	119.52	111.59	105.18	99.91
10000	872.20	454.56	315.68	246.49	205.17	177.79	158.37	143.93	132.80	123.99	116.87	111.01
11000	959.42	500.02	347.25	271.14	225.69	195.57	174.21	158.32	146.08	136.39	128.56	122.11
12000	1046.64	545.47	378.82	295.78	246.20	213.35	190.04	172.71	159.36	148.79	140.24	133.21
13000	1133.86	590.93	410.38	320.43	266.72	231.12	205.88	187.10	172.64	161.19	151.93	144.31
14000	1221.08	636.38	441.95	345.08	287.24	248.90	221.72	201.49	185.92	173.58	163.61	155.41
15000	1308.30	681.84	473.52	369.73	307.75	266.68	237.55	215.89	199.20	185.98	175.30	166.51
16000	1395.52	727.30	505.09	394.38	328.27	284.46	253.39	230.28	212.47	198.38	186.99	177.61
17000	1482.74	772.75	536.65	419.03	348.79	302.24	269.23	244.67	225.75	210.78	198.67	188.71
18000	1569.96	818.21	568.22	443.67	369.30	320.02	285.06	259.06	239.03	223.18	210.36	199.82
19000	1657.18	863.66	599.79	468.32	389.82	337.79	300.90	273.46	252.31	235.58	222.05	210.92
20000	1744.40	909.12	631.36	492.97	410.34	355.57	316.73	287.85	265.59	247.98	233.73	222.02
21000	1831.62	954.57	662.92	517.62	430.85	373.35	332.57	302.24	278.87	260.37	245.42	233.12
22000	1918.84	1000.03	694.49	542.27	451.37	391.13	348.41	316.63	292.15	272.77	257.11	244.22
23000	2006.06	1045.49	726.06	566.92	471.89	408.91	364.24	331.02	305.43	285.17	268.79	255.32
24000	2093.28	1090.94	757.63	591.56	492.40	426.69	380.08	345.42	318.71	297.57	280.48	266.42
25000	2180.50	1136.40	789.19	616.21	512.92	444.46	395.92	359.81	331.99	309.97	292.16	277.52
26000	2267.72	1181.85	820.76	640.86	533.43	462.24	411.75	374.20	345.27	322.37	303.85	288.62
27000	2354.94	1227.31	852.33	665.51	553.95	480.02	427.59	388.59	358.55	334.77	315.54	299.72
28000	2442.16	1272.76	883.90	690.16	574.47	497.80	443.43	402.98	371.83	347.16	327.22	310.82
29000	2529.38	1318.22	915.46	714.81	594.98	515.58	459.26	417.38	385.11	359.56	338.91	321.92
30000	2616.60	1363.68	947.03	739.45	615.50	533.36	475.10	431.77	398.39	371.96	350.60	333.02
31000	2703.82	1409.13	978.60	764.10	636.02	551.13	490.94	446.16	411.66	384.36	362.28	344.12
32000	2791.04	1454.59	1010.17	788.75	656.53	568.91	506.77	460.55	424.94	396.76	373.97	355.22
33000	2878.26	1500.04	1041.73	813.40	677.05	586.69	522.61	474.95	438.22	409.16	385.66	366.32
34000	2965.48	1545.50	1073.30	838.05	697.57	604.47	538.45	489.34	451.50	421.56	397.34	377.42
35000	3052.70	1590.95	1104.87	862.70	718.08	622.25	554.28	503.73	464.78	433.95	409.03	388.52
36000	3139.92	1636.41	1136.44	887.34	738.60	640.03	570.12	518.12	478.06	446.35	420.72	399.63
37000	3227.14	1681.87	1168.00	911.99	759.12	657.81	585.95	532.51	491.34	458.75	432.40	410.73
38000	3314.36	1727.32	1199.57	936.64	779.63	675.58	601.79	546.91	504.62	471.15	444.09	421.83
39000	3401.58	1772.78	1231.14	961.29	800.15	693.36	617.63	561.30	517.90	483.55	455.77	432.93
40000	3488.80	1818.23	1262.71	985.94	820.67	711.14	633.46	575.69	531.18	495.95	467.46	444.03
41000	3576.02	1863.69	1294.27	1010.59	841.18	728.92	649.30	590.08	544.46	508.35	479.15	455.13
42000	3663.24	1909.14	1325.84	1035.23	861.70	746.70	665.14	604.47	557.74	520.74	490.83	466.24
43000	3750.46	1954.60	1357.41	1059.88	882.22	764.48	680.97	618.87	571.02	533.14	502.52	477.33
44000	3837.68	2000.05	1388.98	1084.53	902.73	782.25	696.81	633.26	584.30	545.54	514.21	488.43
45000	3924.90	2045.51	1420.54	1109.18	923.25	800.03	712.65	647.65	597.58	557.94	525.89	499.53
46000	4012.12	2090.97	1452.11	1133.83	943.77	817.81	728.48	662.04	610.86	570.34	537.58	510.63
47000	4099.33	2136.42	1483.68	1158.48	964.28	835.59	744.32	676.44	624.13	582.74	549.27	521.73
48000	4186.55	2181.88	1515.25	1183.12	984.80	853.37	760.16	690.83	637.41	595.14	560.95	532.83
49000	4273.77	2227.33	1546.81	1207.77	1005.32	871.15	775.99	705.22	650.69	607.53	572.64	543.93
50000	4360.99	2272.79	1578.38	1232.42	1025.83	888.92	791.83	719.61	663.97	619.93	584.32	555.03
55000	4797.09	2500.07	1736.22	1355.66	1128.41	977.82	871.01	791.57	730.37	681.93	642.76	610.54
60000	5233.19	2727.35	1894.06	1478.90	1231.00	1066.71	950.19	863.53	796.77	743.92	701.19	666.04
65000	5669.29	2954.62	2051.89	1602.14	1333.58	1155.60	1029.38	935.49	863.16	805.91	759.62	721.54
70000	6105.39	3181.90	2209.73	1725.39	1436.16	1244.49	1108.56	1007.45	929.56	867.90	818.05	777.04
75000	6541.48	3409.18	2367.57	1848.63	1538.74	1333.38	1187.74	1079.41	995.96	929.90	876.48	832.55
80000	6977.59	3636.46	2525.41	1971.87	1641.33	1422.28	1266.92	1151.38	1062.35	991.89	934.92	888.05
85000	7413.69	3863.74	2683.25	2095.11	1743.91	1511.17	1346.11	1223.34	1128.75	1053.88	993.35	943.55
90000	7849.79	4091.02	2841.08	2218.35	1846.49	1600.06	1425.29	1295.30	1195.15	1115.88	1051.78	999.06
95000	8285.88	4318.29	2998.92	2341.59	1949.08	1688.95	1504.47	1367.26	1261.54	1177.87	1110.21	1054.56
100000	8721.98	4545.57	3156.76	2464.84	2051.66	1777.84	1583.65	1439.22	1327.94	1239.86	1168.64	1110.06

30

Table 1

MONTHLY

PAYMENT REQUIRED TO AMORTIZE A LOAN

8.50%

8%

RM UNT	13 YEARS	14 YEARS	15 YEARS	16 YEARS	17 YEARS	18 YEARS	19 YEARS	20 YEARS	25 YEARS	30 YEARS	35 YEARS	40 YEARS
50	.54	.51	.50	.48	.47	.46	.45	.44	.41	.39	.38	.37
100	1.07	1.02	.99	.96	.93	.91	.89	.87	.81	.77	.75	.74
200	2.13	2.04	1.97	1.91	1.86	1.82	1.78	1.74	1.62	1.54	1.50	1.47
300	3.19	3.06	2.96	2.87	2.79	2.72	2.66	2.61	2.42	2.31	2.25	2.20
400	4.25	4.08	3.94	3.82	3.72	3.63	3.55	3.48	3.23	3.08	2.99	2.94
500	5.31	5.10	4.93	4.78	4.65	4.53	4.43	4.34	4.03	3.85	3.74	3.67
600	6.37	6.12	5.91	5.73	5.57	5.44	5.32	5.21	4.84	4.62	4.49	4.40
700	7.43	7.14	6.90	6.69	6.50	6.34	6.20	6.08	5.64	5.39	5.23	5.14
800	8.49	8.16	7.88	7.64	7.43	7.25	7.09	6.95	6.45	6.16	5.98	5.87
900	9.56	9.18	8.87	8.60	8.36	8.15	7.97	7.82	7.25	6.93	6.73	6.60
1000	10.62	10.20	9.85	9.55	9.29	9.06	8.86	8.68	8.06	7.69	7.47	7.34
2000	21.23	20.40	19.70	19.09	18.57	18.11	17.71	17.36	16.11	15.38	14.94	14.67
3000	31.84	30.60	29.55	28.64	27.85	27.17	26.57	26.04	24.16	23.07	22.41	22.00
4000	42.45	40.80	39.39	38.18	37.14	36.22	35.42	34.72	32.21	30.76	29.88	29.33
5000	53.06	51.00	49.24	47.73	46.42	45.28	44.28	43.40	40.27	38.45	37.35	36.66
6000	63.68	61.20	59.09	57.27	55.70	54.33	53.13	52.07	48.32	46.14	44.82	43.99
7000	74.29	71.40	68.94	66.82	64.99	63.39	61.99	60.75	56.37	53.83	52.29	51.32
8000	84.90	81.60	78.78	76.36	74.27	72.44	70.84	69.43	64.42	61.52	59.75	58.65
9000	95.51	91.80	88.63	85.91	83.55	81.50	79.70	78.11	72.48	69.21	67.22	65.98
0000	106.12	102.00	98.48	95.45	92.83	90.55	88.55	86.79	80.53	76.90	74.69	73.31
1000	116.73	112.20	108.33	105.00	102.12	99.61	97.40	95.47	88.58	84.59	82.16	80.65
2000	127.35	122.40	118.17	114.54	111.40	108.66	106.26	104.14	96.63	92.27	89.63	87.98
3000	137.96	132.59	128.02	124.09	120.68	117.71	115.11	112.82	104.68	99.96	97.10	95.31
4000	148.57	142.79	137.87	133.63	129.97	126.77	123.97	121.50	112.74	107.65	104.57	102.64
5000	159.18	152.99	147.72	143.18	139.25	135.82	132.82	130.18	120.79	115.34	112.03	109.97
6000	169.79	163.19	157.56	152.72	148.53	144.88	141.68	138.86	128.84	123.03	119.50	117.30
7000	180.41	173.39	167.41	162.27	157.81	153.93	150.53	147.53	136.89	130.72	126.97	124.63
8000	191.02	183.59	177.26	171.81	167.10	162.99	159.39	156.21	144.95	138.41	134.44	131.96
9000	201.63	193.79	187.11	181.36	176.38	172.04	168.24	164.89	153.00	146.10	141.91	139.29
0000	212.24	203.99	196.95	190.90	185.66	181.10	177.09	173.57	161.05	153.79	149.38	146.62
21000	222.85	214.19	206.80	200.45	194.95	190.15	185.95	182.25	169.10	161.48	156.85	153.95
22000	233.46	224.39	216.65	209.99	204.23	199.21	194.80	190.93	177.15	169.17	164.31	161.29
23000	244.08	234.59	226.50	219.54	213.51	208.26	203.66	199.60	185.21	176.86	171.78	168.62
24000	254.69	244.79	236.34	229.08	222.80	217.31	212.51	208.28	193.26	184.54	179.25	175.95
25000	265.30	254.98	246.19	238.63	232.08	226.37	221.37	216.96	201.31	192.23	186.72	183.28
26000	275.91	265.18	256.04	248.17	241.36	235.42	230.22	225.64	209.36	199.92	194.19	190.61
27000	286.52	275.38	265.88	257.72	250.64	244.48	239.08	234.32	217.42	207.61	201.66	197.94
28000	297.14	285.58	275.73	267.26	259.93	253.53	247.93	243.00	225.47	215.30	209.13	205.27
29000	307.75	295.78	285.58	276.81	269.21	262.59	256.78	251.67	233.52	222.99	216.59	212.60
30000	318.36	305.98	295.43	286.35	278.49	271.64	265.64	260.35	241.57	230.68	224.06	219.93
31000	328.97	316.18	305.27	295.90	287.78	280.70	274.49	269.03	249.63	238.37	231.53	227.26
32000	339.58	326.38	315.12	305.44	297.06	289.75	283.35	277.71	257.68	246.06	239.00	234.60
33000	350.19	336.58	324.97	314.99	306.34	298.81	292.20	286.39	265.73	253.75	246.47	241.93
34000	360.81	346.78	334.82	324.53	315.62	307.86	301.06	295.06	273.78	261.44	253.94	249.26
35000	371.42	356.98	344.66	334.08	324.91	316.92	309.91	303.74	281.83	269.12	261.41	256.59
36000	382.03	367.18	354.51	343.62	334.19	325.97	318.77	312.42	289.89	276.81	268.87	263.92
37000	392.64	377.37	364.36	353.17	343.47	335.02	327.62	321.10	297.94	284.50	276.34	271.25
38000	403.25	387.57	374.21	362.71	352.76	344.08	336.47	329.78	305.99	292.19	283.81	278.58
39000	413.86	397.77	384.05	372.26	362.04	353.13	345.33	338.46	314.04	299.88	291.28	285.91
40000	424.48	407.97	393.90	381.80	371.32	362.19	354.18	347.13	322.10	307.57	298.75	293.24
41000	435.09	418.17	403.75	391.35	380.60	371.24	363.03	355.81	330.15	315.26	306.22	300.57
42000	445.70	428.37	413.60	400.89	389.89	380.30	371.89	364.49	338.20	322.95	313.69	307.90
43000	456.31	438.57	423.44	410.44	399.17	389.35	380.75	373.17	346.25	330.64	321.16	315.24
44000	466.92	448.77	433.29	419.98	408.45	398.41	389.60	381.85	354.30	338.33	328.62	322.57
45000	477.54	458.97	443.14	429.53	417.74	407.46	398.46	390.53	362.36	346.02	336.09	329.90
46000	488.15	469.17	452.99	439.07	427.02	416.52	407.31	399.20	370.41	353.71	343.56	337.23
47000	498.76	479.37	462.83	448.62	436.30	425.57	416.16	407.88	378.46	361.39	351.03	344.56
48000	509.37	489.57	472.68	458.16	445.59	434.62	425.02	416.56	386.51	369.08	358.50	351.89
49000	519.98	499.77	482.53	467.71	454.87	443.68	433.87	425.24	394.57	376.77	365.97	359.22
50000	530.59	509.96	492.37	477.25	464.15	452.73	442.73	433.92	402.62	384.46	373.44	366.55
55000	583.65	560.96	541.61	524.98	510.57	498.01	487.00	477.31	442.88	422.91	410.78	403.21
60000	636.71	611.96	590.85	572.70	556.98	543.28	531.27	520.70	483.14	461.35	448.12	439.86
65000	689.77	662.95	640.09	620.42	603.39	588.55	575.54	564.09	523.40	499.80	485.46	476.52
70000	742.83	713.95	689.32	668.15	649.81	633.83	619.82	607.48	563.66	538.24	522.81	513.17
75000	795.89	764.94	738.56	715.87	696.22	679.10	664.09	650.87	603.93	576.69	560.15	549.83
80000	848.95	815.94	787.80	763.60	742.64	724.37	708.36	694.26	644.19	615.14	597.49	586.48
85000	902.01	866.94	837.03	811.32	789.05	769.64	752.63	737.65	684.45	653.58	634.84	623.13
90000	955.07	917.93	886.27	859.05	835.47	814.92	796.91	781.05	724.71	692.03	672.18	659.79
95000	1008.13	968.93	935.51	906.77	881.88	860.19	841.18	824.44	764.97	730.47	709.52	696.44
00000	1061.18	1019.92	984.74	954.50	928.30	905.46	885.45	867.83	805.23	768.92	746.87	733.10

Table 1

8.75%

MONTHLY
PAYMENT REQUIRED TO AMORTIZE A LOAN

8%

TERM / AMOUNT	1 YEAR	2 YEARS	3 YEARS	4 YEARS	5 YEARS	6 YEARS	7 YEARS	8 YEARS	9 YEARS	10 YEARS	11 YEARS	12 YEAR
50	4.37	2.28	1.59	1.24	1.04	.90	.80	.73	.68	.63	.60	.57
100	8.74	4.56	3.17	2.48	2.07	1.80	1.60	1.46	1.35	1.26	1.19	1.13
200	17.47	9.12	6.34	4.96	4.13	3.59	3.20	2.91	2.69	2.51	2.37	2.25
300	26.21	13.68	9.51	7.43	6.20	5.38	4.79	4.36	4.03	3.76	3.55	3.38
400	34.94	18.23	12.68	9.91	8.26	7.17	6.39	5.81	5.37	5.02	4.73	4.50
500	43.67	22.79	15.85	12.39	10.32	8.96	7.99	7.27	6.71	6.27	5.92	5.62
600	52.41	27.35	19.02	14.86	12.39	10.75	9.58	8.72	8.05	7.52	7.10	6.75
700	61.14	31.90	22.18	17.34	14.45	12.54	11.18	10.17	9.39	8.78	8.28	7.87
800	69.87	36.46	25.35	19.82	16.51	14.33	12.77	11.62	10.73	10.03	9.46	9.00
900	78.61	41.02	28.52	22.29	18.58	16.12	14.37	13.07	12.07	11.28	10.65	10.12
1000	87.34	45.58	31.69	24.77	20.64	17.91	15.97	14.53	13.42	12.54	11.83	11.24
2000	174.68	91.15	63.37	49.54	41.28	35.81	31.93	29.05	26.83	25.07	23.65	22.48
3000	262.01	136.72	95.06	74.30	61.92	53.71	47.89	43.57	40.24	37.60	35.47	33.72
4000	349.35	182.29	126.74	99.07	82.55	71.61	63.85	58.09	53.65	50.14	47.30	44.96
5000	436.68	227.86	158.42	123.84	103.19	89.51	79.82	72.61	67.06	62.67	59.12	56.20
6000	524.02	273.43	190.11	148.60	123.83	107.42	95.78	87.13	80.47	75.20	70.94	67.44
7000	611.35	319.00	221.79	173.37	144.47	125.32	111.74	101.65	93.88	87.73	82.77	78.68
8000	698.69	364.57	253.47	198.14	165.10	143.22	127.70	116.17	107.29	100.27	94.59	89.92
9000	786.03	410.14	285.16	222.90	185.74	161.12	143.67	130.69	120.70	112.80	106.41	101.16
10000	873.36	455.71	316.84	247.67	206.38	179.02	159.63	145.21	134.11	125.33	118.24	112.40
11000	960.70	501.28	348.52	272.44	227.01	196.92	175.59	159.73	147.52	137.86	130.06	123.64
12000	1048.03	546.85	380.21	297.20	247.65	214.83	191.55	174.26	160.93	150.40	141.88	134.88
13000	1135.37	592.42	411.89	321.97	268.29	232.73	207.52	188.78	174.34	162.93	153.71	146.12
14000	1222.70	637.99	443.57	346.74	288.93	250.63	223.48	203.30	187.76	175.46	165.53	157.36
15000	1310.04	683.56	475.26	371.50	309.56	268.53	239.44	217.82	201.17	188.00	177.35	168.60
16000	1397.37	729.13	506.94	396.27	330.20	286.43	255.40	232.34	214.58	200.53	189.18	179.84
17000	1484.71	774.70	538.62	421.04	350.84	304.33	271.37	246.86	227.99	213.06	201.00	191.08
18000	1572.05	820.27	570.31	445.80	371.48	322.24	287.33	261.38	241.40	225.59	212.82	202.32
19000	1659.38	865.84	601.99	470.57	392.11	340.14	303.29	275.90	254.81	238.13	224.65	213.56
20000	1746.72	911.41	633.68	495.34	412.75	358.04	319.25	290.42	268.22	250.66	236.47	224.80
21000	1834.05	956.98	665.36	520.10	433.39	375.94	335.22	304.94	281.63	263.19	248.29	236.04
22000	1921.39	1002.55	697.04	544.87	454.02	393.84	351.18	319.46	295.04	275.72	260.11	247.28
23000	2008.72	1048.12	728.73	569.63	474.66	411.74	367.14	333.98	308.45	288.26	271.94	258.52
24000	2096.06	1093.69	760.41	594.40	495.30	429.65	383.10	348.51	321.86	300.79	283.76	269.76
25000	2183.39	1139.26	792.09	619.17	515.94	447.55	399.07	363.03	335.27	313.32	295.58	281.00
26000	2270.73	1184.83	823.78	643.93	536.57	465.45	415.03	377.55	348.68	325.85	307.41	292.24
27000	2358.07	1230.40	855.46	668.70	557.21	483.35	430.99	392.07	362.10	338.39	319.23	303.48
28000	2445.40	1275.97	887.14	693.47	577.85	501.25	446.95	406.59	375.51	350.92	331.05	314.72
29000	2532.74	1321.54	918.83	718.23	598.48	519.15	462.92	421.11	388.92	363.45	342.88	325.96
30000	2620.07	1367.11	950.51	743.00	619.12	537.06	478.88	435.63	402.33	375.99	354.70	337.20
31000	2707.41	1412.68	982.19	767.77	639.76	554.96	494.84	450.15	415.74	388.52	366.52	348.44
32000	2794.74	1458.25	1013.88	792.53	660.40	572.86	510.80	464.67	429.15	401.05	378.35	359.68
33000	2882.08	1503.82	1045.56	817.30	681.03	590.76	526.77	479.19	442.56	413.58	390.17	370.92
34000	2969.41	1549.39	1077.24	842.07	701.67	608.66	542.73	493.71	455.97	426.12	401.99	382.16
35000	3056.75	1594.96	1108.93	866.83	722.31	626.56	558.69	508.23	469.38	438.65	413.82	393.40
36000	3144.09	1640.53	1140.61	891.60	742.95	644.47	574.65	522.76	482.79	451.18	425.64	404.64
37000	3231.42	1686.10	1172.29	916.37	763.58	662.37	590.62	537.28	496.20	463.71	437.46	415.88
38000	3318.76	1731.67	1203.98	941.13	784.22	680.27	606.58	551.80	509.61	476.25	449.29	427.12
39000	3406.09	1777.24	1235.66	965.90	804.86	698.17	622.54	566.32	523.02	488.78	461.11	438.36
40000	3493.43	1822.81	1267.35	990.67	825.49	716.07	638.50	580.84	536.44	501.31	472.93	449.60
41000	3580.76	1868.38	1299.03	1015.43	846.13	733.98	654.47	595.36	549.85	513.84	484.75	460.84
42000	3668.10	1913.95	1330.71	1040.20	866.77	751.88	670.43	609.88	563.26	526.38	496.58	472.08
43000	3755.44	1959.52	1362.40	1064.96	887.41	769.78	686.39	624.40	576.67	538.91	508.40	483.32
44000	3842.77	2005.09	1394.08	1089.73	908.04	787.68	702.35	638.92	590.08	551.44	520.22	494.56
45000	3930.11	2050.66	1425.76	1114.50	928.68	805.58	718.32	653.44	603.49	563.98	532.05	505.80
46000	4017.44	2096.23	1457.45	1139.26	949.32	823.48	734.28	667.96	616.90	576.51	543.87	517.04
47000	4104.78	2141.80	1489.13	1164.03	969.95	841.39	750.24	682.48	630.31	589.04	555.69	528.28
48000	4192.11	2187.37	1520.81	1188.80	990.59	859.29	766.20	697.01	643.72	601.57	567.52	539.52
49000	4279.45	2232.94	1552.50	1213.56	1011.23	877.19	782.17	711.53	657.13	614.11	579.34	550.76
50000	4366.78	2278.51	1584.18	1238.33	1031.87	895.09	798.13	726.05	670.54	626.64	591.16	562.00
55000	4803.46	2506.36	1742.60	1362.16	1135.05	984.60	877.94	798.65	737.60	689.30	650.28	618.20
60000	5240.14	2734.21	1901.02	1486.00	1238.24	1074.11	957.75	871.26	804.65	751.97	709.40	674.40
65000	5676.82	2962.06	2059.43	1609.83	1341.43	1163.62	1037.57	943.86	871.70	814.63	768.51	730.60
70000	6113.50	3189.91	2217.85	1733.66	1444.61	1253.12	1117.38	1016.46	938.76	877.29	827.63	786.80
75000	6550.17	3417.76	2376.27	1857.49	1547.80	1342.63	1197.19	1089.07	1005.81	939.96	886.74	843.00
80000	6986.85	3645.61	2534.69	1981.33	1650.98	1432.14	1277.00	1161.67	1072.87	1002.62	945.86	899.20
85000	7423.53	3873.47	2693.10	2105.16	1754.17	1521.65	1356.82	1234.28	1139.92	1065.28	1004.97	955.40
90000	7860.21	4101.32	2851.52	2228.99	1857.36	1611.16	1436.63	1306.88	1206.97	1127.95	1064.09	1011.60
95000	8296.89	4329.17	3009.94	2352.82	1960.54	1700.67	1516.44	1379.48	1274.03	1190.61	1123.21	1067.80
100000	8733.56	4557.02	3168.36	2476.66	2063.73	1790.18	1596.25	1452.09	1341.08	1253.27	1182.32	1124.00

Table 1

MONTHLY

8.75%

PAYMENT REQUIRED TO AMORTIZE A LOAN

TERM AMOUNT	13 YEARS	14 YEARS	15 YEARS	16 YEARS	17 YEARS	18 YEARS	19 YEARS	20 YEARS	25 YEARS	30 YEARS	35 YEARS	40 YEARS
50	.54	.52	.50	.49	.48	.47	.46	.45	.42	.40	.39	.38
100	1.08	1.04	1.00	.97	.95	.93	.91	.89	.83	.79	.77	.76
200	2.16	2.07	2.00	1.94	1.89	1.85	1.81	1.77	1.65	1.58	1.54	1.51
300	3.23	3.11	3.00	2.91	2.84	2.77	2.71	2.66	2.47	2.37	2.30	2.26
400	4.31	4.14	4.00	3.88	3.78	3.69	3.61	3.54	3.29	3.15	3.07	3.01
500	5.38	5.18	5.00	4.85	4.72	4.61	4.51	4.42	4.12	3.94	3.83	3.77
600	6.46	6.21	6.00	5.82	5.67	5.53	5.41	5.31	4.94	4.73	4.60	4.52
700	7.53	7.25	7.00	6.79	6.61	6.45	6.31	6.19	5.76	5.51	5.36	5.27
800	8.61	8.28	8.00	7.76	7.55	7.37	7.21	7.07	6.58	6.30	6.13	6.02
900	9.68	9.31	9.00	8.73	8.48	8.29	8.11	7.96	7.40	7.09	6.89	6.77
1000	10.76	10.35	10.00	9.70	9.44	9.21	9.02	8.84	8.23	7.87	7.66	7.53
2000	21.51	20.69	19.99	19.39	18.87	18.42	18.03	17.68	16.45	15.74	15.31	15.05
3000	32.27	31.04	29.99	29.09	28.31	27.63	27.04	26.52	24.67	23.61	22.97	22.57
4000	43.02	41.38	39.98	38.78	37.74	36.84	36.05	35.35	32.89	31.47	30.62	30.09
5000	53.77	51.72	49.98	48.48	47.18	46.05	45.06	44.19	41.11	39.34	38.27	37.61
6000	64.53	62.07	59.97	58.17	56.61	55.26	54.07	53.03	49.33	47.21	45.93	45.14
7000	75.28	72.41	69.97	67.87	66.05	64.47	63.08	61.86	57.56	55.07	53.58	52.66
8000	86.04	82.76	79.96	77.56	75.48	73.68	72.09	70.70	65.78	62.94	61.23	60.18
9000	96.79	93.10	89.96	87.26	84.92	82.89	81.10	79.54	74.00	70.81	68.89	67.70
10000	107.54	103.44	99.95	96.95	94.35	92.09	90.12	88.38	82.22	78.68	76.54	75.22
11000	118.30	113.79	109.94	106.64	103.79	101.30	99.13	97.21	90.44	86.54	84.19	82.74
12000	129.05	124.13	119.94	116.34	113.22	110.51	108.14	106.05	98.66	94.41	91.85	90.27
13000	139.80	134.47	129.93	126.03	122.66	119.72	117.15	114.89	106.88	102.28	99.50	97.79
14000	150.56	144.82	139.93	135.73	132.09	128.93	126.16	123.72	115.11	110.14	107.16	105.31
15000	161.31	155.16	149.92	145.42	141.53	138.14	135.17	132.56	123.33	118.01	114.81	112.83
16000	172.07	165.51	159.92	155.12	150.96	147.35	144.18	141.40	131.55	125.88	122.46	120.35
17000	182.82	175.85	169.91	164.81	160.40	156.56	153.19	150.24	139.77	133.74	130.12	127.87
18000	193.57	186.19	179.91	174.51	169.83	165.77	162.20	159.07	147.99	141.61	137.77	135.40
19000	204.33	196.54	189.90	184.20	179.27	174.97	171.22	167.91	156.21	149.48	145.42	142.92
20000	215.08	206.88	199.89	193.89	188.70	184.18	180.23	176.75	164.43	157.35	153.08	150.44
21000	225.83	217.22	209.89	203.59	198.14	193.39	189.24	185.58	172.66	165.21	160.73	157.96
22000	236.59	227.57	219.88	213.28	207.57	202.60	198.25	194.42	180.88	173.08	168.38	165.48
23000	247.34	237.91	229.88	222.98	217.01	211.81	207.26	203.26	189.10	180.95	176.04	173.00
24000	258.10	248.26	239.87	232.67	226.44	221.02	216.27	212.10	197.32	188.81	183.69	180.53
25000	268.85	258.60	249.87	242.37	235.88	230.23	225.28	220.93	205.54	196.68	191.35	188.05
26000	279.60	268.94	259.86	252.06	245.31	239.44	234.29	229.77	213.76	204.55	199.00	195.57
27000	290.36	279.29	269.86	261.76	254.75	248.65	243.30	238.61	221.98	212.41	206.65	203.09
28000	301.11	289.63	279.85	271.45	264.18	257.85	252.32	247.44	230.21	220.28	214.31	210.61
29000	311.87	299.97	289.85	281.14	273.62	267.06	261.33	256.28	238.43	228.15	221.96	218.13
30000	322.62	310.32	299.84	290.84	283.05	276.27	270.34	265.12	246.65	236.02	229.61	225.66
31000	333.37	320.66	309.83	300.53	292.49	285.48	279.35	273.96	254.87	243.88	237.27	233.18
32000	344.13	331.01	319.83	310.23	301.92	294.69	288.36	282.79	263.09	251.75	244.92	240.70
33000	354.88	341.35	329.82	319.92	311.36	303.90	297.37	291.63	271.31	259.62	252.57	248.22
34000	365.63	351.69	339.82	329.62	320.79	313.11	306.38	300.47	279.53	267.48	260.23	255.74
35000	376.39	362.04	349.81	339.31	330.23	322.32	315.39	309.30	287.76	275.35	267.88	263.26
36000	387.14	372.38	359.81	349.01	339.66	331.53	324.40	318.14	295.98	283.22	275.54	270.79
37000	397.90	382.72	369.80	358.70	349.10	340.73	333.42	326.98	304.20	291.08	283.19	278.31
38000	408.65	393.07	379.80	368.39	358.53	349.94	342.43	335.82	312.42	298.95	290.84	285.83
39000	419.40	403.41	389.79	378.09	367.97	359.15	351.44	344.65	320.64	306.82	298.50	293.35
40000	430.16	413.76	399.78	387.78	377.40	368.36	360.45	353.49	328.86	314.69	306.15	300.87
41000	440.91	424.10	409.78	397.48	386.84	377.57	369.46	362.33	337.08	322.55	313.80	308.39
42000	451.66	434.44	419.77	407.17	396.27	386.78	378.47	371.16	345.31	330.42	321.46	315.92
43000	462.42	444.79	429.77	416.87	405.71	395.99	387.48	380.00	353.53	338.29	329.11	323.44
44000	473.17	455.13	439.76	426.56	415.14	405.20	396.49	388.84	361.75	346.15	336.76	330.96
45000	483.93	465.47	449.76	436.26	424.58	414.41	405.50	397.67	369.97	354.02	344.42	338.48
46000	494.68	475.82	459.75	445.95	434.01	423.61	414.52	406.51	378.19	361.89	352.07	346.00
47000	505.43	486.16	469.75	455.64	443.44	432.82	423.53	415.35	386.41	369.75	359.73	353.53
48000	516.19	496.51	479.74	465.34	452.88	442.03	432.54	424.19	394.63	377.62	367.38	361.05
49000	526.94	506.85	489.73	475.03	462.31	451.24	441.55	433.02	402.86	385.49	375.03	368.57
50000	537.70	517.19	499.73	484.73	471.75	460.45	450.56	441.86	411.08	393.36	382.69	376.09
55000	591.46	568.91	549.70	533.20	518.92	506.49	495.61	486.05	452.18	432.69	420.95	413.70
60000	645.23	620.63	599.67	581.67	566.10	552.54	540.67	530.23	493.29	472.03	459.22	451.31
65000	699.00	672.35	649.65	630.15	613.27	598.58	585.73	574.42	534.40	511.36	497.49	488.92
70000	752.77	724.07	699.62	678.62	660.45	644.63	630.78	618.60	575.51	550.70	535.76	526.52
75000	806.54	775.79	749.59	727.09	707.62	690.67	675.84	662.79	616.61	590.04	574.03	564.13
80000	860.31	827.51	799.56	775.56	754.80	736.72	720.89	706.97	657.72	629.37	612.30	601.74
85000	914.08	879.22	849.54	824.03	801.97	782.76	765.95	751.16	698.83	668.70	650.56	639.35
90000	967.85	930.94	899.51	872.51	849.15	828.81	811.00	795.34	739.93	708.04	688.83	676.96
95000	1021.62	982.66	949.48	920.98	896.32	874.85	856.06	839.53	781.04	747.37	727.10	714.57
100000	1075.39	1034.38	999.45	969.45	943.49	920.90	901.11	883.72	822.15	786.71	765.37	752.18

8%

Table 1

9.00%

MONTHLY

PAYMENT REQUIRED TO AMORTIZE A LOAN

9%

TERM AMOUNT	1 YEAR	2 YEARS	3 YEARS	4 YEARS	5 YEARS	6 YEARS	7 YEARS	8 YEARS	9 YEARS	10 YEARS	11 YEARS	12 YEARS
50	4.38	2.29	1.59	1.25	1.04	.91	.81	.74	.68	.64	.60	.57
100	8.75	4.57	3.18	2.49	2.08	1.81	1.61	1.47	1.36	1.27	1.20	1.14
200	17.50	9.14	6.36	4.98	4.16	3.61	3.22	2.94	2.71	2.54	2.40	2.28
300	26.24	13.71	9.54	7.47	6.23	5.41	4.83	4.40	4.07	3.81	3.59	3.42
400	34.99	18.28	12.72	9.96	8.31	7.22	6.44	5.87	5.42	5.07	4.79	4.56
500	43.73	22.85	15.90	12.45	10.38	9.02	8.05	7.33	6.78	6.34	5.99	5.70
600	52.48	27.42	19.08	14.94	12.46	10.82	9.66	8.80	8.13	7.61	7.18	6.83
700	61.22	31.98	22.26	17.42	14.54	12.62	11.27	10.26	9.49	8.87	8.38	7.97
800	69.97	36.55	25.44	19.91	16.61	14.43	12.88	11.73	10.84	10.14	9.57	9.11
900	78.71	41.12	28.62	22.40	18.69	16.23	14.49	13.19	12.19	11.41	10.77	10.25
1000	87.46	45.69	31.80	24.89	20.76	18.03	16.09	14.66	13.55	12.67	11.97	11.39
2000	174.91	91.37	63.60	49.78	41.52	36.06	32.18	29.31	27.09	25.34	23.93	22.77
3000	262.36	137.06	95.40	74.66	62.28	54.08	48.27	43.96	40.63	38.01	35.89	34.15
4000	349.81	182.74	127.20	99.55	83.04	72.11	64.36	58.61	54.18	50.68	47.85	45.53
5000	437.26	228.43	159.00	124.43	103.80	90.13	80.45	73.26	67.72	63.34	59.81	56.91
6000	524.71	274.11	190.80	149.32	124.56	108.16	96.54	87.91	81.26	76.01	71.77	68.29
7000	612.17	319.80	222.60	174.20	145.31	126.18	112.63	102.56	94.81	88.68	83.73	79.67
8000	699.62	365.48	254.40	199.09	166.07	144.21	128.72	117.21	108.35	101.35	95.69	91.05
9000	787.07	411.17	286.20	223.97	186.83	162.23	144.81	131.86	121.89	114.01	107.65	102.43
10000	874.52	456.85	318.00	248.86	207.59	180.26	160.90	146.51	135.43	126.68	119.61	113.81
11000	961.97	502.54	349.80	273.74	228.35	198.29	176.98	161.16	148.98	139.35	131.57	125.19
12000	1049.42	548.22	381.60	298.63	249.11	216.31	193.07	175.81	162.52	152.02	143.53	136.57
13000	1136.87	593.91	413.40	323.51	269.86	234.34	209.16	190.46	176.06	164.68	155.50	147.95
14000	1224.33	639.59	445.20	348.40	290.62	252.36	225.25	205.11	189.61	177.35	167.46	159.33
15000	1311.78	685.28	477.00	373.28	311.38	270.39	241.34	219.76	203.15	190.02	179.42	170.71
16000	1399.23	730.96	508.80	398.17	332.14	288.41	257.43	234.41	216.69	202.69	191.38	182.09
17000	1486.68	776.65	540.60	423.05	352.90	306.44	273.52	249.06	230.23	215.35	203.34	193.47
18000	1574.13	822.33	572.40	447.94	373.66	324.46	289.61	263.71	243.78	228.02	215.30	204.85
19000	1661.58	868.02	604.20	472.82	394.41	342.49	305.70	278.36	257.32	240.69	227.26	216.23
20000	1749.05	913.70	636.00	497.71	415.17	360.52	321.79	293.01	270.86	253.36	239.22	227.61
21000	1836.49	959.38	667.80	522.59	435.93	378.54	337.88	307.66	284.41	266.02	251.18	238.99
22000	1923.94	1005.07	699.60	547.48	456.69	396.57	353.96	322.31	297.95	278.69	263.14	250.37
23000	2011.39	1050.75	731.40	572.36	477.45	414.59	370.05	336.96	311.49	291.36	275.10	261.75
24000	2098.84	1096.44	763.20	597.25	498.21	432.62	386.14	351.61	325.03	304.03	287.06	273.13
25000	2186.29	1142.12	795.00	622.13	518.96	450.64	402.23	366.26	338.58	316.69	299.03	284.51
26000	2273.74	1187.81	826.80	647.02	539.72	468.67	418.32	380.91	352.12	329.36	310.99	295.89
27000	2361.19	1233.49	858.60	671.90	560.48	486.69	434.41	395.56	365.66	342.03	322.95	307.27
28000	2448.65	1279.18	890.40	696.79	581.24	504.72	450.50	410.21	379.21	354.70	334.91	318.65
29000	2536.10	1324.86	922.20	721.67	602.00	522.75	466.59	424.86	392.75	367.36	346.87	330.03
30000	2623.55	1370.55	954.00	746.56	622.76	540.77	482.68	439.51	406.29	380.03	358.83	341.41
31000	2711.00	1416.23	985.80	771.44	643.51	558.80	498.77	454.15	419.84	392.70	370.79	352.79
32000	2798.45	1461.92	1017.60	796.33	664.27	576.82	514.86	468.81	433.38	405.37	382.75	364.17
33000	2885.90	1507.60	1049.40	821.21	685.03	594.85	530.94	483.46	446.92	418.04	394.71	375.56
34000	2973.36	1553.29	1081.20	846.10	705.79	612.87	547.03	498.11	460.46	430.70	406.67	386.94
35000	3060.81	1598.97	1113.00	870.98	726.55	630.90	563.12	512.76	474.01	443.37	418.63	398.32
36000	3148.26	1644.66	1144.80	895.87	747.31	648.92	579.21	527.41	487.55	456.04	430.59	409.70
37000	3235.71	1690.34	1176.60	920.75	768.06	666.95	595.30	542.06	501.09	468.71	442.55	421.08
38000	3323.16	1736.03	1208.39	945.64	788.82	684.98	611.39	556.71	514.64	481.37	454.52	432.46
39000	3410.61	1781.71	1240.19	970.52	809.58	703.00	627.48	571.36	528.18	494.04	466.48	443.84
40000	3498.06	1827.39	1271.99	995.41	830.34	721.03	643.57	586.01	541.72	506.71	478.44	455.22
41000	3585.52	1873.08	1303.79	1020.29	851.10	739.05	659.66	600.66	555.26	519.38	490.40	466.60
42000	3672.97	1918.76	1335.59	1045.18	871.86	757.08	675.75	615.31	568.81	532.04	502.36	477.98
43000	3760.42	1964.45	1367.39	1070.06	892.61	775.10	691.84	629.96	582.35	544.71	514.32	489.36
44000	3847.87	2010.13	1399.19	1094.95	913.37	793.13	707.92	644.61	595.89	557.38	526.28	500.74
45000	3935.32	2055.82	1430.99	1119.83	934.13	811.15	724.01	659.26	609.44	570.05	538.24	512.12
46000	4022.77	2101.50	1462.79	1144.72	954.89	829.18	740.10	673.91	622.98	582.71	550.20	523.50
47000	4110.22	2147.19	1494.59	1169.60	975.65	847.21	756.19	688.56	636.52	595.38	562.16	534.88
48000	4197.68	2192.87	1526.39	1194.49	996.41	865.23	772.28	703.21	650.06	608.05	574.12	546.26
49000	4285.13	2238.56	1558.19	1219.37	1017.16	883.26	788.37	717.86	663.61	620.72	586.08	557.64
50000	4372.58	2284.24	1589.99	1244.26	1037.92	901.28	804.46	732.52	677.15	633.38	598.05	569.02
55000	4809.84	2512.67	1748.99	1368.68	1141.71	991.41	884.90	805.77	744.86	696.72	657.85	625.92
60000	5247.09	2741.09	1907.99	1493.11	1245.51	1081.54	965.35	879.02	812.58	760.06	717.65	682.82
65000	5684.35	2969.51	2066.99	1617.53	1349.30	1171.66	1045.80	952.27	880.29	823.40	777.46	739.72
70000	6121.61	3197.94	2225.99	1741.96	1453.09	1261.79	1126.24	1025.52	948.01	886.74	837.26	796.63
75000	6558.87	3426.36	2384.98	1866.38	1556.88	1351.92	1206.69	1098.77	1015.72	950.07	897.07	853.53
80000	6996.12	3654.78	2543.98	1990.81	1660.67	1442.05	1287.13	1172.02	1083.44	1013.41	956.87	910.43
85000	7433.38	3883.21	2702.98	2115.23	1764.47	1532.18	1367.58	1245.27	1151.15	1076.75	1016.67	967.33
90000	7870.64	4111.63	2861.98	2239.66	1868.26	1622.30	1448.02	1318.52	1218.87	1140.09	1076.48	1024.23
95000	8307.90	4340.06	3020.98	2364.08	1972.05	1712.43	1528.47	1391.77	1286.58	1203.42	1136.28	1081.13
100000	8745.15	4568.48	3179.98	2488.51	2075.84	1802.56	1608.91	1465.03	1354.30	1266.76	1196.09	1138.04

Table 1

MONTHLY

PAYMENT REQUIRED TO AMORTIZE A LOAN

9.00%

9%

TERM AMOUNT	13 YEARS	14 YEARS	15 YEARS	16 YEARS	17 YEARS	18 YEARS	19 YEARS	20 YEARS	25 YEARS	30 YEARS	35 YEARS	40 YEARS
50	.55	.53	.51	.50	.48	.47	.46	.45	.42	.41	.40	.39
100	1.09	1.05	1.02	.99	.96	.94	.92	.90	.84	.81	.79	.78
200	2.18	2.10	2.03	1.97	1.92	1.88	1.84	1.80	1.68	1.61	1.57	1.55
300	3.27	3.15	3.05	2.96	2.88	2.81	2.76	2.70	2.52	2.42	2.36	2.32
400	4.36	4.20	4.06	3.94	3.84	3.75	3.67	3.60	3.36	3.22	3.14	3.09
500	5.45	5.25	5.08	4.93	4.80	4.69	4.59	4.50	4.20	4.03	3.92	3.86
600	6.54	6.30	6.09	5.91	5.76	5.62	5.51	5.40	5.04	4.83	4.71	4.63
700	7.63	7.35	7.10	6.90	6.72	6.56	6.42	6.30	5.88	5.64	5.49	5.40
800	8.72	8.40	8.12	7.88	7.68	7.50	7.34	7.20	6.72	6.44	6.28	6.18
900	9.81	9.45	9.13	8.87	8.63	8.43	8.26	8.10	7.56	7.25	7.06	6.95
1000	10.90	10.49	10.15	9.85	9.59	9.37	9.17	9.00	8.40	8.05	7.84	7.72
2000	21.80	20.98	20.29	19.70	19.18	18.73	18.34	18.00	16.79	16.10	15.68	15.43
3000	32.70	31.47	30.43	29.54	28.77	28.10	27.51	27.00	25.18	24.14	23.52	23.15
4000	43.59	41.96	40.58	39.39	38.36	37.46	36.68	35.99	33.57	32.19	31.36	30.86
5000	54.49	52.45	50.72	49.23	47.95	46.83	45.85	44.99	41.96	40.24	39.20	38.57
6000	65.39	62.94	60.86	59.08	57.53	56.19	55.02	53.99	50.36	48.28	47.04	46.29
7000	76.28	73.43	71.00	68.92	67.12	65.56	64.19	62.99	58.75	56.33	54.88	54.00
8000	87.18	83.92	81.15	78.77	76.71	74.92	73.36	71.98	67.14	64.37	62.72	61.71
9000	98.08	94.41	91.29	88.61	86.30	84.29	82.53	80.98	75.53	72.42	70.56	69.43
10000	108.97	104.90	101.43	98.46	95.89	93.65	91.69	89.98	83.92	80.47	78.40	77.14
11000	119.87	115.39	111.57	108.30	105.47	103.01	100.86	98.97	92.32	88.51	86.24	84.85
12000	130.77	125.88	121.72	118.15	115.06	112.38	110.03	107.97	100.71	96.56	94.08	92.57
13000	141.66	136.37	131.86	127.99	124.65	121.74	119.20	116.97	109.10	104.61	101.92	100.28
14000	152.56	146.86	142.00	137.84	134.24	131.11	128.37	125.97	117.49	112.65	109.76	108.00
15000	163.46	157.35	152.14	147.68	143.83	140.47	137.54	134.96	125.88	120.70	117.60	115.71
16000	174.35	167.84	162.29	157.53	153.41	149.84	146.71	143.96	134.28	128.74	125.44	123.42
17000	185.25	178.32	172.43	167.37	163.00	159.20	155.88	152.96	142.67	136.79	133.28	131.14
18000	196.15	188.81	182.57	177.22	172.59	168.57	165.05	161.96	151.06	144.84	141.12	138.85
19000	207.04	199.30	192.72	187.06	182.18	177.93	174.22	170.95	159.45	152.88	148.96	146.56
20000	217.94	209.79	202.86	196.91	191.77	187.29	183.38	179.95	167.84	160.93	156.80	154.28
21000	228.84	220.28	213.00	206.75	201.35	196.66	192.55	188.95	176.24	168.98	164.64	161.99
22000	239.73	230.77	223.14	216.60	210.94	206.02	201.72	197.94	184.63	177.02	172.48	169.70
23000	250.63	241.26	233.29	226.44	220.53	215.39	210.89	206.94	193.02	185.07	180.32	177.42
24000	261.53	251.75	243.43	236.29	230.12	224.75	220.06	215.94	201.41	193.11	188.16	185.13
25000	272.43	262.24	253.57	246.13	239.71	234.12	229.23	224.94	209.80	201.16	196.00	192.85
26000	283.32	272.73	263.71	255.98	249.29	243.48	238.40	233.93	218.20	209.21	203.84	200.56
27000	294.22	283.22	273.86	265.82	258.88	252.85	247.57	242.93	226.59	217.25	211.68	208.27
28000	305.12	293.71	284.00	275.67	268.47	262.21	256.74	251.93	234.98	225.30	219.52	215.99
29000	316.01	304.20	294.14	285.51	278.06	271.57	265.91	260.93	243.37	233.35	227.36	223.70
30000	326.91	314.69	304.28	295.36	287.65	280.94	275.07	269.92	251.76	241.39	235.20	231.41
31000	337.81	325.18	314.43	305.20	297.23	290.30	284.24	278.92	260.16	249.44	243.04	239.13
32000	348.70	335.67	324.57	315.05	306.82	299.67	293.41	287.92	268.55	257.48	250.88	246.84
33000	359.60	346.15	334.71	324.90	316.41	309.03	302.58	296.91	276.94	265.53	258.72	254.55
34000	370.50	356.64	344.86	334.74	326.00	318.40	311.75	305.91	285.33	273.58	266.56	262.27
35000	381.39	367.13	355.00	344.59	335.59	327.76	320.92	314.91	293.72	281.62	274.40	269.98
36000	392.29	377.62	365.14	354.43	345.17	337.13	330.09	323.91	302.12	289.67	282.24	277.70
37000	403.19	388.11	375.28	364.28	354.76	346.49	339.26	332.90	310.51	297.72	290.08	285.41
38000	414.08	398.60	385.43	374.12	364.35	355.85	348.43	341.90	318.90	305.76	297.92	293.12
39000	424.98	409.09	395.57	383.97	373.94	365.22	357.59	350.90	327.29	313.81	305.76	300.84
40000	435.88	419.58	405.71	393.81	383.53	374.58	366.76	359.90	335.68	321.85	313.60	308.55
41000	446.77	430.07	415.85	403.66	393.11	383.95	375.93	368.89	344.08	329.90	321.44	316.26
42000	457.67	440.56	426.00	413.50	402.70	393.31	385.10	377.89	352.47	337.95	329.28	323.98
43000	468.57	451.05	436.14	423.35	412.29	402.68	394.27	386.89	360.86	345.59	337.12	331.69
44000	479.46	461.54	446.28	433.19	421.88	412.04	403.44	395.88	369.25	354.04	344.96	339.40
45000	490.36	472.03	456.42	443.04	431.47	421.41	412.61	404.88	377.64	362.09	352.80	347.12
46000	501.26	482.52	466.57	452.88	441.05	430.77	421.78	413.88	386.04	370.13	360.64	354.83
47000	512.15	493.01	476.71	462.73	450.64	440.13	430.95	422.88	394.43	378.18	368.48	362.54
48000	523.05	503.50	486.85	472.57	460.23	449.50	440.12	431.87	402.82	386.22	376.32	370.26
49000	533.95	513.98	497.00	482.42	469.82	458.86	449.28	440.87	411.21	394.27	384.16	377.97
50000	544.85	524.47	507.14	492.26	479.41	468.23	458.45	449.87	419.60	402.32	392.00	385.69
55000	599.33	576.92	557.85	541.49	527.35	515.05	504.30	494.85	461.56	442.55	431.20	424.25
60000	653.81	629.37	608.56	590.71	575.29	561.87	550.14	539.84	503.52	482.78	470.40	462.82
65000	708.30	681.81	659.28	639.94	623.23	608.69	595.99	584.83	545.48	523.01	509.60	501.39
70000	762.78	734.26	709.99	689.17	671.17	655.52	641.83	629.81	587.44	563.24	548.80	539.96
75000	817.27	786.71	760.70	738.39	719.11	702.34	687.68	674.80	629.40	603.47	588.00	578.53
80000	871.75	839.16	811.42	787.62	767.05	749.16	733.52	719.79	671.36	643.70	627.20	617.09
85000	926.23	891.60	862.13	836.84	814.99	795.98	779.37	764.77	713.32	683.93	666.40	655.66
90000	980.72	944.05	912.84	886.07	862.93	842.81	825.21	809.76	755.28	724.17	705.60	694.23
95000	1035.20	996.50	963.56	935.30	910.87	889.63	871.06	854.74	797.24	764.40	744.80	732.80
100000	1089.69	1048.94	1014.27	984.52	958.81	936.45	916.90	899.73	839.20	804.63	784.00	771.37

Table 1

9.25%

MONTHLY
PAYMENT REQUIRED TO AMORTIZE A LOAN

9%

TERM AMOUNT	1 YEAR	2 YEARS	3 YEARS	4 YEARS	5 YEARS	6 YEARS	7 YEARS	8 YEARS	9 YEARS	10 YEARS	11 YEARS	12 YEARS
50	4.38	2.29	1.60	1.26	1.05	.91	.82	.74	.69	.65	.61	.58
100	8.76	4.58	3.20	2.51	2.09	1.82	1.63	1.48	1.37	1.29	1.21	1.16
200	17.52	9.16	6.39	5.01	4.18	3.63	3.25	2.96	2.74	2.57	2.42	2.31
300	26.28	13.74	9.58	7.51	6.27	5.45	4.87	4.44	4.11	3.85	3.63	3.46
400	35.03	18.32	12.77	10.01	8.36	7.26	6.49	5.92	5.48	5.13	4.84	4.61
500	43.79	22.90	15.96	12.51	10.44	9.08	8.11	7.40	6.84	6.41	6.05	5.77
600	52.55	27.48	19.15	15.01	12.53	10.89	9.73	8.87	8.21	7.69	7.26	6.92
700	61.30	32.06	22.35	17.51	14.62	12.71	11.36	10.35	9.58	8.97	8.47	8.07
800	70.06	36.64	25.54	20.01	16.71	14.52	12.98	11.83	10.95	10.25	9.68	9.22
900	78.82	41.22	28.73	22.51	18.80	16.34	14.60	13.31	12.31	11.53	10.89	10.37
1000	87.57	45.80	31.92	25.01	20.88	18.15	16.22	14.79	13.68	12.81	12.10	11.53
2000	175.14	91.60	63.84	50.01	41.76	36.30	32.44	29.57	27.36	25.61	24.20	23.05
3000	262.71	137.40	95.75	75.02	62.64	54.45	48.65	44.35	41.03	38.41	36.30	34.57
4000	350.27	183.20	127.67	100.02	83.52	72.60	64.87	59.13	54.71	51.22	48.40	46.09
5000	437.84	229.00	159.59	125.02	104.40	90.75	81.09	73.91	68.38	64.02	60.50	57.61
6000	525.41	274.80	191.50	150.03	125.28	108.90	97.30	88.69	82.06	76.82	72.60	69.13
7000	612.98	320.60	223.42	175.03	146.16	127.05	113.52	103.47	95.74	89.63	84.70	80.66
8000	700.54	366.40	255.33	200.04	167.04	145.20	129.73	118.25	109.41	102.43	96.80	92.18
9000	788.11	412.20	287.25	225.04	187.92	163.35	145.95	133.03	123.09	115.23	108.90	103.70
10000	875.68	458.00	319.17	250.04	208.80	181.50	162.17	147.81	136.76	128.04	121.00	115.22
11000	963.25	503.80	351.08	275.05	229.68	199.65	178.38	162.59	150.44	140.84	133.10	126.74
12000	1050.81	549.60	383.00	300.05	250.56	217.80	194.60	177.37	164.11	153.64	145.20	138.26
13000	1138.38	595.40	414.92	325.06	271.44	235.95	210.82	192.15	177.79	166.45	157.30	149.79
14000	1225.95	641.20	446.83	350.06	292.32	254.10	227.03	206.93	191.47	179.25	169.40	161.31
15000	1313.52	687.00	478.75	375.06	313.20	272.25	243.25	221.71	205.14	192.05	181.49	172.83
16000	1401.08	732.80	510.66	400.07	334.08	290.40	259.46	236.49	218.82	204.86	193.59	184.35
17000	1488.65	778.60	542.58	425.07	354.96	308.55	275.68	251.27	232.49	217.66	205.69	195.87
18000	1576.22	824.40	574.50	450.08	375.84	326.70	291.90	266.05	246.17	230.46	217.79	207.39
19000	1663.79	870.20	606.41	475.08	396.72	344.85	308.11	280.83	259.84	243.27	229.89	218.91
20000	1751.35	916.00	638.33	500.08	417.60	363.00	324.33	295.61	273.52	256.07	241.99	230.44
21000	1838.92	961.80	670.25	525.09	438.48	381.15	340.55	310.39	287.20	268.87	254.09	241.96
22000	1926.49	1007.59	702.16	550.09	459.36	399.30	356.76	325.17	300.87	281.68	266.19	253.48
23000	2014.06	1053.39	734.08	575.10	480.24	417.45	372.98	339.95	314.55	294.48	278.29	265.00
24000	2101.62	1099.19	765.99	600.10	501.12	435.60	389.19	354.73	328.22	307.28	290.39	276.52
25000	2189.19	1144.99	797.91	625.10	522.00	453.75	405.41	369.51	341.90	320.09	302.49	288.04
26000	2276.76	1190.79	829.83	650.11	542.88	471.90	421.63	384.29	355.58	332.89	314.59	299.57
27000	2364.33	1236.59	861.74	675.11	563.76	490.05	437.84	399.07	369.25	345.69	326.69	311.09
28000	2451.89	1282.39	893.66	700.11	584.64	508.20	454.06	413.85	382.93	358.50	338.79	322.61
29000	2539.46	1328.19	925.58	725.12	605.52	526.35	470.28	428.63	396.60	371.30	350.88	334.13
30000	2627.03	1373.99	957.49	750.12	626.40	544.50	486.49	443.41	410.28	384.10	362.98	345.65
31000	2714.60	1419.79	989.41	775.13	647.28	562.65	502.71	458.19	423.95	396.91	375.08	357.17
32000	2802.16	1465.59	1021.32	800.13	668.16	580.80	518.92	472.97	437.63	409.71	387.18	368.70
33000	2889.73	1511.39	1053.24	825.13	689.04	598.95	535.14	487.75	451.31	422.51	399.28	380.22
34000	2977.30	1557.19	1085.16	850.14	709.92	617.10	551.36	502.53	464.98	435.32	411.38	391.74
35000	3064.87	1602.99	1117.07	875.14	730.80	635.25	567.57	517.31	478.66	448.12	423.48	403.26
36000	3152.43	1648.79	1146.99	900.15	751.68	653.40	583.79	532.09	492.33	460.92	435.58	414.78
37000	3240.00	1694.59	1180.90	925.15	772.56	671.55	600.01	546.87	506.01	473.73	447.68	426.30
38000	3327.57	1740.39	1212.82	950.15	793.44	689.70	616.22	561.65	519.68	486.53	459.78	437.82
39000	3415.14	1786.19	1244.74	975.16	814.32	707.85	632.44	576.43	533.36	499.33	471.88	449.35
40000	3502.70	1831.99	1276.65	1000.16	835.20	726.00	648.65	591.21	547.04	512.14	483.98	460.87
41000	3590.27	1877.79	1308.57	1025.17	856.08	744.15	664.87	605.99	560.71	524.94	496.08	472.39
42000	3677.84	1923.59	1340.49	1050.17	876.96	762.30	681.09	620.77	574.39	537.74	508.18	483.91
43000	3765.41	1969.38	1372.40	1075.17	897.84	780.45	697.30	635.55	588.06	550.55	520.27	495.43
44000	3852.97	2015.18	1404.32	1100.18	918.72	798.60	713.52	650.33	601.74	563.35	532.37	506.95
45000	3940.54	2060.98	1436.23	1125.18	939.60	816.75	729.74	665.11	615.41	576.15	544.47	518.48
46000	4028.11	2106.78	1468.15	1150.19	960.48	834.90	745.95	679.90	629.09	588.96	556.57	530.00
47000	4115.68	2152.58	1500.07	1175.19	981.36	853.05	762.17	694.68	642.77	601.76	568.67	541.52
48000	4203.24	2198.38	1531.98	1200.19	1002.24	871.20	778.38	709.46	656.44	614.56	580.77	553.04
49000	4290.81	2244.18	1563.90	1225.20	1023.12	889.35	794.60	724.24	670.12	627.37	592.87	564.56
50000	4378.38	2289.98	1595.82	1250.20	1044.00	907.50	810.82	739.02	683.79	640.17	604.97	576.08
55000	4816.21	2518.98	1755.40	1375.22	1148.40	998.25	891.90	812.92	752.17	704.18	665.47	633.69
60000	5254.05	2747.98	1914.98	1500.24	1252.80	1089.00	972.98	886.82	820.55	768.20	725.96	691.30
65000	5691.89	2976.97	2074.56	1625.26	1357.20	1179.75	1054.06	960.72	888.93	832.22	786.46	748.91
70000	6129.73	3205.97	2234.14	1750.28	1461.60	1270.50	1135.14	1034.62	957.31	896.23	846.96	806.51
75000	6567.56	3434.97	2393.72	1875.30	1566.00	1361.24	1216.22	1108.52	1025.69	960.25	907.45	864.12
80000	7005.40	3663.97	2553.30	2000.32	1670.40	1451.99	1297.30	1182.42	1094.07	1024.27	967.95	921.73
85000	7443.24	3892.97	2712.88	2125.34	1774.80	1542.74	1378.39	1256.32	1162.45	1088.28	1028.45	979.34
90000	7881.08	4121.96	2872.46	2250.36	1879.20	1633.49	1459.47	1330.22	1230.82	1152.30	1088.94	1036.95
95000	8318.91	4350.96	3032.05	2375.38	1983.60	1724.24	1540.55	1404.13	1299.20	1216.32	1149.44	1094.55
100000	8756.75	4579.96	3191.63	2500.40	2087.99	1814.99	1621.63	1478.03	1367.58	1280.33	1209.93	1152.16

Table 1

MONTHLY 9.25%

PAYMENT REQUIRED TO AMORTIZE A LOAN

TERM AMOUNT	13 YEARS	14 YEARS	15 YEARS	16 YEARS	17 YEARS	18 YEARS	19 YEARS	20 YEARS	25 YEARS	30 YEARS	35 YEARS	40 YEARS
50	.56	.54	.52	.50	.49	.48	.47	.46	.43	.42	.41	.40
100	1.11	1.07	1.03	1.00	.98	.96	.94	.92	.86	.83	.81	.80
200	2.21	2.13	2.06	2.00	1.95	1.91	1.87	1.84	1.72	1.65	1.61	1.59
300	3.32	3.20	3.09	3.00	2.93	2.86	2.80	2.75	2.57	2.47	2.41	2.38
400	4.42	4.26	4.12	4.00	3.90	3.81	3.74	3.67	3.43	3.30	3.22	3.17
500	5.53	5.32	5.15	5.00	4.88	4.77	4.67	4.58	4.29	4.12	4.02	3.96
600	6.63	6.39	6.18	6.00	5.85	5.72	5.60	5.50	5.14	4.94	4.82	4.75
700	7.73	7.45	7.21	7.00	6.82	6.67	6.53	6.42	6.00	5.76	5.62	5.54
800	8.84	8.51	8.24	8.00	7.80	7.62	7.47	7.33	6.86	6.59	6.43	6.33
900	9.94	9.58	9.27	9.00	8.77	8.57	8.40	8.25	7.71	7.41	7.23	7.12
1000	11.05	10.64	10.30	10.00	9.75	9.53	9.33	9.16	8.57	8.23	8.03	7.91
2000	22.09	21.28	20.59	20.00	19.49	19.05	18.66	18.32	17.13	16.46	16.06	15.82
3000	33.13	31.91	30.88	30.00	29.23	28.57	27.99	27.48	25.70	24.69	24.09	23.72
4000	44.17	42.55	41.17	39.99	38.97	38.09	37.32	36.64	34.26	32.91	32.11	31.63
5000	55.21	53.19	51.46	49.99	48.72	47.61	46.65	45.80	42.82	41.14	40.14	39.54
6000	66.25	63.82	61.76	59.99	58.46	57.13	55.97	54.96	51.39	49.37	48.17	47.44
7000	77.29	74.46	72.05	69.98	68.20	66.65	65.30	64.12	59.95	57.59	56.20	55.35
8000	88.33	85.09	82.34	79.98	77.94	76.17	74.63	73.27	68.52	65.82	64.22	63.26
9000	99.37	95.73	92.63	89.98	87.69	85.70	83.96	82.43	77.08	74.05	72.25	71.16
10000	110.41	106.37	102.92	99.97	97.43	95.22	93.29	91.59	85.64	82.27	80.28	79.07
11000	121.45	117.00	113.22	109.97	107.17	104.74	102.61	100.75	94.21	90.50	88.31	86.98
12000	132.49	127.64	123.51	119.97	116.91	114.26	111.94	109.91	102.77	98.73	96.33	94.88
13000	143.54	138.27	133.80	129.97	126.66	123.78	121.27	119.07	111.33	106.95	104.36	102.79
14000	154.58	148.91	144.09	139.96	136.40	133.30	130.60	128.23	119.90	115.18	112.39	110.70
15000	165.62	159.55	154.38	149.96	146.14	142.82	139.93	137.39	128.46	123.41	120.42	118.60
16000	176.66	170.18	164.68	159.96	155.88	152.34	149.25	146.54	137.03	131.63	128.44	126.51
17000	187.70	180.82	174.97	169.95	165.62	161.87	158.58	155.70	145.59	139.86	136.47	134.42
18000	198.74	191.45	185.26	179.95	175.37	171.39	167.91	164.86	154.15	148.09	144.50	142.32
19000	209.78	202.09	195.55	189.95	185.11	180.91	177.24	174.02	162.72	156.31	152.53	150.23
20000	220.82	212.73	205.84	199.94	194.85	190.43	186.57	183.18	171.28	164.54	160.55	158.14
21000	231.86	223.36	216.14	209.94	204.59	199.95	195.89	192.34	179.85	172.77	168.58	166.04
22000	242.90	234.00	226.43	219.94	214.34	209.47	205.22	201.50	188.41	180.99	176.61	173.95
23000	253.94	244.63	236.72	229.94	224.08	218.99	214.55	210.65	196.97	189.22	184.64	181.86
24000	264.98	255.27	247.01	239.93	233.82	228.51	223.88	219.81	205.54	197.45	192.66	189.76
25000	276.02	265.91	257.30	249.93	243.56	238.03	233.21	228.97	214.10	205.67	200.69	197.67
26000	287.07	276.54	267.59	259.93	253.31	247.56	242.54	238.13	222.66	213.90	208.72	205.58
27000	298.11	287.18	277.89	269.92	263.05	257.08	251.86	247.29	231.23	222.13	216.75	213.49
28000	309.15	297.81	288.18	279.92	272.79	266.60	261.19	256.45	239.79	230.35	224.77	221.39
29000	320.19	308.45	298.47	289.92	282.53	276.12	270.52	265.61	248.36	238.58	232.80	229.30
30000	331.23	319.09	308.76	299.91	292.28	285.64	279.85	274.77	256.92	246.81	240.83	237.20
31000	342.27	329.72	319.05	309.91	302.02	295.16	289.18	283.92	265.48	255.03	248.86	245.11
32000	353.31	340.36	329.35	319.91	311.76	304.68	298.50	293.08	274.05	263.26	256.88	253.02
33000	364.35	350.99	339.64	329.91	321.50	314.20	307.83	302.24	282.61	271.49	264.91	260.92
34000	375.39	361.63	349.93	339.90	331.24	323.73	317.16	311.40	291.17	279.71	272.94	268.83
35000	386.43	372.27	360.22	349.90	340.99	333.25	326.49	320.56	299.74	287.94	280.97	276.74
36000	397.47	382.90	370.51	359.90	350.73	342.77	335.82	329.72	308.30	296.17	288.99	284.64
37000	408.51	393.54	380.81	369.89	360.47	352.29	345.14	338.88	316.87	304.39	297.02	292.55
38000	419.55	404.17	391.10	379.89	370.21	361.81	354.47	348.03	325.43	312.62	305.05	300.46
39000	430.60	414.81	401.39	389.89	379.96	371.33	363.80	357.19	333.99	320.85	313.08	308.36
40000	441.64	425.45	411.68	399.88	389.70	380.85	373.13	366.35	342.56	329.08	321.10	316.27
41000	452.68	436.08	421.97	409.88	399.44	390.37	382.46	375.51	351.12	337.30	329.13	324.18
42000	463.72	446.72	432.27	419.88	409.18	399.90	391.78	384.67	359.69	345.53	337.16	332.08
43000	474.76	457.35	442.56	429.87	418.93	409.42	401.11	393.83	368.25	353.76	345.19	339.99
44000	485.80	467.99	452.85	439.87	428.67	418.94	410.44	402.99	376.81	361.98	353.21	347.90
45000	496.84	478.63	463.14	449.87	438.41	428.46	419.77	412.15	385.38	370.21	361.24	355.80
46000	507.88	489.26	473.43	459.87	448.15	437.98	429.10	421.30	393.94	378.44	369.27	363.71
47000	518.92	499.90	483.73	469.86	457.90	447.50	438.42	430.46	402.50	386.66	377.29	371.62
48000	529.96	510.53	494.02	479.86	467.64	457.02	447.75	439.62	411.07	394.89	385.32	379.52
49000	541.00	521.17	504.31	489.86	477.38	466.54	457.08	448.78	419.63	403.12	393.35	387.43
50000	552.04	531.81	514.60	499.85	487.12	476.06	466.41	457.94	428.20	411.34	401.38	395.34
55000	607.25	584.99	566.06	549.84	535.83	523.67	513.05	503.73	471.02	452.48	441.51	434.87
60000	662.45	638.17	617.52	599.82	584.55	571.28	559.69	549.53	513.83	493.61	481.65	474.40
65000	717.66	691.35	668.98	649.81	633.26	618.88	606.33	595.32	556.65	534.74	521.79	513.93
70000	772.86	744.53	720.44	699.79	681.97	666.49	652.97	641.11	599.47	575.88	561.93	553.47
75000	828.06	797.71	771.90	749.78	730.68	714.09	699.61	686.91	642.29	617.01	602.06	593.00
80000	883.27	850.89	823.36	799.76	779.39	761.70	746.25	732.70	685.11	658.15	642.20	632.53
85000	938.47	904.07	874.82	849.75	828.10	809.31	792.89	778.49	727.93	699.28	682.34	672.07
90000	993.68	957.25	926.28	899.73	876.82	856.91	839.53	824.29	770.75	740.41	722.47	711.60
95000	1048.88	1010.43	977.74	949.72	925.53	904.52	886.17	870.08	813.57	781.55	762.61	751.13
100000	1104.08	1063.61	1029.20	999.70	974.24	952.12	932.81	915.87	856.39	822.68	802.75	790.67

9%

37

Table 1

9.50%

MONTHLY
PAYMENT REQUIRED TO AMORTIZE A LOAN

9%

TERM / AMOUNT	1 YEAR	2 YEARS	3 YEARS	4 YEARS	5 YEARS	6 YEARS	7 YEARS	8 YEARS	9 YEARS	10 YEARS	11 YEARS	12 YEARS
50	4.39	2.30	1.61	1.26	1.06	.92	.82	.75	.70	.65	.62	.59
100	8.77	4.60	3.21	2.52	2.11	1.83	1.64	1.50	1.39	1.30	1.23	1.17
200	17.54	9.19	6.41	5.03	4.21	3.66	3.27	2.99	2.77	2.59	2.45	2.34
300	26.31	13.78	9.61	7.54	6.31	5.49	4.91	4.48	4.15	3.89	3.68	3.50
400	35.08	18.37	12.82	10.05	8.41	7.31	6.54	5.97	5.53	5.18	4.90	4.67
500	43.85	22.96	16.02	12.57	10.51	9.14	8.18	7.46	6.91	6.47	6.12	5.84
600	52.62	27.55	19.22	15.08	12.61	10.97	9.81	8.95	8.29	7.77	7.35	7.00
700	61.38	32.15	22.43	17.59	14.71	12.80	11.45	10.44	9.67	9.06	8.57	8.17
800	70.15	36.74	25.63	20.10	16.81	14.62	13.08	11.93	11.05	10.36	9.80	9.34
900	78.92	41.33	28.83	22.62	18.91	16.45	14.71	13.42	12.43	11.65	11.02	10.50
1000	87.69	45.92	32.04	25.13	21.01	18.28	16.35	14.92	13.81	12.94	12.24	11.67
2000	175.37	91.83	64.07	50.25	42.01	36.55	32.69	29.83	27.62	25.88	24.48	23.33
3000	263.06	137.75	96.10	75.37	63.01	54.83	49.04	44.74	41.43	38.82	36.72	35.00
4000	350.74	183.66	128.14	100.50	84.01	73.10	65.38	59.65	55.24	51.76	48.96	46.66
5000	438.42	229.58	160.17	125.62	105.01	91.38	81.72	74.56	69.05	64.70	61.20	58.32
6000	526.11	275.49	192.20	150.74	126.02	109.65	98.07	89.47	82.86	77.64	73.44	69.99
7000	613.79	321.41	224.24	175.87	147.02	127.93	114.41	104.38	96.67	90.58	85.68	81.65
8000	701.47	367.32	256.27	200.99	168.02	146.20	130.76	119.29	110.48	103.52	97.91	93.31
9000	789.16	413.24	288.30	226.11	189.02	164.48	147.10	134.20	124.29	116.46	110.15	104.98
10000	876.84	459.15	320.33	251.24	210.02	182.75	163.44	149.11	138.10	129.40	122.39	116.64
11000	964.52	505.06	352.37	276.36	231.03	201.03	179.79	164.02	151.91	142.34	134.63	128.31
12000	1052.21	550.98	384.40	301.48	252.03	219.30	196.13	178.94	165.72	155.28	146.87	139.97
13000	1139.89	596.89	416.43	326.61	273.03	237.58	212.48	193.85	179.53	168.22	159.11	151.63
14000	1227.57	642.81	448.47	351.73	294.03	255.85	228.82	208.76	193.34	181.16	171.35	163.30
15000	1315.26	688.72	480.50	376.85	315.03	274.13	245.16	223.67	207.15	194.10	183.58	174.96
16000	1402.94	734.64	512.53	401.98	336.03	292.40	261.51	238.58	220.95	207.04	195.82	186.62
17000	1490.62	780.55	544.57	427.10	357.04	310.67	277.85	253.49	234.76	219.98	208.06	198.29
18000	1578.31	826.47	576.60	452.22	378.04	328.95	294.20	268.40	248.57	232.92	220.30	209.95
19000	1665.99	872.38	608.63	477.34	399.04	347.22	310.54	283.31	262.38	245.86	232.54	221.62
20000	1753.68	918.29	640.66	502.47	420.04	365.50	326.88	298.22	276.19	258.80	244.78	233.28
21000	1841.36	964.21	672.70	527.59	441.04	383.77	343.23	313.13	290.00	271.74	257.02	244.94
22000	1929.04	1010.12	704.73	552.71	462.05	402.05	359.57	328.04	303.81	284.68	269.26	256.61
23000	2016.73	1056.04	736.76	577.84	483.05	420.32	375.92	342.96	317.62	297.62	281.49	268.27
24000	2104.41	1101.95	768.80	602.96	504.05	438.60	392.26	357.87	331.43	310.56	293.73	279.93
25000	2192.09	1147.87	800.83	628.08	525.05	456.87	408.60	372.78	345.24	323.50	305.97	291.60
26000	2279.78	1193.78	832.86	653.21	546.05	475.15	424.95	387.69	359.05	336.44	318.21	303.26
27000	2367.46	1239.70	864.89	678.33	567.06	493.42	441.29	402.60	372.86	349.38	330.45	314.93
28000	2455.14	1285.61	896.93	703.45	588.06	511.70	457.64	417.51	386.67	362.32	342.69	326.59
29000	2542.83	1331.53	928.96	728.58	609.06	529.97	473.98	432.42	400.48	375.26	354.93	338.25
30000	2630.51	1377.44	960.99	753.70	630.06	548.25	490.32	447.33	414.29	388.20	367.16	349.92
31000	2718.19	1423.35	993.03	778.82	651.06	566.52	506.67	462.24	428.10	401.14	379.40	361.58
32000	2805.88	1469.27	1025.06	803.95	672.06	584.80	523.01	477.15	441.90	414.08	391.64	373.24
33000	2893.56	1515.18	1057.09	829.07	693.07	603.07	539.36	492.06	455.71	427.02	403.88	384.91
34000	2981.24	1561.10	1089.13	854.19	714.07	621.34	555.70	506.98	469.52	439.96	416.12	396.57
35000	3068.93	1607.01	1121.16	879.31	735.07	639.62	572.04	521.89	483.33	452.90	428.36	408.24
36000	3156.61	1652.93	1153.19	904.44	756.07	657.89	588.39	536.80	497.14	465.84	440.60	419.90
37000	3244.29	1698.84	1185.22	929.56	777.07	676.17	604.73	551.71	510.95	478.78	452.83	431.56
38000	3331.98	1744.76	1217.26	954.68	798.08	694.44	621.08	566.62	524.76	491.72	465.07	443.23
39000	3419.66	1790.67	1249.29	979.81	819.08	712.72	637.42	581.53	538.57	504.66	477.31	454.89
40000	3507.35	1836.58	1281.32	1004.93	840.08	730.99	653.76	596.44	552.38	517.60	489.55	466.55
41000	3595.03	1882.50	1313.36	1030.05	861.08	749.27	670.11	611.35	566.19	530.53	501.79	478.22
42000	3682.71	1928.41	1345.39	1055.18	882.08	767.54	686.45	626.26	580.00	543.47	514.03	489.88
43000	3770.40	1974.33	1377.42	1080.30	903.09	785.82	702.80	641.17	593.81	556.41	526.27	501.55
44000	3858.08	2020.24	1409.45	1105.42	924.09	804.09	719.14	656.08	607.62	569.35	538.51	513.21
45000	3945.76	2066.16	1441.49	1130.55	945.09	822.37	735.48	670.99	621.43	582.29	550.74	524.87
46000	4033.45	2112.07	1473.52	1155.67	966.09	840.64	751.83	685.91	635.24	595.23	562.98	536.54
47000	4121.13	2157.99	1505.55	1180.79	987.09	858.92	768.17	700.82	649.04	608.17	575.22	548.20
48000	4208.81	2203.90	1537.59	1205.92	1008.09	877.19	784.52	715.73	662.85	621.11	587.46	559.86
49000	4296.50	2249.82	1569.62	1231.04	1029.10	895.46	800.86	730.64	676.66	634.05	599.70	571.53
50000	4384.18	2295.73	1601.65	1256.16	1050.10	913.74	817.20	745.55	690.47	646.99	611.94	583.19
55000	4822.60	2525.30	1761.82	1381.78	1155.11	1005.11	898.92	820.10	759.52	711.69	673.13	641.51
60000	5261.02	2754.87	1921.98	1507.39	1260.12	1096.49	980.64	894.66	828.57	776.39	734.32	699.83
65000	5699.43	2984.45	2082.15	1633.01	1365.13	1187.86	1062.36	969.21	897.61	841.09	795.52	758.15
70000	6137.85	3214.02	2242.31	1758.62	1470.14	1279.23	1144.08	1043.77	966.66	905.79	856.71	816.47
75000	6576.27	3443.59	2402.48	1884.24	1575.14	1370.61	1225.80	1118.32	1035.71	970.49	917.90	874.78
80000	7014.69	3673.16	2562.64	2009.86	1680.15	1461.98	1307.52	1192.88	1104.75	1035.19	979.10	933.10
85000	7453.10	3902.74	2722.81	2135.47	1785.16	1553.35	1389.24	1267.43	1173.80	1099.88	1040.29	991.42
90000	7891.52	4132.31	2882.97	2261.09	1890.17	1644.73	1470.96	1341.98	1242.85	1164.58	1101.48	1049.74
95000	8329.94	4361.88	3043.14	2386.70	1995.18	1736.10	1552.68	1416.54	1311.89	1229.28	1162.68	1108.06
100000	8768.36	4591.45	3203.30	2512.32	2100.19	1827.47	1634.40	1491.09	1380.94	1293.98	1223.87	1166.38

Table 1

MONTHLY

9.50%

PAYMENT REQUIRED TO AMORTIZE A LOAN

TERM AMOUNT	13 YEARS	14 YEARS	15 YEARS	16 YEARS	17 YEARS	18 YEARS	19 YEARS	20 YEARS	25 YEARS	30 YEARS	35 YEARS	40 YEARS
50	.56	.54	.53	.51	.50	.49	.48	.47	.44	.43	.42	.41
100	1.12	1.08	1.05	1.02	.99	.97	.95	.94	.88	.85	.83	.82
200	2.24	2.16	2.09	2.03	1.98	1.94	1.90	1.87	1.75	1.69	1.65	1.63
300	3.36	3.24	3.14	3.05	2.97	2.91	2.85	2.80	2.63	2.53	2.47	2.44
400	4.48	4.32	4.18	4.06	3.96	3.88	3.80	3.73	3.50	3.37	3.29	3.25
500	5.60	5.40	5.23	5.08	4.95	4.84	4.75	4.67	4.37	4.21	4.11	4.06
600	6.72	6.48	6.27	6.09	5.94	5.81	5.70	5.60	5.25	5.05	4.93	4.87
700	7.84	7.55	7.31	7.11	6.93	6.78	6.65	6.53	6.12	5.89	5.76	5.68
800	8.95	8.63	8.36	8.12	7.92	7.75	7.60	7.46	6.99	6.73	6.58	6.49
900	10.07	9.71	9.40	9.14	8.91	8.72	8.54	8.39	7.87	7.57	7.40	7.30
1000	11.19	10.79	10.45	10.15	9.90	9.68	9.49	9.33	8.74	8.41	8.22	8.11
2000	22.38	21.57	20.89	20.30	19.80	19.36	18.98	18.65	17.48	16.82	16.44	16.21
3000	33.56	32.36	31.33	30.45	29.70	29.04	28.47	27.97	26.22	25.23	24.65	24.31
4000	44.75	43.14	41.77	40.60	39.60	38.72	37.96	37.29	34.95	33.64	32.87	32.41
5000	55.93	53.92	52.22	50.75	49.49	48.40	47.45	46.61	43.69	42.05	41.09	40.51
6000	67.12	64.71	62.66	60.90	59.39	58.08	56.94	55.93	52.43	50.46	49.30	48.61
7000	78.31	75.49	73.10	71.05	69.29	67.76	66.42	65.25	61.16	58.86	57.52	56.71
8000	89.49	86.27	83.54	81.20	79.19	77.44	75.91	74.58	69.90	67.27	65.73	64.81
9000	100.68	97.06	93.99	91.35	89.09	87.12	85.40	83.90	78.64	75.68	73.95	72.91
10000	111.86	107.84	104.43	101.50	98.98	96.80	94.89	93.22	87.37	84.09	82.17	81.01
11000	123.05	118.63	114.87	111.65	108.88	106.48	104.38	102.54	96.11	92.50	90.38	89.11
12000	134.23	129.41	125.31	121.80	118.78	116.15	113.87	111.86	104.85	100.91	98.60	97.21
13000	145.42	140.19	135.75	131.95	128.68	125.83	123.35	121.18	113.59	109.32	106.81	105.31
14000	156.61	150.98	146.20	142.10	138.57	135.51	132.84	130.50	122.32	117.72	115.03	113.41
15000	167.79	161.76	156.64	152.25	148.47	145.19	142.33	139.82	131.06	126.13	123.25	121.51
16000	178.98	172.54	167.08	162.40	158.37	154.87	151.82	149.15	139.80	134.54	131.46	129.61
17000	190.16	183.33	177.52	172.55	168.27	164.55	161.31	158.47	148.53	142.95	139.68	137.72
18000	201.35	194.11	187.97	182.70	178.17	174.23	170.80	167.79	157.27	151.36	147.90	145.82
19000	212.53	204.89	198.41	192.85	188.06	183.91	180.28	177.11	166.01	159.77	156.11	153.92
20000	223.72	215.68	208.85	203.00	197.96	193.59	189.77	186.43	174.74	168.18	164.33	162.02
21000	234.91	226.46	219.29	213.15	207.86	203.27	199.26	195.75	183.48	176.58	172.54	170.12
22000	246.09	237.25	229.73	223.30	217.76	212.95	208.75	205.07	192.22	184.99	180.76	178.22
23000	257.28	248.03	240.18	233.45	227.65	222.62	218.24	214.40	200.96	193.40	188.98	186.32
24000	268.46	258.81	250.62	243.60	237.55	232.30	227.73	223.72	209.69	201.81	197.19	194.42
25000	279.65	269.60	261.06	253.75	247.45	241.98	237.21	233.04	218.43	210.22	205.41	202.52
26000	290.83	280.38	271.50	263.90	257.35	251.66	246.70	242.36	227.17	218.63	213.62	210.62
27000	302.02	291.16	281.95	274.05	267.25	261.34	256.19	251.68	235.90	227.04	221.84	218.72
28000	313.21	301.95	292.39	284.20	277.14	271.02	265.68	261.00	244.64	235.44	230.06	226.82
29000	324.39	312.73	302.83	294.35	287.04	280.70	275.17	270.32	253.38	243.85	238.27	234.92
30000	335.58	323.52	313.27	304.50	296.94	290.38	284.66	279.64	262.11	252.26	246.49	243.02
31000	346.76	334.30	323.71	314.65	306.84	300.06	294.15	288.97	270.85	260.67	254.70	251.12
32000	357.95	345.08	334.16	324.80	316.73	309.74	303.63	298.29	279.59	269.08	262.92	259.22
33000	369.13	355.87	344.60	334.95	326.63	319.42	313.12	307.61	288.32	277.49	271.14	267.33
34000	380.32	366.65	355.04	345.10	336.53	329.09	322.61	316.93	297.06	285.90	279.35	275.43
35000	391.51	377.43	365.48	355.25	346.43	338.77	332.10	326.25	305.80	294.30	287.57	283.53
36000	402.69	388.22	375.93	365.40	356.33	348.45	341.59	335.57	314.54	302.71	295.79	291.63
37000	413.88	399.00	386.37	375.55	366.22	358.13	351.08	344.89	323.27	311.12	304.00	299.73
38000	425.06	409.78	396.81	385.70	376.12	367.81	360.56	354.21	332.01	319.53	312.22	307.83
39000	436.25	420.57	407.25	395.85	386.02	377.49	370.05	363.54	340.75	327.94	320.43	315.93
40000	447.43	431.35	417.69	406.00	395.92	387.17	379.54	372.86	349.48	336.35	328.65	324.03
41000	458.62	442.14	428.14	416.15	405.82	396.85	389.03	382.18	358.22	344.76	336.87	332.13
42000	469.81	452.92	438.58	426.30	415.71	406.53	398.52	391.50	366.96	353.16	345.08	340.23
43000	480.99	463.70	449.02	436.45	425.61	416.21	408.01	400.82	375.69	361.57	353.30	348.33
44000	492.18	474.49	459.46	446.60	435.51	425.89	417.49	410.14	384.43	369.98	361.51	356.43
45000	503.36	485.27	469.91	456.75	445.41	435.57	426.98	419.46	393.17	378.39	369.73	364.53
46000	514.55	496.05	480.35	466.90	455.30	445.24	436.47	428.79	401.91	386.80	377.95	372.63
47000	525.73	506.84	490.79	477.05	465.20	454.92	445.96	438.11	410.64	395.21	386.16	380.73
48000	536.92	517.62	501.23	487.20	475.10	464.60	455.45	447.43	419.38	403.62	394.38	388.83
49000	548.11	528.41	511.68	497.35	485.00	474.28	464.94	456.75	428.12	412.02	402.59	396.94
50000	559.29	539.19	522.12	507.50	494.90	483.96	474.42	466.07	436.85	420.43	410.81	405.04
55000	615.22	593.11	574.33	558.25	544.38	532.36	521.87	512.68	480.54	462.47	451.89	445.54
60000	671.15	647.03	626.54	609.00	593.87	580.75	569.31	559.28	524.22	504.52	492.97	486.04
65000	727.08	700.94	678.75	659.75	643.36	629.15	616.75	605.89	567.91	546.56	534.05	526.55
70000	783.01	754.86	730.96	710.50	692.85	677.54	664.19	652.50	611.59	588.60	575.13	567.05
75000	838.93	808.78	783.17	761.25	742.34	725.94	711.63	699.10	655.28	630.65	616.21	607.55
80000	894.86	862.70	835.38	812.00	791.83	774.33	759.08	745.71	698.96	672.69	657.29	648.05
85000	950.79	916.62	887.60	862.75	841.32	822.73	806.52	792.32	742.65	714.73	698.37	688.56
90000	1006.72	970.54	939.81	913.50	890.81	871.13	853.96	838.92	786.33	756.77	739.46	729.06
95000	1062.65	1024.45	992.02	964.25	940.30	919.52	901.40	885.53	830.02	798.82	780.54	769.56
100000	1118.58	1078.37	1044.23	1014.99	989.79	967.92	948.84	932.14	873.70	840.86	821.62	810.07

9%

Table 1

9.75%

MONTHLY
PAYMENT REQUIRED TO AMORTIZE A LOAN

9%

TERM / AMOUNT	1 YEAR	2 YEARS	3 YEARS	4 YEARS	5 YEARS	6 YEARS	7 YEARS	8 YEARS	9 YEARS	10 YEARS	11 YEARS	12 YEARS
50	4.39	2.31	1.61	1.27	1.06	.93	.83	.76	.70	.66	.62	.60
100	8.78	4.61	3.22	2.53	2.12	1.85	1.65	1.51	1.40	1.31	1.24	1.19
200	17.56	9.21	6.43	5.05	4.23	3.69	3.30	3.01	2.79	2.62	2.48	2.37
300	26.34	13.81	9.65	7.58	6.34	5.53	4.95	4.52	4.19	3.93	3.72	3.55
400	35.12	18.42	12.86	10.10	8.45	7.37	6.59	6.02	5.58	5.24	4.96	4.73
500	43.90	23.02	16.08	12.63	10.57	9.21	8.24	7.53	6.98	6.54	6.19	5.91
600	52.68	27.62	19.29	15.15	12.68	11.05	9.89	9.03	8.37	7.85	7.43	7.09
700	61.46	32.23	22.51	17.67	14.79	12.89	11.54	10.53	9.77	9.16	8.67	8.27
800	70.24	36.83	25.72	20.20	16.90	14.73	13.18	12.04	11.16	10.47	9.91	9.45
900	79.02	41.43	28.94	22.72	19.02	16.57	14.83	13.54	12.55	11.77	11.15	10.63
1000	87.80	46.03	32.15	25.25	21.13	18.41	16.48	15.05	13.95	13.08	12.38	11.81
2000	175.60	92.06	64.30	50.49	42.25	36.81	32.95	30.09	27.89	26.16	24.76	23.62
3000	263.40	138.09	96.45	75.73	63.38	55.21	49.42	45.13	41.84	39.24	37.14	35.43
4000	351.20	184.12	128.60	100.98	84.50	73.61	65.89	60.17	55.78	52.31	49.52	47.23
5000	439.00	230.15	160.75	126.22	105.63	92.01	82.37	75.22	69.72	65.39	61.90	59.04
6000	526.80	276.18	192.90	151.46	126.75	110.41	98.84	90.26	83.67	78.47	74.28	70.85
7000	614.60	322.21	225.05	176.70	147.87	128.81	115.31	105.30	97.61	91.54	86.66	82.65
8000	702.40	368.24	257.20	201.95	169.00	147.21	131.78	120.34	111.55	104.62	99.04	94.46
9000	790.20	414.27	289.35	227.19	190.12	165.61	148.26	135.38	125.50	117.70	111.41	106.27
10000	878.00	460.30	321.50	252.43	211.25	184.01	164.73	150.43	139.44	130.78	123.79	118.07
11000	965.80	506.33	353.65	277.67	232.37	202.41	181.20	165.47	153.39	143.85	136.17	129.88
12000	1053.60	552.36	385.80	302.92	253.50	220.81	197.67	180.51	167.33	156.93	148.55	141.69
13000	1141.40	598.39	417.95	328.16	274.62	239.21	214.14	195.55	181.27	170.01	160.93	153.49
14000	1229.20	644.42	450.10	353.40	295.74	257.61	230.62	210.60	195.22	183.08	173.31	165.30
15000	1317.00	690.45	482.25	378.65	316.87	276.01	247.09	225.64	209.16	196.16	185.69	177.11
16000	1404.80	736.48	514.40	403.89	337.99	294.41	263.56	240.68	223.10	209.24	198.07	188.91
17000	1492.60	782.51	546.55	429.13	359.12	312.81	280.03	255.72	237.05	222.31	210.45	200.72
18000	1580.40	828.54	578.70	454.37	380.24	331.21	296.51	270.76	250.99	235.39	222.82	212.53
19000	1668.20	874.57	610.85	479.62	401.37	349.61	312.98	285.81	264.93	248.47	235.20	224.33
20000	1756.00	920.60	643.00	504.86	422.49	368.01	329.45	300.85	278.88	261.55	247.58	236.14
21000	1843.80	966.63	675.15	530.10	443.61	386.41	345.92	315.89	292.82	274.62	259.96	247.95
22000	1931.60	1012.66	707.30	555.34	464.74	404.81	362.40	330.93	306.77	287.70	272.34	259.75
23000	2019.40	1058.69	739.45	580.59	485.86	423.21	378.87	345.98	320.71	300.78	284.72	271.56
24000	2107.20	1104.72	771.60	605.83	506.99	441.61	395.34	361.02	334.65	313.85	297.10	283.37
25000	2195.00	1150.75	803.75	631.07	528.11	460.01	411.81	376.06	348.60	326.93	309.48	295.18
26000	2282.80	1196.78	835.90	656.31	549.24	478.41	428.28	391.10	362.54	340.01	321.85	306.98
27000	2370.60	1242.80	868.05	681.56	570.36	496.81	444.76	406.14	376.48	353.08	334.23	318.79
28000	2458.40	1288.83	900.20	706.80	591.48	515.21	461.23	421.19	390.43	366.16	346.61	330.60
29000	2546.20	1334.86	932.35	732.04	612.61	533.61	477.70	436.23	404.37	379.24	358.99	342.40
30000	2633.99	1380.89	964.50	757.29	633.73	552.01	494.17	451.27	418.31	392.32	371.37	354.21
31000	2721.79	1426.92	996.65	782.53	654.86	570.41	510.65	466.31	432.26	405.39	383.75	366.02
32000	2809.59	1472.95	1028.80	807.77	675.98	588.81	527.12	481.36	446.20	418.47	396.13	377.82
33000	2897.39	1518.98	1060.95	833.01	697.11	607.21	543.59	496.40	460.15	431.55	408.51	389.63
34000	2985.19	1565.01	1093.10	858.26	718.23	625.61	560.06	511.44	474.09	444.62	420.89	401.44
35000	3072.99	1611.04	1125.25	883.50	739.35	644.01	576.54	526.48	488.03	457.70	433.26	413.24
36000	3160.79	1657.07	1157.40	908.74	760.48	662.41	593.01	541.52	501.98	470.78	445.64	425.05
37000	3248.59	1703.10	1189.55	933.98	781.60	680.81	609.48	556.57	515.92	483.85	458.02	436.86
38000	3336.39	1749.13	1221.70	959.23	802.73	699.21	625.95	571.61	529.86	496.93	470.40	448.66
39000	3424.19	1795.16	1253.85	984.47	823.85	717.61	642.42	586.65	543.81	510.01	482.78	460.47
40000	3511.99	1841.19	1286.00	1009.71	844.97	736.01	658.90	601.69	557.75	523.09	495.16	472.28
41000	3599.79	1887.22	1318.15	1034.96	866.10	754.41	675.37	616.74	571.70	536.16	507.54	484.08
42000	3687.59	1933.25	1350.30	1060.20	887.22	772.81	691.84	631.78	585.64	549.24	519.92	495.89
43000	3775.39	1979.28	1382.45	1085.44	908.35	791.21	708.31	646.82	599.58	562.32	532.30	507.70
44000	3863.19	2025.31	1414.60	1110.68	929.47	809.61	724.79	661.86	613.53	575.39	544.67	519.50
45000	3950.99	2071.34	1446.75	1135.93	950.60	828.01	741.26	676.90	627.47	588.47	557.05	531.31
46000	4038.79	2117.37	1478.90	1161.17	971.72	846.41	757.73	691.95	641.41	601.55	569.43	543.12
47000	4126.59	2163.40	1511.05	1186.41	992.84	864.81	774.20	706.99	655.36	614.63	581.81	554.92
48000	4214.39	2209.43	1543.20	1211.65	1013.97	883.21	790.68	722.03	669.30	627.70	594.19	566.73
49000	4302.19	2255.46	1575.35	1236.90	1035.09	901.61	807.15	737.07	683.24	640.78	606.57	578.54
50000	4389.99	2301.49	1607.50	1262.14	1056.22	920.01	823.62	752.12	697.19	653.86	618.95	590.35
55000	4828.99	2531.63	1768.25	1388.35	1161.84	1012.01	905.98	827.33	766.91	719.24	680.84	649.38
60000	5267.98	2761.78	1929.00	1514.57	1267.46	1104.01	988.34	902.54	836.62	784.63	742.74	708.41
65000	5706.98	2991.93	2089.75	1640.78	1373.08	1196.01	1070.70	977.75	906.34	850.01	804.63	767.45
70000	6145.98	3222.08	2250.50	1766.99	1478.70	1288.01	1153.07	1052.96	976.06	915.40	866.52	826.48
75000	6584.98	3452.23	2411.25	1893.21	1584.32	1380.01	1235.43	1128.17	1045.78	980.78	928.42	885.52
80000	7023.98	3682.37	2572.00	2019.42	1689.94	1472.01	1317.79	1203.38	1115.50	1046.17	990.31	944.55
85000	7462.98	3912.52	2732.75	2145.63	1795.57	1564.01	1400.15	1278.59	1185.22	1111.55	1052.21	1003.58
90000	7901.97	4142.67	2893.50	2271.85	1901.19	1656.01	1482.51	1353.80	1254.93	1176.94	1114.10	1062.62
95000	8340.97	4372.82	3054.25	2398.06	2006.81	1748.01	1564.87	1429.01	1324.65	1242.32	1175.99	1121.65
100000	8779.97	4602.97	3215.00	2524.27	2112.43	1840.01	1647.23	1504.23	1394.37	1307.71	1237.89	1180.69

Table 1

MONTHLY

9.75%

PAYMENT REQUIRED TO AMORTIZE A LOAN

9%

TERM AMOUNT	13 YEARS	14 YEARS	15 YEARS	16 YEARS	17 YEARS	18 YEARS	19 YEARS	20 YEARS	25 YEARS	30 YEARS	35 YEARS	40 YEARS
50	.57	.55	.53	.52	.51	.50	.49	.48	.45	.43	.43	.42
100	1.14	1.10	1.06	1.04	1.01	.99	.97	.95	.90	.86	.85	.83
200	2.27	2.19	2.12	2.07	2.02	1.97	1.93	1.90	1.79	1.72	1.69	1.66
300	3.40	3.28	3.18	3.10	3.02	2.96	2.90	2.85	2.68	2.58	2.53	2.49
400	4.54	4.38	4.24	4.13	4.03	3.94	3.86	3.80	3.57	3.44	3.37	3.32
500	5.67	5.47	5.30	5.16	5.03	4.92	4.83	4.75	4.46	4.30	4.21	4.15
600	6.80	6.56	6.36	6.19	6.04	5.91	5.79	5.70	5.35	5.16	5.05	4.98
700	7.94	7.66	7.42	7.22	7.04	6.89	6.76	6.64	6.24	6.02	5.89	5.81
800	9.07	8.75	8.48	8.25	8.05	7.88	7.72	7.59	7.13	6.88	6.73	6.64
900	10.20	9.84	9.54	9.28	9.05	8.86	8.69	8.54	8.03	7.74	7.57	7.47
1000	11.34	10.94	10.60	10.31	10.06	9.84	9.65	9.49	8.92	8.60	8.41	8.30
2000	22.67	21.87	21.19	20.61	20.11	19.68	19.30	18.98	17.83	17.19	16.82	16.60
3000	34.00	32.80	31.79	30.92	30.17	29.52	28.95	28.46	26.74	25.78	25.22	24.89
4000	45.33	43.73	42.38	41.22	40.22	39.36	38.60	37.95	35.65	34.37	33.63	33.19
5000	56.66	54.67	52.97	51.52	50.28	49.20	48.25	47.43	44.56	42.96	42.03	41.48
6000	67.99	65.60	63.57	61.83	60.33	59.03	57.90	56.92	53.47	51.55	50.44	49.78
7000	79.33	76.53	74.16	72.13	70.39	68.87	67.55	66.40	62.38	60.15	58.85	58.07
8000	90.66	87.46	84.75	82.44	80.44	78.71	77.20	75.89	71.30	68.74	67.25	66.37
9000	101.99	98.40	95.35	92.74	90.49	88.55	86.85	85.37	80.21	77.33	75.66	74.67
10000	113.32	109.33	105.94	103.04	100.55	98.39	96.50	94.86	89.12	85.92	84.06	82.96
11000	124.65	120.26	116.53	113.35	110.60	108.23	106.15	104.34	98.03	94.51	92.47	91.26
12000	135.98	131.19	127.13	123.65	120.66	118.06	115.80	113.83	106.94	103.10	100.88	99.55
13000	147.32	142.13	137.72	133.96	130.71	127.90	125.45	123.31	115.85	111.70	109.28	107.85
14000	158.65	153.06	148.32	144.26	140.77	137.74	135.10	132.80	124.76	120.29	117.69	116.14
15000	169.98	163.99	158.91	154.56	150.82	147.58	144.75	142.28	133.68	128.88	126.09	124.44
16000	181.31	174.92	169.50	164.87	160.88	157.42	154.40	151.77	142.59	137.47	134.50	132.73
17000	192.64	185.86	180.10	175.17	170.93	167.25	164.05	161.25	151.50	146.06	142.91	141.03
18000	203.97	196.79	190.69	185.48	180.98	177.09	173.70	170.74	160.41	154.65	151.31	149.33
19000	215.31	207.72	201.28	195.78	191.04	186.93	183.35	180.22	169.32	163.24	159.72	157.62
20000	226.64	218.65	211.88	206.08	201.09	196.77	193.00	189.71	178.23	171.84	168.12	165.92
21000	237.97	229.58	222.47	216.39	211.15	206.61	202.65	199.19	187.14	180.43	176.53	174.21
22000	249.30	240.52	233.06	226.69	221.20	216.45	212.30	208.68	196.06	189.02	184.93	182.51
23000	260.63	251.45	243.66	237.00	231.26	226.28	221.95	218.16	204.97	197.61	193.34	190.80
24000	271.96	262.38	254.25	247.30	241.31	236.12	231.60	227.65	213.88	206.20	201.75	199.10
25000	283.30	273.31	264.85	257.60	251.36	245.96	241.25	237.13	222.79	214.79	210.15	207.39
26000	294.63	284.25	275.44	267.91	261.42	255.80	250.90	246.62	231.70	223.39	218.56	215.69
27000	305.96	295.18	286.03	278.21	271.47	265.64	260.55	256.10	240.61	231.98	226.96	223.99
28000	317.29	306.11	296.63	288.51	281.53	275.47	270.20	265.59	249.52	240.57	235.37	232.28
29000	328.62	317.04	307.22	298.82	291.58	285.31	279.85	275.07	258.43	249.16	243.78	240.58
30000	339.95	327.98	317.81	309.12	301.64	295.15	289.50	284.56	267.35	257.75	252.18	248.87
31000	351.29	338.91	328.41	319.43	311.69	304.99	299.15	294.05	276.26	266.34	260.59	257.17
32000	362.62	349.84	339.00	329.73	321.75	314.83	308.80	303.53	285.17	274.93	268.99	265.46
33000	373.95	360.77	349.59	340.03	331.80	324.67	318.45	313.02	294.08	283.53	277.40	273.76
34000	385.28	371.70	360.19	350.34	341.85	334.50	328.10	322.50	302.99	292.12	285.81	282.05
35000	396.61	382.64	370.78	360.64	351.91	344.34	337.75	331.99	311.90	300.71	294.21	290.35
36000	407.94	393.57	381.38	370.95	361.96	354.18	347.40	341.47	320.81	309.30	302.62	298.65
37000	419.28	404.50	391.97	381.25	372.02	364.02	357.05	350.96	329.73	317.89	311.02	306.94
38000	430.61	415.43	402.56	391.55	382.07	373.86	366.70	360.44	338.64	326.48	319.43	315.24
39000	441.94	426.37	413.16	401.86	392.13	383.69	376.35	369.93	347.55	335.08	327.83	323.53
40000	453.27	437.30	423.75	412.16	402.18	393.53	386.00	379.41	356.46	343.67	336.24	331.83
41000	464.60	448.23	434.34	422.47	412.24	403.37	395.65	388.90	365.37	352.26	344.65	340.12
42000	475.93	459.16	444.94	432.77	422.29	413.21	405.30	398.38	374.28	360.85	353.05	348.42
43000	487.26	470.10	455.53	443.07	432.34	423.05	414.95	407.87	383.19	369.44	361.46	356.72
44000	498.60	481.03	466.12	453.38	442.40	432.89	424.60	417.35	392.11	378.03	369.86	365.01
45000	509.93	491.96	476.72	463.68	452.45	442.72	434.25	426.84	401.02	386.62	378.27	373.31
46000	521.26	502.89	487.31	473.99	462.51	452.56	443.90	436.32	409.93	395.22	386.68	381.60
47000	532.59	513.83	497.91	484.29	472.56	462.40	453.55	445.81	418.84	403.81	395.08	389.90
48000	543.92	524.76	508.50	494.59	482.62	472.24	463.20	455.29	427.75	412.40	403.49	398.19
49000	555.25	535.69	519.09	504.90	492.67	482.08	472.85	464.78	436.66	420.99	411.89	406.49
50000	566.59	546.62	529.69	515.20	502.72	491.92	482.50	474.26	445.57	429.58	420.30	414.78
55000	623.24	601.28	582.65	566.72	553.00	541.11	530.75	521.69	490.13	472.54	462.33	456.26
60000	679.90	655.95	635.62	618.24	603.27	590.30	579.00	569.12	534.69	515.50	504.36	497.74
65000	736.56	710.61	688.59	669.76	653.54	639.49	627.25	616.54	579.24	558.46	546.39	539.22
70000	793.22	765.27	741.56	721.28	703.81	688.68	675.50	663.97	623.80	601.41	588.42	580.70
75000	849.88	819.93	794.53	772.80	754.08	737.87	723.75	711.39	668.36	644.37	630.45	622.17
80000	906.54	874.59	847.50	824.32	804.36	787.06	772.00	758.82	712.91	687.33	672.48	663.65
85000	963.19	929.25	900.46	875.84	854.63	836.25	820.25	806.24	757.47	730.29	714.51	705.13
90000	1019.85	983.92	953.43	927.36	904.90	885.44	868.50	853.67	802.03	773.24	756.54	746.61
95000	1076.51	1038.58	1006.40	978.88	955.17	934.63	916.75	901.10	846.59	816.20	798.56	788.09
100000	1133.17	1093.24	1059.37	1030.40	1005.44	983.83	965.00	948.52	891.14	859.16	840.59	829.56

Table 1

10.00%

MONTHLY
PAYMENT REQUIRED TO AMORTIZE A LOAN

10%

TERM / AMOUNT	1 YEAR	2 YEARS	3 YEARS	4 YEARS	5 YEARS	6 YEARS	7 YEARS	8 YEARS	9 YEARS	10 YEARS	11 YEARS	12 YEARS
50	4.40	2.31	1.62	1.27	1.07	.93	.84	.76	.71	.67	.63	.6
100	8.80	4.62	3.23	2.54	2.13	1.86	1.67	1.52	1.41	1.33	1.26	1.20
200	17.59	9.23	6.46	5.08	4.25	3.71	3.33	3.04	2.82	2.65	2.51	2.40
300	26.38	13.85	9.69	7.61	6.38	5.56	4.99	4.56	4.23	3.97	3.76	3.59
400	35.17	18.46	12.91	10.15	8.50	7.42	6.65	6.07	5.64	5.29	5.01	4.7
500	43.96	23.08	16.14	12.69	10.63	9.27	8.31	7.59	7.04	6.61	6.26	5.9
600	52.75	27.69	19.37	15.22	12.75	11.12	9.97	9.11	8.45	7.93	7.52	7.1
700	61.55	32.31	22.59	17.76	14.88	12.97	11.63	10.63	9.86	9.26	8.77	8.3
800	70.34	36.92	25.82	20.30	17.00	14.83	13.29	12.14	11.27	10.58	10.02	9.5
900	79.13	41.54	29.05	22.83	19.13	16.68	14.95	13.66	12.68	11.90	11.27	10.7
1000	87.92	46.15	32.27	25.37	21.25	18.53	16.61	15.18	14.08	13.22	12.52	11.9
2000	175.84	92.29	64.54	50.73	42.50	37.06	33.21	30.35	28.16	26.44	25.04	23.9
3000	263.75	138.44	96.81	76.09	63.75	55.58	49.81	45.53	42.24	39.65	37.56	35.8
4000	351.67	184.58	129.07	101.46	84.99	74.11	66.41	60.70	56.32	52.87	50.08	47.8
5000	439.58	230.73	161.34	126.82	106.24	92.63	83.01	75.88	70.40	66.08	62.60	59.7
6000	527.50	276.87	193.61	152.18	127.49	111.16	99.61	91.05	84.48	79.30	75.12	71.7
7000	615.42	323.02	225.88	177.54	148.73	129.69	116.21	106.22	98.56	92.51	87.64	83.6
8000	703.33	369.16	258.14	202.91	169.98	148.21	132.81	121.40	112.63	105.73	100.16	95.6
9000	791.25	415.31	290.41	228.27	191.23	166.74	149.42	136.57	126.71	118.94	112.68	107.5
10000	879.16	461.45	322.68	253.63	212.48	185.26	166.02	151.75	140.79	132.16	125.20	119.5
11000	967.08	507.60	354.94	278.99	233.72	203.79	182.62	166.92	154.87	145.37	137.72	131.4
12000	1055.00	553.74	387.21	304.36	254.97	222.32	199.22	182.09	168.95	158.59	150.24	143.4
13000	1142.91	599.89	419.48	329.72	276.22	240.84	215.82	197.27	183.03	171.80	162.76	155.3
14000	1230.83	646.03	451.75	355.08	297.46	259.37	232.42	212.44	197.11	185.02	175.28	167.3
15000	1318.74	692.18	484.01	380.44	318.71	277.89	249.02	227.62	211.19	198.23	187.80	179.2
16000	1406.66	738.32	516.28	405.81	339.96	296.42	265.62	242.79	225.26	211.45	200.32	191.2
17000	1494.58	784.47	548.55	431.17	361.20	314.94	282.23	257.97	239.34	224.66	212.84	203.1
18000	1582.49	830.61	580.81	456.53	382.45	333.47	298.83	273.14	253.42	237.88	225.36	215.1
19000	1670.41	876.76	613.08	481.89	403.70	352.00	315.43	288.31	267.50	251.09	237.88	227.0
20000	1758.32	922.90	645.35	507.26	424.95	370.52	332.03	303.49	281.58	264.31	250.40	239.0
21000	1846.24	969.05	677.62	532.62	446.19	389.05	348.63	318.66	295.66	277.52	262.92	250.9
22000	1934.15	1015.19	709.88	557.98	467.44	407.57	365.23	333.84	309.74	290.74	275.44	262.9
23000	2022.07	1061.34	742.15	583.34	488.69	426.10	381.83	349.01	323.81	303.95	287.96	274.8
24000	2109.99	1107.48	774.42	608.71	509.93	444.63	398.43	364.18	337.89	317.17	300.48	286.8
25000	2197.90	1153.63	806.68	634.07	531.18	463.15	415.03	379.36	351.97	330.38	313.00	298.7
26000	2285.82	1199.77	838.95	659.43	552.43	481.68	431.64	394.53	366.05	343.60	325.52	310.73
27000	2373.73	1245.92	871.22	684.79	573.68	500.20	448.24	409.71	380.13	356.81	338.04	322.68
28000	2461.65	1292.06	903.49	710.16	594.92	518.73	464.84	424.88	394.21	370.03	350.56	334.63
29000	2549.57	1338.21	935.75	735.52	616.17	537.25	481.44	440.06	408.29	383.24	363.08	346.58
30000	2637.48	1384.35	968.02	760.88	637.42	555.78	498.04	455.23	422.37	396.46	375.60	358.53
31000	2725.40	1430.50	1000.29	786.25	658.66	574.31	514.64	470.40	436.44	409.67	388.12	370.48
32000	2813.31	1476.64	1032.56	811.61	679.91	592.83	531.24	485.58	450.52	422.89	400.64	382.43
33000	2901.23	1522.79	1064.82	836.97	701.16	611.36	547.84	500.75	464.60	436.10	413.16	394.38
34000	2989.15	1568.93	1097.09	862.33	722.40	629.88	564.45	515.93	478.68	449.32	425.68	406.33
35000	3077.06	1615.08	1129.36	887.70	743.65	648.41	581.05	531.10	492.76	462.53	438.20	418.28
36000	3164.98	1661.22	1161.62	913.06	764.90	666.94	597.65	546.27	506.84	475.75	450.72	430.23
37000	3252.89	1707.37	1193.89	938.42	786.15	685.46	614.25	561.45	520.92	488.96	463.24	442.18
38000	3340.81	1753.51	1226.16	963.78	807.39	703.99	630.85	576.62	535.00	502.18	475.76	454.13
39000	3428.72	1799.66	1258.43	989.15	828.64	722.51	647.45	591.80	549.07	515.39	488.28	466.09
40000	3516.64	1845.80	1290.69	1014.51	849.89	741.04	664.05	606.97	563.15	528.61	500.80	478.04
41000	3604.56	1891.95	1322.96	1039.87	871.13	759.56	680.65	622.15	577.23	541.82	513.32	489.99
42000	3692.47	1938.09	1355.23	1065.23	892.38	778.09	697.25	637.32	591.31	555.04	525.84	501.94
43000	3780.39	1984.24	1387.49	1090.60	913.63	796.62	713.86	652.49	605.39	568.25	538.36	513.89
44000	3868.30	2030.38	1419.76	1115.96	934.87	815.14	730.46	667.67	619.47	581.47	550.88	525.84
45000	3956.22	2076.53	1452.03	1141.32	956.12	833.67	747.06	682.84	633.55	594.68	563.40	537.79
46000	4044.14	2122.67	1484.30	1166.68	977.37	852.19	763.66	698.02	647.62	607.90	575.92	549.74
47000	4132.05	2168.82	1516.56	1192.05	998.62	870.72	780.26	713.19	661.70	621.11	588.44	561.69
48000	4219.97	2214.96	1548.83	1217.41	1019.86	889.25	796.86	728.36	675.78	634.33	600.96	573.64
49000	4307.88	2261.11	1581.10	1242.77	1041.11	907.77	813.46	743.54	689.86	647.54	613.48	585.59
50000	4395.80	2307.25	1613.36	1268.13	1062.36	926.30	830.06	758.71	703.94	660.76	626.00	597.54
55000	4835.38	2537.98	1774.70	1394.95	1168.59	1018.93	913.07	834.58	774.33	726.83	688.60	657.30
60000	5274.96	2768.70	1936.04	1521.76	1274.83	1111.56	996.08	910.45	844.73	792.91	751.20	717.05
65000	5714.54	2999.43	2097.37	1648.57	1381.06	1204.18	1079.08	986.33	915.12	858.98	813.80	776.81
70000	6154.12	3230.15	2258.71	1775.39	1487.30	1296.81	1162.09	1062.20	985.51	925.06	876.40	836.56
75000	6593.70	3460.87	2420.04	1902.20	1593.53	1389.44	1245.09	1138.07	1055.91	991.14	939.00	896.31
80000	7033.28	3691.60	2581.38	2029.01	1699.77	1482.07	1328.10	1213.94	1126.30	1057.21	1001.60	956.07
85000	7472.86	3922.32	2742.72	2155.82	1806.00	1574.70	1411.11	1289.81	1196.69	1123.29	1064.19	1015.82
90000	7912.43	4153.05	2904.05	2282.64	1912.24	1667.33	1494.11	1365.68	1267.09	1189.36	1126.79	1075.57
95000	8352.01	4383.77	3065.39	2409.45	2018.47	1759.96	1577.12	1441.55	1337.48	1255.44	1189.39	1135.33
100000	8791.59	4614.50	3226.72	2536.26	2124.71	1852.59	1660.12	1517.42	1407.87	1321.51	1251.99	1195.08

Table 1

MONTHLY

10.00%

PAYMENT REQUIRED TO AMORTIZE A LOAN

TERM AMOUNT	13 YEARS	14 YEARS	15 YEARS	16 YEARS	17 YEARS	18 YEARS	19 YEARS	20 YEARS	25 YEARS	30 YEARS	35 YEARS	40 YEARS
50	.58	.56	.54	.53	.52	.50	.50	.49	.46	.44	.43	.43
100	1.15	1.11	1.08	1.05	1.03	1.00	.99	.97	.91	.88	.86	.85
200	2.30	2.22	2.15	2.10	2.05	2.00	1.97	1.94	1.82	1.76	1.72	1.70
300	3.45	3.33	3.23	3.14	3.07	3.00	2.95	2.90	2.73	2.64	2.58	2.55
400	4.60	4.44	4.30	4.19	4.09	4.00	3.93	3.87	3.64	3.52	3.44	3.40
500	5.74	5.55	5.38	5.23	5.11	5.00	4.91	4.83	4.55	4.39	4.30	4.25
600	6.89	6.65	6.45	6.28	6.13	6.00	5.89	5.80	5.46	5.27	5.16	5.10
700	8.04	7.76	7.53	7.33	7.15	7.00	6.87	6.76	6.37	6.15	6.02	5.95
800	9.19	8.87	8.60	8.37	8.17	8.00	7.86	7.73	7.27	7.03	6.88	6.80
900	10.34	9.98	9.68	9.42	9.20	9.00	8.84	8.69	8.18	7.90	7.74	7.65
1000	11.48	11.09	10.75	10.46	10.22	10.00	9.82	9.66	9.09	8.78	8.60	8.50
2000	22.96	22.17	21.50	20.92	20.43	20.00	19.63	19.31	18.18	17.56	17.20	16.99
3000	34.44	33.25	32.24	31.38	30.64	30.00	29.44	28.96	27.27	26.33	25.80	25.48
4000	45.92	44.33	42.99	41.84	40.85	40.00	39.26	38.61	36.35	35.11	34.39	33.97
5000	57.40	55.42	53.74	52.30	51.07	50.00	49.07	48.26	45.44	43.88	42.99	42.46
6000	68.88	66.50	64.48	62.76	61.28	60.00	58.88	57.91	54.53	52.66	51.59	50.95
7000	80.35	77.58	75.23	73.22	71.49	69.99	68.69	67.56	63.61	61.44	60.18	59.45
8000	91.83	88.66	85.97	83.68	81.70	79.99	78.51	77.21	72.70	70.21	68.78	67.94
9000	103.31	99.74	96.72	94.14	91.91	89.99	88.32	86.86	81.79	78.99	77.38	76.43
10000	114.79	110.83	107.47	104.60	102.13	99.99	98.13	96.51	90.88	87.76	85.97	84.92
11000	126.27	121.91	118.21	115.05	112.34	109.99	107.94	106.16	99.96	96.54	94.57	93.41
12000	137.75	132.99	128.96	125.51	122.55	119.99	117.76	115.81	109.05	105.31	103.17	101.90
13000	149.23	144.07	139.70	135.97	132.76	129.98	127.57	125.46	118.14	114.09	111.76	110.39
14000	160.70	155.15	150.45	146.43	142.97	139.98	137.38	135.11	127.22	122.87	120.36	118.89
15000	172.18	166.24	161.20	156.89	153.19	149.98	147.19	144.76	136.31	131.64	128.96	127.38
16000	183.66	177.32	171.94	167.35	163.40	159.98	157.01	154.41	145.40	140.42	137.55	135.87
17000	195.14	188.40	182.69	177.81	173.61	169.98	166.82	164.06	154.48	149.19	146.15	144.36
18000	206.62	199.48	193.43	188.27	183.82	179.98	176.63	173.71	163.57	157.97	154.75	152.85
19000	218.10	210.56	204.18	198.73	194.03	189.98	186.44	183.36	172.66	166.74	163.34	161.34
20000	229.57	221.65	214.93	209.19	204.25	199.97	196.26	193.01	181.75	175.52	171.94	169.83
21000	241.05	232.73	225.67	219.64	214.46	209.97	206.07	202.66	190.83	184.30	180.54	178.33
22000	252.53	243.81	236.42	230.10	224.67	219.97	215.88	212.31	199.92	193.07	189.13	186.82
23000	264.01	254.89	247.16	240.56	234.88	229.97	225.69	221.96	209.01	201.85	197.73	195.31
24000	275.49	265.97	257.91	251.02	245.10	239.97	235.51	231.61	218.09	210.62	206.33	203.80
25000	286.97	277.06	268.66	261.48	255.31	249.97	245.32	241.26	227.18	219.40	214.92	212.29
26000	298.45	288.14	279.40	271.94	265.52	259.96	255.13	250.91	236.27	228.17	223.52	220.78
27000	309.92	299.22	290.15	282.40	275.73	269.96	264.94	260.56	245.35	236.95	232.12	229.27
28000	321.40	310.30	300.89	292.86	285.94	279.96	274.76	270.21	254.44	245.73	240.71	237.77
29000	332.88	321.38	311.64	303.32	296.16	289.96	284.57	279.86	263.53	254.50	249.31	246.26
30000	344.36	332.47	322.39	313.78	306.37	299.96	294.38	289.51	272.62	263.28	257.91	254.75
31000	355.84	343.55	333.13	324.23	316.58	309.96	304.20	299.16	281.70	272.05	266.50	263.24
32000	367.32	354.63	343.88	334.69	326.79	319.95	314.01	308.81	290.79	280.83	275.10	271.73
33000	378.79	365.71	354.62	345.15	337.00	329.95	323.82	318.46	299.88	289.60	283.70	280.22
34000	390.27	376.79	365.37	355.61	347.22	339.95	333.63	328.11	308.96	298.38	292.29	288.71
35000	401.75	387.88	376.12	366.07	357.43	349.95	343.45	337.76	318.05	307.16	300.89	297.21
36000	413.23	398.96	386.86	376.53	367.64	359.95	353.26	347.41	327.14	315.93	309.49	305.70
37000	424.71	410.04	397.61	386.99	377.85	369.95	363.07	357.06	336.22	324.71	318.08	314.19
38000	436.19	421.12	408.35	397.45	388.06	379.95	372.88	366.71	345.31	333.48	326.68	322.68
39000	447.67	432.20	419.10	407.91	398.28	389.94	382.70	376.36	354.40	342.26	335.28	331.17
40000	459.14	443.29	429.85	418.37	408.49	399.94	392.51	386.01	363.49	351.03	343.87	339.66
41000	470.62	454.37	440.59	428.82	418.70	409.94	402.32	395.66	372.57	359.81	352.47	348.15
42000	482.10	465.45	451.34	439.28	428.91	419.94	412.13	405.31	381.66	368.59	361.07	356.65
43000	493.58	476.53	462.09	449.74	439.13	429.94	421.95	414.96	390.75	377.36	369.66	365.14
44000	505.06	487.61	472.83	460.20	449.34	439.94	431.76	424.61	399.83	386.14	378.26	373.63
45000	516.54	498.70	483.58	470.66	459.55	449.93	441.57	434.26	408.92	394.91	386.86	382.12
46000	528.02	509.78	494.32	481.12	469.76	459.93	451.38	443.91	418.01	403.69	395.45	390.61
47000	539.49	520.86	505.07	491.58	479.97	469.93	461.20	453.57	427.09	412.46	404.05	399.10
48000	550.97	531.94	515.82	502.04	490.19	479.93	471.01	463.22	436.18	421.24	412.65	407.60
49000	562.45	543.02	526.56	512.50	500.40	489.93	480.82	472.87	445.27	430.02	421.24	416.09
50000	573.93	554.11	537.31	522.96	510.61	499.93	490.63	482.52	454.36	438.79	429.84	424.58
55000	631.32	609.52	591.04	575.25	561.67	549.92	539.70	530.77	499.79	482.67	472.82	467.04
60000	688.71	664.93	644.77	627.55	612.73	599.91	588.76	579.02	545.23	526.55	515.81	509.49
65000	746.11	720.34	698.50	679.84	663.79	649.90	637.82	627.27	590.66	570.43	558.79	551.95
70000	803.50	775.75	752.23	732.14	714.85	699.90	686.89	675.52	636.10	614.31	601.78	594.41
75000	860.89	831.16	805.96	784.43	765.91	749.89	735.95	723.77	681.53	658.18	644.76	636.86
80000	918.28	886.57	859.69	836.73	816.97	799.88	785.01	772.02	726.97	702.06	687.74	679.32
85000	975.68	941.98	913.42	889.02	868.03	849.87	834.08	820.27	772.40	745.94	730.73	721.78
90000	1033.07	997.39	967.15	941.32	919.09	899.86	883.14	868.52	817.84	789.82	773.71	764.24
95000	1090.46	1052.80	1020.88	993.61	970.15	949.86	932.20	916.78	863.27	833.70	816.69	806.69
00000	1147.85	1108.21	1074.61	1045.91	1021.22	999.85	981.26	965.03	908.71	877.58	859.68	849.15

Table 1

10.25%

MONTHLY
PAYMENT REQUIRED TO AMORTIZE A LOAN

10%

TERM AMOUNT	1 YEAR	2 YEARS	3 YEARS	4 YEARS	5 YEARS	6 YEARS	7 YEARS	8 YEARS	9 YEARS	10 YEARS	11 YEARS	12 YEARS
50	4.41	2.32	1.62	1.28	1.07	.94	.84	.77	.72	.67	.64	.61
100	8.81	4.63	3.24	2.55	2.14	1.87	1.68	1.54	1.43	1.34	1.27	1.21
200	17.61	9.26	6.48	5.10	4.28	3.74	3.35	3.07	2.85	2.68	2.54	2.42
300	26.41	13.88	9.72	7.65	6.42	5.60	5.02	4.60	4.27	4.01	3.80	3.63
400	35.22	18.51	12.96	10.20	8.55	7.47	6.70	6.13	5.69	5.35	5.07	4.84
500	44.02	23.14	16.20	12.75	10.69	9.33	8.37	7.66	7.11	6.68	6.34	6.05
600	52.82	27.76	19.44	15.29	12.83	11.20	10.04	9.19	8.53	8.02	7.60	7.26
700	61.63	32.39	22.67	17.84	14.96	13.06	11.72	10.72	9.96	9.35	8.87	8.47
800	70.43	37.01	25.91	20.39	17.10	14.93	13.39	12.25	11.38	10.69	10.13	9.68
900	79.23	41.64	29.15	22.94	19.24	16.79	15.06	13.78	12.80	12.02	11.40	10.89
1000	88.04	46.27	32.39	25.49	21.38	18.66	16.74	15.31	14.22	13.36	12.67	12.10
2000	176.07	92.53	64.77	50.97	42.75	37.31	33.47	30.62	28.43	26.71	25.33	24.20
3000	264.10	138.79	97.16	76.45	64.12	55.96	50.20	45.93	42.65	40.07	37.99	36.29
4000	352.13	185.05	129.54	101.94	85.49	74.61	66.93	61.23	56.86	53.42	50.65	48.39
5000	440.17	231.31	161.93	127.42	106.86	93.27	83.66	76.54	71.08	66.77	63.31	60.48
6000	528.20	277.57	194.31	152.90	128.23	111.92	100.39	91.85	85.29	80.13	75.98	72.58
7000	616.23	323.83	226.70	178.38	149.60	130.57	117.12	107.15	99.51	93.48	88.64	84.67
8000	704.26	370.09	259.08	203.87	170.97	149.22	133.85	122.46	113.72	106.84	101.30	96.77
9000	792.29	416.35	291.47	229.35	192.34	167.87	150.58	137.77	127.93	120.19	113.96	108.87
10000	880.33	462.61	323.85	254.83	213.71	186.53	167.31	153.07	142.15	133.54	126.62	120.96
11000	968.36	508.87	356.24	280.32	235.08	205.18	184.04	168.38	156.36	146.90	139.28	133.06
12000	1056.39	555.13	388.62	305.80	256.45	223.83	200.77	183.69	170.58	160.25	151.95	145.15
13000	1144.42	601.39	421.01	331.28	277.82	242.48	217.50	198.99	184.79	173.61	164.61	157.25
14000	1232.46	647.65	453.39	356.76	299.19	261.14	234.23	214.30	199.01	186.96	177.27	169.34
15000	1320.49	693.91	485.78	382.25	320.56	279.79	250.96	229.61	213.22	200.31	189.93	181.44
16000	1408.52	740.17	518.16	407.73	341.93	298.44	267.70	244.91	227.44	213.67	202.59	193.54
17000	1496.55	786.43	550.54	433.21	363.30	317.09	284.43	260.22	241.65	227.02	215.25	205.63
18000	1584.58	832.69	582.93	458.70	384.67	335.74	301.16	275.53	255.86	240.38	227.92	217.73
19000	1672.62	878.95	615.31	484.18	406.04	354.40	317.89	290.83	270.08	253.73	240.58	229.82
20000	1760.65	925.21	647.70	509.66	427.41	373.05	334.62	306.14	284.29	267.08	253.24	241.92
21000	1848.68	971.47	680.08	535.14	448.78	391.70	351.35	321.45	298.51	280.44	265.90	254.01
22000	1936.71	1017.73	712.47	560.63	470.15	410.35	368.08	336.75	312.72	293.79	278.56	266.11
23000	2024.75	1063.99	744.85	586.11	491.52	429.00	384.81	352.06	326.94	307.14	291.23	278.20
24000	2112.78	1110.25	777.24	611.59	512.89	447.66	401.54	367.37	341.15	320.50	303.89	290.30
25000	2200.81	1156.52	809.62	637.08	534.26	466.31	418.27	382.67	355.37	333.85	316.55	302.40
26000	2288.84	1202.78	842.01	662.56	555.63	484.96	435.00	397.98	369.58	347.21	329.21	314.49
27000	2376.87	1249.04	874.39	688.04	577.00	503.61	451.73	413.29	383.79	360.56	341.87	326.59
28000	2464.91	1295.30	906.78	713.52	598.37	522.27	468.46	428.59	398.01	373.91	354.53	338.68
29000	2552.94	1341.56	939.16	739.01	619.74	540.92	485.19	443.90	412.22	387.27	367.20	350.78
30000	2640.97	1387.82	971.55	764.49	641.11	559.57	501.92	459.21	426.44	400.62	379.86	362.87
31000	2729.00	1434.08	1003.93	789.97	662.48	578.22	518.65	474.51	440.65	413.98	392.52	374.97
32000	2817.04	1480.34	1036.32	815.46	683.85	596.87	535.39	489.82	454.87	427.33	405.18	387.07
33000	2905.07	1526.60	1068.70	840.94	705.22	615.53	552.12	505.13	469.08	440.68	417.84	399.16
34000	2993.10	1572.86	1101.08	866.42	726.59	634.18	568.85	520.44	483.30	454.04	430.50	411.26
35000	3081.13	1619.12	1133.47	891.90	747.96	652.83	585.58	535.74	497.51	467.39	443.17	423.35
36000	3169.16	1665.38	1165.85	917.39	769.33	671.48	602.31	551.05	511.72	480.75	455.83	435.45
37000	3257.20	1711.64	1198.24	942.87	790.70	690.13	619.04	566.36	525.94	494.10	468.49	447.54
38000	3345.23	1757.90	1230.62	968.35	812.08	708.79	635.77	581.66	540.15	507.45	481.15	459.64
39000	3433.26	1804.16	1263.01	993.83	833.45	727.44	652.50	596.97	554.37	520.81	493.81	471.74
40000	3521.29	1850.42	1295.39	1019.32	854.82	746.09	669.23	612.28	568.58	534.16	506.48	483.83
41000	3609.33	1896.68	1327.78	1044.80	876.19	764.74	685.96	627.58	582.80	547.51	519.14	495.93
42000	3697.36	1942.94	1360.16	1070.28	897.56	783.40	702.69	642.89	597.01	560.87	531.80	508.02
43000	3785.39	1989.20	1392.55	1095.77	918.93	802.05	719.42	658.20	611.23	574.22	544.46	520.12
44000	3873.42	2035.46	1424.93	1121.25	940.30	820.70	736.15	673.50	625.44	587.58	557.12	532.21
45000	3961.45	2081.72	1457.32	1146.73	961.67	839.35	752.88	688.81	639.65	600.93	569.78	544.31
46000	4049.49	2127.98	1489.70	1172.21	983.04	858.00	769.61	704.12	653.87	614.28	582.45	556.40
47000	4137.52	2174.24	1522.09	1197.70	1004.41	876.66	786.35	719.42	668.08	627.64	595.11	568.50
48000	4225.55	2220.50	1554.47	1223.18	1025.78	895.31	803.08	734.73	682.30	640.99	607.77	580.60
49000	4313.58	2266.76	1586.85	1248.66	1047.15	913.96	819.81	750.04	696.51	654.35	620.43	592.69
50000	4401.62	2313.02	1619.24	1274.15	1068.52	932.61	836.54	765.34	710.73	667.70	633.09	604.79
55000	4841.78	2544.33	1781.16	1401.56	1175.37	1025.87	920.19	841.88	781.80	734.47	696.40	665.27
60000	5281.94	2775.63	1943.09	1528.97	1282.22	1119.13	1003.84	918.41	852.87	801.24	759.71	725.74
65000	5722.10	3006.93	2105.01	1656.39	1389.07	1212.40	1087.50	994.95	923.94	868.01	823.02	786.22
70000	6162.26	3238.23	2266.93	1783.80	1495.92	1305.66	1171.15	1071.48	995.01	934.78	886.33	846.70
75000	6602.42	3469.53	2428.86	1911.22	1602.77	1398.92	1254.80	1148.01	1066.09	1001.55	949.64	907.18
80000	7042.58	3700.84	2590.78	2038.63	1709.63	1492.18	1338.46	1224.55	1137.16	1068.32	1012.95	967.66
85000	7482.74	3932.14	2752.70	2166.04	1816.48	1585.44	1422.11	1301.08	1208.23	1135.09	1076.26	1028.13
90000	7922.90	4163.44	2914.63	2293.46	1923.33	1678.70	1505.76	1377.61	1279.30	1201.86	1139.56	1088.61
95000	8363.06	4394.74	3076.55	2420.87	2030.18	1771.96	1589.42	1454.15	1350.37	1268.63	1202.87	1149.09
100000	8803.23	4626.04	3238.47	2548.29	2137.03	1865.22	1673.07	1530.68	1421.45	1335.40	1266.18	1209.57

Table 1

MONTHLY

PAYMENT REQUIRED TO AMORTIZE A LOAN

10.25%

10%

ERM / UNT	13 YEARS	14 YEARS	15 YEARS	16 YEARS	17 YEARS	18 YEARS	19 YEARS	20 YEARS	25 YEARS	30 YEARS	35 YEARS	40 YEARS
50	.59	.57	.55	.54	.52	.51	.50	.50	.47	.45	.44	.44
100	1.17	1.13	1.09	1.07	1.04	1.02	1.00	.99	.93	.90	.88	.87
200	2.33	2.25	2.18	2.13	2.08	2.04	2.00	1.97	1.86	1.80	1.76	1.74
300	3.49	3.37	3.27	3.19	3.12	3.05	3.00	2.95	2.78	2.69	2.64	2.61
400	4.66	4.50	4.36	4.25	4.15	4.07	4.00	3.93	3.71	3.59	3.52	3.48
500	5.82	5.62	5.45	5.31	5.19	5.08	4.99	4.91	4.64	4.49	4.40	4.35
600	6.98	6.74	6.54	6.37	6.23	6.10	5.99	5.89	5.56	5.38	5.28	5.22
700	8.14	7.87	7.63	7.44	7.26	7.12	6.99	6.88	6.49	6.28	6.16	6.09
800	9.31	8.99	8.72	8.50	8.30	8.13	7.99	7.86	7.42	7.17	7.04	6.96
900	10.47	10.11	9.81	9.56	9.34	9.15	8.98	8.84	8.34	8.07	7.91	7.82
1000	11.63	11.24	10.90	10.62	10.38	10.16	9.98	9.82	9.27	8.97	8.79	8.69
2000	23.26	22.47	21.80	21.24	20.75	20.32	19.96	19.64	18.53	17.93	17.58	17.38
3000	34.88	33.70	32.70	31.85	31.12	30.48	29.93	29.45	27.80	26.89	26.37	26.07
4000	46.51	44.94	43.60	42.47	41.49	40.64	39.91	39.27	37.06	35.85	35.16	34.76
5000	58.14	56.17	54.50	53.08	51.86	50.80	49.89	49.09	46.32	44.81	43.95	43.45
6000	69.76	67.40	65.40	63.70	62.23	60.96	59.86	58.90	55.59	53.77	52.74	52.13
7000	81.39	78.63	76.30	74.31	72.60	71.12	69.84	68.72	64.85	62.73	61.52	60.82
8000	93.02	89.87	87.20	84.93	82.97	81.28	79.82	78.54	74.12	71.69	70.31	69.51
9000	104.64	101.10	98.10	95.54	93.34	91.44	89.79	88.35	83.38	80.65	79.10	78.20
10000	116.27	112.33	109.00	106.16	103.71	101.60	99.77	98.17	92.64	89.62	87.89	86.89
11000	127.89	123.56	119.90	116.77	114.09	111.76	109.75	107.99	101.91	98.58	96.68	95.58
12000	139.52	134.80	130.80	127.39	124.46	121.92	119.72	117.80	111.17	107.54	105.47	104.26
13000	151.15	146.03	141.70	138.00	134.83	132.08	129.70	127.62	120.43	116.50	114.26	112.95
14000	162.77	157.26	152.60	148.62	145.20	142.24	139.67	137.44	129.70	125.46	123.04	121.64
15000	174.40	168.50	163.50	159.23	155.57	152.40	149.65	147.25	138.96	134.42	131.83	130.33
16000	186.03	179.73	174.40	169.85	165.94	162.56	159.63	157.07	148.23	143.38	140.62	139.02
17000	197.65	190.96	185.30	180.46	176.31	172.72	169.60	166.88	157.49	152.34	149.41	147.70
18000	209.28	202.19	196.20	191.08	186.68	182.88	179.58	176.70	166.75	161.30	158.20	156.39
19000	220.90	213.43	207.10	201.69	197.05	193.04	189.56	186.52	176.02	170.26	166.99	165.08
20000	232.53	224.66	218.00	212.31	207.42	203.20	199.53	196.33	185.28	179.23	175.78	173.77
21000	244.16	235.89	228.89	222.92	217.79	213.36	209.51	206.15	194.55	188.19	184.56	182.46
22000	255.78	247.12	239.79	233.54	228.17	223.52	219.49	215.97	203.81	197.15	193.35	191.15
23000	267.41	258.36	250.69	244.15	238.54	233.68	229.46	225.78	213.07	206.11	202.14	199.83
24000	279.04	269.59	261.59	254.77	248.91	243.84	239.44	235.60	222.34	215.07	210.93	208.52
25000	290.66	280.82	272.49	265.38	259.28	254.00	249.42	245.42	231.60	224.03	219.72	217.21
26000	302.29	292.06	283.39	276.00	269.65	264.16	259.39	255.23	240.86	232.99	228.51	225.90
27000	313.91	303.29	294.29	286.62	280.02	274.32	269.37	265.05	250.13	241.95	237.30	234.59
28000	325.54	314.52	305.19	297.23	290.39	284.48	279.34	274.87	259.39	250.91	246.08	243.27
29000	337.17	325.75	316.09	307.85	300.76	294.64	289.32	284.68	268.66	259.87	254.87	251.96
30000	348.79	336.99	326.99	318.46	311.13	304.80	299.30	294.50	277.92	268.84	263.66	260.65
31000	360.42	348.22	337.89	329.08	321.50	314.96	309.27	304.31	287.18	277.80	272.45	269.34
32000	372.05	359.45	348.79	339.69	331.87	325.12	319.25	314.13	296.45	286.76	281.24	278.03
33000	383.67	370.68	359.69	350.31	342.25	335.28	329.23	323.95	305.71	295.72	290.03	286.72
34000	395.30	381.92	370.59	360.92	352.62	345.44	339.20	333.76	314.98	304.68	298.82	295.40
35000	406.92	393.15	381.49	371.54	362.99	355.60	349.18	343.58	324.24	313.64	307.60	304.09
36000	418.55	404.38	392.39	382.15	373.36	365.76	359.16	353.40	333.50	322.60	316.39	312.78
37000	430.18	415.61	403.29	392.77	383.73	375.92	369.13	363.21	342.77	331.56	325.18	321.47
38000	441.80	426.85	414.19	403.38	394.10	386.08	379.11	373.03	352.03	340.52	333.97	330.16
39000	453.43	438.08	425.09	414.00	404.47	396.24	389.09	382.85	361.29	349.48	342.76	338.84
40000	465.06	449.31	435.99	424.61	414.84	406.40	399.06	392.66	370.56	358.45	351.55	347.53
41000	476.68	460.55	446.88	435.23	425.21	416.56	409.04	402.48	379.82	367.41	360.34	356.22
42000	488.31	471.78	457.78	445.84	435.58	426.72	419.01	412.30	389.09	376.37	369.12	364.91
43000	499.94	483.01	468.68	456.46	445.95	436.88	428.99	422.11	398.35	385.33	377.91	373.60
44000	511.56	494.24	479.58	467.07	456.33	447.04	438.97	431.93	407.61	394.29	386.70	382.29
45000	523.19	505.48	490.48	477.69	466.70	457.20	448.94	441.74	416.88	403.25	395.49	390.97
46000	534.81	516.71	501.38	488.30	477.07	467.36	458.92	451.56	426.14	412.21	404.28	399.66
47000	546.44	527.94	512.28	498.92	487.44	477.52	468.90	461.38	435.41	421.17	413.07	408.35
48000	558.07	539.17	523.18	509.53	497.81	487.68	478.87	471.19	444.67	430.13	421.86	417.04
49000	569.69	550.41	534.08	520.15	508.18	497.84	488.85	481.01	453.93	439.09	430.64	425.73
50000	581.32	561.64	544.98	530.76	518.55	508.00	498.83	490.83	463.20	448.06	439.43	434.41
55000	639.45	617.80	599.48	583.84	570.41	558.79	548.71	539.91	509.52	492.86	483.38	477.86
60000	697.58	673.97	653.97	636.92	622.26	609.59	598.59	588.99	555.83	537.67	527.32	521.30
65000	755.71	730.13	708.47	689.99	674.11	660.39	648.47	638.07	602.15	582.47	571.26	564.74
70000	813.84	786.29	762.97	743.07	725.97	711.19	698.35	687.16	648.47	627.28	615.20	608.18
75000	871.98	842.46	817.47	796.14	777.82	761.99	748.24	736.24	694.79	672.08	659.15	651.62
80000	930.11	898.62	871.97	849.22	829.68	812.79	798.12	785.32	741.11	716.89	703.09	695.06
85000	988.24	954.78	926.46	902.30	881.53	863.59	848.00	834.40	787.43	761.69	747.03	738.50
90000	1046.37	1010.95	980.96	955.37	933.39	914.39	897.88	883.48	833.75	806.50	790.98	781.94
95000	1104.50	1067.11	1035.46	1008.45	985.24	965.19	947.77	932.57	880.07	851.30	834.92	825.38
100000	1162.63	1123.27	1089.96	1061.52	1037.10	1015.99	997.65	981.65	926.39	896.11	878.86	868.82

Table 1

10.50%

MONTHLY

PAYMENT REQUIRED TO AMORTIZE A LOAN

10%

TERM	1 YEAR	2 YEARS	3 YEARS	4 YEARS	5 YEARS	6 YEARS	7 YEARS	8 YEARS	9 YEARS	10 YEARS	11 YEARS	12 YEARS
AMOUNT												
50	4.41	2.32	1.63	1.29	1.08	.94	.85	.78	.72	.68	.65	.62
100	8.82	4.64	3.26	2.57	2.15	1.88	1.69	1.55	1.44	1.35	1.29	1.23
200	17.63	9.28	6.51	5.13	4.30	3.76	3.38	3.09	2.88	2.70	2.57	2.45
300	26.45	13.92	9.76	7.69	6.45	5.64	5.06	4.64	4.31	4.05	3.85	3.68
400	35.26	18.56	13.01	10.25	8.60	7.52	6.75	6.18	5.75	5.40	5.13	4.90
500	44.08	23.19	16.26	12.81	10.75	9.39	8.44	7.73	7.18	6.75	6.41	6.13
600	52.89	27.83	19.51	15.37	12.90	11.27	10.12	9.27	8.62	8.10	7.69	7.35
700	61.71	32.47	22.76	17.93	15.05	13.15	11.81	10.81	10.05	9.45	8.97	8.57
800	70.52	37.11	26.01	20.49	17.20	15.03	13.49	12.36	11.49	10.80	10.25	9.80
900	79.34	41.74	29.26	23.05	19.35	16.91	15.18	13.90	12.92	12.15	11.53	11.02
1000	88.15	46.38	32.51	25.61	21.50	18.78	16.87	15.45	14.36	13.50	12.81	12.25
2000	176.30	92.76	65.01	51.21	42.99	37.56	33.73	30.89	28.71	26.99	25.61	24.49
3000	264.45	139.13	97.51	76.82	64.49	56.34	50.59	46.33	43.06	40.49	38.42	36.73
4000	352.60	185.51	130.01	102.42	85.98	75.12	67.45	61.77	57.41	53.98	51.22	48.97
5000	440.75	231.89	162.52	128.02	107.47	93.90	84.31	77.21	71.76	67.47	64.03	61.21
6000	528.90	278.26	195.02	153.63	128.97	112.68	101.17	92.65	86.11	80.97	76.83	73.45
7000	617.05	324.64	227.52	179.23	150.46	131.46	118.03	108.09	100.46	94.46	89.64	85.69
8000	705.19	371.01	260.02	204.83	171.96	150.24	134.89	123.53	114.81	107.95	102.44	97.94
9000	793.34	417.39	292.53	230.44	193.45	169.02	151.75	138.97	129.16	121.45	115.25	110.18
10000	881.49	463.77	325.03	256.04	214.94	187.79	168.61	154.41	143.51	134.94	128.05	122.42
11000	969.64	510.14	357.53	281.64	236.44	206.57	185.47	169.85	157.86	148.43	140.85	134.66
12000	1057.79	556.52	390.03	307.25	257.93	225.35	202.33	185.29	172.22	161.93	153.66	146.90
13000	1145.94	602.89	422.54	332.85	279.43	244.13	219.19	200.73	186.57	175.42	166.46	159.14
14000	1234.09	649.27	455.04	358.45	300.92	262.91	236.05	216.17	200.92	188.91	179.27	171.38
15000	1322.23	695.65	487.54	384.06	322.41	281.69	252.92	231.61	215.27	202.41	192.07	183.63
16000	1410.38	742.02	520.04	409.66	343.91	300.47	269.78	247.05	229.62	215.90	204.88	195.87
17000	1498.53	788.40	552.55	435.26	365.40	319.25	286.64	262.49	243.97	229.39	217.68	208.11
18000	1586.68	834.77	585.05	460.87	386.90	338.03	303.50	277.93	258.32	242.89	230.49	220.35
19000	1674.83	881.15	617.55	486.47	408.39	356.81	320.36	293.37	272.67	256.38	243.29	232.59
20000	1762.98	927.53	650.05	512.07	429.88	375.58	337.22	308.81	287.02	269.87	256.09	244.83
21000	1851.13	973.90	682.56	537.68	451.38	394.36	354.08	324.25	301.37	283.37	268.90	257.07
22000	1939.27	1020.28	715.06	563.28	472.87	413.14	370.94	339.69	315.72	296.86	281.70	269.32
23000	2027.42	1066.65	747.56	588.88	494.36	431.92	387.80	355.13	330.07	310.36	294.51	281.56
24000	2115.57	1113.03	780.06	614.49	515.86	450.70	404.66	370.57	344.43	323.85	307.31	293.80
25000	2203.72	1159.41	812.57	640.09	537.35	469.48	421.52	386.01	358.78	337.34	320.12	306.04
26000	2291.87	1205.78	845.07	665.69	558.85	488.26	438.38	401.45	373.13	350.84	332.92	318.28
27000	2380.02	1252.16	877.57	691.30	580.34	507.04	455.24	416.89	387.48	364.33	345.73	330.52
28000	2468.17	1298.53	910.07	716.90	601.83	525.82	472.10	432.33	401.83	377.82	358.53	342.76
29000	2556.31	1344.91	942.58	742.50	623.33	544.60	488.96	447.77	416.18	391.32	371.33	355.01
30000	2644.46	1391.29	975.08	768.11	644.82	563.37	505.83	463.21	430.53	404.81	384.14	367.25
31000	2732.61	1437.66	1007.58	793.71	666.32	582.15	522.69	478.65	444.88	418.30	396.94	379.49
32000	2820.76	1484.04	1040.08	819.31	687.81	600.93	539.55	494.09	459.23	431.80	409.75	391.73
33000	2908.91	1530.41	1072.59	844.92	709.30	619.71	556.41	509.53	473.58	445.29	422.55	403.97
34000	2997.06	1576.79	1105.09	870.52	730.80	638.49	573.27	524.97	487.93	458.78	435.36	416.21
35000	3085.21	1623.17	1137.59	896.12	752.29	657.27	590.13	540.41	502.29	472.28	448.16	428.45
36000	3173.35	1669.54	1170.09	921.73	773.79	676.05	606.99	555.85	516.64	485.77	460.97	440.70
37000	3261.50	1715.92	1202.60	947.33	795.28	694.83	623.85	571.29	530.99	499.26	473.77	452.94
38000	3349.65	1762.29	1235.10	972.93	816.77	713.61	640.71	586.73	545.34	512.76	486.57	465.18
39000	3437.80	1808.67	1267.60	998.54	838.27	732.38	657.57	602.17	559.69	526.25	499.38	477.42
40000	3525.95	1855.05	1300.10	1024.14	859.76	751.16	674.43	617.61	574.04	539.74	512.18	489.66
41000	3614.10	1901.42	1332.61	1049.74	881.25	769.94	691.29	633.05	588.39	553.24	524.99	501.90
42000	3702.25	1947.80	1365.11	1075.35	902.75	788.72	708.15	648.49	602.74	566.73	537.79	514.14
43000	3790.39	1994.17	1397.61	1100.95	924.24	807.50	725.01	663.93	617.09	580.23	550.60	526.39
44000	3878.54	2040.55	1430.11	1126.55	945.74	826.28	741.87	679.37	631.44	593.72	563.40	538.63
45000	3966.69	2086.93	1462.61	1152.16	967.23	845.06	758.74	694.81	645.79	607.21	576.21	550.87
46000	4054.84	2133.30	1495.12	1177.76	988.72	863.84	775.60	710.25	660.14	620.71	589.01	563.11
47000	4142.99	2179.68	1527.62	1203.36	1010.22	882.62	792.46	725.69	674.50	634.20	601.81	575.35
48000	4231.14	2226.06	1560.12	1228.97	1031.71	901.40	809.32	741.13	688.85	647.69	614.62	587.59
49000	4319.29	2272.43	1592.62	1254.57	1053.21	920.17	826.18	756.57	703.20	661.19	627.42	599.83
50000	4407.44	2318.81	1625.13	1280.17	1074.70	938.95	843.04	772.01	717.55	674.68	640.23	612.08
55000	4848.18	2550.69	1787.64	1408.19	1182.17	1032.85	927.34	849.21	789.30	742.15	704.25	673.28
60000	5288.92	2782.57	1950.15	1536.21	1289.64	1126.74	1011.65	926.41	861.06	809.61	768.27	734.49
65000	5729.66	3014.45	2112.66	1664.22	1397.11	1220.64	1095.95	1003.61	932.81	877.08	832.29	795.70
70000	6170.41	3246.33	2275.18	1792.24	1504.58	1314.53	1180.25	1080.81	1004.57	944.55	896.32	856.90
75000	6611.15	3478.21	2437.69	1920.26	1612.05	1408.43	1264.56	1158.01	1076.32	1012.02	960.34	918.11
80000	7051.89	3710.09	2600.20	2048.28	1719.52	1502.32	1348.86	1235.21	1148.07	1079.49	1024.36	979.32
85000	7492.64	3941.97	2762.71	2176.29	1826.99	1596.22	1433.16	1312.41	1219.83	1146.95	1088.38	1040.52
90000	7933.38	4173.85	2925.22	2304.31	1934.46	1690.11	1517.47	1389.61	1291.58	1214.42	1152.41	1101.73
95000	8374.12	4405.73	3087.74	2432.33	2041.93	1784.01	1601.77	1466.81	1363.34	1281.89	1216.43	1162.94
100000	8814.87	4637.61	3250.25	2560.34	2149.40	1877.90	1686.07	1544.01	1435.09	1349.36	1280.45	1224.15

Table 1

MONTHLY   10.50%

PAYMENT REQUIRED TO AMORTIZE A LOAN

TERM	13 YEARS	14 YEARS	15 YEARS	16 YEARS	17 YEARS	18 YEARS	19 YEARS	20 YEARS	25 YEARS	30 YEARS	35 YEARS	40 YEARS
50	.59	.57	.56	.54	.53	.52	.51	.50	.48	.46	.45	.45
100	1.18	1.14	1.11	1.08	1.06	1.04	1.02	1.00	.95	.92	.90	.89
200	2.36	2.28	2.22	2.16	2.11	2.07	2.03	2.00	1.89	1.83	1.80	1.78
300	3.54	3.42	3.32	3.24	3.16	3.10	3.05	3.00	2.84	2.75	2.70	2.67
400	4.72	4.56	4.43	4.31	4.22	4.13	4.06	4.00	3.78	3.66	3.60	3.56
500	5.89	5.70	5.53	5.39	5.27	5.17	5.08	5.00	4.73	4.58	4.50	4.45
600	7.07	6.84	6.64	6.47	6.32	6.20	6.09	6.00	5.67	5.49	5.39	5.34
700	8.25	7.97	7.74	7.55	7.38	7.23	7.10	6.99	6.61	6.41	6.29	6.22
800	9.43	9.11	8.85	8.62	8.43	8.26	8.12	7.99	7.56	7.32	7.19	7.11
900	10.60	10.25	9.95	9.70	9.48	9.30	9.13	8.99	8.50	8.24	8.09	8.00
1000	11.78	11.39	11.06	10.78	10.54	10.33	10.15	9.99	9.45	9.15	8.99	8.89
2000	23.56	22.77	22.11	21.55	21.07	20.65	20.29	19.97	18.89	18.30	17.97	17.78
3000	35.33	34.16	33.17	32.32	31.60	30.97	30.43	29.96	28.33	27.45	26.95	26.66
4000	47.11	45.54	44.22	43.09	42.13	41.29	40.57	39.94	37.77	36.59	35.93	35.55
5000	58.88	56.93	55.27	53.87	52.66	51.62	50.71	49.92	47.21	45.74	44.91	44.43
6000	70.66	68.31	66.33	64.64	63.19	61.94	60.85	59.91	56.66	54.89	53.89	53.32
7000	82.43	79.70	77.38	75.41	73.72	72.26	70.99	69.89	66.10	64.04	62.87	62.20
8000	94.21	91.08	88.44	86.18	84.25	82.58	81.14	79.88	75.54	73.18	71.86	71.09
9000	105.98	102.46	99.49	96.96	94.78	92.91	91.28	89.86	84.98	82.33	80.84	79.98
10000	117.76	113.85	110.54	107.73	105.31	103.23	101.42	99.84	94.42	91.48	89.82	88.86
11000	129.53	125.23	121.60	118.50	115.84	113.55	111.56	109.83	103.86	100.63	98.80	97.75
12000	141.31	136.62	132.65	129.27	126.37	123.87	121.70	119.81	113.31	109.77	107.78	106.63
13000	153.08	148.00	143.71	140.05	136.91	134.19	131.84	129.79	122.75	118.92	116.76	115.52
14000	164.86	159.39	154.76	150.82	147.44	144.52	141.98	139.78	132.19	128.07	125.74	124.40
15000	176.63	170.77	165.81	161.59	157.97	154.84	152.13	149.76	141.63	137.22	134.73	133.29
16000	188.41	182.15	176.87	172.36	168.50	165.16	162.27	159.75	151.07	146.36	143.71	142.18
17000	200.18	193.54	187.92	183.14	179.03	175.48	172.41	169.73	160.52	155.51	152.69	151.06
18000	211.96	204.92	198.98	193.91	189.56	185.81	182.55	179.71	169.96	164.66	161.67	159.95
19000	223.73	216.31	210.03	204.68	200.09	196.13	192.69	189.70	179.40	173.81	170.65	168.83
20000	235.51	227.69	221.08	215.45	210.62	206.45	202.83	199.68	188.84	182.95	179.63	177.72
21000	247.28	239.08	232.14	226.23	221.15	216.77	212.97	209.66	198.28	192.10	188.61	186.60
22000	259.06	250.46	243.19	237.00	231.68	227.10	223.12	219.65	207.72	201.25	197.59	195.49
23000	270.83	261.84	254.25	247.77	242.21	237.42	233.26	229.63	217.17	210.40	206.58	204.38
24000	282.61	273.23	265.30	258.54	252.74	247.74	243.40	239.62	226.61	219.54	215.56	213.26
25000	294.38	284.61	276.35	269.32	263.28	258.06	253.54	249.60	236.05	228.69	224.54	222.15
26000	306.16	296.00	287.41	280.09	273.81	268.38	263.68	259.58	245.49	237.84	233.52	231.03
27000	317.93	307.38	298.46	290.86	284.34	278.71	273.82	269.57	254.93	246.98	242.50	239.92
28000	329.71	318.77	309.52	301.63	294.87	289.03	283.96	279.55	264.38	256.13	251.48	248.80
29000	341.48	330.15	320.57	312.41	305.40	299.35	294.11	289.54	273.82	265.28	260.46	257.69
30000	353.26	341.54	331.62	323.18	315.93	309.67	304.25	299.52	283.26	274.43	269.45	266.58
31000	365.03	352.92	342.68	333.95	326.46	320.00	314.39	309.50	292.70	283.57	278.43	275.46
32000	376.81	364.30	353.73	344.72	336.99	330.32	324.53	319.49	302.14	292.72	287.41	284.35
33000	388.58	375.69	364.79	355.50	347.52	340.64	334.67	329.47	311.58	301.87	296.39	293.23
34000	400.36	387.07	375.84	366.27	358.05	350.96	344.81	339.45	321.03	311.02	305.37	302.12
35000	412.13	398.46	386.89	377.04	368.58	361.28	354.95	349.44	330.47	320.16	314.35	311.00
36000	423.91	409.84	397.95	387.81	379.11	371.61	365.10	359.42	339.91	329.31	323.33	319.89
37000	435.68	421.23	409.00	398.58	389.65	381.93	375.24	369.41	349.35	338.46	332.31	328.78
38000	447.46	432.61	420.06	409.36	400.18	392.25	385.38	379.39	358.79	347.61	341.30	337.66
39000	459.23	443.99	431.11	420.13	410.71	402.57	395.52	389.37	368.24	356.75	350.28	346.55
40000	471.01	455.38	442.16	430.90	421.24	412.90	405.66	399.36	377.68	365.90	359.26	355.43
41000	482.78	466.76	453.22	441.67	431.77	423.22	415.80	409.34	387.12	375.05	368.24	364.32
42000	494.56	478.15	464.27	452.45	442.30	433.54	425.94	419.32	396.56	384.20	377.22	373.20
43000	506.33	489.53	475.33	463.22	452.83	443.86	436.08	429.31	406.00	393.34	386.20	382.09
44000	518.11	500.92	486.38	473.99	463.36	454.19	446.23	439.29	415.44	402.49	395.18	390.98
45000	529.88	512.30	497.43	484.76	473.89	464.51	456.37	449.28	424.89	411.64	404.17	399.86
46000	541.66	523.68	508.49	495.54	484.42	474.83	466.51	459.26	434.33	420.79	413.15	408.75
47000	553.43	535.07	519.54	506.31	494.95	485.15	476.65	469.24	443.77	429.93	422.13	417.63
48000	565.21	546.45	530.60	517.08	505.48	495.47	486.79	479.23	453.21	439.08	431.11	426.52
49000	576.98	557.84	541.65	527.85	516.01	505.80	496.93	489.21	462.65	448.23	440.09	435.40
50000	588.76	569.22	552.70	538.63	526.55	516.12	507.07	499.19	472.10	457.37	449.07	444.29
55000	647.63	626.14	607.97	592.49	579.20	567.73	557.78	549.11	519.30	503.11	493.98	488.72
60000	706.51	683.07	663.24	646.35	631.85	619.34	608.49	599.03	566.51	548.85	538.89	533.15
65000	765.38	739.99	718.51	700.21	684.51	670.95	659.20	648.95	613.72	594.59	583.79	577.58
70000	824.26	796.91	773.78	754.07	737.16	722.56	709.90	698.87	660.93	640.32	628.70	622.00
75000	883.13	853.83	829.05	807.94	789.82	774.18	760.61	748.79	708.14	686.06	673.61	666.43
80000	942.01	910.75	884.32	861.80	842.47	825.79	811.32	798.71	755.35	731.80	718.51	710.86
85000	1000.88	967.67	939.59	915.66	895.12	877.40	862.02	848.63	802.56	777.53	763.42	755.29
90000	1059.76	1024.60	994.86	969.52	947.78	929.01	912.73	898.55	849.77	823.27	808.33	799.72
95000	1118.63	1081.52	1050.13	1023.39	1000.43	980.62	963.44	948.47	896.98	869.01	853.23	844.15
100000	1177.51	1138.44	1105.40	1077.25	1053.09	1032.23	1014.14	998.38	944.19	914.74	898.14	888.58

Table 1

10.75%

MONTHLY
PAYMENT REQUIRED TO AMORTIZE A LOAN

10%

TERM AMOUNT	1 YEAR	2 YEARS	3 YEARS	4 YEARS	5 YEARS	6 YEARS	7 YEARS	8 YEARS	9 YEARS	10 YEARS	11 YEARS	12 YEAR
50	4.42	2.33	1.64	1.29	1.09	.95	.85	.78	.73	.69	.65	.62
100	8.83	4.65	3.27	2.58	2.17	1.90	1.70	1.56	1.45	1.37	1.30	1.24
200	17.66	9.30	6.53	5.15	4.33	3.79	3.40	3.12	2.90	2.73	2.59	2.4
300	26.48	13.95	9.79	7.72	6.49	5.68	5.10	4.68	4.35	4.10	3.89	3.7
400	35.31	18.60	13.05	10.29	8.65	7.57	6.80	6.23	5.80	5.46	5.18	4.96
500	44.14	23.25	16.32	12.87	10.81	9.46	8.50	7.79	7.25	6.82	6.48	6.2
600	52.96	27.90	19.58	15.44	12.98	11.35	10.20	9.35	8.70	8.19	7.77	7.4
700	61.79	32.55	22.84	18.01	15.14	13.24	11.90	10.91	10.15	9.55	9.07	8.6
800	70.62	37.20	26.10	20.58	17.30	15.13	13.60	12.46	11.60	10.91	10.36	9.9
900	79.44	41.85	29.36	23.16	19.46	17.02	15.30	14.02	13.04	12.28	11.66	11.15
1000	88.27	46.50	32.63	25.73	21.62	18.91	17.00	15.58	14.49	13.64	12.95	12.39
2000	176.54	92.99	65.25	51.45	43.24	37.82	33.99	31.15	28.98	27.27	25.90	24.78
3000	264.80	139.48	97.87	77.18	64.86	56.72	50.98	46.73	43.47	40.91	38.85	37.1
4000	353.07	185.97	130.49	102.90	86.48	75.63	67.97	62.30	57.96	54.54	51.80	49.56
5000	441.33	232.46	163.11	128.63	108.09	94.54	84.96	77.87	72.45	68.17	64.74	61.95
6000	529.60	278.96	195.73	154.35	129.71	113.44	101.95	93.45	86.93	81.81	77.69	74.3
7000	617.86	325.45	228.35	180.07	151.33	132.35	118.94	109.02	101.42	95.44	90.64	86.72
8000	706.13	371.94	260.97	205.80	172.95	151.26	135.94	124.60	115.91	109.08	103.59	99.11
9000	794.39	418.43	293.59	231.52	194.57	170.16	152.93	140.17	130.40	122.71	116.54	111.56
10000	882.66	464.92	326.21	257.25	216.18	189.07	169.92	155.74	144.89	136.34	129.48	123.89
11000	970.92	511.42	358.83	282.97	237.80	207.97	186.91	171.32	159.37	149.98	142.43	136.27
12000	1059.19	557.91	391.45	308.70	259.42	226.88	203.90	186.89	173.86	163.61	155.38	148.66
13000	1147.45	604.40	424.07	334.42	281.04	245.79	220.89	202.47	188.35	177.25	168.33	161.05
14000	1235.72	650.89	456.69	360.14	302.66	264.69	237.88	218.04	202.84	190.88	181.28	173.44
15000	1323.98	697.38	489.31	385.87	324.27	283.60	254.87	233.61	217.33	204.51	194.22	185.83
16000	1412.25	743.87	521.93	411.59	345.89	302.51	271.87	249.19	231.81	218.15	207.17	198.21
17000	1500.51	790.37	554.55	437.32	367.51	321.41	288.86	264.76	246.30	231.78	220.12	210.60
18000	1588.78	836.86	587.17	463.04	389.13	340.32	305.85	280.34	260.79	245.41	233.07	222.99
19000	1677.04	883.35	619.79	488.77	410.75	359.22	322.84	295.91	275.28	259.05	246.02	235.3
20000	1765.31	929.84	652.41	514.49	432.36	378.13	339.83	311.48	289.77	272.68	258.96	247.77
21000	1853.57	976.33	685.03	540.21	453.98	397.04	356.82	327.06	304.25	286.32	271.91	260.15
22000	1941.84	1022.83	717.65	565.94	475.60	415.94	373.81	342.63	318.74	299.95	284.86	272.54
23000	2030.10	1069.32	750.28	591.66	497.22	434.85	390.80	358.20	333.23	313.58	297.81	284.93
24000	2118.37	1115.81	782.90	617.39	518.84	453.76	407.80	373.78	347.72	327.22	310.76	297.32
25000	2206.63	1162.30	815.52	643.11	540.45	472.66	424.79	389.35	362.21	340.85	323.70	309.71
26000	2294.90	1208.79	848.14	668.84	562.07	491.57	441.78	404.93	376.69	354.49	336.65	322.09
27000	2383.16	1255.29	880.76	694.56	583.69	510.47	458.77	420.50	391.18	368.12	349.60	334.48
28000	2471.43	1301.78	913.38	720.28	605.31	529.38	475.76	436.07	405.67	381.75	362.55	346.87
29000	2559.69	1348.27	946.00	746.01	626.93	548.29	492.75	451.65	420.16	395.39	375.50	359.26
30000	2647.96	1394.76	978.62	771.73	648.54	567.19	509.74	467.22	434.65	409.02	388.44	371.65
31000	2736.22	1441.25	1011.24	797.46	670.16	586.10	526.73	482.80	449.13	422.65	401.39	384.03
32000	2824.49	1487.74	1043.86	823.18	691.78	605.01	543.73	498.37	463.62	436.29	414.34	396.42
33000	2912.75	1534.24	1076.48	848.91	713.40	623.91	560.72	513.94	478.11	449.92	427.29	408.81
34000	3001.02	1580.73	1109.10	874.63	735.02	642.82	577.71	529.52	492.60	463.56	440.24	421.20
35000	3089.28	1627.22	1141.72	900.35	756.63	661.72	594.70	545.09	507.09	477.19	453.18	433.59
36000	3177.55	1673.71	1174.34	926.08	778.25	680.63	611.69	560.67	521.57	490.82	466.13	445.97
37000	3265.81	1720.20	1206.96	951.80	799.87	699.54	628.68	576.24	536.06	504.46	479.08	458.36
38000	3354.08	1766.70	1239.58	977.53	821.49	718.44	645.67	591.81	550.55	518.09	492.03	470.75
39000	3442.34	1813.19	1272.20	1003.25	843.11	737.35	662.66	607.39	565.04	531.73	504.98	483.14
40000	3530.61	1859.68	1304.82	1028.98	864.72	756.26	679.66	622.96	579.53	545.36	517.92	495.53
41000	3618.87	1906.17	1337.44	1054.70	886.34	775.16	696.65	638.54	594.01	558.99	530.87	507.91
42000	3707.14	1952.66	1370.06	1080.42	907.96	794.07	713.64	654.11	608.50	572.63	543.82	520.30
43000	3795.40	1999.15	1402.68	1106.15	929.58	812.97	730.63	669.68	622.99	586.26	556.77	532.69
44000	3883.67	2045.65	1435.30	1131.87	951.19	831.88	747.62	685.26	637.48	599.90	569.72	545.08
45000	3971.93	2092.14	1467.93	1157.60	972.81	850.79	764.61	700.83	651.97	613.53	582.66	557.47
46000	4060.20	2138.63	1500.55	1183.32	994.43	869.69	781.60	716.40	666.45	627.16	595.61	569.85
47000	4148.46	2185.12	1533.17	1209.05	1016.05	888.60	798.59	731.98	680.94	640.80	608.56	582.24
48000	4236.73	2231.61	1565.79	1234.77	1037.67	907.51	815.59	747.55	695.43	654.43	621.51	594.63
49000	4324.99	2278.11	1598.41	1260.49	1059.28	926.41	832.58	763.13	709.92	668.06	634.46	607.02
50000	4413.26	2324.60	1631.03	1286.22	1080.90	945.32	849.57	778.70	724.41	681.70	647.40	619.41
55000	4854.58	2557.06	1794.13	1414.84	1188.99	1039.85	934.52	856.57	796.85	749.87	712.14	681.3
60000	5295.91	2789.52	1957.23	1543.46	1297.08	1134.38	1019.48	934.44	869.29	818.04	776.88	743.29
65000	5737.24	3021.98	2120.33	1672.08	1405.17	1228.91	1104.44	1012.31	941.73	886.21	841.62	805.23
70000	6178.56	3254.43	2283.44	1800.70	1513.26	1323.44	1189.39	1090.18	1014.17	954.38	906.36	867.17
75000	6619.89	3486.89	2446.54	1929.33	1621.35	1417.98	1274.35	1168.05	1086.61	1022.55	971.10	929.11
80000	7061.21	3719.35	2609.64	2057.95	1729.44	1512.51	1359.31	1245.92	1159.05	1090.71	1035.84	991.05
85000	7502.54	3951.81	2772.74	2186.57	1837.53	1607.04	1444.26	1323.79	1231.49	1158.88	1100.58	1052.99
90000	7943.86	4184.27	2935.85	2315.19	1945.62	1701.57	1529.22	1401.66	1303.93	1227.05	1165.32	1114.93
95000	8385.19	4416.73	3098.95	2443.81	2053.71	1796.10	1614.18	1479.53	1376.37	1295.22	1230.06	1176.87
100000	8826.51	4649.19	3262.05	2572.43	2161.80	1890.63	1699.13	1557.40	1448.81	1363.39	1294.80	1238.81

Table 1

MONTHLY

PAYMENT REQUIRED TO AMORTIZE A LOAN

10.75%

10%

TERM AMOUNT	13 YEARS	14 YEARS	15 YEARS	16 YEARS	17 YEARS	18 YEARS	19 YEARS	20 YEARS	25 YEARS	30 YEARS	35 YEARS	40 YEARS
50	.60	.58	.57	.55	.54	.53	.52	.51	.49	.47	.46	.46
100	1.20	1.16	1.13	1.10	1.07	1.05	1.04	1.02	.97	.94	.92	.91
200	2.39	2.31	2.25	2.19	2.14	2.10	2.07	2.04	1.93	1.87	1.84	1.82
300	3.58	3.47	3.37	3.28	3.21	3.15	3.10	3.05	2.89	2.81	2.76	2.73
400	4.77	4.62	4.49	4.38	4.28	4.20	4.13	4.07	3.85	3.74	3.68	3.64
500	5.97	5.77	5.61	5.47	5.35	5.25	5.16	5.08	4.82	4.67	4.59	4.55
600	7.16	6.93	6.73	6.56	6.42	6.30	6.19	6.10	5.78	5.61	5.51	5.46
700	8.35	8.08	7.85	7.66	7.49	7.35	7.22	7.11	6.74	6.54	6.43	6.36
800	9.54	9.23	8.97	8.75	8.56	8.39	8.25	8.13	7.70	7.47	7.35	7.27
900	10.74	10.39	10.09	9.84	9.63	9.44	9.28	9.14	8.66	8.41	8.26	8.18
1000	11.93	11.54	11.21	10.94	10.70	10.49	10.31	10.16	9.63	9.34	9.18	9.09
2000	23.85	23.08	22.42	21.87	21.39	20.98	20.62	20.31	19.25	18.67	18.36	18.17
3000	35.78	34.62	33.63	32.80	32.08	31.46	30.93	30.46	28.87	28.01	27.53	27.26
4000	47.70	46.15	44.84	43.73	42.77	41.95	41.23	40.61	38.49	37.34	36.71	36.34
5000	59.63	57.69	56.05	54.66	53.46	52.43	51.54	50.77	48.11	46.68	45.88	45.42
6000	71.55	69.23	67.26	65.59	64.16	62.92	61.85	60.92	57.73	56.01	55.06	54.51
7000	83.48	80.76	78.47	76.52	74.85	73.41	72.16	71.07	67.35	65.35	64.23	63.59
8000	95.40	92.30	89.68	87.45	85.54	83.89	82.46	81.22	76.97	74.68	73.41	72.68
9000	107.33	103.84	100.89	98.38	96.23	94.38	92.77	91.38	86.59	84.02	82.58	81.76
10000	119.25	115.37	112.10	109.31	106.92	104.86	103.08	101.53	96.21	93.35	91.76	90.84
11000	131.18	126.91	123.31	120.24	117.61	115.35	113.39	111.68	105.84	102.69	100.93	99.93
12000	143.10	138.45	134.52	131.17	128.31	125.84	123.69	121.83	115.46	112.02	110.11	109.01
13000	155.03	149.99	145.73	142.10	139.00	136.32	134.00	131.98	125.08	121.36	119.28	118.10
14000	166.95	161.52	156.94	153.03	149.69	146.81	144.31	142.14	134.70	130.69	128.46	127.18
15000	178.88	173.06	168.15	163.97	160.38	157.29	154.62	152.29	144.32	140.03	137.63	136.26
16000	190.80	184.60	179.36	174.90	171.07	167.78	164.92	162.44	153.94	149.36	146.81	145.35
17000	202.72	196.13	190.57	185.83	181.77	178.26	175.23	172.59	163.56	158.70	155.98	154.43
18000	214.65	207.67	201.78	196.76	192.46	188.75	185.54	182.75	173.18	168.03	165.16	163.52
19000	226.57	219.21	212.99	207.69	203.15	199.24	195.85	192.90	182.80	177.37	174.33	172.60
20000	238.50	230.74	224.19	218.62	213.84	209.72	206.15	203.05	192.42	186.70	183.51	181.68
21000	250.42	242.28	235.40	229.55	224.53	220.21	216.46	213.20	202.04	196.04	192.68	190.77
22000	262.35	253.82	246.61	240.48	235.22	230.69	226.77	223.36	211.67	205.37	201.86	199.85
23000	274.27	265.36	257.82	251.41	245.92	241.18	237.08	233.51	221.29	214.71	211.03	208.94
24000	286.20	276.89	269.03	262.34	256.61	251.67	247.38	243.66	230.91	224.04	220.21	218.02
25000	298.12	288.43	280.24	273.27	267.30	262.15	257.69	253.81	240.53	233.38	229.38	227.10
26000	310.05	299.97	291.45	284.20	277.99	272.64	268.00	263.96	250.15	242.71	238.56	236.19
27000	321.97	311.50	302.66	295.13	288.68	283.12	278.31	274.12	259.77	252.04	247.73	245.27
28000	333.90	323.04	313.87	306.06	299.37	293.61	288.61	284.27	269.39	261.38	256.91	254.36
29000	345.82	334.58	325.08	317.00	310.07	304.09	298.92	294.42	279.01	270.71	266.08	263.44
30000	357.75	346.11	336.29	327.93	320.76	314.58	309.23	304.57	288.63	280.05	275.26	272.52
31000	369.67	357.65	347.50	338.86	331.45	325.07	319.54	314.73	298.25	289.38	284.43	281.61
32000	381.59	369.19	358.71	349.79	342.14	335.55	329.84	324.88	307.87	298.72	293.61	290.69
33000	393.52	380.72	369.92	360.72	352.83	346.04	340.15	335.03	317.50	308.05	302.78	299.78
34000	405.44	392.26	381.13	371.65	363.53	356.52	350.46	345.18	327.12	317.39	311.96	308.86
35000	417.37	403.80	392.34	382.58	374.22	367.01	360.77	355.34	336.74	326.72	321.13	317.94
36000	429.29	415.34	403.55	393.51	384.91	377.50	371.07	365.49	346.36	336.06	330.31	327.03
37000	441.22	426.87	414.76	404.44	395.60	387.98	381.38	375.64	355.98	345.39	339.48	336.11
38000	453.14	438.41	425.97	415.37	406.29	398.47	391.69	385.79	365.60	354.73	348.66	345.20
39000	465.07	449.95	437.17	426.30	416.98	408.95	402.00	395.94	375.22	364.06	357.83	354.28
40000	476.99	461.48	448.38	437.23	427.68	419.44	412.30	406.10	384.84	373.40	367.01	363.36
41000	488.92	473.02	459.59	448.16	438.37	429.92	422.61	416.25	394.46	382.73	376.18	372.45
42000	500.84	484.56	470.80	459.09	449.06	440.41	432.92	426.40	404.08	392.07	385.36	381.53
43000	512.77	496.09	482.01	470.03	459.75	450.90	443.23	436.55	413.70	401.40	394.53	390.62
44000	524.69	507.63	493.22	480.96	470.44	461.38	453.53	446.71	423.33	410.74	403.71	399.70
45000	536.62	519.17	504.43	491.89	481.14	471.87	463.84	456.86	432.95	420.07	412.88	408.78
46000	548.54	530.71	515.64	502.82	491.83	482.35	474.15	467.01	442.57	429.41	422.06	417.87
47000	560.47	542.24	526.85	513.75	502.52	492.84	484.46	477.16	452.19	438.74	431.23	426.95
48000	572.39	553.78	538.06	524.68	513.21	503.33	494.76	487.31	461.81	448.08	440.41	436.04
49000	584.31	565.32	549.27	535.61	523.90	513.81	505.07	497.47	471.43	457.41	449.58	445.12
50000	596.24	576.85	560.48	546.54	534.59	524.30	515.38	507.62	481.05	466.75	458.76	454.20
55000	655.86	634.54	616.53	601.19	588.05	576.73	566.92	558.38	529.16	513.42	504.63	499.62
60000	715.49	692.22	672.57	655.85	641.51	629.16	618.45	609.14	577.26	560.09	550.51	545.04
65000	775.11	749.91	728.62	710.50	694.97	681.59	669.99	659.90	625.37	606.77	596.38	590.46
70000	834.73	807.59	784.67	765.15	748.43	734.01	721.53	710.67	673.47	653.44	642.26	635.88
75000	894.36	865.28	840.72	819.81	801.89	786.44	773.07	761.43	721.57	700.12	688.13	681.30
80000	953.98	922.96	896.76	874.46	855.35	838.87	824.60	812.19	769.68	746.79	734.01	726.72
85000	1013.60	980.65	952.81	929.11	908.81	891.30	876.14	862.95	817.78	793.46	779.88	772.14
90000	1073.23	1038.33	1008.86	983.77	962.27	943.73	927.68	913.71	865.89	840.14	825.76	817.56
95000	1132.85	1096.02	1064.91	1038.42	1015.72	996.16	979.21	964.47	913.99	886.81	871.63	862.98
100000	1192.47	1153.70	1120.95	1093.07	1069.18	1048.59	1030.75	1015.23	962.10	933.49	917.51	908.40

Table 1

11.00% MONTHLY

PAYMENT REQUIRED TO AMORTIZE A LOAN

TERM	1 YEAR	2 YEARS	3 YEARS	4 YEARS	5 YEARS	6 YEARS	7 YEARS	8 YEARS	9 YEARS	10 YEARS	11 YEARS	12 YEARS
AMOUNT												
50	4.42	2.34	1.64	1.30	1.09	.96	.86	.79	.74	.69	.66	.63
100	8.84	4.67	3.28	2.59	2.18	1.91	1.72	1.58	1.47	1.38	1.31	1.26
200	17.68	9.33	6.55	5.17	4.35	3.81	3.43	3.15	2.93	2.76	2.62	2.51
300	26.52	13.99	9.83	7.76	6.53	5.72	5.14	4.72	4.39	4.14	3.93	3.77
400	35.36	18.65	13.10	10.34	8.70	7.62	6.85	6.29	5.86	5.52	5.24	5.02
500	44.20	23.31	16.37	12.93	10.88	9.52	8.57	7.86	7.32	6.89	6.55	6.27
600	53.03	27.97	19.65	15.51	13.05	11.43	10.28	9.43	8.78	8.27	7.86	7.53
700	61.87	32.63	22.92	18.10	15.22	13.33	11.99	11.00	10.24	9.65	9.17	8.78
800	70.71	37.29	26.20	20.68	17.40	15.23	13.70	12.57	11.70	11.03	10.48	10.03
900	79.55	41.95	29.47	23.27	19.57	17.14	15.42	14.14	13.17	12.40	11.79	11.29
1000	88.39	46.61	32.74	25.85	21.75	19.04	17.13	15.71	14.63	13.78	13.10	12.54
2000	176.77	93.22	65.48	51.70	43.49	38.07	34.25	31.42	29.26	27.56	26.19	25.08
3000	265.15	139.83	98.22	77.54	65.23	57.11	51.37	47.13	43.88	41.33	39.28	37.61
4000	353.53	186.44	130.96	103.39	86.97	76.14	68.49	62.84	58.51	55.11	52.37	50.15
5000	441.91	233.04	163.70	129.23	108.72	95.18	85.62	78.55	73.13	68.88	65.47	62.68
6000	530.29	279.65	196.44	155.08	130.46	114.21	102.74	94.26	87.76	82.66	78.56	75.22
7000	618.68	326.26	229.18	180.92	152.20	133.24	119.86	109.96	102.39	96.43	91.65	87.75
8000	707.06	372.87	261.91	206.77	173.94	152.28	136.98	125.67	117.01	110.21	104.74	100.29
9000	795.44	419.48	294.65	232.61	195.69	171.31	154.11	141.38	131.64	123.98	117.84	112.82
10000	883.82	466.08	327.39	258.46	217.43	190.35	171.23	157.09	146.26	137.76	130.93	125.36
11000	972.20	512.69	360.13	284.31	239.17	209.38	188.35	172.80	160.89	151.53	144.02	137.90
12000	1060.58	559.30	392.87	310.15	260.91	228.41	205.47	188.51	175.52	165.31	157.11	150.43
13000	1148.97	605.91	425.61	336.00	282.66	247.45	222.60	204.21	190.14	179.08	170.21	162.97
14000	1237.35	652.51	458.35	361.84	304.40	266.48	239.72	219.92	204.77	192.86	183.30	175.50
15000	1325.73	699.12	491.09	387.69	326.14	285.52	256.84	235.63	219.39	206.63	196.39	188.04
16000	1414.11	745.73	523.82	413.53	347.88	304.55	273.96	251.34	234.02	220.41	209.48	200.57
17000	1502.49	792.34	556.56	439.38	369.63	323.58	291.09	267.05	248.64	234.18	222.57	213.11
18000	1590.87	838.95	589.30	465.22	391.37	342.62	308.21	282.76	263.27	247.96	235.67	225.64
19000	1679.26	885.55	622.04	491.07	413.11	361.65	325.33	298.47	277.90	261.73	248.76	238.18
20000	1767.64	932.16	654.78	516.92	434.85	380.69	342.45	314.17	292.52	275.51	261.85	250.72
21000	1856.02	978.77	687.52	542.76	456.60	399.72	359.58	329.88	307.15	289.28	274.94	263.25
22000	1944.40	1025.38	720.26	568.61	478.34	418.75	376.70	345.59	321.77	303.06	288.04	275.79
23000	2032.78	1071.99	753.00	594.45	500.08	437.79	393.82	361.30	336.40	316.83	301.13	288.32
24000	2121.16	1118.59	785.73	620.30	521.82	456.82	410.94	377.01	351.03	330.61	314.22	300.86
25000	2209.55	1165.20	818.47	646.14	543.57	475.86	428.07	392.72	365.65	344.38	327.31	313.39
26000	2297.93	1211.81	851.21	671.99	565.31	494.89	445.19	408.42	380.28	358.16	340.41	325.93
27000	2386.31	1258.42	883.95	697.83	587.05	513.93	462.31	424.13	394.90	371.93	353.50	338.46
28000	2474.69	1305.02	916.69	723.68	608.79	532.96	479.43	439.84	409.53	385.71	366.59	351.00
29000	2563.07	1351.63	949.43	749.53	630.54	551.99	496.56	455.55	424.15	399.48	379.68	363.54
30000	2651.45	1398.24	982.17	775.37	652.28	571.03	513.68	471.26	438.78	413.26	392.78	376.07
31000	2739.84	1444.85	1014.91	801.22	674.02	590.06	530.80	486.97	453.41	427.03	405.87	388.61
32000	2828.22	1491.46	1047.64	827.06	695.76	609.10	547.92	502.67	468.03	440.81	418.96	401.14
33000	2916.60	1538.06	1080.38	852.91	717.50	628.13	565.05	518.38	482.66	454.58	432.05	413.68
34000	3004.98	1584.67	1113.12	878.75	739.25	647.16	582.17	534.09	497.28	468.36	445.14	426.21
35000	3093.36	1631.28	1145.86	904.60	760.99	666.20	599.29	549.80	511.91	482.13	458.24	438.75
36000	3181.74	1677.89	1178.60	930.44	782.73	685.23	616.41	565.51	526.54	495.91	471.33	451.28
37000	3270.13	1724.50	1211.34	956.29	804.47	704.27	633.54	581.22	541.16	509.68	484.42	463.82
38000	3358.51	1771.10	1244.08	982.13	826.22	723.30	650.66	596.93	555.79	523.46	497.51	476.36
39000	3446.89	1817.71	1276.82	1007.98	847.96	742.33	667.78	612.63	570.41	537.23	510.61	488.89
40000	3535.27	1864.32	1309.55	1033.82	869.70	761.37	684.90	628.34	585.04	551.01	523.70	501.43
41000	3623.65	1910.93	1342.29	1059.67	891.44	780.40	702.02	644.05	599.67	564.78	536.79	513.96
42000	3712.03	1957.53	1375.03	1085.52	913.19	799.44	719.15	659.76	614.29	578.56	549.88	526.50
43000	3800.42	2004.14	1407.77	1111.36	934.93	818.47	736.27	675.47	628.92	592.33	562.98	539.03
44000	3888.80	2050.75	1440.51	1137.21	956.67	837.50	753.39	691.18	643.54	606.11	576.07	551.57
45000	3977.18	2097.36	1473.25	1163.05	978.41	856.54	770.51	706.88	658.17	619.88	589.16	564.10
46000	4065.56	2143.97	1505.99	1188.90	1000.16	875.57	787.64	722.59	672.79	633.66	602.25	576.64
47000	4153.94	2190.57	1538.72	1214.74	1021.90	894.61	804.76	738.30	687.42	647.43	615.35	589.18
48000	4242.32	2237.18	1571.46	1240.59	1043.64	913.64	821.88	754.01	702.05	661.21	628.44	601.71
49000	4330.71	2283.79	1604.20	1266.44	1065.38	932.67	839.00	769.72	716.67	674.98	641.53	614.25
50000	4419.09	2330.40	1636.94	1292.28	1087.13	951.71	856.13	785.43	731.30	688.76	654.62	626.78
55000	4861.00	2563.44	1800.63	1421.51	1195.84	1046.88	941.74	863.97	804.43	757.63	720.08	689.46
60000	5302.90	2796.48	1964.33	1550.74	1304.55	1142.05	1027.35	942.51	877.56	826.51	785.55	752.14
65000	5744.81	3029.51	2128.02	1679.96	1413.26	1237.22	1112.96	1021.05	950.69	895.38	851.01	814.82
70000	6186.72	3262.55	2291.72	1809.19	1521.97	1332.39	1198.58	1099.59	1023.82	964.26	916.47	877.49
75000	6628.63	3495.59	2455.41	1938.42	1630.69	1427.56	1284.19	1178.14	1096.94	1033.13	981.93	940.17
80000	7070.54	3728.63	2619.10	2067.65	1739.40	1522.73	1369.80	1256.68	1170.07	1102.01	1047.39	1002.85
85000	7512.45	3961.67	2782.80	2196.87	1848.11	1617.90	1455.41	1335.22	1243.20	1170.88	1112.85	1065.53
90000	7954.35	4194.71	2946.49	2326.10	1956.82	1713.07	1541.02	1413.76	1316.33	1239.76	1178.32	1128.20
95000	8396.26	4427.75	3110.18	2455.33	2065.54	1808.24	1626.64	1492.31	1389.46	1308.63	1243.78	1190.88
100000	8838.17	4660.79	3273.88	2584.56	2174.25	1903.41	1712.25	1570.85	1462.59	1377.51	1309.24	1253.56

Table 1

MONTHLY   11.00%

PAYMENT REQUIRED TO AMORTIZE A LOAN

TERM ÒUNT	13 YEARS	14 YEARS	15 YEARS	16 YEARS	17 YEARS	18 YEARS	19 YEARS	20 YEARS	25 YEARS	30 YEARS	35 YEARS	40 YEARS
50	.61	.59	.57	.56	.55	.54	.53	.52	.50	.48	.47	.47
100	1.21	1.17	1.14	1.11	1.09	1.07	1.05	1.04	.99	.96	.94	.93
200	2.42	2.34	2.28	2.22	2.18	2.14	2.10	2.07	1.97	1.91	1.88	1.86
300	3.63	3.51	3.41	3.33	3.26	3.20	3.15	3.10	2.95	2.86	2.82	2.79
400	4.84	4.68	4.55	4.44	4.35	4.27	4.19	4.13	3.93	3.81	3.75	3.72
500	6.04	5.85	5.69	5.55	5.43	5.33	5.24	5.17	4.91	4.77	4.69	4.65
600	7.25	7.02	6.82	6.66	6.52	6.40	6.29	6.20	5.89	5.72	5.63	5.57
700	8.46	8.19	7.96	7.77	7.60	7.46	7.34	7.23	6.87	6.67	6.56	6.50
800	9.67	9.36	9.10	8.88	8.69	8.53	8.38	8.26	7.85	7.62	7.50	7.43
900	10.87	10.53	10.23	9.99	9.77	9.59	9.43	9.29	8.83	8.58	8.44	8.36
1000	12.08	11.70	11.37	11.10	10.86	10.66	10.48	10.33	9.81	9.53	9.37	9.29
2000	24.16	23.39	22.74	22.19	21.71	21.31	20.95	20.65	19.61	19.05	18.74	18.57
3000	36.23	35.08	34.10	33.28	32.57	31.96	31.43	30.97	29.41	28.57	28.11	27.85
4000	48.31	46.77	45.47	44.37	43.42	42.61	41.90	41.29	39.21	38.10	37.48	37.14
5000	60.38	58.46	56.83	55.46	54.27	53.26	52.38	51.61	49.01	47.62	46.85	46.42
6000	72.46	70.15	68.20	66.55	65.13	63.91	62.85	61.94	58.81	57.14	56.22	55.70
7000	84.53	81.84	79.57	77.64	75.98	74.56	73.33	72.26	68.61	66.67	65.59	64.99
8000	96.61	93.53	90.93	88.73	86.84	85.21	83.80	82.58	78.41	76.19	74.96	74.27
9000	108.68	105.22	102.30	99.82	97.69	95.86	94.28	92.90	88.22	85.71	84.33	83.55
10000	120.76	116.91	113.66	110.91	108.54	106.51	104.75	103.22	98.02	95.24	93.70	92.83
11000	132.83	128.60	125.03	122.00	119.40	117.16	115.23	113.55	107.82	104.76	103.07	102.12
12000	144.91	140.29	136.40	133.09	130.25	127.81	125.70	123.87	117.62	114.28	112.44	111.40
13000	156.98	151.98	147.76	144.18	141.10	138.46	136.18	134.19	127.42	123.81	121.81	120.68
14000	169.06	163.67	159.13	155.27	151.96	149.11	146.65	144.51	137.22	133.33	131.18	129.97
15000	181.13	175.36	170.49	166.36	162.81	159.76	157.12	154.83	147.02	142.85	140.55	139.25
16000	193.21	187.05	181.86	177.45	173.67	170.41	167.60	165.16	156.82	152.38	149.92	148.53
17000	205.28	198.74	193.23	188.54	184.52	181.06	178.07	175.48	166.62	161.90	159.29	157.82
18000	217.36	210.43	204.59	199.63	195.37	191.71	188.55	185.80	176.43	171.42	168.66	167.10
19000	229.44	222.13	215.96	210.72	206.23	202.36	199.02	196.12	186.23	180.95	178.03	176.38
20000	241.51	233.82	227.32	221.81	217.08	213.01	209.50	206.44	196.03	190.47	187.40	185.66
21000	253.59	245.51	238.69	232.90	227.93	223.67	219.97	216.76	205.83	199.99	196.77	194.95
22000	265.66	257.20	250.06	243.99	238.79	234.32	230.45	227.09	215.63	209.52	206.14	204.23
23000	277.74	268.89	261.42	255.08	249.64	244.97	240.92	237.41	225.43	219.04	215.51	213.51
24000	289.81	280.58	272.79	266.17	260.50	255.62	251.40	247.73	235.23	228.56	224.87	222.80
25000	301.89	292.27	284.15	277.26	271.35	266.27	261.87	258.05	245.03	238.09	234.24	232.08
26000	313.96	303.96	295.52	288.35	282.20	276.92	272.35	268.37	254.83	247.61	243.61	241.36
27000	326.04	315.65	306.89	299.44	293.06	287.57	282.82	278.70	264.64	257.13	252.98	250.64
28000	338.11	327.34	318.25	310.53	303.91	298.22	293.29	289.02	274.44	266.66	262.35	259.93
29000	350.19	339.03	329.62	321.62	314.77	308.87	303.77	299.34	284.24	276.18	271.72	269.21
30000	362.26	350.72	340.98	332.71	325.62	319.52	314.24	309.66	294.04	285.70	281.09	278.49
31000	374.34	362.41	352.35	343.80	336.47	330.17	324.72	319.98	303.84	295.23	290.46	287.78
32000	386.41	374.10	363.72	354.89	347.33	340.82	335.19	330.31	313.64	304.75	299.83	297.06
33000	398.49	385.79	375.08	365.98	358.18	351.47	345.67	340.63	323.44	314.27	309.20	306.34
34000	410.56	397.48	386.45	377.07	369.03	362.12	356.14	350.95	333.24	323.79	318.57	315.63
35000	422.64	409.17	397.81	388.16	379.89	372.77	366.62	361.27	343.04	333.32	327.94	324.91
36000	434.71	420.86	409.18	399.25	390.74	383.42	377.09	371.59	352.85	342.84	337.31	334.19
37000	446.79	432.56	420.55	410.34	401.60	394.07	387.57	381.91	362.65	352.36	346.68	343.47
38000	458.87	444.25	431.91	421.43	412.45	404.72	398.04	392.24	372.45	361.89	356.05	352.76
39000	470.94	455.94	443.28	432.52	423.30	415.37	408.52	402.56	382.25	371.41	365.42	362.04
40000	483.02	467.63	454.64	443.61	434.16	426.02	418.99	412.88	392.05	380.93	374.79	371.32
41000	495.09	479.32	466.01	454.70	445.01	436.68	429.47	423.20	401.85	390.46	384.16	380.61
42000	507.17	491.01	477.38	465.79	455.86	447.33	439.94	433.52	411.65	399.98	393.53	389.89
43000	519.24	502.70	488.74	476.88	466.72	457.98	450.41	443.85	421.45	409.50	402.90	399.17
44000	531.32	514.39	500.11	487.97	477.57	468.63	460.89	454.17	431.25	419.03	412.27	408.45
45000	543.39	526.08	511.47	499.06	488.43	479.28	471.36	464.49	441.06	428.55	421.64	417.74
46000	555.47	537.77	522.84	510.15	499.28	489.93	481.84	474.81	450.86	438.07	431.01	427.02
47000	567.54	549.46	534.21	521.24	510.13	500.58	492.31	485.13	460.66	447.60	440.38	436.30
48000	579.62	561.15	545.57	532.33	520.99	511.23	502.79	495.46	470.46	457.12	449.74	445.59
49000	591.69	572.84	556.94	543.42	531.84	521.88	513.26	505.78	480.26	466.64	459.11	454.87
50000	603.77	584.53	568.30	554.51	542.70	532.53	523.74	516.10	490.06	476.17	468.48	464.15
55000	664.15	642.98	625.13	609.96	596.96	585.78	576.11	567.71	539.07	523.78	515.33	510.57
60000	724.52	701.44	681.96	665.41	651.23	639.03	628.48	619.32	588.07	571.40	562.18	556.98
65000	784.90	759.89	738.79	720.86	705.50	692.29	680.86	670.93	637.08	619.02	609.03	603.40
70000	845.27	818.34	795.62	776.31	759.77	745.54	733.23	722.54	686.08	666.63	655.88	649.81
75000	905.65	876.80	852.45	831.76	814.04	798.79	785.60	774.15	735.09	714.25	702.72	696.23
80000	966.03	935.25	909.28	887.21	868.31	852.04	837.98	825.76	784.10	761.86	749.57	742.64
85000	1026.40	993.70	966.11	942.66	922.58	905.30	890.35	877.37	833.10	809.48	796.42	789.06
90000	1086.78	1052.15	1022.94	998.11	976.85	958.55	942.72	928.97	882.11	857.10	843.27	835.47
95000	1147.16	1110.61	1079.77	1053.56	1031.12	1011.80	995.10	980.58	931.11	904.71	890.11	881.88
100000	1207.53	1169.06	1136.60	1109.01	1085.39	1065.05	1047.47	1032.19	980.12	952.33	936.96	928.30

11%

Table 1

11.25%

MONTHLY
PAYMENT REQUIRED TO AMORTIZE A LOAN

TERM / AMOUNT	1 YEAR	2 YEARS	3 YEARS	4 YEARS	5 YEARS	6 YEARS	7 YEARS	8 YEARS	9 YEARS	10 YEARS	11 YEARS	12 YEARS
50	4.43	2.34	1.65	1.30	1.10	.96	.87	.80	.74	.70	.67	.64
100	8.85	4.68	3.29	2.60	2.19	1.92	1.73	1.59	1.48	1.40	1.33	1.27
200	17.70	9.35	6.58	5.20	4.38	3.84	3.46	3.17	2.96	2.79	2.65	2.54
300	26.55	14.02	9.86	7.80	6.57	5.75	5.18	4.76	4.43	4.18	3.98	3.81
400	35.40	18.69	13.15	10.39	8.75	7.67	6.91	6.34	5.91	5.57	5.30	5.08
500	44.25	23.37	16.43	12.99	10.94	9.59	8.63	7.93	7.39	6.96	6.62	6.35
600	53.10	28.04	19.72	15.59	13.13	11.50	10.36	9.51	8.86	8.36	7.95	7.62
700	61.95	32.71	23.01	18.18	15.31	13.42	12.08	11.10	10.34	9.75	9.27	8.88
800	70.80	37.38	26.29	20.78	17.50	15.33	13.81	12.68	11.82	11.14	10.60	10.15
900	79.65	42.06	29.58	23.38	19.69	17.25	15.53	14.26	13.29	12.53	11.92	11.42
1000	88.50	46.73	32.86	25.97	21.87	19.17	17.26	15.85	14.77	13.92	13.24	12.69
2000	177.00	93.45	65.72	51.94	43.74	38.33	34.51	31.69	29.53	27.84	26.48	25.37
3000	265.50	140.18	98.58	77.91	65.61	57.49	51.77	47.54	44.30	41.76	39.72	38.06
4000	354.00	186.90	131.43	103.87	87.47	76.65	69.02	63.38	59.06	55.67	52.96	50.74
5000	442.50	233.62	164.29	129.84	109.34	95.82	86.28	79.22	73.83	69.59	66.19	63.42
6000	530.99	280.35	197.15	155.81	131.21	114.98	103.53	95.07	88.59	83.51	79.43	76.11
7000	619.49	327.07	230.01	181.77	153.08	134.14	120.78	110.91	103.36	97.42	92.67	88.79
8000	707.99	373.80	262.86	207.74	174.94	153.30	138.04	126.75	118.12	111.34	105.91	101.48
9000	796.49	420.52	295.72	233.71	196.81	172.47	155.29	142.60	132.88	125.26	119.14	114.16
10000	884.99	467.24	328.58	259.68	218.68	191.63	172.55	158.44	147.65	139.17	132.38	126.84
11000	973.49	513.97	361.43	285.64	240.55	210.79	189.80	174.28	162.41	153.09	145.62	139.53
12000	1061.98	560.69	394.29	311.61	262.41	229.95	207.06	190.13	177.18	167.01	158.86	152.21
13000	1150.48	607.42	427.15	337.58	284.28	249.12	224.31	205.97	191.94	180.92	172.09	164.90
14000	1238.98	654.14	460.01	363.54	306.15	268.28	241.56	221.82	206.71	194.84	185.33	177.58
15000	1327.48	700.86	492.86	389.51	328.01	287.44	258.82	237.66	221.47	208.76	198.57	190.26
16000	1415.98	747.59	525.72	415.48	349.88	306.60	276.07	253.50	236.24	222.68	211.81	202.95
17000	1504.48	794.31	558.58	441.45	371.75	325.77	293.33	269.35	251.00	236.59	225.04	215.63
18000	1592.97	841.04	591.44	467.41	393.62	344.93	310.58	285.19	265.76	250.51	238.28	228.32
19000	1681.47	887.76	624.29	493.38	415.48	364.09	327.83	301.03	280.53	264.43	251.52	241.00
20000	1769.97	934.48	657.15	519.35	437.35	383.25	345.09	316.88	295.29	278.34	264.76	253.68
21000	1858.47	981.21	690.01	545.31	459.22	402.41	362.34	332.72	310.06	292.26	277.99	266.37
22000	1946.97	1027.93	722.86	571.28	481.09	421.58	379.60	348.56	324.82	306.18	291.23	279.05
23000	2035.47	1074.66	755.72	597.25	502.95	440.74	396.85	364.41	339.59	320.09	304.47	291.74
24000	2123.96	1121.38	788.58	623.22	524.82	459.90	414.11	380.25	354.35	334.01	317.71	304.42
25000	2212.46	1168.10	821.44	649.18	546.69	479.06	431.36	396.09	369.12	347.93	330.94	317.10
26000	2300.96	1214.83	854.29	675.15	568.56	498.23	448.61	411.94	383.88	361.84	344.18	329.79
27000	2389.46	1261.55	887.15	701.12	590.42	517.39	465.87	427.78	398.64	375.76	357.42	342.47
28000	2477.96	1308.28	920.01	727.08	612.29	536.55	483.12	443.63	413.41	389.68	370.66	355.16
29000	2566.46	1355.00	952.86	753.05	634.16	555.71	500.38	459.47	428.17	403.59	383.89	367.84
30000	2654.95	1401.72	985.72	779.02	656.02	574.88	517.63	475.31	442.94	417.51	397.13	380.52
31000	2743.45	1448.45	1018.58	804.99	677.89	594.04	534.88	491.16	457.70	431.43	410.37	393.21
32000	2831.95	1495.17	1051.44	830.95	699.76	613.20	552.14	507.00	472.47	445.35	423.61	405.89
33000	2920.45	1541.90	1084.29	856.92	721.63	632.36	569.39	522.84	487.23	459.26	436.84	418.57
34000	3008.95	1588.62	1117.15	882.89	743.49	651.53	586.65	538.69	502.00	473.18	450.08	431.26
35000	3097.45	1635.34	1150.01	908.85	765.36	670.69	603.90	554.53	516.76	487.10	463.32	443.94
36000	3185.94	1682.07	1182.87	934.82	787.23	689.85	621.16	570.37	531.52	501.01	476.56	456.63
37000	3274.44	1728.79	1215.72	960.79	809.10	709.01	638.41	586.22	546.29	514.93	489.79	469.31
38000	3362.94	1775.52	1248.58	986.75	830.96	728.18	655.66	602.06	561.05	528.85	503.03	481.99
39000	3451.44	1822.24	1281.44	1012.72	852.83	747.34	672.92	617.90	575.82	542.76	516.27	494.68
40000	3539.94	1868.96	1314.29	1038.69	874.70	766.50	690.17	633.75	590.58	556.68	529.51	507.36
41000	3628.44	1915.69	1347.15	1064.66	896.56	785.66	707.43	649.59	605.35	570.60	542.74	520.05
42000	3716.93	1962.41	1380.01	1090.62	918.43	804.82	724.68	665.44	620.11	584.51	555.98	532.73
43000	3805.43	2009.14	1412.87	1116.59	940.30	823.99	741.93	681.28	634.87	598.43	569.22	545.41
44000	3893.93	2055.86	1445.72	1142.56	962.17	843.15	759.19	697.12	649.64	612.35	582.46	558.10
45000	3982.43	2102.58	1478.58	1168.52	984.03	862.31	776.44	712.97	664.40	626.27	595.69	570.78
46000	4070.93	2149.31	1511.44	1194.49	1005.90	881.47	793.70	728.81	679.17	640.18	608.93	583.47
47000	4159.43	2196.03	1544.30	1220.46	1027.77	900.64	810.95	744.65	693.93	654.10	622.17	596.15
48000	4247.92	2242.76	1577.15	1246.43	1049.64	919.80	828.21	760.50	708.70	668.02	635.41	608.83
49000	4336.42	2289.48	1610.01	1272.39	1071.50	938.96	845.46	776.34	723.46	681.93	648.64	621.52
50000	4424.92	2336.20	1642.87	1298.36	1093.37	958.12	862.71	792.18	738.23	695.85	661.88	634.20
55000	4867.41	2569.82	1807.15	1428.20	1202.71	1053.94	948.98	871.40	812.05	765.43	728.07	697.62
60000	5309.90	2803.44	1971.44	1558.03	1312.04	1149.75	1035.26	950.62	885.87	835.02	794.26	761.04
65000	5752.40	3037.06	2135.73	1687.87	1421.38	1245.56	1121.53	1029.84	959.69	904.60	860.44	824.46
70000	6194.89	3270.68	2300.01	1817.70	1530.72	1341.37	1207.80	1109.06	1033.51	974.19	926.63	887.88
75000	6637.38	3504.30	2464.30	1947.54	1640.05	1437.18	1294.07	1188.27	1107.34	1043.77	992.82	951.30
80000	7079.87	3737.92	2628.58	2077.37	1749.39	1532.99	1380.34	1267.49	1181.16	1113.36	1059.01	1014.72
85000	7522.36	3971.54	2792.87	2207.21	1858.73	1628.81	1466.61	1346.71	1254.98	1182.94	1125.19	1078.14
90000	7964.85	4205.16	2957.16	2337.04	1968.06	1724.62	1552.88	1425.93	1328.80	1252.53	1191.38	1141.56
95000	8407.35	4438.78	3121.44	2466.88	2077.40	1820.43	1639.15	1505.15	1402.62	1322.11	1257.57	1204.98
100000	8849.84	4672.40	3285.73	2596.71	2186.74	1916.24	1725.42	1584.36	1476.45	1391.69	1323.76	1268.40

Table 1

MONTHLY 11.25%

PAYMENT REQUIRED TO AMORTIZE A LOAN

TERM	13 YEARS	14 YEARS	15 YEARS	16 YEARS	17 YEARS	18 YEARS	19 YEARS	20 YEARS	25 YEARS	30 YEARS	35 YEARS	40 YEARS
OUNT												
50	.62	.60	.58	.57	.56	.55	.54	.53	.50	.49	.48	.48
100	1.23	1.19	1.16	1.13	1.11	1.09	1.07	1.05	1.00	.98	.96	.95
200	2.45	2.37	2.31	2.26	2.21	2.17	2.13	2.10	2.00	1.95	1.92	1.90
300	3.67	3.56	3.46	3.38	3.31	3.25	3.20	3.15	3.00	2.92	2.87	2.85
400	4.90	4.74	4.61	4.51	4.41	4.33	4.26	4.20	4.00	3.89	3.83	3.80
500	6.12	5.93	5.77	5.63	5.51	5.41	5.33	5.25	5.00	4.86	4.79	4.75
600	7.34	7.11	6.92	6.76	6.62	6.49	6.39	6.30	5.99	5.83	5.74	5.69
700	8.56	8.30	8.07	7.88	7.72	7.58	7.46	7.35	6.99	6.80	6.70	6.64
800	9.79	9.48	9.22	9.01	8.82	8.66	8.52	8.40	7.99	7.78	7.66	7.59
900	11.01	10.67	10.38	10.13	9.92	9.74	9.58	9.45	8.99	8.75	8.61	8.54
1000	12.23	11.85	11.53	11.26	11.02	10.82	10.65	10.50	9.99	9.72	9.57	9.49
2000	24.46	23.70	23.05	22.51	22.04	21.64	21.29	20.99	19.97	19.43	19.13	18.97
3000	36.69	35.54	34.58	33.76	33.06	32.45	31.93	31.48	29.95	29.14	28.70	28.45
4000	48.91	47.39	46.10	45.01	44.07	43.27	42.58	41.98	39.93	38.86	38.26	37.94
5000	61.14	59.23	57.62	56.26	55.09	54.09	53.22	52.47	49.92	48.57	47.83	47.42
6000	73.37	71.08	69.15	67.51	66.11	64.90	63.86	62.96	59.90	58.28	57.39	56.90
7000	85.59	82.92	80.67	78.76	77.12	75.72	74.51	73.45	69.88	67.99	66.96	66.38
8000	97.82	94.77	92.19	90.01	88.14	86.53	85.15	83.95	79.86	77.71	76.52	75.87
9000	110.05	106.61	103.72	101.26	99.16	97.35	95.79	94.44	89.85	87.42	86.09	85.35
10000	122.27	118.46	115.24	112.51	110.17	108.17	106.43	104.93	99.83	97.13	95.65	94.83
11000	134.50	130.30	126.76	123.76	121.19	118.98	117.08	115.42	109.81	106.84	105.22	104.31
12000	146.73	142.15	138.29	135.01	132.21	129.80	127.72	125.92	119.79	116.56	114.78	113.80
13000	158.95	153.99	149.81	146.26	143.22	140.62	138.36	136.41	129.78	126.27	124.35	123.28
14000	171.18	165.84	161.33	157.51	154.24	151.43	149.01	146.90	139.76	135.98	133.91	132.76
15000	183.41	177.68	172.86	168.76	165.26	162.25	159.65	157.39	149.74	145.69	143.48	142.24
16000	195.63	189.53	184.38	180.01	176.27	173.06	170.29	167.89	159.72	155.41	153.04	151.73
17000	207.86	201.37	195.90	191.26	187.29	183.88	180.93	178.38	169.71	165.12	162.61	161.21
18000	220.09	213.22	207.43	202.51	198.31	194.70	191.58	188.87	179.69	174.83	172.17	170.69
19000	232.31	225.06	218.95	213.76	209.33	205.51	202.22	199.36	189.67	184.54	181.74	180.17
20000	244.54	236.91	230.47	225.01	220.34	216.33	212.86	209.86	199.65	194.26	191.30	189.66
21000	256.77	248.75	242.00	236.26	231.36	227.15	223.51	220.35	209.64	203.97	200.87	199.14
22000	268.99	260.60	253.52	247.51	242.38	237.96	234.15	230.84	219.62	213.68	210.43	208.62
23000	281.22	272.44	265.04	258.76	253.39	248.78	244.79	241.33	229.60	223.40	220.00	218.10
24000	293.45	284.29	276.57	270.01	264.41	259.59	255.43	251.83	239.58	233.11	229.56	227.59
25000	305.67	296.13	288.09	281.26	275.43	270.41	266.08	262.32	249.56	242.82	239.13	237.07
26000	317.90	307.98	299.61	292.51	286.44	281.23	276.72	272.81	259.55	252.53	248.69	246.55
27000	330.13	319.82	311.14	303.76	297.46	292.04	287.36	283.30	269.53	262.25	258.26	256.03
28000	342.35	331.67	322.66	315.01	308.48	302.86	298.01	293.80	279.51	271.96	267.82	265.52
29000	354.58	343.51	334.18	326.26	319.49	313.67	308.65	304.29	289.49	281.67	277.39	275.00
30000	366.81	355.36	345.71	337.51	330.51	324.49	319.29	314.78	299.48	291.38	286.95	284.48
31000	379.03	367.20	357.23	348.77	341.53	335.31	329.93	325.27	309.46	301.10	296.52	293.96
32000	391.26	379.05	368.76	360.02	352.54	346.12	340.58	335.77	319.44	310.81	306.08	303.45
33000	403.49	390.89	380.28	371.27	363.56	356.94	351.22	346.26	329.42	320.52	315.65	312.93
34000	415.72	402.74	391.80	382.52	374.58	367.76	361.86	356.75	339.41	330.23	325.21	322.41
35000	427.94	414.58	403.33	393.77	385.60	378.57	372.51	367.24	349.39	339.95	334.78	331.90
36000	440.17	426.43	414.85	405.02	396.61	389.39	383.15	377.74	359.37	349.66	344.34	341.38
37000	452.40	438.27	426.37	416.27	407.63	400.20	393.79	388.23	369.35	359.37	353.91	350.86
38000	464.62	450.12	437.90	427.52	418.65	411.02	404.43	398.72	379.34	369.08	363.47	360.34
39000	476.85	461.96	449.42	438.77	429.66	421.84	415.08	409.21	389.32	378.80	373.04	369.83
40000	489.08	473.81	460.94	450.02	440.68	432.65	425.72	419.71	399.30	388.51	382.60	379.31
41000	501.30	485.65	472.47	461.27	451.70	443.47	436.36	430.20	409.28	398.22	392.17	388.79
42000	513.53	497.50	483.99	472.52	462.71	454.29	447.01	440.69	419.27	407.93	401.73	398.27
43000	525.76	509.34	495.51	483.77	473.73	465.10	457.65	451.19	429.25	417.65	411.30	407.76
44000	537.98	521.19	507.04	495.02	484.75	475.92	468.29	461.68	439.23	427.36	420.86	417.24
45000	550.21	533.03	518.56	506.27	495.76	486.73	478.93	472.17	449.21	437.07	430.43	426.72
46000	562.44	544.88	530.08	517.52	506.78	497.55	489.58	482.66	459.20	446.79	439.99	436.20
47000	574.66	556.72	541.61	528.77	517.80	508.37	500.22	493.16	469.18	456.50	449.56	445.69
48000	586.89	568.57	553.13	540.02	528.81	519.18	510.86	503.65	479.16	466.21	459.12	455.17
49000	599.12	580.41	564.65	551.27	539.83	530.00	521.51	514.14	489.14	475.92	468.69	464.65
50000	611.34	592.26	576.18	562.52	550.85	540.82	532.15	524.63	499.12	485.64	478.25	474.13
55000	672.48	651.48	633.79	618.77	605.93	594.90	585.36	577.10	549.04	534.20	526.08	521.55
60000	733.61	710.71	691.41	675.02	661.02	648.98	638.58	629.56	598.95	582.76	573.90	568.96
65000	794.75	769.94	749.03	731.28	716.10	703.06	691.79	682.02	648.86	631.32	621.73	616.37
70000	855.88	829.16	806.65	787.53	771.19	757.14	745.01	734.48	698.77	679.89	669.55	663.79
75000	917.01	888.39	864.26	843.78	826.27	811.22	798.22	786.95	748.68	728.45	717.38	711.20
80000	978.15	947.61	921.88	900.03	881.35	865.30	851.44	839.41	798.60	777.01	765.20	758.61
85000	1039.28	1006.84	979.50	956.28	936.44	919.38	904.65	891.87	848.51	825.58	813.02	806.02
90000	1100.41	1066.06	1037.12	1012.53	991.52	973.46	957.86	944.34	898.42	874.14	860.85	853.44
95000	1161.55	1125.29	1094.73	1068.79	1046.61	1027.54	1011.08	996.80	948.33	922.70	908.67	900.85
100000	1222.68	1184.51	1152.35	1125.04	1101.69	1081.63	1064.29	1049.26	998.24	971.27	956.50	948.26

Table 1

11.50%

MONTHLY

PAYMENT REQUIRED TO AMORTIZE A LOAN

TERM	1 YEAR	2 YEARS	3 YEARS	4 YEARS	5 YEARS	6 YEARS	7 YEARS	8 YEARS	9 YEARS	10 YEARS	11 YEARS	12 YEARS
AMOUNT												
50	4.44	2.35	1.65	1.31	1.10	.97	.87	.80	.75	.71	.67	.65
100	8.87	4.69	3.30	2.61	2.20	1.93	1.74	1.60	1.50	1.41	1.34	1.29
200	17.73	9.37	6.60	5.22	4.40	3.86	3.48	3.20	2.99	2.82	2.68	2.57
300	26.59	14.06	9.90	7.83	6.60	5.79	5.22	4.80	4.48	4.22	4.02	3.85
400	35.45	18.74	13.20	10.44	8.80	7.72	6.96	6.40	5.97	5.63	5.36	5.14
500	44.31	23.43	16.49	13.05	11.00	9.65	8.70	7.99	7.46	7.03	6.70	6.42
600	53.17	28.11	19.79	15.66	13.20	11.58	10.44	9.59	8.95	8.44	8.04	7.70
700	62.04	32.79	23.09	18.27	15.40	13.51	12.18	11.19	10.44	9.85	9.37	8.99
800	70.90	37.48	26.39	20.88	17.60	15.44	13.91	12.79	11.93	11.25	10.71	10.27
900	79.76	42.16	29.68	23.49	19.80	17.37	15.65	14.39	13.42	12.66	12.05	11.55
1000	88.62	46.85	32.98	26.09	22.00	19.30	17.39	15.98	14.91	14.06	13.39	12.84
2000	177.24	93.69	65.96	52.18	43.99	38.59	34.78	31.96	29.81	28.12	26.77	25.67
3000	265.85	140.53	98.93	78.27	65.98	57.88	52.16	47.94	44.72	42.18	40.16	38.50
4000	354.47	187.37	131.91	104.36	87.98	77.17	69.55	63.92	59.62	56.24	53.54	51.34
5000	443.08	234.21	164.89	130.45	109.97	96.46	86.94	79.90	74.52	70.30	66.92	64.17
6000	531.70	281.05	197.86	156.54	131.96	115.75	104.32	95.88	89.43	84.36	80.31	77.00
7000	620.31	327.89	230.84	182.63	153.95	135.04	121.71	111.86	104.33	98.42	93.69	89.84
8000	708.93	374.73	263.81	208.72	175.95	154.33	139.10	127.84	119.23	112.48	107.07	102.67
9000	797.54	421.57	296.79	234.81	197.94	173.63	156.48	143.82	134.14	126.54	120.46	115.50
10000	886.16	468.41	329.77	260.90	219.93	192.92	173.87	159.80	149.04	140.60	133.84	128.34
11000	974.77	515.25	362.74	286.98	241.92	212.21	191.26	175.78	163.95	154.66	147.22	141.17
12000	1063.39	562.09	395.72	313.07	263.92	231.50	208.64	191.76	178.85	168.72	160.61	154.00
13000	1152.00	608.93	428.69	339.16	285.91	250.79	226.03	207.74	193.75	182.78	173.99	166.84
14000	1240.62	655.77	461.67	365.25	307.90	270.08	243.42	223.72	208.66	196.84	187.37	179.67
15000	1329.23	702.61	494.65	391.34	329.89	289.37	260.80	239.70	223.56	210.90	200.76	192.50
16000	1417.85	749.45	527.62	417.43	351.89	308.66	278.19	255.67	238.46	224.96	214.14	205.34
17000	1506.46	796.29	560.60	443.52	373.88	327.95	295.57	271.65	253.37	239.02	227.52	218.17
18000	1595.08	843.13	593.57	469.61	395.87	347.25	312.96	287.63	268.27	253.08	240.91	231.00
19000	1683.69	889.97	626.55	495.70	417.86	366.54	330.35	303.61	283.17	267.14	254.29	243.84
20000	1772.31	936.81	659.53	521.79	439.86	385.83	347.73	319.59	298.08	281.20	267.68	256.67
21000	1860.92	983.65	692.50	547.87	461.85	405.12	365.12	335.57	312.98	295.26	281.06	269.50
22000	1949.54	1030.49	725.48	573.96	483.84	424.41	382.51	351.55	327.89	309.31	294.44	282.33
23000	2038.15	1077.33	758.45	600.05	505.83	443.70	399.89	367.53	342.79	323.37	307.83	295.17
24000	2126.77	1124.17	791.43	626.14	527.83	462.99	417.28	383.51	357.69	337.43	321.21	308.00
25000	2215.38	1171.01	824.41	652.23	549.82	482.28	434.67	399.49	372.60	351.49	334.59	320.83
26000	2304.00	1217.85	857.38	678.32	571.81	501.58	452.05	415.47	387.50	365.55	347.98	333.67
27000	2392.61	1264.69	890.36	704.41	593.81	520.87	469.44	431.45	402.40	379.61	361.36	346.50
28000	2481.23	1311.53	923.33	730.50	615.80	540.16	486.83	447.43	417.31	393.67	374.74	359.33
29000	2569.84	1358.37	956.31	756.59	637.79	559.45	504.21	463.41	432.21	407.73	388.13	372.17
30000	2658.46	1405.21	989.29	782.68	659.78	578.74	521.60	479.39	447.11	421.79	401.51	385.00
31000	2747.07	1452.05	1022.26	808.76	681.78	598.03	538.99	495.37	462.02	435.85	414.89	397.83
32000	2835.69	1498.90	1055.24	834.85	703.77	617.32	556.37	511.34	476.92	449.91	428.28	410.67
33000	2924.30	1545.74	1088.21	860.94	725.76	636.61	573.76	527.32	491.83	463.97	441.66	423.50
34000	3012.92	1592.58	1121.19	887.03	747.75	655.90	591.14	543.30	506.73	478.03	455.04	436.33
35000	3101.53	1639.42	1154.17	913.12	769.75	675.20	608.53	559.28	521.63	492.09	468.43	449.17
36000	3190.15	1686.26	1187.14	939.21	791.74	694.49	625.92	575.26	536.54	506.15	481.81	462.00
37000	3278.76	1733.10	1220.12	965.30	813.73	713.78	643.30	591.24	551.44	520.21	495.19	474.83
38000	3367.38	1779.94	1253.09	991.39	835.72	733.07	660.69	607.22	566.34	534.27	508.58	487.67
39000	3455.99	1826.78	1286.07	1017.48	857.72	752.36	678.08	623.20	581.25	548.33	521.96	500.50
40000	3544.61	1873.62	1319.05	1043.57	879.71	771.65	695.46	639.18	596.15	562.39	535.35	513.33
41000	3633.22	1920.46	1352.02	1069.65	901.70	790.94	712.85	655.16	611.06	576.45	548.73	526.16
42000	3721.84	1967.30	1385.00	1095.74	923.69	810.23	730.24	671.14	625.96	590.51	562.11	539.00
43000	3810.45	2014.14	1417.97	1121.83	945.69	829.52	747.62	687.12	640.86	604.57	575.50	551.83
44000	3899.07	2060.98	1450.95	1147.92	967.68	848.82	765.01	703.10	655.77	618.62	588.88	564.66
45000	3987.68	2107.82	1483.93	1174.01	989.67	868.11	782.40	719.08	670.67	632.68	602.26	577.50
46000	4076.30	2154.66	1516.90	1200.10	1011.66	887.40	799.78	735.06	685.57	646.74	615.65	590.33
47000	4164.91	2201.50	1549.88	1226.19	1033.66	906.69	817.17	751.04	700.48	660.80	629.03	603.16
48000	4253.53	2248.34	1582.85	1252.28	1055.65	925.98	834.56	767.01	715.38	674.86	642.41	616.00
49000	4342.14	2295.18	1615.83	1278.37	1077.64	945.27	851.94	782.99	730.28	688.92	655.80	628.83
50000	4430.76	2342.02	1648.81	1304.46	1099.64	964.56	869.33	798.97	745.19	702.98	669.18	641.66
55000	4873.83	2576.22	1813.69	1434.90	1209.60	1061.02	956.26	878.87	819.71	773.28	736.10	705.83
60000	5316.91	2810.42	1978.57	1565.35	1319.56	1157.47	1043.19	958.77	894.22	843.58	803.02	769.99
65000	5759.98	3044.63	2143.45	1695.79	1429.52	1253.93	1130.12	1038.66	968.74	913.88	869.93	834.16
70000	6203.06	3278.83	2308.33	1826.24	1539.49	1350.39	1217.06	1118.56	1043.26	984.17	936.85	898.33
75000	6646.13	3513.03	2473.21	1956.68	1649.45	1446.84	1303.99	1198.46	1117.78	1054.47	1003.77	962.49
80000	7089.21	3747.23	2638.09	2087.13	1759.41	1543.30	1390.92	1278.35	1192.30	1124.77	1070.69	1026.66
85000	7532.28	3981.43	2802.97	2217.57	1869.38	1639.75	1477.85	1358.25	1266.82	1195.07	1137.60	1090.82
90000	7975.36	4215.63	2967.85	2348.02	1979.34	1736.21	1564.79	1438.15	1341.33	1265.36	1204.52	1154.99
95000	8418.44	4449.83	3132.73	2478.46	2089.30	1832.66	1651.72	1518.05	1415.85	1335.66	1271.44	1219.16
100000	8861.51	4684.04	3297.61	2608.91	2199.27	1929.12	1738.65	1597.94	1490.37	1405.96	1338.36	1283.32

Table 1

MONTHLY

11.50%

PAYMENT REQUIRED TO AMORTIZE A LOAN

TERM AMOUNT	13 YEARS	14 YEARS	15 YEARS	16 YEARS	17 YEARS	18 YEARS	19 YEARS	20 YEARS	25 YEARS	30 YEARS	35 YEARS	40 YEARS
50	.62	.61	.59	.58	.56	.55	.55	.54	.51	.50	.49	.49
100	1.24	1.21	1.17	1.15	1.12	1.10	1.09	1.07	1.02	1.00	.98	.97
200	2.48	2.41	2.34	2.29	2.24	2.20	2.17	2.14	2.04	1.99	1.96	1.94
300	3.72	3.61	3.51	3.43	3.36	3.30	3.25	3.20	3.05	2.98	2.93	2.91
400	4.96	4.81	4.68	4.57	4.48	4.40	4.33	4.27	4.07	3.97	3.91	3.88
500	6.19	6.01	5.85	5.71	5.60	5.50	5.41	5.34	5.09	4.96	4.89	4.85
600	7.43	7.21	7.01	6.85	6.71	6.59	6.49	6.40	6.10	5.95	5.86	5.81
700	8.67	8.41	8.18	7.99	7.83	7.69	7.57	7.47	7.12	6.94	6.84	6.78
800	9.91	9.61	9.35	9.13	8.95	8.79	8.65	8.54	8.14	7.93	7.81	7.75
900	11.15	10.81	10.52	10.28	10.07	9.89	9.74	9.60	9.15	8.92	8.79	8.72
1000	12.38	12.01	11.69	11.42	11.19	10.99	10.82	10.67	10.17	9.91	9.77	9.69
2000	24.76	24.01	23.37	22.83	22.37	21.97	21.63	21.33	20.33	19.81	19.53	19.37
3000	37.14	36.01	35.05	34.24	33.55	32.95	32.44	32.00	30.50	29.71	29.29	29.05
4000	49.52	48.01	46.73	45.65	44.73	43.94	43.25	42.66	40.66	39.62	39.05	38.74
5000	61.90	60.01	58.41	57.06	55.91	54.92	54.07	53.33	50.83	49.52	48.81	48.42
6000	74.28	72.01	70.10	68.47	67.09	65.90	64.88	63.99	60.99	59.42	58.57	58.10
7000	86.66	84.01	81.78	79.89	78.27	76.89	75.69	74.66	71.16	69.33	68.33	67.78
8000	99.04	96.01	93.46	91.30	89.45	87.87	86.50	85.32	81.32	79.23	78.09	77.47
9000	111.42	108.01	105.14	102.71	100.63	98.85	97.31	95.98	91.49	89.13	87.85	87.15
10000	123.80	120.01	116.82	114.12	111.81	109.83	108.13	106.65	101.65	99.03	97.62	96.83
11000	136.18	132.01	128.51	125.53	123.00	120.82	118.94	117.31	111.82	108.94	107.38	106.52
12000	148.56	144.01	140.19	136.94	134.18	131.80	129.75	127.98	121.98	118.84	117.14	116.20
13000	160.93	156.01	151.87	148.36	145.36	142.78	140.56	138.64	132.15	128.74	126.90	125.88
14000	173.31	168.01	163.55	159.77	156.54	153.77	151.38	149.31	142.31	138.65	136.66	135.56
15000	185.69	180.01	175.23	171.18	167.72	164.75	162.19	159.97	152.48	148.55	146.42	145.25
16000	198.07	192.01	186.92	182.59	178.90	175.73	173.00	170.63	162.64	158.45	156.18	154.93
17000	210.45	204.01	198.60	194.00	190.08	186.72	183.81	181.30	172.80	168.35	165.94	164.61
18000	222.83	216.01	210.28	205.41	201.26	197.70	194.62	191.96	182.97	178.26	175.70	174.30
19000	235.21	228.02	221.96	216.83	212.44	208.68	205.44	202.63	193.13	188.16	185.47	183.98
20000	247.59	240.02	233.64	228.24	223.62	219.66	216.25	213.29	203.30	198.06	195.23	193.66
21000	259.97	252.02	245.32	239.65	234.81	230.65	227.06	223.96	213.46	207.97	204.99	203.34
22000	272.35	264.02	257.01	251.06	245.99	241.63	237.87	234.62	223.63	217.87	214.75	213.03
23000	284.73	276.02	268.69	262.47	257.17	252.61	248.69	245.28	233.79	227.77	224.51	222.71
24000	297.11	288.02	280.37	273.88	268.35	263.60	259.50	255.95	243.96	237.67	234.27	232.39
25000	309.48	300.02	292.05	285.30	279.53	274.58	270.31	266.61	254.12	247.58	244.03	242.08
26000	321.86	312.02	303.73	296.71	290.71	285.56	281.12	277.28	264.29	257.48	253.79	251.76
27000	334.24	324.02	315.42	308.12	301.89	296.54	291.93	287.94	274.45	267.38	263.55	261.44
28000	346.62	336.02	327.10	319.53	313.07	307.53	302.75	298.61	284.62	277.29	273.32	271.12
29000	359.00	348.02	338.78	330.94	324.25	318.51	313.56	309.27	294.78	287.19	283.08	280.81
30000	371.38	360.02	350.46	342.35	335.43	329.49	324.37	319.93	304.95	297.09	292.84	290.49
31000	383.76	372.02	362.14	353.77	346.61	340.48	335.18	330.60	315.11	307.00	302.60	300.17
32000	396.14	384.02	373.83	365.18	357.80	351.46	345.99	341.26	325.28	316.90	312.36	309.86
33000	408.52	396.02	385.51	376.59	368.98	362.44	356.81	351.93	335.44	326.80	322.12	319.54
34000	420.90	408.02	397.19	388.00	380.16	373.43	367.62	362.59	345.60	336.70	331.88	329.22
35000	433.28	420.02	408.87	399.41	391.34	384.41	378.43	373.26	355.77	346.61	341.64	338.90
36000	445.66	432.02	420.55	410.82	402.52	395.39	389.24	383.92	365.93	356.51	351.40	348.59
37000	458.03	444.03	432.24	422.24	413.70	406.37	400.06	394.58	376.10	366.41	361.16	358.27
38000	470.41	456.03	443.92	433.65	424.88	417.36	410.87	405.25	386.26	376.32	370.93	367.95
39000	482.79	468.03	455.60	445.06	436.06	428.34	421.68	415.91	396.43	386.22	380.69	377.63
40000	495.17	480.03	467.28	456.47	447.24	439.32	432.49	426.58	406.59	396.12	390.45	387.32
41000	507.55	492.03	478.96	467.88	458.42	450.31	443.30	437.24	416.76	406.02	400.21	397.00
42000	519.93	504.03	490.64	479.29	469.61	461.29	454.12	447.91	426.92	415.93	409.97	406.68
43000	532.31	516.03	502.33	490.71	480.79	472.27	464.93	458.57	437.09	425.83	419.73	416.37
44000	544.69	528.03	514.01	502.12	491.97	483.25	475.74	469.23	447.25	435.73	429.49	426.05
45000	557.07	540.03	525.69	513.53	503.15	494.24	486.55	479.90	457.42	445.64	439.25	435.73
46000	569.45	552.03	537.37	524.94	514.33	505.22	497.37	490.56	467.58	455.54	449.01	445.41
47000	581.83	564.03	549.05	536.35	525.51	516.20	508.18	501.23	477.75	465.44	458.78	455.10
48000	594.21	576.03	560.74	547.76	536.69	527.19	518.99	511.89	487.91	475.34	468.54	464.78
49000	606.58	588.03	572.42	559.17	547.87	538.17	529.80	522.56	498.07	485.25	478.30	474.46
50000	618.96	600.03	584.10	570.59	559.05	549.15	540.61	533.22	508.24	495.15	488.06	484.15
55000	680.86	660.04	642.51	627.65	614.96	604.07	594.67	586.54	559.06	544.67	536.86	532.56
60000	742.76	720.04	700.92	684.70	670.86	658.98	648.74	639.86	609.89	594.18	585.67	580.97
65000	804.65	780.04	759.33	741.76	726.77	713.90	702.80	693.18	660.71	643.69	634.47	629.39
70000	866.55	840.04	817.74	798.82	782.67	768.81	756.86	746.51	711.53	693.21	683.28	677.80
75000	928.44	900.05	876.15	855.88	838.58	823.73	810.92	799.83	762.36	742.72	732.09	726.22
80000	990.34	960.05	934.56	912.94	894.48	878.64	864.98	853.15	813.18	792.24	780.89	774.63
85000	1052.24	1020.05	992.97	970.00	950.39	933.56	919.04	906.47	864.00	841.75	829.70	823.04
90000	1114.13	1080.05	1051.38	1027.05	1006.29	988.47	973.10	959.79	914.83	891.27	878.50	871.46
95000	1176.03	1140.06	1109.79	1084.11	1062.20	1043.39	1027.16	1013.11	965.65	940.78	927.31	919.87
100000	1237.92	1200.06	1168.19	1141.17	1118.10	1098.30	1081.22	1066.43	1016.47	990.30	976.11	968.29

11%

Table 1

11.75%

MONTHLY
PAYMENT REQUIRED TO AMORTIZE A LOAN

TERM AMOUNT	1 YEAR	2 YEARS	3 YEARS	4 YEARS	5 YEARS	6 YEARS	7 YEARS	8 YEARS	9 YEARS	10 YEARS	11 YEARS	12 YEARS
50	4.44	2.35	1.66	1.32	1.11	.98	.88	.81	.76	.72	.68	.65
100	8.88	4.70	3.31	2.63	2.22	1.95	1.76	1.62	1.51	1.43	1.36	1.30
200	17.75	9.40	6.62	5.25	4.43	3.89	3.51	3.23	3.01	2.85	2.71	2.60
300	26.62	14.09	9.93	7.87	6.64	5.83	5.26	4.84	4.52	4.27	4.06	3.90
400	35.50	18.79	13.24	10.49	8.85	7.77	7.01	6.45	6.02	5.69	5.42	5.20
500	44.37	23.48	16.55	13.11	11.06	9.72	8.76	8.06	7.53	7.11	6.77	6.50
600	53.24	28.18	19.86	15.73	13.28	11.66	10.52	9.67	9.03	8.53	8.12	7.79
700	62.12	32.87	23.17	18.35	15.49	13.60	12.27	11.29	10.54	9.95	9.48	9.09
800	70.99	37.57	26.48	20.97	17.70	15.54	14.02	12.90	12.04	11.37	10.83	10.39
900	79.86	42.27	29.79	23.60	19.91	17.48	15.77	14.51	13.54	12.79	12.18	11.69
1000	88.74	46.96	33.10	26.22	22.12	19.43	17.52	16.12	15.05	14.21	13.54	12.99
2000	177.47	93.92	66.20	52.43	44.24	38.85	35.04	32.24	30.09	28.41	27.07	25.97
3000	266.20	140.88	99.29	78.64	66.36	58.27	52.56	48.35	45.14	42.61	40.60	38.95
4000	354.93	187.83	132.39	104.85	88.48	77.69	70.08	64.47	60.18	56.82	54.13	51.94
5000	443.66	234.79	165.48	131.06	110.60	97.11	87.60	80.58	75.22	71.02	67.66	64.92
6000	532.40	281.75	198.58	157.27	132.71	116.53	105.12	96.70	90.27	85.22	81.19	77.90
7000	621.13	328.70	231.67	183.48	154.83	135.95	122.64	112.82	105.31	99.43	94.72	90.89
8000	709.86	375.66	264.77	209.70	176.95	155.37	140.16	128.93	120.35	113.63	108.25	103.87
9000	798.59	422.62	297.86	235.91	199.07	174.79	157.68	145.05	135.40	127.83	121.78	116.85
10000	887.32	469.57	330.96	262.12	221.19	194.21	175.20	161.16	150.44	142.03	135.31	129.84
11000	976.06	516.53	364.05	288.33	243.31	213.63	192.72	177.28	165.48	156.24	148.84	142.82
12000	1064.79	563.49	397.15	314.54	265.42	233.05	210.24	193.39	180.53	170.44	162.37	155.80
13000	1153.52	610.44	430.24	340.75	287.54	252.47	227.76	209.51	195.57	184.64	175.90	168.79
14000	1242.25	657.40	463.34	366.96	309.66	271.89	245.28	225.63	210.62	198.85	189.43	181.77
15000	1330.98	704.36	496.43	393.17	331.78	291.31	262.79	241.74	225.66	213.05	202.96	194.75
16000	1419.72	751.31	529.53	419.39	353.90	310.73	280.31	257.86	240.70	227.25	216.49	207.74
17000	1508.45	798.27	562.62	445.60	376.02	330.15	297.83	273.97	255.75	241.46	230.02	220.72
18000	1597.18	845.23	595.72	471.81	398.13	349.57	315.35	290.09	270.79	255.66	243.55	233.70
19000	1685.91	892.18	628.81	498.02	420.25	368.99	332.87	306.21	285.83	269.86	257.08	246.69
20000	1774.64	939.14	661.91	524.23	442.37	388.41	350.39	322.32	300.88	284.06	270.61	259.67
21000	1863.37	986.10	695.00	550.44	464.49	407.83	367.91	338.44	315.92	298.27	284.14	272.65
22000	1952.11	1033.05	728.10	576.65	486.61	427.25	385.43	354.55	330.96	312.47	297.67	285.64
23000	2040.84	1080.01	761.19	602.86	508.73	446.67	402.95	370.67	346.01	326.67	311.20	298.62
24000	2129.57	1126.97	794.29	629.08	530.84	466.10	420.47	386.78	361.05	340.88	324.73	311.60
25000	2218.30	1173.93	827.38	655.29	552.96	485.52	437.99	402.90	376.10	355.08	338.26	324.59
26000	2307.03	1220.88	860.48	681.50	575.08	504.94	455.51	419.02	391.14	369.28	351.79	337.57
27000	2395.77	1267.84	893.57	707.71	597.20	524.36	473.03	435.13	406.18	383.48	365.32	350.55
28000	2484.50	1314.80	926.67	733.92	619.32	543.78	490.55	451.25	421.23	397.69	378.85	363.54
29000	2573.23	1361.75	959.76	760.13	641.44	563.20	508.07	467.36	436.27	411.89	392.38	376.52
30000	2661.96	1408.71	992.86	786.34	663.55	582.62	525.58	483.48	451.31	426.09	405.91	389.50
31000	2750.69	1455.67	1025.95	812.55	685.67	602.04	543.10	499.59	466.36	440.30	419.44	402.49
32000	2839.43	1502.62	1059.05	838.77	707.79	621.46	560.62	515.71	481.40	454.50	432.97	415.47
33000	2928.16	1549.58	1092.14	864.98	729.91	640.88	578.14	531.83	496.44	468.70	446.50	428.45
34000	3016.89	1596.54	1125.24	891.19	752.03	660.30	595.66	547.94	511.49	482.91	460.03	441.44
35000	3105.62	1643.49	1158.33	917.40	774.15	679.72	613.18	564.06	526.53	497.11	473.57	454.42
36000	3194.35	1690.45	1191.43	943.61	796.26	699.14	630.70	580.17	541.57	511.31	487.10	467.40
37000	3283.08	1737.41	1224.52	969.82	818.38	718.56	648.22	596.29	556.62	525.51	500.63	480.39
38000	3371.82	1784.36	1257.62	996.03	840.50	737.98	665.74	612.41	571.66	539.72	514.16	493.37
39000	3460.55	1831.32	1290.71	1022.24	862.62	757.40	683.26	628.52	586.71	553.92	527.69	506.35
40000	3549.28	1878.28	1323.81	1048.46	884.74	776.82	700.78	644.64	601.75	568.12	541.22	519.34
41000	3638.01	1925.23	1356.90	1074.67	906.86	796.24	718.30	660.75	616.79	582.33	554.75	532.32
42000	3726.74	1972.19	1390.00	1100.88	928.97	815.66	735.82	676.87	631.84	596.53	568.28	545.30
43000	3815.48	2019.15	1423.09	1127.09	951.09	835.08	753.34	692.98	646.88	610.73	581.81	558.28
44000	3904.21	2066.10	1456.19	1153.30	973.21	854.50	770.85	709.10	661.92	624.93	595.34	571.27
45000	3992.94	2113.06	1489.28	1179.51	995.33	873.92	788.37	725.22	676.97	639.14	608.87	584.25
46000	4081.67	2160.02	1522.38	1205.72	1017.45	893.34	805.89	741.33	692.01	653.34	622.40	597.23
47000	4170.40	2206.98	1555.47	1231.93	1039.57	912.77	823.41	757.45	707.05	667.54	635.93	610.22
48000	4259.14	2253.93	1588.57	1258.15	1061.68	932.19	840.93	773.56	722.10	681.75	649.46	623.20
49000	4347.87	2300.89	1621.66	1284.36	1083.80	951.61	858.45	789.68	737.14	695.95	662.99	636.18
50000	4436.60	2347.85	1654.76	1310.57	1105.92	971.03	875.97	805.79	752.19	710.15	676.52	649.17
55000	4880.26	2582.63	1820.23	1441.62	1216.51	1068.13	963.57	886.37	827.40	781.15	744.17	714.08
60000	5323.92	2817.41	1985.71	1572.68	1327.10	1165.23	1051.16	966.95	902.62	852.18	811.82	779.00
65000	5767.58	3052.20	2151.18	1703.74	1437.70	1262.33	1138.76	1047.53	977.84	923.20	879.47	843.92
70000	6211.24	3286.98	2316.66	1834.79	1548.29	1359.44	1226.36	1128.11	1053.06	994.21	947.13	908.83
75000	6654.90	3521.77	2482.13	1965.85	1658.88	1456.54	1313.95	1208.69	1128.28	1065.23	1014.78	973.75
80000	7098.56	3756.55	2647.61	2096.91	1769.47	1553.64	1401.55	1289.27	1203.49	1136.24	1082.43	1038.67
85000	7542.21	3991.33	2813.08	2227.96	1880.06	1650.74	1489.15	1369.85	1278.71	1207.26	1150.08	1103.58
90000	7985.87	4226.12	2978.56	2359.02	1990.65	1747.84	1576.74	1450.43	1353.93	1278.27	1217.73	1168.50
95000	8429.53	4460.90	3144.03	2490.07	2101.25	1844.95	1664.34	1531.01	1429.15	1349.28	1285.38	1233.41
100000	8873.19	4695.69	3309.51	2621.13	2211.84	1942.05	1751.94	1611.58	1504.37	1420.30	1353.03	1298.33

56

Table 1

MONTHLY

11.75%

PAYMENT REQUIRED TO AMORTIZE A LOAN

11%

TERM AMOUNT	13 YEARS	14 YEARS	15 YEARS	16 YEARS	17 YEARS	18 YEARS	19 YEARS	20 YEARS	25 YEARS	30 YEARS	35 YEARS	40 YEARS
50	.63	.61	.60	.58	.57	.56	.55	.55	.52	.51	.50	.50
100	1.26	1.22	1.19	1.16	1.14	1.12	1.10	1.09	1.04	1.01	1.00	.99
200	2.51	2.44	2.37	2.32	2.27	2.24	2.20	2.17	2.07	2.02	2.00	1.98
300	3.76	3.65	3.56	3.48	3.41	3.35	3.30	3.26	3.11	3.03	2.99	2.97
400	5.02	4.87	4.74	4.63	4.54	4.47	4.40	4.34	4.14	4.04	3.99	3.96
500	6.27	6.08	5.93	5.79	5.68	5.58	5.50	5.42	5.18	5.05	4.98	4.95
600	7.52	7.30	7.11	6.95	6.81	6.70	6.59	6.51	6.21	6.06	5.98	5.94
700	8.78	8.51	8.29	8.11	7.95	7.81	7.69	7.59	7.25	7.07	6.98	6.92
800	10.03	9.73	9.48	9.26	9.08	8.93	8.79	8.67	8.28	8.08	7.97	7.91
900	11.28	10.95	10.66	10.42	10.22	10.04	9.89	9.76	9.32	9.09	8.97	8.90
1000	12.54	12.16	11.85	11.58	11.35	11.16	10.99	10.84	10.35	10.10	9.96	9.89
2000	25.07	24.32	23.69	23.15	22.70	22.31	21.97	21.68	20.70	20.19	19.92	19.77
3000	37.60	36.48	35.53	34.73	34.04	33.46	32.95	32.52	31.05	30.29	29.88	29.66
4000	50.13	48.63	47.37	46.30	45.39	44.61	43.94	43.35	41.40	40.38	39.84	39.54
5000	62.67	60.79	59.21	57.87	56.74	55.76	54.92	54.19	51.74	50.48	49.79	49.42
6000	75.20	72.95	71.05	69.45	68.08	66.91	65.90	65.03	62.09	60.57	59.75	59.31
7000	87.73	85.10	82.89	81.02	79.43	78.06	76.88	75.86	72.44	70.66	69.71	69.19
8000	100.26	97.26	94.74	92.60	90.77	89.21	87.87	86.70	82.79	80.76	79.67	79.07
9000	112.80	109.42	106.58	104.17	102.12	100.36	98.85	97.54	93.14	90.85	89.63	88.96
10000	125.33	121.57	118.42	115.74	113.47	111.51	109.83	108.38	103.48	100.95	99.58	98.84
11000	137.86	133.73	130.26	127.32	124.81	122.66	120.81	119.21	113.83	111.04	109.54	108.73
12000	150.39	145.89	142.10	138.89	136.16	133.81	131.80	130.05	124.18	121.13	119.50	118.61
13000	162.93	158.05	153.94	150.47	147.50	144.96	142.78	140.89	134.53	131.23	129.46	128.49
14000	175.46	170.20	165.78	162.04	158.85	156.12	153.76	151.72	144.88	141.32	139.42	138.38
15000	187.99	182.36	177.62	173.61	170.20	167.27	164.74	162.56	155.22	151.42	149.37	148.26
16000	200.52	194.52	189.47	185.19	181.54	178.42	175.73	173.40	165.57	161.51	159.33	158.14
17000	213.06	206.67	201.31	196.76	192.89	189.57	186.71	184.24	175.92	171.60	169.29	168.03
18000	225.59	218.83	213.15	208.34	204.23	200.72	197.69	195.07	186.27	181.70	179.25	177.91
19000	238.12	230.99	224.99	219.91	215.58	211.87	208.67	205.91	196.62	191.79	189.21	187.79
20000	250.65	243.14	236.83	231.48	226.93	223.02	219.66	216.75	206.96	201.89	199.16	197.68
21000	263.19	255.30	248.67	243.06	238.27	234.17	230.64	227.58	217.31	211.98	209.12	207.56
22000	275.72	267.46	260.51	254.63	249.62	245.32	241.62	238.42	227.66	222.08	219.08	217.45
23000	288.25	279.62	272.36	266.21	260.96	256.47	252.60	249.26	238.01	232.17	229.04	227.33
24000	300.78	291.77	284.20	277.78	272.31	267.62	263.59	260.09	248.36	242.26	239.00	237.21
25000	313.32	303.93	296.04	289.35	283.66	278.77	274.57	270.93	258.70	252.36	248.95	247.10
26000	325.85	316.09	307.88	300.93	295.00	289.92	285.55	281.77	269.05	262.45	258.91	256.98
27000	338.38	328.24	319.72	312.50	306.35	301.07	296.53	292.61	279.40	272.55	268.87	266.86
28000	350.91	340.40	331.56	324.08	317.69	312.23	307.52	303.44	289.75	282.64	278.83	276.75
29000	363.45	352.56	343.40	335.65	329.04	323.38	318.50	314.28	300.10	292.73	288.79	286.63
30000	375.98	364.71	355.24	347.22	340.39	334.53	329.48	325.12	310.44	302.83	298.74	296.51
31000	388.51	376.87	367.09	358.80	351.73	345.68	340.46	335.95	320.79	312.92	308.70	306.40
32000	401.04	389.03	378.93	370.37	363.08	356.83	351.45	346.79	331.14	323.02	318.66	316.28
33000	413.58	401.18	390.77	381.95	374.43	367.98	362.43	357.63	341.49	333.11	328.62	326.17
34000	426.11	413.34	402.61	393.52	385.77	379.13	373.41	368.47	351.84	343.20	338.57	336.05
35000	438.64	425.50	414.45	405.09	397.12	390.28	384.39	379.30	362.18	353.30	348.53	345.93
36000	451.17	437.66	426.29	416.67	408.46	401.43	395.38	390.14	372.53	363.39	358.49	355.82
37000	463.71	449.81	438.13	428.24	419.81	412.58	406.36	400.98	382.88	373.49	368.45	365.70
38000	476.24	461.97	449.97	439.82	431.16	423.73	417.34	411.81	393.23	383.58	378.41	375.58
39000	488.77	474.13	461.82	451.39	442.50	434.88	428.32	422.65	403.58	393.67	388.36	385.47
40000	501.30	486.28	473.66	462.96	453.85	446.03	439.31	433.49	413.92	403.77	398.32	395.35
41000	513.84	498.44	485.50	474.54	465.19	457.18	450.29	444.32	424.27	413.86	408.28	405.23
42000	526.37	510.60	497.34	486.11	476.54	468.34	461.27	455.16	434.62	423.96	418.24	415.12
43000	538.90	522.75	509.18	497.69	487.89	479.49	472.25	466.00	444.97	434.05	428.20	425.00
44000	551.43	534.91	521.02	509.26	499.23	490.64	483.24	476.84	455.32	444.15	438.15	434.89
45000	563.97	547.07	532.86	520.83	510.58	501.79	494.22	487.67	465.66	454.24	448.11	444.77
46000	576.50	559.23	544.71	532.41	521.92	512.94	505.20	498.51	476.01	464.33	458.07	454.65
47000	589.03	571.38	556.55	543.98	533.27	524.09	516.18	509.35	486.36	474.43	468.03	464.54
48000	601.56	583.54	568.39	555.56	544.62	535.24	527.17	520.18	496.71	484.52	477.99	474.42
49000	614.10	595.70	580.23	567.13	555.96	546.39	538.15	531.02	507.06	494.62	487.94	484.30
50000	626.63	607.85	592.07	578.70	567.31	557.54	549.13	541.86	517.40	504.71	497.90	494.19
55000	689.29	668.64	651.28	636.57	624.04	613.29	604.04	596.04	569.14	555.18	547.69	543.61
60000	751.95	729.42	710.48	694.44	680.77	669.05	658.96	650.23	620.88	605.65	597.48	593.02
65000	814.62	790.21	769.69	752.31	737.50	724.80	713.87	704.41	672.62	656.12	647.27	642.44
70000	877.28	850.99	828.90	810.18	794.23	780.56	768.78	758.60	724.36	706.59	697.06	691.86
75000	939.94	911.78	888.10	868.05	850.96	836.31	823.69	812.79	776.10	757.06	746.85	741.28
80000	1002.60	972.56	947.31	925.92	907.69	892.06	878.61	866.97	827.84	807.53	796.64	790.70
85000	1065.27	1033.35	1006.52	983.79	964.42	947.82	933.52	921.16	879.58	858.00	846.43	840.11
90000	1127.93	1094.13	1065.72	1041.66	1021.15	1003.57	988.43	975.34	931.32	908.47	896.22	889.53
95000	1190.59	1154.92	1124.93	1099.53	1077.88	1059.32	1043.34	1029.53	983.06	958.94	946.01	938.95
100000	1253.25	1215.70	1184.14	1157.40	1134.61	1115.08	1098.26	1083.71	1034.80	1009.41	995.80	988.37

Table 1

12.00%

MONTHLY
PAYMENT REQUIRED TO AMORTIZE A LOAN

12%

TERM / AMOUNT	1 YEAR	2 YEARS	3 YEARS	4 YEARS	5 YEARS	6 YEARS	7 YEARS	8 YEARS	9 YEARS	10 YEARS	11 YEARS	12 YEARS
50	4.45	2.36	1.67	1.32	1.12	.98	.89	.82	.76	.72	.69	.66
100	8.89	4.71	3.33	2.64	2.23	1.96	1.77	1.63	1.52	1.44	1.37	1.32
200	17.77	9.42	6.65	5.27	4.45	3.92	3.54	3.26	3.04	2.87	2.74	2.63
300	26.66	14.13	9.97	7.91	6.68	5.87	5.30	4.88	4.56	4.31	4.11	3.95
400	35.54	18.83	13.29	10.54	8.90	7.83	7.07	6.51	6.08	5.74	5.48	5.26
500	44.43	23.54	16.61	13.17	11.13	9.78	8.83	8.13	7.60	7.18	6.84	6.57
600	53.31	28.25	19.93	15.81	13.35	11.74	10.60	9.76	9.12	8.61	8.21	7.89
700	62.20	32.96	23.26	18.44	15.58	13.69	12.36	11.38	10.63	10.05	9.58	9.20
800	71.08	37.66	26.58	21.07	17.80	15.65	14.13	13.01	12.15	11.48	10.95	10.51
900	79.97	42.37	29.90	23.71	20.03	17.60	15.89	14.63	13.67	12.92	12.32	11.83
1000	88.85	47.08	33.22	26.34	22.25	19.56	17.66	16.26	15.19	14.35	13.68	13.14
2000	177.70	94.15	66.43	52.67	44.49	39.11	35.31	32.51	30.37	28.70	27.36	26.27
3000	266.55	141.23	99.65	79.01	66.74	58.66	52.96	48.76	45.56	43.05	41.04	39.41
4000	355.40	188.30	132.86	105.34	88.98	78.21	70.62	65.02	60.74	57.39	54.72	52.54
5000	444.25	235.37	166.08	131.67	111.23	97.76	88.27	81.27	75.93	71.74	68.39	65.68
6000	533.10	282.45	199.29	158.01	133.47	117.31	105.92	97.52	91.11	86.09	82.07	78.81
7000	621.95	329.52	232.51	184.34	155.72	136.86	123.57	113.77	106.29	100.43	95.75	91.94
8000	710.80	376.59	265.72	210.68	177.96	156.41	141.23	130.03	121.48	114.78	109.43	105.08
9000	799.64	423.67	298.93	237.01	200.21	175.96	158.88	146.28	136.66	129.13	123.11	118.21
10000	888.49	470.74	332.15	263.34	222.45	195.51	176.53	162.53	151.85	143.48	136.78	131.35
11000	977.34	517.81	365.36	289.68	244.69	215.06	194.19	178.79	167.03	157.82	150.46	144.48
12000	1066.19	564.89	398.58	316.01	266.94	234.61	211.84	195.04	182.22	172.17	164.14	157.62
13000	1155.04	611.96	431.79	342.34	289.18	254.16	229.49	211.29	197.40	186.52	177.82	170.75
14000	1243.89	659.03	465.01	368.68	311.43	273.71	247.14	227.54	212.58	200.86	191.50	183.88
15000	1332.74	706.11	498.22	395.01	333.67	293.26	264.80	243.80	227.77	215.21	205.17	197.02
16000	1421.59	753.18	531.43	421.35	355.92	312.81	282.45	260.05	242.95	229.56	218.85	210.15
17000	1510.43	800.25	564.65	447.68	378.16	332.36	300.10	276.30	258.14	243.91	232.53	223.29
18000	1599.28	847.33	597.86	474.01	400.41	351.91	317.75	292.56	273.32	258.25	246.21	236.42
19000	1688.13	894.40	631.08	500.35	422.65	371.46	335.41	308.81	288.51	272.60	259.88	249.55
20000	1776.98	941.47	664.29	526.68	444.89	391.01	353.06	325.06	303.69	286.95	273.56	262.69
21000	1865.83	988.55	697.51	553.02	467.14	410.56	370.71	341.31	318.87	301.29	287.24	275.82
22000	1954.68	1035.62	730.72	579.35	489.38	430.11	388.37	357.57	334.06	315.64	300.92	288.96
23000	2043.53	1082.69	763.93	605.68	511.63	449.66	406.02	373.82	349.24	329.99	314.60	302.09
24000	2132.38	1129.77	797.15	632.02	533.87	469.21	423.67	390.07	364.43	344.34	328.27	315.23
25000	2221.22	1176.84	830.36	658.35	556.12	488.76	441.32	406.33	379.61	358.68	341.95	328.36
26000	2310.07	1223.92	863.58	684.68	578.36	508.31	458.98	422.58	394.80	373.03	355.63	341.49
27000	2398.92	1270.99	896.79	711.02	600.61	527.86	476.63	438.83	409.98	387.38	369.31	354.63
28000	2487.77	1318.06	930.01	737.35	622.85	547.41	494.28	455.08	425.16	401.72	382.99	367.76
29000	2576.62	1365.14	963.22	763.69	645.09	566.96	511.93	471.34	440.35	416.07	396.66	380.90
30000	2665.47	1412.21	996.43	790.02	667.34	586.51	529.59	487.59	455.53	430.42	410.34	394.03
31000	2754.32	1459.28	1029.65	816.35	689.58	606.06	547.24	503.84	470.72	444.76	424.02	407.16
32000	2843.17	1506.36	1062.86	842.69	711.83	625.61	564.89	520.10	485.90	459.11	437.70	420.30
33000	2932.02	1553.43	1096.08	869.02	734.07	645.16	582.55	536.35	501.08	473.46	451.38	433.43
34000	3020.86	1600.50	1129.29	895.36	756.32	664.71	600.20	552.60	516.27	487.81	465.05	446.57
35000	3109.71	1647.58	1162.51	921.69	778.56	684.26	617.85	568.85	531.45	502.15	478.73	459.70
36000	3198.56	1694.65	1195.72	948.02	800.81	703.81	635.50	585.11	546.64	516.50	492.41	472.84
37000	3287.41	1741.72	1228.93	974.36	823.05	723.36	653.16	601.36	561.82	530.85	506.09	485.97
38000	3376.26	1788.80	1262.15	1000.69	845.29	742.91	670.81	617.61	577.01	545.19	519.76	499.11
39000	3465.11	1835.87	1295.36	1027.02	867.54	762.46	688.46	633.87	592.19	559.54	533.44	512.24
40000	3553.96	1882.94	1328.58	1053.36	889.78	782.01	706.11	650.12	607.37	573.89	547.12	525.37
41000	3642.81	1930.02	1361.79	1079.69	912.03	801.56	723.77	666.37	622.56	588.24	560.80	538.51
42000	3731.65	1977.09	1395.01	1106.03	934.27	821.11	741.42	682.62	637.74	602.58	574.48	551.64
43000	3820.50	2024.16	1428.22	1132.36	956.52	840.66	759.07	698.88	652.93	616.93	588.15	564.78
44000	3909.35	2071.24	1461.43	1158.69	978.76	860.21	776.73	715.13	668.11	631.28	601.83	577.91
45000	3998.20	2118.31	1494.65	1185.03	1001.01	879.76	794.38	731.38	683.30	645.62	615.51	591.04
46000	4087.05	2165.38	1527.86	1211.36	1023.25	899.31	812.03	747.64	698.48	659.97	629.19	604.18
47000	4175.90	2212.46	1561.08	1237.70	1045.49	918.86	829.68	763.89	713.66	674.32	642.87	617.31
48000	4264.75	2259.53	1594.29	1264.03	1067.74	938.41	847.34	780.14	728.85	688.67	656.54	630.45
49000	4353.60	2306.61	1627.51	1290.36	1089.98	957.96	864.99	796.39	744.03	703.01	670.22	643.58
50000	4442.44	2353.68	1660.72	1316.70	1112.23	977.51	882.64	812.65	759.22	717.36	683.90	656.71
55000	4886.69	2589.05	1826.79	1448.37	1223.45	1075.27	970.91	893.91	835.14	789.10	752.29	722.39
60000	5330.93	2824.41	1992.86	1580.04	1334.67	1173.02	1059.17	975.18	911.06	860.83	820.68	788.06
65000	5775.18	3059.78	2158.94	1711.70	1445.89	1270.77	1147.43	1056.44	986.98	932.57	889.07	853.73
70000	6219.42	3295.15	2325.01	1843.37	1557.12	1368.52	1235.70	1137.70	1062.90	1004.30	957.46	919.40
75000	6663.66	3530.52	2491.08	1975.04	1668.34	1466.27	1323.96	1218.97	1138.82	1076.04	1025.85	985.07
80000	7107.91	3765.88	2657.15	2106.71	1779.56	1564.02	1412.22	1300.23	1214.74	1147.77	1094.24	1050.74
85000	7552.15	4001.25	2823.22	2238.38	1890.78	1661.77	1500.49	1381.50	1290.66	1219.51	1162.62	1116.41
90000	7996.40	4236.62	2989.29	2370.05	2002.01	1759.52	1588.75	1462.76	1366.59	1291.24	1231.01	1182.08
95000	8440.64	4471.98	3155.36	2501.72	2113.23	1857.27	1677.01	1544.02	1442.51	1362.98	1299.40	1247.75
100000	8884.88	4707.35	3321.44	2633.39	2224.45	1955.02	1765.28	1625.29	1518.43	1434.71	1367.79	1313.42

Table 1

MONTHLY 12.00%

PAYMENT REQUIRED TO AMORTIZE A LOAN

TERM	13 YEARS	14 YEARS	15 YEARS	16 YEARS	17 YEARS	18 YEARS	19 YEARS	20 YEARS	25 YEARS	30 YEARS	35 YEARS	40 YEARS
OUNT												
50	.64	.62	.61	.59	.58	.57	.56	.56	.53	.52	.51	.51
100	1.27	1.24	1.21	1.18	1.16	1.14	1.12	1.11	1.06	1.03	1.02	1.01
200	2.54	2.47	2.41	2.35	2.31	2.27	2.24	2.21	2.11	2.06	2.04	2.02
300	3.81	3.70	3.61	3.53	3.46	3.40	3.35	3.31	3.16	3.09	3.05	3.03
400	5.08	4.93	4.81	4.70	4.61	4.53	4.47	4.41	4.22	4.12	4.07	4.04
500	6.35	6.16	6.01	5.87	5.76	5.66	5.58	5.51	5.27	5.15	5.08	5.05
600	7.62	7.39	7.21	7.05	6.91	6.80	6.70	6.61	6.32	6.18	6.10	6.06
700	8.89	8.63	8.41	8.22	8.06	7.93	7.81	7.71	7.38	7.21	7.11	7.06
800	10.15	9.86	9.61	9.39	9.21	9.06	8.93	8.81	8.43	8.23	8.13	8.07
900	11.42	11.09	10.81	10.57	10.37	10.19	10.04	9.91	9.48	9.26	9.14	9.08
1000	12.69	12.32	12.01	11.74	11.52	11.32	11.16	11.02	10.54	10.29	10.16	10.09
2000	25.38	24.63	24.01	23.48	23.03	22.64	22.31	22.03	21.07	20.58	20.32	20.17
3000	38.06	36.95	36.01	35.22	34.54	33.96	33.47	33.04	31.60	30.86	30.47	30.26
4000	50.75	49.26	48.01	46.95	46.05	45.28	44.62	44.05	42.13	41.15	40.63	40.34
5000	63.44	61.58	60.01	58.69	57.57	56.60	55.77	55.06	52.67	51.44	50.78	50.43
6000	76.12	73.89	72.02	70.43	69.08	67.92	66.93	66.07	63.20	61.72	60.94	60.51
7000	88.81	86.21	84.02	82.17	80.59	79.24	78.08	77.08	73.73	72.01	71.09	70.60
8000	101.50	98.52	96.02	93.90	92.10	90.56	89.24	88.09	84.26	82.29	81.25	80.68
9000	114.18	110.83	108.02	105.64	103.61	101.88	100.39	99.10	94.80	92.58	91.40	90.77
10000	126.87	123.15	120.02	117.38	115.13	113.20	111.54	110.11	105.33	102.87	101.56	100.85
11000	139.56	135.46	132.02	129.11	126.64	124.52	122.70	121.12	115.86	113.15	111.72	110.94
12000	152.24	147.78	144.03	140.85	138.15	135.84	133.85	132.14	126.39	123.44	121.87	121.02
13000	164.93	160.09	156.03	152.59	149.66	147.16	145.01	143.15	136.92	133.72	132.03	131.11
14000	177.62	172.41	168.03	164.33	161.18	158.48	156.16	154.16	147.46	144.01	142.18	141.19
15000	190.30	184.72	180.03	176.06	172.69	169.80	167.31	165.17	157.99	154.30	152.34	151.28
16000	202.99	197.03	192.03	187.80	184.20	181.12	178.47	176.18	168.52	164.58	162.49	161.36
17000	215.68	209.35	204.03	199.54	195.71	192.44	189.62	187.19	179.05	174.87	172.65	171.45
18000	228.36	221.66	216.04	211.28	207.22	203.76	200.77	198.20	189.59	185.16	182.80	181.53
19000	241.05	233.98	228.04	223.01	218.74	215.08	211.93	209.21	200.12	195.44	192.96	191.62
20000	253.74	246.29	240.04	234.75	230.25	226.40	223.08	220.22	210.65	205.73	203.11	201.70
21000	266.42	258.61	252.04	246.49	241.76	237.71	234.24	231.23	221.18	216.01	213.27	211.79
22000	279.11	270.92	264.04	258.22	253.27	249.03	245.39	242.24	231.71	226.30	223.43	221.87
23000	291.80	283.23	276.04	269.96	264.78	260.35	256.54	253.25	242.25	236.59	233.58	231.96
24000	304.48	295.55	288.05	281.70	276.30	271.67	267.70	264.27	252.78	246.87	243.74	242.04
25000	317.17	307.86	300.05	293.44	287.81	282.99	278.85	275.28	263.31	257.16	253.89	252.13
26000	329.86	320.18	312.05	305.17	299.32	294.31	290.01	286.29	273.84	267.44	264.05	262.21
27000	342.54	332.49	324.05	316.91	310.83	305.63	301.16	297.30	284.38	277.73	274.20	272.30
28000	355.23	344.81	336.05	328.65	322.35	316.95	312.31	308.31	294.91	288.02	284.36	282.38
29000	367.92	357.12	348.05	340.39	333.86	328.27	323.47	319.32	305.44	298.30	294.51	292.47
30000	380.60	369.43	360.06	352.12	345.37	339.59	334.62	330.33	315.97	308.59	304.67	302.55
31000	393.29	381.75	372.06	363.86	356.88	350.91	345.77	341.34	326.50	318.87	314.83	312.64
32000	405.98	394.06	384.06	375.60	368.39	362.23	356.93	352.35	337.04	329.16	324.98	322.72
33000	418.66	406.38	396.06	387.33	379.91	373.55	368.08	363.36	347.57	339.45	335.14	332.81
34000	431.35	418.69	408.06	399.07	391.42	384.87	379.24	374.37	358.10	349.73	345.29	342.89
35000	444.04	431.01	420.06	410.81	402.93	396.19	390.39	385.39	368.63	360.02	355.45	352.98
36000	456.72	443.32	432.07	422.55	414.44	4C7.51	401.54	396.40	379.17	370.31	365.60	363.06
37000	469.41	455.63	444.07	434.28	425.95	418.83	412.70	407.41	389.70	380.59	375.76	373.15
38000	482.10	467.95	456.07	446.02	437.47	430.15	423.85	418.42	400.23	390.88	385.91	383.23
39000	494.78	480.26	468.07	457.76	448.98	441.47	435.01	429.43	410.76	401.16	396.07	393.32
40000	507.47	492.58	480.07	469.50	460.49	452.79	446.16	440.44	421.29	411.45	406.22	403.40
41000	520.16	504.89	492.07	481.23	472.00	464.10	457.31	451.45	431.83	421.74	416.38	413.49
42000	532.84	517.21	504.08	492.97	483.52	475.42	468.47	462.46	442.36	432.02	426.54	423.57
43000	545.53	529.52	516.08	504.71	495.03	486.74	479.62	473.47	452.89	442.31	436.69	433.66
44000	558.22	541.83	528.08	516.44	506.54	498.06	490.77	484.48	463.42	452.51	446.85	443.74
45000	570.90	554.15	540.08	528.18	518.05	509.38	501.93	495.49	473.96	462.88	457.00	453.83
46000	583.59	566.46	552.08	539.92	529.56	520.70	513.08	506.50	484.49	473.17	467.16	463.91
47000	596.28	578.78	564.08	551.66	541.08	532.02	524.24	517.52	495.02	483.45	477.31	474.00
48000	608.96	591.09	576.09	563.39	552.59	543.34	535.39	528.53	505.55	493.74	487.47	484.08
49000	621.65	603.41	588.09	575.13	564.10	554.66	546.54	539.54	516.08	504.03	497.62	494.17
50000	634.34	615.72	600.09	586.87	575.61	565.98	557.70	550.55	526.62	514.31	507.78	504.25
55000	697.77	677.29	660.10	645.55	633.17	622.58	613.47	605.60	579.28	565.74	558.56	554.68
60000	761.20	738.86	720.11	704.24	690.73	679.18	669.24	660.66	631.94	617.17	609.33	605.10
65000	824.64	800.43	780.11	762.93	748.30	735.77	725.01	715.71	684.60	668.60	660.11	655.53
70000	888.07	862.01	840.12	821.61	805.86	792.37	780.77	770.77	737.26	720.03	710.89	705.95
75000	951.50	923.58	900.13	880.30	863.42	848.97	836.54	825.82	789.92	771.46	761.67	756.38
80000	1014.94	985.15	960.14	938.99	920.98	905.57	892.31	880.87	842.58	822.90	812.44	806.80
85000	1078.37	1046.72	1020.15	997.67	978.54	962.16	948.08	935.93	895.25	874.33	863.22	857.23
90000	1141.80	1108.29	1080.16	1056.36	1036.10	1018.76	1003.85	990.98	947.91	925.76	914.00	907.65
95000	1205.23	1169.86	1140.16	1115.04	1093.66	1075.36	1059.62	1046.04	1000.57	977.19	964.78	958.08
100000	1268.67	1231.43	1200.17	1173.73	1151.22	1131.96	1115.39	1101.09	1053.23	1028.62	1015.55	1008.50

Table 1

12.25%

MONTHLY
PAYMENT REQUIRED TO AMORTIZE A LOAN

12%

TERM / AMOUNT	1 YEAR	2 YEARS	3 YEARS	4 YEARS	5 YEARS	6 YEARS	7 YEARS	8 YEARS	9 YEARS	10 YEARS	11 YEARS	12 YEARS
50	4.45	2.36	1.67	1.33	1.12	.99	.89	.82	.77	.73	.70	.67
100	8.90	4.72	3.34	2.65	2.24	1.97	1.78	1.64	1.54	1.45	1.39	1.33
200	17.80	9.44	6.67	5.30	4.48	3.94	3.56	3.28	3.07	2.90	2.77	2.66
300	26.69	14.16	10.01	7.94	6.72	5.91	5.34	4.92	4.60	4.35	4.15	3.99
400	35.59	18.88	13.34	10.59	8.95	7.88	7.12	6.56	6.14	5.80	5.54	5.32
500	44.49	23.60	16.67	13.23	11.19	9.85	8.90	8.20	7.67	7.25	6.92	6.65
600	53.38	28.32	20.01	15.88	13.43	11.81	10.68	9.84	9.20	8.70	8.30	7.98
700	62.28	33.04	23.34	18.52	15.66	13.78	12.46	11.48	10.73	10.15	9.68	9.31
800	71.18	37.76	26.67	21.17	17.90	15.75	14.23	13.12	12.27	11.60	11.07	10.63
900	80.07	42.48	30.01	23.82	20.14	17.72	16.01	14.76	13.80	13.05	12.45	11.96
1000	88.97	47.20	33.34	26.46	22.38	19.69	17.79	16.40	15.33	14.50	13.83	13.29
2000	177.94	94.39	66.67	52.92	44.75	39.37	35.58	32.79	30.66	28.99	27.66	26.58
3000	266.90	141.58	100.01	79.38	67.12	59.05	53.37	49.18	45.98	43.48	41.48	39.86
4000	355.87	188.77	133.34	105.83	89.49	78.73	71.15	65.57	61.31	57.97	55.31	53.15
5000	444.83	235.96	166.67	132.29	111.86	98.41	88.94	81.96	76.63	72.46	69.14	66.43
6000	533.80	283.15	200.01	158.75	134.23	118.09	106.73	98.35	91.96	86.96	82.96	79.72
7000	622.77	330.34	233.34	185.20	156.60	137.77	124.51	114.74	107.28	101.45	96.79	93.01
8000	711.73	377.53	266.68	211.66	178.97	157.45	142.30	131.13	122.61	115.94	110.62	106.29
9000	800.70	424.72	300.01	238.12	201.34	177.13	160.09	147.52	137.93	130.43	124.44	119.58
10000	889.66	471.91	333.34	264.57	223.71	196.81	177.87	163.91	153.26	144.92	138.27	132.86
11000	978.63	519.10	366.68	291.03	246.09	216.49	195.66	180.30	168.59	159.42	152.09	146.15
12000	1067.59	566.29	400.01	317.49	268.46	236.17	213.45	196.69	183.91	173.91	165.92	159.44
13000	1156.56	613.48	433.34	343.94	290.83	255.85	231.23	213.08	199.24	188.40	179.75	172.72
14000	1245.53	660.67	466.68	370.40	313.20	275.53	249.02	229.47	214.56	202.89	193.57	186.01
15000	1334.49	707.86	500.01	396.86	335.57	295.21	266.81	245.86	229.89	217.38	207.40	199.29
16000	1423.46	755.05	533.35	423.31	357.94	314.89	284.59	262.25	245.21	231.88	221.23	212.58
17000	1512.42	802.24	566.68	449.77	380.31	334.57	302.38	278.64	260.54	246.37	235.05	225.87
18000	1601.39	849.43	600.01	476.23	402.68	354.25	320.17	295.03	275.86	260.86	248.88	239.15
19000	1690.35	896.62	633.35	502.68	425.05	373.93	337.95	311.42	291.19	275.35	262.70	252.44
20000	1779.32	943.81	666.68	529.14	447.42	393.61	355.74	327.82	306.52	289.84	276.53	265.72
21000	1868.29	991.00	700.02	555.60	469.80	413.29	373.53	344.21	321.84	304.34	290.36	279.01
22000	1957.25	1038.19	733.35	582.05	492.17	432.97	391.31	360.60	337.17	318.83	304.18	292.30
23000	2046.22	1085.38	766.68	608.51	514.54	452.66	409.10	376.99	352.49	333.32	318.01	305.58
24000	2135.18	1132.57	800.02	634.97	536.91	472.34	426.89	393.38	367.82	347.81	331.84	318.87
25000	2224.15	1179.76	833.35	661.42	559.28	492.02	444.67	409.77	383.14	362.30	345.66	332.15
26000	2313.12	1226.95	866.68	687.88	581.65	511.70	462.46	426.16	398.47	376.80	359.49	345.44
27000	2402.08	1274.14	900.02	714.34	604.02	531.38	480.25	442.55	413.79	391.29	373.31	358.73
28000	2491.05	1321.33	933.35	740.79	626.39	551.06	498.03	458.94	429.12	405.78	387.14	372.01
29000	2580.01	1368.52	966.69	767.25	648.76	570.74	515.82	475.33	444.45	420.27	400.97	385.30
30000	2668.98	1415.71	1000.02	793.71	671.13	590.42	533.61	491.72	459.77	434.76	414.79	398.58
31000	2757.94	1462.90	1033.35	820.16	693.51	610.10	551.39	508.11	475.10	449.26	428.62	411.87
32000	2846.91	1510.09	1066.69	846.62	715.88	629.78	569.18	524.50	490.42	463.75	442.45	425.16
33000	2935.88	1557.29	1100.02	873.08	738.25	649.46	586.97	540.89	505.75	478.24	456.27	438.44
34000	3024.84	1604.48	1133.36	899.53	760.62	669.14	604.75	557.28	521.07	492.73	470.10	451.73
35000	3113.81	1651.67	1166.69	925.99	782.99	688.82	622.54	573.67	536.40	507.22	483.92	465.01
36000	3202.77	1698.86	1200.02	952.45	805.36	708.50	640.33	590.06	551.72	521.72	497.75	478.30
37000	3291.74	1746.05	1233.36	978.90	827.73	728.18	658.11	606.45	567.05	536.21	511.58	491.59
38000	3380.70	1793.24	1266.69	1005.36	850.10	747.86	675.90	622.84	582.38	550.70	525.40	504.87
39000	3469.67	1840.43	1300.02	1031.82	872.47	767.54	693.69	639.24	597.70	565.19	539.23	518.16
40000	3558.64	1887.62	1333.36	1058.28	894.84	787.22	711.47	655.63	613.03	579.68	553.06	531.44
41000	3647.60	1934.81	1366.69	1084.73	917.22	806.90	729.26	672.02	628.35	594.18	566.88	544.73
42000	3736.57	1982.00	1400.03	1111.19	939.59	826.58	747.05	688.41	643.68	608.67	580.71	558.02
43000	3825.53	2029.19	1433.36	1137.65	961.96	846.26	764.83	704.80	659.00	623.16	594.53	571.30
44000	3914.50	2076.38	1466.69	1164.10	984.33	865.94	782.62	721.19	674.33	637.65	608.36	584.59
45000	4003.47	2123.57	1500.03	1190.56	1006.70	885.62	800.41	737.58	689.65	652.14	622.19	597.87
46000	4092.43	2170.76	1533.36	1217.02	1029.07	905.31	818.19	753.97	704.98	666.64	636.01	611.16
47000	4181.40	2217.95	1566.70	1243.47	1051.44	924.99	835.98	770.36	720.31	681.13	649.84	624.45
48000	4270.36	2265.14	1600.03	1269.93	1073.81	944.67	853.77	786.75	735.63	695.62	663.67	637.73
49000	4359.33	2312.33	1633.36	1296.39	1096.18	964.35	871.55	803.14	750.96	710.11	677.49	651.02
50000	4448.29	2359.52	1666.70	1322.84	1118.55	984.03	889.34	819.53	766.28	724.60	691.32	664.30
55000	4893.12	2595.47	1833.37	1455.13	1230.41	1082.43	978.27	901.48	842.91	797.06	760.45	730.73
60000	5337.95	2831.42	2000.04	1587.41	1342.26	1180.83	1067.21	983.44	919.54	869.52	829.58	797.16
65000	5782.78	3067.37	2166.70	1719.69	1454.12	1279.23	1156.14	1065.39	996.17	941.98	898.71	863.59
70000	6227.61	3303.33	2333.37	1851.98	1565.97	1377.64	1245.07	1147.34	1072.79	1014.44	967.84	930.02
75000	6672.44	3539.28	2500.04	1984.26	1677.83	1476.04	1334.01	1229.29	1149.42	1086.90	1036.97	996.45
80000	7117.27	3775.23	2666.71	2116.55	1789.68	1574.44	1422.94	1311.25	1226.05	1159.36	1106.11	1062.88
85000	7562.10	4011.18	2833.38	2248.83	1901.54	1672.84	1511.88	1393.20	1302.68	1231.82	1175.24	1129.31
90000	8006.93	4247.13	3000.05	2381.11	2013.39	1771.24	1600.81	1475.15	1379.30	1304.28	1244.37	1195.74
95000	8451.75	4483.08	3166.72	2513.40	2125.25	1869.65	1689.74	1557.10	1455.93	1376.74	1313.50	1262.17
100000	8896.58	4719.04	3333.39	2645.68	2237.10	1968.05	1778.68	1639.06	1532.56	1449.20	1382.63	1328.60

Table 1

MONTHLY

12.25%

PAYMENT REQUIRED TO AMORTIZE A LOAN

TERM	13 YEARS	14 YEARS	15 YEARS	16 YEARS	17 YEARS	18 YEARS	19 YEARS	20 YEARS	25 YEARS	30 YEARS	35 YEARS	40 YEARS
OUNT												
50	.65	.63	.61	.60	.59	.58	.57	.56	.54	.53	.52	.52
100	1.29	1.25	1.22	1.20	1.17	1.15	1.14	1.12	1.08	1.05	1.04	1.03
200	2.57	2.50	2.44	2.39	2.34	2.30	2.27	2.24	2.15	2.10	2.08	2.06
300	3.86	3.75	3.65	3.58	3.51	3.45	3.40	3.36	3.22	3.15	3.11	3.09
400	5.14	4.99	4.87	4.77	4.68	4.60	4.54	4.48	4.29	4.20	4.15	4.12
500	6.43	6.24	6.09	5.96	5.84	5.75	5.67	5.60	5.36	5.24	5.18	5.15
600	7.71	7.49	7.30	7.15	7.01	6.90	6.80	6.72	6.44	6.29	6.22	6.18
700	8.99	8.74	8.52	8.34	8.18	8.05	7.93	7.83	7.51	7.34	7.25	7.21
800	10.28	9.98	9.74	9.53	9.35	9.20	9.07	8.95	8.58	8.39	8.29	8.23
900	11.56	11.23	10.95	10.72	10.52	10.35	10.20	10.07	9.65	9.44	9.32	9.26
1000	12.85	12.48	12.17	11.91	11.68	11.49	11.33	11.19	10.72	10.48	10.36	10.29
2000	25.69	24.95	24.33	23.81	23.36	22.98	22.66	22.38	21.44	20.96	20.71	20.58
3000	38.53	37.42	36.49	35.71	35.04	34.47	33.98	33.56	32.16	31.44	31.07	30.87
4000	51.37	49.90	48.66	47.61	46.72	45.96	45.31	44.75	42.87	41.92	41.42	41.15
5000	64.21	62.37	60.82	59.51	58.40	57.45	56.64	55.93	53.59	52.40	51.77	51.44
6000	77.06	74.84	72.98	71.41	70.08	68.94	67.96	67.12	64.31	62.88	62.13	61.73
7000	89.90	87.31	85.15	83.32	81.76	80.43	79.29	78.30	75.03	73.36	72.48	72.01
8000	102.74	99.79	97.31	95.22	93.44	91.92	90.61	89.49	85.74	83.84	82.83	82.30
9000	115.58	112.26	109.47	107.12	105.12	103.41	101.94	100.68	96.46	94.32	93.19	92.59
10000	128.42	124.73	121.63	119.02	116.80	114.90	113.27	111.86	107.18	104.79	103.54	102.87
11000	141.26	137.20	133.80	130.92	128.48	126.39	124.59	123.05	117.90	115.27	113.90	113.16
12000	154.11	149.68	145.96	142.82	140.16	137.88	135.92	134.23	128.61	125.75	124.25	123.45
13000	166.95	162.15	158.12	154.72	151.83	149.37	147.25	145.42	139.33	136.23	134.60	133.73
14000	179.79	174.62	170.29	166.63	163.51	160.85	158.57	156.60	150.05	146.71	144.96	144.02
15000	192.63	187.09	182.45	178.53	175.19	172.34	169.90	167.79	160.77	157.19	155.31	154.31
16000	205.47	199.57	194.61	190.43	186.87	183.83	181.22	178.98	171.48	167.67	165.66	164.59
17000	218.31	212.04	206.78	202.33	198.55	195.32	192.55	190.16	182.20	178.15	176.02	174.88
18000	231.16	224.51	218.94	214.23	210.23	206.81	203.88	201.35	192.92	188.63	186.37	185.17
19000	244.00	236.98	231.10	226.13	221.91	218.30	215.20	212.53	203.64	199.11	196.73	195.46
20000	256.84	249.46	243.26	238.04	233.59	229.79	226.53	223.72	214.35	209.58	207.08	205.74
21000	269.68	261.93	255.43	249.94	245.27	241.28	237.86	234.90	225.07	220.06	217.43	216.03
22000	282.52	274.40	267.59	261.84	256.95	252.77	249.18	246.09	235.79	230.54	227.79	226.32
23000	295.36	286.87	279.75	273.74	268.63	264.26	260.51	257.27	246.51	241.02	238.14	236.60
24000	308.21	299.35	291.92	285.64	280.31	275.75	271.83	268.46	257.22	251.50	248.49	246.89
25000	321.05	311.82	304.08	297.54	291.99	287.24	283.16	279.65	267.94	261.98	258.85	257.18
26000	333.89	324.29	316.24	309.44	303.66	298.73	294.49	290.83	278.66	272.46	269.20	267.46
27000	346.73	336.76	328.41	321.35	315.34	310.22	305.81	302.02	289.38	282.94	279.56	277.75
28000	359.57	349.24	340.57	335.25	327.02	321.70	317.14	313.20	300.09	293.42	289.91	288.04
29000	372.42	361.71	352.73	345.15	338.70	333.19	328.46	324.39	310.81	303.89	300.26	298.32
30000	385.26	374.18	364.89	357.05	350.38	344.68	339.79	335.57	321.53	314.37	310.62	308.61
31000	398.10	386.65	377.06	368.95	362.06	356.17	351.12	346.76	332.25	324.85	320.97	318.90
32000	410.94	399.13	389.22	380.85	373.74	367.66	362.44	357.95	342.96	335.33	331.32	329.18
33000	423.78	411.60	401.38	392.75	385.42	379.15	373.77	369.13	353.68	345.81	341.68	339.47
34000	436.62	424.07	413.55	404.66	397.10	390.64	385.10	380.32	364.40	356.29	352.03	349.76
35000	449.47	436.54	425.71	416.56	408.78	402.13	396.42	391.50	375.12	366.77	362.38	360.05
36000	462.31	449.02	437.87	428.46	420.46	413.62	407.75	402.69	385.83	377.25	372.74	370.33
37000	475.15	461.49	450.04	440.36	432.14	425.11	419.07	413.87	396.55	387.73	383.09	380.62
38000	487.99	473.96	462.20	452.26	443.82	436.60	430.40	425.06	407.27	398.21	393.45	390.91
39000	500.83	486.43	474.36	464.16	455.49	448.09	441.73	436.25	417.99	408.68	403.80	401.19
40000	513.67	498.91	486.52	476.07	467.17	459.58	453.05	447.43	428.70	419.16	414.15	411.48
41000	526.52	511.38	498.69	487.97	478.85	471.07	464.38	458.62	439.42	429.64	424.51	421.77
42000	539.36	523.85	510.85	499.87	490.53	482.55	475.71	469.80	450.14	440.12	434.86	432.05
43000	552.20	536.32	523.01	511.77	502.21	494.04	487.03	480.99	460.85	450.60	445.21	442.34
44000	565.04	548.80	535.18	523.67	513.89	505.53	498.36	492.17	471.57	461.08	455.57	452.63
45000	577.88	561.27	547.34	535.57	525.57	517.02	509.68	503.36	482.29	471.56	465.92	462.91
46000	590.72	573.74	559.50	547.47	537.25	528.51	521.01	514.54	493.01	482.04	476.28	473.20
47000	603.57	586.21	571.67	559.38	548.93	540.00	532.34	525.73	503.72	492.52	486.63	483.49
48000	616.41	598.69	583.83	571.28	560.61	551.49	543.66	536.92	514.44	503.00	496.98	493.77
49000	629.25	611.16	595.99	583.18	572.29	562.98	554.99	548.10	525.16	513.47	507.34	504.06
50000	642.09	623.63	608.15	595.08	583.97	574.47	566.31	559.29	535.88	523.95	517.69	514.35
55000	706.30	685.99	668.97	654.59	642.36	631.91	622.95	615.22	589.46	576.35	569.46	565.78
60000	770.51	748.36	729.78	714.10	700.76	689.36	679.58	671.14	643.05	628.74	621.23	617.22
65000	834.72	810.72	790.60	773.60	759.15	746.81	736.21	727.07	696.64	681.14	673.00	668.65
70000	898.93	873.08	851.41	833.11	817.55	804.25	792.84	783.00	750.23	733.53	724.76	720.09
75000	963.13	935.45	912.23	892.62	875.95	861.70	849.47	838.93	803.81	785.93	776.53	771.52
80000	1027.34	997.81	973.04	952.13	934.34	919.15	906.10	894.86	857.40	838.32	828.30	822.95
85000	1091.55	1060.17	1033.86	1011.63	992.74	976.59	962.73	950.78	910.99	890.72	880.07	874.39
90000	1155.76	1122.53	1094.67	1071.14	1051.14	1034.04	1019.36	1006.71	964.57	943.11	931.84	925.82
95000	1219.97	1184.90	1155.49	1130.65	1109.53	1091.49	1075.99	1062.64	1018.16	995.51	983.61	977.26
100000	1284.18	1247.26	1216.30	1190.16	1167.93	1148.93	1132.62	1118.57	1071.75	1047.90	1035.38	1028.69

12%

Table 1

12.50%

MONTHLY

PAYMENT REQUIRED TO AMORTIZE A LOAN

12%

TERM AMOUNT	1 YEAR	2 YEARS	3 YEARS	4 YEARS	5 YEARS	6 YEARS	7 YEARS	8 YEARS	9 YEARS	10 YEARS	11 YEARS	12 YEARS
50	4.46	2.37	1.68	1.33	1.13	1.00	.90	.83	.78	.74	.70	.68
100	8.91	4.74	3.35	2.66	2.25	1.99	1.80	1.66	1.55	1.47	1.40	1.35
200	17.82	9.47	6.70	5.32	4.50	3.97	3.59	3.31	3.10	2.93	2.80	2.69
300	26.73	14.20	10.04	7.98	6.75	5.95	5.38	4.96	4.65	4.40	4.20	4.04
400	35.64	18.93	13.39	10.64	9.00	7.93	7.17	6.62	6.19	5.86	5.60	5.38
500	44.55	23.66	16.73	13.29	11.25	9.91	8.97	8.27	7.74	7.32	6.99	6.72
600	53.45	28.39	20.08	15.95	13.50	11.89	10.76	9.92	9.29	8.79	8.39	8.07
700	62.36	33.12	23.42	18.61	15.75	13.87	12.55	11.58	10.83	10.25	9.79	9.41
800	71.27	37.85	26.77	21.27	18.00	15.85	14.34	13.23	12.38	11.72	11.19	10.76
900	80.18	42.58	30.11	23.93	20.25	17.84	16.13	14.88	13.93	13.18	12.58	12.10
1000	89.09	47.31	33.46	26.58	22.50	19.82	17.93	16.53	15.47	14.64	13.98	13.44
2000	178.17	94.62	66.91	53.16	45.00	39.63	35.85	33.06	30.94	29.28	27.96	26.88
3000	267.25	141.93	100.37	79.74	67.50	59.44	53.77	49.59	46.41	43.92	41.93	40.32
4000	356.34	189.23	133.82	106.32	90.00	79.25	71.69	66.12	61.88	58.56	55.91	53.76
5000	445.42	236.54	167.27	132.90	112.49	99.06	89.61	82.65	77.34	73.19	69.88	67.20
6000	534.50	283.85	200.73	159.48	134.99	118.87	107.53	99.18	92.81	87.83	83.86	80.64
7000	623.59	331.16	234.18	186.06	157.49	138.68	125.45	115.71	108.28	102.47	97.83	94.08
8000	712.67	378.46	267.63	212.64	179.99	158.49	143.37	132.24	123.75	117.11	111.81	107.51
9000	801.75	425.77	301.09	239.22	202.49	178.31	161.30	148.76	139.21	131.74	125.78	120.95
10000	890.83	473.08	334.54	265.80	224.98	198.12	179.22	165.29	154.68	146.38	139.76	134.39
11000	979.92	520.39	367.99	292.38	247.48	217.93	197.14	181.82	170.15	161.02	153.73	147.83
12000	1069.00	567.69	401.45	318.96	269.98	237.74	215.06	198.35	185.62	175.66	167.71	161.27
13000	1158.08	615.00	434.90	345.54	292.48	257.55	232.98	214.88	201.08	190.29	181.69	174.71
14000	1247.17	662.31	468.36	372.12	314.98	277.36	250.90	231.41	216.55	204.93	195.66	188.15
15000	1336.25	709.61	501.81	398.70	337.47	297.17	268.82	247.94	232.02	219.57	209.64	201.58
16000	1425.33	756.92	535.26	425.28	359.97	316.98	286.74	264.47	247.49	234.21	223.61	215.02
17000	1514.41	804.23	568.72	451.86	382.47	336.80	304.67	280.99	262.95	248.84	237.59	228.46
18000	1603.50	851.54	602.17	478.44	404.97	356.61	322.59	297.52	278.42	263.48	251.56	241.90
19000	1692.58	898.84	635.62	505.02	427.47	376.42	340.51	314.05	293.89	278.12	265.54	255.34
20000	1781.66	946.15	669.08	531.60	449.96	396.23	358.43	330.58	309.36	292.76	279.51	268.78
21000	1870.75	993.46	702.53	558.18	472.46	416.04	376.35	347.11	324.82	307.39	293.49	282.22
22000	1959.83	1040.77	735.98	584.76	494.96	435.85	394.27	363.64	340.29	322.03	307.46	295.65
23000	2048.91	1088.07	769.44	611.34	517.46	455.66	412.19	380.17	355.76	336.67	321.44	309.09
24000	2137.99	1135.38	802.89	637.92	539.96	475.47	430.11	396.70	371.23	351.31	335.42	322.53
25000	2227.08	1182.69	836.35	664.50	562.45	495.28	448.04	413.23	386.69	365.95	349.39	335.97
26000	2316.16	1230.00	869.80	691.08	584.95	515.10	465.96	429.75	402.16	380.58	363.37	349.41
27000	2405.24	1277.30	903.25	717.66	607.45	534.91	483.88	446.28	417.63	395.22	377.34	362.85
28000	2494.33	1324.61	936.71	744.24	629.95	554.72	501.80	462.81	433.10	409.86	391.32	376.29
29000	2583.41	1371.92	970.16	770.82	652.45	574.53	519.72	479.34	448.56	424.50	405.29	389.72
30000	2672.49	1419.22	1003.61	797.40	674.94	594.34	537.64	495.87	464.03	439.13	419.27	403.16
31000	2761.57	1466.53	1037.07	823.98	697.44	614.15	555.56	512.40	479.50	453.77	433.24	416.60
32000	2850.66	1513.84	1070.52	850.56	719.94	633.96	573.48	528.93	494.97	468.41	447.22	430.04
33000	2939.74	1561.15	1103.97	877.14	742.44	653.77	591.41	545.46	510.43	483.05	461.19	443.48
34000	3028.82	1608.45	1137.43	903.72	764.93	673.59	609.33	561.98	525.90	497.68	475.17	456.92
35000	3117.91	1655.76	1170.88	930.30	787.43	693.40	627.25	578.51	541.37	512.32	489.15	470.36
36000	3206.99	1703.07	1204.34	956.88	809.93	713.21	645.17	595.04	556.84	526.96	503.12	483.79
37000	3296.07	1750.38	1237.79	983.46	832.43	733.02	663.09	611.57	572.30	541.60	517.10	497.23
38000	3385.15	1797.68	1271.24	1010.04	854.93	752.83	681.01	628.10	587.77	556.23	531.07	510.67
39000	3474.24	1844.99	1304.70	1036.63	877.42	772.64	698.93	644.63	603.24	570.87	545.05	524.11
40000	3563.32	1892.30	1338.15	1063.20	899.92	792.45	716.85	661.16	618.71	585.51	559.02	537.55
41000	3652.40	1939.60	1371.60	1089.78	922.42	812.26	734.78	677.69	634.17	600.15	573.00	550.99
42000	3741.49	1986.91	1405.06	1116.36	944.92	832.07	752.70	694.21	649.64	614.78	586.97	564.43
43000	3830.57	2034.22	1438.51	1142.94	967.42	851.89	770.62	710.74	665.11	629.42	600.95	577.86
44000	3919.65	2081.53	1471.96	1169.52	989.91	871.70	788.54	727.27	680.58	644.06	614.92	591.30
45000	4008.73	2128.83	1505.42	1196.10	1012.41	891.51	806.46	743.80	696.04	658.70	628.90	604.74
46000	4097.82	2176.14	1538.87	1222.68	1034.91	911.32	824.38	760.33	711.51	673.34	642.87	618.18
47000	4186.90	2223.45	1572.33	1249.26	1057.41	931.13	842.30	776.86	726.98	687.97	656.85	631.62
48000	4275.98	2270.76	1605.78	1275.84	1079.91	950.94	860.22	793.39	742.45	702.61	670.83	645.06
49000	4365.07	2318.06	1639.23	1302.42	1102.40	970.75	878.15	809.92	757.91	717.25	684.80	658.50
50000	4454.15	2365.37	1672.69	1329.00	1124.90	990.56	896.07	826.45	773.38	731.89	698.78	671.93
55000	4899.56	2601.91	1839.95	1461.90	1237.39	1089.62	985.67	909.09	850.72	805.07	768.65	739.13
60000	5344.98	2838.44	2007.22	1594.80	1349.88	1188.68	1075.28	991.73	928.06	878.26	838.53	806.32
65000	5790.39	3074.98	2174.49	1727.70	1462.37	1287.73	1164.89	1074.38	1005.40	951.45	908.41	873.51
70000	6235.81	3311.52	2341.76	1860.60	1574.86	1386.79	1254.49	1157.02	1082.73	1024.64	978.29	940.71
75000	6681.22	3548.05	2509.03	1993.50	1687.35	1485.84	1344.10	1239.67	1160.07	1097.83	1048.16	1007.90
80000	7126.63	3784.59	2676.30	2126.40	1799.84	1584.90	1433.70	1322.31	1237.41	1171.01	1118.04	1075.09
85000	7572.05	4021.13	2843.56	2259.30	1912.33	1683.96	1523.31	1404.95	1314.75	1244.20	1187.92	1142.28
90000	8017.46	4257.66	3010.83	2392.20	2024.82	1783.01	1612.92	1487.60	1392.08	1317.39	1257.79	1209.48
95000	8462.88	4494.20	3178.10	2525.10	2137.31	1882.07	1702.52	1570.24	1469.42	1390.58	1327.67	1276.67
100000	8908.29	4730.74	3345.37	2658.00	2249.80	1981.12	1792.13	1652.89	1546.76	1463.77	1397.55	1343.86

Table 1

MONTHLY   12.50%

PAYMENT REQUIRED TO AMORTIZE A LOAN

TERM / AMOUNT	13 YEARS	14 YEARS	15 YEARS	16 YEARS	17 YEARS	18 YEARS	19 YEARS	20 YEARS	25 YEARS	30 YEARS	35 YEARS	40 YEARS
50	.65	.64	.62	.61	.60	.59	.58	.57	.55	.54	.53	.53
100	1.30	1.27	1.24	1.21	1.19	1.17	1.15	1.14	1.10	1.07	1.06	1.05
200	2.60	2.53	2.47	2.42	2.37	2.34	2.30	2.28	2.19	2.14	2.12	2.10
300	3.90	3.79	3.70	3.63	3.56	3.50	3.45	3.41	3.28	3.21	3.17	3.15
400	5.20	5.06	4.94	4.83	4.74	4.67	4.60	4.55	4.37	4.27	4.23	4.20
500	6.50	6.32	6.17	6.04	5.93	5.84	5.75	5.69	5.46	5.34	5.28	5.25
600	7.80	7.58	7.40	7.25	7.11	7.00	6.90	6.82	6.55	6.41	6.34	6.30
700	9.10	8.85	8.63	8.45	8.30	8.17	8.05	7.96	7.64	7.48	7.39	7.35
800	10.40	10.11	9.87	9.66	9.48	9.33	9.20	9.09	8.73	8.54	8.45	8.40
900	11.70	11.37	11.10	10.87	10.67	10.50	10.35	10.23	9.82	9.61	9.50	9.45
1000	13.00	12.64	12.33	12.07	11.85	11.67	11.50	11.37	10.91	10.68	10.56	10.49
2000	26.00	25.27	24.66	24.14	23.70	23.33	23.00	22.73	21.81	21.35	21.11	20.98
3000	39.00	37.90	36.98	36.21	35.55	34.99	34.50	34.09	32.72	32.02	31.66	31.47
4000	52.00	50.53	49.31	48.27	47.39	46.65	46.00	45.45	43.62	42.70	42.22	41.96
5000	64.99	63.16	61.63	60.34	59.24	58.31	57.50	56.81	54.52	53.37	52.77	52.45
6000	77.99	75.80	73.96	72.41	71.09	69.97	69.00	68.17	65.43	64.04	63.32	62.94
7000	90.99	88.43	86.28	84.47	82.94	81.63	80.50	79.53	76.33	74.71	73.87	73.43
8000	103.99	101.06	98.61	96.54	94.78	93.29	92.00	90.90	87.23	85.39	84.43	83.92
9000	116.98	113.69	110.93	108.61	106.63	104.95	103.50	102.26	98.14	96.06	94.98	94.41
10000	129.98	126.32	123.26	120.67	118.48	116.61	115.00	113.62	109.04	106.73	105.53	104.90
11000	142.98	138.95	135.58	132.74	130.32	128.27	126.50	124.98	119.94	117.40	116.08	115.39
12000	155.98	151.59	147.91	144.81	142.17	139.93	138.00	136.34	130.85	128.08	126.64	125.88
13000	168.97	164.22	160.23	156.87	154.02	151.59	149.50	147.70	141.75	138.75	137.19	136.36
14000	181.97	176.85	172.56	168.94	165.87	163.25	161.00	159.06	152.65	149.42	147.74	146.85
15000	194.97	189.48	184.88	181.01	177.71	174.91	172.50	170.43	163.56	160.09	158.29	157.34
16000	207.97	202.11	197.21	193.07	189.56	186.57	184.00	181.79	174.46	170.77	168.85	167.83
17000	220.97	214.74	209.53	205.14	201.41	198.23	195.50	193.15	185.37	181.44	179.40	178.32
18000	233.96	227.38	221.86	217.21	213.26	209.89	207.00	204.51	196.27	192.11	189.95	188.81
19000	246.96	240.01	234.18	229.27	225.10	221.55	218.50	215.87	207.17	202.78	200.50	199.30
20000	259.96	252.64	246.51	241.34	236.95	233.21	230.00	227.23	218.08	213.46	211.06	209.79
21000	272.96	265.27	258.83	253.41	248.80	244.87	241.49	238.59	228.98	224.13	221.61	220.28
22000	285.95	277.90	271.16	265.47	260.64	256.53	252.99	249.96	239.88	234.80	232.16	230.77
23000	298.95	290.53	283.49	277.54	272.49	268.19	264.49	261.32	250.79	245.47	242.71	241.26
24000	311.95	303.17	295.81	289.61	284.34	279.85	275.99	272.68	261.69	256.15	253.27	251.75
25000	324.95	315.80	308.14	301.67	296.19	291.51	287.49	284.04	272.59	266.82	263.82	262.23
26000	337.94	328.43	320.46	313.74	308.03	303.17	298.99	295.40	283.50	277.49	274.37	272.72
27000	350.94	341.06	332.79	325.81	319.88	314.83	310.49	306.76	294.40	288.16	284.92	283.21
28000	363.94	353.69	345.11	337.87	331.73	326.49	321.99	318.12	305.30	298.84	295.48	293.70
29000	376.94	366.32	357.44	349.94	343.58	338.15	333.49	329.49	316.21	309.51	306.03	304.19
30000	389.93	378.96	369.76	362.01	355.42	349.81	344.99	340.85	327.11	320.18	316.58	314.68
31000	402.93	391.59	382.09	374.07	367.27	361.47	356.49	352.21	338.01	330.85	327.13	325.17
32000	415.93	404.22	394.41	386.14	379.12	373.13	367.99	363.57	348.92	341.53	337.69	335.66
33000	428.93	416.85	406.74	398.21	390.96	384.79	379.49	374.93	359.82	352.20	348.24	346.15
34000	441.93	429.48	419.06	410.27	402.81	396.45	390.99	386.29	370.73	362.87	358.79	356.64
35000	454.92	442.11	431.39	422.34	414.66	408.11	402.49	397.65	381.63	373.55	369.34	367.13
36000	467.92	454.75	443.71	434.41	426.51	419.77	413.99	409.02	392.53	384.22	379.90	377.62
37000	480.92	467.38	456.04	446.47	438.35	431.43	425.49	420.38	403.44	394.89	390.45	388.11
38000	493.92	480.01	468.36	458.54	450.20	443.09	436.99	431.74	414.34	405.56	401.00	398.59
39000	506.91	492.64	480.69	470.61	462.05	454.75	448.49	443.10	425.24	416.24	411.55	409.08
40000	519.91	505.27	493.01	482.67	473.90	466.41	459.99	454.46	436.15	426.91	422.11	419.57
41000	532.91	517.90	505.34	494.74	485.74	478.07	471.48	465.82	447.05	437.58	432.66	430.06
42000	545.91	530.54	517.66	506.81	497.59	489.73	482.98	477.18	457.95	448.25	443.21	440.55
43000	558.90	543.17	529.99	518.87	509.44	501.39	494.48	488.55	468.86	458.93	453.76	451.04
44000	571.90	555.80	542.31	530.94	521.28	513.05	505.98	499.91	479.76	469.60	464.32	461.53
45000	584.90	568.43	554.64	543.01	533.13	524.71	517.48	511.27	490.66	480.27	474.87	472.02
46000	597.90	581.06	566.97	555.07	544.98	536.37	528.98	522.63	501.57	490.94	485.42	482.51
47000	610.90	593.69	579.29	567.14	556.83	548.03	540.48	533.99	512.47	501.62	495.97	493.00
48000	623.89	606.33	591.62	579.21	568.67	559.69	551.98	545.35	523.37	512.29	506.53	503.49
49000	636.89	618.96	603.94	591.27	580.52	571.35	563.48	556.71	534.28	522.96	517.08	513.98
50000	649.89	631.59	616.27	603.34	592.37	583.01	574.98	568.08	545.18	533.63	527.63	524.46
55000	714.88	694.75	677.89	663.67	651.60	641.31	632.48	624.88	599.70	587.00	580.39	576.91
60000	779.86	757.91	739.52	724.01	710.84	699.61	689.98	681.69	654.22	640.36	633.16	629.36
65000	844.85	821.06	801.14	784.34	770.08	757.91	747.47	738.50	708.74	693.72	685.92	681.80
70000	909.84	884.22	862.77	844.67	829.31	816.21	804.97	795.30	763.25	747.09	738.68	734.25
75000	974.83	947.38	924.40	905.01	888.55	874.51	862.47	852.11	817.77	800.45	791.45	786.69
80000	1039.82	1010.54	986.02	965.34	947.79	932.81	919.97	908.92	872.29	853.81	844.21	839.14
85000	1104.81	1073.70	1047.65	1025.67	1007.02	991.11	977.46	965.72	926.81	907.17	896.97	891.59
90000	1169.79	1136.86	1109.27	1086.01	1066.26	1049.41	1034.96	1022.53	981.32	960.54	949.73	944.03
95000	1234.78	1200.01	1170.90	1146.34	1125.49	1107.71	1092.46	1079.34	1035.84	1013.90	1002.50	996.48
100000	1299.77	1263.17	1232.53	1206.67	1184.73	1166.01	1149.96	1136.15	1090.36	1067.26	1055.26	1048.92

12%

Table 1

12.75%

MONTHLY

PAYMENT REQUIRED TO AMORTIZE A LOAN

12%

TERM AMOUNT	1 YEAR	2 YEARS	3 YEARS	4 YEARS	5 YEARS	6 YEARS	7 YEARS	8 YEARS	9 YEARS	10 YEARS	11 YEARS	12 YEARS
50	4.47	2.38	1.68	1.34	1.14	1.00	.91	.84	.79	.74	.71	.68
100	8.93	4.75	3.36	2.68	2.27	2.00	1.81	1.67	1.57	1.48	1.42	1.36
200	17.85	9.49	6.72	5.35	4.53	3.99	3.62	3.34	3.13	2.96	2.83	2.72
300	26.77	14.23	10.08	8.02	6.79	5.99	5.42	5.01	4.69	4.44	4.24	4.08
400	35.69	18.97	13.43	10.69	9.06	7.98	7.23	6.67	6.25	5.92	5.66	5.44
500	44.61	23.72	16.79	13.36	11.32	9.98	9.03	8.34	7.81	7.40	7.07	6.80
600	53.53	28.46	20.15	16.03	13.58	11.97	10.84	10.01	9.37	8.88	8.48	8.16
700	62.45	33.20	23.51	18.70	15.84	13.96	12.64	11.67	10.93	10.35	9.89	9.52
800	71.37	37.94	26.86	21.37	18.11	15.96	14.45	13.34	12.49	11.83	11.31	10.88
900	80.29	42.69	30.22	24.04	20.37	17.95	16.26	15.01	14.05	13.31	12.72	12.24
1000	89.21	47.43	33.58	26.71	22.63	19.95	18.06	16.67	15.62	14.79	14.13	13.60
2000	178.41	94.85	67.15	53.41	45.26	39.89	36.12	33.34	31.23	29.57	28.26	27.19
3000	267.61	142.28	100.73	80.12	67.88	59.83	54.17	50.01	46.84	44.36	42.38	40.78
4000	356.81	189.70	134.30	106.82	90.51	79.77	72.23	66.68	62.45	59.14	56.51	54.37
5000	446.01	237.13	167.87	133.52	113.13	99.72	90.29	83.34	78.06	73.92	70.63	67.97
6000	535.21	284.55	201.45	160.23	135.76	119.66	108.34	100.01	93.67	88.71	84.76	81.56
7000	624.41	331.98	235.02	186.93	158.38	139.60	126.40	116.68	109.28	103.49	98.88	95.15
8000	713.61	379.40	268.59	213.63	181.01	159.54	144.46	133.35	124.89	118.28	113.01	108.74
9000	802.81	426.83	302.17	240.34	203.63	179.49	162.51	150.01	140.50	133.06	127.13	122.33
10000	892.01	474.25	335.74	267.04	226.26	199.43	180.57	166.68	156.11	147.84	141.26	135.93
11000	981.21	521.67	369.32	293.74	248.88	219.37	198.62	183.35	171.72	162.63	155.38	149.52
12000	1070.41	569.10	402.89	320.45	271.51	239.31	216.68	200.02	187.33	177.41	169.51	163.11
13000	1159.61	616.52	436.46	347.15	294.13	259.26	234.74	216.69	202.94	192.20	183.63	176.70
14000	1248.81	663.95	470.04	373.86	316.76	279.20	252.79	233.35	218.55	206.98	197.76	190.29
15000	1338.01	711.37	503.61	400.56	339.38	299.14	270.85	250.02	234.16	221.76	211.89	203.89
16000	1427.21	758.80	537.18	427.26	362.01	319.08	288.91	266.69	249.77	236.55	226.01	217.48
17000	1516.41	806.22	570.76	453.97	384.64	339.03	306.96	283.36	265.38	251.33	240.14	231.07
18000	1605.61	853.65	604.33	480.67	407.26	358.97	325.02	300.02	280.99	266.12	254.26	244.66
19000	1694.81	901.07	637.90	507.37	429.89	378.91	343.08	316.69	296.60	280.090	268.39	258.25
20000	1784.01	948.49	671.48	534.08	452.51	398.85	361.13	333.36	312.21	295.68	282.51	271.85
21000	1873.21	995.92	705.05	560.78	475.14	418.80	379.19	350.03	327.82	310.47	296.64	285.44
22000	1962.41	1043.34	738.63	587.48	497.76	438.74	397.24	366.69	343.43	325.25	310.76	299.03
23000	2051.61	1090.77	772.20	614.19	520.39	458.68	415.30	383.36	359.04	340.04	324.89	312.62
24000	2140.81	1138.19	805.77	640.89	543.01	478.62	433.36	400.03	374.65	354.82	339.01	326.21
25000	2230.01	1185.62	839.35	667.59	565.64	498.57	451.41	416.70	390.26	369.60	353.14	339.81
26000	2319.21	1233.04	872.92	694.30	588.26	518.51	469.47	433.37	405.87	384.39	367.26	353.40
27000	2408.41	1280.47	906.49	721.00	610.89	538.45	487.53	450.03	421.48	399.17	381.39	366.99
28000	2497.61	1327.89	940.07	747.71	633.51	558.39	505.58	466.70	437.09	413.96	395.52	380.58
29000	2586.81	1375.31	973.64	774.41	656.14	578.33	523.64	483.37	452.70	428.74	409.64	394.17
30000	2676.01	1422.74	1007.21	801.11	678.76	598.28	541.69	500.04	468.31	443.52	423.77	407.77
31000	2765.21	1470.16	1040.79	827.82	701.39	618.22	559.75	516.70	483.92	458.31	437.89	421.36
32000	2854.61	1517.59	1074.36	854.52	724.01	638.16	577.81	533.37	499.53	473.09	452.02	434.95
33000	2943.61	1565.01	1107.94	881.22	746.64	658.10	595.86	550.04	515.14	487.88	466.14	448.54
34000	3032.81	1612.44	1141.51	907.93	769.27	678.05	613.92	566.71	530.75	502.66	480.27	462.13
35000	3122.01	1659.86	1175.08	934.63	791.89	697.99	631.98	583.38	546.36	517.44	494.39	475.73
36000	3211.21	1707.29	1208.66	961.33	814.52	717.93	650.03	600.04	561.97	532.23	508.52	489.32
37000	3300.41	1754.71	1242.23	988.04	837.14	737.87	668.09	616.71	577.58	547.01	522.64	502.91
38000	3389.61	1802.14	1275.80	1014.74	859.77	757.82	686.15	633.38	593.19	561.80	536.77	516.50
39000	3478.81	1849.56	1309.38	1041.44	882.39	777.76	704.20	650.05	608.80	576.58	550.89	530.09
40000	3568.01	1896.98	1342.95	1068.15	905.02	797.70	722.26	666.71	624.41	591.36	565.02	543.69
41000	3657.21	1944.41	1376.53	1094.85	927.64	817.64	740.31	683.38	640.02	606.15	579.15	557.28
42000	3746.41	1991.83	1410.10	1121.56	950.27	837.59	758.37	700.05	655.63	620.93	593.27	570.87
43000	3835.61	2039.26	1443.67	1148.26	972.89	857.53	776.43	716.72	671.24	635.72	607.40	584.46
44000	3924.81	2086.68	1477.25	1174.96	995.52	877.47	794.48	733.38	686.86	650.50	621.52	598.05
45000	4014.01	2134.11	1510.82	1201.67	1018.14	897.41	812.54	750.05	702.47	665.28	635.65	611.65
46000	4103.21	2181.53	1544.39	1228.37	1040.77	917.36	830.60	766.72	718.08	680.07	649.77	625.24
47000	4192.41	2228.96	1577.97	1255.07	1063.39	937.30	848.65	783.39	733.69	694.85	663.90	638.83
48000	4281.61	2276.38	1611.54	1281.78	1086.02	957.24	866.71	800.06	749.30	709.64	678.02	652.42
49000	4370.81	2323.80	1645.11	1308.48	1108.64	977.18	884.76	816.72	764.91	724.42	692.15	666.01
50000	4460.01	2371.23	1678.69	1335.18	1131.27	997.13	902.82	833.39	780.52	739.20	706.27	679.61
55000	4906.01	2608.35	1846.56	1468.70	1244.40	1096.84	993.10	916.73	858.57	813.12	776.90	747.57
60000	5352.01	2845.47	2014.42	1602.22	1357.52	1196.55	1083.38	1000.07	936.62	887.04	847.53	815.53
65000	5798.01	3082.60	2182.29	1735.74	1470.65	1296.26	1173.67	1083.41	1014.67	960.96	918.15	883.49
70000	6244.01	3319.72	2350.16	1869.26	1583.78	1395.97	1263.95	1166.75	1092.72	1034.88	988.78	951.45
75000	6690.01	3556.84	2518.03	2002.77	1696.90	1495.69	1354.23	1250.08	1170.77	1108.80	1059.41	1019.41
80000	7136.01	3793.96	2685.90	2136.29	1810.03	1595.40	1444.51	1333.42	1248.82	1182.72	1130.04	1087.37
85000	7582.01	4031.09	2853.77	2269.81	1923.16	1695.11	1534.79	1416.76	1326.87	1256.64	1200.66	1155.33
90000	8028.01	4268.21	3021.63	2403.33	2036.28	1794.82	1625.07	1500.10	1404.93	1330.56	1271.29	1223.29
95000	8474.01	4505.33	3189.50	2536.85	2149.41	1894.53	1715.36	1583.44	1482.98	1404.48	1341.92	1291.25
100000	8920.01	4742.45	3357.37	2670.36	2262.54	1994.25	1805.64	1666.78	1561.03	1478.40	1412.54	1359.21

Table 1

MONTHLY   12.75%

PAYMENT REQUIRED TO AMORTIZE A LOAN

TERM / AMOUNT	13 YEARS	14 YEARS	15 YEARS	16 YEARS	17 YEARS	18 YEARS	19 YEARS	20 YEARS	25 YEARS	30 YEARS	35 YEARS	40 YEARS
50	.66	.64	.63	.62	.61	.60	.59	.58	.56	.55	.54	.54
100	1.32	1.28	1.25	1.23	1.21	1.19	1.17	1.16	1.11	1.09	1.08	1.07
200	2.64	2.56	2.50	2.45	2.41	2.37	2.34	2.31	2.22	2.18	2.16	2.14
300	3.95	3.84	3.75	3.67	3.61	3.55	3.51	3.47	3.33	3.27	3.23	3.21
400	5.27	5.12	5.00	4.90	4.81	4.74	4.67	4.62	4.44	4.35	4.31	4.28
500	6.58	6.40	6.25	6.12	6.01	5.92	5.84	5.77	5.55	5.44	5.38	5.35
600	7.90	7.68	7.50	7.34	7.21	7.10	7.01	6.93	6.66	6.53	6.46	6.42
700	9.21	8.96	8.75	8.57	8.42	8.29	8.18	8.08	7.77	7.61	7.53	7.49
800	10.53	10.24	10.00	9.79	9.62	9.47	9.34	9.24	8.88	8.70	8.61	8.56
900	11.84	11.52	11.24	11.01	10.82	10.65	10.51	10.39	9.99	9.79	9.68	9.63
1000	13.16	12.80	12.49	12.23	12.02	11.84	11.68	11.54	11.10	10.87	10.76	10.70
2000	26.31	25.59	24.98	24.47	24.04	23.67	23.35	23.08	22.19	21.74	21.51	21.39
3000	39.47	38.38	37.47	36.70	36.05	35.50	35.03	34.62	33.28	32.61	32.26	32.08
4000	52.62	51.17	49.96	48.94	48.07	47.33	46.70	46.16	44.37	43.47	43.01	42.77
5000	65.78	63.96	62.45	61.17	60.09	59.16	58.37	57.70	55.46	54.34	53.76	53.46
6000	78.93	76.76	74.94	73.40	72.10	71.00	70.05	69.23	66.55	65.21	64.52	64.16
7000	92.09	89.55	87.42	85.63	84.12	82.83	81.72	80.77	77.64	76.07	75.27	74.85
8000	105.24	102.34	99.91	97.87	96.13	94.66	93.40	92.31	88.73	86.94	86.02	85.54
9000	118.40	115.13	112.40	110.10	108.15	106.49	105.07	103.85	99.82	97.81	96.77	96.23
10000	131.55	127.92	124.89	122.33	120.17	118.32	116.74	115.39	110.91	108.67	107.52	106.92
11000	144.70	140.71	137.38	134.57	132.18	130.15	128.42	126.92	122.00	119.54	118.28	117.62
12000	157.86	153.51	149.87	146.80	144.20	141.99	140.09	138.46	133.09	130.41	129.03	128.31
13000	171.01	166.30	162.35	159.03	156.22	153.82	151.76	150.00	144.18	141.28	139.78	139.00
14000	184.17	179.09	174.84	171.26	168.23	165.65	163.44	161.54	155.27	152.14	150.53	149.69
15000	197.32	191.88	187.33	183.50	180.25	177.48	175.11	173.08	166.36	163.01	161.28	160.38
16000	210.48	204.67	199.82	195.73	192.26	189.31	186.79	184.61	177.45	173.88	172.04	171.08
17000	223.63	217.46	212.31	207.96	204.28	201.14	198.46	196.15	188.54	184.74	182.79	181.77
18000	236.79	230.26	224.80	220.20	216.30	212.98	210.13	207.69	199.63	195.61	193.54	192.46
19000	249.94	243.05	237.28	232.43	228.31	224.81	221.81	219.23	210.72	206.48	204.29	203.15
20000	263.09	255.84	249.77	244.66	240.33	236.64	233.48	230.77	221.82	217.34	215.04	213.84
21000	276.25	268.63	262.26	256.89	252.35	248.47	245.15	242.31	232.91	228.21	225.80	224.54
22000	289.40	281.42	274.75	269.13	264.36	260.30	256.83	253.84	244.00	239.08	236.55	235.23
23000	302.56	294.21	287.24	281.36	276.38	272.13	268.50	265.38	255.09	249.94	247.30	245.92
24000	315.71	307.01	299.73	293.59	288.39	283.97	280.18	276.92	266.18	260.81	258.05	256.61
25000	328.87	319.80	312.21	305.83	300.41	295.80	291.85	288.46	277.27	271.68	268.80	267.30
26000	342.02	332.59	324.70	318.06	312.43	307.63	303.52	300.00	288.36	282.55	279.56	278.00
27000	355.18	345.38	337.19	330.29	324.44	319.46	315.20	311.53	299.45	293.41	290.31	288.69
28000	368.33	358.17	349.68	342.52	336.46	331.29	326.87	323.07	310.54	304.28	301.06	299.38
29000	381.48	370.96	362.17	354.76	348.48	343.12	338.54	334.61	321.63	315.15	311.81	310.07
30000	394.64	383.76	374.66	366.99	360.49	354.96	350.22	346.15	332.72	326.01	322.56	320.76
31000	407.79	396.55	387.14	379.22	372.51	366.79	361.89	357.69	343.81	336.88	333.32	331.46
32000	420.95	409.34	399.63	391.46	384.52	378.62	373.57	369.22	354.90	347.75	344.07	342.15
33000	434.10	422.13	412.12	403.69	396.54	390.45	385.24	380.76	365.99	358.61	354.82	352.84
34000	447.26	434.92	424.61	415.92	408.56	402.28	396.91	392.30	377.08	369.48	365.57	363.53
35000	460.41	447.72	437.10	428.15	420.57	414.11	408.59	403.84	388.17	380.35	376.32	374.22
36000	473.57	460.51	449.59	440.39	432.59	425.95	420.26	415.38	399.26	391.21	387.08	384.92
37000	486.72	473.30	462.07	452.62	444.61	437.78	431.93	426.92	410.35	402.08	397.83	395.61
38000	499.87	486.09	474.56	464.85	456.62	449.61	443.61	438.45	421.44	412.95	408.58	406.30
39000	513.03	498.88	487.05	477.09	468.64	461.44	455.28	449.99	432.54	423.82	419.33	416.99
40000	526.18	511.67	499.54	489.32	480.65	473.27	466.96	461.53	443.63	434.68	430.08	427.68
41000	539.34	524.47	512.03	501.55	492.67	485.10	478.63	473.07	454.72	445.55	440.84	438.38
42000	552.49	537.26	524.52	513.78	504.69	496.94	490.30	484.61	465.81	456.42	451.59	449.07
43000	565.65	550.05	537.00	526.02	516.70	508.77	501.98	496.14	476.90	467.28	462.34	459.76
44000	578.80	562.84	549.49	538.25	528.72	520.60	513.65	507.68	487.99	478.15	473.09	470.45
45000	591.96	575.63	561.98	550.48	540.74	532.43	525.32	519.22	499.08	489.02	483.84	481.14
46000	605.11	588.42	574.47	562.72	552.75	544.26	537.00	530.76	510.17	499.88	494.60	491.84
47000	618.26	601.22	586.96	574.95	564.77	556.09	548.67	542.30	521.26	510.75	505.35	502.53
48000	631.42	614.01	599.45	587.18	576.78	567.93	560.35	553.83	532.35	521.62	516.10	513.22
49000	644.57	626.80	611.94	599.41	588.80	579.76	572.02	565.37	543.44	532.48	526.85	523.91
50000	657.73	639.59	624.42	611.65	600.82	591.59	583.69	576.91	554.53	543.35	537.60	534.60
55000	723.50	703.55	686.87	672.81	660.90	650.75	642.06	634.60	609.98	597.69	591.36	588.06
60000	789.27	767.51	749.31	733.97	720.98	709.91	700.43	692.29	665.44	652.02	645.12	641.52
65000	855.04	831.47	811.75	795.14	781.06	769.07	758.80	749.98	720.89	706.36	698.88	694.98
70000	920.82	895.43	874.19	856.30	841.14	828.22	817.17	807.67	776.34	760.69	752.64	748.44
75000	986.59	959.38	936.63	917.47	901.22	887.38	875.54	865.36	831.79	815.02	806.40	801.90
80000	1052.36	1023.34	999.07	978.63	961.30	946.54	933.91	923.05	887.25	869.36	860.16	855.36
85000	1118.13	1087.30	1061.52	1039.80	1021.39	1005.70	992.28	980.74	942.70	923.69	913.92	908.82
90000	1183.91	1151.26	1123.96	1100.96	1081.47	1064.86	1050.64	1038.44	998.15	978.03	967.68	962.28
95000	1249.68	1215.22	1186.40	1162.12	1141.55	1124.02	1109.01	1096.13	1053.60	1032.36	1021.44	1015.74
100000	1315.45	1279.18	1248.84	1223.29	1201.63	1183.17	1167.38	1153.82	1109.06	1086.70	1075.20	1069.20

12%

Table 1

13.00%

MONTHLY
PAYMENT REQUIRED TO AMORTIZE A LOAN

TERM AMOUNT	1 YEAR	2 YEARS	3 YEARS	4 YEARS	5 YEARS	6 YEARS	7 YEARS	8 YEARS	9 YEARS	10 YEARS	11 YEARS	12 YEAR
50	4.47	2.38	1.69	1.35	1.14	1.01	.91	.85	.79	.75	.72	.69
100	8.94	4.76	3.37	2.69	2.28	2.01	1.82	1.69	1.58	1.50	1.43	1.38
200	17.87	9.51	6.74	5.37	4.56	4.02	3.64	3.37	3.16	2.99	2.86	2.75
300	26.80	14.27	10.11	8.05	6.83	6.03	5.46	5.05	4.73	4.48	4.29	4.13
400	35.73	19.02	13.48	10.74	9.11	8.03	7.28	6.73	6.31	5.98	5.72	5.50
500	44.66	23.78	16.85	13.42	11.38	10.04	9.10	8.41	7.88	7.47	7.14	6.88
600	53.60	28.53	20.22	16.10	13.66	12.05	10.92	10.09	9.46	8.96	8.57	8.25
700	62.53	33.28	23.59	18.78	15.93	14.06	12.74	11.77	11.03	10.46	10.00	9.63
800	71.46	38.04	26.96	21.47	18.21	16.06	14.56	13.45	12.61	11.95	11.43	11.00
900	80.39	42.79	30.33	24.15	20.48	18.07	16.38	15.13	14.18	13.44	12.85	12.38
1000	89.32	47.55	33.70	26.83	22.76	20.08	18.20	16.81	15.76	14.94	14.28	13.75
2000	178.64	95.09	67.39	53.66	45.51	40.15	36.39	33.62	31.51	29.87	28.56	27.50
3000	267.96	142.63	101.09	80.49	68.26	60.23	54.58	50.43	47.27	44.80	42.83	41.24
4000	357.27	190.17	134.78	107.31	91.02	80.30	72.77	67.23	63.02	59.73	57.11	54.99
5000	446.59	237.71	168.47	134.14	113.77	100.38	90.96	84.04	78.77	74.66	71.39	68.74
6000	535.91	285.26	202.17	160.97	136.52	120.45	109.16	100.85	94.53	89.59	85.66	82.48
7000	625.23	332.80	235.86	187.80	159.28	140.52	127.35	117.66	110.28	104.52	99.94	96.23
8000	714.54	380.34	269.56	214.62	182.03	160.60	145.54	134.46	126.03	119.45	114.21	109.98
9000	803.86	427.88	303.25	241.45	204.78	180.67	163.73	151.27	141.79	134.38	128.49	123.72
10000	893.18	475.42	336.94	268.28	227.54	200.75	181.92	168.08	157.54	149.32	142.77	137.47
11000	982.50	522.97	370.64	295.11	250.29	220.82	200.12	184.88	173.29	164.25	157.04	151.21
12000	1071.81	570.51	404.33	321.93	273.04	240.89	218.31	201.69	189.05	179.18	171.32	164.96
13000	1161.13	618.05	438.03	348.76	295.79	260.97	236.50	218.50	204.80	194.11	185.59	178.71
14000	1250.45	665.59	471.72	375.59	318.55	281.04	254.69	235.31	220.56	209.04	199.87	192.45
15000	1339.76	713.13	505.41	402.42	341.30	301.12	272.88	252.11	236.31	223.97	214.15	206.20
16000	1429.08	760.67	539.11	429.24	364.05	321.19	291.08	268.92	252.06	238.90	228.42	219.95
17000	1518.40	808.22	572.80	456.07	386.81	341.26	309.27	285.73	267.82	253.83	242.70	233.69
18000	1607.72	855.76	606.50	482.90	409.56	361.34	327.46	302.54	283.57	268.76	256.97	247.44
19000	1697.03	903.30	640.19	509.73	432.31	381.41	345.65	319.34	299.32	283.70	271.25	261.18
20000	1786.35	950.84	673.88	536.55	455.07	401.49	363.84	336.15	315.08	298.63	285.53	274.93
21000	1875.67	998.38	707.58	563.38	477.82	421.56	382.04	352.96	330.83	313.56	299.80	288.68
22000	1964.99	1045.93	741.27	590.21	500.57	441.64	400.23	369.76	346.58	328.49	314.08	302.42
23000	2054.30	1093.47	774.97	617.04	523.33	461.71	418.42	386.57	362.34	343.42	328.36	316.17
24000	2143.62	1141.01	808.66	643.86	546.08	481.78	436.61	403.38	378.09	358.35	342.63	329.92
25000	2232.94	1188.55	842.35	670.69	568.83	501.86	454.80	420.19	393.84	373.28	356.91	343.66
26000	2322.25	1236.09	876.05	697.52	591.58	521.93	473.00	436.99	409.60	388.21	371.18	357.41
27000	2411.57	1283.63	909.74	724.35	614.34	542.01	491.19	453.80	425.35	403.14	385.46	371.15
28000	2500.89	1331.18	943.44	751.17	637.09	562.08	509.38	470.61	441.11	418.08	399.74	384.90
29000	2590.21	1378.72	977.13	778.00	659.84	582.15	527.57	487.42	456.86	433.01	414.01	398.65
30000	2679.52	1426.26	1010.82	804.83	682.60	602.23	545.76	504.22	472.61	447.94	428.29	412.39
31000	2768.84	1473.80	1044.52	831.66	705.35	622.30	563.96	521.03	488.37	462.87	442.56	426.14
32000	2858.16	1521.34	1078.21	858.48	728.10	642.38	582.15	537.84	504.12	477.80	456.84	439.89
33000	2947.48	1568.89	1111.91	885.31	750.86	662.45	600.34	554.64	519.87	492.73	471.12	453.63
34000	3036.79	1616.43	1145.60	912.14	773.61	682.52	618.53	571.45	535.63	507.66	485.39	467.38
35000	3126.11	1663.97	1179.29	938.97	796.36	702.60	636.72	588.26	551.38	522.59	499.67	481.12
36000	3215.43	1711.51	1212.99	965.79	819.12	722.67	654.92	605.07	567.13	537.52	513.94	494.87
37000	3304.74	1759.05	1246.68	992.62	841.87	742.75	673.11	621.87	582.89	552.45	528.22	508.62
38000	3394.06	1806.59	1280.38	1019.45	864.62	762.82	691.30	638.68	598.64	567.39	542.50	522.36
39000	3483.38	1854.14	1314.07	1046.28	887.37	782.90	709.49	655.49	614.39	582.32	556.77	536.11
40000	3572.70	1901.68	1347.76	1073.10	910.13	802.97	727.68	672.30	630.15	597.25	571.05	549.86
41000	3662.01	1949.22	1381.46	1099.93	932.88	823.04	745.88	689.10	645.90	612.18	585.33	563.60
42000	3751.33	1996.76	1415.15	1126.76	955.63	843.12	764.07	705.91	661.66	627.11	599.60	577.35
43000	3840.65	2044.30	1448.84	1153.59	978.39	863.19	782.26	722.72	677.41	642.04	613.88	591.09
44000	3929.97	2091.85	1482.54	1180.41	1001.14	883.27	800.45	739.52	693.16	656.97	628.15	604.84
45000	4019.28	2139.39	1516.23	1207.24	1023.89	903.34	818.64	756.33	708.92	671.90	642.43	618.59
46000	4108.60	2186.93	1549.93	1234.07	1046.65	923.41	836.84	773.14	724.67	686.83	656.71	632.33
47000	4197.92	2234.47	1583.62	1260.90	1069.40	943.49	855.03	789.95	740.42	701.77	670.98	646.08
48000	4287.23	2282.01	1617.31	1287.72	1092.15	963.56	873.22	806.75	756.18	716.70	685.26	659.83
49000	4376.55	2329.55	1651.01	1314.55	1114.91	983.64	891.41	823.56	771.93	731.63	699.53	673.57
50000	4465.87	2377.10	1684.70	1341.38	1137.66	1003.71	909.60	840.37	787.68	746.56	713.81	687.32
55000	4912.46	2614.81	1853.17	1475.52	1251.42	1104.08	1000.56	924.40	866.45	821.21	785.19	756.05
60000	5359.04	2852.51	2021.64	1609.65	1365.19	1204.45	1091.52	1008.44	945.22	895.87	856.57	824.78
65000	5805.63	3090.22	2190.11	1743.79	1478.95	1304.82	1182.48	1092.48	1023.99	970.52	927.95	893.51
70000	6252.21	3327.93	2358.58	1877.93	1592.72	1405.19	1273.44	1176.51	1102.76	1045.18	999.33	962.24
75000	6698.80	3565.64	2527.05	2012.07	1706.49	1505.56	1364.40	1260.55	1181.52	1119.84	1070.71	1030.97
80000	7145.39	3803.35	2695.52	2146.20	1820.25	1605.93	1455.36	1344.59	1260.29	1194.49	1142.09	1099.71
85000	7591.97	4041.06	2863.99	2280.34	1934.02	1706.30	1546.32	1428.62	1339.06	1269.15	1213.47	1168.44
90000	8038.56	4278.77	3032.46	2414.48	2047.78	1806.67	1637.28	1512.66	1417.83	1343.80	1284.85	1237.17
95000	8485.15	4516.48	3200.93	2548.62	2161.55	1907.05	1728.24	1596.69	1496.60	1418.46	1356.24	1305.90
100000	8931.73	4754.19	3369.40	2682.75	2275.31	2007.42	1819.20	1680.73	1575.36	1493.11	1427.62	1374.63

13%

66

Table 1

MONTHLY   13.00%
PAYMENT REQUIRED TO AMORTIZE A LOAN

TERM / AMOUNT	13 YEARS	14 YEARS	15 YEARS	16 YEARS	17 YEARS	18 YEARS	19 YEARS	20 YEARS	25 YEARS	30 YEARS	35 YEARS	40 YEARS
50	.67	.65	.64	.62	.61	.61	.60	.59	.57	.56	.55	.55
100	1.34	1.30	1.27	1.24	1.22	1.21	1.19	1.18	1.13	1.11	1.10	1.09
200	2.67	2.60	2.54	2.48	2.44	2.41	2.37	2.35	2.26	2.22	2.20	2.18
300	4.00	3.89	3.80	3.72	3.66	3.61	3.56	3.52	3.39	3.32	3.29	3.27
400	5.33	5.19	5.07	4.96	4.88	4.81	4.74	4.69	4.52	4.43	4.39	4.36
500	6.66	6.48	6.33	6.20	6.10	6.01	5.93	5.86	5.64	5.54	5.48	5.45
600	7.99	7.78	7.60	7.44	7.32	7.21	7.11	7.03	6.77	6.64	6.58	6.54
700	9.32	9.07	8.86	8.68	8.54	8.41	8.30	8.21	7.90	7.75	7.67	7.63
800	10.65	10.37	10.13	9.92	9.75	9.61	9.48	9.38	9.03	8.85	8.77	8.72
900	11.99	11.66	11.39	11.16	10.97	10.81	10.67	10.55	10.16	9.96	9.86	9.81
1000	13.32	12.96	12.66	12.40	12.19	12.01	11.85	11.72	11.28	11.07	10.96	10.90
2000	26.63	25.91	25.31	24.80	24.38	24.01	23.70	23.44	22.56	22.13	21.91	21.80
3000	39.94	38.86	37.96	37.20	36.56	36.02	35.55	35.15	33.84	33.19	32.86	32.69
4000	53.25	51.82	50.61	49.60	48.75	48.02	47.40	46.87	45.12	44.25	43.81	43.59
5000	66.57	64.77	63.27	62.00	60.94	60.03	59.25	58.58	56.40	55.31	54.76	54.48
6000	79.88	77.72	75.92	74.40	73.12	72.03	71.10	70.30	67.68	66.38	65.72	65.38
7000	93.19	90.67	88.57	86.80	85.31	84.04	82.95	82.02	78.95	77.44	76.67	76.27
8000	106.50	103.63	101.22	99.20	97.49	96.04	94.80	93.73	90.23	88.50	87.62	87.17
9000	119.81	116.58	113.88	111.60	109.68	108.04	106.65	105.45	101.51	99.56	98.57	98.06
10000	133.13	129.53	126.53	124.00	121.87	120.05	118.49	117.16	112.79	110.62	109.52	108.96
11000	146.44	142.48	139.18	136.40	134.05	132.05	130.34	128.88	124.07	121.69	120.48	119.85
12000	159.75	155.44	151.83	148.80	146.24	144.06	142.19	140.59	135.35	132.75	131.43	130.75
13000	173.06	168.39	164.49	161.20	158.42	156.06	154.04	152.31	146.62	143.81	142.38	141.64
14000	186.37	181.34	177.14	173.60	170.61	168.07	165.89	164.03	157.90	154.87	153.33	152.54
15000	199.69	194.29	189.79	186.00	182.80	180.07	177.74	175.74	169.18	165.93	164.28	163.43
16000	213.00	207.25	202.44	198.40	194.98	192.07	189.59	187.46	180.46	177.00	175.24	174.33
17000	226.31	220.20	215.10	210.80	207.17	204.08	201.44	199.17	191.74	188.06	186.19	185.22
18000	239.62	233.15	227.75	223.20	219.36	216.08	213.29	210.89	203.02	199.12	197.14	196.12
19000	252.93	246.11	240.40	235.60	231.54	228.09	225.14	222.60	214.29	210.18	208.09	207.01
20000	266.25	259.06	253.05	248.00	243.73	240.09	236.98	234.32	225.57	221.24	219.04	217.91
21000	279.56	272.01	265.71	260.40	255.91	252.10	248.83	246.04	236.85	232.31	230.00	228.80
22000	292.87	284.96	278.36	272.80	268.10	264.10	260.68	257.75	248.13	243.37	240.95	239.70
23000	306.18	297.92	291.01	285.20	280.29	276.10	272.53	269.47	259.41	254.43	251.90	250.59
24000	319.50	310.87	303.66	297.60	292.47	288.11	284.38	281.18	270.69	265.49	262.85	261.49
25000	332.81	323.82	316.32	310.00	304.66	300.11	296.23	292.90	281.96	276.55	273.80	272.38
26000	346.12	336.77	328.97	322.40	316.84	312.12	308.08	304.61	293.24	287.62	284.76	283.28
27000	359.43	349.73	341.62	334.80	329.03	324.12	319.93	316.33	304.52	298.68	295.71	294.17
28000	372.74	362.68	354.27	347.20	341.22	336.13	331.78	328.05	315.80	309.74	306.66	305.07
29000	386.06	375.63	366.93	359.60	353.40	348.13	343.63	339.76	327.08	320.80	317.61	315.96
30000	399.37	388.58	379.58	372.00	365.59	360.13	355.47	351.48	338.36	331.86	328.56	326.86
31000	412.68	401.54	392.23	384.40	377.78	372.14	367.32	363.19	349.63	342.93	339.51	337.75
32000	425.99	414.49	404.88	396.80	389.96	384.14	379.17	374.91	360.91	353.99	350.47	348.65
33000	439.30	427.44	417.53	409.20	402.15	396.15	391.02	386.62	372.19	365.05	361.42	359.54
34000	452.62	440.39	430.19	421.60	414.33	408.15	402.87	398.34	383.47	376.11	372.37	370.44
35000	465.93	453.35	442.84	434.00	426.52	420.16	414.72	410.06	394.75	387.17	383.32	381.33
36000	479.24	466.30	455.49	446.40	438.71	432.16	426.57	421.77	406.03	398.24	394.27	392.23
37000	492.55	479.25	468.14	458.80	450.89	444.17	438.42	433.49	417.30	409.30	405.23	403.13
38000	505.86	492.21	480.80	471.20	463.08	456.17	450.27	445.20	428.58	420.36	416.18	414.02
39000	519.18	505.16	493.45	483.60	475.26	468.17	462.12	456.92	439.86	431.42	427.13	424.92
40000	532.49	518.11	506.10	496.00	487.45	480.18	473.96	468.64	451.14	442.48	438.08	435.81
41000	545.80	531.06	518.75	508.40	499.64	492.18	485.81	480.35	462.42	453.55	449.03	446.71
42000	559.11	544.02	531.41	520.80	511.82	504.19	497.66	492.07	473.70	464.61	459.99	457.60
43000	572.42	556.97	544.06	533.20	524.01	516.19	509.51	503.78	484.97	475.67	470.94	468.50
44000	585.74	569.92	556.71	545.60	536.20	528.20	521.36	515.50	496.25	486.73	481.89	479.39
45000	599.05	582.87	569.36	558.00	548.38	540.20	533.21	527.21	507.53	497.79	492.84	490.29
46000	612.36	595.83	582.02	570.40	560.57	552.20	545.06	538.93	518.81	508.86	503.79	501.18
47000	625.67	608.78	594.67	582.80	572.75	564.21	556.91	550.65	530.09	519.92	514.75	512.08
48000	638.99	621.73	607.32	595.20	584.94	576.21	568.76	562.36	541.37	530.98	525.70	522.97
49000	652.30	634.68	619.97	607.60	597.13	588.22	580.61	574.08	552.64	542.04	536.65	533.87
50000	665.61	647.64	632.63	620.00	609.31	600.22	592.45	585.79	563.92	553.10	547.60	544.76
55000	732.17	712.40	695.89	682.00	670.24	660.24	651.70	644.37	620.31	608.41	602.36	599.24
60000	798.73	777.16	759.15	744.00	731.17	720.26	710.94	702.95	676.71	663.72	657.12	653.71
65000	865.29	841.93	822.41	806.00	792.10	780.29	770.19	761.53	733.10	719.03	711.88	708.19
70000	931.85	906.69	885.67	868.00	853.04	840.31	829.43	820.11	789.49	774.34	766.64	762.66
75000	998.41	971.45	948.94	930.00	913.97	900.33	888.68	878.69	845.88	829.65	821.40	817.14
80000	1064.97	1036.22	1012.20	992.00	974.90	960.35	947.92	937.27	902.27	884.96	876.16	871.62
85000	1131.53	1100.98	1075.46	1053.99	1035.83	1020.37	1007.17	995.84	958.67	940.27	930.92	926.09
90000	1198.09	1165.74	1138.72	1115.99	1096.76	1080.39	1066.41	1054.42	1015.06	995.58	985.68	980.57
95000	1264.65	1230.51	1201.99	1177.99	1157.69	1140.42	1125.66	1113.00	1071.45	1050.89	1040.44	1035.04
00000	1331.22	1295.27	1265.25	1239.99	1218.62	1200.44	1184.90	1171.58	1127.84	1106.20	1095.20	1089.52

13%

67

Table 1

13.25%

MONTHLY
PAYMENT REQUIRED TO AMORTIZE A LOAN

TERM AMOUNT	1 YEAR	2 YEARS	3 YEARS	4 YEARS	5 YEARS	6 YEARS	7 YEARS	8 YEARS	9 YEARS	10 YEARS	11 YEARS	12 YEARS
50	4.48	2.39	1.70	1.35	1.15	1.02	.92	.85	.80	.76	.73	.70
100	8.95	4.77	3.39	2.70	2.29	2.03	1.84	1.70	1.59	1.51	1.45	1.40
200	17.89	9.54	6.77	5.40	4.58	4.05	3.67	3.39	3.18	3.02	2.89	2.79
300	26.84	14.30	10.15	8.09	6.87	6.07	5.50	5.09	4.77	4.53	4.33	4.18
400	35.78	19.07	13.53	10.79	9.16	8.09	7.34	6.78	6.36	6.04	5.78	5.57
500	44.72	23.83	16.91	13.48	11.45	10.11	9.17	8.48	7.95	7.54	7.22	6.96
600	53.67	28.60	20.29	16.18	13.73	12.13	11.00	10.17	9.54	9.05	8.66	8.35
700	62.61	33.37	23.68	18.87	16.02	14.15	12.83	11.87	11.13	10.56	10.10	9.74
800	71.55	38.13	27.06	21.57	18.31	16.17	14.67	13.56	12.72	12.07	11.55	11.13
900	80.50	42.90	30.44	24.26	20.60	18.19	16.50	15.26	14.31	13.58	12.99	12.52
1000	89.44	47.66	33.82	26.96	22.89	20.21	18.33	16.95	15.90	15.08	14.43	13.91
2000	178.87	95.32	67.63	53.91	45.77	40.42	36.66	33.90	31.80	30.16	28.86	27.81
3000	268.31	142.98	101.45	80.86	68.65	60.62	54.99	50.85	47.70	45.24	43.29	41.71
4000	357.74	190.64	135.26	107.81	91.53	80.83	73.32	67.79	63.60	60.32	57.72	55.61
5000	447.18	238.30	169.08	134.76	114.41	101.04	91.65	84.74	79.49	75.40	72.14	69.51
6000	536.61	285.96	202.89	161.72	137.29	121.24	109.97	101.69	95.39	90.48	86.57	83.41
7000	626.05	333.62	236.71	188.67	160.17	141.45	128.30	118.64	111.29	105.56	101.00	97.31
8000	715.48	381.28	270.52	215.62	183.06	161.66	146.63	135.58	127.19	120.64	115.43	111.22
9000	804.92	428.94	304.34	242.57	205.94	181.86	164.96	152.53	143.08	135.72	129.85	125.12
10000	894.35	476.60	338.15	269.52	228.82	202.07	183.29	169.48	158.98	150.79	144.28	139.02
11000	983.79	524.26	371.96	296.47	251.70	222.27	201.61	186.43	174.88	165.87	158.71	152.92
12000	1073.22	571.92	405.78	323.43	274.58	242.48	219.94	203.37	190.78	180.95	173.14	166.82
13000	1162.65	619.58	439.59	350.38	297.46	262.69	238.27	220.32	206.67	196.03	187.56	180.72
14000	1252.09	667.24	473.41	377.33	320.34	282.89	256.60	237.27	222.57	211.11	201.99	194.62
15000	1341.52	714.90	507.22	404.28	343.22	303.10	274.93	254.22	238.47	226.19	216.42	208.52
16000	1430.96	762.55	541.04	431.23	366.11	323.31	293.26	271.16	254.37	241.27	230.85	222.43
17000	1520.39	810.21	574.85	458.18	388.99	343.51	311.58	288.11	270.26	256.35	245.27	236.33
18000	1609.83	857.87	608.67	485.14	411.87	363.72	329.91	305.06	286.16	271.43	259.70	250.23
19000	1699.26	905.53	642.48	512.09	434.75	383.92	348.24	322.01	302.06	286.50	274.13	264.13
20000	1788.70	953.19	676.29	539.04	457.63	404.13	366.57	338.95	317.96	301.58	288.56	278.03
21000	1878.13	1000.85	710.11	565.99	480.51	424.34	384.90	355.90	333.85	316.66	302.98	291.93
22000	1967.57	1048.51	743.92	592.94	503.39	444.54	403.22	372.85	349.75	331.74	317.41	305.83
23000	2057.00	1096.17	777.74	619.90	526.27	464.75	421.55	389.80	365.65	346.82	331.84	319.74
24000	2146.44	1143.83	811.55	646.85	549.16	484.96	439.88	406.74	381.55	361.90	346.27	333.64
25000	2235.87	1191.49	845.37	673.80	572.04	505.16	458.21	423.69	397.45	376.98	360.70	347.54
26000	2325.30	1239.15	879.18	700.75	594.92	525.37	476.54	440.64	413.34	392.06	375.12	361.44
27000	2414.74	1286.81	913.00	727.70	617.80	545.57	494.87	457.58	429.24	407.14	389.55	375.34
28000	2504.17	1334.47	946.81	754.65	640.68	565.78	513.19	474.53	445.14	422.21	403.98	389.24
29000	2593.61	1382.13	980.63	781.61	663.56	585.99	531.52	491.48	461.04	437.29	418.41	403.14
30000	2683.04	1429.79	1014.44	808.56	686.44	606.19	549.85	508.43	476.93	452.37	432.83	417.04
31000	2772.48	1477.44	1048.25	835.51	709.32	626.40	568.18	525.37	492.83	467.45	447.26	430.95
32000	2861.91	1525.10	1082.07	862.46	732.21	646.61	586.51	542.32	508.73	482.53	461.69	444.85
33000	2951.35	1572.76	1115.88	889.41	755.09	666.81	604.83	559.27	524.63	497.61	476.12	458.75
34000	3040.78	1620.42	1149.70	916.36	777.97	687.02	623.16	576.22	540.52	512.69	490.54	472.65
35000	3130.22	1668.08	1183.51	943.32	800.85	707.23	641.49	593.16	556.42	527.77	504.97	486.55
36000	3219.65	1715.74	1217.33	970.27	823.73	727.43	659.82	610.11	572.32	542.85	519.40	500.45
37000	3309.09	1763.40	1251.14	997.22	846.61	747.64	678.15	627.06	588.22	557.92	533.83	514.35
38000	3398.52	1811.06	1284.96	1024.17	869.49	767.84	696.47	644.01	604.11	573.00	548.25	528.25
39000	3487.95	1858.72	1318.77	1051.12	892.37	788.05	714.80	660.95	620.01	588.08	562.68	542.16
40000	3577.39	1906.38	1352.58	1078.07	915.26	808.26	733.13	677.90	635.91	603.16	577.11	556.06
41000	3666.82	1954.04	1386.40	1105.03	938.14	828.46	751.46	694.85	651.81	618.24	591.54	569.96
42000	3756.26	2001.70	1420.21	1131.98	961.02	848.67	769.79	711.80	667.70	633.32	605.96	583.86
43000	3845.69	2049.36	1454.03	1158.93	983.90	868.88	788.12	728.74	683.60	648.40	620.39	597.76
44000	3935.13	2097.02	1487.84	1185.88	1006.78	889.08	806.44	745.69	699.50	663.48	634.82	611.66
45000	4024.56	2144.68	1521.66	1212.83	1029.66	909.29	824.77	762.64	715.40	678.56	649.25	625.56
46000	4114.00	2192.33	1555.47	1239.79	1052.54	929.49	843.10	779.59	731.30	693.63	663.67	639.47
47000	4203.43	2239.99	1589.29	1266.74	1075.42	949.70	861.43	796.53	747.19	708.71	678.10	653.37
48000	4292.87	2287.65	1623.10	1293.69	1098.31	969.91	879.76	813.48	763.09	723.79	692.53	667.27
49000	4382.30	2335.31	1656.92	1320.64	1121.19	990.11	898.08	830.43	778.99	738.87	706.96	681.17
50000	4471.74	2382.97	1690.73	1347.59	1144.07	1010.32	916.41	847.38	794.89	753.95	721.39	695.07
55000	4918.91	2621.27	1859.69	1482.35	1258.47	1111.35	1008.05	932.11	874.37	829.34	793.52	764.58
60000	5366.08	2859.57	2028.87	1617.11	1372.88	1212.38	1099.69	1016.85	953.86	904.74	865.66	834.08
65000	5813.25	3097.86	2197.95	1751.87	1487.29	1313.41	1191.34	1101.59	1033.35	980.13	937.80	903.59
70000	6260.43	3336.16	2367.02	1886.63	1601.69	1414.45	1282.98	1186.32	1112.84	1055.53	1009.94	973.10
75000	6707.60	3574.46	2536.09	2021.39	1716.10	1515.48	1374.62	1271.06	1192.33	1130.92	1082.08	1042.60
80000	7154.77	3812.75	2705.16	2156.14	1830.51	1616.51	1466.26	1355.80	1271.81	1206.32	1154.21	1112.11
85000	7601.95	4051.05	2874.24	2290.90	1944.91	1717.54	1557.90	1440.53	1351.30	1281.71	1226.35	1181.62
90000	8049.12	4289.35	3043.31	2425.66	2059.32	1818.57	1649.54	1525.27	1430.79	1357.11	1298.49	1251.12
95000	8496.29	4527.64	3212.38	2560.42	2173.72	1919.60	1741.18	1610.01	1510.28	1432.50	1370.63	1320.63
100000	8943.47	4765.94	3381.45	2695.18	2288.13	2020.63	1832.82	1694.75	1589.77	1507.89	1442.77	1390.14

Table 1

MONTHLY

13.25%

PAYMENT REQUIRED TO AMORTIZE A LOAN

TERM AMOUNT	13 YEARS	14 YEARS	15 YEARS	16 YEARS	17 YEARS	18 YEARS	19 YEARS	20 YEARS	25 YEARS	30 YEARS	35 YEARS	40 YEARS
50	.68	.66	.65	.63	.62	.61	.61	.60	.58	.57	.56	.56
100	1.35	1.32	1.29	1.26	1.24	1.22	1.21	1.19	1.15	1.13	1.12	1.11
200	2.70	2.63	2.57	2.52	2.48	2.44	2.41	2.38	2.30	2.26	2.24	2.22
300	4.05	3.94	3.85	3.78	3.71	3.66	3.61	3.57	3.45	3.38	3.35	3.33
400	5.39	5.25	5.13	5.03	4.95	4.88	4.82	4.76	4.59	4.51	4.47	4.44
500	6.74	6.56	6.41	6.29	6.18	6.09	6.02	5.95	5.74	5.63	5.58	5.55
600	8.09	7.87	7.70	7.55	7.42	7.31	7.22	7.14	6.89	6.76	6.70	6.66
700	9.43	9.19	8.98	8.80	8.65	8.53	8.42	8.33	8.03	7.89	7.81	7.77
800	10.78	10.50	10.26	10.06	9.89	9.75	9.63	9.52	9.18	9.01	8.93	8.88
900	12.13	11.81	11.54	11.32	11.13	10.97	10.83	10.71	10.33	10.14	10.04	9.99
1000	13.48	13.12	12.82	12.57	12.36	12.18	12.03	11.90	11.47	11.26	11.16	11.10
2000	26.95	26.23	25.64	25.14	24.72	24.36	24.06	23.79	22.94	22.52	22.31	22.20
3000	40.42	39.35	38.46	37.71	37.08	36.54	36.08	35.69	34.41	33.78	33.46	33.30
4000	53.89	52.46	51.27	50.28	49.43	48.72	48.11	47.58	45.87	45.04	44.61	44.40
5000	67.36	65.58	64.09	62.84	61.79	60.89	60.13	59.48	57.34	56.29	55.77	55.50
6000	80.83	78.69	76.91	75.41	74.15	73.07	72.16	71.37	68.81	67.55	66.92	66.60
7000	94.30	91.81	89.73	87.98	86.50	85.25	84.18	83.27	80.27	78.81	78.07	77.70
8000	107.77	104.92	102.54	100.55	98.86	97.43	96.21	95.16	91.74	90.07	89.22	88.79
9000	121.24	118.03	115.36	113.12	111.22	109.61	108.23	107.05	103.21	101.32	100.38	99.89
10000	134.71	131.15	128.18	125.68	123.57	121.78	120.26	118.95	114.68	112.58	111.53	110.99
11000	148.18	144.26	141.00	138.25	135.93	133.96	132.28	130.84	126.14	123.84	122.68	122.09
12000	161.65	157.38	153.81	150.82	148.29	146.14	144.31	142.74	137.61	135.10	133.83	133.19
13000	175.12	170.49	166.63	163.39	160.65	158.32	156.33	154.63	149.08	146.36	144.99	144.29
14000	188.59	183.61	179.45	175.96	173.00	170.50	168.36	166.53	160.54	157.61	156.14	155.39
15000	202.06	196.72	192.27	188.52	185.36	182.67	180.38	178.42	172.01	168.87	167.29	166.49
16000	215.53	209.84	205.08	201.09	197.72	194.85	192.41	190.31	183.48	180.13	178.44	177.58
17000	229.01	222.95	217.90	213.66	210.07	207.03	204.43	202.21	194.94	191.39	189.60	188.68
18000	242.48	236.06	230.72	226.23	222.43	219.21	216.46	214.10	206.41	202.64	200.75	199.78
19000	255.95	249.18	243.53	238.79	234.79	231.38	228.48	226.00	217.88	213.90	211.90	210.88
20000	269.42	262.29	256.35	251.36	247.14	243.56	240.51	237.89	229.35	225.16	223.05	221.98
21000	282.89	275.41	269.17	263.93	259.50	255.74	252.53	249.79	240.81	236.42	234.21	233.08
22000	296.36	288.52	281.99	276.50	271.86	267.92	264.56	261.68	252.28	247.68	245.36	244.18
23000	309.83	301.64	294.80	289.07	284.22	280.10	276.58	273.57	263.75	258.93	256.51	255.28
24000	323.30	314.75	307.62	301.63	296.57	292.27	288.61	285.47	275.21	270.19	267.66	266.37
25000	336.77	327.87	320.44	314.20	308.93	304.45	300.63	297.36	286.68	281.45	278.82	277.47
26000	350.24	340.98	333.26	326.77	321.29	316.63	312.66	309.26	298.15	292.71	289.97	288.57
27000	363.71	354.09	346.07	339.34	333.64	328.81	324.68	321.15	309.61	303.96	301.12	299.67
28000	377.18	367.21	358.89	351.90	346.00	340.99	336.71	333.05	321.08	315.22	312.27	310.77
29000	390.65	380.32	371.71	364.47	358.36	353.16	348.73	344.94	332.55	326.48	323.43	321.87
30000	404.12	393.44	384.53	377.04	370.71	365.34	360.76	356.83	344.02	337.74	334.58	332.97
31000	417.59	406.55	397.34	389.61	383.07	377.52	372.78	368.73	355.48	348.99	345.73	344.06
32000	431.06	419.67	410.16	402.18	395.43	389.70	384.81	380.62	366.95	360.25	356.88	355.16
33000	444.53	432.78	422.98	414.74	407.78	401.87	396.83	392.52	378.42	371.51	368.03	366.26
34000	458.01	445.90	435.80	427.31	420.14	414.05	408.86	404.41	389.88	382.77	379.19	377.36
35000	471.48	459.01	448.61	439.88	432.50	426.23	420.88	416.31	401.35	394.03	390.34	388.46
36000	484.95	472.12	461.43	452.45	444.86	438.41	432.91	428.20	412.82	405.28	401.49	399.56
37000	498.42	485.24	474.25	465.01	457.21	450.59	444.93	440.09	424.28	416.54	412.64	410.66
38000	511.89	498.35	487.06	477.58	469.57	462.76	456.96	451.99	435.75	427.80	423.80	421.76
39000	525.36	511.47	499.88	490.15	481.93	474.94	468.98	463.88	447.22	439.06	434.95	432.85
40000	538.83	524.58	512.70	502.72	494.28	487.12	481.01	475.78	458.69	450.31	446.10	443.95
41000	552.30	537.70	525.52	515.29	506.64	499.30	493.03	487.67	470.15	461.57	457.25	455.05
42000	565.77	550.81	538.33	527.85	519.00	511.48	505.06	499.57	481.62	472.83	468.41	466.15
43000	579.24	563.93	551.15	540.42	531.35	523.65	517.08	511.46	493.09	484.09	479.56	477.25
44000	592.71	577.04	563.97	552.99	543.71	535.83	529.11	523.35	504.55	495.35	490.71	488.35
45000	606.18	590.15	576.79	565.56	556.07	548.01	541.13	535.25	516.02	506.60	501.86	499.45
46000	619.65	603.27	589.60	578.13	568.43	560.19	553.16	547.14	527.49	517.86	513.02	510.55
47000	633.12	616.38	602.42	590.69	580.78	572.36	565.18	559.04	538.95	529.12	524.17	521.64
48000	646.59	629.50	615.24	603.26	593.14	584.54	577.21	570.93	550.42	540.38	535.32	532.74
49000	660.06	642.61	628.06	615.83	605.50	596.72	589.23	582.83	561.89	551.63	546.47	543.84
50000	673.53	655.73	640.87	628.40	617.85	608.90	601.26	594.72	573.36	562.89	557.63	554.94
55000	740.89	721.30	704.96	691.24	679.64	669.79	661.39	654.19	630.69	619.18	613.39	610.43
60000	808.24	786.87	769.05	754.08	741.42	730.68	721.51	713.66	688.03	675.47	669.15	665.93
65000	875.59	852.44	833.13	816.91	803.21	791.57	781.64	773.13	745.36	731.76	724.91	721.42
70000	942.95	918.01	897.22	879.75	864.99	852.46	841.76	832.61	802.70	788.05	780.67	776.91
75000	1010.30	983.59	961.31	942.59	926.78	913.35	901.89	892.08	860.03	844.34	836.44	832.41
80000	1077.65	1049.16	1025.39	1005.43	988.56	974.23	962.01	951.55	917.37	900.62	892.20	887.90
85000	1145.01	1114.73	1089.48	1068.27	1050.35	1035.12	1022.14	1011.02	974.70	956.91	947.96	943.39
90000	1212.36	1180.30	1153.57	1131.11	1112.13	1096.01	1082.26	1070.49	1032.04	1013.20	1003.72	998.89
95000	1279.71	1245.88	1217.65	1193.95	1173.92	1156.90	1142.39	1129.96	1089.37	1069.49	1059.49	1054.38
100000	1347.06	1311.45	1281.74	1256.79	1235.70	1217.79	1202.51	1189.44	1146.71	1125.78	1115.25	1109.88

13%

Table 1

13.50% MONTHLY
PAYMENT REQUIRED TO AMORTIZE A LOAN

TERM AMOUNT	1 YEAR	2 YEARS	3 YEARS	4 YEARS	5 YEARS	6 YEARS	7 YEARS	8 YEARS	9 YEARS	10 YEARS	11 YEARS	12 YEAR
50	4.48	2.39	1.70	1.36	1.16	1.02	.93	.86	.81	.77	.73	.71
100	8.96	4.78	3.40	2.71	2.31	2.04	1.85	1.71	1.61	1.53	1.46	1.41
200	17.92	9.56	6.79	5.42	4.61	4.07	3.70	3.42	3.21	3.05	2.92	2.82
300	26.87	14.34	10.19	8.13	6.91	6.11	5.54	5.13	4.82	4.57	4.38	4.22
400	35.83	19.12	13.58	10.84	9.21	8.14	7.39	6.84	6.42	6.10	5.84	5.63
500	44.78	23.89	16.97	13.54	11.51	10.17	9.24	8.55	8.03	7.62	7.29	7.03
600	53.74	28.67	20.37	16.25	13.81	12.21	11.08	10.26	9.63	9.14	8.75	8.44
700	62.69	33.45	23.76	18.96	16.11	14.24	12.93	11.97	11.23	10.66	10.21	9.85
800	71.65	38.23	27.15	21.67	18.41	16.28	14.78	13.68	12.84	12.19	11.67	11.25
900	80.60	43.00	30.55	24.37	20.71	18.31	16.62	15.38	14.44	13.71	13.13	12.66
1000	89.56	47.78	33.94	27.08	23.01	20.34	18.47	17.09	16.05	15.23	14.58	14.06
2000	179.11	95.56	67.88	54.16	46.02	40.68	36.93	34.18	32.09	30.46	29.16	28.12
3000	268.66	143.34	101.81	81.23	69.03	61.02	55.40	51.27	48.13	45.69	43.74	42.18
4000	358.21	191.11	135.75	108.31	92.04	81.36	73.86	68.36	64.17	60.91	58.32	56.23
5000	447.77	238.89	169.68	135.39	115.05	101.70	92.33	85.45	80.22	76.14	72.90	70.29
6000	537.32	286.67	203.62	162.46	138.06	122.04	110.79	102.53	96.26	91.37	87.48	84.35
7000	626.87	334.44	237.55	189.54	161.07	142.38	129.26	119.62	112.30	106.60	102.06	98.41
8000	716.42	382.22	271.49	216.62	184.08	162.72	147.72	136.71	128.34	121.82	116.64	112.46
9000	805.97	430.00	305.42	243.69	207.09	183.06	166.19	153.80	144.39	137.05	131.22	126.52
10000	895.53	477.78	339.36	270.77	230.10	203.39	184.65	170.89	160.43	152.28	145.80	140.58
11000	985.08	525.55	373.29	297.84	253.11	223.73	203.12	187.97	176.47	167.51	160.38	154.63
12000	1074.63	573.33	407.23	324.92	276.12	244.07	221.58	205.06	192.51	182.73	174.96	168.69
13000	1164.18	621.11	441.16	352.00	299.13	264.41	240.05	222.15	208.56	197.96	189.54	182.75
14000	1253.73	668.88	475.10	379.07	322.14	284.75	258.51	239.24	224.60	213.19	204.12	196.81
15000	1343.29	716.66	509.03	406.15	345.15	305.09	276.98	256.33	240.64	228.42	218.70	210.86
16000	1432.84	764.44	542.97	433.23	368.16	325.43	295.44	273.42	256.68	243.64	233.28	224.92
17000	1522.39	812.21	576.90	460.30	391.17	345.77	313.91	290.50	272.72	258.87	247.86	238.98
18000	1611.94	859.99	610.84	487.38	414.18	366.11	332.37	307.59	288.77	274.10	262.44	253.03
19000	1701.49	907.77	644.78	514.46	437.19	386.45	350.84	324.68	304.81	289.33	277.02	267.09
20000	1791.05	955.55	678.71	541.53	460.20	406.78	369.30	341.77	320.85	304.55	291.60	281.15
21000	1880.60	1003.32	712.65	568.61	483.21	427.12	387.77	358.86	336.89	319.78	306.18	295.21
22000	1970.15	1051.10	746.58	595.68	506.22	447.46	406.23	375.94	352.94	335.01	320.76	309.26
23000	2059.70	1098.88	780.52	622.76	529.23	467.80	424.70	393.03	368.98	350.24	335.34	323.32
24000	2149.25	1146.65	814.45	649.84	552.24	488.14	443.16	410.12	385.02	365.46	349.92	337.38
25000	2238.81	1194.43	848.39	676.91	575.25	508.48	461.63	427.21	401.06	380.69	364.50	351.43
26000	2328.36	1242.21	882.32	703.99	598.26	528.82	480.09	444.30	417.11	395.92	379.08	365.49
27000	2417.91	1289.98	916.26	731.07	621.27	549.16	498.56	461.39	433.15	411.15	393.66	379.55
28000	2507.46	1337.76	950.19	758.14	644.28	569.50	517.02	478.47	449.19	426.37	408.24	393.61
29000	2597.01	1385.54	984.13	785.22	667.29	589.83	535.49	495.56	465.23	441.60	422.82	407.66
30000	2686.57	1433.32	1018.06	812.29	690.30	610.17	553.95	512.65	481.27	456.83	437.40	421.72
31000	2776.12	1481.09	1052.00	839.37	713.31	630.51	572.42	529.74	497.32	472.06	451.98	435.78
32000	2865.67	1528.87	1085.93	866.45	736.32	650.85	590.88	546.83	513.36	487.28	466.56	449.83
33000	2955.22	1576.65	1119.87	893.52	759.33	671.19	609.35	563.91	529.40	502.51	481.14	463.89
34000	3044.77	1624.42	1153.80	920.60	782.34	691.53	627.81	581.00	545.44	517.74	495.72	477.95
35000	3134.33	1672.20	1187.74	947.68	805.35	711.87	646.28	598.09	561.49	532.97	510.30	492.01
36000	3223.88	1719.98	1221.68	974.75	828.36	732.21	664.74	615.18	577.53	548.19	524.88	506.06
37000	3313.43	1767.75	1255.61	1001.83	851.37	752.55	683.21	632.27	593.57	563.42	539.46	520.12
38000	3402.98	1815.53	1289.55	1028.91	874.38	772.89	701.67	649.36	609.61	578.65	554.04	534.18
39000	3492.53	1863.31	1323.48	1055.98	897.39	793.22	720.14	666.44	625.66	593.87	568.62	548.23
40000	3582.09	1911.09	1357.42	1083.06	920.40	813.56	738.60	683.53	641.70	609.10	583.20	562.29
41000	3671.64	1958.86	1391.35	1110.13	943.41	833.90	757.07	700.62	657.74	624.33	597.78	576.35
42000	3761.19	2006.64	1425.29	1137.21	966.42	854.24	775.53	717.71	673.78	639.56	612.36	590.41
43000	3850.74	2054.42	1459.22	1164.29	989.43	874.58	794.00	734.80	689.82	654.78	626.94	604.46
44000	3940.29	2102.19	1493.16	1191.36	1012.44	894.92	812.46	751.88	705.87	670.01	641.52	618.52
45000	4029.85	2149.97	1527.09	1218.44	1035.45	915.26	830.93	768.97	721.91	685.24	656.10	632.58
46000	4119.40	2197.75	1561.03	1245.52	1058.46	935.60	849.39	786.06	737.95	700.47	670.68	646.63
47000	4208.95	2245.52	1594.96	1272.59	1081.47	955.94	867.85	803.15	753.99	715.69	685.26	660.69
48000	4298.50	2293.30	1628.90	1299.67	1104.48	976.28	886.32	820.24	770.04	730.92	699.84	674.75
49000	4388.05	2341.08	1662.83	1326.74	1127.49	996.61	904.78	837.32	786.08	746.15	714.42	688.81
50000	4477.61	2388.86	1696.77	1353.82	1150.50	1016.95	923.25	854.41	802.12	761.38	729.00	702.86
55000	4925.37	2627.74	1866.45	1489.20	1265.55	1118.65	1015.57	939.85	882.33	837.51	801.90	773.15
60000	5373.13	2866.63	2036.12	1624.58	1380.60	1220.34	1107.90	1025.29	962.54	913.65	874.80	843.44
65000	5820.89	3105.51	2205.80	1759.97	1495.65	1322.04	1200.22	1110.74	1042.76	989.79	947.70	913.72
70000	6268.65	3344.40	2375.48	1895.35	1610.69	1423.73	1292.55	1196.18	1122.97	1065.93	1020.60	984.01
75000	6716.41	3583.28	2545.15	2030.73	1725.74	1525.43	1384.87	1281.62	1203.18	1142.06	1093.50	1054.29
80000	7164.17	3822.17	2714.83	2166.11	1840.79	1627.12	1477.20	1367.06	1283.39	1218.20	1166.39	1124.58
85000	7611.93	4061.05	2884.50	2301.49	1955.84	1728.82	1569.52	1452.50	1363.60	1294.34	1239.29	1194.86
90000	8059.69	4299.94	3054.18	2436.87	2070.89	1830.51	1661.85	1537.94	1443.81	1370.47	1312.19	1265.15
95000	8507.45	4538.82	3223.86	2572.26	2185.94	1932.21	1754.17	1623.38	1524.02	1446.61	1385.09	1335.44
100000	8955.21	4777.71	3393.53	2707.64	2300.99	2033.90	1846.49	1708.82	1604.24	1522.75	1457.99	1405.72

13%

Table 1

MONTHLY

13.50%

PAYMENT REQUIRED TO AMORTIZE A LOAN

13%

TERM / AMOUNT	13 YEARS	14 YEARS	15 YEARS	16 YEARS	17 YEARS	18 YEARS	19 YEARS	20 YEARS	25 YEARS	30 YEARS	35 YEARS	40 YEARS
50	.69	.67	.65	.64	.63	.62	.62	.61	.59	.58	.57	.57
100	1.37	1.33	1.30	1.28	1.26	1.24	1.23	1.21	1.17	1.15	1.14	1.14
200	2.73	2.66	2.60	2.55	2.51	2.48	2.45	2.42	2.34	2.30	2.28	2.27
300	4.09	3.99	3.90	3.83	3.76	3.71	3.67	3.63	3.50	3.44	3.41	3.40
400	5.46	5.32	5.20	5.10	5.02	4.95	4.89	4.83	4.67	4.59	4.55	4.53
500	6.82	6.64	6.50	6.37	6.27	6.18	6.11	6.04	5.83	5.73	5.68	5.66
600	8.18	7.97	7.79	7.65	7.52	7.42	7.33	7.25	7.00	6.88	6.82	6.79
700	9.55	9.30	9.09	8.92	8.78	8.65	8.55	8.46	8.16	8.02	7.95	7.92
800	10.91	10.63	10.39	10.19	10.03	9.89	9.77	9.66	9.33	9.17	9.09	9.05
900	12.27	11.95	11.69	11.47	11.28	11.12	10.99	10.87	10.50	10.31	10.22	10.18
1000	13.63	13.28	12.99	12.74	12.53	12.36	12.21	12.08	11.66	11.46	11.36	11.31
2000	27.26	26.56	25.97	25.48	25.06	24.71	24.41	24.15	23.32	22.91	22.71	22.61
3000	40.89	39.84	38.95	38.22	37.59	37.06	36.61	36.23	34.97	34.37	34.07	33.91
4000	54.52	53.11	51.94	50.95	50.12	49.41	48.81	48.30	46.63	45.82	45.42	45.22
5000	68.15	66.39	64.92	63.69	62.65	61.77	61.02	60.37	58.29	57.28	56.77	56.52
6000	81.78	79.67	77.90	76.43	75.18	74.12	73.22	72.45	69.94	68.73	68.13	67.82
7000	95.41	92.94	90.89	89.16	87.71	86.47	85.42	84.52	81.60	80.18	79.48	79.12
8000	109.04	106.22	103.87	101.90	100.23	98.82	97.62	96.59	93.26	91.64	90.83	90.43
9000	122.67	119.50	116.85	114.64	112.76	111.18	109.82	108.67	104.91	103.09	102.19	101.73
10000	136.30	132.78	129.84	127.37	125.29	123.53	122.03	120.74	116.57	114.55	113.54	113.03
11000	149.93	146.05	142.82	140.11	137.82	135.88	134.23	132.82	128.23	126.00	124.89	124.33
12000	163.56	159.33	155.80	152.85	150.35	148.23	146.43	144.89	139.88	137.45	136.25	135.64
13000	177.19	172.61	168.79	165.58	162.88	160.59	158.63	156.96	151.54	148.91	147.60	146.94
14000	190.82	185.88	181.77	178.32	175.41	172.94	170.83	169.04	163.20	160.36	158.95	158.24
15000	204.45	199.16	194.75	191.06	187.94	185.29	183.04	181.11	174.85	171.82	170.31	169.54
16000	218.08	212.44	207.74	203.79	200.46	197.64	195.24	193.18	186.51	183.27	181.66	180.85
17000	231.71	225.72	220.72	216.53	212.99	209.99	207.44	205.26	198.16	194.73	193.01	192.15
18000	245.34	238.99	233.70	229.27	225.52	222.35	219.64	217.33	209.82	206.18	204.37	203.45
19000	258.97	252.27	246.69	242.00	238.05	234.70	231.85	229.41	221.48	217.63	215.72	214.75
20000	272.60	265.55	259.67	254.74	250.58	247.05	244.05	241.48	233.13	229.09	227.07	226.06
21000	286.23	278.82	272.65	267.48	263.11	259.40	256.25	253.55	244.79	240.54	238.43	237.36
22000	299.86	292.10	285.64	280.21	275.64	271.76	268.45	265.63	256.45	252.00	249.78	248.66
23000	313.49	305.38	298.62	292.95	288.16	284.11	280.65	277.70	268.10	263.45	261.13	259.97
24000	327.12	318.65	311.60	305.69	300.69	296.46	292.86	289.77	279.76	274.90	272.49	271.27
25000	340.75	331.93	324.58	318.42	313.22	308.81	305.06	301.85	291.42	286.36	283.84	282.57
26000	354.38	345.21	337.57	331.16	325.75	321.17	317.26	313.92	303.07	297.81	295.19	293.87
27000	368.01	358.49	350.55	343.90	338.28	333.52	329.46	326.00	314.73	309.27	306.55	305.18
28000	381.64	371.76	363.53	356.63	350.81	345.87	341.66	338.07	326.39	320.72	317.90	316.48
29000	395.27	385.04	376.52	369.37	363.34	358.22	353.87	350.14	338.04	332.17	329.25	327.78
30000	408.90	398.32	389.50	382.11	375.87	370.57	366.07	362.22	349.70	343.63	340.61	339.08
31000	422.53	411.59	402.48	394.84	388.39	382.93	378.27	374.29	361.35	355.08	351.96	350.39
32000	436.16	424.87	415.47	407.58	400.92	395.28	390.47	386.36	373.01	366.54	363.31	361.69
33000	449.79	438.15	428.45	420.32	413.45	407.63	402.67	398.44	384.67	377.99	374.67	372.99
34000	463.42	451.43	441.43	433.05	425.98	419.98	414.88	410.51	396.32	389.45	386.02	384.29
35000	477.05	464.70	454.42	445.79	438.51	432.34	427.08	422.59	407.98	400.90	397.37	395.60
36000	490.68	477.98	467.40	458.53	451.04	444.69	439.28	434.66	419.64	412.35	408.73	406.90
37000	504.31	491.26	480.38	471.26	463.57	457.04	451.48	446.73	431.29	423.81	420.08	418.20
38000	517.94	504.53	493.37	484.00	476.10	469.39	463.69	458.81	442.95	435.26	431.43	429.50
39000	531.57	517.81	506.35	496.74	488.62	481.75	475.89	470.88	454.61	446.72	442.79	440.81
40000	545.20	531.09	519.33	509.47	501.15	494.10	488.09	482.95	466.26	458.17	454.14	452.11
41000	558.83	544.36	532.32	522.21	513.68	506.45	500.29	495.03	477.92	469.62	465.49	463.41
42000	572.46	557.64	545.30	534.95	526.21	518.80	512.49	507.10	489.58	481.08	476.85	474.71
43000	586.09	570.92	558.28	547.68	538.74	531.15	524.70	519.18	501.23	492.53	488.20	486.02
44000	599.72	584.20	571.27	560.42	551.27	543.51	536.90	531.25	512.89	503.99	499.55	497.32
45000	613.35	597.47	584.25	573.16	563.80	555.86	549.10	543.32	524.55	515.44	510.91	508.62
46000	626.98	610.75	597.23	585.89	576.32	568.21	561.30	555.40	536.20	526.89	522.26	519.93
47000	640.61	624.03	610.21	598.63	588.85	580.56	573.50	567.47	547.86	538.35	533.62	531.23
48000	654.24	637.30	623.20	611.37	601.38	592.92	585.71	579.54	559.51	549.80	544.97	542.53
49000	667.87	650.58	636.18	624.10	613.91	605.27	597.91	591.62	571.17	561.26	556.32	553.83
50000	681.50	663.86	649.16	636.84	626.44	617.62	610.11	603.69	582.83	572.71	567.68	565.14
55000	749.65	730.24	714.08	700.52	689.08	679.38	671.12	664.06	641.11	629.98	624.44	621.65
60000	817.80	796.63	779.00	764.21	751.73	741.14	732.13	724.43	699.39	687.25	681.21	678.16
65000	885.95	863.01	843.91	827.89	814.37	802.91	793.14	784.80	757.67	744.52	737.98	734.67
70000	954.10	929.40	908.83	891.57	877.01	864.67	854.15	845.17	815.96	801.79	794.74	791.19
75000	1022.25	995.79	973.74	955.26	939.66	926.43	915.16	905.54	874.24	859.06	851.51	847.70
80000	1090.40	1062.17	1038.66	1018.94	1002.30	988.19	976.17	965.90	932.52	916.33	908.28	904.21
85000	1158.55	1128.56	1103.58	1082.62	1064.94	1049.95	1037.18	1026.27	990.80	973.61	965.04	960.73
90000	1226.70	1194.94	1168.49	1146.31	1127.59	1111.71	1098.20	1086.64	1049.09	1030.88	1021.81	1017.24
95000	1294.85	1261.33	1233.41	1209.99	1190.23	1173.47	1159.21	1147.01	1107.37	1088.15	1078.58	1073.75
100000	1363.00	1327.71	1298.32	1273.67	1252.87	1235.24	1220.22	1207.38	1165.65	1145.42	1135.35	1130.27

Table 1

13.75%

MONTHLY

PAYMENT REQUIRED TO AMORTIZE A LOAN

TERM AMOUNT	1 YEAR	2 YEARS	3 YEARS	4 YEARS	5 YEARS	6 YEARS	7 YEARS	8 YEARS	9 YEARS	10 YEARS	11 YEARS	12 YEARS
50	4.49	2.40	1.71	1.37	1.16	1.03	.94	.87	.81	.77	.74	.72
100	8.97	4.79	3.41	2.73	2.32	2.05	1.87	1.73	1.62	1.54	1.48	1.43
200	17.94	9.58	6.82	5.45	4.63	4.10	3.73	3.45	3.24	3.08	2.95	2.85
300	26.91	14.37	10.22	8.17	6.95	6.15	5.59	5.17	4.86	4.62	4.42	4.27
400	35.87	19.16	13.63	10.89	9.26	8.19	7.45	6.90	6.48	6.16	5.90	5.69
500	44.84	23.95	17.03	13.61	11.57	10.24	9.31	8.62	8.10	7.69	7.37	7.11
600	53.81	28.74	20.44	16.33	13.89	12.29	11.17	10.34	9.72	9.23	8.84	8.53
700	62.77	33.53	23.84	19.05	16.20	14.34	13.03	12.07	11.34	10.77	10.32	9.95
800	71.74	38.32	27.25	21.77	18.52	16.38	14.89	13.79	12.96	12.31	11.79	11.38
900	80.71	43.11	30.66	24.49	20.83	18.43	16.75	15.51	14.57	13.84	13.26	12.80
1000	89.67	47.90	34.06	27.21	23.14	20.48	18.61	17.23	16.19	15.38	14.74	14.22
2000	179.34	95.79	68.12	54.41	46.28	40.95	37.21	34.46	32.38	30.76	29.47	28.43
3000	269.01	143.69	102.17	81.61	69.42	61.42	55.81	51.69	48.57	46.14	44.20	42.65
4000	358.68	191.58	136.23	108.81	92.56	81.89	74.41	68.92	64.76	61.51	58.94	56.86
5000	448.35	239.48	170.29	136.01	115.70	102.37	93.02	86.15	80.94	76.89	73.67	71.07
6000	538.02	287.37	204.34	163.21	138.84	122.84	111.62	103.38	97.13	92.27	88.40	85.29
7000	627.69	335.27	238.40	190.41	161.98	143.31	130.22	120.61	113.32	107.64	103.14	99.50
8000	717.36	383.16	272.46	217.61	185.12	163.78	148.82	137.84	129.51	123.02	117.87	113.72
9000	807.03	431.06	306.51	244.82	208.25	184.25	167.42	155.07	145.69	138.40	132.60	127.93
10000	896.70	478.95	340.57	272.02	231.39	204.73	186.03	172.30	161.88	153.77	147.33	142.14
11000	986.37	526.85	374.62	299.22	254.53	225.20	204.63	189.53	178.07	169.15	162.07	156.36
12000	1076.04	574.74	408.68	326.42	277.67	245.67	223.23	206.76	194.26	184.53	176.80	170.57
13000	1165.71	622.64	442.74	353.62	300.81	266.14	241.83	223.99	210.44	199.90	191.53	184.78
14000	1255.38	670.53	476.79	380.82	323.95	286.61	260.44	241.22	226.63	215.28	206.27	199.00
15000	1345.05	718.43	510.85	408.02	347.09	307.09	279.04	258.45	242.82	230.66	221.00	213.21
16000	1434.72	766.32	544.91	435.22	370.23	327.56	297.64	275.68	259.01	246.03	235.73	227.43
17000	1524.39	814.22	578.96	462.43	393.37	348.03	316.24	292.91	275.20	261.41	250.46	241.64
18000	1614.06	862.11	613.02	489.63	416.50	368.50	334.84	310.14	291.38	276.79	265.20	255.85
19000	1703.73	910.01	647.08	516.83	439.64	388.98	353.45	327.37	307.57	292.16	279.93	270.07
20000	1793.40	957.90	681.13	544.03	462.78	409.45	372.05	344.60	323.76	307.54	294.66	284.28
21000	1883.07	1005.80	715.19	571.23	485.92	429.92	390.65	361.83	339.95	322.92	309.40	298.50
22000	1972.73	1053.69	749.24	598.43	509.06	450.39	409.25	379.05	356.13	338.29	324.13	312.71
23000	2062.40	1101.59	783.30	625.63	532.20	470.86	427.86	396.28	372.32	353.67	338.86	326.92
24000	2152.07	1149.48	817.36	652.83	555.34	491.34	446.46	413.51	388.51	369.05	353.59	341.14
25000	2241.74	1197.38	851.41	680.04	578.48	511.81	465.06	430.74	404.70	384.42	368.33	355.35
26000	2331.41	1245.27	885.47	707.24	601.61	532.28	483.66	447.97	420.88	399.80	383.06	369.56
27000	2421.08	1293.17	919.53	734.44	624.75	552.75	502.26	465.20	437.07	415.18	397.79	383.78
28000	2510.75	1341.06	953.58	761.64	647.89	573.22	520.87	482.43	453.26	430.55	412.53	397.99
29000	2600.42	1388.96	987.64	788.84	671.03	593.70	539.47	499.66	469.45	445.93	427.26	412.21
30000	2690.09	1436.85	1021.69	816.04	694.17	614.17	558.07	516.89	485.64	461.31	441.99	426.42
31000	2779.76	1484.75	1055.75	843.24	717.31	634.64	576.67	534.12	501.82	476.68	456.72	440.63
32000	2869.43	1532.64	1089.81	870.44	740.45	655.11	595.27	551.35	518.01	492.06	471.46	454.85
33000	2959.10	1580.54	1123.86	897.65	763.59	675.58	613.88	568.58	534.20	507.44	486.19	469.06
34000	3048.77	1628.43	1157.92	924.85	786.73	696.06	632.48	585.81	550.39	522.81	500.92	483.28
35000	3138.44	1676.33	1191.98	952.05	809.86	716.53	651.08	603.04	566.57	538.19	515.66	497.49
36000	3228.11	1724.22	1226.03	979.25	833.00	737.00	669.68	620.27	582.76	553.57	530.39	511.70
37000	3317.78	1772.12	1260.09	1006.45	856.14	757.47	688.29	637.50	598.95	568.94	545.12	525.92
38000	3407.45	1820.01	1294.15	1033.65	879.28	777.95	706.89	654.73	615.14	584.32	559.85	540.13
39000	3497.12	1867.90	1328.20	1060.85	902.42	798.42	725.49	671.96	631.32	599.70	574.59	554.34
40000	3586.79	1915.80	1362.26	1088.05	925.56	818.89	744.09	689.19	647.51	615.07	589.32	568.56
41000	3676.46	1963.69	1396.31	1115.26	948.70	839.36	762.69	706.42	663.70	630.45	604.05	582.77
42000	3766.13	2011.59	1430.37	1142.46	971.84	859.83	781.30	723.65	679.89	645.83	618.79	596.99
43000	3855.79	2059.48	1464.43	1169.66	994.98	880.31	799.90	740.87	696.08	661.20	633.52	611.20
44000	3945.46	2107.38	1498.48	1196.86	1018.11	900.78	818.50	758.10	712.26	676.58	648.25	625.41
45000	4035.13	2155.27	1532.54	1224.06	1041.25	921.25	837.10	775.33	728.45	691.96	662.98	639.63
46000	4124.80	2203.17	1566.60	1251.26	1064.39	941.72	855.71	792.56	744.64	707.33	677.72	653.84
47000	4214.47	2251.06	1600.65	1278.46	1087.53	962.19	874.31	809.79	760.83	722.71	692.45	668.05
48000	4304.14	2298.96	1634.71	1305.66	1110.67	982.67	892.91	827.02	777.01	738.09	707.18	682.27
49000	4393.81	2346.85	1668.77	1332.87	1133.81	1003.14	911.51	844.25	793.20	753.46	721.92	696.48
50000	4483.48	2394.75	1702.82	1360.07	1156.95	1023.61	930.11	861.48	809.39	768.84	736.65	710.70
55000	4931.83	2634.22	1873.10	1496.07	1272.64	1125.97	1023.12	947.63	890.33	845.72	810.31	781.77
60000	5380.18	2873.70	2043.39	1632.08	1388.34	1228.33	1116.14	1033.78	971.27	922.61	883.98	852.83
65000	5828.52	3113.17	2213.67	1768.09	1504.03	1330.69	1209.15	1119.92	1052.20	999.49	957.64	923.90
70000	6276.87	3352.65	2383.95	1904.09	1619.72	1433.05	1302.16	1206.07	1133.14	1076.37	1031.31	994.97
75000	6725.22	3592.12	2554.23	2040.10	1735.42	1535.41	1395.17	1292.22	1214.08	1153.26	1104.97	1066.04
80000	7173.57	3831.59	2724.51	2176.10	1851.11	1637.77	1488.18	1378.37	1295.02	1230.14	1178.64	1137.11
85000	7621.92	4071.07	2894.79	2312.11	1966.81	1740.13	1581.19	1464.51	1375.96	1307.02	1252.30	1208.18
90000	8070.26	4310.54	3065.07	2448.12	2082.50	1842.50	1674.20	1550.66	1456.90	1383.91	1325.97	1279.25
95000	8518.61	4550.02	3235.36	2584.12	2198.20	1944.86	1767.21	1636.81	1537.83	1460.79	1399.63	1350.32
100000	8966.96	4789.49	3405.64	2720.13	2313.89	2047.22	1860.22	1722.96	1618.77	1537.67	1473.29	1421.39

13%

Table 1

MONTHLY

PAYMENT REQUIRED TO AMORTIZE A LOAN

13.75%

13%

TERM / AMOUNT	13 YEARS	14 YEARS	15 YEARS	16 YEARS	17 YEARS	18 YEARS	19 YEARS	20 YEARS	25 YEARS	30 YEARS	35 YEARS	40 YEARS
50	.69	.68	.66	.65	.64	.63	.62	.62	.60	.59	.58	.58
100	1.38	1.35	1.32	1.30	1.28	1.26	1.24	1.23	1.19	1.17	1.16	1.16
200	2.76	2.69	2.63	2.59	2.55	2.51	2.48	2.46	2.37	2.34	2.32	2.31
300	4.14	4.04	3.95	3.88	3.82	3.76	3.72	3.68	3.56	3.50	3.47	3.46
400	5.52	5.38	5.26	5.17	5.09	5.02	4.96	4.91	4.74	4.67	4.63	4.61
500	6.90	6.73	6.58	6.46	6.36	6.27	6.20	6.13	5.93	5.83	5.78	5.76
600	8.28	8.07	7.89	7.75	7.63	7.52	7.43	7.36	7.11	7.00	6.94	6.91
700	9.66	9.41	9.21	9.04	8.90	8.77	8.67	8.58	8.30	8.16	8.09	8.06
800	11.04	10.76	10.52	10.33	10.17	10.03	9.91	9.81	9.48	9.33	9.25	9.21
900	12.42	12.10	11.84	11.62	11.44	11.28	11.15	11.03	10.67	10.49	10.40	10.36
1000	13.80	13.45	13.15	12.91	12.71	12.53	12.39	12.26	11.85	11.66	11.56	11.51
2000	27.59	26.89	26.30	25.82	25.41	25.06	24.77	24.51	23.70	23.31	23.11	23.02
3000	41.38	40.33	39.45	38.72	38.11	37.59	37.15	36.77	35.54	34.96	34.67	34.53
4000	55.17	53.77	52.60	51.63	50.81	50.12	49.53	49.02	47.39	46.61	46.22	46.03
5000	68.96	67.21	65.75	64.54	63.51	62.64	61.91	61.28	59.24	58.26	57.78	57.54
6000	82.75	80.65	78.90	77.44	76.21	75.17	74.29	73.53	71.08	69.91	69.33	69.05
7000	96.54	94.09	92.05	90.35	88.91	87.70	86.67	85.78	82.93	81.56	80.89	80.55
8000	110.33	107.53	105.20	103.26	101.62	100.23	99.05	98.04	94.78	93.21	92.44	92.06
9000	124.12	120.97	118.35	116.16	114.32	112.75	111.43	110.29	106.62	104.87	104.00	103.57
10000	137.91	134.41	131.50	129.07	127.02	125.28	123.81	122.55	118.47	116.52	115.55	115.07
11000	151.70	147.85	144.65	141.98	139.72	137.81	136.19	134.80	130.32	128.17	127.11	126.58
12000	165.49	161.29	157.80	154.88	152.42	150.34	148.57	147.05	142.16	139.82	138.66	138.09
13000	179.28	174.73	170.95	167.79	165.12	162.86	160.95	159.31	154.01	151.47	150.22	149.59
14000	193.07	188.17	184.10	180.69	177.82	175.39	173.33	171.56	165.86	163.12	161.77	161.10
15000	206.86	201.61	197.25	193.60	190.52	187.92	185.71	183.82	177.70	174.77	173.33	172.61
16000	220.65	215.05	210.40	206.51	203.23	200.45	198.09	196.07	189.55	186.42	184.88	184.11
17000	234.44	228.49	223.55	219.41	215.93	212.97	210.47	208.32	201.40	198.07	196.44	195.62
18000	248.23	241.94	236.70	232.32	228.63	225.50	222.85	220.58	213.24	209.73	207.99	207.13
19000	262.02	255.38	249.85	245.23	241.33	238.03	235.23	232.83	225.09	221.38	219.55	218.64
20000	275.81	268.82	263.00	258.13	254.03	250.56	247.61	245.09	236.94	233.03	231.10	230.14
21000	289.60	282.26	276.15	271.04	266.73	263.09	259.99	257.34	248.78	244.68	242.66	241.65
22000	303.39	295.70	289.30	283.95	279.43	275.61	272.37	269.59	260.63	256.33	254.21	253.16
23000	317.18	309.14	302.45	296.85	292.13	288.14	284.75	281.85	272.48	267.98	265.77	264.66
24000	330.97	322.58	315.60	309.76	304.84	300.67	297.13	294.10	284.32	279.63	277.32	276.17
25000	344.76	336.02	328.75	322.67	317.54	313.20	309.51	306.36	296.17	291.28	288.88	287.68
26000	358.55	349.46	341.90	335.57	330.24	325.72	321.89	318.61	308.02	302.93	300.43	299.18
27000	372.34	362.90	355.05	348.48	342.94	338.25	334.27	330.86	319.86	314.59	311.99	310.69
28000	386.13	376.34	368.20	361.38	355.64	350.78	346.65	343.12	331.71	326.24	323.54	322.20
29000	399.92	389.78	381.35	374.29	368.34	363.31	359.03	355.37	343.56	337.89	335.10	333.70
30000	413.71	403.22	394.50	387.20	381.04	375.83	371.41	367.63	355.40	349.54	346.65	345.21
31000	427.50	416.66	407.65	400.10	393.75	388.36	383.79	379.88	367.25	361.19	358.21	356.72
32000	441.29	430.10	420.80	413.01	406.45	400.89	396.17	392.13	379.10	372.84	369.76	368.22
33000	455.08	443.54	433.95	425.92	419.15	413.42	408.55	404.39	390.94	384.49	381.32	379.73
34000	468.87	456.98	447.10	438.82	431.85	425.94	420.93	416.64	402.79	396.14	392.87	391.24
35000	482.66	470.42	460.25	451.73	444.55	438.47	433.31	428.90	414.64	407.79	404.42	402.74
36000	496.45	483.87	473.40	464.64	457.25	451.00	445.69	441.15	426.48	419.45	415.98	414.25
37000	510.24	497.31	486.55	477.54	469.95	463.53	458.07	453.40	438.33	431.10	427.53	425.76
38000	524.03	510.75	499.70	490.45	482.65	476.06	470.45	465.66	450.18	442.75	439.09	437.27
39000	537.82	524.19	512.85	503.35	495.36	488.58	482.83	477.91	462.02	454.40	450.64	448.77
40000	551.61	537.63	526.00	516.26	508.06	501.11	495.21	490.17	473.87	466.05	462.20	460.28
41000	565.40	551.07	539.15	529.17	520.76	513.64	507.59	502.42	485.72	477.70	473.75	471.79
42000	579.19	564.51	552.30	542.07	533.46	526.17	519.97	514.68	497.56	489.35	485.31	483.29
43000	592.98	577.95	565.45	554.98	546.16	538.69	532.35	526.93	509.41	501.00	496.86	494.80
44000	606.77	591.39	578.60	567.89	558.86	551.22	544.73	539.18	521.26	512.65	508.42	506.31
45000	620.56	604.83	591.75	580.79	571.56	563.75	557.11	551.44	533.10	524.31	519.97	517.81
46000	634.35	618.27	604.90	593.70	584.26	576.28	569.49	563.69	544.95	535.96	531.53	529.32
47000	648.14	631.71	618.05	606.61	596.97	588.80	581.87	575.95	556.80	547.61	543.08	540.83
48000	661.93	645.15	631.20	619.51	609.67	601.33	594.25	588.20	568.64	559.26	554.64	552.33
49000	675.72	658.59	644.35	632.42	622.37	613.86	606.63	600.45	580.49	570.91	566.19	563.84
50000	689.51	672.03	657.50	645.33	635.07	626.39	619.01	612.71	592.34	582.56	577.75	575.35
55000	758.46	739.24	723.25	709.86	698.58	689.03	680.91	673.98	651.57	640.82	635.52	632.88
60000	827.41	806.44	789.00	774.39	762.08	751.66	742.81	735.25	710.80	699.07	693.30	690.42
65000	896.36	873.64	854.75	838.92	825.59	814.30	804.71	796.52	770.04	757.33	751.07	747.95
70000	965.31	940.84	920.50	903.45	889.10	876.94	866.61	857.79	829.27	815.58	808.84	805.48
75000	1034.26	1008.05	986.25	967.99	952.60	939.58	928.51	919.06	888.50	873.84	866.62	863.02
80000	1103.21	1075.25	1051.99	1032.52	1016.11	1002.22	990.41	980.33	947.74	932.10	924.39	920.55
85000	1172.16	1142.45	1117.74	1097.05	1079.61	1064.85	1052.31	1041.60	1006.97	990.35	982.17	978.09
90000	1241.11	1209.66	1183.49	1161.58	1143.12	1127.49	1114.21	1102.87	1066.20	1048.61	1039.94	1035.62
95000	1310.06	1276.86	1249.24	1226.11	1206.63	1190.13	1176.11	1164.14	1125.44	1106.86	1097.72	1093.16
100000	1379.01	1344.06	1314.99	1290.65	1270.13	1252.77	1238.01	1225.41	1184.67	1165.12	1155.49	1150.69

Table 1

14.00%

MONTHLY
PAYMENT REQUIRED TO AMORTIZE A LOAN

14%

TERM / AMOUNT	1 YEAR	2 YEARS	3 YEARS	4 YEARS	5 YEARS	6 YEARS	7 YEARS	8 YEARS	9 YEARS	10 YEARS	11 YEARS	12 YEARS
50	4.49	2.41	1.71	1.37	1.17	1.04	.94	.87	.82	.78	.75	.72
100	8.98	4.81	3.42	2.74	2.33	2.07	1.88	1.74	1.64	1.56	1.49	1.44
200	17.96	9.61	6.84	5.47	4.66	4.13	3.75	3.48	3.27	3.11	2.98	2.88
300	26.94	14.41	10.26	8.20	6.99	6.19	5.63	5.22	4.91	4.66	4.47	4.32
400	35.92	19.21	13.68	10.94	9.31	8.25	7.50	6.95	6.54	6.22	5.96	5.75
500	44.90	24.01	17.09	13.67	11.64	10.31	9.38	8.69	8.17	7.77	7.45	7.19
600	53.88	28.81	20.51	16.40	13.97	12.37	11.25	10.43	9.81	9.32	8.94	8.63
700	62.86	33.61	23.93	19.13	16.29	14.43	13.12	12.17	11.44	10.87	10.43	10.06
800	71.83	38.42	27.35	21.87	18.62	16.49	15.00	13.90	13.07	12.43	11.91	11.50
900	80.81	43.22	30.76	24.60	20.95	18.55	16.87	15.64	14.71	13.98	13.40	12.94
1000	89.79	48.02	34.18	27.33	23.27	20.61	18.75	17.38	16.34	15.53	14.89	14.38
2000	179.58	96.03	68.36	54.66	46.54	41.22	37.49	34.75	32.67	31.06	29.78	28.75
3000	269.37	144.04	102.54	81.98	69.81	61.82	56.23	52.12	49.01	46.58	44.66	43.12
4000	359.15	192.06	136.72	109.31	93.08	82.43	74.97	69.49	65.34	62.11	59.55	57.49
5000	448.94	240.07	170.89	136.64	116.35	103.03	93.71	86.86	81.67	77.64	74.44	71.86
6000	538.73	288.08	205.07	163.96	139.61	123.64	112.45	104.23	98.01	93.16	89.32	86.23
7000	628.51	336.10	239.25	191.29	162.88	144.25	131.19	121.61	114.34	108.69	104.21	100.60
8000	718.30	384.11	273.43	218.62	186.15	164.85	149.93	138.98	130.67	124.22	119.10	114.98
9000	808.09	432.12	307.60	245.94	209.42	185.46	168.67	156.35	147.01	139.74	133.98	129.35
10000	897.88	480.13	341.78	273.27	232.69	206.06	187.41	173.72	163.34	155.27	148.87	143.72
11000	987.66	528.15	375.96	300.60	255.96	226.67	206.15	191.09	179.68	170.80	163.76	158.09
12000	1077.45	576.16	410.14	327.92	279.22	247.27	224.89	208.46	196.01	186.32	178.64	172.46
13000	1167.24	624.17	444.31	355.25	302.49	267.88	243.63	225.83	212.34	201.85	193.53	186.83
14000	1257.02	672.19	478.49	382.58	325.76	288.49	262.37	243.21	228.68	217.38	208.42	201.20
15000	1346.81	720.20	512.67	409.90	349.03	309.09	281.11	260.58	245.01	232.90	223.30	215.57
16000	1436.60	768.21	546.85	437.23	372.30	329.70	299.85	277.95	261.34	248.43	238.19	229.95
17000	1526.39	816.22	581.02	464.56	395.57	350.30	318.59	295.32	277.68	263.96	253.08	244.32
18000	1616.17	864.24	615.20	491.88	418.83	370.91	337.33	312.69	294.01	279.48	267.96	258.69
19000	1705.96	912.25	649.38	519.21	442.10	391.51	356.07	330.06	310.35	295.01	282.85	273.06
20000	1795.75	960.26	683.56	546.53	465.37	412.12	374.81	347.44	326.68	310.54	297.74	287.43
21000	1885.53	1008.28	717.74	573.86	488.64	432.73	393.55	364.81	343.01	326.06	312.62	301.80
22000	1975.32	1056.29	751.91	601.19	511.91	453.33	412.29	382.18	359.35	341.59	327.51	316.17
23000	2065.11	1104.30	786.09	628.51	535.17	473.94	431.03	399.55	375.68	357.12	342.40	330.54
24000	2154.90	1152.31	820.27	655.84	558.44	494.54	449.77	416.92	392.01	372.64	357.28	344.92
25000	2244.68	1200.33	854.45	683.17	581.71	515.15	468.51	434.29	408.35	388.17	372.17	359.29
26000	2334.47	1248.34	888.62	710.49	604.98	535.75	487.25	451.66	424.68	403.70	387.06	373.66
27000	2424.26	1296.35	922.80	737.82	628.25	556.36	505.99	469.04	441.01	419.22	401.94	388.03
28000	2514.04	1344.37	956.98	765.15	651.52	576.97	524.73	486.41	457.35	434.75	416.83	402.40
29000	2603.83	1392.38	991.16	792.47	674.78	597.57	543.47	503.78	473.68	450.28	431.72	416.77
30000	2693.62	1440.39	1025.33	819.80	698.05	618.18	562.21	521.15	490.02	465.80	446.60	431.14
31000	2783.41	1488.40	1059.51	847.13	721.32	638.78	580.95	538.52	506.35	481.33	461.49	445.51
32000	2873.19	1536.42	1093.69	874.45	744.59	659.39	599.69	555.89	522.68	496.86	476.38	459.89
33000	2962.98	1584.43	1127.87	901.78	767.86	679.99	618.43	573.26	539.02	512.38	491.26	474.26
34000	3052.77	1632.44	1162.04	929.11	791.13	700.60	637.17	590.64	555.35	527.91	506.15	488.63
35000	3142.55	1680.46	1196.22	956.43	814.39	721.21	655.91	608.01	571.68	543.44	521.04	503.00
36000	3232.34	1728.47	1230.40	983.76	837.66	741.81	674.65	625.38	588.02	558.96	535.92	517.37
37000	3322.13	1776.48	1264.58	1011.08	860.93	762.42	693.39	642.75	604.35	574.49	550.81	531.74
38000	3411.92	1824.49	1298.75	1038.41	884.20	783.02	712.13	660.12	620.69	590.02	565.70	546.11
39000	3501.70	1872.51	1332.93	1065.74	907.47	803.63	730.87	677.49	637.02	605.54	580.58	560.48
40000	3591.49	1920.52	1367.11	1093.06	930.74	824.23	749.61	694.87	653.35	621.07	595.47	574.86
41000	3681.28	1968.53	1401.29	1120.39	954.00	844.84	768.35	712.24	669.69	636.60	610.36	589.23
42000	3771.06	2016.55	1435.47	1147.72	977.27	865.45	787.09	729.61	686.02	652.12	625.24	603.60
43000	3860.85	2064.56	1469.64	1175.04	1000.54	886.05	805.83	746.98	702.35	667.65	640.13	617.97
44000	3950.64	2112.57	1503.82	1202.37	1023.81	906.66	824.57	764.35	718.69	683.18	655.02	632.34
45000	4040.43	2160.58	1538.00	1229.70	1047.08	927.26	843.31	781.72	735.02	698.70	669.90	646.71
46000	4130.21	2208.60	1572.18	1257.02	1070.34	947.87	862.05	799.09	751.36	714.23	684.79	661.08
47000	4220.00	2256.61	1606.35	1284.35	1093.61	968.47	880.79	816.47	767.69	729.76	699.68	675.45
48000	4309.79	2304.62	1640.53	1311.68	1116.88	989.08	899.53	833.84	784.02	745.28	714.56	689.83
49000	4399.57	2352.64	1674.71	1339.00	1140.15	1009.69	918.27	851.21	800.36	760.81	729.45	704.20
50000	4489.36	2400.65	1708.89	1366.33	1163.42	1030.29	937.01	868.58	816.69	776.34	744.34	718.57
55000	4938.30	2640.71	1879.77	1502.96	1279.76	1133.32	1030.71	955.44	898.36	853.97	818.77	790.42
60000	5387.23	2880.78	2050.66	1639.59	1396.10	1236.35	1124.41	1042.30	980.03	931.60	893.20	862.28
65000	5836.17	3120.84	2221.55	1776.23	1512.44	1339.38	1218.11	1129.15	1061.70	1009.24	967.64	934.14
70000	6285.10	3360.91	2392.44	1912.86	1628.78	1442.41	1311.81	1216.01	1143.36	1086.87	1042.07	1005.99
75000	6734.04	3600.97	2563.33	2049.49	1745.12	1545.44	1405.51	1302.87	1225.03	1164.50	1116.50	1077.85
80000	7182.97	3841.04	2734.22	2186.12	1861.47	1648.46	1499.21	1389.73	1306.70	1242.14	1190.94	1149.71
85000	7631.91	4081.10	2905.10	2322.76	1977.81	1751.49	1592.91	1476.58	1388.37	1319.77	1265.37	1221.56
90000	8080.85	4321.16	3075.99	2459.39	2094.15	1854.52	1686.61	1563.44	1470.04	1397.40	1339.80	1293.42
95000	8529.78	4561.23	3246.88	2596.02	2210.49	1957.55	1780.31	1650.30	1551.71	1475.04	1414.24	1365.28
100000	8978.72	4801.29	3417.77	2732.65	2326.83	2060.58	1874.01	1737.16	1633.38	1552.67	1488.67	1437.13

74

Table 1

MONTHLY 14.00%

PAYMENT REQUIRED TO AMORTIZE A LOAN

TERM / AMOUNT	13 YEARS	14 YEARS	15 YEARS	16 YEARS	17 YEARS	18 YEARS	19 YEARS	20 YEARS	25 YEARS	30 YEARS	35 YEARS	40 YEARS
50	.70	.69	.67	.66	.65	.64	.63	.63	.61	.60	.59	.59
100	1.40	1.37	1.34	1.31	1.29	1.28	1.26	1.25	1.21	1.19	1.18	1.18
200	2.80	2.73	2.67	2.62	2.58	2.55	2.52	2.49	2.41	2.37	2.36	2.35
300	4.19	4.09	4.00	3.93	3.87	3.82	3.77	3.74	3.62	3.56	3.53	3.52
400	5.59	5.45	5.33	5.24	5.15	5.09	5.03	4.98	4.82	4.74	4.71	4.69
500	6.98	6.81	6.66	6.54	6.44	6.36	6.28	6.22	6.02	5.93	5.88	5.86
600	8.38	8.17	8.00	7.85	7.73	7.63	7.54	7.47	7.23	7.11	7.06	7.03
700	9.77	9.53	9.33	9.16	9.02	8.90	8.80	8.71	8.43	8.30	8.23	8.20
800	11.17	10.89	10.66	10.47	10.30	10.17	10.05	9.95	9.64	9.48	9.41	9.37
900	12.56	12.25	11.99	11.77	11.59	11.44	11.31	11.20	10.84	10.67	10.59	10.55
1000	13.96	13.61	13.32	13.08	12.88	12.71	12.56	12.44	12.04	11.85	11.76	11.72
2000	27.91	27.21	26.64	26.16	25.75	25.41	25.12	24.88	24.08	23.70	23.52	23.43
3000	41.86	40.82	39.96	39.24	38.63	38.12	37.68	37.31	36.12	35.55	35.28	35.14
4000	55.81	54.42	53.27	52.31	51.50	50.82	50.24	49.75	48.16	47.40	47.03	46.85
5000	69.76	68.03	66.59	65.39	64.38	63.52	62.80	62.18	60.19	59.25	58.79	58.56
6000	83.71	81.63	79.91	78.47	77.25	76.23	75.36	74.62	72.23	71.10	70.55	70.27
7000	97.66	95.24	93.23	91.54	90.13	88.93	87.92	87.05	84.27	82.95	82.30	81.98
8000	111.61	108.84	106.54	104.62	103.00	101.64	100.48	99.49	96.31	94.79	94.06	93.70
9000	125.56	122.45	119.86	117.70	115.88	114.34	113.03	111.92	108.34	106.64	105.82	105.41
10000	139.52	136.05	133.18	130.77	128.75	127.04	125.59	124.36	120.38	118.49	117.57	117.12
11000	153.47	149.66	146.50	143.85	141.63	139.75	138.15	136.79	132.42	130.34	129.33	128.83
12000	167.42	163.26	159.81	156.93	154.50	152.45	150.71	149.23	144.46	142.19	141.09	140.54
13000	181.37	176.87	173.13	170.01	167.38	165.15	163.27	161.66	156.49	154.04	152.84	152.25
14000	195.32	190.47	186.45	183.08	180.25	177.86	175.83	174.10	168.53	165.89	164.60	163.96
15000	209.27	204.08	199.77	196.16	193.13	190.56	188.39	186.53	180.57	177.74	176.36	175.68
16000	223.22	217.68	213.08	209.24	206.00	203.27	200.95	198.97	192.61	189.58	188.11	187.39
17000	237.17	231.29	226.40	222.31	218.88	215.97	213.50	211.40	204.64	201.43	199.87	199.10
18000	251.12	244.89	239.72	235.39	231.75	228.67	226.06	223.84	216.68	213.28	211.63	210.81
19000	265.07	258.50	253.04	248.47	244.63	241.38	238.62	236.27	228.72	225.13	223.38	222.52
20000	279.03	272.10	266.35	261.54	257.50	254.08	251.18	248.71	240.76	236.98	235.14	234.23
21000	292.98	285.71	279.67	274.62	270.38	266.79	263.74	261.14	252.79	248.83	246.90	245.94
22000	306.93	299.31	292.99	287.70	283.25	279.49	276.30	273.58	264.83	260.68	258.65	257.66
23000	320.88	312.92	306.31	300.78	296.12	292.19	288.86	286.01	276.87	272.53	270.41	269.37
24000	334.83	326.52	319.62	313.85	309.00	304.90	301.42	298.45	288.91	284.37	282.17	281.08
25000	348.78	340.13	332.94	326.93	321.87	317.60	313.97	310.89	300.95	296.22	293.92	292.79
26000	362.73	353.73	346.26	340.01	334.75	330.30	326.53	323.32	312.98	308.07	305.68	304.50
27000	376.68	367.34	359.58	353.08	347.62	343.01	339.09	335.76	325.02	319.92	317.44	316.21
28000	390.63	380.94	372.89	366.16	360.50	355.71	351.65	348.19	337.06	331.77	329.19	327.92
29000	404.58	394.55	386.21	379.24	373.37	368.42	364.21	360.63	349.10	343.62	340.95	339.64
30000	418.54	408.15	399.53	392.31	386.25	381.12	376.77	373.06	361.13	355.47	352.71	351.35
31000	432.49	421.76	412.84	405.39	399.12	393.82	389.33	385.50	373.17	367.32	364.46	363.06
32000	446.44	435.36	426.16	418.47	412.00	406.53	401.89	397.93	385.21	379.16	376.22	374.77
33000	460.39	448.97	439.48	431.55	424.87	419.23	414.44	410.37	397.25	391.01	387.98	386.48
34000	474.34	462.57	452.80	444.62	437.75	431.94	427.00	422.80	409.28	402.86	399.73	398.19
35000	488.29	476.18	466.11	457.70	450.62	444.64	439.56	435.24	421.32	414.71	411.49	409.90
36000	502.24	489.78	479.43	470.78	463.50	457.34	452.12	447.67	433.36	426.56	423.25	421.62
37000	516.19	503.39	492.75	483.85	476.37	470.05	464.68	460.11	445.40	438.41	435.00	433.33
38000	530.14	516.99	506.07	496.93	489.25	482.75	477.24	472.54	457.43	450.26	446.76	445.04
39000	544.10	530.60	519.38	510.01	502.12	495.45	489.80	484.98	469.47	462.10	458.52	456.75
40000	558.05	544.20	532.70	523.08	515.00	508.16	502.36	497.41	481.51	473.95	470.27	468.46
41000	572.00	557.81	546.02	536.16	527.87	520.86	514.91	509.85	493.55	485.80	482.03	480.17
42000	585.95	571.41	559.34	549.24	540.75	533.57	527.47	522.28	505.58	497.65	493.79	491.88
43000	599.90	585.02	572.65	562.32	553.62	546.27	540.03	534.72	517.62	509.50	505.54	503.60
44000	613.85	598.62	585.97	575.39	566.49	558.97	552.59	547.15	529.66	521.35	517.30	515.31
45000	627.80	612.23	599.29	588.47	579.37	571.68	565.15	559.59	541.70	533.20	529.06	527.02
46000	641.75	625.83	612.61	601.55	592.24	584.38	577.71	572.02	553.74	545.05	540.81	538.73
47000	655.70	639.44	625.92	614.62	605.12	597.09	590.27	584.46	565.77	556.89	552.57	550.44
48000	669.65	653.04	639.24	627.70	617.99	609.79	602.83	596.89	577.81	568.74	564.33	562.15
49000	683.61	666.64	652.56	640.78	630.87	622.49	615.38	609.33	589.85	580.59	576.08	573.86
50000	697.56	680.25	665.88	653.85	643.74	635.20	627.94	621.77	601.89	592.44	587.84	585.58
55000	767.31	748.27	732.46	719.24	708.12	698.72	690.74	683.94	662.07	651.68	646.63	644.13
60000	837.07	816.30	799.05	784.62	772.49	762.23	753.53	746.12	722.26	710.93	705.41	702.69
65000	906.82	884.32	865.64	850.01	836.86	825.75	816.32	808.29	782.45	770.17	764.19	761.25
70000	976.58	952.35	932.22	915.39	901.24	889.27	879.12	870.47	842.64	829.42	822.98	819.80
75000	1046.33	1020.37	998.81	980.78	965.61	952.79	941.91	932.65	902.83	888.66	881.76	878.36
80000	1116.09	1088.40	1065.40	1046.16	1029.99	1016.31	1004.71	994.82	963.01	947.90	940.54	936.92
85000	1185.84	1156.42	1131.99	1111.55	1094.36	1079.83	1067.50	1057.00	1023.20	1007.15	999.33	995.47
90000	1255.60	1224.45	1198.57	1176.93	1158.73	1143.35	1130.29	1119.17	1083.39	1066.39	1058.11	1054.03
95000	1325.35	1292.47	1265.16	1242.32	1223.11	1206.87	1193.09	1181.35	1143.58	1125.63	1116.89	1112.59
100000	1395.11	1360.49	1331.75	1307.70	1287.48	1270.39	1255.88	1243.53	1203.77	1184.88	1175.68	1171.15

14%

Table 1

14.25%

MONTHLY

PAYMENT REQUIRED TO AMORTIZE A LOAN

TERM	1 YEAR	2 YEARS	3 YEARS	4 YEARS	5 YEARS	6 YEARS	7 YEARS	8 YEARS	9 YEARS	10 YEARS	11 YEARS	12 YEARS
AMOUNT												
50	4.50	2.41	1.72	1.38	1.17	1.04	.95	.88	.83	.79	.76	.73
100	9.00	4.82	3.43	2.75	2.34	2.08	1.89	1.76	1.65	1.57	1.51	1.46
200	17.99	9.63	6.86	5.50	4.68	4.15	3.78	3.51	3.30	3.14	3.01	2.91
300	26.98	14.44	10.29	8.24	7.02	6.23	5.67	5.26	4.95	4.71	4.52	4.36
400	35.97	19.26	13.72	10.99	9.36	8.30	7.56	7.01	6.60	6.28	6.02	5.82
500	44.96	24.07	17.15	13.73	11.70	10.37	9.44	8.76	8.25	7.84	7.53	7.27
600	53.95	28.88	20.58	16.48	14.04	12.45	11.33	10.51	9.89	9.41	9.03	8.72
700	62.94	33.70	24.01	19.22	16.38	14.52	13.22	12.26	11.54	10.98	10.53	10.18
800	71.93	38.51	27.44	21.97	18.72	16.60	15.11	14.02	13.19	12.55	12.04	11.63
900	80.92	43.32	30.87	24.71	21.06	18.67	17.00	15.77	14.84	14.11	13.54	13.08
1000	89.91	48.14	34.30	27.46	23.40	20.74	18.88	17.52	16.49	15.68	15.05	14.53
2000	179.81	96.27	68.60	54.91	46.80	41.48	37.76	35.03	32.97	31.36	30.09	29.06
3000	269.72	144.40	102.90	82.36	70.20	62.22	56.64	52.55	49.45	47.04	45.13	43.59
4000	359.62	192.53	137.20	109.81	93.60	82.96	75.52	70.06	65.93	62.71	60.17	58.12
5000	449.53	240.66	171.50	137.27	117.00	103.70	94.40	87.58	82.41	78.39	75.21	72.65
6000	539.43	288.79	205.80	164.72	140.39	124.44	113.28	105.09	98.89	94.07	90.25	87.18
7000	629.34	336.92	240.10	192.17	163.79	145.18	132.15	122.60	115.37	109.75	105.29	101.71
8000	719.24	385.05	274.40	219.62	187.19	165.92	151.03	140.12	131.85	125.42	120.33	116.24
9000	809.15	433.18	308.70	247.07	210.59	186.66	169.91	157.63	148.33	141.10	135.38	130.77
10000	899.05	481.32	343.00	274.53	233.99	207.40	188.79	175.15	164.81	156.78	150.42	145.30
11000	988.96	529.45	377.30	301.98	257.38	228.14	207.67	192.66	181.29	172.46	165.46	159.83
12000	1078.86	577.58	411.60	329.43	280.78	248.88	226.55	210.17	197.77	188.13	180.50	174.36
13000	1168.77	625.71	445.89	356.88	304.18	269.62	245.42	227.69	214.25	203.81	195.54	188.89
14000	1258.67	673.84	480.19	384.33	327.58	290.36	264.30	245.20	230.73	219.49	210.58	203.42
15000	1348.58	721.97	514.49	411.79	350.98	311.10	283.18	262.72	247.21	235.16	225.62	217.95
16000	1438.48	770.10	548.79	439.24	374.37	331.84	302.06	280.23	263.69	250.84	240.66	232.48
17000	1528.39	818.23	583.09	466.69	397.77	352.58	320.94	297.74	280.17	266.52	255.71	247.01
18000	1618.29	866.36	617.39	494.14	421.17	373.32	339.82	315.26	296.65	282.20	270.75	261.54
19000	1708.20	914.50	651.69	521.59	444.57	394.06	358.69	332.77	313.13	297.87	285.79	276.07
20000	1798.10	962.63	685.99	549.05	467.97	414.80	377.57	350.29	329.61	313.55	300.83	290.59
21000	1888.01	1010.76	720.29	576.50	491.36	435.54	396.45	367.80	346.09	329.23	315.87	305.12
22000	1977.91	1058.89	754.59	603.95	514.76	456.28	415.33	385.31	362.57	344.91	330.91	319.65
23000	2067.82	1107.02	788.89	631.40	538.16	477.02	434.21	402.83	379.05	360.58	345.95	334.18
24000	2157.72	1155.15	823.19	658.85	561.56	497.76	453.09	420.34	395.53	376.26	360.99	348.71
25000	2247.62	1203.28	857.48	686.31	584.96	518.50	471.96	437.86	412.01	391.94	376.03	363.24
26000	2337.53	1251.41	891.78	713.76	608.35	539.24	490.84	455.37	428.49	407.62	391.08	377.77
27000	2427.43	1299.54	926.08	741.21	631.75	559.98	509.72	472.89	444.98	423.29	406.12	392.30
28000	2517.34	1347.68	960.38	768.66	655.15	580.72	528.60	490.40	461.46	438.97	421.16	406.83
29000	2607.24	1395.81	994.68	796.11	678.55	601.46	547.48	507.91	477.94	454.65	436.20	421.36
30000	2697.15	1443.94	1028.98	823.57	701.95	622.20	566.36	525.43	494.42	470.32	451.24	435.89
31000	2787.05	1492.07	1063.28	851.02	725.34	642.94	585.24	542.94	510.90	486.00	466.28	450.42
32000	2876.96	1540.20	1097.58	878.47	748.74	663.68	604.11	560.46	527.38	501.68	481.32	464.95
33000	2966.86	1588.33	1131.88	905.92	772.14	684.42	622.99	577.97	543.86	517.36	496.36	479.48
34000	3056.77	1636.46	1166.18	933.37	795.54	705.16	641.87	595.48	560.34	533.03	511.41	494.01
35000	3146.67	1684.59	1200.48	960.83	818.94	725.90	660.75	613.00	576.82	548.71	526.45	508.54
36000	3236.58	1732.72	1234.78	988.28	842.34	746.64	679.63	630.51	593.30	564.39	541.49	523.07
37000	3326.48	1780.85	1269.07	1015.73	865.73	767.38	698.51	648.03	609.78	580.07	556.53	537.60
38000	3416.39	1828.99	1303.37	1043.18	889.13	788.12	717.38	665.54	626.26	595.74	571.57	552.13
39000	3506.29	1877.12	1337.67	1070.63	912.53	808.86	736.26	683.05	642.74	611.42	586.61	566.66
40000	3596.20	1925.25	1371.97	1098.09	935.93	829.60	755.14	700.57	659.22	627.10	601.65	581.18
41000	3686.10	1973.38	1406.27	1125.54	959.33	850.34	774.02	718.08	675.70	642.77	616.69	595.71
42000	3776.01	2021.51	1440.57	1152.99	982.72	871.08	792.90	735.60	692.18	658.45	631.73	610.24
43000	3865.91	2069.64	1474.87	1180.44	1006.12	891.82	811.78	753.11	708.66	674.13	646.78	624.77
44000	3955.82	2117.77	1509.17	1207.90	1029.52	912.56	830.65	770.62	725.14	689.81	661.82	639.30
45000	4045.72	2165.90	1543.47	1235.35	1052.92	933.30	849.53	788.14	741.62	705.48	676.86	653.83
46000	4135.63	2214.03	1577.77	1262.80	1076.32	954.04	868.41	805.65	758.10	721.16	691.90	668.36
47000	4225.53	2262.17	1612.07	1290.25	1099.71	974.78	887.29	823.17	774.58	736.84	706.94	682.89
48000	4315.43	2310.30	1646.37	1317.70	1123.11	995.52	906.17	840.68	791.06	752.52	721.98	697.42
49000	4405.34	2358.43	1680.66	1345.16	1146.51	1016.26	925.05	858.19	807.54	768.19	737.02	711.95
50000	4495.24	2406.56	1714.96	1372.61	1169.91	1037.00	943.92	875.71	824.02	783.87	752.06	726.48
55000	4944.77	2647.21	1886.46	1509.87	1286.90	1140.70	1038.32	963.28	906.43	862.26	827.27	799.13
60000	5394.29	2887.87	2057.96	1647.14	1403.89	1244.40	1132.71	1050.85	988.83	940.64	902.48	871.77
65000	5843.82	3128.52	2229.45	1784.39	1520.88	1348.09	1227.10	1138.42	1071.23	1019.03	977.68	944.42
70000	6293.34	3369.18	2400.95	1921.65	1637.87	1451.79	1321.49	1225.99	1153.63	1097.42	1052.89	1017.07
75000	6742.86	3609.84	2572.44	2058.91	1754.86	1555.49	1415.88	1313.56	1236.03	1175.80	1128.09	1089.72
80000	7192.39	3850.49	2743.94	2196.17	1871.85	1659.19	1510.28	1401.13	1318.44	1254.19	1203.30	1162.36
85000	7641.91	4091.15	2915.44	2333.43	1988.84	1762.89	1604.67	1488.70	1400.84	1332.58	1278.51	1235.01
90000	8091.44	4331.80	3086.93	2470.69	2105.83	1866.59	1699.06	1576.27	1483.24	1410.96	1353.71	1307.66
95000	8540.96	4572.46	3258.43	2607.95	2222.82	1970.29	1793.45	1663.84	1565.64	1489.35	1428.92	1380.31
100000	8990.48	4813.11	3429.92	2745.21	2339.81	2073.99	1887.84	1751.41	1648.04	1567.74	1504.12	1452.95

14%

Table 1

MONTHLY

PAYMENT REQUIRED TO AMORTIZE A LOAN

14.25%

TERM	13 YEARS	14 YEARS	15 YEARS	16 YEARS	17 YEARS	18 YEARS	19 YEARS	20 YEARS	25 YEARS	30 YEARS	35 YEARS	40 YEARS
OUNT												
50	.71	.69	.68	.67	.66	.65	.64	.64	.62	.61	.60	.60
100	1.42	1.38	1.35	1.33	1.31	1.29	1.28	1.27	1.23	1.21	1.20	1.20
200	2.83	2.76	2.70	2.65	2.61	2.58	2.55	2.53	2.45	2.41	2.40	2.39
300	4.24	4.14	4.05	3.98	3.92	3.87	3.83	3.79	3.67	3.62	3.59	3.58
400	5.65	5.51	5.40	5.30	5.22	5.16	5.10	5.05	4.90	4.82	4.79	4.77
500	7.06	6.89	6.75	6.63	6.53	6.45	6.37	6.31	6.12	6.03	5.98	5.96
600	8.47	8.27	8.10	7.95	7.83	7.73	7.65	7.58	7.34	7.23	7.18	7.15
700	9.88	9.64	9.45	9.28	9.14	9.02	8.92	8.84	8.57	8.44	8.38	8.35
800	11.30	11.02	10.79	10.60	10.44	10.31	10.20	10.10	9.79	9.64	9.57	9.54
900	12.71	12.40	12.14	11.93	11.75	11.60	11.47	11.36	11.01	10.85	10.77	10.73
1000	14.12	13.78	13.49	13.25	13.05	12.89	12.74	12.62	12.23	12.05	11.96	11.92
2000	28.23	27.55	26.98	26.50	26.10	25.77	25.48	25.24	24.46	24.10	23.92	23.84
3000	42.34	41.32	40.46	39.75	39.15	38.65	38.22	37.86	36.69	36.15	35.88	35.75
4000	56.46	55.09	53.95	53.00	52.20	51.53	50.96	50.47	48.92	48.19	47.84	47.67
5000	70.57	68.86	67.43	66.25	65.25	64.41	63.70	63.09	61.15	60.24	59.80	59.59
6000	84.68	82.63	80.92	79.50	78.30	77.29	76.44	75.71	73.38	72.29	71.76	71.50
7000	98.79	96.40	94.41	92.74	91.35	90.17	89.17	88.33	85.61	84.33	83.72	83.42
8000	112.91	110.17	107.89	105.99	104.40	103.05	101.91	100.94	97.84	96.38	95.68	95.33
9000	127.02	123.94	121.38	119.24	117.45	115.93	114.65	113.56	110.07	108.43	107.64	107.25
10000	141.13	137.71	134.86	132.49	130.50	128.81	127.39	126.18	122.30	120.47	119.60	119.17
11000	155.25	151.48	148.35	145.74	143.54	141.69	140.13	138.79	134.53	132.52	131.55	131.08
12000	169.36	165.25	161.83	158.99	156.59	154.58	152.87	151.41	146.76	144.57	143.51	143.00
13000	183.47	179.02	175.32	172.23	169.64	167.46	165.60	164.03	158.99	156.61	155.47	154.92
14000	197.58	192.79	188.81	185.48	182.69	180.34	178.34	176.65	171.21	168.66	167.43	166.83
15000	211.70	206.56	202.29	198.73	195.74	193.22	191.08	189.26	183.44	180.71	179.39	178.75
16000	225.81	220.33	215.78	211.98	208.79	206.10	203.82	201.88	195.67	192.75	191.35	190.66
17000	239.92	234.10	229.26	225.23	221.84	218.98	216.56	214.50	207.90	204.80	203.31	202.58
18000	254.04	247.87	242.75	238.48	234.89	231.86	229.30	227.11	220.13	216.85	215.27	214.50
19000	268.15	261.64	256.24	251.73	247.94	244.74	242.03	239.73	232.36	228.90	227.23	226.41
20000	282.26	275.41	269.72	264.97	260.99	257.62	254.77	252.35	244.59	240.94	239.19	238.33
21000	296.37	289.18	283.21	278.22	274.04	270.50	267.51	264.97	256.82	252.99	251.14	250.25
22000	310.49	302.95	296.69	291.47	287.08	283.38	280.25	277.58	269.05	265.04	263.10	262.16
23000	324.60	316.72	310.18	304.72	300.13	296.27	292.99	290.20	281.28	277.08	275.06	274.08
24000	338.71	330.49	323.66	317.97	313.18	309.15	305.73	302.82	293.51	289.13	287.02	286.00
25000	352.83	344.26	337.15	331.22	326.23	322.03	318.46	315.43	305.74	301.18	298.98	297.91
26000	366.94	358.03	350.64	344.46	339.28	334.91	331.20	328.05	317.97	313.22	310.94	309.83
27000	381.05	371.80	364.12	357.71	352.33	347.79	343.94	340.67	330.20	325.27	322.90	321.74
28000	395.16	385.57	377.61	370.96	365.38	360.67	356.68	353.29	342.42	337.32	334.86	333.66
29000	409.28	399.34	391.09	384.21	378.43	373.55	369.42	365.90	354.65	349.36	346.82	345.58
30000	423.39	413.11	404.58	397.46	391.48	386.43	382.16	378.52	366.88	361.41	358.78	357.49
31000	437.50	426.88	418.06	410.71	404.53	399.31	394.89	391.14	379.11	373.46	370.73	369.41
32000	451.61	440.65	431.55	423.95	417.58	412.19	407.63	403.76	391.34	385.50	382.69	381.32
33000	465.73	454.42	445.04	437.20	430.62	425.07	420.37	416.37	403.57	397.55	394.65	393.24
34000	479.84	468.19	458.52	450.45	443.67	437.95	433.11	428.99	415.80	409.60	406.61	405.16
35000	493.95	481.96	472.01	463.70	456.72	450.84	445.85	441.61	428.03	421.65	418.57	417.07
36000	508.07	495.73	485.49	476.95	469.77	463.72	458.59	454.22	440.26	433.69	430.53	428.99
37000	522.18	509.50	498.98	490.20	482.82	476.60	471.32	466.84	452.49	445.74	442.49	440.91
38000	536.29	523.27	512.47	503.45	495.87	489.48	484.06	479.46	464.72	457.79	454.45	452.82
39000	550.40	537.04	525.95	516.69	508.92	502.36	496.80	492.08	476.95	469.83	466.41	464.74
40000	564.52	550.81	539.44	529.94	521.97	515.24	509.54	504.69	489.18	481.88	478.37	476.65
41000	578.63	564.58	552.92	543.19	535.02	528.12	522.28	517.31	501.41	493.93	490.33	488.57
42000	592.74	578.35	566.41	556.44	548.07	541.00	535.02	529.93	513.63	505.97	502.28	500.49
43000	606.86	592.12	579.89	569.69	561.12	553.88	547.75	542.54	525.86	518.02	514.24	512.40
44000	620.97	605.89	593.38	582.94	574.16	566.76	560.49	555.16	538.09	530.07	526.20	524.32
45000	635.08	619.66	606.87	596.18	587.21	579.64	573.23	567.78	550.32	542.11	538.16	536.24
46000	649.19	633.43	620.35	609.43	600.26	592.53	585.97	580.40	562.55	554.16	550.12	548.15
47000	663.31	647.20	633.84	622.68	613.31	605.41	598.71	593.01	574.78	566.21	562.08	560.07
48000	677.42	660.97	647.32	635.93	626.36	618.29	611.45	605.63	587.01	578.25	574.04	571.98
49000	691.53	674.74	660.81	649.18	639.41	631.17	624.18	618.25	599.23	590.30	586.00	583.90
50000	705.65	688.51	674.29	662.43	652.46	644.05	636.92	630.86	611.47	602.35	597.96	595.82
55000	776.21	757.36	741.72	728.67	717.70	708.45	700.61	693.95	672.62	662.58	657.75	655.40
60000	846.77	826.21	809.15	794.91	782.95	772.86	764.31	757.04	733.76	722.82	717.55	714.98
65000	917.34	895.06	876.58	861.15	848.20	837.26	828.00	820.12	794.91	783.05	777.34	774.56
70000	987.90	963.91	944.01	927.40	913.44	901.67	891.69	883.21	856.05	843.29	837.14	834.14
75000	1058.47	1032.76	1011.44	993.64	978.69	966.07	955.38	946.29	917.20	903.52	896.93	893.72
80000	1129.03	1101.61	1078.87	1059.88	1043.93	1030.47	1019.07	1009.38	978.35	963.75	956.73	953.30
85000	1199.59	1170.46	1146.30	1126.12	1109.18	1094.88	1082.76	1072.47	1039.49	1023.99	1016.52	1012.88
90000	1270.16	1239.31	1213.73	1192.36	1174.42	1159.28	1146.46	1135.55	1100.64	1084.22	1076.32	1072.47
95000	1340.72	1308.16	1281.16	1258.61	1239.67	1223.69	1210.15	1198.64	1161.79	1144.46	1136.11	1132.05
100000	1411.29	1377.01	1348.58	1324.85	1304.91	1288.09	1273.84	1261.72	1222.93	1204.69	1195.91	1191.63

14%

Table 1

14.50%

MONTHLY
PAYMENT REQUIRED TO AMORTIZE A LOAN

TERM / AMOUNT	1 YEAR	2 YEARS	3 YEARS	4 YEARS	5 YEARS	6 YEARS	7 YEARS	8 YEARS	9 YEARS	10 YEARS	11 YEARS	12 YEARS
50	4.51	2.42	1.73	1.38	1.18	1.05	.96	.89	.84	.80	.76	.74
100	9.01	4.83	3.45	2.76	2.36	2.09	1.91	1.77	1.67	1.59	1.52	1.47
200	18.01	9.65	6.89	5.52	4.71	4.18	3.81	3.54	3.33	3.17	3.04	2.94
300	27.01	14.48	10.33	8.28	7.06	6.27	5.71	5.30	4.99	4.75	4.56	4.41
400	36.01	19.30	13.77	11.04	9.42	8.35	7.61	7.07	6.66	6.34	6.08	5.88
500	45.02	24.13	17.22	13.79	11.77	10.44	9.51	8.83	8.32	7.92	7.60	7.35
600	54.02	28.95	20.66	16.55	14.12	12.53	11.42	10.60	9.98	9.50	9.12	8.82
700	63.02	33.78	24.10	19.31	16.47	14.62	13.32	12.37	11.64	11.09	10.64	10.29
800	72.02	38.60	27.54	22.07	18.83	16.70	15.22	14.13	13.31	12.67	12.16	11.76
900	81.03	43.43	30.98	24.83	21.18	18.79	17.12	15.90	14.97	14.25	13.68	13.22
1000	90.03	48.25	34.43	27.58	23.53	20.88	19.02	17.66	16.63	15.83	15.20	14.69
2000	180.05	96.50	68.85	55.16	47.06	41.75	38.04	35.32	33.26	31.66	30.40	29.38
3000	270.07	144.75	103.27	82.74	70.59	62.63	57.06	52.98	49.89	47.49	45.59	44.07
4000	360.10	193.00	137.69	110.32	94.12	83.50	76.07	70.63	66.52	63.32	60.79	58.76
5000	450.12	241.25	172.11	137.89	117.65	104.38	95.09	88.29	83.14	79.15	75.99	73.45
6000	540.14	289.50	206.53	165.47	141.17	125.25	114.11	105.95	99.77	94.98	91.18	88.14
7000	630.16	337.75	240.95	193.05	164.70	146.13	133.13	123.61	116.40	110.81	106.38	102.82
8000	720.19	386.00	275.37	220.63	188.23	167.00	152.14	141.26	133.03	126.63	121.58	117.51
9000	810.21	434.25	309.79	248.21	211.76	187.87	171.16	158.92	149.65	142.46	136.77	132.20
10000	900.23	482.50	344.21	275.78	235.29	208.75	190.18	176.58	166.28	158.29	151.97	146.89
11000	990.25	530.75	378.64	303.36	258.82	229.62	209.20	194.23	182.91	174.12	167.17	161.58
12000	1080.28	579.00	413.06	330.94	282.34	250.50	228.21	211.89	199.54	189.95	182.36	176.27
13000	1170.30	627.25	447.48	358.52	305.87	271.37	247.23	229.55	216.17	205.78	197.56	190.96
14000	1260.32	675.50	481.90	386.10	329.40	292.25	266.25	247.21	232.79	221.61	212.76	205.64
15000	1350.34	723.75	516.32	413.67	352.93	313.12	285.26	264.86	249.42	237.44	227.95	220.33
16000	1440.37	772.00	550.74	441.25	376.46	334.00	304.28	282.52	266.05	253.26	243.15	235.02
17000	1530.39	820.25	585.16	468.83	399.99	354.87	323.30	300.18	282.68	269.09	258.34	249.71
18000	1620.41	868.49	619.58	496.41	423.51	375.74	342.32	317.84	299.30	284.92	273.54	264.40
19000	1710.43	916.74	654.00	523.99	447.04	396.62	361.33	335.49	315.93	300.75	288.74	279.09
20000	1800.46	964.99	688.42	551.56	470.57	417.49	380.35	353.15	332.56	316.58	303.93	293.77
21000	1890.48	1013.24	722.85	579.14	494.10	438.37	399.37	370.81	349.19	332.41	319.13	308.46
22000	1980.50	1061.49	757.27	606.72	517.63	459.24	418.39	388.46	365.81	348.24	334.33	323.15
23000	2070.52	1109.74	791.69	634.30	541.16	480.12	437.40	406.12	382.44	364.06	349.52	337.84
24000	2160.55	1157.99	826.11	661.88	564.68	500.99	456.42	423.78	399.07	379.89	364.72	352.53
25000	2250.57	1206.24	860.53	689.45	588.21	521.87	475.44	441.44	415.70	395.72	379.92	367.22
26000	2340.59	1254.49	894.95	717.03	611.74	542.74	494.45	459.09	432.33	411.55	395.11	381.91
27000	2430.61	1302.74	929.37	744.61	635.27	563.61	513.47	476.75	448.95	427.38	410.31	396.59
28000	2520.64	1350.99	963.79	772.19	658.80	584.49	532.49	494.41	465.58	443.21	425.51	411.28
29000	2610.66	1399.24	998.21	799.77	682.33	605.36	551.51	512.07	482.21	459.04	440.70	425.97
30000	2700.68	1447.49	1032.63	827.34	705.85	626.24	570.52	529.72	498.84	474.87	455.90	440.66
31000	2790.70	1495.74	1067.06	854.92	729.38	647.11	589.54	547.38	515.46	490.69	471.09	455.35
32000	2880.73	1543.99	1101.48	882.50	752.91	667.99	608.56	565.04	532.09	506.52	486.29	470.04
33000	2970.75	1592.24	1135.90	910.08	776.44	688.86	627.58	582.69	548.72	522.35	501.49	484.73
34000	3060.77	1640.49	1170.32	937.66	799.97	709.74	646.59	600.35	565.35	538.18	516.68	499.41
35000	3150.79	1688.74	1204.74	965.23	823.49	730.61	665.61	618.01	581.98	554.01	531.88	514.10
36000	3240.82	1736.98	1239.16	992.81	847.02	751.48	684.63	635.67	598.60	569.84	547.08	528.79
37000	3330.84	1785.23	1273.58	1020.39	870.55	772.36	703.65	653.32	615.23	585.67	562.27	543.48
38000	3420.86	1833.48	1308.00	1047.99	894.08	793.23	722.66	670.98	631.86	601.49	577.47	558.17
39000	3510.88	1881.73	1342.42	1075.55	917.61	814.11	741.68	688.64	648.49	617.32	592.67	572.86
40000	3600.91	1929.98	1376.84	1103.12	941.14	834.98	760.70	706.30	665.11	633.15	607.86	587.54
41000	3690.93	1978.23	1411.27	1130.70	964.66	855.86	779.71	723.95	681.74	648.98	623.06	602.23
42000	3780.95	2026.48	1445.69	1158.28	988.19	876.73	798.73	741.61	698.37	664.81	638.26	616.92
43000	3870.97	2074.73	1480.11	1185.86	1011.72	897.61	817.75	759.27	715.00	680.64	653.45	631.61
44000	3961.00	2122.98	1514.53	1213.43	1035.25	918.48	836.77	776.92	731.62	696.47	668.65	646.30
45000	4051.02	2171.23	1548.95	1241.01	1058.78	939.35	855.78	794.58	748.25	712.30	683.84	660.99
46000	4141.04	2219.48	1583.37	1268.59	1082.31	960.23	874.80	812.24	764.88	728.12	699.04	675.68
47000	4231.06	2267.73	1617.79	1296.17	1105.83	981.10	893.82	829.90	781.51	743.95	714.24	690.36
48000	4321.09	2315.98	1652.21	1323.75	1129.36	1001.98	912.84	847.55	798.14	759.78	729.43	705.05
49000	4411.11	2364.23	1686.63	1351.32	1152.89	1022.85	931.85	865.21	814.76	775.61	744.63	719.74
50000	4501.13	2412.48	1721.05	1378.90	1176.42	1043.73	950.87	882.87	831.39	791.44	759.83	734.43
55000	4951.25	2653.72	1893.16	1516.79	1294.06	1148.10	1045.96	971.15	914.53	870.58	835.81	807.87
60000	5401.36	2894.97	2065.26	1654.68	1411.70	1252.47	1141.04	1059.44	997.67	949.73	911.79	881.31
65000	5851.47	3136.22	2237.37	1792.57	1529.34	1356.84	1236.13	1147.73	1080.81	1028.87	987.77	954.76
70000	6301.58	3377.46	2409.47	1930.46	1646.98	1461.21	1331.22	1236.01	1163.95	1108.01	1063.76	1028.20
75000	6751.70	3618.71	2581.58	2068.35	1764.63	1565.59	1426.30	1324.30	1247.08	1187.16	1139.74	1101.64
80000	7201.81	3859.96	2753.68	2206.24	1882.27	1669.96	1521.39	1412.59	1330.22	1266.30	1215.72	1175.08
85000	7651.92	4101.21	2925.79	2344.13	1999.91	1774.33	1616.48	1500.87	1413.36	1345.44	1291.70	1248.53
90000	8102.03	4342.45	3097.89	2482.02	2117.55	1878.70	1711.56	1589.16	1496.50	1424.59	1367.68	1321.97
95000	8552.15	4583.70	3270.00	2619.91	2235.19	1983.08	1806.65	1677.44	1579.64	1503.73	1443.67	1395.41
100000	9002.26	4824.95	3442.10	2757.80	2352.83	2087.45	1901.74	1765.73	1662.78	1582.87	1519.65	1468.85

14%

78

Table 1

MONTHLY   14.50%

PAYMENT REQUIRED TO AMORTIZE A LOAN

TERM AMOUNT	13 YEARS	14 YEARS	15 YEARS	16 YEARS	17 YEARS	18 YEARS	19 YEARS	20 YEARS	25 YEARS	30 YEARS	35 YEARS	40 YEARS
50	.72	.70	.69	.68	.67	.66	.65	.64	.63	.62	.61	.61
100	1.43	1.40	1.37	1.35	1.33	1.31	1.30	1.28	1.25	1.23	1.22	1.22
200	2.86	2.79	2.74	2.69	2.65	2.62	2.59	2.56	2.49	2.45	2.44	2.43
300	4.29	4.19	4.10	4.03	3.97	3.92	3.88	3.84	3.73	3.68	3.65	3.64
400	5.72	5.58	5.47	5.37	5.29	5.23	5.17	5.12	4.97	4.90	4.87	4.85
500	7.14	6.97	6.83	6.72	6.62	6.53	6.46	6.40	6.22	6.13	6.09	6.07
600	8.57	8.37	8.20	8.06	7.94	7.84	7.76	7.68	7.46	7.35	7.30	7.28
700	10.00	9.76	9.56	9.40	9.26	9.15	9.05	8.96	8.70	8.58	8.52	8.49
800	11.43	11.15	10.93	10.74	10.58	10.45	10.34	10.24	9.94	9.80	9.73	9.70
900	12.85	12.55	12.29	12.08	11.91	11.76	11.63	11.52	11.18	11.03	10.95	10.91
1000	14.28	13.94	13.66	13.43	13.23	13.06	12.92	12.80	12.43	12.25	12.17	12.13
2000	28.56	27.88	27.32	26.85	26.45	26.12	25.84	25.60	24.85	24.50	24.33	24.25
3000	42.83	41.81	40.97	40.27	39.68	39.18	38.76	38.40	37.27	36.74	36.49	36.37
4000	57.11	55.75	54.63	53.69	52.90	52.24	51.68	51.20	49.69	48.99	48.65	48.49
5000	71.38	69.69	68.28	67.11	66.13	65.30	64.60	64.00	62.11	61.23	60.81	60.61
6000	85.66	83.62	81.94	80.53	79.35	78.36	77.52	76.80	74.53	73.48	72.98	72.73
7000	99.93	97.56	95.59	93.95	92.57	91.42	90.44	89.60	86.96	85.72	85.14	84.85
8000	114.21	111.49	109.25	107.37	105.80	104.47	103.36	102.40	99.38	97.97	97.30	96.98
9000	128.48	125.43	122.90	120.79	119.02	117.53	116.27	115.20	111.80	110.22	109.46	109.10
10000	142.76	139.37	136.56	134.21	132.25	130.59	129.19	128.00	124.22	122.46	121.62	121.22
11000	157.03	153.30	150.21	147.63	145.47	143.65	142.11	140.80	136.64	134.71	133.78	133.34
12000	171.31	167.24	163.87	161.05	158.70	156.71	155.03	153.60	149.06	146.95	145.95	145.46
13000	185.58	181.17	177.52	174.47	171.92	169.77	167.95	166.40	161.49	159.20	158.11	157.58
14000	199.86	195.11	191.18	187.89	185.14	182.83	180.87	179.20	173.91	171.44	170.27	169.70
15000	214.14	209.05	204.83	201.32	198.37	195.89	193.79	192.00	186.33	183.69	182.43	181.82
16000	228.41	222.98	218.49	214.74	211.59	208.94	206.71	204.80	198.75	195.93	194.59	193.95
17000	242.69	236.92	232.14	228.16	224.82	222.00	219.62	217.60	211.17	208.18	206.75	206.07
18000	256.96	250.85	245.80	241.58	238.04	235.06	232.54	230.40	223.59	220.43	218.92	218.19
19000	271.24	264.79	259.45	255.00	251.27	248.12	245.46	243.20	236.02	232.67	231.08	230.31
20000	285.51	278.73	273.11	268.42	264.49	261.18	258.38	256.00	248.44	244.92	243.24	242.43
21000	299.79	292.66	286.76	281.84	277.71	274.24	271.30	268.80	260.86	257.16	255.40	254.55
22000	314.06	306.60	300.42	295.26	290.94	287.30	284.22	281.60	273.28	269.41	267.56	266.67
23000	328.34	320.53	314.07	308.68	304.16	300.36	297.14	294.40	285.70	281.65	279.72	278.80
24000	342.61	334.47	327.73	322.10	317.39	313.41	310.00	307.20	298.12	293.90	291.89	290.92
25000	356.89	348.41	341.38	335.52	330.61	326.47	322.97	320.00	310.55	306.14	304.05	303.04
26000	371.16	362.34	355.04	348.94	343.84	339.53	335.89	332.80	322.97	318.39	316.21	315.16
27000	385.44	376.28	368.69	362.36	357.06	352.59	348.81	345.60	335.39	330.64	328.37	327.28
28000	399.72	390.21	382.35	375.78	370.28	365.65	361.73	358.40	347.81	342.88	340.53	339.40
29000	413.99	404.15	396.00	389.21	383.51	378.71	374.65	371.20	360.23	355.13	352.69	351.52
30000	428.27	418.09	409.66	402.63	396.73	391.77	387.57	384.00	372.65	367.37	364.86	363.64
31000	442.54	432.02	423.31	416.05	409.96	404.83	400.49	396.80	385.08	379.62	377.02	375.77
32000	456.82	445.96	436.97	429.47	423.18	417.88	413.41	409.60	397.50	391.86	389.18	387.89
33000	471.09	459.89	450.62	442.89	436.41	430.94	426.32	422.40	409.92	404.11	401.34	400.01
34000	485.37	473.83	464.28	456.31	449.63	444.00	439.24	435.20	422.34	416.35	413.50	412.13
35000	499.64	487.77	477.93	469.73	462.85	457.06	452.16	448.00	434.76	428.60	425.66	424.25
36000	513.92	501.70	491.59	483.15	476.08	470.12	465.08	460.80	447.18	440.85	437.83	436.37
37000	528.19	515.64	505.24	496.57	489.30	483.18	478.00	473.60	459.61	453.09	449.99	448.49
38000	542.47	529.57	518.90	509.99	502.53	496.24	490.92	486.40	472.03	465.34	462.15	460.62
39000	556.74	543.51	532.55	523.41	515.75	509.30	503.84	499.20	484.45	477.58	474.31	472.74
40000	571.02	557.45	546.21	536.83	528.97	522.35	516.76	512.00	496.87	489.83	486.47	484.86
41000	585.30	571.38	559.86	550.25	542.20	535.41	529.67	524.80	509.29	502.07	498.63	496.98
42000	599.57	585.32	573.52	563.67	555.42	548.47	542.59	537.60	521.71	514.32	510.80	509.10
43000	613.85	599.25	587.17	577.10	568.65	561.53	555.51	550.40	534.14	526.56	522.96	521.22
44000	628.12	613.19	600.83	590.52	581.87	574.59	568.43	563.20	546.56	538.81	535.12	533.34
45000	642.40	627.13	614.48	603.94	595.10	587.65	581.35	576.00	558.98	551.06	547.28	545.46
46000	656.67	641.06	628.14	617.36	608.32	600.71	594.27	588.80	571.40	563.30	559.44	557.59
47000	670.95	655.00	641.79	630.78	621.54	613.77	607.19	601.60	583.82	575.55	571.61	569.71
48000	685.22	668.93	655.45	644.20	634.77	626.82	620.11	614.40	596.24	587.79	583.77	581.83
49000	699.50	682.87	669.10	657.62	647.99	639.88	633.02	627.20	608.66	600.04	595.93	593.95
50000	713.77	696.81	682.76	671.04	661.22	652.94	645.94	640.00	621.09	612.28	608.09	606.07
55000	785.15	766.49	751.03	738.14	727.34	718.24	710.54	704.00	683.19	673.51	668.90	666.68
60000	856.53	836.17	819.31	805.25	793.46	783.53	775.13	768.00	745.30	734.74	729.71	727.28
65000	927.90	905.85	887.58	872.35	859.58	848.82	839.72	832.00	807.41	795.97	790.52	787.89
70000	999.28	975.53	955.86	939.45	925.70	914.12	904.32	896.00	869.52	857.19	851.32	848.50
75000	1070.66	1045.21	1024.13	1006.56	991.82	979.41	968.91	960.00	931.63	918.42	912.13	909.10
80000	1142.04	1114.89	1092.41	1073.66	1057.94	1044.70	1033.51	1024.00	993.74	979.65	972.94	969.71
85000	1213.41	1184.57	1160.68	1140.76	1124.07	1110.00	1098.10	1088.00	1055.84	1040.88	1033.75	1030.32
90000	1284.79	1254.25	1228.96	1207.87	1190.19	1175.29	1162.69	1152.00	1117.95	1102.11	1094.56	1090.92
95000	1356.17	1323.93	1297.23	1274.97	1256.31	1240.59	1227.29	1216.00	1180.06	1163.33	1155.37	1151.53
100000	1427.54	1393.61	1365.51	1342.08	1322.43	1305.88	1291.88	1280.00	1242.17	1224.56	1216.18	1212.14

14%

Table 1

14.75%

MONTHLY

PAYMENT REQUIRED TO AMORTIZE A LOAN

14%

TERM AMOUNT	1 YEAR	2 YEARS	3 YEARS	4 YEARS	5 YEARS	6 YEARS	7 YEARS	8 YEARS	9 YEARS	10 YEARS	11 YEARS	12 YEARS
50	4.51	2.42	1.73	1.39	1.19	1.06	.96	.90	.84	.80	.77	.75
100	9.02	4.84	3.46	2.78	2.37	2.11	1.92	1.79	1.68	1.60	1.54	1.49
200	18.03	9.68	6.91	5.55	4.74	4.21	3.84	3.57	3.36	3.20	3.08	2.97
300	27.05	14.52	10.37	8.32	7.10	6.31	5.75	5.35	5.04	4.80	4.61	4.46
400	36.06	19.35	13.82	11.09	9.47	8.41	7.67	7.13	6.72	6.40	6.15	5.94
500	45.08	24.19	17.28	13.86	11.83	10.51	9.58	8.91	8.39	8.00	7.68	7.43
600	54.09	29.03	20.73	16.63	14.20	12.61	11.50	10.69	10.07	9.59	9.22	8.91
700	63.10	33.86	24.19	19.40	16.57	14.71	13.41	12.47	11.75	11.19	10.75	10.40
800	72.12	38.70	27.64	22.17	18.93	16.81	15.33	14.25	13.43	12.79	12.29	11.88
900	81.13	43.54	31.09	24.94	21.30	18.91	17.25	16.03	15.10	14.39	13.82	13.37
1000	90.15	48.37	34.55	27.71	23.66	21.01	19.16	17.81	16.78	15.99	15.36	14.85
2000	180.29	96.74	69.09	55.41	47.32	42.02	38.32	35.61	33.56	31.97	30.71	29.70
3000	270.43	145.11	103.63	83.12	70.98	63.03	57.48	53.41	50.33	47.95	46.06	44.55
4000	360.57	193.48	138.18	110.82	94.64	84.04	76.63	71.21	67.11	63.93	61.41	59.40
5000	450.71	241.84	172.72	138.53	118.30	105.05	95.79	89.01	83.88	79.91	76.77	74.25
6000	540.85	290.21	207.26	166.23	141.96	126.06	114.95	106.81	100.66	95.89	92.12	89.09
7000	630.99	338.58	241.81	193.93	165.62	147.07	134.10	124.61	117.43	111.87	107.47	103.94
8000	721.13	386.95	276.35	221.64	189.28	168.08	153.26	142.41	134.21	127.85	122.82	118.79
9000	811.27	435.32	310.89	249.34	212.94	189.09	172.42	160.21	150.99	143.83	138.18	133.64
10000	901.41	483.68	345.44	277.05	236.59	210.10	191.57	178.02	167.76	159.81	153.53	148.49
11000	991.55	532.05	379.98	304.75	260.25	231.11	210.73	195.82	184.54	175.79	168.88	163.34
12000	1081.69	580.42	414.52	332.46	283.91	252.12	229.89	213.62	201.31	191.77	184.23	178.18
13000	1171.83	628.79	449.06	360.16	307.57	273.13	249.04	231.42	218.09	207.75	199.59	193.03
14000	1261.97	677.16	483.61	387.86	331.23	294.14	268.20	249.22	234.86	223.74	214.94	207.88
15000	1352.11	725.52	518.15	415.57	354.89	315.15	287.36	267.02	251.64	239.72	230.29	222.73
16000	1442.25	773.89	552.69	443.27	378.55	336.16	306.51	284.82	268.42	255.70	245.64	237.58
17000	1532.39	822.26	587.24	470.98	402.21	357.17	325.67	302.62	285.19	271.68	261.00	252.43
18000	1622.53	870.63	621.78	498.68	425.87	378.18	344.83	320.42	301.97	287.66	276.35	267.27
19000	1712.67	919.00	656.32	526.38	449.52	399.19	363.98	338.22	318.74	303.64	291.70	282.12
20000	1802.81	967.36	690.87	554.09	473.18	420.19	383.14	356.03	335.52	319.62	307.05	296.97
21000	1892.95	1015.73	725.41	581.79	496.84	441.20	402.30	373.83	352.29	335.60	322.41	311.82
22000	1983.09	1064.10	759.95	609.50	520.50	462.21	421.45	391.63	369.07	351.58	337.76	326.67
23000	2073.23	1112.47	794.49	637.20	544.16	483.22	440.61	409.43	385.85	367.56	353.11	341.51
24000	2163.37	1160.84	829.04	664.91	567.82	504.23	459.77	427.23	402.62	383.54	368.46	356.36
25000	2253.51	1209.20	863.58	692.61	591.48	525.24	478.92	445.03	419.40	399.52	383.82	371.21
26000	2343.66	1257.57	898.12	720.31	615.14	546.25	498.08	462.83	436.17	415.50	399.17	386.06
27000	2433.80	1305.94	932.67	748.02	638.80	567.26	517.24	480.63	452.95	431.49	414.52	400.91
28000	2523.94	1354.31	967.21	775.72	662.45	588.27	536.39	498.43	469.72	447.47	429.87	415.76
29000	2614.08	1402.68	1001.75	803.43	686.11	609.28	555.55	516.23	486.50	463.45	445.23	430.60
30000	2704.22	1451.04	1036.30	831.13	709.77	630.29	574.71	534.04	503.28	479.43	460.58	445.45
31000	2794.36	1499.41	1070.84	858.83	733.43	651.30	593.86	551.84	520.05	495.41	475.93	460.30
32000	2884.50	1547.78	1105.38	886.54	757.09	672.31	613.02	569.64	536.83	511.39	491.28	475.15
33000	2974.64	1596.15	1139.92	914.24	780.75	693.32	632.18	587.44	553.60	527.37	506.64	490.00
34000	3064.78	1644.52	1174.47	941.95	804.41	714.33	651.33	605.24	570.38	543.35	521.99	504.85
35000	3154.92	1692.88	1209.01	969.65	828.07	735.34	670.49	623.04	587.15	559.33	537.34	519.69
36000	3245.06	1741.25	1243.55	997.36	851.73	756.35	689.65	640.84	603.93	575.31	552.69	534.54
37000	3335.20	1789.62	1278.10	1025.06	875.38	777.36	708.81	658.64	620.71	591.29	568.04	549.39
38000	3425.34	1837.99	1312.64	1052.76	899.04	798.37	727.96	676.44	637.48	607.27	583.40	564.24
39000	3515.48	1886.36	1347.18	1080.47	922.70	819.37	747.12	694.25	654.26	623.25	598.75	579.09
40000	3605.62	1934.72	1381.73	1108.17	946.36	840.38	766.28	712.05	671.03	639.23	614.10	593.94
41000	3695.76	1983.09	1416.27	1135.88	970.02	861.39	785.43	729.85	687.81	655.22	629.45	608.78
42000	3785.90	2031.46	1450.81	1163.58	993.68	882.40	804.59	747.65	704.58	671.20	644.81	623.63
43000	3876.04	2079.83	1485.36	1191.29	1017.34	903.41	823.75	765.45	721.36	687.18	660.16	638.48
44000	3966.18	2128.19	1519.90	1218.99	1041.00	924.42	842.90	783.25	738.14	703.16	675.51	653.33
45000	4056.32	2176.56	1554.44	1246.69	1064.66	945.43	862.06	801.05	754.91	719.14	690.86	668.18
46000	4146.46	2224.93	1588.98	1274.40	1088.31	966.44	881.22	818.85	771.69	735.12	706.22	683.02
47000	4236.60	2273.30	1623.53	1302.10	1111.97	987.45	900.37	836.65	788.46	751.10	721.57	697.87
48000	4326.74	2321.67	1658.07	1329.81	1135.63	1008.46	919.53	854.45	805.24	767.08	736.92	712.72
49000	4416.88	2370.03	1692.61	1357.51	1159.29	1029.47	938.69	872.26	822.01	783.06	752.27	727.57
50000	4507.02	2418.40	1727.16	1385.21	1182.95	1050.48	957.84	890.06	838.79	799.04	767.63	742.42
55000	4957.73	2660.24	1899.87	1523.74	1301.24	1155.53	1053.63	979.06	922.67	878.95	844.39	816.66
60000	5408.43	2902.08	2072.59	1662.26	1419.54	1260.57	1149.41	1068.07	1006.55	958.85	921.15	890.90
65000	5859.13	3143.92	2245.30	1800.78	1537.83	1365.62	1245.19	1157.07	1090.43	1038.75	997.91	965.14
70000	6309.83	3385.76	2418.02	1939.30	1656.13	1470.67	1340.98	1246.08	1174.30	1118.66	1074.68	1039.38
75000	6760.53	3627.60	2590.73	2077.82	1774.42	1575.72	1436.76	1335.08	1258.18	1198.56	1151.44	1113.62
80000	7211.24	3869.44	2763.45	2216.34	1892.72	1680.76	1532.55	1424.09	1342.06	1278.46	1228.20	1187.87
85000	7661.94	4111.28	2936.16	2354.86	2011.01	1785.81	1628.33	1513.09	1425.94	1358.37	1304.96	1262.11
90000	8112.64	4353.12	3108.88	2493.38	2129.31	1890.86	1724.11	1602.10	1509.82	1438.27	1381.72	1336.35
95000	8563.34	4594.96	3281.59	2631.90	2247.60	1995.91	1819.90	1691.10	1593.70	1518.18	1458.49	1410.59
100000	9014.04	4836.80	3454.31	2770.42	2365.90	2100.95	1915.68	1780.11	1677.58	1598.08	1535.25	1484.83

Table 1

MONTHLY

PAYMENT REQUIRED TO AMORTIZE A LOAN

14.75%

TERM AMOUNT	13 YEARS	14 YEARS	15 YEARS	16 YEARS	17 YEARS	18 YEARS	19 YEARS	20 YEARS	25 YEARS	30 YEARS	35 YEARS	40 YEARS
50	.73	.71	.70	.68	.68	.67	.66	.65	.64	.63	.62	.62
100	1.45	1.42	1.39	1.36	1.35	1.33	1.31	1.30	1.27	1.25	1.24	1.24
200	2.89	2.83	2.77	2.72	2.69	2.65	2.62	2.60	2.53	2.49	2.48	2.47
300	4.34	4.24	4.15	4.08	4.03	3.98	3.93	3.90	3.79	3.74	3.71	3.70
400	5.78	5.65	5.54	5.44	5.37	5.30	5.24	5.20	5.05	4.98	4.95	4.94
500	7.22	7.06	6.92	6.80	6.71	6.62	6.55	6.50	6.31	6.23	6.19	6.17
600	8.67	8.47	8.30	8.16	8.05	7.95	7.86	7.80	7.57	7.47	7.42	7.40
700	10.11	9.88	9.68	9.52	9.39	9.27	9.17	9.09	8.84	8.72	8.66	8.63
800	11.56	11.29	11.07	10.88	10.73	10.59	10.48	10.39	10.10	9.96	9.90	9.87
900	13.00	12.70	12.45	12.24	12.07	11.92	11.79	11.69	11.36	11.21	11.13	11.10
1000	14.44	14.11	13.83	13.60	13.41	13.24	13.10	12.99	12.62	12.45	12.37	12.33
2000	28.88	28.21	27.66	27.19	26.81	26.48	26.20	25.97	25.23	24.89	24.73	24.66
3000	43.32	42.31	41.48	40.79	40.21	39.72	39.30	38.96	37.85	37.34	37.10	36.99
4000	57.76	56.42	55.31	54.38	53.61	52.95	52.40	51.94	50.46	49.78	49.46	49.31
5000	72.20	70.52	69.13	67.97	67.01	66.19	65.50	64.92	63.08	62.23	61.83	61.64
6000	86.64	84.62	82.96	81.57	80.41	79.43	78.60	77.91	75.69	74.67	74.19	73.97
7000	101.08	98.72	96.78	95.16	93.81	92.67	91.70	90.89	88.31	87.12	86.56	86.29
8000	115.51	112.83	110.61	108.76	107.21	105.90	104.80	103.87	100.92	99.56	98.92	98.62
9000	129.95	126.93	124.43	122.35	120.61	119.14	117.90	116.86	113.54	112.01	111.29	110.95
10000	144.39	141.03	138.26	135.94	134.01	132.38	131.00	129.84	126.15	124.45	123.65	123.27
11000	158.83	155.14	152.08	149.54	147.41	145.62	144.10	142.82	138.77	136.90	136.02	135.60
12000	173.27	169.24	165.91	163.13	160.81	158.85	157.20	155.81	151.38	149.34	148.38	147.93
13000	187.71	183.34	179.73	176.72	174.21	172.09	170.30	168.79	164.00	161.79	160.75	160.25
14000	202.15	197.44	193.56	190.32	187.61	185.33	183.40	181.77	176.61	174.23	173.11	172.58
15000	216.59	211.55	207.38	203.91	201.01	198.57	196.50	194.76	189.22	186.68	185.48	184.91
16000	231.02	225.65	221.21	217.51	214.41	211.80	209.60	207.74	201.84	199.12	197.84	197.23
17000	245.46	239.75	235.03	231.10	227.81	225.04	222.70	220.73	214.45	211.57	210.21	209.56
18000	259.90	253.86	248.86	244.69	241.21	238.28	235.80	233.71	227.07	224.01	222.57	221.89
19000	274.34	267.96	262.68	258.29	254.61	251.52	248.90	246.69	239.68	236.46	234.94	234.21
20000	288.78	282.06	276.51	271.88	268.01	264.75	262.00	259.68	252.30	248.90	247.30	246.54
21000	303.22	296.16	290.33	285.47	281.41	277.99	275.10	272.66	264.91	261.34	259.66	258.87
22000	317.66	310.27	304.16	299.07	294.81	291.23	288.20	285.64	277.53	273.79	272.03	271.19
23000	332.10	324.37	317.98	312.66	308.21	304.47	301.30	298.63	290.14	286.23	284.39	283.52
24000	346.53	338.47	331.81	326.26	321.61	317.70	314.40	311.61	302.76	298.68	296.76	295.85
25000	360.97	352.58	345.63	339.85	335.01	330.94	327.50	324.59	315.37	311.12	309.12	308.17
26000	375.41	366.68	359.46	353.44	348.41	344.18	340.60	337.58	327.99	323.57	321.49	320.50
27000	389.85	380.78	373.28	367.04	361.81	357.42	353.70	350.56	340.60	336.01	333.85	332.83
28000	404.29	394.88	387.11	380.63	375.21	370.65	366.80	363.54	353.22	348.46	346.22	345.15
29000	418.73	408.99	400.93	394.23	388.61	383.89	379.90	376.53	365.83	360.90	358.58	357.48
30000	433.17	423.09	414.76	407.82	402.01	397.13	393.00	389.51	378.44	373.35	370.95	369.81
31000	447.61	437.19	428.58	421.41	415.41	410.37	406.10	402.50	391.06	385.79	383.31	382.13
32000	462.04	451.30	442.41	435.01	428.81	423.60	419.20	415.48	403.67	398.24	395.68	394.46
33000	476.48	465.40	456.23	448.60	442.21	436.84	432.30	428.46	416.29	410.68	408.04	406.79
34000	490.92	479.50	470.06	462.19	455.61	450.08	445.40	441.45	428.90	423.13	420.41	419.11
35000	505.36	493.60	483.88	475.79	469.01	463.31	458.50	454.43	441.52	435.57	432.77	431.44
36000	519.80	507.71	497.71	489.38	482.41	476.55	471.60	467.41	454.13	448.02	445.14	443.77
37000	534.24	521.81	511.53	502.98	495.81	489.79	484.70	480.40	466.75	460.46	457.50	456.09
38000	548.68	535.91	525.36	516.57	509.21	503.03	497.80	493.38	479.36	472.91	469.87	468.42
39000	563.12	550.01	539.18	530.16	522.61	516.26	510.90	506.36	491.98	485.35	482.23	480.75
40000	577.55	564.12	553.01	543.76	536.01	529.50	524.00	519.35	504.59	497.80	494.59	493.07
41000	591.99	578.22	566.83	557.35	549.41	542.74	537.10	532.33	517.21	510.24	506.96	505.40
42000	606.43	592.32	580.66	570.94	562.81	555.98	550.20	545.31	529.82	522.68	519.32	517.73
43000	620.87	606.43	594.48	584.54	576.21	569.21	563.30	558.30	542.43	535.13	531.69	530.05
44000	635.31	620.53	608.31	598.13	589.61	582.45	576.40	571.28	555.05	547.57	544.05	542.38
45000	649.75	634.63	622.13	611.73	603.01	595.69	589.50	584.26	567.66	560.02	556.42	554.71
46000	664.19	648.73	635.96	625.32	616.42	608.93	602.60	597.25	580.28	572.46	568.78	567.03
47000	678.63	662.84	649.78	638.91	629.82	622.16	615.70	610.23	592.89	584.91	581.15	579.36
48000	693.06	676.94	663.61	652.51	643.22	635.40	628.80	623.22	605.51	597.35	593.51	591.69
49000	707.50	691.04	677.43	666.10	656.62	648.64	641.90	636.20	618.12	609.80	605.88	604.01
50000	721.94	705.15	691.26	679.69	670.02	661.88	655.00	649.18	630.74	622.24	618.24	616.34
55000	794.14	775.66	760.38	747.66	737.02	728.06	720.50	714.10	693.81	684.47	680.07	677.97
60000	866.33	846.17	829.51	815.63	804.02	794.25	786.00	779.02	756.88	746.69	741.89	739.61
65000	938.52	916.69	898.63	883.60	871.02	860.44	851.50	843.94	819.96	808.91	803.71	801.24
70000	1010.72	987.20	967.76	951.57	938.02	926.62	917.00	908.85	883.03	871.14	865.54	862.87
75000	1082.91	1057.72	1036.88	1019.54	1005.02	992.81	982.50	973.77	946.10	933.36	927.36	924.51
80000	1155.10	1128.23	1106.01	1087.51	1072.02	1059.00	1048.00	1038.69	1009.18	995.59	989.18	986.14
85000	1227.30	1198.74	1175.13	1155.48	1139.02	1125.19	1113.50	1103.61	1072.25	1057.81	1051.01	1047.77
90000	1299.49	1269.26	1244.26	1223.45	1206.02	1191.37	1179.00	1168.52	1135.32	1120.03	1112.83	1109.41
95000	1371.68	1339.77	1313.38	1291.42	1273.03	1257.56	1244.50	1233.44	1198.40	1182.26	1174.66	1171.04
100000	1443.88	1410.29	1382.51	1359.38	1340.03	1323.75	1310.00	1298.36	1261.47	1244.48	1236.48	1232.67

14%

Table 1

15.00%

MONTHLY
PAYMENT REQUIRED TO AMORTIZE A LOAN

TERM	1 YEAR	2 YEARS	3 YEARS	4 YEARS	5 YEARS	6 YEARS	7 YEARS	8 YEARS	9 YEARS	10 YEARS	11 YEARS	12 YEARS
AMOUNT												
50	4.52	2.43	1.74	1.40	1.19	1.06	.97	.90	.85	.81	.78	.76
100	9.03	4.85	3.47	2.79	2.38	2.12	1.93	1.80	1.70	1.62	1.56	1.51
200	18.06	9.70	6.94	5.57	4.76	4.23	3.86	3.59	3.39	3.23	3.11	3.01
300	27.08	14.55	10.40	8.35	7.14	6.35	5.79	5.39	5.08	4.85	4.66	4.51
400	36.11	19.40	13.87	11.14	9.52	8.46	7.72	7.18	6.77	6.46	6.21	6.01
500	45.13	24.25	17.34	13.92	11.90	10.58	9.65	8.98	8.47	8.07	7.76	7.51
600	54.16	29.10	20.80	16.70	14.28	12.69	11.58	10.77	10.16	9.69	9.31	9.01
700	63.19	33.95	24.27	19.49	16.66	14.81	13.51	12.57	11.85	11.30	10.86	10.51
800	72.21	38.79	27.74	22.27	19.04	16.92	15.44	14.36	13.54	12.91	12.41	12.01
900	81.24	43.64	31.20	25.05	21.42	19.04	17.37	16.16	15.24	14.53	13.96	13.51
1000	90.26	48.49	34.67	27.84	23.79	21.15	19.30	17.95	16.93	16.14	15.51	15.01
2000	180.52	96.98	69.34	55.67	47.58	42.30	38.60	35.90	33.85	32.27	31.02	30.02
3000	270.78	145.46	104.00	83.50	71.37	63.44	57.90	53.84	50.78	48.41	46.53	45.03
4000	361.04	193.95	138.67	111.33	95.16	84.59	77.19	71.79	67.70	64.54	62.04	60.04
5000	451.30	242.44	173.33	139.16	118.95	105.73	96.49	89.73	84.63	80.67	77.55	75.05
6000	541.55	290.92	208.00	166.99	142.74	126.88	115.79	107.68	101.55	96.81	93.06	90.06
7000	631.81	339.41	242.66	194.82	166.53	148.02	135.08	125.62	118.48	112.94	108.57	105.07
8000	722.07	387.90	277.33	222.65	190.32	169.17	154.38	143.57	135.40	129.07	124.08	120.08
9000	812.33	436.38	311.99	250.48	214.11	190.31	173.68	161.51	152.32	145.21	139.59	135.08
10000	902.59	484.87	346.66	278.31	237.90	211.46	192.97	179.46	169.25	161.34	155.10	150.09
11000	992.85	533.36	381.32	306.14	261.69	232.60	212.27	197.40	186.17	177.47	170.61	165.10
12000	1083.10	581.84	415.99	333.97	285.48	253.75	231.57	215.35	203.10	193.61	186.11	180.11
13000	1173.36	630.33	450.65	361.80	309.27	274.89	250.86	233.30	220.02	209.74	201.62	195.12
14000	1263.62	678.82	485.32	389.64	333.06	296.04	270.16	251.24	236.95	225.87	217.13	210.13
15000	1353.88	727.30	519.98	417.47	356.85	317.18	289.46	269.19	253.87	242.01	232.64	225.14
16000	1444.14	775.79	554.65	445.30	380.64	338.33	308.75	287.13	270.79	258.14	248.15	240.15
17000	1534.40	824.28	589.32	473.13	404.43	359.47	328.05	305.08	287.72	274.27	263.66	255.15
18000	1624.65	872.76	623.98	500.96	428.22	380.62	347.35	323.02	304.64	290.41	279.17	270.16
19000	1714.91	921.25	658.65	528.79	452.01	401.76	366.64	340.97	321.57	306.54	294.68	285.17
20000	1805.17	969.74	693.31	556.62	475.80	422.91	385.94	358.91	338.49	322.67	310.19	300.18
21000	1895.43	1018.22	727.98	584.45	499.59	444.05	405.24	376.86	355.42	338.81	325.70	315.19
22000	1985.69	1066.71	762.64	612.28	523.38	465.20	424.53	394.80	372.34	354.94	341.21	330.20
23000	2075.95	1115.20	797.31	640.11	547.17	486.34	443.83	412.75	389.26	371.08	356.72	345.21
24000	2166.20	1163.68	831.97	667.94	570.96	507.49	463.13	430.69	406.19	387.21	372.22	360.22
25000	2256.46	1212.17	866.64	695.77	594.75	528.63	482.42	448.64	423.11	403.34	387.73	375.22
26000	2346.72	1260.66	901.30	723.60	618.54	549.78	501.72	466.59	440.04	419.48	403.24	390.23
27000	2436.98	1309.14	935.97	751.44	642.33	570.92	521.02	484.53	456.96	435.61	418.75	405.24
28000	2527.24	1357.63	970.63	779.27	666.12	592.07	540.31	502.48	473.89	451.74	434.26	420.25
29000	2617.50	1406.12	1005.30	807.10	689.91	613.21	559.61	520.42	490.81	467.88	449.77	435.26
30000	2707.75	1454.60	1039.96	834.93	713.70	634.36	578.91	538.37	507.74	484.01	465.28	450.27
31000	2798.01	1503.09	1074.63	862.76	737.49	655.50	598.20	556.31	524.66	500.14	480.79	465.28
32000	2888.27	1551.58	1109.30	890.59	761.28	676.65	617.50	574.26	541.58	516.28	496.30	480.29
33000	2978.53	1600.06	1143.96	918.42	785.07	697.79	636.80	592.20	558.51	532.41	511.81	495.29
34000	3068.79	1648.55	1178.63	946.25	808.86	718.94	656.09	610.15	575.43	548.54	527.32	510.30
35000	3159.05	1697.04	1213.29	974.08	832.65	740.08	675.39	628.09	592.36	564.68	542.83	525.31
36000	3249.30	1745.52	1247.96	1001.91	856.44	761.23	694.69	646.04	609.28	580.81	558.33	540.32
37000	3339.56	1794.01	1282.62	1029.74	880.23	782.37	713.98	663.98	626.21	596.94	573.84	555.33
38000	3429.82	1842.50	1317.29	1057.57	904.02	803.52	733.28	681.93	643.13	613.08	589.35	570.34
39000	3520.08	1890.98	1351.95	1085.40	927.81	824.66	752.58	699.88	660.05	629.21	604.86	585.35
40000	3610.34	1939.47	1386.62	1113.23	951.60	845.81	771.88	717.82	676.98	645.34	620.37	600.36
41000	3700.60	1987.96	1421.28	1141.07	975.39	866.95	791.17	735.77	693.90	661.48	635.88	615.36
42000	3790.85	2036.44	1455.95	1168.90	999.18	888.10	810.47	753.71	710.83	677.61	651.39	630.37
43000	3881.11	2084.93	1490.61	1196.73	1022.97	909.24	829.77	771.66	727.75	693.75	666.90	645.38
44000	3971.37	2133.42	1525.28	1224.56	1046.76	930.39	849.06	789.60	744.68	709.88	682.41	660.39
45000	4061.63	2181.90	1559.94	1252.39	1070.55	951.53	868.36	807.55	761.60	726.01	697.92	675.40
46000	4151.89	2230.39	1594.61	1280.22	1094.34	972.68	887.66	825.49	778.52	742.15	713.43	690.41
47000	4242.15	2278.88	1629.28	1308.05	1118.13	993.82	906.95	843.44	795.45	758.28	728.94	705.42
48000	4332.40	2327.36	1663.94	1335.88	1141.92	1014.97	926.25	861.38	812.37	774.41	744.44	720.43
49000	4422.66	2375.85	1698.61	1363.71	1165.71	1036.11	945.55	879.33	829.30	790.55	759.95	735.43
50000	4512.92	2424.34	1733.27	1391.54	1189.50	1057.26	964.84	897.28	846.22	806.68	775.46	750.44
55000	4964.21	2666.77	1906.60	1530.70	1308.45	1162.98	1061.33	987.00	930.84	887.35	853.01	825.49
60000	5415.50	2909.20	2079.92	1669.85	1427.40	1268.71	1157.81	1076.73	1015.47	968.01	930.55	900.53
65000	5866.80	3151.64	2253.25	1809.00	1546.35	1374.43	1254.29	1166.46	1100.09	1048.68	1008.10	975.57
70000	6318.09	3394.07	2426.58	1948.16	1665.30	1480.16	1350.78	1256.18	1184.71	1129.35	1085.65	1050.62
75000	6769.38	3636.50	2599.90	2087.31	1784.25	1585.88	1447.26	1345.91	1269.33	1210.02	1163.19	1125.66
80000	7220.67	3878.94	2773.23	2226.46	1903.20	1691.61	1543.75	1435.64	1353.95	1290.68	1240.74	1200.71
85000	7671.96	4121.37	2946.56	2365.62	2022.15	1797.33	1640.23	1525.36	1438.57	1371.35	1318.28	1275.75
90000	8123.25	4363.80	3119.88	2504.77	2141.10	1903.06	1736.71	1615.09	1523.20	1452.02	1395.83	1350.79
95000	8574.55	4606.24	3293.21	2643.93	2260.05	2008.78	1833.20	1704.82	1607.82	1532.69	1473.37	1425.84
100000	9025.84	4848.67	3466.54	2783.08	2379.00	2114.51	1929.68	1794.55	1692.44	1613.35	1550.92	1500.88

Table 1

MONTHLY   15.00%
PAYMENT REQUIRED TO AMORTIZE A LOAN

TERM / AMOUNT	13 YEARS	14 YEARS	15 YEARS	16 YEARS	17 YEARS	18 YEARS	19 YEARS	20 YEARS	25 YEARS	30 YEARS	35 YEARS	40 YEARS
50	.74	.72	.70	.69	.68	.68	.67	.66	.65	.64	.63	.63
100	1.47	1.43	1.40	1.38	1.36	1.35	1.33	1.32	1.29	1.27	1.26	1.26
200	2.93	2.86	2.80	2.76	2.72	2.69	2.66	2.64	2.57	2.53	2.52	2.51
300	4.39	4.29	4.20	4.14	4.08	4.03	3.99	3.96	3.85	3.80	3.78	3.76
400	5.85	5.71	5.60	5.51	5.44	5.37	5.32	5.27	5.13	5.06	5.03	5.02
500	7.31	7.14	7.00	6.89	6.79	6.71	6.65	6.59	6.41	6.33	6.29	6.27
600	8.77	8.57	8.40	8.27	8.15	8.06	7.97	7.91	7.69	7.59	7.55	7.52
700	10.23	9.99	9.80	9.64	9.51	9.40	9.30	9.22	8.97	8.86	8.80	8.78
800	11.69	11.42	11.20	11.02	10.87	10.74	10.63	10.54	10.25	10.12	10.06	10.03
900	13.15	12.85	12.60	12.40	12.22	12.08	11.96	11.86	11.53	11.38	11.32	11.28
1000	14.61	14.28	14.00	13.77	13.58	13.42	13.29	13.17	12.81	12.65	12.57	12.54
2000	29.21	28.55	28.00	27.54	27.16	26.84	26.57	26.34	25.62	25.29	25.14	25.07
3000	43.81	42.82	41.99	41.31	40.74	40.26	39.85	39.51	38.43	37.94	37.71	37.60
4000	58.42	57.09	55.99	55.08	54.31	53.67	53.13	52.68	51.24	50.58	50.28	50.13
5000	73.02	71.36	69.98	68.84	67.89	67.09	66.41	65.84	64.05	63.23	62.85	62.67
6000	87.62	85.63	83.98	82.61	81.47	80.51	79.70	79.01	76.85	75.87	75.41	75.20
7000	102.23	99.90	97.98	96.38	95.04	93.92	92.98	92.18	89.66	88.52	87.98	87.73
8000	116.83	114.17	111.97	110.15	108.62	107.34	106.26	105.35	102.47	101.16	100.55	100.26
9000	131.43	128.44	125.97	123.91	122.20	120.76	119.54	118.52	115.28	113.80	113.12	112.80
10000	146.03	142.71	139.96	137.68	135.78	134.17	132.82	131.68	128.09	126.45	125.69	125.33
11000	160.64	156.98	153.96	151.45	149.35	147.59	146.11	144.85	140.90	139.09	138.25	137.86
12000	175.24	171.25	167.96	165.22	162.93	161.01	159.39	158.02	153.70	151.74	150.82	150.39
13000	189.84	185.52	181.95	178.99	176.51	174.42	172.67	171.19	166.51	164.38	163.39	162.92
14000	204.45	199.79	195.95	192.75	190.08	187.84	185.95	184.36	179.32	177.03	175.96	175.46
15000	219.05	214.06	209.94	206.52	203.66	201.26	199.23	197.52	192.13	189.67	188.53	187.99
16000	233.65	228.33	223.94	220.29	217.24	214.68	212.52	210.69	204.94	202.32	201.10	200.52
17000	248.25	242.60	237.93	234.06	230.81	228.09	225.80	223.86	217.75	214.96	213.66	213.05
18000	262.86	256.87	251.93	247.82	244.39	241.51	239.08	237.03	230.55	227.60	226.23	225.59
19000	277.46	271.14	265.93	261.59	257.97	254.93	252.36	250.20	243.36	240.25	238.80	238.12
20000	292.06	285.41	279.92	275.36	271.55	268.34	265.64	263.36	256.17	252.89	251.37	250.65
21000	306.67	299.68	293.92	289.13	285.12	281.76	278.93	276.53	268.98	265.54	263.94	263.18
22000	321.27	313.95	307.91	302.89	298.70	295.18	292.21	289.70	281.79	278.18	276.50	275.71
23000	335.87	328.22	321.91	316.66	312.28	308.59	305.49	302.87	294.60	290.83	289.07	288.25
24000	350.47	342.49	335.91	330.43	325.85	322.01	318.77	316.03	307.40	303.47	301.64	300.78
25000	365.08	356.76	349.90	344.20	339.43	335.43	332.05	329.20	320.21	316.12	314.21	313.31
26000	379.68	371.04	363.90	357.97	353.01	348.84	345.34	342.37	333.02	328.76	326.78	325.84
27000	394.28	385.31	377.89	371.73	366.58	362.26	358.62	355.54	345.83	341.40	339.34	338.38
28000	408.89	399.58	391.89	385.50	380.16	375.68	371.90	368.71	358.64	354.05	351.91	350.91
29000	423.49	413.85	405.89	399.27	393.74	389.10	385.18	381.87	371.45	366.69	364.48	363.44
30000	438.09	428.12	419.88	413.04	407.32	402.51	398.46	395.04	384.25	379.34	377.05	375.97
31000	452.69	442.39	433.88	426.80	420.89	415.93	411.75	408.21	397.06	391.98	389.62	388.50
32000	467.30	456.66	447.87	440.57	434.47	429.35	425.03	421.38	409.87	404.63	402.19	401.04
33000	481.90	470.93	461.87	454.34	448.05	442.76	438.31	434.55	422.68	417.27	414.75	413.57
34000	496.50	485.20	475.86	468.11	461.62	456.18	451.59	447.71	435.49	429.92	427.32	426.10
35000	511.11	499.47	489.86	481.87	475.20	469.60	464.87	460.88	448.30	442.56	439.89	438.63
36000	525.71	513.74	503.86	495.64	488.78	483.01	478.16	474.05	461.10	455.20	452.46	451.17
37000	540.31	528.01	517.85	509.41	502.35	496.43	491.44	487.22	473.91	467.85	465.03	463.70
38000	554.91	542.28	531.85	523.18	515.93	509.85	504.72	500.39	486.72	480.49	477.59	476.23
39000	569.52	556.55	545.84	536.95	529.51	523.26	518.00	513.55	499.53	493.14	490.16	488.76
40000	584.12	570.82	559.84	550.71	543.09	536.68	531.28	526.72	512.34	505.78	502.73	501.29
41000	598.72	585.09	573.84	564.48	556.66	550.10	544.57	539.89	525.15	518.43	515.30	513.83
42000	613.33	599.36	587.83	578.25	570.24	563.52	557.85	553.06	537.95	531.07	527.87	526.36
43000	627.93	613.63	601.83	592.02	583.82	576.93	571.13	566.22	550.76	543.72	540.43	538.89
44000	642.53	627.90	615.82	605.78	597.39	590.35	584.41	579.39	563.57	556.36	553.00	551.42
45000	657.13	642.17	629.82	619.55	610.97	603.77	597.69	592.56	576.38	569.00	565.57	563.96
46000	671.74	656.44	643.82	633.32	624.55	617.18	610.98	605.73	589.19	581.65	578.14	576.49
47000	686.34	670.71	657.81	647.09	638.12	630.60	624.26	618.90	602.00	594.29	590.71	589.02
48000	700.94	684.98	671.81	660.85	651.70	644.02	637.54	632.06	614.80	606.94	603.28	601.55
49000	715.55	699.25	685.80	674.62	665.28	657.43	650.82	645.23	627.61	619.58	615.84	614.08
50000	730.15	713.52	699.80	688.39	678.86	670.85	664.10	658.40	640.42	632.23	628.41	626.62
55000	803.16	784.88	769.78	757.23	746.74	737.93	730.51	724.24	704.46	695.45	691.25	689.28
60000	876.18	856.23	839.76	826.07	814.63	805.02	796.92	790.08	768.50	758.67	754.09	751.94
65000	949.19	927.58	909.74	894.91	882.51	872.10	863.33	855.92	832.54	821.89	816.93	814.60
70000	1022.21	998.93	979.72	963.74	950.40	939.19	929.74	921.76	896.59	885.12	879.77	877.26
75000	1095.22	1070.28	1049.70	1032.58	1018.28	1006.27	996.15	987.60	960.63	948.34	942.61	939.92
80000	1168.24	1141.64	1119.67	1101.42	1086.17	1073.36	1062.56	1053.44	1024.67	1011.56	1005.46	1002.58
85000	1241.25	1212.99	1189.65	1170.26	1154.05	1140.44	1128.97	1119.28	1088.71	1074.78	1068.30	1065.25
90000	1314.26	1284.34	1259.63	1239.10	1221.94	1207.53	1195.38	1185.12	1152.75	1138.00	1131.14	1127.91
95000	1387.28	1355.69	1329.61	1307.94	1289.82	1274.61	1261.79	1250.96	1216.79	1201.23	1193.98	1190.57
100000	1460.29	1427.04	1399.59	1376.77	1357.71	1341.70	1328.20	1316.79	1280.84	1264.45	1256.82	1253.23

15%

Table 1

15.25%

MONTHLY

PAYMENT REQUIRED TO AMORTIZE A LOAN

15%

TERM AMOUNT	1 YEAR	2 YEARS	3 YEARS	4 YEARS	5 YEARS	6 YEARS	7 YEARS	8 YEARS	9 YEARS	10 YEARS	11 YEARS	12 YEARS
50	4.52	2.44	1.74	1.40	1.20	1.07	.98	.91	.86	.82	.79	.76
100	9.04	4.87	3.48	2.80	2.40	2.13	1.95	1.81	1.71	1.63	1.57	1.52
200	18.08	9.73	6.96	5.60	4.79	4.26	3.89	3.62	3.42	3.26	3.14	3.04
300	27.12	14.59	10.44	8.39	7.18	6.39	5.84	5.43	5.13	4.89	4.70	4.56
400	36.16	19.45	13.92	11.19	9.57	8.52	7.78	7.24	6.83	6.52	6.27	6.07
500	45.19	24.31	17.40	13.98	11.97	10.65	9.72	9.05	8.54	8.15	7.84	7.59
600	54.23	29.17	20.88	16.78	14.36	12.77	11.67	10.86	10.25	9.78	9.40	9.11
700	63.27	34.03	24.36	19.58	16.75	14.90	13.61	12.67	11.96	11.41	10.97	10.62
800	72.31	38.89	27.84	22.37	19.14	17.03	15.55	14.48	13.66	13.03	12.54	12.14
900	81.34	43.75	31.31	25.17	21.53	19.16	17.50	16.29	15.37	14.66	14.10	13.66
1000	90.38	48.61	34.79	27.96	23.93	21.29	19.44	18.10	17.08	16.29	15.67	15.18
2000	180.76	97.22	69.58	55.92	47.85	42.57	38.88	36.19	34.15	32.58	31.34	30.35
3000	271.13	145.82	104.37	83.88	71.77	63.85	58.32	54.28	51.23	48.87	47.00	45.52
4000	361.51	194.43	139.16	111.84	95.69	85.13	77.75	72.37	68.30	65.15	62.67	60.69
5000	451.89	243.03	173.94	139.79	119.61	106.41	97.19	90.46	85.37	81.44	78.34	75.86
6000	542.26	291.64	208.73	167.75	143.53	127.69	116.63	108.55	102.45	97.73	94.00	91.03
7000	632.64	340.24	243.52	195.71	167.45	148.97	136.07	126.64	119.52	114.01	109.67	106.20
8000	723.02	388.85	278.31	223.67	191.38	170.25	155.50	144.73	136.59	130.30	125.34	121.37
9000	813.39	437.45	313.10	251.62	215.30	191.53	174.94	162.82	153.67	146.59	141.00	136.54
10000	903.77	486.06	347.88	279.58	239.22	212.82	194.38	180.91	170.74	162.87	156.67	151.71
11000	994.14	534.67	382.67	307.54	263.14	234.10	213.82	199.00	187.81	179.16	172.34	166.88
12000	1084.52	583.27	417.46	335.50	287.06	255.38	233.25	217.09	204.89	195.45	188.00	182.05
13000	1174.90	631.88	452.25	363.45	310.98	276.66	252.69	235.18	221.96	211.74	203.67	197.22
14000	1265.27	680.48	487.04	391.41	334.90	297.94	272.13	253.27	239.04	228.02	219.34	212.39
15000	1355.65	729.09	521.82	419.37	358.83	319.22	291.56	271.36	256.11	244.31	235.00	227.56
16000	1446.03	777.69	556.61	447.33	382.75	340.50	311.00	289.45	273.18	260.60	250.67	242.73
17000	1536.40	826.30	591.40	475.28	406.67	361.78	330.44	307.54	290.26	276.88	266.34	257.90
18000	1626.78	874.90	626.19	503.24	430.59	383.06	349.88	325.63	307.33	293.17	282.00	273.07
19000	1717.16	923.51	660.97	531.20	454.51	404.34	369.31	343.72	324.40	309.46	297.67	288.24
20000	1807.53	972.12	695.76	559.16	478.43	425.63	388.75	361.81	341.48	325.74	313.34	303.41
21000	1897.91	1020.72	730.55	587.12	502.35	446.91	408.19	379.90	358.55	342.03	329.00	318.58
22000	1988.28	1069.33	765.34	615.07	526.27	468.19	427.63	397.99	375.62	358.32	344.67	333.75
23000	2078.66	1117.93	800.13	643.03	550.20	489.47	447.06	416.08	392.70	374.60	360.34	348.92
24000	2169.04	1166.54	834.91	670.99	574.12	510.75	466.50	434.17	409.77	390.89	376.00	364.09
25000	2259.41	1215.14	869.70	698.95	598.04	532.03	485.94	452.26	426.85	407.18	391.67	379.26
26000	2349.79	1263.75	904.49	726.90	621.96	553.31	505.37	470.35	443.92	423.47	407.34	394.43
27000	2440.17	1312.35	939.28	754.86	645.88	574.59	524.81	488.44	460.99	439.75	423.00	409.60
28000	2530.54	1360.96	974.07	782.82	669.80	595.87	544.25	506.54	478.07	456.04	438.67	424.77
29000	2620.92	1409.56	1008.85	810.78	693.72	617.15	563.69	524.63	495.14	472.33	454.34	439.94
30000	2711.29	1458.17	1043.64	838.73	717.65	638.44	583.12	542.72	512.21	488.61	470.00	455.11
31000	2801.67	1506.78	1078.43	866.69	741.57	659.72	602.56	560.81	529.29	504.90	485.67	470.28
32000	2892.05	1555.38	1113.22	894.65	765.49	681.00	622.00	578.90	546.36	521.19	501.34	485.45
33000	2982.42	1603.99	1148.01	922.61	789.41	702.28	641.44	596.99	563.43	537.47	517.00	500.62
34000	3072.80	1652.59	1182.79	950.56	813.33	723.56	660.87	615.08	580.51	553.76	532.67	515.79
35000	3163.18	1701.20	1217.58	978.52	837.25	744.84	680.31	633.17	597.58	570.05	548.34	530.96
36000	3253.55	1749.80	1252.37	1006.48	861.17	766.12	699.75	651.26	614.66	586.33	564.00	546.13
37000	3343.93	1798.41	1287.16	1034.44	885.10	787.40	719.18	669.35	631.73	602.62	579.67	561.30
38000	3434.31	1847.01	1321.94	1062.40	909.02	808.68	738.62	687.44	648.80	618.91	595.34	576.47
39000	3524.68	1895.62	1356.73	1090.35	932.94	829.96	758.06	705.53	665.88	635.20	611.00	591.64
40000	3615.06	1944.23	1391.52	1118.31	956.86	851.25	777.50	723.62	682.95	651.48	626.67	606.81
41000	3705.43	1992.83	1426.31	1146.27	980.78	872.53	796.93	741.71	700.00	667.77	642.34	621.98
42000	3795.81	2041.44	1461.10	1174.23	1004.70	893.81	816.37	759.80	717.10	684.06	658.00	637.15
43000	3886.19	2090.04	1495.88	1202.18	1028.62	915.09	835.81	777.89	734.17	700.34	673.67	652.32
44000	3976.56	2138.65	1530.67	1230.14	1052.54	936.37	855.25	795.98	751.24	716.63	689.33	667.49
45000	4066.94	2187.25	1565.46	1258.10	1076.47	957.65	874.68	814.07	768.32	732.92	705.00	682.66
46000	4157.32	2235.86	1600.25	1286.06	1100.39	978.93	894.12	832.16	785.39	749.20	720.67	697.83
47000	4247.69	2284.46	1635.04	1314.01	1124.31	1000.21	913.56	850.25	802.46	765.49	736.33	713.00
48000	4338.07	2333.07	1669.82	1341.97	1148.23	1021.49	932.99	868.34	819.54	781.78	752.00	728.17
49000	4428.44	2381.68	1704.61	1369.93	1172.15	1042.77	952.43	886.43	836.61	798.06	767.67	743.34
50000	4518.82	2430.28	1739.40	1397.89	1196.07	1064.06	971.87	904.52	853.69	814.35	783.33	758.51
55000	4970.70	2673.31	1913.34	1537.68	1315.68	1170.46	1069.06	994.98	939.05	895.79	861.67	834.36
60000	5422.58	2916.34	2087.28	1677.46	1435.29	1276.87	1166.24	1085.43	1024.42	977.22	940.00	910.21
65000	5874.47	3159.36	2261.22	1817.25	1554.89	1383.27	1263.43	1175.88	1109.79	1058.66	1018.33	986.06
70000	6326.35	3402.39	2435.16	1957.04	1674.50	1489.68	1360.61	1266.33	1195.16	1140.09	1096.67	1061.91
75000	6778.23	3645.42	2609.10	2096.83	1794.11	1596.08	1457.80	1356.78	1280.53	1221.53	1175.00	1137.76
80000	7230.11	3888.45	2783.04	2236.62	1913.71	1702.49	1554.99	1447.23	1365.89	1302.96	1253.33	1213.61
85000	7681.99	4131.47	2956.97	2376.40	2033.32	1808.89	1652.17	1537.69	1451.26	1384.39	1331.67	1289.46
90000	8133.87	4374.50	3130.91	2516.19	2152.93	1915.30	1749.36	1628.14	1536.63	1465.83	1410.00	1365.31
95000	8585.76	4617.53	3304.85	2655.98	2272.53	2021.70	1846.55	1718.59	1622.00	1547.26	1488.33	1441.16
100000	9037.64	4860.56	3478.79	2795.77	2392.14	2128.11	1943.73	1809.04	1707.37	1628.70	1566.66	1517.01

Table 1

MONTHLY

15.25%

PAYMENT REQUIRED TO AMORTIZE A LOAN

TERM / AMOUNT	13 YEARS	14 YEARS	15 YEARS	16 YEARS	17 YEARS	18 YEARS	19 YEARS	20 YEARS	25 YEARS	30 YEARS	35 YEARS	40 YEARS
50	.74	.73	.71	.70	.69	.68	.68	.67	.66	.65	.64	.64
100	1.48	1.45	1.42	1.40	1.38	1.36	1.35	1.34	1.31	1.29	1.28	1.28
200	2.96	2.89	2.84	2.79	2.76	2.72	2.70	2.68	2.61	2.57	2.56	2.55
300	4.44	4.34	4.26	4.19	4.13	4.08	4.04	4.01	3.91	3.86	3.84	3.83
400	5.91	5.78	5.67	5.58	5.51	5.44	5.39	5.35	5.21	5.14	5.11	5.10
500	7.39	7.22	7.09	6.98	6.88	6.80	6.74	6.68	6.51	6.43	6.39	6.37
600	8.87	8.67	8.51	8.37	8.26	8.16	8.08	8.02	7.81	7.71	7.67	7.65
700	10.34	10.11	9.92	9.76	9.63	9.52	9.43	9.35	9.11	9.00	8.95	8.92
800	11.82	11.56	11.34	11.16	11.01	10.88	10.78	10.69	10.41	10.28	10.22	10.20
900	13.30	13.00	12.76	12.55	12.38	12.24	12.12	12.02	11.71	11.57	11.50	11.47
1000	14.77	14.44	14.17	13.95	13.76	13.60	13.47	13.36	13.01	12.85	12.78	12.74
2000	29.54	28.88	28.34	27.89	27.51	27.20	26.93	26.71	26.01	25.69	25.55	25.48
3000	44.31	43.32	42.51	41.83	41.27	40.80	40.40	40.06	39.01	38.54	38.32	38.22
4000	59.08	57.76	56.67	55.77	55.02	54.39	53.86	53.42	52.02	51.38	51.09	50.96
5000	73.84	72.20	70.84	69.72	68.78	67.99	67.33	66.77	65.02	64.23	63.86	63.70
6000	88.61	86.64	85.01	83.66	82.53	81.59	80.79	80.12	78.02	77.07	76.64	76.43
7000	103.38	101.08	99.18	97.60	96.29	95.19	94.26	93.48	91.02	89.92	89.41	89.17
8000	118.15	115.52	113.34	111.54	110.04	108.78	107.72	106.83	104.03	102.76	102.18	101.91
9000	132.92	129.95	127.51	125.49	123.80	122.38	121.19	120.18	117.03	115.61	114.95	114.65
10000	147.68	144.39	141.68	139.43	137.55	135.98	134.65	133.53	130.03	128.45	127.72	127.39
11000	162.45	158.83	155.85	153.37	151.31	149.57	148.12	146.89	143.03	141.30	140.50	140.12
12000	177.22	173.27	170.01	167.31	165.06	163.17	161.58	160.24	156.04	154.14	153.27	152.86
13000	191.99	187.71	184.18	181.26	178.81	176.77	175.05	173.59	169.04	166.98	166.04	165.60
14000	206.75	202.15	198.35	195.20	192.57	190.37	188.51	186.95	182.04	179.83	178.81	178.34
15000	221.52	216.59	212.52	209.14	206.32	203.96	201.98	200.30	195.04	192.67	191.58	191.08
16000	236.29	231.03	226.68	223.08	220.08	217.56	215.44	213.65	208.05	205.52	204.35	203.81
17000	251.06	245.46	240.85	237.03	233.83	231.16	228.91	227.01	221.05	218.36	217.13	216.55
18000	265.83	259.90	255.02	250.97	247.59	244.75	242.37	240.36	234.05	231.21	229.90	229.29
19000	280.59	274.34	269.19	264.91	261.34	258.35	255.84	253.71	247.05	244.05	242.67	242.03
20000	295.36	288.78	283.35	278.85	275.10	271.95	269.30	267.06	260.06	256.90	255.44	254.77
21000	310.13	303.22	297.52	292.80	288.85	285.54	282.76	280.42	273.06	269.74	268.21	267.50
22000	324.90	317.66	311.69	306.74	302.61	299.14	296.23	293.77	286.06	282.59	280.99	280.24
23000	339.66	332.10	325.86	320.68	316.36	312.74	309.69	307.12	299.06	295.43	293.76	292.98
24000	354.43	346.54	340.02	334.62	330.11	326.34	323.16	320.48	312.07	308.28	306.53	305.72
25000	369.20	360.97	354.19	348.56	343.87	339.93	336.62	333.83	325.07	321.12	319.30	318.46
26000	383.97	375.41	368.36	362.51	357.62	353.53	350.09	347.18	338.07	333.96	332.07	331.19
27000	398.74	389.85	382.53	376.45	371.38	367.13	363.55	360.54	351.07	346.81	344.84	343.93
28000	413.50	404.29	396.69	390.39	385.13	380.72	377.02	373.89	364.08	359.65	357.62	356.67
29000	428.27	418.73	410.86	404.33	398.89	394.32	390.48	387.24	377.08	372.50	370.39	369.41
30000	443.04	433.17	425.03	418.28	412.64	407.92	403.95	400.59	390.08	385.34	383.16	382.15
31000	457.81	447.61	439.20	432.22	426.40	421.52	417.41	413.95	403.09	398.19	395.93	394.88
32000	472.57	462.05	453.36	446.16	440.15	435.11	430.88	427.30	416.09	411.03	408.70	407.62
33000	487.34	476.48	467.53	460.10	453.91	448.71	444.34	440.65	429.09	423.88	421.48	420.36
34000	502.11	490.92	481.70	474.05	467.66	462.31	457.81	454.01	442.09	436.72	434.25	433.10
35000	516.88	505.36	495.87	487.99	481.42	475.91	471.27	467.36	455.10	449.57	447.02	445.84
36000	531.65	519.80	510.03	501.93	495.17	489.50	484.74	480.71	468.10	462.41	459.79	458.57
37000	546.41	534.24	524.20	515.87	508.92	503.10	498.20	494.07	481.10	475.25	472.56	471.31
38000	561.18	548.68	538.37	529.82	522.68	516.70	511.67	507.42	494.10	488.10	485.33	484.05
39000	575.95	563.12	552.54	543.76	536.43	530.29	525.13	520.77	507.11	500.94	498.11	496.79
40000	590.72	577.56	566.70	557.70	550.19	543.89	538.59	534.12	520.11	513.79	510.88	509.53
41000	605.48	591.99	580.87	571.64	563.94	557.49	552.06	547.48	533.11	526.63	523.65	522.26
42000	620.25	606.43	595.04	585.59	577.70	571.09	565.52	560.83	546.11	539.48	536.42	535.00
43000	635.02	620.87	609.21	599.53	591.45	584.68	578.99	574.18	559.12	552.32	549.19	547.74
44000	649.79	635.31	623.37	613.47	605.21	598.28	592.45	587.54	572.12	565.17	561.97	560.48
45000	664.56	649.75	637.54	627.41	618.96	611.88	605.92	600.89	585.12	578.01	574.74	573.22
46000	679.32	664.19	651.71	641.36	632.72	625.47	619.38	614.24	598.12	590.86	587.51	585.95
47000	694.09	678.63	665.88	655.30	646.47	639.07	632.85	627.60	611.13	603.70	600.28	598.69
48000	708.86	693.07	680.04	669.24	660.22	652.67	646.31	640.95	624.13	616.55	613.05	611.43
49000	723.63	707.50	694.21	683.18	673.98	666.27	659.78	654.30	637.13	629.39	625.83	624.17
50000	738.39	721.94	708.38	697.12	687.73	679.86	673.24	667.65	650.13	642.23	638.60	636.91
55000	812.23	794.14	779.22	766.84	756.51	747.85	740.57	734.42	715.15	706.46	702.46	700.60
60000	886.07	866.33	850.05	836.55	825.28	815.84	807.89	801.18	780.16	770.68	766.32	764.29
65000	959.91	938.52	920.89	906.26	894.05	883.82	875.21	867.95	845.17	834.90	830.17	827.98
70000	1033.75	1010.72	991.73	975.97	962.83	951.81	942.54	934.71	910.19	899.13	894.03	891.67
75000	1107.59	1082.91	1062.57	1045.68	1031.60	1019.79	1009.86	1001.48	975.20	963.35	957.89	955.36
80000	1181.43	1155.11	1133.40	1115.40	1100.37	1087.78	1077.18	1068.24	1040.21	1027.57	1021.75	1019.05
85000	1255.27	1227.30	1204.24	1185.11	1169.14	1155.76	1144.51	1135.01	1105.22	1091.79	1085.61	1082.74
90000	1329.11	1299.49	1275.08	1254.82	1237.92	1223.75	1211.83	1201.77	1170.24	1156.02	1149.47	1146.43
95000	1402.94	1371.69	1345.92	1324.53	1306.69	1291.74	1279.16	1268.54	1235.25	1220.24	1213.33	1210.12
100000	1476.78	1443.88	1416.75	1394.24	1375.46	1359.72	1346.48	1335.30	1300.26	1284.46	1277.19	1273.81

15%

Table 1

15.50%

MONTHLY
PAYMENT REQUIRED TO AMORTIZE A LOAN

TERM AMOUNT	1 YEAR	2 YEARS	3 YEARS	4 YEARS	5 YEARS	6 YEARS	7 YEARS	8 YEARS	9 YEARS	10 YEARS	11 YEARS	12 YEARS
50	4.53	2.44	1.75	1.41	1.21	1.08	.98	.92	.87	.83	.80	.77
100	9.05	4.88	3.50	2.81	2.41	2.15	1.96	1.83	1.73	1.65	1.59	1.54
200	18.10	9.75	6.99	5.62	4.82	4.29	3.92	3.65	3.45	3.29	3.17	3.07
300	27.15	14.62	10.48	8.43	7.22	6.43	5.88	5.48	5.17	4.94	4.75	4.60
400	36.20	19.49	13.97	11.24	9.63	8.57	7.84	7.30	6.89	6.58	6.33	6.14
500	45.25	24.37	17.46	14.05	12.03	10.71	9.79	9.12	8.62	8.23	7.92	7.67
600	54.30	29.24	20.95	16.86	14.44	12.86	11.75	10.95	10.34	9.87	9.50	9.20
700	63.35	34.11	24.44	19.66	16.84	15.00	13.71	12.77	12.06	11.51	11.08	10.74
800	72.40	38.98	27.93	22.47	19.25	17.14	15.67	14.59	13.78	13.16	12.66	12.27
900	81.45	43.86	31.42	25.28	21.65	19.28	17.63	16.42	15.51	14.80	14.25	13.80
1000	90.50	48.73	34.92	28.09	24.06	21.42	19.58	18.24	17.23	16.45	15.83	15.34
2000	180.99	97.45	69.83	56.17	48.11	42.84	39.16	36.48	34.45	32.89	31.65	30.67
3000	271.49	146.18	104.74	84.26	72.16	64.26	58.74	54.71	51.68	49.33	47.48	46.00
4000	361.98	194.90	139.65	112.34	96.22	85.67	78.32	72.95	68.90	65.77	63.30	61.33
5000	452.48	243.63	174.56	140.43	120.27	107.09	97.90	91.18	86.12	82.21	79.13	76.67
6000	542.97	292.35	209.47	168.51	144.32	128.51	117.48	109.42	103.35	98.65	94.95	92.00
7000	633.47	341.08	244.38	196.60	168.38	149.93	137.05	127.66	120.57	115.09	110.78	107.33
8000	723.96	389.80	279.29	224.68	192.43	171.34	156.63	145.89	137.79	131.53	126.60	122.66
9000	814.45	438.53	314.20	252.77	216.48	192.76	176.21	164.13	155.02	147.97	142.43	137.99
10000	904.95	487.25	349.11	280.85	240.54	214.18	195.79	182.36	172.24	164.42	158.25	153.33
11000	995.44	535.97	384.02	308.94	264.59	235.60	215.37	200.60	189.46	180.86	174.08	168.66
12000	1085.94	584.70	418.93	337.02	288.64	257.01	234.95	218.84	206.69	197.30	189.90	183.99
13000	1176.43	633.42	453.84	365.11	312.70	278.43	254.52	237.07	223.91	213.74	205.73	199.32
14000	1266.93	682.15	488.75	393.19	336.75	299.85	274.10	255.31	241.13	230.18	221.55	214.65
15000	1357.42	730.87	523.67	421.28	360.80	321.27	293.68	273.54	258.36	246.62	237.38	229.99
16000	1447.92	779.60	558.58	449.36	384.86	342.68	313.26	291.78	275.58	263.06	253.20	245.32
17000	1538.41	828.32	593.49	477.45	408.91	364.10	332.84	310.02	292.80	279.50	269.03	260.65
18000	1628.90	877.05	628.40	505.53	432.96	385.52	352.42	328.25	310.03	295.94	284.85	275.98
19000	1719.40	925.77	663.31	533.62	457.02	406.94	371.99	346.49	327.25	312.39	300.68	291.31
20000	1809.89	974.50	698.22	561.70	481.07	428.35	391.57	364.72	344.48	328.83	316.50	306.65
21000	1900.39	1023.22	733.13	589.79	505.12	449.77	411.15	382.96	361.70	345.27	332.32	321.98
22000	1990.88	1071.94	768.04	617.87	529.18	471.19	430.73	401.20	378.92	361.71	348.15	337.31
23000	2081.38	1120.67	802.95	645.96	553.23	492.61	450.31	419.43	396.15	378.15	363.97	352.64
24000	2171.87	1169.39	837.86	674.04	577.28	514.02	469.89	437.67	413.37	394.59	379.80	367.97
25000	2262.37	1218.12	872.77	702.13	601.33	535.44	489.46	455.90	430.59	411.03	395.62	383.31
26000	2352.86	1266.84	907.68	730.21	625.39	556.86	509.04	474.14	447.82	427.47	411.45	398.64
27000	2443.35	1315.57	942.59	758.30	649.44	578.28	528.62	492.37	465.04	443.91	427.27	413.97
28000	2533.85	1364.29	977.50	786.38	673.49	599.69	548.20	510.61	482.26	460.35	443.10	429.30
29000	2624.34	1413.02	1012.41	814.47	697.55	621.11	567.78	528.85	499.49	476.80	458.92	444.63
30000	2714.84	1461.74	1047.33	842.55	721.60	642.53	587.36	547.08	516.71	493.24	474.75	459.97
31000	2805.33	1510.47	1082.24	870.64	745.65	663.95	606.93	565.32	533.93	509.68	490.57	475.30
32000	2895.83	1559.19	1117.15	898.72	769.71	685.36	626.51	583.55	551.16	526.12	506.40	490.63
33000	2986.32	1607.91	1152.06	926.81	793.76	706.78	646.09	601.79	568.38	542.56	522.22	505.96
34000	3076.82	1656.64	1186.97	954.89	817.81	728.20	665.67	620.03	585.60	559.00	538.05	521.29
35000	3167.31	1705.36	1221.88	982.98	841.87	749.62	685.25	638.26	602.83	575.44	553.87	536.63
36000	3257.80	1754.09	1256.79	1011.06	865.92	771.03	704.83	656.50	620.05	591.88	569.70	551.96
37000	3348.30	1802.81	1291.70	1039.14	889.97	792.45	724.40	674.73	637.28	608.32	585.52	567.29
38000	3438.79	1851.54	1326.61	1067.23	914.03	813.87	743.98	692.97	654.50	624.77	601.35	582.62
39000	3529.29	1900.26	1361.52	1095.31	938.08	835.29	763.56	711.21	671.72	641.21	617.17	597.95
40000	3619.78	1948.99	1396.43	1123.40	962.13	856.70	783.14	729.44	688.95	657.65	632.99	613.29
41000	3710.28	1997.71	1431.34	1151.48	986.19	878.12	802.72	747.68	706.17	674.09	648.82	628.62
42000	3800.77	2046.44	1466.25	1179.57	1010.24	899.54	822.30	765.91	723.39	690.53	664.64	643.95
43000	3891.26	2095.16	1501.16	1207.65	1034.29	920.96	841.87	784.15	740.62	706.97	680.47	659.28
44000	3981.76	2143.88	1536.08	1235.74	1058.35	942.37	861.45	802.39	757.84	723.41	696.29	674.61
45000	4072.25	2192.61	1570.99	1263.82	1082.40	963.79	881.03	820.62	775.06	739.85	712.12	689.95
46000	4162.75	2241.33	1605.90	1291.91	1106.45	985.21	900.61	838.86	792.29	756.29	727.94	705.28
47000	4253.24	2290.06	1640.81	1319.99	1130.51	1006.63	920.19	857.09	809.51	772.73	743.77	720.61
48000	4343.74	2338.78	1675.72	1348.08	1154.56	1028.04	939.77	875.33	826.73	789.18	759.59	735.94
49000	4434.23	2387.51	1710.63	1376.16	1178.61	1049.46	959.34	893.57	843.96	805.62	775.42	751.28
50000	4524.73	2436.23	1745.54	1404.25	1202.66	1070.88	978.92	911.80	861.18	822.06	791.24	766.61
55000	4977.20	2679.85	1920.09	1544.67	1322.93	1177.97	1076.81	1002.98	947.30	904.26	870.37	843.27
60000	5429.67	2923.48	2094.65	1685.10	1443.20	1285.05	1174.71	1094.16	1033.42	986.47	949.49	919.93
65000	5882.14	3167.10	2269.20	1825.52	1563.46	1392.14	1272.60	1185.34	1119.53	1068.67	1028.61	996.59
70000	6334.61	3410.72	2443.75	1965.95	1683.73	1499.23	1370.49	1276.52	1205.65	1150.88	1107.74	1073.25
75000	6787.09	3654.35	2618.31	2106.37	1803.99	1606.32	1468.38	1367.70	1291.77	1233.08	1186.86	1149.91
80000	7239.56	3897.97	2792.86	2246.79	1924.26	1713.40	1566.27	1458.88	1377.89	1315.29	1265.98	1226.57
85000	7692.03	4141.59	2967.41	2387.22	2044.53	1820.49	1664.16	1550.06	1464.00	1397.49	1345.11	1303.23
90000	8144.50	4385.21	3141.97	2527.64	2164.79	1927.58	1762.06	1641.24	1550.12	1479.70	1424.23	1379.89
95000	8596.97	4628.84	3316.52	2668.07	2285.06	2034.67	1859.95	1732.42	1636.24	1561.91	1503.36	1456.55
100000	9049.45	4872.46	3491.07	2808.49	2405.32	2141.75	1957.84	1823.60	1722.36	1644.11	1582.48	1533.21

15%

Table 1

MONTHLY 15.50%

PAYMENT REQUIRED TO AMORTIZE A LOAN

TERM AMOUNT	13 YEARS	14 YEARS	15 YEARS	16 YEARS	17 YEARS	18 YEARS	19 YEARS	20 YEARS	25 YEARS	30 YEARS	35 YEARS	40 YEARS
50	.75	.74	.72	.71	.70	.69	.69	.68	.66	.66	.65	.65
100	1.50	1.47	1.44	1.42	1.40	1.38	1.37	1.36	1.32	1.31	1.30	1.30
200	2.99	2.93	2.87	2.83	2.79	2.76	2.73	2.71	2.64	2.61	2.60	2.59
300	4.49	4.39	4.31	4.24	4.18	4.14	4.10	4.07	3.96	3.92	3.90	3.89
400	5.98	5.85	5.74	5.65	5.58	5.52	5.46	5.42	5.28	5.22	5.20	5.18
500	7.47	7.31	7.17	7.06	6.97	6.89	6.83	6.77	6.60	6.53	6.49	6.48
600	8.97	8.77	8.61	8.48	8.36	8.27	8.19	8.13	7.92	7.83	7.79	7.77
700	10.46	10.23	10.04	9.89	9.76	9.65	9.56	9.48	9.24	9.14	9.09	9.07
800	11.95	11.69	11.48	11.30	11.15	11.03	10.92	10.84	10.56	10.44	10.39	10.36
900	13.45	13.15	12.91	12.71	12.54	12.41	12.29	12.19	11.88	11.75	11.68	11.65
1000	14.94	14.61	14.34	14.12	13.94	13.78	13.65	13.54	13.20	13.05	12.98	12.95
2000	29.87	29.22	28.68	28.24	27.87	27.56	27.30	27.08	26.40	26.10	25.96	25.89
3000	44.81	43.83	43.02	42.36	41.80	41.34	40.95	40.62	39.60	39.14	38.93	38.84
4000	59.74	58.44	57.36	56.48	55.74	55.12	54.60	54.16	52.79	52.19	51.91	51.78
5000	74.67	73.04	71.70	70.59	69.67	68.90	68.25	67.70	65.99	65.23	64.88	64.72
6000	89.61	87.65	86.04	84.71	83.60	82.67	81.89	81.24	79.19	78.28	77.86	77.67
7000	104.54	102.26	100.38	98.83	97.54	96.45	95.54	94.78	92.39	91.32	90.84	90.61
8000	119.47	116.87	114.72	112.95	111.47	110.23	109.19	108.32	105.58	104.37	103.81	103.56
9000	134.41	131.48	129.06	127.07	125.40	124.01	122.84	121.85	118.78	117.41	116.79	116.50
10000	149.34	146.08	143.40	141.18	139.33	137.79	136.49	135.39	131.98	130.46	129.76	129.44
11000	164.27	160.69	157.74	155.30	153.27	151.57	150.14	148.93	145.18	143.50	142.74	142.39
12000	179.21	175.30	172.08	169.42	167.20	165.34	163.78	162.47	158.37	156.55	155.72	155.33
13000	194.14	189.91	186.42	183.54	181.13	179.12	177.43	176.01	171.57	169.59	168.69	168.28
14000	209.07	204.52	200.76	197.66	195.07	192.90	191.08	189.55	184.77	182.64	181.67	181.22
15000	224.01	219.12	215.10	211.77	209.00	206.68	204.73	203.09	197.97	195.68	194.64	194.16
16000	238.94	233.73	229.44	225.89	222.93	220.46	218.38	216.63	211.16	208.73	207.62	207.11
17000	253.87	248.34	243.78	240.01	236.86	234.23	232.03	230.16	224.36	221.77	220.59	220.05
18000	268.81	262.95	258.12	254.13	250.80	248.01	245.67	243.70	237.56	234.82	233.57	233.00
19000	283.74	277.56	272.46	268.24	264.73	261.79	259.32	257.24	250.76	247.86	246.55	245.94
20000	298.67	292.16	286.80	282.36	278.66	275.57	272.97	270.78	263.95	260.91	259.52	258.88
21000	313.61	306.77	301.14	296.48	292.60	289.35	286.62	284.32	277.15	273.95	272.50	271.83
22000	328.54	321.38	315.48	310.60	306.53	303.13	300.27	297.86	290.35	287.00	285.47	284.77
23000	343.47	335.99	329.82	324.72	320.46	316.90	313.91	311.40	303.55	300.04	298.45	297.72
24000	358.41	350.59	344.16	338.83	334.40	330.68	327.56	324.94	316.74	313.09	311.43	310.66
25000	373.34	365.20	358.50	352.95	348.33	344.46	341.21	338.48	329.94	326.13	324.40	323.60
26000	388.27	379.81	372.84	367.07	362.26	358.24	354.86	352.01	343.14	339.18	337.38	336.55
27000	403.21	394.42	387.18	381.19	376.19	372.02	368.51	365.55	356.34	352.22	350.35	349.49
28000	418.14	409.03	401.52	395.31	390.13	385.79	382.16	379.09	369.53	365.27	363.33	362.44
29000	433.08	423.63	415.86	409.42	404.06	399.57	395.80	392.63	382.73	378.31	376.30	375.38
30000	448.01	438.24	430.20	423.54	417.99	413.35	409.45	406.17	395.93	391.36	389.28	388.32
31000	462.94	452.85	444.54	437.66	431.93	427.13	423.10	419.71	409.13	404.41	402.26	401.27
32000	477.88	467.46	458.88	451.78	445.86	440.91	436.75	433.25	422.32	415.45	415.23	414.21
33000	492.81	482.07	473.22	465.89	459.79	454.69	450.40	446.79	435.52	430.50	428.21	427.16
34000	507.74	496.67	487.56	480.01	473.72	468.46	464.05	460.32	448.72	443.54	441.18	440.10
35000	522.68	511.28	501.90	494.13	487.66	482.24	477.69	473.86	461.92	456.59	454.16	453.04
36000	537.61	525.89	516.24	508.25	501.59	496.02	491.34	487.40	475.11	469.63	467.14	465.99
37000	552.54	540.50	530.58	522.37	515.52	509.80	504.99	500.94	488.31	482.68	480.11	478.93
38000	567.48	555.11	544.92	536.48	529.46	523.58	518.64	514.48	501.51	495.72	493.09	491.88
39000	582.41	569.71	559.26	550.60	543.39	537.35	532.29	528.02	514.71	508.77	506.06	504.82
40000	597.34	584.32	573.60	564.72	557.32	551.13	545.94	541.56	527.90	521.81	519.04	517.76
41000	612.28	598.93	587.94	578.84	571.25	564.91	559.58	555.10	541.10	534.86	532.01	530.71
42000	627.21	613.54	602.28	592.96	585.19	578.69	573.23	568.63	554.30	547.90	544.99	543.65
43000	642.14	628.14	616.62	607.07	599.12	592.47	586.88	582.17	567.50	560.95	557.97	556.60
44000	657.08	642.75	630.96	621.19	613.05	606.25	600.53	595.71	580.69	573.99	570.94	569.54
45000	672.01	657.36	645.30	635.31	626.99	620.02	614.18	609.25	593.89	587.04	583.92	582.48
46000	686.94	671.97	659.64	649.43	640.92	633.80	627.82	622.79	607.09	600.08	596.89	595.43
47000	701.88	686.58	673.98	663.54	654.85	647.58	641.47	636.33	620.29	613.13	609.87	608.37
48000	716.81	701.18	688.32	677.66	668.79	661.36	655.12	649.87	633.48	626.17	622.85	621.32
49000	731.74	715.79	702.66	691.78	682.72	675.14	668.77	663.41	646.68	639.22	635.82	634.26
50000	746.68	730.40	717.00	705.90	696.65	688.91	682.42	676.95	659.88	652.26	648.80	647.20
55000	821.35	803.44	788.70	776.49	766.32	757.81	750.66	744.64	725.86	717.49	713.68	711.92
60000	896.01	876.48	860.40	847.08	835.98	826.70	818.90	812.33	791.85	782.72	778.56	776.64
65000	970.68	949.52	932.10	917.67	905.65	895.59	887.14	880.03	857.84	847.94	843.44	841.36
70000	1045.35	1022.56	1003.80	988.26	975.31	964.48	955.38	947.72	923.83	913.17	908.31	906.08
75000	1120.01	1095.60	1075.50	1058.85	1044.97	1033.37	1023.62	1015.42	989.81	978.39	973.19	970.80
80000	1194.68	1168.64	1147.20	1129.43	1114.64	1102.26	1091.87	1083.11	1055.80	1043.62	1038.07	1035.52
85000	1269.35	1241.68	1218.90	1200.02	1184.30	1171.15	1160.11	1150.80	1121.79	1108.84	1102.95	1100.24
90000	1344.02	1314.72	1290.60	1270.61	1253.97	1240.04	1228.35	1218.50	1187.78	1174.07	1167.83	1164.97
95000	1418.68	1387.76	1362.30	1341.20	1323.63	1308.93	1296.59	1286.19	1253.76	1239.30	1232.71	1229.68
100000	1493.35	1460.79	1434.00	1411.79	1393.30	1377.82	1364.83	1353.89	1319.75	1304.52	1297.59	1294.40

15%

Table 1

15.75%

MONTHLY

PAYMENT REQUIRED TO AMORTIZE A LOAN

15%

TERM AMOUNT	1 YEAR	2 YEARS	3 YEARS	4 YEARS	5 YEARS	6 YEARS	7 YEARS	8 YEARS	9 YEARS	10 YEARS	11 YEARS	12 YEAR
50	4.54	2.45	1.76	1.42	1.21	1.08	.99	.92	.87	.83	.80	.78
100	9.07	4.89	3.51	2.83	2.42	2.16	1.98	1.84	1.74	1.66	1.60	1.55
200	18.13	9.77	7.01	5.65	4.84	4.32	3.95	3.68	3.48	3.32	3.20	3.10
300	27.19	14.66	10.52	8.47	7.26	6.47	5.92	5.52	5.22	4.98	4.80	4.65
400	36.25	19.54	14.02	11.29	9.68	8.63	7.89	7.36	6.95	6.64	6.40	6.20
500	45.31	24.43	17.52	14.11	12.10	10.78	9.86	9.20	8.69	8.30	8.00	7.75
600	54.37	29.31	21.03	16.93	14.52	12.94	11.84	11.03	10.43	9.96	9.60	9.30
700	63.43	34.20	24.53	19.75	16.93	15.09	13.81	12.87	12.17	11.62	11.19	10.85
800	72.50	39.08	28.03	22.57	19.35	17.25	15.78	14.71	13.90	13.28	12.79	12.40
900	81.56	43.96	31.54	25.40	21.77	19.40	17.75	16.55	15.64	14.94	14.39	13.95
1000	90.62	48.85	35.04	28.22	24.19	21.56	19.72	18.39	17.38	16.60	15.99	15.50
2000	181.23	97.69	70.07	56.43	48.38	43.11	39.44	36.77	34.75	33.20	31.97	30.99
3000	271.84	146.54	105.11	84.64	72.56	64.67	59.16	55.15	52.13	49.79	47.96	46.49
4000	362.46	195.38	140.14	112.85	96.75	86.22	78.88	73.53	69.50	66.39	63.94	61.98
5000	453.07	244.22	175.17	141.07	120.93	107.78	98.60	91.92	86.88	82.98	79.92	77.48
6000	543.68	293.07	210.21	169.28	145.12	129.33	118.32	110.30	104.25	99.58	95.91	92.97
7000	634.29	341.91	245.24	197.49	169.30	150.89	138.04	128.68	121.62	116.18	111.89	108.47
8000	724.91	390.75	280.27	225.70	193.49	172.44	157.76	147.06	139.00	132.77	127.87	123.96
9000	815.52	439.60	315.31	253.92	217.67	193.99	177.48	165.44	156.37	149.37	143.86	139.46
10000	906.13	488.44	350.34	282.13	241.86	215.55	197.20	183.83	173.75	165.96	159.84	154.95
11000	996.74	537.29	385.38	310.34	266.04	237.10	216.92	202.21	191.12	182.56	175.82	170.45
12000	1087.36	586.13	420.41	338.55	290.23	258.66	236.64	220.59	208.49	199.16	191.81	185.94
13000	1177.97	634.97	455.44	366.77	314.42	280.21	256.36	238.97	225.87	215.75	207.79	201.44
14000	1268.58	683.82	490.48	394.98	338.60	301.77	276.08	257.35	243.24	232.35	223.78	216.93
15000	1359.19	732.66	525.51	423.19	362.79	323.32	295.80	275.74	260.62	248.94	239.76	232.43
16000	1449.81	781.50	560.54	451.40	386.97	344.88	315.52	294.12	277.99	265.54	255.74	247.92
17000	1540.42	830.35	595.58	479.62	411.16	366.43	335.24	312.50	295.36	282.13	271.73	263.42
18000	1631.03	879.19	630.61	507.83	435.34	387.98	354.96	330.88	312.74	298.73	287.71	278.91
19000	1721.64	928.04	665.65	536.04	459.53	409.54	374.68	349.26	330.11	315.33	303.69	294.41
20000	1812.26	976.88	700.68	564.25	483.71	431.09	394.40	367.65	347.49	331.92	319.68	309.90
21000	1902.87	1025.72	735.71	592.47	507.90	452.65	414.12	386.03	364.86	348.52	335.66	325.40
22000	1993.48	1074.57	770.75	620.68	532.08	474.20	433.84	404.41	382.23	365.11	351.64	340.89
23000	2084.09	1123.41	805.78	648.89	556.27	495.76	453.56	422.79	399.61	381.71	367.63	356.39
24000	2174.71	1172.25	840.81	677.10	580.46	517.31	473.28	441.17	416.98	398.31	383.61	371.88
25000	2265.32	1221.10	875.85	705.32	604.64	538.87	493.00	459.56	434.36	414.90	399.60	387.37
26000	2355.93	1269.94	910.88	733.53	628.83	560.42	512.72	477.94	451.73	431.50	415.58	402.87
27000	2446.55	1318.79	945.92	761.74	653.01	581.97	532.44	496.32	469.10	448.09	431.56	418.36
28000	2537.16	1367.63	980.95	789.95	677.20	603.53	552.16	514.70	486.48	464.69	447.55	433.86
29000	2627.77	1416.47	1015.98	818.16	701.38	625.08	571.88	533.08	503.85	481.28	463.53	449.35
30000	2718.38	1465.32	1051.02	846.38	725.57	646.64	591.60	551.47	521.23	497.88	479.51	464.85
31000	2809.00	1514.16	1086.05	874.59	749.75	668.19	611.32	569.85	538.60	514.48	495.50	480.34
32000	2899.61	1563.00	1121.08	902.80	773.94	689.75	631.04	588.23	555.98	531.07	511.48	495.84
33000	2990.22	1611.85	1156.12	931.01	798.12	711.30	650.76	606.61	573.35	547.67	527.46	511.33
34000	3080.83	1660.69	1191.15	959.23	822.31	732.86	670.48	625.00	590.72	564.26	543.45	526.83
35000	3171.45	1709.54	1226.19	987.44	846.49	754.41	690.20	643.38	608.10	580.86	559.43	542.32
36000	3262.06	1758.38	1261.22	1015.65	870.68	775.96	709.92	661.76	625.47	597.46	575.41	557.82
37000	3352.67	1807.22	1296.25	1043.86	894.87	797.52	729.64	680.14	642.85	614.05	591.40	573.31
38000	3443.28	1856.07	1331.29	1072.08	919.05	819.07	749.36	698.52	660.22	630.65	607.38	588.81
39000	3533.90	1904.91	1366.32	1100.29	943.24	840.63	769.08	716.91	677.59	647.24	623.37	604.30
40000	3624.51	1953.75	1401.35	1128.50	967.42	862.18	788.80	735.29	694.97	663.84	639.35	619.80
41000	3715.12	2002.60	1436.39	1156.71	991.61	883.74	808.52	753.67	712.34	680.43	655.33	635.29
42000	3805.73	2051.44	1471.42	1184.93	1015.79	905.29	828.24	772.05	729.72	697.03	671.32	650.79
43000	3896.35	2100.29	1506.46	1213.14	1039.98	926.85	847.96	790.43	747.09	713.63	687.30	666.28
44000	3986.96	2149.13	1541.49	1241.35	1064.16	948.40	867.68	808.82	764.46	730.22	703.28	681.78
45000	4077.57	2197.97	1576.52	1269.56	1088.35	969.95	887.40	827.20	781.84	746.82	719.27	697.27
46000	4168.18	2246.82	1611.56	1297.78	1112.53	991.51	907.12	845.58	799.21	763.41	735.25	712.77
47000	4258.80	2295.66	1646.59	1325.99	1136.72	1013.06	926.84	863.96	816.59	780.01	751.23	728.26
48000	4349.41	2344.50	1681.62	1354.20	1160.91	1034.62	946.56	882.34	833.96	796.61	767.22	743.75
49000	4440.02	2393.35	1716.66	1382.41	1185.09	1056.17	966.28	900.73	851.33	813.20	783.20	759.25
50000	4530.63	2442.19	1751.69	1410.63	1209.28	1077.73	986.00	919.11	868.71	829.80	799.19	774.74
55000	4983.70	2686.41	1926.86	1551.69	1330.20	1185.50	1084.60	1011.02	955.58	912.78	879.10	852.22
60000	5436.76	2930.63	2102.03	1692.75	1451.13	1293.27	1183.20	1102.93	1042.45	995.76	959.02	929.69
65000	5889.82	3174.85	2277.20	1833.81	1572.06	1401.04	1281.80	1194.84	1129.32	1078.74	1038.94	1007.17
70000	6342.89	3419.07	2452.37	1974.87	1692.98	1508.82	1380.40	1286.75	1216.19	1161.71	1118.86	1084.64
75000	6795.95	3663.29	2627.53	2115.94	1813.91	1616.59	1479.00	1378.66	1303.06	1244.69	1198.78	1162.11
80000	7249.01	3907.50	2802.70	2257.00	1934.84	1724.36	1577.60	1470.57	1389.93	1327.67	1278.69	1239.59
85000	7702.08	4151.72	2977.87	2398.06	2055.77	1832.13	1676.20	1562.48	1476.80	1410.65	1358.61	1317.06
90000	8155.14	4395.94	3153.04	2539.12	2176.69	1939.90	1774.80	1654.39	1563.67	1493.63	1438.53	1394.54
95000	8608.20	4640.16	3328.21	2680.18	2297.62	2047.68	1873.40	1746.30	1650.54	1576.61	1518.45	1472.01
100000	9061.26	4884.38	3503.38	2821.25	2418.55	2155.45	1972.00	1838.21	1737.41	1659.59	1598.37	1549.48

Table 1

MONTHLY
PAYMENT REQUIRED TO AMORTIZE A LOAN

15.75%

TERM AMOUNT	13 YEARS	14 YEARS	15 YEARS	16 YEARS	17 YEARS	18 YEARS	19 YEARS	20 YEARS	25 YEARS	30 YEARS	35 YEARS	40 YEARS
50	.76	.74	.73	.72	.71	.70	.70	.69	.67	.67	.66	.66
100	1.51	1.48	1.46	1.43	1.42	1.40	1.39	1.38	1.34	1.33	1.32	1.32
200	3.02	2.96	2.91	2.86	2.83	2.80	2.77	2.75	2.68	2.65	2.64	2.64
300	4.53	4.44	4.36	4.29	4.24	4.19	4.15	4.12	4.02	3.98	3.96	3.95
400	6.04	5.92	5.81	5.72	5.65	5.59	5.54	5.50	5.36	5.30	5.28	5.27
500	7.55	7.39	7.26	7.15	7.06	6.98	6.92	6.87	6.70	6.63	6.60	6.58
600	9.06	8.87	8.71	8.58	8.47	8.38	8.30	8.24	8.04	7.95	7.91	7.90
700	10.57	10.35	10.16	10.01	9.88	9.78	9.69	9.61	9.38	9.28	9.23	9.21
800	12.08	11.83	11.62	11.44	11.29	11.17	11.07	10.99	10.72	10.60	10.55	10.53
900	13.59	13.31	13.07	12.87	12.71	12.57	12.45	12.36	12.06	11.93	11.87	11.84
1000	15.10	14.78	14.52	14.30	14.12	13.96	13.84	13.73	13.40	13.25	13.19	13.16
2000	30.20	29.56	29.03	28.59	28.23	27.92	27.67	27.46	26.79	26.50	26.37	26.31
3000	45.30	44.34	43.54	42.89	42.34	41.88	41.50	41.18	40.18	39.74	39.55	39.46
4000	60.40	59.12	58.06	57.18	56.45	55.84	55.34	54.91	53.58	52.99	52.73	52.61
5000	75.50	73.89	72.57	71.48	70.57	69.80	69.17	68.63	66.97	66.24	65.91	65.76
6000	90.60	88.67	87.08	85.77	84.68	83.76	83.00	82.36	80.36	79.48	79.09	78.91
7000	105.70	103.45	101.60	100.06	98.79	97.72	96.83	96.08	93.76	92.73	92.27	92.06
8000	120.80	118.23	116.11	114.36	112.90	111.68	110.67	109.81	107.15	105.97	105.45	105.21
9000	135.90	133.01	130.62	128.65	127.01	125.64	124.50	123.53	120.54	119.22	118.63	118.36
10000	151.00	147.78	145.14	142.95	141.13	139.60	138.33	137.26	133.93	132.47	131.81	131.51
11000	166.10	162.56	159.65	157.24	155.24	153.56	152.16	150.98	147.33	145.71	144.99	144.66
12000	181.20	177.34	174.16	171.53	169.35	167.52	166.00	164.71	160.72	158.96	158.17	157.81
13000	196.30	192.12	188.68	185.83	183.46	181.48	179.83	178.43	174.11	172.21	171.35	170.96
14000	211.40	206.89	203.19	200.12	197.57	195.44	193.66	192.16	187.51	185.45	184.53	184.11
15000	226.50	221.67	217.70	214.42	211.69	209.40	207.49	205.89	200.90	198.70	197.71	197.26
16000	241.60	236.45	232.21	228.71	225.80	223.36	221.33	219.61	214.29	211.94	210.89	210.41
17000	256.70	251.23	246.73	243.00	239.91	237.32	235.16	233.34	227.68	225.19	224.07	223.56
18000	271.80	266.01	261.24	257.30	254.02	251.28	248.99	247.06	241.08	238.44	237.25	236.71
19000	286.90	280.78	275.75	271.59	268.13	265.24	262.82	260.79	254.47	251.68	250.43	249.86
20000	302.00	295.56	290.27	285.89	282.25	279.20	276.66	274.51	267.86	264.93	263.61	263.01
21000	317.10	310.34	304.78	300.18	296.36	293.16	290.49	288.24	281.26	278.17	276.79	276.16
22000	332.20	325.12	319.29	314.48	310.47	307.12	304.32	301.96	294.65	291.42	289.97	289.31
23000	347.30	339.89	333.81	328.77	324.58	321.08	318.15	315.69	308.04	304.67	303.15	302.46
24000	362.40	354.67	348.32	343.06	338.69	335.04	331.99	329.41	321.43	317.91	316.33	315.61
25000	377.50	369.45	362.83	357.36	352.81	349.00	345.82	343.14	334.83	331.16	329.51	328.76
26000	392.60	384.23	377.35	371.65	366.92	362.96	359.65	356.86	348.22	344.41	342.69	341.91
27000	407.70	399.01	391.86	385.95	381.03	376.92	373.48	370.59	361.61	357.65	355.87	355.06
28000	422.80	413.78	406.37	400.24	395.14	390.88	387.32	384.31	375.01	370.90	369.05	368.21
29000	437.90	428.56	420.88	414.53	409.25	404.84	401.15	398.04	388.40	384.14	382.23	381.36
30000	453.00	443.34	435.40	428.83	423.37	418.80	414.98	411.77	401.79	397.39	395.41	394.51
31000	468.10	458.12	449.91	443.12	437.48	432.76	428.81	425.49	415.18	410.64	408.59	407.66
32000	483.20	472.89	464.42	457.42	451.59	446.72	442.65	439.22	428.58	423.88	421.77	420.81
33000	498.30	487.67	478.94	471.71	465.70	460.68	456.48	452.94	441.97	437.13	434.95	433.96
34000	513.40	502.45	493.45	486.00	479.81	474.64	470.31	466.67	455.36	450.37	448.13	447.11
35000	528.50	517.23	507.96	500.30	493.93	488.60	484.14	480.39	468.76	463.62	461.31	460.26
36000	543.60	532.01	522.48	514.59	508.04	502.56	497.98	494.12	482.15	476.87	474.49	473.41
37000	558.70	546.78	536.99	528.89	522.15	516.52	511.81	507.84	495.54	490.11	487.67	486.56
38000	573.80	561.56	551.50	543.18	536.26	530.48	525.64	521.57	508.94	503.36	500.85	499.71
39000	588.90	576.34	566.02	557.48	550.37	544.44	539.47	535.29	522.33	516.61	514.03	512.86
40000	604.00	591.12	580.53	571.77	564.49	558.40	553.31	549.02	535.72	529.85	527.21	526.01
41000	619.10	605.89	595.04	586.06	578.60	572.36	567.14	562.74	549.11	543.10	540.39	539.16
42000	634.20	620.67	609.55	600.36	592.71	586.32	580.97	576.47	562.51	556.34	553.57	552.31
43000	649.30	635.45	624.07	614.65	606.82	600.28	594.80	590.19	575.90	569.59	566.75	565.46
44000	664.40	650.23	638.58	628.95	620.93	614.24	608.64	603.92	589.29	582.84	579.93	578.61
45000	679.50	665.01	653.09	643.24	635.05	628.20	622.47	617.65	602.69	596.08	593.11	591.76
46000	694.60	679.78	667.61	657.53	649.16	642.16	636.30	631.37	616.08	609.33	606.29	604.91
47000	709.70	694.56	682.12	671.83	663.27	656.12	650.13	645.10	629.47	622.58	619.47	618.06
48000	724.80	709.34	696.63	686.12	677.38	670.08	663.97	658.82	642.86	635.82	632.65	631.21
49000	739.90	724.12	711.15	700.42	691.49	684.04	677.80	672.55	656.26	649.07	645.83	644.36
50000	755.00	738.90	725.66	714.71	705.61	698.00	691.63	686.27	669.65	662.31	659.01	657.51
55000	830.50	812.78	798.22	786.18	776.17	767.80	760.79	754.90	736.61	728.54	724.91	723.26
60000	906.00	886.67	870.79	857.65	846.73	837.60	829.96	823.53	803.58	794.78	790.81	789.01
65000	981.50	960.56	943.36	929.12	917.29	907.40	899.12	892.15	870.54	861.01	856.71	854.77
70000	1057.00	1034.45	1015.92	1000.59	987.85	977.20	968.28	960.78	937.51	927.24	922.62	920.52
75000	1132.50	1108.34	1088.49	1072.06	1058.41	1047.00	1037.44	1029.41	1004.47	993.47	988.52	986.27
80000	1208.00	1182.23	1161.05	1143.53	1128.97	1116.80	1106.61	1098.03	1071.44	1059.70	1054.42	1052.02
85000	1283.49	1256.12	1233.62	1215.00	1199.53	1186.60	1175.77	1166.66	1138.40	1125.93	1120.32	1117.77
90000	1358.99	1330.01	1306.18	1286.47	1270.09	1256.40	1244.93	1235.29	1205.37	1192.16	1186.23	1183.52
95000	1434.49	1403.90	1378.75	1357.95	1340.65	1326.20	1314.09	1303.91	1272.33	1258.39	1252.12	1249.27
100000	1509.99	1477.79	1451.31	1429.42	1411.21	1396.00	1383.26	1372.54	1339.29	1324.62	1318.02	1315.02

15%

89

Table 1

16.00%

MONTHLY
PAYMENT REQUIRED TO AMORTIZE A LOAN

TERM AMOUNT	1 YEAR	2 YEARS	3 YEARS	4 YEARS	5 YEARS	6 YEARS	7 YEARS	8 YEARS	9 YEARS	10 YEARS	11 YEARS	12 YEARS
50	4.54	2.45	1.76	1.42	1.22	1.09	1.00	.93	.88	.84	.81	.79
100	9.08	4.90	3.52	2.84	2.44	2.17	1.99	1.86	1.76	1.68	1.62	1.57
200	18.15	9.80	7.04	5.67	4.87	4.34	3.98	3.71	3.51	3.36	3.23	3.14
300	27.22	14.69	10.55	8.51	7.30	6.51	5.96	5.56	5.26	5.03	4.85	4.70
400	36.30	19.59	14.07	11.34	9.73	8.68	7.95	7.42	7.02	6.71	6.46	6.27
500	45.37	24.49	17.58	14.18	12.16	10.85	9.94	9.27	8.77	8.38	8.08	7.83
600	54.44	29.38	21.10	17.01	14.60	13.02	11.92	11.12	10.52	10.06	9.69	9.40
700	63.52	34.28	24.61	19.84	17.03	15.19	13.91	12.98	12.27	11.73	11.31	10.97
800	72.59	39.18	28.13	22.68	19.46	17.36	15.89	14.83	14.03	13.41	12.92	12.53
900	81.66	44.07	31.65	25.51	21.89	19.53	17.88	16.68	15.78	15.08	14.53	14.10
1000	90.74	48.97	35.16	28.35	24.32	21.70	19.87	18.53	17.53	16.76	16.15	15.66
2000	181.47	97.93	70.32	56.69	48.64	43.39	39.73	37.06	35.06	33.51	32.29	31.32
3000	272.20	146.89	105.48	85.03	72.96	65.08	59.59	55.59	52.58	50.26	48.43	46.98
4000	362.93	195.86	140.63	113.37	97.28	86.77	79.45	74.12	70.11	67.01	64.58	62.64
5000	453.66	244.82	175.79	141.71	121.60	108.46	99.32	92.65	87.63	83.76	80.72	78.30
6000	544.39	293.78	210.95	170.05	145.91	130.16	119.18	111.18	105.16	100.51	96.86	93.95
7000	635.12	342.75	246.10	198.39	170.23	151.85	139.04	129.71	122.68	117.26	113.01	109.61
8000	725.85	391.71	281.26	226.73	194.55	173.54	158.90	148.24	140.21	134.02	129.15	125.27
9000	816.58	440.67	316.42	255.07	218.87	195.23	178.76	166.76	157.73	150.77	145.29	140.93
10000	907.31	489.64	351.58	283.41	243.19	216.92	198.63	185.29	175.26	167.52	161.44	156.59
11000	998.04	538.60	386.73	311.75	267.50	238.62	218.49	203.82	192.78	184.27	177.58	172.25
12000	1088.78	587.56	421.89	340.09	291.82	260.31	238.35	222.35	210.31	201.02	193.72	187.90
13000	1179.51	636.53	457.05	368.43	316.14	282.00	258.21	240.88	227.83	217.77	209.87	203.56
14000	1270.24	685.49	492.20	396.77	340.46	303.69	278.07	259.41	245.36	234.52	226.01	219.22
15000	1360.97	734.45	527.36	425.11	364.78	325.38	297.94	277.94	262.88	251.27	242.15	234.88
16000	1451.70	783.41	562.52	453.45	389.09	347.07	317.80	296.47	280.41	268.03	258.30	250.54
17000	1542.43	832.38	597.67	481.79	413.41	368.77	337.66	314.99	297.93	284.78	274.44	266.20
18000	1633.16	881.34	632.83	510.13	437.73	390.46	357.52	333.52	315.46	301.53	290.58	281.85
19000	1723.89	930.30	667.99	538.47	462.05	412.15	377.38	352.05	332.98	318.28	306.73	297.51
20000	1814.62	979.27	703.15	566.81	486.37	433.84	397.25	370.58	350.51	335.03	322.87	313.17
21000	1905.35	1028.23	738.30	595.15	510.68	455.53	417.11	389.11	368.03	351.78	339.01	328.83
22000	1996.08	1077.19	773.46	623.49	535.00	477.23	436.97	407.64	385.56	368.53	355.15	344.49
23000	2086.81	1126.16	808.62	651.83	559.32	498.92	456.83	426.17	403.09	385.29	371.30	360.14
24000	2177.55	1175.12	843.77	680.17	583.64	520.61	476.69	444.70	420.61	402.04	387.44	375.80
25000	2268.28	1224.08	878.93	708.51	607.96	542.30	496.56	463.22	438.14	418.79	403.58	391.46
26000	2359.01	1273.05	914.09	736.85	632.27	563.99	516.42	481.75	455.66	435.54	419.73	407.12
27000	2449.74	1322.01	949.24	765.19	656.59	585.68	536.28	500.28	473.19	452.29	435.87	422.78
28000	2540.47	1370.97	984.40	793.53	680.91	607.38	556.14	518.81	490.71	469.04	452.01	438.44
29000	2631.20	1419.94	1019.56	821.87	705.23	629.07	576.00	537.34	508.24	485.79	468.16	454.09
30000	2721.93	1468.90	1054.72	850.21	729.55	650.76	595.87	555.87	525.76	502.54	484.30	469.75
31000	2812.66	1517.86	1089.87	878.55	753.86	672.45	615.73	574.40	543.29	519.30	500.44	485.41
32000	2903.39	1566.82	1125.03	906.89	778.18	694.14	635.59	592.93	560.81	536.05	516.59	501.07
33000	2994.12	1615.79	1160.19	935.23	802.50	715.84	655.45	611.45	578.34	552.80	532.73	516.73
34000	3084.85	1664.75	1195.34	963.57	826.82	737.53	675.32	629.98	595.86	569.55	548.87	532.39
35000	3175.59	1713.71	1230.50	991.91	851.14	759.22	695.18	648.51	613.39	586.30	565.02	548.04
36000	3266.32	1762.68	1265.66	1020.26	875.46	780.91	715.04	667.04	630.91	603.05	581.16	563.70
37000	3357.05	1811.64	1300.82	1048.60	899.77	802.60	734.90	685.57	648.44	619.80	597.30	579.36
38000	3447.78	1860.60	1335.97	1076.94	924.09	824.29	754.76	704.10	665.96	636.55	613.45	595.02
39000	3538.51	1909.57	1371.13	1105.28	948.41	845.99	774.63	722.63	683.49	653.31	629.59	610.68
40000	3629.24	1958.53	1406.29	1133.62	972.73	867.68	794.49	741.16	701.02	670.06	645.73	626.34
41000	3719.97	2007.49	1441.44	1161.96	997.05	889.37	814.35	759.69	718.54	686.81	661.88	641.99
42000	3810.70	2056.46	1476.60	1190.30	1021.36	911.06	834.21	778.21	736.07	703.56	678.02	657.65
43000	3901.43	2105.42	1511.76	1218.64	1045.68	932.75	854.07	796.74	753.59	720.31	694.16	673.31
44000	3992.16	2154.38	1546.91	1246.98	1070.00	954.45	873.94	815.27	771.12	737.06	710.30	688.97
45000	4082.89	2203.35	1582.07	1275.32	1094.32	976.14	893.80	833.80	788.64	753.81	726.45	704.63
46000	4173.62	2252.31	1617.23	1303.66	1118.64	997.83	913.66	852.33	806.17	770.57	742.59	720.28
47000	4264.36	2301.27	1652.39	1332.00	1142.95	1019.52	933.52	870.86	823.69	787.32	758.73	735.94
48000	4355.09	2350.23	1687.54	1360.34	1167.27	1041.21	953.38	889.39	841.22	804.07	774.88	751.60
49000	4445.82	2399.20	1722.70	1388.68	1191.59	1062.91	973.25	907.92	858.74	820.82	791.02	767.26
50000	4536.55	2448.16	1757.86	1417.02	1215.91	1084.60	993.11	926.44	876.27	837.57	807.16	782.92
55000	4990.20	2692.98	1933.64	1558.72	1337.50	1193.06	1092.42	1019.09	963.89	921.33	887.88	861.21
60000	5443.86	2937.79	2109.43	1700.42	1459.09	1301.52	1191.73	1111.73	1051.52	1005.08	968.60	939.50
65000	5897.51	3182.61	2285.21	1842.12	1580.68	1409.97	1291.04	1204.38	1139.15	1088.84	1049.31	1017.79
70000	6351.17	3427.42	2461.00	1983.82	1702.27	1518.43	1390.35	1297.02	1226.77	1172.60	1130.03	1096.08
75000	6804.82	3672.24	2636.78	2125.53	1823.86	1626.89	1489.66	1389.66	1314.40	1256.35	1210.74	1174.37
80000	7258.47	3917.05	2812.57	2267.23	1945.45	1735.35	1588.97	1482.31	1402.03	1340.11	1291.46	1252.67
85000	7712.13	4161.87	2988.35	2408.93	2067.04	1843.81	1688.28	1574.95	1489.65	1423.87	1372.17	1330.96
90000	8165.78	4406.68	3164.14	2550.63	2188.63	1952.27	1787.59	1667.60	1577.28	1507.62	1452.89	1409.25
95000	8619.44	4651.50	3339.92	2692.33	2310.22	2060.73	1886.90	1760.24	1664.90	1591.38	1533.61	1487.54
100000	9073.09	4896.32	3515.71	2834.03	2431.81	2169.19	1986.21	1852.88	1752.53	1675.14	1614.32	1565.83

16%

90

Table 1

MONTHLY 16.00%

PAYMENT REQUIRED TO AMORTIZE A LOAN

TERM AMOUNT	13 YEARS	14 YEARS	15 YEARS	16 YEARS	17 YEARS	18 YEARS	19 YEARS	20 YEARS	25 YEARS	30 YEARS	35 YEARS	40 YEARS
50	.77	.75	.74	.73	.72	.71	.71	.70	.68	.68	.67	.67
100	1.53	1.50	1.47	1.45	1.43	1.42	1.41	1.40	1.36	1.35	1.34	1.34
200	3.06	2.99	2.94	2.90	2.86	2.83	2.81	2.79	2.72	2.69	2.68	2.68
300	4.59	4.49	4.41	4.35	4.29	4.25	4.21	4.18	4.08	4.04	4.02	4.01
400	6.11	5.98	5.88	5.79	5.72	5.66	5.61	5.57	5.44	5.38	5.36	5.35
500	7.64	7.48	7.35	7.24	7.15	7.08	7.01	6.96	6.80	6.73	6.70	6.68
600	9.17	8.97	8.82	8.69	8.58	8.49	8.42	8.35	8.16	8.07	8.04	8.02
700	10.69	10.47	10.29	10.13	10.01	9.90	9.82	9.74	9.52	9.42	9.37	9.35
800	12.22	11.96	11.75	11.58	11.44	11.32	11.22	11.14	10.88	10.76	10.71	10.69
900	13.75	13.46	13.22	13.03	12.87	12.73	12.62	12.53	12.24	12.11	12.05	12.03
1000	15.27	14.95	14.69	14.48	14.30	14.15	14.02	13.92	13.59	13.45	13.39	13.36
2000	30.54	29.90	29.38	28.95	28.59	28.29	28.04	27.83	27.18	26.90	26.77	26.72
3000	45.81	44.85	44.07	43.42	42.88	42.43	42.06	41.74	40.77	40.35	40.16	40.07
4000	61.07	59.80	58.75	57.89	57.17	56.57	56.07	55.66	54.36	53.80	53.54	53.43
5000	76.34	74.75	73.44	72.36	71.46	70.72	70.09	69.57	67.95	67.24	66.93	66.79
6000	91.61	89.70	88.13	86.83	85.76	84.86	84.11	83.48	81.54	80.69	80.31	80.14
7000	106.87	104.64	102.81	101.30	100.05	99.00	98.13	97.39	95.13	94.14	93.70	93.50
8000	122.14	119.59	117.50	115.77	114.34	113.14	112.14	111.31	108.72	107.59	107.08	106.86
9000	137.41	134.54	132.19	130.24	128.63	127.29	126.16	125.22	122.30	121.03	120.47	120.21
10000	152.68	149.49	146.88	144.72	142.92	141.43	140.18	139.13	135.89	134.48	133.85	133.57
11000	167.94	164.44	161.56	159.19	157.22	155.57	154.20	153.04	149.48	147.93	147.24	146.93
12000	183.21	179.39	176.25	173.66	171.51	169.71	168.21	166.96	163.07	161.38	160.62	160.28
13000	198.48	194.33	190.94	188.13	185.80	183.86	182.23	180.87	176.66	174.82	174.01	173.64
14000	213.74	209.28	205.62	202.60	200.09	198.00	196.25	194.78	190.25	188.27	187.39	187.00
15000	229.01	224.23	220.31	217.07	214.38	212.14	210.27	208.69	203.84	201.72	200.78	200.35
16000	244.28	239.18	235.00	231.54	228.68	226.28	224.28	222.61	217.43	215.17	214.16	213.71
17000	259.54	254.13	249.68	246.01	242.97	240.43	238.30	236.52	231.02	228.61	227.54	227.07
18000	274.81	269.08	264.37	260.48	257.26	254.57	252.32	250.43	244.61	242.06	240.93	240.42
19000	290.08	284.03	279.06	274.96	271.55	268.71	266.34	264.34	258.19	255.51	254.31	253.78
20000	305.35	298.97	293.75	289.43	285.84	282.85	280.35	278.26	271.78	268.96	267.70	267.13
21000	320.61	313.92	308.43	303.90	300.13	297.00	294.37	292.17	285.37	282.40	281.08	280.49
22000	335.88	328.87	323.12	318.37	314.42	311.14	308.39	306.08	298.96	295.85	294.47	293.85
23000	351.15	343.82	337.81	332.84	328.72	325.28	322.41	319.99	312.55	309.30	307.85	307.20
24000	366.41	358.77	352.49	347.31	343.01	339.42	336.42	333.91	326.14	322.75	321.24	320.56
25000	381.68	373.72	367.18	361.78	357.30	353.57	350.44	347.82	339.73	336.19	334.62	333.92
26000	396.95	388.66	381.87	376.25	371.59	367.71	364.46	361.73	353.32	349.64	348.01	347.27
27000	412.22	403.61	396.55	390.72	385.89	381.85	378.48	375.64	366.91	363.09	361.39	360.63
28000	427.48	418.56	411.24	405.20	400.18	395.99	392.49	389.56	380.49	376.54	374.78	373.99
29000	442.75	433.51	425.93	419.67	414.47	410.14	406.51	403.47	394.08	389.98	388.16	387.34
30000	458.02	448.46	440.62	434.14	428.76	424.28	420.53	417.38	407.67	403.43	401.55	400.70
31000	473.28	463.41	455.30	448.61	443.05	438.42	434.55	431.29	421.26	416.88	414.93	414.06
32000	488.55	478.36	469.99	463.08	457.35	452.56	448.56	445.21	434.85	430.33	428.32	427.41
33000	503.82	493.30	484.68	477.55	471.64	466.71	462.58	459.12	448.44	443.77	441.70	440.77
34000	519.08	508.25	499.36	492.02	485.93	480.85	476.60	473.03	462.03	457.22	455.08	454.13
35000	534.35	523.20	514.05	506.49	500.22	494.99	490.62	486.94	475.62	470.67	468.47	467.48
36000	549.62	538.15	528.74	520.96	514.51	509.13	504.63	500.86	489.21	484.12	481.85	480.84
37000	564.89	553.10	543.42	535.44	528.80	523.28	518.65	514.77	502.79	497.57	495.24	494.19
38000	580.15	568.05	558.11	549.91	543.10	537.42	532.67	528.68	516.38	511.01	508.62	507.55
39000	595.42	582.99	572.80	564.38	557.39	551.56	546.69	542.59	529.97	524.46	522.01	520.91
40000	610.69	597.94	587.49	578.85	571.68	565.70	560.70	556.51	543.56	537.91	535.39	534.26
41000	625.95	612.89	602.17	593.32	585.97	579.85	574.72	570.42	557.15	551.36	548.78	547.62
42000	641.22	627.84	616.86	607.79	600.26	593.99	588.74	584.33	570.74	564.80	562.16	560.98
43000	656.49	642.79	631.55	622.26	614.56	608.13	602.76	598.25	584.33	578.25	575.55	574.33
44000	671.75	657.74	646.23	636.73	628.85	622.27	616.77	612.16	597.92	591.70	588.93	587.69
45000	687.02	672.69	660.92	651.20	643.14	636.42	630.79	626.07	611.51	605.15	602.32	601.05
46000	702.29	687.63	675.61	665.68	657.43	650.56	644.81	639.98	625.09	618.59	615.70	614.40
47000	717.56	702.58	690.29	680.15	671.72	664.70	658.83	653.90	638.68	632.04	629.09	627.76
48000	732.82	717.53	704.98	694.62	686.02	678.84	672.84	667.81	652.27	645.49	642.47	641.12
49000	748.09	732.48	719.67	709.09	700.31	692.99	686.86	681.72	665.86	658.94	655.86	654.47
50000	763.36	747.43	734.36	723.56	714.60	707.13	700.88	695.63	679.45	672.38	669.24	667.83
55000	839.69	822.17	807.79	795.92	786.06	777.84	770.97	765.20	747.39	739.62	736.16	734.61
60000	916.03	896.91	881.23	868.27	857.52	848.55	841.05	834.76	815.34	806.86	803.09	801.39
65000	992.36	971.65	954.66	940.63	928.98	919.27	911.14	904.32	883.28	874.10	870.01	868.18
70000	1068.70	1046.40	1028.10	1012.98	1000.44	989.98	981.23	973.88	951.23	941.33	936.93	934.96
75000	1145.03	1121.14	1101.53	1085.34	1071.90	1060.69	1051.31	1043.45	1019.17	1008.57	1003.86	1001.74
80000	1221.37	1195.88	1174.97	1157.69	1143.36	1131.40	1121.40	1113.01	1087.12	1075.81	1070.78	1068.52
85000	1297.70	1270.62	1248.40	1230.05	1214.82	1202.12	1191.49	1182.57	1155.06	1143.05	1137.70	1135.31
90000	1374.04	1345.37	1321.84	1302.40	1286.27	1272.83	1261.58	1252.14	1223.01	1210.29	1204.63	1202.09
95000	1450.37	1420.11	1395.27	1374.76	1357.73	1343.54	1331.66	1321.70	1290.95	1277.52	1271.55	1268.87
100000	1526.71	1494.85	1468.71	1447.12	1429.19	1414.25	1401.75	1391.26	1358.89	1344.76	1338.47	1335.65

16%

Table 1

16.25% MONTHLY
PAYMENT REQUIRED TO AMORTIZE A LOAN

16%

TERM / AMOUNT	1 YEAR	2 YEARS	3 YEARS	4 YEARS	5 YEARS	6 YEARS	7 YEARS	8 YEARS	9 YEARS	10 YEARS	11 YEARS	12 YEARS
50	4.55	2.46	1.77	1.43	1.23	1.10	1.01	.94	.89	.85	.82	.80
100	9.09	4.91	3.53	2.85	2.45	2.19	2.01	1.87	1.77	1.70	1.64	1.59
200	18.17	9.82	7.06	5.70	4.90	4.37	4.01	3.74	3.54	3.39	3.27	3.17
300	27.26	14.73	10.59	8.55	7.34	6.55	6.01	5.61	5.31	5.08	4.90	4.75
400	36.34	19.64	14.12	11.39	9.79	8.74	8.01	7.48	7.08	6.77	6.53	6.33
500	45.43	24.55	17.65	14.24	12.23	10.92	10.01	9.34	8.84	8.46	8.16	7.92
600	54.51	29.45	21.17	17.09	14.68	13.10	12.01	11.21	10.61	10.15	9.79	9.50
700	63.60	34.36	24.70	19.93	17.12	15.29	14.01	13.08	12.38	11.84	11.42	11.08
800	72.68	39.27	28.23	22.78	19.57	17.47	16.01	14.95	14.15	13.53	13.05	12.66
900	81.77	44.18	31.76	25.63	22.01	19.65	18.01	16.81	15.91	15.22	14.68	14.25
1000	90.85	49.09	35.29	28.47	24.46	21.83	20.01	18.68	17.68	16.91	16.31	15.83
2000	181.70	98.17	70.57	56.94	48.91	43.66	40.01	37.36	35.36	33.82	32.61	31.65
3000	272.55	147.25	105.85	85.41	73.36	65.49	60.02	56.03	53.04	50.73	48.92	47.47
4000	363.40	196.34	141.13	113.88	97.81	87.32	80.02	74.71	70.71	67.63	65.22	63.29
5000	454.25	245.42	176.41	142.35	122.26	109.15	100.03	93.39	88.39	84.54	81.52	79.12
6000	545.10	294.50	211.69	170.82	146.71	130.98	120.03	112.06	106.07	101.45	97.83	94.94
7000	635.95	343.58	246.97	199.28	171.16	152.81	140.04	130.74	123.74	118.36	114.13	110.76
8000	726.80	392.67	282.25	227.75	195.61	174.64	160.04	149.41	141.42	135.26	130.43	126.58
9000	817.65	441.75	317.53	256.22	220.06	196.47	180.05	168.09	159.10	152.17	146.74	142.41
10000	908.50	490.83	352.81	284.69	244.52	218.30	200.05	186.77	176.78	169.08	163.04	158.23
11000	999.35	539.91	388.09	313.16	268.97	240.13	220.06	205.44	194.45	185.99	179.34	174.05
12000	1090.20	589.00	423.37	341.63	293.42	261.96	240.06	224.12	212.13	202.89	195.65	189.87
13000	1181.04	638.08	458.65	370.10	317.87	283.79	260.07	242.79	229.81	219.80	211.95	205.70
14000	1271.89	687.16	493.93	398.56	342.32	305.62	280.07	261.47	247.48	236.71	228.25	221.52
15000	1362.74	736.24	529.21	427.03	366.77	327.45	300.08	280.15	265.16	253.62	244.56	237.34
16000	1453.59	785.33	564.49	455.50	391.22	349.28	320.08	298.82	282.84	270.52	260.86	253.16
17000	1544.44	834.41	599.77	483.97	415.67	371.11	340.09	317.50	300.51	287.43	277.16	268.99
18000	1635.29	883.49	635.06	512.44	440.12	392.94	360.09	336.17	318.19	304.34	293.47	284.81
19000	1726.14	932.58	670.34	540.91	464.58	414.77	380.09	354.85	335.87	321.25	309.77	300.63
20000	1816.99	981.66	705.62	569.37	489.03	436.60	400.10	373.53	353.55	338.15	326.07	316.45
21000	1907.84	1030.74	740.90	597.84	513.48	458.43	420.10	392.20	371.22	355.06	342.38	332.28
22000	1998.69	1079.82	776.18	626.31	537.93	480.26	440.11	410.88	388.90	371.97	358.68	348.10
23000	2089.54	1128.91	811.46	654.78	562.38	502.09	460.11	429.56	406.58	388.88	374.98	363.92
24000	2180.39	1177.99	846.74	683.25	586.83	523.92	480.12	448.23	424.25	405.78	391.29	379.74
25000	2271.24	1227.07	882.02	711.72	611.28	545.75	500.12	466.91	441.93	422.69	407.59	395.57
26000	2362.08	1276.15	917.30	740.19	635.73	567.58	520.13	485.58	459.61	439.60	423.89	411.39
27000	2452.93	1325.24	952.58	768.65	660.18	589.41	540.13	504.26	477.29	456.51	440.20	427.21
28000	2543.78	1374.32	987.86	797.12	684.64	611.24	560.14	522.94	494.96	473.41	456.50	443.03
29000	2634.63	1423.40	1023.14	825.59	709.09	633.07	580.14	541.61	512.64	490.32	472.80	458.86
30000	2725.48	1472.48	1058.42	854.06	733.54	654.90	600.15	560.29	530.32	507.23	489.11	474.68
31000	2816.33	1521.57	1093.70	882.53	757.99	676.73	620.15	578.96	547.99	524.14	505.41	490.50
32000	2907.18	1570.65	1128.98	911.00	782.44	698.56	640.16	597.64	565.67	541.04	521.71	506.32
33000	2998.03	1619.73	1164.26	939.46	806.89	720.39	660.16	616.32	583.35	557.95	538.02	522.15
34000	3088.88	1668.82	1199.54	967.93	831.34	742.22	680.17	634.99	601.02	574.86	554.32	537.97
35000	3179.73	1717.90	1234.83	996.40	855.79	764.05	700.17	653.67	618.70	591.77	570.63	553.79
36000	3270.58	1766.98	1270.11	1024.87	880.24	785.87	720.17	672.34	636.38	608.67	586.93	569.61
37000	3361.43	1816.06	1305.39	1053.34	904.70	807.70	740.18	691.02	654.06	625.58	603.23	585.44
38000	3452.27	1865.15	1340.67	1081.81	929.15	829.53	760.18	709.70	671.73	642.49	619.54	601.26
39000	3543.12	1914.23	1375.95	1110.28	953.60	851.36	780.19	728.37	689.41	659.40	635.84	617.08
40000	3633.97	1963.31	1411.23	1138.74	978.05	873.19	800.19	747.05	707.09	676.30	652.14	632.90
41000	3724.82	2012.39	1446.51	1167.21	1002.50	895.02	820.20	765.72	724.76	693.21	668.45	648.73
42000	3815.67	2061.48	1481.79	1195.68	1026.95	916.85	840.20	784.40	742.44	710.12	684.75	664.55
43000	3906.52	2110.56	1517.07	1224.15	1051.40	938.68	860.21	803.08	760.12	727.02	701.05	680.37
44000	3997.37	2159.64	1552.35	1252.62	1075.85	960.51	880.21	821.75	777.80	743.93	717.36	696.19
45000	4088.22	2208.72	1587.63	1281.09	1100.30	982.34	900.22	840.43	795.47	760.84	733.66	712.01
46000	4179.07	2257.81	1622.91	1309.56	1124.76	1004.17	920.22	859.11	813.15	777.75	749.96	727.84
47000	4269.92	2306.89	1658.19	1338.02	1149.21	1026.00	940.23	877.78	830.83	794.65	766.27	743.66
48000	4360.77	2355.97	1693.47	1366.49	1173.66	1047.83	960.23	896.46	848.50	811.56	782.57	759.48
49000	4451.62	2405.05	1728.75	1394.96	1198.11	1069.66	980.24	915.13	866.18	828.47	798.87	775.30
50000	4542.47	2454.14	1764.03	1423.43	1222.56	1091.49	1000.24	933.81	883.86	845.38	815.18	791.13
55000	4996.71	2699.55	1940.44	1565.77	1344.81	1200.64	1100.26	1027.19	972.24	929.91	896.69	870.24
60000	5450.96	2944.96	2116.84	1708.11	1467.07	1309.79	1200.29	1120.57	1060.63	1014.45	978.21	949.35
65000	5905.20	3190.38	2293.24	1850.46	1589.33	1418.94	1300.31	1213.95	1149.01	1098.99	1059.73	1028.46
70000	6359.45	3435.79	2469.65	1992.80	1711.58	1528.09	1400.34	1307.33	1237.40	1183.53	1141.25	1107.58
75000	6813.70	3681.20	2646.05	2135.14	1833.84	1637.23	1500.36	1400.71	1325.78	1268.06	1222.76	1186.69
80000	7267.94	3926.62	2822.45	2277.48	1956.09	1746.38	1600.38	1494.09	1414.17	1352.60	1304.28	1265.80
85000	7722.19	4172.03	2998.85	2419.83	2078.35	1855.53	1700.41	1587.47	1502.55	1437.14	1385.80	1344.91
90000	8176.43	4417.44	3175.26	2562.17	2200.60	1964.68	1800.43	1680.85	1590.94	1521.67	1467.31	1424.02
95000	8630.68	4662.86	3351.66	2704.51	2322.86	2073.83	1900.45	1774.23	1679.33	1606.21	1548.83	1503.14
100000	9084.93	4908.27	3528.06	2846.85	2445.11	2182.98	2000.48	1867.61	1767.71	1690.75	1630.35	1582.25

Table 1

MONTHLY
PAYMENT REQUIRED TO AMORTIZE A LOAN

16.25%

ERM / UNT	13 YEARS	14 YEARS	15 YEARS	16 YEARS	17 YEARS	18 YEARS	19 YEARS	20 YEARS	25 YEARS	30 YEARS	35 YEARS	40 YEARS
50	.78	.76	.75	.74	.73	.72	.72	.71	.69	.69	.68	.68
100	1.55	1.52	1.49	1.47	1.45	1.44	1.43	1.42	1.38	1.37	1.36	1.36
200	3.09	3.03	2.98	2.93	2.90	2.87	2.85	2.83	2.76	2.73	2.72	2.72
300	4.64	4.54	4.46	4.40	4.35	4.30	4.27	4.24	4.14	4.10	4.08	4.07
400	6.18	6.05	5.95	5.86	5.79	5.74	5.69	5.65	5.52	5.46	5.44	5.43
500	7.72	7.56	7.44	7.33	7.24	7.17	7.11	7.06	6.90	6.83	6.80	6.79
600	9.27	9.08	8.92	8.79	8.69	8.60	8.53	8.47	8.28	8.19	8.16	8.14
700	10.81	10.59	10.41	10.26	10.14	10.03	9.95	9.88	9.65	9.56	9.52	9.50
800	12.35	12.10	11.89	11.72	11.58	11.47	11.37	11.29	11.03	10.92	10.88	10.86
900	13.90	13.61	13.38	13.19	13.03	12.90	12.79	12.70	12.41	12.29	12.24	12.21
1000	15.44	15.12	14.87	14.65	14.48	14.33	14.21	14.11	13.79	13.65	13.59	13.57
2000	30.87	30.24	29.73	29.30	28.95	28.66	28.41	28.21	27.58	27.30	27.18	27.13
3000	46.31	45.36	44.59	43.95	43.42	42.98	42.61	42.31	41.36	40.95	40.77	40.69
4000	61.74	60.48	59.45	58.60	57.89	57.31	56.82	56.41	55.15	54.60	54.36	54.26
5000	77.18	75.60	74.31	73.25	72.37	71.63	71.02	70.51	68.93	68.25	67.95	67.82
6000	92.61	90.72	89.18	87.90	86.84	85.96	85.22	84.61	82.72	81.90	81.54	81.38
7000	108.05	105.84	104.04	102.55	101.31	100.28	99.43	98.71	96.50	95.55	95.13	94.95
8000	123.48	120.96	118.90	117.20	115.78	114.61	113.63	112.81	110.29	109.20	108.72	108.51
9000	138.92	136.08	133.76	131.84	130.26	128.94	127.83	126.91	124.07	122.85	122.31	122.07
10000	154.35	151.20	148.62	146.49	144.73	143.26	142.04	141.01	137.86	136.50	135.90	135.63
11000	169.79	166.32	163.48	161.14	159.20	157.59	156.24	155.11	151.64	150.15	149.49	149.20
12000	185.22	181.44	178.35	175.79	173.67	171.91	170.44	169.21	165.43	163.80	163.08	162.76
13000	200.66	196.56	193.21	190.44	188.15	186.24	184.65	183.31	179.22	177.45	176.67	176.32
14000	216.09	211.68	208.07	205.09	202.62	200.56	198.85	197.41	193.00	191.10	190.26	189.89
15000	231.53	226.80	222.93	219.74	217.09	214.89	213.05	211.51	206.79	204.75	203.85	203.45
16000	246.96	241.92	237.79	234.39	231.56	229.22	227.25	225.61	220.57	218.39	217.44	217.01
17000	262.40	257.04	252.65	249.04	246.04	243.54	241.46	239.71	234.36	232.04	231.03	230.58
18000	277.83	272.16	267.52	263.68	260.51	257.87	255.66	253.81	248.14	245.69	244.62	244.14
19000	293.27	287.28	282.38	278.33	274.98	272.19	269.86	267.91	261.93	259.34	258.21	257.70
20000	308.70	302.40	297.24	292.98	289.45	286.52	284.07	282.01	275.71	272.99	271.79	271.26
21000	324.14	317.52	312.10	307.63	303.93	300.84	298.27	296.11	289.50	286.64	285.38	284.83
22000	339.57	332.64	326.96	322.28	318.40	315.17	312.47	310.22	303.28	300.29	298.97	298.39
23000	355.01	347.76	341.82	336.93	332.87	329.50	326.68	324.32	317.07	313.94	312.56	311.95
24000	370.44	362.88	356.69	351.58	347.34	343.82	340.88	338.42	330.85	327.59	326.15	325.52
25000	385.88	378.00	371.55	366.23	361.82	358.15	355.08	352.52	344.64	341.24	339.74	339.08
26000	401.31	393.12	386.41	380.87	376.29	372.47	369.29	366.62	358.43	354.89	353.33	352.64
27000	416.75	408.24	401.27	395.52	390.76	386.80	383.49	380.72	372.21	368.54	366.92	366.21
28000	432.18	423.36	416.13	410.17	405.23	401.12	397.69	394.82	386.00	382.19	380.51	379.77
29000	447.62	438.48	430.99	424.82	419.71	415.45	411.90	408.92	399.78	395.84	394.10	393.33
30000	463.05	453.60	445.86	439.47	434.18	429.78	426.10	423.02	413.57	409.49	407.69	406.89
31000	478.49	468.72	460.72	454.12	448.65	444.10	440.30	437.12	427.35	423.13	421.28	420.46
32000	493.92	483.84	475.58	468.77	463.12	458.43	454.50	451.22	441.14	436.78	434.87	434.02
33000	509.36	498.96	490.44	483.42	477.60	472.75	468.71	465.32	454.92	450.43	448.46	447.58
34000	524.79	514.08	505.30	498.07	492.07	487.08	482.91	479.42	468.71	464.08	462.05	461.15
35000	540.23	529.20	520.16	512.71	506.54	501.40	497.11	493.52	482.49	477.73	475.64	474.71
36000	555.66	544.32	535.03	527.36	521.01	515.73	511.32	507.62	496.28	491.38	489.23	488.27
37000	571.10	559.44	549.89	542.01	535.49	530.06	525.52	521.72	510.07	505.03	502.82	501.83
38000	586.53	574.56	564.75	556.66	549.96	544.38	539.72	535.82	523.85	518.68	516.41	515.40
39000	601.97	589.68	579.61	571.31	564.43	558.71	553.93	549.92	537.64	532.33	530.00	528.96
40000	617.40	604.80	594.47	585.96	578.90	573.03	568.13	564.02	551.42	545.98	543.58	542.52
41000	632.84	619.92	609.33	600.61	593.38	587.36	582.33	578.12	565.21	559.63	557.17	556.09
42000	648.27	635.04	624.20	615.26	607.85	601.68	596.54	592.22	578.99	573.28	570.76	569.65
43000	663.71	650.16	639.06	629.91	622.32	616.01	610.74	606.32	592.78	586.93	584.35	583.21
44000	679.14	665.28	653.92	644.55	636.79	630.34	624.94	620.43	606.56	600.58	597.94	596.78
45000	694.58	680.40	668.78	659.20	651.27	644.66	639.15	634.53	620.35	614.23	611.53	610.34
46000	710.01	695.52	683.64	673.85	665.74	658.99	653.35	648.63	634.13	627.87	625.12	623.90
47000	725.45	710.64	698.50	688.50	680.21	673.31	667.55	662.73	647.92	641.52	638.71	637.46
48000	740.88	725.76	713.37	703.15	694.68	687.64	681.75	676.83	661.70	655.17	652.30	651.03
49000	756.32	740.88	728.23	717.80	709.16	701.96	695.96	690.93	675.49	668.82	665.89	664.59
50000	771.75	756.00	743.09	732.45	723.63	716.29	710.16	705.03	689.28	682.47	679.48	678.15
55000	848.93	831.60	817.40	805.69	795.99	787.92	781.18	775.53	758.20	750.72	747.43	745.97
60000	926.10	907.20	891.71	878.94	868.35	859.55	852.19	846.03	827.13	818.97	815.37	813.78
65000	1003.28	982.80	966.01	952.18	940.72	931.17	923.21	916.53	896.06	887.21	883.32	881.60
70000	1080.45	1058.39	1040.32	1025.42	1013.08	1002.80	994.22	987.04	964.98	955.46	951.27	949.41
75000	1157.63	1133.99	1114.63	1098.67	1085.44	1074.43	1065.24	1057.54	1033.91	1023.71	1019.22	1017.23
80000	1234.80	1209.59	1188.94	1171.91	1157.80	1146.06	1136.25	1128.04	1102.84	1091.95	1087.17	1085.04
85000	1311.98	1285.19	1263.25	1245.16	1230.16	1217.69	1207.27	1198.54	1171.77	1160.20	1155.11	1152.86
90000	1389.15	1360.79	1337.56	1318.40	1302.53	1289.32	1278.29	1269.05	1240.69	1228.45	1223.06	1220.67
95000	1466.32	1436.39	1411.86	1391.64	1374.89	1360.95	1349.30	1339.55	1309.62	1296.69	1291.01	1288.49
100000	1543.50	1511.99	1486.17	1464.89	1447.25	1432.57	1420.32	1410.05	1378.55	1364.94	1358.96	1356.30

16%

93

Table 1

16.50%

MONTHLY
PAYMENT REQUIRED TO AMORTIZE A LOAN

TERM AMOUNT	1 YEAR	2 YEARS	3 YEARS	4 YEARS	5 YEARS	6 YEARS	7 YEARS	8 YEARS	9 YEARS	10 YEARS	11 YEARS	12 YEARS
50	4.55	2.47	1.78	1.43	1.23	1.10	1.01	.95	.90	.86	.83	.80
100	9.10	4.93	3.55	2.86	2.46	2.20	2.02	1.89	1.79	1.71	1.65	1.60
200	18.20	9.85	7.09	5.72	4.92	4.40	4.03	3.77	3.57	3.42	3.30	3.20
300	27.30	14.77	10.63	8.58	7.38	6.60	6.05	5.65	5.35	5.12	4.94	4.80
400	36.39	19.69	14.17	11.44	9.84	8.79	8.06	7.53	7.14	6.83	6.59	6.40
500	45.49	24.61	17.71	14.30	12.30	10.99	10.08	9.42	8.92	8.54	8.24	8.00
600	54.59	29.53	21.25	17.16	14.76	13.19	12.09	11.30	10.70	10.24	9.88	9.60
700	63.68	34.45	24.79	20.02	17.21	15.38	14.11	13.18	12.49	11.95	11.53	11.20
800	72.78	39.37	28.33	22.88	19.67	17.58	16.12	15.06	14.27	13.66	13.18	12.79
900	81.88	44.29	31.87	25.74	22.13	19.78	18.14	16.95	16.05	15.36	14.82	14.39
1000	90.97	49.21	35.41	28.60	24.59	21.97	20.15	18.83	17.83	17.07	16.47	15.99
2000	181.94	98.41	70.81	57.20	49.17	43.94	40.30	37.65	35.66	34.13	32.93	31.98
3000	272.91	147.61	106.22	85.80	73.76	65.91	60.45	56.48	53.49	51.20	49.40	47.97
4000	363.88	196.81	141.62	114.39	98.34	87.88	80.60	75.30	71.32	68.26	65.86	63.95
5000	454.84	246.02	177.03	142.99	122.93	109.85	100.74	94.12	89.15	85.33	82.33	79.94
6000	545.81	295.22	212.43	171.59	147.51	131.81	120.89	112.95	106.98	102.39	98.79	95.93
7000	636.78	344.42	247.84	200.18	172.10	153.78	141.04	131.77	124.81	119.45	115.26	111.92
8000	727.75	393.62	283.24	228.78	196.68	175.75	161.19	150.60	142.64	136.52	131.72	127.90
9000	818.71	442.83	318.64	257.38	221.27	197.72	181.34	169.42	160.47	153.58	148.18	143.89
10000	909.68	492.03	354.05	285.98	245.85	219.69	201.48	188.24	178.30	170.65	164.65	159.88
11000	1000.65	541.23	389.45	314.57	270.43	241.65	221.63	207.07	196.13	187.71	181.11	175.87
12000	1091.62	590.43	424.86	343.17	295.02	263.62	241.78	225.89	213.96	204.78	197.58	191.85
13000	1182.58	639.64	460.26	371.77	319.60	285.59	261.93	244.72	231.79	221.84	214.04	207.84
14000	1273.55	688.84	495.67	400.36	344.19	307.56	282.08	263.54	249.62	238.90	230.51	223.83
15000	1364.52	738.04	531.07	428.96	368.77	329.53	302.22	282.36	267.45	255.97	246.97	239.82
16000	1455.49	787.24	566.48	457.56	393.36	351.49	322.37	301.19	285.28	273.03	263.44	255.80
17000	1546.45	836.44	601.88	486.15	417.94	373.46	342.52	320.01	303.11	290.10	279.90	271.79
18000	1637.42	885.65	637.28	514.75	442.53	395.43	362.67	338.84	320.94	307.16	296.36	287.78
19000	1728.39	934.85	672.69	543.35	467.11	417.40	382.81	357.66	338.77	324.23	312.83	303.76
20000	1819.36	984.05	708.09	571.95	491.70	439.37	402.96	376.48	356.59	341.29	329.29	319.75
21000	1910.33	1033.25	743.50	600.54	516.28	461.33	423.11	395.31	374.42	358.35	345.76	335.74
22000	2001.29	1082.46	778.90	629.14	540.86	483.30	443.26	414.13	392.25	375.42	362.22	351.73
23000	2092.26	1131.66	814.31	657.74	565.45	505.27	463.41	432.96	410.08	392.48	378.69	367.71
24000	2183.23	1180.86	849.71	686.33	590.03	527.24	483.55	451.78	427.91	409.55	395.15	383.70
25000	2274.20	1230.06	885.11	714.93	614.62	549.21	503.70	470.60	445.74	426.61	411.61	399.69
26000	2365.16	1279.27	920.52	743.53	639.20	571.17	523.85	489.43	463.57	443.68	428.08	415.68
27000	2456.13	1328.47	955.92	772.12	663.79	593.14	544.00	508.25	481.40	460.74	444.54	431.66
28000	2547.10	1377.67	991.33	800.72	688.37	615.11	564.15	527.08	499.23	477.80	461.01	447.65
29000	2638.07	1426.87	1026.73	829.32	712.96	637.08	584.29	545.90	517.06	494.87	477.47	463.64
30000	2729.03	1476.08	1062.14	857.92	737.54	659.05	604.44	564.72	534.89	511.93	493.94	479.63
31000	2820.00	1525.28	1097.54	886.51	762.13	681.01	624.59	583.55	552.72	529.00	510.40	495.61
32000	2910.97	1574.48	1132.95	915.11	786.71	702.98	644.74	602.37	570.55	546.06	526.87	511.60
33000	3001.94	1623.68	1168.35	943.71	811.29	724.95	664.89	621.20	588.38	563.12	543.33	527.59
34000	3092.90	1672.88	1203.75	972.30	835.88	746.92	685.03	640.02	606.21	580.19	559.79	543.57
35000	3183.87	1722.09	1239.16	1000.90	860.46	768.89	705.18	658.84	624.04	597.25	576.26	559.56
36000	3274.84	1771.29	1274.56	1029.50	885.05	790.86	725.33	677.67	641.87	614.32	592.72	575.55
37000	3365.81	1820.49	1309.97	1058.09	909.63	812.82	745.48	696.49	659.70	631.38	609.19	591.54
38000	3456.78	1869.69	1345.37	1086.69	934.22	834.79	765.62	715.32	677.53	648.45	625.65	607.52
39000	3547.74	1918.90	1380.78	1115.29	958.80	856.76	785.77	734.14	695.35	665.51	642.12	623.51
40000	3638.71	1968.10	1416.18	1143.89	983.39	878.73	805.92	752.96	713.18	682.57	658.58	639.50
41000	3729.68	2017.30	1451.58	1172.48	1007.97	900.70	826.07	771.79	731.01	699.64	675.04	655.49
42000	3820.65	2066.50	1486.99	1201.08	1032.55	922.66	846.22	790.61	748.84	716.70	691.51	671.47
43000	3911.61	2115.71	1522.39	1229.68	1057.14	944.63	866.36	809.44	766.67	733.77	707.97	687.46
44000	4002.58	2164.91	1557.80	1258.27	1081.72	966.60	886.51	828.26	784.50	750.83	724.44	703.45
45000	4093.55	2214.11	1593.20	1286.87	1106.31	988.57	906.66	847.08	802.33	767.90	740.90	719.44
46000	4184.52	2263.31	1628.61	1315.47	1130.89	1010.54	926.81	865.91	820.16	784.96	757.37	735.42
47000	4275.48	2312.52	1664.01	1344.06	1155.48	1032.50	946.96	884.73	837.99	802.02	773.83	751.41
48000	4366.45	2361.72	1699.42	1372.66	1180.06	1054.47	967.10	903.56	855.82	819.09	790.30	767.40
49000	4457.42	2410.92	1734.82	1401.26	1204.65	1076.44	987.25	922.38	873.65	836.15	806.76	783.38
50000	4548.39	2460.12	1770.22	1429.86	1229.23	1098.41	1007.40	941.20	891.48	853.22	823.22	799.37
55000	5003.23	2706.13	1947.25	1572.84	1352.15	1208.25	1108.14	1035.32	980.63	938.54	905.55	879.31
60000	5458.06	2952.15	2124.27	1715.83	1475.08	1318.09	1208.88	1129.44	1069.77	1023.86	987.87	959.25
65000	5912.90	3198.16	2301.29	1858.81	1598.00	1427.93	1309.62	1223.56	1158.92	1109.18	1070.19	1039.18
70000	6367.74	3444.17	2478.31	2001.80	1720.92	1537.77	1410.36	1317.68	1248.07	1194.50	1152.51	1119.12
75000	6822.58	3690.18	2655.33	2144.78	1843.84	1647.61	1511.10	1411.80	1337.22	1279.82	1234.83	1199.06
80000	7277.42	3936.19	2832.36	2287.77	1966.77	1757.45	1611.84	1505.92	1426.36	1365.14	1317.16	1278.99
85000	7732.25	4182.20	3009.38	2430.75	2089.69	1867.29	1712.58	1600.04	1515.51	1450.46	1399.48	1358.93
90000	8187.09	4428.22	3186.40	2573.74	2212.61	1977.13	1813.32	1694.16	1604.66	1535.79	1481.80	1438.87
95000	8641.93	4674.23	3363.42	2716.72	2335.53	2086.97	1914.05	1788.28	1693.81	1621.11	1564.12	1518.80
100000	9096.77	4920.24	3540.44	2859.71	2458.46	2196.81	2014.79	1882.40	1782.95	1706.43	1646.44	1598.74

Table 1

MONTHLY 16.50%

PAYMENT REQUIRED TO AMORTIZE A LOAN

TERM / AMOUNT	13 YEARS	14 YEARS	15 YEARS	16 YEARS	17 YEARS	18 YEARS	19 YEARS	20 YEARS	25 YEARS	30 YEARS	35 YEARS	40 YEARS
50	.79	.77	.76	.75	.74	.73	.72	.72	.70	.70	.69	.69
100	1.57	1.53	1.51	1.49	1.47	1.46	1.44	1.43	1.40	1.39	1.38	1.38
200	3.13	3.06	3.01	2.97	2.94	2.91	2.88	2.86	2.80	2.78	2.76	2.76
300	4.69	4.59	4.52	4.45	4.40	4.36	4.32	4.29	4.20	4.16	4.14	4.14
400	6.25	6.12	6.02	5.94	5.87	5.81	5.76	5.72	5.60	5.55	5.52	5.51
500	7.81	7.65	7.52	7.42	7.33	7.26	7.20	7.15	7.00	6.93	6.90	6.89
600	9.37	9.18	9.03	8.90	8.80	8.71	8.64	8.58	8.39	8.32	8.28	8.27
700	10.93	10.71	10.53	10.38	10.26	10.16	10.08	10.01	9.79	9.70	9.66	9.64
800	12.49	12.24	12.03	11.87	11.73	11.61	11.52	11.44	11.19	11.09	11.04	11.02
900	14.05	13.77	13.54	13.31	13.19	13.06	12.96	12.87	12.59	12.47	12.42	12.40
1000	15.61	15.30	15.04	14.83	14.66	14.51	14.39	14.29	13.99	13.86	13.80	13.77
2000	31.21	30.59	30.08	29.66	29.31	29.02	28.78	28.58	27.97	27.71	27.59	27.54
3000	46.82	45.88	45.12	44.49	43.97	43.53	43.17	42.87	41.95	41.56	41.39	41.31
4000	62.42	61.17	60.15	59.31	58.62	58.04	57.56	57.16	55.93	55.41	55.18	55.08
5000	78.02	76.46	75.19	74.14	73.27	72.55	71.95	71.45	69.92	69.26	68.98	68.85
6000	93.63	91.76	90.23	88.97	87.93	87.06	86.34	85.74	83.90	83.11	82.77	82.62
7000	109.23	107.05	105.26	103.80	102.58	101.57	100.73	100.03	97.88	96.97	96.57	96.39
8000	124.83	122.34	120.30	118.62	117.24	116.08	115.12	114.32	111.86	110.82	110.36	110.16
9000	140.44	137.63	135.34	133.45	131.89	130.59	129.51	128.61	125.85	124.67	124.16	123.93
10000	156.04	152.92	150.38	148.28	146.54	145.10	143.90	142.90	139.83	138.52	137.95	137.70
11000	171.64	168.22	165.41	163.11	161.20	159.61	158.29	157.18	153.81	152.37	151.74	151.47
12000	187.25	183.51	180.45	177.93	175.85	174.12	172.68	171.47	167.79	166.22	165.54	165.24
13000	202.85	198.80	195.49	192.76	190.50	188.63	187.07	185.76	181.78	180.07	179.33	179.01
14000	218.45	214.09	210.52	207.59	205.16	203.14	201.46	200.05	195.76	193.93	193.13	192.78
15000	234.06	229.38	225.56	222.41	219.81	217.65	215.85	214.34	209.74	207.78	206.92	206.55
16000	249.66	244.68	240.60	237.24	234.47	232.16	230.24	228.63	223.72	221.63	220.72	220.32
17000	265.27	259.97	255.64	252.07	249.12	246.67	244.63	242.92	237.71	235.48	234.51	234.09
18000	280.87	275.26	270.67	266.90	263.77	261.18	259.02	257.21	251.69	249.33	248.31	247.86
19000	296.47	290.55	285.71	281.72	278.43	275.69	273.40	271.50	265.67	263.18	262.10	261.63
20000	312.08	305.84	300.75	296.55	293.08	290.20	287.79	285.79	279.65	277.03	275.90	275.40
21000	327.68	321.14	315.78	311.38	307.73	304.71	302.18	300.07	293.64	290.89	289.69	289.17
22000	343.28	336.43	330.82	326.21	322.39	319.22	316.57	314.36	307.62	304.74	303.48	302.94
23000	358.89	351.72	345.86	341.03	337.04	333.73	330.96	328.65	321.60	318.59	317.28	316.71
24000	374.49	367.01	360.90	355.86	351.70	348.24	345.35	342.94	335.58	332.44	331.07	330.48
25000	390.09	382.30	375.93	370.69	366.35	362.75	359.74	357.23	349.57	346.29	344.87	344.24
26000	405.70	397.60	390.97	385.51	381.00	377.25	374.13	371.52	363.55	360.14	358.66	358.01
27000	421.30	412.89	406.01	400.34	395.66	391.76	388.52	385.81	377.53	373.99	372.46	371.78
28000	436.90	428.18	421.04	415.17	410.31	406.27	402.91	400.10	391.51	387.85	386.25	385.55
29000	452.51	443.47	436.08	430.00	424.96	420.78	417.30	414.39	405.50	401.70	400.05	399.32
30000	468.11	458.76	451.12	444.82	439.62	435.29	431.69	428.68	419.48	415.55	413.84	413.09
31000	483.72	474.06	466.15	459.65	454.27	449.80	446.08	442.96	433.46	429.40	427.64	426.86
32000	499.32	489.35	481.19	474.48	468.93	464.31	460.47	457.25	447.44	443.25	441.43	440.63
33000	514.92	504.64	496.23	489.31	483.58	478.82	474.86	471.54	461.43	457.10	455.22	454.40
34000	530.53	519.93	511.27	504.13	498.23	493.33	489.25	485.83	475.41	470.96	469.02	468.17
35000	546.13	535.22	526.30	518.96	512.89	507.84	503.64	500.12	489.39	484.81	482.81	481.94
36000	561.73	550.52	541.34	533.79	527.54	522.35	518.03	514.41	503.37	498.66	496.61	495.71
37000	577.34	565.81	556.38	548.61	542.19	536.86	532.41	528.70	517.36	512.51	510.40	509.48
38000	592.94	581.10	571.41	563.44	556.85	551.37	546.80	542.99	531.34	526.36	524.20	523.25
39000	608.54	596.39	586.45	578.27	571.50	565.88	561.19	557.28	545.32	540.21	537.99	537.02
40000	624.15	611.68	601.49	593.10	586.16	580.39	575.58	571.57	559.30	554.06	551.79	550.79
41000	639.75	626.98	616.53	607.92	600.81	594.90	589.97	585.85	573.29	567.91	565.58	564.56
42000	655.35	642.27	631.56	622.75	615.46	609.41	604.36	600.14	587.27	581.77	579.38	578.33
43000	670.96	657.56	646.60	637.58	630.12	623.92	618.75	614.43	601.25	595.62	593.17	592.10
44000	686.56	672.85	661.64	652.41	644.77	638.43	633.14	628.72	615.23	609.47	606.96	605.87
45000	702.17	688.14	676.67	667.23	659.42	652.94	647.53	643.01	629.22	623.32	620.76	619.64
46000	717.77	703.44	691.71	682.06	674.08	667.45	661.92	657.30	643.20	637.17	634.55	633.41
47000	733.37	718.73	706.75	696.89	688.73	681.96	676.31	671.59	657.18	651.02	648.35	647.18
48000	748.98	734.02	721.79	711.72	703.39	696.47	690.70	685.88	671.16	664.88	662.14	660.95
49000	764.58	749.31	736.82	726.54	718.04	710.98	705.09	700.17	685.14	678.73	675.94	674.72
50000	780.18	764.60	751.86	741.37	732.69	725.49	719.48	714.46	699.13	692.58	689.73	688.48
55000	858.20	841.06	827.04	815.51	805.96	798.03	791.42	785.90	769.04	761.84	758.70	757.33
60000	936.22	917.52	902.23	889.64	879.23	870.58	863.37	857.35	838.95	831.09	827.68	826.18
65000	1014.24	993.98	977.42	963.78	952.50	943.13	935.32	928.79	908.86	900.35	896.65	895.03
70000	1092.25	1070.44	1052.60	1037.92	1025.77	1015.68	1007.27	1000.24	978.78	969.61	965.62	963.88
75000	1170.27	1146.90	1127.79	1112.05	1099.04	1088.23	1079.21	1071.68	1048.69	1038.87	1034.60	1032.72
80000	1248.29	1223.36	1202.97	1186.19	1172.31	1160.77	1151.16	1143.13	1118.60	1108.12	1103.57	1101.57
85000	1326.31	1299.82	1278.16	1260.33	1245.57	1233.32	1223.11	1214.57	1188.51	1177.38	1172.54	1170.42
90000	1404.33	1376.28	1353.34	1334.46	1318.84	1305.87	1295.06	1286.02	1258.43	1246.64	1241.51	1239.27
95000	1482.34	1452.74	1428.53	1408.60	1392.11	1378.42	1367.00	1357.46	1328.34	1315.90	1310.49	1308.12
100000	1560.36	1529.20	1503.71	1482.73	1465.38	1450.97	1438.95	1428.91	1398.25	1385.15	1379.46	1376.96

16%

Table 1

16.75%

MONTHLY
PAYMENT REQUIRED TO AMORTIZE A LOAN

TERM AMOUNT	1 YEAR	2 YEARS	3 YEARS	4 YEARS	5 YEARS	6 YEARS	7 YEARS	8 YEARS	9 YEARS	10 YEARS	11 YEARS	12 YEARS
50	4.56	2.47	1.78	1.44	1.24	1.11	1.02	.95	.90	.87	.84	.81
100	9.11	4.94	3.56	2.88	2.48	2.22	2.03	1.90	1.80	1.73	1.67	1.62
200	18.22	9.87	7.11	5.75	4.95	4.43	4.06	3.80	3.60	3.45	3.33	3.24
300	27.33	14.80	10.66	8.62	7.42	6.64	6.09	5.70	5.40	5.17	4.99	4.85
400	36.44	19.73	14.22	11.50	9.89	8.85	8.12	7.59	7.20	6.89	6.66	6.47
500	45.55	24.67	17.77	14.37	12.36	11.06	10.15	9.49	9.00	8.62	8.32	8.08
600	54.66	29.60	21.32	17.24	14.84	13.27	12.18	11.39	10.79	10.34	9.98	9.70
700	63.77	34.53	24.87	20.11	17.31	15.48	14.21	13.29	12.59	12.06	11.64	11.31
800	72.87	39.46	28.43	22.99	19.78	17.69	16.24	15.18	14.39	13.78	13.31	12.93
900	81.98	44.40	31.98	25.86	22.25	19.90	18.27	17.08	16.19	15.50	14.97	14.54
1000	91.09	49.33	35.53	28.73	24.72	22.11	20.30	18.98	17.99	17.23	16.63	16.16
2000	182.18	98.65	71.06	57.46	49.44	44.22	40.59	37.95	35.97	34.45	33.26	32.31
3000	273.26	147.97	106.59	86.18	74.16	66.33	60.88	56.92	53.95	51.67	49.88	48.46
4000	364.35	197.29	142.12	114.91	98.88	88.43	81.17	75.89	71.94	68.89	66.51	64.62
5000	455.44	246.62	177.65	143.63	123.60	110.54	101.46	94.87	89.92	86.11	83.14	80.77
6000	546.52	295.94	213.18	172.36	148.32	132.65	121.75	113.84	107.90	103.34	99.76	96.92
7000	637.61	345.26	248.70	201.09	173.03	154.75	142.05	132.81	125.88	120.56	116.39	113.08
8000	728.69	394.58	284.23	229.81	197.75	176.86	162.34	151.78	143.87	137.78	133.01	129.23
9000	819.78	443.91	319.76	258.54	222.47	198.97	182.63	170.76	161.85	155.00	149.64	145.38
10000	910.87	493.23	355.29	287.26	247.19	221.07	202.92	189.73	179.83	172.22	166.27	161.53
11000	1001.95	542.55	390.82	315.99	271.91	243.18	223.21	208.70	197.81	189.44	182.89	177.69
12000	1093.04	591.87	426.35	344.72	296.63	265.29	243.50	227.67	215.80	206.67	199.52	193.84
13000	1184.13	641.19	461.87	373.44	321.34	287.39	263.80	246.65	233.78	223.89	216.14	209.99
14000	1275.21	690.52	497.40	402.17	346.06	309.50	284.09	265.62	251.76	241.11	232.77	226.15
15000	1366.30	739.84	532.93	430.89	370.78	331.61	304.38	284.59	269.74	258.33	249.40	242.30
16000	1457.38	789.16	568.46	459.62	395.50	353.71	324.67	303.56	287.73	275.55	266.02	258.45
17000	1548.47	838.48	603.99	488.34	420.22	375.82	344.96	322.54	305.71	292.77	282.65	274.60
18000	1639.56	887.81	639.52	517.07	444.94	397.93	365.25	341.51	323.69	310.00	299.27	290.76
19000	1730.64	937.13	675.05	545.80	469.65	420.04	385.55	360.48	341.67	327.22	315.90	306.91
20000	1821.73	986.45	710.57	574.52	494.37	442.14	405.84	379.45	359.66	344.44	332.53	323.06
21000	1912.81	1035.77	746.10	603.25	519.09	464.25	426.13	398.43	377.64	361.66	349.15	339.22
22000	2003.90	1085.09	781.63	631.97	543.81	486.36	446.42	417.40	395.62	378.88	365.78	355.37
23000	2094.99	1134.42	817.16	660.70	568.53	508.46	466.71	436.37	413.60	396.10	382.40	371.52
24000	2186.07	1183.74	852.69	689.43	593.25	530.57	487.00	455.34	431.59	413.33	399.03	387.68
25000	2277.16	1233.06	888.22	718.15	617.96	552.68	507.29	474.32	449.57	430.55	415.66	403.83
26000	2368.24	1282.38	923.74	746.88	642.68	574.78	527.59	493.29	467.55	447.77	432.28	419.98
27000	2459.33	1331.71	959.27	775.60	667.40	596.89	547.88	512.26	485.53	464.99	448.91	436.13
28000	2550.42	1381.03	994.80	804.33	692.12	619.00	568.17	531.23	503.52	482.21	465.53	452.29
29000	2641.50	1430.35	1030.33	833.06	716.84	641.10	588.46	550.21	521.50	499.43	482.16	468.44
30000	2732.59	1479.67	1065.86	861.78	741.56	663.21	608.75	569.18	539.48	516.66	498.79	484.59
31000	2823.68	1528.99	1101.39	890.51	766.27	685.32	629.04	588.15	557.46	533.88	515.41	500.75
32000	2914.76	1578.32	1136.91	919.23	790.99	707.42	649.34	607.12	575.45	551.10	532.04	516.90
33000	3005.85	1627.64	1172.44	947.96	815.71	729.53	669.63	626.10	593.43	568.32	548.66	533.05
34000	3096.93	1676.96	1207.97	976.68	840.43	751.64	689.92	645.07	611.41	585.54	565.29	549.20
35000	3188.02	1726.28	1243.50	1005.41	865.15	773.75	710.21	664.04	629.39	602.76	581.92	565.36
36000	3279.11	1775.61	1279.03	1034.14	889.87	795.85	730.50	683.01	647.38	619.99	598.54	581.51
37000	3370.19	1824.93	1314.56	1062.86	914.58	817.96	750.79	701.98	665.36	637.21	615.17	597.66
38000	3461.28	1874.25	1350.09	1091.59	939.30	840.07	771.09	720.96	683.34	654.43	631.79	613.82
39000	3552.36	1923.57	1385.61	1120.31	964.02	862.17	791.38	739.93	701.32	671.65	648.42	629.97
40000	3643.45	1972.89	1421.14	1149.04	988.74	884.28	811.67	758.90	719.31	688.87	665.05	646.12
41000	3734.54	2022.22	1456.67	1177.77	1013.46	906.39	831.96	777.87	737.29	706.09	681.67	662.28
42000	3825.62	2071.54	1492.20	1206.49	1038.18	928.49	852.25	796.85	755.27	723.32	698.30	678.43
43000	3916.71	2120.86	1527.73	1235.22	1062.89	950.60	872.54	815.82	773.25	740.54	714.92	694.58
44000	4007.80	2170.18	1563.26	1263.94	1087.61	972.71	892.83	834.79	791.24	757.76	731.55	710.73
45000	4098.88	2219.51	1598.78	1292.67	1112.33	994.81	913.13	853.76	809.22	774.98	748.18	726.89
46000	4189.97	2268.83	1634.31	1321.39	1137.05	1016.92	933.42	872.74	827.20	792.20	764.80	743.04
47000	4281.05	2318.15	1669.84	1350.12	1161.77	1039.03	953.71	891.71	845.18	809.42	781.43	759.19
48000	4372.14	2367.47	1705.37	1378.85	1186.49	1061.13	974.00	910.68	863.17	826.65	798.05	775.35
49000	4463.23	2416.79	1740.90	1407.57	1211.20	1083.24	994.29	929.65	881.15	843.87	814.68	791.50
50000	4554.31	2466.12	1776.43	1436.30	1235.92	1105.35	1014.58	948.63	899.13	861.09	831.31	807.65
55000	5009.74	2712.73	1954.07	1579.93	1359.51	1215.88	1116.04	1043.49	989.04	947.20	914.44	888.42
60000	5465.17	2959.34	2131.71	1723.56	1483.11	1326.42	1217.50	1138.35	1078.96	1033.31	997.57	969.18
65000	5920.60	3205.95	2309.35	1867.19	1606.70	1436.95	1318.96	1233.21	1168.87	1119.41	1080.70	1049.95
70000	6376.04	3452.56	2487.00	2010.82	1730.29	1547.49	1420.42	1328.07	1258.78	1205.52	1163.83	1130.71
75000	6831.47	3699.17	2664.64	2154.44	1853.88	1658.02	1521.87	1422.94	1348.69	1291.63	1246.96	1211.48
80000	7286.90	3945.78	2842.28	2298.07	1977.47	1768.55	1623.33	1517.80	1438.61	1377.74	1330.09	1292.24
85000	7742.33	4192.39	3019.92	2441.70	2101.06	1879.09	1724.79	1612.66	1528.52	1463.85	1413.22	1373.00
90000	8197.76	4439.01	3197.56	2585.33	2224.66	1989.62	1826.25	1707.52	1618.43	1549.96	1496.35	1453.77
95000	8653.19	4685.62	3375.21	2728.96	2348.25	2100.16	1927.71	1802.39	1708.35	1636.06	1579.48	1534.53
100000	9108.62	4932.23	3552.85	2872.59	2471.84	2210.69	2029.16	1897.25	1798.26	1722.17	1662.61	1615.30

16%

Table 1

MONTHLY
PAYMENT REQUIRED TO AMORTIZE A LOAN

16.75%

16%

TERM AMT	13 YEARS	14 YEARS	15 YEARS	16 YEARS	17 YEARS	18 YEARS	19 YEARS	20 YEARS	25 YEARS	30 YEARS	35 YEARS	40 YEARS
50	.79	.78	.77	.76	.75	.74	.73	.73	.71	.71	.70	.70
100	1.58	1.55	1.53	1.51	1.49	1.47	1.46	1.45	1.42	1.41	1.40	1.40
200	3.16	3.10	3.05	3.01	2.97	2.94	2.92	2.90	2.84	2.82	2.80	2.80
300	4.74	4.64	4.57	4.51	4.46	4.41	4.38	4.35	4.26	4.22	4.20	4.20
400	6.31	6.19	6.09	6.01	5.94	5.88	5.84	5.80	5.68	5.63	5.60	5.60
500	7.89	7.74	7.61	7.51	7.42	7.35	7.29	7.24	7.09	7.03	7.00	6.99
600	9.47	9.28	9.13	9.01	8.91	8.82	8.75	8.69	8.51	8.44	8.40	8.39
700	11.05	10.83	10.65	10.51	10.39	10.29	10.21	10.14	9.93	9.84	9.80	9.79
800	12.62	12.38	12.18	12.01	11.87	11.76	11.67	11.59	11.35	11.25	11.20	11.19
900	14.20	13.92	13.70	13.51	13.36	13.23	13.12	13.04	12.77	12.65	12.60	12.58
1000	15.78	15.47	15.22	15.01	14.84	14.70	14.58	14.48	14.18	14.06	14.00	13.98
2000	31.55	30.93	30.43	30.02	29.68	29.39	29.16	28.96	28.36	28.11	28.00	27.96
3000	47.32	46.40	45.64	45.02	44.51	44.09	43.73	43.44	42.54	42.17	42.00	41.93
4000	63.10	61.86	60.86	60.03	59.35	58.78	58.31	57.92	56.72	56.22	56.00	55.91
5000	78.87	77.33	76.07	75.04	74.18	73.48	72.89	72.40	70.90	70.27	70.00	69.89
6000	94.64	92.79	91.28	90.04	89.02	88.17	87.46	86.87	85.08	84.33	84.00	83.86
7000	110.42	108.26	106.50	105.05	103.86	102.86	102.04	101.35	99.26	98.38	98.00	97.84
8000	126.19	123.72	121.71	120.06	118.69	117.56	116.62	115.83	113.44	112.44	112.00	111.82
9000	141.96	139.19	136.92	135.06	133.53	132.25	131.19	130.31	127.62	126.49	126.00	125.79
10000	157.73	154.65	152.14	150.07	148.36	146.95	145.77	144.79	141.80	140.54	140.00	139.77
11000	173.51	170.12	167.35	165.08	163.20	161.64	160.35	159.27	155.98	154.60	154.00	153.74
12000	189.28	185.58	182.56	180.08	178.03	176.34	174.92	173.74	170.16	168.65	168.00	167.72
13000	205.05	201.05	197.78	195.09	192.87	191.03	189.50	188.22	184.34	182.71	182.00	181.70
14000	220.83	216.51	212.99	210.10	207.71	205.72	204.08	202.70	198.52	196.76	196.00	195.67
15000	236.60	231.98	228.20	225.10	222.54	220.42	218.65	217.18	212.70	210.81	210.00	209.65
16000	252.37	247.44	243.42	240.11	237.38	235.11	233.23	231.66	226.88	224.87	224.00	223.63
17000	268.14	262.91	258.63	255.11	252.21	249.81	247.80	246.13	241.06	238.92	238.00	237.60
18000	283.92	278.37	273.84	270.12	267.05	264.50	262.38	260.61	255.24	252.98	252.00	251.58
19000	299.69	293.84	289.06	285.13	281.88	279.19	276.96	275.09	269.42	267.03	266.00	265.55
20000	315.46	309.30	304.27	300.13	296.72	293.89	291.53	289.57	283.60	281.08	280.00	279.53
21000	331.24	324.77	319.48	315.14	311.56	308.58	306.11	304.05	297.78	295.14	294.00	293.51
22000	347.01	340.23	334.70	330.15	326.39	323.28	320.69	318.53	311.96	309.19	308.00	307.48
23000	362.78	355.70	349.91	345.15	341.23	337.97	335.26	333.00	326.14	323.25	322.00	321.46
24000	378.55	371.16	365.12	360.16	356.06	352.67	349.84	347.48	340.32	337.30	336.00	335.44
25000	394.33	386.63	380.34	375.17	370.90	367.36	364.42	361.96	354.50	351.35	350.00	349.41
26000	410.10	402.09	395.55	390.17	385.73	382.05	378.99	376.44	368.68	365.41	364.00	363.39
27000	425.87	417.56	410.76	405.18	400.57	396.75	393.57	390.92	382.86	379.46	378.00	377.37
28000	441.65	433.02	425.97	420.19	415.41	411.44	408.15	405.39	397.04	393.52	392.00	391.34
29000	457.42	448.48	441.19	435.19	430.24	426.14	422.72	419.87	411.22	407.57	406.00	405.32
30000	473.19	463.95	456.40	450.20	445.08	440.83	437.30	434.35	425.40	421.62	420.00	419.30
31000	488.97	479.41	471.61	465.21	459.91	455.53	451.87	448.83	439.58	435.68	434.00	433.27
32000	504.74	494.88	486.83	480.21	474.75	470.22	466.45	463.31	453.76	449.73	448.00	447.25
33000	520.51	510.34	502.04	495.22	489.58	484.91	481.03	477.79	467.94	463.79	462.00	461.22
34000	536.28	525.81	517.25	510.22	504.42	499.61	495.60	492.26	482.12	477.84	476.00	475.20
35000	552.06	541.27	532.47	525.23	519.26	514.30	510.18	506.74	496.30	491.89	490.00	489.18
36000	567.83	556.74	547.68	540.24	534.09	529.00	524.76	521.22	510.48	505.95	504.00	503.15
37000	583.60	572.20	562.89	555.24	548.93	543.69	539.33	535.70	524.66	520.00	518.00	517.13
38000	599.38	587.67	578.11	570.25	563.76	558.38	553.91	550.18	538.84	534.06	532.00	531.11
39000	615.15	603.13	593.32	585.26	578.60	573.08	568.49	564.65	553.02	548.11	546.00	545.08
40000	630.92	618.60	608.53	600.26	593.44	587.77	583.06	579.13	567.20	562.16	560.00	559.06
41000	646.69	634.06	623.75	615.27	608.27	602.47	597.64	593.61	581.38	576.22	574.00	573.04
42000	662.47	649.53	638.96	630.28	623.11	617.16	612.22	608.09	595.56	590.27	588.00	587.01
43000	678.24	664.99	654.17	645.28	637.94	631.86	626.79	622.57	609.74	604.33	602.00	600.99
44000	694.01	680.46	669.39	660.29	652.78	646.55	641.37	637.05	623.92	618.38	616.00	614.96
45000	709.79	695.92	684.60	675.30	667.61	661.24	655.95	651.52	638.10	632.43	630.00	628.94
46000	725.56	711.39	699.81	690.30	682.45	675.94	670.52	666.00	652.28	646.49	644.00	642.92
47000	741.33	726.85	715.03	705.31	697.29	690.63	685.10	680.48	666.46	660.54	658.00	656.89
48000	757.10	742.32	730.24	720.32	712.12	705.33	699.67	694.96	680.64	674.59	672.00	670.87
49000	772.88	757.78	745.45	735.32	726.96	720.02	714.25	709.44	694.82	688.65	686.00	684.85
50000	788.65	773.25	760.67	750.33	741.79	734.72	728.83	723.91	709.00	702.70	699.99	698.82
55000	867.51	850.57	836.73	825.36	815.97	808.19	801.71	796.31	779.90	772.97	769.99	768.70
60000	946.38	927.89	912.80	900.39	890.15	881.66	874.59	868.70	850.80	843.24	839.99	838.59
65000	1025.24	1005.22	988.86	975.43	964.33	955.13	947.47	941.09	921.70	913.51	909.99	908.47
70000	1104.11	1082.54	1064.93	1050.46	1038.51	1028.60	1020.36	1013.48	992.60	983.78	979.99	978.35
75000	1182.97	1159.87	1141.00	1125.49	1112.69	1102.07	1093.24	1085.87	1063.50	1054.05	1049.99	1048.23
80000	1261.84	1237.19	1217.06	1200.52	1186.87	1175.54	1166.12	1158.26	1134.40	1124.32	1119.99	1118.11
85000	1340.70	1314.52	1293.13	1275.55	1261.04	1249.01	1239.00	1230.65	1205.30	1194.59	1189.99	1188.00
90000	1419.57	1391.84	1369.19	1350.59	1335.22	1322.48	1311.89	1303.04	1276.20	1264.86	1259.99	1257.88
95000	1498.43	1469.16	1445.26	1425.62	1409.40	1395.95	1384.77	1375.43	1347.10	1335.13	1329.99	1327.76
100000	1577.30	1546.49	1521.33	1500.65	1483.58	1469.43	1457.65	1447.82	1418.00	1405.40	1399.98	1397.64

Table 1

17.00%

MONTHLY
PAYMENT REQUIRED TO AMORTIZE A LOAN

TERM / AMOUNT	1 YEAR	2 YEARS	3 YEARS	4 YEARS	5 YEARS	6 YEARS	7 YEARS	8 YEARS	9 YEARS	10 YEARS	11 YEARS	12 YEARS
50	4.57	2.48	1.79	1.45	1.25	1.12	1.03	.96	.91	.87	.84	.8
100	9.13	4.95	3.57	2.89	2.49	2.23	2.05	1.92	1.82	1.74	1.68	1.6
200	18.25	9.89	7.14	5.78	4.98	4.45	4.09	3.83	3.63	3.48	3.36	3.2
300	27.37	14.84	10.70	8.66	7.46	6.68	6.14	5.74	5.45	5.22	5.04	4.9
400	36.49	19.78	14.27	11.55	9.95	8.90	8.18	7.65	7.26	6.96	6.72	6.5
500	45.61	24.73	17.83	14.43	12.43	11.13	10.22	9.57	9.07	8.69	8.40	8.1
600	54.73	29.67	21.40	17.32	14.92	13.35	12.27	11.48	10.89	10.43	10.08	9.8
700	63.85	34.61	24.96	20.20	17.40	15.58	14.31	13.39	12.70	12.17	11.76	11.4
800	72.97	39.56	28.53	23.09	19.89	17.80	16.35	15.30	14.51	13.91	13.44	13.0
900	82.09	44.50	32.09	25.97	22.37	20.03	18.40	17.21	16.33	15.65	15.11	14.6
1000	91.21	49.45	35.66	28.86	24.86	22.25	20.44	19.13	18.14	17.38	16.79	16.3
2000	182.41	98.89	71.31	57.72	49.71	44.50	40.88	38.25	36.28	34.76	33.58	32.6
3000	273.62	148.33	106.96	86.57	74.56	66.74	61.31	57.37	54.41	52.14	50.37	48.9
4000	364.82	197.77	142.62	115.43	99.42	88.99	81.75	76.49	72.55	69.52	67.16	65.2
5000	456.03	247.22	178.27	144.28	124.27	111.24	102.18	95.61	90.69	86.90	83.95	81.6
6000	547.23	296.66	213.92	173.14	149.12	133.48	122.62	114.73	108.82	104.28	100.73	97.9
7000	638.44	346.10	249.57	201.99	173.97	155.73	143.06	133.86	126.96	121.66	117.52	114.2
8000	729.64	395.54	285.23	230.85	198.83	177.97	163.49	152.98	145.09	139.04	134.31	130.5
9000	820.85	444.99	320.88	259.70	223.68	200.22	183.93	172.10	163.23	156.42	151.10	146.8
10000	912.05	494.43	356.53	288.56	248.53	222.47	204.36	191.22	181.37	173.80	167.89	163.2
11000	1003.26	543.87	392.19	317.41	273.38	244.71	224.80	210.34	199.50	191.18	184.68	179.5
12000	1094.46	593.31	427.84	346.27	298.24	266.96	245.23	229.46	217.64	208.56	201.46	195.8
13000	1185.67	642.75	463.49	375.12	323.09	289.20	265.67	248.58	235.78	225.94	218.25	212.1
14000	1276.87	692.20	499.14	403.98	347.94	311.45	286.11	267.71	253.91	243.32	235.04	228.4
15000	1368.08	741.64	534.80	432.83	372.79	333.70	306.54	286.83	272.05	260.70	251.83	244.7
16000	1459.28	791.08	570.45	461.69	397.65	355.94	326.98	305.95	290.18	278.08	268.62	261.1
17000	1550.49	840.52	606.10	490.54	422.50	378.19	347.41	325.07	308.32	295.46	285.41	277.4
18000	1641.69	889.97	641.75	519.40	447.35	400.44	367.85	344.19	326.46	312.84	302.19	293.7
19000	1732.90	939.41	677.41	548.25	472.20	422.68	388.29	363.31	344.59	330.22	318.98	310.0
20000	1824.10	988.85	713.06	577.11	497.06	444.93	408.72	382.43	362.73	347.60	335.77	326.3
21000	1915.30	1038.29	748.71	605.96	521.91	467.17	429.16	401.56	380.86	364.98	352.56	342.7
22000	2006.51	1087.73	784.37	634.82	546.76	489.42	449.59	420.68	399.00	382.36	369.35	359.0
23000	2097.71	1137.18	820.02	663.67	571.61	511.67	470.03	439.80	417.14	399.74	386.14	375.3
24000	2188.92	1186.62	855.67	692.53	596.47	533.91	490.46	458.92	435.27	417.12	402.92	391.6
25000	2280.12	1236.06	891.32	721.38	621.32	556.16	510.90	478.04	453.41	434.50	419.71	407.9
26000	2371.33	1285.50	926.98	750.24	646.17	578.40	531.34	497.16	471.55	451.88	436.50	424.3
27000	2462.53	1334.95	962.63	779.09	671.02	600.65	551.77	516.28	489.68	469.26	453.29	440.6
28000	2553.74	1384.39	998.28	807.95	695.88	622.90	572.21	535.41	507.82	486.64	470.08	456.9
29000	2644.94	1433.83	1033.93	836.80	720.73	645.14	592.64	554.53	525.95	504.02	486.87	473.2
30000	2736.15	1483.27	1069.59	865.66	745.58	667.39	613.08	573.65	544.09	521.40	503.65	489.5
31000	2827.35	1532.72	1105.24	894.51	770.43	689.64	633.51	592.77	562.23	538.78	520.44	505.9
32000	2918.56	1582.16	1140.89	923.37	795.29	711.88	653.95	611.89	580.36	556.16	537.23	522.2
33000	3009.76	1631.60	1176.55	952.22	820.14	734.13	674.39	631.01	598.50	573.54	554.02	538.5
34000	3100.97	1681.04	1212.20	981.08	844.99	756.37	694.82	650.13	616.64	590.92	570.81	554.8
35000	3192.17	1730.48	1247.85	1009.93	869.85	778.62	715.26	669.26	634.77	608.30	587.60	571.1
36000	3283.38	1779.93	1283.50	1038.79	894.70	800.87	735.69	688.38	652.91	625.68	604.38	587.5
37000	3374.58	1829.37	1319.16	1067.64	919.55	823.11	756.13	707.50	671.04	643.06	621.17	603.8
38000	3465.79	1878.81	1354.81	1096.50	944.40	845.36	776.57	726.62	689.18	660.44	637.96	620.1
39000	3556.99	1928.25	1390.46	1125.35	969.26	867.60	797.00	745.74	707.32	677.82	654.75	636.4
40000	3648.20	1977.70	1426.11	1154.21	994.11	889.85	817.44	764.86	725.45	695.20	671.54	652.7
41000	3739.40	2027.14	1461.77	1183.06	1018.96	912.10	837.87	783.98	743.59	712.58	688.33	669.0
42000	3830.60	2076.58	1497.42	1211.92	1043.81	934.34	858.31	803.11	761.72	729.96	705.11	685.4
43000	3921.81	2126.02	1533.07	1240.77	1068.67	956.59	878.74	822.23	779.86	747.33	721.90	701.7
44000	4013.01	2175.46	1568.73	1269.63	1093.52	978.83	899.18	841.35	798.00	764.71	738.69	718.0
45000	4104.22	2224.91	1604.38	1298.48	1118.37	1001.08	919.62	860.47	816.13	782.09	755.48	734.3
46000	4195.42	2274.35	1640.03	1327.34	1143.22	1023.33	940.05	879.59	834.27	799.47	772.27	750.69
47000	4286.63	2323.79	1675.68	1356.19	1168.08	1045.57	960.49	898.71	852.41	816.85	789.06	767.0
48000	4377.83	2373.23	1711.34	1385.05	1192.93	1067.82	980.92	917.83	870.54	834.23	805.84	783.3
49000	4469.04	2422.68	1746.99	1413.90	1217.78	1090.07	1001.36	936.96	888.68	851.61	822.63	799.65
50000	4560.24	2472.12	1782.64	1442.76	1242.63	1112.31	1021.80	956.08	906.81	868.99	839.42	815.9
55000	5016.27	2719.33	1960.91	1587.03	1366.90	1223.54	1123.97	1051.69	997.50	955.89	923.36	897.56
60000	5472.29	2966.54	2139.17	1731.31	1491.16	1334.77	1226.15	1147.29	1088.18	1042.79	1007.30	979.16
65000	5928.31	3213.75	2317.43	1875.58	1615.42	1446.00	1328.33	1242.90	1178.86	1129.69	1091.25	1060.75
70000	6384.34	3460.96	2495.70	2019.86	1739.69	1557.23	1430.51	1338.51	1269.54	1216.59	1175.19	1142.35
75000	6840.36	3708.17	2673.96	2164.13	1863.95	1668.46	1532.69	1434.11	1360.22	1303.49	1259.13	1223.95
80000	7296.39	3955.39	2852.22	2308.41	1988.21	1779.70	1634.87	1529.72	1450.90	1390.39	1343.07	1305.54
85000	7752.41	4202.60	3030.49	2452.68	2112.47	1890.93	1737.05	1625.33	1541.58	1477.29	1427.01	1387.14
90000	8208.43	4449.81	3208.75	2596.96	2236.74	2002.16	1839.23	1720.94	1632.26	1564.18	1510.95	1468.74
95000	8664.46	4697.02	3387.01	2741.23	2361.00	2113.39	1941.41	1816.54	1722.94	1651.08	1594.90	1550.33
100000	9120.48	4944.23	3565.28	2885.51	2485.26	2224.62	2043.59	1912.15	1813.62	1737.98	1678.84	1631.93

Table 1

MONTHLY

17.00%

PAYMENT REQUIRED TO AMORTIZE A LOAN

TERM / AMT	13 YEARS	14 YEARS	15 YEARS	16 YEARS	17 YEARS	18 YEARS	19 YEARS	20 YEARS	25 YEARS	30 YEARS	35 YEARS	40 YEARS
50	.80	.79	.77	.76	.76	.75	.74	.74	.72	.72	.72	.71
100	1.60	1.57	1.54	1.52	1.51	1.49	1.48	1.47	1.44	1.43	1.43	1.42
200	3.19	3.13	3.08	3.04	3.01	2.98	2.96	2.94	2.88	2.86	2.85	2.84
300	4.79	4.70	4.62	4.56	4.51	4.47	4.43	4.41	4.32	4.28	4.27	4.26
400	6.38	6.26	6.16	6.08	6.01	5.96	5.91	5.87	5.76	5.71	5.69	5.68
500	7.98	7.82	7.70	7.60	7.51	7.44	7.39	7.34	7.19	7.13	7.11	7.10
600	9.57	9.39	9.24	9.12	9.02	8.93	8.86	8.81	8.63	8.56	8.53	8.51
700	11.17	10.95	10.78	10.64	10.52	10.42	10.34	10.27	10.07	9.98	9.95	9.93
800	12.76	12.52	12.32	12.15	12.02	11.91	11.82	11.74	11.51	11.41	11.37	11.35
900	14.35	14.08	13.86	13.67	13.52	13.40	13.29	13.21	12.95	12.84	12.79	12.77
1000	15.95	15.64	15.40	15.19	15.02	14.88	14.77	14.67	14.38	14.26	14.21	14.19
2000	31.89	31.28	30.79	30.38	30.04	29.76	29.53	29.34	28.76	28.52	28.42	28.37
3000	47.83	46.92	46.18	45.56	45.06	44.64	44.30	44.01	43.14	42.78	42.62	42.55
4000	63.78	62.56	61.57	60.75	60.08	59.52	59.06	58.68	57.52	57.03	56.83	56.74
5000	79.72	78.20	76.96	75.94	75.10	74.40	73.83	73.35	71.89	71.29	71.03	70.92
6000	95.66	93.84	92.35	91.12	90.12	89.28	88.59	88.01	86.27	85.55	85.24	85.10
7000	111.61	109.47	107.74	106.31	105.13	104.16	103.35	102.68	100.65	99.80	99.44	99.29
8000	127.55	125.11	123.13	121.50	120.15	119.04	118.12	117.35	115.03	114.06	113.65	113.47
9000	143.49	140.75	138.52	136.68	135.17	133.92	132.88	132.02	129.41	128.32	127.85	127.65
10000	159.43	156.39	153.91	151.87	150.19	148.80	147.65	146.69	143.78	142.57	142.06	141.84
11000	175.38	172.03	169.30	167.05	165.21	163.68	162.41	161.35	158.16	156.83	156.26	156.02
12000	191.32	187.67	184.69	182.24	180.23	178.56	177.17	176.02	172.54	171.09	170.47	170.20
13000	207.26	203.30	200.08	197.43	195.24	193.44	191.94	190.69	186.92	185.34	184.67	184.39
14000	223.21	218.94	215.47	212.61	210.26	208.32	206.70	205.36	201.30	199.60	198.88	198.57
15000	239.15	234.58	230.86	227.80	225.28	223.20	221.47	220.03	215.67	213.86	213.08	212.75
16000	255.09	250.22	246.25	242.99	240.30	238.08	236.23	234.69	230.05	228.11	227.29	226.94
17000	271.04	265.86	261.64	258.17	255.32	252.96	250.99	249.36	244.43	242.37	241.49	241.12
18000	286.98	281.50	277.03	273.36	270.34	267.84	265.76	264.03	258.81	256.63	255.70	255.30
19000	302.92	297.13	292.42	288.55	285.36	282.71	280.52	278.70	273.19	270.88	269.90	269.49
20000	318.86	312.77	307.81	303.73	300.37	297.59	295.29	293.37	287.56	285.14	284.11	283.67
21000	334.81	328.41	323.20	318.92	315.39	312.47	310.05	308.03	301.94	299.40	298.32	297.85
22000	350.75	344.05	338.59	334.10	330.41	327.35	324.81	322.70	316.32	313.65	312.52	312.04
23000	366.69	359.69	353.98	349.29	345.43	342.23	339.58	337.37	330.70	327.91	326.73	326.22
24000	382.64	375.33	369.37	364.48	360.45	357.11	354.34	352.04	345.08	342.17	340.93	340.40
25000	398.58	390.96	384.76	379.66	375.47	371.99	369.11	366.71	359.45	356.42	355.14	354.59
26000	414.52	406.60	400.15	394.85	390.48	386.87	383.87	381.37	373.83	370.68	369.34	368.77
27000	430.46	422.24	415.54	410.04	405.50	401.75	398.64	396.04	388.21	384.94	383.55	382.95
28000	446.41	437.88	430.93	425.22	420.52	416.63	413.40	410.71	402.59	399.19	397.75	397.14
29000	462.35	453.52	446.32	440.41	435.54	431.51	428.16	425.38	416.97	413.45	411.96	411.32
30000	478.29	469.16	461.71	455.60	450.56	446.39	442.93	440.05	431.34	427.71	426.16	425.50
31000	494.24	484.79	477.10	470.78	465.58	461.27	457.69	454.71	445.72	441.96	440.37	439.69
32000	510.18	500.43	492.49	485.97	480.59	476.15	472.46	469.38	460.10	456.22	454.57	453.87
33000	526.12	516.07	507.88	501.15	495.61	491.03	487.22	484.05	474.48	470.48	468.78	468.05
34000	542.07	531.71	523.27	516.34	510.63	505.91	501.98	498.72	488.86	484.73	482.98	482.24
35000	558.01	547.35	538.66	531.53	525.65	520.79	516.75	513.39	503.23	498.99	497.19	496.42
36000	573.95	562.99	554.05	546.71	540.67	535.67	531.51	528.05	517.61	513.25	511.39	510.60
37000	589.89	578.63	569.44	561.90	555.69	550.55	546.28	542.72	531.99	527.50	525.60	524.78
38000	605.84	594.26	584.83	577.09	570.71	565.42	561.04	557.39	546.37	541.76	539.80	538.97
39000	621.78	609.90	600.22	592.27	585.72	580.30	575.80	572.06	560.75	556.02	554.01	553.15
40000	637.72	625.54	615.61	607.46	600.74	595.18	590.57	586.73	575.12	570.28	568.22	567.33
41000	653.67	641.18	631.00	622.64	615.76	610.06	605.33	601.39	589.50	584.53	582.42	581.52
42000	669.61	656.82	646.39	637.83	630.78	624.94	620.10	616.06	603.88	598.79	596.63	595.70
43000	685.55	672.46	661.78	653.02	645.80	639.82	634.86	630.73	618.26	613.05	610.83	609.88
44000	701.49	688.09	677.17	668.20	660.82	654.70	649.62	645.40	632.64	627.30	625.04	624.07
45000	717.44	703.73	692.56	683.39	675.83	669.58	664.39	660.07	647.01	641.56	639.24	638.25
46000	733.38	719.37	707.95	698.58	690.85	684.46	679.15	674.73	661.39	655.82	653.45	652.43
47000	749.32	735.01	723.34	713.76	705.87	699.34	693.92	689.40	675.77	670.07	667.65	666.62
48000	765.27	750.65	738.73	728.95	720.89	714.22	708.68	704.07	690.15	684.33	681.86	680.80
49000	781.21	766.29	754.12	744.14	735.91	729.10	723.45	718.74	704.53	698.59	696.06	694.98
50000	797.15	781.92	769.51	759.32	750.93	743.98	738.21	733.41	718.90	712.84	710.27	709.17
55000	876.87	860.12	846.46	835.25	826.02	818.38	812.03	806.75	790.79	784.13	781.29	780.08
60000	956.58	938.31	923.41	911.19	901.11	892.77	885.85	880.09	862.68	855.41	852.32	851.00
65000	1036.30	1016.50	1000.36	987.12	976.20	967.17	959.67	953.43	934.57	926.69	923.35	921.92
70000	1116.01	1094.69	1077.31	1063.05	1051.30	1041.57	1033.49	1026.77	1006.46	997.98	994.37	992.83
75000	1195.73	1172.88	1154.26	1138.98	1126.39	1115.97	1107.31	1100.11	1078.35	1069.26	1065.40	1063.75
80000	1275.44	1251.08	1231.21	1214.91	1201.48	1190.36	1181.13	1173.45	1150.24	1140.55	1136.43	1134.66
85000	1355.16	1329.27	1308.16	1290.84	1276.57	1264.76	1254.95	1246.79	1222.13	1211.83	1207.45	1205.58
90000	1434.87	1407.46	1385.11	1366.78	1351.66	1339.16	1328.77	1320.13	1294.02	1283.11	1278.48	1276.50
95000	1514.59	1485.65	1462.06	1442.71	1426.76	1413.56	1402.59	1393.47	1365.91	1354.40	1349.50	1347.41
100000	1594.30	1563.84	1539.01	1518.64	1501.85	1487.95	1476.41	1466.81	1437.80	1425.68	1420.53	1418.33

17%

Table 1

17.25%

MONTHLY
PAYMENT REQUIRED TO AMORTIZE A LOAN

TERM AMOUNT	1 YEAR	2 YEARS	3 YEARS	4 YEARS	5 YEARS	6 YEARS	7 YEARS	8 YEARS	9 YEARS	10 YEARS	11 YEARS	12 YEARS
50	4.57	2.48	1.79	1.45	1.25	1.12	1.03	.97	.92	.88	.85	.83
100	9.14	4.96	3.58	2.90	2.50	2.24	2.06	1.93	1.83	1.76	1.70	1.65
200	18.27	9.92	7.16	5.80	5.00	4.48	4.12	3.86	3.66	3.51	3.40	3.30
300	27.40	14.87	10.74	8.70	7.50	6.72	6.18	5.79	5.49	5.27	5.09	4.95
400	36.53	19.83	14.32	11.60	10.00	8.96	8.24	7.71	7.32	7.02	6.79	6.60
500	45.67	24.79	17.89	14.50	12.50	11.20	10.30	9.64	9.15	8.77	8.48	8.25
600	54.80	29.74	21.47	17.40	15.00	13.44	12.35	11.57	10.98	10.53	10.18	9.90
700	63.93	34.70	25.05	20.29	17.50	15.68	14.41	13.49	12.81	12.28	11.87	11.55
800	73.06	39.65	28.63	23.19	19.99	17.91	16.47	15.42	14.64	14.04	13.57	13.19
900	82.20	44.61	32.20	26.09	22.49	20.15	18.53	17.35	16.47	15.79	15.26	14.84
1000	91.33	49.57	35.78	28.99	24.99	22.39	20.59	19.28	18.30	17.54	16.96	16.49
2000	182.65	99.13	71.56	57.97	49.98	44.78	41.17	38.55	36.59	35.08	33.91	32.98
3000	273.98	148.69	107.34	86.96	74.97	67.16	61.75	57.82	54.88	52.62	50.86	49.46
4000	365.30	198.25	143.11	115.94	99.95	89.55	82.33	77.09	73.17	70.16	67.81	65.95
5000	456.62	247.82	178.89	144.93	124.94	111.93	102.91	96.36	91.46	87.70	84.76	82.44
6000	547.95	297.38	214.67	173.91	149.93	134.32	123.49	115.63	109.75	105.24	101.71	98.92
7000	639.27	346.94	250.45	202.90	174.92	156.71	144.07	134.90	128.04	122.77	118.66	115.41
8000	730.59	396.50	286.22	231.88	199.90	179.09	164.65	154.17	146.33	140.31	135.62	131.89
9000	821.92	446.07	322.00	260.87	224.89	201.48	185.23	173.44	164.62	157.85	152.57	148.38
10000	913.24	495.63	357.78	289.85	249.88	223.86	205.81	192.72	182.91	175.39	169.52	164.87
11000	1004.56	545.19	393.56	318.84	274.86	246.25	226.39	211.99	201.20	192.93	186.47	181.35
12000	1095.89	594.75	429.33	347.82	299.85	268.64	246.97	231.26	219.49	210.47	203.42	197.84
13000	1187.21	644.32	465.11	376.80	324.84	291.02	267.55	250.53	237.78	228.01	220.37	214.33
14000	1278.53	693.88	500.89	405.79	349.83	313.41	288.13	269.80	256.07	245.54	237.32	230.81
15000	1369.86	743.44	536.66	434.77	374.81	335.79	308.71	289.07	274.36	263.08	254.27	247.30
16000	1461.18	793.00	572.44	463.76	399.80	358.18	329.29	308.34	292.65	280.62	271.23	263.78
17000	1552.50	842.57	608.22	492.74	424.79	380.56	349.87	327.61	310.94	298.16	288.18	280.27
18000	1643.83	892.13	644.00	521.73	449.77	402.95	370.45	346.88	329.23	315.70	305.13	296.76
19000	1735.15	941.69	679.77	550.71	474.76	425.34	391.04	366.15	347.52	333.24	322.08	313.24
20000	1826.47	991.25	715.55	579.70	499.75	447.72	411.62	385.43	365.81	350.78	339.03	329.73
21000	1917.80	1040.82	751.33	608.68	524.74	470.11	432.20	404.70	384.10	368.31	355.98	346.22
22000	2009.12	1090.38	787.11	637.67	549.72	492.49	452.78	423.97	402.40	385.85	372.93	362.70
23000	2100.44	1139.94	822.88	666.65	574.71	514.88	473.36	443.24	420.69	403.39	389.88	379.19
24000	2191.77	1189.50	858.66	695.63	599.70	537.27	493.94	462.51	438.98	420.93	406.84	395.67
25000	2283.09	1239.07	894.44	724.62	624.68	559.65	514.52	481.78	457.27	438.47	423.79	412.16
26000	2374.41	1288.63	930.21	753.60	649.67	582.04	535.10	501.05	475.56	456.01	440.74	428.65
27000	2465.74	1338.19	965.99	782.59	674.66	604.42	555.68	520.32	493.85	473.54	457.69	445.13
28000	2557.06	1387.75	1001.77	811.57	699.65	626.81	576.26	539.59	512.14	491.08	474.64	461.62
29000	2648.38	1437.32	1037.55	840.56	724.63	649.19	596.84	558.87	530.43	508.62	491.59	478.11
30000	2739.71	1486.88	1073.32	869.54	749.62	671.58	617.42	578.14	548.72	526.16	508.54	494.59
31000	2831.03	1536.44	1109.10	898.53	774.61	693.97	638.00	597.41	567.01	543.70	525.50	511.08
32000	2922.35	1586.00	1144.88	927.51	799.60	716.35	658.58	616.68	585.30	561.24	542.45	527.56
33000	3013.68	1635.57	1180.66	956.50	824.58	738.74	679.16	635.95	603.59	578.78	559.40	544.05
34000	3105.00	1685.13	1216.43	985.48	849.57	761.12	699.74	655.22	621.88	596.31	576.35	560.54
35000	3196.33	1734.69	1252.21	1014.46	874.56	783.51	720.32	674.49	640.17	613.85	593.30	577.02
36000	3287.65	1784.25	1287.99	1043.45	899.54	805.90	740.90	693.76	658.46	631.39	610.25	593.51
37000	3378.97	1833.82	1323.76	1072.43	924.53	828.28	761.49	713.03	676.75	648.93	627.20	609.99
38000	3470.30	1883.38	1359.54	1101.42	949.52	850.67	782.07	732.30	695.04	666.47	644.15	626.48
39000	3561.62	1932.94	1395.32	1130.40	974.51	873.05	802.65	751.58	713.33	684.01	661.11	642.97
40000	3652.94	1982.50	1431.10	1159.39	999.49	895.44	823.23	770.85	731.62	701.55	678.06	659.45
41000	3744.27	2032.07	1466.87	1188.37	1024.48	917.83	843.81	790.12	749.91	719.08	695.01	675.94
42000	3835.59	2081.63	1502.65	1217.36	1049.47	940.21	864.39	809.39	768.20	736.62	711.96	692.43
43000	3926.91	2131.19	1538.43	1246.34	1074.45	962.60	884.97	828.66	786.49	754.16	728.91	708.91
44000	4018.24	2180.75	1574.21	1275.33	1099.44	984.98	905.55	847.93	804.79	771.70	745.86	725.40
45000	4109.56	2230.32	1609.98	1304.31	1124.43	1007.37	926.13	867.20	823.08	789.24	762.81	741.88
46000	4200.88	2279.88	1645.76	1333.29	1149.42	1029.75	946.71	886.47	841.37	806.78	779.76	758.37
47000	4292.21	2329.44	1681.54	1362.28	1174.40	1052.14	967.29	905.74	859.66	824.31	796.72	774.86
48000	4383.53	2379.00	1717.31	1391.26	1199.39	1074.53	987.87	925.02	877.95	841.85	813.67	791.34
49000	4474.85	2428.57	1753.09	1420.25	1224.38	1096.91	1008.45	944.29	896.24	859.39	830.62	807.83
50000	4566.18	2478.13	1788.87	1449.23	1249.36	1119.30	1029.03	963.56	914.53	876.93	847.57	824.32
55000	5022.79	2725.94	1967.76	1594.16	1374.30	1231.23	1131.93	1059.91	1005.98	964.62	932.33	906.75
60000	5479.41	2973.75	2146.64	1739.08	1499.24	1343.16	1234.84	1156.27	1097.43	1052.32	1017.08	989.18
65000	5936.03	3221.57	2325.53	1884.00	1624.17	1455.09	1337.74	1252.62	1188.88	1140.01	1101.84	1071.61
70000	6392.65	3469.38	2504.41	2028.92	1749.11	1567.02	1440.64	1348.98	1280.34	1227.70	1186.60	1154.04
75000	6849.26	3717.19	2683.30	2173.85	1874.04	1678.94	1543.55	1445.33	1371.79	1315.39	1271.35	1236.47
80000	7305.88	3965.00	2862.19	2318.77	1998.98	1790.87	1646.45	1541.69	1463.24	1403.09	1356.11	1318.90
85000	7762.50	4212.82	3041.07	2463.69	2123.92	1902.80	1749.35	1638.04	1554.69	1490.78	1440.87	1401.33
90000	8219.11	4460.63	3219.96	2608.61	2248.85	2014.73	1852.25	1734.40	1646.15	1578.47	1525.62	1483.76
95000	8675.73	4708.44	3398.85	2753.54	2373.79	2126.66	1955.16	1830.75	1737.60	1666.16	1610.38	1566.20
100000	9132.35	4956.25	3577.73	2898.46	2498.72	2238.59	2058.06	1927.11	1829.05	1753.86	1695.13	1648.63

17%

Table 1

MONTHLY

17.25%

PAYMENT REQUIRED TO AMORTIZE A LOAN

ERM	13 YEARS	14 YEARS	15 YEARS	16 YEARS	17 YEARS	18 YEARS	19 YEARS	20 YEARS	25 YEARS	30 YEARS	35 YEARS	40 YEARS
UNT												
50	.81	.80	.78	.77	.77	.76	.75	.75	.73	.73	.73	.72
100	1.62	1.59	1.56	1.54	1.53	1.51	1.50	1.49	1.46	1.45	1.45	1.44
200	3.23	3.17	3.12	3.08	3.05	3.02	3.00	2.98	2.92	2.90	2.89	2.88
300	4.84	4.75	4.68	4.62	4.57	4.52	4.49	4.46	4.38	4.34	4.33	4.32
400	6.45	6.33	6.23	6.15	6.09	6.03	5.99	5.95	5.84	5.79	5.77	5.76
500	8.06	7.91	7.79	7.69	7.61	7.54	7.48	7.43	7.29	7.23	7.21	7.20
600	9.67	9.49	9.35	9.23	9.13	9.04	8.98	8.92	8.75	8.68	8.65	8.64
700	11.28	11.07	10.90	10.76	10.65	10.55	10.47	10.41	10.21	10.13	10.09	10.08
800	12.90	12.66	12.46	12.30	12.17	12.06	11.97	11.89	11.67	11.57	11.53	11.52
900	14.51	14.24	14.02	13.84	13.69	13.56	13.46	13.38	13.13	13.02	12.97	12.96
1000	16.12	15.82	15.57	15.37	15.21	15.07	14.96	14.86	14.58	14.46	14.42	14.40
2000	32.23	31.63	31.14	30.74	30.41	30.14	29.91	29.72	29.16	28.92	28.83	28.79
3000	48.35	47.44	46.71	46.11	45.61	45.20	44.86	44.58	43.73	43.38	43.24	43.18
4000	64.46	63.26	62.28	61.47	60.81	60.27	59.81	59.44	58.31	57.84	57.65	57.57
5000	80.57	79.07	77.84	76.84	76.01	75.33	74.77	74.30	72.89	72.30	72.06	71.96
6000	96.69	94.88	93.41	92.21	91.22	90.40	89.72	89.16	87.46	86.76	86.47	86.35
7000	112.80	110.69	108.98	107.57	106.42	105.46	104.67	104.01	102.04	101.22	100.88	100.74
8000	128.91	126.51	124.55	122.94	121.62	120.53	119.62	118.87	116.62	115.68	115.29	115.13
9000	145.03	142.32	140.11	138.31	136.82	135.59	134.58	133.73	131.19	130.14	129.70	129.52
10000	161.14	158.13	155.68	153.67	152.02	150.66	149.53	148.59	145.77	144.60	144.11	143.91
11000	177.26	173.94	171.25	169.04	167.22	165.72	164.48	163.45	160.35	159.06	158.53	158.30
12000	193.37	189.76	186.82	184.41	182.43	180.79	179.43	178.31	174.92	173.52	172.94	172.69
13000	209.48	205.57	202.38	199.77	197.63	195.86	194.39	193.16	189.50	187.98	187.35	187.08
14000	225.60	221.38	217.95	215.14	212.83	210.92	209.34	208.02	204.07	202.44	201.76	201.47
15000	241.71	237.19	233.52	230.51	228.03	225.99	224.29	222.88	218.65	216.90	216.17	215.86
16000	257.82	253.01	249.09	245.88	243.23	241.05	239.24	237.74	233.23	231.36	230.58	230.25
17000	273.94	268.82	264.65	261.24	258.44	256.12	254.20	252.60	247.80	245.82	244.99	244.64
18000	290.05	284.63	280.22	276.61	273.64	271.18	269.15	267.46	262.38	260.28	259.40	259.03
19000	306.17	300.45	295.79	291.98	288.84	286.25	284.10	282.31	276.96	274.74	273.81	273.42
20000	322.28	316.26	311.36	307.34	304.04	301.31	299.05	297.17	291.53	289.20	288.22	287.81
21000	338.39	332.07	326.92	322.71	319.24	316.38	314.00	312.03	306.11	303.66	302.63	302.20
22000	354.51	347.88	342.49	338.08	334.44	331.44	328.96	326.89	320.69	318.12	317.05	316.59
23000	370.62	363.70	358.06	353.44	349.65	346.51	343.91	341.75	335.26	332.58	331.46	330.98
24000	386.73	379.51	373.63	368.81	364.85	361.57	358.86	356.61	349.84	347.04	345.87	345.37
25000	402.85	395.32	389.19	384.18	380.05	376.64	373.81	371.47	364.42	361.50	360.28	359.76
26000	418.96	411.13	404.76	399.54	395.25	391.71	388.77	386.32	378.99	375.96	374.69	374.15
27000	435.07	426.95	420.33	414.91	410.45	406.77	403.72	401.18	393.57	390.42	389.10	388.54
28000	451.19	442.76	435.90	430.28	425.66	421.84	418.67	416.04	408.14	404.88	403.51	402.93
29000	467.30	458.57	451.46	445.65	440.86	436.90	433.62	430.90	422.72	419.34	417.92	417.32
30000	483.42	474.38	467.03	461.01	456.06	451.97	448.58	445.76	437.30	433.80	432.33	431.71
31000	499.53	490.20	482.60	476.38	471.26	467.03	463.53	460.62	451.87	448.26	446.74	446.10
32000	515.64	506.01	498.17	491.75	486.46	482.10	478.48	475.47	466.45	462.72	461.15	460.49
33000	531.76	521.82	513.73	507.11	501.66	497.16	493.43	490.33	481.03	477.18	475.57	474.88
34000	547.87	537.63	529.30	522.48	516.87	512.23	508.39	505.19	495.60	491.64	489.98	489.27
35000	563.98	553.45	544.87	537.85	532.07	527.29	523.34	520.05	510.18	506.10	504.39	503.66
36000	580.10	569.26	560.44	553.21	547.27	542.36	538.29	534.91	524.76	520.56	518.80	518.05
37000	596.21	585.07	576.01	568.58	562.47	557.42	553.24	549.77	539.33	535.02	533.21	532.44
38000	612.33	600.89	591.57	583.95	577.67	572.49	568.19	564.62	553.91	549.48	547.62	546.83
39000	628.44	616.70	607.14	599.31	592.87	587.56	583.15	579.48	568.49	563.94	562.03	561.22
40000	644.55	632.51	622.71	614.68	608.08	602.62	598.10	594.34	583.06	578.40	576.44	575.61
41000	660.67	648.32	638.28	630.05	623.28	617.69	613.05	609.20	597.64	592.86	590.85	590.00
42000	676.78	664.14	653.84	645.41	638.48	632.75	628.00	624.06	612.21	607.32	605.26	604.39
43000	692.89	679.95	669.41	660.78	653.68	647.82	642.96	638.92	626.79	621.78	619.67	618.78
44000	709.01	695.76	684.98	676.15	668.88	662.88	657.91	653.78	641.37	636.24	634.09	633.18
45000	725.12	711.57	700.55	691.52	684.09	677.95	672.86	668.63	655.94	650.70	648.50	647.57
46000	741.23	727.39	716.11	706.88	699.29	693.01	687.81	683.49	670.52	665.16	662.91	661.96
47000	757.35	743.20	731.68	722.25	714.49	708.08	702.77	698.35	685.10	679.62	677.32	676.35
48000	773.46	759.01	747.25	737.62	729.69	723.14	717.72	713.21	699.67	694.08	691.73	690.74
49000	789.58	774.82	762.82	752.98	744.89	738.21	732.67	728.07	714.25	708.54	706.14	705.13
50000	805.69	790.64	778.38	768.35	760.09	753.27	747.62	742.93	728.83	723.00	720.55	719.52
55000	886.26	869.70	856.22	845.18	836.10	828.60	822.38	817.22	801.71	795.30	792.61	791.47
60000	966.83	948.76	934.06	922.02	912.11	903.93	897.15	891.51	874.59	867.60	864.66	863.42
65000	1047.40	1027.83	1011.90	998.85	988.12	979.26	971.91	965.80	947.47	939.90	936.71	935.37
70000	1127.96	1106.89	1089.73	1075.69	1064.13	1054.58	1046.67	1040.09	1020.35	1012.20	1008.77	1007.32
75000	1208.53	1185.95	1167.57	1152.52	1140.14	1129.91	1121.43	1114.39	1093.24	1084.49	1080.82	1079.27
80000	1289.10	1265.02	1245.41	1229.36	1216.15	1205.24	1196.19	1188.68	1166.12	1156.79	1152.88	1151.22
85000	1369.67	1344.08	1323.25	1306.19	1292.16	1280.56	1270.96	1262.97	1239.00	1229.09	1224.93	1223.17
90000	1450.24	1423.14	1401.09	1383.03	1368.17	1355.89	1345.72	1337.26	1311.88	1301.39	1296.99	1295.13
95000	1530.81	1502.21	1478.92	1459.86	1444.17	1431.22	1420.48	1411.55	1384.76	1373.69	1369.04	1367.08
00000	1611.37	1581.27	1556.76	1536.69	1520.18	1506.54	1495.24	1485.85	1457.65	1445.99	1441.10	1439.03

17%

Table 1

17.50%

MONTHLY
PAYMENT REQUIRED TO AMORTIZE A LOAN

TERM	1 YEAR	2 YEARS	3 YEARS	4 YEARS	5 YEARS	6 YEARS	7 YEARS	8 YEARS	9 YEARS	10 YEARS	11 YEARS	12 YEAR.
AMOUNT												
50	4.58	2.49	1.80	1.46	1.26	1.13	1.04	.98	.93	.89	.86	.84
100	9.15	4.97	3.60	2.92	2.52	2.26	2.08	1.95	1.85	1.77	1.72	1.67
200	18.29	9.94	7.19	5.83	5.03	4.51	4.15	3.89	3.69	3.54	3.43	3.34
300	27.44	14.91	10.78	8.74	7.54	6.76	6.22	5.83	5.54	5.31	5.14	5.00
400	36.58	19.88	14.37	11.65	10.05	9.02	8.30	7.77	7.38	7.08	6.85	6.67
500	45.73	24.85	17.96	14.56	12.57	11.27	10.37	9.72	9.23	8.85	8.56	8.33
600	54.87	29.81	21.55	17.47	15.08	13.52	12.44	11.66	11.07	10.62	10.27	10.00
700	64.01	34.78	25.14	20.39	17.59	15.77	14.51	13.60	12.92	12.39	11.99	11.66
800	73.16	39.75	28.73	23.30	20.10	18.03	16.59	15.54	14.76	14.16	13.70	13.33
900	82.30	44.72	32.32	26.21	22.61	20.28	18.66	17.48	16.61	15.93	15.41	14.99
1000	91.45	49.69	35.91	29.12	25.13	22.53	20.73	19.43	18.45	17.70	17.12	16.66
2000	182.89	99.37	71.81	58.23	50.25	45.06	41.46	38.85	36.90	35.40	34.23	33.31
3000	274.33	149.05	107.71	87.35	75.37	67.58	62.18	58.27	55.34	53.10	51.35	49.97
4000	365.77	198.74	143.61	116.46	100.49	90.11	82.91	77.69	73.79	70.80	68.46	66.62
5000	457.22	248.42	179.52	145.58	125.62	112.64	103.63	97.11	92.23	88.49	85.58	83.27
6000	548.66	298.10	215.42	174.69	150.74	135.16	124.36	116.53	110.68	106.19	102.69	99.93
7000	640.10	347.78	251.32	203.81	175.86	157.69	145.09	135.95	129.12	123.89	119.81	116.58
8000	731.54	397.47	287.22	232.92	200.98	180.21	165.81	155.37	147.57	141.59	136.92	133.24
9000	822.98	447.15	323.12	262.03	226.10	202.74	186.54	174.80	166.01	159.29	154.04	149.89
10000	914.43	496.83	359.03	291.15	251.23	225.27	207.26	194.22	184.46	176.98	171.15	166.54
11000	1005.87	546.52	394.93	320.26	276.35	247.79	227.99	213.64	202.90	194.68	188.27	183.20
12000	1097.31	596.20	430.83	349.38	301.47	270.32	248.71	233.06	221.35	212.38	205.38	199.85
13000	1188.75	645.88	466.73	378.49	326.59	292.84	269.44	252.48	239.79	230.08	222.50	216.51
14000	1280.20	695.56	502.63	407.61	351.72	315.37	290.17	271.90	258.24	247.78	239.61	233.16
15000	1371.64	745.25	538.54	436.72	376.84	337.90	310.89	291.32	276.69	265.47	256.73	249.81
16000	1463.08	794.93	574.44	465.83	401.96	360.42	331.62	310.74	295.13	283.17	273.84	266.47
17000	1554.52	844.61	610.34	494.95	427.08	382.95	352.34	330.17	313.58	300.87	290.96	283.12
18000	1645.96	894.30	646.24	524.06	452.20	405.47	373.07	349.59	332.02	318.57	308.07	299.77
19000	1737.41	943.98	682.14	553.18	477.33	428.00	393.80	369.01	350.47	336.26	325.19	316.43
20000	1828.85	993.66	718.05	582.29	502.45	450.53	414.52	388.43	368.91	353.96	342.30	333.08
21000	1920.29	1043.34	753.95	611.41	527.57	473.05	435.25	407.85	387.36	371.66	359.42	349.74
22000	2011.73	1093.03	789.85	640.52	552.69	495.58	455.97	427.27	405.80	389.36	376.53	366.39
23000	2103.18	1142.71	825.75	669.64	577.82	518.10	476.70	446.69	424.25	407.06	393.65	383.04
24000	2194.62	1192.39	861.65	698.75	602.94	540.63	497.42	466.11	442.69	424.75	410.76	399.70
25000	2286.06	1242.08	897.56	727.86	628.06	563.16	518.15	485.54	461.14	442.45	427.88	416.35
26000	2377.50	1291.76	933.46	756.98	653.18	585.68	538.88	504.96	479.58	460.15	444.99	433.01
27000	2468.94	1341.44	969.36	786.09	678.30	608.21	559.60	524.38	498.03	477.85	462.11	449.66
28000	2560.39	1391.12	1005.26	815.21	703.43	630.73	580.33	543.80	516.47	495.55	479.22	466.31
29000	2651.83	1440.81	1041.16	844.32	728.55	653.26	601.05	563.22	534.92	513.24	496.34	482.97
30000	2743.27	1490.49	1077.07	873.44	753.67	675.79	621.78	582.64	553.37	530.94	513.45	499.62
31000	2834.71	1540.17	1112.97	902.55	778.79	698.31	642.50	602.06	571.81	548.64	530.57	516.27
32000	2926.16	1589.86	1148.87	931.66	803.92	720.84	663.23	621.48	590.26	566.34	547.68	532.93
33000	3017.60	1639.54	1184.77	960.78	829.04	743.36	683.96	640.90	608.70	584.03	564.80	549.58
34000	3109.04	1689.22	1220.68	989.89	854.16	765.89	704.68	660.33	627.15	601.73	581.91	566.24
35000	3200.48	1738.90	1256.58	1019.01	879.28	788.42	725.41	679.75	645.59	619.43	599.03	582.89
36000	3291.92	1788.59	1292.48	1048.12	904.40	810.94	746.13	699.17	664.04	637.13	616.14	599.54
37000	3383.37	1838.27	1328.38	1077.24	929.53	833.47	766.86	718.59	682.48	654.83	633.26	616.20
38000	3474.81	1887.95	1364.28	1106.35	954.65	855.99	787.59	738.01	700.93	672.52	650.37	632.85
39000	3566.25	1937.64	1400.19	1135.47	979.77	878.52	808.31	757.43	719.37	690.22	667.49	649.51
40000	3657.69	1987.32	1436.09	1164.58	1004.89	901.05	829.04	776.85	737.82	707.92	684.60	666.16
41000	3749.14	2037.00	1471.99	1193.69	1030.02	923.57	849.76	796.27	756.26	725.62	701.72	682.81
42000	3840.58	2086.68	1507.89	1222.81	1055.14	946.10	870.49	815.70	774.71	743.32	718.83	699.47
43000	3932.02	2136.37	1543.79	1251.92	1080.26	968.62	891.21	835.12	793.15	761.01	735.95	716.12
44000	4023.46	2186.05	1579.70	1281.04	1105.38	991.15	911.94	854.54	811.60	778.71	753.06	732.78
45000	4114.90	2235.73	1615.60	1310.15	1130.50	1013.68	932.67	873.96	830.05	796.41	770.18	749.43
46000	4206.35	2285.42	1651.50	1339.27	1155.63	1036.20	953.39	893.38	848.49	814.11	787.29	766.08
47000	4297.79	2335.10	1687.40	1368.38	1180.75	1058.73	974.12	912.80	866.94	831.81	804.41	782.74
48000	4389.23	2384.78	1723.30	1397.49	1205.87	1081.26	994.84	932.22	885.38	849.50	821.52	799.39
49000	4480.67	2434.46	1759.21	1426.61	1230.99	1103.78	1015.57	951.64	903.83	867.20	838.64	816.04
50000	4572.12	2484.15	1795.11	1455.72	1256.12	1126.31	1036.29	971.07	922.27	884.90	855.75	832.70
55000	5029.33	2732.56	1974.62	1601.30	1381.73	1238.94	1139.92	1068.17	1014.50	973.39	941.33	915.97
60000	5486.54	2980.98	2154.13	1746.87	1507.34	1351.57	1243.55	1165.28	1106.73	1061.88	1026.90	999.24
65000	5943.75	3229.39	2333.64	1892.44	1632.95	1464.20	1347.18	1262.38	1198.95	1150.37	1112.48	1082.51
70000	6400.96	3477.80	2513.15	2038.01	1758.56	1576.83	1450.81	1359.49	1291.18	1238.86	1198.05	1165.78
75000	6858.17	3726.22	2692.66	2183.58	1884.17	1689.46	1554.44	1456.60	1383.41	1327.35	1283.63	1249.05
80000	7315.38	3974.63	2872.17	2329.15	2009.78	1802.09	1658.07	1553.70	1475.63	1415.84	1369.20	1332.31
85000	7772.59	4223.05	3051.68	2474.73	2135.39	1914.72	1761.70	1650.81	1567.86	1504.32	1454.77	1415.58
90000	8229.80	4471.46	3231.19	2620.30	2261.00	2027.35	1865.33	1747.91	1660.09	1592.81	1540.35	1498.85
95000	8687.01	4719.88	3410.70	2765.87	2386.62	2139.98	1968.96	1845.02	1752.31	1681.30	1625.92	1582.12
100000	9144.23	4968.29	3590.21	2911.44	2512.23	2252.61	2072.58	1942.13	1844.54	1769.79	1711.50	1665.39

17%

Table 1

MONTHLY 17.50%

PAYMENT REQUIRED TO AMORTIZE A LOAN

ERM / UNT	13 YEARS	14 YEARS	15 YEARS	16 YEARS	17 YEARS	18 YEARS	19 YEARS	20 YEARS	25 YEARS	30 YEARS	35 YEARS	40 YEARS
50	.82	.80	.79	.78	.77	.77	.76	.76	.74	.74	.74	.73
100	1.63	1.60	1.58	1.56	1.54	1.53	1.52	1.51	1.48	1.47	1.47	1.46
200	3.26	3.20	3.15	3.11	3.08	3.06	3.03	3.01	2.96	2.94	2.93	2.92
300	4.89	4.80	4.73	4.67	4.62	4.58	4.55	4.52	4.44	4.40	4.39	4.38
400	6.52	6.40	6.30	6.22	6.16	6.11	6.06	6.02	5.92	5.87	5.85	5.84
500	8.15	8.00	7.88	7.78	7.70	7.63	7.58	7.53	7.39	7.34	7.31	7.30
600	9.78	9.60	9.45	9.33	9.24	9.16	9.09	9.03	8.87	8.80	8.78	8.76
700	11.40	11.20	11.03	10.89	10.78	10.68	10.60	10.54	10.35	10.27	10.24	10.22
800	13.03	12.80	12.60	12.44	12.31	12.21	12.12	12.04	11.83	11.74	11.70	11.68
900	14.66	14.39	14.18	14.00	13.85	13.73	13.63	13.55	13.30	13.20	13.16	13.14
1000	16.29	15.99	15.75	15.55	15.39	15.26	15.15	15.05	14.78	14.67	14.62	14.60
2000	32.58	31.98	31.50	31.10	30.78	30.51	30.29	30.10	29.56	29.33	29.24	29.20
3000	48.86	47.97	47.24	46.65	46.16	45.76	45.43	45.15	44.33	43.99	43.86	43.80
4000	65.15	63.96	62.99	62.20	61.55	61.01	60.57	60.20	59.11	58.66	58.47	58.39
5000	81.43	79.94	78.73	77.75	76.93	76.26	75.71	75.25	73.88	73.32	73.09	72.99
6000	97.72	95.93	94.48	93.29	92.32	91.52	90.85	90.30	88.66	87.98	87.71	87.59
7000	114.00	111.92	110.23	108.84	107.71	106.77	105.99	105.35	103.43	102.65	102.32	102.19
8000	130.29	127.91	125.97	124.39	123.09	122.02	121.13	120.40	118.21	117.31	116.94	116.78
9000	146.57	143.89	141.72	139.94	138.48	137.27	136.28	135.45	132.98	131.97	131.56	131.38
10000	162.86	159.88	157.46	155.49	153.86	152.52	151.42	150.50	147.76	146.64	146.17	145.98
11000	179.14	175.87	173.21	171.03	169.25	167.78	166.56	165.55	162.53	161.30	160.79	160.58
12000	195.43	191.86	188.95	186.58	184.63	183.03	181.70	180.60	177.31	175.96	175.41	175.17
13000	211.71	207.84	204.70	202.13	200.02	198.28	196.84	195.65	192.08	190.63	190.02	189.77
14000	228.00	223.83	220.45	217.68	215.41	213.53	211.98	210.70	206.86	205.29	204.64	204.37
15000	244.28	239.82	236.19	233.23	230.79	228.78	227.12	225.75	221.63	219.95	219.26	218.97
16000	260.57	255.81	251.94	248.78	246.18	244.04	242.26	240.80	236.41	234.62	233.87	233.56
17000	276.85	271.79	267.68	264.32	261.56	259.29	257.41	255.85	251.19	249.28	248.49	248.16
18000	293.14	287.78	283.43	279.87	276.95	274.54	272.55	270.89	265.96	263.94	263.11	262.76
19000	309.42	303.77	299.17	295.42	292.34	289.79	287.69	285.94	280.74	278.61	277.72	277.35
20000	325.71	319.76	314.92	310.97	307.72	305.04	302.83	300.99	295.51	293.27	292.34	291.95
21000	341.99	335.74	330.67	326.52	323.11	320.30	317.97	316.04	310.29	307.93	306.96	306.55
22000	358.28	351.73	346.41	342.06	338.49	335.55	333.11	331.09	325.06	322.60	321.57	321.15
23000	374.56	367.72	362.16	357.61	353.88	350.80	348.25	346.14	339.84	337.26	336.19	335.74
24000	390.85	383.71	377.90	373.16	369.26	366.05	363.39	361.19	354.61	351.92	350.81	350.34
25000	407.13	399.69	393.65	388.71	384.65	381.30	378.54	376.24	369.39	366.59	365.42	364.94
26000	423.42	415.68	409.40	404.26	400.04	396.56	393.68	391.29	384.16	381.25	380.04	379.54
27000	439.70	431.67	425.14	419.80	415.42	411.81	408.82	406.34	398.94	395.91	394.66	394.13
28000	455.99	447.66	440.89	435.35	430.81	427.06	423.96	421.39	413.71	410.58	409.27	408.73
29000	472.27	463.65	456.63	450.90	446.19	442.31	439.10	436.44	428.49	425.24	423.89	423.33
30000	488.56	479.63	472.38	466.45	461.58	457.56	454.24	451.49	443.26	439.90	438.51	437.93
31000	504.84	495.62	488.12	482.00	476.96	472.82	469.38	466.54	458.04	454.57	453.12	452.52
32000	521.13	511.61	503.87	497.55	492.35	488.07	484.52	481.59	472.81	469.23	467.74	467.12
33000	537.41	527.60	519.62	513.09	507.74	503.32	499.67	496.64	487.59	483.89	482.36	481.72
34000	553.70	543.58	535.36	528.64	523.12	518.57	514.81	511.69	502.37	498.56	496.97	496.31
35000	569.98	559.57	551.11	544.19	538.51	533.82	529.95	526.73	517.14	513.22	511.59	510.91
36000	586.27	575.56	566.85	559.74	553.89	549.08	545.09	541.78	531.92	527.88	526.21	525.51
37000	602.55	591.55	582.60	575.29	569.28	564.33	560.23	556.83	546.69	542.55	540.82	540.11
38000	618.84	607.53	598.34	590.83	584.67	579.58	575.37	571.88	561.47	557.21	555.44	554.70
39000	635.12	623.52	614.09	606.38	600.05	594.83	590.51	586.93	576.24	571.87	570.06	569.30
40000	651.41	639.51	629.84	621.93	615.44	610.08	605.65	601.98	591.02	586.54	584.68	583.90
41000	667.70	655.50	645.58	637.48	630.82	625.33	620.80	617.03	605.79	601.20	599.29	598.50
42000	683.98	671.48	661.33	653.03	646.21	640.59	635.94	632.08	620.57	615.86	613.91	613.09
43000	700.27	687.47	677.07	668.57	661.59	655.84	651.08	647.13	635.34	630.52	628.53	627.69
44000	716.55	703.46	692.82	684.12	676.98	671.09	666.22	662.18	650.12	645.19	643.14	642.29
45000	732.84	719.45	708.57	699.67	692.37	686.34	681.36	677.23	664.89	659.85	657.76	656.89
46000	749.12	735.43	724.31	715.22	707.75	701.59	696.50	692.28	679.67	674.51	672.38	671.48
47000	765.41	751.42	740.06	730.77	723.14	716.85	711.64	707.33	694.44	689.18	686.99	686.08
48000	781.69	767.41	755.80	746.32	738.52	732.10	726.78	722.38	709.22	703.84	701.61	700.68
49000	797.98	783.40	771.55	761.86	753.91	747.35	741.93	737.43	723.99	718.50	716.23	715.27
50000	814.26	799.38	787.29	777.41	769.29	762.60	757.07	752.48	738.77	733.17	730.84	729.87
55000	895.69	879.32	866.02	855.15	846.22	838.86	832.77	827.72	812.65	806.48	803.93	802.86
60000	977.11	959.26	944.75	932.89	923.15	915.12	908.48	902.97	886.52	879.80	877.01	875.85
65000	1058.54	1039.20	1023.48	1010.63	1000.08	991.38	984.19	978.22	960.40	953.12	950.09	948.83
70000	1139.96	1119.14	1102.21	1088.37	1077.01	1067.64	1059.89	1053.46	1034.28	1026.43	1023.18	1021.82
75000	1221.39	1199.07	1180.94	1166.11	1153.94	1143.90	1135.60	1128.71	1108.15	1099.75	1096.26	1094.81
80000	1302.81	1279.01	1259.67	1243.86	1230.87	1220.16	1211.30	1203.96	1182.03	1173.07	1169.35	1167.79
85000	1384.24	1358.95	1338.40	1321.60	1307.80	1296.42	1287.01	1279.21	1255.91	1246.38	1242.43	1240.78
90000	1465.67	1438.89	1417.13	1399.34	1384.73	1372.68	1362.72	1354.45	1329.78	1319.70	1315.51	1313.77
95000	1547.09	1518.83	1495.85	1477.08	1461.66	1448.94	1438.42	1429.70	1403.66	1393.01	1388.60	1386.75
00000	1628.52	1598.76	1574.58	1554.82	1538.58	1525.20	1514.13	1504.95	1477.53	1466.33	1461.68	1459.74

17%

Table 1

17.75%

MONTHLY
PAYMENT REQUIRED TO AMORTIZE A LOAN

TERM AMOUNT	1 YEAR	2 YEARS	3 YEARS	4 YEARS	5 YEARS	6 YEARS	7 YEARS	8 YEARS	9 YEARS	10 YEARS	11 YEARS	12 YEARS
50	4.58	2.50	1.81	1.47	1.27	1.14	1.05	.98	.94	.90	.87	.85
100	9.16	4.99	3.61	2.93	2.53	2.27	2.09	1.96	1.87	1.79	1.73	1.69
200	18.32	9.97	7.21	5.85	5.06	4.54	4.18	3.92	3.73	3.58	3.46	3.37
300	27.47	14.95	10.81	8.78	7.58	6.81	6.27	5.88	5.59	5.36	5.19	5.05
400	36.63	19.93	14.42	11.70	10.11	9.07	8.35	7.83	7.45	7.15	6.92	6.73
500	45.79	24.91	18.02	14.63	12.63	11.34	10.44	9.79	9.31	8.93	8.64	8.42
600	54.94	29.89	21.62	17.55	15.16	13.61	12.53	11.75	11.17	10.72	10.37	10.10
700	64.10	34.87	25.22	20.48	17.69	15.87	14.62	13.71	13.03	12.51	12.10	11.78
800	73.25	39.85	28.83	23.40	20.21	18.14	16.70	15.66	14.89	14.29	13.83	13.46
900	82.41	44.83	32.43	26.33	22.74	20.41	18.79	17.62	16.75	16.08	15.56	15.14
1000	91.57	49.81	36.03	29.25	25.26	22.67	20.88	19.58	18.61	17.86	17.28	16.83
2000	183.13	99.61	72.06	58.49	50.52	45.34	41.75	39.15	37.21	35.72	34.56	33.65
3000	274.69	149.42	108.09	87.74	75.78	68.01	62.62	58.72	55.81	53.58	51.84	50.47
4000	366.25	199.22	144.11	116.98	101.04	90.67	83.49	78.29	74.41	71.44	69.12	67.29
5000	457.81	249.02	180.14	146.23	126.29	113.34	104.36	97.86	93.01	89.29	86.40	84.12
6000	549.37	298.83	216.17	175.47	151.55	136.01	125.23	117.44	111.61	107.15	103.68	100.94
7000	640.93	348.63	252.19	204.72	176.81	158.67	146.11	137.01	130.21	125.01	120.96	117.76
8000	732.49	398.43	288.22	233.96	202.07	181.34	166.98	156.58	148.81	142.87	138.24	134.58
9000	824.05	448.24	324.25	263.21	227.32	204.01	187.85	176.15	167.41	160.73	155.52	151.40
10000	915.62	498.04	360.28	292.45	252.58	226.67	208.72	195.72	186.01	178.58	172.80	168.23
11000	1007.18	547.84	396.30	321.69	277.84	249.34	229.59	215.30	204.61	196.44	190.08	185.05
12000	1098.74	597.65	432.33	350.94	303.10	272.01	250.46	234.87	223.21	214.30	207.36	201.87
13000	1190.30	647.45	468.36	380.18	328.35	294.67	271.34	254.44	241.82	232.16	224.64	218.69
14000	1281.86	697.25	504.38	409.43	353.61	317.34	292.21	274.01	260.42	250.02	241.91	235.52
15000	1373.42	747.06	540.41	438.67	378.87	340.01	313.08	293.58	279.02	267.87	259.19	252.34
16000	1464.98	796.86	576.44	467.92	404.13	362.67	333.95	313.16	297.62	285.73	276.47	269.16
17000	1556.54	846.66	612.47	497.16	429.38	385.34	354.82	332.73	316.22	303.59	293.75	285.98
18000	1648.10	896.47	648.49	526.41	454.64	408.01	375.69	352.30	334.82	321.45	311.03	302.80
19000	1739.67	946.27	684.52	555.65	479.90	430.67	396.56	371.87	353.42	339.30	328.31	319.63
20000	1831.23	996.07	720.55	584.90	505.16	453.34	417.44	391.44	372.02	357.16	345.59	336.45
21000	1922.79	1045.88	756.57	614.14	530.42	476.01	438.31	411.02	390.63	375.02	362.87	353.27
22000	2014.35	1095.68	792.60	643.38	555.67	498.67	459.18	430.59	409.22	392.88	380.15	370.09
23000	2105.91	1145.48	828.63	672.63	580.93	521.34	480.05	450.16	427.82	410.74	397.43	386.92
24000	2197.47	1195.29	864.66	701.87	606.19	544.01	500.92	469.73	446.42	428.59	414.71	403.74
25000	2289.03	1245.09	900.68	731.12	631.45	566.67	521.79	489.30	465.03	446.45	431.99	420.56
26000	2380.59	1294.89	936.71	760.36	656.70	589.34	542.67	508.88	483.63	464.31	449.27	437.38
27000	2472.15	1344.70	972.74	789.61	681.96	612.01	563.54	528.45	502.23	482.17	466.54	454.20
28000	2563.71	1394.50	1008.76	818.85	707.22	634.67	584.41	548.02	520.83	500.03	483.82	471.03
29000	2655.28	1444.30	1044.79	848.10	732.48	657.34	605.28	567.59	539.43	517.88	501.10	487.85
30000	2746.84	1494.11	1080.82	877.34	757.73	680.01	626.15	587.16	558.03	535.74	518.38	504.67
31000	2838.40	1543.91	1116.85	906.59	782.99	702.67	647.02	606.73	576.63	553.60	535.66	521.49
32000	2929.96	1593.71	1152.87	935.83	808.25	725.34	667.89	626.31	595.23	571.46	552.94	538.32
33000	3021.52	1643.52	1188.90	965.07	833.51	748.01	688.77	645.88	613.83	589.32	570.22	555.14
34000	3113.08	1693.32	1224.93	994.32	858.76	770.67	709.64	665.45	632.43	607.17	587.50	571.96
35000	3204.64	1743.12	1260.95	1023.56	884.02	793.34	730.51	685.02	651.03	625.03	604.78	588.78
36000	3296.20	1792.93	1296.98	1052.81	909.28	816.01	751.38	704.59	669.63	642.89	622.06	605.60
37000	3387.76	1842.73	1333.01	1082.05	934.54	838.67	772.25	724.17	688.24	660.75	639.34	622.43
38000	3479.33	1892.53	1369.04	1111.30	959.79	861.34	793.12	743.74	706.84	678.60	656.62	639.25
39000	3570.89	1942.34	1405.06	1140.54	985.05	884.01	814.00	763.31	725.44	696.46	673.90	656.07
40000	3662.45	1992.14	1441.09	1169.79	1010.31	906.67	834.87	782.88	744.04	714.32	691.17	672.89
41000	3754.01	2041.94	1477.12	1199.03	1035.57	929.34	855.74	802.45	762.64	732.18	708.45	689.72
42000	3845.57	2091.75	1513.14	1228.28	1060.83	952.01	876.61	822.03	781.24	750.04	725.73	706.54
43000	3937.13	2141.55	1549.17	1257.52	1086.08	974.67	897.48	841.60	799.84	767.89	743.01	723.36
44000	4028.69	2191.35	1585.20	1286.76	1111.34	997.34	918.35	861.17	818.44	785.75	760.29	740.18
45000	4120.25	2241.16	1621.22	1316.01	1136.60	1020.01	939.23	880.74	837.04	803.61	777.57	757.00
46000	4211.81	2290.96	1657.25	1345.25	1161.86	1042.67	960.10	900.31	855.64	821.47	794.85	773.83
47000	4303.37	2340.76	1693.28	1374.50	1187.11	1065.34	980.97	919.89	874.24	839.33	812.13	790.65
48000	4394.94	2390.57	1729.31	1403.74	1212.37	1088.01	1001.84	939.46	892.84	857.18	829.41	807.47
49000	4486.50	2440.37	1765.33	1432.99	1237.63	1110.67	1022.71	959.03	911.44	875.04	846.69	824.29
50000	4578.06	2490.17	1801.36	1462.23	1262.89	1133.34	1043.58	978.60	930.05	892.90	863.97	841.12
55000	5035.86	2739.19	1981.50	1608.45	1389.17	1246.67	1147.94	1076.46	1023.05	982.19	950.36	925.23
60000	5493.67	2988.21	2161.63	1754.68	1515.46	1360.01	1252.30	1174.32	1116.05	1071.48	1036.76	1009.34
65000	5951.47	3237.23	2341.77	1900.90	1641.75	1473.34	1356.66	1272.18	1209.06	1160.77	1123.16	1093.45
70000	6409.28	3486.24	2521.90	2047.12	1768.04	1586.67	1461.01	1370.04	1302.06	1250.06	1209.55	1177.56
75000	6867.08	3735.26	2702.04	2193.34	1894.33	1700.01	1565.37	1467.90	1395.07	1339.35	1295.95	1261.67
80000	7324.89	3984.28	2882.17	2339.57	2020.61	1813.34	1669.73	1565.76	1488.07	1428.64	1382.34	1345.78
85000	7782.69	4233.29	3062.31	2485.79	2146.90	1926.67	1774.09	1663.62	1581.07	1517.93	1468.74	1429.89
90000	8240.50	4482.31	3242.44	2632.01	2273.19	2040.01	1878.45	1761.48	1674.08	1607.21	1555.14	1514.00
95000	8698.31	4731.33	3422.58	2778.23	2399.48	2153.34	1982.80	1859.34	1767.08	1696.50	1641.53	1598.11
100000	9156.11	4980.34	3602.72	2924.46	2525.77	2266.67	2087.16	1957.20	1860.09	1785.79	1727.93	1682.23

17%

Table 1

MONTHLY 17.75%

PAYMENT REQUIRED TO AMORTIZE A LOAN

TERM AMOUNT	13 YEARS	14 YEARS	15 YEARS	16 YEARS	17 YEARS	18 YEARS	19 YEARS	20 YEARS	25 YEARS	30 YEARS	35 YEARS	40 YEARS
50	.83	.81	.80	.79	.78	.78	.77	.77	.75	.75	.75	.75
100	1.65	1.62	1.60	1.58	1.56	1.55	1.54	1.53	1.50	1.49	1.49	1.49
200	3.30	3.24	3.19	3.15	3.12	3.09	3.07	3.05	3.00	2.98	2.97	2.97
300	4.94	4.85	4.78	4.72	4.68	4.64	4.60	4.58	4.50	4.47	4.45	4.45
400	6.59	6.47	6.37	6.30	6.23	6.18	6.14	6.10	5.99	5.95	5.93	5.93
500	8.23	8.09	7.97	7.87	7.79	7.72	7.67	7.63	7.49	7.44	7.42	7.41
600	9.88	9.70	9.56	9.44	9.35	9.27	9.20	9.15	8.99	8.93	8.90	8.89
700	11.53	11.32	11.15	11.02	10.90	10.81	10.74	10.67	10.49	10.41	10.38	10.37
800	13.17	12.94	12.74	12.59	12.46	12.36	12.27	12.20	11.98	11.90	11.86	11.85
900	14.82	14.55	14.34	14.16	14.02	13.90	13.80	13.72	13.48	13.39	13.35	13.33
1000	16.46	16.17	15.93	15.74	15.58	15.44	15.34	15.25	14.98	14.87	14.83	14.81
2000	32.92	32.33	31.85	31.47	31.15	30.88	30.67	30.49	29.95	29.74	29.65	29.61
3000	49.38	48.49	47.78	47.20	46.72	46.32	46.00	45.73	44.93	44.61	44.47	44.42
4000	65.83	64.66	63.70	62.93	62.29	61.76	61.33	60.97	59.90	59.47	59.30	59.22
5000	82.29	80.82	79.63	78.66	77.86	77.20	76.66	76.21	74.88	74.34	74.12	74.03
6000	98.75	96.98	95.55	94.39	93.43	92.64	91.99	91.45	89.85	89.21	88.94	88.83
7000	115.21	113.15	111.48	110.12	109.00	108.08	107.32	106.69	104.83	104.07	103.76	103.64
8000	131.66	129.31	127.40	125.85	124.57	123.52	122.65	121.93	119.80	118.94	118.59	118.44
9000	148.12	145.47	143.33	141.58	140.14	138.96	137.98	137.17	134.78	133.81	133.41	133.25
10000	164.58	161.64	159.25	157.31	155.71	154.40	153.31	152.41	149.75	148.67	148.23	148.05
11000	181.03	177.80	175.18	173.04	171.28	169.84	168.64	167.66	164.73	163.54	163.06	162.85
12000	197.49	193.96	191.10	188.77	186.85	185.27	183.97	182.90	179.70	178.41	177.88	177.66
13000	213.95	210.13	207.03	204.50	202.42	200.71	199.30	198.14	194.67	193.27	192.70	192.46
14000	230.41	226.29	222.95	220.23	217.99	216.15	214.64	213.38	209.65	208.14	207.52	207.27
15000	246.86	242.45	238.87	235.96	233.56	231.59	229.97	228.62	224.62	223.01	222.35	222.07
16000	263.32	258.62	254.80	251.69	249.13	247.03	245.30	243.86	239.60	237.88	237.17	236.88
17000	279.78	274.78	270.72	267.42	264.70	262.47	260.63	259.10	254.57	252.74	251.99	251.68
18000	296.24	290.94	286.65	283.15	280.27	277.91	275.96	274.34	269.55	267.61	266.81	266.49
19000	312.69	307.11	302.57	298.88	295.84	293.35	291.29	289.58	284.52	282.48	281.64	281.29
20000	329.15	323.27	318.50	314.61	311.41	308.79	306.62	304.82	299.50	297.34	296.46	296.10
21000	345.61	339.43	334.42	330.34	326.98	324.23	321.95	320.07	314.47	312.21	311.28	310.90
22000	362.06	355.60	350.35	346.07	342.55	339.67	337.28	335.31	329.45	327.08	326.11	325.70
23000	378.52	371.76	366.27	361.80	358.13	355.10	352.61	350.55	344.42	341.94	340.93	340.51
24000	394.98	387.92	382.20	377.53	373.70	370.54	367.94	365.79	359.40	356.81	355.75	355.31
25000	411.44	404.09	398.12	393.26	389.27	385.98	383.27	381.03	374.37	371.68	370.57	370.12
26000	427.89	420.25	414.05	408.99	404.84	401.42	398.60	396.27	389.34	386.54	385.40	384.92
27000	444.35	436.41	429.97	424.72	420.41	416.86	413.93	411.51	404.32	401.41	400.22	399.73
28000	460.81	452.57	445.90	440.45	435.98	432.30	429.27	426.75	419.29	416.28	415.04	414.53
29000	477.26	468.74	461.82	456.18	451.55	447.74	444.60	441.99	434.27	431.15	429.86	429.34
30000	493.72	484.90	477.74	471.91	467.12	463.18	459.93	457.23	449.24	446.01	444.69	444.14
31000	510.18	501.06	493.67	487.64	482.69	478.62	475.26	472.48	464.22	460.88	459.51	458.95
32000	526.64	517.23	509.59	503.37	498.26	494.06	490.59	487.72	479.19	475.75	474.33	473.75
33000	543.09	533.39	525.52	519.10	513.83	509.50	505.92	502.96	494.17	490.61	489.16	488.55
34000	559.55	549.55	541.44	534.83	529.40	524.94	521.25	518.20	509.14	505.48	503.98	503.36
35000	576.01	565.72	557.37	550.56	544.97	540.37	536.58	533.44	524.12	520.35	518.80	518.16
36000	592.47	581.88	573.29	566.29	560.54	555.81	551.91	548.68	539.09	535.21	533.62	532.97
37000	608.92	598.04	589.22	582.02	576.11	571.25	567.24	563.92	554.07	550.08	548.45	547.77
38000	625.38	614.21	605.14	597.75	591.68	586.69	582.57	579.16	569.04	564.95	563.27	562.58
39000	641.84	630.37	621.07	613.48	607.25	602.13	597.90	594.40	584.01	579.81	578.09	577.38
40000	658.29	646.53	636.99	629.21	622.82	617.57	613.23	609.64	598.99	594.68	592.92	592.19
41000	674.75	662.70	652.92	644.94	638.39	633.01	628.56	624.89	613.96	609.55	607.74	606.99
42000	691.21	678.86	668.84	660.67	653.96	648.45	643.90	640.13	628.94	624.42	622.56	621.80
43000	707.67	695.02	684.77	676.40	669.53	663.89	659.23	655.37	643.91	639.28	637.38	636.60
44000	724.12	711.19	700.69	692.13	685.10	679.33	674.56	670.61	658.89	654.15	652.21	651.40
45000	740.58	727.35	716.61	707.86	700.68	694.77	689.89	685.85	673.86	669.02	667.03	666.21
46000	757.04	743.51	732.54	723.59	716.25	710.20	705.22	701.09	688.84	683.88	681.85	681.01
47000	773.49	759.68	748.46	739.32	731.82	725.64	720.55	716.33	703.81	698.75	696.67	695.82
48000	789.95	775.84	764.39	755.05	747.39	741.08	735.88	731.57	718.79	713.62	711.50	710.62
49000	806.41	792.00	780.31	770.78	762.96	756.52	751.21	746.81	733.76	728.48	726.32	725.43
50000	822.87	808.17	796.24	786.51	778.53	771.96	766.54	762.05	748.73	743.35	741.14	740.23
55000	905.15	888.98	875.86	865.16	856.38	849.16	843.19	838.26	823.61	817.69	815.26	814.25
60000	987.44	969.80	955.48	943.81	934.23	926.35	919.85	914.46	898.48	892.02	889.37	888.28
65000	1069.73	1050.61	1035.11	1022.46	1012.08	1003.55	996.50	990.67	973.35	966.35	963.48	962.30
70000	1152.01	1131.43	1114.73	1101.11	1089.94	1080.74	1073.16	1066.87	1048.23	1040.69	1037.60	1036.32
75000	1234.30	1212.25	1194.36	1179.76	1167.79	1157.94	1149.81	1143.08	1123.10	1115.02	1111.71	1110.35
80000	1316.58	1293.06	1273.98	1258.41	1245.64	1235.14	1226.46	1219.28	1197.97	1189.36	1185.83	1184.37
85000	1398.87	1373.88	1353.60	1337.06	1323.49	1312.33	1303.12	1295.49	1272.85	1263.69	1259.94	1258.39
90000	1481.16	1454.69	1433.23	1415.71	1401.35	1389.53	1379.77	1371.69	1347.72	1338.03	1334.05	1332.41
95000	1563.44	1535.51	1512.85	1494.36	1479.20	1466.72	1456.42	1447.90	1422.59	1412.36	1408.17	1406.44
100000	1645.73	1616.33	1592.47	1573.01	1557.05	1543.92	1533.08	1524.10	1497.46	1486.70	1482.28	1480.46

17%

Table 1

18.00%

MONTHLY
PAYMENT REQUIRED TO AMORTIZE A LOAN

TERM AMOUNT	1 YEAR	2 YEARS	3 YEARS	4 YEARS	5 YEARS	6 YEARS	7 YEARS	8 YEARS	9 YEARS	10 YEARS	11 YEARS	12 YEARS
50	4.59	2.50	1.81	1.47	1.27	1.15	1.06	.99	.94	.91	.88	.85
100	9.17	5.00	3.62	2.94	2.54	2.29	2.11	1.98	1.88	1.81	1.75	1.70
200	18.34	9.99	7.24	5.88	5.08	4.57	4.21	3.95	3.76	3.61	3.49	3.40
300	27.51	14.98	10.85	8.82	7.62	6.85	6.31	5.92	5.63	5.41	5.24	5.10
400	36.68	19.97	14.47	11.76	10.16	9.13	8.41	7.89	7.51	7.21	6.98	6.80
500	45.84	24.97	18.08	14.69	12.70	11.41	10.51	9.87	9.38	9.01	8.73	8.50
600	55.01	29.96	21.70	17.63	15.24	13.69	12.62	11.84	11.26	10.82	10.47	10.20
700	64.18	34.95	25.31	20.57	17.78	15.97	14.72	13.81	13.13	12.62	12.22	11.90
800	73.35	39.94	28.93	23.51	20.32	18.25	16.82	15.78	15.01	14.42	13.96	13.60
900	82.52	44.94	32.54	26.44	22.86	20.53	18.92	17.76	16.89	16.22	15.70	15.30
1000	91.68	49.93	36.16	29.38	25.40	22.81	21.02	19.73	18.76	18.02	17.45	17.00
2000	183.36	99.85	72.31	58.75	50.79	45.62	42.04	39.45	37.52	36.04	34.89	33.99
3000	275.04	149.78	108.46	88.13	76.19	68.43	63.06	59.17	56.28	54.06	52.34	50.98
4000	366.72	199.70	144.61	117.50	101.58	91.24	84.08	78.90	75.03	72.08	69.78	67.97
5000	458.40	249.63	180.77	146.88	126.97	114.04	105.09	98.62	93.79	90.10	87.23	84.96
6000	550.08	299.55	216.92	176.26	152.37	136.85	126.11	118.34	112.55	108.12	104.67	101.95
7000	641.76	349.47	253.07	205.63	177.76	159.66	147.13	138.07	131.30	126.13	122.11	118.94
8000	733.44	399.40	289.22	235.01	203.15	182.47	168.15	157.79	150.06	144.15	139.56	135.93
9000	825.12	449.32	325.38	264.38	228.55	205.28	189.17	177.51	168.82	162.17	157.00	152.93
10000	916.80	499.25	361.53	293.75	253.94	228.08	210.18	197.24	187.57	180.19	174.45	169.92
11000	1008.48	549.17	397.68	323.13	279.33	250.89	231.20	216.96	206.33	198.21	191.89	186.91
12000	1100.16	599.09	433.83	352.50	304.73	273.70	252.22	236.68	225.09	216.23	209.34	203.90
13000	1191.84	649.02	469.99	381.88	330.12	296.51	273.24	256.41	243.84	234.25	226.78	220.89
14000	1283.52	698.94	506.14	411.25	355.51	319.31	294.25	276.13	262.60	252.26	244.22	237.88
15000	1375.20	748.87	542.29	440.63	380.91	342.12	315.27	295.85	281.36	270.28	261.67	254.87
16000	1466.88	798.79	578.44	470.00	406.30	364.93	336.29	315.58	300.12	288.30	279.11	271.86
17000	1558.56	848.71	614.60	499.38	431.69	387.74	357.31	335.30	318.87	306.32	296.56	288.86
18000	1650.24	898.64	650.75	528.75	457.09	410.55	378.33	355.02	337.63	324.34	314.00	305.85
19000	1741.92	948.56	686.90	558.13	482.48	433.35	399.34	374.75	356.39	342.36	331.44	322.84
20000	1833.60	998.49	723.05	587.50	507.87	456.16	420.36	394.47	375.14	360.38	348.89	339.83
21000	1925.28	1048.41	759.21	616.88	533.27	478.97	441.38	414.19	393.90	378.39	366.33	356.82
22000	2016.96	1098.34	795.36	646.25	558.66	501.78	462.40	433.92	412.66	396.41	383.78	373.81
23000	2108.64	1148.26	831.51	675.63	584.05	524.58	483.42	453.64	431.41	414.43	401.22	390.80
24000	2200.32	1198.18	867.66	705.00	609.45	547.39	504.43	473.36	450.17	432.45	418.67	407.79
25000	2292.00	1248.11	903.81	734.38	634.84	570.20	525.45	493.09	468.93	450.47	436.11	424.78
26000	2383.68	1298.03	939.97	763.75	660.23	593.01	546.47	512.81	487.68	468.49	453.55	441.78
27000	2475.36	1347.96	976.12	793.13	685.63	615.82	567.49	532.53	506.44	486.51	471.00	458.77
28000	2567.04	1397.88	1012.27	822.50	711.02	638.62	588.50	552.25	525.20	504.52	488.44	475.76
29000	2658.72	1447.80	1048.42	851.88	736.41	661.43	609.52	571.98	543.95	522.54	505.89	492.75
30000	2750.40	1497.73	1084.58	881.25	761.81	684.24	630.54	591.70	562.71	540.56	523.33	509.74
31000	2842.08	1547.65	1120.73	910.63	787.20	707.05	651.56	611.42	581.47	558.58	540.77	526.73
32000	2933.76	1597.58	1156.88	940.00	812.59	729.85	672.58	631.15	600.23	576.60	558.22	543.72
33000	3025.44	1647.50	1193.03	969.38	837.99	752.66	693.59	650.87	618.98	594.62	575.66	560.71
34000	3117.12	1697.42	1229.19	998.75	863.38	775.47	714.61	670.59	637.74	612.63	593.11	577.71
35000	3208.80	1747.35	1265.34	1028.13	888.77	798.28	735.63	690.32	656.50	630.65	610.55	594.70
36000	3300.48	1797.27	1301.49	1057.51	914.17	821.09	756.65	710.04	675.25	648.67	628.00	611.69
37000	3392.16	1847.20	1337.64	1086.88	939.56	843.89	777.67	729.76	694.01	666.69	645.44	628.68
38000	3483.84	1897.12	1373.80	1116.26	964.96	866.70	798.68	749.49	712.77	684.71	662.88	645.67
39000	3575.52	1947.05	1409.95	1145.63	990.35	889.51	819.70	769.21	731.52	702.73	680.33	662.66
40000	3667.20	1996.97	1446.10	1175.01	1015.74	912.32	840.72	788.93	750.28	720.75	697.77	679.65
41000	3758.88	2046.89	1482.25	1204.38	1041.14	935.12	861.74	808.66	769.04	738.76	715.22	696.64
42000	3850.56	2096.82	1518.41	1233.76	1066.53	957.93	882.75	828.38	787.79	756.78	732.66	713.64
43000	3942.24	2146.74	1554.56	1263.13	1091.92	980.74	903.77	848.10	806.55	774.80	750.10	730.63
44000	4033.92	2196.67	1590.71	1292.51	1117.32	1003.55	924.79	867.83	825.31	792.82	767.55	747.62
45000	4125.60	2246.59	1626.86	1321.88	1142.71	1026.36	945.81	887.55	844.06	810.84	784.99	764.61
46000	4217.28	2296.51	1663.02	1351.26	1168.10	1049.16	966.83	907.27	862.82	828.86	802.44	781.60
47000	4308.96	2346.44	1699.17	1380.63	1193.50	1071.97	987.84	927.00	881.58	846.88	819.88	798.59
48000	4400.64	2396.36	1735.32	1410.01	1218.89	1094.78	1008.86	946.72	900.34	864.89	837.33	815.58
49000	4492.32	2446.29	1771.47	1439.38	1244.28	1117.59	1029.88	966.44	919.09	882.91	854.77	832.57
50000	4584.00	2496.21	1807.62	1468.76	1269.68	1140.39	1050.90	986.17	937.85	900.93	872.21	849.56
55000	5042.40	2745.83	1988.39	1615.63	1396.64	1254.43	1155.99	1084.78	1031.63	991.02	959.43	934.52
60000	5500.80	2995.45	2169.15	1762.51	1523.61	1368.47	1261.08	1183.40	1125.42	1081.12	1046.66	1019.48
65000	5959.20	3245.07	2349.91	1909.38	1650.58	1482.51	1366.16	1282.01	1219.20	1171.21	1133.88	1104.43
70000	6417.60	3494.69	2530.67	2056.25	1777.54	1596.55	1471.25	1380.63	1312.99	1261.30	1221.10	1189.39
75000	6876.00	3744.31	2711.43	2203.13	1904.51	1710.59	1576.34	1479.25	1406.77	1351.39	1308.32	1274.34
80000	7334.40	3993.93	2892.20	2350.00	2031.48	1824.63	1681.43	1577.86	1500.56	1441.49	1395.54	1359.30
85000	7792.80	4243.55	3072.96	2496.88	2158.45	1938.67	1786.52	1676.48	1594.34	1531.58	1482.76	1444.26
90000	8251.20	4493.17	3253.72	2643.75	2285.41	2052.71	1891.61	1775.09	1688.12	1621.67	1569.98	1529.21
95000	8709.60	4742.79	3434.48	2790.63	2412.38	2166.75	1996.70	1873.71	1781.91	1711.76	1657.20	1614.17
100000	9168.00	4992.42	3615.24	2937.50	2539.35	2280.78	2101.79	1972.33	1875.69	1801.86	1744.42	1699.12

18%

106

Table 1

MONTHLY

18.00%

PAYMENT REQUIRED TO AMORTIZE A LOAN

TERM AMOUNT	13 YEARS	14 YEARS	15 YEARS	16 YEARS	17 YEARS	18 YEARS	19 YEARS	20 YEARS	25 YEARS	30 YEARS	35 YEARS	40 YEARS
50	.84	.82	.81	.80	.79	.79	.78	.78	.76	.76	.76	.76
100	1.67	1.64	1.62	1.60	1.58	1.57	1.56	1.55	1.52	1.51	1.51	1.51
200	3.33	3.27	3.23	3.19	3.16	3.13	3.11	3.09	3.04	3.02	3.01	3.01
300	4.99	4.91	4.84	4.78	4.73	4.69	4.66	4.63	4.56	4.53	4.51	4.51
400	6.66	6.54	6.45	6.37	6.31	6.26	6.21	6.18	6.07	6.03	6.02	6.01
500	8.32	8.17	8.06	7.96	7.88	7.82	7.77	7.72	7.59	7.54	7.52	7.51
600	9.98	9.81	9.67	9.55	9.46	9.38	9.32	9.26	9.11	9.05	9.02	9.01
700	11.65	11.44	11.28	11.14	11.03	10.94	10.87	10.81	10.63	10.55	10.53	10.51
800	13.31	13.08	12.89	12.74	12.61	12.51	12.42	12.35	12.14	12.06	12.03	12.01
900	14.97	14.71	14.50	14.33	14.19	14.07	13.97	13.89	13.66	13.57	13.53	13.52
1000	16.64	16.34	16.11	15.92	15.76	15.63	15.53	15.44	15.18	15.08	15.03	15.02
2000	33.27	32.68	32.21	31.83	31.52	31.26	31.05	30.87	30.35	30.15	30.06	30.03
3000	49.90	49.02	48.32	47.74	47.27	46.89	46.57	46.30	45.53	45.22	45.09	45.04
4000	66.53	65.36	64.42	63.66	63.03	62.51	62.09	61.74	60.70	60.29	60.12	60.05
5000	83.16	81.70	80.53	79.57	78.78	78.14	77.61	77.17	75.88	75.36	75.15	75.06
6000	99.79	98.04	96.63	95.48	94.54	93.77	93.13	92.60	91.05	90.43	90.18	90.08
7000	116.42	114.38	112.73	111.39	110.30	109.39	108.65	108.04	106.23	105.50	105.21	105.09
8000	133.05	130.72	128.84	127.31	126.05	125.02	124.17	123.47	121.40	120.57	120.24	120.10
9000	149.68	147.06	144.94	143.22	141.81	140.65	139.69	138.90	136.57	135.64	135.27	135.11
10000	166.31	163.40	161.05	159.13	157.56	156.27	155.21	154.34	151.75	150.71	150.29	150.12
11000	182.94	179.74	177.15	175.04	173.32	171.90	170.73	169.77	166.92	165.78	165.32	165.14
12000	199.57	196.08	193.26	190.96	189.07	187.53	186.25	185.20	182.10	180.86	180.35	180.15
13000	216.20	212.42	209.36	206.87	204.83	203.15	201.78	200.64	197.27	195.93	195.38	195.16
14000	232.83	228.76	225.46	222.78	220.59	218.78	217.30	216.07	212.45	211.00	210.41	210.17
15000	249.46	245.10	241.57	238.69	236.34	234.41	232.82	231.50	227.62	226.07	225.44	225.18
16000	266.09	261.44	257.67	254.61	252.10	250.04	248.34	246.93	242.79	241.14	240.47	240.19
17000	282.72	277.78	273.78	270.52	267.85	265.66	263.86	262.37	257.97	256.21	255.50	255.21
18000	299.35	294.12	289.88	286.43	283.61	281.29	279.38	277.80	273.14	271.28	270.53	270.22
19000	315.98	310.46	305.99	302.34	299.36	296.92	294.90	293.23	288.32	286.35	285.55	285.23
20000	332.61	326.80	322.09	318.26	315.12	312.54	310.42	308.67	303.49	301.42	300.58	300.24
21000	349.24	343.13	338.19	334.17	330.88	328.17	325.94	324.10	318.67	316.49	315.61	315.25
22000	365.87	359.47	354.30	350.08	346.63	343.80	341.46	339.53	333.84	331.56	330.64	330.27
23000	382.50	375.81	370.40	365.99	362.39	359.42	356.98	354.97	349.01	346.63	345.67	345.28
24000	399.13	392.15	386.51	381.91	378.14	375.05	372.50	370.40	364.19	361.71	360.70	360.29
25000	415.76	408.49	402.61	397.82	393.90	390.68	388.02	385.83	379.36	376.78	375.73	375.30
26000	432.39	424.83	418.71	413.73	409.65	406.30	403.55	401.27	394.54	391.85	390.76	390.31
27000	449.02	441.17	434.82	429.64	425.41	421.93	419.07	416.70	409.71	406.92	405.79	405.32
28000	465.65	457.51	450.92	445.56	441.17	437.56	434.59	432.13	424.89	421.99	420.81	420.34
29000	482.28	473.85	467.03	461.47	456.92	453.19	450.11	447.57	440.06	437.06	435.84	435.35
30000	498.91	490.19	483.13	477.38	472.68	468.81	465.63	463.00	455.23	452.13	450.87	450.36
31000	515.54	506.53	499.24	493.29	488.43	484.44	481.15	478.43	470.41	467.20	465.90	465.37
32000	532.17	522.87	515.34	509.21	504.19	500.07	496.67	493.86	485.58	482.27	480.93	480.38
33000	548.80	539.21	531.44	525.12	519.94	515.69	512.19	509.30	500.76	497.34	495.96	495.40
34000	565.43	555.55	547.55	541.03	535.70	531.32	527.71	524.73	515.93	512.41	510.99	510.41
35000	582.06	571.89	563.65	556.94	551.46	546.95	543.23	540.16	531.11	527.48	526.02	525.42
36000	598.69	588.23	579.76	572.86	567.21	562.57	558.75	555.60	546.28	542.56	541.05	540.43
37000	615.32	604.57	595.86	588.77	582.97	578.20	574.27	571.03	561.45	557.63	556.08	555.44
38000	631.95	620.91	611.96	604.68	598.72	593.83	589.79	586.46	576.63	572.70	571.10	570.45
39000	648.58	637.25	628.07	620.59	614.48	609.45	605.32	601.90	591.80	587.77	586.13	585.47
40000	665.21	653.59	644.17	636.51	630.23	625.08	620.84	617.33	606.98	602.84	601.16	600.48
41000	681.84	669.92	660.28	652.42	645.99	640.71	636.36	632.76	622.15	617.91	616.19	615.49
42000	698.47	686.26	676.38	668.33	661.75	656.34	651.88	648.20	637.33	632.98	631.22	630.50
43000	715.10	702.60	692.49	684.24	677.50	671.96	667.40	663.63	652.50	648.05	646.25	645.51
44000	731.73	718.94	708.59	700.16	693.26	687.59	682.92	679.06	667.67	663.12	661.28	660.53
45000	748.36	735.28	724.69	716.07	709.01	703.22	698.44	694.50	682.85	678.19	676.31	675.54
46000	764.99	751.62	740.80	731.98	724.77	718.84	713.96	709.93	698.02	693.26	691.34	690.55
47000	781.62	767.96	756.90	747.90	740.52	734.47	729.48	725.36	713.20	708.34	706.36	705.56
48000	798.25	784.30	773.01	763.81	756.28	750.10	745.00	740.79	728.37	723.41	721.39	720.57
49000	814.88	800.64	789.11	779.72	772.04	765.72	760.52	756.23	743.55	738.48	736.42	735.58
50000	831.51	816.98	805.22	795.63	787.79	781.35	776.04	771.66	758.72	753.55	751.45	750.60
55000	914.66	898.68	885.74	875.20	866.57	859.49	853.65	848.83	834.59	828.90	826.59	825.66
60000	997.81	980.38	966.26	954.76	945.35	937.62	931.25	925.99	910.46	904.26	901.74	900.71
65000	1080.96	1062.07	1046.78	1034.32	1024.13	1015.75	1008.86	1003.16	986.33	979.61	976.88	975.77
70000	1164.11	1143.77	1127.30	1113.88	1102.91	1093.89	1086.46	1080.32	1062.21	1054.96	1052.03	1050.83
75000	1247.26	1225.47	1207.82	1193.45	1181.68	1172.02	1164.06	1157.49	1138.08	1130.32	1127.17	1125.89
80000	1330.41	1307.17	1288.34	1273.01	1260.46	1250.16	1241.67	1234.65	1213.95	1205.67	1202.32	1200.95
85000	1413.56	1388.86	1368.86	1352.57	1339.24	1328.29	1319.27	1311.82	1289.82	1281.03	1277.46	1276.01
90000	1496.71	1470.56	1449.38	1432.14	1418.02	1406.43	1396.88	1388.99	1365.69	1356.38	1352.61	1351.07
95000	1579.86	1552.26	1529.91	1511.70	1496.80	1484.56	1474.48	1466.15	1441.56	1431.74	1427.75	1426.13
100000	1663.01	1633.96	1610.43	1591.26	1575.58	1562.70	1552.08	1543.32	1517.43	1507.09	1502.90	1501.19

18%

Table 1

18.25%

MONTHLY

PAYMENT REQUIRED TO AMORTIZE A LOAN

TERM / AMOUNT	1 YEAR	2 YEARS	3 YEARS	4 YEARS	5 YEARS	6 YEARS	7 YEARS	8 YEARS	9 YEARS	10 YEARS	11 YEARS	12 YEARS
50	4.59	2.51	1.82	1.48	1.28	1.15	1.06	1.00	.95	.91	.89	.86
100	9.18	5.01	3.63	2.96	2.56	2.30	2.12	1.99	1.90	1.82	1.77	1.72
200	18.36	10.01	7.26	5.91	5.11	4.59	4.24	3.98	3.79	3.64	3.53	3.44
300	27.54	15.02	10.89	8.86	7.66	6.89	6.35	5.97	5.68	5.46	5.29	5.15
400	36.72	20.02	14.52	11.81	10.22	9.18	8.47	7.96	7.57	7.28	7.05	6.87
500	45.90	25.03	18.14	14.76	12.77	11.48	10.59	9.94	9.46	9.09	8.81	8.59
600	55.08	30.03	21.77	17.71	15.32	13.77	12.70	11.93	11.35	10.91	10.57	10.30
700	64.26	35.04	25.40	20.66	17.88	16.07	14.82	13.92	13.24	12.73	12.33	12.02
800	73.44	40.04	29.03	23.61	20.43	18.36	16.94	15.91	15.14	14.55	14.09	13.73
900	82.62	45.05	32.66	26.56	22.98	20.66	19.05	17.89	17.03	16.37	15.85	15.45
1000	91.80	50.05	36.28	29.51	25.53	22.95	21.17	19.88	18.92	18.18	17.61	17.17
2000	183.60	100.09	72.56	59.02	51.06	45.90	42.33	39.76	37.83	36.36	35.22	34.33
3000	275.40	150.14	108.84	88.52	76.59	68.85	63.50	59.63	56.75	54.54	52.83	51.49
4000	367.20	200.18	145.12	118.03	102.12	91.80	84.66	79.51	75.66	72.72	70.44	68.65
5000	459.00	250.23	181.39	147.53	127.65	114.75	105.83	99.38	94.57	90.90	88.05	85.81
6000	550.80	300.27	217.67	177.04	153.18	137.70	126.99	119.26	113.49	109.08	105.66	102.97
7000	642.60	350.32	253.95	206.55	178.71	160.65	148.16	139.13	132.40	127.26	123.27	120.13
8000	734.40	400.36	290.23	236.05	204.24	183.60	169.32	159.01	151.31	145.44	140.88	137.29
9000	826.20	450.41	326.51	265.56	229.77	206.55	190.49	178.88	170.23	163.62	158.49	154.45
10000	918.00	500.45	362.78	295.06	255.30	229.50	211.65	198.76	189.14	181.80	176.10	171.61
11000	1009.79	550.50	399.06	324.57	280.83	252.45	232.82	218.63	208.05	199.98	193.71	188.77
12000	1101.59	600.54	435.34	354.07	306.36	275.40	253.98	238.51	226.97	218.16	211.32	205.94
13000	1193.39	650.59	471.62	383.58	331.89	298.35	275.15	258.38	245.88	236.34	228.93	223.10
14000	1285.19	700.63	507.90	413.09	357.42	321.30	296.31	278.26	264.79	254.52	246.54	240.26
15000	1376.99	750.68	544.17	442.59	382.95	344.25	317.47	298.13	283.71	272.70	264.15	257.42
16000	1468.79	800.72	580.45	472.10	408.48	367.19	338.64	318.01	302.62	290.88	281.76	274.58
17000	1560.59	850.77	616.73	501.60	434.01	390.14	359.80	337.88	321.54	309.06	299.37	291.74
18000	1652.39	900.81	653.01	531.11	459.54	413.09	380.97	357.76	340.45	327.24	316.98	308.90
19000	1744.19	950.86	689.29	560.62	485.07	436.04	402.13	377.63	359.36	345.42	334.59	326.06
20000	1835.99	1000.90	725.56	590.12	510.60	458.99	423.30	397.51	378.28	363.60	352.20	343.22
21000	1927.78	1050.95	761.84	619.63	536.13	481.94	444.46	417.38	397.19	381.78	369.81	360.38
22000	2019.58	1100.99	798.12	649.13	561.66	504.89	465.63	437.26	416.10	399.96	387.42	377.54
23000	2111.38	1151.04	834.40	678.64	587.19	527.84	486.79	457.13	435.02	418.14	405.03	394.70
24000	2203.18	1201.08	870.68	708.14	612.72	550.79	507.96	477.01	453.93	436.32	422.64	411.87
25000	2294.98	1251.13	906.95	737.65	638.25	573.74	529.12	496.88	472.84	454.50	440.25	429.03
26000	2386.78	1301.17	943.23	767.16	663.78	596.69	550.29	516.76	491.76	472.68	457.86	446.19
27000	2478.58	1351.22	979.51	796.66	689.30	619.64	571.45	536.63	510.67	490.86	475.47	463.35
28000	2570.38	1401.26	1015.79	826.17	714.83	642.59	592.61	556.51	529.58	509.04	493.08	480.51
29000	2662.18	1451.31	1052.07	855.67	740.36	665.54	613.78	576.38	548.50	527.22	510.69	497.67
30000	2753.98	1501.35	1088.34	885.18	765.89	688.49	634.94	596.26	567.41	545.40	528.30	514.83
31000	2845.77	1551.40	1124.62	914.68	791.42	711.43	656.11	616.13	586.33	563.58	545.91	531.99
32000	2937.57	1601.44	1160.90	944.19	816.95	734.38	677.27	636.01	605.24	581.76	563.52	549.15
33000	3029.37	1651.49	1197.18	973.70	842.48	757.33	698.44	655.88	624.15	599.94	581.13	566.31
34000	3121.17	1701.53	1233.45	1003.20	868.01	780.28	719.60	675.76	643.07	618.12	598.74	583.47
35000	3212.97	1751.58	1269.73	1032.71	893.54	803.23	740.77	695.63	661.98	636.30	616.35	600.63
36000	3304.77	1801.62	1306.01	1062.21	919.07	826.18	761.93	715.51	680.89	654.48	633.96	617.80
37000	3396.57	1851.67	1342.29	1091.72	944.60	849.13	783.10	735.38	699.81	672.66	651.57	634.96
38000	3488.37	1901.71	1378.57	1121.23	970.13	872.08	804.26	755.26	718.72	690.84	669.18	652.12
39000	3580.17	1951.76	1414.84	1150.73	995.66	895.03	825.43	775.13	737.63	709.02	686.79	669.28
40000	3671.97	2001.80	1451.12	1180.24	1021.19	917.98	846.59	795.01	756.55	727.20	704.40	686.44
41000	3763.76	2051.85	1487.40	1209.74	1046.72	940.93	867.75	814.88	775.46	745.38	722.01	703.60
42000	3855.56	2101.89	1523.68	1239.25	1072.25	963.88	888.92	834.76	794.37	763.56	739.62	720.76
43000	3947.36	2151.94	1559.96	1268.75	1097.78	986.83	910.08	854.63	813.29	781.74	757.22	737.92
44000	4039.16	2201.98	1596.23	1298.26	1123.31	1009.78	931.25	874.51	832.20	799.92	774.83	755.08
45000	4130.96	2252.03	1632.51	1327.77	1148.84	1032.73	952.41	894.38	851.12	818.10	792.44	772.24
46000	4222.76	2302.07	1668.79	1357.27	1174.37	1055.67	973.58	914.26	870.03	836.27	810.05	789.40
47000	4314.56	2352.12	1705.07	1386.78	1199.90	1078.62	994.74	934.13	888.94	854.45	827.66	806.56
48000	4406.36	2402.16	1741.35	1416.28	1225.43	1101.57	1015.91	954.01	907.86	872.63	845.27	823.73
49000	4498.16	2452.21	1777.62	1445.79	1250.96	1124.52	1037.07	973.88	926.77	890.81	862.88	840.89
50000	4589.96	2502.25	1813.90	1475.29	1276.49	1147.47	1058.24	993.76	945.68	908.99	880.49	858.05
55000	5048.95	2752.48	1995.29	1622.82	1404.13	1262.22	1164.06	1093.13	1040.25	999.89	968.54	943.85
60000	5507.95	3002.70	2176.68	1770.35	1531.78	1376.97	1269.88	1192.51	1134.82	1090.79	1056.64	1029.66
65000	5966.94	3252.93	2358.07	1917.88	1659.43	1491.71	1375.71	1291.88	1229.39	1181.69	1144.64	1115.46
70000	6425.94	3503.15	2539.46	2065.41	1787.08	1606.46	1481.53	1391.26	1323.95	1272.59	1232.69	1201.26
75000	6884.93	3753.38	2720.85	2212.94	1914.73	1721.21	1587.35	1490.63	1418.52	1363.49	1320.74	1287.07
80000	7343.93	4003.60	2902.24	2360.47	2042.37	1835.95	1693.18	1590.01	1513.09	1454.39	1408.79	1372.87
85000	7802.92	4253.83	3083.63	2508.00	2170.02	1950.70	1799.00	1689.38	1607.66	1545.29	1496.84	1458.68
90000	8261.92	4504.05	3265.02	2655.53	2297.67	2065.45	1904.82	1788.76	1702.23	1636.19	1584.88	1544.48
95000	8720.91	4754.28	3446.41	2803.06	2425.32	2180.19	2010.64	1888.13	1796.79	1727.08	1672.93	1630.29
100000	9179.91	5004.50	3627.80	2950.58	2552.97	2294.94	2116.47	1987.51	1891.36	1817.98	1760.98	1716.09

18%

Table 1

MONTHLY

18.25%

PAYMENT REQUIRED TO AMORTIZE A LOAN

TERM / OUNT	13 YEARS	14 YEARS	15 YEARS	16 YEARS	17 YEARS	18 YEARS	19 YEARS	20 YEARS	25 YEARS	30 YEARS	35 YEARS	40 YEARS
50	.85	.83	.82	.81	.80	.80	.79	.79	.77	.77	.77	.77
100	1.69	1.66	1.63	1.61	1.60	1.59	1.58	1.57	1.54	1.53	1.53	1.53
200	3.37	3.31	3.26	3.22	3.19	3.17	3.15	3.13	3.08	3.06	3.05	3.05
300	5.05	4.96	4.89	4.83	4.79	4.75	4.72	4.69	4.62	4.59	4.58	4.57
400	6.73	6.61	6.52	6.44	6.38	6.33	6.29	6.26	6.15	6.12	6.10	6.09
500	8.41	8.26	8.15	8.05	7.98	7.91	7.86	7.82	7.69	7.64	7.62	7.61
600	10.09	9.91	9.78	9.66	9.57	9.49	9.43	9.38	9.23	9.17	9.15	9.14
700	11.77	11.57	11.40	11.27	11.16	11.08	11.00	10.94	10.77	10.70	10.67	10.66
800	13.45	13.22	13.03	12.88	12.76	12.66	12.57	12.51	12.30	12.23	12.19	12.18
900	15.13	14.87	14.66	14.49	14.35	14.24	14.15	14.07	13.84	13.75	13.72	13.70
1000	16.81	16.52	16.29	16.10	15.95	15.82	15.72	15.63	15.38	15.28	15.24	15.22
2000	33.61	33.04	32.57	32.20	31.89	31.64	31.43	31.26	30.75	30.56	30.48	30.44
3000	50.42	49.55	48.86	48.29	47.83	47.45	47.14	46.88	46.13	45.83	45.71	45.66
4000	67.22	66.07	65.14	64.39	63.77	63.27	62.85	62.51	61.50	61.11	60.95	60.88
5000	84.02	82.59	81.43	80.48	79.71	79.08	78.56	78.13	76.88	76.38	76.18	76.10
6000	100.83	99.10	97.71	96.58	95.65	94.90	94.27	93.76	92.25	91.66	91.42	91.32
7000	117.63	115.62	114.00	112.68	111.60	110.71	109.98	109.39	107.63	106.93	106.65	106.54
8000	134.43	132.14	130.28	128.77	127.54	126.53	125.70	125.01	123.00	122.21	121.89	121.76
9000	151.24	148.65	146.57	144.87	143.48	142.34	141.41	140.64	138.37	137.48	137.12	136.98
10000	168.04	165.17	162.85	160.96	159.42	158.16	157.12	156.26	153.75	152.76	152.36	152.20
11000	184.84	181.69	179.13	177.06	175.36	173.97	172.83	171.89	169.12	168.03	167.59	167.42
12000	201.65	198.20	195.42	193.15	191.30	189.79	188.54	187.51	184.50	183.31	182.83	182.64
13000	218.45	214.72	211.70	209.25	207.25	205.60	204.25	203.14	199.87	198.58	198.06	197.85
14000	235.25	231.24	227.99	225.35	223.19	221.42	219.96	218.77	215.25	213.86	213.30	213.07
15000	252.06	247.75	244.27	241.44	239.13	237.23	235.68	234.39	230.62	229.13	228.53	228.29
16000	268.86	264.27	260.56	257.54	255.07	253.05	251.39	250.02	246.00	244.41	243.77	243.51
17000	285.66	280.78	276.84	273.63	271.01	268.86	267.10	265.64	261.37	259.68	259.00	258.73
18000	302.47	297.30	293.12	289.73	286.95	284.68	282.81	281.27	276.74	274.96	274.24	273.95
19000	319.27	313.82	309.41	305.82	302.90	300.50	298.52	296.89	292.12	290.23	289.47	289.17
20000	336.07	330.33	325.69	321.92	318.84	316.31	314.23	312.52	307.49	305.51	304.71	304.39
21000	352.88	346.85	341.98	338.02	334.78	332.13	329.94	328.15	322.87	320.78	319.94	319.61
22000	369.68	363.37	358.26	354.11	350.72	347.94	345.66	343.77	338.24	336.06	335.18	334.83
23000	386.48	379.88	374.55	370.21	366.66	363.76	361.37	359.40	353.62	351.33	350.42	350.05
24000	403.29	396.40	390.83	386.30	382.60	379.57	377.08	375.02	368.99	366.61	365.65	365.27
25000	420.09	412.92	407.12	402.40	398.55	395.39	392.79	390.65	384.36	381.88	380.89	380.48
26000	436.89	429.43	423.40	418.49	414.49	411.20	408.50	406.28	399.74	397.16	396.12	395.70
27000	453.70	445.95	439.68	434.59	430.43	427.02	424.21	421.90	415.11	412.43	411.36	410.92
28000	470.50	462.47	455.97	450.69	446.37	442.83	439.92	437.53	430.49	427.71	426.59	426.14
29000	487.30	478.98	472.25	466.78	462.31	458.65	455.64	453.15	445.86	442.98	441.83	441.36
30000	504.11	495.50	488.54	482.88	478.25	474.46	471.35	468.78	461.24	458.26	457.06	456.58
31000	520.91	512.02	504.82	498.97	494.20	490.28	487.06	484.40	476.61	473.53	472.30	471.80
32000	537.72	528.53	521.11	515.07	510.14	506.09	502.77	500.03	491.99	488.81	487.53	487.02
33000	554.52	545.05	537.39	531.16	526.08	521.91	518.48	515.66	507.36	504.08	502.77	502.24
34000	571.32	561.56	553.67	547.26	542.02	537.72	534.19	531.28	522.73	519.36	518.00	517.46
35000	588.13	578.08	569.96	563.36	557.96	553.54	549.90	546.91	538.11	534.63	533.24	532.68
36000	604.93	594.60	586.24	579.45	573.90	569.36	565.62	562.53	553.48	549.91	548.47	547.90
37000	621.73	611.11	602.53	595.55	589.85	585.17	581.33	578.16	568.86	565.18	563.71	563.12
38000	638.54	627.63	618.81	611.64	605.79	600.99	597.04	593.78	584.23	580.46	578.94	578.33
39000	655.34	644.15	635.10	627.74	621.73	616.80	612.75	609.41	599.61	595.73	594.18	593.55
40000	672.14	660.66	651.38	643.83	637.67	632.62	628.46	625.04	614.98	611.01	609.41	608.77
41000	688.95	677.18	667.67	659.93	653.61	648.43	644.17	640.66	630.35	626.28	624.65	623.99
42000	705.75	693.70	683.95	676.03	669.55	664.25	659.88	656.29	645.73	641.56	639.88	639.21
43000	722.55	710.21	700.23	692.12	685.49	680.06	675.60	671.91	661.10	656.83	655.12	654.43
44000	739.36	726.73	716.52	708.22	701.44	695.88	691.31	687.54	676.48	672.11	670.36	669.65
45000	756.16	743.25	732.80	724.31	717.38	711.69	707.02	703.17	691.85	687.38	685.59	684.87
46000	772.96	759.76	749.09	740.41	733.32	727.51	722.73	718.79	707.23	702.66	700.83	700.09
47000	789.77	776.28	765.37	756.50	749.26	743.32	738.44	734.42	722.60	717.93	716.06	715.31
48000	806.57	792.79	781.66	772.60	765.20	759.14	754.15	750.04	737.98	733.21	731.30	730.53
49000	823.37	809.31	797.94	788.70	781.14	774.95	769.86	765.67	753.35	748.48	746.53	745.75
50000	840.18	825.83	814.23	804.79	797.09	790.77	785.58	781.29	768.72	763.76	761.77	760.96
55000	924.19	908.41	895.65	885.27	876.79	869.85	864.13	859.42	845.60	840.13	837.94	837.06
60000	1008.21	990.99	977.07	965.75	956.50	948.92	942.69	937.55	922.47	916.51	914.12	913.16
65000	1092.23	1073.57	1058.49	1046.23	1036.21	1028.00	1021.25	1015.68	999.34	992.88	990.29	989.25
70000	1176.25	1156.16	1139.91	1126.71	1115.92	1107.08	1099.80	1093.81	1076.21	1069.26	1066.47	1065.35
75000	1260.26	1238.74	1221.34	1207.18	1195.63	1186.15	1178.36	1171.94	1153.08	1145.63	1142.65	1141.44
80000	1344.28	1321.32	1302.76	1287.66	1275.34	1265.23	1256.92	1250.07	1229.96	1222.01	1218.82	1217.54
85000	1428.30	1403.90	1384.18	1368.14	1355.04	1344.30	1335.48	1328.20	1306.83	1298.38	1295.00	1293.64
90000	1512.32	1486.49	1465.60	1448.62	1434.75	1423.38	1414.03	1406.33	1383.70	1374.76	1371.18	1369.73
95000	1596.33	1569.07	1547.02	1529.10	1514.46	1502.46	1492.59	1484.45	1460.57	1451.13	1447.35	1445.83
100000	1680.35	1651.65	1628.45	1609.58	1594.17	1581.53	1571.15	1562.58	1537.44	1527.51	1523.53	1521.92

18%

Table 1

18.50%

MONTHLY
PAYMENT REQUIRED TO AMORTIZE A LOAN

TERM AMOUNT	1 YEAR	2 YEARS	3 YEARS	4 YEARS	5 YEARS	6 YEARS	7 YEARS	8 YEARS	9 YEARS	10 YEARS	11 YEARS	12 YEARS
50	4.60	2.51	1.83	1.49	1.29	1.16	1.07	1.01	.96	.92	.89	.87
100	9.20	5.02	3.65	2.97	2.57	2.31	2.14	2.01	1.91	1.84	1.78	1.74
200	18.39	10.04	7.29	5.93	5.14	4.62	4.27	4.01	3.82	3.67	3.56	3.47
300	27.58	15.05	10.93	8.90	7.70	6.93	6.40	6.01	5.73	5.51	5.34	5.20
400	36.77	20.07	14.57	11.86	10.27	9.24	8.53	8.02	7.63	7.34	7.12	6.94
500	45.96	25.09	18.21	14.82	12.84	11.55	10.66	10.02	9.54	9.18	8.89	8.67
600	55.16	30.10	21.85	17.79	15.40	13.86	12.79	12.02	11.45	11.01	10.67	10.40
700	64.35	35.12	25.49	20.75	17.97	16.17	14.92	14.02	13.35	12.84	12.45	12.14
800	73.54	40.14	29.13	23.71	20.54	18.48	17.05	16.03	15.26	14.68	14.23	13.87
900	82.73	45.15	32.77	26.68	23.10	20.79	19.19	18.03	17.17	16.51	16.00	15.60
1000	91.92	50.17	36.41	29.64	25.67	23.10	21.32	20.03	19.08	18.35	17.78	17.34
2000	183.84	100.34	72.81	59.28	51.34	46.19	42.63	40.06	38.15	36.69	35.56	34.67
3000	275.76	150.50	109.22	88.92	77.00	69.28	63.94	60.09	57.22	55.03	53.33	52.00
4000	367.68	200.67	145.62	118.55	102.67	92.37	85.25	80.11	76.29	73.37	71.11	69.33
5000	459.60	250.84	182.02	148.19	128.34	115.46	106.56	100.14	95.36	91.71	88.88	86.66
6000	551.51	301.00	218.43	177.83	154.00	138.55	127.88	120.17	114.43	110.05	106.66	103.99
7000	643.43	351.17	254.83	207.46	179.67	161.64	149.19	140.20	133.50	128.40	124.44	121.32
8000	735.35	401.33	291.23	237.10	205.33	184.74	170.50	160.22	152.57	146.74	142.21	138.65
9000	827.27	451.50	327.64	266.74	231.00	207.83	191.81	180.25	171.64	165.08	159.99	155.99
10000	919.19	501.67	364.04	296.37	256.67	230.92	213.12	200.28	190.71	183.42	177.76	173.32
11000	1011.10	551.83	400.45	326.01	282.33	254.01	234.44	220.31	209.78	201.76	195.54	190.65
12000	1103.02	602.00	436.85	355.65	308.00	277.10	255.75	240.33	228.85	220.10	213.32	207.98
13000	1194.94	652.16	473.25	385.28	333.67	300.19	277.06	260.36	247.93	238.45	231.09	225.31
14000	1286.86	702.33	509.66	414.92	359.33	323.28	298.37	280.39	267.00	256.79	248.87	242.64
15000	1378.78	752.50	546.06	444.56	385.00	346.38	319.68	300.42	286.07	275.13	266.64	259.97
16000	1470.69	802.66	582.46	474.20	410.66	369.47	341.00	320.44	305.14	293.47	284.42	277.30
17000	1562.61	852.83	618.87	503.83	436.33	392.56	362.31	340.47	324.21	311.81	302.20	294.63
18000	1654.53	902.99	655.27	533.47	462.00	415.65	383.62	360.50	343.28	330.15	319.97	311.97
19000	1746.45	953.16	691.68	563.11	487.66	438.74	404.93	380.53	362.35	348.50	337.75	329.30
20000	1838.37	1003.33	728.08	592.74	513.33	461.83	426.24	400.55	381.42	366.84	355.52	346.63
21000	1930.29	1053.49	764.48	622.38	539.00	484.92	447.56	420.58	400.49	385.18	373.30	363.96
22000	2022.20	1103.66	800.89	652.02	564.66	508.01	468.87	440.61	419.56	403.52	391.08	381.29
23000	2114.12	1153.82	837.29	681.65	590.33	531.11	490.18	460.64	438.63	421.86	408.85	398.62
24000	2206.04	1203.99	873.69	711.29	615.99	554.20	511.49	480.66	457.70	440.20	426.63	415.95
25000	2297.96	1254.16	910.10	740.93	641.66	577.29	532.80	500.69	476.78	458.55	444.40	433.28
26000	2389.88	1304.32	946.50	770.56	667.33	600.38	554.11	520.72	495.85	476.89	462.18	450.61
27000	2481.79	1354.49	982.91	800.20	692.99	623.47	575.43	540.75	514.92	495.23	479.96	467.95
28000	2573.71	1404.65	1019.31	829.84	718.66	646.56	596.74	560.77	533.99	513.57	497.73	485.28
29000	2665.63	1454.82	1055.71	859.48	744.33	669.65	618.05	580.80	553.06	531.91	515.51	502.61
30000	2757.55	1504.99	1092.12	889.11	769.99	692.75	639.36	600.83	572.13	550.25	533.28	519.94
31000	2849.47	1555.15	1128.52	918.75	795.66	715.84	660.67	620.86	591.20	568.60	551.06	537.27
32000	2941.38	1605.32	1164.92	948.39	821.32	738.93	681.99	640.88	610.27	586.94	568.84	554.60
33000	3033.30	1655.48	1201.33	978.02	846.99	762.02	703.30	660.91	629.34	605.28	586.61	571.93
34000	3125.22	1705.65	1237.73	1007.66	872.66	785.11	724.61	680.94	648.41	623.62	604.39	589.26
35000	3217.14	1755.82	1274.14	1037.30	898.32	808.20	745.92	700.97	667.48	641.96	622.16	606.59
36000	3309.06	1805.98	1310.54	1066.93	923.99	831.29	767.23	720.99	686.55	660.30	639.94	623.93
37000	3400.98	1856.15	1346.94	1096.57	949.65	854.39	788.55	741.02	705.63	678.65	657.72	641.26
38000	3492.89	1906.31	1383.35	1126.21	975.32	877.48	809.86	761.05	724.70	696.99	675.49	658.59
39000	3584.81	1956.48	1419.75	1155.84	1000.99	900.57	831.17	781.08	743.77	715.33	693.27	675.92
40000	3676.73	2006.65	1456.15	1185.48	1026.65	923.66	852.48	801.10	762.84	733.67	711.04	693.25
41000	3768.65	2056.81	1492.56	1215.12	1052.32	946.75	873.79	821.13	781.91	752.01	728.82	710.58
42000	3860.57	2106.98	1528.96	1244.76	1077.99	969.84	895.11	841.16	800.98	770.35	746.60	727.91
43000	3952.48	2157.14	1565.36	1274.39	1103.65	992.93	916.42	861.18	820.05	788.70	764.37	745.24
44000	4044.40	2207.31	1601.77	1304.03	1129.32	1016.02	937.73	881.21	839.12	807.04	782.15	762.58
45000	4136.32	2257.48	1638.17	1333.67	1154.98	1039.12	959.04	901.24	858.19	825.38	799.92	779.91
46000	4228.24	2307.64	1674.58	1363.30	1180.65	1062.21	980.35	921.27	877.26	843.72	817.70	797.24
47000	4320.16	2357.81	1710.98	1392.94	1206.32	1085.30	1001.67	941.29	896.33	862.06	835.48	814.57
48000	4412.07	2407.97	1747.38	1422.58	1231.98	1108.39	1022.98	961.32	915.40	880.40	853.25	831.90
49000	4503.99	2458.14	1783.79	1452.21	1257.65	1131.48	1044.29	981.35	934.47	898.75	871.03	849.23
50000	4595.91	2508.31	1820.19	1481.85	1283.32	1154.57	1065.60	1001.38	953.55	917.09	888.80	866.56
55000	5055.50	2759.14	2002.21	1630.04	1411.65	1270.03	1172.16	1101.51	1048.90	1008.80	977.68	953.22
60000	5515.09	3009.97	2184.23	1778.22	1539.98	1385.49	1278.72	1201.65	1144.25	1100.50	1066.56	1039.87
65000	5974.68	3260.80	2366.25	1926.40	1668.31	1500.94	1385.28	1301.79	1239.61	1192.21	1155.44	1126.53
70000	6434.27	3511.63	2548.27	2074.59	1796.64	1616.40	1491.84	1401.93	1334.96	1283.92	1244.32	1213.18
75000	6893.86	3762.46	2730.28	2222.77	1924.97	1731.86	1598.40	1502.06	1430.32	1375.63	1333.20	1299.84
80000	7353.45	4013.29	2912.30	2370.96	2053.30	1847.31	1704.96	1602.20	1525.67	1467.34	1422.08	1386.50
85000	7813.05	4264.12	3094.32	2519.14	2181.63	1962.77	1811.52	1702.34	1621.02	1559.05	1510.96	1473.15
90000	8272.64	4514.95	3276.34	2667.33	2309.96	2078.23	1918.08	1802.47	1716.38	1650.75	1599.84	1559.81
95000	8732.23	4765.78	3458.36	2815.51	2438.29	2193.68	2024.64	1902.61	1811.73	1742.46	1688.72	1646.46
100000	9191.82	5016.61	3640.38	2963.70	2566.63	2309.14	2131.20	2002.75	1907.09	1834.17	1777.60	1733.12

Table 1

MONTHLY 18.50%

PAYMENT REQUIRED TO AMORTIZE A LOAN

TERM AMOUNT	13 YEARS	14 YEARS	15 YEARS	16 YEARS	17 YEARS	18 YEARS	19 YEARS	20 YEARS	25 YEARS	30 YEARS	35 YEARS	40 YEARS
50	.85	.84	.83	.82	.81	.81	.80	.80	.78	.78	.78	.78
100	1.70	1.67	1.65	1.63	1.62	1.61	1.60	1.59	1.56	1.55	1.55	1.55
200	3.40	3.34	3.30	3.26	3.23	3.21	3.19	3.17	3.12	3.10	3.09	3.09
300	5.10	5.01	4.94	4.89	4.84	4.81	4.78	4.75	4.68	4.65	4.64	4.63
400	6.80	6.68	6.59	6.52	6.46	6.41	6.37	6.33	6.23	6.20	6.18	6.18
500	8.49	8.35	8.24	8.14	8.07	8.01	7.96	7.91	7.79	7.74	7.73	7.72
600	10.19	10.02	9.88	9.77	9.68	9.61	9.55	9.50	9.35	9.29	9.27	9.26
700	11.89	11.69	11.53	11.40	11.29	11.21	11.14	11.08	10.91	10.84	10.81	10.80
800	13.59	13.36	13.18	13.03	12.91	12.81	12.73	12.66	12.46	12.39	12.36	12.35
900	15.28	15.03	14.82	14.66	14.52	14.41	14.32	14.24	14.02	13.94	13.90	13.89
1000	16.98	16.70	16.47	16.28	16.13	16.01	15.91	15.82	15.58	15.48	15.45	15.43
2000	33.96	33.39	32.94	32.56	32.26	32.01	31.81	31.64	31.15	30.96	30.89	30.86
3000	50.94	50.09	49.40	48.84	48.39	48.02	47.71	47.46	46.73	46.44	46.33	46.28
4000	67.92	66.78	65.87	65.12	64.52	64.02	63.62	63.28	62.30	61.92	61.77	61.71
5000	84.89	83.48	82.33	81.40	80.65	80.03	79.52	79.10	77.88	77.40	77.21	77.14
6000	101.87	100.17	98.80	97.68	96.77	96.03	95.42	94.92	93.45	92.88	92.66	92.56
7000	118.85	116.86	115.26	113.96	112.90	112.03	111.32	110.74	109.03	108.36	108.10	107.99
8000	135.83	133.56	131.73	130.24	129.03	128.04	127.23	126.56	124.60	123.84	123.54	123.42
9000	152.80	150.25	148.19	146.52	145.16	144.04	143.13	142.38	140.18	139.32	138.98	138.84
10000	169.78	166.95	164.66	162.80	161.29	160.05	159.03	158.19	155.75	154.80	154.42	154.27
11000	186.76	183.64	181.12	179.08	177.41	176.05	174.93	174.01	171.33	170.28	169.86	169.70
12000	203.74	200.33	197.59	195.36	193.54	192.06	190.84	189.83	186.90	185.76	185.31	185.12
13000	220.71	217.03	214.05	211.64	209.68	208.06	206.74	205.65	202.48	201.24	200.75	200.55
14000	237.69	233.72	230.52	227.92	225.80	224.06	222.64	221.47	218.05	216.72	216.19	215.98
15000	254.67	250.42	246.98	244.20	241.93	240.07	238.54	237.29	233.63	232.20	231.63	231.40
16000	271.65	267.11	263.45	260.48	258.05	256.07	254.45	253.11	249.20	247.68	247.07	246.83
17000	288.62	283.80	279.91	276.76	274.18	272.08	270.35	268.93	264.78	263.16	262.51	262.26
18000	305.60	300.50	296.38	293.04	290.31	288.08	286.25	284.75	280.35	278.64	277.96	277.68
19000	322.58	317.19	312.84	309.32	306.44	304.09	302.15	300.57	295.93	294.11	293.40	293.11
20000	339.56	333.89	329.31	325.60	322.57	320.09	318.06	316.38	311.50	309.59	308.84	308.54
21000	356.53	350.58	345.77	341.87	338.70	336.09	333.96	332.20	327.08	325.07	324.28	323.96
22000	373.51	367.27	362.24	358.15	354.82	352.10	349.86	348.02	342.65	340.55	339.72	339.39
23000	390.49	383.97	378.71	374.43	370.95	368.10	365.76	363.84	358.23	356.03	355.16	354.82
24000	407.47	400.66	395.17	390.71	387.08	384.11	381.67	379.66	373.80	371.51	370.61	370.24
25000	424.44	417.36	411.64	406.99	403.21	400.11	397.57	395.48	389.38	386.99	386.05	385.67
26000	441.42	434.05	428.10	423.27	419.34	416.12	413.47	411.30	404.95	402.47	401.49	401.10
27000	458.40	450.74	444.57	439.55	435.46	432.12	429.38	427.12	420.53	417.95	416.93	416.52
28000	475.38	467.44	461.03	455.83	451.59	448.12	445.28	442.94	436.10	433.43	432.37	431.95
29000	492.35	484.13	477.50	472.11	467.72	464.13	461.18	458.76	451.68	448.91	447.81	447.38
30000	509.33	500.83	493.96	488.39	483.85	480.13	477.08	474.57	467.25	464.39	463.26	462.80
31000	526.31	517.52	510.43	504.67	499.98	496.14	492.99	490.39	482.83	479.87	478.70	478.23
32000	543.29	534.21	526.89	520.95	516.10	512.14	508.89	506.21	498.40	495.35	494.14	493.66
33000	560.26	550.91	543.36	537.23	532.23	528.15	524.79	522.03	513.97	510.83	509.58	509.08
34000	577.24	567.60	559.82	553.51	548.36	544.15	540.69	537.85	529.55	526.31	525.02	524.51
35000	594.22	584.30	576.29	569.79	564.49	560.15	556.60	553.67	545.12	541.79	540.46	539.94
36000	611.20	600.99	592.75	586.07	580.62	576.16	572.50	569.49	560.70	557.27	555.91	555.36
37000	628.17	617.68	609.22	602.35	596.75	592.16	588.40	585.31	576.27	572.74	571.35	570.79
38000	645.15	634.38	625.68	618.63	612.87	608.17	604.30	601.13	591.85	588.22	586.79	586.22
39000	662.13	651.07	642.15	634.91	629.00	624.17	620.21	616.94	607.42	603.70	602.23	601.64
40000	679.11	667.77	658.61	651.19	645.13	640.17	636.11	632.76	623.00	619.18	617.67	617.07
41000	696.08	684.46	675.08	667.47	661.26	656.18	652.01	648.58	638.57	634.66	633.11	632.50
42000	713.06	701.16	691.54	683.74	677.39	672.18	667.91	664.40	654.15	650.14	648.56	647.92
43000	730.04	717.85	708.01	700.02	693.51	688.19	683.82	680.22	669.72	665.62	664.00	663.35
44000	747.02	734.54	724.48	716.30	709.64	704.19	699.72	696.04	685.30	681.10	679.44	678.78
45000	763.99	751.24	740.94	732.58	725.77	720.20	715.62	711.86	700.87	696.58	694.88	694.20
46000	780.97	767.93	757.41	748.86	741.90	736.20	731.52	727.68	716.45	712.06	710.32	709.63
47000	797.95	784.63	773.87	765.14	758.03	752.20	747.43	743.50	732.02	727.54	725.76	725.06
48000	814.93	801.32	790.34	781.42	774.15	768.21	763.33	759.32	747.60	743.02	741.21	740.48
49000	831.90	818.01	806.80	797.70	790.28	784.21	779.23	775.13	763.17	758.50	756.65	755.91
50000	848.88	834.71	823.27	813.98	806.41	800.22	795.13	790.95	778.75	773.98	772.09	771.34
55000	933.77	918.18	905.59	895.38	887.05	880.24	874.65	870.05	856.62	851.37	849.30	848.47
60000	1018.66	1001.65	987.92	976.78	967.69	960.26	954.16	949.14	934.50	928.77	926.51	925.60
65000	1103.54	1085.12	1070.25	1058.17	1048.33	1040.28	1033.67	1028.24	1012.37	1006.17	1003.71	1002.74
70000	1188.43	1168.59	1152.57	1139.57	1128.97	1120.30	1113.19	1107.33	1090.24	1083.57	1080.92	1079.87
75000	1273.32	1252.06	1234.90	1220.97	1209.61	1200.32	1192.70	1186.43	1168.12	1160.96	1158.13	1157.00
80000	1358.21	1335.53	1317.22	1302.37	1290.26	1280.35	1272.21	1265.52	1245.99	1238.36	1235.34	1234.14
85000	1443.10	1419.00	1399.55	1383.76	1370.90	1360.37	1351.73	1344.62	1323.87	1315.76	1312.55	1311.27
90000	1527.98	1502.47	1481.88	1465.16	1451.54	1440.39	1431.24	1423.71	1401.74	1393.16	1389.76	1388.40
95000	1612.87	1585.94	1564.20	1546.56	1532.18	1520.41	1510.75	1502.81	1479.61	1470.55	1466.96	1465.54
100000	1697.76	1669.41	1646.53	1627.96	1612.82	1600.43	1590.26	1581.90	1557.49	1547.95	1544.17	1542.67

18%

Table 1

18.75%

MONTHLY
PAYMENT REQUIRED TO AMORTIZE A LOAN

TERM / AMOUNT	1 YEAR	2 YEARS	3 YEARS	4 YEARS	5 YEARS	6 YEARS	7 YEARS	8 YEARS	9 YEARS	10 YEARS	11 YEARS	12 YEARS
50	4.61	2.52	1.83	1.49	1.30	1.17	1.08	1.01	.97	.93	.90	.88
100	9.21	5.03	3.66	2.98	2.59	2.33	2.15	2.02	1.93	1.86	1.80	1.76
200	18.41	10.06	7.31	5.96	5.17	4.65	4.30	4.04	3.85	3.71	3.59	3.51
300	27.62	15.09	10.96	8.94	7.75	6.98	6.44	6.06	5.77	5.56	5.39	5.26
400	36.82	20.12	14.62	11.91	10.33	9.30	8.59	8.08	7.70	7.41	7.18	7.01
500	46.02	25.15	18.27	14.89	12.91	11.62	10.73	10.10	9.62	9.26	8.98	8.76
600	55.23	30.18	21.92	17.87	15.49	13.95	12.88	12.11	11.54	11.11	10.77	10.51
700	64.43	35.21	25.58	20.84	18.07	16.27	15.03	14.13	13.47	12.96	12.56	12.26
800	73.63	40.23	29.23	23.82	20.65	18.59	17.17	16.15	15.39	14.81	14.36	14.01
900	82.84	45.26	32.88	26.80	23.23	20.92	19.32	18.17	17.31	16.66	16.15	15.76
1000	92.04	50.29	36.53	29.77	25.81	23.24	21.46	20.19	19.23	18.51	17.95	17.51
2000	184.08	100.58	73.06	59.54	51.61	46.47	42.92	40.37	38.46	37.01	35.89	35.01
3000	276.12	150.87	109.59	89.31	77.41	69.71	64.38	60.55	57.69	55.52	53.83	52.51
4000	368.15	201.15	146.12	119.08	103.22	92.94	85.84	80.73	76.92	74.02	71.78	70.01
5000	460.19	251.44	182.65	148.85	129.02	116.17	107.30	100.91	96.15	92.53	89.72	87.52
6000	552.23	301.73	219.18	178.62	154.82	139.41	128.76	121.09	115.38	111.03	107.66	105.02
7000	644.27	352.02	255.71	208.38	180.63	162.64	150.22	141.27	134.61	129.53	125.60	122.52
8000	736.30	402.30	292.24	238.15	206.43	185.88	171.68	161.45	153.83	148.04	143.55	140.02
9000	828.34	452.59	328.77	267.92	232.23	209.11	193.14	181.63	173.06	166.54	161.49	157.52
10000	920.38	502.88	365.30	297.69	258.04	232.34	214.60	201.81	192.29	185.05	179.43	175.03
11000	1012.42	553.16	401.83	327.46	283.84	255.58	236.06	221.99	211.52	203.55	197.38	192.53
12000	1104.45	603.45	438.36	357.23	309.64	278.81	257.52	242.17	230.75	222.05	215.32	210.03
13000	1196.49	653.74	474.89	386.99	335.45	302.04	278.98	262.35	249.98	240.56	233.26	227.53
14000	1288.53	704.03	511.42	416.76	361.25	325.28	300.44	282.53	269.21	259.06	251.20	245.03
15000	1380.56	754.31	547.95	446.53	387.05	348.51	321.90	302.71	288.43	277.57	269.15	262.54
16000	1472.60	804.60	584.48	476.30	412.86	371.75	343.36	322.89	307.66	296.07	287.09	280.04
17000	1564.64	854.89	621.01	506.07	438.66	394.98	364.82	343.07	326.89	314.58	305.03	297.54
18000	1656.68	905.18	657.54	535.84	464.46	418.21	386.28	363.25	346.12	333.08	322.98	315.04
19000	1748.71	955.46	694.07	565.60	490.27	441.45	407.74	383.43	365.35	351.58	340.92	332.54
20000	1840.75	1005.75	730.60	595.37	516.07	464.68	429.20	403.61	384.58	370.09	358.86	350.05
21000	1932.79	1056.04	767.13	625.14	541.87	487.92	450.66	423.79	403.81	388.59	376.80	367.55
22000	2024.83	1106.32	803.66	654.91	567.68	511.15	472.12	443.97	423.04	407.10	394.75	385.05
23000	2116.86	1156.61	840.19	684.68	593.48	534.38	493.58	464.15	442.26	425.60	412.69	402.55
24000	2208.90	1206.90	876.72	714.45	619.28	557.62	515.04	484.33	461.49	444.10	430.63	420.05
25000	2300.94	1257.19	913.25	744.21	645.08	580.85	536.50	504.51	480.72	462.61	448.58	437.56
26000	2392.97	1307.47	949.78	773.98	670.89	604.08	557.96	524.69	499.95	481.11	466.52	455.06
27000	2485.01	1357.76	986.31	803.75	696.69	627.32	579.42	544.88	519.18	499.62	484.46	472.56
28000	2577.05	1408.05	1022.84	833.52	722.49	650.55	600.88	565.06	538.41	518.12	502.40	490.06
29000	2669.09	1458.33	1059.37	863.29	748.30	673.79	622.34	585.24	557.64	536.63	520.35	507.57
30000	2761.12	1508.62	1095.90	893.06	774.10	697.02	643.80	605.42	576.86	555.13	538.29	525.07
31000	2853.16	1558.91	1132.43	922.82	799.90	720.25	665.26	625.60	596.09	573.63	556.23	542.57
32000	2945.20	1609.20	1168.96	952.59	825.71	743.49	686.72	645.78	615.32	592.14	574.18	560.07
33000	3037.24	1659.48	1205.49	982.36	851.51	766.72	708.18	665.96	634.55	610.64	592.12	577.57
34000	3129.27	1709.77	1242.02	1012.13	877.31	789.95	729.64	686.14	653.78	629.15	610.06	595.08
35000	3221.31	1760.06	1278.55	1041.90	903.12	813.19	751.10	706.32	673.01	647.65	628.00	612.58
36000	3313.35	1810.35	1315.08	1071.67	928.92	836.42	772.55	726.50	692.24	666.15	645.95	630.08
37000	3405.39	1860.63	1351.61	1101.43	954.72	859.66	794.01	746.68	711.47	684.66	663.89	647.58
38000	3497.42	1910.92	1388.14	1131.20	980.53	882.89	815.47	766.86	730.69	703.16	681.83	665.08
39000	3589.46	1961.21	1424.67	1160.97	1006.33	906.12	836.93	787.04	749.92	721.67	699.78	682.59
40000	3681.50	2011.49	1461.19	1190.74	1032.13	929.36	858.39	807.22	769.15	740.17	717.72	700.09
41000	3773.53	2061.78	1497.72	1220.51	1057.94	952.59	879.85	827.40	788.38	758.67	735.66	717.59
42000	3865.57	2112.07	1534.25	1250.28	1083.74	975.83	901.31	847.58	807.61	777.18	753.60	735.09
43000	3957.61	2162.36	1570.78	1280.04	1109.54	999.06	922.77	867.76	826.84	795.68	771.55	752.59
44000	4049.65	2212.64	1607.31	1309.81	1135.35	1022.29	944.23	887.94	846.07	814.19	789.49	770.10
45000	4141.68	2262.93	1643.84	1339.58	1161.15	1045.53	965.69	908.12	865.29	832.69	807.43	787.60
46000	4233.72	2313.22	1680.37	1369.35	1186.95	1068.76	987.15	928.30	884.52	851.20	825.38	805.10
47000	4325.76	2363.51	1716.90	1399.12	1212.75	1091.99	1008.61	948.48	903.75	869.70	843.32	822.60
48000	4417.80	2413.79	1753.43	1428.89	1238.56	1115.23	1030.07	968.66	922.98	888.20	861.26	840.10
49000	4509.83	2464.08	1789.96	1458.65	1264.36	1138.46	1051.53	988.84	942.21	906.71	879.20	857.61
50000	4601.87	2514.37	1826.49	1488.42	1290.16	1161.70	1072.99	1009.02	961.44	925.21	897.15	875.11
55000	5062.06	2765.80	2009.14	1637.26	1419.18	1277.86	1180.29	1109.93	1057.58	1017.73	986.86	962.62
60000	5522.24	3017.24	2191.79	1786.11	1548.20	1394.03	1287.59	1210.83	1153.72	1110.25	1076.58	1050.13
65000	5982.43	3268.68	2374.44	1934.95	1677.21	1510.20	1394.89	1311.73	1249.87	1202.77	1166.29	1137.64
70000	6442.62	3520.11	2557.09	2083.79	1806.23	1626.37	1502.19	1412.63	1346.01	1295.29	1256.00	1225.15
75000	6902.80	3771.55	2739.74	2232.63	1935.24	1742.54	1609.48	1513.53	1442.15	1387.82	1345.72	1312.66
80000	7362.99	4022.98	2922.38	2381.47	2064.26	1858.71	1716.78	1614.44	1538.30	1480.34	1435.43	1400.17
85000	7823.18	4274.42	3105.03	2530.32	2193.28	1974.88	1824.08	1715.34	1634.44	1572.86	1525.15	1487.68
90000	8283.36	4525.86	3287.68	2679.16	2322.29	2091.05	1931.38	1816.24	1730.58	1665.38	1614.86	1575.19
95000	8743.55	4777.29	3470.33	2828.00	2451.31	2207.22	2038.68	1917.14	1826.73	1757.90	1704.58	1662.70
100000	9203.74	5028.73	3652.98	2976.84	2580.32	2323.39	2145.98	2018.04	1922.87	1850.42	1794.29	1750.21

18%

Table 1

MONTHLY

18.75%

PAYMENT REQUIRED TO AMORTIZE A LOAN

TERM	13 YEARS	14 YEARS	15 YEARS	16 YEARS	17 YEARS	18 YEARS	19 YEARS	20 YEARS	25 YEARS	30 YEARS	35 YEARS	40 YEARS
UNT												
50	.86	.85	.84	.83	.82	.81	.81	.81	.79	.79	.79	.79
100	1.72	1.69	1.67	1.65	1.64	1.62	1.61	1.61	1.58	1.57	1.57	1.57
200	3.44	3.38	3.33	3.30	3.27	3.24	3.22	3.21	3.16	3.14	3.13	3.13
300	5.15	5.07	5.00	4.94	4.90	4.86	4.83	4.81	4.74	4.71	4.70	4.70
400	6.87	6.75	6.66	6.59	6.53	6.48	6.44	6.41	6.32	6.28	6.26	6.26
500	8.58	8.44	8.33	8.24	8.16	8.10	8.05	8.01	7.89	7.85	7.83	7.82
600	10.30	10.13	9.99	9.88	9.79	9.72	9.66	9.61	9.47	9.42	9.39	9.39
700	12.01	11.82	11.66	11.53	11.43	11.34	11.27	11.21	11.05	10.98	10.96	10.95
800	13.73	13.50	13.32	13.18	13.06	12.96	12.88	12.82	12.63	12.55	12.52	12.51
900	15.44	15.19	14.99	14.82	14.69	14.58	14.49	14.42	14.20	14.12	14.09	14.08
1000	17.16	16.88	16.65	16.47	16.32	16.20	16.10	16.02	15.78	15.69	15.65	15.64
2000	34.31	33.75	33.30	32.93	32.64	32.39	32.19	32.03	31.56	31.37	31.30	31.27
3000	51.46	50.62	49.95	49.40	48.95	48.59	48.29	48.04	47.33	47.06	46.95	46.91
4000	68.61	67.49	66.59	65.86	65.27	64.78	64.38	64.06	63.11	62.74	62.60	62.54
5000	85.77	84.37	83.24	82.32	81.58	80.97	80.48	80.07	78.88	78.43	78.25	78.18
6000	102.92	101.24	99.89	98.79	97.90	97.17	96.57	96.08	94.66	94.11	93.89	93.81
7000	120.07	118.11	116.53	115.25	114.21	113.36	112.67	112.09	110.43	109.79	109.54	109.44
8000	137.22	134.98	133.18	131.72	130.53	129.56	128.76	128.11	126.21	125.48	125.19	125.08
9000	154.38	151.86	149.83	148.18	146.84	145.75	144.85	144.12	141.99	141.16	140.84	140.71
10000	171.53	168.73	166.47	164.64	163.16	161.94	160.95	160.13	157.76	156.85	156.49	156.35
11000	188.68	185.60	183.12	181.11	179.47	178.14	177.04	176.14	173.54	172.53	172.14	171.98
12000	205.83	202.47	199.77	197.57	195.79	194.33	193.14	192.16	189.31	188.21	187.78	187.61
13000	222.98	219.34	216.41	214.04	212.10	210.52	209.23	208.17	205.09	203.90	203.43	203.25
14000	240.14	236.22	233.06	230.50	228.42	226.72	225.33	224.18	220.86	219.58	219.08	218.88
15000	257.29	253.09	249.71	246.96	244.73	242.91	241.42	240.19	236.64	235.27	234.73	234.52
16000	274.44	269.96	266.35	263.43	261.05	259.11	257.51	256.21	252.42	250.95	250.38	250.15
17000	291.59	286.83	283.00	279.89	277.36	275.30	273.61	272.22	268.19	266.63	266.03	265.79
18000	308.75	303.71	299.65	296.36	293.68	291.49	289.70	288.23	283.97	282.32	281.67	281.42
19000	325.90	320.58	316.29	312.82	309.99	307.69	305.80	304.25	299.74	298.00	297.32	297.05
20000	343.05	337.45	332.94	329.28	326.31	323.88	321.89	320.26	315.52	313.69	312.97	312.69
21000	360.20	354.32	349.59	345.75	342.62	340.07	337.99	336.27	331.29	329.37	328.62	328.32
22000	377.35	371.20	366.23	362.21	358.94	356.27	354.08	352.28	347.07	345.05	344.27	343.96
23000	394.51	388.07	382.88	378.68	375.25	372.46	370.17	368.30	362.84	360.74	359.91	359.59
24000	411.66	404.94	399.53	395.14	391.57	388.66	386.27	384.31	378.62	376.42	375.56	375.22
25000	428.81	421.81	416.17	411.60	407.89	404.85	402.36	400.32	394.40	392.11	391.21	390.86
26000	445.96	438.68	432.82	428.07	424.20	421.04	418.46	416.33	410.17	407.79	406.86	406.49
27000	463.12	455.56	449.47	444.53	440.52	437.24	434.55	432.35	425.95	423.48	422.51	422.13
28000	480.27	472.43	466.11	460.99	456.83	453.43	450.65	448.36	441.72	439.16	438.16	437.76
29000	497.42	489.30	482.76	477.46	473.15	469.62	466.74	464.37	457.50	454.84	453.80	453.40
30000	514.57	506.17	499.41	493.92	489.46	485.82	482.83	480.38	473.27	470.53	469.45	469.03
31000	531.73	523.05	516.05	510.39	505.78	502.01	498.93	496.40	489.05	486.21	485.10	484.66
32000	548.88	539.92	532.70	526.85	522.09	518.21	515.02	512.41	504.83	501.90	500.75	500.30
33000	566.03	556.79	549.35	543.31	538.41	534.40	531.12	528.42	520.60	517.58	516.40	515.93
34000	583.18	573.66	565.99	559.78	554.72	550.59	547.21	544.44	536.38	533.26	532.05	531.57
35000	600.33	590.53	582.64	576.24	571.04	566.79	563.31	560.45	552.15	548.95	547.69	547.20
36000	617.49	607.41	599.29	592.71	587.35	582.98	579.40	576.46	567.93	564.63	563.34	562.83
37000	634.64	624.28	615.93	609.17	603.67	599.17	595.49	592.47	583.70	580.32	578.99	578.47
38000	651.79	641.15	632.58	625.63	619.98	615.37	611.59	608.49	599.48	596.00	594.64	594.10
39000	668.94	658.02	649.23	642.10	636.30	631.56	627.68	624.50	615.26	611.68	610.29	609.74
40000	686.10	674.90	665.87	658.56	652.61	647.76	643.78	640.51	631.03	627.37	625.94	625.37
41000	703.25	691.77	682.52	675.03	668.93	663.95	659.87	656.52	646.81	643.05	641.58	641.01
42000	720.40	708.64	699.17	691.49	685.24	680.14	675.97	672.54	662.58	658.74	657.23	656.64
43000	737.55	725.51	715.81	707.95	701.56	696.34	692.06	688.55	678.36	674.42	672.88	672.27
44000	754.70	742.39	732.46	724.42	717.87	712.53	708.15	704.56	694.13	690.10	688.53	687.91
45000	771.86	759.26	749.11	740.88	734.19	728.72	724.25	720.57	709.91	705.79	704.18	703.54
46000	789.01	776.13	765.75	757.35	750.50	744.92	740.34	736.59	725.68	721.47	719.82	719.18
47000	806.16	793.00	782.40	773.81	766.82	761.11	756.44	752.60	741.46	737.16	735.47	734.81
48000	823.31	809.87	799.05	790.27	783.14	777.31	772.53	768.61	757.24	752.84	751.12	750.44
49000	840.47	826.75	815.69	806.74	799.45	793.50	788.63	784.63	773.01	768.52	766.77	766.08
50000	857.62	843.62	832.34	823.20	815.77	809.69	804.72	800.64	788.79	784.21	782.42	781.71
55000	943.38	927.98	915.57	905.52	897.34	890.66	885.19	880.70	867.67	862.63	860.66	859.88
60000	1029.14	1012.34	998.81	987.84	978.92	971.63	965.66	960.76	946.54	941.05	938.90	938.05
65000	1114.90	1096.70	1082.04	1070.16	1060.49	1052.60	1046.14	1040.83	1025.42	1019.47	1017.14	1016.23
70000	1200.66	1181.06	1165.27	1152.48	1142.07	1133.57	1126.61	1120.89	1104.30	1097.89	1095.38	1094.40
75000	1286.42	1265.43	1248.51	1234.80	1223.65	1214.54	1207.08	1200.95	1183.18	1176.31	1173.62	1172.57
80000	1372.19	1349.79	1331.74	1317.12	1305.22	1295.51	1287.55	1281.02	1262.06	1254.73	1251.87	1250.74
85000	1457.95	1434.15	1414.97	1399.44	1386.80	1376.48	1368.02	1361.08	1340.94	1333.15	1330.11	1328.91
90000	1543.71	1518.51	1498.21	1481.76	1468.37	1457.44	1448.49	1441.14	1419.81	1411.57	1408.35	1407.08
95000	1629.47	1602.87	1581.44	1564.08	1549.95	1538.41	1528.96	1521.21	1498.69	1489.99	1486.59	1485.25
100000	1715.23	1687.23	1664.67	1646.40	1631.53	1619.38	1609.44	1601.27	1577.57	1568.41	1564.83	1563.42

18%

Table 1

19.00%

MONTHLY
PAYMENT REQUIRED TO AMORTIZE A LOAN

TERM	1 YEAR	2 YEARS	3 YEARS	4 YEARS	5 YEARS	6 YEARS	7 YEARS	8 YEARS	9 YEARS	10 YEARS	11 YEARS	12 YEAR.
AMOUNT												
50	4.61	2.53	1.84	1.50	1.30	1.17	1.09	1.02	.97	.94	.91	.89
100	9.22	5.05	3.67	3.00	2.60	2.34	2.17	2.04	1.94	1.87	1.82	1.77
200	18.44	10.09	7.34	5.99	5.19	4.68	4.33	4.07	3.88	3.74	3.63	3.54
300	27.65	15.13	11.00	8.98	7.79	7.02	6.49	6.11	5.82	5.61	5.44	5.31
400	36.87	20.17	14.67	11.97	10.38	9.36	8.65	8.14	7.76	7.47	7.25	7.07
500	46.08	25.21	18.33	14.96	12.98	11.69	10.81	10.17	9.70	9.34	9.06	8.84
600	55.30	30.25	22.00	17.95	15.57	14.03	12.97	12.21	11.64	11.21	10.87	10.61
700	64.51	35.29	25.66	20.94	18.16	16.37	15.13	14.24	13.58	13.07	12.68	12.38
800	73.73	40.33	29.33	23.93	20.76	18.71	17.29	16.27	15.51	14.94	14.49	14.14
900	82.95	45.37	33.00	26.92	23.35	21.04	19.45	18.31	17.45	16.81	16.30	15.91
1000	92.16	50.41	36.66	29.91	25.95	23.38	21.61	20.34	19.39	18.67	18.12	17.68
2000	184.32	100.82	73.32	59.81	51.89	46.76	43.22	40.67	38.78	37.34	36.23	35.35
3000	276.47	151.23	109.97	89.71	77.83	70.14	64.83	61.01	58.17	56.01	54.34	53.03
4000	368.63	201.64	146.63	119.61	103.77	93.51	86.44	81.34	77.55	74.67	72.45	70.70
5000	460.79	252.05	183.29	149.51	129.71	116.89	108.05	101.67	96.94	93.34	90.56	88.37
6000	552.94	302.46	219.94	179.41	155.65	140.27	129.65	122.01	116.33	112.01	108.67	106.05
7000	645.10	352.87	256.60	209.31	181.59	163.64	151.26	142.34	135.71	130.68	126.78	123.72
8000	737.26	403.27	293.25	239.21	207.53	187.02	172.87	162.68	155.10	149.34	144.89	141.39
9000	829.41	453.68	329.91	269.11	233.47	210.40	194.48	183.01	174.49	168.01	163.00	159.07
10000	921.57	504.09	366.57	299.01	259.41	233.77	216.09	203.34	193.88	186.68	181.11	176.74
11000	1013.73	554.50	403.22	328.91	285.35	257.15	237.69	223.68	213.26	205.34	199.22	194.42
12000	1105.88	604.91	439.88	358.81	311.29	280.53	259.30	244.01	232.65	224.01	217.33	212.09
13000	1198.04	655.32	476.53	388.71	337.23	303.90	280.91	264.35	252.04	242.68	235.44	229.76
14000	1290.20	705.73	513.19	418.61	363.17	327.28	302.52	284.68	271.42	261.35	253.55	247.44
15000	1382.35	756.13	549.85	448.51	389.11	350.66	324.13	305.01	290.81	280.01	271.66	265.11
16000	1474.51	806.54	586.50	478.41	415.05	374.03	345.73	325.35	310.20	298.68	289.77	282.78
17000	1566.67	856.95	623.16	508.31	440.99	397.41	367.34	345.68	329.59	317.35	307.88	300.46
18000	1658.82	907.36	659.81	538.21	466.93	420.79	388.95	366.01	348.97	336.02	325.99	318.13
19000	1750.98	957.77	696.47	568.11	492.88	444.16	410.56	386.35	368.36	354.68	349.10	335.80
20000	1843.14	1008.18	733.13	598.01	518.82	467.54	432.17	406.68	387.75	373.35	362.21	353.48
21000	1935.29	1058.59	769.78	627.91	544.76	490.92	453.77	427.02	407.13	392.02	380.32	371.15
22000	2027.45	1108.99	806.44	657.81	570.70	514.29	475.38	447.35	426.52	410.68	398.43	388.83
23000	2119.61	1159.40	843.09	687.71	596.64	537.67	496.99	467.68	445.91	429.35	416.54	406.50
24000	2211.76	1209.81	879.75	717.61	622.58	561.05	518.60	488.02	465.29	448.02	434.65	424.17
25000	2303.92	1260.22	916.41	747.51	648.52	584.42	540.21	508.35	484.68	466.69	452.76	441.85
26000	2396.08	1310.63	953.06	777.41	674.46	607.80	561.81	528.69	504.07	485.35	470.87	459.52
27000	2488.23	1361.04	989.72	807.31	700.40	631.18	583.42	549.02	523.46	504.02	488.98	477.19
28000	2580.39	1411.45	1026.37	837.21	726.34	654.55	605.03	569.35	542.84	522.69	507.09	494.87
29000	2672.55	1461.85	1063.03	867.11	752.28	677.93	626.64	589.69	562.23	541.35	525.20	512.54
30000	2764.70	1512.26	1099.69	897.01	778.22	701.31	648.25	610.02	581.62	560.02	543.31	530.21
31000	2856.86	1562.67	1136.34	926.91	804.16	724.68	669.85	630.35	601.00	578.69	561.43	547.89
32000	2949.02	1613.08	1173.00	956.81	830.10	748.06	691.46	650.69	620.39	597.36	579.54	565.56
33000	3041.17	1663.49	1209.65	986.71	856.04	771.44	713.07	671.02	639.78	616.02	597.65	583.24
34000	3133.33	1713.90	1246.31	1016.61	881.98	794.81	734.68	691.36	659.17	634.69	615.76	600.91
35000	3225.49	1764.31	1282.97	1046.51	907.92	818.19	756.29	711.69	678.55	653.36	633.87	618.58
36000	3317.64	1814.72	1319.62	1076.41	933.86	841.57	777.89	732.02	697.94	672.03	651.98	636.26
37000	3409.80	1865.12	1356.28	1106.31	959.81	864.94	799.50	752.36	717.33	690.69	670.09	653.93
38000	3501.96	1915.53	1392.93	1136.21	985.75	888.32	821.11	772.69	736.71	709.36	688.20	671.60
39000	3594.11	1965.94	1429.59	1166.11	1011.69	911.70	842.72	793.03	756.10	728.03	706.31	689.28
40000	3686.27	2016.35	1466.25	1196.01	1037.63	935.07	864.33	813.36	775.49	746.69	724.42	706.95
41000	3778.42	2066.76	1502.90	1225.91	1063.57	958.45	885.93	833.69	794.88	765.36	742.53	724.62
42000	3870.58	2117.17	1539.56	1255.81	1089.51	981.83	907.54	854.03	814.26	784.03	760.64	742.30
43000	3962.74	2167.58	1576.21	1285.71	1115.45	1005.20	929.15	874.36	833.65	802.70	778.75	759.97
44000	4054.89	2217.98	1612.87	1315.61	1141.39	1028.58	950.76	894.70	853.04	821.36	796.86	777.65
45000	4147.05	2268.39	1649.53	1345.51	1167.33	1051.96	972.37	915.03	872.42	840.03	814.97	795.32
46000	4239.21	2318.80	1686.18	1375.41	1193.27	1075.33	993.97	935.36	891.81	858.70	833.08	812.99
47000	4331.36	2369.21	1722.84	1405.31	1219.21	1098.71	1015.58	955.70	911.20	877.37	851.19	830.67
48000	4423.52	2419.62	1759.49	1435.21	1245.15	1122.09	1037.19	976.03	930.58	896.03	869.30	848.34
49000	4515.68	2470.03	1796.15	1465.11	1271.09	1145.46	1058.80	996.36	949.97	914.70	887.41	866.01
50000	4607.83	2520.44	1832.81	1495.01	1297.03	1168.84	1080.41	1016.70	969.36	933.37	905.52	883.69
55000	5068.62	2772.48	2016.09	1644.51	1426.74	1285.72	1188.45	1118.37	1066.29	1026.70	996.07	972.06
60000	5529.40	3024.52	2199.37	1794.01	1556.44	1402.61	1296.49	1220.04	1163.23	1120.04	1086.62	1060.42
65000	5990.18	3276.57	2382.65	1943.51	1686.14	1519.49	1404.53	1321.71	1260.17	1213.38	1177.18	1148.79
70000	6450.97	3528.61	2565.93	2093.01	1815.84	1636.38	1512.57	1423.38	1357.10	1306.71	1267.73	1237.16
75000	6911.75	3780.65	2749.21	2242.51	1945.55	1753.26	1620.61	1525.04	1454.04	1400.05	1358.28	1325.53
80000	7372.53	4032.69	2932.49	2392.01	2075.25	1870.14	1728.65	1626.71	1550.97	1493.38	1448.83	1413.90
85000	7833.31	4284.74	3115.77	2541.52	2204.95	1987.03	1836.69	1728.38	1647.91	1586.72	1539.38	1502.27
90000	8294.10	4536.78	3299.05	2691.02	2334.65	2103.91	1944.73	1830.05	1744.84	1680.06	1629.93	1590.63
95000	8754.88	4788.82	3482.33	2840.52	2464.36	2220.79	2052.77	1931.72	1841.78	1773.39	1720.49	1679.00
100000	9215.66	5040.87	3665.61	2990.02	2594.06	2337.68	2160.81	2033.39	1938.71	1866.73	1811.04	1767.37

19%

Table 1

MONTHLY   19.00%

PAYMENT REQUIRED TO AMORTIZE A LOAN

TERM / AMOUNT	13 YEARS	14 YEARS	15 YEARS	16 YEARS	17 YEARS	18 YEARS	19 YEARS	20 YEARS	25 YEARS	30 YEARS	35 YEARS	40 YEARS
50	.87	.86	.85	.84	.83	.82	.82	.82	.80	.80	.80	.80
100	1.74	1.71	1.69	1.67	1.66	1.64	1.63	1.63	1.60	1.59	1.59	1.59
200	3.47	3.42	3.37	3.33	3.31	3.28	3.26	3.25	3.20	3.18	3.18	3.17
300	5.20	5.12	5.05	5.00	4.96	4.92	4.89	4.87	4.80	4.77	4.76	4.76
400	6.94	6.83	6.74	6.66	6.61	6.56	6.52	6.49	6.40	6.36	6.35	6.34
500	8.67	8.53	8.42	8.33	8.26	8.20	8.15	8.11	7.99	7.95	7.93	7.93
600	10.40	10.24	10.10	9.99	9.91	9.84	9.78	9.73	9.59	9.54	9.52	9.51
700	12.13	11.94	11.79	11.66	11.56	11.47	11.41	11.35	11.19	11.13	11.10	11.09
800	13.87	13.65	13.47	13.32	13.21	13.11	13.03	12.97	12.79	12.72	12.69	12.68
900	15.60	15.35	15.15	14.99	14.86	14.75	14.66	14.59	14.38	14.31	14.27	14.26
1000	17.33	17.06	16.83	16.65	16.51	16.39	16.29	16.21	15.98	15.89	15.86	15.85
2000	34.66	34.11	33.66	33.30	33.01	32.77	32.58	32.42	31.96	31.78	31.71	31.69
3000	51.99	51.16	50.49	49.95	49.51	49.16	48.86	48.63	47.94	47.67	47.57	47.53
4000	69.32	68.21	67.32	66.60	66.02	65.54	65.15	64.83	63.91	63.56	63.42	63.37
5000	86.64	85.26	84.15	83.25	82.52	81.92	81.44	81.04	79.89	79.45	79.28	79.21
6000	103.97	102.31	100.98	99.90	99.02	98.31	97.72	97.25	95.87	95.34	95.13	95.06
7000	121.30	119.36	117.81	116.55	115.53	114.69	114.01	113.45	111.84	111.23	110.99	110.90
8000	138.63	136.41	134.64	133.20	132.03	131.08	130.30	129.66	127.82	127.12	126.84	126.74
9000	155.95	153.47	151.46	149.85	148.53	147.46	146.58	145.87	143.80	143.01	142.70	142.58
10000	173.28	170.52	168.29	166.49	165.03	163.84	162.87	162.07	159.77	158.89	158.55	158.42
11000	190.61	187.57	185.12	183.14	181.54	180.23	179.16	178.28	175.75	174.78	174.41	174.26
12000	207.94	204.62	201.95	199.79	198.04	196.61	195.44	194.49	191.73	190.67	190.26	190.11
13000	225.26	221.67	218.78	216.44	214.54	212.99	211.73	210.69	207.70	206.56	206.12	205.95
14000	242.59	238.72	235.61	233.09	231.05	229.38	228.02	226.90	223.68	222.45	221.97	221.79
15000	259.92	255.77	252.44	249.74	247.55	245.76	244.30	243.11	239.66	238.34	237.83	237.63
16000	277.25	272.82	269.27	266.39	264.05	262.15	260.59	259.31	255.63	254.23	253.68	253.47
17000	294.57	289.87	286.09	283.04	280.55	278.53	276.88	275.52	271.61	270.12	269.54	269.31
18000	311.90	306.93	302.92	299.69	297.06	294.91	293.16	291.73	287.59	286.01	285.39	285.16
19000	329.23	323.98	319.75	316.33	313.56	311.30	309.45	307.94	303.56	301.89	301.25	301.00
20000	346.56	341.03	336.58	332.98	330.06	327.68	325.74	324.14	319.54	317.78	317.10	316.84
21000	363.89	358.08	353.41	349.63	346.57	344.07	342.02	340.35	335.52	333.67	332.96	332.68
22000	381.21	375.13	370.24	366.28	363.07	360.45	358.31	356.56	351.49	349.56	348.81	348.52
23000	398.54	392.18	387.07	382.93	379.57	376.83	374.60	372.76	367.47	365.45	364.67	364.37
24000	415.87	409.23	403.90	399.58	396.07	393.22	390.88	388.97	383.45	381.34	380.52	380.21
25000	433.20	426.28	420.72	416.23	412.58	409.60	407.17	405.18	399.43	397.23	396.38	396.05
26000	450.52	443.33	437.55	432.88	429.08	425.98	423.46	421.38	415.40	413.12	412.23	411.89
27000	467.85	460.39	454.38	449.53	445.58	442.37	439.74	437.59	431.38	429.01	428.09	427.73
28000	485.18	477.44	471.21	466.17	462.09	458.75	456.03	453.80	447.36	444.89	443.94	443.57
29000	502.51	494.49	488.04	482.82	478.59	475.14	472.32	470.00	463.33	460.78	459.80	459.42
30000	519.83	511.54	504.87	499.47	495.09	491.52	488.60	486.21	479.31	476.67	475.65	475.26
31000	537.16	528.59	521.70	516.12	511.59	507.90	504.89	502.42	495.29	492.56	491.51	491.10
32000	554.49	545.64	538.53	532.77	528.10	524.29	521.17	518.62	511.26	508.45	507.36	506.94
33000	571.82	562.69	555.35	549.42	544.60	540.67	537.46	534.83	527.24	524.34	523.22	522.78
34000	589.14	579.74	572.18	566.07	561.10	557.06	553.75	551.04	543.22	540.23	539.07	538.62
35000	606.47	596.80	589.01	582.72	577.61	573.44	570.03	567.24	559.19	556.12	554.93	554.47
36000	623.80	613.85	605.84	599.37	594.11	589.82	586.32	583.45	575.17	572.01	570.78	570.31
37000	641.13	630.90	622.67	616.02	610.61	606.21	602.61	599.66	591.15	587.90	586.64	586.15
38000	658.45	647.95	639.50	632.66	627.11	622.59	618.89	615.87	607.12	603.78	602.49	601.99
39000	675.78	665.00	656.33	649.31	643.62	638.97	635.18	632.07	623.10	619.67	618.35	617.83
40000	693.11	682.05	673.16	665.96	660.12	655.36	651.47	648.28	639.08	635.56	634.20	633.67
41000	710.44	699.10	689.98	682.61	676.62	671.74	667.75	664.49	655.05	651.45	650.06	649.52
42000	727.77	716.15	706.81	699.26	693.13	688.13	684.04	680.69	671.03	667.34	665.91	665.36
43000	745.09	733.20	723.64	715.91	709.63	704.51	700.33	696.90	687.01	683.23	681.77	681.20
44000	762.42	750.26	740.47	732.56	726.13	720.89	716.61	713.11	702.98	699.12	697.62	697.04
45000	779.75	767.31	757.30	749.21	742.63	737.28	732.90	729.31	718.96	715.01	713.48	712.88
46000	797.08	784.36	774.13	765.86	759.14	753.66	749.19	745.52	734.94	730.90	729.33	728.73
47000	814.40	801.41	790.96	782.50	775.64	770.05	765.47	761.73	750.91	746.78	745.19	744.57
48000	831.73	818.46	807.79	799.15	792.14	786.43	781.76	777.93	766.89	762.67	761.04	760.41
49000	849.06	835.51	824.61	815.80	808.65	802.81	798.05	794.14	782.87	778.56	776.90	776.25
50000	866.39	852.56	841.44	832.45	825.15	819.20	814.33	810.35	798.85	794.45	792.75	792.09
55000	953.02	937.82	925.59	915.70	907.66	901.12	895.77	891.38	878.73	873.90	872.03	871.30
60000	1039.66	1023.07	1009.73	998.94	990.18	983.04	977.20	972.42	958.61	953.34	951.30	950.51
65000	1126.30	1108.33	1093.87	1082.19	1072.69	1064.95	1058.63	1053.45	1038.50	1032.79	1030.58	1029.72
70000	1212.94	1193.59	1178.02	1165.43	1155.21	1146.87	1140.06	1134.48	1118.38	1112.23	1109.85	1108.93
75000	1299.58	1278.84	1262.16	1248.67	1237.72	1228.79	1221.50	1215.52	1198.27	1191.67	1189.13	1188.14
80000	1386.22	1364.10	1346.31	1331.92	1320.24	1310.71	1302.93	1296.55	1278.15	1271.12	1268.40	1267.34
85000	1472.85	1449.35	1430.45	1415.16	1402.75	1392.63	1384.36	1377.59	1358.03	1350.56	1347.68	1346.55
90000	1559.49	1534.61	1514.59	1498.41	1485.26	1474.55	1465.79	1458.62	1437.92	1430.01	1426.95	1425.76
95000	1646.13	1619.86	1598.74	1581.65	1567.78	1556.47	1547.23	1539.66	1517.80	1509.45	1506.23	1504.97
100000	1732.77	1705.12	1682.88	1664.90	1650.29	1638.39	1628.66	1620.69	1597.69	1588.90	1585.50	1584.18

19%

115

Table 1

19.25%

MONTHLY
PAYMENT REQUIRED TO AMORTIZE A LOAN

TERM AMOUNT	1 YEAR	2 YEARS	3 YEARS	4 YEARS	5 YEARS	6 YEARS	7 YEARS	8 YEARS	9 YEARS	10 YEARS	11 YEARS	12 YEARS
50	4.62	2.53	1.84	1.51	1.31	1.18	1.09	1.03	.98	.95	.92	.90
100	9.23	5.06	3.68	3.01	2.61	2.36	2.18	2.05	1.96	1.89	1.83	1.79
200	18.46	10.11	7.36	6.01	5.22	4.71	4.36	4.10	3.91	3.77	3.66	3.57
300	27.69	15.16	11.04	9.01	7.83	7.06	6.53	6.15	5.87	5.65	5.49	5.36
400	36.92	20.22	14.72	12.02	10.44	9.41	8.71	8.20	7.82	7.54	7.32	7.14
500	46.14	25.27	18.40	15.02	13.04	11.77	10.88	10.25	9.78	9.42	9.14	8.93
600	55.37	30.32	22.07	18.02	15.65	14.12	13.06	12.30	11.73	11.30	10.97	10.71
700	64.60	35.38	25.75	21.03	18.26	16.47	15.23	14.35	13.69	13.19	12.80	12.50
800	73.83	40.43	29.43	24.03	20.87	18.82	17.41	16.40	15.64	15.07	14.63	14.28
900	83.05	45.48	33.11	27.03	23.48	21.17	19.59	18.44	17.60	16.95	16.46	16.07
1000	92.28	50.54	36.79	30.04	26.08	23.53	21.76	20.49	19.55	18.84	18.28	17.85
2000	184.56	101.07	73.57	60.07	52.16	47.05	43.52	40.98	39.10	37.67	36.56	35.70
3000	276.83	151.60	110.35	90.10	78.24	70.57	65.28	61.47	58.64	56.50	54.84	53.54
4000	369.11	202.13	147.14	120.13	104.32	94.09	87.03	81.96	78.19	75.33	73.12	71.39
5000	461.38	252.66	183.92	150.17	130.40	117.61	108.79	102.44	97.74	94.16	91.40	89.23
6000	553.66	303.19	220.70	180.20	156.47	141.13	130.55	122.93	117.29	112.99	109.68	107.08
7000	645.94	353.72	257.48	210.23	182.55	164.65	152.30	143.42	136.83	131.82	127.95	124.93
8000	738.21	404.25	294.27	240.26	208.63	188.17	174.06	163.91	156.37	150.65	146.23	142.77
9000	830.49	454.78	331.05	270.29	234.71	211.69	195.82	184.40	175.92	169.48	164.51	160.62
10000	922.76	505.31	367.83	300.33	260.79	235.21	217.57	204.88	195.47	188.31	182.79	178.46
11000	1015.04	555.84	404.61	330.36	286.87	258.73	239.33	225.37	215.01	207.15	201.07	196.31
12000	1107.32	606.37	441.40	360.39	312.94	282.25	261.09	245.86	234.56	225.98	219.35	214.16
13000	1199.59	656.90	478.18	390.42	339.02	305.77	282.84	266.35	254.10	244.81	237.62	232.00
14000	1291.87	707.43	514.96	420.46	365.10	329.29	304.60	286.84	273.65	263.64	255.90	249.85
15000	1384.14	757.96	551.74	450.49	391.18	352.81	326.36	307.32	293.20	282.47	274.18	267.69
16000	1476.42	808.49	588.53	480.52	417.26	376.33	348.11	327.81	312.74	301.30	292.46	285.54
17000	1568.70	859.02	625.31	510.55	443.34	399.85	369.87	348.30	332.29	320.13	310.74	303.38
18000	1660.97	909.55	662.09	540.58	469.41	423.37	391.63	368.79	351.83	338.96	329.02	321.23
19000	1753.25	960.08	698.87	570.62	495.49	446.89	413.38	389.27	371.38	357.79	347.29	339.08
20000	1845.52	1010.61	735.66	600.65	521.57	470.41	435.14	409.76	390.93	376.62	365.57	356.92
21000	1937.80	1061.14	772.44	630.68	547.65	493.93	456.90	430.25	410.47	395.45	383.85	374.77
22000	2030.08	1111.67	809.22	660.71	573.73	517.45	478.66	450.74	430.02	414.29	402.13	392.61
23000	2122.35	1162.20	846.00	690.75	599.81	540.97	500.41	471.23	449.56	433.12	420.41	410.46
24000	2214.63	1212.73	882.79	720.78	625.88	564.49	522.17	491.71	469.11	451.95	438.69	428.31
25000	2306.90	1263.26	919.57	750.81	651.96	588.01	543.93	512.20	488.66	470.78	456.97	446.15
26000	2399.18	1313.79	956.35	780.84	678.04	611.53	565.68	532.69	508.20	489.61	475.24	464.00
27000	2491.46	1364.32	993.13	810.87	704.12	635.05	587.44	553.18	527.75	508.44	493.52	481.84
28000	2583.73	1414.85	1029.92	840.91	730.20	658.57	609.20	573.67	547.30	527.27	511.80	499.69
29000	2676.01	1465.38	1066.70	870.94	756.28	682.09	630.95	594.15	566.84	546.10	530.08	517.53
30000	2768.28	1515.91	1103.48	900.97	782.35	705.61	652.71	614.64	586.39	564.93	548.36	535.38
31000	2860.56	1566.44	1140.26	931.00	808.43	729.13	674.47	635.13	605.93	583.76	566.64	553.23
32000	2952.83	1616.97	1177.05	961.04	834.51	752.65	696.22	655.62	625.48	602.59	584.91	571.07
33000	3045.11	1667.50	1213.83	991.07	860.59	776.17	717.98	676.11	645.03	621.43	603.19	588.92
34000	3137.39	1718.03	1250.61	1021.10	886.67	799.69	739.74	696.59	664.57	640.26	621.47	606.76
35000	3229.66	1768.56	1287.39	1051.13	912.75	823.21	761.49	717.08	684.12	659.09	639.75	624.61
36000	3321.94	1819.09	1324.18	1081.16	938.82	846.73	783.25	737.57	703.66	677.92	658.03	642.46
37000	3414.21	1869.62	1360.96	1111.20	964.90	870.25	805.01	758.06	723.21	696.75	676.31	660.30
38000	3506.49	1920.15	1397.74	1141.23	990.98	893.77	826.76	778.54	742.76	715.58	694.58	678.15
39000	3598.77	1970.68	1434.52	1171.26	1017.06	917.29	848.52	799.03	762.30	734.41	712.86	695.99
40000	3691.04	2021.21	1471.31	1201.29	1043.14	940.81	870.28	819.52	781.85	753.24	731.14	713.84
41000	3783.32	2071.74	1508.09	1231.33	1069.22	964.33	892.03	840.01	801.39	772.07	749.42	731.68
42000	3875.59	2122.27	1544.87	1261.36	1095.29	987.85	913.79	860.50	820.94	790.90	767.70	749.53
43000	3967.87	2172.80	1581.65	1291.39	1121.37	1011.37	935.55	880.98	840.49	809.74	785.98	767.38
44000	4060.15	2223.33	1618.44	1321.42	1147.45	1034.89	957.31	901.47	860.03	828.57	804.26	785.22
45000	4152.42	2273.86	1655.22	1351.45	1173.53	1058.41	979.06	921.96	879.58	847.40	822.53	803.07
46000	4244.70	2324.39	1692.00	1381.49	1199.61	1081.93	1000.82	942.45	899.12	866.23	840.81	820.91
47000	4336.97	2374.92	1728.78	1411.52	1225.69	1105.45	1022.58	962.94	918.67	885.06	859.09	838.76
48000	4429.25	2425.45	1765.57	1441.55	1251.76	1128.97	1044.33	983.42	938.22	903.89	877.37	856.61
49000	4521.53	2475.98	1802.35	1471.58	1277.84	1152.49	1066.09	1003.91	957.76	922.72	895.65	874.45
50000	4613.80	2526.51	1839.13	1501.62	1303.92	1176.01	1087.85	1024.40	977.31	941.55	913.93	892.30
55000	5075.18	2779.16	2023.04	1651.78	1434.31	1293.61	1196.63	1126.84	1075.04	1035.71	1005.32	981.53
60000	5536.56	3031.81	2206.96	1801.94	1564.70	1411.21	1305.41	1229.28	1172.77	1129.86	1096.71	1070.76
65000	5997.94	3284.47	2390.87	1952.10	1695.09	1528.81	1414.20	1331.72	1270.50	1224.02	1188.10	1159.98
70000	6459.32	3537.12	2574.78	2102.26	1825.49	1646.41	1522.98	1434.16	1368.23	1318.17	1279.49	1249.21
75000	6920.70	3789.77	2758.70	2252.42	1955.88	1764.01	1631.77	1536.60	1465.96	1412.33	1370.89	1338.44
80000	7382.08	4042.42	2942.61	2402.58	2086.27	1881.61	1740.55	1639.04	1563.69	1506.48	1462.28	1427.67
85000	7843.46	4295.07	3126.52	2552.74	2216.66	1999.21	1849.33	1741.48	1661.42	1600.63	1553.67	1516.90
90000	8304.84	4547.72	3310.43	2702.90	2347.05	2116.81	1958.12	1843.92	1759.15	1694.79	1645.06	1606.13
95000	8766.22	4800.37	3494.35	2853.06	2477.44	2234.41	2066.90	1946.35	1856.88	1788.94	1736.46	1695.36
100000	9227.60	5053.02	3678.26	3003.23	2607.84	2352.01	2175.69	2048.79	1954.61	1883.10	1827.85	1784.59

19%

Table 1

MONTHLY   19.25%

PAYMENT REQUIRED TO AMORTIZE A LOAN

ERM / ¡UNT	13 YEARS	14 YEARS	15 YEARS	16 YEARS	17 YEARS	18 YEARS	19 YEARS	20 YEARS	25 YEARS	30 YEARS	35 YEARS	40 YEARS
50	.88	.87	.86	.85	.84	.83	.83	.83	.81	.81	.81	.81
100	1.76	1.73	1.71	1.69	1.67	1.66	1.65	1.65	1.62	1.61	1.61	1.61
200	3.51	3.45	3.41	3.37	3.34	3.32	3.30	3.29	3.24	3.22	3.22	3.21
300	5.26	5.17	5.11	5.06	5.01	4.98	4.95	4.93	4.86	4.83	4.82	4.82
400	7.01	6.90	6.81	6.74	6.68	6.63	6.60	6.57	6.48	6.44	6.43	6.42
500	8.76	8.62	8.51	8.42	8.35	8.29	8.24	8.21	8.09	8.05	8.04	8.03
600	10.51	10.34	10.21	10.11	10.02	9.95	9.89	9.85	9.71	9.66	9.64	9.63
700	12.26	12.07	11.91	11.79	11.69	11.61	11.54	11.49	11.33	11.27	11.25	11.24
800	14.01	13.79	13.61	13.47	13.36	13.26	13.19	13.13	12.95	12.88	12.85	12.84
900	15.76	15.51	15.32	15.16	15.03	14.92	14.84	14.77	14.57	14.49	14.46	14.45
1000	17.51	17.24	17.02	16.84	16.70	16.58	16.48	16.41	16.18	16.10	16.07	16.05
2000	35.01	34.47	34.03	33.67	33.39	33.15	32.96	32.81	32.36	32.19	32.13	32.10
3000	52.52	51.70	51.04	50.51	50.08	49.73	49.44	49.21	48.54	48.29	48.19	48.15
4000	70.02	68.93	68.05	67.34	66.77	66.30	65.92	65.61	64.72	64.38	64.25	64.20
5000	87.52	86.16	85.06	84.18	83.46	82.88	82.40	82.01	80.90	80.47	80.31	80.25
6000	105.03	103.39	102.07	101.01	100.15	99.45	98.88	98.41	97.07	96.57	96.38	96.30
7000	122.53	120.62	119.09	117.85	116.84	116.03	115.36	114.82	113.25	112.66	112.44	112.35
8000	140.03	137.85	136.10	134.68	133.53	132.60	131.84	131.22	129.43	128.76	128.50	128.40
9000	157.54	155.08	153.11	151.52	150.22	149.18	148.32	147.62	145.61	144.85	144.56	144.45
10000	175.04	172.31	170.12	168.35	166.92	165.75	164.80	164.02	161.79	160.94	160.62	160.50
11000	192.54	189.54	187.13	185.18	183.61	182.32	181.28	180.42	177.97	177.04	176.68	176.55
12000	210.05	206.77	204.14	202.02	200.30	198.90	197.76	196.82	194.14	193.13	192.75	192.60
13000	227.55	224.00	221.15	218.85	216.99	215.47	214.24	213.22	210.32	209.23	208.81	208.65
14000	245.06	241.23	238.17	235.69	233.68	232.05	230.72	229.63	226.50	225.32	224.87	224.70
15000	262.56	258.46	255.18	252.52	250.37	248.62	247.19	246.03	242.68	241.41	240.93	240.75
16000	280.06	275.69	272.19	269.36	267.06	265.20	263.67	262.43	258.86	257.51	256.99	256.80
17000	297.57	292.93	289.20	286.19	283.75	281.77	280.15	278.83	275.04	273.60	273.05	272.84
18000	315.07	310.16	306.21	303.03	300.44	298.35	296.63	295.23	291.21	289.70	289.12	288.89
19000	332.57	327.39	323.22	319.86	317.14	314.92	313.11	311.63	307.39	305.79	305.18	304.94
20000	350.08	344.62	340.23	336.70	333.83	331.49	329.59	328.04	323.57	321.88	321.24	320.99
21000	367.58	361.85	357.25	353.53	350.52	348.07	346.07	344.44	339.75	337.98	337.30	337.04
22000	385.08	379.08	374.26	370.36	367.21	364.64	362.55	360.84	355.93	354.07	353.36	353.09
23000	402.59	396.31	391.27	387.20	383.90	381.22	379.03	377.24	372.11	370.17	369.43	369.14
24000	420.09	413.54	408.28	404.03	400.59	397.79	395.51	393.64	388.28	386.26	385.49	385.19
25000	437.60	430.77	425.29	420.87	417.28	414.37	411.99	410.04	404.46	402.35	401.55	401.24
26000	455.10	448.00	442.30	437.70	433.97	430.94	428.47	426.44	420.64	418.45	417.61	417.29
27000	472.60	465.23	459.31	454.54	450.66	447.52	444.95	442.85	436.82	434.54	433.67	433.34
28000	490.11	482.46	476.33	471.37	467.36	464.09	461.43	459.25	453.00	450.64	449.73	449.39
29000	507.61	499.69	493.34	488.21	484.05	480.66	477.90	475.65	469.17	466.73	465.80	465.44
30000	525.11	516.92	510.35	505.04	500.74	497.24	494.38	492.05	485.35	482.82	481.86	481.49
31000	542.62	534.15	527.36	521.87	517.43	513.81	510.86	508.45	501.53	498.92	497.92	497.54
32000	560.12	551.38	544.37	538.71	534.12	530.39	527.34	524.85	517.71	515.01	513.98	513.59
33000	577.62	568.62	561.38	555.54	550.81	546.96	543.82	541.26	533.89	531.11	530.04	529.63
34000	595.13	585.85	578.39	572.38	567.50	563.54	560.30	557.66	550.07	547.20	546.10	545.68
35000	612.63	603.08	595.41	589.21	584.19	580.11	576.78	574.06	566.24	563.29	562.17	561.73
36000	630.13	620.31	612.42	606.05	600.88	596.69	593.26	590.46	582.42	579.39	578.23	577.78
37000	647.64	637.54	629.43	622.88	617.58	613.26	609.74	606.86	598.60	595.48	594.29	593.83
38000	665.14	654.77	646.44	639.72	634.27	629.83	626.22	623.26	614.78	611.58	610.35	609.88
39000	682.65	672.00	663.45	656.55	650.96	646.41	642.70	639.66	630.96	627.67	626.41	625.93
40000	700.15	689.23	680.46	673.39	667.65	662.98	659.18	656.07	647.14	643.76	642.48	641.98
41000	717.65	706.46	697.47	690.22	684.34	679.56	675.66	672.47	663.31	659.86	658.54	658.03
42000	735.16	723.69	714.49	707.05	701.03	696.13	692.14	688.87	679.49	675.95	674.60	674.08
43000	752.66	740.92	731.50	723.89	717.72	712.71	708.62	705.27	695.67	692.05	690.66	690.13
44000	770.16	758.15	748.51	740.72	734.41	729.28	725.09	721.67	711.85	708.14	706.72	706.18
45000	787.67	775.38	765.52	757.56	751.10	745.86	741.57	738.07	728.03	724.23	722.78	722.23
46000	805.17	792.61	782.53	774.39	767.80	762.43	758.05	754.47	744.21	740.33	738.85	738.28
47000	822.67	809.84	799.54	791.23	784.49	779.00	774.53	770.88	760.38	756.42	754.91	754.33
48000	840.18	827.07	816.55	808.06	801.18	795.58	791.01	787.28	776.56	772.52	770.97	770.38
49000	857.68	844.31	833.57	824.90	817.87	812.15	807.49	803.68	792.74	788.61	787.03	786.43
50000	875.19	861.54	850.58	841.73	834.56	828.73	823.97	820.08	808.92	804.70	803.09	802.47
55000	962.70	947.69	935.63	925.90	918.02	911.60	906.37	902.09	889.81	885.17	883.40	882.72
60000	1050.22	1033.84	1020.69	1010.08	1001.47	994.47	988.76	984.10	970.70	965.64	963.71	962.97
65000	1137.74	1120.00	1105.75	1094.25	1084.93	1077.34	1071.16	1066.10	1051.59	1046.11	1044.02	1043.22
70000	1225.26	1206.15	1190.81	1178.42	1168.38	1160.22	1153.56	1148.11	1132.48	1126.58	1124.33	1123.46
75000	1312.78	1292.30	1275.86	1262.59	1251.84	1243.09	1235.95	1230.12	1213.38	1207.05	1204.64	1203.71
80000	1400.29	1378.45	1360.92	1346.77	1335.29	1325.96	1318.35	1312.13	1294.27	1287.52	1284.95	1283.96
85000	1487.81	1464.61	1445.98	1430.94	1418.75	1408.83	1400.75	1394.13	1375.16	1367.99	1365.25	1364.20
90000	1575.33	1550.76	1531.03	1515.11	1502.20	1491.71	1483.14	1476.14	1456.05	1448.46	1445.56	1444.45
95000	1662.85	1636.91	1616.09	1599.28	1585.66	1574.58	1565.54	1558.15	1536.94	1528.93	1525.87	1524.70
100000	1750.37	1723.07	1701.15	1683.46	1669.12	1657.45	1647.94	1640.16	1617.83	1609.40	1606.18	1604.94

19%

Table 1

19.50%

MONTHLY
PAYMENT REQUIRED TO AMORTIZE A LOAN

TERM / AMOUNT	1 YEAR	2 YEARS	3 YEARS	4 YEARS	5 YEARS	6 YEARS	7 YEARS	8 YEARS	9 YEARS	10 YEARS	11 YEARS	12 YEARS
50	4.62	2.54	1.85	1.51	1.32	1.19	1.10	1.04	.99	.95	.93	.91
100	9.24	5.07	3.70	3.02	2.63	2.37	2.20	2.07	1.98	1.90	1.85	1.81
200	18.48	10.14	7.39	6.04	5.25	4.74	4.39	4.13	3.95	3.80	3.69	3.61
300	27.72	15.20	11.08	9.05	7.87	7.10	6.58	6.20	5.92	5.70	5.54	5.41
400	36.96	20.27	14.77	12.07	10.49	9.47	8.77	8.26	7.89	7.60	7.38	7.21
500	46.20	25.33	18.46	15.09	13.11	11.84	10.96	10.33	9.86	9.50	9.23	9.01
600	55.44	30.40	22.15	18.10	15.73	14.20	13.15	12.39	11.83	11.40	11.07	10.82
700	64.68	35.46	25.84	21.12	18.36	16.57	15.34	14.45	13.80	13.30	12.92	12.62
800	73.92	40.53	29.53	24.14	20.98	18.94	17.53	16.52	15.77	15.20	14.76	14.42
900	83.16	45.59	33.22	27.15	23.60	21.30	19.72	18.58	17.74	17.10	16.61	16.22
1000	92.40	50.66	36.91	30.17	26.22	23.67	21.91	20.65	19.71	19.00	18.45	18.02
2000	184.80	101.31	73.82	60.33	52.44	47.33	43.82	41.29	39.42	38.00	36.90	36.04
3000	277.19	151.96	110.73	90.50	78.65	71.00	65.72	61.93	59.12	56.99	55.35	54.06
4000	369.59	202.61	147.64	120.66	104.87	94.66	87.63	82.57	78.83	75.99	73.79	72.08
5000	461.98	253.26	184.55	150.83	131.09	118.32	109.54	103.22	98.53	94.98	92.24	90.10
6000	554.38	303.92	221.46	180.99	157.30	141.99	131.44	123.86	118.24	113.98	110.69	108.12
7000	646.77	354.57	258.37	211.16	183.52	165.65	153.35	144.50	137.94	132.97	129.13	126.14
8000	739.17	405.22	295.28	241.32	209.74	189.32	175.25	165.14	157.65	151.97	147.58	1 4.15
9000	831.56	455.87	332.19	271.49	235.95	212.98	197.16	185.79	177.36	170.96	166.03	162.17
10000	923.96	506.52	369.10	301.65	262.17	236.64	219.07	206.43	197.06	189.96	184.48	180.19
11000	1016.35	557.18	406.01	331.82	288.39	260.31	240.97	227.07	216.77	208.95	202.92	198.21
12000	1108.75	607.83	442.92	361.98	314.60	283.97	262.88	247.71	236.47	227.95	221.37	216.23
13000	1201.14	658.48	479.83	392.14	340.82	307.64	284.78	268.36	256.18	246.94	239.82	234.25
14000	1293.54	709.13	516.74	422.31	367.04	331.30	306.69	289.00	275.88	265.94	258.26	252.27
15000	1385.94	759.78	553.64	452.47	393.25	354.96	328.60	309.64	295.59	284.93	276.71	270.28
16000	1478.33	810.44	590.55	482.64	419.47	378.63	350.50	330.28	315.30	303.93	295.16	288.30
17000	1570.73	861.09	627.46	512.80	445.68	402.29	372.41	350.93	335.00	322.92	313.61	306.32
18000	1663.12	911.74	664.37	542.97	471.90	425.95	394.32	371.57	354.71	341.92	332.05	324.34
19000	1755.52	962.39	701.28	573.13	498.12	449.62	416.22	392.21	374.41	360.91	350.50	342.36
20000	1847.91	1013.04	738.19	603.30	524.33	473.28	438.13	412.85	394.12	379.91	368.95	360.38
21000	1940.31	1063.69	775.10	633.46	550.55	496.95	460.03	433.50	413.82	398.90	387.39	378.40
22000	2032.70	1114.35	812.01	663.63	576.77	520.61	481.94	454.14	433.53	417.90	405.84	396.42
23000	2125.10	1165.00	848.92	693.79	602.98	544.27	503.85	474.78	453.24	436.90	424.29	414.43
24000	2217.49	1215.65	885.83	723.96	629.20	567.94	525.75	495.42	472.94	455.89	442.74	432.45
25000	2309.89	1266.30	922.74	754.12	655.42	591.60	547.66	516.07	492.65	474.89	461.18	450.47
26000	2402.28	1316.95	959.65	784.28	681.63	615.27	569.56	536.71	512.35	493.88	479.63	468.49
27000	2494.68	1367.61	996.56	814.45	707.85	638.93	591.47	557.35	532.06	512.88	498.08	486.51
28000	2587.08	1418.26	1033.47	844.61	734.07	662.59	613.38	577.99	551.76	531.87	516.52	504.53
29000	2679.47	1468.91	1070.38	874.78	760.28	686.26	635.28	598.64	571.47	550.87	534.97	522.55
30000	2771.87	1519.56	1107.28	904.94	786.50	709.92	657.19	619.28	591.17	569.86	553.42	540.56
31000	2864.26	1570.21	1144.19	935.11	812.71	733.59	679.09	639.92	610.88	588.86	571.87	558.58
32000	2956.66	1620.87	1181.10	965.27	838.93	757.25	701.00	660.56	630.59	607.85	590.31	576.60
33000	3049.05	1671.52	1218.01	995.44	865.15	780.91	722.91	681.21	650.29	626.85	608.76	594.62
34000	3141.45	1722.17	1254.92	1025.60	891.36	804.58	744.81	701.85	670.00	645.84	627.21	612.64
35000	3233.84	1772.82	1291.83	1055.77	917.58	828.24	766.72	722.49	689.70	664.84	645.65	630.66
36000	3326.24	1823.47	1328.74	1085.93	943.80	851.90	788.63	743.13	709.41	683.83	664.10	648.68
37000	3418.63	1874.12	1365.65	1116.10	970.01	875.57	810.53	763.78	729.11	702.83	682.55	666.70
38000	3511.03	1924.78	1402.56	1146.26	996.23	899.23	832.44	784.42	748.82	721.82	701.00	684.71
39000	3603.42	1975.43	1439.47	1176.42	1022.45	922.90	854.34	805.06	768.53	740.82	719.44	702.73
40000	3695.82	2026.08	1476.38	1206.59	1048.66	946.56	876.25	825.70	788.23	759.81	737.89	720.75
41000	3788.22	2076.73	1513.29	1236.75	1074.88	970.22	898.16	846.35	807.94	778.81	756.34	738.77
42000	3880.61	2127.38	1550.20	1266.92	1101.10	993.89	920.06	866.99	827.64	797.80	774.78	756.79
43000	3973.01	2178.04	1587.11	1297.08	1127.31	1017.55	941.97	887.63	847.35	816.80	793.23	774.81
44000	4065.40	2228.69	1624.01	1327.25	1153.53	1041.22	963.87	908.27	867.05	835.79	811.68	792.83
45000	4157.80	2279.34	1660.92	1357.41	1179.75	1064.88	985.78	928.92	886.76	854.79	830.13	810.84
46000	4250.19	2329.99	1697.83	1387.58	1205.96	1088.54	1007.69	949.56	906.47	873.79	848.57	828.86
47000	4342.59	2380.64	1734.74	1417.74	1232.18	1112.21	1029.59	970.20	926.17	892.78	867.02	846.88
48000	4434.98	2431.30	1771.65	1447.91	1258.39	1135.87	1051.50	990.84	945.88	911.78	885.47	864.90
49000	4527.38	2481.95	1808.56	1478.07	1284.61	1159.54	1073.40	1011.49	965.58	930.77	903.91	882.92
50000	4619.77	2532.60	1845.47	1508.24	1310.83	1183.20	1095.31	1032.13	985.29	949.77	922.36	900.94
55000	5081.75	2785.86	2030.02	1659.06	1441.91	1301.52	1204.84	1135.34	1083.82	1044.74	1014.60	991.03
60000	5543.73	3039.12	2214.56	1809.88	1572.99	1419.84	1314.37	1238.55	1182.34	1139.72	1106.83	1081.12
65000	6005.70	3292.38	2399.11	1960.70	1704.07	1538.16	1423.90	1341.76	1280.87	1234.69	1199.07	1171.22
70000	6467.68	3545.64	2583.66	2111.53	1835.16	1656.48	1533.43	1444.98	1379.40	1329.67	1291.30	1261.31
75000	6929.66	3798.90	2768.20	2262.35	1966.24	1774.80	1642.96	1548.19	1477.93	1424.65	1383.54	1351.40
80000	7391.63	4052.16	2952.75	2413.17	2097.32	1893.12	1752.49	1651.40	1576.46	1519.62	1475.78	1441.50
85000	7853.61	4305.41	3137.30	2564.00	2228.40	2011.44	1862.03	1754.61	1674.99	1614.60	1568.01	1531.59
90000	8315.59	4558.67	3321.84	2714.82	2359.49	2129.75	1971.56	1857.83	1773.51	1709.57	1660.25	1621.68
95000	8777.57	4811.93	3506.39	2865.64	2490.57	2248.07	2081.09	1961.04	1872.04	1804.55	1752.48	1711.78
100000	9239.54	5065.19	3690.94	3016.47	2621.65	2366.39	2190.62	2064.25	1970.57	1899.53	1844.72	1801.87

19%

Table 1

MONTHLY
PAYMENT REQUIRED TO AMORTIZE A LOAN

19.50%

TERM AMOUNT	13 YEARS	14 YEARS	15 YEARS	16 YEARS	17 YEARS	18 YEARS	19 YEARS	20 YEARS	25 YEARS	30 YEARS	35 YEARS	40 YEARS
50	.89	.88	.86	.86	.85	.84	.84	.83	.82	.82	.82	.82
100	1.77	1.75	1.72	1.71	1.69	1.68	1.67	1.66	1.64	1.63	1.63	1.63
200	3.54	3.49	3.44	3.41	3.38	3.36	3.34	3.32	3.28	3.26	3.26	3.26
300	5.31	5.23	5.16	5.11	5.07	5.03	5.01	4.98	4.92	4.89	4.89	4.88
400	7.08	6.97	6.88	6.81	6.76	6.71	6.67	6.64	6.56	6.52	6.51	6.51
500	8.85	8.71	8.60	8.52	8.44	8.39	8.34	8.30	8.20	8.15	8.14	8.13
600	10.61	10.45	10.32	10.22	10.13	10.06	10.01	9.96	9.83	9.78	9.77	9.76
700	12.38	12.19	12.04	11.92	11.82	11.74	11.68	11.62	11.47	11.41	11.39	11.38
800	14.15	13.93	13.76	13.62	13.51	13.42	13.34	13.28	13.11	13.04	13.02	13.01
900	15.92	15.67	15.48	15.32	15.20	15.09	15.01	14.94	14.75	14.67	14.65	14.64
1000	17.69	17.42	17.20	17.03	16.88	16.77	16.68	16.60	16.39	16.30	16.27	16.26
2000	35.37	34.83	34.39	34.05	33.76	33.54	33.35	33.20	32.77	32.60	32.54	32.52
3000	53.05	52.24	51.59	51.07	50.64	50.30	50.02	49.79	49.15	48.90	48.81	48.78
4000	70.73	69.65	68.78	68.09	67.52	67.07	66.70	66.39	65.53	65.20	65.08	65.03
5000	88.41	87.06	85.98	85.11	84.40	83.83	83.37	82.99	81.91	81.50	81.35	81.29
6000	106.09	104.47	103.17	102.13	101.28	100.60	100.04	99.58	98.29	97.80	97.62	97.55
7000	123.77	121.88	120.37	119.15	118.16	117.36	116.71	116.18	114.67	114.10	113.89	113.80
8000	141.45	139.29	137.56	136.17	135.04	134.13	133.39	132.78	131.05	130.40	130.15	130.06
9000	159.13	156.70	154.76	153.19	151.92	150.90	150.06	149.37	147.43	146.70	146.42	146.32
10000	176.81	174.11	171.95	170.21	168.80	167.66	166.73	165.97	163.81	163.00	162.69	162.58
11000	194.49	191.52	189.15	187.23	185.68	184.43	183.40	182.57	180.19	179.30	178.96	178.83
12000	212.17	208.93	206.34	204.25	202.56	201.19	200.08	199.16	196.57	195.60	195.23	195.09
13000	229.85	226.34	223.54	221.27	219.44	217.96	216.75	215.76	212.95	211.89	211.50	211.35
14000	247.53	243.75	240.73	238.29	236.32	234.72	233.42	232.36	229.33	228.19	227.77	227.60
15000	265.21	261.17	257.93	255.32	253.20	251.49	250.09	248.95	245.71	244.49	244.04	243.86
16000	282.89	278.58	275.12	272.34	270.08	268.25	266.77	265.55	262.09	260.79	260.30	260.12
17000	300.57	295.99	292.31	289.36	286.96	285.02	283.44	282.15	278.47	277.09	276.57	276.38
18000	318.25	313.40	309.51	306.38	303.84	301.79	300.11	298.74	294.85	293.39	292.84	292.63
19000	335.93	330.81	326.70	323.40	320.72	318.55	316.78	315.34	311.23	309.69	309.11	308.89
20000	353.61	348.22	343.90	340.42	337.60	335.32	333.46	331.94	327.61	325.99	325.38	325.15
21000	371.29	365.63	361.09	357.44	354.48	352.08	350.13	348.53	343.99	342.29	341.65	341.40
22000	388.97	383.04	378.29	374.46	371.36	368.85	366.80	365.13	360.37	358.59	357.92	357.66
23000	406.65	400.45	395.48	391.48	388.24	385.61	383.47	381.73	376.75	374.89	374.18	373.92
24000	424.33	417.86	412.68	408.50	405.12	402.38	400.15	398.32	393.13	391.19	390.45	390.18
25000	442.01	435.27	429.87	425.52	422.00	419.14	416.82	414.92	409.51	407.49	406.72	406.43
26000	459.69	452.68	447.07	442.54	438.88	435.91	433.49	431.52	425.89	423.78	422.99	422.69
27000	477.37	470.09	464.26	459.56	455.76	452.68	450.16	448.11	442.27	440.08	439.26	438.95
28000	495.05	487.50	481.46	476.58	472.64	469.44	466.84	464.71	458.65	456.38	455.53	455.20
29000	512.73	504.92	498.65	493.60	489.52	486.21	483.51	481.31	475.03	472.68	471.80	471.46
30000	530.41	522.33	515.85	510.63	506.40	502.97	500.18	497.90	491.41	488.98	488.07	487.72
31000	548.09	539.74	533.04	527.65	523.28	519.74	516.85	514.50	507.79	505.28	504.33	503.97
32000	565.77	557.15	550.24	544.67	540.16	536.50	533.53	531.10	524.17	521.58	520.60	520.23
33000	583.45	574.56	567.43	561.69	557.04	553.27	550.20	547.69	540.55	537.88	536.87	536.49
34000	601.13	591.97	584.62	578.71	573.92	570.03	566.87	564.29	556.93	554.18	553.14	552.75
35000	618.81	609.38	601.82	595.73	590.80	586.80	583.54	580.89	573.31	570.48	569.41	569.00
36000	636.49	626.79	619.01	612.75	607.68	603.57	600.22	597.48	589.69	586.78	585.68	585.26
37000	654.17	644.20	636.21	629.77	624.56	620.33	616.89	614.08	606.07	603.08	601.95	601.52
38000	671.85	661.61	653.40	646.79	641.44	637.10	633.56	630.68	622.45	619.37	618.21	617.77
39000	689.53	679.02	670.60	663.81	658.32	653.86	650.23	647.27	638.83	635.67	634.48	634.03
40000	707.21	696.43	687.79	680.83	675.20	670.63	666.91	663.87	655.21	651.97	650.75	650.29
41000	724.89	713.84	704.99	697.85	692.08	687.39	683.58	680.47	671.59	668.27	667.02	666.55
42000	742.57	731.25	722.18	714.87	708.96	704.16	700.25	697.06	687.97	684.57	683.29	682.80
43000	760.25	748.67	739.38	731.89	725.84	720.93	716.92	713.66	704.35	700.87	699.56	699.06
44000	777.93	766.08	756.57	748.91	742.72	737.69	733.60	730.26	720.73	717.17	715.83	715.32
45000	795.61	783.49	773.77	765.94	759.60	754.46	750.27	746.85	737.11	733.47	732.10	731.57
46000	813.29	800.90	790.96	782.96	776.48	771.22	766.94	763.45	753.49	749.77	748.36	747.83
47000	830.97	818.31	808.16	799.98	793.36	787.99	783.61	780.05	769.87	766.07	764.63	764.09
48000	848.66	835.72	825.35	817.00	810.24	804.75	800.29	796.64	786.25	782.37	780.90	780.35
49000	866.34	853.13	842.55	834.02	827.12	821.52	816.96	813.24	802.63	798.67	797.17	796.60
50000	884.02	870.54	859.74	851.04	844.00	838.28	833.63	829.84	819.01	814.97	813.44	812.86
55000	972.42	957.59	945.71	936.14	928.40	922.11	917.00	912.82	900.91	896.46	894.78	894.15
60000	1060.82	1044.65	1031.69	1021.25	1012.80	1005.94	1000.36	995.80	982.81	977.96	976.13	975.43
65000	1149.22	1131.70	1117.66	1106.35	1097.20	1089.77	1083.72	1078.79	1064.71	1059.45	1057.47	1056.72
70000	1237.62	1218.75	1203.63	1191.45	1181.60	1173.60	1167.08	1161.77	1146.61	1140.95	1138.81	1138.00
75000	1326.02	1305.81	1289.61	1276.56	1266.00	1257.42	1250.45	1244.75	1228.51	1222.45	1220.16	1219.29
80000	1414.42	1392.86	1375.58	1361.66	1350.40	1341.25	1333.81	1327.74	1310.41	1303.94	1301.50	1300.57
85000	1502.82	1479.92	1461.55	1446.76	1434.79	1425.08	1417.17	1410.72	1392.31	1385.44	1382.84	1381.86
90000	1591.22	1566.97	1547.53	1531.87	1519.19	1508.91	1500.53	1493.70	1474.21	1466.93	1464.19	1463.14
95000	1679.63	1654.02	1633.50	1616.97	1603.59	1592.74	1583.90	1576.69	1556.11	1548.43	1545.53	1544.43
100000	1768.03	1741.08	1719.48	1702.07	1687.99	1676.56	1667.26	1659.67	1638.01	1629.93	1626.87	1625.71

19%

119

Table 1

19.75%

MONTHLY
PAYMENT REQUIRED TO AMORTIZE A LOAN

TERM AMOUNT	1 YEAR	2 YEARS	3 YEARS	4 YEARS	5 YEARS	6 YEARS	7 YEARS	8 YEARS	9 YEARS	10 YEARS	11 YEARS	12 YEAR.
50	4.63	2.54	1.86	1.52	1.32	1.20	1.11	1.04	1.00	.96	.94	.91
100	9.26	5.08	3.71	3.03	2.64	2.39	2.21	2.08	1.99	1.92	1.87	1.82
200	18.51	10.16	7.41	6.06	5.28	4.77	4.42	4.16	3.98	3.84	3.73	3.64
300	27.76	15.24	11.12	9.09	7.91	7.15	6.62	6.24	5.96	5.75	5.59	5.46
400	37.01	20.31	14.82	12.12	10.55	9.53	8.83	8.32	7.95	7.67	7.45	7.28
500	46.26	25.39	18.52	15.15	13.18	11.91	11.03	10.40	9.94	9.59	9.31	9.10
600	55.51	30.47	22.23	18.18	15.82	14.29	13.24	12.48	11.92	11.50	11.17	10.92
700	64.77	35.55	25.93	21.21	18.45	16.67	15.44	14.56	13.91	13.42	13.04	12.74
800	74.02	40.62	29.63	24.24	21.09	19.05	17.65	16.64	15.90	15.33	14.90	14.56
900	83.27	45.70	33.34	27.27	23.72	21.43	19.86	18.72	17.88	17.25	16.76	16.38
1000	92.52	50.78	37.04	30.30	26.36	23.81	22.06	20.80	19.87	19.17	18.62	18.20
2000	185.03	101.55	74.08	60.60	52.71	47.62	44.12	41.60	39.74	38.33	37.24	36.39
3000	277.55	152.33	111.11	90.90	79.07	71.43	66.17	62.40	59.60	57.49	55.85	54.58
4000	370.06	203.10	148.15	121.19	105.42	95.24	88.23	83.20	79.47	76.65	74.47	72.77
5000	462.58	253.87	185.19	151.49	131.78	119.05	110.28	103.99	99.33	95.81	93.09	90.97
6000	555.09	304.65	222.22	181.79	158.13	142.85	132.34	124.79	119.20	114.97	111.70	109.16
7000	647.61	355.42	259.26	212.09	184.49	166.66	154.40	145.59	139.07	134.13	130.32	127.35
8000	740.12	406.20	296.30	242.38	210.84	190.47	176.45	166.39	158.93	153.29	148.94	145.54
9000	832.64	456.97	333.33	272.68	237.20	214.28	198.51	187.18	178.80	172.45	167.55	163.73
10000	925.15	507.74	370.37	302.98	263.55	238.09	220.56	207.98	198.66	191.61	186.17	181.93
11000	1017.67	558.52	407.40	333.28	289.91	261.89	242.62	228.78	218.53	210.77	204.79	200.12
12000	1110.18	609.29	444.44	363.57	316.26	285.70	264.68	249.58	238.39	229.93	223.40	218.31
13000	1202.70	660.06	481.48	393.87	342.62	309.51	286.73	270.37	258.26	249.09	242.02	236.50
14000	1295.21	710.84	518.51	424.17	368.97	333.32	308.79	291.17	278.13	268.25	260.64	254.69
15000	1387.73	761.61	555.55	454.46	395.33	357.13	330.84	311.97	297.99	287.41	279.25	272.89
16000	1480.24	812.39	592.59	484.76	421.68	380.94	352.90	332.77	317.86	306.57	297.87	291.08
17000	1572.76	863.16	629.62	515.06	448.04	404.74	374.96	353.56	337.72	325.73	316.48	309.27
18000	1665.27	913.93	666.66	545.36	474.39	428.55	397.01	374.36	357.59	344.89	335.10	327.46
19000	1757.79	964.71	703.70	575.65	500.75	452.36	419.07	395.16	377.46	364.05	353.72	345.65
20000	1850.30	1015.48	740.73	605.95	527.10	476.17	441.12	415.96	397.32	383.21	372.33	363.85
21000	1942.82	1066.25	777.77	636.25	553.46	499.98	463.18	436.75	417.19	402.37	390.95	382.04
22000	2035.33	1117.03	814.80	666.55	579.81	523.78	485.24	457.55	437.05	421.53	409.57	400.23
23000	2127.85	1167.80	851.84	696.84	606.17	547.59	507.29	478.35	456.92	440.69	428.18	418.42
24000	2220.36	1218.58	888.88	727.14	632.52	571.40	529.35	499.15	476.78	459.85	446.80	436.61
25000	2312.88	1269.35	925.91	757.44	658.88	595.21	551.40	519.94	496.65	479.01	465.42	454.81
26000	2405.39	1320.12	962.95	787.74	685.23	619.02	573.46	540.74	516.52	498.17	484.03	473.00
27000	2497.91	1370.90	999.99	818.03	711.59	642.82	595.51	561.54	536.38	517.33	502.65	491.19
28000	2590.42	1421.67	1037.02	848.33	737.94	666.63	617.57	582.34	556.25	536.49	521.27	509.38
29000	2682.94	1472.44	1074.06	878.63	764.30	690.44	639.63	603.13	576.11	555.65	539.88	527.57
30000	2775.45	1523.22	1111.09	908.92	790.65	714.25	661.68	623.93	595.98	574.81	558.50	545.77
31000	2867.97	1573.99	1148.13	939.22	817.01	738.06	683.74	644.73	615.84	593.97	577.11	563.96
32000	2960.48	1624.77	1185.17	969.52	843.36	761.87	705.79	665.53	635.71	613.13	595.73	582.15
33000	3053.00	1675.54	1222.20	999.82	869.72	785.67	727.85	686.32	655.58	632.29	614.35	600.34
34000	3145.51	1726.31	1259.24	1030.11	896.07	809.48	749.91	707.12	675.44	651.45	632.96	618.54
35000	3238.03	1777.09	1296.28	1060.41	922.43	833.29	771.96	727.92	695.31	670.61	651.58	636.73
36000	3330.54	1827.86	1333.31	1090.71	948.78	857.10	794.02	748.72	715.17	689.77	670.20	654.92
37000	3423.06	1878.63	1370.35	1121.01	975.14	880.91	816.07	769.51	735.04	708.93	688.81	673.11
38000	3515.57	1929.41	1407.39	1151.30	1001.49	904.71	838.13	790.31	754.91	728.09	707.43	691.30
39000	3608.09	1980.18	1444.42	1181.60	1027.85	928.52	860.19	811.11	774.77	747.25	726.05	709.50
40000	3700.60	2030.96	1481.46	1211.90	1054.20	952.33	882.24	831.91	794.64	766.41	744.66	727.69
41000	3793.12	2081.73	1518.49	1242.20	1080.56	976.14	904.30	852.71	814.50	785.57	763.28	745.88
42000	3885.63	2132.50	1555.53	1272.49	1106.91	999.95	926.35	873.50	834.37	804.73	781.90	764.07
43000	3978.15	2183.28	1592.57	1302.79	1133.27	1023.75	948.41	894.30	854.23	823.89	800.51	782.26
44000	4070.66	2234.05	1629.60	1333.09	1159.62	1047.56	970.47	915.10	874.10	843.05	819.13	800.46
45000	4163.18	2284.82	1666.64	1363.38	1185.98	1071.37	992.52	935.90	893.97	862.21	837.74	818.65
46000	4255.69	2335.60	1703.68	1393.68	1212.33	1095.18	1014.58	956.69	913.83	881.37	856.36	836.84
47000	4348.21	2386.37	1740.71	1423.98	1238.69	1118.99	1036.63	977.49	933.70	900.53	874.98	855.03
48000	4440.72	2437.15	1777.75	1454.28	1265.04	1142.80	1058.69	998.29	953.56	919.69	893.59	873.22
49000	4533.24	2487.92	1814.78	1484.57	1291.40	1166.60	1080.74	1019.09	973.43	938.85	912.21	891.42
50000	4625.75	2538.69	1851.82	1514.87	1317.75	1190.41	1102.80	1039.88	993.29	958.01	930.83	909.61
55000	5088.32	2792.56	2037.00	1666.36	1449.53	1309.45	1213.08	1143.87	1092.62	1053.81	1023.91	1000.57
60000	5550.90	3046.43	2222.18	1817.84	1581.30	1428.49	1323.36	1247.86	1191.95	1149.61	1116.99	1091.53
65000	6013.47	3300.30	2407.37	1969.33	1713.08	1547.53	1433.64	1351.85	1291.28	1245.41	1210.07	1182.49
70000	6476.05	3554.17	2592.55	2120.82	1844.85	1666.57	1543.92	1455.83	1390.61	1341.21	1303.16	1273.45
75000	6938.62	3808.04	2777.73	2272.30	1976.63	1785.62	1654.20	1559.82	1489.94	1437.01	1396.24	1364.41
80000	7401.20	4061.91	2962.91	2423.79	2108.40	1904.66	1764.48	1663.81	1589.27	1532.81	1489.32	1455.37
85000	7863.77	4315.77	3148.09	2575.28	2240.18	2023.70	1874.76	1767.80	1688.60	1628.61	1582.40	1546.33
90000	8326.35	4569.64	3333.27	2726.76	2371.95	2142.74	1985.04	1871.79	1787.93	1724.41	1675.48	1637.29
95000	8788.92	4823.51	3518.46	2878.25	2503.73	2261.78	2095.32	1975.77	1887.26	1820.21	1768.57	1728.25
100000	9251.50	5077.38	3703.64	3029.74	2635.50	2380.82	2205.60	2079.76	1986.58	1916.02	1861.65	1819.21

19%

120

Table 1

MONTHLY
19.75%
PAYMENT REQUIRED TO AMORTIZE A LOAN

TERM AMOUNT	13 YEARS	14 YEARS	15 YEARS	16 YEARS	17 YEARS	18 YEARS	19 YEARS	20 YEARS	25 YEARS	30 YEARS	35 YEARS	40 YEARS
50	.90	.88	.87	.87	.86	.85	.85	.84	.83	.83	.83	.83
100	1.79	1.76	1.74	1.73	1.71	1.70	1.69	1.68	1.66	1.66	1.65	1.65
200	3.58	3.52	3.48	3.45	3.42	3.40	3.38	3.36	3.32	3.31	3.30	3.30
300	5.36	5.28	5.22	5.17	5.13	5.09	5.06	5.04	4.98	4.96	4.95	4.94
400	7.15	7.04	6.96	6.89	6.83	6.79	6.75	6.72	6.64	6.61	6.60	6.59
500	8.93	8.80	8.69	8.61	8.54	8.48	8.44	8.40	8.30	8.26	8.24	8.24
600	10.72	10.56	10.43	10.33	10.25	10.18	10.12	10.08	9.95	9.91	9.89	9.88
700	12.51	12.32	12.17	12.05	11.95	11.88	11.81	11.76	11.61	11.56	11.54	11.53
800	14.29	14.08	13.91	13.77	13.66	13.57	13.50	13.44	13.27	13.21	13.19	13.18
900	16.08	15.84	15.65	15.49	15.37	15.27	15.18	15.12	14.93	14.86	14.83	14.82
1000	17.86	17.60	17.38	17.21	17.07	16.96	16.87	16.80	16.59	16.51	16.48	16.47
2000	35.72	35.19	34.76	34.42	34.14	33.92	33.74	33.59	33.17	33.01	32.96	32.93
3000	53.58	52.78	52.14	51.63	51.21	50.88	50.60	50.38	49.75	49.52	49.43	49.40
4000	71.43	70.37	69.52	68.83	68.28	67.83	67.47	67.17	66.33	66.02	65.91	65.86
5000	89.29	87.96	86.90	86.04	85.35	84.79	84.34	83.97	82.92	82.53	82.38	82.33
6000	107.15	105.55	104.28	103.25	102.42	101.75	101.20	100.76	99.50	99.03	98.86	98.79
7000	125.01	123.14	121.65	120.46	119.49	118.71	118.07	117.55	116.08	115.54	115.33	115.26
8000	142.86	140.74	139.03	137.66	136.56	135.66	134.94	134.34	132.66	132.04	131.81	131.72
9000	160.72	158.33	156.41	154.87	153.63	152.62	151.80	151.14	149.24	148.55	148.29	148.19
10000	178.58	175.92	173.79	172.08	170.70	169.58	168.67	167.93	165.83	165.05	164.76	164.65
11000	196.44	193.51	191.17	189.29	187.77	186.53	185.53	184.72	182.41	181.56	181.24	181.12
12000	214.29	211.10	208.55	206.49	204.84	203.49	202.40	201.51	198.99	198.06	197.71	197.58
13000	232.15	228.69	225.93	223.70	221.90	220.45	219.27	218.30	215.57	214.56	214.19	214.05
14000	250.01	246.28	243.30	240.91	238.97	237.41	236.13	235.10	232.16	231.07	230.66	230.51
15000	267.87	263.88	260.68	258.12	256.04	254.36	253.00	251.89	248.74	247.57	247.14	246.98
16000	285.72	281.47	278.06	275.32	273.11	271.32	269.87	268.68	265.32	264.08	263.62	263.44
17000	303.58	299.06	295.44	292.53	290.18	288.28	286.73	285.47	281.90	280.58	280.09	279.91
18000	321.44	316.65	312.82	309.74	307.25	305.24	303.60	302.27	298.48	297.09	296.57	296.37
19000	339.30	334.24	330.20	326.95	324.32	322.19	320.46	319.06	315.07	313.59	313.04	312.84
20000	357.15	351.83	347.58	344.15	341.39	339.15	337.33	335.85	331.65	330.10	329.52	329.30
21000	375.01	369.42	364.95	361.36	358.46	356.11	354.20	352.64	348.23	346.60	345.99	345.77
22000	392.87	387.02	382.33	378.57	375.53	373.06	371.06	369.43	364.81	363.11	362.47	362.23
23000	410.73	404.61	399.71	395.78	392.60	390.02	387.93	386.23	381.39	379.61	378.95	378.70
24000	428.58	422.20	417.09	412.98	409.67	406.98	404.80	403.02	397.98	396.12	395.42	395.16
25000	446.44	439.79	434.47	430.19	426.73	423.94	421.66	419.81	414.56	412.62	411.90	411.63
26000	464.30	457.38	451.85	447.40	443.80	440.89	438.53	436.60	431.14	429.12	428.37	428.09
27000	482.16	474.97	469.23	464.60	460.87	455.39	455.39	453.40	447.72	445.63	444.85	444.56
28000	500.01	492.56	486.60	481.81	477.94	474.81	472.26	470.19	464.31	462.13	461.32	461.02
29000	517.87	510.16	503.98	499.02	495.01	491.76	489.13	486.98	480.89	478.64	477.80	477.49
30000	535.73	527.75	521.36	516.23	512.08	508.72	505.99	503.77	497.47	495.14	494.28	493.95
31000	553.58	545.34	538.74	533.43	529.15	525.68	522.86	520.56	514.05	511.65	510.75	510.42
32000	571.44	562.93	556.12	550.64	546.22	542.64	539.73	537.36	530.63	528.15	527.23	526.88
33000	589.30	580.52	573.50	567.85	563.29	559.59	556.59	554.15	547.22	544.66	543.70	543.34
34000	607.16	598.11	590.88	585.06	580.36	576.55	573.46	570.94	563.80	561.16	560.18	559.81
35000	625.01	615.70	608.25	602.26	597.43	593.51	590.32	587.73	580.38	577.67	576.65	576.27
36000	642.87	633.29	625.63	619.47	614.50	610.47	607.19	604.53	596.96	594.17	593.13	592.74
37000	660.73	650.89	643.01	636.68	631.56	627.42	624.06	621.32	613.54	610.68	609.61	609.20
38000	678.59	668.48	660.39	653.89	648.63	644.38	640.92	638.11	630.13	627.18	626.08	625.67
39000	696.44	686.07	677.77	671.09	665.70	661.34	657.79	654.90	646.71	643.68	642.56	642.13
40000	714.30	703.66	695.15	688.30	682.77	678.29	674.66	671.69	663.29	660.19	659.03	658.60
41000	732.16	721.25	712.53	705.51	699.84	695.25	691.52	688.49	679.87	676.69	675.51	675.06
42000	750.02	738.84	729.90	722.72	716.91	712.21	708.39	705.28	696.46	693.20	691.98	691.53
43000	767.87	756.43	747.28	739.92	733.98	729.17	725.25	722.07	713.04	709.70	708.46	707.99
44000	785.73	774.03	764.66	757.13	751.05	746.12	742.12	738.86	729.62	726.21	724.93	724.46
45000	803.59	791.62	782.04	774.34	768.12	763.08	758.99	755.66	746.20	742.71	741.41	740.92
46000	821.45	809.21	799.42	791.55	785.19	780.04	775.85	772.45	762.78	759.22	757.89	757.39
47000	839.30	826.80	816.80	808.75	802.26	796.99	792.72	789.24	779.37	775.72	774.36	773.85
48000	857.16	844.39	834.18	825.96	819.33	813.95	809.59	806.03	795.95	792.23	790.84	790.32
49000	875.02	861.98	851.55	843.17	836.40	830.91	826.45	822.82	812.53	808.73	807.31	806.78
50000	892.88	879.57	868.93	860.37	853.46	847.87	843.32	839.62	829.11	825.24	823.79	823.25
55000	982.16	967.53	955.83	946.41	938.81	932.65	927.65	923.58	912.02	907.76	906.17	905.57
60000	1071.45	1055.49	1042.72	1032.45	1024.16	1017.44	1011.98	1007.54	994.93	990.28	988.55	987.90
65000	1160.74	1143.45	1129.61	1118.49	1109.50	1102.22	1096.31	1091.50	1077.84	1072.80	1070.92	1070.22
70000	1250.02	1231.40	1216.50	1204.52	1194.85	1187.01	1180.64	1175.46	1160.76	1155.33	1153.30	1152.54
75000	1339.31	1319.36	1303.40	1290.56	1280.19	1271.80	1264.98	1259.42	1243.67	1237.85	1235.68	1234.87
80000	1428.60	1407.32	1390.29	1376.60	1365.54	1356.58	1349.31	1343.38	1326.58	1320.37	1318.06	1317.19
85000	1517.89	1495.27	1477.18	1462.63	1450.89	1441.37	1433.64	1427.34	1409.49	1402.90	1400.44	1399.52
90000	1607.17	1583.23	1564.07	1548.67	1536.23	1526.16	1517.97	1511.31	1492.40	1485.42	1482.82	1481.84
95000	1696.46	1671.19	1650.97	1634.71	1621.58	1610.94	1602.30	1595.27	1575.31	1567.94	1565.19	1564.17
100000	1785.75	1759.14	1737.86	1720.74	1706.92	1695.73	1686.63	1679.23	1658.22	1650.47	1647.57	1646.49

19%

Table 1

20.00%

MONTHLY
PAYMENT REQUIRED TO AMORTIZE A LOAN

TERM / AMOUNT	1 YEAR	2 YEARS	3 YEARS	4 YEARS	5 YEARS	6 YEARS	7 YEARS	8 YEARS	9 YEARS	10 YEARS	11 YEARS	12 YEARS
50	4.64	2.55	1.86	1.53	1.33	1.20	1.12	1.05	1.01	.97	.94	.92
100	9.27	5.09	3.72	3.05	2.65	2.40	2.23	2.10	2.01	1.94	1.88	1.84
200	18.53	10.18	7.44	6.09	5.30	4.80	4.45	4.20	4.01	3.87	3.76	3.68
300	27.80	15.27	11.15	9.13	7.95	7.19	6.67	6.29	6.01	5.80	5.64	5.51
400	37.06	20.36	14.87	12.18	10.60	9.59	8.89	8.39	8.02	7.74	7.52	7.35
500	46.32	25.45	18.59	15.22	13.25	11.98	11.11	10.48	10.02	9.67	9.40	9.19
600	55.59	30.54	22.30	18.26	15.90	14.38	13.33	12.58	12.02	11.60	11.28	11.02
700	64.85	35.63	26.02	21.31	18.55	16.77	15.55	14.67	14.02	13.53	13.16	12.86
800	74.11	40.72	29.74	24.35	21.20	19.17	17.77	16.77	16.03	15.47	15.03	14.70
900	83.38	45.81	33.45	27.39	23.85	21.56	19.99	18.86	18.03	17.40	16.91	16.53
1000	92.64	50.90	37.17	30.44	26.50	23.96	22.21	20.96	20.03	19.33	18.79	18.37
2000	185.27	101.80	74.33	60.87	52.99	47.91	44.42	41.91	40.06	38.66	37.58	36.74
3000	277.91	152.69	111.50	91.30	79.49	71.86	66.62	62.86	60.08	57.98	56.36	55.10
4000	370.54	203.59	148.66	121.73	105.98	95.82	88.83	83.82	80.11	77.31	75.15	73.47
5000	463.18	254.48	185.82	152.16	132.47	119.77	111.04	104.77	100.14	96.63	93.94	91.84
6000	555.81	305.38	222.99	182.59	158.97	143.72	133.24	125.72	120.16	115.96	112.72	110.20
7000	648.45	356.28	260.15	213.02	185.46	167.67	155.45	146.68	140.19	135.28	131.51	128.57
8000	741.08	407.17	297.31	243.45	211.96	191.63	177.65	167.63	160.22	154.61	150.30	146.93
9000	833.72	458.07	334.48	273.88	238.45	215.58	199.86	188.58	180.24	173.94	169.08	165.30
10000	926.35	508.96	371.64	304.31	264.94	239.53	222.07	209.54	200.27	193.26	187.87	183.67
11000	1018.98	559.86	408.80	334.74	291.44	263.49	244.27	230.49	220.30	212.59	206.65	202.03
12000	1111.62	610.75	445.97	365.17	317.93	287.44	266.48	251.44	240.32	231.91	225.44	220.40
13000	1204.25	661.65	483.13	395.60	344.43	311.39	288.69	272.40	260.35	251.24	244.23	238.76
14000	1296.89	712.55	520.30	426.03	370.92	335.34	310.89	293.35	280.38	270.56	263.01	257.13
15000	1389.52	763.44	557.46	456.46	397.41	359.30	333.10	314.30	300.40	289.89	281.80	275.50
16000	1482.16	814.34	594.62	486.89	423.91	383.25	355.30	335.26	320.43	309.21	300.59	293.86
17000	1574.79	865.23	631.79	517.32	450.40	407.20	377.51	356.21	340.46	328.54	319.37	312.23
18000	1667.43	916.13	668.95	547.75	476.89	431.16	399.72	377.16	360.48	347.87	338.16	330.59
19000	1760.06	967.03	706.11	578.18	503.39	455.11	421.92	398.12	380.51	367.19	356.95	348.96
20000	1852.70	1017.92	743.28	608.61	529.88	479.06	444.13	419.07	400.54	386.52	375.73	367.33
21000	1945.33	1068.82	780.44	639.04	556.38	503.01	466.34	440.02	420.56	405.84	394.52	385.69
22000	2037.96	1119.71	817.60	669.47	582.87	526.97	488.54	460.98	440.59	425.17	413.30	404.06
23000	2130.60	1170.61	854.77	699.90	609.36	550.92	510.75	481.93	460.61	444.49	432.09	422.42
24000	2223.23	1221.50	891.93	730.33	635.86	574.87	532.95	502.88	480.64	463.82	450.88	440.79
25000	2315.87	1272.40	929.09	760.76	662.35	598.83	555.16	523.84	500.67	483.14	469.66	459.16
26000	2408.50	1323.30	966.26	791.19	688.85	622.78	577.37	544.79	520.69	502.47	488.45	477.52
27000	2501.14	1374.19	1003.42	821.62	715.34	646.73	599.57	565.74	540.72	521.80	507.24	495.89
28000	2593.77	1425.09	1040.59	852.06	741.83	670.68	621.78	586.69	560.75	541.12	526.02	514.26
29000	2686.41	1475.98	1077.75	882.49	768.33	694.64	643.98	607.65	580.77	560.45	544.81	532.62
30000	2779.04	1526.88	1114.91	912.92	794.82	718.59	666.19	628.60	600.80	579.77	563.60	550.99
31000	2871.67	1577.77	1152.08	943.35	821.32	742.54	688.40	649.55	620.83	599.10	582.38	569.35
32000	2964.31	1628.67	1189.24	973.78	847.81	766.50	710.60	670.51	640.85	618.42	601.17	587.72
33000	3056.94	1679.57	1226.40	1004.21	874.30	790.45	732.81	691.46	660.88	637.75	619.95	606.09
34000	3149.58	1730.46	1263.57	1034.64	900.80	814.40	755.02	712.41	680.91	657.07	638.74	624.45
35000	3242.21	1781.36	1300.73	1065.07	927.29	838.35	777.22	733.37	700.93	676.40	657.53	642.82
36000	3334.85	1832.25	1337.89	1095.50	953.78	862.31	799.43	754.32	720.96	695.73	676.31	661.18
37000	3427.48	1883.15	1375.06	1125.93	980.28	886.26	821.63	775.27	740.99	715.05	695.10	679.55
38000	3520.12	1934.05	1412.22	1156.36	1006.77	910.21	843.84	796.23	761.01	734.38	713.89	697.92
39000	3612.75	1984.94	1449.38	1186.79	1033.27	934.17	866.05	817.18	781.04	753.70	732.67	716.28
40000	3705.39	2035.84	1486.55	1217.22	1059.76	958.12	888.25	838.13	801.07	773.03	751.46	734.65
41000	3798.02	2086.73	1523.71	1247.65	1086.25	982.07	910.46	859.09	821.09	792.35	770.24	753.01
42000	3890.65	2137.63	1560.88	1278.08	1112.75	1006.02	932.67	880.04	841.12	811.68	789.03	771.38
43000	3983.29	2188.52	1598.04	1308.51	1139.24	1029.98	954.87	900.99	861.14	831.00	807.82	789.75
44000	4075.92	2239.42	1635.20	1338.94	1165.74	1053.93	977.08	921.95	881.17	850.33	826.60	808.11
45000	4168.56	2290.32	1672.37	1369.37	1192.23	1077.88	999.28	942.90	901.20	869.66	845.39	826.48
46000	4261.19	2341.21	1709.53	1399.80	1218.72	1101.84	1021.49	963.85	921.22	888.98	864.18	844.84
47000	4353.83	2392.11	1746.69	1430.23	1245.22	1125.79	1043.70	984.81	941.25	908.31	882.96	863.21
48000	4446.46	2443.00	1783.86	1460.66	1271.71	1149.74	1065.90	1005.76	961.28	927.63	901.75	881.58
49000	4539.10	2493.90	1821.02	1491.09	1298.21	1173.69	1088.11	1026.71	981.30	946.96	920.54	899.94
50000	4631.73	2544.80	1858.18	1521.52	1324.70	1197.65	1110.32	1047.67	1001.33	966.28	939.32	918.31
55000	5094.90	2799.27	2044.00	1673.68	1457.17	1317.41	1221.35	1152.43	1101.46	1062.91	1033.25	1010.14
60000	5558.08	3053.75	2229.82	1825.83	1589.64	1437.17	1332.38	1257.20	1201.60	1159.54	1127.19	1101.97
65000	6021.25	3308.23	2415.64	1977.98	1722.11	1556.94	1443.41	1361.96	1301.73	1256.17	1221.12	1193.80
70000	6484.42	3562.71	2601.46	2130.13	1854.58	1676.70	1554.44	1466.73	1401.86	1352.79	1315.05	1285.63
75000	6947.59	3817.19	2787.27	2282.28	1987.05	1796.47	1665.47	1571.50	1501.99	1449.42	1408.98	1377.46
80000	7410.77	4071.67	2973.09	2434.43	2119.52	1916.23	1776.50	1676.26	1602.13	1546.05	1502.91	1469.29
85000	7873.94	4326.15	3158.91	2586.59	2251.99	2036.00	1887.53	1781.03	1702.26	1642.68	1596.84	1561.12
90000	8337.11	4580.63	3344.73	2738.74	2384.45	2155.76	1998.56	1885.79	1802.39	1739.31	1690.78	1652.95
95000	8800.28	4835.11	3530.55	2890.89	2516.92	2275.52	2109.59	1990.56	1902.52	1835.93	1784.71	1744.78
100000	9263.46	5089.59	3716.36	3043.04	2649.39	2395.29	2220.62	2095.33	2002.66	1932.56	1878.64	1836.61

20%

Table 1

MONTHLY

20.00%

PAYMENT REQUIRED TO AMORTIZE A LOAN

TERM AMOUNT	13 YEARS	14 YEARS	15 YEARS	16 YEARS	17 YEARS	18 YEARS	19 YEARS	20 YEARS	25 YEARS	30 YEARS	35 YEARS	40 YEARS
50	.91	.89	.88	.87	.87	.86	.86	.85	.84	.84	.84	.84
100	1.81	1.78	1.76	1.74	1.73	1.72	1.71	1.70	1.68	1.68	1.67	1.67
200	3.61	3.56	3.52	3.48	3.46	3.43	3.42	3.40	3.36	3.35	3.34	3.34
300	5.42	5.34	5.27	5.22	5.18	5.15	5.12	5.10	5.04	5.02	5.01	5.01
400	7.22	7.11	7.03	6.96	6.91	6.86	6.83	6.80	6.72	6.69	6.68	6.67
500	9.02	8.89	8.79	8.70	8.63	8.58	8.54	8.50	8.40	8.36	8.35	8.34
600	10.83	10.67	10.54	10.44	10.36	10.29	10.24	10.20	10.08	10.03	10.01	10.01
700	12.63	12.45	12.30	12.18	12.09	12.01	11.95	11.90	11.75	11.70	11.68	11.68
800	14.43	14.22	14.06	13.92	13.81	13.72	13.65	13.60	13.43	13.37	13.35	13.34
900	16.24	16.00	15.81	15.66	15.54	15.44	15.36	15.29	15.11	15.04	15.02	15.01
1000	18.04	17.78	17.57	17.40	17.26	17.15	17.07	16.99	16.79	16.72	16.69	16.68
2000	36.08	35.55	35.13	34.79	34.52	34.30	34.13	33.98	33.57	33.43	33.37	33.35
3000	54.11	53.32	52.69	52.19	51.78	51.45	51.19	50.97	50.36	50.14	50.05	50.02
4000	72.15	71.10	70.26	69.58	69.04	68.60	68.25	67.96	67.14	66.85	66.74	66.70
5000	90.18	88.87	87.82	86.98	86.30	85.75	85.31	84.95	83.93	83.56	83.42	83.37
6000	108.22	106.64	105.38	104.37	103.56	102.90	102.37	101.93	100.71	100.27	100.10	100.04
7000	126.25	124.41	122.95	121.77	120.82	120.05	119.43	118.92	117.50	116.98	116.78	116.71
8000	144.29	142.19	140.51	139.16	138.08	137.20	136.49	135.91	134.28	133.69	133.47	133.39
9000	162.32	159.96	158.07	156.56	155.34	154.35	153.55	152.90	151.07	150.40	150.15	150.06
10000	180.36	177.73	175.63	173.95	172.60	171.50	170.61	169.89	167.85	167.11	166.83	166.73
11000	198.39	195.50	193.20	191.35	189.85	188.65	187.67	186.88	184.63	183.82	183.52	183.40
12000	216.43	213.28	210.76	208.74	207.11	205.80	204.73	203.86	201.42	200.53	200.20	200.08
13000	234.46	231.05	228.32	226.14	224.37	222.95	221.79	220.85	218.20	217.24	216.88	216.75
14000	252.50	248.82	245.89	243.53	241.63	240.10	238.85	237.84	234.99	233.95	233.56	233.42
15000	270.53	266.59	263.45	260.92	258.89	257.25	255.91	254.83	251.77	250.66	250.25	250.09
16000	288.57	284.37	281.01	278.32	276.15	274.39	272.97	271.82	268.56	267.37	266.93	266.77
17000	306.60	302.14	298.58	295.71	293.41	291.54	290.03	288.81	285.34	284.08	283.61	283.44
18000	324.64	319.91	316.14	313.11	310.67	308.69	307.09	305.79	302.13	300.79	300.30	300.11
19000	342.67	337.69	333.70	330.50	327.93	325.84	324.15	322.78	318.91	317.50	316.98	316.79
20000	360.71	355.46	351.26	347.90	345.19	342.99	341.21	339.77	335.70	334.21	333.66	333.46
21000	378.74	373.23	368.83	365.29	362.44	360.14	358.27	356.76	352.48	350.92	350.34	350.13
22000	396.78	391.00	386.39	382.69	379.70	377.29	375.34	373.75	369.26	367.63	367.03	366.80
23000	414.82	408.78	403.95	400.08	396.96	394.44	392.40	390.73	386.05	384.34	383.71	383.48
24000	432.85	426.55	421.52	417.48	414.22	411.59	409.46	407.72	402.83	401.05	400.39	400.15
25000	450.89	444.32	439.08	434.87	431.48	428.74	426.52	424.71	419.62	417.76	417.07	416.82
26000	468.92	462.09	456.64	452.27	448.74	445.89	443.58	441.70	436.40	434.47	433.76	433.49
27000	486.96	479.87	474.21	469.66	466.00	463.04	460.64	458.69	453.19	451.18	450.44	450.17
28000	504.99	497.64	491.77	487.06	483.26	480.19	477.70	475.68	469.97	467.89	467.12	466.84
29000	523.03	515.41	509.33	504.45	500.52	497.34	494.76	492.66	486.76	484.60	483.81	483.51
30000	541.06	533.18	526.89	521.84	517.78	514.49	511.82	509.65	503.54	501.31	500.49	500.18
31000	559.10	550.96	544.46	539.24	535.03	531.64	528.88	526.64	520.33	518.02	517.17	516.86
32000	577.13	568.73	562.02	556.63	552.29	548.78	545.94	543.63	537.11	534.73	533.85	533.53
33000	595.17	586.50	579.58	574.03	569.55	565.93	563.00	560.62	553.89	551.44	550.54	550.20
34000	613.20	604.28	597.15	591.42	586.81	583.08	580.06	577.61	570.68	568.15	567.22	566.87
35000	631.24	622.05	614.71	608.82	604.07	600.23	597.12	594.59	587.46	584.86	583.90	583.55
36000	649.27	639.82	632.27	626.21	621.33	617.38	614.18	611.58	604.25	601.57	600.59	600.22
37000	667.31	657.59	649.83	643.61	638.59	634.53	631.24	628.57	621.03	618.28	617.27	616.89
38000	685.34	675.37	667.40	661.00	655.85	651.68	648.30	645.56	637.82	634.99	633.95	633.57
39000	703.38	693.14	684.96	678.40	673.11	668.83	665.36	662.55	654.60	651.70	650.63	650.24
40000	721.41	710.91	702.52	695.79	690.37	685.98	682.42	679.53	671.39	668.41	667.32	666.91
41000	739.45	728.68	720.09	713.19	707.63	703.13	699.48	696.52	688.17	685.12	684.00	683.58
42000	757.48	746.46	737.65	730.58	724.88	720.28	716.54	713.51	704.95	701.83	700.68	700.26
43000	775.52	764.23	755.21	747.98	742.14	737.43	733.60	730.50	721.74	718.54	717.36	716.93
44000	793.55	782.00	772.78	765.37	759.40	754.58	750.67	747.49	738.52	735.25	734.05	733.60
45000	811.59	799.77	790.34	782.76	776.66	771.73	767.73	764.48	755.31	751.96	750.73	750.27
46000	829.63	817.55	807.90	800.16	793.92	788.88	784.79	781.46	772.09	768.67	767.41	766.95
47000	847.66	835.32	825.46	817.55	811.18	806.03	801.85	798.45	788.88	785.38	784.10	783.62
48000	865.70	853.09	843.03	834.95	828.44	823.17	818.91	815.44	805.66	802.09	800.78	800.29
49000	883.73	870.87	860.59	852.34	845.70	840.32	835.97	832.43	822.45	818.80	817.46	816.96
50000	901.77	888.64	878.15	869.74	862.96	857.47	853.03	849.42	839.23	835.51	834.14	833.64
55000	991.94	977.50	965.97	956.71	949.25	943.22	938.33	934.36	923.15	919.07	917.56	917.00
60000	1082.12	1066.36	1053.78	1043.68	1035.55	1028.97	1023.63	1019.30	1007.08	1002.62	1000.97	1000.36
65000	1172.29	1155.23	1141.60	1130.66	1121.84	1114.71	1108.94	1104.24	1091.00	1086.17	1084.39	1083.73
70000	1262.47	1244.09	1229.41	1217.63	1208.14	1200.46	1194.24	1189.18	1174.92	1169.72	1167.80	1167.09
75000	1352.65	1332.95	1317.23	1304.60	1294.43	1286.21	1279.54	1274.12	1258.84	1253.27	1251.21	1250.45
80000	1442.82	1421.82	1405.04	1391.58	1380.73	1371.95	1364.84	1359.06	1342.77	1336.82	1334.63	1333.82
85000	1533.00	1510.68	1492.86	1478.55	1467.02	1457.70	1450.14	1444.01	1426.69	1420.37	1418.04	1417.18
90000	1623.18	1599.54	1580.67	1565.52	1553.32	1543.45	1535.45	1528.95	1510.61	1503.92	1501.46	1500.54
95000	1713.35	1688.41	1668.49	1652.50	1639.61	1629.19	1620.75	1613.89	1594.53	1587.47	1584.87	1583.91
100000	1803.53	1777.27	1756.30	1739.47	1725.91	1714.94	1706.05	1698.83	1678.46	1671.02	1668.28	1667.27

Table 1

20.25%

MONTHLY
PAYMENT REQUIRED TO AMORTIZE A LOAN

TERM	1 YEAR	2 YEARS	3 YEARS	4 YEARS	5 YEARS	6 YEARS	7 YEARS	8 YEARS	9 YEARS	10 YEARS	11 YEARS	12 YEARS
AMOUNT												
50	4.64	2.56	1.87	1.53	1.34	1.21	1.12	1.06	1.01	.98	.95	.93
100	9.28	5.11	3.73	3.06	2.67	2.41	2.24	2.12	2.02	1.95	1.90	1.86
200	18.56	10.21	7.46	6.12	5.33	4.82	4.48	4.23	4.04	3.90	3.80	3.71
300	27.83	15.31	11.19	9.17	7.99	7.23	6.71	6.34	6.06	5.85	5.69	5.57
400	37.11	20.41	14.92	12.23	10.66	9.64	8.95	8.45	8.08	7.80	7.59	7.42
500	46.38	25.51	18.65	15.29	13.32	12.05	11.18	10.56	10.10	9.75	9.48	9.28
600	55.66	30.62	22.38	18.34	15.98	14.46	13.42	12.67	12.12	11.70	11.38	11.13
700	64.93	35.72	26.11	21.40	18.65	16.87	15.65	14.78	14.14	13.65	13.27	12.98
800	74.21	40.82	29.84	24.46	21.31	19.28	17.89	16.89	16.16	15.60	15.17	14.84
900	83.48	45.92	33.57	27.51	23.97	21.69	20.13	19.00	18.17	17.55	17.07	16.69
1000	92.76	51.02	37.30	30.57	26.64	24.10	22.36	21.11	20.19	19.50	18.96	18.55
2000	185.51	102.04	74.59	61.13	53.27	48.20	44.72	42.22	40.38	38.99	37.92	37.09
3000	278.27	153.06	111.88	91.70	79.90	72.30	67.08	63.33	60.57	58.48	56.88	55.63
4000	371.02	204.08	149.17	122.26	106.54	96.40	89.43	84.44	80.76	77.97	75.83	74.17
5000	463.78	255.10	186.46	152.82	133.17	120.49	111.79	105.55	100.94	97.46	94.79	92.71
6000	556.53	306.11	223.75	183.39	159.80	144.59	134.15	126.66	121.13	116.95	113.75	111.25
7000	649.28	357.13	261.04	213.95	186.44	168.69	156.50	147.77	141.32	136.45	132.70	129.79
8000	742.04	408.15	298.33	244.51	213.07	192.79	178.86	168.88	161.51	155.94	151.66	148.33
9000	834.79	459.17	335.62	275.08	239.70	216.89	201.22	189.99	181.69	175.43	170.62	166.87
10000	927.55	510.19	372.92	305.64	266.34	240.98	223.57	211.10	201.88	194.92	189.57	185.41
11000	1020.30	561.20	410.21	336.21	292.97	265.08	245.93	232.21	222.07	214.41	208.53	203.95
12000	1113.06	612.22	447.50	366.77	319.60	289.18	268.29	253.32	242.26	233.90	227.49	222.49
13000	1205.81	663.24	484.79	397.33	346.24	313.28	290.65	274.43	262.45	253.40	246.44	241.03
14000	1298.56	714.26	522.08	427.90	372.87	337.38	313.00	295.54	282.63	272.89	265.40	259.57
15000	1391.32	765.28	559.37	458.46	399.50	361.47	335.36	316.65	302.82	292.38	284.36	278.12
16000	1484.07	816.29	596.66	489.02	426.14	385.57	357.72	337.75	323.01	311.87	303.31	296.66
17000	1576.83	867.31	633.95	519.59	452.77	409.67	380.07	358.86	343.20	331.36	322.27	315.20
18000	1669.58	918.33	671.24	550.15	479.40	433.77	402.43	379.97	363.38	350.85	341.23	333.74
19000	1762.33	969.35	708.54	580.72	506.04	457.87	424.79	401.08	383.57	370.35	360.18	352.28
20000	1855.09	1020.37	745.83	611.28	532.67	481.96	447.14	422.19	403.76	389.84	379.14	370.82
21000	1947.84	1071.38	783.12	641.84	559.30	506.06	469.50	443.30	423.95	409.33	398.10	389.36
22000	2040.60	1122.40	820.41	672.41	585.93	530.16	491.86	464.41	444.14	428.82	417.06	407.90
23000	2133.35	1173.42	857.70	702.97	612.57	554.26	514.22	485.52	464.32	448.31	436.01	426.44
24000	2226.11	1224.44	894.99	733.53	639.20	578.36	536.57	506.63	484.51	467.80	454.97	444.98
25000	2318.86	1275.46	932.28	764.10	665.83	602.45	558.93	527.74	504.70	487.30	473.93	463.52
26000	2411.61	1326.47	969.57	794.66	692.47	626.55	581.29	548.85	524.89	506.79	492.88	482.06
27000	2504.37	1377.49	1006.86	825.23	719.10	650.65	603.64	569.96	545.07	526.28	511.84	500.60
28000	2597.12	1428.51	1044.16	855.79	745.73	674.75	626.00	591.07	565.26	545.77	530.80	519.14
29000	2689.88	1479.53	1081.45	886.35	772.37	698.85	648.36	612.18	585.45	565.26	549.75	537.69
30000	2782.63	1530.55	1118.74	916.92	799.00	722.94	670.71	633.29	605.64	584.75	568.71	556.23
31000	2875.39	1581.56	1156.03	947.48	825.63	747.04	693.07	654.40	625.83	604.24	587.67	574.77
32000	2968.14	1632.58	1193.32	978.04	852.27	771.14	715.43	675.50	646.01	623.74	606.62	593.31
33000	3060.89	1683.60	1230.61	1008.61	878.90	795.24	737.79	696.61	666.20	643.23	625.58	611.85
34000	3153.65	1734.62	1267.90	1039.17	905.53	819.34	760.14	717.72	686.39	662.72	644.54	630.39
35000	3246.40	1785.64	1305.19	1069.74	932.17	843.43	782.50	738.83	706.58	682.21	663.49	648.93
36000	3339.16	1836.65	1342.48	1100.30	958.80	867.53	804.86	759.94	726.76	701.70	682.45	667.47
37000	3431.91	1887.67	1379.78	1130.86	985.43	891.63	827.21	781.05	746.95	721.19	701.41	686.01
38000	3524.66	1938.69	1417.07	1161.43	1012.07	915.73	849.57	802.16	767.14	740.69	720.36	704.55
39000	3617.42	1989.71	1454.36	1191.99	1038.70	939.83	871.93	823.27	787.33	760.18	739.32	723.09
40000	3710.17	2040.73	1491.65	1222.55	1065.33	963.92	894.28	844.38	807.52	779.67	758.28	741.63
41000	3802.93	2091.74	1528.94	1253.12	1091.97	988.02	916.64	865.49	827.70	799.16	777.24	760.17
42000	3895.68	2142.76	1566.23	1283.68	1118.60	1012.12	939.00	886.60	847.89	818.65	796.19	778.71
43000	3988.44	2193.78	1603.52	1314.24	1145.23	1036.22	961.35	907.71	868.08	838.14	815.15	797.25
44000	4081.19	2244.80	1640.81	1344.81	1171.86	1060.32	983.71	928.82	888.27	857.64	834.11	815.80
45000	4173.94	2295.82	1678.10	1375.37	1198.50	1084.41	1006.07	949.93	908.45	877.13	853.06	834.34
46000	4266.70	2346.83	1715.40	1405.94	1225.13	1108.51	1028.43	971.04	928.64	896.62	872.02	852.88
47000	4359.45	2397.85	1752.69	1436.50	1251.76	1132.61	1050.78	992.15	948.83	916.11	890.98	871.42
48000	4452.21	2448.87	1789.98	1467.06	1278.40	1156.71	1073.14	1013.25	969.02	935.60	909.93	889.96
49000	4544.96	2499.89	1827.27	1497.63	1305.03	1180.81	1095.50	1034.36	989.21	955.09	928.89	908.50
50000	4637.71	2550.91	1864.56	1528.19	1331.66	1204.90	1117.85	1055.47	1009.39	974.59	947.85	927.04
55000	5101.49	2806.00	2051.01	1681.01	1464.83	1325.39	1229.64	1161.02	1110.33	1072.04	1042.63	1019.74
60000	5565.26	3061.09	2237.47	1833.83	1598.00	1445.88	1341.42	1266.57	1211.27	1169.50	1137.42	1112.45
65000	6029.03	3316.18	2423.93	1986.65	1731.16	1566.37	1453.21	1372.11	1312.21	1266.96	1232.20	1205.15
70000	6492.80	3571.27	2610.38	2139.47	1864.33	1686.86	1564.99	1477.66	1413.15	1364.42	1326.98	1297.85
75000	6956.57	3826.36	2796.84	2292.28	1997.49	1807.35	1676.78	1583.21	1514.09	1461.88	1421.77	1390.56
80000	7420.34	4081.45	2983.29	2445.10	2130.66	1927.84	1788.56	1688.75	1615.03	1559.33	1516.55	1483.26
85000	7884.11	4336.54	3169.75	2597.92	2263.83	2048.33	1900.35	1794.30	1715.97	1656.79	1611.34	1575.96
90000	8347.88	4591.63	3356.20	2750.74	2396.99	2168.82	2012.13	1899.85	1816.90	1754.25	1706.12	1668.67
95000	8811.65	4846.72	3542.66	2903.56	2530.16	2289.31	2123.92	2005.39	1917.84	1851.71	1800.90	1761.37
100000	9275.43	5101.81	3729.11	3056.38	2663.32	2409.80	2235.70	2110.94	2018.78	1949.17	1895.69	1854.07

20%

Table 1

MONTHLY

PAYMENT REQUIRED TO AMORTIZE A LOAN

20.25%

ERM	13 YEARS	14 YEARS	15 YEARS	16 YEARS	17 YEARS	18 YEARS	19 YEARS	20 YEARS	25 YEARS	30 YEARS	35 YEARS	40 YEARS
OUNT												
50	.92	.90	.89	.88	.88	.87	.87	.86	.85	.85	.85	.85
100	1.83	1.80	1.78	1.76	1.75	1.74	1.73	1.72	1.70	1.70	1.69	1.69
200	3.65	3.60	3.55	3.52	3.49	3.47	3.46	3.44	3.40	3.39	3.38	3.38
300	5.47	5.39	5.33	5.28	5.24	5.21	5.18	5.16	5.10	5.08	5.07	5.07
400	7.29	7.19	7.10	7.04	6.98	6.94	6.91	6.88	6.80	6.77	6.76	6.76
500	9.11	8.98	8.88	8.80	8.73	8.68	8.63	8.60	8.50	8.46	8.45	8.45
600	10.93	10.78	10.65	10.55	10.47	10.41	10.36	10.32	10.20	10.15	10.14	10.13
700	12.75	12.57	12.43	12.31	12.22	12.14	12.08	12.03	11.90	11.85	11.83	11.82
800	14.58	14.37	14.20	14.07	13.96	13.88	13.81	13.75	13.59	13.54	13.52	13.51
900	16.40	16.16	15.98	15.83	15.71	15.61	15.53	15.47	15.29	15.23	15.21	15.20
1000	18.22	17.96	17.75	17.59	17.45	17.35	17.26	17.19	16.99	16.92	16.89	16.89
2000	36.43	35.91	35.50	35.17	34.90	34.69	34.52	34.37	33.98	33.84	33.78	33.77
3000	54.65	53.87	53.25	52.75	52.35	52.03	51.77	51.56	50.97	50.75	50.67	50.65
4000	72.86	71.82	71.00	70.33	69.80	69.37	69.03	68.74	67.95	67.67	67.56	67.53
5000	91.07	89.78	88.74	87.92	87.25	86.71	86.28	85.93	84.94	84.58	84.45	84.41
6000	109.29	107.73	106.49	105.50	104.70	104.06	103.54	103.11	101.93	101.50	101.34	101.29
7000	127.50	125.69	124.24	123.08	122.15	121.40	120.79	120.30	118.92	118.42	118.23	118.17
8000	145.71	143.64	141.99	140.66	139.60	138.74	138.05	137.48	135.90	135.33	135.12	135.05
9000	163.93	161.60	159.74	158.25	157.05	156.08	155.30	154.67	152.89	152.25	152.01	151.93
10000	182.14	179.55	177.48	175.83	174.50	173.42	172.56	171.85	169.88	169.16	168.90	168.81
11000	200.35	197.50	195.23	193.41	191.95	190.77	189.81	189.04	186.86	186.08	185.79	185.69
12000	218.57	215.46	212.98	210.99	209.40	208.11	207.07	206.22	203.85	203.00	202.68	202.57
13000	236.78	233.41	230.73	228.58	226.85	225.45	224.32	223.41	220.84	219.91	219.57	219.45
14000	255.00	251.37	248.48	246.16	244.30	242.79	241.58	240.59	237.83	236.83	236.46	236.33
15000	273.21	269.32	266.22	263.74	261.75	260.13	258.83	257.78	254.81	253.74	253.35	253.21
16000	291.42	287.28	283.97	281.32	279.20	277.48	276.09	274.96	271.80	270.66	270.24	270.09
17000	309.64	305.23	301.72	298.91	296.64	294.82	293.34	292.14	288.79	287.58	287.13	286.97
18000	327.85	323.19	319.47	316.49	314.09	312.16	310.60	309.33	305.77	304.49	304.02	303.85
19000	346.06	341.14	337.22	334.07	331.54	329.50	327.85	326.51	322.76	321.41	320.91	320.73
20000	364.28	359.09	354.96	351.65	348.99	346.84	345.11	343.70	339.75	338.32	337.80	337.61
21000	382.49	377.05	372.71	369.24	366.44	364.19	362.36	360.88	356.74	355.24	354.69	354.50
22000	400.70	395.00	390.46	386.82	383.89	381.53	379.62	378.07	373.72	372.16	371.58	371.38
23000	418.92	412.96	408.21	404.40	401.34	398.87	396.87	395.25	390.71	389.07	388.47	388.26
24000	437.13	430.91	425.96	421.98	418.79	416.21	414.13	412.44	407.70	405.99	405.36	405.14
25000	455.35	448.87	443.70	439.57	436.24	433.55	431.38	429.62	424.68	422.90	422.25	422.02
26000	473.56	466.82	461.45	457.15	453.69	450.90	448.64	446.81	441.67	439.82	439.14	438.90
27000	491.77	484.78	479.20	474.73	471.14	468.24	465.89	463.99	458.66	456.73	456.03	455.78
28000	509.99	502.73	496.95	492.31	488.59	485.58	483.15	481.18	475.65	473.65	472.92	472.66
29000	528.20	520.69	514.70	509.90	506.04	502.92	500.40	498.36	492.63	490.57	489.81	489.54
30000	546.41	538.64	532.44	527.48	523.49	520.26	517.66	515.55	509.62	507.48	506.70	506.42
31000	564.63	556.59	550.19	545.06	540.94	537.61	534.91	532.73	526.61	524.40	523.59	523.30
32000	582.84	574.55	567.94	562.64	558.38	554.95	552.17	549.92	543.59	541.31	540.48	540.19
33000	601.05	592.50	585.69	580.23	575.83	572.29	569.42	567.10	560.58	558.23	557.37	557.06
34000	619.27	610.46	603.44	597.81	593.28	589.63	586.68	584.28	577.57	575.15	574.26	573.94
35000	637.48	628.41	621.18	615.39	610.73	606.97	603.93	601.47	594.56	592.06	591.15	590.82
36000	655.70	646.37	638.93	632.97	628.18	624.32	621.19	618.65	611.54	608.98	608.04	607.70
37000	673.91	664.32	656.68	650.56	645.63	641.66	638.44	635.84	628.53	625.89	624.93	624.58
38000	692.12	682.28	674.43	668.14	663.08	659.00	655.70	653.02	645.52	642.81	641.82	641.46
39000	710.34	700.23	692.17	685.72	680.53	676.34	672.95	670.21	662.50	659.73	658.71	658.34
40000	728.55	718.18	709.92	703.30	697.98	693.68	690.21	687.39	679.49	676.64	675.60	675.22
41000	746.76	736.14	727.67	720.89	715.43	711.03	707.46	704.58	696.48	693.56	692.49	692.10
42000	764.98	754.09	745.42	738.47	732.88	728.37	724.72	721.76	713.47	710.38	709.38	708.99
43000	783.19	772.05	763.17	756.05	750.33	745.71	741.97	738.95	730.45	727.39	726.27	725.87
44000	801.40	790.00	780.91	773.63	767.78	763.05	759.23	756.13	747.44	744.31	743.16	742.75
45000	819.62	807.96	798.66	791.22	785.23	780.39	776.49	773.32	764.43	761.22	760.05	759.63
46000	837.83	825.91	816.41	808.80	802.68	797.74	793.74	790.50	781.41	778.14	776.94	776.51
47000	856.04	843.87	834.16	826.38	820.13	815.08	811.00	807.69	798.40	795.05	793.83	793.39
48000	874.26	861.82	851.91	843.96	837.58	832.42	828.25	824.87	815.39	811.97	810.72	810.27
49000	892.47	879.78	869.65	861.55	855.02	849.76	845.51	842.05	832.38	828.89	827.61	827.15
50000	910.69	897.73	887.40	879.13	872.47	867.10	862.76	859.24	849.36	845.80	844.50	844.03
55000	1001.75	987.50	976.14	967.04	959.72	953.81	949.04	945.16	934.30	930.38	928.95	928.43
60000	1092.82	1077.27	1064.88	1054.95	1046.97	1040.52	1035.31	1031.09	1019.23	1014.96	1013.40	1012.83
65000	1183.89	1167.05	1153.62	1142.87	1134.21	1127.23	1121.59	1117.01	1104.17	1099.54	1097.85	1097.24
70000	1274.96	1256.82	1242.36	1230.78	1221.46	1213.94	1207.86	1202.93	1189.11	1184.12	1182.30	1181.64
75000	1366.03	1346.59	1331.10	1318.69	1308.71	1300.65	1294.14	1288.86	1274.04	1268.70	1266.75	1266.04
80000	1457.09	1436.36	1419.84	1406.60	1395.96	1387.36	1380.41	1374.78	1358.98	1353.28	1351.20	1350.44
85000	1548.16	1526.14	1508.59	1494.51	1483.20	1474.07	1466.69	1460.70	1443.91	1437.86	1435.65	1434.85
90000	1639.23	1615.91	1597.33	1582.43	1570.45	1560.78	1552.97	1546.63	1528.85	1522.44	1520.10	1519.25
95000	1730.30	1705.68	1686.06	1670.34	1657.70	1647.49	1639.24	1632.55	1613.79	1607.02	1604.55	1603.65
100000	1821.37	1795.45	1774.80	1758.25	1744.94	1734.20	1725.52	1718.47	1698.72	1691.60	1689.00	1688.05

20%

Table 1

20.50%

MONTHLY
PAYMENT REQUIRED TO AMORTIZE A LOAN

TERM AMOUNT	1 YEAR	2 YEARS	3 YEARS	4 YEARS	5 YEARS	6 YEARS	7 YEARS	8 YEARS	9 YEARS	10 YEARS	11 YEARS	12 YEARS
50	4.65	2.56	1.88	1.54	1.34	1.22	1.13	1.07	1.02	.99	.96	.94
100	9.29	5.12	3.75	3.07	2.68	2.43	2.26	2.13	2.04	1.97	1.92	1.88
200	18.58	10.23	7.49	6.14	5.36	4.85	4.51	4.26	4.07	3.94	3.83	3.75
300	27.87	15.35	11.23	9.21	8.04	7.28	6.76	6.38	6.11	5.90	5.74	5.62
400	37.15	20.46	14.97	12.28	10.71	9.70	9.01	8.51	8.14	7.87	7.66	7.49
500	46.44	25.58	18.71	15.35	13.39	12.13	11.26	10.64	10.18	9.83	9.57	9.36
600	55.73	30.69	22.46	18.42	16.07	14.55	13.51	12.76	12.21	11.80	11.48	11.23
700	65.02	35.80	26.20	21.49	18.75	16.98	15.76	14.89	14.25	13.77	13.39	13.11
800	74.30	40.92	29.94	24.56	21.42	19.40	18.01	17.02	16.28	15.73	15.31	14.98
900	83.59	46.03	33.68	27.63	24.10	21.82	20.26	19.14	18.32	17.70	17.22	16.85
1000	92.88	51.15	37.42	30.70	26.78	24.25	22.51	21.27	20.35	19.66	19.13	18.72
2000	185.75	102.29	74.84	61.40	53.55	48.49	45.02	42.54	40.70	39.32	38.26	37.44
3000	278.63	153.43	112.26	92.10	80.32	72.74	67.53	63.80	61.05	58.98	57.39	56.15
4000	371.50	204.57	149.68	122.79	107.10	96.98	90.04	85.07	81.40	78.64	76.52	74.87
5000	464.37	255.71	187.10	153.49	133.87	121.22	112.55	106.34	101.75	98.30	95.64	93.58
6000	557.25	306.85	224.52	184.19	160.64	145.47	135.05	127.60	122.10	117.95	114.77	112.30
7000	650.12	357.99	261.94	214.89	187.42	169.71	157.56	148.87	142.45	137.61	133.90	131.02
8000	743.00	409.13	299.36	245.58	214.19	193.95	180.07	170.13	162.80	157.27	153.03	149.73
9000	835.87	460.27	336.77	276.28	240.96	218.20	202.58	191.40	183.15	176.93	172.16	168.45
10000	928.74	511.41	374.19	306.98	267.73	242.44	225.09	212.67	203.50	196.59	191.28	187.16
11000	1021.62	562.55	411.61	337.68	294.51	266.68	247.60	233.93	223.85	216.25	210.41	205.88
12000	1114.49	613.69	449.03	368.37	321.28	290.93	270.10	255.20	244.20	235.90	229.54	224.60
13000	1207.37	664.83	486.45	399.07	348.05	315.17	292.61	276.46	264.55	255.56	248.67	243.31
14000	1300.24	715.97	523.87	429.77	374.83	339.41	315.12	297.73	284.90	275.22	267.80	262.03
15000	1393.11	767.11	561.29	460.47	401.60	363.66	337.63	319.00	305.25	294.88	286.92	280.74
16000	1485.99	818.25	598.71	491.16	428.37	387.90	360.14	340.26	325.60	314.54	306.05	299.46
17000	1578.86	869.39	636.13	521.86	455.14	412.15	382.65	361.53	345.95	334.19	325.18	318.18
18000	1671.74	920.53	673.54	552.56	481.92	436.39	405.15	382.79	366.30	353.85	344.31	336.89
19000	1764.61	971.67	710.96	583.26	508.69	460.63	427.66	404.06	386.65	373.51	363.44	355.61
20000	1857.48	1022.81	748.38	613.95	535.46	484.88	450.17	425.33	407.00	393.17	382.56	374.32
21000	1950.36	1073.95	785.80	644.65	562.24	509.12	472.68	446.59	427.35	412.83	401.69	393.04
22000	2043.23	1125.09	823.22	675.35	589.01	533.36	495.19	467.86	447.70	432.49	420.82	411.75
23000	2136.11	1176.23	860.64	706.05	615.78	557.61	517.69	489.12	468.05	452.14	439.95	430.47
24000	2228.98	1227.37	898.06	736.74	642.55	581.85	540.20	510.39	488.40	471.80	459.07	449.19
25000	2321.85	1278.51	935.48	767.44	669.33	606.09	562.71	531.66	508.74	491.46	478.20	467.90
26000	2414.73	1329.66	972.89	798.14	696.10	630.34	585.22	552.92	529.09	511.12	497.33	486.62
27000	2507.60	1380.80	1010.31	828.83	722.87	654.58	607.73	574.19	549.44	530.78	516.46	505.33
28000	2600.48	1431.94	1047.73	859.53	749.65	678.82	630.24	595.45	569.79	550.44	535.59	524.05
29000	2693.35	1483.08	1085.15	890.23	776.42	703.07	652.74	616.72	590.14	570.09	554.71	542.77
30000	2786.22	1534.22	1122.57	920.93	803.19	727.31	675.25	637.99	610.49	589.75	573.84	561.48
31000	2879.10	1585.36	1159.99	951.62	829.96	751.55	697.76	659.25	630.84	609.41	592.97	580.20
32000	2971.97	1636.50	1197.41	982.32	856.74	775.80	720.27	680.52	651.19	629.07	612.10	598.91
33000	3064.85	1687.64	1234.83	1013.02	883.51	800.04	742.78	701.78	671.54	648.73	631.23	617.63
34000	3157.72	1738.78	1272.25	1043.72	910.28	824.29	765.29	723.05	691.89	668.38	650.35	636.35
35000	3250.59	1789.92	1309.66	1074.41	937.06	848.53	787.79	744.32	712.24	688.04	669.48	655.06
36000	3343.47	1841.06	1347.08	1105.11	963.83	872.77	810.30	765.58	732.59	707.70	688.61	673.78
37000	3436.34	1892.20	1384.50	1135.81	990.60	897.02	832.81	786.85	752.94	727.36	707.74	692.49
38000	3529.22	1943.34	1421.92	1166.51	1017.37	921.26	855.32	808.12	773.29	747.02	726.87	711.21
39000	3622.09	1994.48	1459.34	1197.20	1044.15	945.50	877.83	829.38	793.64	766.68	745.99	729.92
40000	3714.96	2045.62	1496.76	1227.90	1070.92	969.75	900.33	850.65	813.99	786.33	765.12	748.64
41000	3807.84	2096.76	1534.18	1258.60	1097.69	993.99	922.84	871.91	834.34	805.99	784.25	767.36
42000	3900.71	2147.90	1571.60	1289.30	1124.47	1018.23	945.35	893.18	854.69	825.65	803.38	786.07
43000	3993.59	2199.04	1609.02	1319.99	1151.24	1042.48	967.86	914.45	875.04	845.31	822.51	804.79
44000	4086.46	2250.18	1646.43	1350.69	1178.01	1066.72	990.37	935.71	895.39	864.97	841.63	823.50
45000	4179.33	2301.32	1683.85	1381.39	1204.78	1090.96	1012.88	956.98	915.74	884.63	860.76	842.22
46000	4272.21	2352.46	1721.27	1412.09	1231.56	1115.21	1035.38	978.24	936.09	904.28	879.89	860.94
47000	4365.08	2403.60	1758.69	1442.78	1258.33	1139.45	1057.89	999.51	956.44	923.94	899.02	879.65
48000	4457.96	2454.74	1796.11	1473.48	1285.10	1163.69	1080.40	1020.78	976.79	943.60	918.14	898.37
49000	4550.83	2505.88	1833.53	1504.18	1311.88	1187.94	1102.91	1042.04	997.13	963.26	937.27	917.08
50000	4643.70	2557.02	1870.95	1534.87	1338.65	1212.18	1125.42	1063.31	1017.48	982.92	956.40	935.80
55000	5108.07	2812.73	2058.04	1688.36	1472.51	1333.40	1237.96	1169.64	1119.23	1081.21	1052.04	1029.38
60000	5572.44	3068.43	2245.14	1841.85	1606.38	1454.62	1350.50	1275.97	1220.98	1179.50	1147.68	1122.96
65000	6036.81	3324.13	2432.23	1995.34	1740.24	1575.83	1463.04	1382.30	1322.73	1277.79	1243.32	1216.54
70000	6501.18	3579.83	2619.32	2148.82	1874.11	1697.05	1575.58	1488.63	1424.48	1376.08	1338.96	1310.12
75000	6965.55	3835.53	2806.42	2302.31	2007.97	1818.27	1688.12	1594.96	1526.22	1474.37	1434.60	1403.70
80000	7429.92	4091.24	2993.51	2455.80	2141.83	1939.49	1800.66	1701.29	1627.97	1572.66	1530.24	1497.28
85000	7894.29	4346.94	3180.61	2609.28	2275.70	2060.70	1913.21	1807.62	1729.72	1670.95	1625.88	1590.86
90000	8358.66	4602.64	3367.70	2762.77	2409.56	2181.92	2025.75	1913.95	1831.47	1769.25	1721.52	1684.44
95000	8823.03	4858.34	3554.79	2916.26	2543.43	2303.14	2138.29	2020.28	1933.22	1867.54	1817.16	1778.01
100000	9287.40	5114.04	3741.89	3069.74	2677.29	2424.36	2250.83	2126.61	2034.96	1965.83	1912.80	1871.59

20%

Table 1

MONTHLY

20.50%

PAYMENT REQUIRED TO AMORTIZE A LOAN

TERM	13 YEARS	14 YEARS	15 YEARS	16 YEARS	17 YEARS	18 YEARS	19 YEARS	20 YEARS	25 YEARS	30 YEARS	35 YEARS	40 YEARS
OUNT												
50	.92	.91	.90	.89	.89	.88	.88	.87	.86	.86	.86	.86
100	1.84	1.82	1.80	1.78	1.77	1.76	1.75	1.74	1.72	1.72	1.71	1.71
200	3.68	3.63	3.59	3.56	3.53	3.51	3.50	3.48	3.44	3.43	3.42	3.42
300	5.52	5.45	5.39	5.34	5.30	5.27	5.24	5.22	5.16	5.14	5.13	5.13
400	7.36	7.26	7.18	7.11	7.06	7.02	6.99	6.96	6.88	6.85	6.84	6.84
500	9.20	9.07	8.97	8.89	8.83	8.77	8.73	8.70	8.60	8.57	8.55	8.55
600	11.04	10.89	10.77	10.67	10.59	10.53	10.48	10.43	10.32	10.28	10.26	10.26
700	12.88	12.70	12.56	12.44	12.35	12.28	12.22	12.17	12.04	11.99	11.97	11.97
800	14.72	14.51	14.35	14.22	14.12	14.03	13.97	13.91	13.76	13.70	13.68	13.68
900	16.56	16.33	16.15	16.00	15.88	15.79	15.71	15.65	15.48	15.41	15.39	15.38
1000	18.40	18.14	17.94	17.78	17.65	17.54	17.46	17.39	17.20	17.13	17.10	17.09
2000	36.79	36.28	35.87	35.55	35.29	35.08	34.91	34.77	34.39	34.25	34.20	34.18
3000	55.18	54.42	53.81	53.32	52.93	52.61	52.36	52.15	51.58	51.37	51.30	51.27
4000	73.58	72.55	71.74	71.09	70.57	70.15	69.81	69.53	68.77	68.49	68.39	68.36
5000	91.97	90.69	89.67	88.86	88.21	87.68	87.26	86.91	85.96	85.61	85.49	85.45
6000	110.36	108.83	107.61	106.63	105.85	105.22	104.71	104.29	103.15	102.74	102.59	102.54
7000	128.75	126.96	125.54	124.40	123.49	122.75	122.16	121.68	120.34	119.86	119.69	119.62
8000	147.15	145.10	143.47	142.17	141.13	140.29	139.61	139.06	137.53	136.98	136.78	136.71
9000	165.54	163.24	161.41	159.94	158.77	157.82	157.06	156.44	154.72	154.10	153.88	153.80
10000	183.93	181.37	179.34	177.71	176.41	175.36	174.51	173.82	171.91	171.22	170.98	170.89
11000	202.32	199.51	197.27	195.48	194.05	192.89	191.96	191.20	189.10	188.34	188.07	187.98
12000	220.72	217.65	215.21	213.25	211.69	210.43	209.41	208.58	206.29	205.47	205.17	205.07
13000	239.11	235.78	233.14	231.03	229.33	227.96	226.86	225.97	223.48	222.59	222.27	222.15
14000	257.50	253.92	251.07	248.80	246.97	245.50	244.31	243.35	240.67	239.71	239.37	239.24
15000	275.89	272.06	269.01	266.57	264.61	263.03	261.76	260.73	257.86	256.83	256.46	256.33
16000	294.29	290.20	286.94	284.34	282.25	280.57	279.21	278.11	275.05	273.95	273.56	273.42
17000	312.68	308.33	304.87	302.11	299.89	298.10	296.66	295.49	292.24	291.08	290.66	290.51
18000	331.07	326.47	322.81	319.88	317.53	315.64	314.11	312.87	309.43	308.20	307.76	307.60
19000	349.46	344.61	340.74	337.65	335.17	333.17	331.56	330.25	326.62	325.32	324.85	324.68
20000	367.86	362.74	358.67	355.42	352.81	350.71	349.01	347.64	343.81	342.44	341.95	341.77
21000	386.25	380.88	376.61	373.19	370.45	368.24	366.46	365.02	361.00	359.56	359.05	358.86
22000	404.64	399.02	394.54	390.96	388.09	385.78	383.91	382.40	378.19	376.68	376.14	375.95
23000	423.03	417.15	412.47	408.73	405.73	403.31	401.36	399.78	395.38	393.81	393.24	393.04
24000	441.43	435.29	430.41	426.50	423.37	420.85	418.81	417.16	412.57	410.93	410.34	410.13
25000	459.82	453.43	448.34	444.28	441.01	438.38	436.26	434.54	429.76	428.05	427.44	427.21
26000	478.21	471.56	466.28	462.05	458.65	455.92	453.71	451.93	446.95	445.17	444.53	444.30
27000	496.60	489.70	484.21	479.82	476.29	473.45	471.16	469.31	464.14	462.29	461.63	461.39
28000	515.00	507.84	502.14	497.59	493.93	490.99	488.61	486.69	481.33	479.42	478.73	478.48
29000	533.39	525.98	520.08	515.36	511.57	508.52	506.06	504.07	498.52	496.54	495.82	495.57
30000	551.78	544.11	538.01	533.13	529.21	526.06	523.51	521.45	515.71	513.66	512.92	512.66
31000	570.18	562.25	555.94	550.90	546.85	543.59	540.96	538.83	532.90	530.78	530.02	529.74
32000	588.57	580.39	573.88	568.67	564.49	561.13	558.41	556.21	550.09	547.90	547.12	546.83
33000	606.96	598.52	591.81	586.44	582.13	578.66	575.86	573.60	567.28	565.02	564.21	563.92
34000	625.35	616.66	609.74	604.21	599.77	596.20	593.31	590.98	584.47	582.15	581.31	581.01
35000	643.75	634.80	627.68	621.98	617.41	613.73	610.76	608.36	601.66	599.27	598.41	598.10
36000	662.14	652.93	645.61	639.75	635.05	631.27	628.21	625.74	618.85	616.39	615.51	615.19
37000	680.53	671.07	663.54	657.52	652.69	648.80	645.66	643.12	636.04	633.51	632.60	632.27
38000	698.92	689.21	681.48	675.30	670.33	666.34	663.11	660.50	653.23	650.63	649.70	649.36
39000	717.32	707.34	699.41	693.07	687.97	683.87	680.56	677.89	670.42	667.76	666.80	666.45
40000	735.71	725.48	717.34	710.84	705.61	701.41	698.01	695.27	687.61	684.88	683.89	683.54
41000	754.10	743.62	735.28	728.61	723.25	718.94	715.46	712.65	704.80	702.00	700.99	700.63
42000	772.49	761.76	753.21	746.38	740.89	736.48	732.91	730.03	721.99	719.12	718.09	717.72
43000	790.89	779.89	771.14	764.15	758.53	754.01	750.36	747.41	739.18	736.24	735.19	734.80
44000	809.28	798.03	789.08	781.92	776.17	771.55	767.81	764.79	756.37	753.36	752.28	751.89
45000	827.67	816.17	807.01	799.69	793.82	789.08	785.26	782.17	773.56	770.49	769.38	768.98
46000	846.06	834.30	824.94	817.46	811.46	806.62	802.71	799.56	790.75	787.61	786.48	786.07
47000	864.46	852.44	842.88	835.23	829.10	824.15	820.16	816.94	807.94	804.73	803.58	803.16
48000	882.85	870.58	860.81	853.00	846.74	841.69	837.61	834.32	825.13	821.85	820.67	820.25
49000	901.24	888.71	878.74	870.77	864.38	859.22	855.06	851.70	842.32	838.97	837.77	837.33
50000	919.63	906.85	896.68	888.55	882.02	876.76	872.52	869.08	859.51	856.10	854.87	854.42
55000	1011.60	997.53	986.35	977.40	970.22	964.43	959.77	955.99	945.46	941.70	940.35	939.86
60000	1103.56	1088.22	1076.01	1066.25	1058.42	1052.11	1047.02	1042.90	1031.41	1027.31	1025.84	1025.31
65000	1195.52	1178.90	1165.68	1155.11	1146.62	1139.79	1134.27	1129.81	1117.36	1112.92	1111.33	1110.75
70000	1287.49	1269.59	1255.35	1243.96	1234.82	1227.46	1221.52	1216.71	1203.31	1198.53	1196.81	1196.19
75000	1379.45	1360.27	1345.02	1332.82	1323.02	1315.14	1308.77	1303.62	1289.26	1284.14	1282.30	1281.63
80000	1471.41	1450.96	1434.68	1421.67	1411.22	1402.81	1396.02	1390.53	1375.21	1369.75	1367.78	1367.07
85000	1563.37	1541.64	1524.35	1510.52	1499.42	1490.49	1483.27	1477.44	1461.16	1455.36	1453.27	1452.52
90000	1655.34	1632.33	1614.02	1599.38	1587.63	1578.16	1570.52	1564.34	1547.11	1540.97	1538.76	1537.96
95000	1747.30	1723.01	1703.68	1688.23	1675.83	1665.84	1657.77	1651.25	1633.06	1626.58	1624.24	1623.40
100000	1839.26	1813.70	1793.35	1777.09	1764.03	1753.51	1745.03	1738.16	1719.01	1712.19	1709.73	1708.84

20%

Table 1

20.75%

MONTHLY
PAYMENT REQUIRED TO AMORTIZE A LOAN

TERM / AMOUNT	1 YEAR	2 YEARS	3 YEARS	4 YEARS	5 YEARS	6 YEARS	7 YEARS	8 YEARS	9 YEARS	10 YEARS	11 YEARS	12 YEARS
50	4.65	2.57	1.88	1.55	1.35	1.22	1.14	1.08	1.03	1.00	.97	.95
100	9.30	5.13	3.76	3.09	2.70	2.44	2.27	2.15	2.06	1.99	1.93	1.89
200	18.60	10.26	7.51	6.17	5.39	4.88	4.54	4.29	4.11	3.97	3.86	3.78
300	27.90	15.38	11.27	9.25	8.08	7.32	6.80	6.43	6.16	5.95	5.79	5.67
400	37.20	20.51	15.02	12.34	10.77	9.76	9.07	8.57	8.21	7.94	7.72	7.56
500	46.50	25.64	18.78	15.42	13.46	12.20	11.33	10.72	10.26	9.92	9.65	9.45
600	55.80	30.76	22.53	18.50	16.15	14.64	13.60	12.86	12.31	11.90	11.58	11.34
700	65.10	35.89	26.29	21.59	18.84	17.08	15.87	15.00	14.36	13.88	13.51	13.23
800	74.40	41.02	30.04	24.67	21.54	19.52	18.13	17.14	16.41	15.87	15.44	15.12
900	83.70	46.14	33.80	27.75	24.23	21.96	20.40	19.29	18.47	17.85	17.37	17.01
1000	93.00	51.27	37.55	30.84	26.92	24.39	22.66	21.43	20.52	19.83	19.30	18.90
2000	185.99	102.53	75.10	61.67	53.83	48.78	45.32	42.85	41.03	39.66	38.60	37.79
3000	278.99	153.79	112.65	92.50	80.74	73.17	67.98	64.27	61.54	59.48	57.90	56.68
4000	371.98	205.06	150.19	123.33	107.66	97.56	90.64	85.70	82.05	79.31	77.20	75.57
5000	464.97	256.32	187.74	154.16	134.57	121.95	113.30	107.12	102.56	99.13	96.50	94.46
6000	557.97	307.58	225.29	184.99	161.48	146.34	135.96	128.54	123.08	118.96	115.80	113.36
7000	650.96	358.85	262.83	215.82	188.40	170.73	158.62	149.97	143.59	138.78	135.10	132.25
8000	743.96	410.11	300.38	246.66	215.31	195.12	181.28	171.39	164.10	158.61	154.40	151.14
9000	836.95	461.37	337.93	277.49	242.22	219.51	203.94	192.81	184.61	178.43	173.70	170.03
10000	929.94	512.63	375.47	308.32	269.13	243.90	226.60	214.24	205.12	198.26	193.00	188.92
11000	1022.94	563.90	413.02	339.15	296.05	268.29	249.26	235.66	225.64	218.08	212.30	207.81
12000	1115.93	615.16	450.57	369.98	322.96	292.68	271.92	257.08	246.15	237.91	231.60	226.71
13000	1208.92	666.42	488.11	400.81	349.87	317.07	294.58	278.51	266.66	257.74	250.90	245.60
14000	1301.92	717.69	525.66	431.64	376.79	341.46	317.24	299.93	287.17	277.56	270.20	264.49
15000	1394.91	768.95	563.21	462.48	403.70	365.85	339.90	321.35	307.68	297.39	289.50	283.38
16000	1487.91	820.21	600.75	493.31	430.61	390.24	362.56	342.78	328.20	317.21	308.80	302.27
17000	1580.90	871.47	638.30	524.14	457.52	414.63	385.22	364.20	348.71	337.04	328.10	321.16
18000	1673.89	922.74	675.85	554.97	484.44	439.02	407.88	385.62	369.22	356.86	347.40	340.06
19000	1766.89	974.00	713.39	585.80	511.35	463.41	430.54	407.05	389.73	376.69	366.70	358.95
20000	1859.88	1025.26	750.94	616.63	538.26	487.80	453.20	428.47	410.24	396.51	386.00	377.84
21000	1952.88	1076.53	788.49	647.46	565.18	512.19	475.86	449.89	430.76	416.34	405.30	396.73
22000	2045.87	1127.79	826.04	678.30	592.09	536.58	498.52	471.32	451.27	436.16	424.60	415.62
23000	2138.86	1179.05	863.58	709.13	619.00	560.96	521.18	492.74	471.78	455.99	443.90	434.51
24000	2231.86	1230.32	901.13	739.96	645.92	585.35	543.84	514.16	492.29	475.82	463.19	453.41
25000	2324.85	1281.58	938.68	770.79	672.83	609.74	566.50	535.59	512.80	495.64	482.49	472.30
26000	2417.84	1332.84	976.22	801.62	699.74	634.13	589.16	557.01	533.32	515.47	501.79	491.19
27000	2510.84	1384.10	1013.77	832.45	726.65	658.52	611.82	578.43	553.83	535.29	521.09	510.08
28000	2603.83	1435.37	1051.32	863.28	753.57	682.91	634.48	599.86	574.34	555.12	540.39	528.97
29000	2696.83	1486.63	1088.86	894.12	780.48	707.30	657.14	621.28	594.85	574.94	559.69	547.86
30000	2789.82	1537.89	1126.41	924.95	807.39	731.69	679.80	642.70	615.36	594.77	578.99	566.76
31000	2882.81	1589.16	1163.96	955.78	834.31	756.08	702.46	664.13	635.88	614.59	598.29	585.65
32000	2975.81	1640.42	1201.50	986.61	861.22	780.47	725.12	685.55	656.39	634.42	617.59	604.54
33000	3068.80	1691.68	1239.05	1017.44	888.13	804.86	747.78	706.97	676.90	654.24	636.89	623.43
34000	3161.80	1742.94	1276.60	1048.27	915.04	829.25	770.44	728.40	697.41	674.07	656.19	642.32
35000	3254.79	1794.21	1314.14	1079.10	941.96	853.64	793.10	749.82	717.92	693.89	675.49	661.21
36000	3347.78	1845.47	1351.69	1109.93	968.87	878.03	815.76	771.24	738.44	713.72	694.79	680.11
37000	3440.78	1896.73	1389.24	1140.77	995.78	902.42	838.42	792.67	758.95	733.55	714.09	699.00
38000	3533.77	1948.00	1426.78	1171.60	1022.70	926.81	861.08	814.09	779.46	753.37	733.39	717.89
39000	3626.76	1999.26	1464.33	1202.43	1049.61	951.20	883.74	835.51	799.97	773.20	752.69	736.78
40000	3719.76	2050.52	1501.88	1233.26	1076.52	975.59	906.40	856.94	820.48	793.02	771.99	755.67
41000	3812.75	2101.79	1539.43	1264.09	1103.43	999.98	929.06	878.36	841.00	812.85	791.29	774.56
42000	3905.75	2153.05	1576.97	1294.92	1130.35	1024.37	951.72	899.78	861.51	832.67	810.59	793.46
43000	3998.74	2204.31	1614.52	1325.75	1157.26	1048.76	974.38	921.21	882.02	852.50	829.89	812.35
44000	4091.73	2255.57	1652.07	1356.59	1184.17	1073.15	997.04	942.63	902.53	872.32	849.19	831.24
45000	4184.73	2306.84	1689.61	1387.42	1211.09	1097.53	1019.70	964.05	923.04	892.15	868.49	850.13
46000	4277.72	2358.10	1727.16	1418.25	1238.00	1121.92	1042.36	985.48	943.55	911.97	887.79	869.02
47000	4370.72	2409.36	1764.71	1449.08	1264.91	1146.31	1065.02	1006.90	964.07	931.80	907.08	887.91
48000	4463.71	2460.63	1802.25	1479.91	1291.83	1170.70	1087.68	1028.32	984.58	951.63	926.38	906.81
49000	4556.70	2511.89	1839.80	1510.74	1318.74	1195.09	1110.34	1049.75	1005.09	971.45	945.68	925.70
50000	4649.70	2563.15	1877.35	1541.57	1345.65	1219.48	1133.00	1071.17	1025.60	991.28	964.98	944.59
55000	5114.67	2819.47	2065.08	1695.73	1480.22	1341.43	1246.30	1178.29	1128.16	1090.40	1061.48	1039.05
60000	5579.63	3075.78	2252.81	1849.89	1614.78	1463.38	1359.60	1285.40	1230.72	1189.53	1157.98	1133.51
65000	6044.60	3332.10	2440.55	2004.05	1749.34	1585.33	1472.90	1392.52	1333.28	1288.66	1254.48	1227.96
70000	6509.57	3588.41	2628.28	2158.20	1883.91	1707.27	1586.20	1499.63	1435.84	1387.78	1350.98	1322.42
75000	6974.54	3844.73	2816.02	2312.36	2018.47	1829.22	1699.50	1606.75	1538.40	1486.91	1447.47	1416.88
80000	7439.51	4101.04	3003.75	2466.52	2153.04	1951.17	1812.80	1713.87	1640.96	1586.04	1543.97	1511.34
85000	7904.48	4357.35	3191.49	2620.67	2287.60	2073.12	1926.10	1820.98	1743.52	1685.17	1640.47	1605.80
90000	8369.45	4613.67	3379.22	2774.83	2422.17	2195.06	2039.40	1928.10	1846.08	1784.29	1736.97	1700.26
95000	8834.42	4869.98	3566.95	2928.99	2556.73	2317.01	2152.70	2035.22	1948.64	1883.42	1833.46	1794.71
100000	9299.39	5126.30	3754.69	3083.14	2691.30	2438.96	2266.00	2142.33	2051.20	1982.55	1929.96	1889.17

20%

Table 1

MONTHLY 20.75%

PAYMENT REQUIRED TO AMORTIZE A LOAN

TERM / AMOUNT	13 YEARS	14 YEARS	15 YEARS	16 YEARS	17 YEARS	18 YEARS	19 YEARS	20 YEARS	25 YEARS	30 YEARS	35 YEARS	40 YEARS
50	.93	.92	.91	.90	.90	.89	.89	.88	.87	.87	.87	.87
100	1.86	1.84	1.82	1.80	1.79	1.78	1.77	1.76	1.74	1.74	1.74	1.73
200	3.72	3.67	3.63	3.60	3.57	3.55	3.53	3.52	3.48	3.47	3.47	3.46
300	5.58	5.50	5.44	5.39	5.35	5.32	5.30	5.28	5.22	5.20	5.20	5.19
400	7.43	7.33	7.25	7.19	7.14	7.10	7.06	7.04	6.96	6.94	6.93	6.92
500	9.29	9.16	9.06	8.98	8.92	8.87	8.83	8.79	8.70	8.67	8.66	8.65
600	11.15	11.00	10.88	10.78	10.70	10.64	10.59	10.55	10.44	10.40	10.39	10.38
700	13.01	12.83	12.69	12.58	12.49	12.42	12.36	12.31	12.18	12.13	12.12	12.11
800	14.86	14.66	14.50	14.37	14.27	14.19	14.12	14.07	13.92	13.87	13.85	13.84
900	16.72	16.49	16.31	16.17	16.05	15.96	15.89	15.83	15.66	15.60	15.58	15.57
1000	18.58	18.32	18.12	17.96	17.84	17.73	17.65	17.58	17.40	17.33	17.31	17.30
2000	37.15	36.64	36.24	35.92	35.67	35.46	35.30	35.16	34.79	34.66	34.61	34.60
3000	55.72	54.96	54.36	53.88	53.50	53.19	52.94	52.74	52.18	51.99	51.92	51.89
4000	74.29	73.28	72.48	71.84	71.33	70.92	70.59	70.32	69.58	69.32	69.22	69.19
5000	92.87	91.60	90.60	89.80	89.16	88.65	88.23	87.90	86.97	86.64	86.53	86.49
6000	111.44	109.92	108.72	107.76	106.99	106.38	105.88	105.48	104.36	103.97	103.83	103.78
7000	130.01	128.24	126.84	125.72	124.83	124.11	123.53	123.06	121.76	121.30	121.14	121.08
8000	148.58	146.56	144.96	143.68	142.66	141.83	141.17	140.64	139.15	138.63	138.44	138.38
9000	167.15	164.88	163.08	161.64	160.49	159.56	158.82	158.21	156.54	155.96	155.75	155.67
10000	185.73	183.20	181.20	179.60	178.32	177.29	176.46	175.79	173.94	173.28	173.05	172.97
11000	204.30	201.52	199.32	197.56	196.15	195.02	194.11	193.37	191.33	190.61	190.36	190.26
12000	222.87	219.84	217.44	215.52	213.98	212.75	211.75	210.95	208.72	207.94	207.66	207.56
13000	241.44	238.16	235.56	233.48	231.82	230.48	229.40	228.53	226.12	225.27	224.96	224.86
14000	260.01	256.48	253.68	251.44	249.65	248.21	247.05	246.11	243.51	242.59	242.27	242.15
15000	278.59	274.80	271.80	269.40	267.48	265.93	264.69	263.69	260.90	259.92	259.57	259.45
16000	297.16	293.12	289.92	287.36	285.31	283.66	282.34	281.27	278.30	277.25	276.88	276.75
17000	315.73	311.44	308.04	305.32	303.14	301.39	299.98	298.84	295.69	294.58	294.18	294.04
18000	334.30	329.76	326.16	323.28	320.97	319.12	317.63	316.42	313.08	311.91	311.49	311.34
19000	352.88	348.08	344.28	341.24	338.80	336.85	335.27	334.00	330.48	329.23	328.79	328.63
20000	371.45	366.40	362.40	359.20	356.64	354.58	352.92	351.58	347.87	346.56	346.10	345.93
21000	390.02	384.72	380.52	377.16	374.47	372.31	370.57	369.16	365.26	363.89	363.40	363.23
22000	408.59	403.04	398.63	395.12	392.30	390.03	388.21	386.74	382.66	381.22	380.71	380.52
23000	427.16	421.36	416.75	413.08	410.13	407.76	405.86	404.32	400.05	398.55	398.01	397.82
24000	445.74	439.68	434.87	431.04	427.96	425.49	423.50	421.90	417.44	415.87	415.31	415.12
25000	464.31	458.00	452.99	449.00	445.79	443.22	441.15	439.47	434.84	433.20	432.62	432.41
26000	482.88	476.32	471.11	466.96	463.63	460.95	458.79	457.05	452.23	450.53	449.92	449.71
27000	501.45	494.64	489.23	484.92	481.46	478.68	476.44	474.63	469.62	467.86	467.23	467.00
28000	520.02	512.96	507.35	502.88	499.29	496.41	494.09	492.21	487.02	485.18	484.53	484.30
29000	538.60	531.28	525.47	520.83	517.12	514.14	511.73	509.79	504.41	502.51	501.84	501.60
30000	557.17	549.60	543.59	538.79	534.95	531.86	529.38	527.37	521.80	519.84	519.14	518.89
31000	575.74	567.92	561.71	556.75	552.78	549.59	547.02	544.95	539.20	537.17	536.45	536.19
32000	594.31	586.24	579.83	574.71	570.62	567.32	564.67	562.53	556.59	554.50	553.75	553.49
33000	612.89	604.56	597.95	592.67	588.45	585.05	582.31	580.11	573.98	571.82	571.06	570.78
34000	631.46	622.88	616.07	610.63	606.28	602.78	599.96	597.68	591.37	589.15	588.36	588.08
35000	650.03	641.20	634.19	628.59	624.11	620.51	617.61	615.26	608.77	606.48	605.67	605.37
36000	668.60	659.52	652.31	646.55	641.94	638.24	635.25	632.84	626.16	623.81	622.97	622.67
37000	687.17	677.84	670.43	664.51	659.77	655.96	652.90	650.42	643.55	641.14	640.27	639.97
38000	705.75	696.16	688.55	682.47	677.60	673.69	670.54	668.00	660.95	658.46	657.58	657.26
39000	724.32	714.48	706.67	700.43	695.44	691.42	688.19	685.58	678.34	675.79	674.88	674.56
40000	742.89	732.80	724.79	718.39	713.27	709.15	705.83	703.16	695.73	693.12	692.19	691.86
41000	761.46	751.12	742.91	736.35	731.10	726.88	723.48	720.74	713.13	710.45	709.49	709.15
42000	780.03	769.44	761.03	754.31	748.93	744.61	741.13	738.31	730.52	727.77	726.80	726.45
43000	798.61	787.76	779.14	772.27	766.76	762.34	758.77	755.89	747.91	745.10	744.10	743.75
44000	817.18	806.08	797.26	790.23	784.59	780.06	776.42	773.47	765.31	762.43	761.41	761.04
45000	835.75	824.40	815.38	808.19	802.43	797.79	794.06	791.05	782.70	779.76	778.71	778.34
46000	854.32	842.72	833.50	826.15	820.26	815.52	811.71	808.63	800.09	797.09	796.02	795.63
47000	872.89	861.04	851.62	844.11	838.09	833.25	829.35	826.21	817.49	814.41	813.32	812.93
48000	891.47	879.36	869.74	862.07	855.92	850.98	847.00	843.79	834.88	831.74	830.62	830.23
49000	910.04	897.68	887.86	880.03	873.75	868.71	864.65	861.37	852.27	849.07	847.93	847.52
50000	928.61	916.00	905.98	897.99	891.58	886.44	882.29	878.94	869.67	866.40	865.23	864.82
55000	1021.47	1007.60	996.58	987.79	980.74	975.08	970.52	966.84	956.63	953.04	951.76	951.30
60000	1114.33	1099.20	1087.18	1077.58	1069.90	1063.72	1058.75	1054.73	1043.60	1039.68	1038.28	1037.78
65000	1207.19	1190.80	1177.77	1167.38	1159.06	1152.37	1146.98	1142.63	1130.56	1126.31	1124.80	1124.26
70000	1300.05	1282.40	1268.37	1257.18	1248.21	1241.01	1235.21	1230.52	1217.53	1212.95	1211.33	1210.74
75000	1392.91	1374.00	1358.97	1346.98	1337.37	1329.65	1323.43	1318.41	1304.50	1299.59	1297.85	1297.23
80000	1485.78	1465.59	1449.57	1436.78	1426.53	1418.30	1411.66	1406.31	1391.46	1386.23	1384.37	1383.71
85000	1578.64	1557.19	1540.17	1526.58	1515.69	1506.94	1499.89	1494.20	1478.43	1472.87	1470.89	1470.19
90000	1671.50	1648.79	1630.76	1616.37	1604.85	1595.58	1588.12	1582.10	1565.40	1559.51	1557.42	1556.67
95000	1764.36	1740.39	1721.36	1706.17	1694.00	1684.23	1676.35	1669.99	1652.36	1646.15	1643.94	1643.15
100000	1857.22	1831.99	1811.96	1795.97	1783.16	1772.87	1764.58	1757.88	1739.33	1732.79	1730.46	1729.63

20%

Table 1

21.00%

MONTHLY
PAYMENT REQUIRED TO AMORTIZE A LOAN

TERM AMOUNT	1 YEAR	2 YEARS	3 YEARS	4 YEARS	5 YEARS	6 YEARS	7 YEARS	8 YEARS	9 YEARS	10 YEARS	11 YEARS	12 YEARS
50	4.66	2.57	1.89	1.55	1.36	1.23	1.15	1.08	1.04	1.00	.98	.96
100	9.32	5.14	3.77	3.10	2.71	2.46	2.29	2.16	2.07	2.00	1.95	1.91
200	18.63	10.28	7.54	6.20	5.42	4.91	4.57	4.32	4.14	4.00	3.90	3.82
300	27.94	15.42	11.31	9.29	8.12	7.37	6.85	6.48	6.21	6.00	5.85	5.73
400	37.25	20.56	15.08	12.39	10.83	9.82	9.13	8.64	8.27	8.00	7.79	7.63
500	46.56	25.70	18.84	15.49	13.53	12.27	11.41	10.80	10.34	10.00	9.74	9.54
600	55.87	30.84	22.61	18.58	16.24	14.73	13.69	12.95	12.41	12.00	11.69	11.45
700	65.18	35.97	26.38	21.68	18.94	17.18	15.97	15.11	14.48	14.00	13.64	13.35
800	74.50	41.11	30.15	24.78	21.65	19.63	18.25	17.27	16.54	16.00	15.58	15.26
900	83.81	46.25	33.91	27.87	24.35	22.09	20.54	19.43	18.61	18.00	17.53	17.17
1000	93.12	51.39	37.68	30.97	27.06	24.54	22.82	21.59	20.68	20.00	19.48	19.07
2000	186.23	102.78	75.36	61.94	54.11	49.08	45.63	43.17	41.35	39.99	38.95	38.14
3000	279.35	154.16	113.03	92.90	81.17	73.61	68.44	64.75	62.03	59.98	58.42	57.21
4000	372.46	205.55	150.71	123.87	108.22	98.15	91.25	86.33	82.70	79.98	77.89	76.28
5000	465.57	256.93	188.38	154.83	135.27	122.68	114.07	107.91	103.38	99.97	97.36	95.35
6000	558.69	308.32	226.06	185.80	162.33	147.22	136.88	129.49	124.05	119.96	116.84	114.41
7000	651.80	359.70	263.73	216.76	189.38	171.76	159.69	151.07	144.73	139.96	136.31	133.48
8000	744.92	411.09	301.41	247.73	216.43	196.29	182.50	172.65	165.40	159.95	155.78	152.55
9000	838.03	462.48	339.08	278.70	243.49	220.83	205.32	194.23	186.08	179.94	175.25	171.62
10000	931.14	513.86	376.76	309.66	270.54	245.36	228.13	215.82	206.75	199.94	194.72	190.69
11000	1024.26	565.25	414.43	340.63	297.59	269.90	250.94	237.40	227.43	219.93	214.19	209.75
12000	1117.37	616.63	452.11	371.59	324.65	294.44	273.75	258.98	248.10	239.92	233.67	228.82
13000	1210.48	668.02	489.78	402.56	351.70	318.97	296.56	280.56	268.78	259.92	253.14	247.89
14000	1303.60	719.40	527.46	433.52	378.75	343.51	319.38	302.14	289.45	279.91	272.61	266.96
15000	1396.71	770.79	565.13	464.49	405.81	368.04	342.19	323.72	310.13	299.90	292.08	286.03
16000	1489.83	822.18	602.81	495.46	432.86	392.58	365.00	345.30	330.80	319.90	311.55	305.09
17000	1582.94	873.56	640.48	526.42	459.91	417.12	387.81	366.88	351.48	339.89	331.03	324.16
18000	1676.05	924.95	678.16	557.39	486.97	441.65	410.63	388.46	372.15	359.88	350.50	343.23
19000	1769.17	976.33	715.83	588.35	514.02	466.19	433.44	410.04	392.83	379.88	369.97	362.30
20000	1862.28	1027.72	753.51	619.32	541.07	490.72	456.25	431.63	413.50	399.87	389.44	381.37
21000	1955.39	1079.10	791.18	650.28	568.13	515.26	479.06	453.21	434.18	419.86	408.91	400.43
22000	2048.51	1130.49	828.86	681.25	595.18	539.80	501.87	474.79	454.85	439.85	428.38	419.50
23000	2141.62	1181.88	866.53	712.22	622.23	564.33	524.69	496.37	475.53	459.85	447.86	438.57
24000	2234.74	1233.26	904.21	743.18	649.29	588.87	547.50	517.95	496.20	479.84	467.33	457.64
25000	2327.85	1284.65	941.88	774.15	676.34	613.40	570.31	539.53	516.88	499.83	486.80	476.71
26000	2420.96	1336.03	979.56	805.11	703.39	637.94	593.12	561.11	537.55	519.83	506.27	495.77
27000	2514.08	1387.42	1017.23	836.08	730.45	662.48	615.94	582.69	558.23	539.82	525.74	514.84
28000	2607.19	1438.80	1054.91	867.04	757.50	687.01	638.75	604.27	578.90	559.81	545.22	533.91
29000	2700.30	1490.19	1092.58	898.01	784.55	711.55	661.56	625.85	599.58	579.81	564.69	552.98
30000	2793.42	1541.57	1130.26	928.98	811.61	736.08	684.37	647.44	620.25	599.80	584.16	572.05
31000	2886.53	1592.96	1167.93	959.94	838.66	760.62	707.18	669.02	640.93	619.79	603.63	591.11
32000	2979.65	1644.35	1205.61	990.91	865.71	785.16	730.00	690.60	661.60	639.79	623.10	610.18
33000	3072.76	1695.73	1243.28	1021.87	892.77	809.69	752.81	712.18	682.28	659.78	642.57	629.25
34000	3165.87	1747.12	1280.96	1052.84	919.82	834.23	775.62	733.76	702.95	679.77	662.05	648.32
35000	3258.99	1798.50	1318.63	1083.80	946.87	858.76	798.43	755.34	723.63	699.77	681.52	667.39
36000	3352.10	1849.89	1356.31	1114.77	973.93	883.30	821.25	776.92	744.30	719.76	700.99	686.45
37000	3445.21	1901.27	1393.98	1145.74	1000.98	907.84	844.06	798.50	764.98	739.75	720.46	705.52
38000	3538.33	1952.66	1431.66	1176.70	1028.03	932.37	866.87	820.08	785.65	759.75	739.93	724.59
39000	3631.44	2004.05	1469.33	1207.67	1055.09	956.91	889.68	841.66	806.32	779.74	759.41	743.66
40000	3724.56	2055.43	1507.01	1238.63	1082.14	981.44	912.49	863.25	827.00	799.73	778.88	762.73
41000	3817.67	2106.82	1544.68	1269.60	1109.19	1005.98	935.31	884.83	847.67	819.72	798.35	781.79
42000	3910.78	2158.20	1582.36	1300.56	1136.25	1030.52	958.12	906.41	868.35	839.72	817.82	800.86
43000	4003.90	2209.59	1620.03	1331.53	1163.30	1055.05	980.93	927.99	889.02	859.71	837.29	819.93
44000	4097.01	2260.97	1657.71	1362.50	1190.35	1079.59	1003.74	949.57	909.70	879.70	856.76	839.00
45000	4190.12	2312.36	1695.38	1393.46	1217.41	1104.12	1026.56	971.15	930.37	899.70	876.24	858.07
46000	4283.24	2363.74	1733.06	1424.43	1244.46	1128.66	1049.37	992.73	951.05	919.69	895.71	877.13
47000	4376.35	2415.13	1770.73	1455.39	1271.51	1153.20	1072.18	1014.31	971.72	939.68	915.18	896.20
48000	4469.47	2466.52	1808.41	1486.36	1298.57	1177.73	1094.99	1035.89	992.40	959.68	934.65	915.27
49000	4562.58	2517.90	1846.08	1517.32	1325.62	1202.27	1117.80	1057.47	1013.07	979.67	954.12	934.34
50000	4655.69	2569.29	1883.76	1548.29	1352.67	1226.80	1140.62	1079.06	1033.75	999.66	973.60	953.41
55000	5121.26	2826.22	2072.13	1703.12	1487.94	1349.48	1254.68	1186.96	1137.12	1099.63	1070.95	1048.75
60000	5586.83	3083.14	2260.51	1857.95	1623.21	1472.16	1368.74	1294.87	1240.50	1199.60	1168.31	1144.09
65000	6052.40	3340.07	2448.88	2012.78	1758.47	1594.84	1482.80	1402.77	1343.87	1299.56	1265.67	1239.43
70000	6517.97	3597.00	2637.26	2167.60	1893.74	1717.52	1596.86	1510.68	1447.25	1399.53	1363.03	1334.77
75000	6983.54	3853.93	2825.64	2322.43	2029.01	1840.20	1710.92	1618.58	1550.62	1499.49	1460.39	1430.11
80000	7449.11	4110.86	3014.01	2477.26	2164.27	1962.88	1824.98	1726.49	1653.99	1599.46	1557.75	1525.45
85000	7914.68	4367.79	3202.39	2632.09	2299.54	2085.56	1939.04	1834.39	1757.37	1699.42	1655.11	1620.79
90000	8380.25	4624.71	3390.76	2786.92	2434.81	2208.24	2053.11	1942.30	1860.74	1799.39	1752.47	1716.13
95000	8845.81	4881.64	3579.14	2941.75	2570.07	2330.92	2167.17	2050.20	1964.12	1899.36	1849.83	1811.47
100000	9311.38	5138.57	3767.51	3096.57	2705.34	2453.60	2281.23	2158.11	2067.49	1999.32	1947.19	1906.81

21%

Table 1

MONTHLY

PAYMENT REQUIRED TO AMORTIZE A LOAN

21.00%

TERM AMOUNT	13 YEARS	14 YEARS	15 YEARS	16 YEARS	17 YEARS	18 YEARS	19 YEARS	20 YEARS	25 YEARS	30 YEARS	35 YEARS	40 YEARS
50	.94	.93	.92	.91	.91	.90	.90	.89	.88	.88	.88	.88
100	1.88	1.86	1.84	1.82	1.81	1.80	1.79	1.78	1.76	1.76	1.76	1.76
200	3.76	3.71	3.67	3.63	3.61	3.59	3.57	3.56	3.52	3.51	3.51	3.51
300	5.63	5.56	5.50	5.45	5.41	5.38	5.36	5.34	5.28	5.27	5.26	5.26
400	7.51	7.41	7.33	7.26	7.21	7.17	7.14	7.12	7.04	7.02	7.01	7.01
500	9.38	9.26	9.16	9.08	9.02	8.97	8.93	8.89	8.80	8.77	8.76	8.76
600	11.26	11.11	10.99	10.89	10.82	10.76	10.71	10.67	10.56	10.53	10.51	10.51
700	13.13	12.96	12.82	12.71	12.62	12.55	12.49	12.45	12.32	12.28	12.26	12.26
800	15.01	14.81	14.65	14.52	14.42	14.34	14.28	14.23	14.08	14.03	14.01	14.01
900	16.88	16.66	16.48	16.34	16.23	16.14	16.06	16.00	15.84	15.79	15.77	15.76
1000	18.76	18.51	18.31	18.15	18.03	17.93	17.85	17.78	17.60	17.54	17.52	17.51
2000	37.51	37.01	36.62	36.30	36.05	35.85	35.69	35.56	35.20	35.07	35.03	35.01
3000	56.26	55.52	54.92	54.45	54.08	53.77	53.53	53.33	52.79	52.61	52.54	52.52
4000	75.01	74.02	73.23	72.60	72.10	71.70	71.37	71.11	70.39	70.14	70.05	70.02
5000	93.77	92.52	91.54	90.75	90.12	89.62	89.21	88.89	87.99	87.68	87.56	87.53
6000	112.52	111.03	109.84	108.90	108.15	107.54	107.05	106.66	105.58	105.21	105.08	105.03
7000	131.27	129.53	128.15	127.05	126.17	125.46	124.90	124.44	123.18	122.74	122.59	122.53
8000	150.02	148.03	146.45	145.20	144.19	143.39	142.74	142.22	140.78	140.28	140.10	140.04
9000	168.78	166.54	164.76	163.35	162.22	161.31	160.58	159.99	158.37	157.81	157.61	157.54
10000	187.53	185.04	183.07	181.50	180.24	179.23	178.42	177.77	175.97	175.35	175.12	175.05
11000	206.28	203.54	201.37	199.64	198.26	197.15	196.26	195.55	193.57	192.88	192.64	192.55
12000	225.03	222.05	219.68	217.79	216.29	215.08	214.10	213.32	211.16	210.41	210.15	210.06
13000	243.78	240.55	237.98	235.94	234.31	233.00	231.95	231.10	228.76	227.95	227.66	227.56
14000	262.54	259.05	256.29	254.09	252.33	250.92	249.79	248.88	246.36	245.48	245.17	245.06
15000	281.29	277.56	274.60	272.24	270.36	268.84	267.63	266.65	263.95	263.02	262.68	262.57
16000	300.04	296.06	292.90	290.39	288.38	286.77	285.47	284.43	281.55	280.55	280.20	280.07
17000	318.79	314.56	311.21	308.54	306.40	304.69	303.31	302.20	299.15	298.08	297.71	297.58
18000	337.55	333.07	329.52	326.69	324.43	322.61	321.15	319.98	316.74	315.62	315.22	315.08
19000	356.30	351.57	347.82	344.84	342.45	340.54	339.00	337.76	334.34	333.15	332.73	332.59
20000	375.05	370.07	366.13	362.98	360.47	358.46	356.84	355.53	351.94	350.69	350.24	350.09
21000	393.80	388.58	384.43	381.13	378.50	376.38	374.68	373.31	369.53	368.22	367.76	367.59
22000	412.55	407.08	402.74	399.28	396.52	394.30	392.52	391.09	387.13	385.75	385.27	385.10
23000	431.31	425.58	421.05	417.43	414.54	412.23	410.36	408.86	404.73	403.29	402.78	402.60
24000	450.06	444.09	439.35	435.58	432.57	430.15	428.20	426.64	422.32	420.82	420.29	420.11
25000	468.81	462.59	457.66	453.73	450.59	448.07	446.05	444.42	439.92	438.36	437.80	437.61
26000	487.56	481.09	475.96	471.88	468.61	465.99	463.89	462.19	457.52	455.89	455.32	455.12
27000	506.32	499.60	494.27	490.03	486.64	483.92	481.73	479.97	475.11	473.42	472.83	472.62
28000	525.07	518.10	512.58	508.18	504.66	501.84	499.57	497.75	492.71	490.96	490.34	490.12
29000	543.82	536.60	530.88	526.33	522.68	519.76	517.41	515.52	510.31	508.49	507.85	507.63
30000	562.57	555.11	549.19	544.47	540.71	537.68	535.25	533.30	527.90	526.03	525.36	525.13
31000	581.32	573.61	567.49	562.62	558.73	555.61	553.10	551.07	545.50	543.56	542.88	542.64
32000	600.08	592.11	585.80	580.77	576.75	573.53	570.94	568.85	563.10	561.09	560.39	560.14
33000	618.83	610.62	604.11	598.92	594.78	591.45	588.78	586.63	580.69	578.63	577.90	577.64
34000	637.58	629.12	622.41	617.07	612.80	609.37	606.62	604.40	598.29	596.16	595.41	595.15
35000	656.33	647.62	640.72	635.22	630.82	627.30	624.46	622.18	615.89	613.70	612.92	612.65
36000	675.09	666.13	659.03	653.37	648.85	645.22	642.30	639.96	633.48	631.23	630.44	630.16
37000	693.84	684.63	677.33	671.52	666.87	663.14	660.15	657.73	651.08	648.76	647.95	647.66
38000	712.59	703.13	695.64	689.67	684.89	681.07	677.99	675.51	668.68	666.30	665.46	665.17
39000	731.34	721.64	713.94	707.82	702.92	698.99	695.83	693.29	686.27	683.83	682.97	682.67
40000	750.09	740.14	732.25	725.96	720.94	716.91	713.67	711.06	703.87	701.37	700.48	700.17
41000	768.85	758.64	750.56	744.11	738.96	734.83	731.51	728.84	721.47	718.90	718.00	717.68
42000	787.60	777.15	768.86	762.26	756.99	752.76	749.35	746.62	739.06	736.43	735.51	735.18
43000	806.35	795.65	787.17	780.41	775.01	770.68	767.20	764.39	756.66	753.97	753.02	752.69
44000	825.10	814.15	805.47	798.56	793.03	788.60	785.04	782.17	774.26	771.50	770.53	770.19
45000	843.86	832.66	823.78	816.71	811.06	806.52	802.88	799.94	791.85	789.04	788.04	787.70
46000	862.61	851.16	842.09	834.86	829.08	824.45	820.72	817.72	809.45	806.57	805.56	805.20
47000	881.36	869.66	860.39	853.01	847.10	842.37	838.56	835.50	827.05	824.10	823.07	822.70
48000	900.11	888.17	878.70	871.16	865.13	860.29	856.40	853.27	844.64	841.64	840.58	840.21
49000	918.86	906.67	897.01	889.31	883.15	878.21	874.25	871.05	862.24	859.17	858.09	857.71
50000	937.62	925.17	915.31	907.45	901.17	896.14	892.09	888.83	879.84	876.71	875.60	875.22
55000	1031.38	1017.69	1006.84	998.20	991.29	985.75	981.30	977.71	967.82	964.38	963.16	962.74
60000	1125.14	1110.21	1098.37	1088.95	1081.41	1075.36	1070.50	1066.59	1055.80	1052.05	1050.72	1050.26
65000	1218.90	1202.73	1189.90	1179.69	1171.52	1164.98	1159.71	1155.47	1143.79	1139.72	1138.28	1137.78
70000	1312.66	1295.24	1281.43	1270.44	1261.64	1254.59	1248.92	1244.36	1231.77	1227.39	1225.84	1225.30
75000	1406.42	1387.76	1372.96	1361.18	1351.76	1344.20	1338.13	1333.24	1319.75	1315.06	1313.40	1312.82
80000	1500.18	1480.28	1464.49	1451.93	1441.88	1433.82	1427.34	1422.12	1407.74	1402.73	1400.96	1400.34
85000	1593.94	1572.79	1556.03	1542.67	1531.99	1523.43	1516.55	1511.00	1495.72	1490.40	1488.52	1487.86
90000	1687.71	1665.31	1647.56	1633.42	1622.11	1613.04	1605.75	1599.88	1583.70	1578.07	1576.08	1575.39
95000	1781.47	1757.83	1739.09	1724.16	1712.23	1702.66	1694.96	1688.77	1671.68	1665.74	1663.64	1662.91
100000	1875.23	1850.34	1830.62	1814.91	1802.34	1792.27	1784.17	1777.65	1759.67	1753.41	1751.20	1750.43

21%

Table 1

21.25%

MONTHLY

PAYMENT REQUIRED TO AMORTIZE A LOAN

TERM AMOUNT	1 YEAR	2 YEARS	3 YEARS	4 YEARS	5 YEARS	6 YEARS	7 YEARS	8 YEARS	9 YEARS	10 YEARS	11 YEARS	12 YEARS
50	4.67	2.58	1.90	1.56	1.36	1.24	1.15	1.09	1.05	1.01	.99	.97
100	9.33	5.16	3.79	3.12	2.72	2.47	2.30	2.18	2.09	2.02	1.97	1.93
200	18.65	10.31	7.57	6.23	5.44	4.94	4.60	4.35	4.17	4.04	3.93	3.85
300	27.98	15.46	11.35	9.34	8.16	7.41	6.89	6.53	6.26	6.05	5.90	5.78
400	37.30	20.61	15.13	12.45	10.88	9.88	9.19	8.70	8.34	8.07	7.86	7.70
500	46.62	25.76	18.91	15.56	13.60	12.35	11.49	10.87	10.42	10.09	9.83	9.63
600	55.95	30.91	22.69	18.67	16.32	14.81	13.78	13.05	12.51	12.10	11.79	11.55
700	65.27	36.06	26.47	21.78	19.04	17.28	16.08	15.22	14.59	14.12	13.76	13.48
800	74.59	41.21	30.25	24.89	21.76	19.75	18.38	17.40	16.68	16.13	15.72	15.40
900	83.92	46.36	34.03	28.00	24.48	22.22	20.67	19.57	18.76	18.15	17.69	17.33
1000	93.24	51.51	37.81	31.11	27.20	24.69	22.97	21.74	20.84	20.17	19.65	19.25
2000	186.47	103.02	75.61	62.21	54.39	49.37	45.93	43.48	41.68	40.33	39.29	38.49
3000	279.71	154.53	113.42	93.31	81.59	74.05	68.90	65.22	62.52	60.49	58.94	57.74
4000	372.94	206.04	151.22	124.41	108.78	98.74	91.86	86.96	83.36	80.65	78.58	76.98
5000	466.17	257.55	189.02	155.51	135.98	123.42	114.83	108.70	104.20	100.81	98.23	96.23
6000	559.41	309.06	226.83	186.61	163.17	148.10	137.79	130.44	125.03	120.97	117.87	115.47
7000	652.64	360.56	264.63	217.71	190.36	172.79	160.76	152.18	145.87	141.14	137.52	134.72
8000	745.88	412.07	302.43	248.81	217.56	197.47	183.72	173.92	166.71	161.30	157.16	153.96
9000	839.11	463.58	340.24	279.91	244.75	222.15	206.69	195.66	187.55	181.46	176.81	173.21
10000	932.34	515.09	378.04	311.01	271.95	246.83	229.65	217.40	208.39	201.62	196.45	192.45
11000	1025.58	566.60	415.84	342.11	299.14	271.52	252.62	239.14	229.23	221.78	216.10	211.70
12000	1118.81	618.11	453.65	373.21	326.34	296.20	275.58	260.88	250.06	241.94	235.74	230.94
13000	1212.04	669.62	491.45	404.31	353.53	320.88	298.55	282.62	270.90	262.10	255.38	250.19
14000	1305.28	721.12	529.25	435.41	380.72	345.57	321.51	304.35	291.74	282.27	275.03	269.43
15000	1398.51	772.63	567.06	466.51	407.92	370.25	344.48	326.09	312.58	302.43	294.67	288.68
16000	1491.75	824.14	604.86	497.61	435.11	394.93	367.44	347.83	333.42	322.59	314.32	307.92
17000	1584.98	875.65	642.67	528.71	462.31	419.61	390.41	369.57	354.26	342.75	333.96	327.17
18000	1678.21	927.16	680.47	559.81	489.50	444.30	413.37	391.31	375.09	362.91	353.61	346.41
19000	1771.45	978.67	718.27	590.91	516.69	468.98	436.34	413.05	395.93	383.07	373.25	365.66
20000	1864.68	1030.18	756.08	622.01	543.89	493.66	459.30	434.79	416.77	403.23	392.90	384.90
21000	1957.91	1081.68	793.88	653.11	571.08	518.35	482.27	456.53	437.61	423.40	412.54	404.15
22000	2051.15	1133.19	831.68	684.21	598.28	543.03	505.23	478.27	458.45	443.56	432.19	423.39
23000	2144.38	1184.70	869.49	715.31	625.47	567.71	528.20	500.01	479.29	463.72	451.83	442.64
24000	2237.62	1236.21	907.29	746.41	652.67	592.39	551.16	521.75	500.12	483.88	471.48	461.88
25000	2330.85	1287.72	945.09	777.51	679.86	617.08	574.13	543.49	520.96	504.04	491.12	481.13
26000	2424.08	1339.23	982.90	808.61	707.05	641.76	597.09	565.23	541.80	524.20	510.76	500.37
27000	2517.32	1390.74	1020.70	839.71	734.25	666.44	620.06	586.97	562.64	544.36	530.41	519.62
28000	2610.55	1442.24	1058.50	870.81	761.44	691.13	643.02	608.70	583.48	564.53	550.05	538.86
29000	2703.79	1493.75	1096.31	901.91	788.64	715.81	665.99	630.44	604.32	584.69	569.70	558.11
30000	2797.02	1545.26	1134.11	933.01	815.83	740.49	688.95	652.18	625.15	604.85	589.34	577.35
31000	2890.25	1596.77	1171.92	964.11	843.02	765.17	711.92	673.92	645.99	625.01	608.99	596.60
32000	2983.49	1648.28	1209.72	995.22	870.22	789.86	734.88	695.66	666.83	645.17	628.63	615.84
33000	3076.72	1699.79	1247.52	1026.32	897.41	814.54	757.85	717.40	687.67	665.33	648.28	635.09
34000	3169.95	1751.30	1285.33	1057.42	924.61	839.22	780.81	739.14	708.51	685.50	667.92	654.33
35000	3263.19	1802.80	1323.13	1088.52	951.80	863.91	803.78	760.88	729.35	705.66	687.57	673.58
36000	3356.42	1854.31	1360.93	1119.62	979.00	888.59	826.74	782.62	750.18	725.82	707.21	692.82
37000	3449.66	1905.82	1398.74	1150.72	1006.19	913.27	849.71	804.36	771.02	745.98	726.85	712.07
38000	3542.89	1957.33	1436.54	1181.82	1033.38	937.95	872.67	826.10	791.86	766.14	746.50	731.31
39000	3636.12	2008.84	1474.34	1212.92	1060.58	962.64	895.64	847.84	812.70	786.30	766.14	750.56
40000	3729.36	2060.35	1512.15	1244.02	1087.77	987.32	918.60	869.58	833.54	806.46	785.79	769.80
41000	3822.59	2111.85	1549.95	1275.12	1114.97	1012.00	941.57	891.31	854.38	826.63	805.43	789.05
42000	3915.82	2163.36	1587.75	1306.22	1142.16	1036.69	964.53	913.05	875.21	846.79	825.08	808.29
43000	4009.06	2214.87	1625.56	1337.32	1169.35	1061.37	987.50	934.79	896.05	866.95	844.72	827.54
44000	4102.29	2266.38	1663.36	1368.42	1196.55	1086.05	1010.46	956.53	916.89	887.11	864.37	846.78
45000	4195.53	2317.89	1701.16	1399.52	1223.74	1110.73	1033.43	978.27	937.73	907.27	884.01	866.03
46000	4288.76	2369.40	1738.97	1430.62	1250.94	1135.42	1056.39	1000.01	958.57	927.43	903.66	885.27
47000	4381.99	2420.91	1776.77	1461.72	1278.13	1160.10	1079.36	1021.75	979.41	947.59	923.30	904.52
48000	4475.23	2472.41	1814.58	1492.82	1305.33	1184.78	1102.32	1043.49	1000.24	967.76	942.95	923.76
49000	4568.46	2523.92	1852.38	1523.92	1332.52	1209.47	1125.29	1065.23	1021.08	987.92	962.59	943.01
50000	4661.69	2575.43	1890.18	1555.02	1359.71	1234.15	1148.25	1086.97	1041.92	1008.08	982.23	962.25
55000	5127.86	2832.97	2079.20	1710.52	1495.68	1357.56	1263.08	1195.66	1146.11	1108.89	1080.46	1058.48
60000	5594.03	3090.52	2268.22	1866.02	1631.66	1480.98	1377.90	1304.36	1250.30	1209.69	1178.68	1154.70
65000	6060.20	3348.06	2457.24	2021.53	1767.63	1604.39	1492.73	1413.06	1354.50	1310.50	1276.90	1250.92
70000	6526.37	3605.60	2646.25	2177.03	1903.60	1727.81	1607.55	1521.75	1458.69	1411.31	1375.13	1347.15
75000	6992.54	3863.14	2835.27	2332.53	2039.57	1851.22	1722.38	1630.45	1562.88	1512.12	1473.35	1443.37
80000	7458.71	4120.69	3024.29	2488.03	2175.54	1974.64	1837.20	1739.15	1667.07	1612.92	1571.57	1539.60
85000	7924.88	4378.23	3213.31	2643.53	2311.51	2098.05	1952.03	1847.84	1771.26	1713.73	1669.80	1635.82
90000	8391.05	4635.77	3402.32	2799.03	2447.48	2221.46	2066.85	1956.54	1875.45	1814.54	1768.02	1732.05
95000	8857.22	4893.32	3591.34	2954.54	2583.45	2344.88	2181.67	2065.23	1979.65	1915.35	1866.24	1828.27
100000	9323.39	5150.86	3780.36	3110.04	2719.42	2468.29	2296.50	2173.93	2083.84	2016.15	1964.46	1924.50

21%

Table 1

MONTHLY

PAYMENT REQUIRED TO AMORTIZE A LOAN

21.25%

TERM	13 YEARS	14 YEARS	15 YEARS	16 YEARS	17 YEARS	18 YEARS	19 YEARS	20 YEARS	25 YEARS	30 YEARS	35 YEARS	40 YEARS
AMOUNT												
50	.95	.94	.93	.92	.92	.91	.91	.90	.90	.89	.89	.89
100	1.90	1.87	1.85	1.84	1.83	1.82	1.81	1.80	1.79	1.78	1.78	1.78
200	3.79	3.74	3.70	3.67	3.65	3.63	3.61	3.60	3.57	3.55	3.55	3.55
300	5.68	5.61	5.55	5.51	5.47	5.44	5.42	5.40	5.35	5.33	5.32	5.32
400	7.58	7.48	7.40	7.34	7.29	7.25	7.22	7.19	7.13	7.10	7.09	7.09
500	9.47	9.35	9.25	9.17	9.11	9.06	9.02	8.99	8.91	8.88	8.86	8.86
600	11.36	11.22	11.10	11.01	10.93	10.88	10.83	10.79	10.69	10.65	10.64	10.63
700	13.26	13.09	12.95	12.84	12.76	12.69	12.63	12.59	12.47	12.42	12.41	12.40
800	15.15	14.95	14.80	14.68	14.58	14.50	14.44	14.38	14.25	14.20	14.18	14.17
900	17.04	16.82	16.65	16.51	16.40	16.31	16.24	16.18	16.03	15.97	15.95	15.95
1000	18.94	18.69	18.50	18.34	18.22	18.12	18.04	17.98	17.81	17.75	17.72	17.72
2000	37.87	37.38	36.99	36.68	36.44	36.24	36.08	35.95	35.61	35.49	35.44	35.43
3000	56.80	56.07	55.48	55.02	54.65	54.36	54.12	53.93	53.41	53.23	53.16	53.14
4000	75.74	74.75	73.98	73.36	72.87	72.47	72.16	71.90	71.21	70.97	70.88	70.85
5000	94.67	93.44	92.47	91.70	91.08	90.59	90.19	89.88	89.01	88.71	88.60	88.57
6000	113.60	112.13	110.96	110.04	109.30	108.71	108.23	107.85	106.81	106.45	106.32	106.28
7000	132.54	130.82	129.46	128.38	127.51	126.82	126.27	125.83	124.61	124.19	124.04	123.99
8000	151.47	149.50	147.95	146.72	145.73	144.94	144.31	143.80	142.41	141.93	141.76	141.70
9000	170.40	168.19	166.44	165.05	163.95	163.06	162.35	161.77	160.21	159.67	159.48	159.41
10000	189.33	186.88	184.94	183.39	182.16	181.18	180.38	179.75	178.01	177.41	177.20	177.13
11000	208.27	205.57	203.43	201.73	200.38	199.29	198.42	197.72	195.81	195.15	194.92	194.84
12000	227.20	224.25	221.92	220.07	218.59	217.41	216.46	215.70	213.61	212.89	212.64	212.55
13000	246.13	242.94	240.42	238.41	236.81	235.53	234.50	233.67	231.41	230.63	230.36	230.26
14000	265.07	261.63	258.91	256.75	255.02	253.64	252.54	251.65	249.21	248.37	248.08	247.98
15000	284.00	280.32	277.40	275.09	273.24	271.76	270.57	269.62	267.01	266.11	265.80	265.69
16000	302.93	299.00	295.90	293.43	291.46	289.88	288.61	287.60	284.81	283.85	283.52	283.40
17000	321.86	317.69	314.39	311.77	309.67	308.00	306.65	305.57	302.61	301.59	301.24	301.11
18000	340.80	336.38	332.88	330.10	327.89	326.11	324.69	323.54	320.41	319.33	318.96	318.82
19000	359.73	355.07	351.38	348.44	346.10	344.23	342.73	341.52	338.21	337.07	336.67	336.53
20000	378.66	373.75	369.87	366.78	364.32	362.35	360.76	359.49	356.01	354.81	354.39	354.25
21000	397.60	392.44	388.36	385.12	382.53	380.46	378.80	377.47	373.81	372.55	372.11	371.96
22000	416.53	411.13	406.86	403.46	400.75	398.58	396.84	395.44	391.61	390.29	389.83	389.67
23000	435.46	429.82	425.35	421.80	418.97	416.70	414.88	413.42	409.41	408.03	407.55	407.39
24000	454.39	448.50	443.84	440.14	437.18	434.81	432.92	431.39	427.21	425.77	425.27	425.10
25000	473.33	467.19	462.34	458.48	455.40	452.93	450.95	449.37	445.01	443.51	442.99	442.81
26000	492.26	485.88	480.83	476.81	473.61	471.05	468.99	467.34	462.81	461.25	460.71	460.52
27000	511.19	504.57	499.32	495.15	491.83	489.17	487.03	485.31	480.61	478.99	478.43	478.23
28000	530.13	523.25	517.82	513.49	510.04	507.28	505.07	503.29	498.41	496.73	496.15	495.95
29000	549.06	541.94	536.31	531.83	528.26	525.40	523.11	521.26	516.21	514.47	513.87	513.66
30000	567.99	560.63	554.80	550.17	546.47	543.52	541.14	539.24	534.01	532.21	531.59	531.37
31000	586.92	579.32	573.30	568.51	564.69	561.63	559.18	557.21	551.81	549.95	549.31	549.08
32000	605.86	598.00	591.79	586.85	582.91	579.75	577.22	575.19	569.61	567.69	567.03	566.80
33000	624.79	616.69	610.28	605.19	601.12	597.87	595.26	593.16	587.41	585.43	584.75	584.51
34000	643.72	635.38	628.77	623.53	619.34	615.99	613.30	611.14	605.21	603.17	602.47	602.22
35000	662.66	654.07	647.27	641.86	637.55	634.10	631.33	629.11	623.01	620.92	620.19	619.93
36000	681.59	672.75	665.76	660.20	655.77	652.22	649.37	647.08	640.81	638.66	637.91	637.64
37000	700.52	691.44	684.25	678.54	673.98	670.34	667.41	665.06	658.61	656.40	655.63	655.36
38000	719.45	710.13	702.75	696.88	692.20	688.45	685.45	683.03	676.41	674.14	673.34	673.07
39000	738.39	728.82	721.24	715.22	710.42	706.57	703.49	701.01	694.22	691.88	691.06	690.78
40000	757.32	747.50	739.73	733.56	728.63	724.69	721.52	718.98	712.02	709.62	708.78	708.49
41000	776.25	766.19	758.23	751.90	746.85	742.81	739.56	736.96	729.82	727.36	726.50	726.21
42000	795.19	784.88	776.72	770.24	765.06	760.92	757.60	754.93	747.62	745.10	744.22	743.92
43000	814.12	803.56	795.21	788.58	783.28	779.04	775.64	772.91	765.42	762.84	761.94	761.63
44000	833.05	822.25	813.71	806.91	801.49	797.16	793.68	790.88	783.22	780.58	779.66	779.34
45000	851.98	840.94	832.20	825.25	819.71	815.27	811.71	808.85	801.02	798.32	797.38	797.05
46000	870.92	859.63	850.69	843.59	837.93	833.39	829.75	826.83	818.82	816.06	815.10	814.77
47000	889.85	878.31	869.19	861.93	856.14	851.51	847.79	844.80	836.62	833.80	832.82	832.48
48000	908.78	897.00	887.68	880.27	874.36	869.62	865.83	862.78	854.42	851.54	850.54	850.19
49000	927.72	915.69	906.17	898.61	892.57	887.74	883.87	880.75	872.22	869.28	868.26	867.90
50000	946.65	934.38	924.67	916.95	910.79	905.86	901.90	898.73	890.02	887.02	885.98	885.62
55000	1041.31	1027.81	1017.13	1008.64	1001.87	996.44	992.09	988.60	979.02	975.72	974.58	974.18
60000	1135.98	1121.25	1109.60	1100.34	1092.94	1087.03	1082.28	1078.47	1068.02	1064.42	1063.17	1062.74
65000	1230.64	1214.69	1202.07	1192.03	1184.02	1177.61	1172.47	1168.34	1157.02	1153.12	1151.77	1151.30
70000	1325.31	1308.13	1294.53	1283.72	1275.10	1268.20	1262.66	1258.22	1246.02	1241.83	1240.37	1239.86
75000	1419.97	1401.56	1387.00	1375.42	1366.18	1358.79	1352.85	1348.09	1335.02	1330.53	1328.97	1328.42
80000	1514.64	1495.00	1479.46	1467.11	1457.26	1449.37	1443.04	1437.96	1424.03	1419.23	1417.56	1416.98
85000	1609.30	1588.44	1571.93	1558.81	1548.34	1539.96	1533.23	1527.83	1513.03	1507.93	1506.16	1505.54
90000	1703.96	1681.87	1664.40	1650.50	1639.41	1630.54	1623.42	1617.70	1602.03	1596.63	1594.76	1594.10
95000	1798.63	1775.31	1756.86	1742.20	1730.49	1721.13	1713.61	1707.58	1691.03	1685.33	1683.35	1682.67
100000	1893.29	1868.75	1849.33	1833.89	1821.57	1811.71	1803.80	1797.45	1780.03	1774.03	1771.95	1771.23

21%

Table 1

21.50%

MONTHLY
PAYMENT REQUIRED TO AMORTIZE A LOAN

TERM / AMOUNT	1 YEAR	2 YEARS	3 YEARS	4 YEARS	5 YEARS	6 YEARS	7 YEARS	8 YEARS	9 YEARS	10 YEARS	11 YEARS	12 YEARS
50	4.67	2.59	1.90	1.57	1.37	1.25	1.16	1.10	1.06	1.02	1.00	.98
100	9.34	5.17	3.80	3.13	2.74	2.49	2.32	2.19	2.11	2.04	1.99	1.95
200	18.68	10.33	7.59	6.25	5.47	4.97	4.63	4.38	4.21	4.07	3.97	3.89
300	28.01	15.49	11.38	9.38	8.21	7.45	6.94	6.57	6.31	6.10	5.95	5.83
400	37.35	20.66	15.18	12.50	10.94	9.94	9.25	8.76	8.41	8.14	7.93	7.77
500	46.68	25.82	18.97	15.62	13.67	12.42	11.56	10.95	10.51	10.17	9.91	9.72
600	56.02	30.98	22.76	18.75	16.41	14.90	13.88	13.14	12.61	12.20	11.90	11.66
700	65.35	36.15	26.56	21.87	19.14	17.39	16.19	15.33	14.71	14.24	13.88	13.60
800	74.69	41.31	30.35	24.99	21.87	19.87	18.50	17.52	16.81	16.27	15.86	15.54
900	84.02	46.47	34.14	28.12	24.61	22.35	20.81	19.71	18.91	18.30	17.84	17.49
1000	93.36	51.64	37.94	31.24	27.34	24.84	23.12	21.90	21.01	20.34	19.82	19.43
2000	186.71	103.27	75.87	62.48	54.68	49.67	46.24	43.80	42.01	40.67	39.64	38.85
3000	280.07	154.90	113.80	93.71	82.01	74.50	69.36	65.70	63.01	61.00	59.46	58.27
4000	373.42	206.53	151.73	124.95	109.35	99.33	92.48	87.60	84.01	81.33	79.28	77.69
5000	466.77	258.16	189.67	156.18	136.68	124.16	115.60	109.50	105.02	101.66	99.09	97.12
6000	560.13	309.79	227.60	187.42	164.02	148.99	138.71	131.39	126.02	121.99	118.91	116.54
7000	653.48	361.43	265.53	218.65	191.35	173.82	161.83	153.29	147.02	142.32	138.73	135.96
8000	746.84	413.06	303.46	249.89	218.69	198.65	184.95	175.19	168.02	162.65	158.55	155.38
9000	840.19	464.69	341.40	281.12	246.02	223.48	208.07	197.09	189.03	182.98	178.37	174.81
10000	933.54	516.32	379.33	312.36	273.36	248.31	231.19	218.99	210.03	203.31	198.18	194.23
11000	1026.90	567.95	417.26	343.59	300.69	273.14	254.30	240.88	231.03	223.64	218.00	213.65
12000	1120.25	619.58	455.19	374.83	328.03	297.97	277.42	262.78	252.03	243.97	237.82	233.07
13000	1213.61	671.22	493.12	406.06	355.36	322.80	300.54	284.68	273.04	264.30	257.64	252.50
14000	1306.96	722.85	531.06	437.30	382.70	347.63	323.66	306.58	294.04	284.63	277.46	271.92
15000	1400.31	774.48	568.99	468.53	410.04	372.46	346.78	328.48	315.04	304.96	297.27	291.34
16000	1493.67	826.11	606.92	499.77	437.37	397.29	369.90	350.37	336.04	325.29	317.09	310.76
17000	1587.02	877.74	644.85	531.00	464.71	422.12	393.01	372.27	357.04	345.62	336.91	330.19
18000	1680.38	929.37	682.79	562.24	492.04	446.95	416.13	394.17	378.05	365.95	356.73	349.61
19000	1773.73	981.00	720.72	593.47	519.38	471.78	439.25	416.07	399.05	386.28	376.55	369.03
20000	1867.08	1032.64	758.65	624.71	546.71	496.61	462.37	437.97	420.05	406.61	396.36	388.45
21000	1960.44	1084.27	796.58	655.95	574.05	521.44	485.49	459.86	441.05	426.94	416.18	407.87
22000	2053.79	1135.90	834.52	687.18	601.38	546.27	508.60	481.76	462.06	447.27	436.00	427.30
23000	2147.14	1187.53	872.45	718.42	628.72	571.10	531.72	503.66	483.06	467.60	455.82	446.72
24000	2240.50	1239.16	910.38	749.65	656.05	595.93	554.84	525.56	504.06	487.93	475.64	466.14
25000	2333.85	1290.79	948.31	780.89	683.39	620.76	577.96	547.46	525.06	508.26	495.45	485.56
26000	2427.21	1342.43	986.24	812.12	710.72	645.59	601.08	569.35	546.07	528.59	515.27	504.99
27000	2520.56	1394.06	1024.18	843.36	738.06	670.42	624.19	591.25	567.07	548.92	535.09	524.41
28000	2613.91	1445.69	1062.11	874.59	765.40	695.25	647.31	613.15	588.07	569.25	554.91	543.83
29000	2707.27	1497.32	1100.04	905.83	792.73	720.08	670.43	635.05	609.07	589.58	574.73	563.25
30000	2800.62	1548.95	1137.97	937.06	820.07	744.91	693.55	656.95	630.07	609.92	594.54	582.68
31000	2893.98	1600.58	1175.91	968.30	847.40	769.74	716.67	678.84	651.08	630.25	614.36	602.10
32000	2987.33	1652.22	1213.84	999.53	874.74	794.57	739.79	700.74	672.08	650.58	634.18	621.52
33000	3080.68	1703.85	1251.77	1030.77	902.07	819.40	762.90	722.64	693.08	670.91	654.00	640.94
34000	3174.04	1755.48	1289.70	1062.00	929.41	844.23	786.02	744.54	714.08	691.24	673.81	660.37
35000	3267.39	1807.11	1327.63	1093.24	956.74	869.06	809.14	766.44	735.09	711.57	693.63	679.79
36000	3360.75	1858.74	1365.57	1124.47	984.08	893.89	832.26	788.33	756.09	731.90	713.45	699.21
37000	3454.10	1910.37	1403.50	1155.71	1011.41	918.72	855.38	810.23	777.09	752.23	733.27	718.63
38000	3547.45	1962.00	1441.43	1186.94	1038.75	943.55	878.49	832.13	798.09	772.56	753.09	738.06
39000	3640.81	2013.64	1479.36	1218.18	1066.08	968.38	901.61	854.03	819.10	792.89	772.90	757.48
40000	3734.16	2065.27	1517.30	1249.42	1093.42	993.21	924.73	875.93	840.10	813.22	792.72	776.90
41000	3827.52	2116.90	1555.23	1280.65	1120.76	1018.04	947.85	897.82	861.10	833.55	812.54	796.32
42000	3920.87	2168.53	1593.16	1311.89	1148.09	1042.87	970.97	919.72	882.10	853.88	832.36	815.74
43000	4014.22	2220.16	1631.09	1343.12	1175.43	1067.70	994.08	941.62	903.10	874.21	852.18	835.17
44000	4107.58	2271.79	1669.03	1374.36	1202.76	1092.53	1017.20	963.52	924.11	894.54	871.99	854.59
45000	4200.93	2323.43	1706.96	1405.59	1230.10	1117.36	1040.32	985.42	945.11	914.87	891.81	874.01
46000	4294.28	2375.06	1744.89	1436.83	1257.43	1142.19	1063.44	1007.31	966.11	935.20	911.63	893.43
47000	4387.64	2426.69	1782.82	1468.06	1284.77	1167.02	1086.56	1029.21	987.11	955.53	931.45	912.86
48000	4480.99	2478.32	1820.75	1499.30	1312.10	1191.85	1109.68	1051.11	1008.12	975.86	951.27	932.28
49000	4574.35	2529.95	1858.69	1530.53	1339.44	1216.68	1132.79	1073.01	1029.12	996.19	971.08	951.70
50000	4667.70	2581.58	1896.62	1561.77	1366.77	1241.51	1155.91	1094.91	1050.12	1016.52	990.90	971.12
55000	5134.47	2839.74	2086.28	1717.94	1503.45	1365.67	1271.50	1204.40	1155.13	1118.17	1089.99	1068.24
60000	5601.24	3097.90	2275.94	1874.12	1640.13	1489.82	1387.09	1313.89	1260.14	1219.83	1189.08	1165.35
65000	6068.01	3356.06	2465.60	2030.30	1776.80	1613.97	1502.68	1423.38	1365.16	1321.48	1288.17	1262.46
70000	6534.78	3614.22	2655.26	2186.47	1913.48	1738.12	1618.27	1532.87	1470.17	1423.13	1387.26	1359.57
75000	7001.55	3872.37	2844.93	2342.65	2050.16	1862.27	1733.87	1642.36	1575.18	1524.78	1486.35	1456.68
80000	7468.32	4130.53	3034.55	2498.83	2186.84	1986.42	1849.46	1751.85	1680.19	1626.43	1585.44	1553.80
85000	7935.09	4388.69	3224.25	2655.00	2323.51	2110.57	1965.05	1861.34	1785.20	1728.08	1684.53	1650.91
90000	8401.86	4646.85	3413.91	2811.18	2460.19	2234.72	2080.64	1970.83	1890.21	1829.74	1783.62	1748.02
95000	8868.63	4905.00	3603.57	2967.35	2596.87	2358.87	2196.23	2080.32	1995.23	1931.39	1882.71	1845.13
100000	9335.40	5163.16	3793.23	3123.53	2733.54	2483.02	2311.82	2189.81	2100.24	2033.04	1981.80	1942.24

21%

Table 1

MONTHLY

21.50%

PAYMENT REQUIRED TO AMORTIZE A LOAN

TERM OUNT	13 YEARS	14 YEARS	15 YEARS	16 YEARS	17 YEARS	18 YEARS	19 YEARS	20 YEARS	25 YEARS	30 YEARS	35 YEARS	40 YEARS
50	.96	.95	.94	.93	.93	.92	.92	.91	.91	.90	.90	.90
100	1.92	1.89	1.87	1.86	1.85	1.84	1.83	1.82	1.81	1.80	1.80	1.80
200	3.83	3.78	3.74	3.71	3.69	3.67	3.65	3.64	3.61	3.59	3.59	3.59
300	5.74	5.67	5.61	5.56	5.53	5.50	5.48	5.46	5.41	5.39	5.38	5.38
400	7.65	7.55	7.48	7.42	7.37	7.33	7.30	7.27	7.21	7.18	7.18	7.17
500	9.56	9.44	9.35	9.27	9.21	9.16	9.12	9.09	9.01	8.98	8.97	8.97
600	11.47	11.33	11.21	11.12	11.05	10.99	10.95	10.91	10.81	10.77	10.76	10.76
700	13.38	13.22	13.08	12.98	12.89	12.82	12.77	12.73	12.61	12.57	12.55	12.55
800	15.30	15.10	14.95	14.83	14.73	14.65	14.59	14.54	14.41	14.36	14.35	14.34
900	17.21	16.99	16.82	16.68	16.57	16.49	16.42	16.36	16.21	16.16	16.14	16.13
1000	19.12	18.88	18.69	18.53	18.41	18.32	18.24	18.18	18.01	17.95	17.93	17.93
2000	38.23	37.75	37.37	37.06	36.82	36.63	36.47	36.35	36.01	35.90	35.86	35.85
3000	57.35	56.62	56.05	55.59	55.23	54.94	54.71	54.52	54.02	53.85	53.79	53.77
4000	76.46	75.49	74.73	74.12	73.64	73.25	72.94	72.70	72.02	71.79	71.71	71.69
5000	95.58	94.37	93.41	92.65	92.05	91.56	91.18	90.87	90.03	89.74	89.64	89.61
6000	114.69	113.24	112.09	111.18	110.46	109.88	109.41	109.04	108.03	107.69	107.57	107.53
7000	133.80	132.11	130.77	129.71	128.86	128.19	127.65	127.21	126.03	125.63	125.49	125.45
8000	152.92	150.98	149.45	148.24	147.27	146.50	145.88	145.39	144.04	143.58	143.42	143.37
9000	172.03	169.85	168.13	166.77	165.68	164.81	164.12	163.56	162.04	161.53	161.35	161.29
10000	191.15	188.73	186.81	185.30	184.09	183.12	182.35	181.73	180.05	179.47	179.28	179.21
11000	210.26	207.60	205.49	203.83	202.50	201.44	200.59	199.91	198.05	197.42	197.20	197.13
12000	229.37	226.47	224.18	222.36	220.91	219.75	218.82	218.08	216.05	215.37	215.13	215.05
13000	248.49	245.34	242.86	240.88	239.31	238.06	237.06	236.25	234.06	233.31	233.06	232.97
14000	267.60	264.21	261.54	259.41	257.72	256.37	255.29	254.42	252.06	251.26	250.98	250.89
15000	286.72	283.09	280.22	277.94	276.13	274.68	273.53	272.60	270.07	269.21	268.91	268.81
16000	305.83	301.96	298.90	296.47	294.54	293.00	291.76	290.77	288.07	287.15	286.84	286.73
17000	324.94	320.83	317.58	315.00	312.95	311.31	310.00	308.94	306.07	305.10	304.76	304.65
18000	344.06	339.70	336.26	333.53	331.36	329.62	328.23	327.12	324.08	323.05	322.69	322.57
19000	363.17	358.57	354.94	352.06	349.76	347.93	346.46	345.29	342.08	340.99	340.62	340.49
20000	382.29	377.45	373.62	370.59	368.17	366.24	364.70	363.46	360.09	358.94	358.55	358.41
21000	401.40	396.32	392.30	389.12	386.58	384.56	382.93	381.63	378.09	376.89	376.47	376.33
22000	420.51	415.19	410.98	407.65	404.99	402.87	401.17	399.81	396.10	394.83	394.40	394.25
23000	439.63	434.06	429.66	426.18	423.40	421.18	419.40	417.98	414.10	412.78	412.33	412.17
24000	458.74	452.93	448.35	444.71	441.81	439.49	437.64	436.15	432.10	430.73	430.25	430.09
25000	477.86	471.81	467.03	463.23	460.21	457.80	455.87	454.33	450.11	448.67	448.18	448.01
26000	496.97	490.68	485.71	481.76	478.62	476.12	474.11	472.50	468.11	466.62	466.11	465.93
27000	516.09	509.55	504.39	500.29	497.03	494.43	492.34	490.67	486.12	484.57	484.03	483.85
28000	535.20	528.42	523.07	518.82	515.44	512.74	510.58	508.84	504.12	502.51	501.96	501.77
29000	554.31	547.29	541.75	537.35	533.85	531.05	528.81	527.02	522.12	520.46	519.89	519.69
30000	573.43	566.17	560.43	555.88	552.26	549.36	547.05	545.19	540.13	538.41	537.82	537.61
31000	592.54	585.04	579.11	574.41	570.67	567.68	565.28	563.36	558.13	556.35	555.74	555.53
32000	611.66	603.91	597.79	592.94	589.07	585.99	583.52	581.54	576.14	574.30	573.67	573.45
33000	630.77	622.78	616.47	611.47	607.48	604.30	601.75	599.71	594.14	592.25	591.60	591.37
34000	649.88	641.65	635.15	630.00	625.89	622.61	619.99	617.88	612.14	610.19	609.52	609.29
35000	669.00	660.53	653.83	648.53	644.30	640.92	638.22	636.05	630.15	628.14	627.45	627.21
36000	688.11	679.40	672.52	667.06	662.71	659.23	656.46	654.23	648.15	646.09	645.38	645.13
37000	707.23	698.27	691.20	685.58	681.12	677.55	674.69	672.40	666.16	664.03	663.30	663.05
38000	726.34	717.14	709.88	704.11	699.52	695.86	692.92	690.57	684.16	681.98	681.23	680.97
39000	745.45	736.01	728.56	722.64	717.93	714.17	711.16	708.74	702.17	699.93	699.16	698.89
40000	764.57	754.89	747.24	741.17	736.34	732.48	729.39	726.92	720.17	717.87	717.09	716.81
41000	783.68	773.76	765.92	759.70	754.75	750.79	747.63	745.09	738.17	735.82	735.01	734.73
42000	802.80	792.63	784.60	778.23	773.16	769.11	765.86	763.26	756.18	753.77	752.94	752.65
43000	821.91	811.50	803.28	796.76	791.57	787.42	784.10	781.44	774.18	771.71	770.87	770.57
44000	841.02	830.37	821.96	815.29	809.97	805.73	802.33	799.61	792.19	789.66	788.79	788.49
45000	860.14	849.25	840.64	833.82	828.38	824.04	820.57	817.78	810.19	807.61	806.72	806.42
46000	879.25	868.12	859.32	852.35	846.79	842.35	838.80	835.95	828.19	825.55	824.65	824.34
47000	898.37	886.99	878.00	870.88	865.20	860.67	857.04	854.13	846.20	843.50	842.57	842.26
48000	917.48	905.86	896.69	889.41	883.61	878.98	875.27	872.30	864.20	861.45	860.50	860.18
49000	936.60	924.73	915.37	907.93	902.02	897.29	893.51	890.47	882.21	879.39	878.43	878.10
50000	955.71	943.61	934.05	926.46	920.42	915.60	911.74	908.65	900.21	897.34	896.36	896.02
55000	1051.28	1037.97	1027.45	1019.11	1012.47	1007.16	1002.92	999.51	990.23	987.07	985.99	985.62
60000	1146.85	1132.33	1120.86	1111.76	1104.51	1098.72	1094.09	1090.37	1080.25	1076.81	1075.63	1075.22
65000	1242.42	1226.69	1214.26	1204.40	1196.55	1190.28	1185.26	1181.24	1170.27	1166.54	1165.26	1164.82
70000	1337.99	1321.05	1307.66	1297.05	1288.59	1281.84	1276.44	1272.10	1260.29	1256.27	1254.90	1254.42
75000	1433.56	1415.41	1401.07	1389.69	1380.63	1373.40	1367.61	1362.97	1350.31	1346.01	1344.53	1344.02
80000	1529.13	1509.77	1494.47	1482.34	1472.68	1464.96	1458.78	1453.83	1440.33	1435.74	1434.17	1433.62
85000	1624.70	1604.13	1587.88	1574.98	1564.72	1556.52	1549.96	1544.69	1530.35	1525.47	1523.80	1523.22
90000	1720.27	1698.49	1681.28	1667.63	1656.76	1648.08	1641.13	1635.56	1620.37	1615.21	1613.44	1612.83
95000	1815.84	1792.85	1774.69	1760.28	1748.80	1739.64	1732.30	1726.42	1710.40	1704.94	1703.07	1702.43
100000	1911.41	1887.21	1868.09	1852.92	1840.84	1831.20	1823.48	1817.29	1800.42	1794.67	1792.71	1792.03

21%

135

Table 1

21.75%

MONTHLY
PAYMENT REQUIRED TO AMORTIZE A LOAN

TERM / AMOUNT	1 YEAR	2 YEARS	3 YEARS	4 YEARS	5 YEARS	6 YEARS	7 YEARS	8 YEARS	9 YEARS	10 YEARS	11 YEARS	12 YEARS
50	4.68	2.59	1.91	1.57	1.38	1.25	1.17	1.11	1.06	1.03	1.00	.99
100	9.35	5.18	3.81	3.14	2.75	2.50	2.33	2.21	2.12	2.05	2.00	1.97
200	18.70	10.36	7.62	6.28	5.50	5.00	4.66	4.42	4.24	4.10	4.00	3.93
300	28.05	15.53	11.42	9.42	8.25	7.50	6.99	6.62	6.36	6.15	6.00	5.89
400	37.39	20.71	15.23	12.55	11.00	10.00	9.31	8.83	8.47	8.20	8.00	7.85
500	46.74	25.88	19.04	15.69	13.74	12.49	11.64	11.03	10.59	10.25	10.00	9.81
600	56.09	31.06	22.84	18.83	16.49	14.99	13.97	13.24	12.71	12.30	12.00	11.77
700	65.44	36.23	26.65	21.96	19.24	17.49	16.30	15.45	14.82	14.35	14.00	13.73
800	74.78	41.41	30.45	25.10	21.99	19.99	18.62	17.65	16.94	16.40	16.00	15.69
900	84.13	46.58	34.26	28.24	24.73	22.49	20.95	19.86	19.06	18.45	18.00	17.65
1000	93.48	51.76	38.07	31.38	27.48	24.98	23.28	22.06	21.17	20.50	20.00	19.61
2000	186.95	103.51	76.13	62.75	54.96	49.96	46.55	44.12	42.34	41.00	39.99	39.21
3000	280.43	155.27	114.19	94.12	82.44	74.94	69.82	66.18	63.51	61.50	59.98	58.81
4000	373.90	207.02	152.25	125.49	109.91	99.92	93.09	88.23	84.67	82.00	79.97	78.41
5000	467.38	258.78	190.31	156.86	137.39	124.89	116.36	110.29	105.84	102.50	99.96	98.01
6000	560.85	310.53	228.37	188.23	164.87	149.87	139.64	132.35	127.01	123.00	119.96	117.61
7000	654.32	362.29	266.43	219.60	192.34	174.85	162.91	154.41	148.17	143.50	139.95	137.21
8000	747.80	414.04	304.49	250.97	219.82	199.83	186.18	176.46	169.34	164.00	159.94	156.81
9000	841.27	465.80	342.56	282.34	247.30	224.81	209.45	198.52	190.51	184.50	179.93	176.41
10000	934.75	517.55	380.62	313.71	274.77	249.78	232.72	220.58	211.67	205.00	199.92	196.01
11000	1028.22	569.31	418.68	345.08	302.25	274.76	255.99	242.64	232.84	225.50	219.92	215.61
12000	1121.69	621.06	456.74	376.45	329.73	299.74	279.27	264.69	254.01	246.00	239.91	235.21
13000	1215.17	672.82	494.80	407.82	357.21	324.72	302.54	286.75	275.17	266.50	259.90	254.81
14000	1308.64	724.57	532.86	439.19	384.68	349.70	325.81	308.81	296.34	287.00	279.89	274.41
15000	1402.12	776.33	570.92	470.56	412.16	374.67	349.08	330.86	317.51	307.50	299.88	294.01
16000	1495.59	828.08	608.98	501.93	439.64	399.65	372.35	352.92	338.67	328.00	319.87	313.61
17000	1589.06	879.84	647.05	533.30	467.11	424.63	395.63	374.98	359.84	348.50	339.87	333.21
18000	1682.54	931.59	685.11	564.67	494.59	449.61	418.90	397.04	381.01	369.00	359.86	352.81
19000	1776.01	983.35	723.17	596.04	522.07	474.59	442.17	419.09	402.18	389.50	379.85	372.41
20000	1869.49	1035.10	761.23	627.42	549.54	499.56	465.44	441.15	423.34	410.00	399.84	392.01
21000	1962.96	1086.86	799.29	658.79	577.02	524.54	488.71	463.21	444.51	430.50	419.83	411.61
22000	2056.44	1138.61	837.35	690.16	604.50	549.52	511.98	485.27	465.68	451.00	439.83	431.21
23000	2149.91	1190.36	875.41	721.53	631.98	574.50	535.26	507.32	486.84	471.50	459.82	450.81
24000	2243.38	1242.12	913.47	752.90	659.45	599.48	558.53	529.38	508.01	492.00	479.81	470.41
25000	2336.86	1293.87	951.54	784.27	686.93	624.45	581.80	551.44	529.18	512.50	499.80	490.01
26000	2430.33	1345.63	989.60	815.64	714.41	649.43	605.07	573.49	550.34	533.00	519.79	509.62
27000	2523.81	1397.38	1027.66	847.01	741.88	674.41	628.34	595.55	571.51	553.50	539.78	529.22
28000	2617.28	1449.14	1065.72	878.38	769.36	699.39	651.62	617.61	592.68	574.00	559.78	548.82
29000	2710.75	1500.89	1103.78	909.75	796.84	724.37	674.89	639.67	613.84	594.50	579.77	568.42
30000	2804.23	1552.65	1141.84	941.12	824.31	749.34	698.16	661.72	635.01	615.00	599.76	588.02
31000	2897.70	1604.40	1179.90	972.49	851.79	774.32	721.43	683.78	656.18	635.50	619.75	607.62
32000	2991.18	1656.16	1217.96	1003.86	879.27	799.30	744.70	705.84	677.34	656.00	639.74	627.22
33000	3084.65	1707.91	1256.03	1035.23	906.74	824.28	767.97	727.90	698.51	676.50	659.74	646.82
34000	3178.12	1759.67	1294.09	1066.60	934.22	849.26	791.25	749.95	719.68	697.00	679.73	666.42
35000	3271.60	1811.42	1332.15	1097.97	961.70	874.23	814.52	772.01	740.84	717.50	699.72	686.02
36000	3365.07	1863.18	1370.21	1129.34	989.18	899.21	837.79	794.07	762.01	738.00	719.71	705.62
37000	3458.55	1914.93	1408.27	1160.71	1016.65	924.19	861.06	816.13	783.18	758.50	739.70	725.22
38000	3552.02	1966.69	1446.33	1192.08	1044.13	949.17	884.33	838.18	804.35	779.00	759.69	744.82
39000	3645.50	2018.44	1484.39	1223.45	1071.61	974.14	907.61	860.24	825.51	799.49	779.69	764.42
40000	3738.97	2070.20	1522.45	1254.83	1099.08	999.12	930.88	882.30	846.68	819.99	799.68	784.02
41000	3832.44	2121.95	1560.52	1286.20	1126.56	1024.10	954.15	904.35	867.85	840.49	819.67	803.62
42000	3925.92	2173.71	1598.58	1317.57	1154.04	1049.08	977.42	926.41	889.01	860.99	839.66	823.22
43000	4019.39	2225.46	1636.64	1348.94	1181.51	1074.06	1000.69	948.47	910.18	881.49	859.65	842.82
44000	4112.87	2277.22	1674.70	1380.31	1208.99	1099.03	1023.96	970.53	931.35	901.99	879.65	862.42
45000	4206.34	2328.97	1712.76	1411.68	1236.47	1124.01	1047.24	992.58	952.51	922.49	899.64	882.02
46000	4299.81	2380.72	1750.82	1443.05	1263.95	1148.99	1070.51	1014.64	973.68	942.99	919.63	901.62
47000	4393.29	2432.48	1788.88	1474.42	1291.42	1173.97	1093.78	1036.70	994.85	963.49	939.62	921.22
48000	4486.76	2484.23	1826.94	1505.79	1318.90	1198.95	1117.05	1058.76	1016.01	983.99	959.61	940.82
49000	4580.24	2535.99	1865.01	1537.16	1346.38	1223.92	1140.32	1080.81	1037.18	1004.49	979.61	960.42
50000	4673.71	2587.74	1903.07	1568.53	1373.85	1248.90	1163.60	1102.87	1058.35	1024.99	999.60	980.02
55000	5141.08	2846.52	2093.37	1725.38	1511.24	1373.79	1279.95	1213.16	1164.18	1127.49	1099.56	1078.03
60000	5608.45	3105.29	2283.68	1882.24	1648.62	1498.68	1396.31	1323.44	1270.02	1229.99	1199.52	1176.03
65000	6075.82	3364.07	2473.99	2039.09	1786.01	1623.57	1512.67	1433.73	1375.85	1332.49	1299.47	1274.03
70000	6543.19	3622.84	2664.29	2195.94	1923.39	1748.46	1629.03	1544.02	1481.68	1434.99	1399.43	1372.03
75000	7010.56	3881.61	2854.60	2352.79	2060.78	1873.35	1745.39	1654.30	1587.52	1537.49	1499.39	1470.03
80000	7477.93	4140.39	3044.90	2509.65	2198.16	1998.24	1861.75	1764.59	1693.35	1639.98	1599.35	1568.04
85000	7945.30	4399.16	3235.21	2666.50	2335.55	2123.13	1978.11	1874.88	1799.19	1742.48	1699.31	1666.04
90000	8412.67	4657.94	3425.52	2823.35	2472.93	2248.02	2094.47	1985.16	1905.02	1844.98	1799.27	1764.04
95000	8880.05	4916.71	3615.82	2980.20	2610.32	2372.91	2210.83	2095.45	2010.86	1947.48	1899.23	1862.04
100000	9347.42	5175.48	3806.13	3137.06	2747.70	2497.80	2327.19	2205.73	2116.69	2049.98	1999.19	1960.04

21%

136

Table 1

MONTHLY   21.75%

PAYMENT REQUIRED TO AMORTIZE A LOAN

TERM / AMOUNT	13 YEARS	14 YEARS	15 YEARS	16 YEARS	17 YEARS	18 YEARS	19 YEARS	20 YEARS	25 YEARS	30 YEARS	35 YEARS	40 YEARS
50	.97	.96	.95	.94	.94	.93	.93	.92	.92	.91	.91	.91
100	1.93	1.91	1.89	1.88	1.87	1.86	1.85	1.84	1.83	1.82	1.82	1.82
200	3.86	3.82	3.78	3.75	3.73	3.71	3.69	3.68	3.65	3.64	3.63	3.63
300	5.79	5.72	5.67	5.62	5.59	5.56	5.53	5.52	5.47	5.45	5.45	5.44
400	7.72	7.63	7.55	7.49	7.45	7.41	7.38	7.35	7.29	7.27	7.26	7.26
500	9.65	9.53	9.44	9.36	9.31	9.26	9.22	9.19	9.11	9.08	9.07	9.07
600	11.58	11.44	11.33	11.24	11.17	11.11	11.06	11.03	10.93	10.90	10.89	10.88
700	13.51	13.34	13.21	13.11	13.03	12.96	12.91	12.87	12.75	12.71	12.70	12.69
800	15.44	15.25	15.10	14.98	14.89	14.81	14.75	14.70	14.57	14.53	14.51	14.51
900	17.37	17.16	16.99	16.85	16.75	16.66	16.59	16.54	16.39	16.34	16.33	16.32
1000	19.30	19.06	18.87	18.72	18.61	18.51	18.44	18.38	18.21	18.16	18.14	18.13
2000	38.60	38.12	37.74	37.44	37.21	37.02	36.87	36.75	36.42	36.31	36.27	36.26
3000	57.89	57.18	56.61	56.16	55.81	55.53	55.30	55.12	54.63	54.46	54.41	54.39
4000	77.19	76.23	75.48	74.88	74.41	74.03	73.73	73.49	72.84	72.62	72.54	72.52
5000	96.48	95.29	94.35	93.60	93.01	92.54	92.16	91.86	91.05	90.77	90.68	90.65
6000	115.78	114.35	113.22	112.32	111.61	111.05	110.60	110.23	109.25	108.92	108.81	108.77
7000	135.08	133.40	132.09	131.04	130.22	129.56	129.03	128.61	127.46	127.08	126.95	126.90
8000	154.37	152.46	150.96	149.76	148.82	148.06	147.46	146.98	145.67	145.23	145.08	145.03
9000	173.67	171.52	169.83	168.48	167.42	166.57	165.89	165.35	163.88	163.38	163.22	163.16
10000	192.96	190.58	188.69	187.20	186.02	185.08	184.32	183.72	182.09	181.54	181.35	181.29
11000	212.26	209.63	207.56	205.92	204.62	203.58	202.76	202.09	200.29	199.69	199.49	199.42
12000	231.55	228.69	226.43	224.64	223.22	222.09	221.19	220.46	218.50	217.84	217.62	217.54
13000	250.85	247.75	245.30	243.36	241.83	240.60	239.62	238.83	236.71	236.00	235.75	235.67
14000	270.15	266.80	264.17	262.08	260.43	259.11	258.05	257.21	254.92	254.15	253.89	253.80
15000	289.44	285.86	283.04	280.80	279.03	277.61	276.48	275.58	273.13	272.30	272.02	271.93
16000	308.74	304.92	301.91	299.52	297.63	296.12	294.91	293.95	291.34	290.46	290.16	290.06
17000	328.03	323.98	320.78	318.24	316.23	314.63	313.35	312.32	309.54	308.61	308.29	308.19
18000	347.33	343.03	339.65	336.96	334.83	333.13	331.78	330.69	327.75	326.76	326.43	326.31
19000	366.63	362.09	358.52	355.68	353.43	351.64	350.21	349.06	345.96	344.92	344.56	344.44
20000	385.92	381.15	377.38	374.40	372.04	370.15	368.64	367.44	364.17	363.07	362.70	362.57
21000	405.22	400.20	396.25	393.12	390.64	388.66	387.07	385.81	382.38	381.22	380.83	380.70
22000	424.51	419.26	415.12	411.84	409.24	407.16	405.51	404.18	400.58	399.38	398.97	398.83
23000	443.81	438.32	433.99	430.56	427.84	425.67	423.94	422.55	418.79	417.53	417.10	416.96
24000	463.10	457.38	452.86	449.28	446.44	444.18	442.37	440.92	437.00	435.68	435.24	435.09
25000	482.40	476.43	471.73	468.00	465.04	462.69	460.80	459.29	455.21	453.84	453.37	453.21
26000	501.70	495.49	490.60	486.72	483.65	481.19	479.23	477.66	473.42	471.99	471.50	471.34
27000	520.99	514.55	509.47	505.44	502.25	499.70	497.66	496.04	491.63	490.14	489.64	489.47
28000	540.29	533.60	528.34	524.16	520.85	518.21	516.10	514.41	509.83	508.30	507.77	507.60
29000	559.58	552.66	547.20	542.88	539.45	536.71	534.53	532.78	528.04	526.45	525.91	525.72
30000	578.88	571.72	566.07	561.60	558.05	555.22	552.96	551.15	546.25	544.60	544.04	543.85
31000	598.18	590.78	584.94	580.32	576.65	573.73	571.39	569.52	564.46	562.75	562.18	561.98
32000	617.47	609.83	603.81	599.04	595.26	592.24	589.82	587.89	582.67	580.91	580.31	580.11
33000	636.77	628.89	622.68	617.76	613.86	610.74	608.26	606.27	600.87	599.06	598.45	598.24
34000	656.06	647.95	641.55	636.48	632.46	629.25	626.69	624.64	619.08	617.21	616.58	616.37
35000	675.36	667.00	660.42	655.20	651.06	647.76	645.12	643.01	637.29	635.37	634.72	634.49
36000	694.65	686.06	679.29	673.92	669.66	666.26	663.55	661.38	655.50	653.52	652.85	652.62
37000	713.95	705.12	698.16	692.64	688.26	684.77	681.98	679.75	673.71	671.67	670.99	670.75
38000	733.25	724.18	717.03	711.36	706.86	703.28	700.42	698.12	691.92	689.83	689.12	688.88
39000	752.54	743.23	735.89	730.08	725.47	721.79	718.85	716.49	710.12	707.98	707.25	707.01
40000	771.84	762.29	754.76	748.80	744.07	740.29	737.28	734.87	728.33	726.13	725.39	725.14
41000	791.13	781.35	773.63	767.52	762.67	758.80	755.71	753.24	746.54	744.29	743.52	743.26
42000	810.43	800.40	792.50	786.24	781.27	777.31	774.14	771.61	764.75	762.44	761.66	761.39
43000	829.73	819.46	811.37	804.96	799.87	795.82	792.57	789.98	782.96	780.59	779.79	779.52
44000	849.02	838.52	830.24	823.68	818.47	814.32	811.01	808.35	801.16	798.75	797.93	797.65
45000	868.32	857.58	849.11	842.40	837.08	832.83	829.44	826.72	819.37	816.90	816.06	815.78
46000	887.61	876.63	867.98	861.12	855.68	851.34	847.87	845.10	837.58	835.05	834.20	833.91
47000	906.91	895.69	886.85	879.84	874.28	869.84	866.30	863.47	855.79	853.21	852.33	852.03
48000	926.20	914.75	905.72	898.56	892.88	888.35	884.73	881.84	874.00	871.36	870.47	870.16
49000	945.50	933.80	924.58	917.28	911.48	906.86	903.17	900.21	892.21	889.51	888.60	888.29
50000	964.80	952.86	943.45	936.00	930.08	925.37	921.60	918.58	910.41	907.67	906.73	906.42
55000	1061.28	1048.15	1037.80	1029.60	1023.09	1017.90	1013.76	1010.44	1001.45	998.43	997.41	997.06
60000	1157.75	1143.43	1132.14	1123.20	1116.10	1110.44	1105.92	1102.30	1092.49	1089.20	1088.08	1087.70
65000	1254.23	1238.72	1226.49	1216.80	1209.11	1202.97	1198.07	1194.15	1183.54	1179.96	1178.75	1178.34
70000	1350.71	1334.00	1320.83	1310.40	1302.11	1295.51	1290.23	1286.01	1274.58	1270.73	1269.43	1268.98
75000	1447.19	1429.29	1415.18	1404.00	1395.12	1388.05	1382.39	1377.87	1365.62	1361.50	1360.10	1359.62
80000	1543.67	1524.57	1509.52	1497.60	1488.13	1480.58	1474.55	1469.73	1456.66	1452.26	1450.77	1450.27
85000	1640.15	1619.86	1603.87	1591.20	1581.14	1573.12	1566.71	1561.59	1547.70	1543.03	1541.45	1540.91
90000	1736.63	1715.15	1698.21	1684.80	1674.15	1665.65	1658.87	1653.44	1638.74	1633.79	1632.12	1631.55
95000	1833.11	1810.43	1792.56	1778.40	1767.15	1758.19	1751.03	1745.30	1729.78	1724.56	1722.79	1722.19
100000	1929.59	1905.72	1886.90	1872.00	1860.16	1850.73	1843.19	1837.16	1820.82	1815.33	1813.46	1812.83

21%

Table 1

22.00%

MONTHLY
PAYMENT REQUIRED TO AMORTIZE A LOAN

TERM AMOUNT	1 YEAR	2 YEARS	3 YEARS	4 YEARS	5 YEARS	6 YEARS	7 YEARS	8 YEARS	9 YEARS	10 YEARS	11 YEARS	12 YEARS
50	4.68	2.60	1.91	1.58	1.39	1.26	1.18	1.12	1.07	1.04	1.01	.99
100	9.36	5.19	3.82	3.16	2.77	2.52	2.35	2.23	2.14	2.07	2.02	1.98
200	18.72	10.38	7.64	6.31	5.53	5.03	4.69	4.45	4.27	4.14	4.04	3.96
300	28.08	15.57	11.46	9.46	8.29	7.54	7.03	6.67	6.40	6.21	6.05	5.94
400	37.44	20.76	15.28	12.61	11.05	10.06	9.38	8.89	8.54	8.27	8.07	7.92
500	46.80	25.94	19.10	15.76	13.81	12.57	11.72	11.11	10.67	10.34	10.09	9.89
600	56.16	31.13	22.92	18.91	16.58	15.08	14.06	13.34	12.80	12.41	12.10	11.87
700	65.52	36.32	26.74	22.06	19.34	17.59	16.40	15.56	14.94	14.47	14.12	13.85
800	74.88	41.51	30.56	25.21	22.10	20.11	18.75	17.78	17.07	16.54	16.14	15.83
900	84.24	46.70	34.38	28.36	24.86	22.62	21.09	20.00	19.20	18.61	18.15	17.81
1000	93.60	51.88	38.20	31.51	27.62	25.13	23.43	22.22	21.34	20.67	20.17	19.78
2000	187.19	103.76	76.39	63.02	55.24	50.26	46.86	44.44	42.67	41.34	40.34	39.56
3000	280.79	155.64	114.58	94.52	82.86	75.38	70.28	66.66	64.00	62.01	60.50	59.34
4000	374.38	207.52	152.77	126.03	110.48	100.51	93.71	88.87	85.33	82.68	80.67	79.12
5000	467.98	259.40	190.96	157.54	138.10	125.64	117.13	111.09	106.66	103.35	100.84	98.90
6000	561.57	311.27	229.15	189.04	165.72	150.76	140.56	133.31	128.00	124.02	121.00	118.68
7000	655.17	363.15	267.34	220.55	193.34	175.89	163.99	155.52	149.33	144.69	141.17	138.46
8000	748.76	415.03	305.53	252.05	220.96	201.01	187.41	177.74	170.66	165.36	161.34	158.24
9000	842.35	466.91	343.72	283.56	248.58	226.14	210.84	199.96	191.99	186.03	181.50	178.02
10000	935.95	518.79	381.91	315.07	276.19	251.27	234.26	222.18	213.32	206.70	201.67	197.79
11000	1029.54	570.66	420.10	346.57	303.81	276.39	257.69	244.39	234.66	227.37	221.83	217.57
12000	1123.14	622.54	458.29	378.08	331.43	301.52	281.12	266.61	255.99	248.04	242.00	237.35
13000	1216.73	674.42	496.48	409.58	359.05	326.64	304.54	288.83	277.32	268.71	262.17	257.13
14000	1310.33	726.30	534.67	441.09	386.67	351.77	327.97	311.04	298.65	289.38	282.33	276.91
15000	1403.92	778.18	572.86	472.60	414.29	376.90	351.39	333.26	319.98	310.05	302.50	296.69
16000	1497.52	830.06	611.05	504.10	441.91	402.02	374.82	355.48	341.32	330.72	322.67	316.47
17000	1591.11	881.93	649.24	535.61	469.53	427.15	398.25	377.70	362.65	351.39	342.83	336.25
18000	1684.70	933.81	687.43	567.11	497.15	452.28	421.67	399.91	383.98	372.06	363.00	356.03
19000	1778.30	985.69	725.62	598.62	524.76	477.40	445.10	422.13	405.31	392.73	383.16	375.80
20000	1871.89	1037.57	763.81	630.13	552.38	502.53	468.52	444.35	426.64	413.40	403.33	395.58
21000	1965.49	1089.45	802.00	661.63	580.00	527.65	491.95	466.56	447.97	434.07	423.50	415.36
22000	2059.08	1141.32	840.19	693.14	607.62	552.78	515.38	488.78	469.31	454.74	443.66	435.14
23000	2152.68	1193.20	878.39	724.64	635.24	577.91	538.80	511.00	490.64	475.41	463.83	454.92
24000	2246.27	1245.08	916.58	756.15	662.86	603.03	562.23	533.21	511.97	496.08	484.00	474.70
25000	2339.86	1296.96	954.77	787.66	690.48	628.16	585.65	555.43	533.30	516.75	504.16	494.48
26000	2433.46	1348.84	992.96	819.16	718.10	653.28	609.08	577.65	554.63	537.42	524.33	514.26
27000	2527.05	1400.72	1031.15	850.67	745.72	678.41	632.51	599.87	575.97	558.09	544.49	534.04
28000	2620.65	1452.59	1069.34	882.18	773.33	703.54	655.93	622.08	597.30	578.76	564.66	553.82
29000	2714.24	1504.47	1107.53	913.68	800.95	728.66	679.36	644.30	618.63	599.43	584.83	573.59
30000	2807.84	1556.35	1145.72	945.19	828.57	753.79	702.78	666.52	639.96	620.10	604.99	593.37
31000	2901.43	1608.23	1183.91	976.69	856.19	778.91	726.21	688.73	661.29	640.77	625.16	613.15
32000	2995.03	1660.11	1222.10	1008.20	883.81	804.04	749.64	710.95	682.63	661.44	645.33	632.93
33000	3088.62	1711.98	1260.29	1039.71	911.43	829.17	773.06	733.17	703.96	682.10	665.49	652.71
34000	3182.21	1763.86	1298.48	1071.21	939.05	854.29	796.49	755.39	725.29	702.77	685.66	672.49
35000	3275.81	1815.74	1336.67	1102.72	966.67	879.42	819.91	777.60	746.62	723.44	705.83	692.27
36000	3369.40	1867.62	1374.86	1134.22	994.29	904.55	843.34	799.82	767.95	744.11	725.99	712.05
37000	3463.00	1919.50	1413.05	1165.73	1021.90	929.67	866.76	822.04	789.29	764.78	746.16	731.83
38000	3556.59	1971.37	1451.24	1197.24	1049.52	954.80	890.19	844.25	810.62	785.45	766.32	751.60
39000	3650.19	2023.25	1489.43	1228.74	1077.14	979.92	913.62	866.47	831.95	806.12	786.49	771.38
40000	3743.78	2075.13	1527.62	1260.25	1104.76	1005.05	937.04	888.69	853.28	826.79	806.66	791.16
41000	3837.37	2127.01	1565.81	1291.75	1132.38	1030.18	960.47	910.91	874.61	847.46	826.82	810.94
42000	3930.97	2178.89	1604.00	1323.26	1160.00	1055.30	983.89	933.12	895.94	868.13	846.99	830.72
43000	4024.56	2230.77	1642.19	1354.77	1187.62	1080.43	1007.32	955.34	917.28	888.80	867.16	850.50
44000	4118.15	2282.64	1680.38	1386.27	1215.24	1105.55	1030.75	977.56	938.61	909.47	887.32	870.28
45000	4211.75	2334.52	1718.58	1417.78	1242.86	1130.68	1054.17	999.77	959.94	930.14	907.49	890.06
46000	4305.35	2386.40	1756.77	1449.28	1270.47	1155.81	1077.60	1021.99	981.27	950.81	927.65	909.84
47000	4398.94	2438.28	1794.96	1480.79	1298.09	1180.93	1101.02	1044.21	1002.60	971.48	947.82	929.61
48000	4492.54	2490.16	1833.15	1512.30	1325.71	1206.06	1124.45	1066.42	1023.94	992.15	967.99	949.39
49000	4586.13	2542.03	1871.34	1543.80	1353.33	1231.19	1147.88	1088.64	1045.27	1012.82	988.15	969.17
50000	4679.72	2593.91	1909.53	1575.31	1380.95	1256.31	1171.30	1110.86	1066.60	1033.49	1008.32	988.95
55000	5147.70	2853.30	2100.48	1732.84	1519.05	1381.94	1288.43	1221.94	1173.26	1136.84	1109.15	1087.85
60000	5615.67	3112.69	2291.43	1890.37	1657.14	1507.57	1405.56	1333.03	1279.92	1240.19	1209.98	1186.74
65000	6083.64	3372.09	2482.38	2047.90	1795.23	1633.20	1522.69	1444.12	1386.58	1343.53	1310.81	1285.64
70000	6551.61	3631.48	2673.34	2205.43	1933.33	1758.83	1639.82	1555.20	1493.24	1446.88	1411.65	1384.53
75000	7019.58	3890.87	2864.29	2362.96	2071.42	1884.46	1756.95	1666.29	1599.90	1550.23	1512.48	1483.43
80000	7487.56	4150.26	3055.24	2520.49	2209.52	2010.10	1874.08	1777.37	1706.56	1653.58	1613.31	1582.32
85000	7955.53	4409.65	3246.19	2678.02	2347.61	2135.73	1991.21	1888.46	1813.22	1756.93	1714.14	1681.21
90000	8423.50	4669.04	3437.15	2835.55	2485.71	2261.36	2108.34	1999.54	1919.88	1860.28	1814.97	1780.11
95000	8891.47	4928.43	3628.10	2993.08	2623.80	2386.99	2225.47	2110.63	2026.54	1963.63	1915.80	1879.00
100000	9359.44	5187.82	3819.05	3150.61	2761.90	2512.62	2342.60	2221.71	2133.20	2066.97	2016.63	1977.90

22%

Table 1

MONTHLY 22.00%

PAYMENT REQUIRED TO AMORTIZE A LOAN

TERM AMOUNT	13 YEARS	14 YEARS	15 YEARS	16 YEARS	17 YEARS	18 YEARS	19 YEARS	20 YEARS	25 YEARS	30 YEARS	35 YEARS	40 YEARS
50	.98	.97	.96	.95	.94	.94	.94	.93	.93	.92	.92	.92
100	1.95	1.93	1.91	1.90	1.88	1.88	1.87	1.86	1.85	1.84	1.84	1.84
200	3.90	3.85	3.82	3.79	3.76	3.75	3.73	3.72	3.69	3.68	3.67	3.67
300	5.85	5.78	5.72	5.68	5.64	5.62	5.59	5.58	5.53	5.51	5.51	5.51
400	7.80	7.70	7.63	7.57	7.52	7.49	7.46	7.43	7.37	7.35	7.34	7.34
500	9.74	9.63	9.53	9.46	9.40	9.36	9.32	9.29	9.21	9.18	9.18	9.17
600	11.69	11.55	11.44	11.35	11.28	11.23	11.18	11.15	11.05	11.02	11.01	11.01
700	13.64	13.47	13.35	13.24	13.16	13.10	13.05	13.00	12.89	12.86	12.84	12.84
800	15.59	15.40	15.25	15.13	15.04	14.97	14.91	14.86	14.73	14.69	14.68	14.67
900	17.54	17.32	17.16	17.03	16.92	16.84	16.77	16.72	16.58	16.53	16.51	16.51
1000	19.48	19.25	19.06	18.92	18.80	18.71	18.63	18.58	18.42	18.36	18.35	18.34
2000	38.96	38.49	38.12	37.83	37.60	37.41	37.26	37.15	36.83	36.72	36.69	36.68
3000	58.44	57.73	57.18	56.74	56.39	56.11	55.89	55.72	55.24	55.08	55.03	55.01
4000	77.92	76.98	76.24	75.65	75.19	74.82	74.52	74.29	73.65	73.44	73.37	73.35
5000	97.40	96.22	95.29	94.56	93.98	93.52	93.15	92.86	92.07	91.80	91.72	91.69
6000	116.87	115.46	114.35	113.47	112.78	112.22	111.78	111.43	110.48	110.16	110.06	110.02
7000	136.35	134.70	133.41	132.38	131.57	130.93	130.41	130.00	128.89	128.52	128.40	128.36
8000	155.83	153.95	152.47	151.29	150.37	149.63	149.04	148.57	147.30	146.88	146.74	146.70
9000	175.31	173.19	171.52	170.21	169.16	168.33	167.67	167.14	165.72	165.24	165.09	165.03
10000	194.79	192.43	190.58	189.12	187.96	187.03	186.30	185.71	184.13	183.60	183.43	183.37
11000	214.26	211.68	209.64	208.03	206.75	205.74	204.93	204.28	202.54	201.96	201.77	201.70
12000	233.74	230.92	228.70	226.94	225.55	224.44	223.56	222.85	220.95	220.32	220.11	220.04
13000	253.22	250.16	247.75	245.85	244.34	243.14	242.19	241.42	239.37	238.68	238.45	238.38
14000	272.70	269.40	266.81	264.76	263.14	261.85	260.82	259.99	257.78	257.04	256.80	256.71
15000	292.18	288.65	285.87	283.67	281.93	280.55	279.44	278.56	276.19	275.40	275.14	275.05
16000	311.65	307.89	304.93	302.58	300.73	299.25	298.07	297.13	294.60	293.76	293.48	293.39
17000	331.13	327.13	323.98	321.50	319.52	317.95	316.70	315.71	313.02	312.12	311.82	311.72
18000	350.61	346.37	343.04	340.41	338.32	336.66	335.33	334.28	331.43	330.48	330.17	330.06
19000	370.09	365.62	362.10	359.32	357.11	355.36	353.96	352.85	349.84	348.84	348.51	348.40
20000	389.57	384.86	381.16	378.23	375.91	374.06	372.59	371.42	368.25	367.20	366.85	366.73
21000	409.04	404.10	400.21	397.14	394.70	392.77	391.22	389.99	386.67	385.56	385.19	385.07
22000	428.52	423.35	419.27	416.05	413.50	411.47	409.85	408.56	405.08	403.92	403.53	403.40
23000	448.00	442.59	438.33	434.96	432.29	430.17	428.48	427.13	423.49	422.28	421.88	421.74
24000	467.48	461.83	457.39	453.87	451.09	448.87	447.11	445.70	441.90	440.64	440.22	440.08
25000	486.96	481.07	476.44	472.79	469.88	467.58	465.74	464.27	460.32	459.00	458.56	458.41
26000	506.44	500.32	495.50	491.70	488.68	486.28	484.37	482.84	478.73	477.36	476.90	476.75
27000	525.91	519.56	514.56	510.61	507.47	504.98	503.00	501.41	497.14	495.72	495.25	495.09
28000	545.39	538.80	533.62	529.52	526.27	523.69	521.63	519.98	515.55	514.08	513.59	513.42
29000	564.87	558.04	552.67	548.43	545.07	542.39	540.26	538.55	533.97	532.44	531.93	531.76
30000	584.35	577.29	571.73	567.34	563.86	561.09	558.88	557.12	552.38	550.80	550.27	550.09
31000	603.83	596.53	590.79	586.25	582.66	579.79	577.51	575.69	570.79	569.16	568.61	568.43
32000	623.30	615.77	609.85	605.16	601.45	598.50	596.14	594.26	589.20	587.52	586.96	586.77
33000	642.78	635.02	628.90	624.08	620.25	617.20	614.77	612.83	607.61	605.88	605.30	605.10
34000	662.26	654.26	647.96	642.99	639.04	635.90	633.40	631.41	626.03	624.24	623.64	623.44
35000	681.74	673.50	667.02	661.90	657.84	654.61	652.03	649.98	644.44	642.60	641.98	641.78
36000	701.22	692.74	686.08	680.81	676.63	673.31	670.66	668.55	662.85	660.96	660.33	660.11
37000	720.69	711.99	705.13	699.72	695.43	692.01	689.29	687.12	681.26	679.32	678.67	678.45
38000	740.17	731.23	724.19	718.63	714.22	710.71	707.92	705.69	699.68	697.68	697.01	696.79
39000	759.65	750.47	743.25	737.54	733.02	729.42	726.55	724.26	718.09	716.04	715.35	715.12
40000	779.13	769.71	762.31	756.45	751.81	748.12	745.18	742.83	736.50	734.40	733.69	733.46
41000	798.61	788.96	781.36	775.37	770.61	766.82	763.81	761.40	754.91	752.76	752.04	751.79
42000	818.08	808.20	800.42	794.28	789.40	785.53	782.44	779.97	773.33	771.12	770.38	770.13
43000	837.56	827.44	819.48	813.19	808.20	804.23	801.07	798.54	791.74	789.48	788.72	788.47
44000	857.04	846.69	838.54	832.10	826.99	822.93	819.70	817.11	810.15	807.84	807.06	806.80
45000	876.52	865.93	857.60	851.01	845.79	841.63	838.32	835.68	828.56	826.20	825.41	825.14
46000	896.00	885.17	876.65	869.92	864.58	860.34	856.95	854.25	846.98	844.56	843.75	843.48
47000	915.48	904.41	895.71	888.83	883.38	879.04	875.58	872.82	865.39	862.92	862.09	861.81
48000	934.95	923.66	914.77	907.74	902.17	897.74	894.21	891.39	883.80	881.28	880.43	880.15
49000	954.43	942.90	933.83	926.66	920.97	916.45	912.84	909.96	902.21	899.64	898.77	898.48
50000	973.91	962.14	952.88	945.57	939.76	935.15	931.47	928.53	920.63	918.00	917.12	916.82
55000	1071.30	1058.36	1048.17	1040.12	1033.74	1028.66	1024.62	1021.39	1012.69	1009.80	1008.83	1008.50
60000	1168.69	1154.57	1143.46	1134.68	1127.72	1122.18	1117.76	1114.24	1104.75	1101.60	1100.54	1100.18
65000	1266.08	1250.78	1238.75	1229.23	1221.69	1215.69	1210.91	1207.09	1196.81	1193.40	1192.25	1191.87
70000	1363.47	1347.00	1334.03	1323.79	1315.67	1309.21	1304.06	1299.95	1288.87	1285.19	1283.96	1283.55
75000	1460.86	1443.21	1429.32	1418.35	1409.64	1402.72	1397.20	1392.80	1380.94	1376.99	1375.67	1375.23
80000	1558.25	1539.42	1524.61	1512.90	1503.62	1496.24	1490.35	1485.65	1473.00	1468.79	1467.38	1466.91
85000	1655.64	1635.64	1619.90	1607.46	1597.60	1589.75	1583.50	1578.51	1565.06	1560.59	1559.10	1558.59
90000	1753.03	1731.85	1715.19	1702.02	1691.57	1683.26	1676.64	1671.36	1657.12	1652.39	1650.81	1650.27
95000	1850.42	1828.06	1810.47	1796.57	1785.55	1776.78	1769.79	1764.21	1749.19	1744.19	1742.52	1741.96
00000	1947.81	1924.28	1905.76	1891.13	1879.52	1870.29	1862.94	1857.06	1841.25	1835.99	1834.23	1833.64

22%

Table 1

22.25%

MONTHLY
PAYMENT REQUIRED TO AMORTIZE A LOAN

TERM / AMOUNT	1 YEAR	2 YEARS	3 YEARS	4 YEARS	5 YEARS	6 YEARS	7 YEARS	8 YEARS	9 YEARS	10 YEARS	11 YEARS	12 YEARS
50	4.69	2.61	1.92	1.59	1.39	1.27	1.18	1.12	1.08	1.05	1.02	1.00
100	9.38	5.21	3.84	3.17	2.78	2.53	2.36	2.24	2.15	2.09	2.04	2.00
200	18.75	10.41	7.67	6.33	5.56	5.06	4.72	4.48	4.30	4.17	4.07	4.00
300	28.12	15.61	11.50	9.50	8.33	7.59	7.08	6.72	6.45	6.26	6.11	5.99
400	37.49	20.81	15.33	12.66	11.11	10.11	9.44	8.96	8.60	8.34	8.14	7.99
500	46.86	26.01	19.16	15.83	13.89	12.64	11.80	11.19	10.75	10.43	10.18	9.98
600	56.23	31.21	23.00	18.99	16.66	15.17	14.15	13.43	12.90	12.51	12.21	11.98
700	65.61	36.41	26.83	22.15	19.44	17.70	16.51	15.67	15.05	14.59	14.24	13.98
800	74.98	41.61	30.66	25.32	22.21	20.22	18.87	17.91	17.20	16.68	16.28	15.97
900	84.35	46.81	34.49	28.48	24.99	22.75	21.23	20.14	19.35	18.76	18.31	17.97
1000	93.72	52.01	38.32	31.65	27.77	25.28	23.59	22.38	21.50	20.85	20.35	19.96
2000	187.43	104.01	76.64	63.29	55.53	50.55	47.17	44.76	43.00	41.69	40.69	39.92
3000	281.15	156.01	114.96	94.93	83.29	75.83	70.75	67.14	64.50	62.53	61.03	59.88
4000	374.86	208.01	153.28	126.57	111.05	101.10	94.33	89.51	85.99	83.37	81.37	79.84
5000	468.58	260.01	191.60	158.21	138.81	126.38	117.91	111.89	107.49	104.21	101.71	99.80
6000	562.29	312.02	229.92	189.86	166.57	151.65	141.49	134.27	128.99	125.05	122.05	119.75
7000	656.01	364.02	268.24	221.50	194.33	176.93	165.07	156.65	150.49	145.89	142.39	139.71
8000	749.72	416.02	306.56	253.14	222.09	202.20	188.65	179.02	171.98	166.73	162.74	159.67
9000	843.44	468.02	344.88	284.78	249.86	227.48	212.23	201.40	193.48	187.57	183.08	179.63
10000	937.15	520.02	383.20	316.42	277.62	252.75	235.81	223.78	214.98	208.41	203.42	199.59
11000	1030.87	572.02	421.52	348.07	305.38	278.03	259.39	246.16	236.48	229.25	223.76	219.54
12000	1124.58	624.03	459.84	379.71	333.14	303.30	282.97	268.53	257.97	250.09	244.10	239.50
13000	1218.30	676.03	498.16	411.35	360.90	328.58	306.55	290.91	279.47	270.93	264.44	259.46
14000	1312.01	728.03	536.48	442.99	388.66	353.85	330.13	313.29	300.97	291.77	284.78	279.42
15000	1405.73	780.03	574.80	474.63	416.42	379.13	353.71	335.67	322.47	312.61	305.12	299.38
16000	1499.44	832.03	613.12	506.28	444.18	404.40	377.29	358.04	343.96	333.45	325.47	319.33
17000	1593.16	884.03	651.44	537.92	471.95	429.68	400.87	380.42	365.46	354.29	345.81	339.29
18000	1686.87	936.04	689.76	569.56	499.71	454.95	424.46	402.80	386.96	375.13	366.15	359.25
19000	1780.59	988.04	728.08	601.20	527.47	480.22	448.04	425.17	408.46	395.97	386.49	379.21
20000	1874.30	1040.04	766.40	632.84	555.23	505.50	471.62	447.55	429.95	416.81	406.83	399.17
21000	1968.01	1092.04	804.72	664.49	582.99	530.77	495.20	469.93	451.45	437.65	427.17	419.12
22000	2061.73	1144.04	843.04	696.13	610.75	556.05	518.78	492.31	472.95	458.49	447.51	439.08
23000	2155.44	1196.04	881.36	727.77	638.51	581.32	542.36	514.68	494.45	479.33	467.85	459.04
24000	2249.16	1248.05	919.68	759.41	666.27	606.60	565.94	537.06	515.94	500.17	488.20	479.00
25000	2342.87	1300.05	958.00	791.05	694.04	631.87	589.52	559.44	537.44	521.01	508.54	498.96
26000	2436.59	1352.05	996.32	822.70	721.80	657.15	613.10	581.82	558.94	541.85	528.88	518.91
27000	2530.30	1404.05	1034.64	854.34	749.56	682.42	636.68	604.19	580.44	562.69	549.22	538.87
28000	2624.02	1456.05	1072.96	885.98	777.32	707.70	660.26	626.57	601.93	583.53	569.56	558.83
29000	2717.73	1508.05	1111.28	917.62	805.08	732.97	683.84	648.95	623.43	604.37	589.90	578.79
30000	2811.45	1560.06	1149.60	949.26	832.84	758.25	707.42	671.33	644.93	625.21	610.24	598.75
31000	2905.16	1612.06	1187.92	980.91	860.60	783.52	731.00	693.70	666.43	646.05	630.58	618.70
32000	2998.88	1664.06	1226.24	1012.55	888.36	808.80	754.58	716.08	687.92	666.89	650.93	638.66
33000	3092.59	1716.06	1264.56	1044.19	916.13	834.07	778.16	738.46	709.42	687.73	671.27	658.62
34000	3186.31	1768.06	1302.88	1075.83	943.89	859.35	801.74	760.84	730.92	708.57	691.61	678.58
35000	3280.02	1820.06	1341.20	1107.47	971.65	884.62	825.32	783.21	752.42	729.41	711.95	698.54
36000	3373.74	1872.07	1379.52	1139.12	999.41	909.90	848.91	805.59	773.91	750.25	732.29	718.49
37000	3467.45	1924.07	1417.84	1170.76	1027.17	935.17	872.49	827.97	795.41	771.09	752.63	738.45
38000	3561.17	1976.07	1456.16	1202.40	1054.93	960.44	896.07	850.34	816.91	791.93	772.97	758.41
39000	3654.88	2028.07	1494.48	1234.04	1082.69	985.72	919.65	872.72	838.41	812.77	793.31	778.37
40000	3748.59	2080.07	1532.80	1265.68	1110.45	1010.99	943.23	895.10	859.90	833.61	813.66	798.33
41000	3842.31	2132.07	1571.12	1297.33	1138.22	1036.27	966.81	917.48	881.40	854.45	834.00	818.28
42000	3936.02	2184.08	1609.44	1328.97	1165.98	1061.54	990.39	939.85	902.90	875.29	854.34	838.24
43000	4029.74	2236.08	1647.76	1360.61	1193.74	1086.82	1013.97	962.23	924.40	896.13	874.68	858.20
44000	4123.45	2288.08	1686.08	1392.25	1221.50	1112.09	1037.55	984.61	945.89	916.97	895.02	878.16
45000	4217.17	2340.08	1724.40	1423.89	1249.26	1137.37	1061.13	1006.99	967.39	937.81	915.36	898.12
46000	4310.88	2392.08	1762.72	1455.54	1277.02	1162.64	1084.71	1029.36	988.89	958.65	935.70	918.07
47000	4404.60	2444.08	1801.04	1487.18	1304.78	1187.92	1108.29	1051.74	1010.39	979.49	956.04	938.03
48000	4498.31	2496.09	1839.36	1518.82	1332.54	1213.19	1131.87	1074.12	1031.88	1000.33	976.39	957.99
49000	4592.03	2548.09	1877.68	1550.46	1360.31	1238.47	1155.45	1096.50	1053.38	1021.17	996.73	977.95
50000	4685.74	2600.09	1916.00	1582.10	1388.07	1263.74	1179.03	1118.87	1074.88	1042.01	1017.07	997.91
55000	5154.32	2860.10	2107.60	1740.31	1526.87	1390.12	1296.94	1230.76	1182.37	1146.21	1118.77	1097.70
60000	5622.89	3120.11	2299.20	1898.52	1665.68	1516.49	1414.84	1342.65	1289.85	1250.42	1220.48	1197.49
65000	6091.46	3380.12	2490.80	2056.73	1804.49	1642.86	1532.74	1454.53	1397.34	1354.62	1322.19	1297.28
70000	6560.04	3640.12	2682.40	2214.94	1943.29	1769.24	1650.64	1566.42	1504.83	1458.82	1423.89	1397.07
75000	7028.61	3900.13	2874.00	2373.15	2082.10	1895.61	1768.55	1678.31	1612.32	1563.02	1525.60	1496.86
80000	7497.18	4160.14	3065.60	2531.36	2220.90	2021.98	1886.45	1790.19	1719.80	1667.22	1627.31	1596.65
85000	7965.76	4420.15	3257.20	2689.57	2359.71	2148.36	2004.35	1902.08	1827.29	1771.42	1729.01	1696.44
90000	8434.33	4680.16	3448.80	2847.78	2498.52	2274.73	2122.26	2013.97	1934.78	1875.62	1830.72	1796.23
95000	8902.91	4940.17	3640.40	3005.99	2637.32	2401.10	2240.16	2125.85	2042.27	1979.82	1932.43	1896.02
100000	9371.48	5200.17	3832.00	3164.20	2776.13	2527.48	2358.06	2237.74	2149.75	2084.02	2034.13	1995.81

22%

Table 1

MONTHLY 22.25%
PAYMENT REQUIRED TO AMORTIZE A LOAN

TERM AMOUNT	13 YEARS	14 YEARS	15 YEARS	16 YEARS	17 YEARS	18 YEARS	19 YEARS	20 YEARS	25 YEARS	30 YEARS	35 YEARS	40 YEARS
50	.99	.98	.97	.96	.95	.95	.95	.94	.94	.93	.93	.93
100	1.97	1.95	1.93	1.92	1.90	1.89	1.89	1.88	1.87	1.86	1.86	1.86
200	3.94	3.89	3.85	3.83	3.80	3.78	3.77	3.76	3.73	3.72	3.71	3.71
300	5.90	5.83	5.78	5.74	5.70	5.67	5.65	5.64	5.59	5.57	5.57	5.57
400	7.87	7.78	7.70	7.65	7.60	7.56	7.54	7.51	7.45	7.43	7.42	7.42
500	9.84	9.72	9.63	9.56	9.50	9.45	9.42	9.39	9.31	9.29	9.28	9.28
600	11.80	11.66	11.55	11.47	11.40	11.34	11.30	11.27	11.18	11.14	11.13	11.13
700	13.77	13.61	13.48	13.38	13.30	13.23	13.18	13.14	13.04	13.00	12.99	12.99
800	15.73	15.55	15.40	15.29	15.20	15.12	15.07	15.02	14.90	14.86	14.84	14.84
900	17.70	17.49	17.33	17.20	17.10	17.01	16.95	16.90	16.76	16.71	16.70	16.69
1000	19.67	19.43	19.25	19.11	18.99	18.90	18.83	18.77	18.62	18.57	18.55	18.55
2000	39.33	38.86	38.50	38.21	37.98	37.80	37.66	37.54	37.24	37.14	37.10	37.09
3000	58.99	58.29	57.74	57.31	56.97	56.70	56.49	56.31	55.86	55.70	55.65	55.64
4000	78.65	77.72	76.99	76.42	75.96	75.60	75.31	75.08	74.47	74.27	74.20	74.18
5000	98.31	97.15	96.24	95.52	94.95	94.50	94.14	93.85	93.09	92.84	92.75	92.73
6000	117.97	116.58	115.48	114.62	113.94	113.40	112.97	112.62	111.71	111.40	111.30	111.27
7000	137.63	136.01	134.73	133.73	132.93	132.30	131.80	131.39	130.32	129.97	129.85	129.82
8000	157.29	155.44	153.98	152.83	151.92	151.20	150.62	150.16	148.94	148.54	148.40	148.36
9000	176.95	174.86	173.22	171.93	170.91	170.10	169.45	168.93	167.56	167.10	166.95	166.90
10000	196.61	194.29	192.47	191.03	189.90	188.99	188.28	187.70	186.17	185.67	185.50	185.45
11000	216.27	213.72	211.72	210.14	208.89	207.89	207.10	206.47	204.79	204.24	204.05	203.99
12000	235.94	233.15	230.96	229.24	227.88	226.79	225.93	225.24	223.41	222.80	222.60	222.54
13000	255.60	252.58	250.21	248.34	246.86	245.69	244.76	244.01	242.02	241.37	241.15	241.08
14000	275.26	272.01	269.45	267.45	265.85	264.59	263.59	262.78	260.64	259.94	259.70	259.63
15000	294.92	291.44	288.70	286.55	284.84	283.49	282.41	281.55	279.26	278.50	278.25	278.17
16000	314.58	310.87	307.95	305.65	303.83	302.39	301.24	300.32	297.88	297.07	296.80	296.72
17000	334.24	330.30	327.20	324.75	322.82	321.29	320.07	319.09	316.49	315.64	315.35	315.26
18000	353.90	349.72	346.44	343.86	341.81	340.19	338.89	337.86	335.11	334.20	333.90	333.80
19000	373.56	369.15	365.69	362.96	360.80	359.09	357.72	356.63	353.73	352.77	352.45	352.35
20000	393.22	388.58	384.94	382.06	379.79	377.98	376.55	375.40	372.34	371.34	371.00	370.89
21000	412.88	408.01	404.18	401.17	398.78	396.88	395.38	394.17	390.96	389.90	389.55	389.44
22000	432.54	427.44	423.43	420.27	417.77	415.78	414.20	412.94	409.58	408.47	408.10	407.98
23000	452.21	446.87	442.68	439.37	436.76	434.68	433.03	431.71	428.19	427.04	426.65	426.53
24000	471.87	466.30	461.92	458.48	455.75	453.58	451.86	450.48	446.81	445.60	445.20	445.07
25000	491.53	485.73	481.17	477.58	474.74	472.48	470.68	469.25	465.43	464.17	463.75	463.62
26000	511.19	505.15	500.42	496.68	493.72	491.38	489.51	488.02	484.04	482.74	482.30	482.16
27000	530.85	524.58	519.66	515.78	512.71	510.28	508.34	506.79	502.66	501.30	500.85	500.70
28000	550.51	544.01	538.91	534.89	531.70	529.18	527.17	525.56	521.28	519.87	519.40	519.25
29000	570.17	563.44	558.16	553.99	550.69	548.07	545.99	544.33	539.89	538.44	537.95	537.79
30000	589.83	582.87	577.40	573.09	569.68	566.97	564.82	563.10	558.51	557.00	556.50	556.34
31000	609.49	602.30	596.65	592.20	588.67	585.87	583.65	581.87	577.13	575.57	575.05	574.88
32000	629.15	621.73	615.90	611.30	607.66	604.77	602.47	600.64	595.75	594.14	593.60	593.43
33000	648.81	641.16	635.14	630.40	626.65	623.67	621.30	619.41	614.36	612.70	612.15	611.97
34000	668.47	660.59	654.39	649.50	645.64	642.57	640.13	638.18	632.98	631.27	630.70	630.51
35000	688.14	680.01	673.64	668.61	664.63	661.47	658.96	656.95	651.60	649.84	649.25	649.06
36000	707.80	699.44	692.88	687.71	683.62	680.37	677.78	675.72	670.21	668.40	667.80	667.60
37000	727.46	718.87	712.13	706.81	702.61	699.27	696.61	694.49	688.83	686.97	686.35	686.15
38000	747.12	738.30	731.38	725.92	721.59	718.17	715.44	713.26	707.45	705.53	704.90	704.69
39000	766.78	757.73	750.62	745.02	740.58	737.06	734.26	732.03	726.06	724.10	723.45	723.24
40000	786.44	777.16	769.87	764.12	759.57	755.96	753.09	750.80	744.68	742.67	742.00	741.78
41000	806.10	796.59	789.12	783.23	778.56	774.86	771.92	769.57	763.30	761.23	760.55	760.33
42000	825.76	816.02	808.36	802.33	797.55	793.76	790.75	788.34	781.91	779.80	779.10	778.87
43000	845.42	835.45	827.61	821.43	816.54	812.66	809.57	807.11	800.53	798.37	797.65	797.41
44000	865.08	854.87	846.86	840.53	835.53	831.56	828.40	825.88	819.15	816.93	816.20	815.96
45000	884.74	874.30	866.10	859.64	854.52	850.46	847.23	844.65	837.76	835.50	834.75	834.50
46000	904.41	893.73	885.35	878.74	873.51	869.36	866.06	863.42	856.38	854.07	853.30	853.05
47000	924.07	913.16	904.60	897.84	892.50	888.26	884.88	882.19	875.00	872.63	871.85	871.59
48000	943.73	932.59	923.84	916.95	911.49	907.15	903.71	900.96	893.62	891.20	890.40	890.14
49000	963.39	952.02	943.09	936.05	930.48	926.05	922.54	919.73	912.23	909.77	908.95	908.68
50000	983.05	971.45	962.34	955.15	949.47	944.95	941.36	938.50	930.85	928.33	927.50	927.23
55000	1081.35	1068.59	1058.57	1050.67	1044.41	1039.45	1035.50	1032.35	1023.93	1021.17	1020.25	1019.95
60000	1179.66	1165.74	1154.80	1146.18	1139.36	1133.94	1129.64	1126.20	1117.02	1114.00	1113.00	1112.67
65000	1277.96	1262.88	1251.04	1241.70	1234.30	1228.44	1223.77	1220.05	1210.10	1206.83	1205.75	1205.39
70000	1376.27	1360.02	1347.27	1337.21	1329.25	1322.93	1317.91	1313.90	1303.19	1299.67	1298.50	1298.11
75000	1474.57	1457.17	1443.50	1432.73	1424.20	1417.43	1412.04	1407.75	1396.27	1392.50	1391.25	1390.84
80000	1572.87	1554.31	1539.74	1528.24	1519.14	1511.92	1506.18	1501.60	1489.36	1485.33	1484.00	1483.56
85000	1671.18	1651.46	1635.97	1623.75	1614.09	1606.42	1600.31	1595.45	1582.44	1578.16	1576.75	1576.28
90000	1769.48	1748.60	1732.20	1719.27	1709.03	1700.91	1694.45	1689.30	1675.52	1671.00	1669.50	1669.00
95000	1867.79	1845.74	1828.44	1814.78	1803.98	1795.41	1788.59	1783.15	1768.61	1763.83	1762.25	1761.72
100000	1966.09	1942.89	1924.67	1910.30	1898.93	1889.90	1882.72	1877.00	1861.69	1856.66	1855.00	1854.45

22%

Table 1

22.50%

MONTHLY
PAYMENT REQUIRED TO AMORTIZE A LOAN

TERM AMOUNT	1 YEAR	2 YEARS	3 YEARS	4 YEARS	5 YEARS	6 YEARS	7 YEARS	8 YEARS	9 YEARS	10 YEARS	11 YEARS	12 YEARS
50	4.70	2.61	1.93	1.59	1.40	1.28	1.19	1.13	1.09	1.06	1.03	1.01
100	9.39	5.22	3.85	3.18	2.80	2.55	2.38	2.26	2.17	2.11	2.06	2.02
200	18.77	10.43	7.69	6.36	5.59	5.09	4.75	4.51	4.34	4.21	4.11	4.03
300	28.16	15.64	11.54	9.54	8.38	7.63	7.13	6.77	6.50	6.31	6.16	6.05
400	37.54	20.86	15.38	12.72	11.17	10.17	9.50	9.02	8.67	8.41	8.21	8.06
500	46.92	26.07	19.23	15.89	13.96	12.72	11.87	11.27	10.84	10.51	10.26	10.07
600	56.31	31.28	23.07	19.07	16.75	15.26	14.25	13.53	13.00	12.61	12.32	12.09
700	65.69	36.49	26.92	22.25	19.54	17.80	16.62	15.78	15.17	14.71	14.37	14.10
800	75.07	41.71	30.76	25.43	22.33	20.34	18.99	18.04	17.34	16.81	16.42	16.12
900	84.46	46.92	34.61	28.61	25.12	22.89	21.37	20.29	19.50	18.92	18.47	18.13
1000	93.84	52.13	38.45	31.78	27.91	25.43	23.74	22.54	21.67	21.02	20.52	20.14
2000	187.68	104.26	76.90	63.56	55.81	50.85	47.48	45.08	43.33	42.03	41.04	40.28
3000	281.51	156.38	115.35	95.34	83.72	76.28	71.21	67.62	65.00	63.04	61.56	60.42
4000	375.35	208.51	153.80	127.12	111.62	101.70	94.95	90.16	86.66	84.05	82.07	80.56
5000	469.18	260.63	192.25	158.90	139.52	127.12	118.68	112.70	108.32	105.06	102.59	100.69
6000	563.02	312.76	230.70	190.67	167.43	152.55	142.42	135.23	129.99	126.07	123.11	120.83
7000	656.85	364.88	269.15	222.45	195.33	177.97	166.15	157.77	151.65	147.08	143.62	140.97
8000	750.69	417.01	307.60	254.23	223.24	203.40	189.89	180.31	173.31	168.09	164.14	161.11
9000	844.52	469.13	346.05	286.01	251.14	228.82	213.63	202.85	194.98	189.11	184.66	181.24
10000	938.36	521.26	384.50	317.79	279.04	254.24	237.36	225.39	216.64	210.12	205.17	201.38
11000	1032.19	573.38	422.95	349.56	306.95	279.67	261.10	247.92	238.30	231.13	225.69	221.52
12000	1126.03	625.51	461.40	381.34	334.85	305.09	284.83	270.46	259.97	252.14	246.21	241.66
13000	1219.86	677.64	499.85	413.12	362.76	330.51	308.57	293.00	281.63	273.15	266.72	261.79
14000	1313.70	729.76	538.30	444.90	390.66	355.94	332.30	315.54	303.30	294.16	287.24	281.93
15000	1407.53	781.89	576.75	476.68	418.56	381.36	356.04	338.08	324.96	315.17	307.76	302.07
16000	1501.37	834.01	615.20	508.46	446.47	406.79	379.78	360.62	346.63	336.18	328.27	322.21
17000	1595.20	886.14	653.65	540.23	474.37	432.21	403.51	383.15	368.29	357.20	348.79	342.34
18000	1689.04	938.26	692.10	572.01	502.28	457.63	427.25	405.69	389.95	378.21	369.31	362.48
19000	1782.87	990.39	730.55	603.79	530.18	483.06	450.98	428.23	411.61	399.22	389.82	382.62
20000	1876.71	1042.51	769.00	635.57	558.08	508.48	474.72	450.77	433.28	420.23	410.34	402.76
21000	1970.54	1094.64	807.45	667.35	585.99	533.90	498.45	473.31	454.94	441.24	430.86	422.90
22000	2064.38	1146.76	845.90	699.12	613.89	559.33	522.19	495.84	476.60	462.25	451.37	443.03
23000	2158.21	1198.89	884.35	730.90	641.80	584.75	545.92	518.38	498.27	483.26	471.89	463.17
24000	2252.05	1251.01	922.80	762.68	669.70	610.18	569.66	540.92	519.93	504.27	492.41	483.31
25000	2345.88	1303.14	961.25	794.46	697.60	635.60	593.40	563.46	541.59	525.28	512.92	503.45
26000	2439.72	1355.27	999.69	826.24	725.51	661.02	617.13	586.00	563.26	546.30	533.44	523.58
27000	2533.55	1407.39	1038.14	858.02	753.41	686.45	640.87	608.53	584.92	567.31	553.96	543.72
28000	2627.39	1459.52	1076.59	889.79	781.32	711.87	664.60	631.07	606.59	588.32	574.47	563.86
29000	2721.23	1511.64	1115.04	921.57	809.22	737.29	688.34	653.61	628.25	609.33	594.99	584.00
30000	2815.06	1563.77	1153.49	953.35	837.12	762.72	712.07	676.15	649.91	630.34	615.51	604.13
31000	2908.90	1615.89	1191.94	985.13	865.03	788.14	735.81	698.69	671.58	651.35	636.03	624.27
32000	3002.73	1668.02	1230.39	1016.91	892.93	813.57	759.55	721.23	693.24	672.36	656.54	644.41
33000	3096.57	1720.14	1268.84	1048.68	920.84	838.99	783.28	743.76	714.90	693.37	677.06	664.55
34000	3190.40	1772.27	1307.29	1080.46	948.74	864.41	807.02	766.30	736.57	714.39	697.58	684.68
35000	3284.24	1824.39	1345.74	1112.24	976.64	889.84	830.75	788.84	758.23	735.40	718.09	704.82
36000	3378.07	1876.52	1384.19	1144.02	1004.55	915.26	854.49	811.38	779.89	756.41	738.61	724.96
37000	3471.91	1928.64	1422.64	1175.80	1032.45	940.68	878.22	833.92	801.56	777.42	759.13	745.10
38000	3565.74	1980.77	1461.09	1207.57	1060.35	966.11	901.96	856.45	823.22	798.43	779.64	765.23
39000	3659.58	2032.90	1499.54	1239.35	1088.26	991.53	925.69	878.99	844.88	819.44	800.16	785.37
40000	3753.41	2085.02	1537.99	1271.13	1116.16	1016.96	949.43	901.53	866.55	840.45	820.68	805.51
41000	3847.25	2137.15	1576.44	1302.91	1144.07	1042.38	973.17	924.07	888.21	861.46	841.19	825.65
42000	3941.08	2189.27	1614.89	1334.69	1171.97	1067.80	996.90	946.61	909.88	882.47	861.71	845.79
43000	4034.92	2241.40	1653.34	1366.47	1199.87	1093.23	1020.64	969.15	931.54	903.49	882.23	865.92
44000	4128.75	2293.52	1691.79	1398.24	1227.78	1118.65	1044.37	991.68	953.20	924.50	902.74	886.06
45000	4222.59	2345.65	1730.24	1430.02	1255.68	1144.07	1068.11	1014.22	974.87	945.51	923.26	906.20
46000	4316.42	2397.77	1768.69	1461.80	1283.59	1169.50	1091.84	1036.76	996.53	966.52	943.78	926.34
47000	4410.26	2449.90	1807.14	1493.58	1311.49	1194.92	1115.58	1059.30	1018.19	987.53	964.29	946.47
48000	4504.09	2502.02	1845.59	1525.36	1339.39	1220.35	1139.32	1081.84	1039.86	1008.54	984.81	966.61
49000	4597.93	2554.15	1884.04	1557.13	1367.30	1245.77	1163.05	1104.37	1061.52	1029.55	1005.33	986.75
50000	4691.76	2606.28	1922.49	1588.91	1395.20	1271.19	1186.79	1126.91	1083.18	1050.56	1025.84	1006.89
55000	5160.94	2866.90	2114.73	1747.80	1534.72	1398.31	1305.47	1239.60	1191.50	1155.62	1128.43	1107.57
60000	5630.12	3127.53	2306.99	1906.69	1674.24	1525.43	1424.14	1352.29	1299.82	1260.68	1231.01	1208.26
65000	6099.29	3388.16	2499.23	2065.58	1813.76	1652.55	1542.82	1464.98	1408.14	1365.73	1333.60	1308.95
70000	6568.47	3648.78	2691.49	2224.48	1953.28	1779.67	1661.50	1577.68	1516.46	1470.79	1436.18	1409.64
75000	7037.64	3909.41	2883.73	2383.37	2092.80	1906.79	1780.18	1690.37	1624.77	1575.84	1538.76	1510.33
80000	7506.82	4170.04	3075.97	2542.26	2232.32	2033.91	1898.86	1803.06	1733.09	1680.90	1641.35	1611.01
85000	7976.00	4430.66	3268.22	2701.15	2371.84	2161.03	2017.53	1915.75	1841.41	1785.96	1743.93	1711.70
90000	8445.17	4691.29	3460.47	2860.04	2511.36	2288.14	2136.21	2028.44	1949.73	1891.01	1846.52	1812.39
95000	8914.35	4951.92	3652.72	3018.93	2650.88	2415.26	2254.89	2141.13	2058.05	1996.07	1949.10	1913.08
100000	9383.52	5212.55	3844.97	3177.82	2790.40	2542.38	2373.57	2253.82	2166.36	2101.12	2051.68	2013.77

22%

Table 1

MONTHLY 22.50%

PAYMENT REQUIRED TO AMORTIZE A LOAN

TERM AMOUNT	13 YEARS	14 YEARS	15 YEARS	16 YEARS	17 YEARS	18 YEARS	19 YEARS	20 YEARS	25 YEARS	30 YEARS	35 YEARS	40 YEARS
50	1.00	.99	.98	.97	.96	.96	.96	.95	.95	.94	.94	.94
100	1.99	1.97	1.95	1.93	1.92	1.91	1.91	1.90	1.89	1.88	1.88	1.88
200	3.97	3.93	3.89	3.86	3.84	3.82	3.81	3.80	3.77	3.76	3.76	3.76
300	5.96	5.89	5.84	5.79	5.76	5.73	5.71	5.70	5.65	5.64	5.63	5.63
400	7.94	7.85	7.78	7.72	7.68	7.64	7.62	7.59	7.53	7.51	7.51	7.51
500	9.93	9.81	9.72	9.65	9.60	9.55	9.52	9.49	9.42	9.39	9.38	9.38
600	11.91	11.77	11.67	11.58	11.52	11.46	11.42	11.39	11.30	11.27	11.26	11.26
700	13.90	13.74	13.61	13.51	13.43	13.37	13.32	13.28	13.18	13.15	13.14	13.13
800	15.88	15.70	15.55	15.44	15.35	15.28	15.23	15.18	15.06	15.02	15.01	15.01
900	17.86	17.66	17.50	17.37	17.27	17.19	17.13	17.08	16.94	16.90	16.89	16.88
1000	19.85	19.62	19.44	19.30	19.19	19.10	19.03	18.97	18.83	18.78	18.76	18.76
2000	39.69	39.24	38.88	38.60	38.37	38.20	38.06	37.94	37.65	37.55	37.52	37.51
3000	59.54	58.85	58.31	57.89	57.56	57.29	57.08	56.91	56.47	56.33	56.28	56.26
4000	79.38	78.47	77.75	77.19	76.74	76.39	76.11	75.88	75.29	75.10	75.04	75.02
5000	99.23	98.08	97.19	96.48	95.92	95.48	95.13	94.85	94.11	93.87	93.79	93.77
6000	119.07	117.70	116.62	115.78	115.11	114.58	114.16	113.82	112.93	112.65	112.55	112.52
7000	138.91	137.31	136.06	135.07	134.29	133.67	133.18	132.79	131.76	131.42	131.31	131.27
8000	158.76	156.93	155.49	154.37	153.47	152.77	152.21	151.76	150.58	150.19	150.07	150.03
9000	178.60	176.54	174.93	173.66	172.66	171.86	171.23	170.73	169.40	168.97	168.82	168.78
10000	198.45	196.16	194.37	192.96	191.84	190.96	190.26	189.70	188.22	187.74	187.58	187.53
11000	218.29	215.77	213.80	212.25	211.03	210.05	209.28	208.67	207.04	206.51	206.34	206.28
12000	238.14	235.39	233.24	231.55	230.21	229.15	228.31	227.64	225.86	225.29	225.10	225.04
13000	257.98	255.01	252.68	250.84	249.39	248.25	247.33	246.61	244.68	244.06	243.85	243.79
14000	277.82	274.62	272.11	270.14	268.58	267.34	266.36	265.58	263.51	262.83	262.61	262.54
15000	297.67	294.24	291.55	289.43	287.76	286.44	285.39	284.55	282.33	281.61	281.37	281.29
16000	317.51	313.85	310.98	308.73	306.94	305.53	304.41	303.52	301.15	300.38	300.13	300.05
17000	337.36	333.47	330.42	328.02	326.13	324.63	323.44	322.49	319.97	319.15	318.89	318.80
18000	357.20	353.08	349.86	347.32	345.31	343.72	342.46	341.46	338.79	337.93	337.64	337.55
19000	377.04	372.70	369.29	366.61	364.49	362.82	361.49	360.43	357.61	356.70	356.40	356.30
20000	396.89	392.31	388.73	385.91	383.68	381.91	380.51	379.40	376.44	375.47	375.16	375.06
21000	416.73	411.93	408.16	405.20	402.86	401.01	399.54	398.37	395.26	394.25	393.92	393.81
22000	436.58	431.54	427.60	424.50	422.05	420.10	418.56	417.34	414.08	413.02	412.67	412.56
23000	456.42	451.16	447.04	443.79	441.23	439.20	437.59	436.31	432.90	431.79	431.43	431.31
24000	476.27	470.78	466.47	463.09	460.41	458.29	456.61	455.28	451.72	450.57	450.19	450.07
25000	496.11	490.39	485.91	482.38	479.60	477.39	475.64	474.25	470.54	469.34	468.95	468.82
26000	515.95	510.01	505.35	501.68	498.78	496.49	494.66	493.22	489.36	488.11	487.70	487.57
27000	535.80	529.62	524.78	520.97	517.96	515.58	513.69	512.19	508.19	506.89	506.46	506.32
28000	555.64	549.24	544.22	540.27	537.15	534.68	532.72	531.16	527.01	525.66	525.22	525.08
29000	575.49	568.85	563.65	559.56	556.33	553.77	551.74	550.13	545.83	544.43	543.98	543.83
30000	595.33	588.47	583.09	578.86	575.51	572.87	570.77	569.10	564.65	563.21	562.74	562.58
31000	615.17	608.08	602.53	598.15	594.70	591.96	589.79	588.07	583.47	581.98	581.49	581.33
32000	635.02	627.70	621.96	617.45	613.88	611.06	608.82	607.04	602.29	600.75	600.25	600.09
33000	654.86	647.31	641.40	636.74	633.07	630.15	627.84	626.01	621.11	619.53	619.01	618.84
34000	674.71	666.93	660.84	656.04	652.25	649.25	646.87	644.97	639.94	638.30	637.77	637.59
35000	694.55	686.55	680.27	675.33	671.43	668.34	665.89	663.94	658.76	657.07	656.52	656.34
36000	714.40	706.16	699.71	694.63	690.62	687.44	684.92	682.91	677.58	675.85	675.28	675.10
37000	734.24	725.78	719.14	713.92	709.80	706.53	703.94	701.88	696.40	694.62	694.04	693.85
38000	754.08	745.39	738.58	733.22	728.98	725.63	722.97	720.85	715.22	713.39	712.80	712.60
39000	773.93	765.01	758.02	752.51	748.17	744.73	741.99	739.82	734.04	732.17	731.55	731.35
40000	793.77	784.62	777.45	771.81	767.35	763.82	761.02	758.79	752.87	750.94	750.31	750.11
41000	813.62	804.24	796.89	791.10	786.53	782.92	780.05	777.76	771.69	769.71	769.07	768.86
42000	833.46	823.85	816.32	810.40	805.72	802.01	799.07	796.73	790.51	788.49	787.83	787.61
43000	853.30	843.47	835.76	829.69	824.90	821.11	818.10	815.70	809.33	807.26	806.58	806.36
44000	873.15	863.08	855.20	848.99	844.09	840.20	837.12	834.67	828.15	826.03	825.34	825.12
45000	892.99	882.70	874.63	868.28	863.27	859.30	856.15	853.64	846.97	844.81	844.10	843.87
46000	912.84	902.32	894.07	887.58	882.45	878.39	875.17	872.61	865.79	863.58	862.86	862.62
47000	932.68	921.93	913.51	906.87	901.64	897.49	894.20	891.58	884.62	882.35	881.62	881.37
48000	952.53	941.55	932.94	926.17	920.82	916.58	913.22	910.55	903.44	901.13	900.37	900.13
49000	972.37	961.16	952.38	945.46	940.00	935.68	932.25	929.52	922.26	919.90	919.13	918.88
50000	992.21	980.78	971.81	964.76	959.19	954.78	951.27	948.49	941.08	938.67	937.89	937.63
55000	1091.43	1078.85	1069.00	1061.23	1055.11	1050.25	1046.40	1043.34	1035.19	1032.54	1031.68	1031.39
60000	1190.66	1176.93	1166.18	1157.71	1151.02	1145.73	1141.53	1138.19	1129.30	1126.41	1125.47	1125.16
65000	1289.88	1275.01	1263.36	1254.19	1246.94	1241.21	1236.65	1233.04	1223.40	1220.28	1219.25	1218.92
70000	1389.10	1373.09	1360.54	1350.66	1342.86	1336.68	1331.78	1327.88	1317.51	1314.14	1313.04	1312.68
75000	1488.32	1471.16	1457.72	1447.14	1438.78	1432.16	1426.91	1422.73	1411.62	1408.01	1406.83	1406.44
80000	1587.54	1569.24	1554.90	1543.61	1534.70	1527.64	1522.03	1517.58	1505.73	1501.88	1500.62	1500.21
85000	1686.76	1667.32	1652.08	1640.09	1630.62	1623.11	1617.16	1612.43	1599.83	1595.74	1594.41	1593.97
90000	1785.98	1765.39	1749.26	1736.56	1726.53	1718.59	1712.29	1707.28	1693.94	1689.61	1688.20	1687.73
95000	1885.20	1863.47	1846.44	1833.04	1822.45	1814.07	1807.42	1802.13	1788.05	1783.48	1781.98	1781.49
100000	1984.42	1961.55	1943.62	1929.51	1918.37	1909.55	1902.54	1896.98	1882.16	1877.34	1875.77	1875.26

22%

143

Table 1

22.75% MONTHLY

PAYMENT REQUIRED TO AMORTIZE A LOAN

TERM / AMOUNT	1 YEAR	2 YEARS	3 YEARS	4 YEARS	5 YEARS	6 YEARS	7 YEARS	8 YEARS	9 YEARS	10 YEARS	11 YEARS	12 YEARS
50	4.70	2.62	1.93	1.60	1.41	1.28	1.20	1.14	1.10	1.06	1.04	1.02
100	9.40	5.23	3.86	3.20	2.81	2.56	2.39	2.27	2.19	2.12	2.07	2.04
200	18.80	10.45	7.72	6.39	5.61	5.12	4.78	4.54	4.37	4.24	4.14	4.07
300	28.19	15.68	11.58	9.58	8.42	7.68	7.17	6.81	6.55	6.36	6.21	6.10
400	37.59	20.90	15.44	12.77	11.22	10.23	9.56	9.08	8.74	8.48	8.28	8.13
500	46.98	26.13	19.29	15.96	14.03	12.79	11.95	11.35	10.92	10.60	10.35	10.16
600	56.38	31.35	23.15	19.15	16.83	15.35	14.34	13.62	13.10	12.71	12.42	12.20
700	65.77	36.58	27.01	22.35	19.64	17.91	16.73	15.89	15.29	14.83	14.49	14.23
800	75.17	41.80	30.87	25.54	22.44	20.46	19.12	18.16	17.47	16.95	16.56	16.26
900	84.57	47.03	34.73	28.73	25.25	23.02	21.51	20.43	19.65	19.07	18.63	18.29
1000	93.96	52.25	38.58	31.92	28.05	25.58	23.90	22.70	21.84	21.19	20.70	20.32
2000	187.92	104.50	77.16	63.83	56.10	51.15	47.79	45.40	43.67	42.37	41.39	40.64
3000	281.87	156.75	115.74	95.75	84.15	76.72	71.68	68.10	65.50	63.55	62.08	60.96
4000	375.83	209.00	154.32	127.66	112.19	102.30	95.57	90.80	87.33	84.74	82.78	81.28
5000	469.78	261.25	192.90	159.58	140.24	127.87	119.46	113.50	109.16	105.92	103.47	101.59
6000	563.74	313.50	231.48	191.49	168.29	153.44	143.35	136.20	130.99	127.10	124.16	121.91
7000	657.69	365.75	270.06	223.41	196.33	179.02	167.24	158.90	152.82	148.28	144.85	142.23
8000	751.65	418.00	308.64	255.32	224.38	204.59	191.13	181.60	174.65	169.47	165.55	162.55
9000	845.61	470.25	347.22	287.24	252.43	230.16	215.03	204.30	196.48	190.65	186.24	182.86
10000	939.56	522.50	385.80	319.15	280.48	255.74	238.92	227.00	218.31	211.83	206.93	203.18
11000	1033.52	574.75	424.38	351.07	308.52	281.31	262.81	249.70	240.14	233.01	227.63	223.50
12000	1127.47	627.00	462.96	382.98	336.57	306.88	286.70	272.40	261.97	254.20	248.32	243.82
13000	1221.43	679.25	501.54	414.90	364.62	332.46	310.59	295.10	283.80	275.38	269.01	264.14
14000	1315.38	731.49	540.12	446.81	392.66	358.03	334.48	317.80	305.63	296.56	289.70	284.45
15000	1409.34	783.74	578.70	478.72	420.71	383.60	358.37	340.50	327.46	317.75	310.40	304.77
16000	1503.30	835.99	617.28	510.64	448.76	409.18	382.26	363.20	349.29	338.93	331.09	325.09
17000	1597.25	888.24	655.86	542.55	476.80	434.75	406.16	385.90	371.12	360.11	351.78	345.41
18000	1691.21	940.49	694.44	574.47	504.85	460.32	430.05	408.59	392.95	381.29	372.48	365.72
19000	1785.16	992.74	733.02	606.38	532.90	485.90	453.94	431.29	414.78	402.48	393.17	386.04
20000	1879.12	1044.99	771.60	638.30	560.95	511.47	477.83	453.99	436.61	423.66	413.86	406.36
21000	1973.07	1097.24	810.18	670.21	588.99	537.04	501.72	476.69	458.44	444.84	434.55	426.68
22000	2067.03	1149.49	848.75	702.13	617.04	562.62	525.61	499.39	480.27	466.02	455.25	447.00
23000	2160.99	1201.74	887.33	734.04	645.09	588.19	549.50	522.09	502.10	487.21	475.94	467.31
24000	2254.94	1253.99	925.91	765.96	673.13	613.76	573.39	544.79	523.93	508.39	496.63	487.63
25000	2348.90	1306.24	964.49	797.87	701.18	639.34	597.28	567.49	545.76	529.57	517.33	507.95
26000	2442.85	1358.49	1003.07	829.79	729.23	664.91	621.18	590.19	567.59	550.76	538.02	528.27
27000	2536.81	1410.74	1041.65	861.70	757.27	690.48	645.07	612.89	589.42	571.94	558.71	548.58
28000	2630.76	1462.98	1080.23	893.62	785.32	716.06	668.96	635.59	611.25	593.12	579.40	568.90
29000	2724.72	1515.23	1118.81	925.53	813.37	741.63	692.85	658.29	633.08	614.30	600.10	589.22
30000	2818.68	1567.48	1157.39	957.44	841.42	767.20	716.74	680.99	654.91	635.49	620.79	609.54
31000	2912.63	1619.73	1195.97	989.36	869.46	792.78	740.63	703.69	676.74	656.67	641.48	629.86
32000	3006.59	1671.98	1234.55	1021.27	897.51	818.35	764.52	726.39	698.57	677.85	662.18	650.17
33000	3100.54	1724.23	1273.13	1053.19	925.56	843.92	788.41	749.09	720.40	699.03	682.87	670.49
34000	3194.50	1776.48	1311.71	1085.10	953.60	869.49	812.31	771.79	742.23	720.22	703.56	690.81
35000	3288.45	1828.73	1350.29	1117.02	981.65	895.07	836.20	794.48	764.06	741.40	724.25	711.13
36000	3382.41	1880.98	1388.87	1148.93	1009.70	920.64	860.09	817.18	785.89	762.58	744.95	731.44
37000	3476.37	1933.23	1427.45	1180.85	1037.74	946.21	883.98	839.88	807.72	783.77	765.64	751.76
38000	3570.32	1985.48	1466.03	1212.76	1065.79	971.79	907.87	862.58	829.55	804.95	786.33	772.08
39000	3664.28	2037.73	1504.61	1244.68	1093.84	997.36	931.76	885.28	851.38	826.13	807.03	792.40
40000	3758.23	2089.98	1543.19	1276.59	1121.89	1022.93	955.65	907.98	873.21	847.31	827.72	812.71
41000	3852.19	2142.23	1581.77	1308.51	1149.93	1048.51	979.54	930.68	895.04	868.50	848.41	833.03
42000	3946.14	2194.47	1620.35	1340.42	1177.98	1074.08	1003.43	953.38	916.87	889.68	869.10	853.35
43000	4040.10	2246.72	1658.93	1372.34	1206.03	1099.65	1027.33	976.08	938.70	910.86	889.80	873.67
44000	4134.06	2298.97	1697.50	1404.25	1234.07	1125.23	1051.22	998.78	960.53	932.04	910.49	893.99
45000	4228.01	2351.22	1736.08	1436.16	1262.12	1150.80	1075.11	1021.48	982.36	953.23	931.18	914.30
46000	4321.97	2403.47	1774.66	1468.08	1290.17	1176.37	1099.00	1044.18	1004.19	974.41	951.87	934.62
47000	4415.92	2455.72	1813.24	1499.99	1318.22	1201.95	1122.89	1066.88	1026.02	995.59	972.57	954.94
48000	4509.88	2507.97	1851.82	1531.91	1346.26	1227.52	1146.78	1089.58	1047.85	1016.78	993.26	975.26
49000	4603.83	2560.22	1890.40	1563.82	1374.31	1253.09	1170.67	1112.28	1069.68	1037.96	1013.95	995.57
50000	4697.79	2612.47	1928.98	1595.74	1402.36	1278.67	1194.56	1134.98	1091.51	1059.14	1034.65	1015.89
55000	5167.57	2873.71	2121.88	1755.31	1542.59	1406.53	1314.02	1248.47	1200.67	1165.05	1138.11	1117.48
60000	5637.35	3134.96	2314.78	1914.88	1682.83	1534.40	1433.48	1361.97	1309.82	1270.97	1241.57	1219.07
65000	6107.13	3396.21	2507.68	2074.46	1823.06	1662.26	1552.93	1475.47	1418.97	1376.88	1345.04	1320.66
70000	6576.90	3657.45	2700.57	2234.03	1963.30	1790.13	1672.39	1588.96	1528.12	1482.80	1448.50	1422.25
75000	7046.68	3918.70	2893.47	2393.60	2103.53	1918.00	1791.84	1702.46	1637.27	1588.71	1551.97	1523.84
80000	7516.46	4179.95	3086.37	2553.18	2243.77	2045.86	1911.30	1815.96	1746.42	1694.62	1655.43	1625.42
85000	7986.24	4441.19	3279.27	2712.75	2384.00	2173.73	2030.76	1929.46	1855.57	1800.54	1758.89	1727.01
90000	8456.02	4702.44	3472.16	2872.32	2524.24	2301.60	2150.21	2042.95	1964.72	1906.45	1862.36	1828.60
95000	8925.80	4963.69	3665.06	3031.90	2664.47	2429.46	2269.67	2156.45	2073.87	2012.36	1965.82	1930.19
100000	9395.58	5224.93	3857.96	3191.47	2804.71	2557.33	2389.12	2269.95	2183.02	2118.28	2069.29	2031.78

22%

144

Table 1

MONTHLY
PAYMENT REQUIRED TO AMORTIZE A LOAN

22.75%

TERM AMOUNT	13 YEARS	14 YEARS	15 YEARS	16 YEARS	17 YEARS	18 YEARS	19 YEARS	20 YEARS	25 YEARS	30 YEARS	35 YEARS	40 YEARS
50	1.01	1.00	.99	.98	.97	.97	.97	.96	.96	.95	.95	.95
100	2.01	1.99	1.97	1.95	1.94	1.93	1.93	1.92	1.91	1.90	1.90	1.90
200	4.01	3.97	3.93	3.90	3.88	3.86	3.85	3.84	3.81	3.80	3.80	3.80
300	6.01	5.95	5.89	5.85	5.82	5.79	5.77	5.76	5.71	5.70	5.69	5.69
400	8.02	7.93	7.86	7.80	7.76	7.72	7.69	7.67	7.62	7.60	7.59	7.59
500	10.02	9.91	9.82	9.75	9.69	9.65	9.62	9.59	9.52	9.50	9.49	9.49
600	12.02	11.89	11.78	11.70	11.63	11.58	11.54	11.51	11.42	11.39	11.38	11.38
700	14.02	13.87	13.74	13.65	13.57	13.51	13.46	13.42	13.32	13.29	13.28	13.28
800	16.03	15.85	15.71	15.60	15.51	15.44	15.38	15.34	15.23	15.19	15.18	15.17
900	18.03	17.83	17.67	17.54	17.45	17.37	17.31	17.26	17.13	17.09	17.07	17.07
1000	20.03	19.81	19.63	19.49	19.38	19.30	19.23	19.17	19.03	18.99	18.97	18.97
2000	40.06	39.61	39.26	38.98	38.76	38.59	38.45	38.34	38.06	37.97	37.94	37.93
3000	60.09	59.41	58.88	58.47	58.14	57.88	57.68	57.51	57.08	56.95	56.90	56.89
4000	80.12	79.22	78.51	77.96	77.52	77.17	76.90	76.68	76.11	75.93	75.87	75.85
5000	100.14	99.02	98.14	97.44	96.90	96.47	96.12	95.85	95.14	94.91	94.83	94.81
6000	120.17	118.82	117.76	116.93	116.28	115.76	115.35	115.02	114.16	113.89	113.80	113.77
7000	140.20	138.62	137.39	136.42	135.65	135.05	134.57	134.19	133.19	132.87	132.76	132.73
8000	160.23	158.43	157.01	155.91	155.03	154.34	153.80	153.36	152.22	151.85	151.73	151.69
9000	180.26	178.23	176.64	175.39	174.41	173.63	173.02	172.53	171.24	170.83	170.69	170.65
10000	200.28	198.03	196.27	194.88	193.79	192.93	192.24	191.70	190.27	189.81	189.66	189.61
11000	220.31	217.83	215.89	214.37	213.17	212.22	211.47	210.87	209.29	208.79	208.62	208.57
12000	240.34	237.64	235.52	233.86	232.55	231.51	230.69	230.04	228.32	227.77	227.59	227.53
13000	260.37	257.44	255.15	253.34	251.93	250.80	249.92	249.21	247.35	246.75	246.56	246.49
14000	280.40	277.24	274.77	272.83	271.30	270.10	269.14	268.38	266.37	265.73	265.52	265.45
15000	300.42	297.04	294.40	292.32	290.68	289.39	288.36	287.55	285.40	284.71	284.49	284.41
16000	320.45	316.85	314.02	311.81	310.06	308.68	307.59	306.72	304.43	303.69	303.45	303.38
17000	340.48	336.65	333.65	331.30	329.44	327.97	326.81	325.89	323.45	322.67	322.42	322.34
18000	360.51	356.45	353.28	350.78	348.82	347.26	346.04	345.06	342.48	341.65	341.38	341.30
19000	380.54	376.25	372.90	370.27	368.20	366.56	365.26	364.23	361.51	360.63	360.35	360.26
20000	400.56	396.06	392.53	389.76	387.57	385.85	384.48	383.40	380.53	379.61	379.31	379.22
21000	420.59	415.86	412.15	409.25	406.95	405.14	403.71	402.57	399.56	398.59	398.28	398.18
22000	440.62	435.66	431.78	428.73	426.33	424.43	422.93	421.74	418.58	417.57	417.24	417.14
23000	460.65	455.46	451.41	448.22	445.71	443.73	442.15	440.91	437.61	436.55	436.21	436.10
24000	480.68	475.27	471.03	467.71	465.09	463.02	461.38	460.08	456.64	455.53	455.18	455.06
25000	500.70	495.07	490.66	487.20	484.47	482.31	480.60	479.25	475.66	474.51	474.14	474.02
26000	520.73	514.87	510.29	506.68	503.85	501.60	499.83	498.42	494.69	493.49	493.11	492.98
27000	540.76	534.67	529.91	526.17	523.22	520.89	519.05	517.59	513.72	512.47	512.07	511.94
28000	560.79	554.48	549.54	545.66	542.60	540.19	538.27	536.76	532.74	531.45	531.04	530.90
29000	580.82	574.28	569.16	565.15	561.98	559.48	557.50	555.93	551.77	550.43	550.00	549.86
30000	600.84	594.08	588.79	584.63	581.36	578.77	576.72	575.10	570.79	569.41	568.97	568.82
31000	620.87	613.88	608.42	604.12	600.74	598.06	595.95	594.27	589.82	588.39	587.93	587.78
32000	640.90	633.69	628.04	623.61	620.12	617.36	615.17	613.44	608.85	607.37	606.90	606.75
33000	660.93	653.49	647.67	643.10	639.50	636.65	634.39	632.61	627.87	626.36	625.86	625.71
34000	680.96	673.29	667.30	662.59	658.87	655.94	653.62	651.78	646.90	645.34	644.83	644.67
35000	700.98	693.09	686.92	682.07	678.25	675.23	672.84	670.95	665.93	664.32	663.80	663.63
36000	721.01	712.90	706.55	701.56	697.63	694.52	692.07	690.11	684.95	683.30	682.76	682.59
37000	741.04	732.70	726.17	721.05	717.01	713.82	711.29	709.28	703.98	702.28	701.73	701.55
38000	761.07	752.50	745.80	740.54	736.39	733.11	730.51	728.45	723.01	721.26	720.69	720.51
39000	781.10	772.30	765.43	760.02	755.77	752.40	749.74	747.62	742.03	740.24	739.66	739.47
40000	801.12	792.11	785.05	779.51	775.14	771.69	768.96	766.79	761.06	759.22	758.62	758.43
41000	821.15	811.91	804.68	799.00	794.52	790.99	788.18	785.96	780.08	778.20	777.59	777.39
42000	841.18	831.71	824.30	818.49	813.90	810.28	807.41	805.13	799.11	797.18	796.55	796.35
43000	861.21	851.51	843.93	837.97	833.28	829.57	826.63	824.30	818.14	816.16	815.52	815.31
44000	881.24	871.32	863.56	857.46	852.66	848.86	845.86	843.47	837.16	835.14	834.48	834.27
45000	901.26	891.12	883.18	876.95	872.04	868.15	865.08	862.64	856.19	854.12	853.45	853.23
46000	921.29	910.92	902.81	896.44	891.42	887.45	884.30	881.81	875.22	873.10	872.42	872.19
47000	941.32	930.72	922.44	915.93	910.79	906.74	903.53	900.98	894.24	892.08	891.38	891.16
48000	961.35	950.53	942.06	935.41	930.17	926.03	922.75	920.15	913.27	911.06	910.35	910.12
49000	981.38	970.33	961.69	954.90	949.55	945.32	941.98	939.32	932.29	930.04	929.31	929.08
50000	1001.40	990.13	981.31	974.39	968.93	964.62	961.20	958.49	951.32	949.02	948.28	948.04
55000	1101.54	1089.14	1079.45	1071.83	1065.82	1061.08	1057.32	1054.34	1046.45	1043.92	1043.10	1042.84
60000	1201.68	1188.16	1177.58	1169.26	1162.71	1157.54	1153.44	1150.19	1141.58	1138.82	1137.93	1137.64
65000	1301.82	1287.17	1275.71	1266.70	1259.61	1254.00	1249.56	1246.04	1236.72	1233.73	1232.76	1232.45
70000	1401.96	1386.18	1373.84	1364.14	1356.50	1350.46	1345.68	1341.89	1331.85	1328.63	1327.59	1327.25
75000	1502.10	1485.19	1471.97	1461.58	1453.39	1446.92	1441.80	1437.73	1426.98	1423.53	1422.41	1422.05
80000	1602.24	1584.21	1570.10	1559.02	1550.28	1543.38	1537.92	1533.58	1522.11	1518.43	1517.24	1516.86
85000	1702.38	1683.22	1668.23	1656.46	1647.18	1639.84	1634.04	1629.43	1617.24	1613.33	1612.07	1611.66
90000	1802.52	1782.23	1766.36	1753.89	1744.07	1736.30	1730.16	1725.28	1712.37	1708.23	1706.90	1706.46
95000	1902.66	1881.24	1864.49	1851.33	1840.96	1832.77	1826.28	1821.13	1807.51	1803.13	1801.72	1801.27
100000	2002.80	1980.26	1962.62	1948.77	1937.85	1929.23	1922.40	1916.98	1902.64	1898.04	1896.55	1896.07

22%

Table 1

23.00%

MONTHLY

PAYMENT REQUIRED TO AMORTIZE A LOAN

TERM AMOUNT	1 YEAR	2 YEARS	3 YEARS	4 YEARS	5 YEARS	6 YEARS	7 YEARS	8 YEARS	9 YEARS	10 YEARS	11 YEARS	12 YEARS
50	4.71	2.62	1.94	1.61	1.41	1.29	1.21	1.15	1.10	1.07	1.05	1.03
100	9.41	5.24	3.88	3.21	2.82	2.58	2.41	2.29	2.20	2.14	2.09	2.05
200	18.82	10.48	7.75	6.42	5.64	5.15	4.81	4.58	4.40	4.28	4.18	4.10
300	28.23	15.72	11.62	9.62	8.46	7.72	7.22	6.86	6.60	6.41	6.27	6.15
400	37.64	20.95	15.49	12.83	11.28	10.29	9.62	9.15	8.80	8.55	8.35	8.20
500	47.04	26.19	19.36	16.03	14.10	12.87	12.03	11.44	11.00	10.68	10.44	10.25
600	56.45	31.43	23.23	19.24	16.92	15.44	14.43	13.72	13.20	12.82	12.53	12.30
700	65.86	36.67	27.10	22.44	19.74	18.01	16.84	16.01	15.40	14.95	14.61	14.35
800	75.27	41.90	30.97	25.65	22.56	20.58	19.24	18.29	17.60	17.09	16.70	16.40
900	84.67	47.14	34.84	28.85	25.38	23.16	21.65	20.58	19.80	19.22	18.79	18.45
1000	94.08	52.38	38.71	32.06	28.20	25.73	24.05	22.87	22.00	21.36	20.87	20.50
2000	188.16	104.75	77.42	64.11	56.39	51.45	48.10	45.73	44.00	42.71	41.74	41.00
3000	282.23	157.12	116.13	96.16	84.58	77.17	72.15	68.59	66.00	64.07	62.61	61.50
4000	376.31	209.50	154.84	128.21	112.77	102.90	96.19	91.45	87.99	85.42	83.48	82.00
5000	470.39	261.87	193.55	160.26	140.96	128.62	120.24	114.31	109.99	106.78	104.35	102.50
6000	564.46	314.24	232.26	192.31	169.15	154.34	144.29	137.17	131.99	128.13	125.22	123.00
7000	658.54	366.62	270.97	224.37	197.34	180.07	168.34	160.03	153.99	149.49	146.09	143.49
8000	752.62	418.99	309.68	256.42	225.53	205.79	192.38	182.89	175.98	170.84	166.96	163.99
9000	846.69	471.36	348.39	288.47	253.72	231.51	216.43	205.76	197.98	192.20	187.83	184.49
10000	940.77	523.74	387.10	320.52	281.91	257.24	240.48	228.62	219.98	213.55	208.70	204.99
11000	1034.84	576.11	425.81	352.57	310.10	282.96	264.52	251.48	241.98	234.91	229.57	225.49
12000	1128.92	628.48	464.52	384.62	338.29	308.68	288.57	274.34	263.97	256.26	250.44	245.99
13000	1223.00	680.86	503.23	416.67	366.48	334.41	312.62	297.20	285.97	277.62	271.31	266.48
14000	1317.07	733.23	541.94	448.73	394.67	360.13	336.67	320.06	307.97	298.97	292.18	286.98
15000	1411.15	785.60	580.65	480.78	422.86	385.85	360.71	342.92	329.96	320.33	313.05	307.48
16000	1505.23	837.98	619.36	512.83	451.05	411.57	384.76	365.78	351.96	341.68	333.92	327.98
17000	1599.30	890.35	658.07	544.88	479.24	437.30	408.81	388.65	373.96	363.04	354.78	348.48
18000	1693.38	942.72	696.78	576.93	507.43	463.02	432.85	411.51	395.96	384.39	375.65	368.98
19000	1787.46	995.10	735.49	608.98	535.62	488.74	456.90	434.37	417.95	405.75	396.52	389.47
20000	1881.53	1047.47	774.20	641.03	563.81	514.47	480.95	457.23	439.95	427.10	417.39	409.97
21000	1975.61	1099.84	812.91	673.09	592.00	540.19	505.00	480.09	461.95	448.46	438.26	430.47
22000	2069.68	1152.22	851.62	705.14	620.20	565.91	529.04	502.95	483.95	469.81	459.13	450.97
23000	2163.76	1204.59	890.33	737.19	648.39	591.64	553.09	525.81	505.94	491.16	480.00	471.47
24000	2257.84	1256.96	929.04	769.24	676.58	617.36	577.14	548.67	527.94	512.52	500.87	491.97
25000	2351.91	1309.34	967.75	801.29	704.77	643.08	601.18	571.53	549.94	533.87	521.74	512.46
26000	2445.99	1361.71	1006.46	833.34	732.96	668.81	625.23	594.40	571.94	555.23	542.61	532.96
27000	2540.07	1414.08	1045.17	865.39	761.15	694.53	649.28	617.26	593.93	576.58	563.48	553.46
28000	2634.14	1466.46	1083.88	897.45	789.34	720.25	673.33	640.12	615.93	597.94	584.35	573.96
29000	2728.22	1518.83	1122.59	929.50	817.53	745.98	697.37	662.98	637.93	619.29	605.22	594.46
30000	2822.29	1571.20	1161.30	961.55	845.72	771.70	721.42	685.84	659.92	640.65	626.09	614.96
31000	2916.37	1623.58	1200.01	993.60	873.91	797.42	745.47	708.70	681.92	662.00	646.96	635.45
32000	3010.45	1675.95	1238.72	1025.65	902.10	823.14	769.52	731.56	703.92	683.36	667.83	655.95
33000	3104.52	1728.32	1277.43	1057.70	930.29	848.87	793.56	754.42	725.92	704.71	688.69	676.45
34000	3198.60	1780.70	1316.14	1089.76	958.48	874.59	817.61	777.29	747.91	726.07	709.56	696.95
35000	3292.68	1833.07	1354.85	1121.81	986.67	900.31	841.66	800.15	769.91	747.42	730.43	717.45
36000	3386.75	1885.44	1393.56	1153.86	1014.86	926.04	865.70	823.01	791.91	768.78	751.30	737.95
37000	3480.83	1937.82	1432.26	1185.91	1043.05	951.76	889.75	845.87	813.91	790.13	772.17	758.44
38000	3574.91	1990.19	1470.97	1217.96	1071.24	977.48	913.80	868.73	835.90	811.49	793.04	778.94
39000	3668.98	2042.56	1509.68	1250.01	1099.43	1003.21	937.85	891.59	857.90	832.84	813.91	799.44
40000	3763.06	2094.94	1548.39	1282.06	1127.62	1028.93	961.89	914.45	879.90	854.20	834.78	819.94
41000	3857.13	2147.31	1587.10	1314.12	1155.81	1054.65	985.94	937.31	901.90	875.55	855.65	840.44
42000	3951.21	2199.68	1625.81	1346.17	1184.00	1080.38	1009.99	960.18	923.89	896.91	876.52	860.94
43000	4045.29	2252.06	1664.52	1378.22	1212.20	1106.10	1034.03	983.04	945.89	918.26	897.39	881.44
44000	4139.36	2304.43	1703.23	1410.27	1240.39	1131.82	1058.08	1005.90	967.89	939.62	918.26	901.93
45000	4233.44	2356.80	1741.94	1442.32	1268.58	1157.54	1082.13	1028.76	989.88	960.97	939.13	922.43
46000	4327.52	2409.18	1780.65	1474.37	1296.77	1183.27	1106.18	1051.62	1011.88	982.32	960.00	942.93
47000	4421.59	2461.55	1819.36	1506.42	1324.96	1208.99	1130.22	1074.48	1033.88	1003.68	980.87	963.43
48000	4515.67	2513.92	1858.07	1538.48	1353.15	1234.71	1154.27	1097.34	1055.88	1025.03	1001.74	983.93
49000	4609.74	2566.30	1896.78	1570.53	1381.34	1260.44	1178.32	1120.20	1077.87	1046.39	1022.60	1004.43
50000	4703.82	2618.67	1935.49	1602.58	1409.53	1286.16	1202.36	1143.06	1099.87	1067.74	1043.47	1024.92
55000	5174.20	2880.54	2129.04	1762.84	1550.48	1414.78	1322.60	1257.37	1209.86	1174.52	1147.82	1127.42
60000	5644.58	3142.40	2322.59	1923.09	1691.43	1543.39	1442.84	1371.68	1319.84	1281.29	1252.17	1229.91
65000	6114.97	3404.27	2516.14	2083.35	1832.39	1672.01	1563.07	1485.98	1429.83	1388.07	1356.51	1332.40
70000	6585.35	3666.14	2709.69	2243.61	1973.34	1800.62	1683.31	1600.29	1539.82	1494.84	1460.86	1434.89
75000	7055.73	3928.00	2903.23	2403.87	2114.29	1929.24	1803.54	1714.59	1649.80	1601.61	1565.21	1537.38
80000	7526.11	4189.87	3096.78	2564.12	2255.24	2057.85	1923.78	1828.90	1759.79	1708.39	1669.56	1639.88
85000	7996.49	4451.74	3290.33	2724.38	2396.20	2186.47	2044.02	1943.21	1869.78	1815.16	1773.90	1742.37
90000	8466.87	4713.60	3483.88	2884.64	2537.15	2315.08	2164.25	2057.51	1979.76	1921.94	1878.25	1844.86
95000	8937.25	4975.47	3677.43	3044.89	2678.10	2443.70	2284.49	2171.82	2089.75	2028.71	1982.60	1947.35
100000	9407.64	5237.34	3870.98	3205.15	2819.05	2572.32	2404.72	2286.12	2199.74	2135.48	2086.94	2049.84

Table 1

MONTHLY 23.00%

PAYMENT REQUIRED TO AMORTIZE A LOAN

TERM	13 YEARS	14 YEARS	15 YEARS	16 YEARS	17 YEARS	18 YEARS	19 YEARS	20 YEARS	25 YEARS	30 YEARS	35 YEARS	40 YEARS
AMOUNT												
50	1.02	1.00	1.00	.99	.98	.98	.98	.97	.97	.96	.96	.96
100	2.03	2.00	1.99	1.97	1.96	1.95	1.95	1.94	1.93	1.92	1.92	1.92
200	4.05	4.00	3.97	3.94	3.92	3.90	3.89	3.88	3.85	3.84	3.84	3.84
300	6.07	6.00	5.95	5.91	5.88	5.85	5.83	5.82	5.77	5.76	5.76	5.76
400	8.09	8.00	7.93	7.88	7.83	7.80	7.77	7.75	7.70	7.68	7.67	7.67
500	10.11	10.00	9.91	9.85	9.79	9.75	9.72	9.69	9.62	9.60	9.59	9.59
600	12.13	12.00	11.89	11.81	11.75	11.70	11.66	11.63	11.54	11.52	11.51	11.51
700	14.15	14.00	13.88	13.78	13.71	13.65	13.60	13.56	13.47	13.44	13.43	13.42
800	16.17	16.00	15.86	15.75	15.66	15.60	15.54	15.50	15.39	15.35	15.34	15.34
900	18.20	18.00	17.84	17.72	17.62	17.55	17.49	17.44	17.31	17.27	17.26	17.26
1000	20.22	20.00	19.82	19.69	19.58	19.49	19.43	19.38	19.24	19.19	19.18	19.17
2000	40.43	39.99	39.64	39.37	39.15	38.98	38.85	38.75	38.47	38.38	38.35	38.34
3000	60.64	59.98	59.45	59.05	58.73	58.47	58.27	58.12	57.70	57.57	57.52	57.51
4000	80.85	79.97	79.27	78.73	78.30	77.96	77.70	77.49	76.93	76.75	76.70	76.68
5000	101.07	99.96	99.09	98.41	97.87	97.45	97.12	96.86	96.16	95.94	95.87	95.85
6000	121.28	119.95	118.90	118.09	117.45	116.94	116.54	116.23	115.39	115.13	115.04	115.02
7000	141.49	139.94	138.72	137.77	137.02	136.43	135.96	135.60	134.62	134.32	134.22	134.19
8000	161.70	159.93	158.54	157.45	156.59	155.92	155.39	154.97	153.86	153.50	153.39	153.36
9000	181.92	179.92	178.35	177.13	176.17	175.41	174.81	174.34	173.09	172.69	172.56	172.52
10000	202.13	199.91	198.17	196.81	195.74	194.90	194.23	193.71	192.32	191.88	191.74	191.69
11000	222.34	219.90	217.99	216.49	215.32	214.39	213.66	213.08	211.55	211.07	210.91	210.86
12000	242.55	239.89	237.80	236.17	234.89	233.88	233.08	232.45	230.78	230.25	230.08	230.03
13000	262.76	259.88	257.62	255.85	254.46	253.37	252.50	251.82	250.01	249.44	249.26	249.20
14000	282.98	279.87	277.44	275.53	274.04	272.86	271.92	271.19	269.24	268.63	268.43	268.37
15000	303.19	299.86	297.25	295.21	293.61	292.35	291.35	290.56	288.47	287.81	287.60	287.54
16000	323.40	319.85	317.07	314.90	313.18	311.84	310.77	309.93	307.71	307.00	306.78	306.71
17000	343.61	339.84	336.89	334.58	332.76	331.32	330.19	329.30	326.94	326.19	325.95	325.87
18000	363.83	359.83	356.70	354.26	352.33	350.81	349.61	348.67	346.17	345.38	345.12	345.04
19000	384.04	379.82	376.52	373.94	371.91	370.30	369.04	368.04	365.40	364.56	364.30	364.21
20000	404.25	399.81	396.34	393.62	391.48	389.79	388.46	387.41	384.63	383.75	383.47	383.38
21000	424.46	419.80	416.15	413.30	411.05	409.28	407.88	406.78	403.86	402.94	402.64	402.55
22000	444.67	439.79	435.97	432.98	430.63	428.77	427.31	426.15	423.09	422.13	421.82	421.72
23000	464.89	459.78	455.79	452.66	450.20	448.26	446.73	445.52	442.32	441.31	440.99	440.89
24000	485.10	479.77	475.60	472.34	469.77	467.75	466.15	464.89	461.56	460.50	460.16	460.06
25000	505.31	499.76	495.42	492.02	489.35	487.24	485.57	484.26	480.79	479.69	479.34	479.22
26000	525.52	519.75	515.24	511.70	508.92	506.73	505.00	503.63	500.02	498.88	498.51	498.39
27000	545.74	539.74	535.05	531.38	528.50	526.22	524.42	523.00	519.25	518.06	517.68	517.56
28000	565.95	559.73	554.87	551.06	548.07	545.71	543.84	542.37	538.48	537.25	536.86	536.73
29000	586.16	579.72	574.69	570.74	567.64	565.20	563.27	561.74	557.71	556.44	556.03	555.90
30000	606.37	599.71	594.50	590.42	587.22	584.69	582.69	581.11	576.94	575.62	575.20	575.07
31000	626.58	619.70	614.32	610.11	606.79	604.18	602.11	600.48	596.18	594.81	594.38	594.24
32000	646.80	639.69	634.14	629.79	626.36	623.67	621.53	619.85	615.41	614.00	613.55	613.41
33000	667.01	659.68	653.95	649.47	645.94	643.15	640.96	639.22	634.64	633.19	632.72	632.57
34000	687.22	679.67	673.77	669.15	665.51	662.64	660.38	658.59	653.87	652.37	651.90	651.74
35000	707.43	699.66	693.59	688.83	685.09	682.13	679.80	677.96	673.10	671.56	671.07	670.91
36000	727.65	719.65	713.40	708.51	704.66	701.62	699.22	697.33	692.33	690.75	690.24	690.08
37000	747.86	739.64	733.22	728.19	724.23	721.11	718.65	716.70	711.56	709.94	709.42	709.25
38000	768.07	759.63	753.04	747.87	743.81	740.60	738.07	736.07	730.79	729.12	728.59	728.42
39000	788.28	779.62	772.85	767.55	763.38	760.09	757.49	755.44	750.03	748.31	747.76	747.59
40000	808.50	799.61	792.67	787.23	782.95	779.58	776.92	774.81	769.26	767.50	766.94	766.76
41000	828.71	819.60	812.49	806.91	802.53	799.07	796.34	794.18	788.49	786.68	786.11	785.92
42000	848.92	839.59	832.30	826.59	822.10	818.56	815.76	813.55	807.72	805.87	805.28	805.09
43000	869.13	859.58	852.12	846.27	841.67	838.05	835.18	832.92	826.95	825.06	824.46	824.26
44000	889.34	879.57	871.94	865.95	861.25	857.54	854.61	852.29	846.18	844.25	843.63	843.43
45000	909.56	899.56	891.75	885.63	880.82	877.03	874.03	871.66	865.41	863.43	862.80	862.60
46000	929.77	919.55	911.57	905.32	900.40	896.52	893.45	891.03	884.64	882.62	881.98	881.77
47000	949.98	939.54	931.39	925.00	919.97	916.01	912.87	910.40	903.88	901.81	901.15	900.94
48000	970.19	959.53	951.20	944.68	939.54	935.50	932.30	929.77	923.11	921.00	920.32	920.11
49000	990.41	979.52	971.02	964.36	959.12	954.99	951.72	949.14	942.34	940.18	939.50	939.28
50000	1010.62	999.51	990.84	984.04	978.69	974.47	971.14	968.51	961.57	959.37	958.67	958.44
55000	1111.68	1099.46	1089.92	1082.44	1076.56	1071.92	1068.26	1065.36	1057.73	1055.31	1054.53	1054.29
60000	1212.74	1199.41	1189.00	1180.84	1174.43	1169.37	1165.37	1162.21	1153.88	1151.24	1150.40	1150.13
65000	1313.80	1299.36	1288.09	1279.25	1272.30	1266.82	1262.48	1259.06	1250.04	1247.18	1246.27	1245.98
70000	1414.86	1399.31	1387.17	1377.65	1370.17	1364.26	1359.60	1355.91	1346.20	1343.12	1342.13	1341.82
75000	1515.92	1499.26	1486.25	1476.05	1468.03	1461.71	1456.71	1452.76	1442.35	1439.05	1438.00	1437.66
80000	1616.99	1599.21	1585.34	1574.45	1565.90	1559.16	1553.83	1549.61	1538.51	1534.99	1533.87	1533.51
85000	1718.05	1699.16	1684.42	1672.86	1663.77	1656.60	1650.94	1646.46	1634.67	1630.93	1629.73	1629.35
90000	1819.11	1799.11	1783.50	1771.26	1761.64	1754.05	1748.05	1743.31	1730.82	1726.86	1725.60	1725.20
95000	1920.17	1899.06	1882.59	1869.67	1859.51	1851.50	1845.17	1840.16	1826.98	1822.80	1821.47	1821.04
100000	2021.23	1999.01	1981.67	1968.07	1957.38	1948.94	1942.28	1937.01	1923.13	1918.74	1917.33	1916.88

23%

Table 1

23.25%

MONTHLY
PAYMENT REQUIRED TO AMORTIZE A LOAN

TERM AMOUNT	1 YEAR	2 YEARS	3 YEARS	4 YEARS	5 YEARS	6 YEARS	7 YEARS	8 YEARS	9 YEARS	10 YEARS	11 YEARS	12 YEARS
50	4.71	2.63	1.95	1.61	1.42	1.30	1.22	1.16	1.11	1.08	1.06	1.04
100	9.42	5.25	3.89	3.22	2.84	2.59	2.43	2.31	2.22	2.16	2.11	2.07
200	18.84	10.50	7.77	6.44	5.67	5.18	4.85	4.61	4.44	4.31	4.21	4.14
300	28.26	15.75	11.66	9.66	8.51	7.77	7.27	6.91	6.65	6.46	6.32	6.21
400	37.68	21.00	15.54	12.88	11.34	10.35	9.69	9.21	8.87	8.62	8.42	8.28
500	47.10	26.25	19.43	16.10	14.17	12.94	12.11	11.52	11.09	10.77	10.53	10.34
600	56.52	31.50	23.31	19.32	17.01	15.53	14.53	13.82	13.30	12.92	12.63	12.41
700	65.94	36.75	27.19	22.54	19.84	18.12	16.95	16.12	15.52	15.07	14.74	14.48
800	75.36	42.00	31.08	25.76	22.67	20.70	19.37	18.42	17.74	17.23	16.84	16.55
900	84.78	47.25	34.96	28.97	25.51	23.29	21.79	20.73	19.95	19.38	18.95	18.62
1000	94.20	52.50	38.85	32.19	28.34	25.88	24.21	23.03	22.17	21.53	21.05	20.68
2000	188.40	105.00	77.69	64.38	56.67	51.75	48.41	46.05	44.33	43.06	42.10	41.36
3000	282.60	157.50	116.53	96.57	85.01	77.63	72.62	69.08	66.50	64.59	63.14	62.04
4000	376.79	210.00	155.37	128.76	113.34	103.50	96.82	92.10	88.66	86.11	84.19	82.72
5000	470.99	262.49	194.21	160.95	141.68	129.37	121.02	115.12	110.83	107.64	105.24	103.40
6000	565.19	314.99	233.05	193.14	170.01	155.25	145.23	138.15	132.99	129.17	126.28	124.08
7000	659.38	367.49	271.89	225.33	198.35	181.12	169.43	161.17	155.16	150.70	147.33	144.76
8000	753.58	419.99	310.73	257.51	226.68	206.99	193.63	184.19	177.32	172.22	168.38	165.44
9000	847.78	472.48	349.57	289.70	255.01	232.87	217.84	207.22	199.49	193.75	189.42	186.12
10000	941.98	524.98	388.41	321.89	283.35	258.74	242.04	230.24	221.65	215.28	210.47	206.80
11000	1036.17	577.48	427.25	354.08	311.68	284.61	266.25	253.26	243.82	236.81	231.52	227.48
12000	1130.37	629.98	466.09	386.27	340.02	310.49	290.45	276.29	265.98	258.33	252.56	248.16
13000	1224.57	682.47	504.93	418.46	368.35	336.36	314.65	299.31	288.15	279.86	273.61	268.84
14000	1318.76	734.97	543.77	450.65	396.69	362.23	338.86	322.33	310.31	301.39	294.66	289.52
15000	1412.96	787.47	582.61	482.83	425.02	388.11	363.06	345.36	332.48	322.92	315.70	310.20
16000	1507.16	839.97	621.45	515.02	453.35	413.98	387.26	368.38	354.64	344.44	336.75	330.88
17000	1601.35	892.46	660.29	547.21	481.69	439.85	411.47	391.40	376.81	365.97	357.79	351.56
18000	1695.55	944.96	699.13	579.40	510.02	465.73	435.67	414.43	398.97	387.50	378.84	372.24
19000	1789.75	997.46	737.97	611.59	538.36	491.60	459.87	437.45	421.14	409.02	399.89	392.92
20000	1883.95	1049.96	776.81	643.78	566.69	517.47	484.08	460.47	443.30	430.55	420.93	413.60
21000	1978.14	1102.45	815.65	675.97	595.03	543.35	508.28	483.50	465.47	452.08	441.98	434.27
22000	2072.34	1154.95	854.49	708.15	623.36	569.22	532.49	506.52	487.63	473.61	463.03	454.95
23000	2166.54	1207.45	893.33	740.34	651.69	595.09	556.69	529.54	509.80	495.13	484.07	475.63
24000	2260.73	1259.95	932.17	772.53	680.03	620.97	580.89	552.57	531.96	516.66	505.12	496.31
25000	2354.93	1312.44	971.01	804.72	708.36	646.84	605.10	575.59	554.13	538.19	526.17	516.99
26000	2449.13	1364.94	1009.85	836.91	736.70	672.71	629.30	598.61	576.29	559.72	547.21	537.67
27000	2543.32	1417.44	1048.69	869.10	765.03	698.59	653.50	621.64	598.46	581.24	568.26	558.35
28000	2637.52	1469.94	1087.53	901.29	793.37	724.46	677.71	644.66	620.62	602.77	589.31	579.03
29000	2731.72	1522.43	1126.37	933.47	821.70	750.33	701.91	667.69	642.79	624.30	610.35	599.71
30000	2825.92	1574.93	1165.21	965.66	850.03	776.21	726.11	690.71	664.95	645.83	631.40	620.39
31000	2920.11	1627.43	1204.05	997.85	878.37	802.08	750.32	713.73	687.12	667.35	652.44	641.07
32000	3014.31	1679.93	1242.89	1030.04	906.70	827.95	774.52	736.76	709.28	688.88	673.49	661.75
33000	3108.51	1732.42	1281.73	1062.23	935.04	853.83	798.73	759.78	731.45	710.41	694.54	682.43
34000	3202.70	1784.92	1320.57	1094.42	963.37	879.70	822.93	782.80	753.61	731.93	715.58	703.11
35000	3296.90	1837.42	1359.41	1126.61	991.71	905.57	847.13	805.83	775.78	753.46	736.63	723.79
36000	3391.10	1889.92	1398.25	1158.79	1020.04	931.45	871.34	828.85	797.94	774.99	757.68	744.47
37000	3485.29	1942.41	1437.09	1190.98	1048.37	957.32	895.54	851.87	820.11	796.52	778.72	765.15
38000	3579.49	1994.91	1475.93	1223.17	1076.71	983.19	919.74	874.90	842.27	818.04	799.77	785.83
39000	3673.69	2047.41	1514.77	1255.36	1105.04	1009.07	943.95	897.92	864.44	839.57	820.82	806.51
40000	3767.89	2099.91	1553.61	1287.55	1133.38	1034.94	968.15	920.94	886.60	861.10	841.86	827.19
41000	3862.08	2152.40	1592.45	1319.74	1161.71	1060.81	992.36	943.97	908.77	882.63	862.91	847.86
42000	3956.28	2204.90	1631.29	1351.93	1190.05	1086.69	1016.56	966.99	930.93	904.15	883.96	868.54
43000	4050.48	2257.40	1670.13	1384.11	1218.38	1112.56	1040.76	990.01	953.10	925.68	905.00	889.22
44000	4144.67	2309.90	1708.97	1416.30	1246.71	1138.44	1064.97	1013.04	975.26	947.21	926.05	909.90
45000	4238.87	2362.39	1747.81	1448.49	1275.05	1164.31	1089.17	1036.06	997.43	968.74	947.10	930.58
46000	4333.07	2414.89	1786.65	1480.68	1303.38	1190.18	1113.37	1059.08	1019.59	990.26	968.14	951.26
47000	4427.26	2467.39	1825.49	1512.87	1331.72	1216.06	1137.58	1082.11	1041.76	1011.79	989.19	971.94
48000	4521.46	2519.89	1864.33	1545.06	1360.05	1241.93	1161.78	1105.13	1063.92	1033.32	1010.23	992.62
49000	4615.66	2572.38	1903.17	1577.25	1388.39	1267.80	1185.98	1128.15	1086.09	1054.85	1031.28	1013.30
50000	4709.86	2624.88	1942.01	1609.43	1416.72	1293.68	1210.19	1151.18	1108.25	1076.37	1052.33	1033.98
55000	5180.84	2887.37	2136.21	1770.38	1558.39	1423.04	1331.21	1266.29	1219.08	1184.01	1157.56	1137.38
60000	5651.83	3149.86	2330.41	1931.32	1700.06	1552.41	1452.22	1381.41	1329.90	1291.65	1262.79	1240.78
65000	6122.81	3412.34	2524.61	2092.26	1841.73	1681.78	1573.24	1496.53	1440.73	1399.28	1368.02	1344.17
70000	6593.80	3674.83	2718.82	2253.21	1983.41	1811.14	1694.26	1611.65	1551.55	1506.92	1473.26	1447.57
75000	7064.78	3937.32	2913.02	2414.15	2125.08	1940.51	1815.28	1726.76	1662.38	1614.56	1578.49	1550.97
80000	7535.77	4199.81	3107.22	2575.09	2266.75	2069.88	1936.30	1841.88	1773.20	1722.19	1683.72	1654.37
85000	8006.75	4462.29	3301.42	2736.04	2408.42	2199.25	2057.32	1957.00	1884.03	1829.83	1788.95	1757.76
90000	8477.74	4724.78	3495.62	2896.98	2550.09	2328.61	2178.33	2072.12	1994.85	1937.47	1894.19	1861.16
95000	8948.72	4987.27	3689.82	3057.92	2691.76	2457.98	2299.35	2187.23	2105.68	2045.10	1999.42	1964.56
100000	9419.71	5249.76	3884.02	3218.86	2833.43	2587.35	2420.37	2302.35	2216.50	2152.74	2104.65	2067.96

23%

148

Table 1

MONTHLY 23.25%

PAYMENT REQUIRED TO AMORTIZE A LOAN

TERM AMOUNT	13 YEARS	14 YEARS	15 YEARS	16 YEARS	17 YEARS	18 YEARS	19 YEARS	20 YEARS	25 YEARS	30 YEARS	35 YEARS	40 YEARS
50	1.02	1.01	1.01	1.00	.99	.99	.99	.98	.98	.97	.97	.97
100	2.04	2.02	2.01	1.99	1.98	1.97	1.97	1.96	1.95	1.94	1.94	1.94
200	4.08	4.04	4.01	3.98	3.96	3.94	3.93	3.92	3.89	3.88	3.88	3.88
300	6.12	6.06	6.01	5.97	5.94	5.91	5.89	5.88	5.84	5.82	5.82	5.82
400	8.16	8.08	8.01	7.95	7.91	7.88	7.85	7.83	7.78	7.76	7.76	7.76
500	10.20	10.09	10.01	9.94	9.89	9.85	9.82	9.79	9.72	9.70	9.70	9.69
600	12.24	12.11	12.01	11.93	11.87	11.82	11.78	11.75	11.67	11.64	11.63	11.63
700	14.28	14.13	14.01	13.92	13.84	13.79	13.74	13.70	13.61	13.58	13.57	13.57
800	16.32	16.15	16.01	15.90	15.82	15.75	15.70	15.66	15.55	15.52	15.51	15.51
900	18.36	18.17	18.01	17.89	17.80	17.72	17.66	17.62	17.50	17.46	17.45	17.44
1000	20.40	20.18	20.01	19.88	19.77	19.69	19.63	19.58	19.44	19.40	19.39	19.38
2000	40.80	40.36	40.02	39.75	39.54	39.38	39.25	39.15	38.88	38.79	38.77	38.76
3000	61.20	60.54	60.03	59.63	59.31	59.07	58.87	58.72	58.31	58.19	58.15	58.14
4000	81.59	80.72	80.04	79.50	79.08	78.75	78.49	78.29	77.75	77.58	77.53	77.51
5000	101.99	100.90	100.04	99.38	98.85	98.44	98.11	97.86	97.19	96.98	96.91	96.89
6000	122.39	121.07	120.05	119.25	118.62	118.13	117.74	117.43	116.62	116.37	116.29	116.27
7000	142.78	141.25	140.06	139.12	138.39	137.81	137.36	137.00	136.06	135.77	135.67	135.64
8000	163.18	161.43	160.07	159.00	158.16	157.50	156.98	156.57	155.50	155.16	155.05	155.02
9000	183.58	181.61	180.07	178.87	177.93	177.19	176.60	176.14	174.93	174.55	174.44	174.40
10000	203.98	201.79	200.08	198.75	197.70	196.87	196.22	195.71	194.37	193.95	193.82	193.77
11000	224.37	221.96	220.09	218.62	217.47	216.56	215.85	215.28	213.81	213.34	213.20	213.15
12000	244.77	242.14	240.10	238.49	237.24	236.25	235.47	234.85	233.24	232.74	232.58	232.53
13000	265.17	262.32	260.10	258.37	257.01	255.93	255.09	254.42	252.68	252.13	251.96	251.91
14000	285.56	282.50	280.11	278.24	276.78	275.62	274.71	273.99	272.12	271.53	271.34	271.28
15000	305.96	302.68	300.12	298.12	296.54	295.31	294.33	293.56	291.55	290.92	290.72	290.66
16000	326.36	322.85	320.13	317.99	316.31	315.00	313.96	313.14	310.99	310.32	310.10	310.04
17000	346.75	343.03	340.13	337.86	336.08	334.68	333.58	332.71	330.42	329.71	329.48	329.41
18000	367.15	363.21	360.14	357.74	355.85	354.37	353.20	352.28	349.86	349.10	348.87	348.79
19000	387.55	383.39	380.15	377.61	375.62	374.06	372.82	371.85	369.30	368.50	368.25	368.17
20000	407.95	403.57	400.16	397.49	395.39	393.74	392.44	391.42	388.73	387.89	387.63	387.54
21000	428.34	423.75	420.16	417.36	415.16	413.43	412.07	410.99	408.17	407.29	407.01	406.92
22000	448.74	443.92	440.17	437.23	434.93	433.12	431.69	430.56	427.61	426.68	426.39	426.30
23000	469.14	464.10	460.18	457.11	454.70	452.80	451.31	450.13	447.04	446.08	445.77	445.67
24000	489.53	484.28	480.19	476.98	474.47	472.49	470.93	469.70	466.48	465.47	465.15	465.05
25000	509.93	504.46	500.19	496.86	494.24	492.18	490.55	489.27	485.92	484.86	484.53	484.43
26000	530.33	524.64	520.20	516.73	514.01	511.86	510.18	508.84	505.35	504.26	503.91	503.81
27000	550.72	544.81	540.21	536.60	533.78	531.55	529.80	528.41	524.79	523.65	523.30	523.18
28000	571.12	564.99	560.22	556.48	553.55	551.24	549.42	547.98	544.23	543.05	542.68	542.56
29000	591.52	585.17	580.22	576.35	573.32	570.93	569.04	567.55	563.66	562.44	562.06	561.94
30000	611.92	605.35	600.23	596.23	593.08	590.61	588.66	587.12	583.10	581.84	581.44	581.31
31000	632.31	625.53	620.24	616.10	612.85	610.30	608.29	606.69	602.53	601.23	600.82	600.69
32000	652.71	645.70	640.25	635.98	632.62	629.99	627.91	626.27	621.97	620.63	620.20	620.07
33000	673.11	665.88	660.25	655.85	652.39	649.67	647.53	645.84	641.41	640.02	639.58	639.44
34000	693.50	686.06	680.26	675.72	672.16	669.36	665.15	665.41	660.84	659.41	658.96	658.82
35000	713.90	706.24	700.27	695.60	691.93	689.05	686.77	684.98	680.28	678.81	678.34	678.20
36000	734.30	726.42	720.28	715.47	711.70	708.73	706.39	704.55	699.72	698.20	697.73	697.57
37000	754.70	746.59	740.28	735.35	731.47	728.42	726.02	724.12	719.15	717.60	717.11	716.95
38000	775.09	766.77	760.29	755.22	751.24	748.11	745.64	743.69	738.59	736.99	736.49	736.33
39000	795.49	786.95	780.30	775.09	771.01	767.79	765.26	763.26	758.03	756.39	755.87	755.71
40000	815.89	807.13	800.31	794.97	790.78	787.48	784.88	782.83	777.46	775.78	775.25	775.08
41000	836.28	827.31	820.31	814.84	810.55	807.17	804.50	802.40	796.90	795.17	794.63	794.46
42000	856.68	847.49	840.32	834.72	830.32	826.86	824.13	821.97	816.34	814.57	814.01	813.84
43000	877.08	867.66	860.33	854.59	850.09	846.54	843.75	841.54	835.77	833.96	833.39	833.21
44000	897.47	887.84	880.34	874.46	869.86	866.23	863. 7	861.11	855.21	853.36	852.77	852.59
45000	917.87	908.02	900.34	894.34	889.62	885.92	882.59	880.68	874.64	872.75	872.16	871.97
46000	938.27	928.20	920.35	914.21	909.39	905.60	902.61	900.25	894.08	892.15	891.54	891.34
47000	958.67	948.38	940.36	934.09	929.16	925.29	922.24	919.82	913.52	911.54	910.92	910.72
48000	979.06	968.55	960.37	953.96	948.93	944.98	941.86	939.40	932.95	930.94	930.30	930.10
49000	999.46	988.73	980.37	973.83	968.70	964.66	961.48	958.97	952.39	950.33	949.68	949.47
50000	1019.86	1008.91	1000.38	993.71	988.47	984.35	981.10	978.54	971.83	969.72	969.06	968.85
55000	1121.84	1109.80	1100.42	1093.08	1087.32	1082.79	1079.21	1076.39	1069.01	1066.70	1065.97	1065.74
60000	1223.83	1210.69	1200.46	1192.45	1186.16	1181.22	1177.32	1174.24	1166.19	1163.67	1162.87	1162.62
65000	1325.81	1311.58	1300.49	1291.82	1285.01	1279.65	1275.43	1272.10	1263.37	1260.64	1259.78	1259.51
70000	1427.80	1412.47	1400.53	1391.19	1383.86	1378.09	1373.54	1369.95	1360.56	1357.61	1356.68	1356.39
75000	1529.78	1513.36	1500.57	1490.56	1482.71	1476.52	1471.65	1467.80	1457.74	1454.58	1453.59	1453.28
80000	1631.77	1614.25	1600.61	1589.93	1581.55	1574.96	1569.76	1565.66	1554.92	1551.56	1550.50	1550.16
85000	1733.75	1715.14	1700.64	1689.30	1680.40	1673.39	1667.87	1663.51	1652.10	1648.53	1647.40	1647.04
90000	1835.74	1816.03	1800.68	1788.67	1779.24	1771.83	1765.98	1761.36	1749.28	1745.50	1744.31	1743.93
95000	1937.72	1916.92	1900.72	1888.04	1878.09	1870.26	1864.09	1859.22	1846.47	1842.47	1841.21	1840.81
100000	2039.71	2017.82	2000.76	1987.41	1976.94	1968.70	1962.20	1957.07	1943.65	1939.44	1938.12	1937.70

23%

Table 1

23.50%

MONTHLY

PAYMENT REQUIRED TO AMORTIZE A LOAN

TERM AMOUNT	1 YEAR	2 YEARS	3 YEARS	4 YEARS	5 YEARS	6 YEARS	7 YEARS	8 YEARS	9 YEARS	10 YEARS	11 YEARS	12 YEARS
50	4.72	2.64	1.95	1.62	1.43	1.31	1.22	1.16	1.12	1.09	1.07	1.05
100	9.44	5.27	3.90	3.24	2.85	2.61	2.44	2.32	2.24	2.18	2.13	2.09
200	18.87	10.53	7.80	6.47	5.70	5.21	4.88	4.64	4.47	4.35	4.25	4.18
300	28.30	15.79	11.70	9.70	8.55	7.81	7.31	6.96	6.70	6.52	6.37	6.26
400	37.73	21.05	15.59	12.94	11.40	10.41	9.75	9.28	8.94	8.69	8.49	8.35
500	47.16	26.32	19.49	16.17	14.24	13.02	12.19	11.60	11.17	10.86	10.62	10.44
600	56.60	31.58	23.39	19.40	17.09	15.62	14.62	13.92	13.40	13.03	12.74	12.52
700	66.03	36.84	27.28	22.63	19.94	18.22	17.06	16.24	15.64	15.20	14.86	14.61
800	75.46	42.10	31.18	25.87	22.79	20.82	19.49	18.55	17.87	17.37	16.98	16.69
900	84.89	47.36	35.08	29.10	25.64	23.43	21.93	20.87	20.10	19.54	19.11	18.78
1000	94.32	52.63	38.98	32.33	28.48	26.03	24.37	23.19	22.34	21.71	21.23	20.87
2000	188.64	105.25	77.95	64.66	56.96	52.05	48.73	46.38	44.67	43.41	42.45	41.73
3000	282.96	157.87	116.92	96.98	85.44	78.08	73.09	69.56	67.00	65.11	63.68	62.59
4000	377.28	210.49	155.89	129.31	113.92	104.10	97.45	92.75	89.34	86.81	84.90	83.45
5000	471.59	263.11	194.86	161.64	142.40	130.13	121.81	115.94	111.67	108.51	106.13	104.31
6000	565.91	315.74	233.83	193.96	170.88	156.15	146.17	139.12	134.00	130.21	127.35	125.17
7000	660.23	368.36	272.80	226.29	199.35	182.17	170.53	162.31	156.34	151.91	148.57	146.03
8000	754.55	420.98	311.77	258.61	227.83	208.20	194.89	185.49	178.67	173.61	169.80	166.89
9000	848.87	473.60	350.74	290.94	256.31	234.22	219.25	208.68	201.00	195.31	191.02	187.76
10000	943.18	526.22	389.71	323.27	284.79	260.25	243.61	231.87	223.34	217.01	212.25	208.62
11000	1037.50	578.85	428.68	355.59	313.27	286.27	267.97	255.05	245.67	238.71	233.47	229.48
12000	1131.82	631.47	467.65	387.92	341.75	312.29	292.33	278.24	268.00	260.41	254.69	250.34
13000	1226.14	684.09	506.63	420.24	370.23	338.32	316.69	301.43	290.34	282.11	275.92	271.20
14000	1320.45	736.71	545.60	452.57	398.70	364.34	341.05	324.61	312.67	303.81	297.14	292.06
15000	1414.77	789.33	584.57	484.90	427.18	390.37	365.41	347.80	335.00	325.51	318.37	312.92
16000	1509.09	841.95	623.54	517.22	455.66	416.39	389.77	370.98	357.33	347.21	339.59	333.78
17000	1603.41	894.58	662.51	549.55	484.14	442.42	414.14	394.17	379.67	368.91	360.81	354.64
18000	1697.73	947.20	701.48	581.87	512.62	468.44	438.50	417.36	402.00	390.61	382.04	375.51
19000	1792.04	999.82	740.45	614.20	541.10	494.46	462.86	440.54	424.33	412.31	403.26	396.37
20000	1886.36	1052.44	779.42	646.53	569.57	520.49	487.22	463.73	446.67	434.01	424.49	417.23
21000	1980.68	1105.06	818.39	678.85	598.05	546.51	511.58	486.92	469.00	455.71	445.71	438.09
22000	2075.00	1157.69	857.36	711.18	626.53	572.54	535.94	510.10	491.33	477.41	466.93	458.95
23000	2169.31	1210.31	896.33	743.50	655.01	598.56	560.30	533.29	513.67	499.11	488.16	479.81
24000	2263.63	1262.93	935.30	775.83	683.49	624.58	584.66	556.47	536.00	520.82	509.38	500.67
25000	2357.95	1315.55	974.28	808.16	711.97	650.61	609.02	579.66	558.33	542.52	530.61	521.53
26000	2452.27	1368.17	1013.25	840.48	740.45	676.63	633.38	602.85	580.67	564.22	551.83	542.39
27000	2546.59	1420.80	1052.22	872.81	768.92	702.66	657.74	626.03	603.00	585.92	573.05	563.26
28000	2640.90	1473.42	1091.19	905.13	797.40	728.68	682.10	649.22	625.33	607.62	594.28	584.12
29000	2735.22	1526.04	1130.16	937.46	825.88	754.70	706.46	672.40	647.66	629.32	615.50	604.98
30000	2829.54	1578.66	1169.13	969.79	854.36	780.73	730.82	695.59	670.00	651.02	636.73	625.84
31000	2923.86	1631.28	1208.10	1002.11	882.84	806.75	755.18	718.78	692.33	672.72	657.95	646.70
32000	3018.17	1683.90	1247.07	1034.44	911.32	832.78	779.54	741.96	714.66	694.42	679.17	667.56
33000	3112.49	1736.53	1286.04	1066.76	939.79	858.80	803.90	765.15	737.00	716.12	700.40	688.42
34000	3206.81	1789.15	1325.01	1099.09	968.27	884.83	828.27	788.34	759.33	737.82	721.62	709.28
35000	3301.13	1841.77	1363.98	1131.42	996.75	910.85	852.63	811.52	781.66	759.52	742.85	730.14
36000	3395.45	1894.39	1402.95	1163.74	1025.23	936.87	876.99	834.71	804.00	781.22	764.07	751.01
37000	3489.76	1947.01	1441.92	1196.07	1053.71	962.90	901.35	857.89	826.33	802.92	785.29	771.87
38000	3584.08	1999.64	1480.90	1228.39	1082.19	988.92	925.71	881.08	848.66	824.62	806.52	792.73
39000	3678.40	2052.26	1519.87	1260.72	1110.67	1014.95	950.07	904.27	871.00	846.32	827.74	813.59
40000	3772.72	2104.88	1558.84	1293.05	1139.14	1040.97	974.43	927.45	893.33	868.02	848.97	834.45
41000	3867.03	2157.50	1597.81	1325.37	1167.62	1066.99	998.79	950.64	915.66	889.72	870.19	855.31
42000	3961.35	2210.12	1636.78	1357.70	1196.10	1093.02	1023.15	973.83	937.99	911.42	891.41	876.17
43000	4055.67	2262.75	1675.75	1390.02	1224.58	1119.04	1047.51	997.01	960.33	933.12	912.64	897.03
44000	4149.99	2315.37	1714.72	1422.35	1253.06	1145.07	1071.87	1020.20	982.66	954.82	933.86	917.90
45000	4244.31	2367.99	1753.69	1454.68	1281.54	1171.09	1096.23	1043.38	1004.99	976.52	955.09	938.76
46000	4338.62	2420.61	1792.66	1487.00	1310.02	1197.12	1120.59	1066.57	1027.33	998.22	976.31	959.62
47000	4432.94	2473.23	1831.63	1519.33	1338.49	1223.14	1144.95	1089.76	1049.66	1019.93	997.53	980.48
48000	4527.26	2525.85	1870.60	1551.65	1366.97	1249.16	1169.31	1112.94	1071.99	1041.63	1018.76	1001.34
49000	4621.58	2578.48	1909.57	1583.98	1395.45	1275.19	1193.67	1136.13	1094.33	1063.33	1039.98	1022.20
50000	4715.89	2631.10	1948.55	1616.31	1423.93	1301.21	1218.03	1159.31	1116.66	1085.03	1061.21	1043.06
55000	5187.48	2894.21	2143.40	1777.94	1566.32	1431.33	1339.84	1275.25	1228.32	1193.53	1167.33	1147.37
60000	5659.07	3157.32	2338.25	1939.57	1708.71	1561.45	1461.64	1391.18	1339.99	1302.03	1273.45	1251.67
65000	6130.66	3420.43	2533.11	2101.20	1851.11	1691.57	1583.44	1507.11	1451.66	1410.53	1379.57	1355.98
70000	6602.25	3683.54	2727.96	2262.83	1993.50	1821.69	1705.25	1623.04	1563.33	1519.04	1485.69	1460.28
75000	7073.84	3946.65	2922.82	2424.46	2135.89	1951.82	1827.05	1738.97	1674.99	1627.54	1591.81	1564.59
80000	7545.43	4209.75	3117.67	2586.09	2278.28	2081.94	1948.85	1854.90	1786.65	1736.04	1697.93	1668.90
85000	8017.02	4472.86	3312.52	2747.72	2420.68	2212.06	2070.66	1970.83	1898.32	1844.54	1804.05	1773.20
90000	8488.61	4735.97	3507.38	2909.35	2563.07	2342.18	2192.46	2086.76	2009.98	1953.04	1910.17	1877.51
95000	8960.20	4999.08	3702.23	3070.98	2705.46	2472.30	2314.26	2202.69	2121.65	2061.55	2016.29	1981.81
100000	9431.78	5262.19	3897.09	3232.61	2847.85	2602.42	2436.06	2318.62	2233.31	2170.05	2122.41	2086.12

23%

Table 1

MONTHLY

23.50%

PAYMENT REQUIRED TO AMORTIZE A LOAN

ERM ꞮUNT	13 YEARS	14 YEARS	15 YEARS	16 YEARS	17 YEARS	18 YEARS	19 YEARS	20 YEARS	25 YEARS	30 YEARS	35 YEARS	40 YEARS
50	1.03	1.02	1.01	1.01	1.00	1.00	1.00	.99	.99	.99	.98	.98
100	2.06	2.04	2.02	2.01	2.00	1.99	1.99	1.98	1.97	1.97	1.96	1.96
200	4.12	4.08	4.04	4.02	4.00	3.98	3.97	3.96	3.93	3.93	3.92	3.92
300	6.18	6.11	6.06	6.03	5.99	5.97	5.95	5.94	5.90	5.89	5.88	5.88
400	8.24	8.15	8.08	8.03	7.99	7.96	7.93	7.91	7.86	7.85	7.84	7.84
500	10.30	10.19	10.10	10.04	9.99	9.95	9.92	9.89	9.83	9.81	9.80	9.80
600	12.35	12.22	12.12	12.05	11.98	11.94	11.90	11.87	11.79	11.77	11.76	11.76
700	14.41	14.26	14.14	14.05	13.98	13.92	13.88	13.85	13.75	13.73	13.72	13.71
800	16.47	16.30	16.16	16.06	15.98	15.91	15.86	15.82	15.72	15.69	15.68	15.67
900	18.53	18.33	18.18	18.07	17.97	17.90	17.84	17.80	17.68	17.65	17.64	17.63
1000	20.59	20.37	20.20	20.07	19.97	19.89	19.83	19.78	19.65	19.61	19.59	19.59
2000	41.17	40.74	40.40	40.14	39.94	39.77	39.65	39.55	39.29	39.21	39.18	39.18
3000	61.75	61.10	60.60	60.21	59.90	59.66	59.47	59.32	58.93	58.81	58.77	58.76
4000	82.33	81.47	80.80	80.28	79.87	79.54	79.29	79.09	78.57	78.41	78.36	78.35
5000	102.92	101.84	101.00	100.34	99.83	99.43	99.11	98.86	98.21	98.01	97.95	97.93
6000	123.50	122.20	121.20	120.41	119.80	119.31	118.93	118.63	117.86	117.61	117.54	117.52
7000	144.08	142.57	141.40	140.48	139.76	139.20	138.76	138.41	137.50	137.22	137.13	137.10
8000	164.66	162.94	161.60	160.55	159.73	159.08	158.58	158.18	157.14	156.82	156.72	156.69
9000	185.25	183.30	181.79	180.62	179.69	178.97	178.40	177.95	176.78	176.42	176.31	176.27
10000	205.83	203.67	201.99	200.68	199.66	198.85	198.22	197.72	196.42	196.02	195.90	195.86
11000	226.41	224.04	222.19	220.75	219.62	218.74	218.04	217.49	216.06	215.62	215.48	215.44
12000	246.99	244.40	242.39	240.82	239.59	238.62	237.86	237.26	235.71	235.22	235.07	235.03
13000	267.57	264.77	262.59	260.89	259.55	258.51	257.68	257.03	255.35	254.82	254.66	254.61
14000	288.16	285.14	282.79	280.96	279.52	278.39	277.51	276.81	274.99	274.43	274.25	274.20
15000	308.74	305.50	302.99	301.02	299.48	298.28	297.33	296.58	294.63	294.03	293.84	293.78
16000	329.32	325.87	323.19	321.09	319.45	318.16	317.15	316.35	314.27	313.63	313.43	313.37
17000	349.90	346.24	343.39	341.16	339.42	338.05	336.97	336.12	333.91	333.23	333.02	332.95
18000	370.49	366.60	363.58	361.23	359.38	357.93	356.79	355.89	353.56	352.83	352.61	352.54
19000	391.07	386.97	383.78	381.29	379.35	377.82	376.61	375.66	373.20	372.43	372.20	372.12
20000	411.65	407.34	403.98	401.36	399.31	397.70	396.43	395.44	392.84	392.04	391.79	391.71
21000	432.23	427.70	424.18	421.43	419.28	417.59	416.26	415.21	412.48	411.64	411.37	411.29
22000	452.82	448.07	444.38	441.50	439.24	437.47	436.08	434.98	432.12	431.24	430.96	430.88
23000	473.40	468.44	464.58	461.57	459.21	457.35	455.90	454.75	451.76	450.84	450.55	450.46
24000	493.98	488.80	484.78	481.63	479.17	477.24	475.72	474.52	471.41	470.44	470.14	470.05
25000	514.56	509.17	504.98	501.70	499.14	497.12	495.54	494.29	491.05	490.04	489.73	489.63
26000	535.14	529.54	525.17	521.77	519.10	517.01	515.36	514.06	510.69	509.64	509.32	509.22
27000	555.73	549.90	545.37	541.84	539.07	536.89	535.18	533.84	530.33	529.25	528.91	528.80
28000	576.31	570.27	565.57	561.91	559.03	556.78	555.01	553.61	549.97	548.85	548.50	548.39
29000	596.89	590.64	585.77	581.97	579.00	576.66	574.83	573.38	569.62	568.45	568.09	567.97
30000	617.47	611.00	605.97	602.04	598.96	596.55	594.65	593.15	589.26	588.05	587.68	587.56
31000	638.06	631.37	626.17	622.11	618.93	616.43	614.47	612.92	608.90	607.65	607.26	607.14
32000	658.64	651.74	646.37	642.18	638.90	636.32	634.29	632.69	628.54	627.25	626.85	626.73
33000	679.22	672.10	666.57	662.25	658.86	656.20	654.11	652.47	648.18	646.86	646.44	646.31
34000	699.80	692.47	686.77	682.31	678.83	676.09	673.93	672.24	667.82	666.46	666.03	665.90
35000	720.39	712.84	706.96	702.38	698.79	695.97	693.76	692.01	687.47	686.06	685.62	685.48
36000	740.97	733.20	727.16	722.45	718.76	715.86	713.58	711.78	707.11	705.66	705.21	705.07
37000	761.55	753.57	747.36	742.52	738.72	735.74	733.40	731.55	726.75	725.26	724.80	724.65
38000	782.13	773.94	767.56	762.58	758.69	755.63	753.22	751.32	746.39	744.86	744.39	744.24
39000	802.71	794.30	787.76	782.65	778.65	775.51	773.04	771.09	766.03	764.46	763.98	763.82
40000	823.30	814.67	807.96	802.72	798.62	795.40	792.86	790.87	785.67	784.07	783.57	783.41
41000	843.88	835.03	828.16	822.79	818.58	815.28	812.68	810.64	805.32	803.67	803.15	802.99
42000	864.46	855.40	848.36	842.86	838.55	835.17	832.51	830.41	824.96	823.27	822.74	822.58
43000	885.04	875.77	868.56	862.92	858.51	855.05	852.33	850.18	844.60	842.87	842.33	842.16
44000	905.63	896.13	888.75	882.99	878.48	874.94	872.15	869.95	864.24	862.47	861.92	861.75
45000	926.21	916.50	908.95	903.06	898.44	894.82	891.97	889.72	883.88	882.07	881.51	881.33
46000	946.79	936.87	929.15	923.13	918.41	914.70	911.79	909.49	903.52	901.68	901.10	900.92
47000	967.37	957.23	949.35	943.20	938.37	934.59	931.61	929.27	923.17	921.28	920.69	920.51
48000	987.96	977.60	969.55	963.26	958.34	954.47	951.43	949.04	942.81	940.88	940.28	940.09
49000	1008.54	997.97	989.75	983.33	978.31	974.36	971.26	968.81	962.45	960.48	959.87	959.68
50000	1029.12	1018.33	1009.95	1003.40	998.27	994.24	991.08	988.58	982.09	980.08	979.46	979.26
55000	1132.03	1120.17	1110.94	1103.74	1098.10	1093.67	1090.18	1087.44	1080.30	1078.09	1077.40	1077.19
60000	1234.94	1222.00	1211.94	1204.08	1197.92	1193.09	1189.29	1186.30	1178.51	1176.10	1175.35	1175.11
65000	1337.85	1323.83	1312.93	1304.42	1297.75	1292.52	1288.40	1285.15	1276.72	1274.10	1273.29	1273.04
70000	1440.77	1425.67	1413.92	1404.76	1397.58	1391.94	1387.51	1384.01	1374.93	1372.11	1371.24	1370.96
75000	1543.68	1527.50	1514.92	1505.10	1497.40	1491.36	1486.61	1482.87	1473.13	1470.12	1469.18	1468.89
80000	1646.59	1629.33	1615.91	1605.44	1597.23	1590.79	1585.72	1581.73	1571.34	1568.13	1567.13	1566.81
85000	1749.50	1731.16	1716.91	1705.78	1697.06	1690.21	1684.83	1680.58	1669.55	1666.14	1665.07	1664.74
90000	1852.41	1833.00	1817.90	1806.11	1796.88	1789.64	1783.93	1779.44	1767.76	1764.15	1763.02	1762.66
95000	1955.32	1934.83	1918.90	1906.45	1896.71	1889.06	1883.04	1878.30	1865.97	1862.15	1860.96	1860.59
100000	2058.23	2036.66	2019.89	2006.79	1996.54	1988.48	1982.15	1977.16	1964.18	1960.16	1958.91	1958.52

23%

Table 1

23.75%

MONTHLY

PAYMENT REQUIRED TO AMORTIZE A LOAN

TERM AMOUNT	1 YEAR	2 YEARS	3 YEARS	4 YEARS	5 YEARS	6 YEARS	7 YEARS	8 YEARS	9 YEARS	10 YEARS	11 YEARS	12 YEARS
50	4.73	2.64	1.96	1.63	1.44	1.31	1.23	1.17	1.13	1.10	1.08	1.06
100	9.45	5.28	3.92	3.25	2.87	2.62	2.46	2.34	2.26	2.19	2.15	2.11
200	18.89	10.55	7.83	6.50	5.73	5.24	4.91	4.67	4.51	4.38	4.29	4.21
300	28.34	15.83	11.74	9.74	8.59	7.86	7.36	7.01	6.76	6.57	6.43	6.32
400	37.78	21.10	15.65	12.99	11.45	10.48	9.81	9.34	9.01	8.75	8.57	8.42
500	47.22	26.38	19.56	16.24	14.32	13.09	12.26	11.68	11.26	10.94	10.71	10.53
600	56.67	31.65	23.47	19.48	17.18	15.71	14.72	14.01	13.51	13.13	12.85	12.63
700	66.11	36.93	27.38	22.73	20.04	18.33	17.17	16.35	15.76	15.32	14.99	14.74
800	75.56	42.20	31.29	25.98	22.90	20.95	19.62	18.68	18.01	17.50	17.13	16.84
900	85.00	47.48	35.20	29.22	25.77	23.56	22.07	21.02	20.26	19.69	19.27	18.94
1000	94.44	52.75	39.11	32.47	28.63	26.18	24.52	23.35	22.51	21.88	21.41	21.05
2000	188.88	105.50	78.21	64.93	57.25	52.36	49.04	46.70	45.01	43.75	42.81	42.09
3000	283.32	158.24	117.31	97.40	85.87	78.53	73.56	70.05	67.51	65.63	64.21	63.13
4000	377.76	210.99	156.41	129.86	114.50	104.71	98.08	93.40	90.01	87.50	85.61	84.18
5000	472.20	263.74	195.51	162.32	143.12	130.88	122.59	116.75	112.51	109.38	107.02	105.22
6000	566.64	316.48	234.62	194.79	171.74	157.06	147.11	140.10	135.02	131.25	128.42	126.26
7000	661.08	369.23	273.72	227.25	200.37	183.23	171.63	163.45	157.52	153.12	149.82	147.31
8000	755.51	421.98	312.82	259.72	228.99	209.41	196.15	186.80	180.02	175.00	171.22	168.35
9000	849.95	474.72	351.92	292.18	257.61	235.58	220.67	210.15	202.52	196.87	192.62	189.39
10000	944.39	527.47	391.02	324.64	286.24	261.76	245.18	233.50	225.02	218.75	214.03	210.44
11000	1038.83	580.22	430.12	357.11	314.86	287.93	269.70	256.85	247.52	240.62	235.43	231.48
12000	1133.27	632.96	469.23	389.57	343.48	314.11	294.22	280.20	270.03	262.49	256.83	252.52
13000	1227.71	685.71	508.33	422.03	372.10	340.28	318.74	303.55	292.53	284.37	278.23	273.57
14000	1322.15	738.45	547.43	454.50	400.73	366.46	343.26	326.90	315.03	306.24	299.63	294.61
15000	1416.58	791.20	586.53	486.96	429.35	392.63	367.77	350.25	337.53	328.12	321.04	315.65
16000	1511.02	843.95	625.63	519.43	457.97	418.81	392.29	373.60	360.03	349.99	342.44	336.70
17000	1605.46	896.69	664.73	551.89	486.60	444.98	416.81	396.95	382.53	371.86	363.84	357.74
18000	1699.90	949.44	703.84	584.35	515.22	471.16	441.33	420.29	405.04	393.74	385.24	378.78
19000	1794.34	1002.19	742.94	616.82	543.84	497.34	465.85	443.64	427.54	415.61	406.64	399.83
20000	1888.78	1054.93	782.04	649.28	572.47	523.51	490.36	466.99	450.04	437.49	428.05	420.87
21000	1983.22	1107.68	821.14	681.74	601.09	549.69	514.88	490.34	472.54	459.36	449.45	441.91
22000	2077.66	1160.43	860.24	714.21	629.71	575.86	539.40	513.69	495.04	481.23	470.85	462.96
23000	2172.09	1213.17	899.34	746.67	658.33	602.04	563.92	537.04	517.54	503.11	492.25	484.00
24000	2266.53	1265.92	938.45	779.14	686.96	628.21	588.44	560.39	540.05	524.98	513.66	505.04
25000	2360.97	1318.67	977.55	811.60	715.58	654.39	612.95	583.74	562.55	546.86	535.06	526.09
26000	2455.41	1371.41	1016.65	844.06	744.20	680.56	637.47	607.09	585.05	568.73	556.46	547.13
27000	2549.85	1424.16	1055.75	876.53	772.83	706.74	661.99	630.44	607.55	590.60	577.86	568.17
28000	2644.29	1476.90	1094.85	908.99	801.45	732.91	686.51	653.79	630.05	612.48	599.26	589.22
29000	2738.73	1529.65	1133.95	941.45	830.07	759.09	711.03	677.14	652.55	634.35	620.67	610.26
30000	2833.16	1582.40	1173.06	973.92	858.70	785.26	735.54	700.49	675.06	656.23	642.07	631.30
31000	2927.60	1635.14	1212.16	1006.38	887.32	811.44	760.06	723.84	697.56	678.10	663.47	652.35
32000	3022.04	1687.89	1251.26	1038.85	915.94	837.61	784.58	747.19	720.06	699.97	684.87	673.39
33000	3116.48	1740.64	1290.36	1071.31	944.57	863.79	809.10	770.54	742.56	721.85	706.27	694.43
34000	3210.92	1793.38	1329.46	1103.77	973.19	889.96	833.62	793.89	765.06	743.72	727.68	715.48
35000	3305.36	1846.13	1368.56	1136.24	1001.81	916.14	858.13	817.23	787.57	765.60	749.08	736.52
36000	3399.80	1898.88	1407.67	1168.70	1030.43	942.31	882.65	840.58	810.07	787.47	770.48	757.56
37000	3494.24	1951.62	1446.77	1201.16	1059.06	968.49	907.17	863.93	832.57	809.34	791.88	778.61
38000	3588.67	2004.37	1485.87	1233.63	1087.68	994.67	931.69	887.28	855.07	831.22	813.28	799.65
39000	3683.11	2057.11	1524.97	1266.09	1116.30	1020.84	956.21	910.63	877.57	853.09	834.69	820.69
40000	3777.55	2109.86	1564.07	1298.56	1144.93	1047.02	980.72	933.98	900.07	874.97	856.09	841.74
41000	3871.99	2162.61	1603.18	1331.02	1173.55	1073.19	1005.24	957.33	922.58	896.84	877.49	862.78
42000	3966.43	2215.35	1642.28	1363.48	1202.17	1099.37	1029.76	980.68	945.08	918.71	898.89	883.82
43000	4060.87	2268.10	1681.38	1395.95	1230.80	1125.54	1054.28	1004.03	967.58	940.59	920.30	904.87
44000	4155.31	2320.85	1720.48	1428.41	1259.42	1151.72	1078.80	1027.38	990.08	962.46	941.70	925.91
45000	4249.74	2373.59	1759.58	1460.88	1288.04	1177.89	1103.31	1050.73	1012.58	984.34	963.10	946.95
46000	4344.18	2426.34	1798.68	1493.34	1316.66	1204.07	1127.83	1074.08	1035.08	1006.21	984.50	967.99
47000	4438.62	2479.09	1837.79	1525.80	1345.29	1230.24	1152.35	1097.43	1057.59	1028.08	1005.90	989.04
48000	4533.06	2531.83	1876.89	1558.27	1373.91	1256.42	1176.87	1120.78	1080.09	1049.96	1027.31	1010.08
49000	4627.50	2584.58	1915.99	1590.73	1402.53	1282.59	1201.39	1144.13	1102.59	1071.83	1048.71	1031.12
50000	4721.94	2637.33	1955.09	1623.19	1431.16	1308.77	1225.90	1167.48	1125.09	1093.71	1070.11	1052.17
55000	5194.13	2901.06	2150.60	1785.51	1574.27	1439.65	1348.49	1284.22	1237.60	1203.08	1177.12	1157.38
60000	5666.32	3164.79	2346.11	1947.83	1717.39	1570.52	1471.08	1400.97	1350.11	1312.45	1284.13	1262.60
65000	6138.52	3428.52	2541.62	2110.15	1860.50	1701.40	1593.67	1517.72	1462.62	1421.82	1391.14	1367.82
70000	6610.71	3692.25	2737.12	2272.47	2003.62	1832.27	1716.26	1634.46	1575.13	1531.19	1498.15	1473.03
75000	7082.90	3955.99	2932.63	2434.79	2146.73	1963.15	1838.85	1751.21	1687.63	1640.56	1605.16	1578.25
80000	7555.10	4219.72	3128.14	2597.11	2289.85	2094.03	1961.44	1867.96	1800.14	1749.93	1712.17	1683.47
85000	8027.29	4483.45	3323.65	2759.43	2432.96	2224.90	2084.03	1984.71	1912.65	1859.30	1819.18	1788.68
90000	8499.48	4747.18	3519.16	2921.75	2576.08	2355.78	2206.62	2101.45	2025.16	1968.67	1926.19	1893.90
95000	8971.68	5010.91	3714.67	3084.06	2719.19	2486.66	2329.21	2218.20	2137.67	2078.04	2033.20	1999.11
100000	9443.87	5274.65	3910.18	3246.38	2862.31	2617.53	2451.80	2334.95	2250.18	2187.41	2140.22	2104.33

23%

Table 1

MONTHLY

23.75%

PAYMENT REQUIRED TO AMORTIZE A LOAN

TERM AMOUNT	13 YEARS	14 YEARS	15 YEARS	16 YEARS	17 YEARS	18 YEARS	19 YEARS	20 YEARS	25 YEARS	30 YEARS	35 YEARS	40 YEARS
50	1.04	1.03	1.02	1.02	1.01	1.01	1.01	1.00	1.00	1.00	.99	.99
100	2.08	2.06	2.04	2.03	2.02	2.01	2.01	2.00	1.99	1.99	1.98	1.98
200	4.16	4.12	4.08	4.06	4.04	4.02	4.01	4.00	3.97	3.97	3.96	3.96
300	6.24	6.17	6.12	6.08	6.05	6.03	6.01	6.00	5.96	5.95	5.94	5.94
400	8.31	8.23	8.16	8.11	8.07	8.04	8.01	7.99	7.94	7.93	7.92	7.92
500	10.39	10.28	10.20	10.14	10.09	10.05	10.02	9.99	9.93	9.91	9.90	9.90
600	12.47	12.34	12.24	12.16	12.10	12.05	12.02	11.99	11.91	11.89	11.88	11.88
700	14.54	14.39	14.28	14.19	14.12	14.06	14.02	13.99	13.90	13.87	13.86	13.86
800	16.62	16.45	16.32	16.21	16.13	16.07	16.02	15.98	15.88	15.85	15.84	15.84
900	18.70	18.50	18.36	18.24	18.15	18.08	18.02	17.98	17.87	17.83	17.82	17.82
1000	20.77	20.56	20.40	20.27	20.17	20.09	20.03	19.98	19.85	19.81	19.80	19.80
2000	41.54	41.12	40.79	40.53	40.33	40.17	40.05	39.95	39.70	39.62	39.60	39.59
3000	62.31	61.67	61.18	60.79	60.49	60.25	60.07	59.92	59.55	59.43	59.40	59.38
4000	83.08	82.23	81.57	81.05	80.65	80.34	80.09	79.90	79.39	79.24	79.19	79.18
5000	103.85	102.78	101.96	101.32	100.81	100.42	100.11	99.87	99.24	99.05	98.99	98.97
6000	124.61	123.34	122.35	121.58	120.97	120.50	120.13	119.84	119.09	118.86	118.79	118.76
7000	145.38	143.89	142.74	141.84	141.14	140.59	140.15	139.81	138.94	138.67	138.58	138.56
8000	166.15	164.45	163.13	162.10	161.30	160.67	160.17	159.79	158.78	158.48	158.38	158.35
9000	186.92	185.00	183.52	182.36	181.46	180.75	180.20	179.76	178.63	178.28	178.18	178.14
10000	207.69	205.56	203.91	202.63	201.62	200.83	200.22	199.73	198.48	198.09	197.97	197.94
11000	228.45	226.12	224.30	222.89	221.78	220.92	220.24	219.70	218.32	217.90	217.77	217.73
12000	249.22	246.67	244.69	243.15	241.94	241.00	240.26	239.68	238.17	237.71	237.57	237.52
13000	269.99	267.23	265.08	263.41	262.11	261.08	260.28	259.65	258.02	257.52	257.37	257.32
14000	290.76	287.78	285.47	283.67	282.27	281.17	280.30	279.62	277.87	277.33	277.16	277.11
15000	311.53	308.34	305.86	303.94	302.43	301.25	300.32	299.60	297.71	297.14	296.96	296.90
16000	332.29	328.89	326.25	324.20	322.59	321.33	320.34	319.57	317.56	316.95	316.76	316.70
17000	353.06	349.45	346.64	344.46	342.75	341.42	340.37	339.54	337.41	336.75	336.55	336.49
18000	373.83	370.00	367.04	364.72	362.91	361.50	360.39	359.51	357.25	356.56	356.35	356.28
19000	394.60	390.56	387.43	384.98	383.08	381.58	380.41	379.49	377.10	376.37	376.15	376.08
20000	415.37	411.12	407.82	405.25	403.24	401.66	400.43	399.46	396.95	396.18	395.94	395.87
21000	436.13	431.67	428.21	425.51	423.40	421.75	420.45	419.43	416.80	415.99	415.74	415.66
22000	456.90	452.23	448.60	445.77	443.56	441.83	440.47	439.40	436.64	435.80	435.54	435.46
23000	477.67	472.78	468.99	466.03	463.72	461.91	460.49	459.38	456.49	455.61	455.33	455.25
24000	498.44	493.34	489.38	486.30	483.88	482.00	480.51	479.35	476.34	475.42	475.13	475.04
25000	519.21	513.89	509.77	506.56	504.05	502.08	500.54	499.32	496.18	495.22	494.93	494.84
26000	539.97	534.45	530.16	526.82	524.21	522.16	520.56	519.29	516.03	515.03	514.73	514.63
27000	560.74	555.00	550.55	547.08	544.37	542.25	540.58	539.27	535.88	534.84	534.52	534.42
28000	581.51	575.56	570.94	567.34	564.53	562.33	560.60	559.24	555.73	554.65	554.32	554.22
29000	602.28	596.11	591.33	587.61	584.69	582.41	580.62	579.21	575.57	574.46	574.12	574.01
30000	623.05	616.67	611.72	607.87	604.85	602.49	600.64	599.19	595.42	594.27	593.91	593.80
31000	643.81	637.23	632.11	628.13	625.02	622.58	620.66	619.16	615.27	614.08	613.71	613.60
32000	664.58	657.78	652.50	648.39	645.18	642.66	640.68	639.13	635.11	633.89	633.51	633.39
33000	685.35	678.34	672.89	668.65	665.34	662.74	660.71	659.10	654.96	653.69	653.30	653.18
34000	706.12	698.89	693.28	688.92	685.50	682.83	680.73	679.08	674.81	673.50	673.10	672.98
35000	726.89	719.45	713.68	709.18	705.66	702.91	700.75	699.05	694.66	693.31	692.90	692.77
36000	747.65	740.00	734.07	729.44	725.82	722.99	720.77	719.02	714.50	713.12	712.69	712.56
37000	768.42	760.56	754.46	749.70	745.99	743.08	740.79	738.99	734.35	732.93	732.49	732.36
38000	789.19	781.11	774.85	769.96	766.15	763.16	760.81	758.97	754.20	752.74	752.29	752.15
39000	809.96	801.67	795.24	790.23	786.31	783.24	780.83	778.94	774.04	772.55	772.09	771.94
40000	830.73	822.23	815.63	810.49	806.47	803.32	800.85	798.91	793.89	792.36	791.88	791.74
41000	851.49	842.78	836.02	830.75	826.63	823.41	820.87	818.88	813.74	812.16	811.68	811.53
42000	872.26	863.34	856.41	851.01	846.79	843.49	840.90	838.86	833.59	831.97	831.48	831.32
43000	893.03	883.89	876.80	871.27	866.96	863.57	860.92	858.83	853.43	851.78	851.27	851.12
44000	913.80	904.45	897.19	891.54	887.12	883.66	880.94	878.80	873.28	871.59	871.07	870.91
45000	934.57	925.00	917.58	911.80	907.28	903.74	900.96	898.78	893.13	891.40	890.87	890.70
46000	955.33	945.56	937.97	932.06	927.44	923.82	920.98	918.75	912.97	911.21	910.66	910.50
47000	976.10	966.11	958.36	952.32	947.60	943.90	941.00	938.72	932.82	931.02	930.46	930.29
48000	996.87	986.67	978.75	972.59	967.76	963.99	961.02	958.69	952.67	950.83	950.26	950.08
49000	1017.64	1007.22	999.14	992.85	987.93	984.07	981.04	978.67	972.52	970.63	970.05	969.88
50000	1038.41	1027.78	1019.53	1013.11	1008.09	1004.15	1001.07	998.64	992.36	990.44	989.85	989.67
55000	1142.25	1130.56	1121.49	1114.42	1108.90	1104.57	1101.17	1098.50	1091.60	1089.49	1088.84	1088.64
60000	1246.09	1233.34	1223.44	1215.73	1209.70	1204.98	1201.28	1198.37	1190.83	1188.53	1187.82	1187.60
65000	1349.93	1336.11	1325.39	1317.04	1310.51	1305.40	1301.38	1298.23	1290.07	1287.57	1286.81	1286.57
70000	1453.77	1438.89	1427.35	1418.35	1411.32	1405.81	1401.49	1398.09	1389.31	1386.62	1385.79	1385.54
75000	1557.61	1541.67	1529.30	1519.66	1512.13	1506.23	1501.60	1497.96	1488.54	1485.66	1484.78	1484.50
80000	1661.45	1644.45	1631.25	1620.97	1612.94	1606.64	1601.70	1597.82	1587.78	1584.71	1583.76	1583.47
85000	1765.29	1747.22	1733.20	1722.28	1713.75	1707.06	1701.81	1697.68	1687.01	1683.75	1682.74	1682.43
90000	1869.13	1850.00	1835.16	1823.59	1814.55	1807.47	1801.91	1797.55	1786.25	1782.79	1781.73	1781.40
95000	1972.97	1952.78	1937.11	1924.90	1915.36	1907.89	1902.02	1897.41	1885.49	1881.84	1880.71	1880.37
100000	2076.81	2055.56	2039.06	2026.21	2016.17	2008.30	2002.13	1997.27	1984.72	1980.88	1979.70	1979.33

23%

Table 1

MONTHLY

PAYMENT REQUIRED TO AMORTIZE A LOAN

24.00%

TERM AMOUNT	1 YEAR	2 YEARS	3 YEARS	4 YEARS	5 YEARS	6 YEARS	7 YEARS	8 YEARS	9 YEARS	10 YEARS	11 YEARS	12 YEARS
50	4.73	2.65	1.97	1.64	1.44	1.32	1.24	1.18	1.14	1.11	1.08	1.07
100	9.46	5.29	3.93	3.27	2.88	2.64	2.47	2.36	2.27	2.21	2.16	2.13
200	18.92	10.58	7.85	6.53	5.76	5.27	4.94	4.71	4.54	4.41	4.32	4.25
300	28.37	15.87	11.77	9.79	8.64	7.90	7.41	7.06	6.81	6.62	6.48	6.37
400	37.83	21.15	15.70	13.05	11.51	10.54	9.88	9.41	9.07	8.82	8.64	8.50
500	47.28	26.44	19.62	16.31	14.39	13.17	12.34	11.76	11.34	11.03	10.80	10.62
600	56.74	31.73	23.54	19.57	17.27	15.80	14.81	14.11	13.61	13.23	12.95	12.74
700	66.20	37.01	27.47	22.83	20.14	18.43	17.28	16.46	15.87	15.44	15.11	14.86
800	75.65	42.30	31.39	26.09	23.02	21.07	19.75	18.82	18.14	17.64	17.27	16.99
900	85.11	47.59	35.31	29.35	25.90	23.70	22.21	21.17	20.41	19.85	19.43	19.11
1000	94.56	52.88	39.24	32.61	28.77	26.33	24.68	23.52	22.68	22.05	21.59	21.23
2000	189.12	105.75	78.47	65.21	57.54	52.66	49.36	47.03	45.35	44.10	43.17	42.46
3000	283.68	158.62	117.70	97.81	86.31	78.99	74.03	70.54	68.02	66.15	64.75	63.68
4000	378.24	211.49	156.94	130.41	115.08	105.31	98.71	94.06	90.69	88.20	86.33	84.91
5000	472.80	264.36	196.17	163.01	143.84	131.64	123.38	117.57	113.36	110.25	107.91	106.13
6000	567.36	317.23	235.40	195.62	172.61	157.97	148.06	141.08	136.03	132.29	129.49	127.36
7000	661.92	370.10	274.63	228.22	201.38	184.29	172.74	164.60	158.70	154.34	151.07	148.59
8000	756.48	422.97	313.87	260.82	230.15	210.62	197.41	188.11	181.37	176.39	172.65	169.81
9000	851.04	475.84	353.10	293.42	258.92	236.95	222.09	211.62	204.04	198.44	194.23	191.04
10000	945.60	528.72	392.33	326.02	287.68	263.27	246.76	235.14	226.71	220.49	215.81	212.26
11000	1040.16	581.59	431.57	358.63	316.45	289.60	271.44	258.65	249.38	242.53	237.39	233.49
12000	1134.72	634.46	470.80	391.23	345.22	315.93	296.11	282.16	272.06	264.58	258.97	254.72
13000	1229.28	687.33	510.03	423.83	373.99	342.25	320.79	305.68	294.73	286.63	280.55	275.94
14000	1323.84	740.20	549.26	456.43	402.76	368.58	345.47	329.19	317.40	308.68	302.13	297.17
15000	1418.40	793.07	588.50	489.03	431.52	394.91	370.14	352.70	340.07	330.73	323.72	318.39
16000	1512.96	845.94	627.73	521.63	460.29	421.23	394.82	376.22	362.74	352.77	345.30	339.62
17000	1607.52	898.81	666.96	554.24	489.06	447.56	419.49	399.73	385.41	374.82	366.88	360.84
18000	1702.08	951.68	706.20	586.84	517.83	473.89	444.17	423.24	408.08	396.87	388.46	382.07
19000	1796.64	1004.56	745.43	619.44	546.60	500.21	468.85	446.75	430.75	418.92	410.04	403.30
20000	1891.20	1057.43	784.66	652.04	575.36	526.54	493.52	470.27	453.42	440.97	431.62	424.52
21000	1985.76	1110.30	823.89	684.64	604.13	552.87	518.20	493.78	476.09	463.02	453.20	445.75
22000	2080.32	1163.17	863.13	717.25	632.90	579.20	542.87	517.29	498.76	485.06	474.78	466.97
23000	2174.88	1216.04	902.36	749.85	661.67	605.52	567.55	540.81	521.43	507.11	496.36	488.20
24000	2269.44	1268.91	941.59	782.45	690.44	631.85	592.22	564.32	544.11	529.16	517.94	509.43
25000	2363.99	1321.78	980.83	815.05	719.20	658.18	616.90	587.83	566.78	551.21	539.52	530.65
26000	2458.55	1374.65	1020.06	847.65	747.97	684.50	641.58	611.35	589.45	573.26	561.10	551.88
27000	2553.11	1427.52	1059.29	880.25	776.74	710.83	666.25	634.86	612.12	595.30	582.68	573.10
28000	2647.67	1480.40	1098.52	912.86	805.51	737.16	690.93	658.37	634.79	617.35	604.26	594.33
29000	2742.23	1533.27	1137.76	945.46	834.28	763.48	715.60	681.89	657.46	639.40	625.84	615.55
30000	2836.79	1586.14	1176.99	978.06	863.04	789.81	740.28	705.40	680.13	661.45	647.43	636.78
31000	2931.35	1639.01	1216.22	1010.66	891.81	816.14	764.96	728.91	702.80	683.50	669.01	658.01
32000	3025.91	1691.88	1255.46	1043.26	920.58	842.46	789.63	752.43	725.47	705.54	690.59	679.23
33000	3120.47	1744.75	1294.69	1075.87	949.35	868.79	814.31	775.94	748.14	727.59	712.17	700.46
34000	3215.03	1797.62	1333.92	1108.47	978.12	895.12	838.98	799.45	770.81	749.64	733.75	721.68
35000	3309.59	1850.49	1373.15	1141.07	1006.88	921.44	863.66	822.96	793.48	771.69	755.33	742.91
36000	3404.15	1903.36	1412.39	1173.67	1035.65	947.77	888.33	846.48	816.16	793.74	776.91	764.14
37000	3498.71	1956.24	1451.62	1206.27	1064.42	974.10	913.01	869.99	838.83	815.78	798.49	785.36
38000	3593.27	2009.11	1490.85	1238.87	1093.19	1000.42	937.69	893.50	861.50	837.83	820.07	806.59
39000	3687.83	2061.98	1530.09	1271.48	1121.96	1026.75	962.36	917.02	884.17	859.88	841.65	827.81
40000	3782.39	2114.85	1569.32	1304.08	1150.72	1053.08	987.04	940.53	906.84	881.93	863.23	849.04
41000	3876.95	2167.72	1608.55	1336.68	1179.49	1079.41	1011.71	964.04	929.51	903.98	884.81	870.27
42000	3971.51	2220.59	1647.78	1369.28	1208.26	1105.73	1036.39	987.56	952.18	926.03	906.39	891.49
43000	4066.07	2273.46	1687.02	1401.88	1237.03	1132.06	1061.06	1011.07	974.85	948.07	927.97	912.72
44000	4160.63	2326.33	1726.25	1434.49	1265.80	1158.39	1085.74	1034.58	997.52	970.12	949.55	933.94
45000	4255.19	2379.20	1765.48	1467.09	1294.56	1184.71	1110.42	1058.10	1020.19	992.17	971.14	955.17
46000	4349.75	2432.08	1804.72	1499.69	1323.33	1211.04	1135.09	1081.61	1042.86	1014.22	992.72	976.39
47000	4444.31	2484.95	1843.95	1532.29	1352.10	1237.37	1159.77	1105.12	1065.53	1036.27	1014.30	997.62
48000	4538.87	2537.82	1883.18	1564.89	1380.87	1263.69	1184.44	1128.64	1088.21	1058.31	1035.88	1018.85
49000	4633.43	2590.69	1922.41	1597.49	1409.64	1290.02	1209.12	1152.15	1110.88	1080.36	1057.46	1040.07
50000	4727.98	2643.56	1961.65	1630.10	1438.40	1316.35	1233.80	1175.66	1133.55	1102.41	1079.04	1061.30
55000	5200.78	2907.92	2157.81	1793.11	1582.24	1447.98	1357.17	1293.23	1246.90	1212.65	1186.94	1167.43
60000	5673.58	3172.27	2353.98	1956.12	1726.08	1579.61	1480.55	1410.79	1360.26	1322.89	1294.85	1273.56
65000	6146.38	3436.63	2550.14	2119.12	1869.92	1711.25	1603.93	1528.36	1473.61	1433.13	1402.75	1379.69
70000	6619.18	3700.98	2746.30	2282.13	2013.76	1842.88	1727.31	1645.92	1586.96	1543.37	1510.65	1485.82
75000	7091.97	3965.34	2942.47	2445.14	2157.60	1974.52	1850.69	1763.49	1700.32	1653.61	1618.56	1591.94
80000	7564.77	4229.69	3138.63	2608.15	2301.44	2106.15	1974.07	1881.06	1813.67	1763.85	1726.46	1698.07
85000	8037.57	4494.05	3334.80	2771.16	2445.28	2237.79	2097.45	1998.62	1927.03	1874.09	1834.36	1804.20
90000	8510.37	4758.40	3530.96	2934.17	2589.12	2369.42	2220.83	2116.19	2040.38	1984.33	1942.27	1910.33
95000	8983.17	5022.76	3727.13	3097.18	2732.96	2501.05	2344.21	2233.75	2153.74	2094.57	2050.17	2016.46
100000	9455.97	5287.11	3923.29	3260.19	2876.80	2632.69	2467.59	2351.32	2267.09	2204.81	2158.07	2122.59

24%

154

Table 1

MONTHLY

PAYMENT REQUIRED TO AMORTIZE A LOAN

24.00%

TERM	13 YEARS	14 YEARS	15 YEARS	16 YEARS	17 YEARS	18 YEARS	19 YEARS	20 YEARS	25 YEARS	30 YEARS	35 YEARS	40 YEARS
AMOUNT												
50	1.05	1.04	1.03	1.03	1.02	1.02	1.02	1.01	1.01	1.01	1.01	1.01
100	2.10	2.08	2.06	2.05	2.04	2.03	2.03	2.02	2.01	2.01	2.01	2.01
200	4.20	4.15	4.12	4.10	4.08	4.06	4.05	4.04	4.02	4.01	4.01	4.01
300	6.29	6.23	6.18	6.14	6.11	6.09	6.07	6.06	6.02	6.01	6.01	6.01
400	8.39	8.30	8.24	8.19	8.15	8.12	8.09	8.07	8.03	8.01	8.01	8.01
500	10.48	10.38	10.30	10.23	10.18	10.15	10.12	10.09	10.03	10.01	10.01	10.01
600	12.58	12.45	12.35	12.28	12.22	12.17	12.14	12.11	12.04	12.01	12.01	12.01
700	14.67	14.53	14.41	14.32	14.26	14.20	14.16	14.13	14.04	14.02	14.01	14.01
800	16.77	16.60	16.47	16.37	16.29	16.23	16.18	16.14	16.05	16.02	16.01	16.01
900	18.86	18.68	18.53	18.42	18.33	18.26	18.20	18.16	18.05	18.02	18.01	18.01
1000	20.96	20.75	20.59	20.46	20.36	20.29	20.23	20.18	20.06	20.02	20.01	20.01
2000	41.91	41.49	41.17	40.92	40.72	40.57	40.45	40.35	40.11	40.04	40.01	40.01
3000	62.87	62.24	61.75	61.38	61.08	60.85	60.67	60.53	60.16	60.05	60.02	60.01
4000	83.82	82.98	82.34	81.83	81.44	81.13	80.89	80.70	80.22	80.07	80.02	80.01
5000	104.78	103.73	102.92	102.29	101.80	101.41	101.11	100.88	100.27	100.09	100.03	100.01
6000	125.73	124.47	123.50	122.75	122.16	121.69	121.33	121.05	120.32	120.10	120.03	120.01
7000	146.68	145.22	144.08	143.20	142.51	141.98	141.55	141.22	140.37	140.12	140.04	140.02
8000	167.64	165.96	164.67	163.66	162.87	162.26	161.78	161.40	160.43	160.13	160.04	160.02
9000	188.59	186.71	185.25	184.12	183.23	182.54	182.00	181.57	180.48	180.15	180.05	180.02
10000	209.55	207.45	205.83	204.57	203.59	202.82	202.22	201.75	200.53	200.17	200.05	200.02
11000	230.50	228.20	226.42	225.03	223.95	223.10	222.44	221.92	220.59	220.18	220.06	220.02
12000	251.46	248.94	247.00	245.49	244.31	243.38	242.66	242.09	240.64	240.20	240.06	240.02
13000	272.41	269.69	267.58	265.94	264.66	263.66	262.88	262.27	260.69	260.21	260.07	260.02
14000	293.36	290.43	288.16	286.40	285.02	283.95	283.10	282.44	280.74	280.23	280.07	280.03
15000	314.32	311.18	308.75	306.86	305.38	304.23	303.32	302.62	300.80	300.25	300.08	300.03
16000	335.27	331.92	329.33	327.31	325.74	324.51	323.55	322.79	320.85	320.26	320.08	320.03
17000	356.23	352.67	349.91	347.77	346.10	344.79	343.77	342.96	340.90	340.28	340.09	340.03
18000	377.18	373.41	370.49	368.23	366.46	365.07	363.99	363.14	360.95	360.29	360.09	360.03
19000	398.14	394.16	391.08	388.68	386.81	385.35	384.21	383.31	381.01	380.31	380.10	380.03
20000	419.09	414.90	411.66	409.14	407.17	405.63	404.43	403.49	401.06	400.33	400.10	400.03
21000	440.04	435.65	432.24	429.60	427.53	425.92	424.65	423.66	421.11	420.34	420.11	420.04
22000	461.00	456.39	452.83	450.05	447.89	446.20	444.87	443.83	441.17	440.36	440.11	440.04
23000	481.95	477.14	473.41	470.51	468.25	466.48	465.09	464.01	461.22	460.37	460.12	460.04
24000	502.91	497.88	493.99	490.97	488.61	486.76	485.32	484.18	481.27	480.39	480.12	480.04
25000	523.86	518.63	514.57	511.42	508.96	507.04	505.54	504.36	501.32	500.41	500.13	500.04
26000	544.81	539.37	535.16	531.88	529.32	527.32	525.76	524.53	521.38	520.42	520.13	520.04
27000	565.77	560.12	555.74	552.34	549.68	547.61	546.98	544.71	541.43	540.44	540.14	540.05
28000	586.72	580.86	576.32	572.79	570.04	567.89	566.20	564.88	561.48	560.45	560.14	560.05
29000	607.68	601.61	596.90	593.25	590.40	588.17	586.42	585.05	581.53	580.47	580.15	580.05
30000	628.63	622.35	617.49	613.71	610.76	608.45	606.64	605.23	601.59	600.49	600.15	600.05
31000	649.59	643.10	638.07	634.16	631.11	628.73	626.87	625.40	621.64	620.50	620.16	620.05
32000	670.54	663.84	658.65	654.62	651.47	649.01	647.09	645.58	641.69	640.52	640.16	640.05
33000	691.49	684.59	679.24	675.08	671.83	669.29	667.31	665.75	661.75	660.53	660.17	660.05
34000	712.45	705.33	699.82	695.53	692.19	689.58	687.53	685.92	681.80	680.55	680.17	680.06
35000	733.40	726.08	720.40	715.99	712.55	709.86	707.75	706.10	701.85	700.57	700.18	700.06
36000	754.36	746.82	740.98	736.45	732.91	730.14	727.97	726.27	721.90	720.58	720.18	720.06
37000	775.31	767.57	761.57	756.90	753.26	750.42	748.19	746.45	741.96	740.60	740.19	740.06
38000	796.27	788.31	782.15	777.36	773.62	770.70	768.41	766.62	762.01	760.61	760.19	760.06
39000	817.22	809.06	802.73	797.82	793.98	790.98	788.64	786.79	782.06	780.63	780.20	780.06
40000	838.17	829.80	823.31	818.27	814.34	811.26	808.86	806.97	802.11	800.65	800.20	800.06
41000	859.13	850.54	843.90	838.73	834.70	831.55	829.08	827.14	822.17	820.66	820.21	820.07
42000	880.08	871.29	864.48	859.19	855.06	851.83	849.30	847.32	842.22	840.68	840.21	840.07
43000	901.04	892.03	885.06	879.64	875.41	872.11	869.52	867.49	862.27	860.69	860.22	860.07
44000	921.99	912.78	905.65	900.10	895.77	892.39	889.74	887.66	882.33	880.71	880.22	880.07
45000	942.94	933.52	926.23	920.56	916.13	912.67	909.96	907.84	902.38	900.73	900.22	900.07
46000	963.90	954.27	946.81	941.01	936.49	932.95	930.18	928.01	922.43	920.74	920.23	920.07
47000	984.85	975.01	967.39	961.47	956.85	953.24	950.41	948.19	942.48	940.76	940.23	940.07
48000	1005.81	995.76	987.98	981.93	977.21	973.52	970.63	968.36	962.54	960.78	960.24	960.08
49000	1026.76	1016.50	1008.56	1002.38	997.56	993.80	990.85	988.53	982.59	980.79	980.24	980.08
50000	1047.72	1037.25	1029.14	1022.84	1017.92	1014.08	1011.07	1008.71	1002.64	1000.81	1000.25	1000.08
55000	1152.49	1140.97	1132.06	1125.12	1119.71	1115.49	1112.18	1109.58	1102.91	1100.89	1100.27	1100.09
60000	1257.26	1244.70	1234.97	1227.41	1221.51	1216.89	1213.28	1210.45	1203.17	1200.97	1200.30	1200.09
65000	1362.03	1348.42	1337.88	1329.69	1323.30	1318.30	1314.39	1311.32	1303.43	1301.05	1300.32	1300.10
70000	1466.80	1452.15	1440.80	1431.97	1425.09	1419.71	1415.50	1412.19	1403.70	1401.13	1400.35	1400.11
75000	1571.57	1555.87	1543.71	1534.26	1526.88	1521.12	1516.60	1513.06	1503.96	1501.21	1500.37	1500.12
80000	1676.34	1659.59	1646.62	1636.54	1628.67	1622.52	1617.71	1613.93	1604.22	1601.29	1600.40	1600.12
85000	1781.11	1763.32	1749.54	1738.82	1730.46	1723.93	1718.82	1714.80	1704.49	1701.37	1700.42	1700.13
90000	1885.88	1867.04	1852.45	1841.11	1832.26	1825.34	1819.92	1815.67	1804.75	1801.45	1800.44	1800.14
95000	1990.66	1970.77	1955.37	1943.39	1934.05	1926.75	1921.03	1916.54	1905.02	1901.53	1900.47	1900.15
100000	2095.43	2074.49	2058.28	2045.67	2035.84	2028.15	2022.13	2017.41	2005.28	2001.61	2000.49	2000.15

24%

Table 1

24.25%

MONTHLY
PAYMENT REQUIRED TO AMORTIZE A LOAN

TERM AMOUNT	1 YEAR	2 YEARS	3 YEARS	4 YEARS	5 YEARS	6 YEARS	7 YEARS	8 YEARS	9 YEARS	10 YEARS	11 YEARS	12 YEAR.
50	4.74	2.65	1.97	1.64	1.45	1.33	1.25	1.19	1.15	1.12	1.09	1.08
100	9.47	5.30	3.94	3.28	2.90	2.65	2.49	2.37	2.29	2.23	2.18	2.15
200	18.94	10.60	7.88	6.55	5.79	5.30	4.97	4.74	4.57	4.45	4.36	4.29
300	28.41	15.90	11.81	9.83	8.68	7.95	7.46	7.11	6.86	6.67	6.53	6.43
400	37.88	21.20	15.75	13.10	11.57	10.60	9.94	9.48	9.14	8.89	8.71	8.57
500	47.35	26.50	19.69	16.38	14.46	13.24	12.42	11.84	11.43	11.12	10.88	10.71
600	56.81	31.80	23.62	19.65	17.35	15.89	14.91	14.21	13.71	13.34	13.06	12.85
700	66.28	37.10	27.56	22.92	20.24	18.54	17.39	16.58	15.99	15.56	15.24	14.99
800	75.75	42.40	31.50	26.20	23.14	21.19	19.87	18.95	18.28	17.78	17.41	17.13
900	85.22	47.70	35.43	29.47	26.03	23.84	22.36	21.31	20.56	20.01	19.59	19.27
1000	94.69	53.00	39.37	32.75	28.92	26.48	24.84	23.68	22.85	22.23	21.76	21.41
2000	189.37	106.00	78.73	65.49	57.83	52.96	49.67	47.36	45.69	44.45	43.52	42.82
3000	284.05	158.99	118.10	98.23	79.44	79.44	74.51	71.04	68.53	66.67	65.28	64.23
4000	378.73	211.99	157.46	130.97	115.66	105.92	99.34	94.71	91.37	88.90	87.04	85.64
5000	473.41	264.98	196.83	163.71	144.57	132.40	124.18	118.39	114.21	111.12	108.80	107.05
6000	568.09	317.98	236.19	196.45	173.48	158.88	149.01	142.07	137.05	133.34	130.56	128.46
7000	662.77	370.98	275.55	229.19	202.40	185.36	173.84	165.75	159.89	155.56	152.32	149.87
8000	757.45	423.97	314.92	261.93	231.31	211.84	198.68	189.42	182.73	177.79	174.08	171.28
9000	852.13	476.97	354.28	294.67	260.22	238.31	223.51	213.10	205.57	200.01	195.84	192.69
10000	946.81	529.96	393.65	327.41	289.14	264.79	248.35	236.78	228.41	222.23	217.60	214.09
11000	1041.49	582.96	433.01	360.15	318.05	291.27	273.18	260.46	251.25	244.45	239.36	235.50
12000	1136.17	635.96	472.38	392.89	346.96	317.75	298.01	284.13	274.09	266.68	261.12	256.91
13000	1230.85	688.95	511.74	425.63	375.88	344.23	322.85	307.81	296.93	288.90	282.88	278.32
14000	1325.53	741.95	551.10	458.37	404.79	370.71	347.68	331.49	319.77	311.12	304.64	299.73
15000	1420.21	794.94	590.47	491.11	433.70	397.19	372.52	355.16	342.61	333.35	326.40	321.14
16000	1514.90	847.94	629.83	523.85	462.62	423.67	397.35	378.84	365.45	355.57	348.16	342.55
17000	1609.58	900.94	669.20	556.59	491.53	450.14	422.18	402.52	388.29	377.79	369.92	363.96
18000	1704.26	953.93	708.56	589.33	520.44	476.62	447.02	426.20	411.13	400.01	391.68	385.37
19000	1798.94	1006.93	747.93	622.07	549.36	503.10	471.85	449.87	433.97	422.24	413.44	406.77
20000	1893.62	1059.92	787.29	654.81	578.27	529.58	496.69	473.55	456.81	444.46	435.20	428.18
21000	1988.30	1112.92	826.65	687.55	607.18	556.06	521.52	497.23	479.65	466.68	456.96	449.59
22000	2082.98	1165.92	866.02	720.29	636.10	582.54	546.36	520.91	502.50	488.90	478.72	471.00
23000	2177.66	1218.91	905.38	753.03	665.01	609.02	571.19	544.58	525.34	511.13	500.48	492.41
24000	2272.34	1271.91	944.75	785.77	693.92	635.50	596.02	568.26	548.18	533.35	522.24	513.82
25000	2367.02	1324.90	984.11	818.51	722.84	661.98	620.86	591.94	571.02	555.57	544.00	535.23
26000	2461.70	1377.90	1023.48	851.25	751.75	688.45	645.69	615.62	593.86	577.79	565.76	556.64
27000	2556.38	1430.90	1062.84	883.99	780.66	714.93	670.53	639.29	616.70	600.02	587.52	578.05
28000	2651.06	1483.89	1102.20	916.73	809.58	741.41	695.36	662.97	639.54	622.24	609.28	599.46
29000	2745.74	1536.89	1141.57	949.47	838.49	767.89	720.19	686.65	662.38	644.46	631.04	620.86
30000	2840.42	1589.88	1180.93	982.21	867.40	794.37	745.03	710.32	685.22	666.69	652.80	642.27
31000	2935.11	1642.88	1220.30	1014.95	896.32	820.85	769.86	734.00	708.06	688.91	674.56	663.68
32000	3029.78	1695.88	1259.66	1047.69	925.23	847.33	794.70	757.68	730.90	711.13	696.32	685.09
33000	3124.47	1748.87	1299.02	1080.43	954.14	873.81	819.53	781.36	753.74	733.35	718.08	706.50
34000	3219.15	1801.87	1338.39	1113.17	983.06	900.28	844.36	805.03	776.58	755.58	739.84	727.91
35000	3313.83	1854.86	1377.75	1145.91	1011.97	926.76	869.20	828.71	799.42	777.80	761.60	749.32
36000	3408.51	1907.86	1417.12	1178.65	1040.88	953.24	894.03	852.39	822.26	800.02	783.36	770.73
37000	3503.19	1960.86	1456.48	1211.39	1069.80	979.72	918.87	876.07	845.10	822.24	805.12	792.14
38000	3597.87	2013.85	1495.85	1244.13	1098.71	1006.20	943.70	899.74	867.94	844.47	826.87	813.54
39000	3692.55	2066.85	1535.21	1276.87	1127.62	1032.68	968.53	923.42	890.78	866.69	848.63	834.95
40000	3787.23	2119.84	1574.57	1309.61	1156.54	1059.16	993.37	947.10	913.62	888.91	870.39	856.36
41000	3881.91	2172.84	1613.94	1342.35	1185.45	1085.64	1018.20	970.77	936.46	911.13	892.15	877.77
42000	3976.59	2225.84	1653.30	1375.09	1214.36	1112.11	1043.04	994.45	959.30	933.36	913.91	899.18
43000	4071.27	2278.83	1692.67	1407.83	1243.28	1138.59	1067.87	1018.13	982.14	955.58	935.67	920.59
44000	4165.95	2331.83	1732.03	1440.57	1272.19	1165.07	1092.71	1041.81	1004.99	977.80	957.43	942.00
45000	4260.63	2384.82	1771.40	1473.31	1301.10	1191.55	1117.54	1065.48	1027.83	1000.03	979.19	963.41
46000	4355.31	2437.82	1810.76	1506.05	1330.01	1218.03	1142.37	1089.16	1050.67	1022.25	1000.95	984.82
47000	4449.99	2490.81	1850.12	1538.79	1358.93	1244.51	1167.21	1112.84	1073.51	1044.47	1022.71	1006.22
48000	4544.67	2543.81	1889.49	1571.53	1387.84	1270.99	1192.04	1136.52	1096.35	1066.69	1044.47	1027.63
49000	4639.36	2596.81	1928.85	1604.27	1416.75	1297.47	1216.88	1160.19	1119.19	1088.92	1066.23	1049.04
50000	4734.04	2649.80	1968.22	1637.01	1445.67	1323.95	1241.71	1183.87	1142.03	1111.14	1087.99	1070.45
55000	5207.44	2914.78	2165.04	1800.72	1590.23	1456.34	1365.88	1302.26	1256.23	1222.25	1196.79	1177.50
60000	5680.84	3179.76	2361.86	1964.42	1734.80	1588.73	1490.05	1420.64	1370.43	1333.37	1305.59	1284.54
65000	6154.25	3444.74	2558.68	2128.12	1879.37	1721.13	1614.22	1539.03	1484.64	1444.48	1414.39	1391.59
70000	6627.65	3709.72	2755.50	2291.82	2023.93	1853.52	1738.39	1657.42	1598.84	1555.59	1523.19	1498.63
75000	7101.05	3974.70	2952.32	2455.52	2168.50	1985.92	1862.56	1775.80	1713.04	1666.71	1631.98	1605.68
80000	7574.45	4239.68	3149.14	2619.22	2313.07	2118.31	1986.73	1894.19	1827.24	1777.82	1740.78	1712.72
85000	8047.86	4504.66	3345.97	2782.92	2457.63	2250.70	2110.90	2012.58	1941.44	1888.93	1849.58	1819.76
90000	8521.26	4769.64	3542.79	2946.62	2602.20	2383.10	2235.07	2130.96	2055.65	2000.05	1958.38	1926.81
95000	8994.66	5034.62	3739.61	3110.32	2746.76	2515.49	2359.24	2249.35	2169.85	2111.16	2067.18	2033.85
100000	9468.07	5299.60	3936.43	3274.02	2891.33	2647.89	2483.41	2367.74	2284.05	2222.27	2175.98	2140.90

24%

Table 1

MONKLY 24.25%

PAYMENT REQUIRED TO AMORTIZE A LOAN

TERM AMOUNT	13 YEARS	14 YEARS	15 YEARS	16 YEARS	17 YEARS	18 YEARS	19 YEARS	20 YEARS	25 YEARS	30 YEARS	35 YEARS	40 YEARS
50	1.06	1.05	1.04	1.04	1.03	1.03	1.03	1.02	1.02	1.02	1.02	1.02
100	2.12	2.10	2.08	2.07	2.06	2.05	2.05	2.04	2.03	2.03	2.03	2.03
200	4.23	4.19	4.16	4.14	4.12	4.10	4.09	4.08	4.06	4.05	4.05	4.05
300	6.35	6.29	6.24	6.20	6.17	6.15	6.13	6.12	6.08	6.07	6.07	6.07
400	8.46	8.38	8.32	8.27	8.23	8.20	8.17	8.16	8.11	8.09	8.09	8.09
500	10.58	10.47	10.39	10.33	10.28	10.25	10.22	10.19	10.13	10.12	10.11	10.11
600	12.69	12.57	12.47	12.40	12.34	12.29	12.26	12.23	12.16	12.14	12.13	12.13
700	14.80	14.66	14.55	14.46	14.39	14.34	14.30	14.27	14.19	14.16	14.15	14.15
800	16.92	16.75	16.63	16.53	16.45	16.39	16.34	16.31	16.21	16.18	16.18	16.17
900	19.03	18.85	18.70	18.59	18.50	18.44	18.38	18.34	18.24	18.21	18.20	18.19
1000	21.15	20.94	20.70	20.66	20.56	20.49	20.43	20.38	20.26	20.23	20.22	20.21
2000	42.29	41.87	41.56	41.31	41.12	40.97	40.85	40.76	40.52	40.45	40.43	40.42
3000	63.43	62.81	62.33	61.96	61.67	61.45	61.27	61.13	60.78	60.68	60.64	60.63
4000	84.57	83.74	83.11	82.61	82.23	81.93	81.69	81.51	81.04	80.90	80.86	80.84
5000	105.71	104.68	103.88	103.26	102.78	102.41	102.11	101.88	101.30	101.12	101.07	101.05
6000	126.85	125.61	124.66	123.91	123.34	122.89	122.53	122.26	121.56	121.35	121.28	121.26
7000	147.99	146.55	145.43	144.57	143.89	143.37	142.96	142.64	141.81	141.57	141.50	141.47
8000	169.13	167.48	166.21	165.22	164.45	163.85	163.38	163.01	162.07	161.79	161.71	161.68
9000	190.27	188.42	186.98	185.87	185.00	184.33	183.80	183.39	182.33	182.02	181.92	181.89
10000	211.41	209.35	207.76	206.52	205.56	204.81	204.22	203.76	202.59	202.24	202.13	202.10
11000	232.55	230.29	228.53	227.17	226.11	225.29	224.64	224.14	222.85	222.46	222.35	222.31
12000	253.70	251.22	249.31	247.82	246.67	245.77	245.06	244.51	243.11	242.69	242.56	242.52
13000	274.84	272.16	270.08	268.48	267.23	266.25	265.49	264.89	263.36	262.91	262.77	262.73
14000	295.98	293.09	290.86	289.13	287.78	286.73	285.91	285.27	283.62	283.13	282.99	282.94
15000	317.12	314.03	311.63	309.78	308.34	307.21	306.33	305.64	303.88	303.36	303.20	303.15
16000	338.26	334.96	332.41	330.43	328.89	327.69	326.75	326.02	324.14	323.58	323.41	323.36
17000	359.40	355.89	353.18	351.08	349.45	348.17	347.17	346.39	344.40	343.80	343.62	343.57
18000	380.54	376.83	373.96	371.73	370.00	368.65	367.59	366.77	364.66	364.03	363.84	363.78
19000	401.68	397.76	394.74	392.39	390.56	389.13	388.02	387.14	384.92	384.25	384.05	383.99
20000	422.82	418.70	415.51	413.04	411.11	409.61	408.44	407.52	405.17	404.47	404.26	404.20
21000	443.96	439.63	436.29	433.69	431.67	430.09	428.86	427.90	425.43	424.70	424.48	424.41
22000	465.10	460.57	457.06	454.34	452.22	450.57	449.28	448.27	445.69	444.92	444.69	444.62
23000	486.24	481.50	477.84	474.99	472.78	471.05	469.70	468.65	465.95	465.14	464.90	464.83
24000	507.39	502.44	498.61	495.64	493.33	491.53	490.12	489.02	486.21	485.37	485.11	485.04
25000	528.53	523.37	519.39	516.30	513.89	512.01	510.55	509.40	506.47	505.59	505.33	505.25
26000	549.67	544.31	540.16	536.95	534.45	532.49	530.97	529.77	526.72	525.81	525.54	525.46
27000	570.81	565.24	560.94	557.60	555.00	552.97	551.39	550.15	546.98	546.04	545.75	545.67
28000	591.95	586.18	581.71	578.25	575.56	573.45	571.81	570.53	567.24	566.26	565.97	565.88
29000	613.09	607.11	602.49	598.90	596.11	593.93	592.23	590.90	587.50	586.48	586.18	586.09
30000	634.23	628.05	623.26	619.55	616.67	614.41	612.65	611.28	607.76	606.71	606.39	606.30
31000	655.37	648.98	644.04	640.21	637.22	634.89	633.08	631.65	628.02	626.93	626.60	626.51
32000	676.51	669.91	664.81	660.86	657.78	655.38	653.50	652.03	648.28	647.15	646.82	646.72
33000	697.65	690.85	685.59	681.51	678.33	675.86	673.92	672.40	668.53	667.38	667.03	666.93
34000	718.79	711.78	706.36	702.16	698.89	696.34	694.34	692.78	688.79	687.60	687.24	687.13
35000	739.93	732.72	727.14	722.81	719.44	716.82	714.76	713.16	709.05	707.82	707.46	707.34
36000	761.08	753.65	747.92	743.46	740.00	737.30	735.18	733.53	729.31	728.05	727.67	727.55
37000	782.22	774.59	768.69	764.12	760.55	757.78	755.61	753.91	749.57	748.27	747.88	747.76
38000	803.36	795.52	789.47	784.77	781.11	778.26	776.03	774.28	769.83	768.49	768.09	767.97
39000	824.50	816.46	810.24	805.42	801.67	798.74	796.45	794.66	790.08	788.72	788.31	788.18
40000	845.64	837.39	831.02	826.07	822.22	819.22	816.87	815.03	810.34	808.94	808.52	808.39
41000	866.78	858.33	851.79	846.72	842.78	839.70	837.29	835.41	830.60	829.16	828.73	828.60
42000	887.92	879.26	872.57	867.37	863.33	860.18	857.71	855.79	850.86	849.39	848.95	848.81
43000	909.06	900.20	893.34	888.02	883.89	880.66	878.14	876.16	871.12	869.61	869.16	869.02
44000	930.20	921.13	914.12	908.68	904.44	901.14	898.56	896.54	891.38	889.83	889.37	889.23
45000	951.34	942.07	934.89	929.33	925.00	921.62	918.98	916.91	911.64	910.06	909.58	909.44
46000	972.48	963.00	955.67	949.98	945.55	942.10	939.40	937.29	931.89	930.28	929.80	929.65
47000	993.63	983.93	976.44	970.63	966.11	962.58	959.82	957.67	952.15	950.50	950.01	949.86
48000	1014.77	1004.87	997.22	991.28	986.66	983.06	980.24	978.04	972.41	970.73	970.22	970.07
49000	1035.91	1025.80	1017.99	1011.93	1007.22	1003.54	1000.67	998.42	992.67	990.95	990.44	990.28
50000	1057.05	1046.74	1038.77	1032.59	1027.77	1024.02	1021.09	1018.79	1012.93	1011.17	1010.65	1010.49
55000	1162.75	1151.41	1142.65	1135.84	1130.55	1126.42	1123.20	1120.67	1114.22	1112.29	1111.71	1111.54
60000	1268.46	1256.09	1246.52	1239.10	1233.33	1228.82	1225.30	1222.55	1215.51	1213.41	1212.78	1212.59
65000	1374.16	1360.76	1350.40	1342.36	1336.11	1331.23	1327.41	1324.43	1316.80	1314.53	1313.84	1313.64
70000	1479.86	1465.43	1454.28	1445.62	1438.88	1433.63	1429.52	1426.31	1418.10	1415.64	1414.91	1414.68
75000	1585.57	1570.11	1558.15	1548.88	1541.66	1536.03	1531.63	1528.19	1519.39	1516.76	1515.97	1515.73
80000	1691.27	1674.78	1662.03	1652.14	1644.44	1638.43	1633.74	1630.06	1620.68	1617.88	1617.03	1616.78
85000	1796.98	1779.45	1765.90	1755.39	1747.21	1740.83	1735.85	1731.94	1721.97	1718.99	1718.10	1717.83
90000	1902.68	1884.13	1869.78	1858.65	1849.99	1843.23	1837.95	1833.82	1823.27	1820.11	1819.16	1818.88
95000	2008.39	1988.80	1973.66	1961.91	1952.77	1945.64	1940.06	1935.70	1924.56	1921.23	1920.23	1919.93
100000	2114.09	2093.47	2077.53	2065.17	2055.54	2048.04	2042.17	2037.58	2025.85	2022.34	2021.29	2020.97

24%

Table 1

24.50%

MONTHLY

PAYMENT REQUIRED TO AMORTIZE A LOAN

TERM AMOUNT	1 YEAR	2 YEARS	3 YEARS	4 YEARS	5 YEARS	6 YEARS	7 YEARS	8 YEARS	9 YEARS	10 YEARS	11 YEARS	12 YEARS
50	4.75	2.66	1.98	1.65	1.46	1.34	1.25	1.20	1.16	1.12	1.10	1.08
100	9.49	5.32	3.95	3.29	2.91	2.67	2.50	2.39	2.31	2.24	2.20	2.16
200	18.97	10.63	7.90	6.58	5.82	5.33	5.00	4.77	4.61	4.48	4.39	4.32
300	28.45	15.94	11.85	9.87	8.72	7.99	7.50	7.16	6.91	6.72	6.59	6.48
400	37.93	21.25	15.80	13.16	11.63	10.66	10.00	9.54	9.21	8.96	8.78	8.64
500	47.41	26.57	19.75	16.44	14.53	13.32	12.50	11.93	11.51	11.20	10.97	10.80
600	56.89	31.88	23.70	19.73	17.44	15.98	15.00	14.31	13.81	13.44	13.17	12.96
700	66.37	37.19	27.65	23.02	20.35	18.65	17.50	16.69	16.11	15.68	15.36	15.12
800	75.85	42.50	31.60	26.31	23.25	21.31	20.00	19.08	18.41	17.92	17.56	17.28
900	85.33	47.81	35.55	29.60	26.16	23.97	22.50	21.46	20.71	20.16	19.75	19.44
1000	94.81	53.13	39.50	32.88	29.06	26.64	25.00	23.85	23.02	22.40	21.94	21.60
2000	189.61	106.25	79.00	65.76	58.12	53.27	49.99	47.69	46.03	44.80	43.88	43.19
3000	284.41	159.37	118.49	98.64	87.18	79.90	74.98	71.53	69.04	67.20	65.82	64.78
4000	379.21	212.49	157.99	131.52	116.24	106.53	99.98	95.37	92.05	89.60	87.76	86.37
5000	474.01	265.61	197.48	164.40	145.30	133.16	124.97	119.21	115.06	111.99	109.70	107.97
6000	568.82	318.73	236.98	197.28	174.36	159.79	149.96	143.06	138.07	134.39	131.64	129.56
7000	663.62	371.85	276.48	230.16	203.42	186.42	174.95	166.90	161.08	156.79	153.58	151.15
8000	758.42	424.97	315.97	263.04	232.48	213.05	199.95	190.74	184.09	179.19	175.52	172.74
9000	853.22	478.09	355.47	295.91	261.54	239.69	224.94	214.58	207.10	201.58	197.46	194.34
10000	948.02	531.21	394.96	328.79	290.59	266.32	249.93	238.42	230.11	223.98	219.40	215.93
11000	1042.82	584.34	434.46	361.67	319.65	292.95	274.93	262.27	253.12	246.38	241.34	237.52
12000	1137.63	637.46	473.96	394.55	348.71	319.58	299.92	286.11	276.13	268.78	263.28	259.11
13000	1232.43	690.58	513.45	427.43	377.77	346.21	324.91	309.95	299.14	291.18	285.22	280.71
14000	1327.23	743.70	552.95	460.31	406.83	372.84	349.90	333.79	322.15	313.57	307.15	302.30
15000	1422.03	796.82	592.44	493.19	435.89	399.47	374.90	357.63	345.16	335.97	329.09	323.89
16000	1516.83	849.94	631.94	526.07	464.95	426.10	399.89	381.48	368.17	358.37	351.03	345.48
17000	1611.63	903.06	671.43	558.95	494.01	452.74	424.88	405.32	391.18	380.77	372.97	367.08
18000	1706.44	956.18	710.93	591.82	523.07	479.37	449.88	429.16	414.20	403.16	394.91	388.67
19000	1801.24	1009.30	750.43	624.70	552.12	506.00	474.87	453.00	437.21	425.56	416.85	410.26
20000	1896.04	1062.42	789.92	657.58	581.18	532.63	499.86	476.84	460.22	447.96	438.79	431.85
21000	1990.84	1115.55	829.42	690.46	610.24	559.26	524.85	500.69	483.23	470.36	460.73	453.45
22000	2085.64	1168.67	868.91	723.34	639.30	585.89	549.85	524.53	506.24	492.76	482.67	475.04
23000	2180.44	1221.79	908.41	756.22	668.36	612.52	574.84	548.37	529.25	515.15	504.61	496.63
24000	2275.25	1274.91	947.91	789.10	697.42	639.15	599.83	572.21	552.26	537.55	526.55	518.22
25000	2370.05	1328.03	987.40	821.98	726.48	665.78	624.83	596.05	575.27	559.95	548.49	539.82
26000	2464.85	1381.15	1026.90	854.86	755.54	692.42	649.82	619.90	598.28	582.35	570.43	561.41
27000	2559.65	1434.27	1066.39	887.73	784.60	719.05	674.81	643.74	621.29	604.74	592.37	583.00
28000	2654.45	1487.39	1105.89	920.61	813.65	745.68	699.80	667.58	644.30	627.14	614.30	604.59
29000	2749.26	1540.51	1145.38	953.49	842.71	772.31	724.80	691.42	667.31	649.54	636.24	626.19
30000	2844.06	1593.63	1184.88	986.37	871.77	798.94	749.79	715.26	690.32	671.94	658.18	647.78
31000	2938.86	1646.76	1224.38	1019.25	900.83	825.57	774.78	739.11	713.33	694.33	680.12	669.37
32000	3033.66	1699.88	1263.87	1052.13	929.89	852.20	799.78	762.95	736.34	716.73	702.06	690.96
33000	3128.46	1753.00	1303.37	1085.01	958.95	878.83	824.77	786.79	759.35	739.13	724.00	712.56
34000	3223.26	1806.12	1342.86	1117.89	988.01	905.47	849.76	810.63	782.36	761.53	745.94	734.15
35000	3318.07	1859.24	1382.36	1150.77	1017.07	932.10	874.75	834.47	805.37	783.93	767.88	755.74
36000	3412.87	1912.36	1421.86	1183.64	1046.13	958.73	899.75	858.32	828.39	806.32	789.82	777.33
37000	3507.67	1965.48	1461.35	1216.52	1075.18	985.36	924.74	882.16	851.40	828.72	811.76	798.93
38000	3602.47	2018.60	1500.85	1249.40	1104.24	1011.99	949.73	906.00	874.41	851.12	833.70	820.52
39000	3697.27	2071.72	1540.34	1282.28	1133.30	1038.62	974.73	929.84	897.42	873.52	855.64	842.11
40000	3792.07	2124.84	1579.84	1315.16	1162.36	1065.25	999.72	953.68	920.43	895.91	877.58	863.70
41000	3886.88	2177.97	1619.34	1348.04	1191.42	1091.88	1024.71	977.53	943.44	918.31	899.52	885.30
42000	3981.68	2231.09	1658.83	1380.92	1220.48	1118.51	1049.70	1001.37	966.45	940.71	921.45	906.89
43000	4076.48	2284.21	1698.33	1413.80	1249.54	1145.15	1074.70	1025.21	989.46	963.11	943.39	928.48
44000	4171.28	2337.33	1737.82	1446.68	1278.60	1171.78	1099.69	1049.05	1012.47	985.51	965.33	950.07
45000	4266.08	2390.45	1777.32	1479.55	1307.66	1198.41	1124.68	1072.89	1035.48	1007.90	987.27	971.67
46000	4360.88	2443.57	1816.81	1512.43	1336.72	1225.04	1149.68	1096.74	1058.49	1030.30	1009.21	993.26
47000	4455.69	2496.69	1856.31	1545.31	1365.77	1251.67	1174.67	1120.58	1081.50	1052.70	1031.15	1014.85
48000	4550.49	2549.81	1895.81	1578.19	1394.83	1278.30	1199.66	1144.42	1104.51	1075.10	1053.09	1036.44
49000	4645.29	2602.93	1935.30	1611.07	1423.89	1304.93	1224.65	1168.26	1127.52	1097.49	1075.03	1058.04
50000	4740.09	2656.05	1974.80	1643.95	1452.95	1331.57	1249.65	1192.10	1150.53	1119.89	1096.97	1079.63
55000	5214.10	2921.66	2172.28	1808.34	1598.25	1464.72	1374.61	1311.31	1265.59	1231.88	1206.66	1187.59
60000	5688.11	3187.26	2369.76	1972.74	1743.54	1597.88	1499.58	1430.52	1380.64	1343.87	1316.36	1295.55
65000	6162.12	3452.87	2567.24	2137.13	1888.83	1731.03	1624.54	1549.73	1495.69	1455.86	1426.06	1403.52
70000	6636.13	3718.47	2764.72	2301.53	2034.13	1864.19	1749.50	1668.94	1610.74	1567.85	1535.75	1511.48
75000	7110.14	3984.08	2962.19	2465.92	2179.42	1997.34	1874.47	1788.15	1725.80	1679.83	1645.45	1619.44
80000	7584.14	4249.68	3159.67	2630.31	2324.72	2130.50	1999.43	1907.36	1840.85	1791.82	1755.15	1727.40
85000	8058.15	4515.29	3357.15	2794.71	2470.01	2263.66	2124.40	2026.57	1955.90	1903.81	1864.84	1835.37
90000	8532.16	4780.89	3554.63	2959.10	2615.31	2396.81	2249.36	2145.78	2070.96	2015.80	1974.54	1943.33
95000	9006.17	5046.50	3752.11	3123.50	2760.60	2529.97	2374.32	2264.99	2186.01	2127.79	2084.24	2051.29
100000	9480.18	5312.10	3949.59	3287.89	2905.90	2663.12	2499.29	2384.20	2301.06	2239.78	2193.93	2159.25

24%

Table 1

MONTHLY

24.50%

PAYMENT REQUIRED TO AMORTIZE A LOAN

TERM / AMOUNT	13 YEARS	14 YEARS	15 YEARS	16 YEARS	17 YEARS	18 YEARS	19 YEARS	20 YEARS	25 YEARS	30 YEARS	35 YEARS	40 YEARS
50	1.07	1.06	1.05	1.05	1.04	1.04	1.04	1.03	1.03	1.03	1.03	1.03
100	2.14	2.12	2.10	2.09	2.08	2.07	2.07	2.06	2.05	2.05	2.05	2.05
200	4.27	4.23	4.20	4.17	4.16	4.14	4.13	4.12	4.10	4.09	4.09	4.09
300	6.40	6.34	6.30	6.26	6.23	6.21	6.19	6.18	6.14	6.13	6.13	6.13
400	8.54	8.45	8.39	8.34	8.31	8.28	8.25	8.24	8.19	8.18	8.17	8.17
500	10.67	10.57	10.49	10.43	10.38	10.34	10.32	10.29	10.24	10.22	10.22	10.21
600	12.80	12.68	12.59	12.51	12.46	12.41	12.38	12.35	12.28	12.26	12.26	12.26
700	14.93	14.79	14.68	14.60	14.53	14.48	14.44	14.41	14.33	14.31	14.30	14.30
800	17.07	16.90	16.78	16.68	16.61	16.55	16.50	16.47	16.38	16.35	16.34	16.34
900	19.20	19.02	18.88	18.77	18.68	18.62	18.57	18.52	18.42	18.39	18.38	18.38
1000	21.33	21.13	20.97	20.85	20.76	20.68	20.63	20.58	20.47	20.44	20.43	20.42
2000	42.66	42.25	41.94	41.70	41.51	41.36	41.25	41.16	40.93	40.87	40.85	40.84
3000	63.99	63.38	62.91	62.55	62.26	62.04	61.87	61.74	61.40	61.30	61.27	61.26
4000	85.32	84.50	83.88	83.39	83.02	82.72	82.49	82.32	81.86	81.73	81.69	81.68
5000	106.64	105.63	104.85	104.24	103.77	103.40	103.12	102.89	102.33	102.16	102.11	102.09
6000	127.97	126.75	125.81	125.09	124.52	124.08	123.74	123.47	122.79	122.59	122.53	122.51
7000	149.30	147.88	146.78	145.93	145.27	144.76	144.36	144.05	143.25	143.02	142.95	142.93
8000	170.63	169.00	167.75	166.78	166.03	165.44	164.98	164.63	163.72	163.45	163.37	163.35
9000	191.96	190.13	188.72	187.63	186.78	186.12	185.61	185.20	184.18	183.88	183.79	183.77
10000	213.28	211.25	209.69	208.47	207.53	206.80	206.23	205.78	204.65	204.31	204.21	204.18
11000	234.61	232.38	230.66	229.32	228.29	227.48	226.85	226.36	225.11	224.74	224.63	224.60
12000	255.94	253.50	251.62	250.17	249.04	248.16	247.47	246.94	245.58	245.17	245.06	245.02
13000	277.27	274.63	272.59	271.02	269.79	268.84	268.09	267.51	266.04	265.61	265.48	265.44
14000	298.60	295.75	293.56	291.86	290.54	289.52	288.72	288.09	286.50	286.04	285.90	285.86
15000	319.92	316.88	314.53	312.71	311.30	310.20	309.34	308.67	306.97	306.47	306.32	306.27
16000	341.25	338.00	335.50	333.56	332.05	330.88	329.96	329.25	327.43	326.90	326.74	326.69
17000	362.58	359.13	356.47	354.40	352.80	351.56	350.58	349.83	347.90	347.33	347.16	347.11
18000	383.91	380.25	377.43	375.25	373.55	372.24	371.21	370.40	368.36	367.76	367.58	367.53
19000	405.24	401.38	398.40	396.10	394.31	392.91	391.83	390.98	388.83	388.19	388.00	387.95
20000	426.56	422.50	419.37	416.94	415.06	413.59	412.45	411.56	409.29	408.62	408.42	408.36
21000	447.89	443.63	440.34	437.79	435.81	434.27	433.07	432.14	429.75	429.05	428.84	428.78
22000	469.22	464.75	461.31	458.64	456.57	454.95	453.70	452.71	450.22	449.48	449.26	449.20
23000	490.55	485.88	482.27	479.48	477.32	475.63	474.32	473.29	470.68	469.91	469.68	469.62
24000	511.88	507.00	503.24	500.33	498.07	496.31	494.94	493.87	491.15	490.34	490.11	490.04
25000	533.20	528.13	524.21	521.18	518.82	516.99	515.56	514.45	511.61	510.78	510.53	510.45
26000	554.53	549.25	545.18	542.03	539.58	537.67	536.18	535.02	532.08	531.21	530.95	530.87
27000	575.86	570.38	566.15	562.87	560.33	558.35	556.81	555.60	552.54	551.64	551.37	551.29
28000	597.19	591.50	587.12	583.72	581.08	579.03	577.43	576.18	573.00	572.07	571.79	571.71
29000	618.52	612.63	608.08	604.57	601.83	599.71	598.05	596.76	593.47	592.50	592.21	592.12
30000	639.84	633.75	629.05	625.41	622.59	620.39	618.67	617.33	613.93	612.93	612.63	612.54
31000	661.17	654.88	650.02	646.26	643.34	641.07	639.30	637.91	634.40	633.36	633.05	632.96
32000	682.50	676.00	670.99	667.11	664.09	661.75	659.92	658.49	654.86	653.79	653.47	653.38
33000	703.83	697.13	691.96	687.95	684.85	682.43	680.54	679.07	675.33	674.22	673.89	673.80
34000	725.16	718.25	712.93	708.80	705.60	703.11	701.16	699.65	695.79	694.65	694.31	694.22
35000	746.48	739.38	733.89	729.65	726.35	723.79	721.78	720.22	716.25	715.08	714.74	714.63
36000	767.81	760.50	754.86	750.50	747.10	744.47	742.41	740.80	736.72	735.51	735.16	735.05
37000	789.14	781.63	775.83	771.34	767.86	765.14	763.03	761.38	757.18	755.94	755.58	755.47
38000	810.47	802.75	796.80	792.19	788.61	785.82	783.65	781.96	777.65	776.38	776.00	775.89
39000	831.79	823.88	817.77	813.04	809.36	806.50	804.27	802.53	798.11	796.81	796.42	796.30
40000	853.12	845.00	838.73	833.88	830.12	827.18	824.90	823.11	818.58	817.24	816.84	816.72
41000	874.45	866.13	859.70	854.73	850.87	847.86	845.52	843.69	839.04	837.67	837.26	837.14
42000	895.78	887.25	880.67	875.58	871.62	868.54	866.14	864.27	859.50	858.10	857.68	857.56
43000	917.11	908.38	901.64	896.42	892.37	889.22	886.76	884.84	879.97	878.53	878.10	877.98
44000	938.43	929.50	922.61	917.27	913.13	909.90	907.39	905.42	900.43	898.96	898.52	898.39
45000	959.76	950.62	943.58	938.12	933.88	930.58	928.01	926.00	920.90	919.39	918.94	918.81
46000	981.09	971.75	964.54	958.96	954.63	951.26	948.63	946.58	941.36	939.82	939.36	939.23
47000	1002.42	992.87	985.51	979.81	975.38	971.94	969.25	967.15	961.83	960.25	959.79	959.65
48000	1023.75	1014.00	1006.48	1000.66	996.14	992.62	989.87	987.73	982.29	980.68	980.21	980.06
49000	1045.07	1035.12	1027.45	1021.51	1016.89	1013.30	1010.50	1008.31	1002.75	1001.11	1000.63	1000.48
50000	1066.40	1056.25	1048.42	1042.35	1037.64	1033.98	1031.12	1028.89	1023.22	1021.55	1021.05	1020.90
55000	1173.04	1161.87	1153.26	1146.59	1141.41	1137.37	1134.23	1131.78	1125.54	1123.70	1123.15	1122.99
60000	1279.68	1267.50	1258.10	1250.82	1245.17	1240.77	1237.34	1234.66	1227.86	1225.85	1225.26	1225.08
65000	1386.32	1373.12	1362.94	1355.06	1348.93	1344.17	1340.45	1337.55	1330.18	1328.01	1327.36	1327.17
70000	1492.96	1478.75	1467.78	1459.29	1452.70	1447.57	1443.56	1440.44	1432.50	1430.16	1429.47	1429.26
75000	1599.60	1584.37	1572.62	1563.53	1556.46	1550.96	1546.68	1543.33	1534.83	1532.32	1531.57	1531.35
80000	1706.24	1690.00	1677.46	1667.76	1660.23	1654.36	1649.79	1646.22	1637.15	1634.47	1633.67	1633.44
85000	1812.88	1795.62	1782.31	1772.00	1763.99	1757.76	1752.90	1749.11	1739.47	1736.62	1735.78	1735.53
90000	1919.52	1901.24	1887.15	1876.23	1867.75	1861.16	1856.01	1851.99	1841.79	1838.78	1837.88	1837.62
95000	2026.16	2006.87	1991.99	1980.47	1971.52	1964.55	1959.12	1954.88	1944.11	1940.93	1939.99	1939.71
100000	2132.80	2112.49	2096.83	2084.70	2075.28	2067.95	2062.23	2057.77	2046.43	2043.09	2042.09	2041.80

24%

Table 1

24.75%

MONTHLY
PAYMENT REQUIRED TO AMORTIZE A LOAN

TERM AMOUNT	1 YEAR	2 YEARS	3 YEARS	4 YEARS	5 YEARS	6 YEARS	7 YEARS	8 YEARS	9 YEARS	10 YEARS	11 YEARS	12 YEARS
50	4.75	2.67	1.99	1.66	1.47	1.34	1.26	1.21	1.16	1.13	1.11	1.09
100	9.50	5.33	3.97	3.31	2.93	2.68	2.52	2.41	2.32	2.26	2.22	2.18
200	18.99	10.65	7.93	6.61	5.85	5.36	5.04	4.81	4.64	4.52	4.43	4.36
300	28.48	15.98	11.89	9.91	8.77	8.04	7.55	7.21	6.96	6.78	6.64	6.54
400	37.97	21.30	15.86	13.21	11.69	10.72	10.07	9.61	9.28	9.03	8.85	8.72
500	47.47	26.63	19.82	16.51	14.61	13.40	12.58	12.01	11.60	11.29	11.06	10.89
600	56.96	31.95	23.78	19.82	17.53	16.08	15.10	14.41	13.91	13.55	13.28	13.07
700	66.45	37.28	27.74	23.12	20.45	18.75	17.61	16.81	16.23	15.81	15.49	15.25
800	75.94	42.60	31.71	26.42	23.37	21.43	20.13	19.21	18.55	18.06	17.70	17.43
900	85.44	47.93	35.67	29.72	26.29	24.11	22.64	21.61	20.87	20.32	19.91	19.60
1000	94.93	53.25	39.63	33.02	29.21	26.79	25.16	24.01	23.19	22.58	22.12	21.78
2000	189.85	106.50	79.26	66.04	58.41	53.57	50.31	48.02	46.37	45.15	44.24	43.56
3000	284.77	159.74	118.89	99.06	87.62	80.36	75.46	72.03	69.55	67.72	66.36	65.33
4000	379.70	212.99	158.52	132.08	116.82	107.14	100.61	96.03	92.73	90.30	88.48	87.11
5000	474.62	266.24	198.14	165.09	146.03	133.92	125.77	120.04	115.91	112.87	110.60	108.89
6000	569.54	319.48	237.77	198.11	175.23	160.71	150.92	144.05	139.09	135.44	132.72	130.66
7000	664.47	372.73	277.40	231.13	204.44	187.49	176.07	168.05	162.27	158.02	154.84	152.44
8000	759.39	425.97	317.03	264.15	233.64	214.28	201.22	192.06	185.45	180.59	176.96	174.22
9000	854.31	479.22	356.65	297.17	262.85	241.06	226.37	216.07	208.64	203.16	199.08	195.99
10000	949.23	532.47	396.28	330.18	292.05	267.84	251.53	240.08	231.82	225.74	221.20	217.77
11000	1044.16	585.71	435.91	363.20	321.26	294.63	276.68	264.08	255.00	248.31	243.32	239.55
12000	1139.08	638.96	475.54	396.22	350.46	321.41	301.83	288.09	278.18	270.88	265.44	261.32
13000	1234.00	692.21	515.17	429.24	379.67	348.20	326.98	312.10	301.36	293.46	287.56	283.10
14000	1328.93	745.45	554.79	462.25	408.87	374.98	352.13	336.10	324.54	316.03	309.67	304.88
15000	1423.85	798.70	594.42	495.27	438.08	401.76	377.29	360.11	347.72	338.60	331.79	326.65
16000	1518.77	851.94	634.05	528.29	467.28	428.55	402.44	384.12	370.90	361.18	353.91	348.43
17000	1613.69	905.19	673.68	561.31	496.49	455.33	427.59	408.13	394.08	383.75	376.03	370.21
18000	1708.62	958.44	713.30	594.33	525.69	482.12	452.74	432.13	417.27	406.32	398.15	391.98
19000	1803.54	1011.68	752.93	627.34	554.90	508.90	477.89	456.14	440.45	428.90	420.27	413.76
20000	1898.46	1064.93	792.56	660.36	584.10	535.68	503.05	480.15	463.63	451.47	442.39	435.53
21000	1993.39	1118.17	832.19	693.38	613.31	562.47	528.20	504.15	486.81	474.04	464.51	457.31
22000	2088.31	1171.42	871.81	726.40	642.51	589.25	553.35	528.16	509.99	496.62	486.63	479.09
23000	2183.23	1224.67	911.44	759.42	671.72	616.04	578.50	552.17	533.17	519.19	508.75	500.86
24000	2278.16	1277.91	951.07	792.43	700.92	642.82	603.65	576.17	556.35	541.76	530.87	522.64
25000	2373.08	1331.16	990.70	825.45	730.13	669.60	628.81	600.18	579.53	564.34	552.99	544.42
26000	2468.00	1384.41	1030.33	858.47	759.33	696.39	653.96	624.19	602.71	586.91	575.11	566.19
27000	2562.92	1437.65	1069.95	891.49	788.54	723.17	679.11	648.20	625.90	609.48	597.23	587.97
28000	2657.85	1490.90	1109.58	924.50	817.74	749.96	704.26	672.20	649.08	632.06	619.34	609.75
29000	2752.77	1544.15	1149.21	957.52	846.95	776.74	729.41	696.21	672.26	654.63	641.46	631.52
30000	2847.69	1597.39	1188.84	990.54	876.15	803.52	754.57	720.22	695.44	677.20	663.58	653.30
31000	2942.62	1650.64	1228.46	1023.56	905.36	830.31	779.72	744.22	718.62	699.78	685.70	675.08
32000	3037.54	1703.88	1268.09	1056.58	934.56	857.09	804.87	768.23	741.80	722.35	707.82	696.85
33000	3132.46	1757.13	1307.72	1089.59	963.77	883.88	830.02	792.24	764.98	744.92	729.94	718.63
34000	3227.38	1810.37	1347.35	1122.61	992.97	910.66	855.17	816.25	788.16	767.50	752.06	740.41
35000	3322.31	1863.62	1386.98	1155.63	1022.18	937.44	880.33	840.25	811.34	790.07	774.18	762.18
36000	3417.23	1916.87	1426.60	1188.65	1051.38	964.23	905.48	864.26	834.53	812.64	796.30	783.96
37000	3512.15	1970.11	1466.23	1221.67	1080.59	991.01	930.63	888.27	857.71	835.22	818.42	805.73
38000	3607.08	2023.36	1505.86	1254.68	1109.79	1017.80	955.78	912.27	880.89	857.79	840.54	827.51
39000	3702.00	2076.61	1545.49	1287.70	1139.00	1044.58	980.93	936.28	904.07	880.36	862.66	849.29
40000	3796.92	2129.85	1585.11	1320.72	1168.20	1071.36	1006.09	960.29	927.25	902.94	884.78	871.06
41000	3891.85	2183.10	1624.74	1353.74	1197.41	1098.15	1031.24	984.30	950.43	925.51	906.90	892.84
42000	3986.77	2236.34	1664.37	1386.75	1226.61	1124.93	1056.39	1008.30	973.61	948.09	929.01	914.62
43000	4081.69	2289.59	1704.00	1419.77	1255.82	1151.72	1081.54	1032.31	996.79	970.66	951.13	936.39
44000	4176.61	2342.84	1743.62	1452.79	1285.02	1178.50	1106.69	1056.32	1019.98	993.23	973.25	958.17
45000	4271.54	2396.08	1783.25	1485.81	1314.23	1205.28	1131.85	1080.32	1043.16	1015.80	995.37	979.95
46000	4366.46	2449.33	1822.88	1518.83	1343.43	1232.07	1157.00	1104.33	1066.34	1038.38	1017.49	1001.72
47000	4461.38	2502.57	1862.51	1551.84	1372.64	1258.85	1182.15	1128.34	1089.52	1060.95	1039.61	1023.50
48000	4556.31	2555.82	1902.14	1584.86	1401.84	1285.64	1207.30	1152.34	1112.70	1083.52	1061.73	1045.28
49000	4651.23	2609.07	1941.76	1617.88	1431.05	1312.42	1232.45	1176.35	1135.88	1106.10	1083.85	1067.05
50000	4746.15	2662.31	1981.39	1650.90	1460.25	1339.20	1257.61	1200.36	1159.06	1128.67	1105.97	1088.83
55000	5220.77	2928.54	2179.53	1815.99	1606.28	1473.12	1383.37	1320.39	1274.97	1241.54	1216.57	1197.71
60000	5695.38	3194.78	2377.67	1981.08	1752.30	1607.04	1509.13	1440.43	1390.87	1354.40	1327.16	1306.59
65000	6170.00	3461.01	2575.81	2146.16	1898.33	1740.96	1634.89	1560.47	1506.78	1467.27	1437.76	1415.48
70000	6644.61	3727.24	2773.95	2311.25	2044.35	1874.88	1760.65	1680.50	1622.69	1580.13	1548.35	1524.36
75000	7119.22	3993.47	2972.08	2476.34	2190.38	2008.80	1886.41	1800.54	1738.59	1693.00	1658.95	1633.24
80000	7593.84	4259.70	3170.22	2641.43	2336.40	2142.72	2012.17	1920.57	1854.50	1805.87	1769.55	1742.12
85000	8068.45	4525.93	3368.36	2806.52	2482.42	2276.64	2137.93	2040.61	1970.40	1918.73	1880.14	1851.01
90000	8543.07	4792.16	3566.50	2971.61	2628.45	2410.56	2263.69	2160.64	2086.31	2031.60	1990.74	1959.89
95000	9017.68	5058.39	3764.64	3136.70	2774.47	2544.48	2389.45	2280.68	2202.21	2144.47	2101.34	2068.77
100000	9492.30	5324.62	3962.78	3301.79	2920.50	2678.40	2515.21	2400.71	2318.12	2257.33	2211.93	2177.65

24%

160

Table 1

MONTHLY   24.75%

PAYMENT REQUIRED TO AMORTIZE A LOAN

TERM AMOUNT	13 YEARS	14 YEARS	15 YEARS	16 YEARS	17 YEARS	18 YEARS	19 YEARS	20 YEARS	25 YEARS	30 YEARS	35 YEARS	40 YEARS
50	1.08	1.07	1.06	1.06	1.05	1.05	1.05	1.04	1.04	1.04	1.04	1.04
100	2.16	2.14	2.12	2.11	2.10	2.09	2.09	2.08	2.07	2.07	2.07	2.07
200	4.31	4.27	4.24	4.21	4.20	4.18	4.17	4.16	4.14	4.13	4.13	4.13
300	6.46	6.40	6.35	6.32	6.29	6.27	6.25	6.24	6.21	6.20	6.19	6.19
400	8.61	8.53	8.47	8.42	8.39	8.36	8.33	8.32	8.27	8.26	8.26	8.26
500	10.76	10.66	10.59	10.53	10.48	10.44	10.42	10.39	10.34	10.32	10.32	10.32
600	12.91	12.79	12.70	12.63	12.58	12.53	12.50	12.47	12.41	12.39	12.38	12.38
700	15.07	14.93	14.82	14.73	14.67	14.62	14.58	14.55	14.47	14.45	14.45	14.44
800	17.22	17.06	16.93	16.84	16.77	16.71	16.66	16.63	16.54	16.52	16.51	16.51
900	19.37	19.19	19.05	18.94	18.86	18.80	18.75	18.71	18.61	18.58	18.57	18.57
1000	21.52	21.32	21.17	21.05	20.96	20.88	20.83	20.78	20.68	20.64	20.63	20.63
2000	43.04	42.64	42.33	42.09	41.91	41.76	41.65	41.56	41.35	41.28	41.26	41.26
3000	64.55	63.95	63.49	63.13	62.86	62.64	62.47	62.34	62.02	61.92	61.89	61.88
4000	86.07	85.27	84.65	84.18	83.81	83.52	83.30	83.12	82.69	82.56	82.52	82.51
5000	107.58	106.58	105.81	105.22	104.76	104.40	104.12	103.90	103.36	103.20	103.15	103.14
6000	129.10	127.90	126.97	126.26	125.71	125.28	124.94	124.68	124.03	123.83	123.78	123.76
7000	150.61	149.21	148.14	147.30	146.66	146.16	145.77	145.46	144.70	144.47	144.41	144.39
8000	172.13	170.53	169.30	168.35	167.61	167.04	166.59	166.24	165.37	165.11	165.04	165.01
9000	193.64	191.84	190.46	189.39	188.56	187.91	187.41	187.02	186.04	185.75	185.67	185.64
10000	215.16	213.16	211.62	210.43	209.51	208.79	208.24	207.80	206.71	206.39	206.29	206.27
11000	236.68	234.48	232.78	231.47	230.46	229.67	229.06	228.58	227.38	227.03	226.92	226.89
12000	258.19	255.79	253.94	252.52	251.41	250.55	249.88	249.36	248.05	247.66	247.55	247.52
13000	279.71	277.11	275.11	273.56	272.36	271.43	270.71	270.14	268.72	268.30	268.18	268.14
14000	301.22	298.42	296.27	294.60	293.31	292.31	291.53	290.92	289.39	288.94	288.81	288.77
15000	322.74	319.74	317.43	315.64	314.26	313.19	312.35	311.70	310.06	309.58	309.44	309.40
16000	344.25	341.05	338.59	336.69	335.21	334.07	333.18	332.48	330.73	330.22	330.07	330.02
17000	365.77	362.37	359.75	357.73	356.16	354.95	354.00	353.26	351.40	350.86	350.70	350.65
18000	387.28	383.68	380.91	378.77	377.11	375.82	374.82	374.04	372.07	371.49	371.33	371.28
19000	408.80	405.00	402.07	399.81	398.06	396.70	395.65	394.82	392.74	392.13	391.96	391.90
20000	430.31	426.32	423.24	420.86	419.01	417.58	416.47	415.60	413.41	412.77	412.58	412.53
21000	451.83	447.63	444.40	441.90	439.96	438.46	437.29	436.38	434.08	433.41	433.21	433.15
22000	473.35	468.95	465.56	462.94	460.91	459.34	458.11	457.16	454.75	454.05	453.84	453.78
23000	494.86	490.26	486.72	483.99	481.87	480.22	478.94	477.94	475.42	474.69	474.47	474.41
24000	516.38	511.58	507.88	505.03	502.82	501.10	499.76	498.72	496.09	495.32	495.10	495.03
25000	537.89	532.89	529.04	526.07	523.77	521.98	520.58	519.50	516.76	515.96	515.73	515.66
26000	559.41	554.21	550.21	547.11	544.72	542.86	541.41	540.28	537.43	536.60	536.36	536.28
27000	580.92	575.52	571.37	568.16	565.67	563.73	562.23	561.06	558.10	557.24	556.99	556.91
28000	602.44	596.84	592.53	589.20	586.62	584.61	583.05	581.84	578.77	577.88	577.61	577.54
29000	623.95	618.15	613.69	610.24	607.57	605.49	603.88	602.62	599.44	598.51	598.24	598.16
30000	645.47	639.47	634.85	631.28	628.52	626.37	624.70	623.40	620.11	619.15	618.87	618.79
31000	666.98	660.79	656.01	652.33	649.47	647.25	645.52	644.18	640.78	639.79	639.50	639.42
32000	688.50	682.10	677.18	673.37	670.42	668.13	666.35	664.96	661.45	660.43	660.13	660.04
33000	710.02	703.42	698.34	694.41	691.37	689.01	687.17	685.74	682.12	681.07	680.76	680.67
34000	731.53	724.73	719.50	715.45	712.32	709.89	707.99	706.52	702.79	701.71	701.39	701.29
35000	753.05	746.05	740.66	736.50	733.27	730.77	728.82	727.30	723.46	722.34	722.02	721.92
36000	774.56	767.36	761.82	757.54	754.22	751.64	749.64	748.08	744.13	742.98	742.65	742.55
37000	796.08	788.68	782.98	778.58	775.17	772.52	770.46	768.86	764.80	763.62	763.27	763.17
38000	817.59	809.99	804.14	799.62	796.12	793.40	791.29	789.64	785.47	784.26	783.90	783.80
39000	839.11	831.31	825.31	820.67	817.07	814.28	812.11	810.42	806.14	804.90	804.53	804.42
40000	860.62	852.63	846.47	841.71	838.02	835.16	832.93	831.20	826.81	825.54	825.16	825.05
41000	882.14	873.94	867.63	862.75	858.97	856.04	853.76	851.98	847.48	846.17	845.79	845.68
42000	903.66	895.26	888.79	883.80	879.92	876.92	874.58	872.76	868.15	866.81	866.42	866.30
43000	925.17	916.57	909.95	904.84	900.87	897.80	895.40	893.54	888.83	887.45	887.05	886.93
44000	946.69	937.89	931.11	925.88	921.82	918.68	916.22	914.32	909.50	908.09	907.68	907.56
45000	968.20	959.20	952.28	946.92	942.78	939.55	937.05	935.10	930.17	928.73	928.31	928.18
46000	989.72	980.52	973.44	967.97	963.73	960.43	957.87	955.88	950.84	949.37	948.93	948.81
47000	1011.23	1001.83	994.60	989.01	984.68	981.31	978.69	976.66	971.51	970.00	969.56	969.43
48000	1032.75	1023.15	1015.76	1010.05	1005.63	1002.19	999.52	997.44	992.18	990.64	990.19	990.06
49000	1054.26	1044.47	1036.92	1031.09	1026.58	1023.07	1020.34	1018.21	1012.85	1011.28	1010.82	1010.69
50000	1075.78	1065.78	1058.08	1052.14	1047.53	1043.95	1041.16	1038.99	1033.52	1031.92	1031.45	1031.31
55000	1183.36	1172.36	1163.89	1157.35	1152.28	1148.34	1145.28	1142.89	1136.87	1135.11	1134.59	1134.44
60000	1290.93	1278.94	1269.70	1262.56	1257.03	1252.74	1249.40	1246.79	1240.22	1238.30	1237.74	1237.57
65000	1398.51	1385.51	1375.51	1367.78	1361.78	1357.13	1353.51	1350.69	1343.57	1341.49	1340.88	1340.70
70000	1506.09	1492.09	1481.32	1472.99	1466.54	1461.53	1457.63	1454.59	1446.92	1444.68	1444.03	1443.84
75000	1613.67	1598.67	1587.12	1578.20	1571.29	1565.92	1561.74	1558.49	1550.27	1547.88	1547.17	1546.97
80000	1721.24	1705.25	1692.93	1683.42	1676.04	1670.31	1665.86	1662.39	1653.62	1651.07	1650.32	1650.10
85000	1828.82	1811.82	1798.74	1788.63	1780.79	1774.71	1769.98	1766.29	1756.98	1754.26	1753.46	1753.23
90000	1936.40	1918.40	1904.55	1893.84	1885.55	1879.10	1874.09	1870.19	1860.33	1857.45	1856.61	1856.36
95000	2043.98	2024.98	2010.35	1999.05	1990.30	1983.50	1978.21	1974.09	1963.68	1960.64	1959.75	1959.49
100000	2151.55	2131.56	2116.16	2104.27	2095.05	2087.89	2082.32	2077.98	2067.03	2063.83	2062.89	2062.62

24%

Table 1

25.00%

MONTHLY
PAYMENT REQUIRED TO AMORTIZE A LOAN

TERM AMOUNT	1 YEAR	2 YEARS	3 YEARS	4 YEARS	5 YEARS	6 YEARS	7 YEARS	8 YEARS	9 YEARS	10 YEARS	11 YEARS	12 YEAR
50	4.76	2.67	1.99	1.66	1.47	1.35	1.27	1.21	1.17	1.14	1.12	1.10
100	9.51	5.34	3.98	3.32	2.94	2.70	2.54	2.42	2.34	2.28	2.23	2.20
200	19.01	10.68	7.96	6.64	5.88	5.39	5.07	4.84	4.68	4.55	4.46	4.40
300	28.52	16.02	11.93	9.95	8.81	8.09	7.60	7.26	7.01	6.83	6.69	6.59
400	38.02	21.35	15.91	13.27	11.75	10.78	10.13	9.67	9.35	9.10	8.92	8.79
500	47.53	26.69	19.88	16.58	14.68	13.47	12.66	12.09	11.68	11.38	11.15	10.99
600	57.03	32.03	23.86	19.90	17.62	16.17	15.19	14.51	14.02	13.65	13.38	13.18
700	66.54	37.37	27.84	23.21	20.55	18.86	17.72	16.93	16.35	15.93	15.61	15.38
800	76.04	42.70	31.81	26.53	23.49	21.55	20.25	19.34	18.69	18.20	17.84	17.57
900	85.54	48.04	35.79	29.85	26.42	24.25	22.79	21.76	21.02	20.48	20.07	19.77
1000	95.05	53.38	39.76	33.16	29.36	26.94	25.32	24.18	23.36	22.75	22.30	21.97
2000	190.09	106.75	79.52	66.32	58.71	53.88	50.63	48.35	46.71	45.50	44.60	43.93
3000	285.14	160.12	119.28	99.48	88.06	80.82	75.94	72.52	70.06	68.25	66.90	65.89
4000	380.18	213.49	159.04	132.63	117.41	107.75	101.25	96.70	93.41	91.00	89.20	87.85
5000	475.23	266.86	198.80	165.79	146.76	134.69	126.56	120.87	116.77	113.75	111.50	109.81
6000	570.27	320.23	238.56	198.95	176.11	161.63	151.87	145.04	140.12	136.50	133.80	131.77
7000	665.31	373.61	278.32	232.10	205.46	188.57	177.19	169.21	163.47	159.25	156.10	153.73
8000	760.36	426.98	318.08	265.26	234.82	215.50	202.50	193.39	186.82	182.00	178.40	175.69
9000	855.40	480.35	357.84	298.42	264.17	242.44	227.81	217.56	210.17	204.75	200.70	197.65
10000	950.45	533.72	397.60	331.58	293.52	269.38	253.12	241.73	233.53	227.50	223.00	219.61
11000	1045.49	587.09	437.36	364.73	322.87	296.31	278.43	265.90	256.88	250.25	245.30	241.58
12000	1140.54	640.46	477.12	397.89	352.22	323.25	303.74	290.08	280.23	273.00	267.60	263.54
13000	1235.58	693.83	516.88	431.05	381.57	350.19	329.06	314.25	303.58	295.75	289.90	285.50
14000	1330.62	747.21	556.64	464.20	410.92	377.13	354.37	338.42	326.94	318.50	312.20	307.46
15000	1425.67	800.58	596.40	497.36	440.27	404.06	379.68	362.59	350.29	341.24	334.50	329.42
16000	1520.71	853.95	636.16	530.52	469.63	431.00	404.99	386.77	373.64	363.99	356.80	351.38
17000	1615.76	907.32	675.92	563.68	498.98	457.94	430.30	410.94	396.99	386.74	379.10	373.34
18000	1710.80	960.69	715.68	596.83	528.33	484.87	455.61	435.11	420.34	409.49	401.40	395.30
19000	1805.84	1014.06	755.44	629.99	557.68	511.81	480.93	459.29	443.70	432.24	423.70	417.26
20000	1900.89	1067.44	795.20	663.15	587.03	538.75	506.24	483.46	467.05	454.99	446.00	439.22
21000	1995.93	1120.81	834.96	696.30	616.38	565.69	531.55	507.63	490.40	477.74	468.30	461.18
22000	2090.98	1174.18	874.72	729.46	645.73	592.62	556.86	531.80	513.75	500.49	490.60	483.15
23000	2186.02	1227.55	914.48	762.62	675.09	619.56	582.17	555.98	537.11	523.24	512.90	505.11
24000	2281.07	1280.92	954.24	795.78	704.44	646.50	607.48	580.15	560.46	545.99	535.20	527.07
25000	2376.11	1334.29	994.00	828.93	733.79	673.43	632.80	604.32	583.81	568.74	557.50	549.03
26000	2471.15	1387.66	1033.76	862.09	763.14	700.37	658.11	628.49	607.16	591.49	579.80	570.99
27000	2566.20	1441.04	1073.52	895.25	792.49	727.31	683.42	652.67	630.51	614.24	602.10	592.95
28000	2661.24	1494.41	1113.28	928.40	821.84	754.25	708.73	676.84	653.87	636.99	624.40	614.91
29000	2756.29	1547.78	1153.04	961.56	851.19	781.18	734.04	701.01	677.22	659.73	646.70	636.87
30000	2851.33	1601.15	1192.80	994.72	880.54	808.12	759.35	725.18	700.57	682.48	669.00	658.83
31000	2946.38	1654.52	1232.56	1027.88	909.90	835.06	784.67	749.36	723.92	705.23	691.30	680.79
32000	3041.42	1707.89	1272.32	1061.03	939.25	861.99	809.98	773.53	747.28	727.98	713.60	702.75
33000	3136.46	1761.27	1312.08	1094.19	968.60	888.93	835.29	797.70	770.63	750.73	735.90	724.72
34000	3231.51	1814.64	1351.84	1127.35	997.95	915.87	860.60	821.88	793.98	773.48	758.20	746.68
35000	3326.55	1868.01	1391.60	1160.50	1027.30	942.81	885.91	846.05	817.33	796.23	780.50	768.64
36000	3421.60	1921.38	1431.36	1193.66	1056.65	969.74	911.22	870.22	840.68	818.98	802.80	790.60
37000	3516.64	1974.75	1471.12	1226.82	1086.00	996.68	936.54	894.39	864.04	841.73	825.10	812.56
38000	3611.68	2028.12	1510.88	1259.98	1115.36	1023.62	961.85	918.57	887.39	864.48	847.40	834.52
39000	3706.73	2081.49	1550.64	1293.13	1144.71	1050.55	987.16	942.74	910.74	887.23	869.70	856.48
40000	3801.77	2134.87	1590.40	1326.29	1174.06	1077.49	1012.47	966.91	934.09	909.98	892.00	878.44
41000	3896.82	2188.24	1630.16	1359.45	1203.41	1104.43	1037.78	991.08	957.45	932.73	914.30	900.40
42000	3991.86	2241.61	1669.92	1392.60	1232.76	1131.37	1063.09	1015.26	980.80	955.48	936.60	922.36
43000	4086.91	2294.98	1709.68	1425.76	1262.11	1158.30	1088.41	1039.43	1004.15	978.22	958.89	944.32
44000	4181.95	2348.35	1749.44	1458.92	1291.46	1185.24	1113.72	1063.60	1027.50	1000.97	981.19	966.29
45000	4276.99	2401.72	1789.20	1492.08	1320.81	1212.18	1139.03	1087.77	1050.85	1023.72	1003.49	988.25
46000	4372.04	2455.09	1828.96	1525.23	1350.17	1239.12	1164.34	1111.95	1074.21	1046.47	1025.79	1010.21
47000	4467.08	2508.47	1868.72	1558.39	1379.52	1266.05	1189.65	1136.12	1097.56	1069.22	1048.09	1032.17
48000	4562.13	2561.84	1908.48	1591.55	1408.87	1292.99	1214.96	1160.29	1120.91	1091.97	1070.39	1054.13
49000	4657.17	2615.21	1948.24	1624.70	1438.22	1319.93	1240.28	1184.47	1144.26	1114.72	1092.69	1076.09
50000	4752.22	2668.58	1988.00	1657.86	1467.57	1346.86	1265.59	1208.64	1167.61	1137.47	1114.99	1098.05
55000	5227.44	2935.44	2186.80	1823.65	1614.33	1481.55	1392.15	1329.50	1284.38	1251.22	1226.49	1207.86
60000	5702.66	3202.30	2385.59	1989.43	1761.08	1616.24	1518.70	1450.36	1401.14	1364.96	1337.99	1317.66
65000	6177.88	3469.15	2584.39	2155.22	1907.84	1750.92	1645.26	1571.23	1517.90	1478.71	1449.49	1427.47
70000	6653.10	3736.01	2783.19	2321.00	2054.60	1885.61	1771.82	1692.09	1634.66	1592.46	1560.99	1537.27
75000	7128.32	4002.87	2981.99	2486.79	2201.35	2020.29	1898.38	1812.95	1751.42	1706.20	1672.49	1647.07
80000	7603.54	4269.73	3180.79	2652.58	2348.11	2154.98	2024.94	1933.82	1868.18	1819.95	1783.99	1756.88
85000	8078.76	4536.58	3379.59	2818.36	2494.87	2289.67	2151.49	2054.68	1984.94	1933.70	1895.48	1866.68
90000	8553.98	4803.44	3578.39	2984.15	2641.62	2424.35	2278.05	2175.54	2101.70	2047.44	2006.98	1976.49
95000	9029.20	5070.30	3777.19	3149.93	2788.38	2559.04	2404.61	2296.41	2218.46	2161.19	2118.48	2086.29
100000	9504.43	5337.16	3975.99	3315.72	2935.14	2693.72	2531.17	2417.27	2335.22	2274.93	2229.98	2196.10

Table 1

MONTHLY

PAYMENT REQUIRED TO AMORTIZE A LOAN

25.00%

TERM AMOUNT	13 YEARS	14 YEARS	15 YEARS	16 YEARS	17 YEARS	18 YEARS	19 YEARS	20 YEARS	25 YEARS	30 YEARS	35 YEARS	40 YEARS
50	1.09	1.08	1.07	1.07	1.06	1.06	1.06	1.05	1.05	1.05	1.05	1.05
100	2.18	2.16	2.14	2.13	2.12	2.11	2.11	2.10	2.09	2.09	2.09	2.09
200	4.35	4.31	4.28	4.25	4.23	4.22	4.21	4.20	4.18	4.17	4.17	4.17
300	6.52	6.46	6.41	6.38	6.35	6.33	6.31	6.30	6.27	6.26	6.26	6.26
400	8.69	8.61	8.55	8.50	8.46	8.44	8.41	8.40	8.36	8.34	8.34	8.34
500	10.86	10.76	10.68	10.62	10.58	10.54	10.52	10.50	10.44	10.43	10.42	10.42
600	13.03	12.91	12.82	12.75	12.69	12.65	12.62	12.59	12.53	12.51	12.51	12.51
700	15.20	15.06	14.95	14.87	14.81	14.76	14.72	14.69	14.62	14.60	14.59	14.59
800	17.37	17.21	17.09	17.00	16.92	16.87	16.82	16.79	16.71	16.68	16.67	16.67
900	19.54	19.36	19.22	19.12	19.04	18.98	18.93	18.89	18.79	18.77	18.76	18.76
1000	21.71	21.51	21.36	21.24	21.15	21.08	21.03	20.99	20.88	20.85	20.84	20.84
2000	43.41	43.02	42.72	42.48	42.30	42.16	42.05	41.97	41.76	41.70	41.68	41.67
3000	65.12	64.52	64.07	63.72	63.45	63.24	63.08	62.95	62.63	62.54	62.52	62.51
4000	86.82	86.03	85.43	84.96	84.60	84.32	84.10	83.93	83.51	83.39	83.35	83.34
5000	108.52	107.54	106.78	106.20	105.75	105.40	105.13	104.92	104.39	104.23	104.19	104.18
6000	130.23	129.04	128.14	127.44	126.90	126.48	126.15	125.90	125.26	125.08	125.03	125.01
7000	151.93	150.55	149.49	148.68	148.04	147.56	147.18	146.88	146.14	145.93	145.86	145.85
8000	173.63	172.06	170.85	169.91	169.19	168.63	168.20	167.86	167.02	166.77	166.70	166.68
9000	195.34	193.56	192.20	191.15	190.34	189.71	189.22	188.84	187.89	187.62	187.54	187.51
10000	217.04	215.07	213.56	212.39	211.49	210.79	210.25	209.83	208.77	208.46	208.37	208.35
11000	238.74	236.58	234.91	233.63	232.64	231.87	231.27	230.81	229.64	229.31	229.21	229.18
12000	260.45	258.08	256.27	254.87	253.79	252.95	252.30	251.79	250.52	250.15	250.05	250.02
13000	282.15	279.59	277.62	276.11	274.94	274.03	273.32	272.77	271.40	271.00	270.89	270.85
14000	303.85	301.10	298.98	297.35	296.08	295.11	294.35	293.76	292.27	291.85	291.72	291.69
15000	325.56	322.60	320.33	318.58	317.23	316.18	315.37	314.74	313.15	312.69	312.56	312.52
16000	347.26	344.11	341.69	339.82	338.38	337.26	336.39	335.72	334.03	333.54	333.40	333.36
17000	368.96	365.62	363.04	361.06	359.53	358.34	357.42	356.70	354.90	354.38	354.23	354.19
18000	390.67	387.12	384.40	382.30	380.68	379.42	378.44	377.68	375.78	375.23	375.07	375.02
19000	412.37	408.63	405.76	403.54	401.83	400.50	399.47	398.67	396.65	396.07	395.91	395.86
20000	434.07	430.14	427.11	424.78	422.97	421.58	420.49	419.65	417.53	416.92	416.74	416.69
21000	455.78	451.64	448.47	446.02	444.12	442.66	441.52	440.63	438.41	437.77	437.58	437.53
22000	477.48	473.15	469.82	467.26	465.27	463.73	462.54	461.61	459.28	458.61	458.42	458.36
23000	499.18	494.66	491.18	488.49	486.42	484.81	483.56	482.59	480.16	479.46	479.25	479.20
24000	520.89	516.16	512.53	509.73	507.57	505.89	504.59	503.58	501.04	500.30	500.09	500.03
25000	542.59	537.67	533.89	530.97	528.72	526.97	525.61	524.56	521.91	521.15	520.93	520.86
26000	564.29	559.18	555.24	552.21	549.87	548.05	546.64	545.54	542.79	542.00	541.77	541.70
27000	586.00	580.68	576.60	573.45	571.01	569.13	567.66	566.52	563.67	562.84	562.60	562.53
28000	607.70	602.19	597.95	594.69	592.16	590.21	588.69	587.51	584.54	583.69	583.44	583.37
29000	629.40	623.70	619.31	615.93	613.31	611.28	609.71	608.49	605.42	604.53	604.28	604.20
30000	651.11	645.20	640.66	637.16	634.46	632.36	630.73	629.47	626.29	625.38	625.11	625.04
31000	672.81	666.71	662.02	658.40	655.61	653.44	651.76	650.45	647.17	646.22	645.95	645.87
32000	694.52	688.21	683.37	679.64	676.76	674.52	672.78	671.43	668.05	667.07	666.79	666.71
33000	716.22	709.72	704.73	700.88	697.90	695.60	693.81	692.42	688.92	687.92	687.62	687.54
34000	737.92	731.23	726.08	722.12	719.05	716.68	714.83	713.40	709.80	708.76	708.46	708.37
35000	759.63	752.73	747.44	743.36	740.20	737.76	735.86	734.38	730.68	729.61	729.30	729.21
36000	781.33	774.24	768.80	764.60	761.35	758.83	756.88	755.36	751.55	750.45	750.14	750.04
37000	803.03	795.75	790.15	785.84	782.50	779.91	777.91	776.35	772.43	771.30	770.97	770.88
38000	824.74	817.25	811.51	807.07	803.65	800.99	798.93	797.33	793.30	792.14	791.81	791.71
39000	846.44	838.76	832.86	828.31	824.80	822.07	819.95	818.31	814.18	812.99	812.65	812.55
40000	868.14	860.27	854.22	849.55	845.94	843.15	840.98	839.29	835.06	833.84	833.48	833.38
41000	889.85	881.77	875.57	870.79	867.09	864.23	862.00	860.27	855.93	854.68	854.32	854.21
42000	911.55	903.28	896.93	892.03	888.24	885.31	883.03	881.26	876.81	875.53	875.16	875.05
43000	933.25	924.79	918.28	913.27	909.39	906.38	904.05	902.24	897.69	896.37	895.99	895.88
44000	954.96	946.29	939.64	934.51	930.54	927.46	925.08	923.22	918.56	917.22	916.83	916.72
45000	976.66	967.80	960.99	955.74	951.69	948.54	946.10	944.20	939.44	938.07	937.67	937.55
46000	998.36	989.31	982.35	976.98	972.83	969.62	967.12	965.18	960.32	958.91	958.50	958.39
47000	1020.07	1010.81	1003.70	998.22	993.98	990.70	988.15	986.17	981.19	979.76	979.34	979.22
48000	1041.77	1032.32	1025.06	1019.46	1015.13	1011.78	1009.17	1007.15	1002.07	1000.60	1000.18	1000.06
49000	1063.47	1053.83	1046.41	1040.70	1036.28	1032.86	1030.20	1028.13	1022.94	1021.45	1021.02	1020.89
50000	1085.18	1075.33	1067.77	1061.94	1057.43	1053.93	1051.22	1049.11	1043.82	1042.29	1041.85	1041.72
55000	1193.69	1182.87	1174.55	1168.13	1163.17	1159.33	1156.34	1154.02	1148.20	1146.52	1146.04	1145.90
60000	1302.21	1290.40	1281.32	1274.32	1268.91	1264.72	1261.46	1258.93	1252.58	1250.75	1250.22	1250.07
65000	1410.73	1397.93	1388.10	1380.52	1374.66	1370.11	1366.59	1363.85	1356.96	1354.98	1354.41	1354.24
70000	1519.25	1505.46	1494.88	1486.71	1480.40	1475.51	1471.71	1468.76	1461.35	1459.21	1458.59	1458.41
75000	1627.76	1613.00	1601.65	1592.90	1586.14	1580.90	1576.83	1573.67	1565.73	1563.44	1562.78	1562.58
80000	1736.28	1720.53	1708.43	1699.10	1691.88	1686.29	1681.95	1678.58	1670.11	1667.67	1666.96	1666.76
85000	1844.80	1828.06	1815.20	1805.29	1797.62	1791.68	1787.07	1783.49	1774.49	1771.90	1771.15	1770.93
90000	1953.31	1935.59	1921.98	1911.48	1903.37	1897.08	1892.19	1888.40	1878.87	1876.13	1875.33	1875.10
95000	2061.83	2043.13	2028.76	2017.68	2009.11	2002.47	1997.32	1993.31	1983.25	1980.35	1979.51	1979.27
100000	2170.35	2150.66	2135.53	2123.87	2114.85	2107.86	2102.44	2098.22	2087.64	2084.58	2083.70	2083.44

25%

Table 1

25.25%

MONTHLY
PAYMENT REQUIRED TO AMORTIZE A LOAN

TERM AMOUNT	1 YEAR	2 YEARS	3 YEARS	4 YEARS	5 YEARS	6 YEARS	7 YEARS	8 YEARS	9 YEARS	10 YEARS	11 YEARS	12 YEARS
50	4.76	2.68	2.00	1.67	1.48	1.36	1.28	1.22	1.18	1.15	1.13	1.11
100	9.52	5.35	3.99	3.33	2.95	2.71	2.55	2.44	2.36	2.30	2.25	2.22
200	19.04	10.70	7.98	6.66	5.90	5.42	5.10	4.87	4.71	4.59	4.50	4.43
300	28.55	16.05	11.97	9.99	8.85	8.13	7.65	7.31	7.06	6.88	6.75	6.65
400	38.07	21.40	15.96	13.32	11.80	10.84	10.19	9.74	9.41	9.18	9.00	8.86
500	47.59	26.75	19.95	16.65	14.75	13.55	12.74	12.17	11.77	11.47	11.25	11.08
600	57.10	32.10	23.94	19.98	17.70	16.26	15.29	14.61	14.12	13.76	13.49	13.29
700	66.62	37.45	27.93	23.31	20.65	18.97	17.84	17.04	16.47	16.05	15.74	15.51
800	76.14	42.80	31.92	26.64	23.60	21.68	20.38	19.48	18.82	18.35	17.99	17.72
900	85.65	48.15	35.91	29.97	26.55	24.39	22.93	21.91	21.18	20.64	20.24	19.94
1000	95.17	53.50	39.90	33.30	29.50	27.10	25.48	24.34	23.53	22.93	22.49	22.15
2000	190.34	107.00	79.79	66.60	59.00	54.19	50.95	48.68	47.05	45.86	44.97	44.30
3000	285.50	160.50	119.68	99.90	88.50	81.28	76.42	73.02	70.58	68.78	67.45	66.44
4000	380.67	213.99	159.57	133.19	118.00	108.37	101.89	97.36	94.10	91.71	89.93	88.59
5000	475.83	267.49	199.47	166.49	147.50	135.46	127.36	121.70	117.62	114.63	112.41	110.73
6000	571.00	320.99	239.36	199.79	176.99	162.55	152.84	146.04	141.15	137.56	134.89	132.88
7000	666.16	374.48	279.25	233.08	206.49	189.64	178.31	170.38	164.67	160.49	157.37	155.03
8000	761.33	427.98	319.14	266.38	235.99	216.73	203.78	194.71	188.19	183.41	179.85	177.17
9000	856.50	481.48	359.03	299.68	265.49	243.82	229.25	219.05	211.72	206.34	202.33	199.32
10000	951.66	534.98	398.93	332.97	294.99	270.91	254.72	243.39	235.24	229.26	224.81	221.46
11000	1046.83	588.47	438.82	366.27	324.49	298.00	280.19	267.73	258.77	252.19	247.29	243.61
12000	1141.99	641.97	478.71	399.57	353.98	325.09	305.67	292.07	282.29	275.11	269.77	265.75
13000	1237.16	695.47	518.60	432.86	383.48	352.19	331.14	316.41	305.81	298.04	292.25	287.90
14000	1332.32	748.96	558.50	466.16	412.98	379.28	356.61	340.75	329.34	320.97	314.73	310.05
15000	1427.49	802.46	598.39	499.46	442.48	406.37	382.08	365.09	352.86	343.89	337.22	332.19
16000	1522.65	855.96	638.28	532.75	471.97	433.46	407.55	389.42	376.38	366.82	359.70	354.34
17000	1617.82	909.45	678.17	566.05	501.47	460.55	433.02	413.76	399.91	389.74	382.18	376.48
18000	1712.99	962.95	718.06	599.35	530.97	487.64	458.50	438.10	423.43	412.67	404.66	398.63
19000	1808.15	1016.45	757.96	632.64	560.47	514.73	483.97	462.44	446.96	435.59	427.14	420.78
20000	1903.32	1069.95	797.85	665.94	589.97	541.82	509.44	486.78	470.48	458.52	449.62	442.92
21000	1998.48	1123.44	837.74	699.24	619.46	568.91	534.91	511.12	494.00	481.45	472.10	465.07
22000	2093.65	1176.94	877.63	732.53	648.96	596.00	560.38	535.46	517.53	504.37	494.58	487.21
23000	2188.81	1230.44	917.52	765.83	678.46	623.09	585.85	559.80	541.05	527.30	517.06	509.36
24000	2283.98	1283.93	957.42	799.13	707.96	650.18	611.33	584.13	564.57	550.22	539.54	531.50
25000	2379.14	1337.43	997.31	832.42	737.46	677.27	636.80	608.47	588.10	573.15	562.02	553.65
26000	2474.31	1390.93	1037.20	865.72	766.95	704.37	662.27	632.81	611.62	596.08	584.50	575.80
27000	2569.48	1444.43	1077.09	899.02	796.45	731.46	687.74	657.15	635.15	619.00	606.98	597.94
28000	2664.64	1497.92	1116.99	932.31	825.95	758.55	713.21	681.49	658.67	641.93	629.46	620.09
29000	2759.81	1551.42	1156.88	965.61	855.45	785.64	738.68	705.83	682.19	664.85	651.95	642.23
30000	2854.97	1604.92	1196.77	998.91	884.95	812.73	764.16	730.17	705.72	687.78	674.43	664.38
31000	2950.14	1658.41	1236.66	1032.20	914.45	839.82	789.63	754.51	729.24	710.70	696.91	686.53
32000	3045.30	1711.91	1276.55	1065.50	943.94	866.91	815.10	778.84	752.76	733.63	719.39	708.67
33000	3140.47	1765.41	1316.45	1098.80	973.44	894.00	840.57	803.18	776.29	756.56	741.87	730.82
34000	3235.63	1818.90	1356.34	1132.09	1002.94	921.09	866.04	827.52	799.81	779.48	764.35	752.96
35000	3330.80	1872.40	1396.23	1165.39	1032.44	948.18	891.51	851.86	823.34	802.41	786.83	775.11
36000	3425.97	1925.90	1436.12	1198.69	1061.94	975.27	916.99	876.20	846.86	825.33	809.31	797.25
37000	3521.13	1979.40	1476.02	1231.98	1091.43	1002.36	942.46	900.54	870.38	848.26	831.79	819.40
38000	3616.30	2032.89	1515.91	1265.28	1120.93	1029.45	967.93	924.88	893.91	871.18	854.27	841.55
39000	3711.46	2086.39	1555.80	1298.58	1150.43	1056.55	993.40	949.21	917.43	894.11	876.75	863.69
40000	3806.63	2139.89	1595.69	1331.87	1179.93	1083.64	1018.87	973.55	940.95	917.04	899.23	885.84
41000	3901.79	2193.38	1635.58	1365.17	1209.43	1110.73	1044.34	997.89	964.48	939.96	921.71	907.98
42000	3996.96	2246.88	1675.48	1398.47	1238.92	1137.82	1069.82	1022.23	988.00	962.89	944.19	930.13
43000	4092.12	2300.38	1715.37	1431.76	1268.42	1164.91	1095.29	1046.57	1011.53	985.81	966.68	952.28
44000	4187.29	2353.87	1755.26	1465.06	1297.92	1192.00	1120.76	1070.91	1035.05	1008.74	989.16	974.42
45000	4282.46	2407.37	1795.15	1498.36	1327.42	1219.09	1146.23	1095.25	1058.57	1031.67	1011.64	996.57
46000	4377.62	2460.87	1835.04	1531.65	1356.92	1246.18	1171.70	1119.59	1082.10	1054.59	1034.12	1018.71
47000	4472.79	2514.37	1874.94	1564.95	1386.41	1273.27	1197.17	1143.92	1105.62	1077.52	1056.60	1040.86
48000	4567.95	2567.86	1914.83	1598.25	1415.91	1300.36	1222.65	1168.26	1129.14	1100.44	1079.08	1063.00
49000	4663.12	2621.36	1954.72	1631.54	1445.41	1327.45	1248.12	1192.60	1152.67	1123.37	1101.56	1085.15
50000	4758.28	2674.86	1994.61	1664.84	1474.91	1354.54	1273.59	1216.94	1176.19	1146.29	1124.04	1107.30
55000	5234.11	2942.34	2194.07	1831.32	1622.40	1490.00	1400.95	1338.63	1293.81	1260.92	1236.44	1218.03
60000	5709.94	3209.83	2393.54	1997.81	1769.89	1625.45	1528.31	1460.33	1411.43	1375.55	1348.85	1328.75
65000	6185.77	3477.31	2593.00	2164.29	1917.38	1760.91	1655.67	1582.02	1529.05	1490.18	1461.25	1439.48
70000	6661.59	3744.80	2792.46	2330.78	2064.87	1896.36	1783.02	1703.71	1646.67	1604.81	1573.65	1550.21
75000	7137.42	4012.28	2991.92	2497.26	2212.36	2031.81	1910.38	1825.41	1764.28	1719.44	1686.06	1660.94
80000	7613.25	4279.77	3191.38	2663.74	2359.85	2167.27	2037.74	1947.10	1881.90	1834.07	1798.46	1771.67
85000	8089.08	4547.25	3390.84	2830.23	2507.34	2302.72	2165.10	2068.80	1999.52	1948.70	1910.87	1882.40
90000	8564.91	4814.74	3590.30	2996.71	2654.83	2438.18	2292.46	2190.49	2117.14	2063.33	2023.27	1993.13
95000	9040.73	5082.22	3789.76	3163.19	2802.32	2573.63	2419.82	2312.18	2234.76	2177.95	2135.67	2103.86
100000	9516.56	5349.71	3989.22	3329.68	2949.81	2709.08	2547.17	2433.88	2352.38	2292.58	2248.08	2214.59

Table 1

MONTHLY
PAYMENT REQUIRED TO AMORTIZE A LOAN

25.25%

TERM AMOUNT	13 YEARS	14 YEARS	15 YEARS	16 YEARS	17 YEARS	18 YEARS	19 YEARS	20 YEARS	25 YEARS	30 YEARS	35 YEARS	40 YEARS
50	1.10	1.09	1.08	1.08	1.07	1.07	1.07	1.06	1.06	1.06	1.06	1.06
100	2.19	2.17	2.16	2.15	2.14	2.13	2.13	2.12	2.11	2.11	2.11	2.11
200	4.38	4.34	4.31	4.29	4.27	4.26	4.25	4.24	4.22	4.22	4.21	4.21
300	6.57	6.51	6.47	6.44	6.41	6.39	6.37	6.36	6.33	6.32	6.32	6.32
400	8.76	8.68	8.62	8.58	8.54	8.52	8.50	8.48	8.44	8.43	8.42	8.42
500	10.95	10.85	10.78	10.72	10.68	10.64	10.62	10.60	10.55	10.53	10.53	10.53
600	13.14	13.02	12.93	12.87	12.81	12.77	12.74	12.72	12.65	12.64	12.63	12.63
700	15.33	15.19	15.09	15.01	14.95	14.90	14.86	14.83	14.76	14.74	14.74	14.73
800	17.52	17.36	17.24	17.15	17.08	17.03	16.99	16.95	16.87	16.85	16.84	16.84
900	19.71	19.53	19.40	19.30	19.22	19.16	19.11	19.07	18.98	18.95	18.95	18.94
1000	21.90	21.70	21.55	21.44	21.35	21.28	21.23	21.19	21.09	21.06	21.05	21.05
2000	43.79	43.40	43.10	42.88	42.70	42.56	42.46	42.37	42.17	42.11	42.10	42.09
3000	65.68	65.10	64.65	64.31	64.05	63.84	63.68	63.56	63.25	63.17	63.14	63.13
4000	87.57	86.80	86.20	85.75	85.39	85.12	84.91	84.74	84.33	84.22	84.19	84.18
5000	109.46	108.49	107.75	107.18	106.74	106.40	106.13	105.93	105.42	105.27	105.23	105.22
6000	131.36	130.19	129.30	128.62	128.09	127.68	127.36	127.11	126.50	126.33	126.28	126.26
7000	153.25	151.89	150.85	150.05	149.43	148.95	148.59	148.30	147.58	147.38	147.32	147.30
8000	175.14	173.59	172.40	171.49	170.78	170.23	169.81	169.48	168.66	168.43	168.37	168.35
9000	197.03	195.29	193.95	192.92	192.13	191.51	191.04	190.67	189.75	189.48	189.41	189.39
10000	218.92	216.98	215.50	214.36	213.47	212.79	212.26	211.85	210.83	210.54	210.46	210.43
11000	240.82	238.68	237.05	235.79	234.82	234.07	233.49	233.04	231.91	231.59	231.50	231.47
12000	262.71	260.38	258.60	257.23	256.17	255.35	254.71	254.22	252.99	252.65	252.55	252.52
13000	284.60	282.08	280.15	278.66	277.51	276.63	275.94	275.41	274.08	273.70	273.59	273.56
14000	306.49	303.78	301.70	300.10	298.86	297.90	297.17	296.59	295.16	294.75	294.64	294.60
15000	328.38	325.47	323.25	321.53	320.21	319.18	318.39	317.78	316.24	315.81	315.68	315.64
16000	350.27	347.17	344.79	342.97	341.55	340.46	339.62	338.96	337.32	336.86	336.73	336.69
17000	372.17	368.87	366.34	364.40	362.90	361.74	360.84	360.15	358.41	357.91	357.77	357.73
18000	394.06	390.57	387.89	385.84	384.25	383.02	382.07	381.33	379.49	378.97	378.82	378.77
19000	415.95	412.27	409.44	407.27	405.59	404.30	403.29	402.52	400.57	400.02	399.86	399.81
20000	437.84	433.96	430.99	428.71	426.94	425.58	424.52	423.70	421.65	421.07	420.91	420.86
21000	459.73	455.66	452.54	450.14	448.29	446.85	445.75	444.88	442.74	442.13	441.95	441.90
22000	481.63	477.36	474.09	471.58	469.63	468.13	466.97	466.07	463.82	463.18	463.00	462.94
23000	503.52	499.06	495.64	493.01	490.98	489.41	488.20	487.25	484.90	484.24	484.04	483.99
24000	525.41	520.76	517.19	514.45	512.33	510.69	509.42	508.44	505.99	505.29	505.09	505.03
25000	547.30	542.45	538.74	535.88	533.67	531.97	530.65	529.62	527.07	526.34	526.13	526.07
26000	569.19	564.15	560.29	557.32	555.02	553.25	551.87	550.81	548.15	547.39	547.18	547.11
27000	591.08	585.85	581.84	578.75	576.37	574.53	573.10	571.99	569.23	568.45	568.22	568.16
28000	612.98	607.55	603.39	600.19	597.71	595.80	594.33	593.18	590.31	589.50	589.27	589.20
29000	634.87	629.25	624.94	621.62	619.06	617.08	615.55	614.36	611.40	610.55	610.31	610.24
30000	656.76	650.94	646.49	643.06	640.41	638.36	636.78	635.55	632.48	631.61	631.36	631.28
31000	678.65	672.64	668.04	664.49	661.76	659.64	658.00	656.73	653.56	652.66	652.40	652.33
32000	700.54	694.34	689.58	685.93	683.10	680.92	679.23	677.92	674.64	673.71	673.45	673.37
33000	722.44	716.04	711.13	707.36	704.45	702.20	700.45	699.10	695.73	694.77	694.49	694.41
34000	744.33	737.74	732.68	728.80	725.80	723.48	721.68	720.29	716.81	715.82	715.54	715.45
35000	766.22	759.43	754.23	750.23	747.14	744.75	742.91	741.47	737.89	736.87	736.58	736.50
36000	788.11	781.13	775.78	771.67	768.49	766.03	764.13	762.66	758.97	757.93	757.63	757.54
37000	810.00	802.83	797.33	793.10	789.84	787.31	785.36	783.84	780.06	778.98	778.67	778.58
38000	831.89	824.53	818.88	814.54	811.18	808.59	806.58	805.03	801.14	800.03	799.72	799.62
39000	853.79	846.23	840.43	835.97	832.53	829.87	827.81	826.21	822.22	821.09	820.76	820.67
40000	875.68	867.92	861.98	857.41	853.88	851.15	849.03	847.40	843.30	842.14	841.81	841.71
41000	897.57	889.62	883.53	878.84	875.22	872.43	870.26	868.58	864.39	863.19	862.85	862.75
42000	919.46	911.32	905.08	900.28	896.57	893.70	891.49	889.76	885.47	884.25	883.90	883.80
43000	941.35	933.02	926.63	921.71	917.92	914.98	912.71	910.95	906.55	905.30	904.94	904.84
44000	963.25	954.72	948.18	943.15	939.26	936.26	933.94	932.13	927.63	926.35	925.99	925.88
45000	985.14	976.41	969.73	964.58	960.61	957.54	955.16	953.32	948.72	947.41	947.03	946.92
46000	1007.03	998.11	991.28	986.02	981.96	978.82	976.39	974.50	969.80	968.46	968.08	967.97
47000	1028.92	1019.81	1012.83	1007.45	1003.30	1000.10	997.61	995.69	990.88	989.51	989.12	989.01
48000	1050.81	1041.51	1034.37	1028.89	1024.65	1021.38	1018.84	1016.87	1011.96	1010.57	1010.17	1010.05
49000	1072.70	1063.21	1055.92	1050.32	1046.00	1042.65	1040.07	1038.06	1033.05	1031.62	1031.21	1031.09
50000	1094.60	1084.90	1077.47	1071.76	1067.34	1063.93	1061.29	1059.24	1054.13	1052.67	1052.26	1052.14
55000	1204.06	1193.39	1185.22	1178.93	1174.08	1170.33	1167.42	1165.17	1159.54	1157.94	1157.48	1157.35
60000	1313.51	1301.88	1292.97	1286.11	1280.81	1276.72	1273.55	1271.09	1264.95	1263.21	1262.71	1262.56
65000	1422.97	1410.37	1400.71	1393.28	1387.55	1383.11	1379.68	1377.01	1370.37	1368.47	1367.93	1367.78
70000	1532.43	1518.86	1508.46	1500.46	1494.28	1489.50	1485.81	1482.94	1475.78	1473.74	1473.16	1472.99
75000	1641.89	1627.35	1616.21	1607.63	1601.01	1595.90	1591.93	1588.86	1581.19	1579.01	1578.38	1578.20
80000	1751.35	1735.84	1723.95	1714.81	1707.75	1702.29	1698.06	1694.79	1686.60	1684.27	1683.61	1683.42
85000	1860.81	1844.33	1831.70	1821.98	1814.48	1808.68	1804.19	1800.71	1792.02	1789.54	1788.83	1788.63
90000	1970.27	1952.82	1939.45	1929.16	1921.22	1915.08	1910.32	1906.63	1897.43	1894.81	1894.06	1893.84
95000	2079.73	2061.31	2047.20	2036.33	2027.95	2021.47	2016.45	2012.56	2002.84	2000.07	1999.28	1999.05
100000	2189.19	2169.80	2154.94	2143.51	2134.68	2127.86	2122.58	2118.48	2108.25	2105.34	2104.51	2104.27

25%

Table 1

25.50%

MONTHLY
PAYMENT REQUIRED TO AMORTIZE A LOAN

TERM AMOUNT	1 YEAR	2 YEARS	3 YEARS	4 YEARS	5 YEARS	6 YEARS	7 YEARS	8 YEARS	9 YEARS	10 YEARS	11 YEARS	12 YEARS
50	4.77	2.69	2.01	1.68	1.49	1.37	1.29	1.23	1.19	1.16	1.14	1.12
100	9.53	5.37	4.01	3.35	2.97	2.73	2.57	2.46	2.37	2.32	2.27	2.24
200	19.06	10.73	8.01	6.69	5.93	5.45	5.13	4.91	4.74	4.63	4.54	4.47
300	28.59	16.09	12.01	10.04	8.90	8.18	7.69	7.36	7.11	6.94	6.80	6.70
400	38.12	21.45	16.01	13.38	11.86	10.90	10.26	9.81	9.48	9.25	9.07	8.94
500	47.65	26.82	20.02	16.72	14.83	13.63	12.82	12.26	11.85	11.56	11.34	11.17
600	57.18	32.18	24.02	20.07	17.79	16.35	15.38	14.71	14.22	13.87	13.60	13.40
700	66.71	37.54	28.02	23.41	20.76	19.08	17.95	17.16	16.59	16.18	15.87	15.64
800	76.23	42.90	32.02	26.75	23.72	21.80	20.51	19.61	18.96	18.49	18.13	17.87
900	85.76	48.27	36.03	30.10	26.69	24.53	23.07	22.06	21.33	20.80	20.40	20.10
1000	95.29	53.63	40.03	33.44	29.65	27.25	25.64	24.51	23.70	23.11	22.67	22.34
2000	190.58	107.25	80.05	66.88	59.30	54.49	51.27	49.02	47.40	46.21	45.33	44.67
3000	285.87	160.87	120.08	100.31	88.94	81.74	76.90	73.52	71.09	69.31	67.99	67.00
4000	381.15	214.50	160.10	133.75	118.59	108.98	102.53	98.03	94.79	92.42	90.65	89.33
5000	476.44	268.12	200.13	167.19	148.23	136.23	128.17	122.53	118.48	115.52	113.32	111.66
6000	571.73	321.74	240.15	200.62	177.88	163.47	153.80	147.04	142.18	138.62	135.98	133.99
7000	667.01	375.36	280.18	234.06	207.52	190.72	179.43	171.54	165.88	161.72	158.64	156.32
8000	762.30	428.99	320.20	267.50	237.17	217.96	205.06	196.05	189.57	184.83	181.30	178.65
9000	857.59	482.61	360.23	300.93	266.81	245.21	230.69	220.55	213.27	207.93	203.96	200.99
10000	952.88	536.23	400.25	334.37	296.46	272.45	256.33	245.06	236.96	231.03	226.63	223.32
11000	1048.16	589.85	440.28	367.81	326.10	299.70	281.96	269.56	260.66	254.14	249.29	245.65
12000	1143.45	643.48	480.30	401.24	355.75	326.94	307.59	294.07	284.35	277.24	271.95	267.98
13000	1238.74	697.10	520.33	434.68	385.39	354.19	333.22	318.57	308.05	300.34	294.61	290.31
14000	1334.02	750.72	560.35	468.12	415.04	381.43	358.86	343.08	331.75	323.44	317.27	312.64
15000	1429.31	804.35	600.38	501.55	444.68	408.68	384.49	367.58	355.44	346.55	339.94	334.97
16000	1524.60	857.97	640.40	534.99	474.33	435.92	410.12	392.09	379.14	369.65	362.60	357.30
17000	1619.88	911.59	680.43	568.43	503.97	463.17	435.75	416.59	402.83	392.75	385.26	379.63
18000	1715.17	965.21	720.45	601.86	533.62	490.41	461.38	441.10	426.53	415.85	407.92	401.97
19000	1810.46	1018.84	760.48	635.30	563.26	517.66	487.02	465.60	450.22	438.96	430.59	424.30
20000	1905.75	1072.46	800.50	668.74	592.91	544.90	512.65	490.11	473.92	462.06	453.25	446.63
21000	2001.03	1126.08	840.52	702.17	622.55	572.15	538.28	514.61	497.62	485.16	475.91	468.96
22000	2096.32	1179.70	880.55	735.61	652.20	599.39	563.91	539.12	521.31	508.27	498.57	491.29
23000	2191.61	1233.33	920.57	769.05	681.84	626.64	589.55	563.62	545.01	531.37	521.23	513.62
24000	2286.89	1286.95	960.60	802.48	711.49	653.88	615.18	588.13	568.70	554.47	543.90	535.95
25000	2382.18	1340.57	1000.62	835.92	741.13	681.12	640.81	612.64	592.40	577.57	566.56	558.28
26000	2477.47	1394.20	1040.65	869.36	770.78	708.37	666.44	637.14	616.09	600.68	589.22	580.62
27000	2572.75	1447.82	1080.67	902.79	800.42	735.61	692.07	661.65	639.79	623.78	611.88	602.95
28000	2668.04	1501.44	1120.70	936.23	830.07	762.86	717.71	686.15	663.49	646.88	634.54	625.28
29000	2763.33	1555.06	1160.72	969.67	859.72	790.10	743.34	710.66	687.18	669.98	657.21	647.61
30000	2858.62	1608.69	1200.75	1003.10	889.36	817.35	768.97	735.16	710.88	693.09	679.87	669.94
31000	2953.90	1662.31	1240.77	1036.54	919.01	844.59	794.60	759.67	734.57	716.19	702.53	692.27
32000	3049.19	1715.93	1280.80	1069.98	948.65	871.84	820.24	784.17	758.27	739.29	725.19	714.60
33000	3144.48	1769.55	1320.82	1103.41	978.30	899.08	845.87	808.68	781.96	762.40	747.85	736.93
34000	3239.76	1823.18	1360.85	1136.85	1007.94	926.33	871.50	833.18	805.66	785.50	770.52	759.26
35000	3335.05	1876.80	1400.87	1170.29	1037.59	953.57	897.13	857.69	829.36	808.60	793.18	781.60
36000	3430.34	1930.42	1440.90	1203.72	1067.23	980.82	922.76	882.19	853.05	831.70	815.84	803.93
37000	3525.62	1984.05	1480.92	1237.16	1096.88	1008.06	948.40	906.70	876.75	854.81	838.50	826.26
38000	3620.91	2037.67	1520.95	1270.60	1126.52	1035.31	974.03	931.20	900.44	877.91	861.16	848.59
39000	3716.20	2091.29	1560.97	1304.03	1156.17	1062.55	999.66	955.71	924.14	901.01	883.83	870.92
40000	3811.49	2144.91	1600.99	1337.47	1185.81	1089.80	1025.29	980.21	947.83	924.11	906.49	893.25
41000	3906.77	2198.54	1641.02	1370.91	1215.46	1117.04	1050.93	1004.72	971.53	947.22	929.15	915.58
42000	4002.06	2252.16	1681.04	1404.34	1245.10	1144.29	1076.56	1029.22	995.23	970.32	951.81	937.91
43000	4097.35	2305.78	1721.07	1437.78	1274.75	1171.53	1102.19	1053.73	1018.92	993.42	974.48	960.25
44000	4192.63	2359.40	1761.09	1471.22	1304.39	1198.78	1127.82	1078.23	1042.62	1016.53	997.14	982.58
45000	4287.92	2413.03	1801.12	1504.65	1334.04	1226.02	1153.45	1102.74	1066.31	1039.63	1019.80	1004.91
46000	4383.21	2466.65	1841.14	1538.09	1363.68	1253.27	1179.09	1127.24	1090.01	1062.73	1042.46	1027.24
47000	4478.49	2520.27	1881.17	1571.53	1393.33	1280.51	1204.72	1151.75	1113.70	1085.83	1065.12	1049.57
48000	4573.78	2573.90	1921.19	1604.96	1422.97	1307.76	1230.35	1176.26	1137.40	1108.94	1087.79	1071.90
49000	4669.07	2627.52	1961.22	1638.40	1452.62	1335.00	1255.98	1200.76	1161.10	1132.04	1110.45	1094.23
50000	4764.36	2681.14	2001.24	1671.84	1482.26	1362.24	1281.61	1225.27	1184.79	1155.14	1133.11	1116.56
55000	5240.79	2949.25	2201.37	1839.02	1630.49	1498.47	1409.78	1347.79	1303.27	1270.66	1246.42	1228.22
60000	5717.23	3217.37	2401.49	2006.20	1778.72	1634.69	1537.94	1470.32	1421.75	1386.17	1359.73	1339.88
65000	6193.66	3485.48	2601.61	2173.38	1926.94	1770.92	1666.10	1592.84	1540.23	1501.68	1473.04	1451.53
70000	6670.10	3753.60	2801.74	2340.57	2075.17	1907.14	1794.26	1715.37	1658.71	1617.20	1586.35	1563.19
75000	7146.53	4021.71	3001.86	2507.75	2223.39	2043.36	1922.42	1837.90	1777.18	1732.71	1699.66	1674.84
80000	7622.97	4289.82	3201.98	2674.93	2371.62	2179.59	2050.58	1960.42	1895.66	1848.22	1812.97	1786.50
85000	8099.40	4557.94	3402.11	2842.12	2519.85	2315.81	2178.74	2082.95	2014.14	1963.74	1926.28	1898.15
90000	8575.84	4826.05	3602.23	3009.30	2668.07	2452.04	2306.90	2205.47	2132.62	2079.25	2039.59	2009.81
95000	9052.27	5094.16	3802.36	3176.48	2816.30	2588.26	2435.06	2328.00	2251.10	2194.77	2152.91	2121.47
100000	9528.71	5362.28	4002.48	3343.67	2964.52	2724.48	2563.22	2450.53	2369.58	2310.28	2266.22	2233.12

25%

Table 1

MONTHLY

PAYMENT REQUIRED TO AMORTIZE A LOAN

25.50%

TERM / AMOUNT	13 YEARS	14 YEARS	15 YEARS	16 YEARS	17 YEARS	18 YEARS	19 YEARS	20 YEARS	25 YEARS	30 YEARS	35 YEARS	40 YEARS
50	1.11	1.10	1.09	1.09	1.08	1.08	1.08	1.07	1.07	1.07	1.07	1.07
100	2.21	2.19	2.18	2.17	2.16	2.15	2.15	2.14	2.13	2.13	2.13	2.13
200	4.42	4.38	4.35	4.33	4.31	4.30	4.29	4.28	4.26	4.26	4.26	4.26
300	6.63	6.57	6.53	6.49	6.47	6.45	6.43	6.42	6.39	6.38	6.38	6.38
400	8.84	8.76	8.70	8.66	8.62	8.60	8.58	8.56	8.52	8.51	8.51	8.51
500	11.05	10.95	10.88	10.82	10.78	10.74	10.72	10.70	10.65	10.64	10.63	10.63
600	13.25	13.14	13.05	12.98	12.93	12.89	12.86	12.84	12.78	12.76	12.76	12.76
700	15.46	15.33	15.23	15.15	15.09	15.04	15.00	14.98	14.91	14.89	14.88	14.88
800	17.67	17.52	17.40	17.31	17.24	17.19	17.15	17.12	17.04	17.01	17.01	17.01
900	19.88	19.71	19.57	19.47	19.40	19.34	19.29	19.25	19.16	19.14	19.13	19.13
1000	22.09	21.89	21.75	21.64	21.55	21.48	21.43	21.39	21.29	21.27	21.26	21.26
2000	44.17	43.78	43.49	43.27	43.10	42.96	42.86	42.78	42.58	42.53	42.51	42.51
3000	66.25	65.67	65.24	64.90	64.64	64.44	64.29	64.17	63.87	63.79	63.76	63.76
4000	88.33	87.56	86.98	86.53	86.19	85.92	85.71	85.56	85.16	85.05	85.02	85.01
5000	110.41	109.45	108.72	108.16	107.73	107.40	107.14	106.94	106.45	106.31	106.27	106.26
6000	132.49	131.34	130.47	129.80	129.28	128.88	128.57	128.33	127.74	127.57	127.52	127.51
7000	154.57	153.23	152.21	151.43	150.82	150.36	150.00	149.72	149.03	148.83	148.78	148.76
8000	176.65	175.12	173.96	173.06	172.37	171.84	171.42	171.11	170.32	170.09	170.03	170.01
9000	198.73	197.01	195.70	194.69	193.91	193.31	192.85	192.49	191.60	191.35	191.28	191.26
10000	220.81	218.90	217.44	216.32	215.46	214.79	214.28	213.88	212.89	212.61	212.54	212.51
11000	242.89	240.79	239.19	237.95	237.00	236.27	235.71	235.27	234.18	233.88	233.79	233.76
12000	264.97	262.68	260.93	259.59	258.55	257.75	257.13	256.66	255.47	255.14	255.04	255.02
13000	287.05	284.57	282.67	281.22	280.10	279.23	278.56	278.04	276.76	276.40	276.30	276.27
14000	309.13	306.46	304.42	302.85	301.64	300.71	299.99	299.43	298.05	297.66	297.55	297.52
15000	331.21	328.35	326.16	324.48	323.19	322.19	321.42	320.82	319.34	318.92	318.80	318.77
16000	353.30	350.24	347.91	346.11	344.73	343.67	342.84	342.21	340.63	340.18	340.05	340.02
17000	375.38	372.13	369.65	367.74	366.28	365.14	364.27	363.59	361.91	361.44	361.31	361.27
18000	397.46	394.02	391.39	389.38	387.82	386.62	385.70	384.98	383.20	382.70	382.56	382.52
19000	419.54	415.91	413.14	411.01	409.37	408.10	407.12	406.37	404.49	403.96	403.81	403.77
20000	441.62	437.80	434.88	432.64	430.91	429.58	428.55	427.76	425.78	425.22	425.07	425.02
21000	463.70	459.69	456.63	454.27	452.46	451.06	449.98	449.14	447.07	446.49	446.32	446.27
22000	485.78	481.58	478.37	475.90	474.00	472.54	471.41	470.53	468.36	467.75	467.57	467.52
23000	507.86	503.47	500.11	497.53	495.55	494.02	492.83	491.92	489.65	489.01	488.83	488.78
24000	529.94	525.36	521.86	519.17	517.09	515.50	514.26	513.31	510.94	510.27	510.08	510.03
25000	552.02	547.25	543.60	540.80	538.64	536.98	535.69	534.69	532.22	531.53	531.33	531.28
26000	574.10	569.14	565.35	562.43	560.19	558.45	557.12	556.08	553.51	552.79	552.59	552.53
27000	596.18	591.03	587.09	584.06	581.73	579.93	578.54	577.47	574.80	574.05	573.84	573.78
28000	618.26	612.92	608.83	605.69	603.28	601.41	599.97	598.86	596.09	595.31	595.09	595.03
29000	640.34	634.81	630.58	627.32	624.82	622.89	621.40	620.24	617.38	616.57	616.35	616.28
30000	662.42	656.70	652.32	648.96	646.37	644.37	642.83	641.63	638.67	637.83	637.60	637.53
31000	684.50	678.59	674.06	670.59	667.91	665.85	664.25	663.02	659.96	659.09	658.85	658.78
32000	706.59	700.48	695.81	692.22	689.46	687.33	685.68	684.41	681.25	680.36	680.10	680.03
33000	728.67	722.37	717.55	713.85	711.00	708.81	707.11	705.79	702.53	701.62	701.36	701.28
34000	750.75	744.26	739.29	735.48	732.55	730.28	728.54	727.18	723.82	722.88	722.61	722.53
35000	772.83	766.15	761.04	757.11	754.09	751.76	749.96	748.57	745.11	744.14	743.86	743.79
36000	794.91	788.04	782.78	778.75	775.64	773.24	771.39	769.96	766.40	765.40	765.12	765.04
37000	816.99	809.93	804.53	800.38	797.18	794.72	792.82	791.34	787.69	786.66	786.37	786.29
38000	839.07	831.82	826.27	822.01	818.73	816.20	814.24	812.73	808.98	807.92	807.62	807.54
39000	861.15	853.71	848.01	843.64	840.28	837.68	835.67	834.12	830.27	829.18	828.88	828.79
40000	883.23	875.60	869.76	865.27	861.82	859.16	857.10	855.51	851.56	850.44	850.13	850.04
41000	905.31	897.49	891.50	886.91	883.37	880.64	878.53	876.89	872.84	871.70	871.38	871.29
42000	927.39	919.38	913.25	908.54	904.91	902.12	899.95	898.28	894.13	892.97	892.64	892.54
43000	949.47	941.27	934.99	930.17	926.46	923.59	921.38	919.67	915.42	914.23	913.89	913.79
44000	971.55	963.16	956.73	951.80	948.00	945.07	942.81	941.06	936.71	935.49	935.14	935.04
45000	993.63	985.05	978.48	973.43	969.55	966.55	964.24	962.44	958.00	956.75	956.39	956.29
46000	1015.71	1006.94	1000.22	995.06	991.09	988.03	985.66	983.83	979.29	978.01	977.65	977.55
47000	1037.79	1028.83	1021.96	1016.70	1012.64	1009.51	1007.09	1005.22	1000.58	999.27	998.90	998.80
48000	1059.88	1050.72	1043.71	1038.33	1034.18	1030.99	1028.52	1026.61	1021.87	1020.53	1020.15	1020.05
49000	1081.96	1072.61	1065.45	1059.96	1055.73	1052.47	1049.95	1048.00	1043.15	1041.79	1041.41	1041.30
50000	1104.04	1094.50	1087.20	1081.59	1077.28	1073.95	1071.37	1069.38	1064.44	1063.05	1062.66	1062.55
55000	1214.44	1203.94	1195.91	1189.75	1185.00	1181.34	1178.51	1176.32	1170.89	1169.36	1168.93	1168.80
60000	1324.84	1313.39	1304.63	1297.91	1292.73	1288.73	1285.65	1283.26	1277.33	1275.66	1275.19	1275.06
65000	1435.25	1422.84	1413.35	1406.07	1400.46	1396.13	1392.78	1390.20	1383.78	1381.97	1381.46	1381.31
70000	1545.65	1532.29	1522.07	1514.22	1508.18	1503.52	1499.92	1497.13	1490.22	1488.27	1487.72	1487.57
75000	1656.05	1641.74	1630.79	1622.38	1615.91	1610.92	1607.06	1604.07	1596.66	1594.58	1593.99	1593.82
80000	1766.46	1751.19	1739.51	1730.54	1723.64	1718.31	1714.19	1711.01	1703.11	1700.88	1700.25	1700.08
85000	1876.86	1860.64	1848.23	1838.70	1831.36	1825.70	1821.33	1817.95	1809.55	1807.19	1806.52	1806.33
90000	1987.26	1970.09	1956.95	1946.86	1939.09	1933.10	1928.47	1924.88	1915.99	1913.49	1912.78	1912.58
95000	2097.67	2079.54	2065.67	2055.02	2046.82	2040.49	2035.60	2031.82	2022.44	2019.80	2019.05	2018.84
100000	2208.07	2188.99	2174.39	2163.18	2154.55	2147.89	2142.74	2138.76	2128.88	2126.10	2125.32	2125.09

167

25%

Table 1

25.75%

MONTHLY
PAYMENT REQUIRED TO AMORTIZE A LOAN

TERM AMOUNT	1 YEAR	2 YEARS	3 YEARS	4 YEARS	5 YEARS	6 YEARS	7 YEARS	8 YEARS	9 YEARS	10 YEARS	11 YEARS	12 YEARS
50	4.78	2.69	2.01	1.68	1.49	1.37	1.29	1.24	1.20	1.17	1.15	1.13
100	9.55	5.38	4.02	3.36	2.98	2.74	2.58	2.47	2.39	2.33	2.29	2.26
200	19.09	10.75	8.04	6.72	5.96	5.48	5.16	4.94	4.78	4.66	4.57	4.51
300	28.63	16.13	12.05	10.08	8.94	8.22	7.74	7.41	7.17	6.99	6.86	6.76
400	38.17	21.50	16.07	13.44	11.92	10.96	10.32	9.87	9.55	9.32	9.14	9.01
500	47.71	26.88	20.08	16.79	14.90	13.70	12.90	12.34	11.94	11.65	11.43	11.26
600	57.25	32.25	24.10	20.15	17.88	16.44	15.48	14.81	14.33	13.97	13.71	13.52
700	66.79	37.63	28.12	23.51	20.86	19.18	18.06	17.28	16.71	16.30	16.00	15.77
800	76.33	43.00	32.13	26.87	23.84	21.92	20.64	19.74	19.10	18.63	18.28	18.02
900	85.87	48.38	36.15	30.23	26.82	24.66	23.22	22.21	21.49	20.96	20.56	20.27
1000	95.41	53.75	40.16	33.58	29.80	27.40	25.80	24.68	23.87	23.29	22.85	22.52
2000	190.82	107.50	80.32	67.16	59.59	54.80	51.59	49.35	47.74	46.57	45.69	45.04
3000	286.23	161.25	120.48	100.74	89.38	82.20	77.38	74.02	71.61	69.85	68.54	67.56
4000	381.64	215.00	160.64	134.31	119.18	109.60	103.18	98.69	95.48	93.13	91.38	90.07
5000	477.05	268.75	200.79	167.89	148.97	137.00	128.97	123.37	119.35	116.41	114.22	112.59
6000	572.46	322.50	240.95	201.47	178.76	164.40	154.76	148.04	143.21	139.69	137.07	135.11
7000	667.86	376.24	281.11	235.04	208.55	191.80	180.56	172.71	167.08	162.97	159.91	157.62
8000	763.27	429.99	321.27	268.62	238.35	219.20	206.35	197.38	190.95	186.25	182.76	180.14
9000	858.68	483.74	361.42	302.20	268.14	246.60	232.14	222.05	214.82	209.53	205.60	202.66
10000	954.09	537.49	401.58	335.77	297.93	274.00	257.94	246.73	238.69	232.81	228.44	225.17
11000	1049.50	591.24	441.74	369.35	327.72	301.40	283.73	271.40	262.55	256.09	251.29	247.69
12000	1144.91	644.99	481.90	402.93	357.52	328.80	309.52	296.07	286.42	279.37	274.13	270.21
13000	1240.32	698.74	522.05	436.50	387.31	356.19	335.32	320.74	310.29	302.65	296.98	292.73
14000	1335.72	752.48	562.21	470.08	417.10	383.59	361.11	345.42	334.16	325.93	319.82	315.24
15000	1431.13	806.23	602.37	503.66	446.89	410.99	386.90	370.09	358.03	349.21	342.66	337.76
16000	1526.54	859.98	642.53	537.23	476.69	438.39	412.70	394.76	381.90	372.49	365.51	360.28
17000	1621.95	913.73	682.68	570.81	506.48	465.79	438.49	419.43	405.76	395.77	388.35	382.79
18000	1717.36	967.48	722.84	604.39	536.27	493.19	464.28	444.10	429.63	419.05	411.20	405.31
19000	1812.77	1021.23	763.00	637.96	566.07	520.59	490.07	468.78	453.50	442.33	434.04	427.83
20000	1908.18	1074.98	803.16	671.54	595.86	547.99	515.87	493.45	477.37	465.61	456.88	450.34
21000	2003.58	1128.72	843.31	705.12	625.65	575.39	541.66	518.12	501.24	488.89	479.73	472.86
22000	2098.99	1182.47	883.47	738.69	655.44	602.79	567.45	542.79	525.10	512.17	502.57	495.38
23000	2194.40	1236.22	923.63	772.27	685.24	630.19	593.25	567.47	548.97	535.45	525.42	517.89
24000	2289.81	1289.97	963.79	805.85	715.03	657.59	619.04	592.14	572.84	558.73	548.26	540.41
25000	2385.22	1343.72	1003.94	839.43	744.82	684.99	644.83	616.81	596.71	582.01	571.10	562.93
26000	2480.63	1397.47	1044.10	873.00	774.61	712.38	670.63	641.48	620.58	605.29	593.95	585.45
27000	2576.04	1451.22	1084.26	906.58	804.41	739.78	696.42	666.15	644.45	628.57	616.79	607.96
28000	2671.44	1504.96	1124.42	940.16	834.20	767.18	722.21	690.83	668.31	651.85	639.64	630.48
29000	2766.85	1558.71	1164.57	973.73	863.99	794.58	748.01	715.50	692.18	675.13	662.48	653.00
30000	2862.26	1612.46	1204.73	1007.31	893.78	821.98	773.80	740.17	716.05	698.41	685.32	675.51
31000	2957.67	1666.21	1244.89	1040.89	923.58	849.38	799.59	764.84	739.92	721.69	708.17	698.03
32000	3053.08	1719.96	1285.05	1074.46	953.37	876.78	825.39	789.51	763.79	744.97	731.01	720.55
33000	3148.49	1773.71	1325.20	1108.04	983.16	904.18	851.18	814.19	787.65	768.25	753.86	743.06
34000	3243.90	1827.46	1365.36	1141.62	1012.95	931.58	876.97	838.86	811.52	791.53	776.70	765.58
35000	3339.30	1881.20	1405.52	1175.19	1042.75	958.98	902.76	863.53	835.39	814.81	799.54	788.10
36000	3434.71	1934.95	1445.68	1208.77	1072.54	986.38	928.56	888.20	859.26	838.09	822.39	810.61
37000	3530.12	1988.70	1485.83	1242.35	1102.33	1013.78	954.35	912.88	883.13	861.37	845.23	833.13
38000	3625.53	2042.45	1525.99	1275.92	1132.13	1041.18	980.14	937.55	907.00	884.65	868.08	855.65
39000	3720.94	2096.20	1566.15	1309.50	1161.92	1068.57	1005.94	962.22	930.86	907.93	890.92	878.17
40000	3816.35	2149.95	1606.31	1343.08	1191.71	1095.97	1031.73	986.89	954.73	931.21	913.76	900.68
41000	3911.75	2203.70	1646.47	1376.65	1221.50	1123.37	1057.52	1011.56	978.60	954.49	936.61	923.20
42000	4007.16	2257.44	1686.62	1410.23	1251.30	1150.77	1083.32	1036.24	1002.47	977.77	959.45	945.72
43000	4102.57	2311.19	1726.78	1443.81	1281.09	1178.17	1109.11	1060.91	1026.34	1001.05	982.30	968.23
44000	4197.98	2364.94	1766.94	1477.38	1310.88	1205.57	1134.90	1085.58	1050.20	1024.33	1005.14	990.75
45000	4293.39	2418.69	1807.10	1510.96	1340.67	1232.97	1160.70	1110.25	1074.07	1047.61	1027.98	1013.27
46000	4388.80	2472.44	1847.25	1544.54	1370.47	1260.37	1186.49	1134.93	1097.94	1120.89	1050.83	1035.78
47000	4484.21	2526.19	1887.41	1578.11	1400.26	1287.77	1212.28	1159.60	1121.81	1094.17	1073.67	1058.30
48000	4579.61	2579.94	1927.57	1611.69	1430.05	1315.17	1238.08	1184.27	1145.68	1117.45	1096.51	1080.82
49000	4675.02	2633.68	1967.73	1645.27	1459.84	1342.57	1263.87	1208.94	1169.55	1140.73	1119.36	1103.34
50000	4770.43	2687.43	2007.88	1678.85	1489.64	1369.97	1289.66	1233.61	1193.41	1164.01	1142.20	1125.85
55000	5247.47	2956.18	2208.67	1846.73	1638.60	1506.96	1418.63	1356.97	1312.75	1280.41	1256.42	1238.44
60000	5724.52	3224.92	2409.46	2014.61	1787.56	1643.96	1547.59	1480.34	1432.10	1396.81	1370.64	1351.02
65000	6201.56	3493.66	2610.25	2182.50	1936.53	1780.95	1676.56	1603.70	1551.44	1513.22	1484.86	1463.61
70000	6678.60	3762.40	2811.03	2350.38	2085.49	1917.95	1805.52	1727.06	1670.78	1629.62	1599.08	1576.19
75000	7155.64	4031.15	3011.82	2518.27	2234.45	2054.95	1934.49	1850.42	1790.12	1746.02	1713.30	1688.78
80000	7632.69	4299.89	3212.61	2686.15	2383.42	2191.94	2063.46	1973.78	1909.46	1862.42	1827.52	1801.36
85000	8109.73	4568.63	3413.40	2854.03	2532.38	2328.94	2192.42	2097.14	2028.80	1978.82	1941.74	1913.95
90000	8586.77	4837.38	3614.19	3021.92	2681.34	2465.93	2321.39	2220.50	2148.14	2095.22	2055.96	2026.53
95000	9063.82	5106.12	3814.97	3189.80	2830.31	2602.93	2450.35	2343.86	2267.48	2211.62	2170.18	2139.11
100000	9540.86	5374.86	4015.76	3357.69	2979.27	2739.93	2579.32	2467.22	2386.82	2328.02	2284.40	2251.70

25%

Table 1

MONTHLY
25.75%

PAYMENT REQUIRED TO AMORTIZE A LOAN

TERM AMOUNT	13 YEARS	14 YEARS	15 YEARS	16 YEARS	17 YEARS	18 YEARS	19 YEARS	20 YEARS	25 YEARS	30 YEARS	35 YEARS	40 YEARS
50	1.12	1.11	1.10	1.10	1.09	1.09	1.09	1.08	1.08	1.08	1.08	1.08
100	2.23	2.21	2.20	2.19	2.18	2.17	2.17	2.16	2.15	2.15	2.15	2.15
200	4.46	4.42	4.39	4.37	4.35	4.34	4.33	4.32	4.30	4.30	4.30	4.30
300	6.69	6.63	6.59	6.55	6.53	6.51	6.49	6.48	6.45	6.45	6.44	6.44
400	8.91	8.84	8.78	8.74	8.70	8.68	8.66	8.64	8.60	8.59	8.59	8.59
500	11.14	11.05	10.97	10.92	10.88	10.84	10.82	10.80	10.75	10.74	10.74	10.73
600	13.37	13.25	13.17	13.10	13.05	13.01	12.98	12.96	12.90	12.89	12.88	12.88
700	15.59	15.46	15.36	15.29	15.23	15.18	15.15	15.12	15.05	15.03	15.03	15.03
800	17.82	17.67	17.56	17.47	17.40	17.35	17.31	17.27	17.20	17.18	17.17	17.17
900	20.05	19.88	19.75	19.65	19.57	19.52	19.47	19.44	19.35	19.33	19.32	19.32
1000	22.27	22.09	21.94	21.83	21.75	21.68	21.63	21.60	21.50	21.47	21.47	21.46
2000	44.54	44.17	43.88	43.66	43.49	43.36	43.26	43.19	43.00	42.94	42.93	42.92
3000	66.81	66.25	65.82	65.49	65.24	65.04	64.89	64.78	64.49	64.41	64.39	64.38
4000	89.08	88.33	87.76	87.32	86.98	86.72	86.52	86.37	85.99	85.88	85.85	85.84
5000	111.35	110.42	109.70	109.15	108.73	108.40	108.15	107.96	107.48	107.35	107.31	107.30
6000	133.62	132.50	131.64	130.98	130.47	130.08	129.78	129.55	128.98	128.82	128.77	128.76
7000	155.89	154.58	153.58	152.81	152.22	151.76	151.41	151.14	150.47	150.29	150.23	150.22
8000	178.16	176.66	175.51	174.63	173.96	173.44	173.04	172.73	171.97	171.75	171.69	171.68
9000	200.43	198.74	197.45	196.46	195.70	195.12	194.67	194.32	193.46	193.22	193.16	193.14
10000	222.70	220.83	219.39	218.29	217.45	216.80	216.30	215.91	214.96	214.69	214.62	214.60
11000	244.97	242.91	241.33	240.12	239.19	238.48	237.93	237.50	236.45	236.16	236.08	236.06
12000	267.24	264.99	263.27	261.95	260.94	260.16	259.56	259.09	257.95	257.63	257.54	257.51
13000	289.51	287.07	285.21	283.78	282.68	281.84	281.18	280.68	279.44	279.10	279.00	278.97
14000	311.78	309.15	307.15	305.61	304.43	303.52	302.81	302.27	300.94	300.57	300.46	300.43
15000	334.05	331.24	329.08	327.44	326.17	325.19	324.44	323.86	322.43	322.03	321.92	321.89
16000	356.32	353.32	351.02	349.26	347.91	346.87	346.07	345.45	343.93	343.50	343.38	343.35
17000	378.59	375.40	372.96	371.09	369.66	368.55	367.70	367.04	365.42	364.97	364.85	364.81
18000	400.86	397.48	394.90	392.92	391.40	390.23	389.33	388.64	386.92	386.44	386.31	386.27
19000	423.13	419.56	416.84	414.75	413.15	411.91	410.96	410.23	408.41	407.91	407.77	407.73
20000	445.40	441.65	438.78	436.58	434.89	433.59	432.59	431.82	429.91	429.38	429.23	429.19
21000	467.67	463.73	460.72	458.41	456.64	455.27	454.22	453.41	451.40	450.85	450.69	450.65
22000	489.94	485.81	482.65	480.24	478.38	476.95	475.85	475.00	472.90	472.31	472.15	472.11
23000	512.21	507.89	504.59	502.07	500.12	498.63	497.48	496.59	494.39	493.78	493.61	493.57
24000	534.48	529.97	526.53	523.89	521.87	520.31	519.11	518.18	515.89	515.25	515.07	515.02
25000	556.75	552.06	548.47	545.72	543.61	541.99	540.74	539.77	537.38	536.72	536.54	536.48
26000	579.02	574.14	570.41	567.55	565.36	563.67	562.36	561.36	558.88	558.19	558.00	557.94
27000	601.29	596.22	592.35	589.38	587.10	585.35	583.99	582.95	580.37	579.66	579.46	579.40
28000	623.56	618.30	614.29	611.21	608.85	607.03	605.62	604.54	601.87	601.13	600.92	600.86
29000	645.83	640.38	636.22	633.04	630.59	628.71	627.25	626.13	623.36	622.60	622.38	622.32
30000	668.10	662.47	658.16	654.87	652.33	650.38	648.88	647.72	644.86	644.06	643.84	643.78
31000	690.37	684.55	680.10	676.70	674.08	672.06	670.51	669.31	666.35	665.53	665.30	665.24
32000	712.64	706.63	702.04	698.52	695.82	693.74	692.14	690.90	687.85	687.00	686.76	686.70
33000	734.91	728.71	723.98	720.35	717.57	715.42	713.77	712.49	709.35	708.47	708.22	708.16
34000	757.18	750.79	745.92	742.18	739.31	737.10	735.40	734.08	730.84	729.94	729.69	729.62
35000	779.45	772.88	767.86	764.01	761.06	758.78	757.03	755.67	752.34	751.41	751.15	751.07
36000	801.72	794.96	789.79	785.84	782.80	780.46	778.66	777.27	773.83	772.88	772.61	772.53
37000	823.99	817.04	811.73	807.67	804.54	802.14	800.29	798.86	795.33	794.34	794.07	793.99
38000	846.26	839.12	833.67	829.50	826.29	823.82	821.92	820.45	816.82	815.81	815.53	815.45
39000	868.53	861.20	855.61	851.33	848.03	845.50	843.54	842.04	838.32	837.28	836.99	836.91
40000	890.80	883.29	877.55	873.15	869.78	867.18	865.17	863.63	859.81	858.75	858.45	858.37
41000	913.07	905.37	899.49	894.98	891.52	888.86	886.80	885.22	881.31	880.22	879.91	879.83
42000	935.34	927.45	921.43	916.81	913.27	910.54	908.43	906.81	902.80	901.69	901.38	901.29
43000	957.61	949.53	943.37	938.64	935.01	932.22	930.06	928.40	924.30	923.16	922.84	922.75
44000	979.88	971.61	965.30	960.47	956.75	953.90	951.69	949.99	945.79	944.62	944.30	944.21
45000	1002.15	993.70	987.24	982.30	978.50	975.57	973.32	971.58	967.29	966.09	965.76	965.67
46000	1024.42	1015.78	1009.18	1004.13	1000.24	997.25	994.95	993.17	988.78	987.56	987.22	987.13
47000	1046.69	1037.86	1031.12	1025.96	1021.99	1018.93	1016.58	1014.76	1010.28	1009.03	1008.68	1008.58
48000	1068.96	1059.94	1053.06	1047.78	1043.73	1040.61	1038.21	1036.35	1031.77	1030.50	1030.14	1030.04
49000	1091.23	1082.02	1075.00	1069.61	1065.48	1062.29	1059.84	1057.94	1053.27	1051.97	1051.60	1051.50
50000	1113.50	1104.11	1096.94	1091.44	1087.22	1083.97	1081.47	1079.53	1074.76	1073.43	1073.07	1072.96
55000	1224.85	1214.52	1206.63	1200.58	1195.94	1192.37	1189.61	1187.49	1182.24	1180.78	1180.37	1180.26
60000	1336.20	1324.93	1316.32	1309.73	1304.66	1300.76	1297.76	1295.44	1289.71	1288.12	1287.68	1287.55
65000	1447.54	1435.34	1426.01	1418.87	1413.39	1409.16	1405.90	1403.39	1397.19	1395.47	1394.98	1394.85
70000	1558.89	1545.75	1535.71	1528.02	1522.11	1517.56	1514.05	1511.34	1504.67	1502.81	1502.29	1502.14
75000	1670.24	1656.16	1645.40	1637.16	1630.83	1625.95	1622.20	1619.30	1612.14	1610.15	1609.60	1609.44
80000	1781.59	1766.57	1755.09	1746.30	1739.55	1734.35	1730.34	1727.25	1719.62	1717.49	1716.90	1716.74
85000	1892.94	1876.98	1864.79	1855.45	1848.27	1842.75	1838.49	1835.20	1827.09	1824.84	1824.21	1824.03
90000	2004.29	1987.39	1974.48	1964.59	1956.99	1951.14	1946.64	1943.16	1934.57	1932.18	1931.51	1931.33
95000	2115.64	2097.80	2084.17	2073.73	2065.71	2059.54	2054.78	2051.11	2042.05	2039.52	2038.82	2038.62
100000	2226.99	2208.21	2193.87	2182.88	2174.44	2167.94	2162.93	2159.06	2149.52	2146.87	2146.13	2145.92

169

25%

Table 2 PAYMENT REQUIRED TO AMORTIZE A $1,000 LOAN

These tables for monthly, quarterly, semi-annual and annual payments show the combined principal and interest payment required to amortize a loan of $1,000 at a specified rate of interest by the end of the term shown.

Examples:

1. What would be the monthly principal and interest payment required to amortize a loan of $8,000 at 8.25 percent interest in 2.5 years?

   Ans. By following the 8.25 percent column down to 2.5 years you will find the payment required to be $37.01 per $1,000. For $8,000,

   $$\$37.01 \times 8 = \$296.08 \text{ (total monthly payment)}$$

2. What would be the quarterly principal and interest payment required to amortize a loan of $18,650 at 9.00 percent per annum in 22 years?

   Ans. By following the 9.00 percent column for quarterly payments down to 22 years you will find the payment required to be $26.20 per $1,000. For $18,650,

   $$\$26.20 \times 18.65 = \$488.63 \text{ (total quarterly payment)}$$

Table 2

MONTHLY

PAYMENT REQUIRED TO AMORTIZE A $1000.00 LOAN

INTEREST	5.00%	5.25%	5.50%	5.75%	6.00%	6.25%	6.50%	6.75%	7.00%	7.25%	7.50%	7.75%
YEARS												
.5	169.11	169.23	169.36	169.48	169.60	169.72	169.85	169.97	170.09	170.21	170.34	17C.46
1.0	85.61	85.73	85.84	85.96	86.07	86.19	86.30	86.42	86.53	86.65	86.76	86.88
1.5	57.79	57.90	58.01	58.12	58.24	58.35	58.46	58.58	58.69	58.80	58.92	59.03
2.0	43.88	43.99	44.10	44.21	44.33	44.44	44.55	44.66	44.78	44.89	45.00	45.12
2.5	35.53	35.65	35.76	35.87	35.98	36.10	36.21	36.32	36.44	36.55	36.66	36.78
3.0	29.98	30.09	30.20	30.31	30.43	30.54	30.65	30.77	30.88	31.00	31.11	31.23
3.5	26.01	26.12	26.23	26.35	26.46	26.58	26.69	26.80	26.92	27.03	27.15	27.27
4.0	23.03	23.15	23.26	23.38	23.49	23.60	23.72	23.84	23.95	24.07	24.18	24.30
4.5	20.72	20.84	20.95	21.07	21.18	21.30	21.41	21.53	21.65	21.76	21.88	22.00
5.0	18.88	18.99	19.11	19.22	19.34	19.45	19.57	19.69	19.81	19.92	20.04	20.16
5.5	17.37	17.48	17.60	17.71	17.83	17.95	18.07	18.18	18.30	18.42	18.54	18.66
6.0	16.11	16.23	16.34	16.46	16.58	16.70	16.81	16.93	17.05	17.17	17.30	17.42
6.5	15.05	15.16	15.28	15.40	15.52	15.64	15.76	15.88	16.00	16.12	16.24	16.37
7.0	14.14	14.26	14.38	14.49	14.61	14.73	14.85	14.98	15.10	15.22	15.34	15.47
7.5	13.35	13.47	13.59	13.71	13.83	13.95	14.07	14.20	14.32	14.44	14.57	14.69
8.0	12.66	12.78	12.90	13.03	13.15	13.27	13.39	13.51	13.64	13.76	13.89	14.01
8.5	12.06	12.18	12.30	12.42	12.54	12.67	12.79	12.92	13.04	13.17	13.29	13.42
9.0	11.52	11.64	11.76	11.89	12.01	12.13	12.26	12.39	12.51	12.64	12.77	12.89
9.5	11.04	11.16	11.29	11.41	11.53	11.66	11.79	11.91	12.04	12.17	12.30	12.43
10.0	10.61	10.73	10.86	10.98	11.11	11.23	11.36	11.49	11.62	11.75	11.88	12.01
10.5	10.22	10.35	10.47	10.60	10.72	10.85	10.98	11.10	11.23	11.36	11.50	11.63
11.0	9.87	9.99	10.12	10.25	10.37	10.50	10.63	10.76	10.89	11.02	11.15	11.29
11.5	9.55	9.67	9.80	9.93	10.05	10.18	10.31	10.44	10.58	10.71	10.84	10.98
12.0	9.25	9.38	9.51	9.63	9.76	9.89	10.02	10.16	10.29	10.42	10.56	10.69
12.5	8.98	9.11	9.24	9.37	9.50	9.63	9.76	9.89	10.03	10.16	10.30	10.43
13.0	8.74	8.86	8.99	9.12	9.25	9.38	9.52	9.65	9.79	9.92	10.06	10.20
13.5	8.51	8.63	8.76	8.89	9.03	9.16	9.29	9.43	9.56	9.70	9.84	9.98
14.0	8.29	8.42	8.55	8.68	8.82	8.95	9.09	9.22	9.36	9.50	9.64	9.78
14.5	8.10	8.23	8.36	8.49	8.62	8.76	8.89	9.03	9.17	9.31	9.45	9.59
15.0	7.91	8.04	8.18	8.31	8.44	8.58	8.72	8.85	8.99	9.13	9.28	9.42
15.5	7.74	7.87	8.01	8.14	8.28	8.41	8.55	8.69	8.83	8.97	9.11	9.26
16.0	7.58	7.71	7.85	7.98	8.12	8.26	8.40	8.54	8.68	8.82	8.96	9.11
16.5	7.43	7.57	7.70	7.84	7.97	8.11	8.25	8.39	8.53	8.68	8.82	8.97
17.0	7.29	7.43	7.56	7.70	7.84	7.98	8.12	8.26	8.40	8.55	8.69	8.84
17.5	7.16	7.29	7.43	7.57	7.71	7.85	7.99	8.13	8.28	8.42	8.57	8.72
18.0	7.04	7.17	7.31	7.45	7.59	7.73	7.87	8.01	8.16	8.31	8.45	8.60
18.5	6.92	7.05	7.19	7.33	7.47	7.62	7.76	7.90	8.05	8.20	8.35	8.50
19.0	6.81	6.95	7.08	7.22	7.37	7.51	7.65	7.80	7.95	8.10	8.25	8.40
19.5	6.70	6.84	6.98	7.12	7.26	7.41	7.55	7.70	7.85	8.00	8.15	8.30
20.0	6.60	6.74	6.88	7.03	7.17	7.31	7.46	7.61	7.76	7.91	8.06	8.21
20.5	6.51	6.65	6.79	6.93	7.08	7.22	7.37	7.52	7.67	7.82	7.98	8.13
21.0	6.42	6.56	6.70	6.85	6.99	7.14	7.29	7.44	7.59	7.74	7.90	8.05
21.5	6.34	6.48	6.62	6.77	6.91	7.06	7.21	7.36	7.51	7.67	7.82	7.98
22.0	6.26	6.40	6.54	6.69	6.84	6.98	7.13	7.29	7.44	7.59	7.75	7.91
22.5	6.18	6.32	6.47	6.62	6.76	6.91	7.06	7.22	7.37	7.53	7.68	7.84
23.0	6.11	6.25	6.40	6.54	6.69	6.84	7.00	7.15	7.30	7.46	7.62	7.78
23.5	6.04	6.18	6.33	6.48	6.63	6.78	6.93	7.09	7.24	7.40	7.56	7.72
24.0	5.97	6.12	6.27	6.41	6.56	6.72	6.87	7.03	7.18	7.34	7.50	7.66
24.5	5.91	6.06	6.20	6.35	6.50	6.66	6.81	6.97	7.13	7.29	7.45	7.61
25.0	5.85	6.00	6.15	6.30	6.45	6.60	6.76	6.91	7.07	7.23	7.39	7.56
25.5	5.79	5.94	6.09	6.24	6.39	6.55	6.70	6.86	7.02	7.18	7.35	7.51
26.0	5.74	5.89	6.04	6.19	6.34	6.50	6.65	6.81	6.97	7.14	7.30	7.46
26.5	5.69	5.83	5.99	6.14	6.29	6.45	6.61	6.77	6.93	7.09	7.25	7.42
27.0	5.64	5.78	5.94	6.09	6.24	6.40	6.56	6.72	6.88	7.05	7.21	7.38
27.5	5.59	5.74	5.89	6.04	6.20	6.36	6.52	6.68	6.84	7.01	7.17	7.34
28.0	5.54	5.69	5.84	6.00	6.16	6.31	6.48	6.64	6.80	6.97	7.13	7.30
28.5	5.50	5.65	5.80	5.96	6.11	6.27	6.44	6.60	6.76	6.93	7.10	7.27
29.0	5.45	5.61	5.76	5.92	6.08	6.24	6.40	6.56	6.73	6.89	7.06	7.23
29.5	5.41	5.57	5.72	5.88	6.04	6.20	6.36	6.53	6.69	6.86	7.03	7.20
30.0	5.37	5.53	5.68	5.84	6.00	6.16	6.33	6.49	6.66	6.83	7.00	7.17
35	5.05	5.21	5.38	5.54	5.71	5.88	6.05	6.22	6.39	6.57	6.75	6.93
40	4.83	4.99	5.16	5.33	5.51	5.68	5.86	6.04	6.22	6.40	6.59	6.77

Table 2

MONTHLY

PAYMENT REQUIRED TO AMORTIZE A $1000.00 LOAN

INTEREST	8.00%	8.25%	8.50%	8.75%	9.00%	9.25%	9.50%	9.75%	10.00%	10.25%	10.50%	10.75%
YEARS												
.5	170.58	170.70	170.83	170.95	171.07	171.20	171.32	171.44	171.57	171.69	171.81	171.94
1.0	86.99	87.11	87.22	87.34	87.46	87.57	87.69	87.80	87.92	88.04	88.15	88.27
1.5	59.15	59.26	59.37	59.49	59.60	59.72	59.83	59.95	60.06	60.18	60.29	60.41
2.0	45.23	45.35	45.46	45.58	45.69	45.80	45.92	46.03	46.15	46.27	46.38	46.50
2.5	36.89	37.01	37.12	37.24	37.35	37.47	37.58	37.70	37.82	37.93	38.05	38.17
3.0	31.34	31.46	31.57	31.69	31.80	31.92	32.04	32.15	32.27	32.39	32.51	32.63
3.5	27.38	27.50	27.62	27.73	27.85	27.97	28.09	28.20	28.32	28.44	28.56	28.68
4.0	24.42	24.54	24.65	24.77	24.89	25.01	25.13	25.25	25.37	25.49	25.61	25.73
4.5	22.12	22.24	22.36	22.47	22.59	22.71	22.84	22.96	23.08	23.20	23.32	23.44
5.0	20.28	20.40	20.52	20.64	20.76	20.88	21.01	21.13	21.25	21.38	21.50	21.62
5.5	18.78	18.90	19.03	19.15	19.27	19.39	19.52	19.64	19.76	19.89	20.01	20.14
6.0	17.54	17.66	17.78	17.91	18.03	18.15	18.28	18.41	18.53	18.66	18.78	18.91
6.5	16.49	16.61	16.74	16.86	16.99	17.11	17.24	17.36	17.49	17.62	17.75	17.88
7.0	15.59	15.72	15.84	15.97	16.09	16.22	16.35	16.48	16.61	16.74	16.87	17.00
7.5	14.82	14.94	15.07	15.20	15.32	15.45	15.58	15.71	15.84	15.97	16.11	16.24
8.0	14.14	14.27	14.40	14.53	14.66	14.79	14.92	15.05	15.18	15.31	15.45	15.58
8.5	13.55	13.68	13.81	13.94	14.07	14.20	14.33	14.46	14.60	14.73	14.87	15.00
9.0	13.02	13.15	13.28	13.42	13.55	13.68	13.81	13.95	14.08	14.22	14.36	14.49
9.5	12.56	12.69	12.82	12.95	13.09	13.22	13.36	13.49	13.63	13.76	13.90	14.04
10.0	12.14	12.27	12.40	12.54	12.67	12.81	12.94	13.08	13.22	13.36	13.50	13.64
10.5	11.76	11.89	12.03	12.16	12.30	12.44	12.58	12.71	12.85	12.99	13.14	13.28
11.0	11.42	11.56	11.69	11.83	11.97	12.10	12.24	12.38	12.52	12.67	12.81	12.95
11.5	11.11	11.25	11.38	11.52	11.66	11.80	11.94	12.08	12.23	12.37	12.51	12.66
12.0	10.83	10.97	11.11	11.24	11.39	11.53	11.67	11.81	11.96	12.10	12.25	12.39
12.5	10.57	10.71	10.85	10.99	11.13	11.28	11.42	11.56	11.71	11.86	12.00	12.15
13.0	10.34	10.48	10.62	10.76	10.90	11.05	11.19	11.34	11.48	11.63	11.78	11.93
13.5	10.12	10.26	10.40	10.55	10.69	10.83	10.98	11.13	11.28	11.43	11.58	11.73
14.0	9.92	10.06	10.20	10.35	10.49	10.64	10.79	10.94	11.09	11.24	11.39	11.54
14.5	9.73	9.88	10.02	10.17	10.31	10.46	10.61	10.76	10.91	11.06	11.22	11.37
15.0	9.56	9.71	9.85	10.00	10.15	10.30	10.45	10.60	10.75	10.90	11.06	11.21
15.5	9.40	9.55	9.70	9.84	9.99	10.14	10.30	10.45	10.60	10.76	10.91	11.07
16.0	9.25	9.40	9.55	9.70	9.85	10.00	10.15	10.31	10.46	10.62	10.78	10.94
16.5	9.12	9.26	9.41	9.57	9.72	9.87	10.02	10.18	10.34	10.49	10.65	10.81
17.0	8.99	9.14	9.29	9.44	9.59	9.75	9.90	10.06	10.22	10.38	10.54	10.70
17.5	8.87	9.02	9.17	9.32	9.48	9.63	9.79	9.95	10.11	10.27	10.43	10.59
18.0	8.75	8.91	9.06	9.21	9.37	9.53	9.68	9.84	10.00	10.16	10.33	10.49
18.5	8.65	8.80	8.96	9.11	9.27	9.43	9.59	9.75	9.91	10.07	10.23	10.40
19.0	8.55	8.70	8.86	9.02	9.17	9.33	9.49	9.65	9.82	9.98	10.15	10.31
19.5	8.46	8.61	8.77	8.93	9.09	9.25	9.41	9.57	9.73	9.90	10.06	10.23
20.0	8.37	8.53	8.68	8.84	9.00	9.16	9.33	9.49	9.66	9.82	9.99	10.16
20.5	8.29	8.44	8.60	8.76	8.92	9.09	9.25	9.42	9.58	9.75	9.92	10.09
21.0	8.21	8.37	8.53	8.69	8.85	9.01	9.18	9.35	9.51	9.68	9.85	10.02
21.5	8.14	8.30	8.46	8.62	8.78	8.95	9.11	9.28	9.45	9.62	9.79	9.96
22.0	8.07	8.23	8.39	8.55	8.72	8.88	9.05	9.22	9.39	9.56	9.73	9.90
22.5	8.00	8.16	8.33	8.49	8.66	8.82	8.99	9.16	9.33	9.50	9.68	9.85
23.0	7.94	8.10	8.27	8.43	8.60	8.77	8.93	9.11	9.28	9.45	9.62	9.80
23.5	7.88	8.04	8.21	8.38	8.54	8.71	8.88	9.05	9.23	9.40	9.58	9.75
24.0	7.83	7.99	8.16	8.32	8.49	8.66	8.83	9.01	9.18	9.35	9.53	9.71
24.5	7.77	7.94	8.11	8.27	8.44	8.61	8.79	8.96	9.13	9.31	9.49	9.67
25.0	7.72	7.89	8.06	8.23	8.40	8.57	8.74	8.92	9.09	9.27	9.45	9.63
25.5	7.68	7.84	8.01	8.18	8.35	8.53	8.70	8.88	9.05	9.23	9.41	9.59
26.0	7.63	7.80	7.97	8.14	8.31	8.49	8.66	8.84	9.01	9.19	9.37	9.55
26.5	7.59	7.76	7.93	8.10	8.27	8.45	8.62	8.80	8.98	9.16	9.34	9.52
27.0	7.55	7.72	7.89	8.06	8.24	8.41	8.59	8.77	8.95	9.13	9.31	9.49
27.5	7.51	7.68	7.85	8.03	8.20	8.38	8.56	8.73	8.91	9.10	9.28	9.46
28.0	7.47	7.64	7.82	7.99	8.17	8.35	8.52	8.70	8.88	9.07	9.25	9.43
28.5	7.44	7.61	7.78	7.96	8.14	8.31	8.49	8.67	8.86	9.04	9.22	9.41
29.0	7.40	7.58	7.75	7.93	8.11	8.29	8.47	8.65	8.83	9.01	9.20	9.38
29.5	7.37	7.55	7.72	7.90	8.08	8.26	8.44	8.62	8.80	8.99	9.17	9.36
30.0	7.34	7.52	7.69	7.87	8.05	8.23	8.41	8.60	8.78	8.97	9.15	9.34
35	7.11	7.29	7.47	7.66	7.84	8.03	8.22	8.41	8.60	8.79	8.99	9.18
40	6.96	7.15	7.34	7.53	7.72	7.91	8.11	8.30	8.50	8.69	8.89	9.09

Table 2

MONTHLY

PAYMENT REQUIRED TO AMORTIZE A $1000.00 LOAN

INTEREST YEARS	11.00%	11.25%	11.50%	11.75%	12.00%	12.25%	12.50%	12.75%	13.00%	13.25%	13.50%	13.75%
.5	172.06	172.18	172.31	172.43	172.55	172.68	172.80	172.92	173.05	173.17	173.30	173.42
1.0	88.39	88.50	88.62	88.74	88.85	88.97	89.09	89.21	89.32	89.44	89.56	89.67
1.5	60.52	60.64	60.76	60.87	60.99	61.10	61.22	61.34	61.45	61.57	61.69	61.80
2.0	46.61	46.73	46.85	46.96	47.08	47.20	47.31	47.43	47.55	47.66	47.78	47.90
2.5	38.28	38.40	38.52	38.64	38.75	38.87	38.99	39.11	39.23	39.35	39.46	39.58
3.0	32.74	32.86	32.98	33.10	33.22	33.34	33.46	33.58	33.70	33.82	33.94	34.06
3.5	28.80	28.92	29.04	29.16	29.28	29.40	29.52	29.65	29.77	29.89	30.01	30.14
4.0	25.85	25.97	26.09	26.22	26.34	26.46	26.58	26.71	26.83	26.96	27.08	27.21
4.5	23.57	23.69	23.81	23.94	24.06	24.19	24.31	24.44	24.56	24.69	24.82	24.94
5.0	21.75	21.87	22.00	22.12	22.25	22.38	22.50	22.63	22.76	22.89	23.01	23.14
5.5	20.27	20.39	20.52	20.65	20.78	20.90	21.03	21.16	21.29	21.42	21.55	21.68
6.0	19.04	19.17	19.30	19.43	19.56	19.69	19.82	19.95	20.08	20.21	20.34	20.48
6.5	18.01	18.14	18.27	18.40	18.53	18.66	18.79	18.93	19.06	19.20	19.33	19.47
7.0	17.13	17.26	17.39	17.52	17.66	17.79	17.93	18.06	18.20	18.33	18.47	18.61
7.5	16.37	16.50	16.64	16.77	16.91	17.04	17.18	17.32	17.45	17.59	17.73	17.87
8.0	15.71	15.85	15.98	16.12	16.26	16.40	16.53	16.67	16.81	16.95	17.09	17.23
8.5	15.14	15.27	15.41	15.55	15.69	15.83	15.97	16.11	16.25	16.39	16.54	16.68
9.0	14.63	14.77	14.91	15.05	15.19	15.33	15.47	15.62	15.76	15.90	16.05	16.19
9.5	14.18	14.32	14.46	14.60	14.75	14.89	15.03	15.18	15.32	15.47	15.62	15.76
10.0	13.78	13.92	14.06	14.21	14.35	14.50	14.64	14.79	14.94	15.08	15.23	15.38
10.5	13.42	13.56	13.71	13.85	14.00	14.15	14.29	14.44	14.59	14.74	14.89	15.04
11.0	13.10	13.24	13.39	13.54	13.68	13.83	13.98	14.13	14.28	14.43	14.58	14.74
11.5	12.81	12.95	13.10	13.25	13.40	13.55	13.70	13.85	14.00	14.16	14.31	14.46
12.0	12.54	12.69	12.84	12.99	13.14	13.29	13.44	13.60	13.75	13.91	14.06	14.22
12.5	12.30	12.45	12.60	12.75	12.90	13.06	13.21	13.37	13.52	13.68	13.84	14.00
13.0	12.08	12.23	12.38	12.54	12.69	12.85	13.00	13.16	13.32	13.48	13.63	13.80
13.5	11.88	12.03	12.19	12.34	12.50	12.65	12.81	12.97	13.13	13.29	13.45	13.61
14.0	11.70	11.85	12.01	12.16	12.32	12.48	12.64	12.80	12.96	13.12	13.28	13.45
14.5	11.53	11.68	11.84	12.00	12.16	12.32	12.48	12.64	12.80	12.96	13.13	13.29
15.0	11.37	11.53	11.69	11.85	12.01	12.17	12.33	12.49	12.66	12.82	12.99	13.15
15.5	11.23	11.39	11.55	11.71	11.87	12.03	12.20	12.36	12.53	12.69	12.86	13.03
16.0	11.10	11.26	11.42	11.58	11.74	11.91	12.07	12.24	12.40	12.57	12.74	12.91
16.5	10.97	11.13	11.30	11.46	11.63	11.79	11.96	12.13	12.29	12.46	12.63	12.80
17.0	10.86	11.02	11.19	11.35	11.52	11.68	11.85	12.02	12.19	12.36	12.53	12.71
17.5	10.75	10.92	11.08	11.25	11.42	11.59	11.75	11.93	12.10	12.27	12.44	12.62
18.0	10.66	10.82	10.99	11.16	11.32	11.49	11.67	11.84	12.01	12.18	12.36	12.53
18.5	10.56	10.73	10.90	11.07	11.24	11.41	11.58	11.75	11.93	12.10	12.28	12.46
19.0	10.48	10.65	10.82	10.99	11.16	11.33	11.50	11.68	11.85	12.03	12.21	12.39
19.5	10.40	10.57	10.74	10.91	11.08	11.26	11.43	11.61	11.78	11.96	12.14	12.32
20.0	10.33	10.50	10.67	10.84	11.02	11.19	11.37	11.54	11.72	11.90	12.08	12.26
20.5	10.26	10.43	10.60	10.78	10.95	11.13	11.30	11.48	11.66	11.84	12.02	12.20
21.0	10.19	10.37	10.54	10.72	10.89	11.07	11.25	11.43	11.61	11.79	11.97	12.15
21.5	10.13	10.31	10.48	10.66	10.84	11.01	11.19	11.37	11.55	11.74	11.92	12.10
22.0	10.08	10.25	10.43	10.61	10.78	10.96	11.14	11.33	11.51	11.69	11.87	12.06
22.5	10.02	10.20	10.38	10.56	10.74	10.92	11.10	11.28	11.46	11.65	11.83	12.02
23.0	9.98	10.15	10.33	10.51	10.69	10.87	11.05	11.24	11.42	11.61	11.79	11.98
23.5	9.93	10.11	10.29	10.47	10.65	10.83	11.01	11.20	11.38	11.57	11.76	11.94
24.0	9.89	10.06	10.25	10.43	10.61	10.79	10.98	11.16	11.35	11.53	11.72	11.91
24.5	9.84	10.02	10.21	10.39	10.57	10.76	10.94	11.13	11.31	11.50	11.69	11.88
25.0	9.81	9.99	10.17	10.35	10.54	10.72	10.91	11.10	11.28	11.47	11.66	11.85
25.5	9.77	9.95	10.14	10.32	10.50	10.69	10.88	11.07	11.25	11.44	11.63	11.83
26.0	9.74	9.92	10.10	10.29	10.47	10.66	10.85	11.04	11.23	11.42	11.61	11.80
26.5	9.70	9.89	10.07	10.26	10.45	10.63	10.82	11.01	11.20	11.39	11.59	11.78
27.0	9.67	9.86	10.05	10.23	10.42	10.61	10.80	10.99	11.18	11.37	11.56	11.76
27.5	9.65	9.83	10.02	10.21	10.39	10.58	10.77	10.97	11.16	11.35	11.54	11.74
28.0	9.62	9.81	9.99	10.18	10.37	10.56	10.75	10.94	11.14	11.33	11.52	11.72
28.5	9.59	9.78	9.97	10.16	10.35	10.54	10.73	10.92	11.12	11.31	11.51	11.70
29.0	9.57	9.76	9.95	10.14	10.33	10.52	10.71	10.91	11.10	11.29	11.49	11.68
29.5	9.55	9.74	9.93	10.12	10.31	10.50	10.69	10.89	11.08	11.28	11.47	11.67
30.0	9.53	9.72	9.91	10.10	10.29	10.48	10.68	10.87	11.07	11.26	11.46	11.66
35	9.37	9.57	9.77	9.96	10.16	10.36	10.56	10.76	10.96	11.16	11.36	11.56
40	9.29	9.49	9.69	9.89	10.09	10.29	10.49	10.70	10.90	11.10	11.31	11.51

Table 2

MONTHLY

PAYMENT REQUIRED TO AMORTIZE A $1000.00 LOAN

TEREST YEARS	14.00%	14.25%	14.50%	14.75%	15.00%	15.25%	15.50%	15.75%	16.00%	16.25%	16.50%	16.75%
.5	173.54	173.67	173.79	173.91	174.04	174.16	174.29	174.41	174.54	174.66	174.78	174.91
1.0	89.79	89.91	90.03	90.15	90.26	90.38	90.50	90.62	90.74	90.85	90.97	91.09
1.5	61.92	62.04	62.15	62.27	62.39	62.51	62.63	62.74	62.86	62.98	63.10	63.22
2.0	48.02	48.14	48.25	48.37	48.49	48.61	48.73	48.85	48.97	49.09	49.21	49.33
2.5	39.70	39.82	39.94	40.06	40.18	40.30	40.42	40.55	40.67	40.79	40.91	41.03
3.0	34.18	34.30	34.43	34.55	34.67	34.79	34.92	35.04	35.16	35.29	35.41	35.53
3.5	30.26	30.38	30.51	30.63	30.75	30.88	31.00	31.13	31.25	31.38	31.51	31.63
4.0	27.33	27.46	27.58	27.71	27.84	27.96	28.09	28.22	28.35	28.47	28.60	28.73
4.5	25.07	25.20	25.33	25.45	25.58	25.71	25.84	25.97	26.10	26.23	26.36	26.49
5.0	23.27	23.40	23.53	23.66	23.79	23.93	24.06	24.19	24.32	24.46	24.59	24.72
5.5	21.82	21.95	22.08	22.21	22.35	22.48	22.61	22.75	22.88	23.02	23.15	23.29
6.0	20.61	20.74	20.88	21.01	21.15	21.29	21.42	21.56	21.70	21.83	21.97	22.11
6.5	19.60	19.74	19.87	20.01	20.15	20.29	20.43	20.57	20.71	20.85	20.99	21.13
7.0	18.75	18.88	19.02	19.16	19.30	19.44	19.58	19.72	19.87	20.01	20.15	20.30
7.5	18.01	18.15	18.29	18.43	18.58	18.72	18.86	19.01	19.15	19.30	19.44	19.59
8.0	17.38	17.52	17.66	17.81	17.95	18.10	18.24	18.39	18.53	18.68	18.83	18.98
8.5	16.82	16.97	17.11	17.26	17.41	17.55	17.70	17.85	18.00	18.15	18.30	18.45
9.0	16.34	16.49	16.63	16.78	16.93	17.08	17.23	17.38	17.53	17.68	17.83	17.99
9.5	15.91	16.06	16.21	16.36	16.51	16.66	16.81	16.97	17.12	17.27	17.43	17.58
10.0	15.53	15.68	15.83	15.99	16.14	16.29	16.45	16.60	16.76	16.91	17.07	17.23
10.5	15.19	15.35	15.50	15.65	15.81	15.96	16.12	16.28	16.43	16.59	16.75	16.91
11.0	14.89	15.05	15.20	15.36	15.51	15.67	15.83	15.99	16.15	16.31	16.47	16.63
11.5	14.62	14.78	14.93	15.09	15.25	15.41	15.57	15.73	15.89	16.05	16.22	16.38
12.0	14.38	14.53	14.69	14.85	15.01	15.18	15.34	15.50	15.66	15.83	15.99	16.16
12.5	14.16	14.32	14.48	14.64	14.80	14.96	15.13	15.29	15.46	15.62	15.79	15.96
13.0	13.96	14.12	14.28	14.44	14.61	14.77	14.94	15.10	15.27	15.44	15.61	15.78
13.5	13.77	13.94	14.10	14.27	14.43	14.60	14.77	14.94	15.10	15.27	15.44	15.62
14.0	13.61	13.78	13.94	14.11	14.28	14.44	14.61	14.78	14.95	15.12	15.30	15.47
14.5	13.46	13.63	13.79	13.96	14.13	14.30	14.47	14.64	14.82	14.99	15.16	15.34
15.0	13.32	13.49	13.66	13.83	14.00	14.17	14.34	14.52	14.69	14.87	15.04	15.22
15.5	13.20	13.37	13.54	13.71	13.88	14.05	14.23	14.40	14.58	14.76	14.93	15.11
16.0	13.08	13.25	13.43	13.60	13.77	13.95	14.12	14.30	14.48	14.65	14.83	15.01
16.5	12.98	13.15	13.32	13.50	13.67	13.85	14.03	14.20	14.38	14.56	14.74	14.92
17.0	12.88	13.05	13.23	13.41	13.58	13.76	13.94	14.12	14.30	14.48	14.66	14.84
17.5	12.79	12.97	13.14	13.32	13.50	13.68	13.86	14.04	14.22	14.40	14.58	14.77
18.0	12.71	12.89	13.06	13.24	13.42	13.60	13.78	13.96	14.15	14.33	14.51	14.70
18.5	12.63	12.81	12.99	13.17	13.35	13.53	13.72	13.90	14.08	14.27	14.45	14.64
19.0	12.56	12.74	12.92	13.10	13.29	13.47	13.65	13.84	14.02	14.21	14.39	14.58
19.5	12.50	12.68	12.86	13.04	13.23	13.41	13.60	13.78	13.97	14.15	14.34	14.53
20.0	12.44	12.62	12.80	12.99	13.17	13.36	13.54	13.73	13.92	14.11	14.29	14.48
20.5	12.39	12.57	12.75	12.94	13.12	13.31	13.50	13.68	13.87	14.06	14.25	14.44
21.0	12.33	12.52	12.70	12.89	13.08	13.26	13.45	13.64	13.83	14.02	14.21	14.40
21.5	12.29	12.47	12.66	12.85	13.03	13.22	13.41	13.60	13.79	13.98	14.17	14.37
22.0	12.24	12.43	12.62	12.81	12.99	13.18	13.37	13.56	13.75	13.95	14.14	14.33
22.5	12.20	12.39	12.58	12.77	12.96	13.15	13.34	13.53	13.72	13.91	14.11	14.30
23.0	12.17	12.35	12.54	12.73	12.92	13.12	13.31	13.50	13.69	13.89	14.08	14.27
23.5	12.13	12.32	12.51	12.70	12.89	13.08	13.28	13.47	13.66	13.86	14.05	14.25
24.0	12.10	12.29	12.48	12.67	12.86	13.06	13.25	13.44	13.64	13.83	14.03	14.23
24.5	12.07	12.26	12.45	12.64	12.84	13.03	13.23	13.42	13.62	13.81	14.01	14.20
25.0	12.04	12.23	12.43	12.62	12.81	13.01	13.20	13.40	13.59	13.79	13.99	14.18
25.5	12.02	12.21	12.40	12.60	12.79	12.99	13.18	13.38	13.57	13.77	13.97	14.17
26.0	11.99	12.19	12.38	12.57	12.77	12.97	13.16	13.36	13.56	13.75	13.95	14.15
26.5	11.97	12.16	12.36	12.55	12.75	12.95	13.14	13.34	13.54	13.74	13.94	14.14
27.0	11.95	12.14	12.34	12.54	12.73	12.93	13.13	13.32	13.52	13.72	13.92	14.12
27.5	11.93	12.13	12.32	12.52	12.72	12.91	13.11	13.31	13.51	13.71	13.91	14.11
28.0	11.91	12.11	12.31	12.50	12.70	12.90	13.10	13.30	13.50	13.70	13.90	14.10
28.5	11.90	12.09	12.29	12.49	12.69	12.88	13.08	13.28	13.48	13.68	13.89	14.09
29.0	11.88	12.08	12.28	12.47	12.67	12.87	13.07	13.27	13.47	13.67	13.87	14.08
29.5	11.87	12.06	12.26	12.46	12.66	12.86	13.06	13.26	13.46	13.66	13.87	14.07
30.0	11.85	12.05	12.25	12.45	12.65	12.85	13.05	13.25	13.45	13.65	13.86	14.06
35	11.76	11.96	12.17	12.37	12.57	12.78	12.98	13.19	13.39	13.59	13.80	14.00
40	11.72	11.92	12.13	12.33	12.54	12.74	12.95	13.16	13.36	13.57	13.77	13.98

Table 2

MONTHLY

PAYMENT REQUIRED TO AMORTIZE A $1000.00 LOAN

INTEREST	17.00%	17.25%	17.50%	17.75%	18.00%	18.25%	18.50%	18.75%	19.00%	19.25%	19.50%	19.75%
YEARS												
.5	175.03	175.16	175.28	175.41	175.53	175.65	175.78	175.90	176.03	176.15	176.28	176.40
1.0	91.21	91.33	91.45	91.57	91.68	91.80	91.92	92.04	92.16	92.28	92.40	92.52
1.5	63.34	63.45	63.57	63.69	63.81	63.93	64.05	64.17	64.29	64.41	64.53	64.65
2.0	49.45	49.57	49.69	49.81	49.93	50.05	50.17	50.29	50.41	50.54	50.66	50.78
2.5	41.15	41.28	41.40	41.52	41.64	41.77	41.89	42.01	42.14	42.26	42.39	42.51
3.0	35.66	35.78	35.91	36.03	36.16	36.28	36.41	36.53	36.66	36.79	36.91	37.04
3.5	31.76	31.89	32.01	32.14	32.27	32.40	32.53	32.65	32.78	32.91	33.04	33.17
4.0	28.86	28.99	29.12	29.25	29.38	29.51	29.64	29.77	29.91	30.04	30.17	30.30
4.5	26.63	26.76	26.89	27.02	27.16	27.29	27.42	27.56	27.69	27.83	27.96	28.10
5.0	24.86	24.99	25.13	25.26	25.40	25.53	25.67	25.81	25.95	26.08	26.22	26.36
5.5	23.43	23.56	23.70	23.84	23.98	24.12	24.26	24.40	24.54	24.68	24.82	24.96
6.0	22.25	22.39	22.53	22.67	22.81	22.95	23.10	23.24	23.38	23.53	23.67	23.81
6.5	21.27	21.41	21.55	21.70	21.84	21.99	22.13	22.28	22.42	22.57	22.71	22.86
7.0	20.44	20.59	20.73	20.88	21.02	21.17	21.32	21.46	21.61	21.76	21.91	22.06
7.5	19.73	19.88	20.03	20.18	20.33	20.48	20.63	20.78	20.93	21.08	21.23	21.38
8.0	19.13	19.28	19.43	19.58	19.73	19.88	20.03	20.19	20.34	20.49	20.65	20.80
8.5	18.60	18.75	18.90	19.06	19.21	19.37	19.52	19.68	19.83	19.99	20.15	20.30
9.0	18.14	18.30	18.45	18.61	18.76	18.92	19.08	19.23	19.39	19.55	19.71	19.87
9.5	17.74	17.90	18.05	18.21	18.37	18.53	18.69	18.85	19.01	19.17	19.33	19.49
10.0	17.38	17.54	17.70	17.86	18.02	18.18	18.35	18.51	18.67	18.84	19.00	19.17
10.5	17.07	17.23	17.39	17.56	17.72	17.88	18.05	18.21	18.38	18.54	18.71	18.88
11.0	16.79	16.96	17.12	17.28	17.45	17.61	17.78	17.95	18.12	18.28	18.45	18.62
11.5	16.55	16.71	16.88	17.04	17.21	17.38	17.55	17.71	17.88	18.05	18.23	18.40
12.0	16.32	16.49	16.66	16.83	17.00	17.17	17.34	17.51	17.68	17.85	18.02	18.20
12.5	16.13	16.29	16.46	16.63	16.81	16.98	17.15	17.32	17.50	17.67	17.84	18.02
13.0	15.95	16.12	16.29	16.46	16.64	16.81	16.98	17.16	17.33	17.51	17.69	17.86
13.5	15.79	15.96	16.13	16.31	16.48	16.66	16.83	17.01	17.19	17.36	17.54	17.72
14.0	15.64	15.82	15.99	16.17	16.34	16.52	16.70	16.88	17.06	17.24	17.42	17.60
14.5	15.51	15.69	15.87	16.04	16.22	16.40	16.58	16.76	16.94	17.12	17.30	17.48
15.0	15.40	15.57	15.75	15.93	16.11	16.29	16.47	16.65	16.83	17.02	17.20	17.38
15.5	15.29	15.47	15.65	15.83	16.01	16.19	16.37	16.56	16.74	16.92	17.11	17.29
16.0	15.19	15.37	15.55	15.74	15.92	16.10	16.28	16.47	16.65	16.84	17.03	17.21
16.5	15.10	15.29	15.47	15.65	15.84	16.02	16.20	16.39	16.58	16.76	16.95	17.14
17.0	15.02	15.21	15.39	15.58	15.76	15.95	16.13	16.32	16.51	16.70	16.88	17.07
17.5	14.95	15.14	15.32	15.51	15.69	15.88	16.07	16.26	16.45	16.63	16.82	17.02
18.0	14.88	15.07	15.26	15.44	15.63	15.82	16.01	16.20	16.39	16.58	16.77	16.96
18.5	14.82	15.01	15.20	15.39	15.58	15.77	15.96	16.15	16.34	16.53	16.72	16.91
19.0	14.77	14.96	15.15	15.34	15.53	15.72	15.91	16.10	16.29	16.48	16.68	16.87
19.5	14.72	14.91	15.10	15.29	15.48	15.67	15.86	16.06	16.25	16.44	16.64	16.83
20.0	14.67	14.86	15.05	15.25	15.44	15.63	15.82	16.02	16.21	16.41	16.60	16.80
20.5	14.63	14.82	15.01	15.21	15.40	15.59	15.79	15.98	16.18	16.37	16.57	16.77
21.0	14.59	14.79	14.98	15.17	15.37	15.56	15.76	15.95	16.15	16.34	16.54	16.74
21.5	14.56	14.75	14.94	15.14	15.33	15.53	15.73	15.92	16.12	16.32	16.51	16.71
22.0	14.53	14.72	14.91	15.11	15.31	15.50	15.70	15.90	16.09	16.29	16.49	16.69
22.5	14.50	14.69	14.89	15.08	15.28	15.48	15.67	15.87	16.07	16.27	16.47	16.67
23.0	14.47	14.67	14.86	15.06	15.26	15.45	15.65	15.85	16.05	16.25	16.45	16.65
23.5	14.45	14.64	14.84	15.04	15.23	15.43	15.63	15.83	16.03	16.23	16.43	16.63
24.0	14.42	14.62	14.82	15.02	15.21	15.41	15.61	15.81	16.01	16.21	16.41	16.61
24.5	14.40	14.60	14.80	15.00	15.20	15.40	15.60	15.80	16.00	16.20	16.40	16.60
25.0	14.38	14.58	14.78	14.98	15.18	15.38	15.58	15.78	15.98	16.18	16.39	16.59
25.5	14.37	14.56	14.76	14.96	15.16	15.36	15.57	15.77	15.97	16.17	16.37	16.58
26.0	14.35	14.55	14.75	14.95	15.15	15.35	15.55	15.75	15.96	16.16	16.36	16.56
26.5	14.34	14.54	14.74	14.94	15.14	15.34	15.54	15.74	15.95	16.15	16.35	16.56
27.0	14.32	14.52	14.72	14.92	15.13	15.33	15.53	15.73	15.94	16.14	16.34	16.55
27.5	14.31	14.51	14.71	14.91	15.12	15.32	15.52	15.72	15.93	16.13	16.33	16.54
28.0	14.30	14.50	14.70	14.90	15.11	15.31	15.51	15.72	15.92	16.12	16.33	16.53
28.5	14.29	14.49	14.69	14.89	15.10	15.30	15.50	15.71	15.91	16.12	16.32	16.53
29.0	14.28	14.48	14.68	14.89	15.09	15.29	15.50	15.70	15.91	16.11	16.31	16.52
29.5	14.27	14.47	14.68	14.88	15.08	15.29	15.49	15.69	15.90	16.10	16.31	16.51
30.0	14.26	14.46	14.67	14.87	15.08	15.28	15.48	15.69	15.89	16.10	16.30	16.51
35	14.21	14.42	14.62	14.83	15.03	15.24	15.45	15.65	15.86	16.07	16.27	16.48
40	14.19	14.40	14.60	14.81	15.02	15.22	15.43	15.64	15.85	16.05	16.26	16.47

Table 2

MONTHLY

PAYMENT REQUIRED TO AMORTIZE A $1000.00 LOAN

INTEREST	20.00%	20.25%	20.50%	20.75%	21.00%	21.25%	21.50%	21.75%	22.00%	22.25%	22.50%	22.75%
YEARS												
.5	176.53	176.65	176.78	176.90	177.03	177.15	177.28	177.40	177.53	177.65	177.78	177.90
1.0	92.64	92.76	92.88	93.00	93.12	93.24	93.36	93.48	93.60	93.72	93.84	93.96
1.5	64.77	64.89	65.01	65.13	65.25	65.37	65.49	65.61	65.73	65.85	65.98	66.10
2.0	50.90	51.02	51.15	51.27	51.39	51.51	51.64	51.76	51.88	52.01	52.13	52.25
2.5	42.63	42.76	42.88	43.01	43.13	43.26	43.39	43.51	43.64	43.76	43.89	44.02
3.0	37.17	37.30	37.42	37.55	37.68	37.81	37.94	38.07	38.20	38.32	38.45	38.58
3.5	33.30	33.43	33.56	33.69	33.83	33.96	34.09	34.22	34.35	34.49	34.62	34.75
4.0	30.44	30.57	30.70	30.84	30.97	31.11	31.24	31.38	31.51	31.65	31.78	31.92
4.5	28.23	28.37	28.51	28.64	28.78	28.92	29.06	29.20	29.33	29.47	29.61	29.75
5.0	26.50	26.64	26.78	26.92	27.06	27.20	27.34	27.48	27.62	27.77	27.91	28.05
5.5	25.10	25.24	25.39	25.53	25.67	25.82	25.96	26.11	26.25	26.40	26.54	26.69
6.0	23.96	24.10	24.25	24.39	24.54	24.69	24.84	24.98	25.13	25.28	25.43	25.58
6.5	23.01	23.16	23.30	23.45	23.60	23.75	23.90	24.05	24.21	24.36	24.51	24.66
7.0	22.21	22.36	22.51	22.66	22.82	22.97	23.12	23.28	23.43	23.59	23.74	23.90
7.5	21.54	21.69	21.84	22.00	22.15	22.31	22.46	22.62	22.78	22.94	23.09	23.25
8.0	20.96	21.11	21.27	21.43	21.59	21.74	21.90	22.06	22.22	22.38	22.54	22.70
8.5	20.46	20.62	20.78	20.94	21.10	21.26	21.42	21.58	21.75	21.91	22.07	22.24
9.0	20.03	20.19	20.35	20.52	20.68	20.84	21.01	21.17	21.34	21.50	21.67	21.84
9.5	19.66	19.82	19.99	20.15	20.32	20.48	20.65	20.82	20.98	21.15	21.32	21.49
10.0	19.33	19.50	19.66	19.83	20.00	20.17	20.34	20.50	20.67	20.85	21.02	21.19
10.5	19.04	19.21	19.38	19.55	19.72	19.89	20.06	20.23	20.41	20.58	20.75	20.93
11.0	18.79	18.96	19.13	19.30	19.48	19.65	19.82	20.00	20.17	20.35	20.52	20.70
11.5	18.57	18.74	18.91	19.09	19.26	19.44	19.61	19.79	19.97	20.14	20.32	20.50
12.0	18.37	18.55	18.72	18.90	19.07	19.25	19.43	19.61	19.78	19.96	20.14	20.32
12.5	18.20	18.37	18.55	18.73	18.91	19.08	19.26	19.44	19.62	19.81	19.99	20.17
13.0	18.04	18.22	18.40	18.58	18.76	18.94	19.12	19.30	19.48	19.67	19.85	20.03
13.5	17.90	18.08	18.26	18.44	18.63	18.81	18.99	19.17	19.36	19.54	19.73	19.91
14.0	17.78	17.96	18.14	18.32	18.51	18.69	18.88	19.06	19.25	19.43	19.62	19.81
14.5	17.67	17.85	18.03	18.22	18.40	18.59	18.78	18.96	19.15	19.34	19.53	19.71
15.0	17.57	17.75	17.94	18.12	18.31	18.50	18.69	18.87	19.06	19.25	19.44	19.63
15.5	17.48	17.67	17.85	18.04	18.23	18.42	18.61	18.80	18.99	19.18	19.37	19.56
16.0	17.40	17.59	17.78	17.96	18.15	18.34	18.53	18.72	18.92	19.11	19.30	19.49
16.5	17.33	17.52	17.71	17.90	18.09	18.28	18.47	18.66	18.85	19.05	19.24	19.43
17.0	17.26	17.45	17.65	17.84	18.03	18.22	18.41	18.61	18.80	18.99	19.19	19.38
17.5	17.21	17.40	17.59	17.78	17.98	18.17	18.36	18.56	18.75	18.95	19.14	19.34
18.0	17.15	17.35	17.54	17.73	17.93	18.12	18.32	18.51	18.71	18.90	19.10	19.30
18.5	17.11	17.30	17.50	17.69	17.88	18.08	18.28	18.47	18.67	18.87	19.06	19.26
19.0	17.07	17.26	17.46	17.65	17.85	18.04	18.24	18.44	18.63	18.83	19.03	19.23
19.5	17.03	17.22	17.42	17.62	17.81	18.01	18.21	18.41	18.60	18.80	19.00	19.20
20.0	16.99	17.19	17.39	17.58	17.78	17.98	18.18	18.38	18.58	18.77	18.97	19.17
20.5	16.96	17.16	17.36	17.56	17.75	17.95	18.15	18.35	18.55	18.75	18.95	19.15
21.0	16.93	17.13	17.33	17.53	17.73	17.93	18.13	18.33	18.53	18.73	18.93	19.13
21.5	16.91	17.11	17.31	17.51	17.71	17.91	18.11	18.31	18.51	18.71	18.91	19.11
22.0	16.89	17.09	17.29	17.49	17.69	17.89	18.09	18.29	18.49	18.69	18.90	19.10
22.5	16.87	17.07	17.27	17.47	17.67	17.87	18.07	18.27	18.48	18.68	18.88	19.08
23.0	16.85	17.05	17.25	17.45	17.65	17.85	18.06	18.26	18.46	18.66	18.87	19.07
23.5	16.83	17.03	17.23	17.44	17.64	17.84	18.04	18.25	18.45	18.65	18.86	19.06
24.0	16.82	17.02	17.22	17.42	17.62	17.83	18.03	18.23	18.44	18.64	18.84	19.05
24.5	16.80	17.00	17.21	17.41	17.61	17.82	18.02	18.22	18.43	18.63	18.83	19.04
25.0	16.79	16.99	17.20	17.40	17.60	17.81	18.01	18.21	18.42	18.62	18.83	19.03
25.5	16.78	16.98	17.18	17.39	17.59	17.80	18.00	18.20	18.41	18.61	18.82	19.02
26.0	16.77	16.97	17.18	17.38	17.58	17.79	17.99	18.20	18.40	18.61	18.81	19.02
26.5	16.76	16.96	17.17	17.37	17.58	17.78	17.99	18.19	18.40	18.60	18.81	19.01
27.0	16.75	16.95	17.16	17.36	17.57	17.77	17.98	18.18	18.39	18.59	18.80	19.01
27.5	16.76	16.95	17.15	17.36	17.56	17.77	17.97	18.18	18.38	18.59	18.80	19.00
28.0	16.74	16.94	17.15	17.35	17.56	17.76	17.97	18.17	18.38	18.59	18.79	19.00
28.5	16.73	16.94	17.14	17.35	17.55	17.76	17.96	18.17	18.38	18.58	18.79	18.99
29.0	16.72	16.93	17.14	17.34	17.55	17.75	17.96	18.17	18.37	18.58	18.78	18.99
29.5	16.72	16.93	17.13	17.34	17.54	17.75	17.96	18.16	18.37	18.57	18.78	18.99
30.0	16.72	16.92	17.13	17.33	17.54	17.75	17.95	18.16	18.36	18.57	18.78	18.99
35	16.69	16.89	17.10	17.31	17.52	17.72	17.93	18.14	18.35	18.55	18.76	18.97
40	16.68	16.89	17.09	17.30	17.51	17.72	17.93	18.13	18.34	18.55	18.76	18.97

Table 2

MONTHLY

PAYMENT REQUIRED TO AMORTIZE A $1000.00 LOAN

INTEREST YEARS	23.00%	23.25%	23.50%	23.75%	24.00%	24.25%	24.50%	24.75%	25.00%	25.25%	25.50%	25.75%
.5	178.03	178.15	178.28	178.41	178.53	178.66	178.78	178.91	179.03	179.16	179.28	179.41
1.0	94.08	94.20	94.32	94.44	94.56	94.69	94.81	94.93	95.05	95.17	95.29	95.41
1.5	66.22	66.34	66.46	66.58	66.71	66.83	66.95	67.07	67.20	67.32	67.44	67.57
2.0	52.38	52.50	52.63	52.75	52.88	53.00	53.13	53.25	53.38	53.50	53.63	53.75
2.5	44.14	44.27	44.40	44.53	44.65	44.78	44.91	45.04	45.17	45.30	45.43	45.56
3.0	38.71	38.85	38.98	39.11	39.24	39.37	39.50	39.63	39.76	39.90	40.03	40.16
3.5	34.89	35.02	35.15	35.29	35.42	35.56	35.69	35.83	35.96	36.10	36.24	36.37
4.0	32.06	32.19	32.33	32.47	32.61	32.75	32.88	33.02	33.16	33.30	33.44	33.58
4.5	29.89	30.03	30.17	30.32	30.46	30.60	30.74	30.88	31.03	31.17	31.31	31.46
5.0	28.20	28.34	28.48	28.63	28.77	28.92	29.06	29.21	29.36	29.50	29.65	29.80
5.5	26.84	26.98	27.13	27.28	27.43	27.57	27.72	27.87	28.02	28.17	28.32	28.48
6.0	25.73	25.88	26.03	26.18	26.33	26.48	26.64	26.79	26.94	27.10	27.25	27.40
6.5	24.81	24.97	25.12	25.28	25.43	25.59	25.74	25.90	26.05	26.21	26.37	26.53
7.0	24.05	24.21	24.37	24.52	24.68	24.84	25.00	25.16	25.32	25.48	25.64	25.80
7.5	23.41	23.57	23.73	23.89	24.05	24.21	24.37	24.54	24.70	24.86	25.03	25.19
8.0	22.87	23.03	23.19	23.35	23.52	23.68	23.85	24.01	24.18	24.34	24.51	24.68
8.5	22.40	22.57	22.73	22.90	23.06	23.23	23.40	23.57	23.74	23.90	24.07	24.24
9.0	22.00	22.17	22.34	22.51	22.68	22.85	23.02	23.19	23.36	23.53	23.70	23.87
9.5	21.66	21.83	22.00	22.17	22.34	22.51	22.69	22.86	23.03	23.21	23.38	23.56
10.0	21.36	21.53	21.71	21.88	22.05	22.23	22.40	22.58	22.75	22.93	23.11	23.29
10.5	21.10	21.28	21.45	21.63	21.80	21.98	22.16	22.34	22.51	22.69	22.87	23.05
11.0	20.87	21.05	21.23	21.41	21.59	21.76	21.94	22.12	22.30	22.49	22.67	22.85
11.5	20.68	20.86	21.04	21.22	21.40	21.58	21.76	21.94	22.12	22.31	22.49	22.67
12.0	20.50	20.68	20.87	21.05	21.23	21.41	21.60	21.78	21.97	22.15	22.34	22.52
12.5	20.35	20.53	20.72	20.90	21.09	21.27	21.46	21.64	21.83	22.02	22.20	22.39
13.0	20.22	20.40	20.59	20.77	20.96	21.15	21.33	21.52	21.71	21.90	22.09	22.27
13.5	20.10	20.29	20.47	20.66	20.85	21.04	21.22	21.41	21.60	21.79	21.98	22.17
14.0	20.00	20.18	20.37	20.56	20.75	20.94	21.13	21.32	21.51	21.70	21.89	22.09
14.5	19.90	20.09	20.28	20.47	20.66	20.85	21.05	21.24	21.43	21.62	21.82	22.01
15.0	19.82	20.01	20.20	20.40	20.59	20.78	20.97	21.17	21.36	21.55	21.75	21.94
15.5	19.75	19.94	20.13	20.33	20.52	20.71	20.91	21.10	21.30	21.49	21.69	21.89
16.0	19.69	19.88	20.07	20.27	20.46	20.66	20.85	21.05	21.24	21.44	21.64	21.83
16.5	19.63	19.82	20.02	20.21	20.41	20.61	20.80	21.00	21.20	21.39	21.59	21.79
17.0	19.58	19.77	19.97	20.17	20.36	20.56	20.76	20.96	21.15	21.35	21.55	21.75
17.5	19.53	19.73	19.93	20.12	20.32	20.52	20.72	20.92	21.12	21.32	21.51	21.71
18.0	19.49	19.69	19.89	20.09	20.29	20.49	20.68	20.88	21.08	21.28	21.48	21.68
18.5	19.46	19.66	19.86	20.06	20.25	20.45	20.65	20.85	21.05	21.26	21.46	21.66
19.0	19.43	19.63	19.83	20.03	20.23	20.43	20.63	20.83	21.03	21.23	21.43	21.63
19.5	19.40	19.60	19.80	20.00	20.20	20.40	20.60	20.81	21.01	21.21	21.41	21.61
20.0	19.38	19.58	19.78	19.98	20.18	20.38	20.58	20.78	20.99	21.19	21.39	21.60
20.5	19.35	19.55	19.76	19.96	20.16	20.36	20.56	20.77	20.97	21.17	21.38	21.58
21.0	19.33	19.54	19.74	19.94	20.14	20.34	20.55	20.75	20.95	21.16	21.36	21.57
21.5	19.32	19.52	19.72	19.92	20.13	20.33	20.53	20.74	20.94	21.14	21.35	21.55
22.0	19.30	19.50	19.71	19.91	20.11	20.32	20.52	20.72	20.93	21.13	21.34	21.54
22.5	19.29	19.49	19.69	19.90	20.10	20.30	20.51	20.71	20.92	21.12	21.33	21.53
23.0	19.27	19.48	19.68	19.89	20.09	20.29	20.50	20.70	20.91	21.11	21.32	21.52
23.5	19.26	19.47	19.67	19.88	20.08	20.29	20.49	20.70	20.90	21.11	21.31	21.52
24.0	19.25	19.46	19.66	19.87	20.07	20.28	20.48	20.69	20.89	21.10	21.30	21.51
24.5	19.24	19.45	19.65	19.86	20.06	20.27	20.48	20.68	20.89	21.09	21.30	21.51
25.0	19.24	19.44	19.65	19.85	20.06	20.26	20.47	20.68	20.88	21.09	21.29	21.50
25.5	19.23	19.43	19.64	19.85	20.05	20.26	20.46	20.67	20.88	21.08	21.29	21.50
26.0	19.22	19.43	19.63	19.84	20.05	20.25	20.46	20.67	20.87	21.08	21.29	21.49
26.5	19.22	19.42	19.63	19.84	20.04	20.25	20.45	20.66	20.87	21.07	21.28	21.49
27.0	19.21	19.42	19.62	19.83	20.04	20.24	20.45	20.66	20.86	21.07	21.28	21.49
27.5	19.21	19.41	19.62	19.83	20.03	20.24	20.45	20.65	20.86	21.07	21.28	21.48
28.0	19.20	19.41	19.62	19.82	20.03	20.24	20.44	20.65	20.86	21.07	21.27	21.48
28.5	19.20	19.41	19.61	19.82	20.03	20.23	20.44	20.65	20.86	21.06	21.27	21.48
29.0	19.20	19.40	19.61	19.82	20.03	20.23	20.44	20.65	20.85	21.06	21.27	21.48
29.5	19.19	19.40	19.61	19.82	20.02	20.23	20.44	20.64	20.85	21.06	21.27	21.47
30.0	19.19	19.40	19.61	19.81	20.02	20.23	20.43	20.64	20.85	21.06	21.27	21.47
35	19.18	19.39	19.59	19.80	20.01	20.22	20.43	20.63	20.84	21.05	21.26	21.47
40	19.17	19.38	19.59	19.80	20.01	20.21	20.42	20.63	20.84	21.05	21.26	21.46

Table 2

QUARTERLY

PAYMENT REQUIRED TO AMORTIZE A $1000.00 LOAN

TEREST	5.00%	5.25%	5.50%	5.75%	6.00%	6.25%	6.50%	6.75%	7.00%	7.25%	7.50%	7.75%
YEARS
.5	509.40	509.87	510.34	510.81	511.28	511.75	512.23	512.70	513.17	513.64	514.11	514.58
1.0	257.87	258.26	258.66	259.05	259.45	259.85	260.24	260.64	261.04	261.43	261.83	262.23
1.5	174.04	174.41	174.78	175.16	175.53	175.90	176.28	176.65	177.03	177.40	177.78	178.15
2.0	132.14	132.50	132.86	133.23	133.59	133.95	134.32	134.68	135.05	135.41	135.78	136.15
2.5	107.01	107.36	107.72	108.08	108.44	108.80	109.16	109.52	109.88	110.24	110.60	110.97
3.0	90.26	90.62	90.97	91.33	91.68	92.04	92.40	92.76	93.12	93.48	93.84	94.20
3.5	78.31	78.66	79.02	79.37	79.73	80.09	80.44	80.80	81.16	81.52	81.88	82.24
4.0	69.35	69.70	70.06	70.41	70.77	71.13	71.49	71.84	72.20	72.57	72.93	73.29
4.5	62.39	62.74	63.10	63.45	63.81	64.17	64.53	64.89	65.25	65.61	65.98	66.34
5.0	56.83	57.18	57.54	57.89	58.25	58.61	58.97	59.33	59.70	60.06	60.43	60.79
5.5	52.28	52.63	52.99	53.35	53.71	54.07	54.43	54.80	55.16	55.53	55.90	56.27
6.0	48.49	48.85	49.21	49.57	49.93	50.29	50.66	51.02	51.39	51.76	52.13	52.50
6.5	45.29	45.65	46.01	46.37	46.74	47.10	47.47	47.84	48.21	48.58	48.95	49.33
7.0	42.55	42.91	43.28	43.64	44.01	44.37	44.74	45.11	45.49	45.86	46.24	46.62
7.5	40.18	40.55	40.91	41.28	41.64	42.01	42.39	42.76	43.13	43.51	43.89	44.27
8.0	38.11	38.48	38.84	39.21	39.58	39.95	40.33	40.70	41.08	41.46	41.85	42.23
8.5	36.29	36.66	37.02	37.39	37.77	38.14	38.52	38.90	39.28	39.66	40.05	40.43
9.0	34.67	35.04	35.41	35.78	36.16	36.53	36.91	37.30	37.68	38.07	38.45	38.85
9.5	33.22	33.60	33.97	34.34	34.72	35.10	35.48	35.87	36.25	36.64	37.04	37.43
10.0	31.93	32.30	32.67	33.05	33.43	33.81	34.20	34.59	34.98	35.37	35.76	36.16
10.5	30.75	31.13	31.51	31.89	32.27	32.65	33.04	33.43	33.83	34.22	34.62	35.02
11.0	29.69	30.07	30.45	30.83	31.22	31.60	31.99	32.39	32.78	33.18	33.58	33.99
11.5	28.72	29.10	29.48	29.87	30.26	30.65	31.04	31.44	31.84	32.24	32.64	33.05
12.0	27.84	28.22	28.60	28.99	29.38	29.77	30.17	30.57	30.97	31.38	31.78	32.19
12.5	27.02	27.41	27.79	28.18	28.58	28.97	29.37	29.77	30.18	30.59	31.00	31.41
13.0	26.27	26.66	27.05	27.44	27.84	28.24	28.64	29.04	29.45	29.86	30.28	30.69
13.5	25.58	25.97	26.36	26.76	27.16	27.56	27.96	28.37	28.78	29.20	29.61	30.03
14.0	24.94	25.33	25.73	26.13	26.53	26.93	27.34	27.75	28.16	28.58	29.00	29.42
14.5	24.35	24.74	25.14	25.54	25.94	26.35	26.76	27.17	27.59	28.01	28.43	28.86
15.0	23.79	24.19	24.59	24.99	25.40	25.81	26.22	26.64	27.06	27.48	27.91	28.34
15.5	23.28	23.68	24.08	24.48	24.89	25.30	25.72	26.14	26.56	26.99	27.42	27.85
16.0	22.80	23.20	23.60	24.01	24.42	24.84	25.25	25.68	26.10	26.53	26.97	27.40
16.5	22.35	22.75	23.15	23.56	23.98	24.40	24.82	25.24	25.67	26.11	26.54	26.98
17.0	21.92	22.33	22.74	23.15	23.57	23.99	24.41	24.84	25.27	25.71	26.15	26.59
17.5	21.52	21.93	22.34	22.76	23.18	23.60	24.03	24.46	24.89	25.33	25.78	26.22
18.0	21.15	21.56	21.97	22.39	22.81	23.24	23.67	24.10	24.54	24.98	25.43	25.88
18.5	20.80	21.21	21.62	22.05	22.47	22.90	23.33	23.77	24.21	24.65	25.10	25.56
19.0	20.46	20.88	21.30	21.72	22.15	22.58	23.01	23.45	23.90	24.34	24.80	25.25
19.5	20.15	20.57	20.99	21.41	21.84	22.28	22.71	23.16	23.60	24.05	24.51	24.97
20.0	19.85	20.27	20.69	21.12	21.55	21.99	22.43	22.88	23.33	23.78	24.24	24.70
20.5	19.57	19.99	20.42	20.85	21.28	21.72	22.16	22.61	23.06	23.52	23.98	24.45
21.0	19.30	19.72	20.15	20.59	21.02	21.46	21.91	22.36	22.82	23.28	23.74	24.21
21.5	19.05	19.47	19.90	20.34	20.78	21.22	21.67	22.13	22.58	23.05	23.51	23.98
22.0	18.81	19.23	19.67	20.10	20.55	20.99	21.45	21.90	22.36	22.83	23.30	23.77
22.5	18.58	19.01	19.44	19.88	20.33	20.78	21.23	21.69	22.15	22.62	23.09	23.57
23.0	18.36	18.79	19.23	19.67	20.12	20.57	21.03	21.49	21.95	22.42	22.90	23.38
23.5	18.15	18.58	19.02	19.47	19.92	20.37	20.83	21.30	21.77	22.24	22.72	23.20
24.0	17.95	18.39	18.83	19.28	19.73	20.19	20.65	21.11	21.59	22.06	22.54	23.03
24.5	17.76	18.20	18.64	19.09	19.55	20.01	20.47	20.94	21.42	21.89	22.38	22.87
25.0	17.58	18.02	18.47	18.92	19.38	19.84	20.30	20.78	21.25	21.74	22.22	22.71
25.5	17.41	17.85	18.30	18.75	19.21	19.68	20.15	20.62	21.10	21.58	22.07	22.57
26.0	17.24	17.69	18.14	18.59	19.05	19.52	19.99	20.47	20.95	21.44	21.93	22.43
26.5	17.08	17.53	17.98	18.44	18.90	19.37	19.85	20.33	20.81	21.30	21.80	22.30
27.0	16.93	17.38	17.83	18.30	18.76	19.23	19.71	20.19	20.68	21.17	21.67	22.17
27.5	16.78	17.24	17.69	18.16	18.63	19.10	19.58	20.06	20.55	21.05	21.55	22.05
28.0	16.64	17.10	17.56	18.02	18.49	18.97	19.45	19.94	20.43	20.93	21.43	21.94
28.5	16.51	16.97	17.43	17.90	18.37	18.85	19.33	19.82	20.32	20.82	21.32	21.83
29.0	16.38	16.84	17.30	17.77	18.25	18.73	19.22	19.71	20.20	20.71	21.21	21.72
29.5	16.26	16.72	17.18	17.66	18.13	18.62	19.11	19.60	20.10	20.60	21.11	21.63
30.0	16.14	16.60	17.07	17.54	18.02	18.51	19.00	19.50	20.00	20.50	21.02	21.53
35	15.17	15.65	16.14	16.63	17.14	17.64	18.16	18.67	19.20	19.72	20.26	20.80
40	14.49	14.99	15.50	16.01	16.53	17.06	17.59	18.13	18.67	19.21	19.77	20.32

Table 2

QUARTERLY

PAYMENT REQUIRED TO AMORTIZE A $1000.00 LOAN

INTEREST	8.00%	8.25%	8.50%	8.75%	9.00%	9.25%	9.50%	9.75%	10.00%	10.25%	10.50%	10.75%
YEARS												
.5	515.05	515.53	516.00	516.47	516.94	517.41	517.89	518.36	518.83	519.30	519.78	520.25
1.0	262.63	263.03	263.43	263.82	264.22	264.62	265.02	265.42	265.82	266.22	266.62	267.02
1.5	178.53	178.91	179.28	179.66	180.04	180.42	180.80	181.18	181.55	181.93	182.31	182.70
2.0	136.51	136.88	137.25	137.62	137.99	138.36	138.73	139.10	139.47	139.84	140.22	140.59
2.5	111.33	111.70	112.06	112.43	112.79	113.16	113.53	113.90	114.26	114.63	115.00	115.37
3.0	94.56	94.93	95.29	95.66	96.02	96.39	96.76	97.12	97.49	97.86	98.23	98.60
3.5	82.61	82.97	83.34	83.70	84.07	84.43	84.80	85.17	85.54	85.91	86.28	86.66
4.0	73.66	74.02	74.39	74.75	75.12	75.49	75.86	76.23	76.60	76.98	77.35	77.73
4.5	66.71	67.07	67.44	67.81	68.18	68.55	68.93	69.30	69.68	70.05	70.43	70.81
5.0	61.16	61.53	61.90	62.27	62.65	63.02	63.40	63.77	64.15	64.53	64.91	65.29
5.5	56.64	57.01	57.38	57.76	58.13	58.51	58.89	59.27	59.65	60.03	60.42	60.80
6.0	52.88	53.25	53.63	54.01	54.39	54.77	55.15	55.53	55.92	56.30	56.69	57.08
6.5	49.70	50.08	50.46	50.84	51.23	51.61	52.00	52.38	52.77	53.16	53.56	53.95
7.0	46.99	47.38	47.76	48.14	48.53	48.92	49.31	49.70	50.09	50.49	50.88	51.28
7.5	44.65	45.04	45.43	45.81	46.20	46.60	46.99	47.39	47.78	48.18	48.58	48.99
8.0	42.62	43.00	43.39	43.79	44.18	44.57	44.97	45.37	45.77	46.18	46.58	46.99
8.5	40.82	41.22	41.61	42.00	42.40	42.80	43.20	43.61	44.01	44.42	44.83	45.24
9.0	39.24	39.63	40.03	40.43	40.83	41.23	41.64	42.05	42.46	42.87	43.28	43.70
9.5	37.83	38.22	38.62	39.03	39.43	39.84	40.25	40.66	41.08	41.49	41.91	42.33
10.0	36.56	36.96	37.37	37.77	38.18	38.59	39.01	39.42	39.84	40.26	40.68	41.11
10.5	35.42	35.83	36.24	36.65	37.06	37.47	37.89	38.31	38.73	39.16	39.59	40.02
11.0	34.39	34.80	35.21	35.63	36.04	36.46	36.88	37.31	37.74	38.16	38.60	39.03
11.5	33.46	33.87	34.29	34.70	35.12	35.55	35.97	36.40	36.83	37.27	37.70	38.14
12.0	32.61	33.02	33.44	33.86	34.29	34.71	35.14	35.58	36.01	36.45	36.89	37.33
12.5	31.83	32.25	32.67	33.10	33.52	33.95	34.39	34.82	35.26	35.70	36.15	36.60
13.0	31.11	31.54	31.96	32.39	32.82	33.26	33.70	34.14	34.58	35.03	35.47	35.93
13.5	30.46	30.88	31.31	31.75	32.18	32.62	33.06	33.51	33.95	34.40	34.86	35.31
14.0	29.85	30.28	30.71	31.15	31.59	32.03	32.48	32.93	33.38	33.83	34.29	34.75
14.5	29.29	29.73	30.16	30.60	31.04	31.49	31.94	32.39	32.85	33.31	33.77	34.23
15.0	28.77	29.21	29.65	30.09	30.54	30.99	31.44	31.90	32.36	32.82	33.29	33.75
15.5	28.29	28.73	29.18	29.62	30.07	30.53	30.98	31.44	31.91	32.37	32.84	33.31
16.0	27.84	28.29	28.73	29.19	29.64	30.10	30.56	31.02	31.49	31.96	32.43	32.91
16.5	27.43	27.87	28.32	28.78	29.24	29.70	30.16	30.63	31.10	31.57	32.05	32.53
17.0	27.04	27.49	27.94	28.40	28.86	29.32	29.79	30.26	30.74	31.22	31.70	32.18
17.5	26.67	27.13	27.58	28.05	28.51	28.98	29.45	29.92	30.40	30.88	31.37	31.86
18.0	26.33	26.79	27.25	27.71	28.18	28.65	29.13	29.61	30.09	30.57	31.06	31.55
18.5	26.01	26.47	26.94	27.40	27.88	28.35	28.83	29.31	29.80	30.29	30.78	31.27
19.0	25.71	26.18	26.64	27.11	27.59	28.07	28.55	29.04	29.52	30.02	30.51	31.01
19.5	25.43	25.90	26.37	26.84	27.32	27.80	28.29	28.78	29.27	29.77	30.26	30.77
20.0	25.17	25.64	26.11	26.59	27.07	27.55	28.04	28.54	29.03	29.53	30.03	30.54
20.5	24.92	25.39	25.87	26.35	26.83	27.32	27.81	28.31	28.81	29.31	29.82	30.33
21.0	24.68	25.16	25.64	26.12	26.61	27.10	27.60	28.10	28.60	29.10	29.61	30.13
21.5	24.46	24.94	25.42	25.91	26.40	26.89	27.39	27.90	28.40	28.91	29.42	29.94
22.0	24.25	24.73	25.22	25.71	26.20	26.70	27.20	27.71	28.22	28.73	29.25	29.76
22.5	24.05	24.54	25.03	25.52	26.02	26.52	27.02	27.53	28.04	28.56	29.08	29.60
23.0	23.86	24.35	24.84	25.34	25.84	26.34	26.85	27.36	27.88	28.40	28.92	29.45
23.5	23.69	24.18	24.67	25.17	25.68	26.18	26.69	27.21	27.73	28.25	28.77	29.30
24.0	23.52	24.01	24.51	25.01	25.52	26.03	26.54	27.06	27.58	28.11	28.63	29.17
24.5	23.36	23.86	24.36	24.86	25.37	25.88	26.40	26.92	27.45	27.97	28.50	29.04
25.0	23.21	23.71	24.21	24.72	25.23	25.75	26.27	26.79	27.32	27.85	28.38	28.92
25.5	23.06	23.57	24.07	24.58	25.10	25.62	26.14	26.67	27.20	27.73	28.27	28.81
26.0	22.93	23.43	23.94	24.46	24.97	25.49	26.02	26.55	27.08	27.62	28.16	28.70
26.5	22.80	23.31	23.82	24.33	24.85	25.38	25.91	26.44	26.97	27.51	28.05	28.60
27.0	22.68	23.19	23.70	24.22	24.74	25.27	25.80	26.33	26.87	27.41	27.96	28.51
27.5	22.56	23.07	23.59	24.11	24.64	25.16	25.70	26.23	26.78	27.32	27.87	28.42
28.0	22.45	22.96	23.48	24.01	24.53	25.07	25.60	26.14	26.68	27.23	27.78	28.33
28.5	22.34	22.86	23.38	23.91	24.44	24.97	25.51	26.05	26.60	27.15	27.70	28.25
29.0	22.24	22.76	23.29	23.81	24.35	24.88	25.42	25.97	26.52	27.07	27.62	28.18
29.5	22.14	22.67	23.19	23.73	24.26	24.80	25.34	25.89	26.44	26.99	27.55	28.11
30.0	22.05	22.58	23.11	23.64	24.18	24.72	25.27	25.81	26.37	26.92	27.48	28.04
35	21.34	21.89	22.44	22.99	23.55	24.11	24.68	25.25	25.82	26.39	26.97	27.55
40	20.88	21.45	22.02	22.59	23.16	23.74	24.32	24.91	25.50	26.09	26.68	27.27

Table 2

QUARTERLY

PAYMENT REQUIRED TO AMORTIZE A $1000.00 LOAN

INTEREST	11.00%	11.25%	11.50%	11.75%	12.00%	12.25%	12.50%	12.75%	13.00%	13.25%	13.50%	13.75%
YEARS												
.5	520.72	521.20	521.67	522.14	522.62	523.09	523.56	524.04	524.51	524.98	525.46	525.93
1.0	267.43	267.83	268.23	268.63	269.03	269.43	269.84	270.24	270.64	271.05	271.45	271.85
1.5	183.08	183.46	183.84	184.22	184.60	184.99	185.37	185.75	186.13	186.52	186.90	187.29
2.0	140.96	141.34	141.71	142.09	142.46	142.84	143.21	143.59	143.97	144.35	144.72	145.10
2.5	115.74	116.12	116.49	116.86	117.24	117.61	117.98	118.36	118.74	119.11	119.49	119.87
3.0	98.97	99.35	99.72	100.09	100.47	100.84	101.22	101.59	101.97	102.35	102.73	103.11
3.5	87.03	87.40	87.78	88.15	88.53	88.91	89.29	89.67	90.05	90.43	90.81	91.19
4.0	78.10	78.48	78.86	79.24	79.62	80.00	80.38	80.76	81.15	81.53	81.92	82.30
4.5	71.19	71.57	71.95	72.33	72.71	73.10	73.48	73.87	74.26	74.65	75.04	75.43
5.0	65.68	66.06	66.45	66.83	67.22	67.61	68.00	68.39	68.78	69.18	69.57	69.97
5.5	61.19	61.58	61.97	62.36	62.75	63.15	63.54	63.94	64.33	64.73	65.13	65.53
6.0	57.47	57.87	58.26	58.66	59.05	59.45	59.85	60.25	60.65	61.06	61.46	61.87
6.5	54.35	54.74	55.14	55.54	55.94	56.35	56.75	57.16	57.56	57.97	58.38	58.80
7.0	51.68	52.08	52.49	52.89	53.30	53.71	54.12	54.53	54.94	55.35	55.77	56.19
7.5	49.39	49.80	50.20	50.61	51.02	51.44	51.85	52.27	52.69	53.11	53.53	53.95
8.0	47.40	47.81	48.22	48.64	49.05	49.47	49.89	50.31	50.73	51.16	51.59	52.02
8.5	45.65	46.07	46.49	46.91	47.33	47.75	48.18	48.60	49.03	49.46	49.89	50.33
9.0	44.12	44.54	44.96	45.38	45.81	46.24	46.67	47.10	47.53	47.97	48.41	48.85
9.5	42.75	43.18	43.60	44.03	44.46	44.90	45.33	45.77	46.21	46.65	47.09	47.54
10.0	41.54	41.97	42.40	42.83	43.27	43.71	44.15	44.59	45.03	45.48	45.93	46.38
10.5	40.45	40.88	41.32	41.76	42.20	42.64	43.09	43.53	43.98	44.43	44.89	45.34
11.0	39.47	39.90	40.35	40.79	41.23	41.68	42.13	42.59	43.04	43.50	43.96	44.42
11.5	38.58	39.02	39.47	39.92	40.37	40.82	41.28	41.73	42.19	42.66	43.12	43.59
12.0	37.78	38.22	38.67	39.13	39.58	40.04	40.50	40.96	41.43	41.90	42.37	42.84
12.5	37.05	37.50	37.95	38.41	38.87	39.33	39.80	40.27	40.74	41.21	41.68	42.16
13.0	36.38	36.84	37.30	37.76	38.22	38.69	39.16	39.63	40.11	40.58	41.06	41.54
13.5	35.77	36.23	36.69	37.16	37.63	38.10	38.58	39.05	39.53	40.02	40.50	40.99
14.0	35.21	35.68	36.14	36.62	37.09	37.57	38.04	38.53	39.01	39.50	39.99	40.48
14.5	34.70	35.17	35.64	36.12	36.59	37.07	37.56	38.04	38.53	39.02	39.52	40.01
15.0	34.23	34.70	35.18	35.66	36.14	36.62	37.11	37.60	38.09	38.59	39.09	39.59
15.5	33.79	34.27	34.75	35.23	35.72	36.21	36.70	37.20	37.69	38.19	38.70	39.20
16.0	33.39	33.87	34.35	34.84	35.33	35.83	36.32	36.82	37.32	37.83	38.34	38.85
16.5	33.01	33.50	33.99	34.48	34.98	35.47	35.97	36.48	36.98	37.49	38.00	38.52
17.0	32.67	33.16	33.65	34.15	34.65	35.15	35.65	36.16	36.67	37.18	37.70	38.22
17.5	32.35	32.84	33.34	33.84	34.34	34.85	35.36	35.87	36.38	36.90	37.42	37.94
18.0	32.05	32.55	33.05	33.55	34.06	34.57	35.08	35.60	36.12	36.64	37.16	37.69
18.5	31.77	32.27	32.78	33.29	33.80	34.31	34.83	35.35	35.87	36.39	36.92	37.45
19.0	31.51	32.02	32.53	33.04	33.55	34.07	34.59	35.11	35.64	36.17	36.70	37.23
19.5	31.27	31.78	32.29	32.81	33.33	33.85	34.37	34.90	35.43	35.96	36.50	37.03
20.0	31.05	31.56	32.08	32.60	33.12	33.64	34.17	34.70	35.23	35.77	36.31	36.85
20.5	30.84	31.35	31.87	32.40	32.92	33.45	33.98	34.51	35.05	35.59	36.13	36.67
21.0	30.64	31.16	31.68	32.21	32.74	33.27	33.80	34.34	34.88	35.42	35.97	36.52
21.5	30.46	30.98	31.51	32.04	32.57	33.10	33.64	34.18	34.72	35.27	35.82	36.37
22.0	30.29	30.81	31.34	31.87	32.41	32.95	33.49	34.03	34.58	35.13	35.68	36.23
22.5	30.13	30.66	31.19	31.72	32.26	32.80	33.35	33.89	34.44	34.99	35.55	36.10
23.0	29.98	30.51	31.04	31.58	32.12	32.67	33.21	33.76	34.31	34.87	35.43	35.99
23.5	29.83	30.37	30.91	31.45	31.99	32.54	33.09	33.64	34.20	34.75	35.31	35.88
24.0	29.70	30.24	30.78	31.32	31.87	32.42	32.97	33.53	34.09	34.65	35.21	35.77
24.5	29.58	30.12	30.66	31.21	31.76	32.31	32.87	33.42	33.98	34.55	35.11	35.68
25.0	29.46	30.00	30.55	31.10	31.65	32.21	32.76	33.33	33.89	34.45	35.02	35.59
25.5	29.35	29.90	30.44	31.00	31.55	32.11	32.67	33.23	33.80	34.37	34.94	35.51
26.0	29.25	29.79	30.35	30.90	31.46	32.02	32.58	33.15	33.72	34.29	34.86	35.43
26.5	29.15	29.70	30.25	30.81	31.37	31.93	32.50	33.07	33.64	34.21	34.79	35.36
27.0	29.06	29.61	30.17	30.73	31.29	31.86	32.42	32.99	33.57	34.14	34.72	35.30
27.5	28.97	29.53	30.09	30.65	31.21	31.78	32.35	32.92	33.50	34.08	34.65	35.24
28.0	28.89	29.45	30.01	30.57	31.14	31.71	32.28	32.86	33.43	34.01	34.60	35.18
28.5	28.81	29.37	29.94	30.50	31.07	31.65	32.22	32.80	33.38	33.96	34.54	35.13
29.0	28.74	29.30	29.87	30.44	31.01	31.58	32.16	32.74	33.32	33.90	34.49	35.08
29.5	28.67	29.24	29.81	30.38	30.95	31.53	32.11	32.69	33.27	33.85	34.44	35.03
30.0	28.61	29.18	29.75	30.32	30.89	31.47	32.05	32.64	33.22	33.81	34.40	34.99
35	28.14	28.72	29.31	29.90	30.49	31.09	31.68	32.28	32.88	33.48	34.08	34.69
40	27.87	28.47	29.07	29.67	30.27	30.88	31.48	32.09	32.70	33.31	33.92	34.53

Table 2

QUARTERLY

PAYMENT REQUIRED TO AMORTIZE A $1000.00 LOAN

INTEREST	14.00%	14.25%	14.50%	14.75%	15.00%	15.25%	15.50%	15.75%	16.00%	16.25%	16.50%	16.75%
YEARS												
.5	526.41	526.88	527.35	527.83	528.30	528.78	529.25	529.73	530.20	530.68	531.15	531.63
1.0	272.26	272.66	273.06	273.47	273.87	274.28	274.68	275.09	275.50	275.90	276.31	276.71
1.5	187.67	188.06	188.44	188.83	189.22	189.60	189.99	190.38	190.77	191.16	191.54	191.93
2.0	145.48	145.86	146.24	146.62	147.00	147.39	147.77	148.15	148.53	148.92	149.30	149.68
2.5	120.25	120.63	121.01	121.39	121.77	122.15	122.53	122.91	123.30	123.68	124.06	124.45
3.0	103.49	103.87	104.25	104.63	105.02	105.40	105.79	106.17	106.56	106.94	107.33	107.72
3.5	91.58	91.96	92.35	92.73	93.12	93.51	93.89	94.28	94.67	95.07	95.46	95.85
4.0	82.69	83.08	83.47	83.86	84.25	84.64	85.04	85.43	85.82	86.22	86.62	87.02
4.5	75.82	76.22	76.61	77.01	77.40	77.80	78.20	78.60	79.00	79.40	79.80	80.21
5.0	70.37	70.76	71.16	71.57	71.97	72.37	72.77	73.18	73.59	73.99	74.40	74.81
5.5	65.94	66.34	66.75	67.15	67.56	67.97	68.38	68.79	69.20	69.62	70.03	70.45
6.0	62.28	62.69	63.10	63.51	63.92	64.34	64.76	65.17	65.59	66.01	66.43	66.86
6.5	59.21	59.63	60.04	60.46	60.88	61.30	61.72	62.15	62.57	63.00	63.43	63.86
7.0	56.61	57.03	57.45	57.87	58.30	58.73	59.16	59.59	60.02	60.45	60.89	61.32
7.5	54.38	54.80	55.23	55.66	56.09	56.53	56.96	57.40	57.84	58.27	58.72	59.16
8.0	52.45	52.88	53.31	53.75	54.19	54.63	55.07	55.51	55.95	56.40	56.85	57.30
8.5	50.76	51.20	51.64	52.08	52.53	52.97	53.42	53.87	54.32	54.77	55.23	55.68
9.0	49.29	49.73	50.18	50.63	51.08	51.53	51.98	52.44	52.89	53.35	53.81	54.27
9.5	47.99	48.44	48.89	49.34	49.80	50.25	50.71	51.17	51.64	52.10	52.57	53.04
10.0	46.83	47.29	47.74	48.20	48.66	49.13	49.59	50.06	50.53	51.00	51.47	51.95
10.5	45.80	46.26	46.73	47.19	47.66	48.13	48.60	49.07	49.55	50.02	50.50	50.98
11.0	44.88	45.35	45.82	46.29	46.76	47.23	47.71	48.19	48.67	49.15	49.64	50.12
11.5	44.06	44.53	45.00	45.48	45.95	46.43	46.92	47.40	47.89	48.38	48.87	49.36
12.0	43.31	43.79	44.27	44.75	45.23	45.72	46.20	46.69	47.19	47.68	48.18	48.67
12.5	42.64	43.12	43.60	44.09	44.58	45.07	45.56	46.06	46.56	47.05	47.56	48.06
13.0	42.03	42.52	43.01	43.50	43.99	44.49	44.98	45.48	45.99	46.49	47.00	47.51
13.5	41.48	41.97	42.46	42.96	43.46	43.96	44.46	44.97	45.47	45.98	46.50	47.01
14.0	40.97	41.47	41.97	42.47	42.97	43.48	43.99	44.50	45.01	45.52	46.04	46.56
14.5	40.51	41.01	41.52	42.02	42.53	43.04	43.56	44.07	44.59	45.11	45.63	46.15
15.0	40.09	40.60	41.11	41.62	42.13	42.65	43.16	43.68	44.21	44.73	45.26	45.79
15.5	39.71	40.22	40.73	41.25	41.77	42.29	42.81	43.33	43.86	44.39	44.92	45.45
16.0	39.36	39.87	40.39	40.91	41.43	41.96	42.48	43.01	43.54	44.08	44.61	45.15
16.5	39.04	39.55	40.08	40.60	41.13	41.65	42.19	42.72	43.25	43.79	44.33	44.87
17.0	38.74	39.26	39.79	40.32	40.85	41.38	41.91	42.45	42.99	43.53	44.08	44.62
17.5	38.47	38.99	39.52	40.06	40.59	41.13	41.67	42.21	42.75	43.30	43.84	44.39
18.0	38.21	38.75	39.28	39.82	40.35	40.89	41.44	41.98	42.53	43.08	43.63	44.18
18.5	37.98	38.52	39.06	39.60	40.14	40.68	41.23	41.78	42.33	42.88	43.44	43.99
19.0	37.77	38.31	38.85	39.39	39.94	40.49	41.04	41.59	42.14	42.70	43.26	43.82
19.5	37.57	38.11	38.66	39.21	39.76	40.31	40.86	41.42	41.97	42.53	43.10	43.66
20.0	37.39	37.94	38.48	39.03	39.59	40.14	40.70	41.26	41.82	42.38	42.95	43.51
20.5	37.22	37.77	38.32	38.88	39.43	39.99	40.55	41.11	41.68	42.24	42.81	43.38
21.0	37.07	37.62	38.17	38.73	39.29	39.85	40.41	40.98	41.55	42.11	42.69	43.26
21.5	36.92	37.48	38.03	38.59	39.16	39.72	40.29	40.85	41.43	42.00	42.57	43.15
22.0	36.79	37.35	37.91	38.47	39.03	39.60	40.17	40.74	41.31	41.89	42.47	43.04
22.5	36.66	37.22	37.79	38.35	38.92	39.49	40.06	40.64	41.21	41.79	42.37	42.95
23.0	36.55	37.11	37.68	38.25	38.82	39.39	39.96	40.54	41.12	41.70	42.28	42.86
23.5	36.44	37.01	37.58	38.15	38.72	39.30	39.87	40.45	41.03	41.62	42.20	42.78
24.0	36.34	36.91	37.48	38.06	38.63	39.21	39.79	40.37	40.95	41.54	42.12	42.71
24.5	36.25	36.82	37.40	37.97	38.55	39.13	39.71	40.30	40.88	41.47	42.06	42.65
25.0	36.16	36.74	37.32	37.89	38.47	39.06	39.64	40.23	40.81	41.40	41.99	42.58
25.5	36.08	36.66	37.24	37.82	38.40	38.99	39.57	40.16	40.75	41.34	41.93	42.53
26.0	36.01	36.59	37.17	37.75	38.34	38.92	39.51	40.10	40.69	41.29	41.88	42.48
26.5	35.94	36.52	37.11	37.69	38.28	38.87	39.46	40.05	40.64	41.24	41.83	42.43
27.0	35.88	36.46	37.05	37.63	38.22	38.81	39.40	40.00	40.59	41.19	41.79	42.38
27.5	35.82	36.40	36.99	37.58	38.17	38.76	39.36	39.95	40.55	41.15	41.74	42.34
28.0	35.76	36.35	36.94	37.53	38.12	38.72	39.31	39.91	40.51	41.11	41.71	42.31
28.5	35.71	36.30	36.89	37.48	38.08	38.67	39.27	39.87	40.47	41.07	41.67	42.27
29.0	35.66	36.25	36.85	37.44	38.04	38.63	39.23	39.83	40.43	41.03	41.64	42.24
29.5	35.62	36.21	36.81	37.40	38.00	38.60	39.20	39.80	40.40	41.00	41.61	42.21
30.0	35.58	36.17	36.77	37.36	37.96	38.56	39.16	39.77	40.37	40.97	41.58	42.19
35	35.29	35.90	36.50	37.11	37.72	38.33	38.95	39.56	40.17	40.78	41.40	42.01
40	35.15	35.76	36.38	36.99	37.61	38.23	38.84	39.46	40.08	40.70	41.32	41.94

Table 2

QUARTERLY

PAYMENT REQUIRED TO AMORTIZE A $1000.00 LOAN

EREST	17.00%	17.25%	17.50%	17.75%	18.00%	18.25%	18.50%	18.75%	19.00%	19.25%	19.50%	19.75%
YEARS												
.5	532.10	532.58	533.05	533.53	534.00	534.48	534.95	535.43	535.91	536.38	536.86	537.33
1.0	277.12	277.53	277.93	278.34	278.75	279.16	279.56	279.97	280.38	280.79	281.20	281.61
1.5	192.32	192.71	193.10	193.49	193.88	194.27	194.67	195.06	195.45	195.84	196.24	196.63
2.0	150.07	150.46	150.84	151.23	151.61	152.00	152.39	152.78	153.17	153.56	153.95	154.34
2.5	124.84	125.22	125.61	126.00	126.38	126.77	127.16	127.55	127.94	128.33	128.72	129.12
3.0	108.11	108.50	108.89	109.28	109.67	110.06	110.46	110.85	111.25	111.64	112.04	112.43
3.5	96.24	96.64	97.03	97.43	97.83	98.22	98.62	99.02	99.42	99.82	100.22	100.63
4.0	87.42	87.82	88.22	88.62	89.02	89.42	89.83	90.23	90.64	91.05	91.46	91.86
4.5	80.61	81.02	81.42	81.83	82.24	82.65	83.06	83.48	83.89	84.30	84.72	85.13
5.0	75.22	75.64	76.05	76.47	76.88	77.30	77.72	78.14	78.56	78.98	79.40	79.82
5.5	70.87	71.29	71.71	72.13	72.55	72.97	73.40	73.83	74.25	74.68	75.11	75.54
6.0	67.28	67.71	68.13	68.56	68.99	69.42	69.86	70.29	70.72	71.16	71.60	72.04
6.5	64.29	64.72	65.15	65.59	66.03	66.46	66.90	67.34	67.79	68.23	68.68	69.12
7.0	61.76	62.20	62.64	63.08	63.53	63.97	64.42	64.87	65.32	65.77	66.22	66.67
7.5	59.60	60.05	60.50	60.95	61.40	61.85	62.30	62.76	63.21	63.67	64.13	64.59
8.0	57.75	58.20	58.65	59.11	59.57	60.03	60.49	60.95	61.41	61.88	62.35	62.82
8.5	56.14	56.60	57.06	57.52	57.99	58.45	58.92	59.39	59.86	60.33	60.81	61.28
9.0	54.74	55.20	55.67	56.14	56.61	57.08	57.56	58.03	58.51	58.99	59.47	59.96
9.5	53.51	53.98	54.45	54.93	55.41	55.89	56.37	56.85	57.33	57.82	58.31	58.80
10.0	52.42	52.90	53.38	53.86	54.35	54.83	55.32	55.81	56.30	56.79	57.29	57.79
10.5	51.46	51.95	52.44	52.92	53.41	53.91	54.40	54.90	55.39	55.89	56.39	56.90
11.0	50.61	51.10	51.60	52.09	52.59	53.08	53.58	54.09	54.59	55.09	55.60	56.11
11.5	49.85	50.35	50.85	51.35	51.85	52.35	52.86	53.37	53.88	54.39	54.90	55.42
12.0	49.17	49.68	50.18	50.69	51.19	51.70	52.22	52.73	53.24	53.76	54.28	54.80
12.5	48.57	49.07	49.58	50.09	50.61	51.12	51.64	52.16	52.68	53.20	53.73	54.25
13.0	48.02	48.53	49.05	49.56	50.08	50.60	51.13	51.65	52.18	52.70	53.23	53.77
13.5	47.53	48.04	48.56	49.09	49.61	50.14	50.66	51.19	51.73	52.26	52.79	53.33
14.0	47.08	47.60	48.13	48.66	49.19	49.72	50.25	50.78	51.32	51.86	52.40	52.94
14.5	46.68	47.21	47.74	48.27	48.80	49.34	49.88	50.42	50.96	51.50	52.05	52.59
15.0	46.32	46.85	47.38	47.92	48.46	49.00	49.54	50.09	50.63	51.18	51.73	52.28
15.5	45.99	46.52	47.06	47.60	48.15	48.69	49.24	49.79	50.34	50.89	51.44	52.00
16.0	45.69	46.23	46.77	47.32	47.87	48.42	48.97	49.52	50.07	50.63	51.19	51.75
16.5	45.42	45.96	46.51	47.06	47.61	48.16	48.72	49.28	49.83	50.40	50.96	51.52
17.0	45.17	45.72	46.27	46.82	47.38	47.94	48.50	49.06	49.62	50.18	50.75	51.32
17.5	44.94	45.50	46.05	46.61	47.17	47.73	48.29	48.86	49.42	49.99	50.56	51.13
18.0	44.74	45.30	45.86	46.42	46.98	47.54	48.11	48.68	49.25	49.82	50.39	50.97
18.5	44.55	45.11	45.68	46.24	46.81	47.37	47.94	48.52	49.09	49.66	50.24	50.82
19.0	44.38	44.95	45.51	46.08	46.65	47.22	47.79	48.37	48.94	49.52	50.10	50.68
19.5	44.23	44.79	45.36	45.93	46.51	47.08	47.66	48.23	48.81	49.39	49.97	50.56
20.0	44.08	44.65	45.23	45.80	46.38	46.95	47.53	48.11	48.69	49.28	49.86	50.45
20.5	43.95	44.53	45.10	45.68	46.26	46.84	47.42	48.00	48.59	49.17	49.76	50.35
21.0	43.83	44.41	44.99	45.57	46.15	46.73	47.32	47.90	48.49	49.08	49.67	50.26
21.5	43.72	44.30	44.88	45.47	46.05	46.64	47.22	47.81	48.40	48.99	49.58	50.18
22.0	43.62	44.21	44.79	45.37	45.96	46.55	47.14	47.73	48.32	48.91	49.51	50.10
22.5	43.53	44.12	44.70	45.29	45.88	46.47	47.06	47.65	48.25	48.84	49.44	50.03
23.0	43.45	44.04	44.62	45.21	45.80	46.40	46.99	47.58	48.18	48.78	49.37	49.97
23.5	43.37	43.96	44.55	45.14	45.73	46.33	46.92	47.52	48.12	48.72	49.32	49.92
24.0	43.30	43.89	44.48	45.08	45.67	46.27	46.87	47.46	48.06	48.66	49.27	49.87
24.5	43.24	43.83	44.42	45.02	45.62	46.21	46.81	47.41	48.01	48.62	49.22	49.82
25.0	43.18	43.77	44.37	44.97	45.56	46.16	46.76	47.37	47.97	48.57	49.18	49.78
25.5	43.12	43.72	44.32	44.92	45.52	46.12	46.72	47.32	47.93	48.53	49.14	49.74
26.0	43.07	43.67	44.27	44.87	45.47	46.07	46.68	47.28	47.89	48.50	49.10	49.71
26.5	43.03	43.63	44.23	44.83	45.43	46.04	46.64	47.25	47.85	48.46	49.07	49.68
27.0	42.98	43.59	44.19	44.79	45.40	46.00	46.61	47.22	47.82	48.43	49.04	49.65
27.5	42.94	43.55	44.15	44.76	45.36	45.97	46.58	47.19	47.79	48.41	49.02	49.63
28.0	42.91	43.51	44.12	44.73	45.33	45.94	46.55	47.16	47.77	48.38	48.99	49.60
28.5	42.88	43.48	44.09	44.70	45.30	45.91	46.52	47.13	47.75	48.36	48.97	49.58
29.0	42.85	43.45	44.06	44.67	45.28	45.89	46.50	47.11	47.72	48.34	48.95	49.56
29.5	42.82	43.43	44.04	44.65	45.26	45.87	46.48	47.09	47.70	48.32	48.93	49.55
30.0	42.79	43.40	44.01	44.62	45.23	45.85	46.46	47.07	47.69	48.30	48.92	49.53
35	42.63	43.25	43.86	44.48	45.10	45.72	46.34	46.96	47.58	48.20	48.82	49.44
40	42.56	43.18	43.80	44.42	45.04	45.67	46.29	46.91	47.53	48.16	48.78	49.40

Table 2

QUARTERLY

PAYMENT REQUIRED TO AMORTIZE A $1000.00 LOAN

INTEREST	20.00%	20.25%	20.50%	20.75%	21.00%	21.25%	21.50%	21.75%	22.00%	22.25%	22.50%	22.75%
YEARS
.5	537.81	538.29	538.76	539.24	539.72	540.19	540.67	541.15	541.62	542.10	542.58	543.05
1.0	282.02	282.43	282.84	283.25	283.66	284.07	284.48	284.89	285.30	285.71	286.12	286.53
1.5	197.02	197.42	197.81	198.21	198.60	199.00	199.39	199.79	200.18	200.58	200.98	201.38
2.0	154.73	155.12	155.51	155.90	156.29	156.69	157.08	157.47	157.87	158.26	158.66	159.06
2.5	129.51	129.90	130.30	130.69	131.09	131.48	131.88	132.28	132.67	133.07	133.47	133.87
3.0	112.83	113.23	113.63	114.03	114.43	114.83	115.23	115.63	116.03	116.44	116.84	117.25
3.5	101.03	101.43	101.84	102.24	102.65	103.06	103.47	103.87	104.28	104.69	105.11	105.52
4.0	92.27	92.69	93.10	93.51	93.92	94.34	94.75	95.17	95.59	96.01	96.42	96.84
4.5	85.55	85.97	86.39	86.81	87.23	87.65	88.08	88.50	88.92	89.35	89.78	90.21
5.0	80.25	80.67	81.10	81.53	81.96	82.39	82.82	83.25	83.68	84.12	84.55	84.99
5.5	75.98	76.41	76.84	77.28	77.72	78.15	78.59	79.03	79.48	79.92	80.36	80.81
6.0	72.48	72.92	73.36	73.80	74.25	74.69	75.14	75.59	76.04	76.49	76.94	77.40
6.5	69.57	70.02	70.47	70.92	71.37	71.83	72.28	72.74	73.20	73.66	74.12	74.58
7.0	67.13	67.58	68.04	68.50	68.96	69.42	69.89	70.35	70.82	71.29	71.76	72.23
7.5	65.06	65.52	65.99	66.45	66.92	67.39	67.86	68.34	68.81	69.29	69.76	70.24
8.0	63.29	63.76	64.23	64.70	65.18	65.66	66.14	66.62	67.10	67.58	68.07	68.55
8.5	61.76	62.24	62.72	63.20	63.69	64.17	64.66	65.15	65.63	66.13	66.62	67.11
9.0	60.44	60.93	61.41	61.90	62.39	62.89	63.38	63.87	64.37	64.87	65.37	65.87
9.5	59.29	59.78	60.28	60.77	61.27	61.77	62.27	62.77	63.28	63.78	64.29	64.80
10.0	58.28	58.78	59.28	59.79	60.29	60.80	61.31	61.81	62.33	62.84	63.35	63.87
10.5	57.40	57.91	58.41	58.92	59.43	59.95	60.46	60.98	61.49	62.01	62.53	63.06
11.0	56.62	57.13	57.65	58.16	58.68	59.20	59.72	60.24	60.77	61.29	61.82	62.35
11.5	55.93	56.45	56.97	57.49	58.02	58.54	59.07	59.60	60.13	60.66	61.19	61.73
12.0	55.32	55.85	56.37	56.90	57.43	57.96	58.49	59.03	59.56	60.10	60.64	61.18
12.5	54.78	55.31	55.84	56.38	56.91	57.45	57.99	58.53	59.07	59.61	60.15	60.70
13.0	54.30	54.83	55.37	55.91	56.45	56.99	57.54	58.08	58.63	59.17	59.72	60.28
13.5	53.87	54.41	54.95	55.50	56.04	56.59	57.14	57.69	58.24	58.79	59.34	59.90
14.0	53.49	54.03	54.58	55.13	55.68	56.23	56.78	57.34	57.89	58.45	59.01	59.57
14.5	53.14	53.69	54.24	54.80	55.35	55.91	56.46	57.02	57.59	58.15	58.71	59.28
15.0	52.83	53.39	53.94	54.50	55.06	55.62	56.18	56.75	57.31	57.88	58.45	59.02
15.5	52.56	53.12	53.68	54.24	54.80	55.37	55.93	56.50	57.07	57.64	58.21	58.78
16.0	52.31	52.87	53.44	54.00	54.57	55.14	55.71	56.28	56.85	57.43	58.00	58.58
16.5	52.09	52.65	53.22	53.79	54.36	54.93	55.51	56.08	56.66	57.24	57.82	58.40
17.0	51.88	52.46	53.03	53.60	54.17	54.75	55.33	55.91	56.49	57.07	57.65	58.23
17.5	51.70	52.28	52.85	53.43	54.01	54.59	55.17	55.75	56.33	56.92	57.50	58.09
18.0	51.54	52.12	52.70	53.28	53.86	54.44	55.02	55.61	56.19	56.78	57.37	57.96
18.5	51.39	51.97	52.56	53.14	53.72	54.31	54.90	55.48	56.07	56.66	57.25	57.84
19.0	51.26	51.85	52.43	53.02	53.60	54.19	54.78	55.37	55.96	56.55	57.15	57.74
19.5	51.14	51.73	52.32	52.90	53.49	54.08	54.68	55.27	55.86	56.46	57.05	57.65
20.0	51.03	51.62	52.21	52.80	53.40	53.99	54.58	55.18	55.77	56.37	56.97	57.57
20.5	50.94	51.53	52.12	52.71	53.31	53.90	54.50	55.10	55.70	56.29	56.89	57.50
21.0	50.85	51.44	52.04	52.63	53.23	53.83	54.42	55.02	55.62	56.23	56.83	57.43
21.5	50.77	51.36	51.96	52.56	53.16	53.76	54.36	54.96	55.56	56.16	56.77	57.37
22.0	50.70	51.29	51.89	52.49	53.09	53.69	54.30	54.90	55.50	56.11	56.71	57.32
22.5	50.63	51.23	51.83	52.43	53.04	53.64	54.24	54.85	55.45	56.06	56.67	57.27
23.0	50.57	51.17	51.78	52.38	52.98	53.59	54.19	54.80	55.41	56.01	56.62	57.23
23.5	50.52	51.12	51.73	52.33	52.94	53.54	54.15	54.76	55.37	55.98	56.59	57.20
24.0	50.47	51.08	51.68	52.29	52.89	53.50	54.11	54.72	55.33	55.94	56.55	57.16
24.5	50.43	51.03	51.64	52.25	52.86	53.46	54.07	54.69	55.30	55.91	56.52	57.13
25.0	50.39	51.00	51.60	52.21	52.82	53.43	54.04	54.65	55.27	55.88	56.49	57.11
25.5	50.35	50.96	51.57	52.18	52.79	53.40	54.01	54.63	55.24	55.85	56.47	57.08
26.0	50.32	50.93	51.54	52.15	52.76	53.38	53.99	54.60	55.22	55.83	56.45	57.06
26.5	50.29	50.90	51.51	52.12	52.74	53.35	53.96	54.58	55.19	55.81	56.43	57.04
27.0	50.26	50.88	51.49	52.10	52.71	53.33	53.94	54.56	55.17	55.79	56.41	57.03
27.5	50.24	50.85	51.47	52.08	52.69	53.31	53.93	54.54	55.16	55.77	56.39	57.01
28.0	50.22	50.83	51.45	52.06	52.68	53.29	53.91	54.52	55.14	55.76	56.38	57.00
28.5	50.20	50.81	51.43	52.04	52.66	53.28	53.89	54.51	55.13	55.75	56.37	56.98
29.0	50.18	50.80	51.41	52.03	52.64	53.26	53.88	54.50	55.12	55.73	56.35	56.97
29.5	50.16	50.78	51.40	52.01	52.63	53.25	53.87	54.49	55.10	55.72	56.34	56.96
30.0	50.15	50.77	51.38	52.00	52.62	53.24	53.86	54.47	55.09	55.71	56.33	56.95
35	50.06	50.68	51.30	51.92	52.55	53.17	53.79	54.41	55.04	55.66	56.28	56.90
40	50.03	50.65	51.27	51.90	52.52	53.14	53.77	54.39	55.02	55.64	56.26	56.89

Table 2

QUARTERLY

PAYMENT REQUIRED TO AMORTIZE A $1000.00 LOAN

TEREST	23.00%	23.25%	23.50%	23.75%	24.00%	24.25%	24.50%	24.75%	25.00%	25.25%	25.50%	25.75%
YEARS
.5	543.53	544.01	544.49	544.96	545.44	545.92	546.40	546.88	547.35	547.83	548.31	548.79
1.0	286.95	287.36	287.77	288.18	288.60	289.01	289.42	289.84	290.25	290.66	291.08	291.49
1.5	201.77	202.17	202.57	202.97	203.37	203.77	204.17	204.57	204.97	205.37	205.77	206.17
2.0	159.45	159.85	160.25	160.64	161.04	161.44	161.84	162.24	162.64	163.04	163.44	163.84
2.5	134.27	134.67	135.07	135.47	135.87	136.28	136.68	137.08	137.49	137.89	138.30	138.70
3.0	117.65	118.06	118.47	118.87	119.28	119.69	120.10	120.51	120.92	121.33	121.75	122.16
3.5	105.93	106.34	106.76	107.17	107.59	108.01	108.42	108.84	109.26	109.68	110.10	110.52
4.0	97.27	97.69	98.11	98.53	98.96	99.38	99.81	100.24	100.66	101.09	101.52	101.95
4.5	90.64	91.07	91.50	91.93	92.36	92.80	93.23	93.67	94.10	94.54	94.98	95.42
5.0	85.43	85.87	86.31	86.75	87.19	87.63	88.08	88.52	88.97	89.41	89.86	90.31
5.5	81.25	81.70	82.15	82.60	83.05	83.50	83.96	84.41	84.86	85.32	85.78	86.24
6.0	77.85	78.31	78.77	79.22	79.68	80.14	80.61	81.07	81.53	82.00	82.47	82.93
6.5	75.04	75.51	75.97	76.44	76.91	77.38	77.85	78.32	78.79	79.27	79.74	80.22
7.0	72.70	73.17	73.65	74.12	74.60	75.08	75.56	76.04	76.52	77.00	77.49	77.97
7.5	70.72	71.20	71.68	72.17	72.65	73.14	73.63	74.12	74.61	75.10	75.59	76.09
8.0	69.04	69.53	70.02	70.51	71.01	71.50	72.00	72.50	72.99	73.49	74.00	74.50
8.5	67.61	68.10	68.60	69.10	69.60	70.11	70.61	71.11	71.62	72.13	72.64	73.15
9.0	66.37	66.88	67.38	67.89	68.40	68.91	69.42	69.93	70.45	70.96	71.48	72.00
9.5	65.31	65.82	66.33	66.85	67.36	67.88	68.40	68.92	69.44	69.96	70.49	71.01
10.0	64.38	64.90	65.42	65.94	66.47	66.99	67.52	68.04	68.57	69.10	69.63	70.16
10.5	63.58	64.10	64.63	65.16	65.69	66.22	66.75	67.29	67.82	68.36	68.89	69.43
11.0	62.88	63.41	63.94	64.48	65.01	65.55	66.09	66.63	67.17	67.71	68.25	68.80
11.5	62.26	62.80	63.34	63.88	64.42	64.96	65.51	66.05	66.60	67.15	67.70	68.25
12.0	61.72	62.26	62.81	63.36	63.90	64.45	65.00	65.55	66.11	66.66	67.22	67.77
12.5	61.25	61.79	62.35	62.90	63.45	64.00	64.56	65.12	65.67	66.23	66.79	67.36
13.0	60.83	61.38	61.94	62.49	63.05	63.61	64.17	64.73	65.30	65.86	66.43	66.99
13.5	60.46	61.02	61.58	62.14	62.70	63.27	63.83	64.40	64.96	65.53	66.10	66.68
14.0	60.13	60.69	61.26	61.83	62.39	62.96	63.53	64.10	64.67	65.25	65.82	66.40
14.5	59.84	60.41	60.98	61.55	62.12	62.69	63.27	63.84	64.42	65.00	65.57	66.15
15.0	59.59	60.16	60.73	61.31	61.88	62.46	63.04	63.61	64.19	64.78	65.36	65.94
15.5	59.36	59.93	60.51	61.09	61.67	62.25	62.83	63.41	64.00	64.58	65.17	65.75
16.0	59.16	59.74	60.32	60.90	61.48	62.07	62.65	63.24	63.82	64.41	65.00	65.59
16.5	58.98	59.56	60.14	60.73	61.32	61.90	62.49	63.08	63.67	64.26	64.85	65.45
17.0	58.82	59.40	59.99	60.58	61.17	61.76	62.35	62.94	63.53	64.13	64.72	65.32
17.5	58.68	59.27	59.86	60.45	61.04	61.63	62.22	62.82	63.42	64.01	64.61	65.21
18.0	58.55	59.14	59.73	60.33	60.92	61.52	62.11	62.71	63.31	63.91	64.51	65.11
18.5	58.44	59.03	59.63	60.22	60.82	61.42	62.02	62.62	63.22	63.82	64.42	65.02
19.0	58.34	58.93	59.53	60.13	60.73	61.33	61.93	62.53	63.13	63.74	64.34	64.95
19.5	58.25	58.85	59.45	60.05	60.65	61.25	61.85	62.46	63.06	63.67	64.27	64.88
20.0	58.17	58.77	59.37	59.97	60.58	61.18	61.79	62.39	63.00	63.61	64.21	64.82
20.5	58.10	58.70	59.30	59.91	60.51	61.12	61.73	62.33	62.94	63.55	64.16	64.77
21.0	58.03	58.64	59.24	59.85	60.46	61.07	61.67	62.28	62.89	63.50	64.11	64.72
21.5	57.98	58.58	59.19	59.80	60.41	61.02	61.63	62.24	62.85	63.46	64.07	64.68
22.0	57.93	58.54	59.14	59.75	60.36	60.97	61.58	62.20	62.81	63.42	64.03	64.65
22.5	57.88	58.49	59.10	59.71	60.32	60.93	61.55	62.16	62.77	63.39	64.00	64.62
23.0	57.84	58.45	59.06	59.68	60.29	60.90	61.51	62.13	62.74	63.36	63.97	64.59
23.5	57.81	58.42	59.03	59.64	60.26	60.87	61.49	62.10	62.72	63.33	63.95	64.56
24.0	57.77	58.39	59.00	59.61	60.23	60.84	61.46	62.07	62.69	63.31	63.92	64.54
24.5	57.75	58.36	58.97	59.59	60.20	60.82	61.44	62.05	62.67	63.29	63.90	64.52
25.0	57.72	58.34	58.95	59.57	60.18	60.80	61.42	62.03	62.65	63.27	63.89	64.51
25.5	57.70	58.31	58.93	59.55	60.16	60.78	61.40	62.02	62.63	63.25	63.87	64.49
26.0	57.68	58.29	58.91	59.53	60.15	60.76	61.38	62.00	62.62	63.24	63.86	64.48
26.5	57.66	58.28	58.89	59.51	60.13	60.75	61.37	61.99	62.61	63.23	63.85	64.47
27.0	57.64	58.26	58.88	59.50	60.12	60.74	61.35	61.97	62.59	63.22	63.84	64.46
27.5	57.63	58.25	58.87	59.48	60.10	60.72	61.34	61.96	62.58	63.21	63.83	64.45
28.0	57.61	58.23	58.85	59.47	60.09	60.71	61.33	61.95	62.58	63.20	63.82	64.44
28.5	57.60	58.22	58.84	59.46	60.08	60.70	61.32	61.95	62.57	63.19	63.81	64.43
29.0	57.59	58.21	58.83	59.45	60.07	60.70	61.32	61.94	62.56	63.18	63.80	64.43
29.5	57.58	58.20	58.82	59.45	60.07	60.69	61.31	61.93	62.55	63.18	63.80	64.42
30.0	57.58	58.20	58.82	59.44	60.06	60.68	61.30	61.93	62.55	63.17	63.79	64.42
35	57.53	58.15	58.77	59.40	60.02	60.65	61.27	61.89	62.52	63.14	63.77	64.39
40	57.51	58.14	58.76	59.39	60.01	60.63	61.26	61.88	62.51	63.13	63.76	64.38

Table 2

SEMI-ANNUAL

PAYMENT REQUIRED TO AMORTIZE A $1000.00 LOAN

INTEREST	5.00%	5.25%	5.50%	5.75%	6.00%	6.25%	6.50%	6.75%	7.00%	7.25%	7.50%	7.75%
YEARS												
.5	1025.00	1026.25	1027.50	1028.75	1030.00	1031.25	1032.50	1033.75	1035.00	1036.25	1037.50	1038.75
1.0	518.83	519.78	520.72	521.67	522.62	523.56	524.51	525.46	526.41	527.35	528.30	529.25
1.5	350.14	350.99	351.84	352.69	353.54	354.39	355.24	356.09	356.94	357.79	358.65	359.50
2.0	265.82	266.62	267.43	268.23	269.03	269.84	270.64	271.45	272.26	273.06	273.87	274.68
2.5	215.25	216.03	216.80	217.58	218.36	219.14	219.92	220.70	221.49	222.27	223.06	223.84
3.0	181.55	182.31	183.08	183.84	184.60	185.37	186.13	186.90	187.67	188.44	189.22	189.99
3.5	157.50	158.25	159.00	159.76	160.51	161.27	162.03	162.79	163.55	164.31	165.08	165.85
4.0	139.47	140.22	140.96	141.71	142.46	143.21	143.97	144.72	145.48	146.24	147.00	147.77
4.5	125.46	126.20	126.95	127.69	128.44	129.19	129.94	130.69	131.45	132.21	132.97	133.73
5.0	114.26	115.00	115.74	116.49	117.24	117.98	118.74	119.49	120.25	121.01	121.77	122.53
5.5	105.11	105.85	106.59	107.34	108.08	108.83	109.58	110.34	111.10	111.86	112.62	113.39
6.0	97.49	98.23	98.97	99.72	100.47	101.22	101.97	102.73	103.49	104.25	105.02	105.79
6.5	91.05	91.79	92.54	93.28	94.03	94.79	95.54	96.30	97.07	97.83	98.60	99.37
7.0	85.54	86.28	87.03	87.78	88.53	89.29	90.05	90.81	91.58	92.35	93.12	93.89
7.5	80.77	81.52	82.26	83.02	83.77	84.53	85.29	86.06	86.83	87.60	88.38	89.16
8.0	76.60	77.35	78.10	78.86	79.62	80.38	81.15	81.92	82.69	83.47	84.25	85.04
8.5	72.93	73.68	74.44	75.20	75.96	76.72	77.49	78.27	79.05	79.83	80.62	81.41
9.0	69.68	70.43	71.19	71.95	72.71	73.48	74.26	75.04	75.82	76.61	77.40	78.20
9.5	66.77	67.52	68.28	69.05	69.82	70.59	71.37	72.16	72.95	73.74	74.54	75.34
10.0	64.15	64.91	65.68	66.45	67.22	68.00	68.78	69.57	70.37	71.16	71.97	72.77
10.5	61.79	62.56	63.32	64.10	64.88	65.66	66.45	67.24	68.04	68.85	69.65	70.47
11.0	59.65	60.42	61.19	61.97	62.75	63.54	64.33	65.13	65.94	66.75	67.56	68.38
11.5	57.70	58.47	59.25	60.03	60.82	61.61	62.41	63.21	64.02	64.84	65.66	66.48
12.0	55.92	56.69	57.47	58.26	59.05	59.85	60.65	61.46	62.28	63.10	63.92	64.76
12.5	54.28	55.06	55.84	56.64	57.43	58.24	59.04	59.86	60.68	61.51	62.34	63.17
13.0	52.77	53.56	54.35	55.14	55.94	56.75	57.56	58.38	59.21	60.04	60.88	61.72
13.5	51.38	52.17	52.96	53.76	54.57	55.38	56.20	57.03	57.86	58.69	59.54	60.39
14.0	50.09	50.88	51.68	52.49	53.30	54.12	54.94	55.77	56.61	57.45	58.30	59.16
14.5	48.90	49.69	50.49	51.30	52.12	52.94	53.77	54.61	55.45	56.30	57.15	58.02
15.0	47.78	48.58	49.39	50.20	51.02	51.85	52.69	53.53	54.38	55.23	56.09	56.96
15.5	46.74	47.55	48.36	49.18	50.00	50.84	51.68	52.52	53.38	54.24	55.11	55.98
16.0	45.77	46.58	47.40	48.22	49.05	49.89	50.73	51.59	52.45	53.31	54.19	55.07
16.5	44.86	45.68	46.50	47.33	48.16	49.00	49.85	50.71	51.58	52.45	53.33	54.22
17.0	44.01	44.83	45.65	46.49	47.33	48.18	49.03	49.89	50.76	51.64	52.53	53.42
17.5	43.21	44.03	44.86	45.70	46.54	47.40	48.26	49.13	50.00	50.89	51.78	52.68
18.0	42.46	43.28	44.12	44.96	45.81	46.67	47.53	48.41	49.29	50.18	51.08	51.98
18.5	41.75	42.58	43.41	44.26	45.12	45.98	46.85	47.73	48.62	49.51	50.42	51.33
19.0	41.08	41.91	42.75	43.60	44.46	45.33	46.21	47.09	47.99	48.89	49.80	50.71
19.5	40.44	41.28	42.13	42.98	43.85	44.72	45.60	46.49	47.39	48.30	49.21	50.14
20.0	39.84	40.68	41.54	42.40	43.27	44.15	45.03	45.93	46.83	47.74	48.66	49.59
20.5	39.27	40.12	40.98	41.84	42.72	43.60	44.49	45.39	46.30	47.22	48.15	49.08
21.0	38.73	39.59	40.45	41.32	42.20	43.09	43.98	44.89	45.80	46.73	47.66	48.60
21.5	38.22	39.08	39.94	40.82	41.70	42.60	43.50	44.41	45.33	46.26	47.20	48.14
22.0	37.74	38.60	39.47	40.35	41.23	42.13	43.04	43.96	44.88	45.82	46.76	47.71
22.5	37.27	38.14	39.01	39.90	40.79	41.69	42.61	43.53	44.46	45.40	46.35	47.30
23.0	36.83	37.70	38.58	39.47	40.37	41.28	42.19	43.12	44.06	45.00	45.95	46.92
23.5	36.41	37.29	38.17	39.06	39.97	40.88	41.80	42.73	43.67	44.62	45.58	46.55
24.0	36.01	36.89	37.78	38.67	39.58	40.50	41.43	42.37	43.31	44.27	45.23	46.20
24.5	35.63	36.51	37.40	38.31	39.22	40.14	41.07	42.02	42.97	43.93	44.90	45.88
25.0	35.26	36.15	37.05	37.95	38.87	39.80	40.74	41.68	42.64	43.60	44.58	45.56
25.5	34.91	35.80	36.71	37.62	38.54	39.47	40.41	41.37	42.33	43.30	44.28	45.27
26.0	34.58	35.47	36.38	37.30	38.22	39.16	40.11	41.06	42.03	43.01	43.99	44.98
26.5	34.26	35.16	36.07	36.99	37.92	38.86	39.81	40.77	41.75	42.73	43.72	44.72
27.0	33.95	34.86	35.77	36.69	37.63	38.58	39.53	40.50	41.48	42.46	43.46	44.46
27.5	33.66	34.57	35.48	36.41	37.35	38.30	39.27	40.24	41.22	42.21	43.21	44.22
28.0	33.38	34.29	35.21	36.14	37.09	38.04	39.01	39.99	40.97	41.97	42.97	43.99
28.5	33.11	34.02	34.95	35.89	36.84	37.80	38.77	39.75	40.74	41.74	42.75	43.77
29.0	32.85	33.77	34.70	35.64	36.59	37.56	38.53	39.52	40.51	41.52	42.53	43.56
29.5	32.60	33.52	34.46	35.40	36.36	37.33	38.31	39.30	40.30	41.31	42.33	43.36
30.0	32.36	33.29	34.23	35.18	36.14	37.11	38.09	39.09	40.09	41.11	42.13	43.16
35	30.40	31.37	32.35	33.34	34.34	35.36	36.38	37.42	38.47	39.52	40.59	41.67
40	29.03	30.03	31.05	32.08	33.12	34.17	35.23	36.31	37.39	38.48	39.59	40.70

Table 2

SEMI-ANNUAL

PAYMENT REQUIRED TO AMORTIZE A $1000.00 LOAN

INTEREST	8.00%	8.25%	8.50%	8.75%	9.00%	9.25%	9.50%	9.75%	10.00%	10.25%	10.50%	10.75%
YEARS												
.5	1040.00	1041.25	1042.50	1043.75	1045.00	1046.25	1047.50	1048.75	1050.00	1051.25	1052.50	1053.75
1.0	530.20	531.15	532.10	533.05	534.00	534.95	535.91	536.86	537.81	538.76	539.72	540.67
1.5	360.35	361.21	362.06	362.92	363.78	364.64	365.49	366.35	367.21	368.07	368.94	369.80
2.0	275.50	276.31	277.12	277.93	278.75	279.56	280.38	281.20	282.02	282.84	283.66	284.48
2.5	224.63	225.42	226.21	227.00	227.80	228.59	229.39	230.18	230.98	231.78	232.58	233.38
3.0	190.77	191.54	192.32	193.10	193.88	194.67	195.45	196.24	197.02	197.81	198.60	199.39
3.5	166.61	167.39	168.16	168.93	169.71	170.48	171.26	172.04	172.82	173.61	174.39	175.18
4.0	148.53	149.30	150.07	150.84	151.61	152.39	153.17	153.95	154.73	155.51	156.29	157.08
4.5	134.50	135.27	136.03	136.81	137.58	138.36	139.13	139.91	140.70	141.48	142.27	143.05
5.0	123.30	124.06	124.84	125.61	126.38	127.16	127.94	128.72	129.51	130.30	131.09	131.88
5.5	114.15	114.92	115.70	116.47	117.25	118.03	118.82	119.60	120.39	121.19	121.98	122.78
6.0	106.56	107.33	108.11	108.89	109.67	110.46	111.25	112.04	112.83	113.63	114.43	115.23
6.5	100.15	100.93	101.71	102.49	103.28	104.07	104.86	105.66	106.46	107.26	108.07	108.88
7.0	94.67	95.46	96.24	97.03	97.83	98.62	99.42	100.22	101.03	101.84	102.65	103.47
7.5	89.95	90.73	91.53	92.32	93.12	93.92	94.73	95.53	96.35	97.16	97.98	98.80
8.0	85.82	86.62	87.42	88.22	89.02	89.83	90.64	91.46	92.27	93.10	93.92	94.75
8.5	82.20	83.00	83.81	84.61	85.42	86.24	87.06	87.88	88.70	89.53	90.37	91.21
9.0	79.00	79.80	80.61	81.42	82.24	83.06	83.89	84.72	85.55	86.39	87.23	88.08
9.5	76.14	76.95	77.77	78.59	79.41	80.24	81.07	81.91	82.75	83.60	84.44	85.30
10.0	73.59	74.40	75.22	76.05	76.88	77.72	78.56	79.40	80.25	81.10	81.96	82.82
10.5	71.29	72.11	72.94	73.77	74.61	75.45	76.29	77.15	78.00	78.86	79.73	80.60
11.0	69.20	70.03	70.87	71.71	72.55	73.40	74.25	75.11	75.98	76.84	77.72	78.59
11.5	67.31	68.15	68.99	69.84	70.69	71.54	72.40	73.27	74.14	75.02	75.90	76.78
12.0	65.59	66.43	67.28	68.13	68.99	69.86	70.72	71.60	72.48	73.36	74.25	75.14
12.5	64.02	64.87	65.72	66.58	67.44	68.32	69.19	70.07	70.96	71.85	72.75	73.65
13.0	62.57	63.43	64.29	65.15	66.03	66.90	67.79	68.68	69.57	70.47	71.37	72.28
13.5	61.24	62.11	62.97	63.85	64.72	65.61	66.50	67.40	68.30	69.20	70.12	71.03
14.0	60.02	60.89	61.76	62.64	63.53	64.42	65.32	66.22	67.13	68.04	68.96	69.89
14.5	58.88	59.76	60.64	61.53	62.42	63.32	64.22	65.13	66.05	66.97	67.90	68.83
15.0	57.84	58.72	59.60	60.50	61.40	62.30	63.21	64.13	65.06	65.99	66.92	67.86
15.5	56.86	57.75	58.64	59.54	60.45	61.36	62.28	63.21	64.14	65.07	66.02	66.97
16.0	55.95	56.85	57.75	58.65	59.57	60.49	61.41	62.35	63.29	64.23	65.18	66.14
16.5	55.11	56.01	56.92	57.83	58.75	59.68	60.61	61.55	62.50	63.45	64.41	65.37
17.0	54.32	55.23	56.14	57.06	57.99	58.92	59.86	60.81	61.76	62.72	63.69	64.66
17.5	53.58	54.50	55.41	56.34	57.28	58.22	59.16	60.12	61.08	62.04	63.02	63.99
18.0	52.89	53.81	54.74	55.67	56.61	57.56	58.51	59.47	60.44	61.41	62.39	63.38
18.5	52.24	53.17	54.10	55.04	55.99	56.94	57.90	58.87	59.84	60.83	61.81	62.81
19.0	51.64	52.57	53.51	54.45	55.41	56.37	57.33	58.31	59.29	60.28	61.27	62.27
19.5	51.07	52.00	52.95	53.90	54.86	55.83	56.80	57.78	58.77	59.76	60.76	61.77
20.0	50.53	51.47	52.42	53.38	54.35	55.32	56.30	57.29	58.28	59.28	60.29	61.31
20.5	50.02	50.97	51.93	52.89	53.87	54.85	55.83	56.83	57.83	58.83	59.85	60.87
21.0	49.55	50.50	51.46	52.44	53.41	54.40	55.39	56.39	57.40	58.41	59.43	60.46
21.5	49.09	50.06	51.03	52.00	52.99	53.98	54.98	55.98	57.00	58.02	59.05	60.08
22.0	48.67	49.64	50.61	51.60	52.59	53.58	54.59	55.60	56.62	57.65	58.68	59.72
22.5	48.27	49.24	50.22	51.21	52.21	53.21	54.22	55.24	56.27	57.30	58.34	59.38
23.0	47.89	48.87	49.85	50.85	51.85	52.86	53.88	54.90	55.93	56.97	58.02	59.07
23.5	47.53	48.51	49.50	50.50	51.51	52.53	53.55	54.58	55.62	56.66	57.71	58.77
24.0	47.19	48.18	49.17	50.18	51.19	52.22	53.24	54.28	55.32	56.37	57.43	58.49
24.5	46.86	47.86	48.86	49.87	50.89	51.92	52.95	54.00	55.04	56.10	57.16	58.23
25.0	46.56	47.56	48.57	49.58	50.61	51.64	52.68	53.73	54.78	55.84	56.91	57.99
25.5	46.26	47.27	48.28	49.31	50.34	51.38	52.42	53.47	54.53	55.60	56.67	57.75
26.0	45.99	47.00	48.02	49.05	50.08	51.13	52.18	53.23	54.30	55.37	56.45	57.54
26.5	45.72	46.74	47.77	48.80	49.84	50.89	51.94	53.01	54.08	55.16	56.24	57.33
27.0	45.47	46.50	47.53	48.56	49.61	50.66	51.73	52.79	53.87	54.95	56.04	57.14
27.5	45.24	46.26	47.30	48.34	49.39	50.45	51.52	52.59	53.67	54.76	55.85	56.95
28.0	45.01	46.04	47.08	48.13	49.19	50.25	51.32	52.40	53.49	54.58	55.68	56.78
28.5	44.79	45.83	46.88	47.93	48.99	50.06	51.13	52.22	53.31	54.41	55.51	56.62
29.0	44.59	45.63	46.68	47.74	48.80	49.88	50.96	52.05	53.14	54.24	55.35	56.46
29.5	44.39	45.44	46.49	47.56	48.63	49.71	50.79	51.88	52.98	54.09	55.20	56.32
30.0	44.21	45.26	46.32	47.38	48.46	49.54	50.63	51.73	52.83	53.94	55.06	56.18
35	42.75	43.84	44.94	46.05	47.17	48.29	49.42	50.56	51.70	52.85	54.01	55.17
40	41.82	42.95	44.08	45.23	46.38	47.53	48.69	49.86	51.03	52.21	53.40	54.58

Table 2

SEMI-ANNUAL

PAYMENT REQUIRED TO AMORTIZE A $1000.00 LOAN

INTEREST	11.00%	11.25%	11.50%	11.75%	12.00%	12.25%	12.50%	12.75%	13.00%	13.25%	13.50%	13.75%
YEARS												
.5	1055.00	1056.25	1057.50	1C58.75	1060.00	1061.25	1062.50	1063.75	1065.00	1066.25	1067.50	1068.75
1.0	541.62	542.58	543.53	544.49	545.44	546.40	547.35	548.31	549.27	550.22	551.18	552.14
1.5	370.66	371.52	372.39	373.25	374.11	374.98	375.85	376.71	377.58	378.45	379.32	380.19
2.0	285.30	286.12	286.95	287.77	288.60	289.42	290.25	291.08	291.91	292.74	293.57	294.40
2.5	234.18	234.98	235.79	236.59	237.40	238.21	239.02	239.83	240.64	241.45	242.27	243.08
3.0	200.18	200.98	201.77	202.57	203.37	204.17	204.97	205.77	206.57	207.38	208.18	208.99
3.5	175.97	176.76	177.55	178.34	179.14	179.94	180.73	181.53	182.34	183.14	183.94	184.75
4.0	157.87	158.66	159.45	160.25	161.04	161.84	162.64	163.44	164.24	165.05	165.85	166.66
4.5	143.84	144.64	145.43	146.23	147.03	147.83	148.63	149.44	150.24	151.05	151.86	152.68
5.0	132.67	133.47	134.27	135.07	135.87	136.68	137.49	138.30	139.11	139.92	140.74	141.56
5.5	123.58	124.38	125.18	125.99	126.80	127.61	128.42	129.24	130.06	130.88	131.71	132.53
6.0	116.03	116.84	117.65	118.47	119.28	120.10	120.92	121.75	122.57	123.40	124.23	125.07
6.5	109.69	110.50	111.32	112.14	112.97	113.79	114.62	115.45	116.29	117.13	117.97	118.81
7.0	104.28	105.11	105.93	106.76	107.59	108.42	109.26	110.10	110.95	111.79	112.64	113.49
7.5	99.63	100.46	101.29	102.13	102.97	103.81	104.66	105.51	106.36	107.21	108.07	108.93
8.0	95.59	96.42	97.27	98.11	98.96	99.81	100.66	101.52	102.38	103.25	104.12	104.99
8.5	92.05	92.89	93.74	94.59	95.45	96.31	97.17	98.04	98.91	99.79	100.66	101.55
9.0	88.92	89.78	90.64	91.50	92.36	93.23	94.10	94.98	95.86	96.74	97.63	98.52
9.5	86.16	87.02	87.88	88.75	89.63	90.50	91.39	92.27	93.16	94.05	94.95	95.85
10.0	83.68	84.55	85.43	86.31	87.19	88.08	88.97	89.86	90.76	91.66	92.57	93.48
10.5	81.47	82.35	83.23	84.12	85.01	85.91	86.81	87.71	88.62	89.53	90.45	91.37
11.0	79.48	80.36	81.25	82.15	83.05	83.96	84.86	85.78	86.70	87.62	88.55	89.48
11.5	77.67	78.57	79.47	80.37	81.28	82.20	83.12	84.04	84.97	85.90	86.83	87.77
12.0	76.04	76.94	77.85	78.77	79.68	80.61	81.53	82.47	83.40	84.34	85.29	86.24
12.5	74.55	75.47	76.38	77.30	78.23	79.16	80.10	81.04	81.99	82.94	83.89	84.85
13.0	73.20	74.12	75.04	75.97	76.91	77.85	78.79	79.74	80.70	81.66	82.62	83.59
13.5	71.96	72.89	73.82	74.76	75.70	76.65	77.61	78.56	79.53	80.50	81.47	82.45
14.0	70.82	71.76	72.70	73.65	74.60	75.56	76.52	77.49	78.46	79.44	80.42	81.41
14.5	69.77	70.72	71.67	72.62	73.58	74.55	75.52	76.50	77.48	78.47	79.46	80.45
15.0	68.81	69.76	70.72	71.68	72.65	73.63	74.61	75.59	76.58	77.58	78.58	79.58
15.5	67.92	68.88	69.85	70.82	71.80	72.78	73.77	74.76	75.76	76.76	77.77	78.78
16.0	67.10	68.07	69.04	70.02	71.01	72.00	72.99	74.00	75.00	76.01	77.03	78.05
16.5	66.34	67.32	68.30	69.28	70.28	71.28	72.28	73.29	74.30	75.32	76.35	77.38
17.0	65.63	66.62	67.61	68.60	69.60	70.61	71.62	72.64	73.66	74.69	75.72	76.76
17.5	64.97	65.97	-66.97	67.97	68.98	69.99	71.01	72.04	73.07	74.10	75.14	76.19
18.0	64.37	65.37	66.37	67.38	68.40	69.42	70.45	71.48	72.52	73.56	74.61	75.66
18.5	63.80	64.81	65.82	66.84	67.86	68.89	69.93	70.97	72.01	73.06	74.12	75.18
19.0	63.28	64.29	65.31	66.33	67.36	68.40	69.44	70.49	71.54	72.60	73.66	74.73
19.5	62.78	63.80	64.83	65.86	66.90	67.94	68.99	70.04	71.10	72.17	73.24	74.31
20.0	62.33	63.35	64.38	65.42	66.47	67.52	68.57	69.63	70.70	71.77	72.85	73.93
20.5	61.90	62.93	63.97	65.01	66.06	67.12	68.18	69.25	70.32	71.40	72.48	73.57
21.0	61.49	62.53	63.58	64.63	65.69	66.75	67.82	68.89	69.97	71.06	72.15	73.24
21.5	61.12	62.16	63.22	64.27	65.34	66.41	67.48	68.56	69.65	70.74	71.83	72.94
22.0	60.77	61.82	62.88	63.94	65.01	66.09	67.17	68.25	69.35	70.44	71.54	72.65
22.5	60.44	61.49	62.56	63.63	64.71	65.79	66.87	67.97	69.06	70.17	71.28	72.39
23.0	60.13	61.19	62.26	63.34	64.42	65.51	66.60	67.70	68.80	69.91	71.02	72.14
23.5	59.84	60.91	61.98	63.06	64.15	65.25	66.34	67.45	68.56	69.67	70.79	71.91
24.0	59.56	60.64	61.72	62.81	63.90	65.00	66.11	67.22	68.33	69.45	70.57	71.70
24.5	59.31	60.39	61.48	62.57	63.67	64.77	65.88	67.00	68.12	69.24	70.37	71.51
25.0	59.07	60.15	61.25	62.35	63.45	64.56	65.67	66.79	67.92	69.05	70.18	71.32
25.5	58.84	59.93	61.03	62.13	63.24	64.36	65.48	66.60	67.73	68.87	70.01	71.15
26.0	58.63	59.72	60.83	61.94	63.05	64.17	65.30	66.43	67.56	68.70	69.84	70.99
26.5	58.43	59.53	60.64	61.75	62.87	64.00	65.12	66.26	67.40	68.54	69.69	70.84
27.0	58.24	59.34	60.46	61.58	62.70	63.83	64.96	66.10	67.25	68.40	69.55	70.71
27.5	58.06	59.17	60.29	61.41	62.54	63.68	64.81	65.96	67.11	68.26	69.42	70.58
28.0	57.89	59.01	60.13	61.26	62.39	63.53	64.67	65.82	66.97	68.13	69.29	70.46
28.5	57.73	58.86	59.98	61.11	62.25	63.39	64.54	65.69	66.85	68.01	69.18	70.34
29.0	57.59	58.71	59.84	60.98	62.12	63.27	64.42	65.57	66.73	67.90	69.07	70.24
29.5	57.44	58.57	59.71	60.85	62.00	63.15	64.30	65.46	66.63	67.79	68.97	70.14
30.0	57.31	58.45	59.59	60.73	61.88	63.04	64.19	65.36	66.53	67.70	68.87	70.05
35	56.33	57.50	58.68	59.86	61.04	62.22	63.42	64.61	65.81	67.01	68.21	69.42
40	55.77	56.97	58.17	59.37	60.58	61.79	63.00	64.21	65.43	66.65	67.87	69.09

Table 2

SEMI-ANNUAL

PAYMENT REQUIRED TO AMORTIZE A $1000.00 LOAN

TEREST	14.00%	14.25%	14.50%	14.75%	15.00%	15.25%	15.50%	15.75%	16.00%	16.25%	16.50%	16.75%
YEARS												
.5	1070.00	1071.25	1072.50	1073.75	1075.00	1076.25	1077.50	1078.75	1080.00	1081.25	1082.50	1083.75
1.0	553.10	554.06	555.01	555.97	556.93	557.89	558.85	559.81	560.77	561.74	562.70	563.66
1.5	381.06	381.93	382.80	383.67	384.54	385.42	386.29	387.16	388.04	388.91	389.79	390.67
2.0	295.23	296.07	296.90	297.74	298.57	299.41	300.25	301.09	301.93	302.77	303.61	304.45
2.5	243.90	244.71	245.53	246.35	247.17	247.99	248.81	249.64	250.46	251.29	252.11	252.94
3.0	209.80	210.61	211.42	212.24	213.05	213.87	214.68	215.50	216.32	217.14	217.96	218.79
3.5	185.56	186.37	187.18	187.99	188.81	189.62	190.44	191.26	192.08	192.90	193.72	194.55
4.0	167.47	168.28	169.10	169.91	170.73	171.55	172.37	173.20	174.02	174.85	175.67	176.50
4.5	153.49	154.31	155.13	155.95	156.77	157.60	158.42	159.25	160.08	160.92	161.75	162.59
5.0	142.38	143.21	144.03	144.86	145.69	146.52	147.36	148.20	149.03	149.88	150.72	151.56
5.5	133.36	134.19	135.03	135.86	136.70	137.54	138.39	139.23	140.08	140.93	141.78	142.64
6.0	125.91	126.75	127.59	128.43	129.28	130.13	130.99	131.84	132.70	133.56	134.42	135.29
6.5	119.66	120.50	121.36	122.21	123.07	123.93	124.79	125.66	126.53	127.40	128.27	129.15
7.0	114.35	115.21	116.07	116.93	117.80	118.67	119.55	120.42	121.30	122.18	123.07	123.96
7.5	109.80	110.67	111.54	112.41	113.29	114.17	115.06	115.94	116.83	117.73	118.62	119.52
8.0	105.86	106.74	107.62	108.51	109.40	110.29	111.18	112.08	112.98	113.89	114.79	115.70
8.5	102.43	103.32	104.21	105.11	106.01	106.91	107.81	108.72	109.63	110.55	111.47	112.39
9.0	99.42	100.32	101.22	102.12	103.03	103.95	104.86	105.78	106.71	107.63	108.56	109.50
9.5	96.76	97.67	98.58	99.50	100.42	101.34	102.27	103.20	104.13	105.07	106.01	106.96
10.0	94.40	95.32	96.24	97.17	98.10	99.03	99.97	100.91	101.86	102.81	103.76	104.72
10.5	92.29	93.22	94.16	95.09	96.03	96.98	97.93	98.88	99.84	100.80	101.76	102.73
11.0	90.41	91.35	92.29	93.24	94.19	95.15	96.11	97.07	98.04	99.01	99.98	100.96
11.5	88.72	89.67	90.62	91.58	92.54	93.51	94.48	95.45	96.43	97.41	98.39	99.38
12.0	87.19	88.15	89.12	90.08	91.06	92.03	93.01	93.99	94.98	95.98	96.97	97.97
12.5	85.82	86.78	87.76	88.73	89.72	90.70	91.69	92.69	93.68	94.69	95.69	96.70
13.0	84.57	85.54	86.53	87.51	88.50	89.50	90.50	91.50	92.51	93.52	94.54	95.56
13.5	83.43	84.42	85.41	86.41	87.41	88.41	89.42	90.44	91.45	92.48	93.50	94.53
14.0	82.40	83.39	84.39	85.40	86.41	87.42	88.44	89.47	90.49	91.53	92.56	93.60
14.5	81.45	82.46	83.47	84.48	85.50	86.53	87.55	88.59	89.62	90.66	91.71	92.76
15.0	80.59	81.61	82.62	83.65	84.68	85.71	86.75	87.79	88.83	89.88	90.94	91.99
15.5	79.80	80.82	81.85	82.88	83.92	84.96	86.01	87.06	88.11	89.17	90.23	91.30
16.0	79.08	80.11	81.15	82.19	83.23	84.28	85.33	86.39	87.46	88.52	89.59	90.67
16.5	78.41	79.45	80.50	81.55	82.60	83.66	84.72	85.79	86.86	87.93	89.01	90.09
17.0	77.80	78.85	79.90	80.96	82.02	83.09	84.16	85.23	86.31	87.39	88.48	89.57
17.5	77.24	78.29	79.35	80.42	81.49	82.56	83.64	84.72	85.81	86.90	87.99	89.09
18.0	76.72	77.78	78.85	79.92	81.00	82.08	83.17	84.26	85.35	86.45	87.55	88.66
18.5	76.24	77.31	78.39	79.47	80.55	81.64	82.73	83.83	84.93	86.03	87.14	88.26
19.0	75.80	76.88	77.96	79.05	80.14	81.23	82.33	83.44	84.54	85.66	86.77	87.89
19.5	75.39	76.48	77.56	78.66	79.76	80.86	81.96	83.08	84.19	85.31	86.43	87.56
20.0	75.01	76.11	77.20	78.30	79.41	80.51	81.63	82.74	83.87	84.99	86.12	87.25
20.5	74.66	75.76	76.86	77.97	79.08	80.20	81.32	82.44	83.57	84.70	85.83	86.97
21.0	74.34	75.44	76.55	77.67	78.78	79.90	81.03	82.16	83.29	84.43	85.57	86.71
21.5	74.04	75.15	76.27	77.38	78.51	79.63	80.77	81.90	83.04	84.18	85.33	86.48
22.0	73.76	74.88	76.00	77.12	78.25	79.38	80.52	81.66	82.81	83.95	85.11	86.26
22.5	73.50	74.63	75.75	76.88	78.02	79.15	80.30	81.44	82.59	83.75	84.90	86.06
23.0	73.26	74.39	75.52	76.66	77.80	78.94	80.09	81.24	82.39	83.55	84.71	85.88
23.5	73.04	74.17	75.31	76.45	77.60	78.75	79.90	81.05	82.21	83.38	84.54	85.71
24.0	72.84	73.97	75.11	76.26	77.41	78.56	79.72	80.88	82.05	83.21	84.38	85.56
24.5	72.64	73.79	74.93	76.08	77.24	78.40	79.56	80.72	81.89	83.06	84.24	85.41
25.0	72.46	73.61	74.76	75.92	77.08	78.24	79.41	80.58	81.75	82.92	84.10	85.28
25.5	72.30	73.45	74.61	75.77	76.93	78.10	79.27	80.44	81.62	82.80	83.98	85.16
26.0	72.14	73.30	74.46	75.62	76.79	77.96	79.14	80.31	81.49	82.68	83.86	85.05
26.5	72.00	73.16	74.32	75.49	76.66	77.84	79.02	80.20	81.38	82.57	83.76	84.95
27.0	71.87	73.03	74.20	75.37	76.55	77.72	78.91	80.09	81.28	82.47	83.66	84.86
27.5	71.74	72.91	74.08	75.26	76.44	77.62	78.80	79.99	81.18	82.38	83.57	84.77
28.0	71.63	72.80	73.97	75.15	76.33	77.52	78.71	79.90	81.09	82.29	83.49	84.69
28.5	71.52	72.69	73.87	75.05	76.24	77.43	78.62	79.82	81.01	82.21	83.41	84.62
29.0	71.42	72.60	73.78	74.96	76.15	77.35	78.54	79.74	80.94	82.14	83.34	84.55
29.5	71.32	72.50	73.69	74.88	76.07	77.27	78.46	79.66	80.87	82.07	83.28	84.49
30.0	71.23	72.42	73.61	74.80	76.00	77.19	78.39	79.60	80.80	82.01	83.22	84.43
35	70.62	71.84	73.05	74.26	75.48	76.70	77.92	79.15	80.37	81.60	82.83	84.06
40	70.32	71.55	72.77	74.00	75.24	76.47	77.70	78.94	80.17	81.41	82.65	83.89

Table 2

SEMI-ANNUAL

PAYMENT REQUIRED TO AMORTIZE A $1000.00 LOAN

INTEREST	17.00%	17.25%	17.50%	17.75%	18.00%	18.25%	18.50%	18.75%	19.00%	19.25%	19.50%	19.75%
YEARS												
.5	1085.00	1086.25	1087.50	1088.75	1090.00	1091.25	1092.50	1093.75	1095.00	1096.25	1097.50	1098.75
1.0	564.62	565.58	566.55	567.51	568.47	569.44	570.40	571.37	572.33	573.30	574.26	575.23
1.5	391.54	392.42	393.30	394.18	395.06	395.94	396.82	397.70	398.58	399.47	400.35	401.24
2.0	305.29	306.14	306.98	307.83	308.67	309.52	310.37	311.22	312.07	312.92	313.77	314.62
2.5	253.77	254.60	255.43	256.26	257.10	257.93	258.77	259.60	260.44	261.28	262.12	262.96
3.0	219.61	220.44	221.27	222.09	222.92	223.76	224.59	225.42	226.26	227.09	227.93	228.77
3.5	195.37	196.20	197.03	197.86	198.70	199.53	200.37	201.20	202.04	202.88	203.72	204.57
4.0	177.34	178.17	179.00	179.84	180.68	181.52	182.36	183.21	184.05	184.90	185.75	186.60
4.5	163.43	164.27	165.11	165.96	166.80	167.65	168.50	169.36	170.21	171.07	171.92	172.78
5.0	152.41	153.26	154.11	154.97	155.83	156.68	157.54	158.41	159.27	160.14	161.01	161.88
5.5	143.50	144.36	145.22	146.08	146.95	147.82	148.69	149.57	150.44	151.32	152.20	153.08
6.0	136.16	137.03	137.90	138.78	139.66	140.54	141.42	142.30	143.19	144.08	144.98	145.87
6.5	130.03	130.91	131.79	132.68	133.57	134.46	135.36	136.26	137.16	138.06	138.97	139.87
7.0	124.85	125.74	126.64	127.54	128.44	129.34	130.25	131.16	132.07	132.99	133.91	134.83
7.5	120.43	121.33	122.24	123.15	124.06	124.98	125.90	126.82	127.75	128.68	129.61	130.54
8.0	116.62	117.54	118.46	119.38	120.30	121.23	122.17	123.10	124.04	124.98	125.92	126.87
8.5	113.32	114.25	115.18	116.11	117.05	117.99	118.94	119.89	120.84	121.79	122.75	123.71
9.0	110.44	111.38	112.32	113.27	114.22	115.17	116.13	117.09	118.05	119.02	119.99	120.96
9.5	107.91	108.86	109.81	110.77	111.74	112.70	113.67	114.64	115.62	116.60	117.58	118.56
10.0	105.68	106.64	107.61	108.58	109.55	110.53	111.51	112.49	113.48	114.47	115.47	116.46
10.5	103.70	104.68	105.65	106.64	107.62	108.61	109.60	110.60	111.60	112.60	113.61	114.62
11.0	101.94	102.93	103.92	104.91	105.91	106.91	107.91	108.92	109.93	110.95	111.96	112.99
11.5	100.38	101.37	102.37	103.38	104.39	105.40	106.41	107.43	108.45	109.48	110.51	111.54
12.0	98.97	99.98	100.99	102.01	103.03	104.05	105.08	106.11	107.14	108.18	109.21	110.26
12.5	97.72	98.73	99.76	100.78	101.81	102.84	103.88	104.92	105.96	107.01	108.06	109.12
13.0	96.59	97.61	98.65	99.68	100.72	101.76	102.81	103.86	104.91	105.97	107.03	108.10
13.5	95.57	96.60	97.64	98.69	99.74	100.79	101.85	102.91	103.97	105.04	106.11	107.19
14.0	94.64	95.69	96.74	97.80	98.86	99.92	100.99	102.06	103.13	104.21	105.29	106.37
14.5	93.81	94.87	95.93	96.99	98.06	99.13	100.21	101.29	102.37	103.46	104.54	105.64
15.0	93.06	94.12	95.19	96.26	97.34	98.42	99.51	100.59	101.69	102.78	103.88	104.98
15.5	92.37	93.44	94.52	95.60	96.69	97.78	98.87	99.97	101.07	102.17	103.28	104.39
16.0	91.75	92.83	93.92	95.01	96.10	97.20	98.30	99.40	100.51	101.62	102.74	103.86
16.5	91.18	92.27	93.37	94.46	95.57	96.67	97.78	98.89	100.01	101.13	102.25	103.38
17.0	90.66	91.76	92.87	93.97	95.08	96.19	97.31	98.43	99.55	100.68	101.81	102.94
17.5	90.19	91.30	92.41	93.52	94.64	95.76	96.89	98.01	99.14	100.28	101.41	102.55
18.0	89.77	90.88	92.00	93.12	94.24	95.37	96.50	97.63	98.77	99.91	101.05	102.20
18.5	89.37	90.49	91.62	92.74	93.88	95.01	96.15	97.29	98.43	99.58	100.73	101.88
19.0	89.01	90.14	91.27	92.41	93.54	94.68	95.83	96.97	98.12	99.28	100.43	101.59
19.5	88.69	89.82	90.96	92.10	93.24	94.39	95.54	96.69	97.85	99.00	100.17	101.33
20.0	88.39	89.53	90.67	91.82	92.96	94.12	95.27	96.43	97.59	98.76	99.92	101.09
20.5	88.11	89.26	90.41	91.56	92.71	93.87	95.03	96.20	97.36	98.53	99.70	100.88
21.0	87.86	89.01	90.17	91.32	92.48	93.65	94.81	95.98	97.15	98.33	99.50	100.68
21.5	87.63	88.79	89.95	91.11	92.27	93.44	94.61	95.79	96.96	98.14	99.32	100.51
22.0	87.42	88.58	89.74	90.91	92.08	93.25	94.43	95.61	96.79	97.97	99.16	100.35
22.5	87.22	88.39	89.56	90.73	91.91	93.08	94.26	95.45	96.63	97.82	99.01	100.20
23.0	87.05	88.22	89.39	90.57	91.75	92.93	94.11	95.30	96.49	97.68	98.87	100.07
23.5	86.88	88.06	89.24	90.42	91.60	92.79	93.97	95.17	96.36	97.55	98.75	99.95
24.0	86.73	87.91	89.09	90.28	91.47	92.66	93.85	95.04	96.24	97.44	98.64	99.84
24.5	86.60	87.78	88.96	90.15	91.34	92.54	93.73	94.93	96.13	97.33	98.54	99.74
25.0	86.47	87.66	88.85	90.04	91.23	92.43	93.63	94.83	96.03	97.24	98.44	99.65
25.5	86.35	87.54	88.74	89.93	91.13	92.33	93.53	94.74	95.94	97.15	98.36	99.57
26.0	86.24	87.44	88.64	89.83	91.04	92.24	93.44	94.65	95.86	97.07	98.28	99.50
26.5	86.15	87.34	88.54	89.75	90.95	92.16	93.36	94.57	95.79	97.00	98.21	99.43
27.0	86.06	87.26	88.46	89.66	90.87	92.08	93.29	94.50	95.72	96.93	98.15	99.37
27.5	85.97	87.18	88.38	89.59	90.80	92.01	93.22	94.44	95.65	96.87	98.09	99.31
28.0	85.90	87.10	88.31	89.52	90.73	91.95	93.16	94.38	95.60	96.82	98.04	99.26
28.5	85.83	87.03	88.24	89.46	90.67	91.89	93.11	94.33	95.55	96.77	97.99	99.22
29.0	85.76	86.97	88.18	89.40	90.62	91.83	93.05	94.28	95.50	96.72	97.95	99.18
29.5	85.70	86.91	88.13	89.35	90.57	91.79	93.01	94.23	95.46	96.68	97.91	99.14
30.0	85.65	86.86	88.08	89.30	90.52	91.74	92.97	94.19	95.42	96.64	97.87	99.10
35.0	85.29	86.52	87.75	88.99	90.22	91.46	92.69	93.93	95.17	96.41	97.65	98.89
40.0	85.13	86.37	87.61	88.85	90.10	91.34	92.58	93.83	95.07	96.32	97.56	98.81

Table 2

SEMI-ANNUAL

PAYMENT REQUIRED TO AMORTIZE A $1000.00 LOAN

INTEREST	20.00%	20.25%	20.50%	20.75%	21.00%	21.25%	21.50%	21.75%	22.00%	22.25%	22.50%	22.75%
YEARS												
.5	1100.00	1101.25	1102.50	1103.75	1105.00	1106.25	1107.50	1108.75	1110.00	1111.25	1112.50	1113.75
1.0	576.20	577.16	578.13	579.10	580.06	581.03	582.00	582.97	583.94	584.91	585.88	586.85
1.5	402.12	403.01	403.89	404.78	405.66	406.55	407.44	408.33	409.22	410.11	411.00	411.89
2.0	315.48	316.33	317.18	318.04	318.90	319.75	320.61	321.47	322.33	323.19	324.05	324.92
2.5	263.80	264.65	265.49	266.33	267.18	268.03	268.88	269.73	270.58	271.43	272.28	273.13
3.0	229.61	230.45	231.30	232.14	232.99	233.83	234.68	235.53	236.38	237.23	238.09	238.94
3.5	205.41	206.26	207.10	207.95	208.80	209.66	210.51	211.36	212.22	213.08	213.94	214.80
4.0	187.45	188.30	189.16	190.02	190.87	191.73	192.60	193.46	194.33	195.19	196.06	196.93
4.5	173.65	174.51	175.37	176.24	177.11	177.98	178.86	179.73	180.61	181.49	182.37	183.25
5.0	162.75	163.63	164.50	165.38	166.26	167.15	168.03	168.92	169.81	170.70	171.59	172.49
5.5	153.97	154.86	155.74	156.64	157.53	158.43	159.32	160.22	161.13	162.03	162.94	163.85
6.0	146.77	147.67	148.57	149.47	150.38	151.29	152.20	153.12	154.03	154.95	155.87	156.79
6.5	140.78	141.70	142.61	143.53	144.45	145.37	146.30	147.23	148.16	149.09	150.02	150.96
7.0	135.75	136.68	137.61	138.54	139.47	140.41	141.35	142.29	143.23	144.18	145.13	146.08
7.5	131.48	132.42	133.36	134.31	135.25	136.20	137.16	138.11	139.07	140.03	140.99	141.96
8.0	127.82	128.77	129.73	130.69	131.65	132.61	133.58	134.55	135.52	136.50	137.47	138.45
8.5	124.67	125.63	126.60	127.58	128.55	129.53	130.51	131.49	132.48	133.47	134.46	135.45
9.0	121.94	122.91	123.90	124.88	125.87	126.86	127.85	128.85	129.85	130.85	131.85	132.86
9.5	119.55	120.54	121.54	122.54	123.54	124.54	125.55	126.56	127.57	128.58	129.60	130.62
10.0	117.46	118.47	119.48	120.49	121.50	122.51	123.53	124.56	125.58	126.61	127.64	128.67
10.5	115.63	116.65	117.66	118.69	119.71	120.74	121.77	122.81	123.84	124.88	125.93	126.97
11.0	114.01	115.04	116.07	117.10	118.14	119.18	120.22	121.27	122.32	123.37	124.43	125.48
11.5	112.58	113.62	114.66	115.70	116.75	117.80	118.86	119.92	120.98	122.04	123.11	124.18
12.0	111.30	112.35	113.41	114.46	115.52	116.59	117.65	118.72	119.79	120.87	121.94	123.02
12.5	110.17	111.23	112.30	113.36	114.43	115.51	116.58	117.66	118.75	119.83	120.92	122.01
13.0	109.16	110.23	111.31	112.39	113.47	114.55	115.64	116.73	117.82	118.91	120.01	121.11
13.5	108.26	109.34	110.43	111.51	112.60	113.70	114.79	115.89	116.99	118.10	119.21	120.32
14.0	107.46	108.55	109.64	110.74	111.83	112.94	114.04	115.15	116.26	117.38	118.49	119.61
14.5	106.73	107.83	108.93	110.04	111.15	112.26	113.37	114.49	115.61	116.73	117.86	118.99
15.0	106.08	107.19	108.30	109.42	110.53	111.65	112.78	113.90	115.03	116.16	117.29	118.43
15.5	105.50	106.62	107.74	108.86	109.98	111.11	112.24	113.38	114.51	115.65	116.79	117.94
16.0	104.98	106.10	107.23	108.36	109.49	110.63	111.76	112.90	114.05	115.19	116.34	117.49
16.5	104.50	105.64	106.77	107.91	109.05	110.19	111.34	112.48	113.63	114.79	115.94	117.10
17.0	104.08	105.22	106.36	107.50	108.65	109.80	110.95	112.11	113.26	114.42	115.59	116.75
17.5	103.69	104.84	105.99	107.14	108.29	109.45	110.61	111.77	112.93	114.10	115.27	116.44
18.0	103.35	104.50	105.65	106.81	107.97	109.13	110.30	111.47	112.64	113.81	114.98	116.16
18.5	103.03	104.19	105.35	106.52	107.68	108.85	110.02	111.19	112.37	113.55	114.73	115.91
19.0	102.75	103.92	105.08	106.25	107.42	108.60	109.77	110.95	112.13	113.31	114.50	115.68
19.5	102.50	103.67	104.84	106.01	107.19	108.37	109.55	110.73	111.92	113.10	114.29	115.48
20.0	102.26	103.44	104.62	105.79	106.98	108.16	109.35	110.53	111.72	112.92	114.11	115.30
20.5	102.05	103.23	104.42	105.60	106.79	107.97	109.16	110.36	111.55	112.75	113.95	115.14
21.0	101.86	103.05	104.24	105.42	106.61	107.81	109.00	110.20	111.40	112.60	113.80	115.00
21.5	101.69	102.88	104.07	105.26	106.46	107.66	108.85	110.05	111.26	112.46	113.67	114.87
22.0	101.54	102.73	103.92	105.12	106.32	107.52	108.72	109.93	111.13	112.34	113.55	114.76
22.5	101.40	102.59	103.79	104.99	106.19	107.40	108.60	109.81	111.02	112.23	113.44	114.65
23.0	101.27	102.47	103.67	104.87	106.08	107.29	108.49	109.71	110.92	112.13	113.35	114.56
23.5	101.15	102.36	103.56	104.77	105.98	107.19	108.40	109.61	110.83	112.04	113.26	114.48
24.0	101.05	102.25	103.46	104.67	105.88	107.10	108.31	109.53	110.74	111.96	113.18	114.40
24.5	100.95	102.16	103.37	104.58	105.80	107.01	108.23	109.45	110.67	111.89	113.11	114.34
25.0	100.86	102.08	103.29	104.51	105.72	106.94	108.16	109.38	110.60	111.83	113.05	114.28
25.5	100.79	102.00	103.22	104.43	105.65	106.87	108.10	109.32	110.54	111.77	113.00	114.22
26.0	100.71	101.93	103.15	104.37	105.59	106.82	108.04	109.26	110.49	111.72	112.95	114.18
26.5	100.65	101.87	103.09	104.31	105.54	106.76	107.99	109.21	110.44	111.67	112.90	114.13
27.0	100.59	101.81	103.04	104.26	105.49	106.71	107.94	109.17	110.40	111.63	112.86	114.09
27.5	100.54	101.76	102.99	104.21	105.44	106.67	107.90	109.13	110.36	111.59	112.83	114.06
28.0	100.49	101.71	102.94	104.17	105.40	106.63	107.86	109.09	110.32	111.56	112.79	114.03
28.5	100.44	101.67	102.90	104.13	105.36	106.59	107.82	109.06	110.29	111.53	112.76	114.00
29.0	100.40	101.63	102.86	104.09	105.33	106.56	107.79	109.03	110.26	111.50	112.74	113.98
29.5	100.37	101.60	102.83	104.06	105.30	106.53	107.77	109.00	110.24	111.48	112.71	113.95
30.0	100.33	101.57	102.80	104.03	105.27	106.50	107.74	108.98	110.22	111.45	112.69	113.93
35	100.13	101.37	102.62	103.86	105.10	106.35	107.59	108.83	110.08	111.32	112.57	113.82
40	100.05	101.30	102.55	103.79	105.04	106.29	107.54	108.78	110.03	111.28	112.53	113.78

Table 2

SEMI-ANNUAL

PAYMENT REQUIRED TO AMORTIZE A $1000.00 LOAN

INTEREST	23.00%	23.25%	23.50%	23.75%	24.00%	24.25%	24.50%	24.75%	25.00%	25.25%	25.50%	25.75%
YEARS												
.5	1115.00	1116.25	1117.50	1118.75	1120.00	1121.25	1122.50	1123.75	1125.00	1126.25	1127.50	1128.75
1.0	587.82	588.79	589.76	590.73	591.70	592.68	593.65	594.62	595.59	596.57	597.54	598.51
1.5	412.78	413.67	414.57	415.46	416.35	417.25	418.14	419.04	419.94	420.83	421.73	422.63
2.0	325.78	326.64	327.51	328.37	329.24	330.11	330.97	331.84	332.71	333.58	334.45	335.33
2.5	273.99	274.84	275.70	276.56	277.41	278.27	279.13	280.00	280.86	281.72	282.59	283.45
3.0	239.80	240.65	241.51	242.37	243.23	244.09	244.96	245.82	246.68	247.55	248.42	249.29
3.5	215.66	216.52	217.39	218.25	219.12	219.99	220.86	221.73	222.61	223.48	224.36	225.24
4.0	197.80	198.68	199.55	200.43	201.31	202.19	203.07	203.95	204.84	205.72	206.61	207.50
4.5	184.13	185.02	185.90	186.79	187.68	188.58	189.47	190.37	191.27	192.16	193.07	193.97
5.0	173.38	174.28	175.18	176.08	176.99	177.90	178.80	179.71	180.63	181.54	182.46	183.37
5.5	164.76	165.67	166.58	167.50	168.42	169.34	170.26	171.19	172.12	173.05	173.98	174.91
6.0	157.72	158.65	159.58	160.51	161.44	162.38	163.32	164.26	165.20	166.14	167.09	168.04
6.5	151.90	152.84	153.79	154.73	155.68	156.63	157.59	158.54	159.50	160.46	161.42	162.39
7.0	147.04	147.99	148.95	149.91	150.88	151.84	152.81	153.78	154.76	155.73	156.71	157.69
7.5	142.93	143.90	144.87	145.85	146.83	147.81	148.79	149.78	150.77	151.76	152.75	153.75
8.0	139.44	140.42	141.41	142.40	143.40	144.39	145.39	146.39	147.39	148.40	149.41	150.42
8.5	136.45	137.45	138.45	139.45	140.46	141.47	142.48	143.50	144.52	145.54	146.56	147.59
9.0	133.87	134.89	135.90	136.92	137.94	138.97	139.99	141.02	142.05	143.09	144.12	145.16
9.5	131.65	132.67	133.70	134.73	135.77	136.81	137.85	138.89	139.93	140.98	142.03	143.08
10.0	129.71	130.75	131.79	132.84	133.88	134.93	135.99	137.04	138.10	139.16	140.22	141.29
10.5	128.02	129.07	130.13	131.19	132.25	133.31	134.37	135.44	136.51	137.58	138.66	139.74
11.0	126.54	127.61	128.67	129.74	130.82	131.89	132.97	134.05	135.13	136.21	137.30	138.39
11.5	125.25	126.32	127.40	128.48	129.56	130.65	131.74	132.83	133.92	135.02	136.12	137.22
12.0	124.11	125.19	126.28	127.37	128.47	129.57	130.66	131.77	132.87	133.98	135.09	136.20
12.5	123.10	124.20	125.30	126.40	127.50	128.61	129.72	130.83	131.95	133.07	134.18	135.31
13.0	122.22	123.32	124.43	125.54	126.66	127.77	128.89	130.01	131.14	132.27	133.39	134.53
13.5	121.43	122.55	123.66	124.79	125.91	127.04	128.16	129.29	130.43	131.56	132.70	133.84
14.0	120.73	121.86	122.99	124.12	125.25	126.38	127.52	128.66	129.80	130.95	132.09	133.24
14.5	120.12	121.25	122.39	123.52	124.67	125.81	126.95	128.10	129.25	130.40	131.56	132.71
15.0	119.57	120.71	121.85	123.00	124.15	125.30	126.45	127.61	128.77	129.92	131.09	132.25
15.5	119.08	120.23	121.38	122.54	123.69	124.85	126.01	127.17	128.34	129.50	130.67	131.84
16.0	118.65	119.80	120.96	122.12	123.29	124.45	125.62	126.79	127.96	129.13	130.31	131.48
16.5	118.26	119.42	120.59	121.76	122.93	124.10	125.27	126.45	127.62	128.80	129.98	131.17
17.0	117.92	119.09	120.26	121.43	122.61	123.78	124.96	126.14	127.33	128.51	129.70	130.89
17.5	117.61	118.78	119.96	121.14	122.32	123.50	124.69	125.88	127.06	128.25	129.45	130.64
18.0	117.34	118.52	119.70	120.88	122.07	123.26	124.45	125.64	126.83	128.03	129.22	130.42
18.5	117.09	118.28	119.46	120.65	121.84	123.04	124.23	125.43	126.63	127.83	129.03	130.23
19.0	116.87	118.06	119.26	120.45	121.64	122.84	124.04	125.24	126.44	127.65	128.85	130.06
19.5	116.68	117.87	119.07	120.27	121.47	122.67	123.87	125.08	126.28	127.49	128.70	129.91
20.0	116.50	117.70	118.90	120.10	121.31	122.51	123.72	124.93	126.14	127.35	128.56	129.78
20.5	116.35	117.55	118.75	119.96	121.17	122.38	123.59	124.80	126.01	127.23	128.44	129.66
21.0	116.21	117.41	118.62	119.83	121.04	122.25	123.47	124.68	125.90	127.12	128.34	129.56
21.5	116.08	117.29	118.50	119.72	120.93	122.15	123.36	124.58	125.80	127.02	128.24	129.46
22.0	115.97	117.18	118.40	119.61	120.83	122.05	123.27	124.49	125.71	126.93	128.16	129.38
22.5	115.87	117.09	118.30	119.52	120.74	121.96	123.18	124.41	125.63	126.86	128.08	129.31
23.0	115.78	117.00	118.22	119.44	120.66	121.89	123.11	124.34	125.56	126.79	128.02	129.25
23.5	115.70	116.92	118.14	119.37	120.59	121.82	123.04	124.27	125.50	126.73	127.96	129.19
24.0	115.63	116.85	118.08	119.30	120.53	121.76	122.98	124.21	125.44	126.68	127.91	129.14
24.5	115.56	116.79	118.02	119.24	120.47	121.70	122.93	124.16	125.40	126.63	127.86	129.10
25.0	115.50	116.73	117.96	119.19	120.42	121.65	122.89	124.12	125.35	126.59	127.82	129.06
25.5	115.45	116.68	117.91	119.14	120.38	121.61	122.84	124.08	125.31	126.55	127.79	129.02
26.0	115.41	116.64	117.87	119.10	120.34	121.57	122.81	124.04	125.28	126.52	127.75	128.99
26.5	115.37	116.60	117.83	119.07	120.30	121.54	122.77	124.01	125.25	126.49	127.73	128.97
27.0	115.33	116.56	117.80	119.03	120.27	121.51	122.74	123.98	125.22	126.46	127.70	128.94
27.5	115.29	116.53	117.77	119.00	120.24	121.48	122.72	123.96	125.20	126.44	127.68	128.92
28.0	115.26	116.50	117.74	118.98	120.22	121.46	122.69	123.94	125.18	126.42	127.66	128.90
28.5	115.24	116.48	117.71	118.95	120.19	121.43	122.67	123.92	125.16	126.40	127.64	128.88
29.0	115.21	116.45	117.69	118.93	120.17	121.41	122.66	123.90	125.14	126.38	127.63	128.87
29.5	115.19	116.43	117.67	118.91	120.15	121.40	122.64	123.88	125.13	126.37	127.61	128.86
30.0	115.17	116.41	117.65	118.90	120.14	121.38	122.62	123.87	125.11	126.36	127.60	128.84
35	115.06	116.31	117.55	118.80	120.05	121.30	122.54	123.79	125.04	126.29	127.53	128.78
40	115.02	116.27	117.52	118.77	120.02	121.27	122.52	123.77	125.02	126.26	127.51	128.76

Table 2

ANNUAL
PAYMENT REQUIRED TO AMORTIZE A $1000.00 LOAN

EREST YEARS	5.00%	5.25%	5.50%	5.75%	6.00%	6.25%	6.50%	6.75%	7.00%	7.25%	7.50%	7.75%
1.0	1050.00	1052.50	1055.00	1057.50	1060.00	1062.50	1065.00	1067.50	1070.00	1072.50	1075.00	1077.50
2.0	537.81	539.72	541.62	543.53	545.44	547.35	549.27	551.18	553.10	555.01	556.93	558.85
3.0	367.21	368.94	370.66	372.39	374.11	375.85	377.58	379.32	381.06	382.80	384.54	386.29
4.0	282.02	283.66	285.30	286.95	288.60	290.25	291.91	293.57	295.23	296.90	298.57	300.25
5.0	230.98	232.58	234.18	235.79	237.40	239.02	240.64	242.27	243.90	245.53	247.17	248.81
6.0	197.02	198.60	200.18	201.77	203.37	204.97	206.57	208.18	209.80	211.42	213.05	214.68
7.0	172.82	174.39	175.97	177.55	179.14	180.73	182.34	183.94	185.56	187.18	188.81	190.44
8.0	154.73	156.29	157.87	159.45	161.04	162.64	164.24	165.85	167.47	169.10	170.73	172.37
9.0	140.70	142.27	143.84	145.43	147.03	148.63	150.24	151.86	153.49	155.13	156.77	158.42
10.0	129.51	131.09	132.67	134.27	135.87	137.49	139.11	140.74	142.38	144.03	145.69	147.36
11.0	120.39	121.98	123.58	125.18	126.80	128.42	130.06	131.71	133.36	135.03	136.70	138.39
12.0	112.83	114.43	116.03	117.65	119.28	120.92	122.57	124.23	125.91	127.59	129.28	130.99
13.0	106.46	108.07	109.69	111.32	112.97	114.62	116.29	117.97	119.66	121.36	123.07	124.79
14.0	101.03	102.65	104.28	105.93	107.59	109.26	110.95	112.64	114.35	116.07	117.80	119.55
15.0	96.35	97.98	99.63	101.29	102.97	104.66	106.36	108.07	109.80	111.54	113.29	115.06
16.0	92.27	93.92	95.59	97.27	98.96	100.66	102.38	104.12	105.86	107.62	109.40	111.18
17.0	88.70	90.37	92.05	93.74	95.45	97.17	98.91	100.66	102.43	104.21	106.01	107.81
18.0	85.55	87.23	88.92	90.64	92.36	94.10	95.86	97.63	99.42	101.22	103.03	104.86
19.0	82.75	84.44	86.16	87.88	89.63	91.39	93.16	94.95	96.76	98.58	100.42	102.27
20.0	80.25	81.96	83.68	85.43	87.19	88.97	90.76	92.57	94.40	96.24	98.10	99.97
21.0	78.00	79.73	81.47	83.23	85.01	86.81	88.62	90.45	92.29	94.16	96.03	97.93
22.0	75.98	77.72	79.48	81.25	83.05	84.86	86.70	88.55	90.41	92.29	94.19	96.11
23.0	74.14	75.90	77.67	79.47	81.28	83.12	84.97	86.83	88.72	90.62	92.54	94.48
24.0	72.48	74.25	76.04	77.85	79.68	81.53	83.40	85.29	87.19	89.12	91.06	93.01
25.0	70.96	72.75	74.55	76.38	78.23	80.10	81.99	83.89	85.82	87.76	89.72	91.69
26.0	69.57	71.37	73.20	75.04	76.91	78.79	80.70	82.62	84.57	86.53	88.50	90.50
27.0	68.30	70.12	71.96	73.82	75.70	77.61	79.53	81.47	83.43	85.41	87.41	89.42
28.0	67.13	68.96	70.82	72.70	74.60	76.52	78.46	80.42	82.40	84.39	86.41	88.44
29.0	66.05	67.90	69.77	71.67	73.58	75.52	77.48	79.46	81.45	83.47	85.50	87.55
30.0	65.06	66.92	68.81	70.72	72.65	74.61	76.58	78.58	80.59	82.62	84.68	86.75
31.0	64.14	66.02	67.92	69.85	71.80	73.77	75.76	77.77	79.80	81.85	83.92	86.01
32.0	63.29	65.18	67.10	69.04	71.01	72.99	75.00	77.03	79.08	81.15	83.23	85.33
33.0	62.50	64.41	66.34	68.30	70.28	72.28	74.30	76.35	78.41	80.50	82.60	84.72
34.0	61.76	63.69	65.63	67.61	69.60	71.62	73.66	75.72	77.80	79.90	82.02	84.16
35.0	61.08	63.02	64.98	66.97	68.98	71.01	73.07	75.14	77.24	79.35	81.49	83.64
36.0	60.44	62.39	64.37	66.37	68.40	70.45	72.52	74.61	76.72	78.85	81.00	83.17
37.0	59.84	61.81	63.80	65.82	67.86	69.93	72.01	74.12	76.24	78.39	80.55	82.73
38.0	59.29	61.27	63.28	65.31	67.36	69.44	71.54	73.66	75.80	77.96	80.14	82.33
39.0	58.77	60.76	62.78	64.83	66.90	68.99	71.10	73.24	75.39	77.56	79.76	81.96
40.0	58.28	60.29	62.33	64.38	66.47	68.57	70.70	72.85	75.01	77.20	79.41	81.63
41.0	57.83	59.85	61.90	63.97	66.06	68.18	70.32	72.48	74.66	76.86	79.08	81.32
42.0	57.40	59.43	61.49	63.58	65.69	67.82	69.97	72.15	74.34	76.55	78.78	81.03
43.0	57.00	59.05	61.12	63.22	65.34	67.48	69.65	71.83	74.04	76.27	78.51	80.77
44.0	56.62	58.68	60.77	62.88	65.01	67.17	69.35	71.54	73.76	76.00	78.25	80.52
45.0	56.27	58.34	60.44	62.56	64.71	66.87	69.06	71.28	73.50	75.75	78.02	80.30
46.0	55.93	58.02	60.13	62.26	64.42	66.60	68.80	71.02	73.26	75.52	77.80	80.09
47.0	55.62	57.71	59.84	61.98	64.15	66.34	68.56	70.79	73.04	75.31	77.60	79.90
48.0	55.32	57.43	59.56	61.72	63.90	66.11	68.33	70.57	72.84	75.11	77.41	79.72
49.0	55.04	57.16	59.31	61.48	63.67	65.88	68.12	70.37	72.64	74.93	77.24	79.56
50.0	54.78	56.91	59.07	61.25	63.45	65.67	67.92	70.18	72.46	74.76	77.08	79.41

Table 2

ANNUAL

PAYMENT REQUIRED TO AMORTIZE A $1000.00 LOAN

INTEREST YEARS	8.00%	8.25%	8.50%	8.75%	9.00%	9.25%	9.50%	9.75%	10.00%	10.25%	10.50%	10.75%
1.0	1080.00	1082.50	1085.00	1087.50	1090.00	1092.50	1095.00	1097.50	1100.00	1102.50	1105.00	1107.50
2.0	560.77	562.70	564.62	566.55	568.47	570.40	572.33	574.26	576.20	578.13	580.06	582.00
3.0	388.04	389.79	391.54	393.30	395.06	396.82	398.58	400.35	402.12	403.89	405.66	407.44
4.0	301.93	303.61	305.29	306.98	308.67	310.37	312.07	313.77	315.48	317.18	318.90	320.61
5.0	250.46	252.11	253.77	255.43	257.10	258.77	260.44	262.12	263.80	265.49	267.18	268.88
6.0	216.32	217.96	219.61	221.27	222.92	224.59	226.26	227.93	229.61	231.30	232.99	234.68
7.0	192.08	193.72	195.37	197.03	198.70	200.37	202.04	203.72	205.41	207.10	208.80	210.51
8.0	174.02	175.67	177.34	179.00	180.68	182.36	184.05	185.75	187.45	189.16	190.87	192.60
9.0	160.08	161.75	163.43	165.11	166.80	168.50	170.21	171.92	173.65	175.37	177.11	178.86
10.0	149.03	150.72	152.41	154.11	155.83	157.54	159.27	161.01	162.75	164.50	166.26	168.03
11.0	140.08	141.78	143.50	145.22	146.95	148.69	150.44	152.20	153.97	155.74	157.53	159.32
12.0	132.70	134.42	136.16	137.90	139.66	141.42	143.19	144.98	146.77	148.57	150.38	152.20
13.0	126.53	128.27	130.03	131.79	133.57	135.36	137.16	138.97	140.78	142.61	144.45	146.30
14.0	121.30	123.07	124.85	126.64	128.44	130.25	132.07	133.91	135.75	137.61	139.47	141.35
15.0	116.83	118.62	120.43	122.24	124.06	125.90	127.75	129.61	131.48	133.36	135.25	137.16
16.0	112.98	114.79	116.62	118.46	120.30	122.17	124.04	125.92	127.82	129.73	131.65	133.58
17.0	109.63	111.47	113.32	115.18	117.05	118.94	120.84	122.75	124.67	126.60	128.55	130.51
18.0	106.71	108.56	110.44	112.32	114.22	116.13	118.05	119.99	121.94	123.90	125.87	127.85
19.0	104.13	106.01	107.91	109.81	111.74	113.67	115.62	117.58	119.55	121.54	123.54	125.55
20.0	101.86	103.76	105.68	107.61	109.55	111.51	113.48	115.47	117.46	119.48	121.50	123.53
21.0	99.84	101.76	103.70	105.65	107.62	109.60	111.60	113.61	115.63	117.66	119.71	121.77
22.0	98.04	99.98	101.94	103.92	105.91	107.91	109.93	111.96	114.01	116.07	118.14	120.22
23.0	96.43	98.39	100.38	102.37	104.39	106.41	108.45	110.51	112.58	114.66	116.75	118.86
24.0	94.98	96.97	98.97	100.99	103.03	105.08	107.14	109.21	111.30	113.41	115.52	117.65
25.0	93.68	95.69	97.72	99.76	101.81	103.88	105.96	108.06	110.17	112.30	114.43	116.58
26.0	92.51	94.54	96.59	98.65	100.72	102.81	104.91	107.03	109.16	111.31	113.47	115.64
27.0	91.45	93.50	95.57	97.64	99.74	101.85	103.97	106.11	108.26	110.43	112.60	114.79
28.0	90.49	92.56	94.64	96.74	98.86	100.99	103.13	105.29	107.46	109.64	111.83	114.04
29.0	89.62	91.71	93.81	95.93	98.06	100.21	102.37	104.54	106.73	108.93	111.15	113.37
30.0	88.83	90.94	93.06	95.19	97.34	99.51	101.69	103.88	106.08	108.30	110.53	112.78
31.0	88.11	90.23	92.37	94.52	96.69	98.87	101.07	103.28	105.50	107.74	109.98	112.24
32.0	87.46	89.59	91.75	93.92	96.10	98.30	100.51	102.74	104.98	107.23	109.49	111.76
33.0	86.86	89.01	91.18	93.37	95.57	97.78	100.01	102.25	104.50	106.77	109.05	111.34
34.0	86.31	88.48	90.66	92.87	95.08	97.31	99.55	101.81	104.08	106.36	108.65	110.95
35.0	85.81	87.99	90.19	92.41	94.64	96.89	99.14	101.41	103.69	105.99	108.29	110.61
36.0	85.35	87.55	89.77	92.00	94.24	96.50	98.77	101.05	103.35	105.65	107.97	110.30
37.0	84.93	87.14	89.37	91.62	93.88	96.15	98.43	100.73	103.03	105.35	107.68	110.02
38.0	84.54	86.77	89.01	91.27	93.54	95.83	98.12	100.43	102.75	105.08	107.42	109.77
39.0	84.19	86.43	88.69	90.96	93.24	95.54	97.85	100.17	102.50	104.84	107.19	109.55
40.0	83.87	86.12	88.39	90.67	92.96	95.27	97.59	99.92	102.26	104.62	106.98	109.35
41.0	83.57	85.83	88.11	90.41	92.71	95.03	97.36	99.70	102.05	104.42	106.79	109.16
42.0	83.29	85.57	87.86	90.17	92.48	94.81	97.15	99.50	101.86	104.24	106.61	109.00
43.0	83.04	85.33	87.63	89.95	92.27	94.61	96.96	99.32	101.69	104.07	106.46	108.85
44.0	82.81	85.11	87.42	89.74	92.08	94.43	96.79	99.16	101.54	103.92	106.32	108.72
45.0	82.59	84.90	87.22	89.56	91.91	94.26	96.63	99.01	101.40	103.79	106.19	108.60
46.0	82.39	84.71	87.05	89.39	91.75	94.11	96.49	98.87	101.27	103.67	106.08	108.49
47.0	82.21	84.54	86.88	89.24	91.60	93.97	96.36	98.75	101.15	103.56	105.98	108.40
48.0	82.05	84.38	86.73	89.09	91.47	93.85	96.24	98.64	101.05	103.46	105.88	108.31
49.0	81.89	84.24	86.60	88.96	91.34	93.73	96.13	98.54	100.95	103.37	105.80	108.23
50.0	81.75	84.10	86.47	88.85	91.23	93.63	96.03	98.44	100.86	103.29	105.72	108.16

Table 2

ANNUAL

PAYMENT REQUIRED TO AMORTIZE A $1000.00 LOAN

INTEREST YEARS	11.00%	11.25%	11.50%	11.75%	12.00%	12.25%	12.50%	12.75%	13.00%	13.25%	13.50%	13.75%
1.0	1110.00	1112.50	1115.00	1117.50	1120.00	1122.50	1125.00	1127.50	1130.00	1132.50	1135.00	1137.50
2.0	583.94	585.88	587.82	589.76	591.70	593.65	595.59	597.54	599.49	601.44	603.39	605.34
3.0	409.22	411.00	412.78	414.57	416.35	418.14	419.94	421.73	423.53	425.33	427.13	428.93
4.0	322.33	324.05	325.78	327.51	329.24	330.97	332.71	334.45	336.20	337.95	339.70	341.45
5.0	270.58	272.28	273.99	275.70	277.41	279.13	280.86	282.59	284.32	286.06	287.80	289.54
6.0	236.38	238.09	239.80	241.51	243.23	244.96	246.68	248.42	250.16	251.90	253.65	255.40
7.0	212.22	213.94	215.66	217.39	219.12	220.86	222.61	224.36	226.12	227.88	229.65	231.42
8.0	194.33	196.06	197.80	199.55	201.31	203.07	204.84	206.61	208.39	210.18	211.97	213.77
9.0	180.61	182.37	184.13	185.90	187.68	189.47	191.27	193.07	194.87	196.69	198.51	200.34
10.0	169.81	171.59	173.38	175.18	176.99	178.80	180.63	182.46	184.29	186.14	187.99	189.85
11.0	161.13	162.94	164.76	166.58	168.42	170.26	172.12	173.98	175.85	177.72	179.61	181.50
12.0	154.03	155.87	157.72	159.58	161.44	163.32	165.20	167.09	168.99	170.90	172.82	174.74
13.0	148.16	150.02	151.90	153.79	155.68	157.59	159.50	161.42	163.36	165.30	167.24	169.20
14.0	143.23	145.13	147.04	148.95	150.88	152.81	154.76	156.71	158.67	160.64	162.63	164.62
15.0	139.07	140.99	142.93	144.87	146.83	148.79	150.77	152.75	154.75	156.75	158.76	160.78
16.0	135.52	137.47	139.44	141.41	143.40	145.39	147.39	149.41	151.43	153.46	155.51	157.56
17.0	132.48	134.46	136.45	138.45	140.46	142.48	144.52	146.56	148.61	150.68	152.75	154.83
18.0	129.85	131.85	133.87	135.90	137.94	139.99	142.05	144.12	146.21	148.30	150.40	152.51
19.0	127.57	129.60	131.65	133.70	135.77	137.85	139.93	142.03	144.14	146.26	148.38	150.52
20.0	125.58	127.64	129.71	131.79	133.88	135.99	138.10	140.22	142.36	144.50	146.66	148.82
21.0	123.84	125.93	128.02	130.13	132.25	134.37	136.51	138.66	140.82	142.99	145.17	147.35
22.0	122.32	124.43	126.54	128.67	130.82	132.97	135.13	137.30	139.48	141.68	143.88	146.09
23.0	120.98	123.11	125.25	127.40	129.56	131.74	133.92	136.12	138.32	140.54	142.76	144.99
24.0	119.79	121.94	124.11	126.28	128.47	130.66	132.87	135.09	137.31	139.55	141.79	144.05
25.0	118.75	120.92	123.10	125.30	127.50	129.72	131.95	134.18	136.43	138.69	140.95	143.22
26.0	117.82	120.01	122.22	124.43	126.66	128.89	131.14	133.39	135.66	137.93	140.22	142.51
27.0	116.99	119.21	121.43	123.66	125.91	128.16	130.43	132.70	134.98	137.28	139.57	141.88
28.0	116.26	118.49	120.73	122.99	125.25	127.52	129.80	132.09	134.39	136.70	139.02	141.34
29.0	115.61	117.86	120.12	122.39	124.67	126.95	129.25	131.56	133.87	136.20	138.53	140.86
30.0	115.03	117.29	119.57	121.85	124.15	126.45	128.77	131.09	133.42	135.75	138.10	140.45
31.0	114.51	116.79	119.08	121.38	123.69	126.01	128.34	130.67	133.01	135.36	137.72	140.09
32.0	114.05	116.34	118.65	120.96	123.29	125.62	127.96	130.31	132.66	135.02	137.39	139.77
33.0	113.63	115.94	118.26	120.59	122.93	125.27	127.62	129.98	132.35	134.72	137.10	139.49
34.0	113.26	115.59	117.92	120.26	122.61	124.96	127.33	129.70	132.08	134.46	136.85	139.25
35.0	112.93	115.27	117.61	119.96	122.32	124.69	127.06	129.45	131.83	134.23	136.63	139.04
36.0	112.64	114.98	117.34	119.70	122.07	124.45	126.83	129.22	131.62	134.02	136.43	138.85
37.0	112.37	114.73	117.09	119.46	121.84	124.23	126.63	129.03	131.43	133.85	136.26	138.68
38.0	112.13	114.50	116.87	119.26	121.64	124.04	126.44	128.85	131.27	133.69	136.11	138.54
39.0	111.92	114.29	116.68	119.07	121.47	123.87	126.28	128.70	131.12	133.55	135.98	138.42
40.0	111.72	114.11	116.50	118.90	121.31	123.72	126.14	128.56	130.99	133.42	135.86	138.30
41.0	111.55	113.95	116.35	118.75	121.17	123.59	126.01	128.44	130.88	133.32	135.76	138.21
42.0	111.40	113.80	116.21	118.62	121.04	123.47	125.90	128.34	130.78	133.22	135.67	138.12
43.0	111.26	113.67	116.08	118.50	120.93	123.36	125.80	128.24	130.69	133.14	135.59	138.05
44.0	111.13	113.55	115.97	118.40	120.83	123.27	125.71	128.16	130.61	133.06	135.52	137.98
45.0	111.02	113.44	115.87	118.30	120.74	123.18	125.63	128.08	130.54	133.00	135.46	137.92
46.0	110.92	113.35	115.78	118.22	120.66	123.11	125.56	128.02	130.48	132.94	135.40	137.87
47.0	110.83	113.26	115.70	118.14	120.59	123.04	125.50	127.96	130.42	132.89	135.36	137.83
48.0	110.74	113.18	115.63	118.08	120.53	122.98	125.44	127.91	130.37	132.84	135.32	137.79
49.0	110.67	113.11	115.56	118.02	120.47	122.93	125.40	127.86	130.33	132.80	135.28	137.75
50.0	110.60	113.05	115.50	117.96	120.42	122.89	125.35	127.82	130.29	132.77	135.25	137.72

Table 2

ANNUAL

PAYMENT REQUIRED TO AMORTIZE A $1000.00 LOAN

INTEREST YEARS	14.00%	14.25%	14.50%	14.75%	15.00%	15.25%	15.50%	15.75%	16.00%	16.25%	16.50%	16.75%
1.0	1140.00	1142.50	1145.00	1147.50	1150.00	1152.50	1155.00	1157.50	1160.00	1162.50	1165.00	1167.50
2.0	607.29	609.25	611.21	613.16	615.12	617.08	619.04	621.00	622.97	624.93	626.90	628.87
3.0	430.74	432.54	434.35	436.17	437.98	439.80	441.62	443.44	445.26	447.09	448.92	450.75
4.0	343.21	344.97	346.73	348.50	350.27	352.04	353.82	355.60	357.38	359.17	360.95	362.74
5.0	291.29	293.04	294.80	296.56	298.32	300.09	301.86	303.64	305.41	307.20	308.98	310.77
6.0	257.16	258.93	260.69	262.47	264.24	266.02	267.81	269.60	271.39	273.19	275.00	276.81
7.0	233.20	234.98	236.77	238.57	240.37	242.17	243.98	245.80	247.62	249.44	251.27	253.11
8.0	215.58	217.39	219.20	221.03	222.86	224.69	226.53	228.38	230.23	232.09	233.95	235.82
9.0	202.17	204.01	205.86	207.72	209.58	211.45	213.32	215.20	217.09	218.98	220.88	222.78
10.0	191.72	193.59	195.47	197.36	199.26	201.16	203.07	204.98	206.91	208.84	210.77	212.71
11.0	183.40	185.31	187.22	189.14	191.07	193.01	194.96	196.91	198.87	200.83	202.80	204.78
12.0	176.67	178.62	180.56	182.52	184.49	186.46	188.44	190.43	192.42	194.42	196.43	198.45
13.0	171.17	173.14	175.13	177.12	179.12	181.12	183.14	185.16	187.19	189.23	191.27	193.32
14.0	166.61	168.62	170.64	172.66	174.69	176.73	178.78	180.84	182.90	184.97	187.05	189.14
15.0	162.81	164.85	166.90	168.96	171.02	173.10	175.18	177.27	179.36	181.47	183.58	185.70
16.0	159.62	161.69	163.77	165.86	167.95	170.06	172.17	174.29	176.42	178.55	180.70	182.85
17.0	156.92	159.02	161.13	163.25	165.37	167.51	169.65	171.80	173.96	176.12	178.30	180.48
18.0	154.63	156.75	158.89	161.04	163.19	165.35	167.52	169.70	171.89	174.08	176.29	178.49
19.0	152.67	154.82	156.99	159.16	161.34	163.53	165.73	167.93	170.15	172.37	174.60	176.83
20.0	150.99	153.17	155.36	157.56	159.77	161.98	164.20	166.43	168.67	170.92	173.17	175.43
21.0	149.55	151.76	153.97	156.19	158.42	160.66	162.91	165.16	167.42	169.69	171.96	174.25
22.0	148.31	150.54	152.77	155.02	157.27	159.53	161.80	164.08	166.36	168.65	170.94	253.11
23.0	147.24	149.49	151.74	154.01	156.28	158.56	160.85	163.15	165.45	167.76	170.08	172.40
24.0	146.31	148.58	150.86	153.14	155.43	157.74	160.04	162.36	164.68	167.01	169.34	171.68
25.0	145.50	147.79	150.09	152.39	154.70	157.02	159.35	161.68	164.02	166.36	168.71	171.07
26.0	144.81	147.11	149.43	151.75	154.07	156.41	158.75	161.10	163.45	165.81	168.18	170.55
27.0	144.20	146.52	148.85	151.19	153.53	155.88	158.24	160.60	162.97	165.34	167.72	170.10
28.0	143.67	146.01	148.35	150.70	153.06	155.43	157.80	160.17	162.55	164.94	167.33	169.73
29.0	143.21	145.56	147.92	150.29	152.66	155.03	157.42	159.80	162.20	164.59	167.00	169.40
30.0	142.81	145.17	147.54	149.92	152.31	154.69	157.09	159.49	161.89	164.30	166.71	169.13
31.0	142.46	144.83	147.22	149.61	152.00	154.40	156.81	159.21	161.63	164.05	166.47	168.89
32.0	142.15	144.54	146.93	149.33	151.74	154.15	156.56	158.98	161.40	163.83	166.26	168.69
33.0	141.88	144.28	146.69	149.10	151.51	153.93	156.35	158.78	161.21	163.64	166.08	168.52
34.0	141.65	144.06	146.47	148.89	151.31	153.74	156.17	158.60	161.04	163.48	165.93	168.38
35.0	141.45	143.86	146.28	148.71	151.14	153.57	156.01	158.45	160.90	163.35	165.80	168.25
36.0	141.27	143.69	146.12	148.55	150.99	153.43	155.88	158.32	160.77	163.23	165.68	168.14
37.0	141.11	143.54	145.98	148.42	150.86	153.31	155.76	158.21	160.67	163.13	165.59	168.05
38.0	140.97	143.41	145.85	148.30	150.75	153.20	155.66	158.11	160.58	163.04	165.50	167.97
39.0	140.86	143.30	145.75	148.20	150.65	153.11	155.57	158.03	160.50	162.96	165.43	167.90
40.0	140.75	143.20	145.65	148.11	150.57	153.03	155.49	157.96	160.43	162.90	165.37	167.85
41.0	140.66	143.11	145.57	148.03	150.49	152.96	155.43	157.90	160.37	162.84	165.32	167.80
42.0	140.58	143.04	145.50	147.96	150.43	152.90	155.37	157.84	160.32	162.80	165.28	167.76
43.0	140.51	142.97	145.44	147.90	150.37	152.85	155.32	157.80	160.28	162.76	165.24	167.72
44.0	140.45	142.91	145.38	147.85	150.33	152.80	155.28	157.76	160.24	162.72	165.20	167.69
45.0	140.39	142.86	145.33	147.81	150.28	152.76	155.24	157.72	160.21	162.69	165.18	167.66
46.0	140.34	142.82	145.29	147.77	150.25	152.73	155.21	157.69	160.18	162.66	165.15	167.64
47.0	140.30	142.78	145.26	147.73	150.22	152.70	155.18	157.67	160.15	162.64	165.13	167.62
48.0	140.27	142.74	145.22	147.71	150.19	152.67	155.16	157.65	160.13	162.62	165.11	167.60
49.0	140.23	142.71	145.20	147.68	150.16	152.65	155.14	157.63	160.12	162.61	165.10	167.59
50.0	140.21	142.69	145.17	147.66	150.14	152.63	155.12	157.61	160.10	162.59	165.08	167.58

Table 2

ANNUAL

PAYMENT REQUIRED TO AMORTIZE A $1000.00 LOAN

INTEREST YEARS	17.00%	17.25%	17.50%	17.75%	18.00%	18.25%	18.50%	18.75%	19.00%	19.25%	19.50%	19.75%
1.0	1170.00	1172.50	1175.00	1177.50	1180.00	1182.50	1185.00	1187.50	1190.00	1192.50	1195.00	1197.50
2.0	630.83	632.80	634.78	636.75	638.72	640.70	642.67	644.65	646.63	648.61	650.59	652.57
3.0	452.58	454.41	456.25	458.09	459.93	461.77	463.62	465.46	467.31	469.16	471.02	472.87
4.0	364.54	366.34	368.14	369.94	371.74	373.55	375.36	377.18	379.00	380.82	382.64	384.47
5.0	312.57	314.37	316.17	317.97	319.78	321.60	323.41	325.23	327.06	328.88	330.71	332.55
6.0	278.62	280.44	282.26	284.08	285.92	287.75	289.59	291.43	293.28	295.13	296.99	298.85
7.0	254.95	256.80	258.65	260.51	262.37	264.23	266.10	267.98	269.86	271.75	273.64	275.53
8.0	237.69	239.58	241.46	243.35	245.25	247.15	249.06	250.97	252.89	254.81	256.74	258.68
9.0	224.70	226.61	228.54	230.46	232.40	234.34	236.29	238.24	240.20	242.16	244.13	246.10
10.0	214.66	216.62	218.58	220.55	222.52	224.50	226.49	228.48	230.48	232.48	234.49	236.51
11.0	206.77	208.76	210.76	212.77	214.78	216.80	218.83	220.86	222.90	224.94	226.99	229.05
12.0	200.47	202.50	204.54	206.58	208.63	210.69	212.75	214.82	216.90	218.98	221.07	223.17
13.0	195.38	197.45	199.52	201.60	203.69	205.79	207.89	209.99	212.11	214.23	216.35	218.49
14.0	191.24	193.34	195.45	197.56	199.68	201.81	203.95	206.09	208.24	210.39	212.56	214.72
15.0	187.83	189.96	192.10	194.25	196.41	198.57	200.74	202.91	205.10	207.29	209.48	211.68
16.0	185.01	187.18	189.35	191.53	193.72	195.91	198.11	200.32	202.53	204.75	206.97	209.20
17.0	182.67	184.86	187.06	189.27	191.49	193.71	195.94	198.18	200.42	202.67	204.92	207.18
18.0	180.71	182.93	185.16	187.40	189.64	191.89	194.15	196.41	198.68	200.95	203.23	205.52
19.0	179.07	181.32	183.58	185.84	188.11	190.38	192.66	194.95	197.24	199.54	201.84	204.15
20.0	177.70	179.97	182.25	184.53	186.82	189.12	191.43	193.74	196.05	198.37	200.70	203.03
21.0	176.54	178.83	181.13	183.44	185.75	188.07	190.39	192.72	195.06	197.40	199.74	202.09
22.0	175.56	177.87	180.19	182.52	184.85	187.19	189.53	191.88	194.23	196.59	198.96	201.32
23.0	174.73	177.06	179.40	181.74	184.10	186.45	188.81	191.18	193.55	195.92	198.30	200.68
24.0	174.02	176.38	178.73	181.09	183.46	185.83	188.21	190.59	192.97	195.36	197.75	200.15
25.0	173.43	175.79	178.17	180.54	182.92	185.31	187.70	190.09	192.49	194.89	197.30	199.71
26.0	172.92	175.30	177.69	180.08	182.47	184.87	187.27	189.68	192.09	194.50	196.92	199.34
27.0	172.49	174.89	177.28	179.69	182.09	184.50	186.92	189.33	191.75	194.18	196.61	199.04
28.0	172.13	174.53	176.94	179.35	181.77	184.19	186.61	189.04	191.47	193.91	196.34	198.78
29.0	171.81	174.23	176.65	179.07	181.50	183.93	186.36	188.80	191.24	193.68	196.12	198.57
30.0	171.55	173.97	176.40	178.83	181.27	183.71	186.15	188.59	191.04	193.49	195.94	198.39
31.0	171.32	173.76	176.19	178.63	181.08	183.52	185.97	188.42	190.87	193.33	195.79	198.25
32.0	171.13	173.57	176.02	178.46	180.91	183.36	185.82	188.28	190.73	193.20	195.66	198.12
33.0	170.97	173.41	175.86	178.32	180.77	183.23	185.69	188.15	190.62	193.08	195.55	198.02
34.0	170.83	173.28	175.74	178.19	180.65	183.12	185.58	188.05	190.52	192.99	195.46	197.94
35.0	170.71	173.16	175.63	178.09	180.56	183.02	185.49	187.96	190.44	192.91	195.39	197.87
36.0	170.60	173.07	175.53	178.00	180.47	182.94	185.42	187.89	190.37	192.85	195.33	197.81
37.0	170.52	172.98	175.45	177.93	180.40	182.88	185.35	187.83	190.31	192.79	195.27	197.76
38.0	170.44	172.91	175.39	177.86	180.34	182.82	185.30	187.78	190.26	192.74	195.23	197.71
39.0	170.38	172.85	175.33	177.81	180.29	182.77	185.25	187.74	190.22	192.71	195.19	197.68
40.0	170.32	172.80	175.28	177.76	180.25	182.73	185.21	187.70	190.19	192.67	195.16	197.65
41.0	170.28	172.76	175.24	177.72	180.21	182.69	185.18	187.67	190.16	192.65	195.14	197.63
42.0	170.24	172.72	175.21	177.69	180.18	182.66	185.15	187.64	190.13	192.62	195.11	197.61
43.0	170.20	172.69	175.18	177.66	180.15	182.64	185.13	187.62	190.11	192.60	195.10	197.59
44.0	170.18	172.66	175.15	177.64	180.13	182.61	185.11	187.60	190.10	192.59	195.08	197.58
45.0	170.15	172.64	175.13	177.62	180.11	182.60	185.09	187.59	190.08	192.57	195.07	197.56
46.0	170.13	172.62	175.11	177.60	180.09	182.59	185.08	187.57	190.07	192.56	195.06	197.55
47.0	170.11	172.60	175.09	177.59	180.08	182.57	185.07	187.56	190.06	192.55	195.05	197.55
48.0	170.10	172.59	175.08	177.57	180.07	182.56	185.06	187.55	190.05	192.55	195.04	197.54
49.0	170.08	172.58	175.07	177.56	180.06	182.55	185.05	187.55	190.04	192.54	195.04	197.53
50.0	170.07	172.57	175.06	177.56	180.05	182.55	185.04	187.54	190.04	192.53	195.03	197.53

Table 2

ANNUAL

PAYMENT REQUIRED TO AMORTIZE A $1000.00 LOAN

INTEREST YEARS	20.00%	20.25%	20.50%	20.75%	21.00%	21.25%	21.50%	21.75%	22.00%	22.25%	22.50%	22.75%
1.0	1200.00	1202.50	1205.00	1207.50	1210.00	1212.50	1215.00	1217.50	1220.00	1222.50	1225.00	1227.50
2.0	654.55	656.53	658.52	660.51	662.49	664.48	666.47	668.46	670.46	672.45	674.44	676.44
3.0	474.73	476.59	478.45	480.31	482.18	484.05	485.92	487.79	489.66	491.54	493.42	495.30
4.0	386.29	388.13	389.96	391.80	393.64	395.48	397.33	399.17	401.03	402.88	404.74	406.59
5.0	334.38	336.23	338.07	339.92	341.77	343.63	345.48	347.35	349.21	351.08	352.95	354.83
6.0	300.71	302.58	304.45	306.33	308.21	310.09	311.98	313.87	315.77	317.67	319.57	321.48
7.0	277.43	279.33	281.24	283.15	285.07	286.99	288.92	290.85	292.79	294.73	296.67	298.62
8.0	260.61	262.56	264.51	266.46	268.42	270.38	272.35	274.33	276.30	278.29	280.27	282.27
9.0	248.08	250.07	252.06	254.06	256.06	258.07	260.08	262.09	264.12	266.14	268.18	270.21
10.0	238.53	240.55	242.59	244.63	246.67	248.72	250.77	252.83	254.90	256.97	259.05	261.13
11.0	231.11	233.18	235.25	237.33	239.42	241.51	243.60	245.70	247.81	249.92	252.04	254.17
12.0	225.27	227.38	229.49	231.61	233.73	235.87	238.00	240.14	242.29	244.44	246.60	248.76
13.0	220.63	222.77	224.92	227.08	229.24	231.41	233.58	235.76	237.94	240.13	242.33	244.53
14.0	216.90	219.08	221.26	223.45	225.65	227.85	230.06	232.28	234.50	236.72	238.95	241.18
15.0	213.89	216.10	218.32	220.54	222.77	225.01	227.25	229.49	231.74	234.00	236.26	238.53
16.0	211.44	213.68	215.93	218.19	220.45	222.71	224.98	227.25	229.53	231.82	234.11	236.40
17.0	209.45	211.72	213.99	216.27	218.56	220.85	223.15	225.45	227.76	230.07	232.38	234.70
18.0	207.81	210.11	212.41	214.71	217.03	219.34	221.66	223.99	226.32	228.65	230.99	233.33
19.0	206.47	208.79	211.11	213.44	215.77	218.11	220.45	222.80	225.15	227.51	229.87	232.23
20.0	205.36	207.70	210.05	212.40	214.75	217.11	219.47	221.84	224.21	226.58	228.96	231.34
21.0	204.45	206.81	209.17	211.54	213.91	216.29	218.67	221.05	223.44	225.83	228.22	230.62
22.0	203.69	206.07	208.45	210.83	213.22	215.61	218.01	220.41	222.81	225.22	227.62	230.04
23.0	203.07	205.46	207.86	210.25	212.66	215.06	217.47	219.88	222.30	224.72	227.14	229.56
24.0	202.55	204.96	207.37	209.78	212.19	214.61	217.03	219.46	221.88	224.31	226.74	229.18
25.0	202.12	204.54	206.96	209.38	211.81	214.24	216.67	219.10	221.54	223.98	226.42	228.87
26.0	201.77	204.19	206.62	209.06	211.49	213.93	216.37	218.82	221.26	223.71	226.16	228.61
27.0	201.47	203.91	206.35	208.79	211.23	213.68	216.13	218.58	221.03	223.49	225.95	228.41
28.0	201.23	203.67	206.12	208.57	211.02	213.47	215.93	218.39	220.85	223.31	225.77	228.24
29.0	201.02	203.47	205.93	208.38	210.84	213.30	215.77	218.23	220.70	223.16	225.63	228.10
30.0	200.85	203.31	205.77	208.23	210.70	213.16	215.63	218.10	220.57	223.04	225.52	227.99
31.0	200.71	203.17	205.64	208.11	210.58	213.05	215.52	217.99	220.47	222.95	225.42	227.90
32.0	200.59	203.06	205.53	208.00	210.48	212.95	215.43	217.91	220.38	222.86	225.35	227.83
33.0	200.49	202.97	205.44	207.92	210.40	212.87	215.35	217.83	220.32	222.80	225.28	227.77
34.0	200.41	202.89	205.37	207.85	210.33	212.81	215.29	217.78	220.26	222.75	225.23	227.72
35.0	200.34	202.82	205.31	207.79	210.27	212.76	215.24	217.73	220.21	222.70	225.19	227.68
36.0	200.29	202.77	205.25	207.74	210.22	212.71	215.20	217.69	220.18	222.67	225.16	227.65
37.0	200.24	202.73	205.21	207.70	210.19	212.68	215.16	217.65	220.15	222.64	225.13	227.62
38.0	200.20	202.69	205.18	207.67	210.16	212.65	215.14	217.63	220.12	222.61	225.11	227.60
39.0	200.17	202.66	205.15	207.64	210.13	212.62	215.11	217.61	220.10	222.59	225.09	227.58
40.0	200.14	202.63	205.12	207.62	210.11	212.60	215.09	217.59	220.08	222.58	225.07	227.57
41.0	200.12	202.61	205.10	207.60	210.09	212.58	215.08	217.57	220.07	222.56	225.06	227.56
42.0	200.10	202.59	205.09	207.58	210.08	212.57	215.07	217.56	220.06	222.55	225.05	227.55
43.0	200.08	202.58	205.07	207.57	210.06	212.56	215.05	217.55	220.05	222.54	225.04	227.54
44.0	200.07	202.57	205.06	207.56	210.05	212.55	215.05	217.54	220.04	222.54	225.03	227.53
45.0	200.06	202.56	205.05	207.55	210.04	212.54	215.04	217.54	220.03	222.53	225.03	227.53
46.0	200.05	202.55	205.04	207.54	210.04	212.54	215.03	217.53	220.03	222.53	225.02	227.52
47.0	200.04	202.54	205.04	207.53	210.03	212.53	215.03	217.53	220.02	222.52	225.02	227.52
48.0	200.04	202.53	205.03	207.53	210.03	212.53	215.02	217.52	220.02	222.52	225.02	227.52
49.0	200.03	202.53	205.03	207.53	210.02	212.52	215.02	217.52	220.02	222.52	225.02	227.51
50.0	200.03	202.53	205.02	207.52	210.02	212.52	215.02	217.52	220.02	222.51	225.01	227.51

Table 2

ANNUAL

PAYMENT REQUIRED TO AMORTIZE A $1000.00 LOAN

EREST YEARS	23.00%	23.25%	23.50%	23.75%	24.00%	24.25%	24.50%	24.75%	25.00%	25.25%	25.50%	25.75%
1.0	1230.00	1232.50	1235.00	1237.50	1240.00	1242.50	1245.00	1247.50	1250.00	1252.50	1255.00	1257.50
2.0	678.44	680.43	682.43	684.43	686.43	688.44	690.44	692.44	694.45	696.46	698.46	700.47
3.0	497.18	499.06	500.95	502.83	504.72	506.61	508.51	510.40	512.30	514.20	516.10	518.00
4.0	408.46	410.32	412.19	414.06	415.93	417.81	419.68	421.56	423.45	425.33	427.22	429.11
5.0	356.71	358.59	360.47	362.36	364.25	366.15	368.05	369.95	371.85	373.76	375.67	377.58
6.0	323.39	325.31	327.23	329.15	331.08	333.01	334.94	336.88	338.82	340.77	342.72	344.67
7.0	300.57	302.53	304.49	306.46	308.43	310.40	312.38	314.36	316.35	318.34	320.33	322.33
8.0	284.26	286.27	288.27	290.28	292.30	294.32	296.34	298.37	300.40	302.44	304.48	306.53
9.0	272.25	274.30	276.35	278.41	280.47	282.54	284.61	286.68	288.76	290.85	292.93	295.03
10.0	263.21	265.30	267.40	269.50	271.61	273.72	275.83	277.95	280.08	282.21	284.34	286.48
11.0	256.29	258.43	260.57	262.71	264.86	267.01	269.17	271.33	273.50	275.67	277.85	280.03
12.0	250.93	253.10	255.28	257.47	259.65	261.85	264.04	266.25	268.45	270.66	272.88	275.10
13.0	246.73	248.94	251.16	253.38	255.60	257.83	260.07	262.31	264.55	266.80	269.05	271.30
14.0	243.42	245.67	247.92	250.17	252.43	254.69	256.96	259.23	261.51	263.79	266.07	268.36
15.0	240.80	243.07	245.35	247.64	249.92	252.22	254.51	256.82	259.12	261.43	263.75	266.06
16.0	238.70	241.01	243.31	245.62	247.94	250.26	252.59	254.91	257.25	259.58	261.92	264.26
17.0	237.03	239.35	241.69	244.02	246.36	248.71	251.06	253.41	255.76	258.12	260.49	262.85
18.0	235.68	238.03	240.39	242.74	245.11	247.47	249.84	252.22	254.59	256.97	259.35	261.74
19.0	234.60	236.97	239.34	241.72	244.10	246.49	248.88	251.27	253.66	256.06	258.46	260.86
20.0	233.73	236.11	238.51	240.90	243.30	245.70	248.10	250.51	252.92	255.33	257.75	260.17
21.0	233.02	235.42	237.83	240.24	242.65	245.07	247.49	249.91	252.33	254.76	257.19	259.62
22.0	232.45	234.87	237.29	239.71	242.14	244.56	247.00	249.43	251.86	254.30	256.74	259.18
23.0	231.99	234.42	236.85	239.28	241.72	244.16	246.60	249.04	251.49	253.94	256.39	258.84
24.0	231.62	234.06	236.50	238.94	241.39	243.84	246.29	248.74	251.19	253.65	256.10	258.56
25.0	231.31	233.76	236.21	238.66	241.12	243.57	246.03	248.49	250.95	253.42	255.88	258.35
26.0	231.07	233.52	235.98	238.44	240.90	243.37	245.83	248.30	250.76	253.23	255.70	258.17
27.0	230.87	233.33	235.79	238.26	240.73	243.20	245.67	248.14	250.61	253.08	255.56	258.04
28.0	230.71	233.17	235.64	238.12	240.59	243.06	245.54	248.01	250.49	252.97	255.45	257.93
29.0	230.57	233.05	235.52	238.00	240.47	242.95	245.43	247.91	250.39	252.87	255.36	257.84
30.0	230.47	232.95	235.42	237.90	240.38	242.87	245.35	247.83	250.31	252.80	255.29	257.77
31.0	230.38	232.86	235.34	237.83	240.31	242.79	245.28	247.77	250.25	252.74	255.23	257.72
32.0	230.31	232.79	235.28	237.76	240.25	242.74	245.23	247.71	250.20	252.69	255.18	257.67
33.0	230.25	232.74	235.23	237.71	240.20	242.69	245.18	247.67	250.16	252.65	255.15	257.64
34.0	230.21	232.70	235.18	237.67	240.17	242.66	245.15	247.64	250.13	252.62	255.12	257.61
35.0	230.17	232.66	235.15	237.64	240.13	242.63	245.12	247.61	250.11	252.60	255.09	257.59
36.0	230.14	232.63	235.12	237.62	240.11	242.60	245.10	247.59	250.09	252.58	255.08	257.57
37.0	230.11	232.61	235.10	237.59	240.09	242.58	245.08	247.57	250.07	252.57	255.06	257.56
38.0	230.09	232.59	235.08	237.58	240.07	242.57	245.06	247.56	250.06	252.55	255.05	257.55
39.0	230.08	232.57	235.07	237.56	240.06	242.55	245.05	247.55	250.05	252.54	255.04	257.54
40.0	230.06	232.56	235.06	237.55	240.05	242.55	245.04	247.54	250.04	252.54	255.03	257.53
41.0	230.05	232.55	235.05	237.54	240.04	242.54	245.04	247.53	250.03	252.53	255.03	257.53
42.0	230.04	232.54	235.04	237.54	240.03	242.53	245.03	247.53	250.03	252.52	255.02	257.52
43.0	230.04	232.53	235.03	237.53	240.03	242.53	245.02	247.52	250.02	252.52	255.02	257.52
44.0	230.03	232.53	235.03	237.53	240.02	242.52	245.02	247.52	250.02	252.52	255.02	257.52
45.0	230.03	232.52	235.02	237.52	240.02	242.52	245.02	247.52	250.02	252.52	255.01	257.51
46.0	230.02	232.52	235.02	237.52	240.02	242.52	245.02	247.51	250.01	252.51	255.01	257.51
47.0	230.02	232.52	235.02	237.52	240.01	242.51	245.01	247.51	250.01	252.51	255.01	257.51
48.0	230.02	232.52	235.01	237.51	240.01	242.51	245.01	247.51	250.01	252.51	255.01	257.51
49.0	230.01	232.51	235.01	237.51	240.01	242.51	245.01	247.51	250.01	252.51	255.01	257.51
50.0	230.01	232.51	235.01	237.51	240.01	242.51	245.01	247.51	250.01	252.51	255.01	257.51

Table 3
REMAINING BALANCE TABLES
(Percentage of Original Loan Unpaid)

These tables give the percentage of the original loan which remains unpaid at the end of the various time periods shown.

The exact payment necessary (to 14 decimals) to amortize a loan during the term shown was used to prepare these tables. Because monthly payments are always rounded up for any part of a cent, some variations can result, especially for combinations of low loan amounts, high interest rates and long-term loans. These variations are slight and usually occur at the fourth decimal place only—which is probably the reason most tables of this sort are only presented to three decimal places.

Example:

1. What is the unpaid balance of an original 25-year $30,000 loan at 5.00 percent per annum, after 10 years?

   Ans. Locate the 25-year column under original loan term and follow it down to opposite 10 years. The percentage is 73.92. This is multiplied by the original loan,

   $0.7392 \times \$30,000 = \$22,176.00$ (unpaid balance)

The ***** which appear in the one- to three-year rows at 21.50 percent and higher indicate there has been no significant reduction of the loan.

Table 3

REMAINING BALANCE TABLES

ORIGINAL TERM IN YEARS

5.00%

AGE OF LOAN	1	2	3	4	5	6	7	8	9	10	15	20	25	30	35	40
1	0.	51.25	68.32	76.84	81.94	85.34	87.76	89.57	90.97	92.09	95.41	97.01	97.94	98.52	98.92	99.20
2		0.	35.01	52.49	62.97	69.93	74.90	78.61	81.49	83.78	90.58	93.87	95.77	96.97	97.78	98.35
3			0.	26.90	43.01	53.74	61.37	67.09	71.51	75.04	85.50	90.57	93.49	95.34	96.59	97.46
4				0.	22.04	36.71	47.16	54.97	61.03	65.86	80.17	87.10	91.10	93.63	95.33	96.53
5					0.	18.81	32.22	42.24	50.01	56.20	74.56	83.45	88.58	91.83	94.01	95.54
6						0.	16.51	28.86	38.43	46.06	68.66	79.62	85.93	89.94	92.63	94.51
7							0.	14.79	26.25	35.39	62.46	75.59	83.15	87.95	91.17	93.43
8								0.	13.45	24.18	55.95	71.36	80.23	85.85	89.64	92.28
9									0.	12.39	49.10	66.90	77.16	83.65	88.03	91.09
10										0.	41.90	62.22	73.92	81.34	86.33	89.82
11										0.	34.34	57.30	70.53	78.91	84.55	88.50
12										0.	26.39	52.13	66.96	76.36	82.68	87.11
13										0.	18.03	46.69	63.21	73.67	80.71	85.64
14										0.	9.24	40.98	59.26	70.85	78.65	84.10
15											0.	34.97	55.12	67.88	76.47	82.48
16											0.	28.66	50.76	64.77	74.19	80.78
17											0.	22.02	46.18	61.49	71.79	79.00
18											0.	15.04	41.36	58.04	69.26	77.12
19											0.	7.71	36.30	54.42	66.61	75.14
20												0.	30.98	50.61	63.82	73.06
21												0.	25.38	46.61	60.89	70.88
22												0.	19.51	42.40	57.81	68.59
23												0.	13.33	37.98	54.57	66.18
24												0.	6.83	33.33	51.16	63.64
25													0.	28.45	47.58	60.98
26													0.	23.31	43.82	58.18
27													0.	17.91	39.86	55.23
28													0.	12.24	35.71	52.14
29													0.	6.27	31.34	48.88
30														0.	26.74	45.46
35															0.	25.55
40																0.

5.25%

AGE OF LOAN	1	2	3	4	5	6	7	8	9	10	15	20	25	30	35	40
1	0.	51.31	68.40	76.93	82.04	85.44	87.86	89.67	91.07	92.19	95.50	97.09	98.01	98.59	98.98	99.25
2		0.	35.09	52.62	63.11	70.09	75.06	78.78	81.66	83.96	90.75	94.03	95.92	97.10	97.90	98.45
3			0.	27.00	43.17	53.92	61.58	67.31	71.75	75.28	85.75	90.81	93.71	95.54	96.76	97.61
4				0.	22.15	36.88	47.37	55.22	61.30	66.14	80.48	87.41	91.38	93.89	95.56	96.73
5					0.	18.92	32.40	42.48	50.29	56.51	74.92	83.82	88.93	92.15	94.30	95.80
6						0.	16.63	29.05	38.69	46.36	69.07	80.05	86.35	90.32	92.97	94.82
7							0.	14.91	26.46	35.66	62.90	76.07	83.62	88.39	91.57	93.79
8								0.	13.58	24.39	56.41	71.88	80.75	86.35	90.10	92.70
9									0.	12.52	49.56	67.46	77.73	84.21	88.54	91.55
10										0.	42.34	62.80	74.54	81.95	86.90	90.34
11										0.	34.74	57.90	71.19	79.57	85.17	89.07
12										0.	26.72	52.73	67.65	77.06	83.35	87.73
13										0.	18.28	47.28	63.92	74.41	81.43	86.31
14										0.	9.38	41.54	59.99	71.63	79.41	84.82
15											0.	35.49	55.85	68.69	77.28	83.25
16											0.	29.12	51.49	65.60	75.03	81.59
17											0.	22.40	46.89	62.34	72.67	79.85
18											0.	15.32	42.05	58.90	70.17	78.01
19											0.	7.86	36.94	55.28	67.55	76.07
20												0.	31.56	51.47	64.78	74.03
21												0.	25.89	47.45	61.86	71.88
22												0.	19.92	43.21	58.79	69.62
23												0.	13.62	38.75	55.55	67.23
24												0.	6.99	34.04	52.13	64.71
25													0.	29.08	48.54	62.06
26													0.	23.86	44.74	59.26
27													0.	18.36	40.75	56.32
28													0.	12.55	36.54	53.21
29													0.	6.44	32.10	49.94
30														0.	27.43	46.50
35															0.	26.28
40																0.

Table 3

REMAINING BALANCE TABLES

ORIGINAL TERM IN YEARS

5.50%

AGE OF LOAN	1	2	3	4	5	6	7	8	9	10	15	20	25	30	35	40
1	0.	51.37	68.48	77.02	82.13	85.53	87.96	89.77	91.17	92.28	95.58	97.17	98.08	98.65	99.03	99.29
2		0.	35.18	52.74	63.26	70.25	75.23	78.95	81.84	84.13	90.92	94.19	96.06	97.23	98.01	98.55
3			0.	27.09	43.32	54.11	61.79	67.53	71.98	75.52	85.99	91.04	93.92	95.73	96.93	97.76
4				0.	22.25	37.05	47.59	55.47	61.57	66.43	80.79	87.71	91.66	94.14	95.79	96.92
5					0.	19.03	32.59	42.72	50.57	56.82	75.29	84.19	89.27	92.46	94.58	96.04
6						0.	16.74	29.25	38.95	46.66	69.48	80.47	86.75	90.69	93.31	95.11
7							0.	15.03	26.67	35.94	63.34	76.54	84.09	88.82	91.96	94.13
8								0.	13.70	24.61	56.86	72.40	81.27	86.84	90.54	93.09
9									0.	12.64	50.01	68.01	78.30	84.75	89.04	92.00
10										0.	42.78	63.38	75.16	82.54	87.45	90.84
11										0.	35.13	58.49	71.84	80.21	85.77	89.61
12										0.	27.06	53.33	68.33	77.75	84.00	88.32
13										0.	18.53	47.87	64.63	75.14	82.13	86.96
14										0.	9.52	42.10	60.72	72.39	80.16	85.51
15											0.	36.01	56.58	69.49	78.07	83.99
16											0.	29.58	52.22	66.42	75.86	82.38
17											0.	22.78	47.61	63.18	73.53	80.68
18											0.	15.60	42.73	59.76	71.07	78.88
19											0.	8.01	37.59	56.14	68.47	76.98
20												0.	32.15	52.32	65.72	74.98
21												0.	26.41	48.28	62.82	72.86
22												0.	20.34	44.02	59.76	70.62
23												0.	13.93	39.51	56.52	68.26
24												0.	7.15	34.75	53.10	65.76
25													0.	29.73	49.48	63.12
26													0.	24.41	45.66	60.34
27													0.	18.80	41.63	57.39
28													0.	12.88	37.37	54.28
29													0.	6.61	32.87	51.00
30														0.	28.11	47.52
35															0.	27.00
40																0.

5.75%

AGE OF LOAN	1	2	3	4	5	6	7	8	9	10	15	20	25	30	35	40
1	0.	51.43	68.56	77.11	82.23	85.63	88.05	89.86	91.26	92.38	95.67	97.25	98.15	98.71	99.08	99.34
2		0.	35.26	52.86	63.40	70.41	75.40	79.12	82.01	84.31	91.09	94.34	96.20	97.35	98.11	98.64
3			0.	27.19	43.47	54.29	62.00	67.75	72.21	75.76	86.23	91.26	94.12	95.91	97.09	97.89
4				0.	22.36	37.22	47.80	55.71	61.83	66.71	81.09	88.00	91.93	94.38	96.00	97.11
5					0.	19.14	32.77	42.96	50.84	57.12	75.65	84.55	89.61	92.76	94.85	96.28
6						0.	16.86	29.45	39.20	46.97	69.89	80.89	87.14	91.05	93.63	95.39
7							0.	15.15	26.88	36.22	63.78	77.01	84.54	89.23	92.33	94.46
8								0.	13.82	24.83	57.31	72.91	81.78	87.31	90.97	93.47
9									0.	12.77	50.47	68.56	78.85	85.28	89.52	92.42
10										0.	43.21	63.96	75.76	83.12	87.98	91.31
11										0.	35.53	59.09	72.48	80.84	86.36	90.14
12										0.	27.40	53.92	69.01	78.42	84.64	88.90
13										0.	18.78	48.46	65.33	75.86	82.81	87.58
14										0.	9.66	42.67	61.44	73.15	80.88	86.18
15											0.	36.53	57.31	70.28	78.84	84.71
16											0.	30.04	52.94	67.23	76.67	83.14
17											0.	23.16	48.32	64.01	74.38	81.48
18											0.	15.88	43.42	60.60	71.95	79.73
19											0.	8.17	38.23	56.99	69.38	77.87
20												0.	32.74	53.16	66.65	75.90
21												0.	26.92	49.11	63.77	73.82
22												0.	20.76	44.82	60.71	71.61
23												0.	14.23	40.28	57.48	69.27
24												0.	7.32	35.46	54.05	66.79
25													0.	30.37	50.42	64.17
26													0.	24.97	46.58	61.39
27													0.	19.25	42.51	58.45
28													0.	13.20	38.20	55.34
29													0.	6.79	33.64	52.04
30														0.	28.80	48.55
35															0.	27.73
40																0.

Table 3

REMAINING BALANCE TABLES

ORIGINAL TERM IN YEARS

6.00%

AGE OF LOAN	1	2	3	4	5	6	7	8	9	10	15	20	25	30	35	40
1	0.	51.50	68.64	77.20	82.32	85.72	88.15	89.96	91.36	92.47	95.76	97.33	98.22	98.77	99.13	99.38
2		0.	35.35	52.99	63.55	70.57	75.56	79.29	82.18	84.48	91.26	94.50	96.33	97.47	98.21	98.72
3			0.	27.29	43.62	54.48	62.20	67.97	72.44	76.00	86.47	91.49	94.32	96.08	97.24	98.02
4				0.	22.46	37.39	48.02	55.96	62.10	66.99	81.40	88.29	92.19	94.61	96.20	97.28
5					0.	19.26	32.96	43.20	51.12	57.43	76.01	84.90	89.93	93.05	95.10	96.50
6						0.	16.97	29.65	39.46	47.27	70.29	81.30	87.53	91.40	93.93	95.66
7							0.	15.27	27.09	36.49	64.21	77.48	84.98	89.64	92.70	94.77
8								0.	13.95	25.05	57.76	73.42	82.28	87.77	91.38	93.83
9									0.	12.90	50.92	69.11	79.40	85.79	89.98	92.83
10										0.	43.65	64.53	76.35	83.69	88.50	91.77
11										0.	35.93	59.67	73.11	81.45	86.92	90.64
12										0.	27.54	54.52	69.68	79.08	85.25	89.45
13										0.	19.04	49.04	66.02	76.56	83.47	88.18
14										0.	9.80	43.23	62.15	73.89	81.59	86.83
15											0.	37.06	58.03	71.05	79.59	85.40
16											0.	30.51	53.67	68.04	77.46	83.88
17											0.	23.55	49.03	64.84	75.21	82.26
18											0.	16.16	44.10	61.44	72.81	80.55
19											0.	8.32	38.88	57.83	70.27	78.73
20												0.	33.33	54.00	67.57	76.80
21												0.	27.43	49.94	64.70	74.75
22												0.	21.18	45.62	61.66	72.57
23												0.	14.54	41.04	58.43	70.26
24												0.	7.49	36.18	55.00	67.81
25													0.	31.01	51.36	65.20
26													0.	25.53	47.49	62.44
27													0.	19.71	43.39	59.50
28													0.	13.53	39.03	56.38
29													0.	6.97	34.40	53.07
30														0.	29.49	49.56
35															0.	28.46
40																0.

6.25%

AGE OF LOAN	1	2	3	4	5	6	7	8	9	10	15	20	25	30	35	40
1	0.	51.56	68.72	77.29	82.41	85.82	88.24	90.05	91.45	92.57	95.84	97.41	98.29	98.83	99.18	99.42
2		0.	35.43	53.11	63.69	70.73	75.73	79.46	82.35	84.65	91.42	94.64	96.46	97.58	98.31	98.80
3			0.	27.38	43.77	54.66	62.41	68.20	72.67	76.23	86.71	91.70	94.52	96.25	97.38	98.15
4				0.	22.57	37.56	48.23	56.20	62.37	67.27	81.70	88.58	92.45	94.84	96.40	97.45
5					0.	19.37	33.15	43.44	51.40	57.73	76.36	85.25	90.25	93.34	95.35	96.71
6						0.	17.09	29.85	39.72	47.58	70.69	81.70	87.91	91.74	94.23	95.92
7							0.	15.39	27.30	36.77	64.65	77.93	85.42	90.03	93.04	95.07
8								0.	14.07	25.27	58.21	73.92	82.76	88.22	91.78	94.18
9									0.	13.03	51.37	69.65	79.94	86.29	90.43	93.22
10										0.	44.09	65.10	76.94	84.24	89.00	92.21
11										0.	36.33	60.26	73.74	82.05	87.47	91.13
12										0.	28.08	55.11	70.33	79.73	85.85	89.98
13										0.	19.30	49.63	66.71	77.25	84.12	88.75
14										0.	9.95	43.79	62.86	74.61	82.28	87.45
15											0.	37.58	58.75	71.81	80.32	86.06
16											0.	30.97	54.38	68.83	78.24	84.59
17											0.	23.94	49.74	65.65	76.02	83.02
18											0.	16.45	44.79	62.27	73.66	81.35
19											0.	8.48	39.52	58.67	71.14	79.57
20												0.	33.92	54.84	68.47	77.67
21												0.	27.95	50.76	65.62	75.66
22												0.	21.60	46.42	62.59	73.51
23												0.	14.85	41.80	59.37	71.23
24												0.	7.65	36.89	55.94	68.80
25													0.	31.66	52.29	66.21
26													0.	26.09	48.40	63.46
27													0.	20.16	44.26	60.53
28													0.	13.86	39.86	57.41
29													0.	7.14	35.17	54.10
30														0.	30.19	50.56
35															0.	29.19
40																0.

Table 3

REMAINING BALANCE TABLES

ORIGINAL TERM IN YEARS

6.50%

AGE OF LOAN	1	2	3	4	5	6	7	8	9	10	15	20	25	30	35	40
1	0.	51.62	68.80	77.38	82.51	85.91	88.34	90.15	91.55	92.66	95.93	97.48	98.35	98.88	99.23	99.46
2		0.	35.52	53.24	63.84	70.88	75.89	79.63	82.53	84.82	91.58	94.79	96.59	97.69	98.40	98.88
3			0.	27.48	43.92	54.85	62.62	68.42	72.90	76.47	86.94	91.92	94.71	96.42	97.52	98.26
4				0.	22.67	37.74	48.45	56.45	62.63	67.55	82.00	88.86	92.70	95.06	96.59	97.61
5					0.	19.48	33.33	43.68	51.67	58.03	76.72	85.59	90.56	93.61	95.58	96.91
6						0.	17.21	30.05	39.98	47.88	71.08	82.10	88.28	92.07	94.52	96.16
7							0.	15.51	27.51	37.05	65.07	78.38	85.84	90.42	93.38	95.36
8								0.	14.20	25.49	58.66	74.41	83.24	88.66	92.16	94.51
9									0.	13.16	51.82	70.18	80.47	86.78	90.86	93.60
10										0.	44.52	65.66	77.51	84.78	89.48	92.63
11										0.	36.73	60.84	74.35	82.64	88.00	91.59
12										0.	28.42	55.70	70.99	80.36	86.42	90.49
13										0.	19.56	50.21	67.39	77.93	84.74	89.31
14										0.	10.09	44.35	63.56	75.33	82.95	88.05
15											0.	38.11	59.46	72.56	81.03	86.71
16											0.	31.44	55.10	69.60	78.99	85.28
17											0.	24.33	50.44	66.45	76.81	83.75
18											0.	16.74	45.47	63.09	74.48	82.12
19											0.	8.64	40.17	59.50	72.00	80.38
20												0.	34.51	55.67	69.35	78.52
21												0.	28.47	51.58	66.53	76.54
22												0.	22.03	47.22	63.52	74.43
23												0.	15.16	42.57	60.30	72.18
24												0.	7.82	37.60	56.87	69.77
25													0.	32.30	53.21	67.21
26													0.	26.65	49.30	64.47
27													0.	20.62	45.13	61.55
28													0.	14.19	40.69	58.43
29													0.	7.32	35.94	55.11
30														0.	30.88	51.56
35															0.	29.92
40																0.

6.75%

AGE OF LOAN	1	2	3	4	5	6	7	8	9	10	15	20	25	30	35	40
1	0.	51.68	68.88	77.46	82.60	86.01	88.43	90.24	91.64	92.75	96.01	97.55	98.41	98.93	99.27	99.49
2		0.	35.60	53.36	63.98	71.04	76.06	79.80	82.69	84.99	91.74	94.93	96.71	97.79	98.49	98.95
3			0.	27.58	44.07	55.03	62.82	68.63	73.13	76.70	87.17	92.13	94.89	96.57	97.66	98.37
4				0.	22.78	37.91	48.66	56.69	62.90	67.83	82.29	89.13	92.95	95.27	96.76	97.76
5					0.	19.59	33.52	43.92	51.95	58.34	77.07	85.93	90.87	93.88	95.81	97.09
6						0.	17.32	30.25	40.24	48.18	71.48	82.50	88.64	92.38	94.79	96.39
7							0.	15.63	27.72	37.33	65.50	78.83	86.26	90.79	93.70	95.63
8								0.	14.33	25.71	59.11	74.91	83.71	89.08	92.53	94.82
9									0.	13.29	52.27	70.71	80.99	87.25	91.28	93.95
10										0.	44.96	66.22	78.08	85.30	89.94	93.02
11										0.	37.13	61.42	74.96	83.21	88.51	92.03
12										0.	28.77	56.28	71.63	80.98	86.98	90.97
13										0.	19.81	50.79	68.06	78.59	85.35	89.84
14										0.	10.24	44.91	64.25	76.03	83.60	88.63
15											0.	38.63	60.17	73.30	81.73	87.33
16											0.	31.91	55.81	70.37	79.72	85.94
17											0.	24.72	51.14	67.24	77.58	84.45
18											0.	17.03	46.15	63.89	75.29	82.87
19											0.	8.80	40.81	60.32	72.84	81.17
20												0.	35.10	56.49	70.22	79.35
21												0.	28.99	52.39	67.42	77.41
22												0.	22.46	48.01	64.42	75.33
23												0.	15.47	43.32	61.22	73.11
24												0.	8.00	38.31	57.79	70.73
25													0.	32.95	54.12	68.18
26													0.	27.22	50.20	65.46
27													0.	21.08	46.00	62.55
28													0.	14.52	41.51	59.44
29													0.	7.51	36.71	56.11
30														0.	31.57	52.55
35															0.	30.65
40																0.

Table 3

REMAINING BALANCE TABLES

ORIGINAL TERM IN YEARS

7.00%

AGE OF LOAN	1	2	3	4	5	6	7	8	9	10	15	20	25	30	35	40
1	0.	51.74	68.96	77.55	82.69	86.10	88.53	90.33	91.73	92.84	96.09	97.62	98.47	98.98	99.31	99.53
2		0.	35.69	53.48	64.13	71.20	76.22	79.97	82.86	85.16	91.90	95.07	96.83	97.89	98.57	99.02
3			0.	27.67	44.23	55.22	63.03	68.85	73.35	76.93	87.40	92.33	95.07	96.73	97.78	98.48
4				0.	22.88	38.08	48.88	56.93	63.16	68.10	82.58	89.40	93.18	95.47	96.93	97.90
5					0.	19.70	33.71	44.15	52.23	58.64	77.41	86.26	91.16	94.13	96.02	97.27
6						0.	17.44	30.45	40.50	48.49	71.87	82.88	88.99	92.69	95.05	96.60
7							0.	15.76	27.93	37.60	65.93	79.27	86.67	91.15	94.00	95.89
8								0.	14.45	25.93	59.55	75.39	84.17	89.49	92.88	95.12
9									0.	13.42	52.72	71.23	81.50	87.72	91.68	94.29
10										0.	45.39	66.77	78.63	85.81	90.39	93.41
11										0.	37.54	61.99	75.56	83.77	89.01	92.46
12										0.	29.11	56.87	72.26	81.58	87.52	91.44
13										0.	20.08	51.37	68.73	79.23	85.93	90.35
14										0.	10.39	45.47	64.94	76.72	84.23	89.18
15											0.	39.15	60.87	74.02	82.40	87.92
16											0.	32.38	56.51	71.12	80.44	86.58
17											0.	25.11	51.84	68.02	78.34	85.14
18											0.	17.32	46.83	64.69	76.09	83.59
19											0.	8.96	41.46	61.13	73.67	81.93
20												0.	35.69	57.30	71.08	80.15
21												0.	29.52	53.20	68.30	78.25
22												0.	22.89	48.80	65.32	76.20
23												0.	15.79	44.08	62.12	74.01
24												0.	8.17	39.02	58.70	71.66
25													0.	33.60	55.02	69.14
26													0.	27.78	51.08	66.43
27													0.	21.55	46.86	63.54
28													0.	14.86	42.33	60.43
29													0.	7.69	37.47	57.10
30														0.	32.26	53.52
35															0.	31.38
40																0.

7.25%

AGE OF LOAN	1	2	3	4	5	6	7	8	9	10	15	20	25	30	35	40
1	0.	51.81	69.04	77.64	82.78	86.19	88.62	90.43	91.82	92.93	96.17	97.69	98.53	99.03	99.35	99.56
2		0.	35.77	53.61	64.27	71.35	76.38	80.13	83.03	85.33	92.05	95.21	96.95	97.99	98.65	99.09
3			0.	27.77	44.38	55.40	63.23	69.07	73.58	77.16	87.63	92.54	95.24	96.87	97.90	98.58
4				0.	22.99	38.25	49.09	57.18	63.42	68.38	82.87	89.67	93.42	95.67	97.10	98.03
5					0.	19.82	33.90	44.39	52.50	58.94	77.76	86.58	91.45	94.38	96.23	97.44
6						0.	17.56	30.65	40.76	48.79	72.26	83.27	89.34	92.99	95.30	96.81
7							0.	15.88	28.15	37.88	66.35	79.70	87.07	91.50	94.30	96.13
8								0.	14.58	26.16	60.00	75.87	84.63	89.89	93.22	95.40
9									0.	13.55	53.17	71.75	82.00	88.17	92.07	94.61
10										0.	45.83	67.32	79.18	86.31	90.82	93.77
11										0.	37.94	62.56	76.15	84.32	89.49	92.86
12										0.	29.46	57.45	72.89	82.17	88.05	91.89
13										0.	20.34	51.95	69.38	79.87	86.50	90.84
14										0.	10.54	46.03	65.62	77.39	84.84	89.71
15											0.	39.68	61.57	74.73	83.06	88.50
16											0.	32.85	57.21	71.87	81.14	87.20
17											0.	25.50	52.54	68.79	79.08	85.80
18											0.	17.61	47.51	65.48	76.86	84.29
19											0.	9.12	42.10	61.93	74.48	82.67
20												0.	36.29	58.11	71.91	80.93
21												0.	30.04	54.00	69.16	79.06
22												0.	23.32	49.58	66.20	77.05
23												0.	16.10	44.84	63.02	74.89
24												0.	8.34	39.73	59.59	72.57
25													0.	34.25	55.92	70.07
26													0.	28.35	51.96	67.39
27													0.	22.01	47.71	64.50
28													0.	15.20	43.15	61.40
29													0.	7.87	38.23	58.07
30														0.	32.96	54.49
35															0.	32.11
40																0.

Table 3

REMAINING BALANCE TABLES

ORIGINAL TERM IN YEARS

7.50%

AGE OF LOAN	1	2	3	4	5	6	7	8	9	10	15	20	25	30	35	40
1	0.	51.87	69.13	77.73	82.87	86.29	88.71	90.52	91.91	93.02	96.25	97.76	98.58	99.08	99.39	99.59
2		0.	35.85	53.73	64.42	71.51	76.55	80.30	83.20	85.50	92.21	95.34	97.06	98.08	98.73	99.15
3			0.	27.87	44.53	55.58	63.44	69.29	73.81	77.39	87.85	92.73	95.41	97.01	98.02	98.67
4				0.	23.10	38.42	49.31	57.42	63.68	68.65	83.15	89.93	93.64	95.86	97.25	98.16
5					0.	19.93	34.09	44.63	52.78	59.24	78.10	86.90	91.73	94.62	96.43	97.60
6						0.	17.68	30.85	41.02	49.09	72.64	83.64	89.67	93.28	95.54	97.00
7							0.	16.00	28.36	38.16	66.77	80.13	87.46	91.83	94.58	96.36
8								0.	14.71	26.38	60.44	76.34	85.07	90.28	93.55	95.67
9									0.	13.68	53.62	72.26	82.49	88.60	92.44	94.92
10										0.	46.26	67.87	79.72	86.79	91.24	94.12
11										0.	38.34	63.13	76.73	84.85	89.95	93.25
12										0.	29.80	58.02	73.50	82.75	88.55	92.31
13										0.	20.60	52.52	70.03	80.49	87.05	91.31
14										0.	10.69	46.59	66.29	78.05	85.44	90.22
15											0.	40.20	62.26	75.43	83.70	89.05
16											0.	33.32	57.91	72.60	81.82	87.79
17											0.	25.90	53.23	69.55	79.79	86.43
18											0.	17.90	48.18	66.26	77.61	84.97
19											0.	9.29	42.74	62.72	75.26	83.39
20												0.	36.88	58.91	72.73	81.69
21												0.	30.56	54.79	70.00	79.86
22												0.	23.76	50.36	67.06	77.88
23												0.	16.42	45.59	63.90	75.75
24												0.	8.52	40.44	60.48	73.46
25													0.	34.89	56.80	70.99
26													0.	28.92	52.84	68.33
27													0.	22.48	48.56	65.46
28													0.	15.54	43.96	62.36
29													0.	8.06	39.00	59.03
30														0.	33.65	55.44
35															0.	32.84
40																0.

7.75%

AGE OF LOAN	1	2	3	4	5	6	7	8	9	10	15	20	25	30	35	40
1	0.	51.93	69.21	77.82	82.96	86.38	88.80	90.61	92.00	93.11	96.33	97.82	98.64	99.12	99.42	99.62
2		0.	35.94	53.85	64.56	71.66	76.71	80.46	83.36	85.66	92.36	95.47	97.17	98.17	98.80	99.20
3			0.	27.97	44.68	55.77	63.64	69.50	74.03	77.62	88.07	92.93	95.58	97.15	98.13	98.76
4				0.	23.20	38.59	49.52	57.66	63.95	68.93	83.44	90.18	93.86	96.04	97.40	98.27
5					0.	20.04	34.27	44.87	53.05	59.54	78.43	87.22	92.01	94.85	96.62	97.75
6						0.	17.80	31.05	41.28	49.40	73.03	84.01	90.00	93.56	95.77	97.19
7							0.	16.13	28.57	38.44	67.19	80.55	87.84	92.16	94.85	96.58
8								0.	14.84	26.60	60.88	76.81	85.50	90.65	93.86	95.92
9									0.	13.81	54.06	72.77	82.97	89.03	92.79	95.21
10										0.	46.70	68.41	80.25	87.27	91.64	94.45
11										0.	38.74	63.69	77.30	85.37	90.39	93.62
12										0.	30.15	58.60	74.11	83.31	89.04	92.72
13										0.	20.86	53.09	70.67	81.10	87.59	91.75
14										0.	10.84	47.15	66.95	78.70	86.01	90.71
15											0.	40.73	62.94	76.11	84.31	89.58
16											0.	33.79	58.60	73.31	82.48	88.36
17											0.	26.29	53.91	70.29	80.49	87.04
18											0.	18.20	48.85	67.03	78.35	85.62
19											0.	9.45	43.38	63.50	76.04	84.08
20												0.	37.47	59.70	73.54	82.42
21												0.	31.09	55.58	70.83	80.62
22												0.	24.19	51.14	67.92	78.69
23												0.	16.74	46.33	64.76	76.59
24												0.	8.69	41.15	61.36	74.33
25													0.	35.54	57.68	71.88
26													0.	29.49	53.70	69.24
27													0.	22.95	49.41	66.39
28													0.	15.88	44.77	63.31
29													0.	8.25	39.75	59.98
30														0.	34.34	56.38
35															0.	33.57
40																0.

Table 3

REMAINING BALANCE TABLES

ORIGINAL TERM IN YEARS

8.00%

AGE OF LOAN	1	2	3	4	5	6	7	8	9	10	15	20	25	30	35	40
1	0.	51.99	69.29	77.91	83.06	86.47	88.90	90.70	92.09	93.19	96.40	97.89	98.69	99.16	99.46	99.64
2		0.	36.02	53.98	64.71	71.82	76.87	80.63	83.53	85.82	92.51	95.60	97.27	98.26	98.87	99.26
3			0.	28.06	44.83	55.95	63.84	69.72	74.25	77.84	88.29	93.12	95.74	97.28	98.23	98.84
4				0.	23.31	38.77	49.74	57.91	64.21	69.20	83.72	90.43	94.07	96.22	97.54	98.39
5					0.	20.16	34.46	45.11	53.33	59.84	78.77	87.53	92.27	95.07	96.80	97.90
6						0.	17.92	31.26	41.55	49.70	73.41	84.38	90.32	93.83	95.99	97.36
7							0.	16.25	28.79	38.72	67.60	80.97	88.21	92.48	95.11	96.79
8								0.	14.97	26.83	61.31	77.27	85.92	91.02	94.16	96.17
9									0.	13.95	54.51	73.27	83.45	89.44	93.14	95.49
10										0.	47.13	68.94	80.76	87.72	92.02	94.76
11										0.	39.15	64.25	77.86	85.87	90.82	93.97
12										0.	30.50	59.17	74.71	83.86	89.52	93.11
13										0.	21.13	53.67	71.30	81.69	88.10	92.18
14										0.	10.99	47.71	67.61	79.33	86.57	91.18
15											0.	41.25	63.61	76.78	84.91	90.09
16											0.	34.26	59.29	74.02	83.12	88.91
17											0.	26.69	54.60	71.03	81.18	87.63
18											0.	18.49	49.52	67.79	79.07	86.25
19											0.	9.62	44.02	64.28	76.79	84.75
20												0.	38.06	60.48	74.32	83.13
21												0.	31.62	56.36	71.65	81.37
22												0.	24.63	51.91	68.75	79.47
23												0.	17.07	47.08	65.62	77.41
24												0.	8.87	41.85	62.22	75.17
25													0.	36.19	58.54	72.76
26													0.	30.06	54.56	70.14
27													0.	23.42	50.24	67.31
28													0.	16.22	45.57	64.23
29													0.	8.44	40.51	60.91
30														0.	35.03	57.31
35															0.	34.29
40																0.

8.25%

AGE OF LOAN	1	2	3	4	5	6	7	8	9	10	15	20	25	30	35	40
1	0.	52.05	69.37	77.99	83.15	86.56	88.99	90.79	92.18	93.28	96.48	97.95	98.74	99.21	99.49	99.67
2		0.	36.11	54.10	64.85	71.97	77.03	80.79	83.69	85.99	92.65	95.72	97.38	98.34	98.93	99.31
3			0.	28.16	44.98	56.14	64.05	69.93	74.47	78.07	88.50	93.30	95.89	97.41	98.33	98.92
4				0.	23.42	38.94	49.95	58.15	64.47	69.47	83.99	90.68	94.28	96.39	97.68	98.49
5					0.	20.27	34.65	45.35	53.60	60.13	79.10	87.83	92.53	95.28	96.97	98.03
6						0.	18.04	31.46	41.81	50.00	73.78	84.73	90.64	94.09	96.20	97.53
7							0.	16.38	29.00	39.00	68.01	81.38	88.58	92.78	95.36	96.99
8								0.	15.10	27.05	61.75	77.73	86.34	91.37	94.45	96.39
9									0.	14.08	54.95	73.77	83.91	89.84	93.47	95.75
10										0.	47.56	69.47	81.27	88.17	92.40	95.06
11										0.	39.55	64.80	78.41	86.36	91.23	94.30
12										0.	30.85	59.74	75.30	84.40	89.97	93.48
13										0.	21.40	54.23	71.93	82.27	88.60	92.59
14										0.	11.14	48.26	68.26	79.95	87.11	91.62
15											0.	41.78	64.28	77.44	85.50	90.58
16											0.	34.74	59.96	74.71	83.74	89.44
17											0.	27.09	55.28	71.75	81.84	88.20
18											0.	18.79	50.18	68.53	79.77	86.85
19											0.	9.78	44.66	65.04	77.53	85.40
20												0.	38.66	61.25	75.09	83.81
21												0.	32.14	57.14	72.45	82.09
22												0.	25.07	52.67	69.57	80.23
23												0.	17.39	47.82	66.46	78.20
24												0.	9.05	42.55	63.07	76.00
25													0.	36.83	59.39	73.61
26													0.	30.63	55.40	71.02
27													0.	23.89	51.07	68.20
28													0.	16.57	46.37	65.15
29													0.	8.62	41.26	61.83
30														0.	35.72	58.22
35															0.	35.01
40																0.

Table 3

REMAINING BALANCE TABLES

ORIGINAL TERM IN YEARS

8.50%

AGE OF LOAN	1	2	3	4	5	6	7	8	9	10	15	20	25	30	35	40
1	0.	52.12	69.45	78.08	83.24	86.65	89.08	90.88	92.27	93.37	96.55	98.01	98.79	99.24	99.52	99.69
2		0.	36.19	54.22	64.99	72.13	77.19	80.95	83.85	86.15	92.80	95.84	97.47	98.42	99.00	99.35
3			0.	28.26	45.14	56.32	64.25	70.15	74.69	78.29	88.71	93.49	96.04	97.53	98.43	98.99
4				0.	23.52	39.11	50.17	58.39	64.73	69.74	84.26	90.92	94.48	96.55	97.81	98.59
5					0.	20.38	34.84	45.59	53.88	60.43	79.42	88.13	92.79	95.49	97.13	98.16
6						0.	18.16	31.66	42.07	50.30	74.16	85.09	90.94	94.34	96.40	97.68
7							0.	16.50	29.21	39.28	68.42	81.78	88.93	93.08	95.60	97.17
8								0.	15.23	27.28	62.18	78.18	86.74	91.71	94.73	96.61
9									0.	14.22	55.39	74.26	84.36	90.22	93.78	96.00
10										0.	48.00	69.99	81.77	88.60	92.75	95.34
11										0.	39.95	65.35	78.95	86.84	91.63	94.62
12										0.	31.19	60.30	75.88	84.92	90.41	93.84
13										0.	21.66	54.80	72.54	82.83	89.08	92.98
14										0.	11.29	48.81	68.90	80.56	87.64	92.05
15											0.	42.30	64.95	78.08	86.06	91.04
16											0.	35.21	60.64	75.39	84.35	89.94
17											0.	27.49	55.95	72.46	82.48	88.74
18											0.	19.09	50.85	69.27	80.46	87.44
19											0.	9.95	45.29	65.80	78.25	86.02
20												0.	39.25	62.02	75.84	84.48
21												0.	32.67	57.90	73.23	82.79
22												0.	25.51	53.43	70.38	80.96
23												0.	17.71	48.55	67.28	78.97
24												0.	9.23	43.25	63.91	76.80
25													0.	37.48	60.24	74.45
26													0.	31.20	56.24	71.88
27													0.	24.36	51.89	69.08
28													0.	16.92	47.16	66.04
29													0.	8.82	42.01	62.73
30														0.	36.40	59.13
35															0.	35.73
40																0.

8.75%

AGE OF LOAN	1	2	3	4	5	6	7	8	9	10	15	20	25	30	35	40
1	0.	52.18	69.53	78.17	83.33	86.74	89.17	90.97	92.36	93.45	96.62	98.07	98.84	99.28	99.55	99.71
2		0.	36.28	54.35	65.14	72.28	77.35	81.11	84.01	86.31	92.94	95.96	97.57	98.50	99.05	99.40
3			0.	28.36	45.29	56.50	64.45	70.36	74.91	78.51	88.92	93.66	96.19	97.64	98.52	99.06
4				0.	23.63	39.28	50.38	58.63	64.98	70.01	84.53	91.16	94.68	96.71	97.93	98.68
5					0.	20.50	35.03	45.83	54.15	60.73	79.75	88.42	93.03	95.69	97.29	98.28
6						0.	18.28	31.86	42.33	50.60	74.53	85.43	91.24	94.58	96.59	97.83
7							0.	16.63	29.43	39.56	68.83	82.18	89.28	93.36	95.83	97.35
8								0.	15.36	27.50	62.61	78.62	87.14	92.04	94.99	96.82
9									0.	14.35	55.83	74.74	84.81	90.60	94.08	96.24
10										0.	48.43	70.51	82.26	89.02	93.09	95.61
11										0.	40.35	65.90	79.48	87.30	92.01	94.92
12										0.	31.54	60.86	76.45	85.43	90.83	94.17
13										0.	21.93	55.36	73.14	83.38	89.55	93.36
14										0.	11.44	49.36	69.54	81.15	88.14	92.46
15											0.	42.82	65.60	78.71	86.61	91.49
16											0.	35.68	61.30	76.06	84.94	90.43
17											0.	27.89	56.62	73.16	83.11	89.27
18											0.	19.39	51.50	69.99	81.12	88.00
19											0.	10.12	45.93	66.54	78.95	86.62
20												0.	39.84	62.77	76.58	85.12
21												0.	33.20	58.66	73.99	83.47
22												0.	25.95	54.18	71.17	81.68
23												0.	18.04	49.28	68.09	79.72
24												0.	9.41	43.95	64.73	77.59
25													0.	38.12	61.07	75.26
26													0.	31.76	57.07	72.72
27													0.	24.83	52.71	69.94
28													0.	17.26	47.95	66.92
29													0.	9.01	42.75	63.62
30														0.	37.09	60.02
35															0.	36.45
40																0.

Table 3

REMAINING BALANCE TABLES

ORIGINAL TERM IN YEARS

9.00%

AGE OF LOAN	1	2	3	4	5	6	7	8	9	10	15	20	25	30	35	40
1	0.	52.24	69.61	78.26	83.42	86.84	89.26	91.06	92.44	93.54	96.69	98.13	98.88	99.32	99.57	99.73
2		0.	36.36	54.47	65.28	72.44	77.51	81.27	84.17	86.47	93.08	96.08	97.66	98.57	99.11	99.44
3			0.	28.46	45.44	56.68	64.65	70.57	75.13	78.73	89.12	93.84	96.33	97.75	98.60	99.12
4				0.	23.74	39.46	50.60	58.87	65.24	70.28	84.80	91.39	94.87	96.86	98.04	98.77
5					0.	20.61	35.22	46.07	54.42	61.02	80.07	88.71	93.27	95.88	97.44	98.39
6						0.	18.40	32.07	42.59	50.90	74.89	85.77	91.53	94.81	96.77	97.97
7							0.	16.75	29.64	39.84	69.23	82.57	89.62	93.64	96.04	97.51
8								0.	15.49	27.73	63.04	79.06	87.53	92.36	95.25	97.01
9									0.	14.49	56.27	75.22	85.24	90.96	94.37	96.47
10										0.	48.86	71.03	82.74	89.43	93.42	95.87
11										0.	40.76	66.44	80.00	87.75	92.38	95.21
12										0.	31.90	61.41	77.01	85.92	91.24	94.49
13										0.	22.20	55.92	73.74	83.92	89.99	93.71
14										0.	11.60	49.91	70.16	81.73	88.63	92.85
15											0.	43.34	66.25	79.33	87.14	91.92
16											0.	36.16	61.97	76.71	85.51	90.89
17											0.	28.29	57.28	73.84	83.72	89.77
18											0.	19.69	52.16	70.70	81.77	88.54
19											0.	10.29	46.56	67.27	79.63	87.20
20												0.	40.43	63.52	77.30	85.73
21												0.	33.72	59.41	74.74	84.13
22												0.	26.39	54.92	71.95	82.37
23												0.	18.37	50.01	68.89	80.45
24												0.	9.60	44.64	65.55	78.35
25													0.	38.76	61.89	76.05
26													0.	32.33	57.89	73.54
27													0.	25.30	53.51	70.79
28													0.	17.61	48.73	67.78
29													0.	9.20	43.49	64.49
30														0.	37.77	60.89
35															0.	37.16
40																0.

9.25%

AGE OF LOAN	1	2	3	4	5	6	7	8	9	10	15	20	25	30	35	40
1	0.	52.30	69.69	78.34	83.51	86.93	89.35	91.14	92.53	93.62	96.76	98.18	98.93	99.35	99.60	99.75
2		0.	36.45	54.59	65.42	72.59	77.66	81.43	84.33	86.62	93.22	96.19	97.75	98.64	99.16	99.48
3			0.	28.55	45.59	56.87	64.85	70.79	75.35	78.95	89.33	94.01	96.47	97.86	98.68	99.18
4				0.	23.84	39.63	50.81	59.11	65.50	70.54	85.06	91.61	95.05	97.00	98.15	98.85
5					0.	20.73	35.41	46.31	54.69	61.32	80.39	88.99	93.51	96.06	97.58	98.49
6						0.	18.52	32.27	42.85	51.21	75.26	86.11	91.81	95.04	96.94	98.10
7							0.	16.88	29.86	40.12	69.63	82.95	89.94	93.91	96.25	97.67
8								0.	15.62	27.96	63.47	79.49	87.90	92.67	95.49	97.20
9									0.	14.62	56.71	75.70	85.66	91.31	94.65	96.68
10										0.	49.29	71.53	83.21	89.82	93.74	96.11
11										0.	41.16	66.97	80.52	88.19	92.73	95.48
12										0.	32.25	61.97	77.57	86.40	91.63	94.80
13										0.	22.47	56.48	74.33	84.44	90.42	94.05
14										0.	11.75	50.46	70.78	82.29	89.10	93.23
15											0.	43.86	66.89	79.93	87.65	92.33
16											0.	36.63	62.62	77.35	86.06	91.34
17											0.	28.70	57.94	74.51	84.31	90.25
18											0.	20.00	52.81	71.40	82.40	89.06
19											0.	10.46	47.18	67.99	80.30	87.76
20												0.	41.01	64.26	78.00	86.33
21												0.	34.25	60.16	75.47	84.76
22												0.	26.83	55.66	72.71	83.04
23												0.	18.70	50.73	69.67	81.16
24												0.	9.78	45.33	66.35	79.09
25													0.	39.40	62.70	76.82
26													0.	32.90	58.70	74.34
27													0.	25.78	54.31	71.61
28													0.	17.96	49.50	68.62
29													0.	9.39	44.23	65.35
30														0.	38.45	61.75
35															0.	37.87
40																0.

Table 3

REMAINING BALANCE TABLES

ORIGINAL TERM IN YEARS

9.50%

AGE OF LOAN	1	2	3	4	5	6	7	8	9	10	15	20	25	30	35	40
1	0.	52.36	69.77	78.43	83.60	87.01	89.44	91.23	92.61	93.70	96.83	98.24	98.97	99.38	99.62	99.77
2		0.	36.53	54.72	65.56	72.74	77.82	81.59	84.49	86.78	93.35	96.30	97.84	98.71	99.21	99.52
3			0.	28.65	45.74	57.05	65.06	71.00	75.57	79.17	89.53	94.18	96.60	97.96	98.76	99.24
4				0.	23.95	39.80	51.02	59.35	65.75	70.81	85.32	91.84	95.23	97.14	98.26	98.93
5					0.	20.84	35.60	46.55	54.97	61.61	80.70	89.27	93.73	96.24	97.71	98.59
6						0.	18.64	32.48	43.11	51.51	75.62	86.44	92.08	95.25	97.11	98.22
7							0.	17.01	30.08	40.40	70.03	83.33	90.27	94.16	96.45	97.82
8								0.	15.75	28.18	63.89	79.92	88.27	92.97	95.72	97.37
9									0.	14.76	57.14	76.16	86.08	91.65	94.92	96.88
10										0.	49.72	72.04	83.67	90.21	94.04	96.34
11										0.	41.56	67.50	81.02	88.62	93.07	95.74
12										0.	32.60	62.51	78.11	86.87	92.01	95.09
13										0.	22.74	57.03	74.91	84.95	90.84	94.37
14										0.	11.91	51.01	71.39	82.84	89.56	93.58
15											0.	44.38	67.52	80.52	88.14	92.72
16											0.	37.10	63.27	77.97	86.59	91.76
17											0.	29.10	58.59	75.17	84.88	90.71
18											0.	20.30	53.46	72.09	83.01	89.56
19											0.	10.63	47.81	68.70	80.95	88.30
20												0.	41.60	64.98	78.68	86.90
21												0.	34.78	60.89	76.19	85.37
22												0.	27.27	56.39	73.45	83.69
23												0.	19.03	51.45	70.44	81.84
24												0.	9.96	46.01	67.13	79.81
25													0.	40.04	63.50	77.58
26													0.	33.47	59.50	75.12
27													0.	26.25	55.10	72.42
28													0.	18.31	50.27	69.45
29													0.	9.59	44.96	66.19
30														0.	39.12	62.60
35															0.	38.57
40																0.

9.75%

AGE OF LOAN	1	2	3	4	5	6	7	8	9	10	15	20	25	30	35	40
1	0.	52.43	69.85	78.52	83.68	87.10	89.52	91.32	92.70	93.78	96.90	98.29	99.01	99.41	99.65	99.79
2		0.	36.62	54.84	65.71	72.89	77.98	81.75	84.65	86.94	93.49	96.41	97.93	98.77	99.26	99.55
3			0.	28.75	45.89	57.23	65.26	71.21	75.78	79.39	89.72	94.34	96.73	98.06	98.83	99.29
4				0.	24.06	39.97	51.24	59.59	66.01	71.07	85.58	92.05	95.41	97.27	98.36	99.00
5					0.	20.96	35.79	46.79	55.24	61.91	81.01	89.54	93.95	96.41	97.84	98.69
6						0.	18.76	32.68	43.37	51.81	75.97	86.76	92.35	95.46	97.27	98.34
7							0.	17.13	30.29	40.68	70.43	83.71	90.58	94.41	96.63	97.96
8								0.	15.88	28.41	64.31	80.34	88.63	93.26	95.94	97.53
9									0.	14.89	57.57	76.62	86.49	91.98	95.17	97.07
10										0.	50.15	72.53	84.12	90.58	94.33	96.56
11										0.	41.97	68.02	81.51	89.03	93.40	95.99
12										0.	32.95	63.06	78.64	87.33	92.37	95.37
13										0.	23.01	57.58	75.48	85.45	91.24	94.68
14										0.	12.07	51.55	71.99	83.38	89.99	93.92
15											0.	44.90	68.15	81.10	88.62	93.09
16											0.	37.58	63.91	78.59	87.11	92.17
17											0.	29.50	59.24	75.82	85.44	91.16
18											0.	20.61	54.10	72.77	83.60	90.04
19											0.	10.80	48.43	69.41	81.58	88.81
20												0.	42.19	65.70	79.35	87.46
21												0.	35.30	61.62	76.89	85.97
22												0.	27.72	57.12	74.18	84.32
23												0.	19.36	52.16	71.20	82.51
24												0.	10.15	46.69	67.91	80.51
25													0.	40.67	64.28	78.31
26													0.	34.04	60.28	75.88
27													0.	26.72	55.88	73.21
28													0.	18.67	51.03	70.26
29													0.	9.79	45.68	67.01
30														0.	39.79	63.44
35															0.	39.27
40																0.

Table 3

REMAINING BALANCE TABLES

ORIGINAL TERM IN YEARS

10.00%

AGE OF LOAN	1	2	3	4	5	6	7	8	9	10	15	20	25	30	35	40
1	0.	52.49	69.93	78.60	83.77	87.19	89.61	91.40	92.78	93.87	96.97	98.35	99.05	99.44	99.67	99.80
2		0.	36.70	54.96	65.85	73.04	78.13	81.91	84.81	87.09	93.62	96.52	98.01	98.83	99.30	99.58
3			0.	28.85	46.04	57.41	65.46	71.42	75.99	79.60	89.92	94.50	96.85	98.15	98.90	99.34
4				0.	24.17	40.15	51.45	59.83	66.26	71.33	85.83	92.27	95.57	97.40	98.45	99.07
5					0.	21.07	35.98	47.03	55.51	62.20	81.32	89.80	94.16	96.57	97.96	98.78
6						0.	18.88	32.88	43.63	52.10	76.33	87.08	92.61	95.66	97.42	98.45
7							0.	17.26	30.51	40.96	70.82	84.07	90.88	94.65	96.81	98.09
8								0.	16.01	28.64	64.73	80.75	88.98	93.53	96.15	97.69
9									0.	15.03	58.01	77.08	86.88	92.30	95.42	97.25
10										0.	50.58	73.02	84.56	90.94	94.60	96.76
11											42.37	68.54	82.00	89.43	93.71	96.22
12											33.30	63.60	79.17	87.77	92.72	95.63
13											23.29	58.13	76.04	85.93	91.63	94.97
14											12.22	52.09	72.58	83.91	90.42	94.25
15											0.	45.42	68.76	81.66	89.08	93.45
16												38.05	64.54	79.19	87.61	92.56
17												29.91	59.88	76.45	85.98	91.58
18												20.91	54.74	73.43	84.18	90.50
19												10.98	49.05	70.09	82.19	89.31
20												0.	42.77	66.41	80.00	87.99
21													35.83	62.33	77.57	86.54
22													28.16	57.83	74.89	84.93
23													19.69	52.86	71.93	83.15
24													10.34	47.37	68.66	81.19
25													0.	41.30	65.05	79.02
26														34.60	61.06	76.62
27														27.20	56.65	73.98
28														19.02	51.78	71.05
29														9.98	46.40	67.82
30														0.	40.46	64.26
35															0.	39.97
40																0.

10.25%

AGE OF LOAN	1	2	3	4	5	6	7	8	9	10	15	20	25	30	35	40
1	0.	52.55	70.01	78.69	83.86	87.28	89.70	91.49	92.86	93.95	97.03	98.40	99.09	99.47	99.69	99.82
2		0.	36.79	55.09	65.99	73.20	78.29	82.06	84.96	87.24	93.75	96.62	98.09	98.89	99.35	99.61
3			0.	28.95	46.20	57.60	65.65	71.63	76.21	79.82	90.11	94.65	96.97	98.24	98.96	99.39
4				0.	24.28	40.32	51.66	60.07	66.51	71.59	86.08	92.48	95.74	97.52	98.54	99.14
5					0.	21.19	36.17	47.27	55.78	62.49	81.62	90.06	94.37	96.73	98.08	98.86
6						0.	19.01	33.09	43.89	52.40	76.68	87.39	92.86	95.85	97.56	98.55
7							0.	17.39	30.73	41.24	71.21	84.43	91.18	94.88	96.99	98.21
8								0.	16.15	28.87	65.15	81.16	89.33	93.80	96.35	97.83
9									0.	15.17	58.44	77.53	87.27	92.61	95.65	97.42
10										0.	51.00	73.51	84.99	91.29	94.87	96.96
11											42.77	69.06	82.47	89.82	94.01	96.44
12											33.66	64.13	79.68	88.20	93.05	95.88
13											23.56	58.67	76.59	86.41	92.00	95.25
14											12.38	52.63	73.16	84.42	90.83	94.56
15											0.	45.94	69.37	82.21	89.53	93.79
16												38.52	65.17	79.78	88.09	92.93
17												30.31	60.52	77.08	86.50	91.99
18												21.22	55.37	74.08	84.74	90.95
19												11.15	49.67	70.77	82.79	89.79
20												0.	43.35	67.10	80.63	88.51
21													36.35	63.04	78.24	87.09
22													28.61	58.54	75.59	85.52
23													20.03	53.56	72.66	83.77
24													10.52	48.04	69.41	81.85
25													0.	41.93	65.81	79.71
26														35.16	61.83	77.35
27														27.67	57.42	74.73
28														19.37	52.53	71.83
29														10.18	47.12	68.62
30														0.	41.13	65.06
35															0.	40.66
40																0.

Table 3

REMAINING BALANCE TABLES

ORIGINAL TERM IN YEARS

10.50%

AGE OF LOAN

Age	1	2	3	4	5	6	7	8	9	10	15	20	25	30	35	40
1	0.	52.61	70.08	78.77	83.95	87.37	89.78	91.57	92.95	94.03	97.10	98.45	99.13	99.50	99.71	99.83
2		0.	36.87	55.21	66.13	73.35	78.44	82.22	85.11	87.39	93.88	96.72	98.16	98.94	99.39	99.64
3			0.	29.05	46.35	57.78	65.85	71.83	76.42	80.03	90.30	94.81	97.09	98.33	99.03	99.43
4				0.	24.38	40.49	51.88	60.30	66.77	71.85	86.33	92.68	95.90	97.64	98.63	99.19
5					0.	21.30	36.36	47.50	56.05	62.78	81.92	90.32	94.57	96.88	98.18	98.94
6						0.	19.13	33.29	44.15	52.70	77.03	87.70	93.10	96.04	97.69	98.65
7							0.	17.52	30.94	41.52	71.59	84.79	91.47	95.10	97.15	98.33
8								0.	16.28	29.10	65.56	81.56	89.66	94.06	96.54	97.97
9									0.	15.31	58.86	77.97	87.65	92.90	95.87	97.58
10										0.	51.43	73.99	85.42	91.62	95.12	97.14
11										0.	43.17	69.57	82.94	90.20	94.29	96.65
12										0.	34.01	64.66	80.19	88.62	93.37	96.11
13										0.	23.84	59.21	77.13	86.86	92.35	95.51
14										0.	12.54	53.16	73.74	84.91	91.22	94.85
15											0.	46.45	69.97	82.75	89.96	94.11
16											0.	38.99	65.79	80.35	88.56	93.29
17											0.	30.72	61.15	77.68	87.01	92.38
18											0.	21.53	56.00	74.73	85.29	91.37
19											0.	11.33	50.28	71.44	83.37	90.25
20												0.	43.93	67.79	81.25	89.00
21												0.	36.88	63.74	78.89	87.62
22												0.	29.05	59.24	76.27	86.08
23												0.	20.36	54.25	73.37	84.38
24												0.	10.71	48.71	70.14	82.49
25													0.	42.56	66.56	80.38
26													0.	35.73	62.58	78.05
27													0.	28.14	58.17	75.46
28													0.	19.72	53.27	72.59
29													0.	10.38	47.83	69.40
30														0.	41.79	65.85
35															0.	41.34
40																0.

10.75%

AGE OF LOAN

Age	1	2	3	4	5	6	7	8	9	10	15	20	25	30	35	40
1	0.	52.67	70.16	78.86	84.04	87.46	89.87	91.66	93.03	94.10	97.16	98.49	99.16	99.53	99.73	99.84
2		0.	36.96	55.33	66.27	73.50	78.60	82.37	85.27	87.54	94.00	96.82	98.23	99.00	99.42	99.67
3			0.	29.14	46.50	57.96	66.05	72.04	76.63	80.24	90.49	94.95	97.20	98.41	99.08	99.47
4				0.	24.49	40.67	52.09	60.54	67.02	72.11	86.57	92.88	96.05	97.75	98.71	99.25
5					0.	21.42	36.55	47.74	56.32	63.07	82.22	90.57	94.77	97.03	98.29	99.01
6						0.	19.25	33.50	44.41	53.00	77.37	88.00	93.34	96.22	97.82	98.74
7							0.	17.64	31.16	41.80	71.98	85.14	91.75	95.31	97.30	98.44
8								0.	16.41	29.33	65.97	81.95	89.98	94.31	96.72	98.10
9									0.	15.45	59.29	78.41	88.02	93.19	96.08	97.73
10										0.	51.85	74.46	85.83	91.95	95.37	97.31
11										0.	43.58	70.07	83.39	90.56	94.57	96.85
12										0.	34.36	65.19	80.68	89.02	93.68	96.34
13										0.	24.11	59.75	77.66	87.31	92.69	95.76
14										0.	12.70	53.70	74.30	85.40	91.60	95.13
15											0.	46.96	70.57	83.28	90.37	94.42
16											0.	39.47	66.41	80.91	89.01	93.63
17											0.	31.12	61.78	78.28	87.50	92.75
18											0.	21.84	56.62	75.35	85.81	91.77
19											0.	11.50	50.89	72.09	83.94	90.69
20												0.	44.50	68.47	81.85	89.48
21												0.	37.40	64.43	79.53	88.13
22												0.	29.49	59.94	76.94	86.63
23												0.	20.69	54.94	74.06	84.96
24												0.	10.90	49.37	70.86	83.11
25													0.	43.18	67.30	81.04
26													0.	36.29	63.33	78.74
27													0.	28.62	58.91	76.18
28													0.	20.08	54.00	73.33
29													0.	10.58	48.53	70.16
30														0.	42.44	66.63
35															0.	42.02
40																0.

Table 3

REMAINING BALANCE TABLES

ORIGINAL TERM IN YEARS

11.00%

AGE OF LOAN	1	2	3	4	5	6	7	8	9	10	15	20	25	30	35	40
1	0.	52.73	70.24	78.94	84.12	87.54	89.96	91.74	93.11	94.18	97.22	98.54	99.20	99.55	99.74	99.85
2		0.	37.04	55.45	66.41	73.65	78.75	82.53	85.42	87.69	94.13	96.91	98.31	99.05	99.46	99.69
3			0.	29.24	46.65	58.14	66.25	72.25	76.84	80.45	90.67	95.10	97.31	98.49	99.14	99.51
4				0.	24.60	40.84	52.30	60.78	67.27	72.37	86.81	93.07	96.20	97.86	98.78	99.30
5					0.	21.54	36.74	47.98	56.59	63.36	82.51	90.81	94.95	97.16	98.39	99.08
6						0.	19.37	33.70	44.67	53.30	77.71	88.29	93.57	96.39	97.94	98.82
7							0.	17.77	31.38	42.08	72.36	85.48	92.03	95.52	97.45	98.54
8								0.	16.55	29.56	66.38	82.34	90.30	94.55	96.90	98.22
9									0.	15.59	59.71	78.84	88.38	93.47	96.28	97.87
10										0.	52.28	74.93	86.23	92.26	95.60	97.48
11										0.	43.98	70.57	83.84	90.92	94.83	97.04
12										0.	34.72	65.71	81.17	89.42	93.98	96.55
13										0.	24.39	60.28	78.19	87.74	93.02	96.00
14										0.	12.86	54.23	74.86	85.87	91.96	95.39
15											0.	47.47	71.15	83.79	90.77	94.71
16											0.	39.94	67.01	81.46	89.45	93.95
17											0.	31.53	62.39	78.87	87.97	93.11
18											0.	22.15	57.24	75.97	86.33	92.16
19											0.	11.68	51.49	72.74	84.49	91.11
20												0.	45.08	69.13	82.44	89.93
21												0.	37.92	65.11	80.15	88.62
22												0.	29.94	60.63	77.59	87.16
23												0.	21.03	55.62	74.74	85.53
24												0.	11.09	50.03	71.57	83.71
25													0.	43.80	68.02	81.67
26													0.	36.85	64.06	79.41
27													0.	29.09	59.65	76.88
28													0.	20.43	54.72	74.05
29													0.	10.78	49.23	70.90
30														0.	43.09	67.39
35															0.	42.70
40																0.

11.25%

AGE OF LOAN	1	2	3	4	5	6	7	8	9	10	15	20	25	30	35	40
1	0.	52.80	70.32	79.03	84.21	87.63	90.04	91.82	93.19	94.26	97.28	98.59	99.23	99.57	99.76	99.86
2		0.	37.13	55.58	66.55	73.79	78.90	82.68	85.57	87.84	94.25	97.01	98.37	99.10	99.49	99.71
3			0.	29.34	46.80	58.32	66.45	72.45	77.05	80.66	90.85	95.24	97.41	98.56	99.19	99.54
4				0.	24.71	41.01	52.51	61.01	67.52	72.63	87.05	93.26	96.34	97.97	98.86	99.35
5					0.	21.65	36.93	48.22	56.86	63.64	82.80	91.05	95.14	97.30	98.48	99.14
6						0.	19.50	33.91	44.94	53.59	78.05	88.58	93.79	96.55	98.06	98.90
7							0.	17.90	31.60	42.36	72.73	85.82	92.29	95.72	97.59	98.63
8								0.	16.68	29.79	66.79	82.72	90.61	94.78	97.06	98.34
9									0.	15.73	60.14	79.26	88.73	93.74	96.48	98.00
10										0.	52.70	75.39	86.63	92.57	95.82	97.63
11										0.	44.38	71.07	84.27	91.26	95.08	97.21
12										0.	35.07	66.23	81.64	89.80	94.26	96.75
13										0.	24.66	60.81	78.70	88.16	93.34	96.23
14										0.	13.02	54.76	75.41	86.33	92.31	95.64
15											0.	47.98	71.73	84.29	91.16	94.99
16											0.	40.41	67.57	82.00	89.87	94.26
17											0.	31.93	63.01	79.44	88.43	93.45
18											0.	22.46	57.85	76.57	86.82	92.54
19											0.	11.86	52.09	73.37	85.02	91.52
20												0.	45.65	69.79	83.00	90.37
21												0.	38.44	65.78	80.75	89.10
22												0.	30.38	61.30	78.23	87.67
23												0.	21.36	56.29	75.41	86.07
24												0.	11.28	50.69	72.26	84.29
25													0.	44.42	68.73	82.29
26													0.	37.40	64.78	80.05
27													0.	29.56	60.37	77.56
28													0.	20.79	55.44	74.76
29													0.	10.97	49.92	71.63
30														0.	43.74	68.14
35															0.	43.36
40																0.

Table 3

REMAINING BALANCE TABLES

ORIGINAL TERM IN YEARS

11.50%

OF N	1	2	3	4	5	6	7	8	9	10	15	20	25	30	35	40
1	0.	52.86	70.40	79.12	84.30	87.72	90.13	91.91	93.27	94.34	97.34	98.63	99.26	99.60	99.78	99.87
2		0.	37.21	55.70	66.69	73.94	79.06	82.83	85.72	87.99	94.37	97.10	98.44	99.14	99.52	99.73
3			0.	29.44	46.95	58.50	66.64	72.66	77.26	80.86	91.03	95.38	97.51	98.63	99.24	99.57
4				0.	24.82	41.18	52.72	61.25	67.77	72.88	87.29	93.45	96.48	98.06	98.92	99.40
5					0.	21.77	37.12	48.46	57.13	63.93	83.09	91.29	95.32	97.42	98.57	99.20
6						0.	19.62	34.11	45.20	53.89	78.38	88.87	94.01	96.71	98.17	98.98
7							0.	18.03	31.82	42.64	73.11	86.15	92.55	95.90	97.72	98.73
8								0.	16.82	30.02	67.19	83.10	90.91	95.00	97.22	98.44
9									0.	15.87	60.56	79.68	89.07	93.99	96.66	98.13
10										0.	53.12	75.85	87.01	92.86	96.03	97.78
11										0.	44.78	71.55	84.70	91.59	95.32	97.38
12										0.	35.43	66.74	82.11	90.17	94.53	96.94
13										0.	24.94	61.34	79.21	88.57	93.64	96.44
14										0.	13.18	55.28	75.95	86.78	92.65	95.88
15											0.	48.49	72.30	84.77	91.53	95.26
16											0.	40.88	68.20	82.52	90.28	94.56
17											0.	32.34	63.61	80.00	88.87	93.77
18											0.	22.77	58.46	77.17	87.30	92.89
19											0.	12.03	52.69	73.99	85.54	91.90
20												0.	46.22	70.44	83.56	90.80
21												0.	38.96	66.45	81.34	89.55
22												0.	30.82	61.97	78.85	88.16
23												0.	21.70	56.96	76.06	86.60
24												0.	11.47	51.33	72.93	84.85
25													0.	45.03	69.43	82.89
26													0.	37.96	65.49	80.69
27													0.	30.03	61.09	78.22
28													0.	21.14	56.14	75.45
29													0.	11.18	50.60	72.35
30														0.	44.38	68.87
35															0.	44.03
40																0.

11.75%

OF N	1	2	3	4	5	6	7	8	9	10	15	20	25	30	35	40
1	0.	52.92	70.48	79.20	84.38	87.80	90.21	91.99	93.35	94.41	97.40	98.68	99.30	99.62	99.79	99.88
2		0.	37.30	55.82	66.83	74.09	79.21	82.98	85.87	88.13	94.49	97.19	98.50	99.19	99.55	99.75
3			0.	29.54	47.10	58.68	66.84	72.86	77.46	81.07	91.20	95.51	97.61	98.70	99.29	99.61
4				0.	24.93	41.36	52.94	61.48	68.01	73.13	87.52	93.63	96.61	98.16	98.99	99.44
5					0.	21.89	37.31	48.70	57.39	64.21	83.37	91.52	95.49	97.55	98.65	99.25
6						0.	19.74	34.32	45.46	54.19	78.71	89.14	94.22	96.86	98.27	99.04
7							0.	18.16	32.04	42.92	73.48	86.47	92.80	96.09	97.85	98.81
8								0.	16.95	30.25	67.59	83.47	91.20	95.22	97.37	98.55
9									0.	16.01	60.97	80.09	89.41	94.24	96.83	98.25
10										0.	53.54	76.30	87.39	93.14	96.23	97.92
11										0.	45.18	72.04	85.12	91.91	95.55	97.54
12										0.	35.78	67.25	82.57	90.52	94.79	97.12
13										0.	25.22	61.86	79.70	88.97	93.93	96.64
14										0.	13.35	55.80	76.48	87.21	92.97	96.11
15											0.	49.00	72.86	85.24	91.89	95.51
16											0.	41.35	68.79	83.03	90.67	94.84
17											0.	32.75	64.21	80.54	89.30	94.08
18											0.	23.08	59.07	77.75	87.77	93.23
19											0.	12.21	53.28	74.60	86.04	92.28
20												0.	46.78	71.07	84.09	91.20
21												0.	39.48	67.10	81.91	89.99
22												0.	31.27	62.63	79.46	88.64
23												0.	22.04	57.62	76.70	87.11
24												0.	11.66	51.98	73.60	85.40
25													0.	45.64	70.11	83.47
26													0.	38.51	66.19	81.30
27													0.	30.50	61.79	78.86
28													0.	21.50	56.84	76.13
29													0.	11.38	51.28	73.05
30														0.	45.02	69.59
35															0.	44.69
40																0.

Table 3

REMAINING BALANCE TABLES

ORIGINAL TERM IN YEARS

12.00%

AGE OF LOAN	1	2	3	4	5	6	7	8	9	10	15	20	25	30	35	40
1	0.	52.98	70.56	79.28	84.47	87.89	90.29	92.07	93.43	94.49	97.46	98.72	99.32	99.64	99.80	99.89
2		0.	37.38	55.94	66.97	74.24	79.36	83.13	86.02	88.27	94.60	97.27	98.56	99.23	99.58	99.77
3			0.	29.64	47.25	58.86	67.03	73.06	77.67	81.27	91.38	95.65	97.71	98.77	99.33	99.63
4				0.	25.04	41.53	53.15	61.72	68.26	73.39	87.75	93.81	96.74	98.25	99.05	99.48
5					0.	22.00	37.50	48.93	57.66	64.50	83.65	91.74	95.65	97.66	98.73	99.31
6						0.	19.87	34.53	45.72	54.48	79.04	89.42	94.43	97.00	98.37	99.11
7							0.	18.29	32.26	43.20	73.84	86.79	93.05	96.26	97.97	98.89
8								0.	17.09	30.48	67.99	83.83	91.49	95.42	97.51	98.64
9									0.	16.15	61.39	80.50	89.73	94.48	97.00	98.36
10										0.	53.95	76.75	87.76	93.42	96.42	98.04
11										0.	45.58	72.52	85.53	92.22	95.77	97.69
12										0.	36.13	67.75	83.02	90.87	95.04	97.29
13										0.	25.50	62.37	80.19	89.35	94.21	96.84
14										0.	13.51	56.32	77.00	88.21	93.28	96.33
15											0.	49.50	73.41	85.71	92.23	95.75
16											0.	41.81	69.36	83.53	91.05	95.11
17											0.	33.15	64.80	81.08	89.72	94.38
18											0.	23.39	59.66	78.32	88.22	93.56
19											0.	12.39	53.87	75.20	86.52	92.63
20												0.	47.35	71.69	84.62	91.59
21												0.	40.00	67.74	82.47	90.42
22												0.	31.71	63.29	80.05	89.09
23												0.	22.37	58.27	77.32	87.60
24												0.	11.85	52.61	74.25	85.92
25													0.	46.24	70.78	84.03
26													0.	39.06	66.88	81.90
27													0.	30.97	62.48	79.49
28													0.	21.85	57.53	76.78
29													0.	11.58	51.95	73.73
30														0.	45.65	70.29
35															0.	45.34
40																0.

12.25%

AGE OF LOAN	1	2	3	4	5	6	7	8	9	10	15	20	25	30	35	40
1	0.	53.04	70.64	79.37	84.56	87.97	90.38	92.15	93.50	94.56	97.52	98.76	99.35	99.66	99.82	99.90
2		0.	37.47	56.06	67.11	74.39	79.51	83.28	86.16	88.42	94.71	97.36	98.62	99.27	99.61	99.79
3			0.	29.74	47.41	59.04	67.23	73.27	77.87	81.48	91.55	95.77	97.80	98.83	99.37	99.66
4				0.	25.15	41.70	53.36	61.95	68.51	73.64	87.97	93.99	96.87	98.33	99.11	99.52
5					0.	22.12	37.69	49.17	57.93	64.78	83.93	91.96	95.81	97.77	98.80	99.35
6						0.	19.94	34.73	45.98	54.78	79.36	89.68	94.63	97.14	98.47	99.17
7							0.	18.42	32.48	43.48	74.21	87.10	93.28	96.43	98.08	98.96
8								0.	17.23	30.71	68.38	84.19	91.76	95.62	97.65	98.73
9									0.	16.29	61.80	80.90	90.05	94.71	97.16	98.47
10										0.	54.37	77.19	88.12	93.68	96.61	98.17
11										0.	45.97	72.99	85.93	92.52	95.98	97.83
12										0.	36.49	68.24	83.46	91.21	95.28	97.45
13										0.	25.77	62.89	80.67	89.72	94.48	97.02
14										0.	13.67	56.84	77.52	88.05	93.58	96.53
15											0.	50.00	73.95	86.15	92.56	95.98
16											0.	42.28	69.93	84.02	91.41	95.36
17											0.	33.56	65.39	81.60	90.12	94.66
18											0.	23.70	60.26	78.87	88.65	93.87
19											0.	12.57	54.46	75.79	87.00	92.98
20												0.	47.91	72.31	85.12	91.96
21												0.	40.51	68.38	83.01	90.82
22												0.	32.15	63.93	80.63	89.53
23												0.	22.71	58.91	77.93	88.00
24												0.	12.05	53.25	74.88	86.43
25													0.	46.84	71.44	84.58
26													0.	39.61	67.56	82.48
27													0.	31.44	63.17	80.10
28													0.	22.21	58.21	77.43
29													0.	11.78	52.61	74.40
30														0.	46.28	70.98
35															0.	45.98
40																0.

Table 3

REMAINING BALANCE TABLES

ORIGINAL TERM IN YEARS

12.50%

AGE OF LOAN	1	2	3	4	5	6	7	8	9	10	15	20	25	30	35	40
1	0.	53.10	70.72	79.45	84.64	88.06	90.46	92.23	93.58	94.63	97.57	98.80	99.38	99.67	99.83	99.91
2		0.	37.55	56.19	67.25	74.53	79.66	83.43	86.31	88.56	94.83	97.44	98.68	99.31	99.63	99.80
3			0.	29.84	47.56	59.22	67.42	73.47	78.07	81.68	91.72	95.90	97.89	98.89	99.41	99.69
4				0.	25.26	41.88	53.57	62.19	68.75	73.89	88.19	94.16	96.99	98.42	99.16	99.55
5					0.	22.24	37.88	49.41	58.19	65.06	84.20	92.18	95.97	97.88	98.88	99.40
6						0.	20.12	34.94	46.24	55.07	79.68	89.94	94.82	97.28	98.55	99.23
7							0.	18.55	32.70	43.75	74.57	87.41	93.51	96.59	98.19	99.03
8								0.	17.36	30.94	68.77	84.54	92.03	95.81	97.78	98.81
9									0.	16.43	62.21	81.30	90.36	94.93	97.31	98.56
10										0.	54.78	77.62	88.47	93.94	96.78	98.28
11										0.	46.37	73.45	86.32	92.81	96.18	97.96
12										0.	36.84	68.74	83.89	91.53	95.50	97.60
13										0.	26.05	63.40	81.14	90.08	94.74	97.19
14										0.	13.84	57.35	78.02	88.45	93.87	96.73
15											0.	50.50	74.49	86.59	92.88	96.20
16											0.	42.74	70.49	84.49	91.77	95.60
17											0.	33.96	65.97	82.11	90.50	94.93
18											0.	24.02	60.84	79.42	89.07	94.17
19											0.	12.75	55.04	76.37	87.45	93.30
20												0.	48.46	72.91	85.62	92.32
21												0.	41.02	69.00	83.54	91.21
22												0.	32.59	64.57	81.19	89.96
23												0.	23.05	59.55	78.52	88.54
24												0.	12.24	53.87	75.51	86.93
25													0.	47.44	72.09	85.10
26													0.	40.15	68.22	83.04
27													0.	31.90	63.84	80.70
28													0.	22.56	58.88	78.05
29													0.	11.98	53.27	75.05
30														0.	46.90	71.66
35															0.	46.62
40																0.

12.75%

AGE OF LOAN	1	2	3	4	5	6	7	8	9	10	15	20	25	30	35	40
1	0.	53.17	70.79	79.54	84.73	88.14	90.54	92.31	93.66	94.71	97.63	98.84	99.41	99.69	99.84	99.91
2		0.	37.64	56.31	67.39	74.68	79.81	83.58	86.45	88.70	94.94	97.52	98.73	99.34	99.65	99.82
3			0.	29.94	47.71	59.40	67.62	73.67	78.28	81.88	91.88	96.02	97.97	98.95	99.45	99.71
4				0.	25.36	42.05	53.78	62.42	68.99	74.13	88.41	94.32	97.10	98.50	99.21	99.58
5					0.	22.36	38.07	49.65	58.46	65.34	84.47	92.39	96.12	97.98	98.94	99.44
6						0.	20.24	35.15	46.50	55.36	80.00	90.20	95.00	97.41	98.64	99.28
7							0.	18.69	32.92	44.03	74.93	87.71	93.74	96.74	98.29	99.10
8								0.	17.50	31.17	69.16	84.89	92.30	96.00	97.90	98.89
9									0.	16.57	62.62	81.68	90.66	95.15	97.45	98.66
10										0.	55.20	78.04	88.81	94.18	96.95	98.39
11										0.	46.77	73.91	86.70	93.09	96.37	98.09
12										0.	37.20	69.22	84.31	91.85	95.72	97.74
13										0.	26.33	63.90	81.60	90.44	94.98	97.35
14										0.	14.00	57.86	78.51	88.83	94.14	96.91
15											0.	51.00	75.02	87.02	93.19	96.41
16											0.	43.21	71.05	84.95	92.10	95.84
17											0.	34.37	66.54	82.61	90.87	95.19
18											0.	24.33	61.42	79.95	89.48	94.45
19											0.	12.94	55.61	76.93	87.89	93.62
20												0.	49.02	73.50	86.10	92.67
21												0.	41.53	69.61	84.05	91.59
22												0.	33.03	65.20	81.74	90.37
23												0.	23.39	60.18	79.11	88.98
24												0.	12.43	54.49	76.12	87.40
25													0.	48.03	72.73	85.62
26													0.	40.69	68.88	83.59
27													0.	32.37	64.51	81.28
28													0.	22.91	59.55	78.66
29													0.	12.18	53.92	75.69
30														0.	47.52	72.32
35															0.	47.26
40																0.

Table 3

REMAINING BALANCE TABLES

ORIGINAL TERM IN YEARS

13.00%

AGE OF LOAN	1	2	3	4	5	6	7	8	9	10	15	20	25	30	35	40
1	0.	53.23	70.87	79.62	84.81	88.23	90.62	92.39	93.73	94.78	97.68	98.88	99.43	99.71	99.85	99.92
2		0.	37.72	56.43	67.53	74.83	79.95	83.73	86.60	88.84	95.04	97.60	98.79	99.38	99.68	99.83
3			0.	30.04	47.86	59.58	67.81	73.87	78.48	82.08	92.04	96.14	98.05	99.00	99.48	99.73
4				0.	25.47	42.22	53.99	62.65	69.24	74.38	88.63	94.48	97.22	98.57	99.26	99.61
5					0.	22.48	38.27	49.88	58.72	65.62	84.74	92.60	96.27	98.08	99.01	99.48
6						0.	20.37	35.35	46.75	55.66	80.31	90.45	95.18	97.53	98.72	99.33
7							0.	18.82	33.14	44.31	75.28	88.01	93.95	96.89	98.39	99.16
8								0.	17.64	31.41	69.55	85.23	92.55	96.17	98.01	98.97
9									0.	16.72	63.03	82.07	90.96	95.35	97.59	98.74
10										0.	55.61	78.47	89.14	94.42	97.11	98.49
11										0.	47.16	74.37	87.07	93.36	96.56	98.20
12										0.	37.55	69.71	84.72	92.15	95.93	97.88
13										0.	26.61	64.40	82.05	90.78	95.22	97.51
14										0.	14.17	58.36	79.00	89.21	94.40	97.08
15											0.	51.49	75.54	87.43	93.48	96.60
16											0.	43.67	71.59	85.40	92.43	96.C5
17											0.	34.77	67.10	83.10	91.23	95.43
18											0.	24.64	62.00	80.47	89.87	94.72
19											0.	13.12	56.18	77.49	88.32	93.91
20												0.	49.57	74.09	86.56	93.00
21												0.	42.04	70.22	84.55	91.95
22												0.	33.47	65.82	82.27	90.76
23												0.	23.72	60.81	79.67	89.41
24												0.	12.63	55.11	76.72	87.86
25													0.	48.62	73.35	86.11
26													0.	41.23	69.52	84.12
27													0.	32.83	65.16	81.84
28													0.	23.27	60.20	79.26
29													0.	12.39	54.56	76.32
30														0.	48.13	72.97
35															0.	47.88
40																0.

13.25%

AGE OF LOAN	1	2	3	4	5	6	7	8	9	10	15	20	25	30	35	40
1	0.	53.29	70.95	79.70	84.90	88.31	90.71	92.47	93.81	94.85	97.73	98.91	99.46	99.72	99.86	99.93
2		0.	37.81	56.55	67.67	74.97	80.10	83.87	86.74	88.97	95.15	97.67	98.84	99.41	99.70	99.84
3			0.	30.14	48.01	59.76	68.00	74.07	78.68	82.27	92.20	96.26	98.13	99.05	99.51	99.75
4				0.	25.58	42.40	54.20	62.88	69.48	74.62	88.84	94.64	97.33	98.64	99.30	99.64
5					0.	22.59	38.46	50.12	58.99	65.90	85.00	92.80	96.41	98.18	99.06	99.52
6						0.	20.49	35.56	47.01	55.95	80.62	90.70	95.36	97.64	98.79	99.38
7							0.	18.95	33.36	44.59	75.63	88.30	94.16	97.03	98.48	99.22
8								0.	17.78	31.64	69.93	85.56	92.80	96.34	98.12	99.03
9									0.	16.86	63.43	82.44	91.24	95.55	97.72	98.83
10										0.	56.02	78.88	89.46	94.65	97.26	98.59
11										0.	47.56	74.82	87.44	93.62	96.73	98.32
12										0.	37.90	70.18	85.13	92.44	96.13	98.01
13										0.	26.89	64.90	82.49	91.10	95.44	97.65
14										0.	14.33	58.86	79.48	89.58	94.66	97.25
15											0.	51.98	76.05	87.83	93.76	96.79
16											0.	44.13	72.13	85.84	92.74	96.26
17											0.	35.18	67.66	83.57	91.58	95.66
18											0.	24.96	62.56	80.98	90.25	94.98
19											0.	13.30	56.75	78.03	88.74	94.20
20												0.	50.12	74.66	87.01	93.31
21												0.	42.55	70.81	85.04	92.30
22												0.	33.91	66.43	82.79	91.14
23												0.	24.06	61.42	80.23	89.82
24												0.	12.82	55.71	77.30	88.31
25													0.	49.20	73.96	86.59
26													0.	41.77	70.15	84.63
27													0.	33.29	65.81	82.39
28													0.	23.62	60.85	79.84
29													0.	12.59	55.19	76.93
30														0.	48.74	73.60
35															0.	48.51
40																0.

Table 3

REMAINING BALANCE TABLES

13.50%

% OF LOAN	1	2	3	4	5	6	7	8	9	10	15	20	25	30	35	40
1	0.	53.35	71.03	79.79	84.98	88.39	90.79	92.54	93.88	94.92	97.79	98.95	99.48	99.74	99.87	99.93
2		0.	37.89	56.67	67.81	75.12	80.25	84.02	86.88	89.11	95.26	97.74	98.89	99.44	99.72	99.86
3			0.	30.24	48.16	59.93	68.20	74.26	78.87	82.47	92.36	96.37	98.21	99.10	99.54	99.77
4				0.	25.69	42.57	54.41	63.11	69.72	74.87	89.05	94.80	97.43	98.71	99.35	99.67
5					0.	22.71	38.65	50.36	59.25	66.18	85.26	93.00	96.54	98.26	99.12	99.55
6						0.	20.62	35.77	47.27	56.24	80.93	90.94	95.53	97.75	98.86	99.42
7							0.	19.08	33.58	44.87	75.98	88.58	94.37	97.17	98.57	99.27
8								0.	17.91	31.87	70.31	85.89	93.04	96.50	98.23	99.10
9									0.	17.00	63.83	82.81	91.52	95.74	97.84	98.90
10										0.	56.42	79.29	89.78	94.87	97.40	98.68
11										0.	47.95	75.26	87.79	93.87	96.89	98.42
12										0.	38.26	70.66	85.52	92.73	96.32	98.13
13										0.	27.17	65.39	82.92	91.42	95.66	97.79
14										0.	14.50	59.36	79.95	89.93	94.90	97.40
15											0.	52.47	76.55	88.22	94.03	96.96
16											0.	44.59	72.66	86.27	93.04	96.46
17											0.	35.58	68.21	84.04	91.91	95.89
18											0.	25.27	63.13	81.48	90.62	95.23
19											0.	13.48	57.31	78.56	89.14	94.47
20												0.	50.66	75.22	87.45	93.61
21												0.	43.05	71.40	85.51	92.63
22												0.	34.35	67.03	83.30	91.50
23												0.	24.40	62.03	80.77	90.21
24												0.	13.02	56.32	77.87	88.74
25													0.	49.78	74.56	87.06
26													0.	42.30	70.77	85.13
27													0.	33.75	66.44	82.93
28													0.	23.97	61.49	80.40
29													0.	12.79	55.82	77.52
30														0.	49.34	74.23
35															0.	49.12
40																0.

13.75%

% OF LOAN	1	2	3	4	5	6	7	8	9	10	15	20	25	30	35	40
1	0.	53.41	71.11	79.87	85.07	88.48	90.87	92.62	93.95	94.99	97.84	98.98	99.50	99.75	99.88	99.94
2		0.	37.98	56.79	67.94	75.26	80.39	84.16	87.02	89.25	95.36	97.82	98.93	99.47	99.74	99.87
3			0.	30.33	48.31	60.11	68.39	74.46	79.07	82.66	92.51	96.48	98.28	99.15	99.57	99.79
4				0.	25.80	42.74	54.62	63.34	69.96	75.11	89.26	94.95	97.53	98.78	99.39	99.69
5					0.	22.83	38.84	50.59	59.51	66.45	85.52	93.19	96.68	98.35	99.17	99.58
6						0.	20.75	35.97	47.53	56.53	81.23	91.17	95.69	97.86	98.93	99.46
7							0.	19.21	33.80	45.15	76.32	88.86	94.56	97.30	98.65	99.32
8								0.	18.05	32.11	70.69	86.21	93.27	96.66	98.33	99.16
9									0.	17.15	64.23	83.17	91.79	95.92	97.96	98.97
10										0.	56.83	79.69	90.09	95.08	97.54	98.76
11										0.	48.34	75.70	88.14	94.11	97.05	98.52
12										0.	38.61	71.12	85.91	93.00	96.50	98.24
13										0.	27.46	65.87	83.35	91.73	95.86	97.92
14										0.	14.66	59.86	80.41	90.27	95.13	97.55
15											0.	52.96	77.04	88.60	94.29	97.13
16											0.	45.05	73.18	86.69	93.33	96.65
17											0.	35.98	68.76	84.49	92.23	96.10
18											0.	25.59	63.68	81.97	90.97	95.46
19											0.	13.67	57.87	79.08	89.53	94.74
20												0.	51.20	75.77	87.87	93.90
21												0.	43.55	71.98	85.97	92.95
22												0.	34.79	67.62	83.79	91.85
23												0.	24.73	62.63	81.29	90.60
24												0.	13.21	56.91	78.43	89.16
25													0.	50.35	75.15	87.51
26													0.	42.83	71.38	85.61
27													0.	34.21	67.06	83.44
28													0.	24.33	62.12	80.96
29													0.	12.99	56.44	78.10
30														0.	49.94	74.83
35															0.	49.73
40																0.

Table 3

REMAINING BALANCE TABLES

ORIGINAL TERM IN YEARS

14.00%

AGE OF LOAN	1	2	3	4	5	6	7	8	9	10	15	20	25	30	35	40
1	0.	53.47	71.18	79.95	85.15	88.56	90.95	92.70	94.03	95.06	97.89	99.02	99.53	99.77	99.88	99.94
2		0.	38.07	56.91	68.08	75.41	80.54	84.30	87.16	89.38	95.46	97.89	98.98	99.50	99.75	99.88
3			0.	30.43	48.46	60.29	68.58	74.66	79.27	82.85	92.67	96.59	98.35	99.19	99.60	99.80
4				0.	25.91	42.92	54.83	63.57	70.20	75.35	89.46	95.09	97.63	98.84	99.42	99.71
5					0.	22.95	39.03	50.83	59.77	66.73	85.77	93.38	96.80	98.43	99.22	99.61
6						0.	20.87	36.18	47.79	56.82	81.53	91.40	95.85	97.96	98.99	99.50
7							0.	19.35	34.02	45.43	76.66	89.13	94.76	97.43	98.73	99.37
8								0.	18.19	32.34	71.06	86.53	93.50	96.81	98.42	99.22
9									0.	17.29	64.63	83.53	92.05	96.10	98.07	99.04
10										0.	57.23	80.09	90.39	95.28	97.67	98.84
11										0.	48.73	76.13	88.48	94.35	97.20	98.61
12										0.	38.97	71.58	86.28	93.27	96.67	98.35
13										0.	27.14	66.36	83.76	92.03	96.06	98.04
14										0.	14.83	60.35	80.86	90.61	95.35	97.69
15											0.	53.44	77.53	88.97	94.54	97.29
16											0.	45.51	73.70	87.09	93.61	96.83
17											0.	36.38	69.30	84.93	92.54	96.30
18											0.	25.90	64.23	82.45	91.32	95.69
19											0.	13.85	58.42	79.59	89.90	94.99
20												0.	51.73	76.31	88.28	94.18
21												0.	44.05	72.54	86.42	93.25
22												0.	35.22	68.21	84.27	92.19
23												0.	25.07	63.23	81.81	90.96
24												0.	13.41	57.50	78.97	89.56
25													0.	50.92	75.72	87.94
26													0.	43.36	71.98	86.08
27													0.	34.67	67.68	83.95
28													0.	24.68	62.74	81.49
29													0.	13.20	57.06	78.67
30														0.	50.53	75.43
35															0.	50.33
40																0.

14.25%

AGE OF LOAN	1	2	3	4	5	6	7	8	9	10	15	20	25	30	35	40
1	0.	53.54	71.26	80.04	85.23	88.64	91.02	92.77	94.10	95.13	97.94	99.05	99.55	99.78	99.89	99.95
2		0.	38.15	57.04	68.22	75.55	80.68	84.45	87.30	89.51	95.56	97.95	99.02	99.53	99.77	99.89
3			0.	30.53	48.61	60.47	68.77	74.85	79.46	83.04	92.82	96.69	98.42	99.23	99.63	99.82
4				0.	26.03	43.09	55.04	63.80	70.43	75.59	89.66	95.24	97.73	98.90	99.46	99.74
5					0.	23.07	39.22	51.06	60.03	67.00	86.02	93.56	96.93	98.51	99.27	99.64
6						0.	21.00	36.39	48.05	57.11	81.83	91.63	96.00	98.06	99.05	99.53
7							0.	19.48	34.24	45.71	77.00	89.40	94.94	97.55	98.80	99.41
8								0.	18.33	32.57	71.44	86.84	93.72	96.95	98.51	99.27
9									0.	17.44	65.02	83.88	92.31	96.27	98.18	99.10
10										0.	57.64	80.48	90.68	95.48	97.79	98.92
11										0.	49.12	76.56	88.81	94.57	97.35	98.70
12										0.	39.32	72.04	86.65	93.53	96.83	98.45
13										0.	28.02	66.83	84.17	92.32	96.25	98.16
14										0.	15.00	60.84	81.31	90.93	95.57	97.82
15											0.	53.92	78.01	89.33	94.78	97.44
16											0.	45.96	74.21	87.49	93.88	97.00
17											0.	36.79	69.83	85.36	92.84	96.49
18											0.	26.21	64.78	82.91	91.65	95.90
19											0.	14.03	58.97	80.09	90.27	95.22
20												0.	52.27	76.84	88.68	94.44
21												0.	44.55	73.10	86.85	93.55
22												0.	35.65	68.78	84.74	92.51
23												0.	25.41	63.81	82.31	91.32
24												0.	13.60	58.09	79.51	89.94
25													0.	51.49	76.28	88.36
26													0.	43.88	72.57	86.54
27													0.	35.12	68.28	84.44
28													0.	25.03	63.35	82.01
29													0.	13.40	57.66	79.22
30														0.	51.11	76.01
35															0.	50.93
40																0.

Table 3

REMAINING BALANCE TABLES

ORIGINAL TERM IN YEARS

AGE OF LOAN

14.50%

Age	1	2	3	4	5	6	7	8	9	10	15	20	25	30	35	40
1	0.	53.60	71.34	80.12	85.32	88.72	91.10	92.85	94.17	95.19	97.98	99.08	99.57	99.79	99.90	99.95
2		0.	38.24	57.16	68.35	75.69	80.83	84.59	87.43	89.64	95.65	98.02	99.06	99.55	99.78	99.89
3			0.	30.63	48.76	60.64	68.96	75.05	79.66	83.23	92.96	96.79	98.49	99.27	99.65	99.83
4				0.	26.14	43.26	55.25	64.03	70.67	75.83	89.86	95.37	97.82	98.95	99.49	99.75
5					0.	23.19	39.41	51.30	60.29	67.28	86.27	93.74	97.04	98.58	99.32	99.67
6						0.	21.13	36.60	48.31	57.40	82.12	91.85	96.15	98.15	99.11	99.57
7							0.	19.61	34.46	45.99	77.33	89.66	95.12	97.66	98.87	99.45
8								0.	18.47	32.81	71.80	87.14	93.93	97.09	98.59	99.32
9									0.	17.58	65.42	84.23	92.56	96.43	98.28	99.16
10										0.	58.04	80.87	90.97	95.67	97.91	98.99
11										0.	49.51	76.98	89.13	94.79	97.48	98.78
12										0.	39.67	72.49	87.01	93.77	96.99	98.54
13										0.	28.30	67.31	84.57	92.60	96.42	98.27
14										0.	15.17	61.32	81.74	91.24	95.77	97.95
15											0.	54.40	78.48	89.68	95.01	97.58
16											0.	46.41	74.70	87.87	94.14	97.16
17											0.	37.19	70.35	85.78	93.13	96.67
18											0.	26.53	65.32	83.37	91.97	96.10
19											0.	14.22	59.51	80.58	90.62	95.45
20												0.	52.79	77.36	89.06	94.70
21												0.	45.04	73.65	87.27	93.83
22												0.	36.09	69.35	85.19	92.82
23												0.	25.74	64.39	82.80	91.66
24												0.	13.80	58.66	80.03	90.32
25													0.	52.05	76.83	88.77
26													0.	44.40	73.14	86.98
27													0.	35.58	68.88	84.91
28													0.	25.38	63.95	82.52
29													0.	13.60	58.26	79.76
30														0.	51.69	76.58
35															0.	51.52
40																0.

14.75%

Age	1	2	3	4	5	6	7	8	9	10	15	20	25	30	35	40
1	0.	53.66	71.42	80.20	85.40	88.80	91.18	92.92	94.24	95.26	98.03	99.11	99.59	99.80	99.91	99.96
2		0.	38.32	57.28	68.49	75.84	80.97	84.73	87.57	89.77	95.75	98.08	99.10	99.58	99.80	99.90
3			0.	30.73	48.91	60.82	69.15	75.24	79.85	83.42	93.11	96.89	98.55	99.31	99.67	99.84
4				0.	26.25	43.44	55.46	64.25	70.91	76.06	90.05	95.51	97.90	99.01	99.53	99.77
5					0.	23.31	39.61	51.53	60.55	67.55	86.51	93.91	97.16	98.65	99.36	99.69
6						0.	21.25	36.80	48.56	57.68	82.41	92.06	96.30	98.24	99.16	99.60
7							0.	19.75	34.68	46.26	77.66	89.92	95.30	97.77	98.94	99.49
8								0.	18.61	33.04	72.17	87.44	94.14	97.22	98.67	99.36
9									0.	17.73	65.80	84.57	92.80	96.59	98.37	99.22
10										0.	58.43	81.24	91.24	95.85	98.02	99.05
11										0.	49.90	77.39	89.45	95.00	97.61	98.86
12										0.	40.02	72.94	87.37	94.01	97.14	98.63
13										0.	28.58	67.78	84.96	92.87	96.60	98.37
14										0.	15.34	61.80	82.17	91.55	95.96	98.07
15											0.	54.88	78.94	90.02	95.23	97.72
16											0.	46.86	75.20	88.24	94.39	97.31
17											0.	37.59	70.86	86.19	93.41	96.84
18											0.	26.84	65.85	83.81	92.27	96.30
19											0.	14.40	60.04	81.06	90.96	95.67
20												0.	53.32	77.87	89.44	94.94
21												0.	45.53	74.18	87.68	94.10
22												0.	36.52	69.91	85.64	93.12
23												0.	26.08	64.96	83.27	91.99
24												0.	13.99	59.23	80.54	90.68
25													0.	52.60	77.37	89.16
26													0.	44.92	73.71	87.41
27													0.	36.03	69.46	85.37
28													0.	25.73	64.55	83.02
29													0.	13.81	58.85	80.29
30														0.	52.26	77.13
35															0.	52.10
40																0.

Table 3

REMAINING BALANCE TABLES

ORIGINAL TERM IN YEARS

15.00%

AGE OF LOAN	1	2	3	4	5	6	7	8	9	10	15	20	25	30	35	40
1	0.	53.72	71.49	80.28	85.48	88.88	91.26	93.00	94.31	95.33	98.08	99.14	99.60	99.81	99.91	99.96
2		0.	38.41	57.40	68.63	75.98	81.11	84.87	87.71	89.90	95.84	98.14	99.14	99.60	99.81	99.91
3			0.	30.83	49.06	61.00	69.34	75.43	80.04	83.61	93.25	96.99	98.61	99.35	99.69	99.85
4				0.	26.36	43.61	55.67	64.48	71.14	76.30	90.24	95.64	97.99	99.06	99.56	99.79
5					0.	23.43	39.80	51.77	60.81	67.82	86.75	94.08	97.27	98.72	99.40	99.71
6						0.	21.38	37.01	48.82	57.97	82.70	92.27	96.43	98.33	99.21	99.63
7							0.	19.88	34.91	46.54	77.99	90.17	95.46	97.87	99.00	99.53
8								0.	18.75	33.27	72.53	87.73	94.34	97.35	98.75	99.41
9									0.	17.87	66.19	84.90	93.03	96.74	98.46	99.27
10										0.	58.83	81.62	91.51	96.02	98.12	99.11
11										0.	50.29	77.80	89.75	95.20	97.74	98.93
12										0.	40.37	73.38	87.71	94.24	97.28	98.71
13										0.	28.87	68.24	85.34	93.13	96.76	98.47
14										0.	15.51	62.27	82.59	91.84	96.15	98.18
15											0.	55.35	79.39	90.34	95.45	97.84
16											0.	47.31	75.68	88.61	94.63	97.46
17											0.	37.99	71.37	86.59	93.67	97.01
18											0.	27.16	66.38	84.25	92.57	96.48
19											0.	14.59	60.57	81.53	91.29	95.88
20												0.	53.84	78.37	89.80	95.17
21												0.	46.02	74.71	88.07	94.36
22												0.	36.95	70.46	86.07	93.41
23												0.	26.42	65.53	83.74	92.30
24												0.	14.19	59.80	81.04	91.03
25													0.	53.15	77.90	89.54
26													0.	45.43	74.26	87.82
27													0.	36.48	70.04	85.82
28													0.	26.08	65.13	83.50
29													0.	14.01	59.44	80.81
30														0.	52.83	77.68
35															0.	52.68
40																0.

15.25%

AGE OF LOAN	1	2	3	4	5	6	7	8	9	10	15	20	25	30	35	40
1	0.	53.78	71.57	80.37	85.56	88.96	91.34	93.07	94.38	95.39	98.12	99.17	99.62	99.82	99.92	99.96
2		0.	38.49	57.52	68.76	76.12	81.25	85.01	87.84	90.03	95.94	98.20	99.18	99.62	99.82	99.92
3			0.	30.93	49.22	61.17	69.52	75.62	80.23	83.79	93.39	97.08	98.67	99.38	99.71	99.87
4				0.	26.47	43.78	55.87	64.71	71.37	76.53	90.43	95.77	98.07	99.11	99.58	99.81
5					0.	23.55	39.99	52.00	61.07	68.09	86.99	94.25	97.38	98.78	99.43	99.74
6						0.	21.51	37.22	49.08	58.26	82.98	92.48	96.57	98.41	99.26	99.65
7							0.	20.02	35.13	46.82	78.32	90.42	95.63	97.98	99.06	99.56
8								0.	18.89	33.51	72.89	88.02	94.53	97.47	98.82	99.45
9									0.	18.02	66.57	85.23	93.26	96.88	98.55	99.32
10										0.	59.23	81.99	91.78	96.19	98.23	99.17
11										0.	50.67	78.21	90.05	95.39	97.85	99.00
12										0.	40.73	73.81	88.05	94.47	97.42	98.79
13										0.	29.15	68.70	85.71	93.38	96.92	98.56
14										0.	15.68	62.75	83.00	92.13	96.33	98.28
15											0.	55.82	79.83	90.66	95.65	97.97
16											0.	47.76	76.16	88.96	94.85	97.59
17											0.	38.38	71.88	86.98	93.93	97.16
18											0.	27.47	66.90	84.67	92.86	96.66
19											0.	14.77	61.10	81.99	91.60	96.08
20												0.	54.36	78.86	90.15	95.39
21												0.	46.51	75.23	88.46	94.60
22												0.	37.38	71.00	86.48	93.68
23												0.	26.75	66.08	84.19	92.61
24												0.	14.39	60.36	81.52	91.36
25													0.	53.70	78.42	89.91
26													0.	45.94	74.80	88.22
27													0.	36.92	70.60	86.26
28													0.	26.43	65.71	83.97
29													0.	14.21	60.02	81.31
30														0.	53.39	78.21
35															0.	53.25
40																0.

Table 3

REMAINING BALANCE TABLES

ORIGINAL TERM IN YEARS

15.50%

AGE OF LOAN	1	2	3	4	5	6	7	8	9	10	15	20	25	30	35	40
1	0.	53.84	71.65	80.45	85.64	89.04	91.41	93.14	94.45	95.46	98.17	99.20	99.64	99.83	99.92	99.96
2		0.	38.58	57.64	68.90	76.26	81.40	85.15	87.97	90.16	96.03	98.26	99.22	99.64	99.83	99.92
3			0.	31.03	49.37	61.35	69.71	75.81	80.42	83.98	93.53	97.17	98.72	99.42	99.73	99.88
4				0.	26.58	43.96	56.08	64.93	71.61	76.76	90.62	95.90	98.15	99.15	99.61	99.82
5					0.	23.67	40.18	52.24	61.33	68.35	87.22	94.41	97.48	98.85	99.47	99.75
6						0.	21.63	37.43	49.34	58.54	83.26	92.68	96.70	98.49	99.30	99.68
7							0.	20.15	35.35	47.09	78.64	90.66	95.79	98.07	99.11	99.59
8								0.	19.03	33.74	73.24	88.30	94.72	97.58	98.89	99.49
9									0.	18.17	66.95	85.55	93.48	97.02	98.63	99.37
10										0.	59.62	82.35	92.03	96.35	98.32	99.22
11										0.	51.06	78.61	90.34	95.58	97.96	99.06
12										0.	41.08	74.24	88.38	94.68	97.55	98.87
13										0.	29.43	69.15	86.08	93.63	97.07	98.64
14										0.	15.85	63.21	83.40	92.40	96.50	98.38
15											0.	56.29	80.27	90.97	95.84	98.08
16											0.	48.21	76.62	89.30	95.07	97.72
17											0.	38.78	72.37	87.36	94.18	97.31
18											0.	27.79	67.41	85.08	93.13	96.83
19											0.	14.96	61.62	82.44	91.91	96.26
20												0.	54.87	79.35	90.49	95.61
21												0.	46.99	75.74	88.83	94.84
22												0.	37.80	71.54	86.89	93.95
23												0.	27.09	66.63	84.63	92.90
24												0.	14.58	60.91	82.00	91.69
25													0.	54.23	78.92	90.27
26													0.	46.45	75.34	88.61
27													0.	37.37	71.16	86.68
28													0.	26.77	66.28	84.42
29													0.	14.42	60.59	81.80
30														0.	53.95	78.73
35															0.	53.81
40																0.

15.75%

AGE OF LOAN	1	2	3	4	5	6	7	8	9	10	15	20	25	30	35	40
1	0.	53.90	71.73	80.53	85.73	89.12	91.49	93.22	94.52	95.52	98.21	99.23	99.65	99.84	99.93	99.97
2		0.	38.66	57.76	69.03	76.40	81.54	85.28	88.10	90.28	96.11	98.32	99.25	99.66	99.85	99.93
3			0.	31.14	49.52	61.52	69.90	76.00	80.61	84.16	93.66	97.26	98.78	99.45	99.75	99.89
4				0.	26.69	44.13	56.29	65.16	71.84	77.00	90.80	96.02	98.22	99.20	99.63	99.83
5					0.	23.79	40.37	52.47	61.58	68.62	87.45	94.57	97.58	98.90	99.50	99.77
6						0.	21.76	37.63	49.59	58.82	83.53	92.88	96.82	98.56	99.35	99.70
7							0.	20.29	35.57	47.37	78.95	90.90	95.94	98.16	99.16	99.62
8								0.	19.17	33.98	73.60	88.58	94.90	97.70	98.95	99.52
9									0.	18.32	67.33	85.87	93.70	97.15	98.70	99.41
10										0.	60.01	82.70	92.28	96.51	98.41	99.28
11										0.	51.44	79.00	90.63	95.76	98.07	99.12
12										0.	41.43	74.67	88.70	94.89	97.67	98.94
13										0.	29.71	69.60	86.43	93.86	97.21	98.73
14										0.	16.02	63.68	83.79	92.67	96.66	98.48
15											0.	56.75	80.70	91.27	96.03	98.19
16											0.	48.65	77.09	89.64	95.28	97.85
17											0.	39.18	72.86	87.72	94.41	97.45
18											0.	28.10	67.92	85.49	93.40	96.99
19											0.	15.15	62.14	82.87	92.21	96.44
20												0.	55.38	79.82	90.82	95.81
21												0.	47.47	76.24	89.19	95.07
22												0.	38.23	72.06	87.29	94.20
23												0.	27.42	67.17	85.06	93.18
24												0.	14.78	61.45	82.46	92.00
25													0.	54.77	79.42	90.61
26													0.	46.95	75.86	88.99
27													0.	37.81	71.70	87.09
28													0.	27.12	66.84	84.87
29													0.	14.62	61.15	82.27
30														0.	54.50	79.24
35															0.	54.37
40																0.

Table 3

REMAINING BALANCE TABLES

ORIGINAL TERM IN YEARS

16.00%

AGE OF LOAN	1	2	3	4	5	6	7	8	9	10	15	20	25	30	35	40
1	0.	53.97	71.80	80.61	85.81	89.20	91.56	93.29	94.58	95.58	98.25	99.25	99.67	99.85	99.93	99.97
2		0.	38.75	57.88	69.17	76.54	81.68	85.42	88.23	90.41	96.20	98.37	99.28	99.68	99.86	99.94
3			0.	31.24	49.67	61.70	70.08	76.19	80.79	84.34	93.80	97.35	98.83	99.48	99.76	99.89
4				0.	26.80	44.30	56.50	65.38	72.07	77.22	90.98	96.14	98.30	99.24	99.66	99.85
5					0.	23.91	40.57	52.70	61.84	68.88	87.68	94.73	97.67	98.96	99.53	99.79
6						0.	21.89	37.84	49.85	59.11	83.80	93.07	96.94	98.63	99.39	99.72
7							0.	20.42	35.79	47.65	79.27	91.13	96.09	98.25	99.21	99.65
8								0.	19.32	34.21	73.95	88.85	95.08	97.80	99.01	99.55
9									0.	18.46	67.71	86.18	93.90	97.27	98.77	99.45
10										0.	60.40	83.05	92.52	96.66	98.50	99.32
11										0.	51.82	79.39	90.90	95.93	98.17	99.18
12										0.	41.78	75.09	89.01	95.09	97.79	99.00
13										0.	30.00	70.05	86.78	94.09	97.34	98.80
14										0.	16.19	64.14	84.18	92.93	96.82	98.57
15											0.	57.21	81.12	91.56	96.21	98.29
16											0.	49.09	77.54	89.96	95.49	97.97
17											0.	39.57	73.34	88.08	94.64	97.58
18											0.	28.41	68.42	85.88	93.65	97.14
19											0.	15.33	62.65	83.30	92.49	96.62
20												0.	55.88	80.28	91.13	96.00
21												0.	47.95	76.73	89.54	95.28
22												0.	38.65	72.58	87.67	94.44
23												0.	27.75	67.70	85.48	93.46
24												0.	14.98	61.99	82.91	92.30
25													0.	55.30	79.90	90.94
26													0.	47.45	76.37	89.35
27													0.	38.25	72.24	87.49
28													0.	27.46	67.39	85.30
29													0.	14.82	61.70	82.74
30														0.	55.04	79.79
35															0.	54.92
40																0.

16.25%

AGE OF LOAN	1	2	3	4	5	6	7	8	9	10	15	20	25	30	35	40
1	0.	54.03	71.88	80.69	85.89	89.28	91.64	93.36	94.65	95.65	98.29	99.28	99.68	99.86	99.94	99.97
2		0.	38.83	58.00	69.30	76.68	81.82	85.55	88.36	90.53	96.29	98.43	99.31	99.70	99.87	99.94
3			0.	31.34	49.82	61.87	70.27	76.38	80.98	84.52	93.93	97.43	98.88	99.50	99.78	99.90
4				0.	26.91	44.48	56.70	65.60	72.30	77.45	91.16	96.26	98.37	99.28	99.68	99.86
5					0.	24.03	40.76	52.94	62.09	69.15	87.90	94.88	97.77	99.01	99.56	99.80
6						0.	22.02	38.05	50.10	59.39	84.07	93.26	97.06	98.70	99.42	99.74
7							0.	20.56	36.01	47.92	79.58	91.35	96.23	98.33	99.26	99.67
8								0.	19.46	34.45	74.29	89.12	95.25	97.90	99.07	99.59
9									0.	18.61	68.08	86.49	94.11	97.40	98.84	99.48
10										0.	60.78	83.40	92.76	96.80	98.58	99.37
11										0.	52.20	79.77	91.17	96.10	98.27	99.23
12										0.	42.12	75.50	89.31	95.28	97.90	99.07
13										0.	30.28	70.49	87.13	94.31	97.47	98.87
14										0.	16.36	64.59	84.56	93.18	96.97	98.65
15											0.	57.67	81.53	91.84	96.38	98.39
16											0.	49.53	77.98	90.27	95.68	98.08
17											0.	39.97	73.81	88.43	94.86	97.71
18											0.	28.73	68.91	86.27	93.90	97.28
19											0.	15.52	63.15	83.72	92.77	96.78
20												0.	56.38	80.73	91.44	96.19
21												0.	48.42	77.22	89.88	95.49
22												0.	39.07	73.08	88.04	94.68
23												0.	28.09	68.23	85.89	93.72
24												0.	15.17	62.53	83.35	92.59
25													0.	55.82	80.38	91.26
26													0.	47.95	76.88	89.70
27													0.	38.69	72.76	87.87
28													0.	27.81	67.93	85.72
29													0.	15.02	62.25	83.19
30														0.	55.58	80.22
35															0.	55.47
40																0.

Table 3

REMAINING BALANCE TABLES

ORIGINAL TERM IN YEARS

16.50%

OF N	1	2	3	4	5	6	7	8	9	10	15	20	25	30	35	40
1	0.	54.09	71.96	80.77	85.97	89.36	91.71	93.43	94.72	95.71	98.33	99.30	99.70	99.87	99.94	99.97
2		0.	38.92	58.12	69.44	76.82	81.95	85.69	88.49	90.65	96.37	98.48	99.34	99.71	99.87	99.94
3			0.	31.44	49.97	62.05	70.45	76.57	81.16	84.69	94.06	97.51	98.93	99.53	99.79	99.91
4				0.	27.03	44.65	56.91	65.82	72.52	77.68	91.33	96.37	98.43	99.32	99.70	99.87
5					0.	24.15	40.95	53.17	62.35	69.41	88.12	95.03	97.85	99.06	99.59	99.82
6						0.	22.15	38.26	50.36	59.67	84.34	93.44	97.17	98.77	99.46	99.76
7							0.	20.69	36.24	48.20	79.88	91.58	96.37	98.41	99.30	99.69
8								0.	19.60	34.68	74.63	89.38	95.42	98.00	99.12	99.61
9									0.	18.76	68.45	86.79	94.30	97.51	98.91	99.52
10										0.	61.16	83.74	92.99	96.94	98.66	99.41
11										0.	52.58	80.14	91.44	96.26	98.36	99.28
12										0.	42.47	75.91	89.61	95.46	98.01	99.12
13										0.	30.56	70.92	87.46	94.53	97.60	98.94
14										0.	16.53	65.04	84.93	93.42	97.11	98.73
15											0.	58.12	81.94	92.12	96.54	98.48
16											0.	49.97	78.42	90.58	95.87	98.18
17											0.	40.36	74.28	88.77	95.07	97.83
18											0.	29.04	69.40	86.64	94.14	97.42
19											0.	15.71	63.65	84.13	93.03	96.94
20												0.	56.88	81.17	91.74	96.36
21												0.	48.89	77.69	90.21	95.69
22												0.	39.49	73.58	88.41	94.90
23												0.	28.42	68.75	86.28	93.97
24												0.	15.37	63.05	83.78	92.87
25													0.	56.34	80.84	91.57
26													0.	48.44	77.37	90.04
27													0.	39.12	73.28	88.25
28													0.	28.15	68.47	86.13
29													0.	15.23	62.79	83.63
30														0.	56.11	80.69
35															0.	56.01
40																0.

16.75%

OF N	1	2	3	4	5	6	7	8	9	10	15	20	25	30	35	40
1	0.	54.15	72.03	80.85	86.05	89.44	91.79	93.50	94.78	95.77	98.37	99.33	99.71	99.88	99.95	99.98
2		0.	39.01	58.24	69.57	76.96	82.09	85.82	88.62	90.77	96.45	98.53	99.37	99.73	99.88	99.95
3			0.	31.54	50.12	62.22	70.64	76.75	81.34	84.87	94.18	97.59	98.97	99.56	99.81	99.92
4				0.	27.14	44.82	57.11	66.05	72.75	77.90	91.50	96.48	98.50	99.35	99.72	99.88
5					0.	24.27	41.14	53.40	62.60	69.67	88.34	95.17	97.94	99.11	99.61	99.83
6						0.	22.28	38.47	50.61	59.95	84.60	93.62	97.28	98.83	99.49	99.78
7							0.	20.83	36.46	48.47	80.19	91.79	96.50	98.49	99.35	99.72
8								0.	19.74	34.92	74.97	89.63	95.58	98.09	99.17	99.64
9									0.	18.91	68.82	87.08	94.49	97.62	98.97	99.55
10										0.	61.55	84.07	93.21	97.07	98.73	99.45
11										0.	52.96	80.51	91.69	96.42	98.45	99.32
12										0.	42.82	76.31	89.90	95.64	98.11	99.18
13										0.	30.84	71.35	87.79	94.73	97.71	99.01
14										0.	16.70	65.49	85.29	93.65	97.25	98.80
15											0.	58.57	82.34	92.38	96.70	98.56
16											0.	50.40	78.85	90.88	96.04	98.28
17											0.	40.75	74.74	89.10	95.27	97.95
18											0.	29.35	69.88	87.01	94.37	97.55
19											0.	15.90	64.14	84.53	93.29	97.08
20												0.	57.37	81.61	92.02	96.53
21												0.	49.36	78.15	90.53	95.88
22												0.	39.91	74.08	88.76	95.11
23												0.	28.75	69.26	86.67	94.21
24												0.	15.57	63.57	84.20	93.14
25													0.	56.86	81.29	91.87
26													0.	48.92	77.85	90.38
27													0.	39.56	73.79	88.61
28													0.	28.49	68.99	86.53
29													0.	15.43	63.33	84.06
30														0.	56.64	81.16
35															0.	56.54
40																0.

Table 3

REMAINING BALANCE TABLES

ORIGINAL TERM IN YEARS

17.00%

AGE OF LOAN	1	2	3	4	5	6	7	8	9	10	15	20	25	30	35	40
1	0.	54.21	72.11	80.93	86.13	89.51	91.86	93.57	94.85	95.83	98.41	99.35	99.73	99.88	99.95	99.98
2		0.	39.09	58.36	69.71	77.10	82.23	85.95	88.75	90.89	96.58	98.58	99.40	99.74	99.89	99.95
3			0.	31.64	50.27	62.40	70.82	76.94	81.53	85.05	94.31	97.67	99.02	99.58	99.82	99.92
4				0.	27.25	44.99	57.32	66.27	72.98	78.12	91.67	96.59	98.56	99.39	99.74	99.89
5					0.	24.39	41.33	53.63	62.85	69.93	88.55	95.31	98.02	99.16	99.64	99.84
6						0.	22.41	38.67	50.87	60.23	84.86	93.79	97.38	98.88	99.52	99.79
7							0.	20.97	36.68	48.75	80.49	92.00	96.63	98.56	99.38	99.74
8								0.	19.89	35.15	75.31	89.88	95.74	98.18	99.22	99.67
9									0.	19.06	69.18	87.37	94.68	97.73	99.03	99.58
10										0.	61.93	84.40	93.42	97.20	98.80	99.48
11										0.	53.34	80.88	91.94	96.56	98.53	99.37
12										0.	43.17	76.71	90.18	95.81	98.21	99.23
13										0.	31.13	71.78	88.10	94.93	97.83	99.07
14										0.	16.87	65.94	85.64	93.88	97.38	98.87
15											0.	59.02	82.73	92.64	96.85	98.65
16											0.	50.83	79.28	91.17	96.21	98.38
17											0.	41.14	75.19	89.42	95.47	98.05
18											0.	29.67	70.36	87.36	94.59	97.68
19											0.	16.08	64.63	84.92	93.54	97.23
20												0.	57.85	82.03	92.30	96.70
21												0.	49.83	78.61	90.84	96.07
22												0.	40.33	74.56	89.10	95.32
23												0.	29.08	69.76	87.05	94.44
24												0.	15.76	64.09	84.61	93.39
25													0.	57.37	81.73	92.16
26													0.	49.41	78.33	90.70
27													0.	39.99	74.29	88.96
28													0.	28.84	69.51	86.91
29													0.	15.63	63.85	84.48
30														0.	57.16	81.61
35															0.	57.07
40																0.

17.25%

AGE OF LOAN	1	2	3	4	5	6	7	8	9	10	15	20	25	30	35	40
1	0.	54.27	72.19	81.01	86.21	89.59	91.94	93.64	94.91	95.89	98.45	99.37	99.74	99.89	99.95	99.98
2		0.	39.18	58.48	69.84	77.23	82.36	86.09	88.87	91.01	96.61	98.63	99.43	99.76	99.90	99.96
3			0.	31.74	50.42	62.57	71.01	77.12	81.71	85.22	94.43	97.74	99.06	99.60	99.83	99.93
4				0.	27.36	45.17	57.52	66.49	73.20	78.35	91.84	96.69	98.62	99.42	99.75	99.90
5					0.	24.51	41.52	53.86	63.10	70.19	88.76	95.44	98.10	99.20	99.66	99.86
6						0.	22.54	38.88	51.12	60.51	85.11	93.97	97.49	98.94	99.55	99.81
7							0.	21.10	36.90	49.02	80.78	92.21	96.75	98.63	99.42	99.75
8								0.	20.03	35.39	75.64	90.13	95.89	98.27	99.27	99.69
9									0.	19.20	69.54	87.65	94.86	97.83	99.08	99.61
10										0.	62.30	84.72	93.63	97.32	98.86	99.52
11										0.	53.71	81.24	92.18	96.71	98.61	99.41
12										0.	43.51	77.10	90.46	95.98	98.30	99.28
13										0.	31.41	72.20	88.42	95.12	97.93	99.12
14										0.	17.05	66.37	85.99	94.10	97.50	98.94
15											0.	59.46	83.11	92.88	96.99	98.72
16											0.	51.26	79.69	91.44	96.38	98.46
17											0.	41.53	75.64	89.74	95.66	98.16
18											0.	29.98	70.83	87.71	94.80	97.79
19											0.	16.27	65.11	85.30	93.78	97.36
20												0.	58.34	82.45	92.57	96.85
21												0.	50.29	79.06	91.14	96.24
22												0.	40.74	75.03	89.43	95.52
23												0.	29.41	70.26	87.41	94.66
24												0.	15.96	64.59	85.01	93.64
25													0.	57.87	82.17	92.44
26													0.	49.89	78.79	91.00
27													0.	40.42	74.78	89.30
28													0.	29.18	70.02	87.29
29													0.	15.83	64.38	84.89
30														0.	57.67	82.05
35															0.	57.59
40																0.

Table 3

REMAINING BALANCE TABLES

ORIGINAL TERM IN YEARS

17.50%

AGE OF LOAN	1	2	3	4	5	6	7	8	9	10	15	20	25	30	35	40
1	0.	54.33	72.26	81.09	86.29	89.67	92.01	93.71	94.98	95.95	98.49	99.39	99.75	99.90	99.96	99.98
2		0.	39.26	58.60	69.97	77.37	82.50	86.22	89.00	91.13	96.69	98.67	99.45	99.77	99.90	99.96
3			0.	31.84	50.57	62.74	71.19	77.31	81.88	85.39	94.55	97.81	99.10	99.63	99.84	99.93
4				0.	27.47	45.34	57.73	66.71	73.42	78.57	92.00	96.79	98.68	99.45	99.77	99.90
5					0.	24.63	41.72	54.09	63.35	70.45	88.97	95.58	98.18	99.24	99.68	99.87
6						0.	22.67	39.09	51.38	60.79	85.36	94.13	97.58	98.99	99.58	99.82
7							0.	21.24	37.13	49.29	81.08	92.41	96.87	98.70	99.46	99.77
8								0.	20.17	35.62	75.97	90.37	96.03	98.35	99.31	99.71
9									0.	19.35	69.90	87.93	95.03	97.93	99.13	99.64
10										0.	62.68	85.04	93.84	97.43	98.93	99.55
11										0.	54.08	81.59	92.42	96.84	98.68	99.45
12										0.	43.86	77.49	90.73	96.14	98.39	99.32
13										0.	31.69	72.61	88.72	95.30	98.04	99.18
14										0.	17.22	66.81	86.33	94.31	97.62	99.00
15											0.	59.90	83.49	93.12	97.13	98.80
16											0.	51.69	80.10	91.72	96.54	98.55
17											0.	41.92	76.08	90.04	95.84	98.26
18											0.	30.29	71.29	88.05	95.00	97.91
19											0.	16.46	65.59	85.68	94.01	97.49
20												0.	58.81	82.85	92.83	97.00
21												0.	50.75	79.50	91.43	96.41
22												0.	41.15	75.50	89.76	95.71
23												0.	29.74	70.75	87.77	94.88
24												0.	16.16	65.09	85.40	93.88
25													0.	58.37	82.59	92.71
26													0.	50.36	79.24	91.30
27													0.	40.84	75.26	89.64
28													0.	29.51	72.52	87.65
29													0.	16.04	64.89	85.29
30														0.	58.18	82.48
35															0.	58.11
40																0.

17.75%

AGE OF LOAN	1	2	3	4	5	6	7	8	9	10	15	20	25	30	35	40
1	0.	54.39	72.34	81.17	86.37	89.74	92.08	93.77	95.04	96.01	98.52	99.41	99.76	99.90	99.96	99.98
2		0.	39.35	58.72	70.11	77.51	82.63	86.35	89.12	91.24	96.76	98.72	99.48	99.79	99.91	99.96
3			0.	31.94	50.71	62.92	71.37	77.49	82.06	85.56	94.66	97.88	99.14	99.65	99.85	99.94
4				0.	27.59	45.51	57.93	66.93	73.64	78.78	92.16	96.89	98.73	99.48	99.78	99.91
5					0.	24.76	41.91	54.33	63.60	70.70	89.17	95.71	98.25	99.28	99.70	99.88
6						0.	22.80	39.30	51.63	61.06	85.61	94.29	97.68	99.04	99.61	99.84
7							0.	21.38	37.35	49.57	81.36	92.61	96.99	98.76	99.49	99.79
8								0.	20.32	35.86	76.30	90.60	96.17	98.43	99.35	99.73
9									0.	19.50	70.26	88.20	95.20	98.02	99.18	99.66
10										0.	63.05	85.35	94.03	97.55	98.99	99.58
11										0.	54.45	81.94	92.65	96.97	98.75	99.48
12										0.	44.20	77.87	90.99	96.29	98.47	99.37
13										0.	31.98	73.02	89.02	95.48	98.13	99.23
14										0.	17.39	67.24	86.66	94.51	97.73	99.06
15											0.	60.34	83.85	93.36	97.26	98.86
16											0.	52.12	80.51	91.98	96.69	98.63
17											0.	42.30	76.51	90.34	96.01	98.35
18											0.	30.60	71.75	88.38	95.20	98.01
19											0.	16.65	66.06	86.04	94.23	97.61
20												0.	59.29	83.25	93.08	97.14
21												0.	51.20	79.93	91.71	96.57
22												0.	41.56	75.96	90.07	95.89
23												0.	30.07	71.23	88.11	95.08
24												0.	16.35	65.59	85.78	94.12
25													0.	58.86	83.00	92.97
26													0.	50.84	79.69	91.59
27													0.	41.27	75.73	89.96
28													0.	29.85	71.02	88.01
29													0.	16.24	65.39	85.68
30														0.	58.69	82.90
35															0.	58.61
40																0.

Table 3

REMAINING BALANCE TABLES

ORIGINAL TERM IN YEARS

18.00%

AGE OF LOAN	1	2	3	4	5	6	7	8	9	10	15	20	25	30	35	40
1	0.	54.45	72.41	81.25	86.45	89.82	92.15	93.84	95.10	96.06	98.56	99.44	99.77	99.91	99.96	99.98
2		0.	39.43	58.84	70.24	77.64	82.77	86.48	89.24	91.36	96.84	98.76	99.50	99.80	99.92	99.97
3			0.	32.04	50.86	63.09	71.55	77.67	82.24	85.73	94.78	97.95	99.18	99.67	99.86	99.94
4				0.	27.70	45.68	58.14	67.14	73.87	79.00	92.32	96.99	98.79	99.51	99.80	99.92
5					0.	24.88	42.10	54.56	63.85	70.96	89.38	95.83	98.32	99.32	99.72	99.89
6						0.	22.93	39.51	51.88	61.34	85.86	94.45	97.77	99.09	99.63	99.85
7							0.	21.51	37.57	49.84	81.65	92.80	97.10	98.82	99.52	99.80
8								0.	20.46	36.09	76.62	90.83	96.31	98.50	99.39	99.75
9									0.	19.65	70.61	88.47	95.36	98.11	99.23	99.69
10										0.	63.42	85.65	94.23	97.65	99.04	99.61
11										0.	54.82	82.28	92.87	97.10	98.82	99.52
12										0.	44.55	78.25	91.25	96.44	98.55	99.41
13										0.	32.26	73.43	89.31	95.65	98.23	99.27
14										0.	17.57	67.67	86.99	94.71	97.84	99.12
15											0.	60.78	84.22	93.58	97.38	98.93
16											0.	52.54	80.90	92.24	96.83	98.70
17											0.	42.69	76.94	90.62	96.17	98.44
18											0.	30.91	72.20	88.70	95.39	98.11
19											0.	16.83	66.53	86.39	94.45	97.73
20												0.	59.76	83.64	93.32	97.27
21												0.	51.66	80.35	91.98	96.72
22												0.	41.97	76.41	90.37	96.06
23												0.	30.39	71.71	88.45	95.28
24												0.	16.55	66.08	86.15	94.34
25													0.	59.35	83.41	93.22
26													0.	51.31	80.12	91.87
27													0.	41.69	76.20	90.27
28													0.	30.19	71.51	88.35
29													0.	16.44	65.89	86.06
30														0.	59.18	83.31
35															0.	59.12
40																0.

18.25%

AGE OF LOAN	1	2	3	4	5	6	7	8	9	10	15	20	25	30	35	40
1	0.	54.52	72.49	81.33	86.52	89.89	92.22	93.91	95.16	96.12	98.60	99.45	99.78	99.91	99.96	99.99
2		0.	39.52	58.96	70.37	77.78	82.90	86.60	89.36	91.47	96.91	98.80	99.52	99.81	99.92	99.97
3			0.	32.14	51.01	63.26	71.73	77.85	82.41	85.90	94.89	98.02	99.21	99.68	99.87	99.95
4				0.	27.81	45.86	58.34	67.36	74.08	79.22	92.47	97.08	98.84	99.53	99.81	99.92
5					0.	25.00	42.29	54.79	64.10	71.21	89.57	95.96	98.39	99.35	99.74	99.89
6						0.	23.06	39.71	52.14	61.61	86.19	94.61	97.85	99.14	99.65	99.86
7							0.	21.65	37.79	50.11	81.93	92.99	97.21	98.88	99.55	99.82
8								0.	20.60	36.33	76.94	91.05	96.44	98.57	99.42	99.77
9									0.	19.80	70.96	88.73	95.52	98.20	99.27	99.71
10										0.	63.79	85.95	94.41	97.76	99.09	99.63
11										0.	55.19	82.62	93.09	97.22	98.88	99.55
12										0.	44.89	78.62	91.50	96.58	98.62	99.44
13										0.	32.54	73.83	89.59	95.82	98.31	99.32
14										0.	17.74	68.09	87.31	94.90	97.94	99.17
15											0.	61.21	84.57	93.80	97.50	98.99
16											0.	52.96	81.29	92.48	96.97	98.78
17											0.	43.07	77.36	90.90	96.33	98.52
18											0.	31.22	72.64	89.01	95.57	98.21
19											0.	17.02	66.99	86.74	94.65	97.84
20												0.	60.22	84.02	93.56	97.40
21												0.	52.11	80.76	92.24	96.87
22												0.	42.38	76.86	90.67	96.23
23												0.	30.72	72.17	88.78	95.47
24												0.	16.75	66.56	86.52	94.55
25													0.	59.83	83.80	93.46
26													0.	51.77	80.55	92.15
27													0.	42.11	76.66	90.57
28													0.	30.52	71.98	88.69
29													0.	16.64	66.39	86.42
30														0.	59.68	83.71
35															0.	59.61
40																0.

Table 3

REMAINING BALANCE TABLES

ORIGINAL TERM IN YEARS

18.50%

AGE OF LOAN	1	2	3	4	5	6	7	8	9	10	15	20	25	30	35	40
1	0.	54.58	72.57	81.41	86.60	89.97	92.29	93.97	95.22	96.18	98.63	99.47	99.79	99.92	99.97	99.99
2		0.	39.60	59.08	70.50	77.91	83.03	86.73	89.48	91.58	96.98	98.84	99.54	99.82	99.93	99.97
3			0.	32.24	51.16	63.43	71.91	78.03	82.59	86.06	95.00	98.08	99.25	99.70	99.88	99.95
4				0.	27.92	46.03	58.54	67.58	74.30	79.43	92.63	97.17	98.89	99.56	99.82	99.93
5					0.	25.12	42.48	55.01	64.35	71.46	89.77	96.07	98.46	99.39	99.76	99.90
6						0.	23.19	39.92	52.39	61.89	86.34	94.76	97.94	99.18	99.67	99.87
7							0.	21.79	38.02	50.38	82.21	93.18	97.32	98.94	99.58	99.83
8								0.	20.75	36.56	77.26	91.27	96.57	98.64	99.46	99.78
9									0.	19.95	71.30	88.99	95.67	98.28	99.32	99.73
10										0.	64.15	86.25	94.59	97.85	99.14	99.66
11										0.	55.56	82.95	93.30	97.34	98.94	99.58
12										0.	45.23	78.99	91.74	96.72	98.69	99.48
13										0.	32.82	74.23	89.87	95.98	98.40	99.36
14										0.	17.91	68.51	87.62	95.09	98.04	99.22
15											0.	61.63	84.92	94.01	97.61	99.05
16											0.	53.38	81.67	92.72	97.10	98.84
17											0.	43.45	77.77	91.18	96.48	98.60
18											0.	31.53	73.08	89.32	95.74	98.30
19											0.	17.21	67.45	87.08	94.85	97.95
20												0.	60.68	84.40	93.78	97.52
21												0.	52.55	81.17	92.50	97.01
22												0.	42.78	77.29	90.95	96.39
23												0.	31.05	72.63	89.10	95.65
24												0.	16.94	67.04	86.87	94.76
25													0.	60.31	84.19	93.69
26													0.	52.23	80.97	92.41
27													0.	42.52	77.10	90.87
28													0.	30.86	72.46	89.01
29													0.	16.84	66.87	86.78
30														0.	60.16	84.11
35															0.	60.10
40																0.

18.75%

AGE OF LOAN	1	2	3	4	5	6	7	8	9	10	15	20	25	30	35	40
1	0.	54.64	72.64	81.49	86.68	90.04	92.36	94.04	95.28	96.23	98.66	99.49	99.80	99.92	99.97	99.99
2		0.	39.69	59.20	70.64	78.05	83.17	86.86	89.60	91.69	97.05	98.88	99.57	99.83	99.93	99.97
3			0.	32.34	51.31	63.60	72.09	78.21	82.76	86.23	95.11	98.15	99.28	99.72	99.89	99.96
4				0.	28.04	46.20	58.75	67.79	74.52	79.64	92.78	97.26	98.93	99.58	99.84	99.94
5					0.	25.24	42.67	55.24	64.59	71.71	89.96	96.19	98.52	99.42	99.77	99.91
6						0.	23.32	40.13	52.64	62.16	86.57	94.91	98.02	99.22	99.69	99.88
7							0.	21.93	38.24	50.65	82.49	93.36	97.42	98.99	99.60	99.84
8								0.	20.89	36.80	77.57	91.49	96.69	98.70	99.49	99.80
9									0.	20.11	71.65	89.24	95.82	98.36	99.35	99.75
10										0.	64.51	86.54	94.77	97.95	99.19	99.68
11										0.	55.92	83.27	93.50	97.45	99.00	99.60
12										0.	45.57	79.35	91.97	96.85	98.76	99.51
13										0.	33.10	74.62	90.14	96.13	98.48	99.40
14										0.	18.09	68.92	87.92	95.26	98.14	99.27
15											0.	62.06	85.25	94.22	97.72	99.10
16											0.	53.79	82.04	92.96	97.23	98.91
17											0.	43.83	78.17	91.44	96.63	98.67
18											0.	31.84	73.51	89.61	95.91	98.39
19											0.	17.40	67.90	87.41	95.05	98.05
20												0.	61.14	84.76	94.00	97.64
21												0.	52.99	81.57	92.75	97.14
22												0.	43.19	77.72	91.23	96.54
23												0.	31.37	73.09	89.41	95.83
24												0.	17.14	67.51	87.21	94.96
25													0.	60.78	84.57	93.92
26													0.	52.69	81.38	92.66
27													0.	42.94	77.54	91.15
28													0.	31.19	72.92	89.33
29													0.	17.04	67.35	87.13
30														0.	60.64	84.49
35															0.	60.59
40																0.

Table 3

REMAINING BALANCE TABLES

ORIGINAL TERM IN YEARS

19.00%

AGE OF LOAN	1	2	3	4	5	6	7	8	9	10	15	20	25	30	35	40
1	0.	54.70	72.72	81.57	86.76	90.12	92.43	94.10	95.34	96.29	98.70	99.51	99.81	99.93	99.97	99.99
2		0.	39.78	59.32	70.77	78.18	83.30	86.98	89.72	91.80	97.12	98.92	99.59	99.84	99.94	99.98
3			0.	32.44	51.46	63.77	72.27	78.39	82.93	86.39	95.22	98.21	99.31	99.73	99.90	99.96
4				0.	28.15	46.37	58.95	68.01	74.74	79.85	92.97	97.34	98.98	99.60	99.85	99.94
5					0.	25.37	42.87	55.47	64.84	71.96	90.15	96.30	98.58	99.45	99.79	99.92
6						0.	23.45	40.34	52.89	62.43	86.80	95.05	98.10	99.26	99.71	99.89
7							0.	22.06	38.46	50.93	82.76	93.53	97.52	99.04	99.63	99.85
8								0.	21.04	37.03	77.88	91.70	96.81	98.76	99.52	99.81
9									0.	20.26	71.99	89.49	95.96	98.44	99.39	99.76
10										0.	64.87	86.82	94.94	98.04	99.24	99.70
11										0.	56.28	83.60	93.70	97.56	99.05	99.63
12										0.	45.91	79.70	92.20	96.98	98.83	99.54
13										0.	33.38	75.00	90.40	96.28	98.55	99.44
14										0.	18.26	69.33	88.22	95.44	98.23	99.31
15											0.	62.48	85.59	94.42	97.83	99.15
16											0.	54.20	82.41	93.18	97.35	98.97
17											0.	44.21	78.57	91.70	96.77	98.74
18											0.	32.15	73.94	89.90	96.07	98.47
19											0.	17.59	68.34	87.73	95.23	98.14
20												0.	61.59	85.12	94.21	97.75
21												0.	53.43	81.96	92.98	97.27
22												0.	43.59	78.14	91.50	96.69
23												0.	31.69	73.53	89.71	95.99
24												0.	17.34	67.97	87.55	95.15
25													0.	61.25	84.93	94.13
26													0.	53.14	81.78	92.91
27													0.	43.35	77.97	91.42
28													0.	31.52	73.38	89.63
29													0.	17.24	67.82	87.47
30														0.	61.12	84.86
35															0.	61.07
40																0.

19.25%

AGE OF LOAN	1	2	3	4	5	6	7	8	9	10	15	20	25	30	35	40
1	0.	54.76	72.79	81.65	86.83	90.19	92.50	94.17	95.40	96.34	98.73	99.53	99.82	99.93	99.97	99.99
2		0.	39.86	59.43	70.90	78.32	83.43	87.11	89.84	91.91	97.19	98.96	99.60	99.85	99.94	99.98
3			0.	32.55	51.61	63.94	72.44	78.56	83.10	86.55	95.32	98.27	99.34	99.75	99.90	99.96
4				0.	28.26	46.55	59.15	68.22	74.95	80.06	93.07	97.43	99.02	99.63	99.86	99.94
5					0.	25.49	43.06	55.70	65.08	72.21	90.34	96.41	98.64	99.48	99.80	99.92
6						0.	23.58	40.55	53.14	62.70	87.03	95.19	98.17	99.30	99.73	99.90
7							0.	22.20	38.68	51.20	83.03	93.70	97.61	99.08	99.65	99.86
8								0.	21.18	37.27	78.19	91.91	96.93	98.82	99.55	99.83
9									0.	20.41	72.33	89.73	96.10	98.51	99.43	99.78
10										0.	65.23	87.10	95.10	98.12	99.28	99.72
11										0.	56.64	83.91	93.89	97.66	99.10	99.65
12										0.	46.25	80.05	92.43	97.10	98.89	99.57
13										0.	33.67	75.39	90.66	96.42	98.63	99.47
14										0.	18.44	69.73	88.51	95.60	98.31	99.35
15											0.	62.89	85.91	94.61	97.93	99.20
16											0.	54.61	82.77	93.40	97.47	99.03
17											0.	44.59	78.97	91.95	96.91	98.81
18											0.	32.46	74.36	90.18	96.23	98.55
19											0.	17.77	68.78	88.05	95.41	98.23
20												0.	62.04	85.47	94.42	97.85
21												0.	53.87	82.34	93.22	97.39
22												0.	43.98	78.55	91.76	96.83
23												0.	32.02	73.97	90.00	96.16
24												0.	17.53	68.43	87.87	95.34
25													0.	61.71	85.29	94.34
26													0.	53.59	82.17	93.14
27													0.	43.75	78.40	91.69
28													0.	31.85	73.82	89.93
29													0.	17.44	68.29	87.81
30														0.	61.59	85.23
35															0.	61.54
40																0.

Table 3
REMAINING BALANCE TABLES

ORIGINAL TERM IN YEARS

19.50%

OF N	1	2	3	4	5	6	7	8	9	10	15	20	25	30	35	40
1	0.	54.82	72.87	81.73	86.91	90.26	92.57	94.23	95.46	96.39	98.76	99.54	99.83	99.94	99.98	99.99
2		0.	39.95	59.55	71.03	78.45	83.56	87.23	89.96	92.02	97.25	98.99	99.62	99.86	99.95	99.98
3			0.	32.65	51.76	64.11	72.62	78.74	83.27	86.71	95.43	98.32	99.37	99.76	99.91	99.97
4				0.	28.37	46.72	59.35	68.43	75.17	80.27	93.21	97.51	99.07	99.65	99.87	99.95
5					0.	25.61	43.25	55.93	65.33	72.46	90.52	96.52	98.70	99.51	99.81	99.93
6						0.	23.71	40.75	53.39	62.97	87.26	95.32	98.25	99.34	99.75	99.90
7							0.	22.34	38.90	51.46	83.30	93.87	97.70	99.13	99.67	99.87
8								0.	21.33	37.50	78.49	92.11	97.04	98.88	99.57	99.84
9									0.	20.56	72.66	89.97	96.24	98.58	99.46	99.79
10										0.	65.59	87.37	95.26	98.21	99.32	99.74
11										0.	57.00	84.22	94.08	97.76	99.15	99.68
12										0.	46.59	80.40	92.65	97.22	98.94	99.60
13										0.	33.95	75.76	90.91	96.56	98.69	99.50
14										0.	18.61	70.13	88.79	95.76	98.39	99.39
15											0.	63.31	86.23	94.79	98.02	99.25
16											0.	55.02	83.12	93.62	97.58	99.08
17											0.	44.97	79.35	92.19	97.04	98.87
18											0.	32.77	74.77	90.46	96.38	98.62
19											0.	17.96	69.22	88.36	95.58	98.32
20												0.	62.48	85.81	94.61	97.95
21												0.	54.30	82.71	93.44	97.51
22												0.	44.38	78.96	92.02	96.97
23												0.	32.34	74.40	90.29	96.31
24												0.	17.73	68.88	88.19	95.51
25													0.	62.17	85.65	94.55
26													0.	54.03	82.56	93.37
27													0.	44.16	78.81	91.95
28													0.	32.18	74.27	90.22
29													0.	17.64	68.75	88.13
30														0.	62.06	85.59
35															0.	62.01
40																0.

19.75%

OF N	1	2	3	4	5	6	7	8	9	10	15	20	25	30	35	40
1	0.	54.88	72.94	81.80	86.99	90.34	92.64	94.29	95.52	96.45	98.79	99.56	99.84	99.94	99.98	99.99
2		0.	40.03	59.67	71.16	78.58	83.69	87.35	90.07	92.13	97.32	99.03	99.64	99.87	99.95	99.98
3			0.	32.75	51.91	64.28	72.80	78.91	83.44	86.87	95.53	98.38	99.40	99.78	99.92	99.97
4				0.	28.49	46.89	59.55	68.64	75.38	80.48	93.35	97.59	99.11	99.67	99.87	99.95
5					0.	25.73	43.44	56.15	65.57	72.70	90.70	96.63	98.75	99.53	99.82	99.93
6						0.	23.84	40.96	53.64	63.24	87.48	95.46	98.32	99.37	99.76	99.91
7							0.	22.48	39.13	51.73	83.56	94.04	97.79	99.17	99.69	99.88
8								0.	21.47	37.74	78.79	92.31	97.15	98.93	99.60	99.85
9									0.	20.71	72.99	90.20	96.37	98.64	99.49	99.81
10										0.	65.94	87.64	95.42	98.29	99.36	99.76
11										0.	57.36	84.53	94.26	97.86	99.20	99.70
12										0.	46.92	80.74	92.86	97.33	99.00	99.62
13										0.	34.23	76.13	91.15	96.69	98.76	99.53
14										0.	18.78	70.53	89.07	95.92	98.47	99.43
15											0.	63.72	86.55	94.97	98.11	99.29
16											0.	55.42	83.47	93.82	97.68	99.13
17											0.	45.34	79.73	92.42	97.16	98.93
18											0.	33.07	75.18	90.72	96.52	98.70
19											0.	18.15	69.65	88.66	95.75	98.40
20												0.	62.92	86.14	94.80	98.05
21												0.	54.73	83.08	93.66	97.62
22												0.	44.77	79.36	92.26	97.10
23												0.	32.66	74.83	90.57	96.46
24												0.	17.92	69.32	88.50	95.68
25													0.	62.62	85.99	94.74
26													0.	54.48	82.93	93.60
27													0.	44.56	79.22	92.20
28													0.	32.51	74.70	90.51
29													0.	17.84	69.20	88.44
30														0.	62.51	85.93
35															0.	62.47
40																0.

Table 3

REMAINING BALANCE TABLES

ORIGINAL TERM IN YEARS

20.00%

AGE OF LOAN	1	2	3	4	5	6	7	8	9	10	15	20	25	30	35	40
1	0.	54.94	73.02	81.88	87.06	90.41	92.71	94.36	95.58	96.50	98.82	99.58	99.84	99.94	99.98	99.99
2		0.	40.12	59.79	71.29	78.71	83.82	87.48	90.18	92.23	97.38	99.06	99.66	99.87	99.95	99.98
3			0.	32.85	52.06	64.45	72.97	79.09	83.61	87.03	95.63	98.43	99.43	99.79	99.92	99.97
4				0.	28.60	47.06	59.75	68.86	75.59	80.68	93.49	97.66	99.14	99.68	99.88	99.96
5					0.	25.86	43.63	56.38	65.81	72.94	90.88	96.73	98.80	99.56	99.84	99.94
6						0.	23.97	41.17	53.89	63.51	87.70	95.59	98.38	99.40	99.78	99.92
7							0.	22.62	39.35	52.00	83.82	94.19	97.87	99.21	99.71	99.89
8								0.	21.62	37.97	79.09	92.50	97.25	98.98	99.62	99.86
9									0.	20.86	73.32	90.43	96.49	98.70	99.52	99.82
10										0.	66.29	87.91	95.57	98.36	99.39	99.78
11										0.	57.72	84.83	94.44	97.95	99.24	99.72
12										0.	47.26	81.08	93.07	97.44	99.05	99.65
13										0.	34.51	76.50	91.39	96.82	98.82	99.56
14										0.	18.96	70.92	89.34	96.07	98.54	99.46
15											0.	64.12	86.85	95.14	98.20	99.33
16											0.	55.83	83.81	94.02	97.79	99.18
17											0.	45.71	80.10	92.65	97.28	98.99
18											0.	33.38	75.58	90.98	96.66	98.76
19											0.	18.34	70.07	88.95	95.91	98.48
20												0.	63.35	86.47	94.99	98.14
21												0.	55.16	83.44	93.87	97.73
22												0.	45.16	79.75	92.50	97.22
23												0.	32.98	75.25	90.83	96.60
24												0.	18.12	69.76	88.80	95.85
25													0.	63.07	86.32	94.93
26													0.	54.91	83.30	93.81
27													0.	44.96	79.62	92.44
28													0.	32.83	75.13	90.78
29													0.	18.04	69.65	88.75
30														0.	62.97	86.27
35															0.	62.93
40																0.

20.25%

AGE OF LOAN	1	2	3	4	5	6	7	8	9	10	15	20	25	30	35	40
1	0.	55.00	73.09	81.96	87.14	90.48	92.78	94.42	95.63	96.55	98.85	99.59	99.85	99.95	99.98	99.99
2		0.	40.20	59.91	71.42	78.84	83.94	87.60	90.30	92.34	97.44	99.09	99.67	99.88	99.96	99.98
3			0.	32.95	52.20	64.62	73.15	79.26	83.77	87.18	95.72	98.48	99.45	99.80	99.93	99.97
4				0.	28.71	47.23	59.95	69.07	75.80	80.88	93.62	97.74	99.18	99.70	99.89	99.96
5					0.	25.98	43.82	56.61	66.05	73.19	91.05	96.83	98.85	99.58	99.85	99.94
6						0.	24.10	41.38	54.14	63.77	87.91	95.71	98.45	99.43	99.79	99.92
7							0.	22.76	39.57	52.27	84.08	94.35	97.95	99.25	99.73	99.90
8								0.	21.76	38.21	79.38	92.69	97.35	99.03	99.65	99.87
9									0.	21.01	73.65	90.65	96.61	98.76	99.55	99.83
10										0.	66.64	88.16	95.71	98.44	99.43	99.79
11										0.	58.07	85.12	94.61	98.03	99.28	99.74
12										0.	47.59	81.41	93.27	97.54	99.10	99.67
13										0.	34.79	76.86	91.62	96.94	98.88	99.59
14										0.	19.13	71.31	89.61	96.21	98.61	99.49
15											0.	64.52	87.15	95.31	98.29	99.37
16											0.	56.23	84.15	94.22	97.88	99.23
17											0.	46.08	80.47	92.88	97.39	99.05
18											0.	33.68	75.98	91.24	96.79	98.83
19											0.	18.53	70.49	89.23	96.06	98.56
20												0.	63.78	86.79	95.17	98.23
21												0.	55.58	83.79	94.07	97.83
22												0.	45.55	80.13	92.73	97.34
23												0.	33.30	75.66	91.10	96.74
24												0.	18.31	70.20	89.10	96.01
25													0.	63.51	86.65	95.11
26													0.	55.35	83.66	94.02
27													0.	45.36	80.01	92.68
28													0.	33.16	75.55	91.05
29													0.	18.24	70.09	89.05
30														0.	63.42	86.60
35															0.	63.38
40																0.

Table 3

REMAINING BALANCE TABLES

ORIGINAL TERM IN YEARS

20.50%

AGE OF LOAN

Age	1	2	3	4	5	6	7	8	9	10	15	20	25	30	35	40
1	0.	55.06	73.17	82.04	87.22	90.55	92.84	94.48	95.69	96.60	98.88	99.61	99.86	99.95	99.98	99.99
2		0.	40.29	60.03	71.55	78.98	84.07	87.72	90.41	92.44	97.50	99.12	99.69	99.89	99.96	99.99
3			0.	33.05	52.35	64.79	73.32	79.43	83.94	87.34	95.82	98.53	99.48	99.81	99.93	99.98
4				0.	28.83	47.41	60.15	69.28	76.01	81.09	93.76	97.81	99.22	99.72	99.90	99.96
5					0.	26.10	44.01	56.83	66.29	73.43	91.23	96.92	98.90	99.60	99.86	99.95
6						0.	24.24	41.58	54.38	64.04	88.13	95.84	98.51	99.46	99.81	99.93
7							0.	22.90	39.79	52.54	84.33	94.50	98.03	99.29	99.74	99.91
8								0.	21.91	38.44	79.68	92.87	97.45	99.08	99.67	99.88
9									0.	21.17	73.97	90.87	96.73	98.82	99.57	99.85
10										0.	66.98	88.42	95.85	98.51	99.46	99.80
11										0.	58.42	85.41	94.78	98.12	99.32	99.75
12										0.	47.93	81.73	93.46	97.64	99.15	99.69
13										0.	35.07	77.22	91.85	97.06	98.94	99.62
14										0.	19.31	71.70	89.87	96.35	98.68	99.52
15											0.	64.92	87.44	95.47	98.36	99.41
16											0.	56.62	84.47	94.40	97.98	99.27
17											0.	46.45	80.83	93.09	97.50	99.10
18											0.	33.99	76.37	91.48	96.92	98.89
19											0.	18.72	70.91	89.51	96.21	98.63
20												0.	64.21	87.10	95.34	98.31
21												0.	56.00	84.14	94.27	97.93
22												0.	45.94	80.51	92.96	97.45
23												0.	33.61	76.07	91.35	96.87
24												0.	18.51	70.62	89.38	96.16
25													0.	63.95	86.97	95.29
26													0.	55.78	84.02	94.22
27													0.	45.76	80.40	92.91
28													0.	33.48	75.96	91.30
29													0.	18.44	70.52	89.34
30														0.	63.86	86.93
35															0.	63.83
40																0.

20.75%

Age	1	2	3	4	5	6	7	8	9	10	15	20	25	30	35	40
1	0.	55.13	73.24	82.11	87.29	90.62	92.91	94.54	95.75	96.65	98.91	99.62	99.87	99.95	99.98	99.99
2		0.	40.38	60.14	71.68	79.11	84.20	87.84	90.52	92.54	97.56	99.15	99.70	99.89	99.96	99.99
3			0.	33.15	52.50	64.96	73.50	79.60	84.10	87.49	95.91	98.58	99.50	99.82	99.94	99.98
4				0.	28.94	47.58	60.35	69.49	76.22	81.29	93.89	97.88	99.25	99.73	99.90	99.97
5					0.	26.23	44.20	57.06	66.53	73.67	91.40	97.02	98.94	99.62	99.87	99.95
6						0.	24.37	41.79	54.63	64.30	88.34	95.95	98.57	99.49	99.82	99.93
7							0.	23.04	40.01	52.80	84.58	94.65	98.11	99.33	99.76	99.91
8								0.	22.06	38.67	79.96	93.05	97.54	99.12	99.69	99.89
9									0.	21.32	74.29	91.08	96.85	98.88	99.60	99.86
10										0.	67.33	88.67	95.99	98.57	99.49	99.82
11										0.	58.77	85.70	94.94	98.20	99.36	99.77
12										0.	48.26	82.05	93.65	97.74	99.19	99.71
13										0.	35.35	77.58	92.07	97.18	98.99	99.64
14										0.	19.48	72.08	90.12	96.48	98.74	99.55
15											0.	65.32	87.73	95.63	98.44	99.44
16											0.	57.02	84.80	94.58	98.07	99.31
17											0.	46.82	81.19	93.30	97.61	99.15
18											0.	34.29	76.76	91.72	97.04	98.94
19											0.	18.90	71.31	89.78	96.35	98.70
20												0.	64.63	87.40	95.50	98.39
21												0.	56.41	84.48	94.46	98.02
22												0.	46.32	80.88	93.18	97.56
23												0.	33.93	76.47	91.60	97.00
24												0.	18.70	71.05	89.66	96.31
25													0.	64.38	87.28	95.46
26													0.	56.20	84.36	94.41
27													0.	46.15	80.77	93.13
28													0.	33.80	76.37	91.56
29													0.	18.63	70.95	89.62
30														0.	64.30	87.24
35															0.	64.27
40																0.

Table 3

REMAINING BALANCE TABLES

ORIGINAL TERM IN YEARS

21.00%

AGE OF LOAN	1	2	3	4	5	6	7	8	9	10	15	20	25	30	35	40
1	0.	55.19	73.32	82.19	87.37	90.69	92.97	94.60	95.80	96.70	98.93	99.63	99.87	99.96	99.98	99.99
2		0.	40.46	60.26	71.81	79.24	84.32	87.96	90.63	92.64	97.62	99.18	99.71	99.90	99.96	99.99
3			0.	33.26	52.65	65.13	73.67	79.77	84.26	87.64	96.00	98.63	99.52	99.83	99.94	99.98
4				0.	29.05	47.75	60.55	69.69	76.42	81.49	94.01	97.95	99.28	99.75	99.91	99.97
5					0.	26.35	44.39	57.28	66.77	73.90	91.56	97.11	98.99	99.64	99.87	99.96
6						0.	24.50	42.00	54.88	64.57	88.54	96.07	98.63	99.52	99.83	99.94
7							0.	23.18	40.23	53.07	84.83	94.80	98.18	99.36	99.77	99.92
8								0.	22.20	38.91	80.25	93.23	97.63	99.17	99.71	99.90
9									0.	21.47	74.61	91.29	96.96	98.93	99.62	99.87
10										0.	67.67	88.91	96.12	98.64	99.52	99.83
11										0.	59.12	85.98	95.10	98.28	99.39	99.79
12										0.	48.59	82.37	93.84	97.83	99.24	99.73
13										0.	35.62	77.93	92.28	97.28	99.04	99.66
14										0.	19.66	72.45	90.37	96.61	98.80	99.58
15											0.	65.71	88.01	95.78	98.51	99.47
16											0.	57.41	85.11	94.76	98.15	99.35
17											0.	47.18	81.54	93.50	97.71	99.19
18											0.	34.59	77.14	91.96	97.16	99.00
19											0.	19.09	71.72	90.05	96.49	98.76
20												0.	65.04	87.70	95.66	98.47
21												0.	56.83	84.81	94.64	98.11
22												0.	46.71	81.25	93.39	97.67
23												0.	34.24	76.86	91.84	97.12
24												0.	18.90	71.46	89.94	96.45
25													0.	64.81	87.59	95.62
26													0.	56.62	84.70	94.60
27													0.	46.54	81.15	93.34
28													0.	34.12	76.77	91.80
29													0.	18.83	71.37	89.90
30														0.	64.73	87.55
35															0.	64.70
40																0.

21.25%

AGE OF LOAN	1	2	3	4	5	6	7	8	9	10	15	20	25	30	35	40
1	0.	55.25	73.39	82.27	87.44	90.77	93.04	94.66	95.86	96.75	98.96	99.65	99.88	99.96	99.99	99.99
2		0.	40.55	60.38	71.94	79.37	84.45	88.07	90.74	92.74	97.68	99.21	99.73	99.91	99.97	99.99
3			0.	33.36	52.80	65.29	73.84	79.94	84.42	87.79	96.09	98.68	99.54	99.84	99.94	99.98
4				0.	29.17	47.92	60.75	69.90	76.63	81.68	94.14	98.01	99.31	99.76	99.92	99.97
5					0.	26.47	44.58	57.51	67.00	74.14	91.73	97.19	99.03	99.66	99.88	99.96
6						0.	24.63	42.21	55.12	64.83	88.75	96.18	98.68	99.54	99.84	99.94
7							0.	23.32	40.46	53.33	85.07	94.94	98.25	99.39	99.79	99.93
8								0.	22.35	39.14	80.53	93.40	97.72	99.21	99.72	99.90
9									0.	21.62	74.92	91.50	97.06	98.98	99.64	99.88
10										0.	68.00	89.15	96.25	98.70	99.55	99.84
11										0.	59.46	86.26	95.25	98.35	99.42	99.80
12										0.	48.92	82.68	94.02	97.92	99.28	99.75
13										0.	35.90	78.27	92.49	97.39	99.09	99.68
14										0.	19.84	72.82	90.61	96.74	98.86	99.60
15											0.	66.10	88.29	95.93	98.58	99.51
16											0.	57.80	85.42	94.93	98.23	99.38
17											0.	47.55	81.88	93.70	97.81	99.23
18											0.	34.90	77.51	92.18	97.28	99.05
19											0.	19.28	72.12	90.31	96.62	98.82
20												0.	65.46	87.99	95.82	98.54
21												0.	57.23	85.13	94.82	98.19
22												0.	47.09	81.60	93.59	97.77
23												0.	34.56	77.25	92.07	97.24
24												0.	19.09	71.87	90.20	96.58
25													0.	65.24	87.89	95.78
26													0.	57.04	85.03	94.78
27													0.	46.93	81.51	93.55
28													0.	34.44	77.16	92.04
29													0.	19.03	71.79	90.16
30														0.	65.16	87.85
35															0.	65.13
40																0.

Table 3

REMAINING BALANCE TABLES

ORIGINAL TERM IN YEARS

21.50%

AGE OF LOAN

Age	1	2	3	4	5	6	7	8	9	10	15	20	25	30	35	40
1	0.	55.31	73.47	82.34	87.51	90.84	93.10	94.72	95.91	96.80	98.99	99.66	99.88	99.96	99.99	*****
2		0.	40.63	60.50	72.06	79.49	84.57	88.19	90.85	92.84	97.73	99.24	99.74	99.91	99.97	99.99
3			0.	33.46	52.94	65.46	74.01	80.11	84.58	87.94	96.18	98.72	99.56	99.85	99.95	99.98
4				0.	29.28	48.09	60.95	70.11	76.83	81.88	94.26	98.08	99.34	99.77	99.92	99.97
5					0.	26.60	44.78	57.73	67.24	74.37	91.89	97.28	99.07	99.68	99.89	99.96
6						0.	24.76	42.41	55.37	65.09	88.95	96.30	98.74	99.57	99.85	99.95
7							0.	23.46	40.68	53.60	85.31	95.08	98.32	99.42	99.80	99.93
8								0.	22.50	39.38	80.81	93.57	97.80	99.25	99.74	99.91
9									0.	21.78	75.23	91.70	97.17	99.03	99.67	99.88
10										0.	68.34	89.39	96.38	98.76	99.57	99.85
11										0.	59.81	86.53	95.40	98.42	99.46	99.81
12										0.	49.25	82.99	94.19	98.01	99.31	99.76
13										0.	36.18	78.61	92.70	97.49	99.14	99.70
14										0.	20.01	73.19	90.85	96.86	98.92	99.63
15											0.	66.48	88.56	96.07	98.65	99.53
16											0.	58.18	85.72	95.10	98.31	99.42
17											0.	47.91	82.22	93.89	97.90	99.28
18											0.	35.20	77.88	92.40	97.38	99.10
19											0.	19.47	72.51	90.56	96.75	98.88
20												0.	65.86	88.28	95.96	98.61
21												0.	57.64	85.45	94.99	98.28
22												0.	47.46	81.96	93.79	97.86
23												0.	34.87	77.63	92.30	97.35
24												0.	19.29	72.28	90.46	96.71
25													0.	65.65	88.18	95.93
26													0.	57.46	85.36	94.96
27													0.	47.31	81.87	93.75
28													0.	34.76	77.55	92.27
29													0.	19.22	72.20	90.42
30														0.	65.58	88.15
35															0.	65.56
40																0.

21.75%

Age	1	2	3	4	5	6	7	8	9	10	15	20	25	30	35	40
1	0.	55.37	73.54	82.42	87.59	90.91	93.17	94.78	95.96	96.85	99.01	99.67	99.89	99.96	99.99	*****
2		0.	40.72	60.61	72.19	79.62	84.70	88.31	90.95	92.94	97.79	99.27	99.75	99.92	99.97	99.99
3			0.	33.56	53.09	65.63	74.18	80.28	84.74	88.09	96.27	98.76	99.58	99.86	99.95	99.98
4				0.	29.40	48.26	61.14	70.31	77.03	82.07	94.38	98.14	99.37	99.79	99.93	99.98
5					0.	26.72	44.97	57.95	67.47	74.61	92.04	97.36	99.11	99.70	99.90	99.97
6						0.	24.90	42.62	55.65	65.35	89.14	96.40	98.79	99.59	99.86	99.95
7							0.	23.60	40.90	53.86	85.55	95.21	98.38	99.45	99.81	99.94
8								0.	22.64	39.61	81.08	93.73	97.89	99.28	99.76	99.92
9									0.	21.93	75.54	91.90	97.27	99.07	99.68	99.89
10										0.	68.67	89.62	96.50	98.81	99.60	99.86
11										0.	60.15	86.79	95.55	98.49	99.49	99.83
12										0.	49.58	83.29	94.36	98.09	99.35	99.78
13										0.	36.46	78.94	92.90	97.59	99.18	99.72
14										0.	20.19	73.55	91.08	96.97	98.97	99.65
15											0.	66.86	88.82	96.21	98.71	99.56
16											0.	58.56	86.02	95.26	98.39	99.45
17											0.	48.27	82.55	94.08	97.99	99.31
18											0.	35.50	78.24	92.62	97.49	99.15
19											0.	19.65	72.90	90.80	96.87	98.94
20												0.	66.27	88.55	96.11	98.68
21												0.	58.04	85.76	95.16	98.35
22												0.	47.84	82.30	93.98	97.95
23												0.	35.18	78.01	92.52	97.46
24												0.	19.48	72.68	90.71	96.84
25													0.	66.07	88.46	96.07
26													0.	57.87	85.67	95.13
27													0.	47.69	82.22	93.95
28													0.	35.08	77.93	92.49
29													0.	19.42	72.60	90.68
30														0.	66.00	88.43
35															0.	65.98
40																0.

Table 3

REMAINING BALANCE TABLES

ORIGINAL TERM IN YEARS

22.00%

AGE OF LOAN	1	2	3	4	5	6	7	8	9	10	15	20	25	30	35	40
1	0.	55.43	73.62	82.50	87.66	90.97	93.23	94.84	96.02	96.90	99.04	99.68	99.89	99.96	99.99	*****
2		0.	40.80	60.73	72.32	79.75	84.82	88.42	91.06	93.04	97.84	99.29	99.76	99.92	99.97	99.99
3			0.	33.66	53.24	65.79	74.35	80.44	84.90	88.23	96.35	98.81	99.60	99.87	99.96	99.98
4				0.	29.51	48.43	61.34	70.52	77.24	82.26	94.50	98.20	99.40	99.80	99.93	99.98
5					0.	26.85	45.16	58.17	67.71	74.84	92.20	97.44	99.15	99.71	99.90	99.97
6						0.	25.03	42.83	55.86	65.61	89.34	96.51	98.84	99.61	99.87	99.96
7							0.	23.74	41.12	54.12	85.78	95.34	98.45	99.48	99.83	99.94
8								0.	22.79	39.84	81.35	93.89	97.96	99.32	99.77	99.92
9									0.	22.08	75.85	92.09	97.36	99.12	99.70	99.90
10										0.	69.00	89.84	96.61	98.87	99.62	99.87
11										0.	60.49	87.06	95.69	98.55	99.51	99.84
12										0.	49.90	83.59	94.53	98.17	99.38	99.79
13										0.	36.74	79.27	93.09	97.68	99.22	99.74
14										0.	20.36	73.91	91.30	97.08	99.02	99.67
15											0.	67.24	89.08	96.34	98.77	99.59
16											0.	58.94	86.31	95.41	98.46	99.48
17											0.	48.63	82.88	94.26	98.07	99.35
18											0.	35.80	78.60	92.83	97.59	99.19
19											0.	19.84	73.28	91.04	96.99	98.99
20												0.	66.67	88.82	96.25	98.74
21												0.	58.44	86.07	95.32	98.43
22												0.	48.21	82.64	94.17	98.04
23												0.	35.49	78.37	92.74	97.56
24												0.	19.67	73.07	90.95	96.96
25													0.	66.48	88.74	96.22
26													0.	58.27	85.99	95.29
27													0.	48.07	82.56	94.14
28													0.	35.39	78.30	92.71
29													0.	19.62	73.00	90.93
30														0.	66.41	88.71
35															0.	66.39
40																0.

22.25%

AGE OF LOAN	1	2	3	4	5	6	7	8	9	10	15	20	25	30	35	40
1	0.	55.49	73.69	82.57	87.74	91.04	93.30	94.90	96.07	96.94	99.06	99.70	99.90	99.97	99.99	*****
2		0.	40.89	60.85	72.45	79.88	84.94	88.54	91.17	93.13	97.89	99.32	99.78	99.93	99.98	99.99
3			0.	33.76	53.39	65.96	74.52	80.61	85.06	88.38	96.44	98.85	99.62	99.87	99.96	99.99
4				0.	29.62	48.60	61.54	70.72	77.44	82.45	94.62	98.26	99.43	99.81	99.94	99.98
5					0.	26.97	45.35	58.40	67.94	75.07	92.35	97.52	99.18	99.73	99.91	99.97
6						0.	25.16	43.03	56.10	65.86	89.53	96.61	98.88	99.63	99.88	99.96
7							0.	23.88	41.34	54.38	86.01	95.47	98.51	99.51	99.84	99.95
8								0.	22.94	40.08	81.62	94.05	98.04	99.35	99.78	99.93
9									0.	22.24	76.15	92.28	97.46	99.16	99.72	99.91
10										0.	69.33	90.07	96.73	98.92	99.64	99.88
11										0.	60.83	87.31	95.82	98.62	99.54	99.85
12										0.	50.23	83.88	94.69	98.24	99.42	99.81
13										0.	37.01	79.60	93.28	97.77	99.26	99.75
14										0.	20.54	74.26	91.52	97.19	99.07	99.69
15											0.	67.61	89.33	96.47	98.83	99.61
16											0.	59.32	86.60	95.56	98.53	99.51
17											0.	48.98	83.20	94.43	98.15	99.39
18											0.	36.09	78.95	93.03	97.69	99.23
19											0.	20.03	73.66	91.28	97.11	99.04
20												0.	67.06	89.09	96.38	98.80
21												0.	58.84	86.37	95.48	98.50
22												0.	48.58	82.97	94.35	98.12
23												0.	35.80	78.74	92.94	97.66
24												0.	19.87	73.46	91.19	97.08
25													0.	66.88	89.01	96.35
26													0.	58.68	86.29	95.45
27													0.	48.45	82.90	94.32
28													0.	35.70	78.67	92.92
29													0.	19.81	73.39	91.17
30														0.	66.82	88.98
35															0.	66.80
40																0.

Table 3

REMAINING BALANCE TABLES

ORIGINAL TERM IN YEARS

22.50%

AGE OF LOAN	1	2	3	4	5	6	7	8	9	10	15	20	25	30	35	40
1	0.	55.55	73.76	82.65	87.81	91.11	93.36	94.95	96.12	96.99	99.09	99.71	99.90	99.97	99.99	*****
2		0.	40.98	60.96	72.57	80.00	85.06	88.65	91.27	93.22	97.94	99.34	99.79	99.93	99.98	99.99
3			0.	33.87	53.53	66.12	74.69	80.77	85.21	88.52	96.52	98.88	99.64	99.88	99.96	99.99
4				0.	29.74	48.77	61.73	70.92	77.64	82.64	94.73	98.31	99.45	99.82	99.94	99.98
5					0.	27.09	45.54	58.62	68.17	75.30	92.50	97.60	99.22	99.74	99.92	99.97
6						0.	25.30	43.24	56.34	66.12	89.72	96.71	98.93	99.65	99.89	99.96
7							0.	24.02	41.56	54.65	86.24	95.59	98.57	99.53	99.85	99.95
8								0.	23.09	40.31	81.89	94.20	98.11	99.38	99.80	99.93
9									0.	22.39	76.45	92.46	97.55	99.20	99.74	99.91
10										0.	69.65	90.28	96.84	98.97	99.66	99.89
11										0.	61.16	87.56	95.95	98.68	99.57	99.86
12										0.	50.55	84.17	94.85	98.31	99.45	99.82
13										0.	37.29	79.92	93.46	97.86	99.30	99.77
14										0.	20.71	74.61	91.74	97.30	99.11	99.71
15											0.	67.98	89.58	96.59	98.88	99.63
16											0.	59.69	86.88	95.71	98.59	99.54
17											0.	49.34	83.51	94.60	98.23	99.42
18											0.	36.39	79.30	93.23	97.78	99.27
19											0.	20.22	74.03	91.50	97.21	99.09
20												0.	67.45	89.35	96.51	98.86
21												0.	59.23	86.66	95.63	98.57
22												0.	48.95	83.30	94.52	98.20
23												0.	36.11	79.09	93.15	97.75
24												0.	20.06	73.84	91.43	97.19
25													0.	67.28	89.27	96.48
26													0.	59.08	86.59	95.60
27													0.	48.83	83.23	94.50
28													0.	36.02	79.03	93.12
29													0.	20.01	73.78	91.40
30														0.	67.22	89.25
35															0.	67.20
40																0.

22.75%

AGE OF LOAN	1	2	3	4	5	6	7	8	9	10	15	20	25	30	35	40
1	0.	55.61	73.84	82.72	87.88	91.18	93.42	95.01	96.17	97.03	99.11	99.72	99.91	99.97	99.99	*****
2		0.	41.06	61.08	72.70	80.13	85.18	88.76	91.37	93.32	97.99	99.37	99.80	99.93	99.98	99.99
3			0.	33.97	53.68	66.29	74.86	80.93	85.36	88.66	96.60	98.92	99.65	99.89	99.96	99.99
4				0.	29.85	48.94	61.93	71.13	77.83	82.83	94.85	98.37	99.48	99.83	99.95	99.98
5					0.	27.22	45.73	58.84	68.40	75.53	92.65	97.67	99.25	99.76	99.92	99.97
6						0.	25.43	43.44	56.58	66.37	89.90	96.80	98.97	99.67	99.89	99.97
7							0.	24.16	41.78	54.91	86.46	95.71	98.62	99.55	99.86	99.95
8								0.	23.23	40.54	82.15	94.35	98.18	99.41	99.81	99.94
9									0.	22.55	76.75	92.64	97.63	99.23	99.75	99.92
10										0.	69.98	90.50	96.94	99.01	99.68	99.90
11										0.	61.50	87.81	96.08	98.73	99.59	99.87
12										0.	50.87	84.45	95.00	98.38	99.48	99.83
13										0.	37.56	80.24	93.64	97.95	99.33	99.78
14										0.	20.89	74.96	91.95	97.40	99.16	99.73
15											0.	68.35	89.82	96.71	98.93	99.65
16											0.	60.07	87.16	95.85	98.66	99.56
17											0.	49.69	83.82	94.77	98.31	99.45
18											0.	36.69	79.64	93.42	97.87	99.31
19											0.	20.40	74.40	91.72	97.32	99.13
20												0.	67.84	89.60	96.63	98.91
21												0.	59.62	86.95	95.77	98.63
22												0.	49.32	83.62	94.69	98.28
23												0.	36.41	79.44	93.34	97.84
24												0.	20.25	74.22	91.65	97.30
25													0.	67.67	89.53	96.61
26													0.	59.47	86.88	95.75
27													0.	49.20	83.55	94.67
28													0.	36.33	79.38	93.32
29													0.	20.20	74.16	91.63
30														0.	67.62	89.51
35															0.	67.60
40																0.

Table 3

REMAINING BALANCE TABLES

ORIGINAL TERM IN YEARS

23.00%

AGE OF LOAN	1	2	3	4	5	6	7	8	9	10	15	20	25	30	35	40
1	0.	55.67	73.91	82.80	87.95	91.25	93.48	95.07	96.22	97.08	99.13	99.73	99.91	99.97	99.99	*****
2		0.	41.15	61.20	72.83	80.26	85.30	88.87	91.48	93.41	98.04	99.39	99.81	99.94	99.98	99.99
3			0.	34.07	53.83	66.45	75.03	81.10	85.52	88.80	96.67	98.96	99.67	99.89	99.97	99.99
4				0.	29.97	49.11	62.12	71.33	78.03	83.02	94.96	98.42	99.50	99.84	99.95	99.98
5					0.	27.34	45.91	59.06	68.63	75.75	92.80	97.75	99.28	99.77	99.93	99.98
6						0.	25.56	43.65	56.83	66.63	90.09	96.90	99.01	99.69	99.90	99.97
7							0.	24.30	42.00	55.17	86.68	95.83	98.68	99.58	99.86	99.96
8								0.	23.38	40.77	82.41	94.50	98.25	99.44	99.82	99.94
9									0.	22.70	77.04	92.82	97.72	99.27	99.77	99.93
10										0.	70.30	90.71	97.05	99.06	99.70	99.90
11										0.	61.83	88.06	96.20	98.79	99.61	99.88
12										0.	51.19	84.73	95.15	98.45	99.50	99.84
13										0.	37.84	80.55	93.82	98.03	99.37	99.80
14										0.	21.06	75.30	92.15	97.49	99.20	99.74
15											0.	68.71	90.06	96.82	98.98	99.67
16											0.	60.43	87.43	95.98	98.72	99.59
17											0.	50.04	84.12	94.93	98.38	99.48
18											0.	36.98	79.97	93.60	97.95	99.35
19											0.	20.59	74.76	91.94	97.42	99.17
20												0.	68.22	89.85	96.75	98.96
21												0.	60.00	87.23	95.91	98.69
22												0.	49.68	83.93	94.86	98.35
23												0.	36.72	79.79	93.54	97.93
24												0.	20.44	74.59	91.87	97.40
25													0.	68.06	89.78	96.73
26													0.	59.86	87.16	95.89
27													0.	49.57	83.87	94.84
28													0.	36.64	79.73	93.51
29													0.	20.40	74.54	91.85
30														0.	68.01	89.76
35															0.	68.00
40																0.

23.25%

AGE OF LOAN	1	2	3	4	5	6	7	8	9	10	15	20	25	30	35	40
1	0.	55.73	73.98	82.87	88.03	91.31	93.55	95.12	96.27	97.12	99.15	99.74	99.92	99.97	99.99	*****
2		0.	41.23	61.31	72.95	80.38	85.42	88.98	91.58	93.50	98.09	99.41	99.81	99.94	99.98	99.99
3			0.	34.17	53.97	66.62	75.19	81.26	85.67	88.94	96.75	98.99	99.68	99.90	99.97	99.99
4				0.	30.08	49.29	62.32	71.53	78.23	83.20	95.06	98.47	99.52	99.85	99.95	99.98
5					0.	27.47	46.10	59.28	68.86	75.98	92.94	97.82	99.31	99.78	99.93	99.98
6						0.	25.69	43.86	57.07	66.88	90.27	96.99	99.05	99.70	99.91	99.97
7							0.	24.44	42.22	55.43	86.90	95.95	98.73	99.60	99.87	99.96
8								0.	23.53	41.01	82.66	94.64	98.32	99.47	99.83	99.95
9									0.	22.85	77.33	92.99	97.80	99.31	99.78	99.93
10										0.	70.61	90.91	97.15	99.10	99.72	99.91
11										0.	62.16	88.30	96.32	98.84	99.63	99.88
12										0.	51.51	85.00	95.29	98.51	99.53	99.85
13										0.	38.11	80.86	93.99	98.10	99.40	99.81
14										0.	21.24	75.64	92.35	97.59	99.24	99.76
15											0.	69.07	90.29	96.94	99.03	99.69
16											0.	60.80	87.69	96.12	98.77	99.61
17											0.	50.39	84.42	95.08	98.45	99.51
18											0.	37.28	80.30	93.79	98.04	99.38
19											0.	20.78	75.12	92.15	97.52	99.22
20												0.	68.60	90.09	96.87	99.01
21												0.	60.38	87.50	96.05	98.75
22												0.	50.04	84.24	95.02	98.43
23												0.	37.02	80.13	93.72	98.02
24												0.	20.63	74.96	92.09	97.50
25													0.	68.45	90.03	96.85
26													0.	60.25	87.44	96.03
27													0.	49.93	84.18	95.00
28													0.	36.94	80.08	93.70
29													0.	20.59	74.91	92.07
30														0.	68.40	90.01
35															0.	68.39
40																0.

Table 3

REMAINING BALANCE TABLES

ORIGINAL TERM IN YEARS

23.50%

AGE OF LOAN	1	2	3	4	5	6	7	8	9	10	15	20	25	30	35	40
1	0.	55.79	74.06	82.95	88.10	91.38	93.61	95.18	96.32	97.17	99.18	99.75	99.92	99.98	99.99	*****
2		0.	41.32	61.43	73.08	80.51	85.54	89.09	91.68	93.59	98.14	99.43	99.82	99.94	99.98	99.99
3			0.	34.27	54.12	66.78	75.36	81.42	85.82	89.08	96.83	99.03	99.70	99.91	99.97	99.99
4				0.	30.19	49.45	62.51	71.73	78.42	83.39	95.17	98.52	99.54	99.86	99.96	99.99
5					0.	27.59	46.29	59.50	69.09	76.20	93.08	97.88	99.34	99.80	99.94	99.98
6						0.	25.83	44.06	57.31	67.13	90.44	97.08	99.09	99.72	99.91	99.97
7							0.	24.58	42.44	55.68	87.12	96.06	98.78	99.62	99.88	99.96
8								0.	23.68	41.24	82.92	94.78	98.38	99.49	99.84	99.95
9									0.	23.01	77.62	93.16	97.88	99.34	99.79	99.94
10										0.	70.93	91.11	97.24	99.14	99.73	99.92
11										0.	62.48	88.53	96.44	98.89	99.65	99.89
12										0.	51.83	85.27	95.43	98.58	99.56	99.86
13										0.	38.38	81.16	94.15	98.18	99.43	99.82
14										0.	21.42	75.97	92.54	97.68	99.27	99.77
15											0.	69.43	90.51	97.04	99.08	99.71
16											0.	61.16	87.95	96.24	98.83	99.63
17											0.	50.73	84.71	95.23	98.51	99.54
18											0.	37.57	80.63	93.96	98.12	99.41
19											0.	20.96	75.48	92.36	97.61	99.25
20												0.	68.97	90.33	96.98	99.06
21												0.	60.76	87.77	96.18	98.81
22												0.	50.40	84.54	95.17	98.49
23												0.	37.33	80.46	93.90	98.10
24												0.	20.83	75.32	92.30	97.59
25													0.	68.83	90.27	96.96
26													0.	60.64	87.71	96.16
27													0.	50.30	84.49	95.16
28													0.	37.25	80.41	93.88
29													0.	20.78	75.27	92.28
30														0.	68.79	90.25
35															0.	68.77
40																0.

23.75%

AGE OF LOAN	1	2	3	4	5	6	7	8	9	10	15	20	25	30	35	40
1	0.	55.85	74.13	83.02	88.17	91.45	93.67	95.23	96.37	97.21	99.20	99.76	99.93	99.98	99.99	*****
2		0.	41.40	61.55	73.20	80.63	85.66	89.20	91.78	93.68	98.18	99.45	99.83	99.95	99.98	*****
3			0.	34.38	54.27	66.94	75.52	81.58	85.97	89.22	96.90	99.06	99.71	99.91	99.97	99.99
4				0.	30.31	49.62	62.70	71.92	78.61	83.57	95.27	98.57	99.56	99.87	99.96	99.99
5					0.	27.72	46.48	59.71	69.31	76.42	93.22	97.95	99.37	99.81	99.94	99.98
6						0.	25.96	44.27	57.55	67.38	90.62	97.16	99.13	99.73	99.92	99.97
7							0.	24.72	42.66	55.94	87.33	96.17	98.83	99.64	99.89	99.97
8								0.	23.83	41.47	83.17	94.91	98.44	99.52	99.85	99.95
9									0.	23.16	77.90	93.32	97.95	99.37	99.81	99.94
10										0.	71.24	91.31	97.33	99.18	99.75	99.92
11										0.	62.81	88.76	96.55	98.94	99.67	99.90
12										0.	52.15	85.54	95.57	98.63	99.58	99.87
13										0.	38.66	81.46	94.32	98.25	99.46	99.83
14										0.	21.59	76.30	92.73	97.76	99.31	99.79
15											0.	69.78	90.73	97.15	99.12	99.73
16											0.	61.52	88.20	96.37	98.88	99.65
17											0.	51.08	85.00	95.38	98.58	99.56
18											0.	37.87	80.95	94.13	98.19	99.44
19											0.	21.15	75.82	92.56	97.70	99.29
20												0.	69.34	90.56	97.09	99.10
21												0.	61.14	88.03	96.31	98.86
22												0.	50.76	84.84	95.32	98.56
23												0.	37.63	80.79	94.08	98.17
24												0.	21.02	75.68	92.50	97.69
25													0.	69.21	90.50	97.07
26													0.	61.02	87.98	96.29
27													0.	50.66	84.79	95.31
28													0.	37.55	80.74	94.06
29													0.	20.98	75.63	92.48
30														0.	69.16	90.49
35															0.	69.15
40																0.

Table 3

REMAINING BALANCE TABLES

ORIGINAL TERM IN YEARS

24.00%

AGE OF LOAN	1	2	3	4	5	6	7	8	9	10	15	20	25	30	35	40
1	0.	55.91	74.20	83.10	88.24	91.51	93.73	95.29	96.42	97.25	99.22	99.77	99.93	99.98	99.99	*****
2		0.	41.49	61.66	73.33	80.75	85.78	89.31	91.87	93.77	98.23	99.47	99.84	99.95	99.99	*****
3			0.	34.48	54.41	67.10	75.69	81.73	86.11	89.35	96.97	99.09	99.73	99.92	99.97	99.99
4				0.	30.42	49.79	62.90	72.12	78.81	83.75	95.38	98.62	99.58	99.87	99.96	99.99
5					0.	27.84	46.67	59.93	69.54	76.64	93.35	98.01	99.40	99.82	99.94	99.98
6						0.	26.10	44.47	57.79	67.63	90.79	97.25	99.17	99.75	99.92	99.98
7							0.	24.87	42.88	56.20	87.54	96.28	98.87	99.66	99.90	99.97
8								0.	23.98	41.70	83.41	95.04	98.50	99.54	99.86	99.96
9									0.	23.32	78.18	93.48	98.03	99.40	99.82	99.94
10										0.	71.55	91.50	97.43	99.22	99.76	99.93
11										0.	63.13	88.99	96.66	98.98	99.69	99.91
12										0.	52.46	85.80	95.70	98.69	99.60	99.88
13										0.	38.93	81.76	94.47	98.32	99.49	99.84
14										0.	21.77	76.63	92.92	97.85	99.34	99.80
15											0.	70.13	90.95	97.25	99.16	99.74
16											0.	61.88	88.45	96.49	98.93	99.67
17											0.	51.42	85.28	95.52	98.64	99.58
18											0.	38.16	81.26	94.30	98.26	99.47
19											0.	21.33	76.17	92.75	97.79	99.33
20												0.	69.71	90.78	97.19	99.14
21												0.	61.51	88.29	96.43	98.91
22												0.	51.11	85.13	95.47	98.62
23												0.	37.93	81.12	94.25	98.25
24												0.	21.21	76.03	92.70	97.77
25													0.	69.58	90.73	97.18
26													0.	61.40	88.24	96.42
27													0.	51.02	85.08	95.45
28													0.	37.86	81.07	94.23
29													0.	21.17	75.99	92.68
30														0.	69.54	90.72
35															0.	69.53
40																0.

24.25%

AGE OF LOAN	1	2	3	4	5	6	7	8	9	10	15	20	25	30	35	40
1	0.	55.97	74.28	83.17	88.31	91.58	93.79	95.34	96.47	97.30	99.24	99.78	99.93	99.98	99.99	*****
2		0.	41.58	61.78	73.45	80.88	85.89	89.42	91.97	93.86	98.27	99.49	99.85	99.95	99.99	*****
3			0.	34.58	54.56	67.27	75.85	81.89	86.26	89.48	97.04	99.13	99.74	99.92	99.98	99.99
4				0.	30.54	49.96	63.09	72.32	79.00	83.93	95.48	98.66	99.60	99.88	99.96	99.99
5					0.	27.97	46.86	60.15	69.76	76.86	93.49	98.08	99.42	99.83	99.95	99.98
6						0.	26.23	44.68	58.02	67.88	90.96	97.33	99.20	99.76	99.93	99.98
7							0.	25.01	43.10	56.45	87.74	96.38	98.92	99.67	99.90	99.97
8								0.	24.12	41.93	83.66	95.17	98.56	99.57	99.87	99.96
9									0.	23.47	78.46	93.64	98.10	99.43	99.83	99.95
10										0.	71.85	91.69	97.51	99.25	99.78	99.93
11										0.	63.45	89.21	96.77	99.03	99.71	99.91
12										0.	52.78	86.06	95.83	98.75	99.62	99.89
13										0.	39.20	82.05	94.63	98.38	99.51	99.85
14										0.	21.94	76.95	93.10	97.93	99.38	99.81
15											0.	70.47	91.16	97.34	99.20	99.76
16											0.	62.23	88.70	96.60	98.98	99.69
17											0.	51.76	85.56	95.66	98.69	99.61
18											0.	38.45	81.58	94.46	98.33	99.50
19											0.	21.52	76.51	92.94	97.88	99.36
20												0.	70.07	91.00	97.29	99.19
21												0.	61.88	88.54	96.55	98.96
22												0.	51.46	85.41	95.61	98.68
23												0.	38.23	81.43	94.41	98.32
24												0.	21.40	76.38	92.89	97.86
25													0.	69.95	90.96	97.28
26													0.	61.77	88.50	96.54
27													0.	51.38	85.37	95.60
28													0.	38.16	81.39	94.40
29													0.	21.36	76.34	92.88
30														0.	69.91	90.94
35															0.	69.90
40																0.

Table 3

REMAINING BALANCE TABLES

ORIGINAL TERM IN YEARS

24.50%

AGE OF LOAN	1	2	3	4	5	6	7	8	9	10	15	20	25	30	35	40
1	0.	56.03	74.35	83.25	88.38	91.65	93.85	95.40	96.51	97.34	99.26	99.78	99.94	99.98	99.99	*****
2		0.	41.66	61.89	73.57	81.00	86.01	89.53	92.07	93.94	98.31	99.51	99.85	99.96	99.99	*****
3			0.	34.68	54.70	67.43	76.01	82.05	86.40	89.62	97.11	99.16	99.75	99.93	99.98	99.99
4				0.	30.65	50.13	63.28	72.51	79.19	84.10	95.57	98.71	99.62	99.89	99.97	99.99
5					0.	28.09	47.05	60.37	69.99	77.08	93.62	98.14	99.45	99.84	99.95	99.99
6						0.	26.36	44.88	58.26	68.12	91.12	97.41	99.23	99.77	99.93	99.98
7							0.	25.15	43.32	56.71	87.95	96.48	98.96	99.69	99.91	99.97
8								0.	24.27	42.16	83.90	95.30	98.61	99.59	99.88	99.96
9									0.	23.63	78.74	93.79	98.16	99.45	99.84	99.95
10										0.	72.16	91.87	97.60	99.29	99.79	99.94
11										0.	63.77	89.43	96.87	99.07	99.72	99.92
12										0.	53.09	86.31	95.95	98.80	99.64	99.89
13										0.	39.47	82.33	94.78	98.45	99.54	99.86
14										0.	22.12	77.27	93.28	98.00	99.41	99.82
15											0.	70.81	91.37	97.44	99.24	99.77
16											0.	62.59	88.93	96.71	99.02	99.71
17											0.	52.10	85.83	95.79	98.75	99.63
18											0.	38.74	81.88	94.62	98.40	99.52
19											0.	21.71	76.84	93.12	97.96	99.39
20												0.	70.42	91.22	97.39	99.22
21												0.	62.24	88.79	96.67	99.01
22												0.	51.81	85.69	95.75	98.74
23												0.	38.52	81.75	94.57	98.39
24												0.	21.59	76.72	93.08	97.94
25													0.	70.31	91.17	97.38
26													0.	62.14	88.75	96.65
27													0.	51.73	85.65	95.73
28													0.	38.46	81.71	94.56
29													0.	21.55	76.68	93.07
30														0.	70.27	91.16
35															0.	70.26
40																0.

24.75%

AGE OF LOAN	1	2	3	4	5	6	7	8	9	10	15	20	25	30	35	40
1	0.	56.09	74.42	83.32	88.45	91.71	93.91	95.45	96.56	97.38	99.28	99.79	99.94	99.98	99.99	*****
2		0.	41.75	62.01	73.70	81.12	86.12	89.63	92.16	94.03	98.36	99.53	99.86	99.96	99.99	*****
3			0.	34.78	54.85	67.59	76.18	82.20	86.55	89.75	97.18	99.19	99.76	99.93	99.98	99.99
4				0.	30.77	50.30	63.47	72.71	79.37	84.28	95.67	98.75	99.63	99.89	99.97	99.99
5					0.	28.22	47.24	60.58	70.21	77.29	93.75	98.20	99.47	99.85	99.95	99.99
6						0.	26.50	45.09	58.50	68.37	91.29	97.49	99.27	99.78	99.94	99.98
7							0.	25.29	43.54	56.96	88.15	96.58	99.00	99.71	99.91	99.97
8								0.	24.42	42.39	84.13	95.42	98.66	99.61	99.88	99.97
9									0.	23.78	79.01	93.94	98.23	99.48	99.85	99.96
10										0.	72.46	92.05	97.68	99.32	99.80	99.94
11										0.	64.09	89.64	96.97	99.11	99.74	99.92
12										0.	53.40	86.56	96.07	98.85	99.66	99.90
13										0.	39.74	82.62	94.92	98.51	99.56	99.87
14										0.	22.29	77.58	93.45	98.08	99.44	99.83
15											0.	71.15	91.57	97.53	99.27	99.79
16											0.	62.94	89.17	96.82	99.07	99.73
17											0.	52.44	86.10	95.92	98.80	99.65
18											0.	39.03	82.18	94.77	98.47	99.55
19											0.	21.89	77.17	93.30	98.03	99.42
20												0.	70.78	91.43	97.48	99.26
21												0.	62.60	89.03	96.78	99.05
22												0.	52.16	85.97	95.88	98.79
23												0.	38.82	82.05	94.73	98.45
24												0.	21.78	77.05	93.26	98.02
25													0.	70.67	91.39	97.47
26													0.	62.51	88.99	96.77
27													0.	52.08	85.93	95.87
28													0.	38.76	82.02	94.72
29													0.	21.74	77.02	93.25
30														0.	70.63	91.37
35															0.	70.63
40																0.

Table 3

REMAINING BALANCE TABLES

ORIGINAL TERM IN YEARS

AGE OF LOAN

25.00%

Age	1	2	3	4	5	6	7	8	9	10	15	20	25	30	35	40
1	0.	56.15	74.50	83.39	88.52	91.78	93.97	95.50	96.61	97.42	99.30	99.80	99.94	99.98	*****	*****
2		0.	41.83	62.13	73.82	81.24	86.24	89.74	92.26	94.11	98.40	99.54	99.87	99.96	99.99	*****
3			0.	34.89	54.99	67.75	76.34	82.36	86.69	89.88	97.24	99.21	99.77	99.93	99.98	99.99
4				0.	30.88	50.47	63.66	72.90	79.56	84.45	95.76	98.79	99.65	99.90	99.97	99.99
5					0.	28.34	47.43	60.80	70.43	77.51	93.87	98.25	99.50	99.85	99.96	99.99
6						0.	26.63	45.29	58.73	68.61	91.45	97.56	99.30	99.80	99.94	99.98
7							0.	25.43	43.75	57.22	88.34	96.68	99.04	99.72	99.92	99.98
8								0.	24.57	42.62	84.37	95.54	98.71	99.63	99.89	99.97
9									0.	23.94	79.28	94.09	98.29	99.51	99.86	99.96
10										0.	72.76	92.23	97.76	99.35	99.81	99.95
11										0.	64.41	89.85	97.07	99.15	99.75	99.93
12										0.	53.71	86.80	96.19	98.90	99.68	99.91
13										0.	40.01	82.90	95.06	98.57	99.58	99.88
14										0.	22.47	77.89	93.62	98.15	99.46	99.84
15											0.	71.49	91.77	97.61	99.31	99.80
16											0.	63.28	89.40	96.93	99.11	99.74
17											0.	52.77	86.36	96.05	98.85	99.67
18											0.	39.31	82.48	94.92	98.53	99.57
19											0.	22.08	77.50	93.48	98.11	99.45
20												0.	71.13	91.63	97.57	99.30
21												0.	62.96	89.27	96.89	99.10
22												0.	52.51	86.24	96.01	98.84
23												0.	39.12	82.36	94.88	98.51
24												0.	21.96	77.39	93.44	98.10
25													0.	71.02	91.59	97.56
26													0.	62.87	89.23	96.87
27													0.	52.43	86.20	96.00
28													0.	39.06	82.32	94.87
29													0.	21.93	77.35	93.43
30														0.	70.99	91.58
35															0.	70.98
40																0.

25.25%

Age	1	2	3	4	5	6	7	8	9	10	15	20	25	30	35	40
1	0.	56.21	74.57	83.47	88.59	91.84	94.02	95.55	96.65	97.46	99.32	99.81	99.94	99.98	*****	*****
2		0.	41.92	62.24	73.94	81.36	86.35	89.84	92.35	94.19	98.44	99.56	99.87	99.96	99.99	*****
3			0.	34.99	55.14	67.91	76.50	82.51	86.83	90.00	97.31	99.24	99.78	99.93	99.98	99.99
4				0.	31.00	50.64	63.85	73.10	79.75	84.63	95.86	98.83	99.67	99.90	99.97	99.99
5					0.	28.47	47.61	61.01	70.65	77.72	94.00	98.31	99.52	99.86	99.96	99.99
6						0.	26.77	45.50	58.97	68.85	91.61	97.63	99.33	99.81	99.94	99.98
7							0.	25.58	43.97	57.47	88.54	96.77	99.08	99.74	99.92	99.98
8								0.	24.72	42.85	84.60	95.66	98.76	99.65	99.90	99.97
9									0.	24.09	79.55	94.24	98.36	99.53	99.87	99.96
10										0.	73.05	92.41	97.83	99.38	99.82	99.95
11										0.	64.72	90.06	97.16	99.19	99.77	99.93
12										0.	54.02	87.04	96.30	98.94	99.70	99.91
13										0.	40.28	83.17	95.20	98.63	99.61	99.89
14										0.	22.64	78.20	93.78	98.22	99.49	99.85
15											0.	71.82	91.96	97.70	99.34	99.81
16											0.	63.62	89.62	97.03	99.15	99.76
17											0.	53.11	86.62	96.17	98.90	99.69
18											0.	39.60	82.77	95.07	98.59	99.59
19											0.	22.26	77.82	93.65	98.18	99.48
20												0.	71.47	91.83	97.66	99.33
21												0.	63.32	89.50	96.99	99.14
22												0.	52.85	86.50	96.13	98.89
23												0.	39.41	82.65	95.03	98.58
24												0.	22.15	77.71	93.61	98.17
25													0.	71.37	91.80	97.65
26													0.	63.23	89.46	96.98
27													0.	52.78	86.47	96.12
28													0.	39.35	82.62	95.02
29													0.	22.12	77.68	93.60
30														0.	71.34	91.79
35															0.	71.34
40	0.															0.

Table 3

REMAINING BALANCE TABLES

ORIGINAL TERM IN YEARS

AGE OF LOAN

25.50%

Age	1	2	3	4	5	6	7	8	9	10	15	20	25	30	35	40
1	0.	56.27	74.64	83.54	88.66	91.90	94.08	95.60	96.70	97.50	99.33	99.81	99.95	99.99	*****	*****
2		0.	42.00	62.36	74.07	81.48	86.46	89.94	92.45	94.28	98.47	99.58	99.88	99.97	99.99	*****
3			0.	35.09	55.28	68.07	76.66	82.66	86.97	90.13	97.37	99.27	99.79	99.94	99.98	*****
4				0.	31.11	50.81	64.04	73.29	79.93	84.80	95.95	98.87	99.68	99.91	99.97	99.99
5					0.	28.59	47.80	61.23	70.87	77.93	94.12	98.36	99.54	99.87	99.96	99.99
6						0.	26.90	45.70	59.20	69.09	91.76	97.71	99.35	99.82	99.95	99.99
7							0.	25.72	44.19	57.72	88.73	96.86	99.12	99.75	99.93	99.98
8								0.	24.87	43.08	84.83	95.77	98.81	99.66	99.90	99.97
9									0.	24.25	79.81	94.38	98.41	99.55	99.87	99.96
10										0.	73.35	92.58	97.91	99.41	99.83	99.95
11										0.	65.03	90.26	97.25	99.22	99.78	99.94
12										0.	54.33	87.28	96.41	98.99	99.71	99.92
13										0.	40.55	83.44	95.33	98.68	99.63	99.89
14										0.	22.82	78.50	93.94	98.29	99.51	99.86
15											0.	72.15	92.15	97.78	99.37	99.82
16											0.	63.96	89.84	97.13	99.19	99.77
17											0.	53.44	86.87	96.29	98.95	99.70
18											0.	39.89	83.05	95.21	98.64	99.62
19											0.	22.45	78.14	93.82	98.25	99.50
20												0.	71.81	92.03	97.74	99.36
21												0.	63.67	89.72	97.09	99.18
22												0.	53.19	86.76	96.25	98.94
23												0.	39.70	82.95	95.17	98.63
24												0.	22.34	78.04	93.78	98.24
25													0.	71.72	91.99	97.73
26													0.	63.59	89.69	97.08
27													0.	53.12	86.73	96.24
28													0.	39.65	82.92	95.16
29													0.	22.31	78.01	93.77
30														0.	71.69	91.98
35															0.	71.68
40																0.

25.75%

Age	1	2	3	4	5	6	7	8	9	10	15	20	25	30	35	40
1	0.	56.34	74.71	83.61	88.73	91.97	94.14	95.65	96.74	97.54	99.35	99.82	99.95	99.99	*****	*****
2		0.	42.09	62.47	74.19	81.60	86.58	90.05	92.54	94.36	98.51	99.59	99.89	99.97	99.99	*****
3			0.	35.19	55.43	68.23	76.82	82.81	87.11	90.26	97.43	99.29	99.80	99.94	99.98	*****
4				0.	31.23	50.98	64.23	73.48	80.11	84.97	96.04	98.91	99.70	99.92	99.98	99.99
5					0.	28.72	47.99	61.44	71.09	78.14	94.24	98.41	99.56	99.88	99.97	99.99
6						0.	27.03	45.90	59.44	69.33	91.92	97.77	99.38	99.83	99.95	99.99
7							0.	25.86	44.41	57.97	88.92	96.95	99.15	99.76	99.93	99.98
8								0.	25.02	43.31	85.06	95.89	98.85	99.68	99.91	99.97
9									0.	24.40	80.07	94.51	98.47	99.57	99.88	99.97
10										0.	73.64	92.74	97.98	99.44	99.84	99.96
11										0.	65.34	90.46	97.34	99.26	99.79	99.94
12										0.	54.63	87.51	96.52	99.03	99.73	99.92
13										0.	40.82	83.71	95.46	98.73	99.65	99.90
14										0.	22.99	78.80	94.10	98.35	99.54	99.87
15											0.	72.47	92.33	97.86	99.40	99.83
16											0.	64.30	90.06	97.22	99.22	99.78
17											0.	53.76	87.12	96.40	98.99	99.72
18											0.	40.17	83.34	95.34	98.70	99.64
19											0.	22.63	78.45	93.98	98.32	99.53
20												0.	72.15	92.22	97.82	99.39
21												0.	64.02	89.95	97.19	99.21
22												0.	53.53	87.02	96.37	98.98
23												0.	39.99	83.23	95.31	98.69
24												0.	22.53	78.35	93.95	98.31
25													0.	72.06	92.19	97.81
26													0.	63.94	89.92	97.18
27													0.	53.46	86.99	96.36
28													0.	39.94	83.21	95.30
29													0.	22.50	78.33	93.94
30														0.	72.04	92.18
35															0.	72.03
40																0.

Table 4   MONTHLY-DAILY
INTEREST FACTORS

The normal procedure to compute monthly interest payments is to multiply the current loan amount by the annual interest rate, then divide by 12 months. This procedure can be shortened by the use of monthly interest factors obtained by dividing the annual interest rate by 12 months, then multiplying the loan amount by the monthly interest factor. This same method can be used to obtain daily interest rates based on 365-day and 360-day years.

Example:

1. Given a loan balance of $15,000 at 7.25 percent annual interest (365-day year) with monthly payments of $170.00, what is the interest portion of the payment?

    Ans. By referring to the 365-day year table, you will find the monthly interest factor corresponding to 7.25 percent interest to be 0.6042 percent. Then,

    $$0.6042\% \times \$15,000 = \$90.63 \quad \begin{array}{l}\text{(interest portion of}\\ \text{monthly loan payment)}\end{array}$$

Table 4

MONTHLY-DAILY
INTEREST FACTORS
365-DAY YEAR

ANNUAL INTEREST	MONTHLY INTEREST	DAILY INTEREST	ANNUAL INTEREST	MONTHLY INTEREST	DAILY INTEREST	ANNUAL INTEREST	MONTHLY INTEREST	DAILY INTEREST
5.00%	.4167%	.0137%	12.00%	1.0000%	.0329%	19.00%	1.5833%	.0521%
5.25	.4375	.0144	12.25	1.0208	.0336	19.25	1.6042	.0527
5.50	.4583	.0151	12.50	1.0417	.0342	19.50	1.6250	.0534
5.75	.4792	.0158	12.75	1.0625	.0349	19.75	1.6458	.0541
6.00	.5000	.0164	13.00	1.0833	.0356	20.00	1.6667	.0548
6.25	.5208	.0171	13.25	1.1042	.0363	20.25	1.6875	.0555
6.50	.5417	.0178	13.50	1.1250	.0370	20.50	1.7083	.0562
6.75	.5625	.0185	13.75	1.1458	.0377	20.75	1.7292	.0568
7.00	.5833	.0192	14.00	1.1667	.0384	21.00	1.7500	.0575
7.25	.6042	.0199	14.25	1.1875	.0390	21.25	1.7708	.0582
7.50	.6250	.0205	14.50	1.2083	.0397	21.50	1.7917	.0589
7.75	.6458	.0212	14.75	1.2292	.0404	21.75	1.8125	.0596
8.00	.6667	.0219	15.00	1.2500	.0411	22.00	1.8333	.0603
8.25	.6875	.0226	15.25	1.2708	.0418	22.25	1.8542	.0610
8.50	.7083	.0233	15.50	1.2917	.0425	22.50	1.8750	.0616
8.75	.7292	.0240	15.75	1.3125	.0432	22.75	1.8958	.0623
9.00	.7500	.0247	16.00	1.3333	.0438	23.00	1.9167	.0630
9.25	.7708	.0253	16.25	1.3542	.0445	23.25	1.9375	.0637
9.50	.7917	.0260	16.50	1.3750	.0452	23.50	1.9583	.0644
9.75	.8125	.0267	16.75	1.3958	.0459	23.75	1.9792	.0651
10.00	.8333	.0274	17.00	1.4167	.0466	24.00	2.0000	.0658
10.25	.8542	.0281	17.25	1.4375	.0473	24.25	2.0208	.0664
10.50	.8750	.0288	17.50	1.4583	.0479	24.50	2.0417	.0671
10.75	.8958	.0295	17.75	1.4792	.0486	24.75	2.0625	.0678
11.00	.9167	.0301	18.00	1.5000	.0493	25.00	2.0833	.0685
11.25	.9375	.0308	18.25	1.5208	.0500	25.25	2.1042	.0692
11.50	.9583	.0315	18.50	1.5417	.0507	25.50	2.1250	.0699
11.75	.9792	.0322	18.75	1.5625	.0514	25.75	2.1458	.0705

Table 4

MONTHLY-DAILY
INTEREST FACTORS
360-DAY YEAR

ANNUAL INTEREST	MONTHLY INTEREST	DAILY INTEREST	ANNUAL INTEREST	MONTHLY INTEREST	DAILY INTEREST	ANNUAL INTEREST	MONTHLY INTEREST	DAILY INTEREST
5.00%	.4167%	.0139%	12.00%	1.0000%	.0333%	19.00%	1.5833%	.0528%
5.25	.4375	.0146	12.25	1.0208	.0340	19.25	1.6042	.0535
5.50	.4583	.0153	12.50	1.0417	.0347	19.50	1.6250	.0542
5.75	.4792	.0160	12.75	1.0625	.0354	19.75	1.6458	.0549
6.00	.5000	.0167	13.00	1.0833	.0361	20.00	1.6667	.0556
6.25	.5208	.0174	13.25	1.1042	.0368	20.25	1.6875	.0563
6.50	.5417	.0181	13.50	1.1250	.0375	20.50	1.7083	.0569
6.75	.5625	.0188	13.75	1.1458	.0382	20.75	1.7292	.0576
7.00	.5833	.0194	14.00	1.1667	.0389	21.00	1.7500	.0583
7.25	.6042	.0201	14.25	1.1875	.0396	21.25	1.7708	.0590
7.50	.6250	.0208	14.50	1.2083	.0403	21.50	1.7917	.0597
7.75	.6458	.0215	14.75	1.2292	.0410	21.75	1.8125	.0604
8.00	.6667	.0222	15.00	1.2500	.0417	22.00	1.8333	.0611
8.25	.6875	.0229	15.25	1.2708	.0424	22.25	1.8542	.0618
8.50	.7083	.0236	15.50	1.2917	.0431	22.50	1.8750	.0625
8.75	.7292	.0243	15.75	1.3125	.0438	22.75	1.8958	.0632
9.00	.7500	.0250	16.00	1.3333	.0444	23.00	1.9167	.0639
9.25	.7708	.0257	16.25	1.3542	.0451	23.25	1.9375	.0646
9.50	.7917	.0264	16.50	1.3750	.0458	23.50	1.9583	.0653
9.75	.8125	.0271	16.75	1.3958	.0465	23.75	1.9792	.0660
10.00	.8333	.0278	17.00	1.4167	.0472	24.00	2.0000	.0667
10.25	.8542	.0285	17.25	1.4375	.0479	24.25	2.0208	.0674
10.50	.8750	.0292	17.50	1.4583	.0486	24.50	2.0417	.0681
10.75	.8958	.0299	17.75	1.4792	.0493	24.75	2.0625	.0688
11.00	.9167	.0306	18.00	1.5000	.0500	25.00	2.0833	.0694
11.25	.9375	.0313	18.25	1.5208	.0507	25.25	2.1042	.0701
11.50	.9583	.0319	18.50	1.5417	.0514	25.50	2.1250	.0708
11.75	.9792	.0326	18.75	1.5625	.0521	25.75	2.1458	.0715

Catalog

If you are interested in a list of fine Paperback
books, covering a wide range of subjects
and interests, send your name and address,
requesting your free catalog, to:

McGraw-Hill Paperbacks
1221 Avenue of Americas
New York, N.Y. 10020